Handbook of Organizational Communication

Handbook of Organizational Communication

An Interdisciplinary Perspective

Editors

FREDRIC M. JABLIN
LINDA L. PUTNAM
KARLENE H. ROBERTS
LYMAN W. PORTER

SAGE PUBLICATIONS
The International Professional Publishers
Newbury Park London New Delhi

For information address:

SAGE Publications, Inc.
2455 Teller Road
Newbury Park, California 91320
E-mail: order@sagepub.com

SAGE Publications Ltd.
6 Bonhill Street
London EC2A 4PU
United Kingdom

SAGE Publications India Pvt. Ltd.
M-32 Market
Greater Kailash I
New Delhi 110 048 India

Printed in the United States of America

Library of Congress Cataloging-in-Publication Data

Handbook of organizational communication.

   Bibliography: p.
   Includes indexes.
      1. Communication in management.   2. Communication
in organizations.   I. Jablin, Fredric M.
HD30.3.H3575 1987   658.4'5   87-23417
ISBN 0-8039-2387-2

96 97 98 99 00 01 02 11 10 9 8 7 6 5 4

CONTENTS

PREFACE

The idea for doing this handbook grew out of a series of discussions that the publisher began several years ago with the set of individuals who eventually became the coeditors. Each of us came to these discussions with more or less the same initial perspective, which was further reinforced by our joint conversations (interactive communication!): namely, the belief that sufficient developments had occurred over the last decade or so in both the field of communication studies and the field of organizational studies to warrant the effort of bringing together a collection of forward-looking review chapters on the rapidly evolving and intersecting area of *organizational communication.*

As two of the editors (the older ones) can testify, such a project would have been impossible as recently as the mid-1970s. The reason they know this is that when they were drafting a review of this topic area for Dunnette's *Handbook of Industrial and Organizational Psychology* in the early 1970s they were hard-pressed to find enough relevant material in the field of organizational studies for that chapter-length piece. In like fashion, research in organizational communication was so sparse in the field of communication studies that it was not until 1972, with the publication of Redding's *Communication Within the Organization* that a comprehensive review and interpretation of the literature was available. In the past 15 years the situation has drastically changed, and a major problem of editing a handbook on this subject is now deciding— reluctantly—where to set the limits and which topics or areas to *exclude.* This is no less a problem for the authors of individual chapters than it is for the editors. There has been, during this brief time period, what can only be called an enormous expansion of research and conceptualization on topics in the communication and organization fields that relate directly or indirectly to organizational communication. This burgeoning of scholarly efforts relevant to the focus of the handbook does not necessarily mean that equally substantial advances in knowledge or understanding have occurred in each of the areas covered in this volume, but it does (and did) confront authors with tough choices about which particular issues to analyze and which studies to cite and, conversely, what must be omitted. The fact that these choices are so difficult is a good sign that the field of organizational communication has emerged with a great deal of vitality. We have tried to capture a sense of that vigor in this handbook.

Any handbook venture presents the editor with the challenge of how to organize this kind of volume. In our early deliberations we considered a number of alternative structures but gradually came to a consensus on the one that the reader will find within. We were unanimous in our belief that the opening section should focus on the theoretical underpinnings of the field. Without conceptual frameworks within which to place the various research studies that have been carried out on topics central and adjacent to organizational communication, the field could come to resemble, if not an empirical dust bowl, something even worse—an empirical swamp. Therefore, we start with theory and conceptualization. The following section on contexts attempts to highlight some of the more important features of both the external and the internal environment that so strongly affect the nature, types, and outcomes of communication that take place in organizational settings. The final two sections concentrate attention on the fundamental elements (as it were) of organizational anatomy and physiology—structure and processes— as they relate to communication issues. The topics in these two sections together constitute much of what is ordinarily regarded as the central core of organizational communication.

It is our hope that this handbook will help to pull together many loose threads in the various strands of thinking and research about organizational communication and, especially, will help to point toward new theory and empirical work that can further advance this young and energetic field. In order to enhance the possibility of meeting these ends, we asked authors in preparing their chapters to analyze from a multidisciplinary perspective research and theory pertaining to their topics, to consider wherever possible communication phenomena at multiple levels of analysis (dyadic, group, organizational, and extraorganizational), and to speculate freely on directions for future research and theory in their respective areas.

Any chance at fulfilling our aspirations for the handbook obviously would not have been possible without the talent, dedicated effort, extensive cooperation, and patience of our authors. Not only have they written chapters for this book but, more important, many of them have the distinction of having been some of the leading pioneers that helped shape and strongly influence an emerging area of academic scholarship and organizational applications. We salute them for their past achievements and for their present contributions to this volume.

Our work as editors has been encouraged and nurtured by four outstanding publishing professionals at Sage who have presided over the various stages of the planning and preparation of this handbook: Sara Miller McCune, Ann West, Alfred W. Goodyear, and Lisa Freeman-Miller. We thank them for the quantity and quality of their efforts and skills. Without both, this book would have remained merely a vision rather than becoming a reality. In addition, we would like to express appreciation to the University of Texas Research Institute for financial support to prepare the indexes, and to Don Hudson and Mary Frye, who assisted in checking references, preparing the indexes, and processing other loose ends associated with the book manuscript. To the numerous scholars who provided feedback and suggestions to authors of chapters in the handbook, and to our colleagues who helped the editors in shaping the book, we are indebted. Gratitude is also due to our spouses and families, who endured many late night phone calls and other disruptions associated with this project.

Finally, we can only conclude by saying that the four of us have enjoyed immensely our own interactions in attempting to bring this project to fruition, and in a perverse sort of way we almost hate to see it come to an end. During the period we have been working on it, we met in some exotic and less than exotic places, such as Yosemite National Park, Beverly Hills, and Chicago, but whatever the surroundings the process has been stimulating. We hope the product will be, too.

—Fredric M. Jablin
—Linda L. Putnam
—Karlene H. Roberts
—Lyman W. Porter

I

THEORETICAL ISSUES

Although empirical research exploring organizational communication processes has burgeoned over the last several decades, critics frequently assail researchers for concentrating on data gathering in the absence of articulated theories of organizational communication. Given that the study of organizational communication is a relatively new area of social science inquiry, scholars often respond to this charge by proclaiming that theories will evolve from observation. To date, however, few theories of organizational communication have been developed. Moreover, those frameworks that have been produced rarely present fully enunciated theories of organizational communication. While numerous reasons can be postulated for this dearth of theory building, it is apparent that one source of the problem rests in the necessity of those who build theories to be broadly versed in *both* organization theory and communication theory. Unfortunately, few of us can claim such expertise. At best, most scholars are familiar with a select group of organization and communication theories.

The first part of this book is designed to introduce those who are interested in building and understanding organizational communication theories to a wide variety of approaches to the study of communication and organizations. The manner in which existing research has integrated communication theories and organization theories to formulate frameworks for exploring organizational communication is also examined. In addition, the chapters in this section suggest concepts, metaphors, and styles of thinking that may be useful in improving extant theories of organizational communication and in constructing new ones. Reading these chapters, however, will not make one an expert in either communication theory or organization theory, but we believe can lay a foundation for better appreciating the contributions of each theoretical perspective to the study of organizational communication.

The chapters included in Part I focus on a diverse set of theoretical issues associated with the study of organizational communication. The four chapters that this section comprises progress from an explication of communication theories and their application in organizational communication research to a discussion of the implications of organization theories for the study of organizational communication, to a treatise exploring symbolism and rhetoric as the "substance" of organizing, to a decomposition of the process of theorizing about organizational communication. Clearly, these chapters introduce the reader to different approaches, assumptions, and issues associated with research and theory building in organizational communication.

The book begins with a chapter by Krone, Jablin, and Putnam that attempts to illustrate how the questions organizational communication researchers choose to explore are direct consequences of the perspectives they assume concerning the general process of human communication. Although they recognize that there are numerous conceptual approaches to human communication, Krone et al. focus on four "fairly comprehensive yet parsimonious" perspectives: mechanistic, psychological, interpretive-symbolic, and systems-interaction. They further observe that while each perspective focuses on different "loci" of the communication process, the approaches are not mutually exclusive—compatible perspectives are frequently combined in studies.

The greater part of the chapter describes the assumptions, key concepts, and implications of each of the four perspectives and provides examples of their application in organizational communication research. Krone et al. distinguish among the perspectives by demonstrating that the locus of communication (where communication is centered) differs across the four perspectives. They assert that the mechanistic perspective focuses on issues associated with communication channels and message transmission, the psychological perspective on the conceptual filters that affect how individuals respond to their information environments, the interpretive-symbolic approach on how shared meanings are created among communicators through role-taking processes, and the systems-interaction perspective on patterns of contiguous communication acts and interacts. To facilitate comprehension of the distinctions among the perspectives, the communication loci, typical research areas, and implications of each of the perspectives are compared in Table 1.1.

Of even greater significance, Krone et al. illustrate how the various perspectives can employ the same communication elements and concepts, yet conceptualize these factors and empirically operationalize them in distinctive ways. For instance, they show that a researcher adhering to the mechanistic perspective might define "feedback" as the amount of messages a source might send a receiver, whereas the same concept viewed from the psychological perspective might be defined as reinforcement achieved through the administration of negative and positive messages. In contrast, in exploring the notion of feedback from an interpretive-symbolic perspective, the concept might be defined as the evaluation of one's own actions by taking the role of a "generalized other," while from a systems-interaction approach feedback could be defined as interacts or double interacts in a sequence of messages.

Although Krone et al. attempt to illustrate the different perspectives through examples such as the one described above, they also argue that though it may be possible to study the same communication concepts from each of the different perspectives, particular approaches may be more or less suitable for certain concepts. Thus they caution researchers that perspectives should be combined only when the constructs under investigation are "conceptualized compatibly" across the approaches being merged.

In concluding their discussion of alternative perspectives to human communication, Krone et al. suggest that communication encompasses all of the perspectives. They propose that the usefulness of any of the approaches rests in the questions they lead us to ask about organizational communication. One perspective is not right and another perspective wrong. Each perspective considers different aspects of the communication process as critical, and thus "obscures other features that are significant to a complete understanding of communication." As a consequence, Krone et al. see value in exploring communication from a variety of perspectives, and propose that the explanatory power of current organizational communication theories and our ability to generate new ones may lie in comprehending and synthesizing different perspectives to human communication.

The second chapter in this section, by Euske and Roberts, builds upon the Krone et al. chapter in that it summarizes various traditional and contemporary organization theories and links them to the four perspectives of communication described above. Since most organization theories consider communication issues tangentially, the goal of this chapter is to glean implications about communication from these theories. Inferences with respect to organizational communication are derived by examining communication-related studies that are derivative of organization theories; suggestions for future research with respect to each theory are also provided.

The first part of the chapter explores communication implications of traditional organization theories. Four categories of theory are considered: classical structural (for example, Taylor, Fayol, and Weber), human relations (for example, Mayo, McGregor, and Likert), behavioral decision (for example, Simon, Cyert, and March), and systems theory (for example, Burns and Stalker, Katz and Kahn). With respect to classical theories, Euske and Roberts observe that communication is generally treated from the mechanistic perspective—classical theories center on formal communication control structures and related message transmission processes and attributes (downward communication, written messages). In contrast, they suggest that human relations theories tend to consider communication from mechanistic and psychological perspectives. Studies exploring informal communication networks and rumors illustrate research from the mechanistic approach, while investigations of communication climate and openness and trust in superior-subordinate interaction exemplify the psychological perspective. In analyzing behavioral decision theory, they conclude that early studies were frequently based on the mechanistic and psychological perspectives—research centered on transmission of decision premises and information flow in decision making (mechanistic), or the cognitive processing of decision-related information (psychological). However, they propose that in more recent years behavioral decision studies have assumed more of an interpretive-symbolic perspective to communication. Research examining decision making as ritual and as nonrational, symbolic activity illustrate this newer approach. In turn, Euske and Roberts suggest that within systems theory communication has most typically been considered from the mechanistic and psychological perspectives—research exploring how organizations adapt to environmental information reflects the mechanistic view, while studies of perceived environmental uncertainty exemplify the psychological perspective.

The latter half of Chapter 2 explores the communication implications of three contemporary "macro" environment-organization theories: resource dependency theory, population ecology and the organizational life cycle model, and institutionalization theory. Euske and Roberts argue that these theories represent "substantial advancements over traditional approaches" since they conceptualize organizations as complex interactive systems, and incorporate organizational change into their theoretical frameworks. Resource dependency theory posits that environments are complex pools of scarce resources, while organizations are coalitions that alter their patterns of behavior and structure to acquire resources necessary for survival. Population ecology and life cycle approaches focus, respectively, on the dynamics by which organizational forms rise and fall as a result of competition, and how particular "focal" organizations are born, change, and disappear. In contrast, institutionalization theory is based on the assumption that "shared views" exist in the environment concerning how organizations should be operated and structured, and that successful organizations conform to these environmental expectations.

Although these theories have been the object of very little communication-related research, Euske and Roberts maintain that the theories may be relevant to the study of organizational communication processes because they imply that organizations must adapt their internal and external communication systems if they are to endure in the turbulent environments that characterize contemporary organizations. Since little communication-related research has explored the theories, Euske and Roberts do not distinguish particular communication perspectives that may be of greater or lesser value in examining each theory. However, they do offer numerous communication implications of the theories that may be adapted for research from a variety of perspectives. Euske and Roberts conclude by presenting a table comparing the organization theories they have discussed with respect to their theoretical characteristics, communication foci, and conceptualizations of the environment.

The following chapter by Tompkins transposes to some degree the theme of the Euske and Roberts essay, and attempts to show how communication is central versus tangential to organization and management theory. While acknowledging that communication has borrowed concepts and theories from organization theory, Tompkins contends that organization theory is but "an extension or outgrowth of the classical concerns of rhetorical theory." In essence, he argues that classical and contemporary organization theories are rooted in the premise that symbolic action is the "substance" of organizing— that without symbolism, rhetoric, and persuasion, we would have no organizations.

In his chapter, Tompkins reviews a variety of classical organization theories and presents evidence supporting his contention that early theorists implicitly and explicitly incorporated communication issues within their theories. Among the various classical writers he considers is the young Karl Marx, who has rarely been associated with organization theory. Yet, as Tompkins demonstrates, Marx advanced several concepts about bureaucracy and communication that are relevant to contemporary approaches to organizational analysis. Tompkins recognizes, however, that though communication has been considered in extant organization theories, the field of organizational communication has liberally appropriated and "translated" ideas and concepts from numerous other disciplines. At the same time, he argues that assimilating and reinterpreting the ideas of other disciplines within one's own field typifies the organization and social sciences generally.

In attempting to show that organizational theory is an extension of the classical concerns of rhetorical theory, Tompkins provides an in-depth analysis of the writings of Max Weber. He compares Weber's notions of legitimate authority and bureaucracy to Aristotle's concepts of persuasive proofs and rhetorical syllogisms (enthymemes) in order to illustrate that Weber's sociology of organizations was an outgrowth of the study of persuasion. Turning to more contemporary theories of organizing, he illustrates through an analysis of six exemplars that recent theories are consistent with the "new rhetoric" of symbolic action. Relying heavily on Kenneth Burke's ideas on dramatism, identification, and scapegoating in his critique of recent environment-oriented organization theories, Tompkins maintains that the essence of organizations is symbolism, or in Burke's terms "the use of language as a symbolic means of inducing cooperation in beings that by nature respond to symbols" (cited in Tompkins). Consequently, he suggests that to divide the actions of organizations into "substantive" and "symbolic" components, as proposed by many recent organizational theorists, is misleading since much of the "substantive" world is dependent on symbolism for its existence.

The chapter culminates by demonstrating that economics, the "hardest," most "objective" of the social sciences, depends on communication concepts in its theories and empirical discourse. Among other points, Tompkins argues that corporate economic strategy is shaped by communication and rhetoric. Building on Alfred Chandler's classic study of strategy and structure in organizations, he posits that the verbalizing of strategy has important consequences for the shape and structure of organizations—corporate economic strategy is "a symbolic precursor to action." In concluding his chapter, Tompkins even offers a brief critique of the language and mathematics of the scholarly writing of economists to substantiate his thesis that economic discourse is founded in symbolism, persuasion, and rhetoric.

Part I closes with a chapter by Weick that explores the process as compared to the "substance" of theorizing about organizational communication. In particular, the chapter focuses on the process of theorizing about organizational communication through unfolding the communication implications of organization theories. In the first part of the chapter Weick highlights, through an example of an action-research study, what he believes are six basic characteristics of theories and the activity of theorizing: (1) theorizing is an active process, (2) devices (such as flow charts and hypothetical models) are often needed to "hold separate phenomena together" long enough to perceive, understand, and alter their relationships, (3) theories must be able to predict how each of their elements will affect the values of other elements contained within them, (4) theories should be capable of gradual transformation from the specific-implicit to the general-explicit, (5) theories are "invented rather than discovered," and (6) theories are symbolic entities that extend beyond themselves for denotation—we learn what a theory is about by determining when, why, and where the theory is true.

Weick's use of an action-research study to demonstrate characteristics of theorizing illustrates the importance he places on "relevance" in theorizing. He maintains that relevant theories are high in usefulness, operational validity, timeliness, goal relevance (focus on outcomes that people want to influence), and nonobviousness. Thus relevant theories are likely to be accurate and general, facilitate additional theory development, and suggest other ways of exploring objects and activities.

Subsequently, Weick uses Burns and Stalker's theory of mechanistic and organic systems to illustrate how organizational communication researchers can take organization theories and "denotate" them by interpreting them from a communication perspective. In the process, he also demonstrates that "what a theory means is often discovered a posteriori rather than known a priori," and shows how a theory can meet the characteristics of theorizing and relevance that he posits are essential ingredients in theory construction.

The concluding sections of the chapter explore the products of the theorizing process. In contrast to other theorists, Weick is not dismayed that the results of theorizing are often just fragments of theory (as compared to "unified" theories). Rather, he suggests that fragmented theories are inevitable (but still of value). His position is based on several reasons, including the belief that a "true unifying theory" of human behavior is not possible. At the same time, however, he also claims that because knowledge is a collective social product, what appear as fragments of theory may actually cohere within a field's "collective omniscience." Further, he posits that a unifying theory may be unattainable because of limits on generalizing human behavior across multiple levels of analysis and because the literary style of published organizational research usually requires readers to project their own meanings onto data, a phenomenon Weick refers to as "imaginative interpretation."

In closing his chapter, Weick observes that flaws in the products of our theorizing can be attributed to three sources: (1) inadequate methodological techniques, (2) researchers who are "incompetent," "poorly trained," and more concerned about their careers than the substance of their research, and (3) a subject matter that cannot be explained by any forms of theory. To remedy these problems he suggests, respectively, three solutions: "beef up," "grow up," or "give up." The existence of this book reflects the fact that many researchers have *not* given up.

1 Communication Theory and Organizational Communication: Multiple Perspectives

KATHLEEN J. KRONE
Ohio State University

FREDRIC M. JABLIN
University of Texas at Austin

LINDA L. PUTNAM
Purdue University

The Perspectives
   Basic Components of Communication/The Mechanistic Perspective/The Psychological Perspective/The Interpretive-Symbolic Perspective/The Systems-Interaction Perspective
The Perspectives in Perspective
   Hypothetical Research Examples/Utility of the Perspectives
Conclusion

PERHAPS more than any other area of communication inquiry, organizational communication stands defenseless against claims that researchers fail to articulate theoretical frameworks underlying their work (Richetto, 1977), and are negligent in their use of theoretical models to integrate research results involving numerous and often disparate variables (Redding, 1979). Moreover, as recent comprehensive reviews of organizational communication research indicate (Jablin, 1978; Putnam & Cheney, 1983, 1985; Richetto, 1977), scholars in the area frequently perceive the essence of communication somewhat differently from one another, yet wittingly or unwittingly fail to tender the communication perspectives and related assumptions that underlie their research. Though certainly unintended, prima facie proof of this point is evident in many of the chapters that follow in this book.

Given the remissive proclivities of organizational communication scholars in designating the *communicative* theoretical foundations of their research, the primary purpose of this chapter is to emphasize the importance of clearly recognizing the manner in which one's (stated or unstated) perspective on human communication affects what, and how one studies organizational communication phenomena. In brief, our goal is to demonstrate a very simple yet often forgotten point: The questions we as organizational communication researchers choose to explore (and often the methods we use to analyze our data) are direct extensions of the perspectives we use to view human communication (Fisher, 1978).

Our discussion of perspectives on the study of human communication is guided by the work of the late B. Aubrey Fisher (1978), who proposed that scholars tend to assume one of four basic conceptual approaches to the study of human communication. For the purposes of this chapter, we have adopted a variation of these four perspectives in the form of (1) mechanistic, (2) psychological, (3) interpretive-symbolic, and (4) systems-interaction perspectives. As we shall demonstrate, each of these perspectives models the process of communication from a relatively distinct point of view. As a consequence, what constitutes the essence of communication changes sometimes subtly, sometimes dramatically, among perspectives. Given the complexity of human communication, we will not advocate the general superiority of any one perspective of communication over another. Rather, we see theoretical value in embracing a variety of perspectives, since each makes potentially unique contributions to an overall understanding of communication in organizations.

Similar to Fisher (1978), we acknowledge that the four previously mentioned perspectives do not exhaust all possible conceptual approaches to the study of human communication. However, we do argue that they represent the most comprehensive and influential frameworks used in organizational communication to date. Moreover, while other philosophical frameworks may be used generally to categorize social science research (see Burrell & Morgan, 1979; Habermas, 1971), none is as explicitly communicative as the Fisher (1978) model. Taken as a whole, Fisher's four perspectives provide at once a fairly comprehensive yet parsimonious view of human communication. Taken separately, each of the perspectives points to essentially different concepts and relationships as being critical to the communication process. Thus, although any one of the four perspectives adequately covers the overall communication process, each perspective simultaneously obscures other features that are significant to a complete understanding of communication. In short, we posit that only by comprehending and synthesizing organizational communication research conducted from a variety of theoretical perspectives (one of the aims of this book), can we hope to increase the explanatory power of current theories and generate new ones.

In summary, in many respects this chapter is designed as a primer in the various perspectives of the study of human communication that are explicitly and implicitly applied in organizational communication research, and referred to in subsequent chapters of this book. Specifically, the first section briefly summarizes the mechanistic, psychological, interpretive-symbolic, and systems-interaction perspectives of human communication and discusses how each is generally reflected in studies of organizational communication. In turn, the second section compares the perspectives to one another by presenting hypothetical illustrations of how the same organizational communication concepts, upward influence and feedback, could be investigated from each of the four perspectives. In addition, this section highlights the utility of the approaches for understanding and conducting organizational communication research.

THE PERSPECTIVES

In what has become a classic graduate-level communication theory text, Fisher (1978) proposes four perspectives of the study of human communication. Our discussion of the four perspectives adopts his basic framework, but adapts the four to research in organizational communication. Thus we have altered both the names and the orientations of the four perspectives to fit the purposes of this chapter. In this section we briefly describe the underlying assumptions and key communication concepts of the mechanistic, psychological, interpretive-symbolic, and systems-interaction perspectives. Following our discussion of how each perspective views human communication in general, specific examples are provided to illustrate the use of each perspective in organizational communication research in particular. For the most part, an attempt will be made to provide research examples that fall squarely within one perspective or another rather than those that reflect assumptions underlying more than one framework.

Several issues should be recognized with respect to the following discussion. First, while the labels of the perspectives reflect their broader philosophical foundations, it is important to realize that "the psychological perspective of communication is not psychology" (Fisher, 1978, p. 95). In like manner the interpretive-symbolic perspective embraces but is not synonymous with symbolic interactionism, and the systems-interaction perspective is not the same as general systems theory. Second, even though the four perspectives draw from different assumptions about communication, emphasize different concepts as critical to the process, and potentially yield unique research findings and explanations, they are not mutually exclusive. In fact, the great bulk of theoretical and conceptual scholarship in organizational communication reflects combinations of the perspectives, and in particular the merger of mechanistic and psychological approaches. At the same time, however, the locus of communication differs across the four perspectives and determines which elements of the communication process receive primary emphasis for a given perspective. Locus refers to "the central location of where communication takes place" (Fisher, 1978, p. 95). It constitutes the place to look in order to explain the communication process or the phenomena deemed most critical to understanding communication. Since each perspective centers on different loci, combining perspectives may increase confusion, and utilizing all four perspectives becomes theoretically contradictory if not empirically impossible (Fisher, 1978, p. 96). Third, the four perspectives are not arranged in a linear progression; that is the four *do not build* on each other in increasing complexity. Since the four incorporate many of the same components, they represent distinct perspectives for examining relationships among elements of the communication process.

Basic Components of Communication

Introductory courses in human communication typically identify the major ingredients of the communication process. This is usually presented through the use of different communication models that map out the relationships between the components. Although the exact nature and definition of these characteristics vary across perspectives, each of the four recognizes and incorporates to some extent these elements: message, channel, sender/receiver, transmission, encoding/decoding, meaning, feedback, and communication effects. The specific nuances of each component vary across the four perspectives; however, general definitions can be offered to frame our understanding of the communication process.

Message typically refers to the verbal and nonverbal cues each communicator conveys, while *channel* is the vehicle or medium in which a message travels. Thus channels range from light waves for nonverbal cues to radio or computers as modes for transmitting sound and visual messages. The *sender* refers to the individual who sends a message or the generalized source of a message, while *receiver* typically denotes a message's destination or the person who receives and deciphers a message. Since communication typically involves a continuous exchange of messages, however, the sender also acts simultaneously as a receiver and the receiver also serves as a message source. *Transmission* refers to the actual sending and receiving of messages through designated channels, whereas *encoding and decoding* denote the process of creating, transforming, and deciphering messages. Through the encoding and decoding process, individuals formulate *meaning* by interpreting or making sense of the message. Interpreting a message is facilitated through the use of *feedback,* a message sent in response to the initial message. *Communication effects* has a broad array of specific definitions but typically refers to the outcome or general results of the message exchange processes. Precise definitions, emphasis, and relationships among these components, however, differ across the four perspectives. Also, new components are added to each perspective, ones that are consistent with the assumptions and loci of a particular perspective.

The Mechanistic Perspective

From a mechanistic perspective, human communication is viewed as a *transmission process* in which a message travels across space (a channel) from one point to another. The locus of communication is the channel; that is, explanations of the communication process emanate from the channel. Transmission occurs through the channel; communicators are linked together via channels; channels also link the encoding and decoding functions within each communicator. As Fisher (1978, p. 112) notes, "From the mechanistic point of view . . . events or functions occurring on the channel become the fodder for research and theorizing."

This emphasis on channel and the transmission of messages emanates from four fundamental assumptions that underlie the mechanistic perspective: quasi-causality, transitivity of communication functions, conceptual material- ism, and reductionism (Fisher, 1978). Researchers who adopt a mechanistic perspective, either explicitly or implicitly, assume that communication concepts are causally or at least quasi-causally related. By treating "A" as causing "B," researchers focus on the link between antecedent conditions and future consequences; more specifically, they assume the source affects or does something to the receiver through messages sent via the channel. Thus the mechanistic perspective implies a linear connection between communicators, with the channel serving as a directional linkage between the two.

A second assumption underlying the mechanistic framework is transitivity of communication functions; that is, communication concepts are linked together in a chainlike relationship. Thus it is believed that the way in which "A" functions leads directly to how "B" functions, which in turn leads to how "C" functions, and so on. As an illustration of this transitive relationship, the mechanistic perspective posits that a source affects a message-sending process, which in turn impacts on message clarity, which subsequently shapes message reception. An implication of this assumption is that breakdowns in communication occur easily when a barrier blocks message transmission and reception.

Third, the mechanistic perspective also treats communication as material- istic, that is, a message becomes a concrete substance with spatial and physical properties (for example, message frequency and/or duration). Materialism also conceptualizes time as being of constant duration and therefore emphasizes (1) physical time versus symbolic time and (2) the notion that time is beyond human manipulation—that is, we cannot speed time up nor can we slow it down. This emphasis on the tangible dimension of communication directs the researcher to concrete representation of messages that frequently merge channel with message codes, for example, written memorandum, computer-generated messages, and bulletin boards. Finally, the mechanistic framework assumes that communication is capable of being broken into smaller and smaller units. Operating from a reductionist perspective implies that communication concepts can best be understood by reducing the whole of a given concept into its smallest parts, identifying and measuring the parts, then testing the linear causal chains among the parts.

Through its emphasis on the channel and the transmission of messages, the mechanistic approach also adds special components to the basic model of communication—namely, fidelity, noise, breakdowns, barriers, and gate-keepers. Message *fidelity* refers to the extent to which a message is similar at two points on the channel. The mechanistic approach centers on reaching a high degree of "accuracy" between the message sent and the message received. Anything that interferes with the message sending and message receiving processes reduces the fidelity of the message and is referred to as *noise*. Noise may occur as static in the channel, like a disturbance in the telephone line, or as misunderstanding between communicators, in the form of unintended problems in encoding or decoding messages.

Barriers and breakdowns involve the success of message transmission. *Breakdowns* refer to those problems along the channel that cause communication to stop completely, while *barriers* refer to obstacles that simply impede or slow down the message transmission process. Relatedly, noise in the transmission process along the channel can lead to breakdowns and barriers to communication. Finally, *gatekeepers* function to receive information from a source and relay that information to a receiver. As such, they serve a filtering function and exercise considerable control over the information flow to all subsequent receivers.

In summary, a mechanistic perspective views communication as a transmission process in which messages travel across a channel from one point to another. From this perspective, communication is best understood in terms of a "conduit" (Axley, 1984), which focuses on (1) the channel or vehicle for transmitting messages; (2) a linear, causal, and chainlike relationship between parts of the process; (3) the effects of the source on the receiver; (4) the concrete or physical nature of messages; and (5) the role of noise and gatekeeping in preventing communication breakdowns and in achieving message fidelity.

Research illustrations. With few exceptions (for example, Albrecht & Ropp, 1982), organizational communication network research is almost entirely mechanistic since it focuses primarily on the channels that allow communication to flow among individuals. Specifically, network analysis uses data about communication flow to analyze interpersonal linkages and to identify the communication structures of large systems (see Monge and Eisenberg, Chapter 10, this volume; Rogers & Agarwala-Rogers, 1976). For example, in a study of three military organizations, Roberts and O'Reilly (1978) obtained information (for instance, the names and frequency of contacts) regarding expertise, social, and formal authority networks. They report that employees rarely follow formal authority networks/channels of communication, but rather communicate in task-focused clusters. By focusing on communication channels and on the transmission process of senders, this research reflects the mechanistic perspective of organizational communication.

Early organizational communication research that examined the effectiveness of downward-directed media in transmitting company information to employees (see Baker, Ballantine, & True, 1949; Dahle, 1953; Peterson & Jenkins, 1948) illustrates the mechanistic perspective. The majority of this work focuses primarily on the concrete properties of messages (for example, their readability), the methods by which messages are transmitted (for instance, oral versus written), and message effects (that is, the success of transmission between sender and receiver). These studies reveal the factors that impair or form barriers to the readability of company publications (see Baker, Ballantine, & True, 1949; Peterson & Jenkins, 1948) and reduce fidelity in disseminating particular types of company information (see, for example, Dahle, 1953). Thus this line of research exemplifies the mechanistic perspective through its focus on the material aspects of messages; its emphasis on linear, causal relationships among source, message, and receiver; and its attention to fidelity and communication effects.

A final illustration of the mechanistic perspective is research conducted on downward message transmission between superiors and subordinates. For example, in an investigation of downward filtering, Davis (1968) traces the flow of information across five hierarchical levels in two similarly structured manufacturing departments of an organization. In the design of the study, top-level managers receive oral information about either a production-oriented or a non-production-oriented event and are asked to pass this information through the chain of command as quickly as possible. Davis uses a technique known as ECCO Analysis (Davis, 1953) to identify each lower-level manager's source of the transmitted information. He reports that transmission tends to stop at level 3 in the hierarchy (general foremen) for both types of information, however, fidelity declines to an even greater extent for the non-production-oriented information. Based on these findings, Davis concludes that non-production-oriented messages may be better suited for written channels, whereas production-related information may be handled more effectively through oral communication. This research illustrates the mechanistic approach because of its focus on message transmission in a chainlike pattern of the administrative hierarchy and its attempt to locate the points in the hierarchy in which communication breakdowns occur. Davis (1968) also specifies identifiable message sources (top manager) and receivers (subordinate managers) and speculates on the fidelity of downward transmission of different types of oral and written information. Hence, Davis's research focuses squarely on the channel of communication and on the movement of a message from one point to another.

The Psychological Perspective

While the mechanistic perspective toward human communication places primary emphasis on the channels that link communicators, the psychological perspective focuses specifically on how characteristics of individuals affect their communication. From a psychologically oriented viewpoint, individual communicators are presumably located within an informational environment that includes stimuli far too numerous to process. Consequently the "conceptual filters" of individuals become the locus of the communication process since they act to structure a potentially chaotic stimulus field. According to Fisher (1978), conceptual filters consist of communicators' attitudes, cognitions, and perceptions. In brief, conceptual filters include all of those unobservable internal states of individuals that significantly affect not only *what* information is attended to, conveyed, and interpreted but also *how* this information is processed.

The psychological perspective also embraces assumptions of linear causality, transitivity of communication functions, and reductionism. But unlike the mechanistic approach, the psychological perspective locates communication in the conceptual filters that encode and decode information and stimuli from the environment. The materialism, transmission effects, and emphasis on channels that characterized the mechanistic view are subjugated to internal cognitive processes of senders and receivers. Components like encoding-decoding, barriers, gatekeeping, and noise stem from psychological processes in interpreting message stimuli rather than message transmission effects. Barriers and gatekeeping become forms of selective exposure rather than obstacles in the transmission process.

Since conceptual filters are internal and therefore unobservable (that is, they are black box concepts), explanations of communication concepts are restricted to direct observation of inputs and outputs only. Communication shifts from a sender-transmission focus in the mechanistic approach to a receiver-orientation in the psychological perspective. For example, it is believed that among other things employment interviewers attend to stimuli or information about job applicants such as nonverbal behavior (McGovern & Tinsley, 1978), level of vocal activity (Diboye & Wiley, 1978), and rhetorical communication strategies (Einhorn, 1981). From a psychological perspective on communication, it is the manner in which interviewers attend to and process such types of applicant-related information (inputs) that is expected to subsequently affect their judgments about applicants' suitability for employment (outputs).

In summary, the psychological perspective of organizational communication concentrates on explaining the *informational environments* in which individuals are located and the range of *stimuli* to which they respond using a variety of *conceptual filters*. In addition, as Fisher (1978, p. 145) suggests, the psychological perspective on communication differs somewhat from psychological models of other behaviors in that "the communicative situation implies some degree of purposiveness or instrumentality on the part of the behavioral stimuli produced by communicators, and that purposiveness is oriented toward another communicator."

Research illustrations. In contrast to the other three approaches, the psychological view conceptualizes organizational communication almost exclusively at the intraindividual level of analysis. Jablin's (1982a) integrative analysis of social cognition, organization communication, and the assimilation of organizational newcomers clearly illustrates this focus on intraindividual processes. Specifically, in his study the job seeker, organizational newcomer, and assimilated organizational member are viewed to some extent as sophisticated information processors whose conceptual filters (for example, self-concepts, perceptions of locus of control, self-monitoring predispositions, and work expectations) affect the occupational and organizational information they seek, interpret, and act upon. Thus from a psychological perspective organizational assimilation can be conceptualized in terms of the intra-personal-related activities of organizational members over time.

Research that focuses on the interpretation of messages by organizational members across levels in the hierarchy also reflects the psychological perspective since traditionally it examines how one's level in the formal organizational structure affects conceptual filtering and related communication activities. For example, in a study of over 800 subordinates from 15 different organizations, Jablin (1982b) found that subordinates in the lowest levels of their organization hierarchies perceive significantly less openness in superior-subordinate communication than do those subordinates at the highest levels of their hierarchies.

Perceptual differences across hierarchical levels have been conceptualized in terms of "disparity" (Browne & Neitzel, 1952), "semantic barriers" (Weaver, 1958), "semantic information-distance" (Tompkins, 1962), and "congruence" (Minter, 1969). Regardless of terminology, however, the general focus of studies exploring these phenomena has been to identify differences in perceptions (one type of conceptual filter) across organizational levels and to point out resulting problems. For example, Webber (1970) has shown that supervisors perceive that they communicate more with their subordinates than their subordinates perceive they do. Similarly, he reports that subordinates perceive that they send more messages to their supervisors than their supervisors perceive they do. In turn, it is not surprising that Webber's findings also indicate that both parties perceive that the other fails to keep them adequately informed. Moreover, other researchers have found that supervisors and subordinates even experience difficulty in agreeing on their perceptions of the basic job duties and demands facing subordinates (see Maier, Hoffman, Hooven, & Read, 1961). Summarizing the research examples cited above, breakdowns in communication result from perceptual differences between supervisors and subordinates. Thus these studies clearly reflect the psychological perspective in that conceptual filters of organizational communicators are given central importance.

A final example of the psychological perspective is evident in studies of upward distortion in hierarchical relationships. For instance, Fulk and Mani

(1986) investigated how subordinates' perceptions of their supervisors' downward communication behavior and perceptions of role stress affect subordinates' perceptions of their own tendencies to distort upward communication. In contrast to the studies reviewed for the mechanistic approach, in this research subordinates or the message receivers were asked to provide self-reports of their own and their superiors' communication; these self-reports then became the basis for modeling a subordinate's proclivity to distort upward communication. Thus, consistent with the psychological perspective, the Fulk and Mani (1986) research suggests that perceptual and cognitive processes within subordinates determine whether and to what extent subordinates will distort upward communication.

In closing, since researchers are unable to observe the conceptual filters that are of primary interest to the psychological perspective, they tend to operationalize and measure identical concepts somewhat differently, leading to a proliferation of measuring instruments (Fisher, 1978). Thus it is not surprising to see a concept like perceptual differences operationalized in at least five different ways in little over a decade. This too is a distinguishing characteristic of the psychological approach to organizational communication.

The Interpretive-Symbolic Perspective

When organizational communication is conceptualized mechanistically or psychologically, the organization takes on the qualities of a "container" within which interaction occurs (Hawes, 1974). Relatedly, each of these perspectives implicitly assumes that organizational characteristics determine communication process (see Hage, Aiken, & Marrett, 1971). In other words, organizational properties are assumed to determine communication process to a greater extent than communication processes are thought to shape organizational characteristics. As a consequence, research designs that view organizations as containers treat communication almost exclusively as a dependent variable. When viewed from an interpretive perspective, however, organizational communications consist of patterns of coordinated behaviors that have the capacity to create, maintain, and dissolve organizations (see Daft & Weick, 1984; Hawes, 1974; Weick, 1979). Thus, rather than passively submitting to some organizationally determined view of the workplace, the interpretive-symbolic perspective posits that by virtue of their ability to communicate, individuals are capable of creating and shaping their own social reality.

Probably the most humanistic of the four perspectives, the interpretive-symbolic approach adopts a view of human communication that resembles symbolic interactionism (Blumer, 1969; Mead, 1934) in the assumptions it makes about the self, shared meanings, and social behavior. The locus of communication in the interpretive-symbolic perspective is role-taking and shared meaning. *Role-taking* consists of a reaching out to form mutual understanding through empathic bonding with others. Role-taking also leads to the creation of *shared meanings* for common events and actions. Unlike the mechanistic and the psychological perspectives, the meanings of words and actions must be interpreted symbolically through the mutuality of experience itself rather than through the sender's intent or the conceptual filters of the receiver. "The result is a sharing of behavior to form a new entity not present and not possible in each person's behavior taken in isolation" (Fisher, 1978, pp. 184-185). In the psychological perspective, the individual interprets messages through an internalized "set" of conceptual filters, for example, motives, attitudes, values, and expectations, which change very slowly over time. But in the interpretive-symbolic perspective, the self is reflected through social interaction as an individual aligns his or her behaviors with others (Cooley, 1964). Thus behavior is not simply the response of conceptual filters to information stimuli; rather, it develops through social interaction and it changes as the social context changes.

The interpretive perspective also draws distinctions among symbolic, nonsymbolic, and social action. *Nonsymbolic action* involves reflex or automatic responses that do not require interpretation. In contrast, *symbolic action* requires self-indication (that is, action *and* interpretation), implying that individuals respond to others based upon their understanding of what the other's words and actions mean. *Social action* is directly tied to the meanings that individuals construct for events and activities. "First, human beings act toward things on the basis of the meanings that the things have for them. Second, those meanings are directly attributable to the social interaction that one has with [others]. Third, these meanings are created, maintained, and modified through an interpretative process used by the person in dealing with the things he encounters" (Fisher, 1978, p. 173).

In addition to the concepts of symbolic and nonsymbolic action, several other components of the interpretive-symbolic perspective warrant elaboration, namely, congruence and cultural context. *Congruence* in the interpretive-symbolic perspective differs from the concept of *fidelity* in the mechanistic tradition and *similarity* in the psychological approach. Congruence refers to a consensus of meaning in interpreting events rather than to accuracy in message transmission or to similarity in conceptual filters between communicators. Because the meaning of various verbal and nonverbal symbols is greatly affected by context, the interpretive-symbolic approach emphasizes how *cultural factors* have an impact on the interpretive process. Culture generally "refers to all the accepted and patterned ways of behavior of a given people. It is a body of common understandings . . . the sum total and the organization or arrangement of all the group's ways of thinking, feeling and acting" (Brown, 1963, pp. 3-4). Within the interactional framework in particular, culture is viewed less as something an organization *has* (that is, a set of variables that determine communication), and more as something an organization *is* (see Smircich and Calás, Chapter 8, this volume). Thus in contrast to the organization as "container" approach, which focuses on identifying specific dimensions of the organizational culture, the interpretive-symbolic paradigm searches for the way consensual meanings constitute culture.

Consistent with the tenets described above, research that adopts the interpretive perspective usually seeks to explain communication from the viewpoint of organizational members. Unlike research within the mechanistic and psychological frameworks, which typically examines only three or four organizational variables in a study, interpretive-symbolic approaches yield dense theories that have the capacity to explain a larger portion of organizational reality (Glaser & Strauss, 1967). Rather than attempting to control their subjective impressions of organizational communication, researchers who adopt the interpretive-symbolic perspective acknowledge their subjectivity and incorporate it into their research methods, such as participant observation, ethnomethodology, and naturalistic inquiry (Putnam & Pacanowsky, 1983).

In summary, the interpretive-symbolic perspective focuses on role-taking and shared meanings as forming organizations. Thus patterns of coordinated activities create, maintain, and dissolve organizations. Individuals respond to others based on role-taking and shared meanings for words and actions. These meanings are derived symbolically through the mutuality of experience and through negotiating consensual interpretations of organizational events and activities. Organizational culture develops from and in turn shapes consensual meanings; thus culture is what an organization *is* rather than what it *has.*

Research illustrations. Two studies illustrate the interpretive-symbolic perspective of the study of organizational communication. In the first study, Maryan Schall (1983) explores communication rules within work groups and the way these rules depict an organizational culture. Communication rules are "tacit understandings (generally unwritten and unspoken) about appropriate ways to interact (communicate) with others in given roles and situations; they are choices, not laws . . . and they allow interactors to interpret behavior in similar ways (to share meanings)" (Schall, 1983, p. 560). Schall collects data on communication rules via multiple qualitative and quantitative techniques to compare organizational insiders' descriptions of their work group's communication rules to the formally sanctioned rules espoused by management. Results of the study demonstrate the value of the rules approach in describing organizational cultures and reveal that the rules based on insiders' descriptions are more accurate depictions of group culture than those that management prescribes. Schall's research adheres to the interpretive-symbolic perspective in its emphasis on the shared meanings of rules, its assumptions about social meaning residing in the mutuality of experience, and its attempt to understand how consensual meanings constitute work group subcultures. Organizational communication in this study is the symbolic meaning of communication rules as derived from members' interpretations of work group and organization activities.

A second illustration of the interpretive-symbolic approach to organizational communication is Trujillo's (1983) work on managerial communication as performance. Drawing from Mintzberg's (1973) research on the characteristics of managerial roles, Trujillo employs naturalistic research methods to describe the way managers perform interpersonal, informational, and decisional roles in a new and used car dealership. In particular, Trujillo demonstrates how organizational role performances reflect and create congruence in interpreting organizational experiences. Through an analysis of dialogues between managers and subordinates, Trujillo observes how interpersonal performances create the appearance of harmonious working relationships, how informational performances constitute a system of social knowledge used to interpret organizational events, and how decisional performances project the appearance of rationality. This study exemplifies the interpretive-symbolic approach to organizational communication through its examination of the role-taking functions of managers, the way shared meanings guide behaviors and social interactions, and the way congruence in interpretations of managerial performances constitute organizational reality. Also, in his data-gathering methods Trujillo integrates in the conclusions of this study members' interpretations of organizational reality with the researcher's subjective understandings of that reality.

The Systems-Interaction Perspective

Unlike the interpretive-symbolic approach, research from the systems-interaction perspective concentrates on *external behaviors* as the fundamental units of analysis. In contrast with the psychological view, the overall communication system rather than conceptual filters determines organizational behavior. The locus of communication in the systems-interaction perspective is *patterned sequential behavior*, that is, the grouping of sequences of communicative behaviors rather than in an individual's conceptual filters or in shared interpretations of events and activities. In this perspective, communication is examined through a qualitative method known as interaction analysis that tracks recurring sequences of contiguous acts or interacts over time. Thus researchers who embrace the systems-interaction view concentrate on the categories, forms, and sequential patterns of message behavior rather than on the cause-and-effect relationships between communication variables, as seen in the mechanistic and psychological perspectives.

Studying social interaction from this perspective also entails the use of *stochastic probability* (determining the redundancy or the probability of a subsequent state from an antecedent state) rather than the use of more standard statistical inference techniques. Based on information theory, *redundancy* is the repetition of behaviors over time. As redundancy increases, uncertainty decreases; thus through tracking the repetition of behaviors over time, researchers can ascertain patterns of message behavior and the probability that a sequence of behaviors will recur.

These patterns take place within a communication system and serve to define that system. Consistent with the tenets of general system theory, the communication process is greater than the sum of its parts and changes in behaviors within the system alter the character of the entire system. Thus the pattern of sequential messages is more salient than any one message at a point in time. This assumption stands in contrast to the reductionistic notions of the mechanistic and psychological perspectives. Concepts of structure, function, and evolution from general system theory are also central to the systems-interaction perspective. *Structure* refers to spatial relationships or sequential patterns of messages, while *function* addresses the relationship between message patterns and communication events. Hence, unlike the psychological perspective, the individual is not the central component of action; rather, the behaviors that he or she performs in relation to others constitutes social events. Moreover, structural and functional relationships gradually *evolve* or change with the passage of time.

In summary, the locus of communication within the systems-interaction perspective is patterns of sequential behaviors or the recurrence of contiguous acts and interacts. This perspective is distinguished by its emphasis on: (1) time, namely that communication acts recur in meaningful ways and change gradually over time; (2) communicative acts, interacts, and double interacts, that is, a recurring sequence of three contiguous messages exchanged by communicators; (3) the probabilities with which sequences of interacts and double interacts occur in social interaction (a measure of the structure and function of the communication system) and (4) phases or patterns of interaction and recurring cycles. In essence, while the mechanistic and psychological perspectives conceptualize communication as something one "does" (that is, send/receive messages, perceive activities/objects), the systems-interaction view treats communications as an act of participation (Fisher, 1978). Along these lines, Fisher cites Birdwhistell (1959, p. 104), who astutely observes, "An individual doesn't 'do' communication, he/[she] becomes a part of communication."

Research illustrations. In recent years the frequency with which organizational communication studies have adopted the systems-interaction perspective has increased. In particular, studies of superior-subordinate communication and labor-management bargaining have adopted this perspective. In a laboratory investigation of interaction patterns Watson (1982) tracks the communication interacts of 16 leader-subordinate goal-setting dyads. Each act is coded with respect to the preceding one using a category system of relational communication. Watson reports that during the goal-setting process leaders tend to resist subordinates' attempts to control their relationship (as evidenced by symmetrical interaction patterns), while subordinates tend to comply with supervisors' efforts to control their relationship (as evidenced by complementary interaction patterns). Thus role differences exist in the goal-setting process as manifested in the way that leaders exercise greater relationship options than their subordinates do.

In a field study that employs relational coding, Fairhurst, Rogers, and Sarr (1987) combine the psychological and the systems-interaction perspectives to examine dominance patterns of manager-subordinate interactions. Their study reveals that managers who demonstrate a high frequency of dominant interacts perceive less subordinate interest in decision involvement and rate their subordinates lower in performance than do managers who use fewer controlling communication patterns. Gioia and Sims (1986) also combine the psychological and systems-interaction perspectives to examine leader-subordinate interactions and attributions of past work in simulated performance appraisal interviews. They employ the Organizational Verbal Behavior (OVB) category system to code the verbal messages of participants and use a form of interaction analysis to determine interacts and double interacts. Their analysis reveals that managers react to poor performance with requests for causal attributions or with negative evaluation. This pattern, however, changes over time with subordinates receiving fewer negative attributions for failure and more credit for success.

In bargaining research, Putnam and Jones (1982) employ the Bargaining Process Analysis (BPAII) to differentiate the communication roles of labor and management and to determine sequential patterns that distinguish settlement from impasse dyads. Using lag sequential analysis, their study reveals that labor specializes in offensive maneuvers such as attacking arguments and threats, while management relies on defensive tactics such as commitments and self-supporting arguments. A recurring exchange of these specialized tactics or a pattern of management giving offensive statements followed by labor providing information appears to prevent uncontrolled escalation of conflict. However, the matching of tactics between labor and management in a one-upmanship pattern leads to cycles of high conflict and to bargaining impasse.

In these studies, researchers embrace the systems-interaction perspective through their focus on sequential communicative acts and interacts, their analysis of message behaviors over time, and their attempts to isolate patterns of recurring behaviors that explain the communication system. Each of the studies incorporates assumptions of redundancy, tests for probabilities of recurrence of behaviors, and examines the structure and function of communication systems.

In summary, the unique attributes of the four perspectives and the corresponding areas of organizational communication research in which they are frequently applied are highlighted in Table 1.1.

TABLE 1.1

Alternative Perspectives to Organizational Communication

Perspective	Locus of Communication	Frequent Research Foci	Characteristics/Implications
Mechanistic	Channel and message transmission	—Communication structures —Communication effects —Source and message variables —Communication barriers, breakdowns and gatekeeping —Mediated versus non-mediated communication systems; —Diffusion of information	—Focus on conveying information and accuracy of message reception —Message-sending/receiving considered to be linear, transitive process —Somewhat dehumanizing; little attention to receiver and role of meaning in communication —Tendency to oversimplify and/or reify the communication process —Can lead to believing there is only one "right way" to communicate
Psychological	Conceptual filters	—Individual as information processor —Distortion in upward communication —Communication climate —Perceptions of leader communication style —Semantic-information distance —Communication-job satisfaction relationships	—Receiver is cast in active role of message interpreter —Emphasizes intentions and human aspects of communication —Accents role of selective exposure and enactment processes —Frequent assumption of linear relations between cognitions and behaviors —"Black box" concepts may lead to proliferation of measurement instruments
Interpretive-symbolic	Role-taking	—Communication "rules" —Organizational culture —Organizational myths, stories and humor —Management of meaning —Power and politics	—Considers role of self and collective—cultural context of communication —Focus on communicating (action) —Emphasis on symbols and "shared" meaning —Often difficult to draw generalizations from results of case studies —Researcher impressions may bias results—need to verify with participants' view
Systems-interaction	Sequences of communication behavior	—Feedback patterns —Conflict management —Work group development —Relational communication —Decision-making phases	—Treats communication as evolving system —Focus on types of message sequences, functions, and behaviors —Utilizes coding of actual verbal and nonverbal behaviors —Analyses micro-analytic; meaning and saliency of messages for participants often ignored —Analyses often based on stochastic versus inferential statistical assumptions

33

THE PERSPECTIVES IN PERSPECTIVE

In order to clarify further how the study of organizational communication varies depending upon the perspective one assumes toward human communication, this section (a) presents a series of hypothetical illustrations of how each of the perspectives might explore the same basic organizational concepts, upward influence and feedback, and (b) discusses briefly the utility of the perspectives for understanding and exploring organizational communication.

Hypothetical Research Examples

The four perspectives, as noted in the first portion of this chapter, can represent different ways of studying similar organizational communication phenomena. Although combinations of several perspectives in one study are quite common, this section demonstrates how organizational communication concepts would vary if each were cast in a particular perspective. Specifically, this section illustrates hypothetical examples of four different studies that employ the same organizational communication concepts, upward influence and feedback on task performance, but adopt different perspectives on the role of communication. Each study will address the relationship between managerial upward influence and the feedback managers give to their superiors. Each hypothetical study demonstrates how operational definitions, research questions, design, and research methods would vary across the four investigations.

Mechanistic perspective. A study that adheres to the mechanistic perspective might define upward influence as a network structure characterized by a high frequency of messages, symmetrical exchanges, and high density of contacts between a manager and his or her superiors in the hierarchy. Treating influence as a network structure would center on the message transmission activity of managers and on the channels or contacts in the communication structure. Consistent with the mechanistic approach, feedback could be defined as the amount of messages from the receiver (target manager) to the source (superior) about task performance. This concept could be operationalized by ascertaining the number of feedback messages sent to superiors via written versus oral channels. Thus feedback would take on a materialistic quality by reducing it to the number of task response messages transmitted through specific channels. In keeping with the quasi-causality assumption of the mechanistic approach, the researcher could hypothesize that the greater the upward influence, the lower the frequency of feedback messages, especially for oral channels of communication. The design of the study could distinguish managers with high-influence networks from those with low-influence networks and could test for differences in reported amount of feedback for written and oral channels. Methods of data collection might include self-report communication diaries that ascertain frequency of contacts with superiors and frequencies of feedback messages via written and oral channels.

Psychological perspective. The same study cast in the mold of the psychological perspective might center on perceived upward influence and on the evaluative nature of feedback. Upward influence could be defined as the superior's perceptions of a target manager's influence in the organization. Feedback could be treated as psychological reinforcement through the giving of positive or negative messages. Both concepts would be defined and measured through the conceptual filters of organizational members. In a field study, the researcher could test the relationship between the degree of perceived upward influence and the giving of positive or negative feedback. In a laboratory study, the researcher could test for the effects of high and low managerial influence on perceptions of evaluative messages of task performance given to superiors. This design would employ questionnaire data to tap perceptions of abstract concepts and would center on a receiver-oriented rather than a sender-oriented view of communication.

Interpretive-symbolic perspective. Research within the interpretive-symbolic perspective could define upward influence as the actions that exert the greatest impact in shaping and creating organizational reality. Upward influence then becomes a construct defined by symbolic action and mutuality of organizational experience. Upward influence could also be synonymous with specific roles in defining an organization's culture, namely, entrepreneurs, dominant coalitions, and organizational sages. Consistent with Kanter's definition of power, organizational members with high levels of upward influence would be able to mobilize resources to control definitions of organizational life or be able to influence others to adopt their interpretations of organizational experiences. Feedback might be viewed as the way individuals or collectivities evaluate their own actions by taking the role of a generalized other. Hence, organizational members rely on empathic bonding to provide positive and negative assessment of their actions. Feedback could be examined in both the creation and dissolution of organizational cultures. A study within this perspective could focus on the way shared meanings of upward influence—that is, actions that exert the greatest impact in shaping organizational reality—evolve from positive and negative assessment of past organizational experiences. The study could employ naturalistic research methods and collect data through participant observation of organizational activities and interviews that focus on the meanings and evaluation of current and past events.

Systems-interaction perspective. In contrast to the other perspectives, in the systems-interaction approach upward influence could be defined as the pattern of sequential messages that characterizes persuasive communication with superiors. Thus the researcher could employ a compliance gaining or influence strategy category system and code persuasive messages exchanged between managers and their superiors. Then the researcher could determine the probability that these behaviors would recur over time. Patterns of sequential strategies could reveal characteristic ways that managers and their superiors work together to create an influence system. In this perspective, influence would be the joint production of both manager and superiors, not simply the efforts of one individual. Feedback could be examined through categories of positive and negative evaluation; hence, each message in the persuasive interaction could be double coded, once for influence attempts and once for implicit or explicit evaluation of task performance. Sequences of feedback messages could be examined to determine the joint patterns of task evaluation produced in the message system. In this design, sender and receiver would interchange roles and feedback would be any evaluative message about task performance rather than a response to the source's initial message. This study would explore the relationship between sequential patterns of influence strategies and patterns of positive and negative feedback. In another design consistent with this perspective, feedback could be operationalized as the interact or the double interact in the sequence of influence messages that managers and their superiors exchange. In this design, the absence of feedback would be the lack of sufficient redundancy to decipher a recognizable pattern of influence sequences. This study might examine the way different antecedent strategies yield subsequent influence patterns and cycles. Both designs might employ content or interaction analysis of audio or videotapes of manager-superior communication.

In summary, as the above hypothetical studies illustrate, contingent on whether the locus of communication is the message channel (mechanistic perspective), conceptual filters of communication (psychological perspective), the role-taking process (interpretive-symbolic perspective), or sequential communication behaviors (systems-interaction perspective), our understanding of the same essential communication concepts varies considerably.

Utility of the Perspectives

Although it may be possible for researchers to study the same communication concept from each of the perspectives, certain approaches are more suitable for studying particular communication concepts. For example, mechanistic approaches are especially congruent with research aimed at comparing channels or determining transmission effects, while interpretive-symbolic perspectives are better suited for examining meaning than are some of the other orientations. Research on the properties of a single message may be more appropriate from psychological and mechanistic approaches than from the interpretive-symbolic or the systems-interaction views. Even though the latter perspectives can accommodate research on message, they recast the concept into symbols and into sequences of message patterns, respectively. In the interpretive-symbolic approach, messages per se are not the basis for understanding communication; messages do not "link" or couple organizational members together. They merely activate culturally based rules or assumptions which, in turn, function to bond communicators. With respect to the systems-interaction perspective, Fisher (1978, p. 281) observes that "only in the pattern or in the sequence or in the behavioral program of ongoing human communication does the single act assume significance—and only then if it exhibits sufficient redundancy."

To summarize, in most cases a researcher would not examine the same concept from all four perspectives. In fact, some concepts may be incompatible with the underlying theoretical assumptions of a particular perspective. In contrast, combining several approaches in any particular investigation may be possible and even advantageous, but only if the constructs under study are conceptualized compatibly across the perspectives being merged. Ultimately, the utility of any perspective for the study of organizational communication lies in the questions its leads us to ask. As a consequence, in choosing a particular perspective

> we need to be aware of what questions are askable, and hence, answerable within that perspective. We need to know what questions are *un*askable and, hence, *un*answerable as well. We need to know what we need to know and how to utilize the perspective that will be the most likely one to lead us to that knowledge. (Fisher, 1978, p. 323)

CONCLUSION

This chapter purports that research and even application in the field of organizational communication espouses, either explicitly or implicitly, a particular view of communication. This view shapes the way people see organizational communication and the way they interpret what they see. A manager who insists, "My subordinate just doesn't listen to me. I sent him that message several days ago" exemplifies the mechanistic approach to communication. Researchers who adopt this view see communication as materialistic substance that travels through computers, memos, telephones, and other concrete substances. In contrast, managers who view communication from a psychological perspective concentrate on the perceptions of the receiver. Effective communication, in this perspective, stems from adapting one's needs to meet the values and attitudes of the respondent. Researchers who operate from this perspective center on the cognitions and personality traits of communicators. Rarely do managers have conceptualizations grounded in the interpretive-symbolic perspective. If they do, the manager would concentrate on how employees and superiors are interpreting the events in their organizational environment and how he or she can influence the consensual meanings that organizational members socially construct. Researchers who espouse this perspective focus on symbols, but not as artifacts of the organization; rather, they attempt to decipher how these symbols represent the ways individuals socially construct their organization life. Finally, in the systems-interaction view of communication, managers concentrate on the patterns, routines, and sequences of interaction that define their relationships with others. They realize that these patterns can become self-sustaining over time since they are typically not in our awareness. Researchers make sequential behaviors and message patterns the primary focus of their investigations. They aim to determine how individuals get into ruts and routines through the way message patterns define their organizational environment.

As we mentioned in the first part of this chapter, no one perspective is right or wrong. As Table 1.1 demonstrates, the four yield different insights about communication. In effect, communication encompasses all of the four perspectives. From a practitioner's view, however, the perspectives that encompass more communication variables and more complexity in understanding message processing yield the greatest practical value in managing communication problems. From a researcher's view, the approaches or combinations of approaches that advance our knowledge of communication in organizations would be the most useful. In applying a particular perspective, however, researchers need to operationalize variables and execute studies in a manner congruent with the perspective's underlying communication assumptions. Hence, we advocate recognition and understanding of the different perspectives that ground the multifaceted research pursuits in organizational communication.

REFERENCES

Albrecht, T. L., & Ropp, V. A. (1982). The study of network structuring in organizations through the use of triangulation. *Western Journal of Speech Communication, 46,* 146-178.

Axley, S. R. (1984). Managerial and organizational communication in terms of the conduit metaphor. *Academy of Management Review, 9,* 428-437.

Baker, H., Ballantine, J. W., & True, J. M. (1949). *Transmitting information through management and union channels: Two case studies.* Princeton, NJ: Princeton University, Industrial Relations Section.

Birdwhistell, R. L. (1959). Contributions of linguistic-kinesic studies to understanding of schizophrenia. In A. Auerback (Ed.), *Schizophrenia: An integrated approach* (pp. 99-123). New York: Ronald Press.

Blumer, H. (1969). *Symbolic interactionism: Perspective and method.* Englewood Cliffs, NJ: Prentice-Hall.

Brown, I. C. (1963). *Understanding other cultures.* Englewood Cliffs, NJ: Prentice-Hall.

Browne, G. G., & Neitzel, B. J. (1952). Communication, supervision and morale. *Journal of Applied Psychology 36,* 86-91.

Burrell, G., & Morgan, G. (1979). *Sociological paradigms and organizational analysis.* London: Heinemann Press.

Cooley, C. H. (1964). *Human nature and social order.* New York: Schocken.

Daft, R. L., & Weick, K. E. (1984). Toward a model of organizations as interpretation systems. *Academy of Management Review, 9,* 284-295.

Dahle, T. L. (1953). *An experimental study of communication in business.* Unpublished doctoral dissertation, Purdue University, Indiana.

Davis, K. (1953). A method of studying communication patterns in organizations. *Personnel Psychology 6,* 301-312.

Davis, K. (1968). Success of chain-of-command oral communication in a manufacturing management group. *Academy of Management Journal, 11,* 379-387.

Diboye, R. L., & Wiley, J. W. (1978). Reactions of male raters to interviewee self-presentation style and sex: Extensions of previous research. *Journal of Vocational Behavior, 13,* 192-203.

Einhorn, L. J. (1981). An inner view of the job interview: An investigation of successful communicative behavior. *Communication Education, 30,* 217-228.

Fairhurst, G. T., Rogers, L. E., & Sarr, R. A. (1987). Manager-subordinate control patterns and judgments about the relationship. In M. L. McLaughlin (Ed.), *Communication yearbook 10* (pp. 395-415). Newbury Park, CA: Sage.

Fisher, B. A. (1978). *Perspectives on human communication.* New York: Macmillan.

Fulk, J., & Mani, S. (1986). Distortion of communication in hierarchical relationships. In M. L. McLaughlin (Ed.), *Communication yearbook 9* (pp. 483-510). Newbury Park, CA: Sage.

Gioia, D. A., & Sims, H. P. (1986). Cognitive-behavior connections: Attribution and verbal behavior in leader-subordinate interactions. *Organizational Behavior and Human Decision Processes, 37,* 197-229.

Glaser, B. G., & Strauss, A. L. (1967). *The discovery of grounded theory: Strategies for qualitative research.* Chicago: Aldine.

Habermas, J. (1971). *Knowledge and human interests.* (J. J. Shapiro, Trans.). Boston: Beacon Press.

Hage, J., Aiken, M., & Marrett, C. B. (1971). Organization structure and communication. *American Sociological Review, 36,* 860-871.

Hawes, L. C. (1974). Social collectivities as communication: Perspectives on organizational behavior. *Quarterly Journal of Speech, 60,* 497-502.

Jablin, F. M. (1978). *Research priorities in organizational communication.* Paper presented at the annual convention of the Speech Communication Association, Minneapolis.

Jablin, F. M. (1982a). Organizational communication: An assimilation approach. In M. Roloff & C. Berger (Eds.), *Social cognition and communication* (pp. 255-286). Newbury Park, CA: Sage.

Jablin, F. M. (1982b). Formal structural characteristics of organizations and superior-subordinate communication. *Human Communication Research, 8,* 338-347.

Kanter, R. M. (1977). *Men and women of the corporation.* New York: Basic Books.

Maier, N.R.F., Hoffman, R. L., Hooven, J. L., & Read, W. H. (1961). Superior-subordinate communication: A statistical research project. *American Management Research Studies, 52,* 9-30.

McGovern, T. V., & Tinsley, H.E.A. (1978). Interviewers evaluations of interviewee nonverbal behavior. *Journal of Vocational Behavior, 13,* 163-171.

Mead, G. H. (1934). *Mind, self and society.* Chicago: University of Chicago Press.

Minter, R. L. (1969). *A comparative analysis of managerial communication in two divisions of a large manufacturing company.* Unpublished doctoral dissertation, Purdue University, Indiana.

Mintzberg, H. (1973). *The nature of managerial work.* New York: Harper & Row.

Peterson, D., & Jenkins, J. (1948). Communication between management and workers. *Journal of Applied Psychology, 32,* 71-80.

Putnam, L. L., & Cheney, G. (1983). A critical review of research traditions in organizational communication. In M. Mander (Ed.), *Communication in transition* (pp. 206-224). New York: Praeger.

Putnam, L. L., & Cheney, G. (1985). Organizational communications: Historical development and future directions. In T. W. Benson (Ed.), *Speech communication in the 20th century* (pp. 130-156). Carbondale, IL: Southern Illinois University Press.

Putnam, L. L., & Jones, T. (1982). Reciprocity in negotiations: An analysis of bargaining interaction. *Communication Monographs, 49,* 171-191.

Putnam, L. L., & Pacanowsky, M. E. (Eds.). (1983). *Communication and organizations: An interpretive approach.* Newbury Park, CA: Sage.

Richetto, G. M. (1977). Organizational communication theory and research: An overview. In B. D. Ruben (Ed.), *Communication yearbook 1* (pp. 331-346). New Brunswick, NJ: Transaction.

Redding, W. C. (1979). Organizational communication theory and ideology: An overview. In D. Nimmo (Ed.), *Communication yearbook 3* (pp. 309-341). New Brunswick, NJ: Transaction.

Roberts, K. H., & O'Reilly, C. A. (1978). Organizations as communication structures: An empirical approach. *Human Communication Research, 4,* 283-293.

Rogers, E., & Agarwala-Rogers, R. (1976). *Communication in organizations.* New York: Free Press.

Schall, M. S. (1983). A communication-rules approach to organizational culture. *Administrative Science Quarterly, 28,* 557-581.

Tompkins, P. K. (1962). *An analysis of communication between headquarters and selected units of a national labor union.* Unpublished doctoral dissertation, Purdue University, Indiana.

Trujillo, N. (1983). "Performing" Mintzberg's roles: The nature of managerial communication. In L. L. Putnam & M. E. Pacanowsky (Eds.), *Communication and organizations: An interpretive approach.* (pp. 73-97). Newbury Park, CA: Sage.

Watson, K. M. (1982). An analysis of communication patterns: A method for discriminating leader and subordinate roles. *Academy of Management Journal, 25,* 107-120.

Weaver, C. H. (1958). The quantification of the frame of reference in labor-management communication. *Journal of Applied Psychology, 42,* 1-9.

Webber, R. A. (1970). Perceptions of interactions between superiors and subordinates. *Human Relations, 23,* 235-248.

Weick, K. E. (1979). *The social psychology of organizing* (2nd ed.). Reading, MA: Addison-Wesley.

2 Evolving Perspectives in Organization Theory: Communication Implications

NANCY A. EUSKE
KARLENE H. ROBERTS
University of California, Berkeley

P HILOSOPHERS since ancient times have speculated on the nature of organizations and their role in society. These philosophical positions, often crossing a variety of disciplinary boundaries, have led to the development of multiple schools of organizational theory. Theories about organizations typically treat communication in an implicit or a tangential manner. Close examination of the various schools of organizational thought, however, uncovers implications for communication research. This chapter summarizes the major traditions in organizational theory and draws out their implications for organizational communication research.

As evident in Chapter 1 by Krone, Jablin, and Putnam, any assessment of organizational theory reflects diverse perspectives on the study of human communication. Some theorists conceive of communication as written versus oral channels or the transmission of messages. These approaches fall into the mechanistic perspective discussed in Chapter 1. Other theorists view organizational communication through the locus of message effects, filtered through

AUTHORS' NOTE: We wish to express appreciation to Fred Jablin and Linda Putnam for their comments and suggestions on an earlier draft of this chapter.

cognitive processes of senders and receivers. Other theorists, although fewer in number, treat communication as the interpretation of information, the meaning of symbols, or the redundancy of message patterns. Differences in defining communication make it difficult to determine how communication surfaces in organizational theory. Most definitions offered by organizational theorists are vague shorthand statements that lack precision and specificity in determining which variables should be the focus of message exchange.

In its broadest sense, communication is the social glue that ties members, subunits, and organizations together. That is, communication underlies most organizational processes, contributes to both the development and the enactment of structures, and is shaped by a number of organizational and individual characteristics, including size, department, autonomy, and upward aspirations. Without communication, organizing could not occur.

Definitions of organizational communication have also been confounded by research at multiple levels of analysis. Past definitions of organizational communication often reveal different definitions across interpersonal subunits, and organizational-environmental interactions. However, the ideal in integrating organizational and communication theory is to employ similar definitions of organizational communication across multiple levels.

Definitions of organizational communication also reflect the growth and evolution of organizational theory. Over the years theorists have developed increasingly complex theories of organizations, reflecting a growing awareness of the complexity of the phenomenon under study. Early theories of organizations focused primarily on internal features of organizations and failed to give serious treatment to the claims that organizations were influenced by and exerted influence upon their surrounding environments. Theories that have surfaced in recent years treat environment as a significant feature of organizational life, one that directly affects and is shaped by organizational behavior. To cover the broad range of developments in organizational theory, the first section of this chapter briefly summarizes the role of communication in the traditional theories of organizations, while the remainder of the chapter centers on recent theories and the implications of these theories for organizational communication. This very general overview of select organizational theories highlights key concepts that relate to communication and links these concepts to the four communication perspectives presented in Chapter 1. The final section of this chapter offers general observations about both of these literatures and about their implications for research developments.

TRADITIONAL ORGANIZATIONAL THEORIES

Roberts, O'Reilly, Bretton, and Porter (1974) differentiate four basic categories of organizational theory development: classical structural, human relations, behavioral decision, and systems theory. These four and the key authors that contributed to each category are reviewed in this chapter. This chapter also taps into writing that have recently examined the role of communication in traditional organizational theory (Conrad, 1985; Jablin, 1986; Putnam & Cheney, 1985; Tompkins, 1984).

Classical Organizational Theories

Taylor (1911) and Weber (1957), the founders of the classical structural approach to organizations, viewed organizations as authority structures in which span of control and work specialization were dominant features. Taylor set forth a "mental revolution" in management based on scientific design of work, improved worker motivation through increased economic rewards, and cooperation between labor and management. However, managers who did not share Taylor's "mental revolution" often implemented his techniques without the use of effective superior-subordinate communication; consequently, most modern descriptions of scientific management view it as a technique for economic gain, one that often dehumanizes the work force. In actuality, Taylor showed great concern for the welfare of workers and a desire to reduce the arbitrary, capricious treatment of workers through scientific selection and training of workers.

Whereas Taylor (1911) concentrated on scientific management, Weber (1957) focused on authority structures. The ideal type of authority, in Weber's view, was a bureaucracy complete with hierarchical positions, formal lines of communication, specialization of function, and replaceability of individuals. Work was accomplished through strict adherence to formal rules and regulations, made permanent through written policies, and enforced through formal control systems. Organizations were closed, formal, and static systems. Other classical theorists who viewed organizations from the perspective of administrative functions emphasized the structural relationships between units of production and distribution (Fayol, 1949; Gulick & Urwick, 1937; Mooney & Reiley, 1939). By focusing on the key activities of managing, Fayol (1949) modified the formal chain of command by initiating the "gangplank" as a form of horizontal communication between subunits of the organization.

Classical structural approaches, then, centered on formal structures, administrative functions, worker efficiency, and managerial control systems as the key elements for designing and operating organizations. Classical theorists also differed in their views of communication. Taylor (1911) introduced the role of upward communication and downward persuasive strategies in implementing his "mental revolution," while Weber centered his efforts on translation of rules and regulations in written downwardly directed communication (Tompkins, 1984). Fayol (1949) relied on communication more directly than the other theorists by demonstrating how his management principles could be codified and communicated, by establishing a system for giving orders through unity of command, by legitimating "bypassing" of the scalar chain through the gangplank or horizontal communication, and by stressing the primacy of oral face-to-face communication (Tompkins, 1984). Although the classical theorists differed in their view of communication, they typically concentrated on communication channels and transmission processes, thus embracing a mechanistic view of the phenomenon (see Krone et al., Chapter 1, this volume, for a discussion of the mechanistic perspective). Formal control structures and tasks served as independent variables, while efficiency and performance were the primary outcome variables.

Classical theory laid the groundwork for research on formal channels of communication, directionality of message flow, and communication networks. Exhaustive research on formal channels was conducted by the early network researchers (for example, Bavelas, 1950; Guetzkow & Simon, 1955; Leavitt, 1951; Shaw, 1954). Since most of this research employed laboratory, experimental groups, the findings of these early studies did not parallel network patterns in actual organizations. Other research linked formal control structures to communication aspects of organizations (Julian, 1966; Smith & Brown, 1964). Research on the uses and effectiveness of downward, upward, and horizontal flow of messages also emanates from classical views of formal communication channels (Downs, 1967; Hage, 1974; Katz & Kahn, 1966).

Very little research was conducted on the way that type of organization, timing, and content of messages affected formal communication structures. Adhering to formal lines of communication might enhance performance only in certain types of organizations. For example, effective operation of a highly complex weapons system might hinge on adherence to formal lines of communication, while effective performance in investment banking might rely on informal as well as formal communication channels. During times of change, adherence to formal lines of communication might have different consequences than during periods of calm (Tushman & Romanelli, 1985; Weick, 1986). Although network researchers have examined task, social, and innovative messages, only a modicum of studies focused on the content of communication in formal channels. More attention should be devoted to the type, function, and characteristics of messages transmitted through formal channels. Issues such as syntax of messages, ties with organizational functions, and relevancy or ambiguity of information need further investigation. Finally, researchers might examine the way coordination and control mechanisms are related to content and directionality of information flow.

Human Relations Approaches

Human relations approaches centered on the social and psychological features of the individual and the work group rather then on formal roles and macro-structures of organizations. Organizational efficiency, then, hinged on the effectiveness of the individual and social needs of workers instead of adherence to the formal structure. Both the classical and the human relations approaches viewed organizations as closed systems that had little interaction with external environments, but the human relations theorists cast organizations as internally dynamic.

Early human relations writers focused on work groups and the importance of informal interaction in organizations (Lewin, 1943; Mayo, 1960; Roethlisberger & Dickson, 1939). McGregor's (1960) Theory Y management emphasized the independence, responsibility, and growth of individuals in organizations. From this work grew concern for improving superior-subordinate communication through openness, trust, and mutual respect; for establishing supportive organizational climates, and for sharing power through participatory decision making. Theorists reasoned that improving relational communication would increase job satisfaction and worker involvement thus leading to higher productivity.

Research, however, demonstrated that the links between communication, job satisfaction, and performance were more complex than the human relations theorists believed. Even though relational communication was strongly related to job satisfaction, job satisfaction did not necessarily lead to increased performance. Thus research adhered to some tenets of the human relations school in that the most satisfied employees had "supervisors who were perceived as employee-centered; supportive; understanding; tolerant of disagreement; . . . willing to listen to their subordinates and who provided their subordinates with information and [with opportunities for] legitimate decision making" (Conrad, 1985, p. 116).

Another group of human relations theorists (Argyris, 1957; Bennis, 1969; Blake & Mouton, 1964; Schein, 1965; Tannenbaum, 1966) concentrated on individual motivation and the frustration between conflicting individual and organizational needs. Frustration that ensued from this conflict was believed to result in maladaptive behavior that had direct corollaries to communication through withdrawal, sabotage, and resistance to the formal organization. Thus building supportive communication climates and meeting individual needs were aimed at enhancing commitment to company goals and norms.

Another aspect of the human relations movement surfaced in Likert's (1967) work on overlapping group membership, participative decision making, and communication "linking pins." Likert placed the work group in a more dominant role than did classical theorists. Organizations consisted of multiple overlapping groups with some individuals belonging to and linking different groups. In his efforts to enhance group leadership and participatory decision making, Likert developed an elaborate system of leadership style complete with measures of open communication within and between groups and with assessments of a supervisors' upward influence in the organization (Tompkins, 1984).

Research in the human relations tradition exemplified both mechanistic and psychological views of communication (see Krone et al., Chapter 1, this volume). The mechanistic approach was evident in the research on informal communication, especially emergent communication networks and rumor studies. Informal communication became a dominant concern in the human relations tradition because the formal channels were too slow, laborious, and ineffectual for meeting certain individual needs. This work tracked the patterns of informal linkages that provided individuals with ways to meet unanticipated needs, to manage crises, to convey detailed information, and to share personal information (Tichy, Tushman, & Fombrun, 1979). Research on rumors and grapevines as forms of informal communication traced the speed, accuracy, and pattern of rumor transmission (Davis, 1953; Sutton & Porter, 1968; Weinshall, 1966). In contrast to the mechanistic topics, the psychological perspective was employed in the research on upward communication distortion, openness and trust in superior-subordinate relationships, and communication climate. These human relations topics were assessed through the use of perceptual measures of communication.

The classical and the human relations writers differed primarily in the ways that they addressed the same phenomena. Both classical and human relations theorists examined the formal structure—the classical writers from the view of authority and control mechanisms and the human relation theorists from the perspective of interpersonal relationships. Both schools aimed at enhancing organizational efficiency and performance. The classical theorists turned to scientific management, rules and regulations, and managerial functions as ways of promoting efficiency, while the human relations theorists stressed increased job satisfaction, worker involvement, and individual motivation as ways of improving performance. The two schools differed in their foci of communication: classical theorists centered on formal channels, downward information flow, and written versus face-to-face communication; whereas the human relations writers concentrated on informal networks, supportive communication climates, relational communication, and communication patterns in participatory decision making. Human relations researchers inferred that the lack of trust and openness between superiors and subordinates influenced the accuracy, distortion, and interpretation of message exchanges.

Behavioral Decision Theories

The behavioral decision theorists, like the classical writers, concentrated on the formal characteristics of organizations, specifically on decision making and specialization. They presented a more complex picture of organizations than did the classical and human relations writers—one characterized by human limitations in information processing and by the need for information from internal and external environments.

Behavioral decision theory was based on the premise that organizational decision making is less rational than classical theorists had predicted (Cyert & March, 1963; March & Simon, 1958; Simon, 1945). The procedure of rational decision making entailed collecting all available options, evaluating each one based on set criteria, comparing the probable outcomes of each, and opting for the best solution. However, due to individual and organizational limitations, participants were unable to obtain all available options and process them; hence, decision theorists viewed rationality as restricted or bounded.

Decision makers, then, "satisficed" by making satisfactory rather than optimal solutions and by employing relatively simple criteria to evaluate potential outcomes. Decision theorists contended that the design of organizational environments facilitated effective decision making. That is, use of such procedures as defining roles, specifying subgoals, establishing rules and information channels, transmitting decision premises, and training individuals to accomplish organizational objectives reduced the range of available options, thus simplifying the decision-making process and keeping satisficing solutions consistent with organizational goals.

Use of these organizational mechanisms, however, had inadvertent consequences for information flow. As information flowed through the organization, successive editing occurred and members drew inferences in accordance with organizational goals. Inferences rather than information were transmitted—a process known as "uncertainty absorption" (March & Simon, 1958). As a result, incomplete information typically influenced decision making. Decision makers generated categories to minimize lost information, transmitted decision premises, substituted programs for overloaded channels, and used shorthand telegraphic signals to replace large amounts of data.

Research on uncertainty absorption as a form of message modification revealed that organizational members altered messages as ways of casting the sender in a favorable light; reducing stress on the receiver; or adapting messages to the sender's prior expectations, biases, and attitudes (Campbell, 1958; Downs, 1967; O'Reilly & Roberts, 1974; Rosen & Tesser, 1970). Formulating inferences provided ways of evaluating and integrating information into the sender's perceptions of the receiver's needs (Ference, 1970).

The behavioral decision theorists also examined the impact of formal organizational structure on decision making. Researchers demonstrated that organizational structure directs information flow in the delegation of decision making (Blankenship & Miles, 1968). Complex formal networks conceived of as groups embedded within larger groups had an impact on information processing in decision systems (Fombrun, 1983; Tushman, 1979). Organizations typically relied on diffuse, multiperson networks to process information on ill-structured decisions (Connolly, 1977). This work might be extended to include hierarchical information transmission, information absorption across different functional specializations, channel utilization, and information content.

Behavioral decision theorists employed both mechanistic and psychological perspectives on communication (Krone et al., Chapter 1, this volume). That is, decision theorists treated communication as the mechanistic transmission of decision premises from management to workers, the amount and direction of information flow in decision making, and the use of communication networks to process decision information. The psychological view of communication surfaced in research on cognitive aspects of information processing in organizations, particularly selective perception of information, inference deduction from messages, and perceptions of information adequacy and overload.

Recent research on information processing in decision making illustrates a more symbolic view of communication than did the early decision theorists. Tompkins and Cheney (1982, 1985) examined the evolution of decision premises as an enthymemic process inculcated by controlling members of organizations. Decision making in Weick's (1979) model functioned symbolically as "retrospective thinking" or justifications for past actions that could guide future behavior. Organizations, then, condensed decision information into symbolic systems that captured rich meanings of past organizational experiences (Daft & MacIntosh, 1981). Reacting with a nonrationalistic view, Feldman and March (1981) concluded that information processing in decision making symbolized social efficiency and organizational surveillance, not the use of data to make a rational choice. In this perspective, organizational decision making became a ritualistic process in which members demonstrated their competence, power, and commitment to the organization instead of their decision-making skills.

Systems Approaches

Organizational theorists who adopted general systems models directed attention away from single bivariate independent-dependent variables to research that focused on multiple factors simultaneously. Systems theory provided an overall framework for integrating this array of factors. Three concepts made up the core of systems theory: process, wholeness, and boundary. Katz and Kahn (1966) employed open systems theory as a way of integrating the small group dynamics literature with organizational context research, a logical extension of the human relations tradition.

Open systems theory posited that every organization was dependent on its environment to keep it viable; that is, the environment provided raw materials and other essential organizational inputs and organizations produced outputs that defined the nature of their environments. Systems theory, unlike classical and decision theorist approaches, focused on the *processes* that shaped patterned activity into stable but changing organizational structures. Organizations reached the same objectives through a number of different processes and decision paths—a principle known as equifinality. Moreover, the concept of *wholeness* suggested that each organization was part of a larger system and composed of smaller subsystems. Changes in one part of the system or subsystem reverberated throughout the entire system; thus each system influenced the actions of each subsystem and of the larger supersystem.

The concept of *boundary* referred to the relationship between an organization and its environment. Organizations that were very open had more permeable boundaries than closed ones that had restricted amounts of information crossing organizational perimeters. Information functioned as an input from the environment and as a by-product of organizing. Information flowed in restricted communication networks that defined and integrated the subsystems of an organization.

Since systems theory was developed at such an abstract level and was difficult to test, it was operationalized through a number of approaches that isolated different aspects of the framework. Conrad (1985) suggested that the principle of equifinality and the concepts of wholeness and boundary spawned different contingency theories that fell under the rubric of the systems approach. Two general classes of contingency theories that had direct implications for communication were environment and production technology.

Burns and Stalker (1961) distinguished between mechanistic and organic types of organizations based on their adaptation to stable or unstable environments. Mechanistic organizations with definite structures, high task specialization, clear hierarchy of control, and reliance on vertical communication and directives were better suited for stable conditions in the environment, while organic organizations with continual readjustment in structures, changes in task specialization, and reliance on information and advice were well-equipped to adapt to unstable conditions in the environment. In stable conditions, organizations engaged in less information search and in less extensive management of perceived ambiguity than in unstable situations (see Conrad, 1985; Huber and Daft, Chapter 5, this volume). Lawrence and Lorsch (1967) also studied the way that subunits differentiated and integrated reactions to their environments. Communication entered into their approach in the form of responses to information uncertainty and management of conflict between subsystems. They concurred with Burns and Stalker (1961) that the appropriate organization structure depended on environmental demands.

Contingency theories also centered on production technologies, specifically on the links between different types of technologies and the communication structures of organizations. Woodward (1965) distinguished among three types of task systems: small-batch, large-batch, and process technologies. Small-batch and process technologies relied on supportive climate and group-centered structures, while large-batch technologies adhered to vertical communication patterns and use of directives. Moreover, effectiveness for all three organizational types hinged on the development of structures consistent with the information-processing needs of their technologies. In general, nonroutine technologies relied more frequently on informal communication networks, decentralized decision making, and equal distribution of power than did routine production technologies.

The role of communication within the systems approach crossed a number of perspectives, but generally adhered to assumptions of the mechanistic and psychological views. The mechanistic notions were embedded in the way organizations processed and adapted to environmental information and the psychological views surfaced in research on information flow and perceptions of environmental uncertainty (see Huber and Daft, Chapter 5, this volume, for a review of the environmental uncertainty literature). Communication issues that emerged in systems theory included how information was developed in the environment; what communication channels were most effective for transmitting information into the organization; and how information was routed, summarized, and interpreted within the organization.

One of the problems in adopting systems theory into organizational communication research was correspondence between the dynamic, recursive models of organizing and the linear, static views of communication that researchers typically employed (Monge, 1982). Current views of organizational communication as process provide alternatives for assessing organizational variables over time (Monge, Farace, Eisenberg, Miller, & White, 1984). Also, research on control patterns of superiors and subordinates (Watson, 1982) and interaction systems of bargainers (Putnam & Jones, 1982) reflected efforts to apply systems views of communication to subsystems of organizational relationships.

Summary

Early classical and human relations theorists conceived of organizations either as structures in which individuals were passive participants or as individual needs in which structures and roles were secondary. Classical theorists treated communication as instruments of control systems, while human relations theorists centered on individual perceptions of supportiveness, superior-subordinate relationships. and participation in decision making. These theories, however, ignored the critical role of environment in shaping internal and external organizational processes; hence, they drew incomplete pictures of organizational life. Decision theorists in turn viewed communication as the processing of decision-relevant information. Systems theorists concentrated on the types of communication structures and subsystems that affect adaptation to organizational environments. Although it was difficult to operationalize systems theory, research efforts on contingency models laid a foundation for examining both communication and organizations as dynamic processes that interface with their environments.

ORGANIZATION-ENVIRONMENT THEORIES

Since the introduction of systems theory, a number of theoretical frameworks have been proposed to explain organizations as dynamic processes that interface with their environments. Three widely accepted contemporary approaches have particular relevance to the study of organizational communication: resource dependency theory, population ecology and the organizational life cycle model, and institutionalization theory. These theories represent substantial advances over traditional approaches with respect to their conceptualizations of organizational environments, their focus on organizations over time, and the research approaches they advocate for studying organizational issues (see Pfeffer, 1982; Scott, 1981). In particular, each theory treats the relationship between the environment and organization as complex and interactive, and considers how social and legal environment dimensions, as well as traditional technical and economic dimensions, affect and are affected by organizational phenomena. In addition, by incorporating the notion of organizational change into their respective theoretical foundations, each theory stresses the role of longitudinal research in exploring organization-environment relations.

Although each of the above theories views the environment as central to understanding organizational behavior/communication, the theories vary with respect to the relative importance they place on intraorganizational as compared to environmental factors in understanding phenomena. Moreover, the theories differ in their specific conceptualization of the notion of environment, and whether or not the environment should be viewed from an objective versus subjective perspective. With respect to conceptualization, the theories consider environments in one of two ways: as a source of information or as a resource pool. Theorists who view the environment as a source of information are concerned with the certainty/uncertainty of environments. Those who conceptualize the environment as a resource pool are concerned with power relationships. As the discussion in this section will demonstrate, how the environment is conceptualized is important because it directs researchers to distinctive communication-related environmental variables.

As noted above, there is little consensus among theorists concerning whether or not the environment should be viewed as a subjective or objective phenomenon (see Huber and Daft, Chapter 5, this volume). Those who assume the former perspective (for example, Dill, 1958; Duncan, 1972) argue that one should consider the environment subjectively because individuals can only respond to factors they can perceive. Weick (1969, 1979) takes this argument further by proposing that organizational members "enact" their environments—environments become what members perceive them to be. In stark contrast, other theorists (for example, Pfeffer and Salancik, 1978) take an objective view of the environment. They argue that the environment influences organizations whether or not individual members perceive it "correctly." Clearly, the perspective one assumes about the objectivity-subjectivity of the environment will affect how communication is operationalized and studied in organization-environment relations.

Finally, it is important to realize that the theories differ in their orientations to the process of organizational adaptation. Specifically, the theories can be differentiated by the extent to which they emphasize the adaptation/change process as a deterministic (environmentally determined) versus voluntaristic (proactive, self-directing) phenomenon (Astley & Van de Ven, 1983). Thus resource dependency theory assumes that to some degree an organization can proactively adapt its internal form and even change its environment, while the population ecology approach suggests that the environment "selects out" obsolete organizational forms and thereby determines internal adaptation. Analogously, one perspective implies that organization-environment communication and related information processing can be viewed as a proactive process, while the other approach denotes communication and information processing as a passive/reactive activity.

In light of the above issues, the following sections explicate the three theories—resource dependency, population ecology and organizational life cycle, and institutionalization theory—and considers their implications for organizational communication research. Since each theory focuses on the "macro" environments of organizations, this discussion will emphasize the manner in which macro environments may be related to "micro," internal organizational and interorganizational communication processes.

Resource Dependency Theory

The intellectual roots of resource dependency theory can be traced to both open systems theory and sociology (Emerson, 1962; Selznick, 1949; Thompson, 1967; Zald, 1970). The theory is founded on the assumption that organizations are dependent on their environments for resources and services required for survival. Thus the environment is viewed as a complex pool of scarce and vital resources, while organizations are conceptualized as coalitions that alter their structures and patterns of behavior to acquire needed resources. In this milieu, a manager's job is to improve or maintain his or her organization's resource exchange posture vis-à-vis other exchange partners.

Organizational uncertainty and interdependence are two critical variables in the resource dependency perspective. Pfeffer and Salancik (1978) argue that focal organizations can alter their interdependence with other elements in the environment in two ways: (1) they can absorb the other entities or (2) they can coordinate with other organizations to achieve mutual interdependence. Absorption of interdependence is usually achieved through merger, vertical integration, and diversification. In turn, coordination occurs when two or more organizations share power and develop social agreements that stabilize and coordinate mutual interdependence (Pfeffer & Salancik, 1978). Although total control of relationships with exchange partners is always the most desirable position for a focal organization, when control is not possible (for example, through vertical integration), achieving a high state of predictability with the exchange partner is the second best alternative. Essentially, it is assumed that the more members of different organizations interact, the more information and understanding they gain about each other. As a consequence, uncertainty is reduced and a predictable exchange pattern can develop. Coordination strategies include joint ventures, cooptation (for instance, interlocking boards of directors), normative control, and the development of trade associations.

Although largely couched in terms of environment-organization relationships, resource dependency theory also considers how environmental conditions affect intraorganizational political processes and structures. Pfeffer and Salancik (1978) argue that the environment influences the organization through its impact on the distribution of power inside the organization. This power distribution in turn influences who succeeds to administrative positions and therefore influences the character of the organization's decision making. The content of these decisions in turn affects the actions and structure of the organization. Thus, in contrast to the traditional management emphasis on formal control and consensus of goals, the focus in resource dependency theory is on social control. In other words, while the environment sets the stage for the distribution of power in organizations, it is through the interplay of various coalitions and interest groups within the organization that power is actually exercised. This view makes it important to understand the causes and consequences of coalition formation in organizations.

Communication implications. The resource dependency perspective suggests a variety of communication processes that should be examined in organizational research. In particular, communication processes associated with the management of interdependence represent an important focus for future research. With respect to absorption strategies, studies might explore the process of acquiring other organizations. Along these lines, researchers might consider how important (meaningful) and unimportant messages are differentiated from one another by members of acquiring and acquired organizations, how organizations with very different cultures find an acceptable communication "style," and how power relationships are negotiated between members of merged organizations.

Since most coordination strategies are founded on the notion of building and maintaining communication networks, the communication dynamics of coordination strategies are an obvious focus for research (see Eisenberg et al., 1985). For example, although *joint ventures* (the creation of a new organization by two parent companies) are in part designed to facilitate information exchange between organizations, few studies have examined (1) the communication process that characterize joint ventures or (2) the impact of joint ventures on other forms of communication between parent organizations. Another coordination strategy, *cooptation* (incorporating powerful, external persons into the organization's decision-making structure; see Selznick, 1949), requires additional communication research. In particular, studies might explore the communication network patterns of the most common form of cooptation, interlocking boards of directors (Burt, 1980; Pennings, 1981). The manner in which organizations accomplish *normative control* by transferring executives and other employees across organizational boundaries represents another relevant area for communication research. Not only can this strategy create vast communication networks for an organization, but it also may serve as a mechanism for communicating norms and values throughout a firm (Edstrom & Galbraith, 1977). Likewise, *trade associations*, which are designed to organize industries by creating communication networks among member firms, have been the focus of scant communication research. For example, studies could determine the manner in which competition among trade association members affects the information exchange process and communication networks among member firms. Relatedly, the communication strategies that associations use to exert political influence in their environments remains relatively unexplored.

As noted earlier, resource dependency theory proposes that the environment affects the internal dynamics of an organization through its impact on the distribution of power within an organization (Pfeffer & Salancik, 1978). Thus central to the theory are studies exploring the manner in which environmental information is sought or found by organizational members and utilized to affect internal power distributions. Along these lines, a number of studies have already investigated the strategies of power acquisition and use by coalitions in organizations. These strategies include controlling information used in decision making (Pettigrew, 1972), maintaining secrecy over the information used in decision making (Salancik & Pfeffer, 1978), advocating decision criteria favoring one's subunit (Pfeffer & Salancik, 1977), and altering the agenda of meetings by manipulating the order in which decisions are considered (Plott & Levine, 1978). Other studies have explored how boundary-spanning roles/groups within organizations acquire and use environmental information to increase their power in organizations (Adams, 1980).

Additional communication-related research is needed, however. Such studies should explore the communication dynamics of coalition formation, and consider the process by which common "meanings" are negotiated and shared across groups forming coalitions. These inquiries might build upon recent work exploring the social psychology of conflict, coalitions, and bargaining in organizations (see Bacharach & Lawler, 1980; Komorita, 1984; Putnam and Poole, Chapter 16, this volume). A recent theoretical framework proposed by Cook, Emerson, Gilmore, & Yamagish (1984) may also be useful in directing future research in this area. This framework is based on an exchange approach (Emerson, 1962), in which coalition formation is viewed as a power-gaining mechanism that has consequences for ongoing communication networks. By linking coalition formation, power processes, and social networks, the framework can be utilized to examine information exchanges between coalitions in organizations from a resource dependency perspective.

Population Ecology and Life Cycle Approaches

The intellectual roots of population ecology are in two disciplines, sociology (Hawley, 1950; Stinchcombe, 1965) and biology (Levins, 1964). The influence of biology distinguishes it the most from other organization-environment approaches; population ecologists have explicitly adopted a biological metaphor as a way to conceptualize changes in populations of organizations. In like fashion, life cycle theorists (for example, Kimberly, 1980) have adopted the same biological metaphor to understand the dynamics by which individual organizations are born, change, and disappear. Concomitantly, the two approaches hold in common the notion that organizations depend on their environments for needed resources. In other words, the environment is seen as a potent force that powerfully shapes the structure and functioning of the organization. The two theories, however, differ with respect to a number of other issues. Life cycle researchers cast their theories at the organizational level of analysis, whereas population ecologists focus on the rise and fall of forms/populations of organizations. In addition, while life cycle theorists assume that organizations are highly adaptive and that internal processes affect an organization's structure and ultimate survival, population ecologists assert that organizations are not adaptive but inertial. In their view the key mechanism of change is the natural selection process: "the differential reproduction and survival of organizations depending on competitive advantages" (Freeman, 1982, p. 2).

To summarize, population ecologists assume that external events determine organization characteristics, whereas life cycle theorists assume intra- and extraorganizational causes of change. Although the theories are couched at different levels of analysis, they both take a longitudinal perspective in which change is the focus of study. Population ecologists are interested in the net mortality of populations of organizations, and as a consequence explore the political (Carroll & Delacroix, 1982), economic (Freeman & Hannan, 1983), and social (Carroll & Huo, 1986) factors that effect the net mortality of populations of organizations in various niches or industries. In contrast, life cycle theorists are interested in the change and development of particular "focal" organizations (Cameron & Whetten, 1981).

Generally speaking, population ecologists and life cycle theorists have payed little attention to how the central constructs of their theories may influence the behavior of individuals and groups *inside* organizations (Sutton & Zald, 1985). Two exceptions to this trend are studies of organizational birth and death. Although the influence of organizational birth on the behavior of individuals and groups inside organizations is relatively unexplored, some evidence does indicate that the birth period has important and lasting influences on behavior in organizations (Stinchcombe, 1965). For instance, Boeker (1986) and Kimberly (1979) have found that background characteristics Of organizational founders have long-term effects on the structure, balance of power, and values of organizations. Similarly, the process of organizational death has been shown to affect individual and group behavior in organizations (Harris & Sutton, 1986; Taber, Walsh, & Cooke, 1979; Whetton, 1980). Sutton (1984), for example, found that during the process of organizational death an organization's best employees "jump ship" first, rumors are rampant, and that many employees have trouble accepting the death of their organization. Relatedly, Harris and Sutton (1986) report that parting ceremonies prior to the closing of organizations create environments in which employees can exchange mutual emotional support, and reconstruct a variety of schemas associated with their work lives.

Communication implications. The population ecology and organizational life cycle approaches offer numerous opportunities for organizational communication research (Jablin & Krone, 1987). With respect to organizational life cycles, scholars might devote attention to examining the communication components of organizational birth and death. For example, it would be valuable to know how founders use communication to develop and transmit the norms, values, and ideologies of their organizations to internal and external audiences (Miller, 1984). In turn, the manner in which communication processes change as organizations move from periods of growth and/or stability into periods of decline represents an important area of research. Studies along these lines might assess how the content of rumors, grapevine communication, volume of communication, and formal and informal communication structures vary as organizations proceed through life cycle phases (see Jablin, Chapter 12, and Monge and Eisenberg, Chapter 10, this volume).

Another issue that could be examined from a communication perspective is why organizations attempt to adapt to their environments by reorganizing their structures. Freeman and Hannan (1983) argue that reorganization may increase the probability of organizational death because it reduces performance reliability and generally increases internal and external uncertainty. Based on this reasoning, one could hypothesize that the longer an organization is undergoing reorganization, the more internal conflict it is experiencing, and, as a consequence, the higher the probability of organizational death. Research could explore the communication dynamics of the reorganizational process, and in particular assess (1) the communication patterns of top management during periods of reorganization, (2) communication processes associated with the escalation or deescalation of conflict among groups vying for control of the reorganization, and (3) the communication characteristics of "successful" as compared to "unsuccessful" reorganizations.

A number of Greiner's (1972) notions concerning phases of organizational growth and development are also amenable to communication research. Specifically, Greiner (1972) argues that growing organizations move through several phases of development, each of which contains a calm period of growth consummated by a period of crisis (which the leaders of the organization must resolve). Phase 1, for example, is the creativity period. According to Greiner, during this phase a company's leadership is usually entrepreneurially oriented. Communication among employees and owners is frequent and informal. This phase ends with a leadership crisis; entrepreneurial energies and skills are no longer sufficient for directing and controlling a larger and more complex organization. Researchers might conceptualize this crisis as a "breakdown" in the organization's communication system. Greiner argues that organizations typically survive the first phase by replacing the entrepreneur with a new manger who institutes formal control and communication procedures. According to Greiner (1972), subsequent phases alternate between an emphasis on formal and informal control systems and, by implication, communication systems. Obviously, each of these phases could be analyzed from a communication perspective. For example, the frequency, formality, type, and intensity of information exchange could be studied and linked to important issues of control, rewards, and survival in different industries over time.

Although still an infant area of study, population ecology has numerous implications for communication research. For example, while the concept of environmental niche is central to population ecology, we know little about the communication processes that facilitate or inhibit individuals and organizations from identifying "new" niches. Relatedly, researchers need to consider how different types of environmental niches constrain the formal and informal communication structures of organizations. Population ecologists frequently distinguish between two basic organization forms: specialists (organizations that serve a narrow range of markets) and generalists (organizations that offer a diversified range of products or services; Hannan & Freeman, 1977). The specific communication characteristics of specialist and generalist organizations, however, remain to be determined. Moreover, researchers should explore how interorganizational communication networks are used to diffuse variations in organizational forms within and between environmental niches (Katz, Levin, & Hamilton, 1963). In addition, the manner in which organizations use formalization of communication as a mechanism for retaining existing organization forms and structures deserves investigation (Aldrich, 1979). Research along these lines might also explore the communication strategies that powerful subunits within organizations use to resist the organizational adaptation process.

Institutionalization Theory

"Institutionalization involves the processes by which social processes, obligations, or actualities come to take on a rule-like status in social thought and action" (Meyer & Rowan, 1977, p. 341). As applied to organizations, "institutionalization operates to produce common understandings about what is appropriate and, fundamentally, meaningful behavior"(Zucker, 1983, p. 6). Specifically, institutionalization theory posits that organizations conform to the expectations of the environment by adapting "appropriate" (rational) structures and behaviors. In response, the organization is deemed legitimate by its environment and receives needed resources (financial support, generalized acceptance).

Institutionalization theorists argue that all organizations are required by society to conform to norms and expectations. However, for expositional purposes we suggest that there are two "ideal types" of organizations, technical and institutional. Technical organizations use structure to make work efficient; institutional organizations use structure to demonstrate conformity to social and cultural expectations/"myths" of what is rational and efficient. Whether or not an institutionalized organization is perceived of as legitimate by social, legal, and cultural forces in its environment determines its survival, not technical efficiency. The most important way that an organization communicates legitimacy is through its structure. Generally, structure includes size, shape, span of control, and staff makeup (see Jablin, Chapter 12, this volume). Organizations that appear rational via appropriate organizational structures will survive.

A fundamental argument of the theory is that an organization's structure does not necessarily support the work that goes on in the organization. Thus, in contrast to functionalist approaches to organizations (Chandler, 1966; Parsons, 1951), institutionalization theory does not support the notion that the multidivisional form of organization structure is desirable because of its superior coordinating and control capabilities. Rather, institutionalization theorists would reason that the multidivisional form is superior because society has deemed it efficient and rational. In essence, institutionalization theorists propose that because "shared" views concerning how an organization should be structured and operated exist in the environment,

> organizations import the form, if not the substance, of these rules and incorporate them in their structures, rules and reporting requirements. However, since such rules and structures may have little to do with how the work can or should get performed, in fact there is little impact on task performance and the behavior of those organizational members who actually do the work. (Pfeffer, 1982, p. 245)

To summarize, in general terms institutionalization theory is a theory of information acquisition, manipulation, and use. The core assumption of the theory is that the environment specifies the way rational organizations should look. In turn, a successful organization responds by developing a structure that is deemed appropriate/rational by its environment. An organization is considered legitimate and successful to the extent that it communicates to the environment that it is a modern, rational organization. Along these lines, Meyer and Rowan (1977) suggest that the success and survival of an organization in highly institutionalized environments is often due to the ability of top management to legitimize the organization with its external environment. Similarly, Pfeffer (1981) argues that in addition to legitimizing the organization externally, management must also develop systems of shared meanings and beliefs that legitimate and rationalize organizational decisions and policies internally. Pfeffer refers to this process of external and internal legitimation as symbolic management and views it as necessary not only to ensure support from the organization's environment, but also to ensure continued participation, compliance, and commitment on the part of organizational members.

To date, the theoretical and empirical focus of institutionalization theory has been on understanding the development of organizational structures, positions, and practices in terms of matching or fulfilling the expectations of the larger society (Ritti & Silver, 1986). In contrast, relatively little attention has been paid to exploring the implications of this process for analyzing and understanding intraorganizational behavior. However, results from the few studies in this area (Zucker, 1977, 1983) are generally supportive of the notion that "social knowledge once institutionalized exists as a fact, a part of objective reality, and can be transmitted directly on that basis" (Zucker, 1977, p. 726). As a consequence, institutionalized understandings may be associated with individual reactions to work environments (Lincoln, Hanada, & Olson, 1981), and normative control in the interactions of organizational members.

Communication implications. The institutionalizational perspective suggests a number of interesting directions for future communication research. One area particularly ripe for empirical research in organizations is symbolic management. Although there is a growing body of theoretical work in this area (see Pondy, Frost, Morgan, & Dandridge, 1983; Putnam & Pacanowsky, 1983), empirical research has not kept pace. Since most theorists argue that a primary activity of managers is explaining, legitimating, and rationalizing their organizations to intra- and extraorganizational audiences, studies need to explore the communication-based skills and processes associated with these activities (for a discussion of public relations and issue management strategies, see Cheney and Vibbert, Chapter 6, this volume). For instance, one time period when the communicative aspects of symbolic management are likely to be most pronounced and interesting is during organizational crises (such as a hostile takeover attempt). During these periods symbolic management is likely to be critical because of the need to reassure internal and external constituents that the organization is structured and operated in a rational and competent manner.

Organizations also attempt to manage the appearance of competence and rationality in more subtle ways. For example, analyses of annual reports

(Bettman & Weitz, 1983; Staw, McKechnie, & Puffer, 1983) indicate that organizations take credit for performance successes but attribute failures to external, uncontrollable factors in order to justify their performance to outside constituencies. Analysis of the language used in annual reports and other organization documents can provide valuable data about how organizations symbolically portray themselves to various internal and external audiences (see Cheney, 1983; Martin, Feldman, Hatch, & Sitkin, 1983). At the same time, studies exploring available documents from companies in the same industry might provide insight into how organizations are socialized into particular industries, how organizations make sense of their environments, and how organizations respond to sectors of their environments (e.g., Scott & Meyer, 1983).

Differences in the overall level of institutionalization of beliefs and activities within a group, organization, or industry may also have important implications for the nature of communication in these systems. One could hypothesize that the greater the degree of institutionalization, the more parsimonious, specialized, and potentially efficient the communication within an organization. At the same time, organizations high in institutionalization of beliefs and activities might be characterized by frequent interactions among employees. In other words, in these types of organizations communication would be facilitated because members would consensually share organizational and situational "meanings" (Brown & Lenneberg, 1954; Pfeffer & Moore, 1979; Zucker, 1983). Relatedly, these types of organizations may be extremely effective in assimilating organizational newcomers because of the consistency of information communicated to recruits by other members (Jablin, 1985; see also Jablin, Chapter 19, this volume).

The manner in which organizations characterized by different forms and levels of institutionalization communicate with one another also represents an important area of study. Seemingly, to the extent that shared definitions and understandings of two systems are similar, one would predict that communication between the systems would be parsimonious, efficient, and perhaps frequent (though frequency may vary over time). Conversely, communication between organizations with different levels and forms of institutionalization might exhibit more conflict. For example, more conflict may exist in business departments than in traditional academic departments (such as psychology or economics) since business professors come from diverse "meaning systems"/backgrounds (such as psychology, accounting, economics). Of course, there are potential negative consequences of shared definitions and meaning systems, such as groupthink (Janis, 1972) and reduced creativity (Nemeth, 1986).

A final area of research relevant to institutionalization theory and communication is concerned with the diffusion of innovations. Meyer and Rowan (1977) suggest that once an innovation is institutionalized by the environment, it is adopted and accepted by organizations not only because of its rational and technical properties, but because elements in the environment expect rational organizations to do so. As a consequence, Pfeffer (1982) observes that prior to its institutionalization the adoption of an innovation can "be predicted from rational or technical considerations but that after the innovation has been institutionalized, such factors account for less (if any) of the variance in adoption and acceptance" (p. 246). This view of the diffusion of innovations implies that researchers exploring communication networks associated with the diffusion process need to consider how the stage of innovation institutionalization may be affecting resulting network patterns. Such research might build upon distinctions between "early" and "late" adopters of innovations reported by Rogers and Shoemaker (1971).

Summary

In contrast to most of the traditional organization theories reviewed in the first section of this chapter, the three approaches discussed in this section—resource dependency theory, population ecology and the life cycle model, and institutionalization theory—explain organizations as dynamic processes that interface with their environments. However, although the theories all view the environment as an essential ingredient for understanding organizations, each theory assumes a somewhat unique approach to conceptualizing and studying the environment and its relationship to the organizing process. As evident form the preceding review, very little research has focused on exploring communication processes, attitudes, and behaviors that may be related to each of the theories. Consequently, we attempted to suggest avenues for communication research. In particular, our research suggestions emphasized the manner in which the "macro" environment variables associated with each theory may be related to "micro" intra- and extraorganizational communication processes. These research recommendations should be considered speculative in nature since the theories do not always directly consider communication-related issues. In addition, it should be noted that since communication research exploring each of the theories is still in its formative stages, we did not identify particular communication perspectives that might be more or less suitable for studying each theory. We believe each of the communication perspectives discussed by Krone et al. in Chapter 1 to be useful in examining various aspects of the theories.

CONCLUSION

This chapter has considered a wide range of organization theories and their implications for organizational communication research. In Table 2.1 we attempt to illustrate some of the important features of this literature. The seven theories covered in the chapter are listed in the rows of the table, and

TABLE 2.1

Comparison of Organizational Theories: Dimension

Theory	Characteristics	Communication	Environment
Classical	Authority structures Scientific management Specialization and formal roles Chain of command Formal rules and regulations	Formal channels and networks Downward-directed messages Unity of command Mechanistic perspective	Closed, formal, static systems
Human relations	Individual and social needs Work groups linking pins Job satisfaction	Informal interaction; supportive communication Participatory decision making Improving superior-subordinate communication; openness and trust Mechanistic and psychological perspectives	Internally dynamic Externally closed
Behavioral decision theorists	Specialization Limitations of rational decision making Uncertainty absorption Formal structure	Transmission of subunit goals and decision premises Incomplete information Filtered information; transmission of inferences Formal networks; diffuse networks Mechanistic, psychological, symbolic-interpretive perspectives	

Perspective		Communication	
Systems	Boundary Wholeness Process	Information as input from environment and output to environment Embedded, interdependent networks of subunits Patterned communication activities; processing environmental information Mechanistic, psychological and systems perspectives	Stable and unstable; open and closed Technical and economic Uncertainty
Resource dependency	Systems views Shifting coalitions Maximize exchange posture through absorption and coordination	Communication focused on reducing dependence Patterned communication activities Interorganizational networks Bargaining and negotiating All communication perspectives	Multi-dimensional Complex pool of resources
Population ecology	Systems view Optimal form survives Change over time Reorganizing Specialists versus generalists	Adaption of communication system to external demands Seeking information about niches Changes in communication structures over time Diffusion of organizational forms All communication perspectives	Multidimensional Selects organizations through competitive process Extends concept of uncertainty (frequency and amplitude)
Institutional	Systems view Formal structure "decoupled" from internal processes Adapt structure to form considered rational by society	Shared meanings "Legitimate" communication networks and procedures Myth-making and symbolic management Use of language Diffusion of innovations All communication perspectives	Multidimensional (social, legal, cultural, technical, and economic) Resource and information pool Source of legitimacy

three aspects of each theoretical framework—theory characteristics, communication, and environment—are described in the columns. The three dimensions differ substantially from theory to theory. It is these differences that we feel present the most fruitful issues for research. For example, within the "communication" dimension of classical theory, formal networks and channels of communication are important because they enhance control in organizations. Similarly, human relations theory focuses on networks, but emphasizes informal networks and channels of communication; these theorists consider networks to be important because they facilitate trust and commitment among organization members. In contrast, institutionalization theory focuses on both formal and informal communication networks, but shows little concern for the internal communication structure of organizations. Rather, institutionalization theory draws attention to organization-environment communication networks because such linkages serve to legitimate the organization. On the other hand, resource dependency theory focuses attention on how organizations adjust their communication networks and structure to reduce dependency on environmental elements. We hope that the above examples, extrapolated from Table 2.1 and based on the review presented in this chapter, demonstrate how comparing and contrasting the organization theories with one another can suggest important foci for communication-related research. Obviously, Table 2.1 does not present an exhaustive list of issues and variables, but it does illustrate an approach that may be useful for guiding future research.

To summarize, in exploring the communication implications of organization theories we have emphasized the importance of viewing organizations as dynamic processes that interface with their environments. Although many traditional theories did not include the environment as a relevant variable associated with organizational processes, more recent theories have recognized the impact of the environment on organizations. It is hoped that the communication implications we have drawn from these macro-oriented organization-environment theories will provide valuable directions for communication research exploring organization-environment relationships.

REFERENCES

Adams, J. S. (1980). Interorganizational processes and organizational boundary activities. In B. M. Staw & L. L. Cummings (Eds.), *Research in organizational behavior* (Vol. 2, pp. 321-355). Greenwich, CT: JAI Press.

Aldrich, H. E. (1979). *Organizations and environments.* Englewood Cliffs, NJ: Prentice-Hall.

Argyris, C. (1957). *Personality and organization.* New York: Harper & Row.

Astley, W. G., & Van de Ven, A. H. (1983). Central perspectives and debates in organizational theory. *Administrative Science Quarterly, 28,* 245-273.

Bacharach, S. B., & Lawler, E. J. (1980). *Power and politics in organizations.* San Francisco: Jossey-Bass.

Bavelas, A. (1950). Communication patterns in task oriented groups. *Journal of the Acoustical Society of America, 22,* 725-730.

Bennis, W. (1969). *Organizational development: Its nature, origins, and prospects.* Reading, MA: Addison-Wesley.

Bettman, J. R., & Weitz, B. A. (1983). Attributions in the board room—causal reasoning in corporate annual reports. *Administrative Science Quarterly, 28,* 165-183.

Blake, R., & Mouton, J. (1964). *The managerial grid.* Houston: Gulf.

Blankenship, L. V., & Miles, R. E. (1986). Organizational structure and managerial decision behavior. *Administrative Science Quarterly, 13,* 106-120.

Boeker, W. (1986). *Organizational origins: Effects of firm founding on organizational strategy and inter-departmental influences.* Unpublished doctoral dissertation, University of California, Berkeley.

Brown, R., & Lennenberg, E. H. (1954). A study in language and cognition. *Journal of Abnormal and Social Psychology, 59,* 454-462.

Burns, T., & Stalker, G. M. (1961). *The managment of innovation.* London: Tavistock.

Burt, R. S. (1980). Cooptive corporate actor networks. *Administrative Science Quarterly, 25,* 557-582.

Cameron, K. S., & Whetten, D. A. (1981). Perceptions of organizational effectiveness over the life cycle. *Administrative Science Quarterly, 26,* 525-544.

Campbell, D. T. (1958). Systematic error on the part of human links in communication systems. *Information and Control, 1,* 334-369.

Carroll, G. R., & Delacroix, J. (1982). Organizational mortality in the newspaper industries of Argentina and Ireland: An ecological approach. *Administrative Science Quarterly, 27,* 169-198.

Carroll, G. R., & Huo, Y. P. (1986). Organizational task and institutional environments in ecological perspective: Findings from the local newspaper industry. *American Journal of Sociology, 91,* 838-873.

Chandler, A. D., Jr. (1966). *Strategy and structure.* Garden City, NY: Doubleday, Anchor Books.

Cheney, G. (1983). The rhetoric of identification and the study of organizational communication. *Quarterly Journal of Speech, 69,* 143-158.

Cook, K. S., R. M. Emerson, M. R. Gillmore, & Yamagisha, T. (1983). The distribution of power in exchange networks—theory and experimental results. *American Journal of Sociology, 89,* 275-305.

Connolly, T. (1977). Information processing and decision making in organizations. In B. M. Staw & G. R. Salancik (Eds.), *New directions in organizational behavior* (pp. 205-234). Chicago: St. Clair Press.

Conrad, C. (1985). *Strategic organizational communication: Cultures, situations, and adaptation.* New York: Holt, Rinehart, & Winston.

Cyert, R. M. & March, J. G. (1963). *A behavioral theory of the firm.* Englewood Cliffs, NJ: Prentice-Hall.

Daft, R. L., & MacIntosh, N. B. (1981). A tentative exploration into the amount and equivocality of information processing organizational work units. *Administrative Science Quarterly, 26,* 207-224.

Davis, K. (1953). Management communication and the grapevine. *Harvard Business Review, 31*(5), 43-49.

Dill, W. (1958). Environments as an influence on managerial autonomy. *Administrative Science Quarterly, 2,* 409-443.

Downs, A. (1967). *Inside bureaucracy.* Boston: Little, Brown.

Duncan, R. B. (1972). Characteristics of organizational environments and perceived environmental uncertainty. *Administrative Science Quarterly, 17,* 313-327.

Edstrom, A., & Galbraith, J. R. (1977). Transfer of managers as a coordination and control strategy in multinational organizations. *Administrative Science Quarterly, 22,* 248-263.

Eisenberg, E. M., Farace, R. V., Monge, P. R., Bettinghaus, E. P., Kurchner-Hawkins, R., Miller, K. I., & Rothman, L. (1985). Communication linkages in interorganizational systems: Review and synthesis. In B. Dervin & M. Voight (Eds.), *Progress in communication sciences* (Vol. 6, pp. 231-262). New York: Ablex.

Emerson, R. M. (1962). Power-dependence relations. *American Sociological Review, 27*, 31-41.

Fayol, H. (1949). *General and industrial management* (C. Storrs, Trans.). London: Pitman.

Feldman, M. S., & March, J. G. (1981). Information in organizations as signal and symbol. *Administrative Science Quarterly, 26*, 171-186.

Ference, T. P. (1970). Organizational communications systems and the decision process. *Management Science, 17*, B83-B96.

Fombrun, C. (1983). Attributions of power across a social network. *Human Relations, 36*, 493-508.

Freeman, J. (1982). Organizational life cycles and natural selection processes. In B. M. Staw & L. L. Cummings (Eds.), *Research in organizational behavior* (Vol. 4, pp. 1-32). Greenwich, CT: JAI Press.

Freeman, J., & Hannan, M. T. (1983). Niche width and the dynamics of organizational populations. *American Journal of Sociology, 88*, 1116-1145.

Greiner, L. E. (1972). Patterns of organization change. *Harvard Business Review, 45*(4), 119-130.

Guetzkow, H., & Simon, H. A. (1955). The impact of certain communication nets upon organization and performance in task-oriented groups. *Management Science, 1*, 233-250.

Gulick. L., & Urwick, L. (Eds.). (1937). *Papers on the science of administration.* New York: Columbia University, Institute of Public Administration.

Hage, J. (1974). *Communication and organizational control: Cybernetics in health and welfare settings.* New York: John Wiley.

Hannan, M. T., & Freeman, J. H. (1977). The population ecology of organizations. *American Journal of Sociology, 82*, 929-964.

Harris, S. G., & Sutton, R. I. (1986). Functions of parting ceremonies in dying organizations. *Academy of Management Journal, 29*, 5-30.

Hawley, A. (1950). *Human ecology.* New York: Ronald Press.

Jablin, F. M. (1985). Task/work relationships: A life-span perspective. In M. L. Knapp & G. R. Miller (Eds.), *Handbook of interpersonal communication* (pp. 615-654). Newbury Park, CA: Sage.

Jablin, F. M. (1986). The study of organizational communication: Its evolution and future. In N.C.F Collado & G. L. Dahnke (Eds.), *La Comunicacion Humana Coma Ciencis Social [The Social Science of Communication]* (pp. 111-142). Mexico City: McGraw Hill de Mexico.

Jablin, F. M. & Krone, K. (1987). Organizational assimilation and levels of analysis in organizational communication research. In C. R. Berger & S. H. Chaffee (Eds.), *Handbook of communication science* (pp. 711-746). Newbury Park, CA: Sage.

Janis, I. L. (1972). *Victims of groupthink.* Boston: Houghton Mifflin.

Julian, J. (1966). Compliance patterns and communication blocks in complex organizations. *American Sociological Review, 31*, 382-387.

Katz, D., & Kahn, R. (1966). *The social psychology of organizations.* New York: John Wiley.

Katz, E., Levin, M. L., & Hamilton, H. (1963). Traditions of research on the diffusion of innovation. *American Sociological Review, 28*, 237-252.

Kimberly, J. R. (1979). Issues in the creation of organizations: Initiation, innovation, and institutionalization. *Academy of Management Journal, 22*, 437-457.

Kimberly, J. R. (1980). The life cycle analogy and the study of organizations. In J. R. Kimberly, R. H. Miles, & associates (Eds.), *The organizational life cycle* (pp. 1-17). San Francisco: Jossey-Bass.

Komorita, S. S. (1984). Effects of alternatives in coalition bargaining. *Journal of Experimental Psychology, 20*, 116-136.

Lawrence, R. R., & Lorsch, J. W. (1967). *Organization and environment: Managing differentiation and integration.* Cambridge, MA: Harvard University Press.

Leavitt, H. J. (1951). Some effects of certain communication patterns on group performance. *Journal of Abnormal and Social Psychology, 46*, 38-50.

Levins, R. (1964). Theory of fitness in a heterogeneous environment: The fitness set and adaptative function. *American Naturalist, 96*, 361-78.

Lewin, K. (1943). Psychology and the process of group living. *Journal of Social Psychology, 17*, 119-129.

Likert, R. (1967). *The human organization*. New York: McGraw-Hill.

Lincoln, J. R., Hanada, M., & Olson, J. (1981). Cultural orientations and individual reactions to organizations: A study of employees of Japanese-owned firms. *Administrative Science Quarterly, 26*, 93-115.

March, J. G., & Simon, H. A. (1958). *Organizations*. New York: John Wiley.

Martin, J., Feldman, M., Hatch, M., & Sitkin, S. (1983). The uniqueness paradox in organizational stories. *Administrative Science Quarterly, 28*, 438-453.

Mayo, E. (1960). *The social problems of an industrial civilization*. New York: Viking.

McGregor, D. (1960). *The human side of enterprise*. New York: McGraw-Hill.

Meyer, J. W., & Rowan, B. (1977). Institutionalized organizations: Formal structure as myth and ceremony. *American Journal of Sociology, 83*, 340-363.

Miller, V. D. (1984, May). *Ideology, communication, and the life cycle of organizations*. Paper presented at the annual meeting of the International Communication Association, Dallas.

Monge, P. R. (1982). Systems theory and research in the study of organizational communication: The correspondence problem. *Human Communication Research, 8*, 245-261.

Monge, P. R., Farace, R. V., Eisenberg, E. M., Miller, K. I., & White, L. L. (1984). The process of studying process in organizational communication. *Journal of Communication, 34*, 22-43.

Mooney, J. D., & Reiley, A. C. (1939). *The principles of organization*. New York: Harper & Row.

Nemeth, C. J. (1986). Differential contributions of majority and minority influence. *Psychological Review, 93*, 23-32.

O'Reilly, C. A., & Roberts, K. H. (1974). Information filtration in organization: Three experiments. *Organizational Behavior and Human Performance, 11*, 253-265.

Parsons, T. (1951). *The social system*. New York: Free Press.

Pennings, J. M. (1981). Strategically interdependent organizations. In P. C. Nystrom & W. H. Starbuck (Eds.), *Handbook of organizational design* (Vol. 1, pp. 443-455). London: Oxford University Press.

Pettigrew, A. M. (1972). Information control as a power resource. *Sociology, 6*, 187-204.

Pfeffer, J. (1981). Management as symbolic action: The creation and maintenance of organizational paradigms. In L. L. Cummings & B. M. Staw (Eds.), *Research in organizational behavior* (Vol. 3, pp. 1-52). Greenwich, CT: JAI Press.

Pfeffer, J. (1982). *Organizations and organization theory*. Boston: Pitman.

Pfeffer, J., & Salancik, G. R. (1977). Administrator effectiveness: The effects of advocacy and information on resource allocations. *Human Relations, 30*, 641-656.

Pfeffer, J., & Salancik, G. R. (1978). *The external control of organizations: A resource dependence perspective*. New York: Harper & Row.

Pfeffer, J., & Moore, W. L. (1979). Average tenure of academic department heads—the effects of paradigm, size and departmental demography. *Administrative Science Quarterly, 25*, 387-406.

Plott, C. R., & Levine, M. E. (1978). A model of agenda influence on committee decisions. *American Economic Review, 68*, 146-160.

Pondy, L. R., Frost, P. J., Morgan, G., & Dandridge, T. C. (Eds.). (1983). *Organizational symbolism*. Greenwich, CT: JAI Press.

Putnam, L. L., & Cheney, G. (1985). Organizational communication: Historical development and future directions. In T. W. Benson (Ed.), *Speech communication in the 20th century* (pp. 130-156). Carbondale: Southern Illinois University Press.

Putnam, L. L., & Jones, T. S. (1982). Reciprocity in negotiations: An analysis of bargaining interaction. *Communication Monographs, 49*, 171-191.

Putnam, L. L., & Pacanowsky, M. E. (Eds.). (1983). *Communication and organizations: An interpretive approach.* Newbury Park, CA: Sage.

Ritti, R. R., & Silver, J. H. (1986). Early processes of institutionalization: The dramaturgy of exchange in interorganizational relations. *Administrative Science Quarterly, 31,* 25-41.

Roberts, K. H., & O'Reilly, C. A., Bretton, G. E., & Porter, L. W. (1974). Organizational theory and organizational communication: A communication failure. *Human Relations, 27,* 501-524.

Roethlisberger, F. J., & Dickson, W. J. (1939). *Management and the worker.* Cambridge, MA: Harvard University Press.

Rogers, E., & Shormaker, F. (1971). *Communication of innovation.* New York: Free Press.

Rose (1965). AEto comeAF

Rosen, S., & Tesser, A. (1970). On reluctance to communicate undersirable information: The MUM effect. *Sociometry, 33,* 253-263.

Salancik, G. R., & Pfeffer, J. (1978). Uncertainty, secrecy, and the choice of similar others. *Social Psychology, 41,* 246-255.

Schein, E. (1965). *Organizational psychology.* Englewood Cliffs, NJ: Prentice-Hall.

Scott, W. R. (1981). *Organizations: Rational, natural, and open systems.* Englewood Cliffs, NJ: Prentice-Hall.

Scott, W. R., & Meyer, J. W. (1983). The organization of societal sectors. In J. W. Meyer & W. R. Scott (Eds.), *Organizational environments,* (pp. 129-154). Newbury Park, Ca: Sage.

Selznick, P. (1949). *TVA and the grass roots.* Berkeley: University of California Press.

Shaw, M. C. (1954). Group structure and the behavior of individuals in small groups. *Journal of Psychology, 38,* 139-149.

Simon, H. (1945). *Administrative behavior.* New York: Macmillan.

Smith, C. G., & Brown, M. E. (1964). Communication structure and control structure in a voluntary association. *Sociometry, 27,* 449-468.

Staw, B., McKechnie, P., & Puffer, S. (1983). The justification of organizational performance. *Administrative Science Quarterly, 28,* 582-600.

Stinchcombe, A. L. (1965). Social structures and organizations. In J. G. March (Ed.), *Handbook or Organizations* (pp. 142-193). Chicago: Rand McNally.

Sutton, R. I. (1984). *Organizational death.* Unpublished doctoral dissertation, University of Michigan, Ann Arbor.

Sutton, R. I., & Porter, L. W. (1968). A study of the grapevine in a governmental organization. *Personal Psychology, 21,* 223-230.

Sutton, R. I., & Zald, M. N. (1984). *The demise of couples, organizations, communities, and regimes: a multi-level analysis.* Paper presented at the American Sociological Association, Washington, D.C.

Taber, T. D., Walsh, J. T., & Cooke, R. A. (1979). Developing a community-based program for reducing the social impact of a plant closing. *Journal of Applied Behavior, 15,* 133-155.

Tannenbaum, A. (1966). *Social psychology of the work organization.* Belmont, CA: Wadsworth.

Taylor, F. W. (1911). *Scientific management.* New York: Harper.

Thompson, J. (1967). *Organizations in action.* New York: McGraw-Hill.

Tichy, N., Tushman, M., & Fombrun, C. (1979). Social network analysis for organizations. *Academy of Management Review, 4,* 507-519.

Tompkins, P. K. (1984). Functions of communication in organizations. In C. Arnold & J. W. Bowers (Eds.), *Handbook of rhetorical and communication theory* (pp. 659-713). Boston: Allyn & Bacon.

Tompkins, P. K., & Cheney, G. (1982, November). *Toward a theory of unobtrusive control in contemporary organizations.* Paper presented at the annual meeting of the Speech Communication Association, Louisville, KY.

Tompkins, P. K., & Cheney, G. (1985). Communication and unobtrusive control in contemporary organizations. In R. D. McPhee & P. K. Tompkins (Eds.), *Organizational communication: Traditional themes and new directions* (pp. 179-210). Newbury Park, CA: Sage.

Tushman, M. L. (1979). Impacts of perceived environmental variability on patterns of work related communication. *Academy of Management Journal, 22*, 482-500.

Tushman, M. L., & Romanelli, E. (1985). Organizational evolution: A metamorphosis model of convergence and reorientation. In L. L. Cummings & B. M. Staw (Eds.), *Research in organizational behavior* (Vol. 7, pp. 171-222). Greenwich, CT: JAI Press.

Watson, K. M. (1982). An analysis of communication patterns: A method for discriminating leader and subordinate roles. *Academy of Management Journal, 25*, 107-120.

Weber, M. (1957). *The theory of social and economic organization.* New York: Free Press.

Weick, K. (1969). *The social psychology of organizing.* Reading, MA: Addison-Wesley.

Weick, K. E. (1979). *The social psychology of organizing* (2nd ed.). Reading, MA: Addison-Wesley.

Weick, K. E. (1986). *Interpretive sources of high reliability: Remedies for normal accidents.* Working paper, Graduate School of Business, University of Texas at Austin.

Weinshall, T. (1966). The communicogram. In J. R. Lawrence (Ed.), *Operational research and the social sciences* (pp. 533-619). London: Tavistock.

Whetton, D. A. (1980). Organizational decline: A neglected topic in organizational science. *Academy of Management Review, 4*, 577-788.

Woodward, J. (1965). *Industrial organization: theory and practice.* Oxford, England: Oxford University Press.

Zald, M. N. (1970). Political economy: A framework for comparative analysis. In M. N. Zald (Ed.), *Power in organizations* (pp. 221-261). Nashville, TN: Vanderbilt University Press.

Zammuto, R. F., & Cameron, K. S. (1985). Environmental decline and organizational response. In L. L. Cummings & B. M. Staw (Eds.), *Research in organizational behavior* (Vol. 7, pp. 223-262). Greenwich, CT: JAI Press.

Zucker, L. G. (1977). The role of institutionalization in cultural persistence. *American Sociological Review, 42* 726-743.

Zucker, L. G. (1983). Organizations as institutions. In S. B. Bacharach (Ed.), *Research in the sociology of organizations* (Vol 2, pp. 1-47). Greenwich, CT: JAI Press.

3 Translating Organizational Theory: Symbolism Over Substance

PHILLIP K. TOMPKINS
University of Colorado, Boulder

> Is it certain that there corresponds to the word *communication* a unique, univocal concept, a concept that can be rigorously grasped and transmitted: a communicable concept? Following a strange figure of discourse, one first must ask whether the word or signifier "communication" communicates a determined content, an identifiable meaning, a describable value. But in order to articulate and to propose this question, I already had to anticipate the meaning of the word *communication:* I have had to predetermine communication as the vehicle, transport, or site of passage of a *meaning,* and a meaning that is *one.* (Derrida, 1982, p. 309)

The question posed here by Derrida is important, difficult, basic, even foundational. It is important to the entire book of which this chapter is but a small part; it is crucial to this chapter because the assignment given me by the editors was this: Show the extent and the manner in which the concept of communication is central—even if *implicit*—in the genealogy of texts we refer to collectively as organization/management theory. The assignment itself, like Derrida's question, anticipated and predetermined that *communication* is itself a communicable concept of an identifiable meaning. By accepting the assignment I accepted the anticipation and predetermination of communication.

Nonetheless, the answer to Derrida's question must be both yes and no.

"Yes" is the answer given by the editors and the writers who have contributed to this book. "No" is the answer any reader must give after searching out the explicit and sometimes implicit definitions of communication used throughout this book. Communication is a polysemic word, a concept of multiple meanings. This chapter acknowledges this polysemic condition and urges the reader to be sensitive to the subtle and not-so-subtle differences in meaning suggested by the range of terms used by authors of organizational theory as well as by authors of communication theory. To anticipate just a few of the different terms used by organization/management theorists that we shall encounter, I preview these: communication, command, control, persuasion, propaganda, hegemony, information processing, bargaining, negotiations, coordination, and feedback. Other terms will enter into this discussion of our polysemic concept and it is useful at this point to warn the reader of distinctions that make a *difference* in meaning: Indeed, even the meanings of *meaning* will be seen to be the many, not *one*.

This chapter unfolds in the following sequence: (1) a review of the explicit (and implicit) reliance on the concept of communication in organization/management theories; (2) the placement of organization/management theory in the history of thought concerning communication and its ancestor, rhetorical theory; (3) the testing of ontological and epistemological conclusions drawn from the first two points in the sequence by application to the "hardest," most "metrical" of the social sciences—economics; and (4) a summary and peroration.

COMING TO TERMS WITH ORGANIZATION THEORY

Dewey, Wittgenstein, and Heidegger . . . hammer away at the holistic point that words take their meanings from other words rather than by virtue of their representative character, and the corollary that vocabularies acquire their privileges from the men who use them rather than from their transparency to the real. (Rorty, 1979, p. 368)

The history of the field of organizational communication has recently been set forth by Redding (1985) and Tompkins and Redding (in press); it will not be rehearsed here. It is noteworthy, however, that long before there was such a field as organizational communication, organization and management theorists incorporated communication as a central concept in their theories. My arguments in support of this assertion are available elsewhere (Tompkins, 1984) and there is no need to repeat them. It will suffice to repeat the 11 communication propositions derived from the work of Fayol (1925/1949), Taylor (1911/1947), Weber (1947), Mayo (1933, 1949), Roethlisberger and Dickson (1939), Follett (1941), Argyris (1957), McGregor (1960), Likert (1961), Simon (1957), and Barnard (1938/1968) as illustrative of this stance:

(1) Organizational communication principles—like management principles—can be isolated, codified, and communicated to organizational members (Fayol, Barnard, and others).

(2) Unity of command—a member should receive orders from a single superior—is the prevailing principle (Fayol and others), even though plurality of command—as with functional supervision—has been vigorously espoused (Taylor).

(3) Oral, face-to-face communication is preferred in most cases because of speed (Fayol and others), morale or esprit de corps (Fayol), and immediate feedback (or "circular behavior" in Follett).

(4) Communicative situations—particularly those involving the superior-subordinate dyad—are constantly evolving, creating the need for both parties to adjust to the environment as well as to each other (Follett).

(5) Written communication (committing oral interactions to memoranda [as an "external memory"] is favored as a means of establishing organizational continuity, if not permanence (Weber).

(6) Organizational persuasion is necessary to bring about radical changes in work procedures (Taylor), to recruit new members and inculcate motives (Barnard), and to represent work groups "upward" and "downward" (Likert).

(7) Upward communication serves several necessary functions—for example, in discovering members' practices (as in attitudes and norms [the Harvard group], and in discovering work-group positions on task questions [Likert]).

(8) The formal channels of communication help create and maintain authority, as well as give authenticity to messages (Barnard), but they also inhibit communication; indeed, they alienate members (Argyris and others).

(9) Partly in response to principle 8, members develop informal norms and informal channels that are at odds with the formal channels (the Harvard group); yet it is the informal system that gives rise to formal organization, which provides necessary support for formal organization (Barnard).

(10) Decision making in organizations is determined by the communication of premises, factual and value (Simon), and by the degree to which all members participate (Likert).

(11) Two contradictory constellations of principles have emerged on the basic issue of centralization-decentralization. Like rhetorical theorists, the writers surveyed here defined the audience—those people who are to be organized or managed—in different ways. The classical writers assumed that humans require close scrutiny; the modern or humanistic theorists assumed that organization members are capable of self-direction and self-scrutiny. I hold that the degree of heterogeneity represented by the organization members of our culture alone—those who people such organizations as construction companies, sanitation departments, and universities—provides validity to both constellations of principles [Tompkins, P. K. (1984). The functions of human communication in organization. In C. Arnold and J. W. Bowers (Eds.), *Handbook of rhetorical and communication theory* (pp. 659-713). Boston: Allyn & Bacon. Copyright 1984 by Phillip K. Tompkins. Reprinted by permission of the author].

This synthesis, originally written in 1977, does in fact measure many of the lexical variations of our central concept: communication, command, feedback, persuasion and its variant rhetoric, as well as such ancillary terms as *channels* and *audiences*. It even anticipates a highly fashionable word connected to organizational studies in the 1980s: culture. I would modify proposition 5 so as to acknowledge the later realization that Weber probably stressed written communication over oral for its *rationality* as well as its permanence (see his attribution of the potential for irrationality and prerationality to the practice of oral communication, especially oratory and charismatic discourse; Weber, 1978).

Another classical writer, Karl Marx (1843/1967)—more famous for his macroscopic analysis of political and economic forces—also lent his genius to the analysis of bureaucracy and, yes, even organization as communication. In his Feuerbachian "Critique of Hegel's Philosophy of the State," written in 1843, Marx challenges Hegel's treatment of democracy, bureaucracy, and voting.

Hierarchy of Information

Marx's analysis of bureaucracy, that organizational apparatus of civil society as well as the state, seems almost a century and a half later a freshly modern, perhaps even postmodern, treatment; I shall put it under the general heading of "Hierarchy of Information," a phrase embedded in his prose. Notice the argument: "Bureaucracy is a circle no one can leave. Its hierarchy is a hierarchy of information. The top entrusts the lower circles with an insight into details, while the lower circles entrust the top with an insight into what is universal, and thus they mutually deceive each other" (Marx, 1843/1967, pp. 185-186). His concept of the circular hierarchy of information has a modern appeal to both academic theorists and corporate consultants. Marx emphasizes that "the universal spirit of bureaucracy is the secret, the mystery sustained within bureaucracy itself by hierarchy and maintained on the outside as a closed corporation" (p. 186). This universal spirit, the secret, is a category of information intended for internal organizational communicative consumption but banned from external communication.

Marx (1843/1967) methodically scatters insights into and observations about both bureaucracy and bureaucrats in his critique:

[It] is obvious that "bureaucracy" is a web of practical illusions. (p. 185)

For the individual bureaucrat the state's purpose becomes his private purpose of hunting for higher positions and making a career for himself. (p. 186)

Everything has a double meaning, a real and a bureaucratic meaning. (p. 186)

And indeed bureaucracy is only the "formalism" of a content lying outside. (p. 184)

These aphorisms have traction with contemporary theoretical issues. For example, the metaphor of organization as "web of practical illusions" can stand as an adumbration of the organizational culturalists' favorite figure, the web. For a second example, Marx's comments about the tendency toward the transformation of a public, collective purpose into a private, individual purpose has been asserted by numerous writers, most exhaustively by Georgiou (1973/1981). For a third example, the distinction between *a real meaning* and *a bureaucratic meaning* foreshadowed still another concept of interest to theorists in communication, criticism, cognitive science, anthropology, and the "symbols and meaning" school of organizational culture. After Rorty's (1979) critique of the correspondence philosophy of knowledge, however, we cannot today accept Marx's use of the term *real meaning.* I suggest a distinction between *bureaucratic* meaning and *individualistic* meaning (with the latter being the meaning assigned to events as perceived from any position other than a formal organizational role). And while bureaucratic meaning may not be limited to language or vocabulary, *it is at least a system of signifiers.* Nearly all languages have disrupted into dialectics; so it is with organizational languages. Dialects help define the subcultures of department, division, and the informal organization. Dialects also help define the counterculture of unions and other hostile subgroups. We learn meaning by learning words and "words take their meanings from other words" (Rorty, 1979, p. 368).

It is Marx's characterization of organization as a "circular" hierarchy of information, however, that could well be used to make a transition to the quasi-phenomenological theorizing of a writer of considerable influence on organizational communication, Karl Weick (1979). Recall Weick's characterization of organizations as loops or circles, whether virtuous or vicious, the content of which is not so important as their patterns. Despite being the author of a book titled *The Social Psychology of Organizing,* if Weick has not written a treatise on our "communicable concept" of communication, he has certainly fooled the professors of organizational communication.

Appropriating Concepts

In this section, I contend that influential ideas in the field of communication have been appropriated and translated from other disciplines. Why do organizational communication scholars tend to borrow concepts from other organizational sciences? The answer lies in the notion of common intertextualities. To demonstrate this point we trace the borrowing of the concept of "retrospective meaning." Johnson's (1977) *Communication: The Process of Organizing* is derivative of Weick's (1969/1979) *The Social Psychology of Organizing.* The influence can be seen in the titles of the two books. Johnson substitutes communication for social psychology and claims that her central signifier is "the one process" of organizing. Johnson places the concept of meaning at the center of her text and her heading, "Retrospection and Meaning," is derivative of Weick's "Retrospective Sense-Making," which in turn is derivative of Schutz's (1967) phenomenology.

Schutz's phenomenological approach itself has starting points, summarized by the author of the introduction to the English translation of *The Phenomenology of the Social World* (1967) in this succinct statement: "Now, since Schutz agrees with Weber that action is defined through meaning, the first positive step of his theory is to formulate a concept of meaning. At this stage he relies heavily upon Husserl" (Walsh, 1967, p. xxiii). Thus our trail of intertextual influences runs thus: Weber (and Husserl) → Schutz → Weick → Johnson. Note that these writers claimed to be declaring allegiance to this pattern: Sociology → Philosophy → Social Psychology → Organizational Communication. It is a hazardous game—if at all even playable—to identify ideas, conceptualizations, and theories with one branch or another of contemporary organizational studies, if not the whole of the contemporary "human sciences."

This is not to say that Johnson failed to give a communicative twist to her treatment of retrospective meaning. And that may be the gist of disciplinary distinctiveness today—a disciplinary twist or linguistic perspective on ideas, conceptualizations, and theories that circulate freely between and among the disciplines. Ideas common to the different fields within organizational studies are given a "bureaucratic meaning" by each separate field. Communication as a field, as opposed to the concept, appears to be a perspective, an angle, a point of view capable of assimilating and reinterpreting almost any idea generated in sister disciplines.

The point can be illustrated in another way by a more recent textbook influenced by Weick: Gary L. Kreps's (1986) *Organizational Communication: Theory and Practice*. Weick's influence is suggested in the first chapter title—"Communicating and Organizing"—and is demonstrated in the title of chapter 6—"Weick's Model of Organizing." Notice how Kreps is able to appropriate Weick's social psychological theory to his own, his *communication* purpose.

> In 1969, Karl Weick published his influential book, *The Social Psychology of Organizing,* in which he presented a process-oriented model of organizing, stressing human interaction as the central phenomenon of organization. Weick contends that organizations do not exist but are in the process of existing through continual streams of organized human activities. Communication is the crucial process performed by organization members to enable this ongoing organization to occur. In the theory, Weick traces the specific communicative activities in which individuals engage to demonstrate organization and describes the information-processing functions of organizing. (Kreps, 1986, p. 112)

Kreps reduces Weick's theory to "three primary components: sociocultural evolutionary theory, information theory, and systems theory" (p. 112). These components add up to the "crucial process" of communicating as organizing, despite the fact that evolutionary theory is inconsistent with a meaning-centered approach (Cheney, 1986). How Weick feels about being appropriated in this way by another field is not important. It is important that our concept of communication is capable of transforming an eclectic approach developed under the rubric of social psychology into something of its own. Organizational communication gives indication of an imperial, if not imperious, attitude.

Kreps also takes over the Weber-Schutz-Weick position on "retrospective meanings" and adds "prospective meanings," explaining that the former "interpret what has happened in the organization," while the latter "develop visions of where the organization will go and what organization members should do" (Kreps, 1986, p. 147). Weick, then, has been interpreted in such a way that makes his work central to organizational communication. I hasten to add *interpreted*. With our distinction between bureaucratic meaning and individualistic meaning, it could be argued that academic fields qua bureaucracies assign meaning to ideas, concepts, and theories in different ways, with twists and flourishes unique to the central perspectives of the field. In any case, an individual can be said to have been successfully "socialized" into an organization when he or she can assign a double meaning to "messages," the bureaucratic as well as the individualistic meaning.

Johnson's and Kreps's textbooks are not alone in using Weick in the interest of organizational communication. Bantz and Smith (1977) made an "experimental test" of Weick's communication theory. Kreps's (1979) dissertation took the title "Human Communication and Weick's Model of Organizing: A Field Experimental Test and Revaluation." One of the editors of this book also used Weick's textbook as as inspiration for an empirical study of organizational communication (Putnam & Sorenson, 1982). Lest any of the writers identified above feel victimized by this account, it must be acknowledged that Tompkins and Cheney (1985) took over and redefined Weick's notion of the double interact as the double interact of communicative control. Weick in turn got the double interact from Hollander and Willis (1967), who in turn got it from . . . And thus runs the complex network of intertextuality we call organizational studies.

My examples may have created a false impression. By arguing that communication theorists have turned to a social psychologist for ideas about communication—a social psychologist who in turn got those ideas from phenomenology, interpretive sociology, and biology—is not to deny that Weick has written creatively about communication. I believe he has. And Weick's participation in numerous conferences sponsored by communication associations suggests he is at home with such ideas. The point is that the existence of separate disciplines in such applied fields as organizational studies is in large part a matter of administrative convenience, that *ideas do not respect the boundaries drawn in respect to that convenience*, and that influential ideas and studies done in one field will be appropriated and "translated" into the unique terministic perspectives of other fields. In conclusion, the membranes separating the various departments and fields devoted to organizational analysis are permeable. It must be admitted that the very young field of communication has taken more from sister disciplines than it has given. That is understandable in this "synchronic" reading of theory produced in the past 80 years or so, a period in which organizational communication is a mere infant, barely learning to speak, in comparison to its more mature siblings in sociology, social psychology, economics, and management. The next section, by taking a "diachronic" view of the subject, promises to turn this conclusion upside down.

SYMBOLISM AS THE
"SUBSTANCE" OF ORGANIZATION

Man, *qua* man, is a symbol user. In this respect, every aspect of his "reality" is likely to be seen through a fog of symbols. And not even the hard reality of basic economic facts is sufficient to pierce this symbolic veil (which is intrinsic to the human mind). One may seek to organize a set of images, another may strive for order among his ideas, a third may feel goaded to make himself head of some political or commercial empire, but however different the situations resulting from these various modes of action, there are purely symbolic motives behind them all. (Burke, 1950/1969, p. 136)

This second section will take a diachronic view of communication and organizational theory. It will, as promised, turn the conclusion of the previous section upside down. As further evidence that influential ideas in one field will be appropriated and translated into other disciplines, I make the bold claim that much of what is today called organizational theory (as well as management and administration) is an extension of the classical concerns of rhetorical theory.

Rhetorical Origins of Organization Theory

Before establishing what those classical concerns were, it is necessary in a diachronic view to mark the beginning of organization/management theory. Setting aside organizational practice, most would accept that *systematic* theorizing about organizations did not begin until the late nineteenth or early twentieth centuries, most notable with the work of Max Weber (1947). The other two theorists usually grouped with Weber in the "classical trinity," Fayol (1925/1949) and Taylor (1912/1947), were of course more oriented to management than organizational theorizing, and as practicing managers did not try to write "academic" theories. That leaves Weber as the first academic/scientific theorist of organizations.

What was Weber's discipline? Any undergraduate can answer that it was sociology. Or was it? There was no established field of sociology when Weber entered the academic world and when he called himself, rather late in his career, a sociologist. One could argue that his self-characterization did much to guarantee the legitimation if not the actual birth of the offspring. It has been argued, furthermore, that sociology did not enter the world to fill a void so much as it replaced one of the original liberal arts that had fallen into disuse.

Although the classical trinity is typically cited as the origins of management and organizational theory, rhetoricians that date back to Aristotle (Cooper, 1932) have introduced concepts frequently employed in organizational writings. One particular rhetorician, Kenneth Burke, presents a learned reclamation of the traditional principles of rhetoric and expands the modern scope of communication in his text *A Rhetoric of Motives* (1950/1969).

The connection between rhetoric and organizational theory is established in Burke's definition of the "realistic function" of rhetoric: [rhetoric is] *"rooted in an essential function of language itself, a function that is wholly realistic, and is continually born anew; the use of language as a symbolic means of inducing cooperation in beings that by nature respond to symbols"* (Burke, 1950/1969, p. 43). The term *cooperation* makes explicit the close link between rhetoric and organization; cooperation is, for example, the central term in Barnard's (1938/1968) communication-centered theory of organization. By beginning with texts typically treated as "pure poetry," Burke emerges with a new term for modern rhetoric—*identification.*

> Thereafter, with this term [identification] as instrument, we seek to mark off the areas of rhetoric, by showing how a rhetorical motive is often present where it is not usually recognized, or thought to belong. In part we would but rediscover rhetorical elements that had become obscured when rhetoric as a term fell into disuse, and other specialized disciplines such as esthetics, anthropology, psychoanalysis, and sociology came to the fore. (Burke, 1950/1969, p. xiii)

Although Burke does not give dates for the rise of aesthetics and its attempt to outlaw rhetoric, it had to happen after the midpoint of the eighteenth century. ("The word aesthetics was first used by Baumgarten about 1750, to imply the science of sensuous knowledge, whose aim is beauty, as contrasted with logic, whose aim is truth" [Runes, 1962, p. 6].) Rhetoric, by virtue of its central place in classical education, had served admirably as ancient Rome's theory of *management, decision making,* and *public relations.* Burke then shows how the social sciences took over the rich rhetorical elements banned by aesthetics.

Burke's analysis of psychoanalysis, for example, reveals the centrality of the audience, the "addressed." The audience is again revealed by Burke to be central in anthropological studies of the Tanala of Madagascar and of Navaho witchcraft. *Cultural anthropology* was a British invention of the nineteenth century and was, as an extension of rhetoric, valued because it made colonial people easier to understand, persuade, rule. From the very beginning, then, cultural studies of the audience or "addressed" have had value to managers and administrators. As Burke (1950/1969, p. 40), concludes: "Precisely at a time when the *term* 'rhetoric' had fallen into greatest neglect and disrepute, writers in the 'social sciences' were, under many guises, making good contributions to the New Rhetoric."

One wishes that, having shown how psychoanalysis and anthropology were created out of rhetorical ingredients, Burke had dealt similarly with Weber (1947) as the founder of modern sociology and its central topic: the sociology of organization, that is, bureaucracy. I will try to show that Weber's work dealing with organization theory, bureaucracy, is an extension of the classical concerns of rhetorical theory.

As a student of law and history, Weber was drawn to those "rich rhetorical elements" that are now assumed to be proper sociological concerns. For example, "the central practical interests, public and private, of his life" were reduced by MacRae (1974, p. 75) to this question: "What is the basis of political obligation, of our uncoerced obedience to the state?" Before we consider Weber's answer, recall that Aristotle (Cooper, 1932) also answered this question in his discussion of *persuasion*, the key term of classical rhetoric. Aristotle took notice of coercion in his *Rhetoric*; he called it "inartistic" persuasion and identified its techniques as oaths and tortures. Uncoerced obedience, however, was secured by "artistic" persuasion, which was divided into three main categories of *pisteis* or "proofs": *ethos, pathos, logos.* Weber (1947), however, gave a more tautological answer than Aristotle in saying that uncoerced obedience was secured by "legitimate" authority, which was subdivided into the now familiar categories of traditional, charismatic, and rational-legal. Weber's biographer and advocate, Reinhard Bendix, has acknowledged the circularity of the typology:

> Like the other types of authority, legal domination [a synonym for authority] rests upon the belief in its legitimacy, and every such belief is in a sense question-begging. Charismatic authority exists only as long as it "proves" itself, and such "proof" is either believed by the followers or rejected. The belief in the legitimacy of a legal order has a similarly circular quality... in other words, laws are legitimate if they have been enacted; and the enactment is legitimate if it has occurred in conformity with the laws prescribing the procedures to be followed. This circularity is intentional. Weber explicitly rejected definitions of the modern state and its legal order that focus on either the "purpose" of this political community or some specific value judgments that inspire the belief in its legitimacy. (Bendix, 1977, pp. 418-419)

The references to proof and the binary opposition of either believed or rejected should be proof at another level that Weber was mining rich rhetorical ore. In fact, there is a strong similarity between Aristotle's three kinds of proof and Weber's three types of authority. Aristotle's first form of proof, ethos, "the speaker's power of evincing a personal character... which will make his speech credible" (Aristotle, 1954, p. 3), or source credibility, as one might say today, is of course comparable to Weber's charismatic or personal authority. In reporting one of my NASA studies I suggested the similarity between the two concepts in analyzing von Braun's commanding presence in the organization: "it was obvious that his organizational 'audience' conferred on him a status . . . which seemed to fall somewhere in that unexplored territory between Aristotle's concept of *ethos* and Weber's concept of charisma" (Tompkins, 1977, p. 6). Aristotle's second type, pathos, "his power of stirring the emotions . . . of his hearers" (Aristotle, 1954, p. 3) is similar to Weber's traditional authority, particularly when one concedes that commitments to the old ways and routines are more dependent on emotions or a quasi-religious frame of mind than on reason and argument. Aristotle's third type of proof, logos, "his power of proving a truth, or an apparent truth, by means of persuasive arguments," (p. 3) is comparable to Weber's rational-legal authority.

Indeed, Aristotle's proofs are less metaphysical than Weber's types of authority for it is *persons* who exercise authority or domination, not abstract, bloodless qualities such as "tradition" and "charisma." Aristotle made this explicit by defining the proofs as techniques employed by a *speaker* in a *speech* to an *audience*. Weber's explanation of authority strips away his own metaphysical categories by falling back on the conduct of the ruled in determining the degree of influence of a ruler's command (Bendix, 1977, p. 291).

Beyond the parallel between Aristotle's speaker/speech/audience and Weber's ruler/command/ruled, Weber's definition of authority contains another striking similarity to Aristotle's rhetorical analysis. Under the heading of logos, Aristotle discussed the example and the enthymeme, which today we would call, respectively, inductive and deductive argument. The enthymeme is thought to be a discovery of Aristotle's and is defined by him as a "rhetorical syllogism." To be effective as proof, however, the premise of the enthymeme must be drawn from the opinions of the audience. As the speaker and hearer proceed through the deductive, syllogistic form of argument, *both participate in the construction of the proof* by which the listener is persuaded. The speaker participates by designing and uttering the argument, the listener by providing the opinion or premise from which the conclusion is drawn.

Pertinent to this discussion of Weber's definition of authority is the fact that *maxims* are part of the listeners' opinions from which the speaker (and listener) can draw the desired conclusion. Aristotle conducts a close analysis of maxims in the *Rhetoric* because they come under the heading of the enthymeme: "A premise or conclusion of an enthymeme is a maxim" (Cooper, 1932, p. 150). In short, listeners successfully persuaded by means of an enthymeme would act, as Weber suggests, " in such a way that their conduct to a socially relevant degree occurs as if the ruled had made the content of the command the maxim of their conduct for its very own sake" (Bendix, 1977, p. 291).

Maxims have had an uneven life in organization theory: Taylor sought to replace the workers' "rules of thumb" with his own, or what he euphemistically called scientific principles; Fayol (1925/1949) promoted proverbs and maxims that in turn were ridiculed by March and Simon (1958); Weick (1979, pp. 39-44) has half-heartedly attempted to revive maxims under the heading of "aphorisms" as an alternative to deductions; and Tompkins and Cheney (1985) see maxims as the essence of the corporately generated enthymemes used deductively to effect unobtrusive control in modern organizations.

Weber's (1947) discussion of bureaucracy, in addition to his views of legitimate authority and organizational maxims, can be traced back to rhetorical theory. Weber's theory of bureaucracy was developed under the heading of rational-legal authority or domination. Bendix (1977) has summarized the four most important attributes and consequences of bureaucracy in the modern world. We condense these in turn into the following: (1) bureaucracy is "technically superior to all other forms of administration" in terms of precision, speed, continuity, and calculability (or predictability); (2) it is distributed throughout most large-scale organizations, including the government, the army, political parties, and universities, as well as business corporations; (3) the replacement of amateur administrators by trained and salaried experts has a leveling effect on social and economic differences; and (4) a "fully developed bureaucracy implements a system of authority relationships that is practically indestructible," indispensable, and oppressive (Bendix, 1977, pp. 426-30). All of this led Weber to predict the emergence of a "dictatorship of the bureaucrats" rather than a "dictatorship of the proletariat" (Bendix, 1977, p. 459).

The essence of Weber's bureaucracy is, if reduced to a word, *hierarchy.* Whether or not one accepts Weber's claim that bureaucracy has a leveling effect on social and economic differences in society, no one would deny that hierarchy, a system of authority [rhetorical, persuasive, communicative] relationships, creates *new sets of differences* (Bendix, 1977, p. 459). In rhetorical theory, hierarchy is viewed as a defining characteristic of humans (Burke, 1945/1969). The existence of hierarchy generates the universal motivation to transcend this state of *segregation* by attempts to achieve *congregation.* Appeals are made up and down the line in this regard; they are obtrusive as well as unobtrusive, obvious as well as subtle. The result is the demonstration that Burke's (1950/1969) term, *identification,* is but an accessory rather than a substitute for the key term, *persuasion.* That Burke had modern organizations in mind in making this distinction between persuasion and identification is made clear in his triple review of Sargant's (1956) *Battle for the Mind,* Packard's (1957) *The Hidden Persuaders,* and Whyte's (1956) *The Organization Man.* About the latter he said:

From the standpoint of my own notions about rhetoric, I would say that this third book [Whyte's *The Organization Man*] shifts the emphasis from persuasion to identification. For it is concerned with the ways in which a class of sub-executives both spontaneously identify themselves with the company they work for and are selected by personnel directors who, with the help of personality tests, seek to make such identification the be-all and end-all of the "'trainees'" lives. (Burke, 1957-1958, p. 631)

Indeed, I contend that Burke is subtler and more profound than Weber on the topic of bureaucracy. As Burke (1950/1969, p. 118) observes: "'Hierarchy' is the old, eulogistic word for 'bureaucracy,' with each stage employing a rhetoric of obeisance to the stage above it, and a rhetoric of charitable condescension to the stage beneath it, in sum, a rhetoric of courtship." Burke is not content with a mere description of the status ladder of bureaucracy; characteristically, he presses the idea of hierarchy to discover the *complete* essence of the underlying motives:

> The hierarchic principle is not complete in the social realm, for instance, in the mere arrangement whereby each rank is overlord to its underlings and underling to its overlords. It is complete only when each rank accepts the principle of gradation itself, and in thus "universalizing" the principle, makes a spiritual *reversal* of the ranks just as meaningful as their actual material arrangement. (Burke, 1950/1969, p. 138)

The division into ranks produces a kind of mystery or mystification between and among them, even at lower levels. As Burke (1950/1969, p. 115) illustrates:

> Thus even the story of relations between the petty clerk and the office manager, however realistically told, draws upon the wells of mystery for its appeal, since the social distinction makes them subtly mysterious to each other, not merely two different people, but representing two different *classes* (or "kinds") of people. The clerk and the manager are identified with and by different social *principles*.

He states the general proposition that is derived from this analysis: "Mystery arises at that point where different kinds of beings are in communication. In mystery there must be *strangeness*; but the estranged must also be thought of as in some way capable of communion" (Burke, 1950/1969, p. 115).

The sources of other bureaucratic "dysfunctions" are analyzed as the very consequences of the hierarchic necessity. Hierarchy in general is inevitable; bureaucracies in particular can crumble, dissolve, disappear. The hierarchic principle, however, is indigenous to all human thinking and interaction. It reminds students of organization, upon hearing talk of participatory decision making, quality circles, requests for "input," and other appearances of equality, to ask this basic question: "Just how does the hierarchic principle work in this particular scheme of equality?" (Burke, 1950/1969, p. 141).

Burke's reading of Castiglione's *The Book of the Courtier* (1528/1561) not as a handbook of etiquette or manners but as a paradigm for bureaucratic courtship, leads to some of the most frequently noted problems in upward-directed communication: How can a subordinate, a courtier, communicate unpalatable truths to a superior, a prince? Frequently complicating this process of upward-directed communication is the superiors' vices of ignorance and vanity, coupled with the willingness of other subordinates to curry favor by telling the superior what he or she would like to hear. The situation is not unlike that of consultants today, "who are hired to serve the interests of local financial or industrial sovereigns" (Burke, 1950/1969), p. 230). A problematic communicative situation is created by the contradictory motives of wanting, on the one hand, to observe the purely professional interest in the truth, and wanting, on the other hand, to please the superior. Castiglione, a contemporary of Machiavelli therefore produced a rhetoric of bureaucratic courtship, a paradigm of superior-subordinate communication that is applicable today.

In sum, this section has sought to show that the "birth" of the social sciences was but, under new labels and in new nomenclatures, the extension of the classical concerns of rhetorical theory. Even the particular case of Weber's sociology of organization (bureaucratization) was shown to be an outgrowth of the study of persuasion (that is, "authority"). The frequent use of such terms as *persuasion, rhetoric*, and *communication* in relation to bureaucracy (or hierarchy) indicate their centrality. If there is to be hierarchy there must be division; if there is to be organization there must be communication (rhetoric, persuasion, identification) and *symbolism* by which to compensate for and occasionally transcend the division.

Contemporary Organizational Theories as Studies of Symbolic Action

How can we illustrate more fully the implications of symbolic action for organizational studies? The person who organizes a new firm will see every aspect of reality through a "fog of symbols," will even be goaded by "purely symbolic motives," to repeat phrases from the epigraph at the head of this section. Symbolism, in short, *creates* organizational realities and environments as well as the motives of those who act. Burke long ago adumbrated an emphasis on symbolism that has recently been manifested in organizational studies such as those of Ranson, Hinings, and Greenwood (1980); Feldman and March (1981); Pfeffer (1981); Meyer (1982); Berg (1985); and Schein (1985).

Collectively, these texts, except for Berg's, divide the world into "substantive action" and "symbolic action," to illustrate the binary oppositions drawn by Pfeffer (1981). Ranson et al. (1980, p. 9) pose a distinction between "provinces of meaning" or "interpretive schemes," and between "environmental and organizational constraints." Meyer (1982, p. 515) similarly distinguishes between "interpretations within organizations" and "environmental jolts."

Schein (1985, p. 242) shows how organizational founders shape cultures by communicating "both explicitly and implicitly the assumptions they really hold"; this rhetorical or symbolic action is distinguished from the "actual environment" (as implied in the expression, "actual dangers in the external environment"[Schein, 1985, p. 230]). Feldman and March (1981, p. 171) also divide the world into information (as signal and symbol) and that which it is about, "environmental uncertainty and risk" or, to use another dialectic, "symbolic significance" and "instrumental importance" (p. 184). Note that the authors seem to have confounded their binary oppositions by using two defining characteristics in dividing up the world: the symbolic versus the substantive, the organization versus the environment. These constructs thus suggest an internal symbolicity and an external actuality. Such a view is, of course, misleading and unproductive, a view that can probably be traced to the reduction of an organization to the perspective of the individual organism. For the individual organism the metaphor of internality/externality has greater validity than it does with a complex organization.

Dismissing the external/internal opposition and concentrating instead on the substantive/symbolic opposition, it seems fair to say that the theorists have placed the symbolic in the superior or privileged position in relation to the substantive. For example, Pfeffer (1981, p. 47) finds discussions of the two realms confused, and because the substantive is constrained, "the symbolic role of the manager is probably the more important one." Indeed, Pfeffer concludes that this insight threatens the status quo by calling "into question the legitimacy of the administrative activity itself and, by extension, its study and teaching" (p. 48). Similarly, Meyer (1982, p. 543) concludes that "ideological and strategic variables [the symbolic] were better predictors of organizational perceptions, responses, and consequences than structural variables of organizational slack [the substantive]." Schein attributes a message value to nearly everything about organizational life in diagnosing how culture is transmitted by leaders. Even though an actual environment "may or may not" exist, it occupies a secondary position in relation to the symbolic. Ranson et al. (1980) also seem to be arguing that a meaning-based theory can accommodate structure and conceptual restraints. The position of Feldman and March (1981, p. 171) on the issue seems clear from their very definition of organization: "Organizations are consumers, managers, and purveyors of information."

The theory that most fully approximates Burke's symbolic action perspective is Berg's (1985) cultural approach to organizations as "symbolic fields." The symbolic field is a "holographic pattern of clustered symbolic representation which constitute reality in the organization" (Berg, 1985, p. 285). The symbolic field has three important characteristics: (1) it consists of coded and stored experiences; (2) it is the result of the transformation of experienced reality into symbolic reality; and (3) it is the collective symbolization of reality.

Organizational change can thus be seen "as a transformation of the underlying symbolic field" (Berg, 1985, p. 289). By implication, (1) organizational environments are described as the symbolic context that gives meaning to members; (2) structure becomes the "collective meanings or structures existing in the mind of the organizations' members" (p. 295); and (3) strategy "in a symbolic perspective becomes nothing but a conscious formulation of (a part of) the underlying corporate myth. A strategy is not seen as a plan but as a collective image than can be acted upon" (p. 295).

Even if these organizational theorists have moved toward Burke's (1950/1969) position of privileging symbolism over substance, it is necessary to consider the nature of the concept of substance. Both Lentricchia (1983) and Tompkins (1985) have argued that Burke antedated the poststructuralists in performing a thoroughgoing "deconstruction" of the concept of substance. The argument is long and complex and only a condensed version can be reproduced here. Any attempt to define substance must proceed by means of symbols, unmistakably *not* the thing being defined; substance thus designates a thing in terms of what it is *not*—that is, something intrinsic to a thing is outside or extrinsic to it, as suggested etymologically by *sub*stance, a foundation or a standing under. The paradox of substance thus destabilizes the very meaning of the term; there can be no secure footing here.

Given the paradox of substance, it would be advisable to drop the distinction between symbolic action and substantive action, substituting for this pair symbolic/nonsymbolic or symbolic/extrasymbolic. The attempt to draw a line between the symbolic and nonsymbolic will allow us to see with greater clarity how the symbolic dominates organizational life.

Take away symbolism and how much do we know about an organization's past? And as for the present, each member of an organization has directly experienced only a tiny "sliver" of the nonsymbolic; each member's overall picture is but a construct provided by the symbol systems of words, numbers, and nomenclatures. Refusing to see or acknowledge the dominating role of symbolicity in shaping notions of "reality" is to cling "to a kind of naive verbal realism" (Burke, 1966, p. 5). The symbolic serves as a link between organizational members and the nonsymbolic, but it also serves as a terministic screen that separates us from it. Moreover, much of the nonsymbolic would not exist if it were not for the symbolic. "Even if any given terminology is a *reflection* of reality, by its very nature as a terminology it must be a *selection* of reality; and to this extent it must function also as a *deflection* of reality" (Burke, 1966, p. 45). Or as he put the idea more precisely, "Many of [our] 'observations' are but implications of the particular terminology in which the observations are made" (Burke, 1966, p. 46).

Of the five theorists cited as moving toward a symbolic approach to organizations, most could benefit from a greater familiarity with Burke's work. For example, the subtlest and most provocative text in the group is probably that of Pfeffer's (1981). The key terms in his title (and analysis) are "Symbolic Action." Yet there is no reference to the fact that symbolic action has been a kind of "trade name" of Burke's for at least 20 years. Specifically, Pfeffer could profit by referring to *drama, identification,* and *scapegoating.* The same can be said about Meyer's (1982, p. 532) use of such expressions as "administrative drama" and an administrator who was "scapegoated."

Burke's theories could also go a long way in disabusing Feldman and March (1981, p. 175) of what might be called a kind of "naive rhetorical realism," the belief that a sharp line can be drawn between information and persuasion, between science and public relations. I refer here to their observations that "much of the information used in organizational life is subject to strategic misrepresentation," which is unpacked and supported by the subsequent assertion, among others, that "often information is produced in order to persuade someone to do something" (Feldman & March, 1981, p. 176). Schein (1985) does not manifest naive rhetorical realism in his analysis of how leaders transmit culture. Nor does Weick (1979); the epigraph for his chapter 9 is a long quote from Kenneth Burke's *Counter-Statement* (1931/1953) about the difference between pamphleteering and inquiry, and the "indeterminate wavering" between the two; indeed, Weick follows up with the acknowledgment that his own book wavers between the two, and we would note that he gives pamphleteering the position of primacy (Weick, 1979, p. 233). And does not the following line sound Weickian? "Perception must be grounded in enactment, by participation in some local role, so that the understanding of the total order is reached through this partial involvement" (Burke, 1950/1969, p. 195). Or should I instead have asked: Doesn't Weick's stress on enactment now sound Burkean?

In conclusion, organizational theory is but an extension of the classical concerns of rhetorical theory. Moreover, the recent turns toward culture and symbolism are consistent with the "new rhetoric" of symbolic action. To those left wondering whether the stress on symbolism implies a new nominalism devoid of references, I do believe that organizations make things, do good, poison the populace, and often crush individuals as well as reward them. I must even confess to thinking there might be a substance out here, but it takes symbolism to "see" it, talk about it, and transform it. The essence (if not the substance) of organization is symbolism, or to quote again by way of reprise, "the use of language as a symbolic means of inducing cooperating in beings that by nature respond to symbols" (Burke, 1950/1969, p. 43). That these six exemplars of recent organizational studies have caught up with—even are capable of being improved by—the rhetorical-symbolic tradition is perhaps the best evidence that the thesis of this second section has been redeemed.

ECONOMICS AND COMMUNICATION

If translated into English, most of the ways economists talk among themselves would sound plausible enough to poets, journalists, businesspeople, and other thoughtful though noneconomical folk. Like serious talk anywhere—among boat designers and baseball fans, say—the talk is hard to follow when one has not made a habit of listening to it for a while. The culture of the conversation makes the words arcane . . . Underneath it all (the economist's favorite phrase) conversational habits are similar. Economics uses mathematical models and statistical tests and market arguments, all of which look alien to the literary eye. But looked at closely they are not so alien. They may be seen as figures of speech—metaphors, analogies, and appeals to authority. (McCloskey, 1985, p. xvii)

The controversy between symbolism and substance, while apparent in organizational studies, is only beginning to surface in the "hardest" of social sciences, economics. Indeed, the mathematical models and "objective" statistical tests typically preclude consideration of persuasion and communication. Symbolic discourse, however, lies at the very core of market analysis and economic thought. Two main claims will be stated and supported in this section: (1) the economic theories of organizational and social life in general are finding it increasingly necessary to appeal to such noneconomical concepts as communication and persuasion in order to explain human action; and (2) even economists are coming to understand that their own theoretical and empirical discourse is symbolic, even rhetorical in nature.

The economic perspective was singled out for analysis because it is thought by most to be the least susceptible to a communicative or symbolic analysis. The most positivistic of the social sciences of organizational studies, economics has prided itself in looking "underneath it all" for the bottom line; in the process it created a caricature of humans as cold, calculating maximizers. This section considers both the *ontology* and the *epistemology* of modernist and postmodernist economics. Alfred D. Chandler (1962), for example, has been almost totally ignored by students of communication despite the centrality of our signifier communication in his prize-winning work on economic history and organizational theory. Chandler describes the redoubled role of communication in his study of structural innovations in the historical development of such organizations as Du Pont, General Motors, Standard Oil, and Sears Roebuck. Finding similarities and differences between and among these firms, he claims that the very structure of major corporations is determined by the strategies articulated and implemented by the "visible hand" of professional managers.

Communication as Ontology

Does it labor the point to make clear that a corporate *strategy* can only be created in communication? That strategy is a symbolic precursor to action? And that such strategies must be expressed and communicated to employees as a precondition to implementation? Perhaps, but this claim differs from the argument that communication constitutes organization (or that organization is reproduced in the day-to-day interactions of employees). This claim steps back to say that the verbalizing of organizational strategy determines the *shape or structure* that in turn is reproduced in routine interactions. It is the organizational variation of the lore that form follows function. A *defensive* strategy protects hard-won advantages by means of vertical integration with customers and suppliers. A *positive* strategy is manifested in the attempt to sell new products in new markets. Both strategies pursue growth, which in turn leads to longer and more complex scalar chains of communication.

In all of this the problem of centralization-decentralization is crucial because if the proper balance is not achieved, the hazards of insufficient control and insufficient time for managerial "strategizing" and planning provide the Scylla and Charybdis for those at the helm. Chandler (1962) delineates four other functions of communication in strategy formulation: (1) communication channels reshape authority relationships between companies that develop new markets and new products (pp. 385, 388); (2) telegraphic commmunication between branch plants, buyers, and central offices aids in allocating supply to meet demand, almost instantaneously (p. 389); (3) communication networks that link facilities with customers promote the rapid delivery of products and the adjustment of output volume to market changes (p. 390); and (4) clear lines of communication and authority between firms provide accurate and meaningful data to allocate resources in a systematic and rational way (p. 396).

These functions illustrate Chandler's thesis that strategy dictated communicative/authoritative structure in the development of the largest corporations; that communication guided the *visible* hand of the new manager; that innovation in communication technologies helped resolve the dilemma of centralization-decentralization; that network analysis could be conducted by research into historical documents and texts; and that innovations in communication/authority structures allowed for organizational growth while minimizing the haphazard and intuitive. All of this growth, however, comes at a high human cost.

Schumacher (1973) laments the master strategy of organizational growth chronicled by Chandler and calls for an effort to achieve a humane "smallness" within the impersonal efficiency of "largeness." Mergers and vertical integration in capitalist countries, nationalization and centralization in socialist countries, create "the devastating effects of remote control on an individual who gropes within the system to find what is what and who is who, perpetually mystified and confused" (Pugh, Hickson, & Hinings, 1985, p. 226).

Schumacher, like Follett (1941) before him, saw as the central problematic of organizational practice the giving of orders, commands, and directives. After lamenting the "brave new world sharply divided between *us* and *them*, torn by mutual suspicion, with a hatred of authority from below and a contempt of people from above," Schumacher unites the interests of organizational and interpersonal communication in a passage of uncommon humaneness. "Undoubtedly this is all a problem of communications. But the only really effective communication is from man to man, face to face," (Schumacher, 1973, p. 227). He shows the "devastating effects of remote control" by summarizing Kafka's (1926/1930) nightmarish novel, *The Castle.* Mr. K., a land surveyor, has been hired by the authorities, but no one understands why. He tries to get his job clarified but everyone he meets tells him there is no need for his services. He makes an effort, every effort, to meet authority face to face; but others tell him he has not met the real authorities, tell him instead his contacts have been illusory. He completes no meaningful work yet he receives written feedback in the form of praise for his surveying, as well as pep talks urging him not to slacken in his efforts. The moral that Schumacher derives from this hierarchical exercise of impersonal, remote control is expressed in this way:

> Nobody really likes large-scale organization; nobody likes to take orders from a superior who takes orders . . . Even if the rules devised by bureaucracy are outstandingly humane, nobody likes to be ruled by rules, that is to say, by people whose answer to every complaint is: "I did not make the rules: I am merely applying them."

> Yet, it seems, large-scale organization is here to stay. Therefore it is all the more necessary to think about it and to theorize about it. The stronger the current, the greater the need for skillful navigation . . . The fundamental task is to achieve smallness within large organization. (Schumacher, 1973, pp. 227-228)

Schumacher's subtitle, *Economics as if People Mattered,* indicates why his work marked something of a break from the center of his field and, simultaneously, why his theorizing values face-to-face communication. The preceding quotation illustrates his ideal for superior-subordinate communication as well as its inhumane opposite. The following quotation illustrates his ideal (and its opposite) for organizational communication; notice the skillful opposition of metaphors, first the metaphor prescribed for the future, second the metaphoric reality of the here and now:

> The structure of the organization can then be symbolized by a man holding a large number of balloons in his hand. Each of the balloons has its own buoyancy and lift, and the man himself does not lord it over the balloons, but stands beneath them, yet holding all the strings firmly in his hands. Every balloon is not only an administrative but also an *entrepreneurial* unit. The monolithic organization, by contrast, might be symbolized by a Christmas tree, with a star at the top and a lot of nuts and other useful things underneath. Everything derives from the top and depends on it. Real freedom and *entrepreneurship* can exist only at the top. (Schumacher, 1973, p. 231)

Schumacher's identification with smallness may obscure the fact that he seems to think the central problem in organizational theory is that of *control.* Put another way, Schumacher seeks the optimal balance between the conflicting needs for orderly control and disorderly freedom. The amount and manner in which control is effected is a topic that most writers on management/organization theory have had to confront directly. Is *control* an acceptable synonym for our central signifier *communication*? I submit that most communication scholars would answer "yes" because of at least two arguments: (1) reasons of disciplinary development (advanced in the previous section); and (2) the reason that the modernist communication model of Message → Feedback → Adaptation is and has been best described as a "mechanism" of control. Even Simon's (1957) text *Administrative Behavior* shows how control is tied to the communication of decision premises. As a 1978 winner of the Nobel Prize in Economics, he made explicit ties between economics, communication, and identification.

How would the pecuniary motive compare with the communicative or rhetorical motive in an economist's theory of motivation? Galbraith (1978) has in fact presented what he calls rather grandly "The General Theory of Motivation." After finding the existing theory of motivation in economics unsatisfactory, Galbraith (following Barnard) introduces the central concept "coordinated"; it is stressed to show that "participating individuals are *persuaded* to set aside their individual purposes or goals and pursue those of the organization"(Galbraith, 1978, p. 120). I added the emphasis to the word *persuaded* and fear I cannot exaggerate enough the fact that an economist would reduce organization itself to the central term of classical rhetoric— persuasion. Moreover, Galbraith then places the *pecuniary* motive below the *communicative* or *rhetorical* motive; indeed, the pecuniary motive is only one step above *compulsion*. The four steps of the general theory are: (1) compulsion, (2) pecuniary motivation, (3) identification, and (4) adaptation.

Only the fourth term, adaptation, requires elaboration. It is defined as "the pursuit of the goals of organization because of the prospect or in the hope of accommodating these goals more closely to the participant's preference" (p. 122). Adaptation, whether on its own or as another form of identification, has much to do with the lust for power or control that figures so prominently in the noneconomic theories of organization. Ironically, it is the economic theorists of organization who see the communicative, rhetorical impulses as sometimes stronger than the pecuniary, as the motivation "underneath it all." Galbraith calls it the paradox of pecuniary motivation.

> Here is the paradox of pecuniary motivation. In general, the higher the amount, the less its importance in relation to other motivations. With higher income there is, under most circumstances, a lessened dependence on a particular employment. So there is a lessened element of compulsion, and this paves the way for identification and adaptation. These supplement and may transcend pecuniary compensation in their importance in the motivational system. (Galbraith, 1976, p. 127)

With an equally valid warrant, this could be called the *paradox of identification*: The lower the amount of income, the greater the element of compulsion and the lower the identification with others. By whatever paradox we call this relationship, it clearly supports the argument of symbolism as substance in acknowledging that somewhere above the economic level of subsistence the rhetorical/communicative motives transcend the pecuniary and vice versa.

This paradox of control and pecuniary motivation also affects the origins of organizations in economic systems. Williamson (1975) looks "underneath it all" to ask why we create organizations. His answer is that they lower transaction costs. Williamson's transactional paradigm assumes society is a network of transactions between formal organizations. Suppose we set up a new corporation and have the need for a team of skilled corporate lawyers. Shall we go into the market and retain a law firm? Or shall we create a legal department?

There are at least four major factors that Williamson thinks should be considered, but I stress the one that conforms best to pecuniary motives. Hierarchies, as opposed to markets, do exercise control. That is the lesson we have learned again and again from noneconomic as well as economic theories. Which motives, or combinations of motives, would most efficiently provide us with satisfactory legal counsel?

A fee paid to a law firm may seem cheap or costly, but if either or both parties lack information about the actual cost of the transaction, the model of the marketplace may be problematic. We can supply little motivation to the external law firm other than the pecuniary. The hierarchy has a greater repertoire of motives under its control, namely, compulsion, pecuniary, identification, and adaptation. Again we see that the communicative motives must enter into our economic calculations of efficiency.

Rhetoric as Epistemology

The economists' appropriation of rhetorical concepts has not been limited to matters of ontology; rather, attention has been drawn to epistemological issues, to the rhetorical aspects of economic discourse, even its equations. Economists are beginning to understand that although equations may a science make, they are modernist expressions of ancient rhetorical figures and are the more persuasive for that fact. Take, for example, Solow's (1957) aggregate production function:

$$Q = A(+) f(K,L)$$

McCloskey (1985, p. 84) shows how the four rhetorical figures (metaphor, metonymy, synecdoche, and irony) discussed in Burke (1950/1969) are at work here. The equation as argument depends at once on the metaphor that organizational work is like a mathematical function. "The jumble of responsibility, habit, conflict, ambition, intrigue, and ceremony that is our working life is supposed to be similar to a chalked curve on a blackboard. Economists are habituated to such figures of speech, as I have said, to the point of not recognizing that they are, but noneconomists will agree that they are bold" (McCloskey, 1985, p. 84).

McCloskey then shows that the K and L in the equation are metonymies, reducing a thing in question to a quality associated with it. L is an hour of work, "a mere emblem, *no more the substance of the matter* that the heart is of emotions" (McCloskey, 1985, p. 84; emphasis added). The K refers to the quantity of capital. The A(+) is a synecdoche, taking a part for the whole, representing technical change, and is a mere "measure of our ignorance" (McCloskey, 1985, p. 85). McCloskey says Solow (1957) has persuaded most economists by the symmetry of the mathematics and the appeal to the authority of scientific traditions in economics, and with the four figures of speech. He also shows that history persuades by means of irony. The most sophisticated economists, like the most sophisticated novelists, favor the dialectical figure of speech. Economic figures and tropes are not stylistic frills.

McCloskey contends that the school of economics with which one is identified—whether Keynesian, Monetarist, or Marxist—influences the statistics one gathers as well as their meanings. Even statistics drawn by the canon of positivist methods, if presented as undermining one of these schools, will be greeted by its adherents with hoots and shouts such as, "I don't believe them" or "Something must be wrong here." McCloskey cites articles that point this out, articles referencing previous articles that have shown the same effect (for example, see Cooley & LeRoy, 1981). So it is clear that one's identification with a school is not determined by considering all the data. Perhaps beneath it all it is the school's root metaphor or perspective that explains such attachments.

McCloskey's (1985) chapter "The Rhetoric of Significance Tests" illustrates that statistical methods as well as economic equations rely on persuasion and symbolic discourse. Sampling statistics are rarely applied to samples in economics; they are applied to populations. The question "How large is large?" often plagues economists, and the situation seems if anything to be worse in the field of communication. The very signifier "significance," instead of such alternatives as "adequate" or "consistent," and the almost religious beauty of the phrase "analysis of variance," are persuasive forms of symbolic discourse. "Is it too cynical to think that the lovely term—half-mystery, half-promise—and the orderly tables helped to win acceptance, quite apart from the underlying theory?" (Kruskal, 1978, as quoted in McCloskey, 1985, p. 164). McCloskey does not want to eliminate statistical tests and statistics themselves, although he makes detailed and particular suggestions for reforming the teachings, executing, reporting, and reading of significance tests. The statistical approach has had a great democratizing effect on social science.

McCloskey's main message is not about methods, it is about epistemology. The neurosis of modernism—we do not know anything until it has been quantified—can be cured by realizing that the social sciences cling to a philosophy of knowledge they violate every day in the reporting of research, a philosophy no longer accepted even by philosophers. McCloskey (1985, pp. 15-16) has been persuaded, after realizing on his own that "prediction is not possible." It is no longer meaningful to speak of the truth or of science as the mirror of nature. Instead, we engage in conversation, in dialogue, and attempt to persuade each other of our claims. This acknowledgment might even make research in economics more persuasive. It is ironic that the major impact of speech-communication on economics and the empirical social sciences is more likely to have been accomplished by the humanists and rhetoricians, such as Scott (1967), who influenced McCloskey's (1985) thinking, than by the empiricists. In any case, there is no alternative to rhetoric, persuasion, communication—except compulsion.

Economics, the hardest of the social sciences, has had to use our central signifier—communication—in explaining how organizations work and change. Economists also appeal to persuasion and its modern counterpart, *identification* in their theoretical discourse. If people in business organizations practice communication and identification, it is likely that economists themselves will use "all the available means" in trying to persuade each other. McCloskey has shown that economists *are not different* from the organizational actors they attempt to explain. By allowing rhetoric and communication to enter into both their epistemological and ontological conversations, they have begun to demonstrate a consistency and universality that could be a sign of maturity, and they demonstrate that symbolic action is, indeed, the substance of organizations and organizational theory.

SUMMARY AND PERORATION

Even if there is not a unique, univocal concept associated with our central signifier, communication, it does (along with its family of variants) occupy a central place in classical and contemporary theory of organization. Communication has borrowed more from other fields than it has lent when conceived synchronically. Diachronically conceived, however, organization theory is but an extension or outgrowth of the classical concerns of rhetorical theory. Indeed, six exemplars drawn from recent organizational study were shown to merge with the "new rhetoric" by adopting symbolic action as the substance of organizing. An examination of the most "metrical" and scientific of the approaches to organization—economics—revealed that at both the ontological and epistemological levels there is a move, if not a paradigm shift, toward a more rhetorical view of theory *and* method.

The editors of this book put two foundational questions before me as I began the final draft of this chapter. Why is it important to say what you have said in this chapter? What implications does your analysis have for theory and research? My considered answer is that the argument has revolutionary implications for theory and research, not to mention education. It matters profoundly to realize that our departmentalized theorizing is but a genealogy of intertextualities. It matters to realize that we present more or less persuasive research findings—in *symbolic form*—rather than the *truth*. It matters that students are taught to realize that they will manage symbols, not substance. It also matters that it takes symbols to say this—or refute it; that there is nothing outside of symbolism we can talk about—without symbolism.

The most fatal mistake one could make in pursuing symbolism as substance, however, would be to hold out the promise of a "new truth or new certainty." As Rorty (1979, p. 157) posits: "Our certainty will be a matter of conversation between persons, rather than a matter of interaction with nonhuman reality . . . [w]e shall be looking for an airtight case rather than an unshakable foundation." In the interest of continuing the conversation about the substance of organizing, symbolic action, I cannot resist observing that conversation or dialogue itself is an important part of the meaning of life: "Life is an unending dialogue; when we enter, it's already going on; we try to get the drift of it; we leave before it's over" (Burke, 1978, p. 33).

REFERENCES

Argyris, C. (1957). *Personality and organization.* New York: Harper & Row.
Aristotle (1954). *Rhetoric and poetics* (W. R. Roberts & J. Bywater, Trans.). New York: Random House.
Bantz, C., & Smith, D. (1977). A critique and experimental test of Weick's model of organizing. *Communication Monographs, 44,* 171-184.
Barnard, C. I. (1968). *The functions of the executive.* Cambridge, MA: Harvard University Press. (Original work published 1938)
Bendix, R. (1977). *Max Weber: An intellectual portrait.* Berkeley: University of California Press.
Berg, P. (1985). Organization change as a symbolic transformation process. In P. J. Frost, L. F. Moore, M. R. Louis, C. C. Lundberg, J. Montese (Eds.), *Organizational culture* (pp. 281-299). Newbury Park, CA: Sage.
Burke, K. (1953) *Counter-statement.* Los Altos, CA: Hermes. (Original work published 1931)
Burke, K. (1957-1958). The carrot and the stick, or . . . *The Hudson Review, 10,* 627-633.
Burke, K. (1966). *Language as symbolic action: Essays on life, literature and method.* Berkeley: University of California Press.
Burke, K. (1969). *A grammar of motives.* Berkeley: University of California Press. (Original work published 1945)
Burke, K. (1969). *A rhetoric of motives.* Berkeley: University of California Press. (Original work published 1950)
Burke, K. (1978). Rhetoric, poetics, and philosophy. In D. Burks (Ed.), *Rhetoric, philosophy, and literature:* An exploration (pp. 15-34). West Lafayette, IN: Purdue University Press.
Castiglione, B. (1561). *The book of the courtier* (Sir Thomas Hoby, Trans.). London: J.M. Dent. (Original work published 1528)

Chandler, A. D., Jr. (1962). *Strategy and Structure.* Cambridge: MIT Press.

Cheney, G. (1986, April). *The importance of organization as a locus of investigation in communication research.* Paper presented at the annual convention of the Central States Speech Association, Cincinnati, OH.

Cooley, T., & LeRoy, S. (1981). Identification and estimation of money demand. *American Economic Review, 71,* 825-844.

Cooper, L. (1932). *The rhetoric of Aristotle.* New York: Appleton-Century-Crofts.

Derrida, J. (1982). *Margins of philosophy.* Chicago: University of Chicago Press.

Fayol, H. (1949). *General and industrial management.* New York: Pitman. (Original Work published 1925)

Feldman, M. S., & March, J. G. (1981). Information in organizations as signal and symbol. *Administrative Science Quarterly, 26,* 171-186.

Follett, M. P. (1941). Constructive conflict. In H. C. Metcalf & L. Urwick (Eds.), *Dynamic administration: The collected papers of Mary Parker Follett* (pp. 30-49). New York: Harper & Brothers.

Galbraith, J. K. (1978). *The new industrial state* (3rd. ed.). New York: Signet.

Georgiou, P. (1981). The goal paradigm and notes toward a counter paradigm. In M. Zey-Ferrell and M. Aiken (Eds.), *Complex organizations: Critical perspectives* (pp. 69-88). Glenview, IL: Scott, Foresman. (Original work published 1973)

Hollander, E., & Wilis, R. (1967). *Some current issues in the psychology of conformity and nonconformity. Psychological Bulletin, 68,* 62-76.

Johnson, B. (1977) *Communication: The process of organizing.* Boston: Allyn & Bacon.

Kafka, F. (1930). *The castle* (E. Muir & W. W. Muir, Trans.). New York: Knopf. (Original work published 1926)

Kreps, G. (1979). Human communication and Weick's model of organizing: A field experimental test and reevaluation. Unpublished doctoral dissertation, University of Southern California.

Kreps, G. (1986). *Organizational communication: Theory and practice.* New York: Longman.

Kruskal, W. (1978). Formulas, numbers, words, statistics in prose. *The American Scholar, 47,* 233-229.

Lentricchia, F. (1983). *Criticism and social change.* Chicago: University of Chicago Press.

Likert, R. (1961). *New patterns of management.* New York: McGraw-Hill.

MacRae, D. G. (1974). *Max Weber.* New York: Viking.

March, J. G., & Simon, H. A. (1958). *Organizations.* New York: John Wiley.

Marx, K. (1967). *Writings of the young Marx on philosophy and society.* Garden City, NY: Doubleday. (Original work published 1843)

Mayo, E. (1933). *The human problems of an industrial civilization.* Boston: Harvard University, Graduate School of Business Administration.

Mayo, E. (1949). *The social problems of industrial civilization.* Boston: Harvard University, Graduate School of Business Administration.

McCloskey, D. (1985). *The rhetoric of economics.* Madison: University of Wisconsin Press.

McGregor, D. (1960). *The human side of enterprise.* New York: McGraw-Hill.

Meyer, A. D. (1982). Adapting to environmental jolts. *Administrative Science Quarterly, 27,* 515-537.

Packard, V. (1957). *The hidden persuaders.* New York: David McKay.

Pfeffer, J. (1981). Management as symbolic action: The creation and maintenance of organizational paradigms. In L. L. Cummings & B. M. Staw (Eds.), *Research in organizational behavior* (Vol. 3, pp. 1-52). Greenwich, CT: JAI Press.

Pierce, J. R. (1961). *Symbols, signals and noises: The nature and process of communication.* New York: Harper & Row.

Pugh, D., D. Hickson, & Hinings, C. (1985). *Writers on organizations.* Newbury Park, CA: Sage.

Putnam, L., & Sorenson, R. (1982). Equivocal messages in organizations. *Human Communication Research, 8,* 114-132.

Ranson, S., Hinings, B., & Greenwood, R. (1980). The structuring of organizational structures. *Administrative Science Quarterly, 25*, 1-17.

Redding, W. C. (1985). Stumbling toward identity. In R. McPhee and P. Tompkins (Eds.), *Organizational communication: Traditional themes and new directions* (pp. 15-54). Newbury Park, CA: Sage.

Roethlisberger, F. J., & Dickson, W. J. (1939) *Management and the worker.* Cambridge, MA: Harvard University Press.

Rorty, R. (1979). *Philosophy and the mirror of nature.* Princeton, NJ: Princeton University Press.

Runes, D. D. (Ed.). (1962). *Dictionary of philosophy.* Totowa, NJ: Littlefield, Adams.

Sargant, W. (1956). *Battle for the mind.* Garden City, NY: Doubleday.

Schein, E. H. (1985). *Organizational culture and leadership: A dynamic view.* San Francisco: Jossey-Bass.

Schumacher, E. (1973). *Small is beautiful: Economics as if people mattered.* New York: Harper & Row.

Schutz, A. (1967). *The phenomenology of the social world.* Evanston, IL: Northwestern University Press.

Scott, R. (1967). On viewing rhetoric as epistemic. *Central States Speech Journal, 18*, 9-17.

Simon, H. A. (1957). *Administrative behavior.* New York: Free Press.

Solow, R. (1957). Technical change and the aggregate production function. *Review of Economics and Statistics, 39*, 312-320.

Taylor, F. W. (1947). *Principles of scientific management.* New York: Harper. (Original work published 1911)

Tompkins, P. K. (1977). Management qua communication in rocket research and development. *Communication Monographs, 44*, 1-26.

Thompkins, P. K. (1984). The functions of human communication in organization. In C. Arnold and J. W. Bowers (Eds.), *Handbook of rhetorical and communication theory* (pp. 659-713). Boston: Allyn & Bacon.

Tompkins, P. K. (1985). On hegemony—"He gave it no name"—And critical structuralism in the work of Kenneth Burke. *Quarterly Journal of Speech, 71*, 119-131.

Tompkins, P., & Cheney, G. (1985). Communication and unobtrusive control. In R. McPhee and P. Tompkins (Eds.), *Organizational communication: Traditional themes and new directions* (pp. 179-210). Newbury Park, CA: Sage.

Tompkins, P., & Redding, W. C. (in press). Organizational communication: Past and present tenses. In G. Goldhaber & G. Barnett (Ed.), *Handbook of organizational communication.* Norwood, NJ: Ablex.

Walsh, G. (1967). Introduction. In A. Schutz (Ed.), *The phenomenology of the social world* (pp. xv-xxix). Evanston, IL: Northwestern University Press.

Weber, M. (1947). *The theory of social and economic organization.* New York: Free Press.

Weber, M. (1978). *Economy and society.* Berkeley: University of California Press.

Weick, K. (1969). *The social psychology of organizing.* Reading, MA: Addison-Wesley.

Weick, K. (1979). *The social psychology of organizing* (2nd ed.). Reading, MA: Addison-Wesley.

Whyte, W. H., Jr. (1956). *The organization man.* Garden City, NY: Doubleday.

Williamson, O. (1975). *Markets and hierarchies: Analysis and antitrust implications.* New York: Free Press.

4   Theorizing About
Organizational Communication

KARL E. WEICK
University of Texas at Austin

A N outsider attending a recent European conference on organizations
looked at the several flow charts and organizational diagrams filled
with boxes, circles, and arrows, and said, "Ye Gods! Your field
looks like plumbing diagrams for an old Scottish castle."

That person may be right: Everything seems to affect everything else when
we depict organizations. But as organizational scholars, when we look more
closely at ongoing organizations, we see that interdependence is a variable
rather than a constant, largely due to the limits and opportunities inherent in
human communication.

OVERVIEW OF ORGANIZATIONAL COMMUNICATION

Interpersonal communication is the essence of organization because it
creates structures that then affect what else gets said and done and by whom.

AUTHOR'S NOTE: I am indebted to George Huber and Larry Browning for their comments on
an early draft of this chapter.

Structures form when communication uncovers shared occupational special-ties, shared social characteristics, or shared values that people want to preserve and expand. The structures themselves create additional resources for communication such as hierarchical levels, common tasks, exchangeable commodities, and negotiable dependencies. These additional resources constrain subsequent contacts and define more precisely the legitimate topics for further communication.

Even though organizations are built out of direct interaction, as they grow larger and more complex they are known by their inhabitants less through direct experience than through indirect images. These images both guide the social construction of reality and register what is constructed. They provide explanations for what has happened and anticipations of what comes next. These representations have been called cognitive maps (Axelrod, 1976) or cause maps (Hall, 1984; Weick & Bougon, 1986) and they essentially store heavily edited summaries of communication.

Cause maps transform communication into stable collective structures and environments through processes similar to those associated with self-fulfilling prophecies (Snyder, 1984). This transformation occurs because organizations are loosely coupled systems where indeterminacies between events are filled in by thought and interaction.

Managers often resolve indeterminacy by presuming on the basis of cause maps that there is some order "out there." The anticipation of order lures the manager to act even though there is indeterminacy. That action often creates the orderly relations that originally were mere presumptions summarized in a cause map.

Thus language trappings of organizations such as strategic plans are important components in the process of creating order. They hold events together long enough and tightly enough in people's heads so that they act in the belief that their actions will be influential and make sense. The importance of presumptions, expectations, justifications, and commitments is that they span the breaks in a loosely coupled system and encourage confident actions that tighten systems and create order. The conditions for order in organiza-tions exist as much in the mind as they do in the rationalized procedures. That is why culture, which affects the mind through meaning, is often more important than structure (Meyer, 1982).

OVERVIEW OF THEORIZING
ABOUT ORGANIZATIONAL COMMUNICATION

Ideas such as the preceding gain their value from what they allow us to see in organizations. Evocative ideas need to be cultivated by theorists from the beginning because belief, not skepticism, precedes observation. Since beliefs prefigure what we see, intentional choice of what we will impose and discover can improve the quality of understanding at the point where quality is most influenceable.

If believing affects seeing, and if theories are significant beliefs that affect what we see, then theories should be adopted more to maximize what we will see than to summarize what we have already seen. Usually, what we have already seen merely confirms what we expected to see. To theorize better, theorists need to expect more in whatever they will observe.

When scholars of communication sort through organizational theories and choose ideas to pursue, they should pay close attention to how the ideas will affect observing and worry less about how well the ideas explain what has already been observed. Theories that explain past observations are imposed on data that have already been limited by beliefs. Both surprise and scope have been removed from past observations and neither is likely to be restored when these limited theories are imposed on the future and discovered once again. To improve the quality of theories about organizational communication, scholars must be aware both of the substance of organizational theory and of the process by which ideas from organizational theory can be used to improve the understanding of communication. Since most other chapters in this handbook discuss theoretical substance, the present chapter will provide a contrasting focus on the process by which theoretical substance is built and used.

Process issues in organizational theorizing will be highlighted in the following manner. First, six characteristics of the activity of theorizing will be identified in the context of an organizational study in which low control and low communication produced mass psychogenic illness. The study shows the close interplay between theory building and theory application. Then the psychogenic study is used to address the issue of relevance in theorizing. It is argued that when scholars focus on relevance defined by five criteria, the quality of their theorizing gets better.

The discussion of theorizing is then deepened through a more extended example of the ways in which theories reach beyond themselves for denotation. We use a durable organizational theory, Burns and Stalker's (1961) distinction between mechanistic and organic systems, to illustrate the point that what a theory means is often discovered a posteriori rather than known a priori. It is less accurate to say that communication scholars know what mechanistic-organic means and want to see if it is true and more accurate to say that scholars know this distinction is true, but they do not know what it means. Each characteristic originally identified by Burns and Stalker is interpreted using ideas associated with communication. The result is an enriched view of what the distinction between mechanistic and organic means for organizational communication scholars.

The chapter concludes by showing that theorizing often results in fragments of theory rather than unified theories, but that this outcome is less troublesome than it looks.

The Process of Theorizing

A theory is defined as an inference from data that is offered as a formula to explain the abstract and general principle that lies behind them as their cause, their method of operation, or their relation to other phenomena. While a hypothesis implies tentativeness, a theory implies more supporting evidence and a wider range of applications (after *Webster's Dictionary of Synonyms,* 1951, p. 420).

An example of organizational theorizing is Pasmore and Friedlander's (1982) attempt to understand an extremely high incidence of work-related injuries (209 separate reports made by 104 employees who had visited the infirmary) at an electronics plant employing 335 people. These injuries, which consisted of damage to muscles in the wrist, forearm, and shoulder (tenosynovitis), had increased sharply among the mostly female workers over a five-year period despite efforts to control and correct the problem. There were 13 employees involved in 18 surgical operations, over 20% of the employees were receiving worker's compensation, and at least one person reported loss of the use of her right hand.

As part of an action-research program, the authors used a 134-item Likert-type scale to survey 312 employees, of whom 183 had reported soreness (some of whom had not reported soreness before the questionnaire was administered). When responses for the high-soreness group were compared with responses from the low-soreness group, significant differences occurred on the 28 items listed in Table 4.1.

These differences are the raw material from which theory is created. But the numbers themselves change their meaning as they are seen in the light of whatever theory emerges. The meaning of data is created, not discovered, and the same holds true for theory.

Readers are urged to look for their own patterns in the numbers to compare with patterns mentioned by the authors. Pasmore and Friedlander propose the following theory to explain what lies behind the complaints of soreness. (See Figure 4.1, where the theory is summarized.)

> We found that tools out of adjustment, poor raw materials, high pressure to produce, strict supervision and repetitive tasks created a high stress environment which left the low status but highly loyal and dependent female workforce in an extremely stressful situation with few alternatives for relief from the stress they experienced. Leaving the situation was impossible, as their families needed the income from their employment and few other jobs were available. Complaining to their supervisors about the situation would have been regarded as improper and ungrateful as evidenced by the votes against unionization. The original triggering event of one worker being injured presented a plausible way out of the situation for those who could neither complain nor leave. The belief that they could be injured caused them to tense their muscles as they worked; this, combined with the repetitive motions using machinery which was slightly out of

TABLE 4.1

t-Tests for Items Discriminating Between High and Low Soreness

Survey Item	Mean for High Soreness Group*	Mean for Low Soreness Group†	t (two-tailed test)
1. Do you feel steady muscle tension in your body as you work?	4.16	2.65	10.53 $^{\infty\infty}$
2. Do you feel relaxed on your job?	2.41	3.29	6.55 $^{\infty}$
3. Do you feel stress on your job?	3.46	2.62	6.24 $^{\infty}$
4. Do you think all cases of soreness are for real?	3.97	3.29	4.65 $^{\infty}$
5. To what extent do you think repetitive motions caused it?	4.08	3.42	4.47 $^{\infty}$
6. Does your job call for you to make repetitive body motions?	4.45	3.83	4.31 $^{\infty}$
7. To what extent do you think stress caused your soreness?	3.25	2.53	4.09 $^{\infty}$
8. Do you feel pressure for producing more?	3.42	2.81	3.90 $^{\infty}$
9. Is your job boring?	4.13	3.54	8.82 $^{\infty}$
10. Do tools out of adjustment cause you to use more pressure than you would normally use?	3.86	3.29	3.80 $^{\infty}$
11. Are you rushed and under pressure to get work out?	3.64	3.11	3.69 $^{\infty}$
12. Were you adequately trained for your job?	2.95	3.48	3.53 $^{\infty}$
13. To what extent do production rates cause stress?	3.42	2.92	3.18 $^{\infty}$
14. To what extent do you think production rates caused it?	3.33	2.74	3.18 $^{\infty}$
15. To what extent does your own pressure to produce more cause stress?	3.17	2.77	2.68 $^{\infty}$
16. Does your foreman help develop your talents and abilities by coaching and counseling you?	1.70	2.02	2.68 $^{\infty}$
17. To what extent do you think inadequate training caused it?	2.04	1.60	2.61 $^{\infty}$
18. Are there conflicting orders given by different people in the plant?	3.36	2.99	2.59 $^{\infty}$
19. Are you notified in advance when changes are to be made in any part of your job?	2.11	2.40	2.27 $^{\circ}$
20. Are you afraid to speak out about your gripes and frustrations?	2.32	1.97	2.23 $^{\circ}$
21. Is management willing to find and try new ways of doing things?	2.62	2.88	2.18 $^{\circ}$
22. To what extent does pressure from the foreman to produce more cause stress?	2.91	2.56	2.17 $^{\circ}$
23. Does your foreman give you feedback concerning your performance?	2.69	2.37	2.14 $^{\circ}$
24. Does management give your suggestions serious consideration?	2.22	2.46	2.11 $^{\circ}$
25. To what extent do you think inadequate materials caused it?	2.43	2.06	2.08 $^{\circ}$
26. Are you given authority to handle day-to-day problems and situations?	1.87	2.15	2.07 $^{\circ}$

(continued)

TABLE 4.1   Continued

Survey Item	Mean for High Soreness Group*	Mean for Low Soreness Group†	t (two-tailed test)
27. Is there ill-feeling among machine operators?	2.72	2.43	2.06°
28. Do you think the overall working environment is good?	2.55	2.82	2.02°
29. Are the production rates on your job attainable?	3.22	2.53	2.13°

SOURCE: Reprinted from "An action-research program for increasing employee involvement in problem solving," by W. Pasmore and F. Friedlander, published in *Administrative Science Quarterly, 27*(3), p. 354, by permission of *Administrative Science Quarterly.* © Administrative Science Quarterly, 1982.

°$p < .05$; °°$p < .01$.
*Experience soreness always or to a large extent.
†Experience some soreness or no soreness at all.

adjustment, induced the tenosynovitis symptoms which, in the final analysis, were very real for those affected. It is interesting to note that while most workers believed that high production rates caused their injuries, explanations involving the new lighting in the plant or possible contamination in the water continued to persist even after the environmental analyses were completed. Such explanations were probably preferred because they didn't point the finger at management but instead viewed everyone in the plant as innocent victims of some unknown condition beyond anyone's control. (Pasmore, 1983, p. 12)

This pattern resembles the pattern of mass psychogenic illness (MPI) that McGrath (1982) summarized:

(1) MPI is one of a number of possible alternative reactions to high levels of stress.
(2) MPI occurs when some or all of the following negative features are present in work situations:
    (a) undesirable physical conditions;
    (b) few motivating factors in the job itself; and
    (c) unfavorable conditions in the social environment.
(3) MPI occurs only for low-status persons in the work environment.
(4) MPI will increasingly and inevitably become the coping mechanism of choice, resulting in somatization, when stress increases, status is low, and other options become unavailable.
(5) An event will trigger MPI only if it is a noticeable, rational, and efficient plausible explanation of cause and effect in a given situation. In this way the triggering event:
    (a) gets the person out of a stressful situation, at least temporarily;
    (b) does so with no blame to the individual;
    (c) places the responsibility for the situation on management; and
    (d) expresses one's empathy with one's peers.
(6) Women are more often affected because they make up a larger percentage of those low-status/high-stress positions.

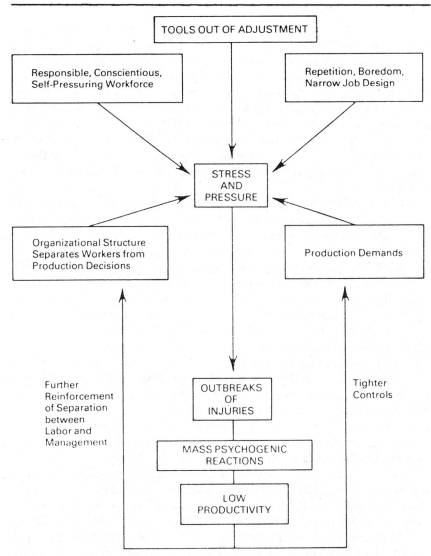

SOURCE: Reprinted from "An action-research program for increasing employee involvement in problem solving," by W. Pasmore and F. Friedlander, published in *Administrative Science Quarterly*, 27(3), p. 355, by permission of *Administrative Science Quarterly*. © Administrative Science Quarterly, 1982.

Figure 4.1 A Model of the Injury Process

Interventions on the basis of this theory led to a drop in soreness complaints from a high of 75 injuries reported when the team entered in the fifth year, to a low of five injuries reported during the ninth year.

The Activity of Theorizing

Several characteristics of theorizing are illustrated by Pasmore and Friedlander's work.

First, theorizing is an active process. A theory is good not just because it portrays the shape of the territory, but because it helps observers discover what that shape is. The soreness data became more meaningful as they were tied to a handful of principles, but these principles themselves became more meaningful as they were "seen" in more of the data. It is less critical that theories be accurate than that they reduce uncertainty and guide further questioning. In J. J. Thomson's phrase, a theory is a "policy rather than a creed." Theories suggest, stimulate, and direct movement from one flow chart to another.

The flow chart drawn by Pasmore and Friedlander resembles much of what passes for theory in organizational studies, and this introduces a second point. A flow chart can be useful because it holds separate phenomena together long enough for people to see where the chart is wrong. In this sense, the chart is like a hypothetical model that participants alter when they add their own perceptions of cause-effect relations in a problem like muscle damage. A flow chart also shows where communication occurs (connections) and where uncertainty is created if connections are weak, lagged, or intermittent.

Third, Pasmore and Friedlander's theory is self-contained in the sense that the only thing that can be predicted from it is the value or magnitude of other units in that same model. Essentially what they can say to practitioners is, "If our model accurately reflects the characteristics of soreness complaints, then we predict the following things will happen should any of the elements we've included change their values" (Dubin, 1976, p. 35).

Pasmore and Friedlander's work illustrates a fourth property of theorizing, the gradual transformation of specific-implicit employee theories into general-explicit theories that are more open to alteration and extension (Dutton & Starbuck, 1963). Specific-implicit theories are based on limited experience and have an unreflective, solitary origin that buries assumptions and logic. These theories are difficult to communicate, difficult to tear apart, and difficult to disentangle from current folklore. General-explicit theories, the type of theory represented in Pasmore and Friedlander's diagram, are based on extensive experience that has a reflective, collective origin and makes visible both assumptions and logic. The resulting theory is communicable, easy to tear apart, and extends beyond the specific cultural theories in which lay explanations for the soreness originated.

While it is implicit in the preceding four points, a fifth characteristic is that the abstract version of the injury process in the flow chart represents a creation, not a discovery. Individual laws may be discovered, but the theories that combine them are invented. It is difficult to realize that theories are invented rather than discovered because we often mistake projection for apprehension. "There is a class of puzzles which depends on the difficulty we all have in becoming aware of a mode of representation, which we project onto what is experienced as fact. The next number in the sequence 4, 14, 34, 42, . . . , is 59; these are express stops on the eighth avenue subway, as every New Yorker will tell you—if he thinks of it. The next letter in the sequence O, T, T, F, F, . . . , is S; these are the initial letters of the number words 'one,' 'two,' 'three,'... We have been tricked because we were looking for properties of the thing-in-itself, and not of something constituted by the forms of the knowing mind" (Kaplan, 1964, p. 309).

Pasmore and Friedlander impose a pattern of their own invention on the answers to the survey, a pattern that can be altered or replaced by a different one (for example, as chronological age decreases, complaints of soreness increase). Their model is neither inherent in the answers nor was it discovered.

The sixth and final property of theorizing illustrated by the example is that the theory itself is a symbolic construction that reaches beyond itself for denotation. We usually think that people know pretty well what a theory means and they want to know if it is true. In actual practice, that sequence is less common than its reverse—people know pretty well that a theory is true, but they want to know what it means (Weick, 1985, p. 583). A theory reaches beyond itself for denotation in the sense that people treat it as true, even though they are not sure why or where or for whom it is true. Those questions get answered when the observer treats every event as if it affirmed the theory, and then looks closely at particulars that do not fit. Continued articulation of where the theory works and where it does not gradually tells the observer what the theory is about. The question is not, Is the theory true? All theories are true (McGuire, 1983). The question is, When and where is the theory true?

The Role of Relevance in Theorizing

Our use of an action-research study to illustrate key properties of theory construction implies that relevance is woven into theorizing from the start. That implication is intentional. "Theory is of practice, and must stand or fall with its practicality, provided only that the mode and contexts of its application are suitably specified" (Kaplan, 1964, p. 196).

If relevance is a property of theorizing, then how do we improve relevance, so that we can improve theorizing? A useful way to think through the question is Thomas and Tymon's (1982) discussion of five necessary properties of relevant research.

The first characteristic of useful ideas is that they have descriptive relevance. They incorporate phenomena practitioners actually encounter, which means "war stories" are signal, not noise.

Useful ideas also focus on outcomes or goals that practitioners want to influence (the second criterion of goal relevance). This criterion does not mean that organizational theories are limited to issues of cost-effectiveness and performance, because constituencies have more diverse interests than this.

The third criterion, operational validity, refers to whether the causal variables in the theory can be controlled by practitioners. This is the most interesting of the five criteria because it is the most open to debate. Control of variables in organizations is tied to issues of accountability, blame, responsibility, status, and authority, which means that practitioners often either deny they have control over variables that theorists think are controllable or they claim control that seems unlikely. Furthermore, theoretical observations often extend the range of what might be controllable in a situation. Thus theorists and practitioners will usually disagree on the amount of operational validity that theories have. The combination of multiple sign-offs, steep hierarchies, reactive roles, standard operating procedures, and risk aversion will usually lead practitioners to say they control fewer variables than theorists say they do. As a result, practitioners will generally claim that theories have less relevance than theorists claim they have.

The fourth criterion, nonobviousness, means that useful theories meet or exceed the complexity of the commonsense theories that practitioners already use. Most practitioners work with theories that contain more than two variables, so this criterion is not as easy to meet as it looks. March (1984) contends that good theories complement common sense and make contributions at the margin, which is another way of saying that relevant theory is not redundant with common sense.

March argues that people in most organizations have a great deal of context-specific knowledge, but there are limits to what this knowledge covers. For example, fast learners often become fixed on the first behavior they find that is rewarding. But the first behavior that works is often poorer than one that would have been discovered had the search continued past the point of the first reinforcement. Thus good theories contribute when they add supplements that are not redundant with context-specific knowledge.

Finally, relevant theories are timely and are developed soon enough to deal with current problems. Timely theories tend to have limited generality because they are tied to specific times, places, and values (for example, so-called theories of sex discrimination or urban growth). Timely theories are usually little more than empirical descriptions of places where one might test more generic theories (Turner, 1979, p. 430).

The five determinants of relevance proposed by Thomas and Tymon demand even more of a theory than do conventional criteria such as refutability, parsimony, and logical coherence. Since theories are abstract, they can incorporate goal relevance, operational validity, and nonobviousness. But this very abstractness also makes it harder for them to incorporate detail, descriptive relevance, and timeliness.

Pasmore and Friedlander's model is of special interest because it seems not to have had a problem with descriptive relevance (it included features that are found in the electronics plant) or timeliness (it addressed and reduced a pressing problem). At the same time the theory also has goal relevance (management wanted to reduce injuries and raise productivity), operational validity (management had the capability to reduce demands, change raw materials, and improve the adjustment of tools), and nonobviousness (management's response to the problem created a vicious circle that made the problem worse and management did not see this). The important lesson in Pasmore and Friedlander's work is that timeliness need not preclude timelessness.

Lewin, an action-researcher much like Pasmore and Friedlander, made essentially the same point when he said, "There is nothing so practical as a good theory." Lewin's well-worn assertion has gained new meaning on the basis of John Miner's (1984) fascinating discovery that out of 32 theories in organizational science, the 4 judged to be most useful and valid by 100 scholars were theories developed by scholars who were trained the same way Lewin was trained, in psychology. These 4 high-validity, high usefulness theories were all motivational and included theories of job characteristics (Hackman), goal setting (Locke), achievement (McClelland), and role-motivation (Miner).

Theories of special interest are those whose validity exceeds their usefulness, because this combination runs contrary to Lewin's maxim. There were 11 instances in which the validity rating exceeded the usefulness rating, and four of these have a pronounced discrepancy (high validity, low usefulness). These 4 theories included the work of March and Simon, J. Stacy Adams, Tannenbaum, and Graen (Miner, 1984, p. 301). Miner suggests that we need to cultivate "applications theorists" who can take good theories such as these four and extend them into the world of practice. One recent effort to do this is Grandori's (1984) prescriptions for decision making built from work like March and Simon's (1958).

An alternative strategy to that of applying valid theories that already exist is to act like an applications theorist from the beginning, a strategy that is implied by Pasmore and Friedlander's experience. The nature of this alternative strategy is suggested by the 8 theories in Miner's sample that achieved a higher rating on usefulness than on validity. These 8 included the work of Likert, Skinner, Trist, Lawrence and Lorsch, Herzberg, McGregor, Bennis, and Fayol. What is intriguing about all of these theories is that when they have been applied, their "applications have often detached themselves from the underlying theory, developing further in large part through a process of trial and error. Thus, although the theory was a catalyst that set the application in motion, the application came to achieve an independent identity of its own" (Miner, 1984, p. 300). The same process undoubtedly occurs with theories that have low validity and low usefulness.

Thomas and Tymon seem to assume that practitioners keep the same theory throughout the application process and therefore the theory guides them at every step. This is why it is so important for the theory to have timeliness and descriptive relevance. Miner, however, suggests that a theory can also serve as a catalyst that sets action in motion. But once action is set in motion, the theory can then be set aside in favor of trial and error and close scrutiny of tight feedback loops that are sensitive to local conditions. Timeliness and descriptive relevance are added later by trial and error; they do not need to be in the theory itself. This possibility extends dramatically the number of theories that now become useful and valid because it trims the criteria for relevance from five to three—goal relevance, operational validity, nonobviousness.

Thus a concern with relevance can improve theory in one of two ways. First, if the five criteria of relevance are salient from the start, as in Lewin's work, Pasmore and Friedlander's work, and much action-research, then the theory is general and accurate from the outset. Second, if the theory catalyzes an understanding of what might be happening in a specific situation and then triggers diagnostic action that is detached from the theory, this sequence activates three criteria immediately, and the other two criteria later during diagnosis and implementation. If the understanding that develops later during diagnosis and implementation is then used to revise and generalize the original theory, then that theory again becomes stronger.

THE PROCESS OF THEORIZING
ABOUT ORGANIZATIONAL COMMUNICATION

We have seen that theories are tools of inquiry that direct, suggest, and stimulate observation. Theories are valued, not just because their concepts correspond to real objects but because they facilitate exploration of objects. This instrumental view of theorizing is important because organizational researchers are often affected by the paradox of conceptualization: "The proper concepts are needed to formulate a good theory, but we need a good theory to arrive at proper concepts . . . the paradox is resolved by a process of approximation: the better our concepts, the better the theory we can formulate with them, and, in turn, the better the concepts available for the next improved theory" (Kaplan, 1964, pp. 53-54).

Successive rounds of clarification and improvement are what we meant earlier by the phrase "a theory reaches beyond itself for denotation." This is the process we wish to explore more fully in this section. We will look at the concepts of mechanistic and organic systems and at the theory that the mechanistic form is rational in a stable environment but irrational in an unstable environment, while the organic form shows the opposite pattern.

Burns and Stalker's formal descriptions of these two systems do not specify how communication mediates the predicted outcomes. What we have assumed in the following discussion is that each property of mechanistic-organic systems contains tacit assumptions about communication that need to be made explicit. They need to be made explicit because they are among the reasons each property has the effects it does; the assumptions are part of the denotation and meaning of that property.

To make the assumptions explicit, we apply the property as originally stated to actual or imagined organizations and pay close attention to where it fits, where it fails to fit, and what adjustments, additions, and specifications we must make to improve its fit. Those adjustments, additions, and specifications are clues to conditions that must be met if the property is to have its predicted effects (Greenwald, Tratkanis, Leippe, & Baumgardner, 1986).

The communication assumptions we will discuss were uncovered when each mechanistic or organic property was "set in motion" in a hypothesized organization characterized by the interactions, cause maps, presumptions, and actions described in the beginning of this chapter. When each property was examined in the context of this communication-rich prototype, several communication assumptions were suggested. These suggestions have been inserted after each property in the form of "comments."

These comments are eclectic interpretations of the exact words Burns and Stalker used. These interpretations are grounded in a selective reading of the organizational communication literature, a social psychological perspective on organizations similar to that used in the introduction of this chapter, and intuition. Nevertheless, they illustrate the nature of ongoing theorizing.

These comments illustrate theorizing because specific organizational properties are linked with underlying ideas about communication, which then flesh out the property, which then strengthens the underlying ideas, and so on. In this process of successive definition, denotation becomes more explicit, the property itself is understood more fully, and its relevance to communication scholars becomes more apparent.

If beliefs prefigure observation, as we have argued they do, then by adding communication properties to the denotation of ideas like mechanistic and organic systems, more will be seen and understood when the ideas are imposed to label, connect, and coordinate the phenomena of organizations. When the theorist works with this communication-enriched theory, and sees where it works, where it does not, and why, that person will have a clearer idea what the theory is about. That clearer idea in turn should facilitate the addition of newer, more powerful concepts and relationships.

Before we discuss specific communication assumptions linked with Burns and Stalker, we should say more about why we chose this formulation to illustrate theorizing. Aside from its prominence in the field of organizational studies, this formulation illustrates the activity of theorizing and it addresses all five issues of relevance.

The theory illustrates each of the six characteristics associated with theorizing viewed as an activity. The theory aids discovery because its properties take on new meaning when they are linked with communication variables. The theory holds diverse phenomena of structure, process, and environment together and contains sufficient variables that it can generate self-contained predictions. The theory is an effort to turn specific-implicit ideas into general-explicit theories. The theory is a creation rather than a discovery in the sense that many other contingency theories supposedly interpret the same problem Burns and Stalker are interested in but use none of the language and concepts they do. Finally, the theory gains meaning through use. It is not so much confirmed or falsified as made denotatively clearer when it is used.

The theory was also chosen because it illustrates the five grounds of relevance mentioned earlier. The theory has descriptive validity because it is derived from case studies of electronics firms and describes problems actually encountered in such firms. It has goal validity because it is a theory about outcomes that are of interest to practicing managers: efficiency, predictability, innovation. The theory has operational validity because it describes levers that managers can manipulate, levers such as job descriptions, organizational design, content of instructions, reporting relationships, and access to information. The theory is nonobvious in the sense that it contains relationships not normally included in lay theories (that is, mechanistic systems are local rather than cosmopolitan, organic systems have multiple hierarchies). Finally, the theory has timeliness because environmental turbulence is a salient contemporary problem, especially for electronics firms, which are the focus of this theory.

Thus the distinction between mechanistic and organic systems is attractive to study because it has a good track record, it has been in the literature for 25 years, and it captures a fundamental property of organizations. And yet with all of this staying power, there are ways in which we can gain new insights into this basic distinction if we spell out more of the communication assumptions it incorporates.

The key ideas for Burns and Stalker are these. The distinction between organic and mechanistic refers to management systems. Management systems are assumed to be affected by three variables: (1) the rate of technical or market change; (2) the strength of individual commitments to political or status-gaining ends; and (3) the capacity of directors to lead, interpret, and prescribe. The core idea is that as the rate of change varies, different systems of control, information conveyance, and authorization are needed (Burns and Stalker, 1961, p. 97). The underlying argument is that the mechanistic form is rational in a stable environment because stability allows tasks to be programmed. When there is instability, not only can one not program "but innovation requires a team approach where each member is equally important, although the direction shifts from member to member depending on the task at hand" (Hage, 1980, p. 34). The rational structure under conditions of instability is the organic form.

The distinction between organic and mechanistic is not a dichotomy; rather, these two forms represent the extreme points on a continuum. This means that there are intermediate stages and that organizations can oscillate between these forms as the rate of change varies. Burns and Stalker are concerned not only with the outcomes that were important to Weber—efficiency, predictability, and calculability of action—but also with innovation, the key word in the title of their book.

MECHANISTIC SYSTEMS

Mechanistic systems have the following characteristics:

"(a) the specialized differentiation of functional tasks into which the problems and tasks facing the concern as a whole are broken down";

Comment: "Functional tasks" are differentiated according to specialties and skills that the organization has, which means that how it labels its specialties will affect which tasks it designs. "Differentiation" is a key aspect of cognitive complexity (Bartunek, Gordon, & Weathersby, 1983), which suggests that task design will vary as a function of the cognitive complexity of the designer. Characteristic "a" also suggests that the organization will see the external world through the lens of the tasks it has differentiated (Dearborn & Simon, 1958). What an organization thinks it can do is what it will see needs to be done in the world. External problems are labeled and sorted into internal categories defined by tasks the organization can perform.

"(b) the abstract nature of each individual task, which is pursued with techniques and purposes more or less distinct from those of the concern as a whole; i.e., the functionaries tend to pursue the technical improvement of means, rather than the accomplishment of the ends of the concern";

Comment: Tasks are defined as individual, stand-alone assignments, which means that in a mechanistic system, dependencies will be underestimated or neglected and responsibility will be hard to assign and often meaningless. If dependencies are underestimated, frustration should be high because it is hard to diagnose adverse influences on performance. People who view themselves as independent are not likely to feel that their problems are caused by the action of someone else. To describe individual tasks as "abstract" is to suggest that they are artificial without some meaningful context provided by their placement in a means-ends chain, and therefore they are subject to meaninglessness and goal displacement (Scott, 1981, pp. 299-300).

"(c) the reconciliation, for each level of the hierarchy, of these distinct performances by the immediate superiors, who are also, in turn, responsible for seeing that each is relevant in his own special part of the main task";

Comment: Description of the superior's activity as "reconciliation" is a provocative choice of word. The superior brings the several distinct and potentially conflicting performances into harmony so they are seen as relevant to whatever he or she is held responsible for. Thus the superior engages in both conflict resolution and uncertainty absorption. Coordination is done by the superior, not by work flows or subordinates. Since the same process of reconciliation occurs "for each level in the hierarchy," there is a communication chain with several links. Finally, to describe work as a "performance" is to invite analysis by those communication scholars who have focused on performance as metaphor (Pacanowsky & O'Donnell-Trujillo, 1983) and as activity (Fine & Speer, 1977).

"(d) the precise definition of rights and obligations and technical methods attached to each functional role";

"(e) The translation of rights and obligations and methods into the responsibilities of functional position";

Comment: Characteristics "d" and "e" both suggests that most communication in a mechanistic organization is job related. Communication clarity seems important in a mechanistic system as is suggested by the emphasis on "precise" definition, although it is not clear in whose view precision is being defined. To say that definitions are "attached to" a role suggests a somewhat arbitrary assignment of rights, obligations, and methods that rules out participation by the subordinate in defining what the job is.

"(f) Hierarchic structure of control, authority, and communication";

Comment: This is the first explicit mention of "communication" in Burns and Stalker's description of a mechanistic system. Its inclusion here with authority and control suggests that all three are similarly structured and reinforce one another. Communication, in other words, tends to flow along the lines of authority and control in a mechanistic system. Since communication tends to create structure, it is likely that authority and control will follow the lines first laid down by regularities in communication.

"(g) A reinforcement of the hierarchic structure by the location of knowledge of actualities exclusively at the top of the hierarchy, where the final reconciliation of distinct tasks and assessment of relevance is made";

Comment: In a footnote, Burns and Stalker note that this attribute "often takes on a clearly expressive aspect" (p. 120), by which they mean that omniscience at the top is dramatized visibly and repeatedly. They cite the example of one firm in which "all correspondence was delivered to the managing director, who would thereafter distribute excerpts to members of the staff, synthesizing their replies into the letter of reply which he eventually sent." Peters (1978) and Pfeffer (1981) have described the symbolic importance of agendas, calendars, and memos to dramatize and exert influence. If all information moves toward the top of the organization, then the top will become overloaded unless there is trustworthy uncertainty absorption throughout the chain of communication. Since trust is rare in mechanistic systems, the probability of overload should be high.

"(h) A tendency for interaction between members of the concern to be vertical, e.g., between superior and subordinate";

Comment: Vertical interaction is one of the better documented aspects of organizational communication (Jablin, 1982). Upward influence, formal communication, and the refinements of vertical communication developed by Graen (1976) through his vertical dyad linkage model all are relevant to this characteristic.

"(i) A tendency for operations and working behaviour to be governed by the instructions and decisions issued by superiors";

Comment: This description of communication is similar to Leavitt and Mueller's (1951) description of one-way communication since the superior's instructions "govern" what the subordinate does. There is more emphasis on the direction and limiting of action than on feedback and negotiation. Again we see that authority and participation in decision making is focused rather than dispersed.

"(j) Insistence on loyalty to the concern and obedience to superiors as a condition of membership";

Comment: Loyalty is often recast as "identification" by communication scholars (Cheney, 1983) but they usually mean identification with the mission of an organization, not with the place itself. This is the only defining characteristic in which the relatively harsh word *obedience* is used to indicate the form of compliance that is expected. The communication issues for someone who is expected to "obey" are relatively simple and clear-cut, namely, do what you are told or you will be punished.

"(k) A greater importance and prestige attaching to internal (local) than to general (cosmopolitan) knowledge, experience, and skill";

Comment: If the organization operates in a stable environment, then local knowledge is sufficient because once something is learned, it does not change.

Forecasting, anticipation, and planning are all relatively unimportant when the rate of change is slow. Since uncertainties that do arise originate in local conditions, people with more detailed knowledge of local conditions will be in a better position to resolve those uncertainties and to gain power (Salancik & Pfeffer, 1977). Mechanistic organizations should have a limited worldview, maintain relatively crude stereotypes (Levine & Campbell, 1972), overestimate their distinctive competence, and be slow to sense when their advantage is disappearing.

Summary of Mechanistic Systems

To summarize, the essence of a mechanistic system is definition and dependence. The more definition that is given, the more omniscient top management has to be or seem to be so that no function is left out, left uninformed, or left with insufficient authority. Among the management personnel in a mechanistic system there is rivalry for resources, which means that top management becomes a "court of appeal" where conflicting interests get reconciled (Burns & Stalker, 1961, pp. 124-125). That is relevant for communication scholars because it suggests that the main thing mechanistic firms do is argue (Weick & Browning, 1986).

Mechanistic systems (for example, automobile assembly plants) tend to be efficient but relatively weak in product innovation and morale. Paradoxically, "mechanical organizations, which have low rates of change, are also places where radical innovation can occur, because they are more likely to have crises as well as a structure that is more tolerant of dictatorial practices" (Hage, 1980, p. 243). Legitimacy is a more salient basis of authority than is competence in mechanistic systems.

ORGANIC SYSTEMS

Organic organizational forms (for example, law firms), which are more appropriate for changing conditions are described by the following characteristics:

"(a) the contributive nature of special knowledge and experience to the common task of the concern";

Comment: In an organic system, the images shift from those of obedience, dependence, and definition to those of volition, interdependence, and improvisation. Initiative shifts from the supervisor to the person who possesses the skill. To describe a system as "contributive" is to imply that if people have relevant experiences for a problem, they should offer it whether the supervisor asks for it or not. Since supervisors are less visible and influential in organic systems, voluntary contribution becomes more crucial.

"(b) The 'realistic' nature of the individual task, which is seen as set by the total situation of the concern";

Comment: Tasks are set by people, not by total situations, but in an organic system people identify more closely with the mission of the firm, which means they speak on behalf of the firm when they set tasks. People become the channel through which the shared mission is translated into "realistic" activities. No longer are tasks described mechanistically as arbitrary collections of rights, obligations, and methods assembled independently of the mission. Instead, tasks change when people agree that the mission has changed. The very fact that tasks are thought to be "realistic" makes compliance with their requirements more likely.

"(c) The adjustment and continual re-definition of individual tasks through interactions with others";

Comment: Task design is a process of interpersonal negotiation. Since tasks are adjusted and redefined, perceptions of tasks are crucial and may outweigh physical characteristics in determining performance (Thomas & Griffin, 1983). A system in which tasks are redefined continually resembles a self-designing organization (Nystrom, Hedberg, & Starbuck, 1976).

"(d) the shedding of 'responsibility' as a limited field of rights, obligations and methods. (Problems may not be posted upwards, downwards, or sideways as being someone else's responsibility)";

Comment: This characteristic is an interesting twist on the concept of "diffusion of responsibility." When used in the context of the group decision making, the concept means that responsibility becomes diffused among group members so that no one takes full responsibility for the group's decisions and action. However, when used in the context of organic systems, the concept of responsibility diffusion means just the opposite: Everybody is responsible for everything. Because people identify with the firm, it is everyone's responsibility to do what is needed to help the firm survive. The very structure (or lack of it) in an organic system makes it hard to assign responsibility because there are no stable public sets of rights, obligations, and methods. Blaming should be relatively uncommon in an organic system and so should the defense "It's not my job."

"(e) the spread of commitment to the concern beyond any technical definition";

Comment: "Commitment to the concern" resembles commitment to a clan (Ouchi & Price, 1978) where one's professional identification is subordinated to the setting within which the profession is practiced.

"(f) a network structure of control, authority, and communication. The sanctions which apply to the individual's conduct in his working role derive more from presumed community of interest with the rest of the working organization in the survival and growth of the firm, and less from a contractual relationship between himself and a non-personal corporation, represented for him by an immediate supervisor";

Comment: Network structures are among the most common structures discussed within the communication literature (Fine & Kleinman, 1983). The hub of a wheel network, in an organic organization, shifts as the problem shifts. In network structure decisions move back and forth between relevant points rather than in a single hierarchic pattern. Authority, communication, and control are problem-specific and change as the relevant expertise changes (Blau & Alba, 1982).

"(g) omniscience is no longer imputed to the head of the concern; knowledge about the technical or commercial nature of the here and now task may be located anywhere in the network; this location becoming the ad hoc centre of control, authority, and communication";

Comment: Again we see that there is no top management in an organic organization. The top instead is an ad hoc center defined by specialized knowledge that is relevant to the task.

"(h) a lateral rather than a vertical direction of communication through the organization, communication between people of different rank, also resembling consultation rather than command";

Comment: This descriptor is explicitly about communication and describes communication among equals, partly because the vertical dimension in many organic systems essentially disappears. While organic systems do not have a hierarchy, they do have stratification because people are differentiated on the basis of their knowledge about the problem being faced. To "consult" is to offer options, listen, paraphrase, question, advise, and then let the target of the consultation make whatever decision seems sensible. People who consult can control inputs but not outcomes. In contrast, people who *command* can control inputs and, at least, short-term outcomes.

"(i) a content of communication which consists of information and advice rather than instructions and decisions";

Comment: Information and advice, when compared with instruction and decisions, resemble an incomplete syllogism or an enthymeme (Bitzer, 1959) whose final premise awaits completion by the person who gathers information.

Gossip (March & Sevon, 1982) is an important source of information and one would expect to see gossip valued more highly in organic systems than in mechanistic ones. The provision of information and advice suggests more give and take and more two-way communication than in a mechanistic system.

"(j) commitment to the concern's tasks and to the 'technological ethos' of material progress and expansion is more highly valued than loyalty and obedience";

Comment: Ideology (Beyer, 1981) is an important source of cohesion within the organic organization, and the ideology of progress and expansion is common in unstable environments. A commitment to progress and expansion is a commitment to change, self-design, innovation, and learning. Ideology is a crude substitute for decision rationality. A narrow, clear, complex ideology can energize action and also provide a modestly rational criterion against which alternatives can be assessed without losing motivation and commitment. The ideology does the deliberating without weakening action. It may be that quality which makes ideology so crucial in organic systems.

"(k) importance and prestige attach to affiliations and expertise valid in the industrial and technical commercial milieux external to the firm";

Comment: External reference groups, contacts, and networks are sources of experience and information for organic systems and are valued and cultivated rather than ignored. External resources may be able to resolve uncertainties internal to the organization, which means that the person who links the outside resource with the inside problem effectively reduces uncertainty and therefore should acquire power. Whether one actually reduces uncertainty or is merely the agent through which uncertainty is reduced should make little difference in the acquisition of prestige and importance.

Summary of Organic Systems

In summary, the organic system institutionalizes a steady state built around the creation of new products to meet particularistic needs. Organic systems tend to be weak in the area of cost cutting. Surprisingly, organic systems exhibit an incremental rather than radical approach to change because power is diffused among so many specialists. Interest groups in an organic system tend to form around occupations and value preferences.

Since an organic system is a management system that facilitates nonprogrammed decision making, it works only if it has a "dependably constant system of shared beliefs about the common interests of the working community and about the standards and criteria used in it to judge achievement, individual contributions, expertise and other matters by which a person or a combination of people are evaluated" (Burns & Stalker, 1961, p. 119). This system of shared beliefs is called a "code of conduct," but bears a close resemblance to what is now called corporate culture. (Schein, 1985).

That resemblance suggests the interesting possibility that the seeming burst of interest in corporate culture during the 1980s may not be due so much to the Japanese influence or the influence of entrepreneurs and high-tech firms. Instead, it may be explained by the fact that as environmental change has accelerated, a relatively greater number of organic organizations held together by culture have survived. This is why we see more culture and judge it to be more important. There is not more culture, there simply are more organic systems.

THE PRODUCT OF THEORIZING PROCESSES

Current organizational theory is often described as fragmented (Whitley, 1984, p. 376). That impression will be reinforced for people who read this book. However, fragments are inevitable and they need not reduce the value of a theory.

Fragments are inevitable for several reasons. First, the search for one true unifying theory that explains organized human behavior is fruitless because there is no such theory. Furthermore, it is hard to cumulate organizational theories when there are multiple levels of analysis, when the open systems that are studied are not of our own construction (Henshel, 1971), when professional rewards go to innovators rather than to cumulators and synthesizers, and when old theories are ignored rather than remade when new theories are proposed (Newton-Smith, 1981).

When all these forces converge on the individual theorist who is subject to overload, it is not surprising that the field contains many theories that do not cohere.

While this diversity is confusing to individuals, that is largely irrelevant because the locus of scientific knowledge is social, not solitary. Knowledge is a collective social product only imperfectly represented in any one mind. Therefore, properties of a field such as its theoretical power, record of verification, and integration are social products that are imperfectly represented in the work of any one scientist (Campbell, 1969).

If I cannot see the coherence in organizational theory, and neither can Whitley (1984), McGuire (1982), or Astley (1984), that does not mean it is not there. Coherence may exist collectively even though our limited rationality cannot grasp it. If individuals can never know their field in its entirety, then theorizing boils down to an act of faith that collective omniscience is significant and growing. Faith is required because no one will ever know for sure whether it is. Thus whether to give up or proceed in the face of diverse theories comes down to an existential choice, the validity of which lies in the path of the action.

In this context, filling the gaps between theories improves collective omniscience since it extends coverage. March's (1984) concern with nonobvious theory, discussed earlier, can now be seen to make sense for both basic and applied research since the field "knows more" as it achieves increased nonredundancy with common sense.

Second, changes in level of analysis may cause theory fragmentation (Roberts, Hulin, & Rousseau, 1978; Glick, 1985). This possibility was suggested by Hage (1980): "Micro-sociological hypotheses usually require limits. The human scale is much smaller than the organizational one—at least as far as hypotheses are concerned. Beyond this the 'world' of the individual appears to be dominated by normal curves where too much of a good thing is as bad as too little. In contrast, linearity appears to be a good first approximation in the organizational 'world'" (p. 202).

Most micro level hypotheses are curvilinear, most macro level hypotheses are linear. For example, McGuire's (1968) model of individual persuasion is curvilinear and predicts that people with moderately high intelligence are more persuasible than those with either high intelligence or low intelligence. Pelz and Andrews (1966) show that individuals become more creative as they are given more autonomy, but only up to a point, after which more freedom leads to lower creativity. As the size of a peer group increases, individuals become more creative until they get too many conflicting inputs, and thereafter individual creativity declines. Group creativity, however, increases steadily as more ideas, more people, more inputs, and more information are added (McGrath, 1984, pp. 132-133).

Finally, problems created by theoretical diversity often are magnified because much organizational research is presented in a literary style that makes demands on the reader for imaginative interpretation. The difficulty with that style is that the reader shares in the process of interpretation, which means it is hard to know how much understanding is shared with the author and how much is the reader's own projection onto the data (for example, much of Gregory Bateson's later writing seems to be appreciated both for reasons of sharing and reasons of projection). The problem is not likely to go away since much organizational research often boils down to storytelling (Postman, 1984) and glossing (Weick, 1981). But the problem need not be serious as long as the interpretation is done systematically and with precision, in ways that are open to consensual validation.

Thus the products of theorizing may be flawed, but the flaws need not be fatal. Existing flaws in the process and substance of theorizing can be remedied in one of three ways (Foddy & Thorngate, 1978).

First, the flaws may be assigned to methodological sources. Thus we could argue that theorizing is flawed because data gathering and data analytic techniques in organizational science are insensitive to important features of data bases such as level of analysis and context dependency. The remedy is to beef up the field by improving technique.

Second, the flaws could be assigned to normative sources such as personal and social influences. Thus theorizing is flawed because researchers are incompetent, poorly trained, or so concerned with professional advancement that they favor style over substance, quantity over quality, and easy/trivial problems over hard/important ones. The remedy is for the field to grow up.

Third, the flaws in theorizing may simply reflect flaws in the subject matter. Organizations are overdetermined, generally disorganized, and have continually shifting causes and structures that can only be explained with context-specific ideas, not by theories. Since there is nothing stable to study, the advice is to give up.

Beef up. Grow up. Give up. Those are the three choices organizational communication scholars have whenever they fear their work is little better than a plumbing diagram for a Scottish castle.

REFERENCES

Astley, W. G. (1984) Subjectivity, sophistry and symbolism in management science. *Journal of Management Studies, 21*, 259-272.

Axelrod, R. (1976) *The structure of decision: The cognitive maps of political elites.* Princeton, NJ: Princeton University Press.

Bartunek, J. M., Gordon, J. R., & Weathersby, R. P. (1983). Developing "complicated" understanding in administrators. *Academy of Management Review, 8,* 273-284.

Beyer, J. M. (1981). Ideologies, values, and decision making in organizations. In P. C. Nystrom and W. H. Starbuck (Eds.), *Handbook of organizational design* (Vol. 2, pp. 166-202). New York: Oxford University Press.

Bitzer, L. (1959). Aristotle's enthymeme revisited. *Quarterly Journal of Speech, 45,* 399-408.

Blau, J. R., & Alba, R. D. (1982). Empowering nets of participation. *Administrative Science Quarterly, 27,* 363-379.

Burns, T., & Stalker, G. M. (1961). *The management of innovation.* London: Tavistock.

Campbell, D. T. (1969). Ethnocentrism of disciplines and the fish-scale model of omniscience. In M. Sherif and C. W. Sherif (Eds.), *Interdisciplinary relationships in the social sciences* (pp. 328-384). Chicago: Aldine.

Cheney, G. (1983). The rhetoric of identification and the study of organizational communication. *Quarterly Journal of Speech, 69,* 143-158.

Dearborn, D. C., & Simon, H. A. (1958). Selective perception: A note on the departmental identification of executives. *Sociometry, 21,* 140-144.

Dubin, R. (1976). Theory building in applied areas. In M. D. Dunnette (Ed.), *Handbook of industrial and organization psychology* (pp. 17-39). Chicago: Rand McNally.

Dutton, J. M., & Starbuck, W. H. (1963). On managers and theories. *Management International, 6,* 1-11.

Fine, E. C., & Speer, J. H. (1977). A new look at performance. *Communication Monographs, 44,* 373-389.

Fine, G. A., & Kleinman, S. (1983). Network and meaning: An interactionist approach to structure. *Symbolic Interaction, 6,* 97-110.

Foddy, M., & Thorngate, W. (1978). *Theory, method, and practice in social psychology.* Unpublished manuscript, Carleton University, Ottawa, Ontario.

Glick, W. H. (1985). Conceptualizing and measuring organizational and psychological climate: Pitfalls in multilevel research. *Academy of Management Review, 10,* 601-616.

Graen, G. (1976). Role-making processes within complex organizations. In M. D. Dunnette (Ed.), *Handbook of industrial and organizational psychology* (pp. 1201-1245). Chicago: Rand McNally.

Grandori, A. (1984). A prescriptive contingency view of organizational decision making. *Administrative Science Quarterly, 29,* 192-209.

Greenwald, A. G., Tratkanis, A. R., Leippe, M. R., & Baumgardener, M. H. (1986). Under what conditions does theory obstruct research progress? *Psychological Review, 93,* 216-229.

Hage, J. (1980). *Theories of organization.* New York: Wiley.

Hall, R. I. (1984). The natural logic of management policy making: Its implications for the survival of an organization. *Management Science, 30,* 905-927.

Henshel, R. L. (1971). Sociology and prediction. *American Sociologist, 6,* 213-220.

Jablin, F. M. (1982). Formal structural characteristics of organizations and superior-subordinate communication. *Human Communication Research, 8,* 338-347.

Kaplan, A. (1964). *The conduct of inquiry.* New York: Harper & Row.

Leavitt, H. J., & Mueller, R.A.H. (1951). Some effects of feedback on communication. *Human Relations, 4,* 401-410.

Levine, R. A., & Campbell, D. T. (1972). *Ethnocentrism.* New York: John Wiley.

March, J. G. (1984, August). *Organizational consultants and organizational research.* Speech delivered at the Academy of Management, Boston.

March, J. G., & Sevon, G. (1982). Gossip, information, and decision making. In L. S. Sproull & P. D. Larkey (Eds.), *Advances in information processing in organizations* (Vol. 1). Greenwich, CT: JAI Press.

March, J. G., & Simon, H. A. (1958). *Organizations.* New York: John Wiley.

McGrath, J. E. (1982). Complexities, cautions and concepts in research on mass psychogenic illness. In M. J. Colligan, J. W. Pennebaker, & L. R. Murphy (Eds.), *Mass psychogenic illness: A social psychological analysis* (pp. 57-85). Hillsdale, NJ: Lawrence Erlbaum.

McGrath, J. E. (1984). *Groups: Interaction and performance.* Englewood Cliffs, NJ: Prentice-Hall.

McGuire, J. W. (1982). Management theory: Retreat to the academy. *Business Horizons, 25*(4), 31-37.

McGuire, W. J. (1968). Personality and susceptibility to social influence. In E. F. Borgatta & W. W. Lambert (Eds.), *Handbook of personality theory and research* (pp. 1130-1187). Chicago: Rand McNally.

McGuire, W. J. (1983). A contextualist theory of knowledge: Its implications for innovations and reform in psychological research. In L. Berkowitz (Ed.), *Advances in experimental social psychology* (Vol. 16, pp. 1-47). New York: Academic Press.

Meyer, A. D. (1982). Adapting to environmental jolts. *Administrative Science Quarterly, 27,* 515-537.

Miner, J. B. (1984). The validity and usefulness of theories in an emerging organizational science. *Academy of Management Review, 9,* 296-306.

Newton-Smith, W. H. (1981). *The rationality of science.* Boston: Routledge & Kegan Paul.

Nystrom, P. C., Hedberg, B.L.T., & Starbuck, W. H. (1976). Interacting processes as organization designs. In R. H. Kilmann, L. R. Pondy, & D. P. Sleven (Eds.), *The management of organization design* (Vol. 1, pp. 209-230). New York: Elsevier North-Holland.

Ouchi, W. G., & Price, R. L. (1978). Hierarchies, clans, and theory Z: A new perspective on organization development. *Organizational Dynamics, 7*(2), 25-44.

Pacanowsky, M. E., & O'Donnell-Trujillo, N. (1983). Organizational communication as cultural performance. *Communication Monographs, 50,* 126-147.

Pasmore, W. A. (1983). *Improving worker morale and reducing days lost from work: Mass psychogenic illness can make you sick.* Paper prepared for the 43rd annual AMA Congress on Occupational Health.

Pasmore, W., & Friedlander, F. (1982). An action-research program for increasing employee involvement in problem solving. *Administrative Science Quarterly, 27,* 343-362.

Pelz, D. C., & Andrews, F. M. (1966). Scientists in organizations: Productive climates of research and development. New York: John Wiley.

Peters, T. J. (1978, Fall). Symbols, patterns, and settings: An optimistic case for getting things done. *Organizational Dynamics, 7*, 3-23.

Pfeffer, J. (1981). *Power in organizations.* Marshfield, MA: Pittman.

Postman, N. (1984). Social science as theology. *ETC, 41,* 22-32.

Roberts, K. H., Hulin, C. L., & Rousseau, D. M. (1978). Developing an interdisciplinary science of organizations. San Francisco: Jossey-Bass.

Salancik, G. R., & Pfeffer, J. (1977, Winter). Who gets power—and how they hold on to it: A strategic-contingency model of power. *Organizational Dynamics,* 3-21.

Schein, E. H. (1985). *Organizational culture and leadership.* San Francisco: Jossey-Bass.

Scott, W. R. (1981). *Organizations: Rational, natural, and open systems.* Englewood Cliffs, NJ: Prentice-Hall.

Snyder, M. (1984). When belief becomes reality. In L. Berkowitz (Ed.), *Advances in experimental social psychology* (Vol. 18, pp. 47-305). New York: Academic Press.

Thomas, J., & Griffin, R. (1983). The social information processing model of task design: A review of the literature. *Academy of Management Review, 8,* 672-682.

Thomas, K. W., & Tymon, W. G., Jr. (1982). Necessary properties of relevant research: Lessons from recent criticisms of the organizational sciences. *Academy of Management Review, 7,* 345-352.

Turner, J. H. (1979). Sociology as a theory building enterprise. *Pacific Sociological Review, 22,* 427-456.

Webster's dictionary of synonyms (1st ed.) (1951). Springfield, MA: G. & C. Merriam.

Weick, K. E. (1981). Psychology as gloss: Reflections on usefulness and application. In P. A. Kasschau & C. N. Cofer (Eds.), *Psychology's second century: Enduring issues* (pp. 110-132). New York: Praeger.

Weick, K. E. (1985). Systematic observational methods. In G. Lindzey & E. Aronson (Eds.), *The handbook of social psychology: Vol. 1* (Third Ed.) (pp. 567-634). New York: Random.

Weick, K. E., & Bougon, M. G. (1986). Organizations as cognitive maps: Charting ways to success and failure. In H. P. Sims, Jr. & D. A. Gioia (Eds.), *Social cognition in organizations.* San Francisco: Jossey-Bass.

Weick, K. E., & Browning, L. D. (1986). Argument and narration in organizational communication. *Journal of Management, 12,* 243-259.

Whitley, R. (1984). The scientific status of management research as a practially-oriented social science. *Journal of Management Studies, 21,* 369-390.

II

CONTEXT: INTERNAL AND EXTERNAL ENVIRONMENTS

The second part of this book centers on the context of organizations, specifically, on the role of internal and external environments in shaping communication processes. Context differs from structure in that it serves as the backdrop rather than the building blocks of organizational life. Context is the framework that embeds behavioral and structural aspects of organizations. As noted in the first section of this book, context plays a secondary role in organizational communication and organizational theory; its emergence as a salient construct parallels shifts in the development of organizational theory.

Early research on the directionality of message flow, communication channels, and networks centered almost exclusively on organization structure as the determinant of communication processes. With the advent of systems theory, context moved into the mainstream of organizatonal behavior and into the foreground of communication research. Indeed, as Euske and Roberts in Chapter 2 of this book suggest, organizations cannot be studied without reference to the relationship between organizations and their environments. Although *environment* typically refers to those activities outside organizational boundaries, conceptualizations of organizational environment differ in the phenomenon that emerges as salient (for example, information, resources, symbols, images), in the objective or subjective nature of external events, in the boundaries and links between internal and external environments, and in the proactive or reactive relationship between organizations and external events. Environment, then, can be characterized as a macro level construct that shapes and is shaped by the processes and structures within and between organizations.

The five chapters in Part II center on the role of communication in understanding the complex and interactive relationship between organizations and their environments. The chapters included in this section focus on the following topics: information and environments, public relations and issues management, communication climate, organizational culture, and cross-cultural organizations. This order of chapters reflects a movement from environmental-organizational interfaces to internal environments to societal-cultural influences on organizational life. Each chapter taps into the debate on enacted versus objective environments and on proactive versus reactive relationships between organizations and their environments.

The first chapter in this part, "Information Environments" by Huber and Daft, examines the role of organizational sense-making units in gathering, processing, and interpreting information about environments. This chapter centers on the relationship between information environments and organizational communication as illustrated through the literature on characteristics of environments, perceived environmental uncertainty, information logistics, and information interpretation. By contrasting resource dependency and information processing as disparate views of environmental research, Huber and Daft treat information, not the "objective" environment itself, as the raw material for organizational activities. Hence, they see organizations as proactive entities that choose their environments by searching for and selecting out certain physical and societal cues. Their discussion of the environmental, structural, and personal determinants of perceived environmental uncertainty culminates with the conclusion that uncertainty is a function of both the perceiver and the environment.

The "objective" environment contributes to uncertainty through changes in complexity, turbulence, and information load. Information, in this logistics literature, takes on the characteristic of a physical property that varies in quantity, ambiguity, and variety. The authors contend that information is actively acquired when organizations scan and probe external events. Their review suggests that members of organizational units are most "proactive" when they can recognize a problem and can justify the costs and payoffs of the information search process, either for decision making or for legitimating the grounds of decisions.

Huber and Daft link external to internal environments through the way that organizational units transmit information. They review the research on routing, summarizing, delaying, and modifying as ways of processing environmental information internally. The final portion of this chapter adds a refreshing twist to this literature by examining "subjective" construction of the environment through interpretations or enactments of meaning. They suggest that the meaning of environmental information is socially constructed through the interactions of organizational members, often triggered by an equivocal or ambiguous event. Communication channels, such as telephones, face-to-face communication, and electronic mail, used to process information could impact on interpretations that members give to environmental messages.

In effect, Huber and Daft's chapter reviews the state of knowledge about the relationship between organizations and information environments. They see information as a photograph or representation of the environment itself, one that is processed internally through organizational communication. Their review pays tribute to both the objective and the subjective views of the environment and to the proactive role of organizations in acquiring environmental information. They conclude that information can increase or decrease environmental uncertainty, depending on the way that organizational units process and interpret messages. Their review culminates with suggestions of ways to integrate information logistics and perceived environmental uncertainty and with ideas for tying perceived environmental uncertainty to the interpretations that members make about their environments.

The chapter by Cheney and Vibbert, "Corporate Discourse: Public Relations and Issue Management," accents the proactive and reactive nature of the organization-environment interface. Their chapter tracks the historical development of public relations, identifies key terminology in this arena, links public relations to environmental monitoring, and describes the functions of contemporary public relations. Cheney and Vibbert define public relations as "the art of adjusting organizations to environments and environments to organizations." Their definition, then, highlights the proactive nature of organizations in monitoring and shaping their environments.

The historical development of public relations, however, reflected a reactive, almost passive role, that organizations played in response to environmental changes and to unfavorable public opinion. Fluctuations in the economy, conflicts between business and government, wartime activities, and political events exemplified "objective" phenomena that organizations reacted to in defense of their actions. But public relations messages in the 1960s began to shape public images through appeals to publicly held values and through references to unique organizational identities. Public relations then resembled a boundary-spanning function that not only monitored the degree of fit between organizations and their environments but also controlled the form and issues of public persuasion.

Communication plays a central role in formulating public messages and in controlling the internal and external agendas of public debate. Persuasive and rhetorical strategies constitute public messages and determine which issues and values merit debate. Thus Cheney and Vibbert contend that corporate discourse functions symbolically to shape the identity of an organization and its boundaries. This position, although similar to Huber and Daft's interpretive level of information environments, treats communication as a symbolic activity that shapes organizational identities and creates corporate environments. The symbolic nature of communication, rather than the processing of information, accounts for the way organizations acquire information and generate public messages.

Cheney and Vibbert also link external to internal environments through the way that organizations create messages for different "publics." Thus internal corporate communications, such as employee handbooks and company newsletters, also promote select values, issues, and images that not only respond to environmental information but also shape perceptions of the environment. In many cases, organizations shape internal environments by disseminating to employees the same messages that they send to external publics. This view of the relationship between internal and external environments moves a step beyond Huber and Daft's focus on the internal processing of information about external events.

In the final portion of this chapter, Cheney and Vibbert demonstrate how public relations strategies serve rhetorical, identity-management, and political functions. The rhetorical aspects of corporate discourse center on shaping the image of an organization, especially during times of crisis management. The identity-management function of public relations shapes perceptions of the dividing lines between organizations and their environment. Finally, the political function of corporate discourse focuses on the advocacy role of messages, often in response to political or legal aspects of the environment.

Thus public opinion is treated in the Cheney and Vibbert chapter as a specific component of an organization's environment, one that stimulates corporate discourse and reacts to the discourse it creates. Hence, corporate discourse functions proactively to influence organizational images and to advocate political and social action and reactively to respond to environmental crises. Cheney and Vibbert adopt a subjective view of organizational environments, tracking the changing role of corporate discourse from its reactive to proactive nature and viewing corporate messages as directed to both internal and external publics. A chief contribution of this chapter lies in its treatment of the symbolic rather than the informational aspects of organizational messages.

The third chapter in this part, "Organizational Communication Climate" by Falcione, Sussman, and Herden, moves the foci of context from the external to the internal organizational environment. Since communication climate frames organizational structures and processes, it can be viewed as a context variable. Climate is defined as a molar construct or an enduring quality of the internal environment of an organization. Environment in this chapter refers to the internal atmosphere or the set of characteristics that constitute the organization's practices and procedures. Climate is also shaped by and affects external events such as economic and political trends, sociocultural norms, and technological developments.

This chapter reviews the theoretical issues that underlie conceptualizations of climate; the dimensions and measurement of communication climate; and the research findings on individual, group, and organizational climate. Theoretical debates on the definition of climate point out diverse treatments of the objective-subjective and the proactive-reactive nature of this construct.

The attribute approach treats climate as an objective phenomenon that endures over time and shapes organizational processes. The attribute-perceptual approach sees climate as an objective organizational attribute but one studied through the subjective perceptions of organizational members, while the perceptual approach views climate subjectively as the perceptions of individual encounters with the organization. The first approach adopts a reactive view of climate, while the other two see individuals as creating their own climates in a proactive way.

All three perspectives, however, treat climate as an external property rather than as the result of members' interactions aimed at making sense of organizational life. Falcione et al. argue for conceptualizing climate as an intersubjective phenomenon, a joint collaboration of individuals as they interact with organizational environments. In their view, communication is the medium for constituting climate; thus to understand climate researchers must focus on the rules and resources embodied in the communication that produces and reproduces subsystems. As an intersubjective phenomenon, communication climate becomes a way of integrating subsystems. The climate of the larger system influences individual and group atmospheres; the production and reproduction of climate at subsystem level shape the development of this construct at the suprasystem level.

An important element in climate research is matching the unit of analysis with an appropriate theoretical unit. Research on the interpersonal and group levels of analysis assumes organizations enact multiple climates that differ in task and socioeconomic qualities. Climate emerges as an outgrowth of dyadic exchanges and group characteristics. A significant contribution of this chapter is its model that accounts for the development and perceptions of communication climate. This model suggests that we know only a modicum about the external forces that have an impact on organizational communication climate. Moreover, Falcione et al. call for research on the interface between different levels of analysis and on the way communication processes produce and reproduce this molar construct.

The fourth chapter in Part II, "Organizational Culture: A Critical Assessment" by Smircich and Calás, also centers on the internal context of the organization, but the authors illustrate why organizational culture research should import social and political knowledge from the external environment to understand the cultural literature. This chapter compares and contrasts three frameworks—themes, paradigms, and interests—used to describe and synthesize the content of the organizational culture literature. Schools of cultural research within each framework differ in their treatments of the objective versus subjective nature of culture. For example, within the framework of "themes," comparative management and corporate culture treat culture as an objective variable or an entity that resembles the attribute approach to organizational climate. Organizations are tools or organisms that respond to their environments in a reactive way. The symbolic, cognitive, and unconscious processes "themes," however, view culture as something that an organization *is* rather than what it *has.* Culture becomes a subjective phenomenon created symbolically through the social construction of meanings that constitute an organization's ideology.

The role of communication in this research also hinges on the way culture is conceptualized. In the comparative management and corporate culture "themes" symbols such as stories, rituals, and myths become ways of transmitting messages about organizational practices. The meaning of these symbols frames the communicative elements of most research. In the symbolic, cognitive, and unconscious processes "themes" the meanings of messages do not reside in artifacts of the culture; instead they reside in social interaction and in the sense-making activities of organizational members. Thus communication extends beyond the meaning of cultural symbols into the way interaction patterns create and recreate the culture.

Using the "theme" framework, Smircich and Calás review and critique the organizational culture literature, drawing out meta-assumptions embodied in exemplars of this work. Then they reexamine the corpus of this literature by questioning its meaning and role in organizational theory and research. They posit that interpretive approaches to cultural research stand in opposition to most traditional organizational work; moreover, this literature has been appropriated into the very positivist and technical interests that it opposes. They support their argument through claims that the "oppositional" brand of cultural research surfaces only in special issues of journals; that "culture" has become a vacuous concept used to examine almost any organizational phenomenon; and that the culture research that opposes traditional positivist literature functions as a modernist movement that has failed.

To revitalize interpretive cultural research, scholars need to view cultural literature as resistance, examining the way culture represents or stands for something else. Representation, as an outgrowth of postmodernism, reveals which presence constitutes reality for a given cultural study. Smircich and Calás urge us to read cultural literature differently, as textual representations of social and political reality. By questioning what a cultural study does, how it is said, who says it, and what ideological message sustains it, researchers engage in producing meta-commentaries on the multiple meanings of organizational culture literature.

The fifth and final chapter in Part II, "Cross-Cultural Perspectives" by Triandis and Albert, examines organizational context at the societal level. In effect, this chapter expands upon and casts a different light on the comparative management culture reviewed by Smircich and Calás. That is, it examines the research on organizational communication that taps into cultural differences between organizations or intercultural communication within organizations. This chapter differs from the view of culture set forth by Smircich and Calás. Triandis and Albert treat culture as a societal rather than an organizational variable, one grounded in cognitive and value differences rather than in symbols and sense-making activities of organizational members. Employing an ingroup-outgroup model, Triandis and Albert adopt a subjective view of culture based on shared meanings and norms rather than an objective view defined by such factors as dress, tools, and languages.

Triandis and Albert lay out a cognitive framework for the dimensions that shape cultural differences in encoding and decoding organizational messages. The cognitive frameworks of significance to organizational research include different emphases on people, ideas, and actions; diverse value systems; and different patterns of information processing. Since these elements are embedded in the culture, communication across cultures may occur reactively by relying on the context for encoding and decoding messages or it may occur proactively by defining one's concepts before communicating.

The remainder of this chapter reviews the literature on organizational communication cross-culturally, between organizations in two or more different countries, and interculturally, between two or more cultures within the same organization. The cross-cultural literature summarizes the structural, value, and motive factors that affect organizational communication differences between countries. Cultural differences in decision making and conflict resolution also distinguish message systems of particular cultures. The intercultural literature focuses on communication between organizational members with different cultural backgrounds. Ignorance of appropriate social rituals, different nonverbal communication systems, and reliance on stereotypes are cited as communication problems linked to cultural differences within organizations.

Triandis and Albert conclude their chapter with a number of testable propositions on the relationship between cultural variables and communication in organizations. They begin with the external or societal level of culture and show how differences in cognitive frameworks across cultures have implications for organizational communication. Their work makes an important contribution by highlighting the societal variables that shape communication outcomes.

5 The Information Environments of Organizations

GEORGE P. HUBER
University of Texas at Austin

RICHARD L. DAFT
Texas A&M University

I NFORMATION environments are important subjects of study for social scientists. For example, information about actors and events in the external environment prompts or affects many task-related organizational communications and thus is important to scientists and scholars interested in organizational communication. Similarly, information about threats and opportunities in the environment initiates or influences many organizational actions, and consequently is important to organization theorists interested in organizational intelligence, learning, adaptation, and strategic choice. It is information about the organization's environment, as contrasted with the environment itself, that constitutes the raw material of organizational communications and actions.

AUTHORS' NOTE: We are indebted to William Glick, Vernon Miller, Linda Putnam, and John Slocum for their constructive suggestions on earlier drafts of this chapter. Preparation of this chapter was supported in part by the Army Research Institute for the Behavioral and Social Sciences through contracts MDA-903-83-K-0440 and MDA-903-85-K-0404.

The chapter focuses on relationships between information environments and organizational communications.[1] These relationships have been explored in literatures having as their respective foci (1) organizational environments, (2) perceived environmental uncertainty, (3) information logistics, and (4) information interpretation. The chapter is organized around these four literatures. We begin with a discussion of external organizational environments and examine the literature bearing on the three principal environmental characteristics of complexity, turbulence, and information load. For each of these characteristics we describe its changing nature and the ways in which these changes impact organizational communication. We then turn to perceived environment uncertainty, an important variable that links the objective and felt environments and that in multiple ways is linked to communication behavior. The third subject, information logistics, is examined in the context of five processes that occur when information about the external environment is gathered and processed by the organization's environment-sensing units. Finally, we discuss information interpretation, since organizations are ultimately faced with the task of interpreting their environment, and draw upon symbolic interactionism and communication theory to identify the crucial role of communication media in the effectiveness of information interpretation.

In the next four sections of the chapter we examine these four subjects in detail and review the key items in the corresponding literatures. In the last section we suggest the nature of the research required to advance our understanding of information environments and their relationships with organizational communications. We turn now to the literature on the external environments of organizations.

ORGANIZATIONAL ENVIRONMENTS

Discussions of organizational environments tend to emphasize the fact that an organization's environment contains opportunities and problems and that information about these opportunities and problems is sought and used by the organization to create and maintain desirable relationships between itself and its environment (Aldrich, 1979; Aldrich & Pfeffer, 1976; Meyer & Scott, 1983; Starbuck, 1976). Many individual writings in the organizational science literature reflect just one of the two primary perspectives on external organizational environments, either the resource-dependency perspective or the information-processing perspective (see Aldrich & Mindlin, 1978).

The focus of the *resource-dependency perspective* or the *resource perspective* is that organizational environments contain resources upon which the organization depends for achieving its goals, such as survival (Hannan & Freeman, 1977; Ulrich & Barney, 1984). The availability and accessibility of these resources have considerable influence on the organization's nature. For example, from the resource-dependency perspective, an organization's size would be explained by the number of customers available in the environment and its technology would be explained by the availability and cost of alternative technologies. As a result, the ready availability and accessibility of resources in the environment, or the *munificence* of the environment, is an environmental characteristic frequently examined by proponents of this perspective. Closely related to this perspective is the view of the organization's environment as a network of interorganizational relationships (Benson, 1978; Pennings, 1981; Porter, 1985). This view assumes that other organizations constituting the relevant external environment because they influence access to critical resources (Van de Ven & Walker, 1984). For example, competitors influence access to customers, suppliers influence access to technology, and government agencies influence access to land. As a consequence of such dependencies, *hostility* and *competitiveness/cooperativeness* are environmental characteristics of interest to those who focus on interorganizational relationships (Miles, 1986; Schermerhorn, 1975). The resource-dependency perspective reminds us that the entities and events in an organization's environment necessarily make up or influence the *content* of most work-related communication.

In contrast, the *information-processing perspective* or *information perspective* focuses on the *processes* through which the environment influences an organization's structure and processes, especially its communications. More generally this perspective focuses on the fact that organizations extract, process, and act on information from their environment.[2] Three classic works of the early 1970s established the perspective of organizations as information processing systems. James G. Miller devoted an entire issue of *Behavioral Science*, 182 pages, to portraying organizations as "living systems" made up of "matter-energy processing subsystems" and "information processing subsystems" (Miller, 1972). Herbert Simon described in a convincing manner the need to design future organizations as if they were primarily information-processing and decision-making systems, rather than goods-and-services-producing systems (Simon, 1973). Jay Galbraith synthesized disparate and diffuse research findings to set forth guidelines for designing organizations to process information (Galbraith, 1973). Related works are those by Thayer (1967), Wilensky (1967), Tushman and Nadler (1978), O'Reilly and Pondy (1979), and Huber (1982). The relationships between organizational information processing, or communication, and its ultimate impact on organizational decision making have been examined by Huber and McDaniel (1986) and O'Reilly, Chatman, and Anderson (Chapter 17, this volume).

Organizational scientists have created typologies of characteristics for describing external organizational environments (Emery & Trist, 1965; Jurkovich, 1974; Kilman, 1983; Miles, Snow, & Pfeffer, 1974; Scott, 1981). Pioneering conceptualizations were those of Emery and Trist (1965) and Terreberry (1968), and a factor-analytic classification was undertaken by Dess and Beard (1984). The environmental characteristics most often discussed in these works are environmental *complexity* and *turbulence*. A third environmental characteristic, *information load*, has been treated outside of the typology-building literature (Driver & Steufert, 1969; Huber, 1984; Simon, 1971, 1973). In the next few pages we examine the nature of these three environmental characteristics and describe in some detail the changes occurring in each.

Information Load

Information load is a function of those characteristics of the environmental information that affect the difficulty of information processing and use, for example, *quantity, ambiguity,* and *variety.* Quantity of information refers to the number of symbols or messages received per unit of time. Ambiguity refers to the potential for multiple interpretations of a symbol or message. Variety refers to the complexity and turbulence of the information stream and will be better understood after our discussion of complexity and turbulence in later paragraphs.

It is clear that the quantity of information in the environments of most organizations is increasing, and will continue to increase. Consider, for example, the quantity of scientific information. The first two scientific journals appeared in the mid-seventeenth century (de Solla Price, 1963). By the middle of the eighteenth century there were 10 scientific journals, by 1800 about 100, by 1850 perhaps 1,000. Near the end of the 1970s estimates of the number ranged between 30,000 and 100,000 (Bell, 1979). Nor is this growth of information likely to diminish in the intermediate future. Since information feeds on itself, we can expect that the absolute quantity of information will continue to rise. That is, even when (or if) the rate of increase declines, the existing information base will be so large that absolute increases in units of information per unit of time will remain large throughout at least the first half of the next century and very likely beyond that.

Of equal importance is that communication and computing technologies will greatly increase the availability of any information produced. Since these two technologies are in their early stages in terms of both effectiveness and adoption, we can anticipate rapid increases in the availability of existing information as the technologies mature and become widely used. The increased adoption of information distribution technologies, superimposed on the geometrically increasing information base, will cause tomorrow's organizations to encounter quantities and varieties of information that are much greater than are today's. An important consequence of this fact is that the number and variety of internal organizational communications will increase dramatically (Huber, 1984; Simon, 1973).

The effects of information load on organizational structures and processes are thought to be akin to the effects of information load on the coping behaviors of individuals (Miller, 1978). Example effects include specialization of environment-sensing units according to the type of information received and prioritization of information inputs so that more important information is dealt with first or more effectively (Driver & Steufert, 1969; Farace, Monge, & Russell, 1977; Miller, 1972). The few empirical studies conducted support this belief (Meier, 1963; Staw, Sandelands, & Dutton, 1981).

Complexity

Complexity, as a characteristic of environment, can be conceptualized as having three components: (1) *numerosity*, (2) *diversity*, and (3) *interdependence*. "Numerosity" refers to the number of relevant actors or components in the environment, such as the number of competitors, suppliers, markets, and so forth. For many organizations, the "numerosity" of their environment is increasing. Whether or not environmental entities in general will become more numerous is unclear, in spite of current short-term tendencies for some types to increase. Aside from whether or not the actual number of components will be greater, however, it seems clear that improved communication and transportation technologies will cause the effective number of environmental components to be greater. Entities that previously could not "reach" the organization will be able to do so readily, and will thus contribute to the complexity of the organization's environment.

The major increases in the complexity of organizational environments will not, however, arise from or depend on increases in "numerosity." Instead they will follow from increases in diversity and interdependency. Diversity refers to the differences among the markets served. The large increase in available information discussed earlier will lead to a large increase in environmental diversity, as it will enable the creators of organizations to identify and exploit a larger number of technological, economic, and social niches in which organizations can be founded and survive, and therefore become an additional component in the environment of other organizations. Thus we can anticipate more and increasing diversity and consequently complexity as a result of more and increasing societal information, whether or not there is an increase in the "numerosity" of environmental components.

Finally, let us turn to the interdependence component of environmental complexity. The specialization that follows from increases in information will result in greater interdependencies among the organizations that make up the environment of any one organization. This will occur because as living systems such as organizations (Miller, 1972) specialize, they give up certain capabilities (or do not achieve commensurate growth in certain capabilities) and must rely on other systems for the resources that they themselves can no longer provide.

The complexity of an organization's environment has a considerable impact on organizational communication. If an organization's environment has numerous elements that are or could be relevant, then the organization must generally allocate more resources to environmental scanning. If the environment is composed of diverse elements, the organization's scanning units will generally be more specialized as the organization attempts to match the environment's diversity—Ashby's Law of Requisite Variety (Ashby, 1956; Schmidt & Cummings, 1976). Specialization, of course, increases the difficulty of effective organizational communication as each unit develops its own language. If the environmental elements have interdependencies that are important to the organization, then the organization's intelligence system (Wilensky, 1967) must possess a significant interpretive capability. This interpretive capability is largely determined by the distribution and effectiveness of organizational communication (Daft & Huber, 1986), as we will make clear at a later point.

The classic study reported by Emery and Trist (1965) captures the essence of both interdependence and inability to interpret interdependence, and was summarily described by "the changed texture of the environment was not recognized by an able but traditional management until it was too late. They failed entirely to appreciate that a number of outside events were becoming connected with each other in a way that was leading up to irreversible general change" (Emery & Trist, 1965, p. 24).

Turbulence

The third characteristic of organizational environments is *turbulence*. Turbulence can be thought of as having two components: (1) *instability* and (2) *randomness*. Instability refers to the frequency of change. Randomness refers to the unpredictability of both the frequency and direction of change. When their environments are turbulent, organizations attempt to protect their core technology—the primary process with which they produce goods or services—from the consequences of this turbulence (Thompson, 1967). They also create processes and structures that maintain their ability to adapt to changes. Thus we have the literature on organic structures (Burns & Stalker, 1961; Lawrence & Lorsch, 1967), which are thought to be more adaptation-prone, and on experimenting organizations (Hedberg, Nystrom, & Starbuck, 1976, 1977), which are thought to identify more quickly the appropriate new processes and structures.

The turbulence of organizational environments is increasing and will continue to increase. Increases in turbulence will follow from increases in the swiftness of individual events. Recall that organizational environments in the future will be characterized by more and increasing information. This information will be used to make many technologies more effective. An important consequence of the increase in technological effectiveness will be that individual events will transpire more quickly. For example, improvements in R&D technology, in mass communication technology, and in transportation technology will enable competitors to steal markets even more quickly than they can today, and some high-technology military engagements will be subject to completion in a matter of moments. The role of geographical distance and even cultural differences as "time buffers" will be greatly diminished as improved communication and transportation technologies are implemented. Since shorter events permit more events per unit of time, the effect of the increased information, discussed earlier, is increased turbulence.

Environmental turbulence would seem to have three important effects on organizational communication. One is that it increases the number of formal communications directed from the organization's environmental sensing units to information users such as decision makers, as there is more news to report (Huber, 1984; Simon, 1973). The second and third effects are more speculative, and in need of empirical investigation. Because turbulence causes there to be more action in the organization's environment and thus provides more common-interest material to talk about with coworkers, it may increase the number of work-related informal communications (and perhaps also the ratio of work-related informal communication to non-work-related informal communications).

The third effect of turbulence is more subtle than the first two. Organizations use task specialization and mechanistic processes and structures to attain efficiency in the communication of routine information (Galbraith, 1977). But turbulence results in nonroutine information, and nonroutine information tends to be handled inefficiently by specialized and mechanistic organizations. The consequences of this dilemma have not been determined by either organization theory researchers or organizational communication researchers. We suggest that one consequence, one effect of environmental turbulence, is greatly increased downward communication. Such communication would inform the organization's environmental sensing units and the intermediate message processing units about the organization's current and anticipated goals, domains, structures, and processes. These downward communications would serve not only the conventional purpose of enhancing the motivation and esprit de corps of lower-level personnel, but would also enhance understanding and judgment about how to recognize and route relevant nonroutine information.

In summary, the environmental characteristics of information load, complexity, and turbulence are increasing, and these increases will affect organizational communication. Let us move on now to examining the three literatures that deal with the relationships between information environments and organizational communication: (1) the perceived environmental uncertainty literature, (2) the information logistics literature, and (3) the information interpretation literature. In the next several pages we describe each of these literatures and the role of organizational communication within the perspectives that the literatures engender.

PERCEIVED ENVIRONMENTAL UNCERTAINTY

Our discussion to this point has not made clear that to a great extent organizations choose their environments, and by so doing they can cause themselves to be faced with quite different levels of environmental characteristics. For example, if a firm explicitly chooses to compete on the basis of being first with new products or services in newly created markets, it will tend to encounter higher levels of environmental complexity, turbulence and information load than will a firm that chooses to compete on the basis of delivering high-quality, low-cost goods and services to old, well-known customers (Miles & Snow, 1978). Perrow (1970) takes the argument one step further and notes the importance of the perceived task environment as well as the physical and societal environments. For example, if a prison implicitly views its task as one of serving as a custodian, it will tend to see its environment as relatively certain. On the other hand, if the prison views its task as rehabilitation, it will tend to view its environment as more uncertain. One consequence of such choices is *perceived environmental uncertainty,* the uncertainty that the organization's members perceive as characterizing the external environment.

"Uncertainty is a term which is used daily in a variety of ways. This everyday acquaintance with uncertainty can be seductive in that it is all too easy to *assume* that one knows what he is talking about. This problem is not new to organizational research" (Downey, & Slocum, 1975, p. 562). Since this statement was made, organizational scientists have made modest progress in advancing their understanding of uncertainty.

Conceptual Issues

It seems reasonable that characteristics of an organization's environment affect an observer's feelings about how certain he or she is concerning what will happen in the environment or why something did happen. Some authorities have used the concept of environmental uncertainty as if it were a characteristic of the environment itself (Thompson, 1967). Others have used it in reference to the perceptions that individual organizational members have about the environment (Duncan, 1972; Galbraith, 1977), in which case it is generally referred to as *perceived environmental uncertainty* (PEU). The latter conceptualization of uncertainty, as a function both of the environment and of the perceiver, seems more useful in light of three nearly universal findings. The first of these is that basic environmental characteristics, such as complexity, turbulence, and information load influence PEU. The second is that PEU is affected by organizational structures and processes. The third finding is that PEU is affected by personal characteristics.

A second conceptual issue is apparent from the two approaches used to assess PEU. One approach has been to focus on the construct of information as a counterpart of uncertainty and thus to assess PEU using the classic information theory measure of uncertainty in which "uncertainty and information have a clear and inverse relationship" (Gifford, Bobbitt, & Slocum, 1979, p. 460). Using this approach, uncertainty is an algebraic function of the probabilities of the several possible environmental states (see Huber, O'Connell, & Cummings, 1975; Leblebici & Salancik, 1981).[3] The other approach has been to use Likert-type scales to assess organizational members' feelings or confidence about how well they could predict or explain the environment (see Downey et al., 1975; Duncan, 1972). The approach using (subjective) probabilities would seem to obtain more cognitively based responses; the Likert-scale approach would seem to obtain more affectively based responses.

Should PEU be assessed as a subjective estimate of an environmental characteristic or as an expression of a state of mind? This is clearly an important conceptual issue, similar to the issue of objective versus enacted environments (Smircich & Stubbart, 1985; Weick, 1979). Bearing on these issues is Bourgeois's (1985) finding that a poor match between true environmental uncertainty and top management's perceived environmental uncertainty was associated with low economic performance by the firm.

Let us turn now from highlighting conceptual issues to examining some of the empirical findings. The literature contains studies of three possible determinants of PEU: (1) the characteristics of the organization's external environment; (2) the structure of the organization; and (3) the characteristics of the perceiver.

Environmental Determinants of PEU

Environmental characteristics examined for their possible effect on PEU include complexity, turbulence, routineness of problem/opportunity states, and information load. With respect to the first two of these characteristics, in his early and often referenced study, Duncan (1972) found that high levels of complexity and high levels of turbulence were associated with high levels of PEU, with turbulence having more effect than complexity. Tung (1979) replicated Duncan's (1972) findings concerning complexity and turbulence and, in addition, investigated the routineness of problem/opportunity states and found a positive relationship between this routineness and PEU. It appears, however, that the component measures of PEU may have been summed incorrectly in both of these studies (Downey, Hellriegel, & Slocum, 1975). A study specifically designed to replicate Duncan's results obtained quite different results (Downey et al., 1975).

In their well-known study, Lawrence and Lorsch (1967) judgmentally inferred an association between external environmental uncertainty and a composite measure of internal organizational uncertainty. However, in their analysis of the Lawrence and Lorsch (1967) composite measure and its three subscales, Tosi, Aldag, and Storey (1973) found numerous negative associations between three objective measures of external environmental volatility and the Lawrence and Lorsch subscales. As noted by Downey et al. (1975), methodological issues make it difficult to draw firm conclusions about the results of either of these studies. Leblebici and Salancik (1981), in their field study, did find PEU to be correlated with an objective measure of environmental turbulence.

Two laboratory simulations of decision situations lend general support to the idea that characteristics of the external environment influence perceived environmental uncertainty. Huber et al. (1975) found that both the amount of information about the environment and the specificity of messages about the environment affected PEU, and Gifford et al. (1979) found that the higher the quality of messages about the environment, the lower was the resultant PEU. Overall, in spite of methodological problems of unknown effect in some of the relevant studies, the preponderance of evidence is congruent with one's intuition—the organization's external environment, or more precisely the information environment representing the external environment, is a determinant of PEU.

Structural Determinants of PEU

It is commonly believed that organizations adapt their structure to their environment, that PEU determines structure. For example, if its environment is turbulent, the organization would adopt an organic structure (Burns & Stalker, 1961; Miles, Snow, Meyer, & Coleman, 1978). The belief is supported in cross-sectional studies in which correlations were found between PEU and organizational processes (Conrath, 1967) or organizational structures (Duncan, 1973, 1974). Such correlations could, however, be a consequence of structure determining PEU. In a war-game simulation involving ROTC cadets and Air Force Academy cadets, Huber et al. (1975) found that experimental manipulation of structure did in fact affect PEU. In tightly structured groups, whose members received specialized information about the environment and whose communications were restricted, members perceived more uncertainty about the environment than in loosely structured groups whose members were able to share information freely.

A subsequent cross-sectional field study using partial correlational analyses of data on PEU, structure, and process also suggested that structure affects PEU, but that the members from tightly structured organizations perceived less uncertainty about the environment (Leifer & Huber, 1977). Possible explanations for these conflicting findings are that tight structures buffer some organizational members from information and that loose structures facilitate informal communication processes, and that in both cases there came to be either an increase or a decrease in PEU depending on the specificity of the information exchanged (Daft & Lengel, 1984; O'Connell, Cummings, & Huber, 1975). Shifting focus from the tightness of structure to structural differentiation, Schmidt and Cummings (1976) found that the top administrators of more differentiated organizations perceived less environmental uncertainty than did top administrators of less differentiated organizations. Thus overall the available evidence does indicate that structure affects PEU.

Personal Determinants of PEU

Strong arguments can be made that the characteristics of individuals affect their perceptions of their environments (Downey & Slocum, 1975; Kiesler & Sproull, 1982). Hunsaker (1973) and Downey, Hellriegel, and Slocum (1977) found cognitive constructs such as tolerance for ambiguity and cognitive complexity to be positively related to PEU, although Gifford et al. (1979) did not. It appears that such personal characteristics are related to PEU when the global organization environment is assessed, but that the effect of personal characteristics on PEU is considerably less when the person's task-related environment is the environment assessed (Lorenzi, Sims, & Slocum, 1981).

Consideration of individual difference determinants of perceived environmental uncertainty brings to the surface the issue of the unit of analysis under discussion. Why in this section on the external environments of organizations are we discussing personal determinants of PEU? Downey and Slocum (1975) respond to this question in depth. We quote just the opening sentences of their discussion:

> This perceptual view of uncertainty raises the issues of how total organizations relate to uncertainty. Zaltman, Duncan, and Holker (1973), while discussing innovation, suggest that all those factors which influence individual perceptions directly or indirectly influence the organization's perceptions. The present authors would tentatively take this one step further and suggest that an organization's perceptions (as some type of summative concept) are subject to these same individual influences because the organization's perceptions are a result of the perceptions of individual organization members. (Downey & Slocum, 1975, p. 568)

In summary, although it seems reasonable that the organization's external environment, as an information environment, provides raw data that affect PEU, exactly how this occurs is not well understood. It also appears that organizational structures moderate whatever linkages exist between this information environment and PEU, probably by influencing the social processing of information (Daft & Huber, 1986). Finally, it appears that personal characteristics moderate these linkages, probably by influencing the cognitive processing of information. Some support is given to this hypothesis by Downey and Slocum's (1982) finding that cognitive complexity moderated the negative relationship between a manager's perceived uncertainty and performance.

Our discussions to this point have examined PEU primarily as a dependent variable. Perceptions of environments and PEU have also been examined as independent variables, as determinants of organizational structure and processes.

Effects of Perceptions of Environments and Uncertainty

Perceptions of external information environments, and in particular perceptions of external environmental uncertainty, are important because they influence the organizational choices that create the structure and process of the organizations in which we participate or that otherwise affect our lives. For example, Duncan (1973, 1974) found that organizational units varied the membership of their decision-making teams more extensively when they perceived high levels of either environmental uncertainty or of control over their environment, and that this feature was more pronounced in the more effective organizations.

More recent studies have examined these same variables. Gordon and Narayanan (1984) found that perceptions of the environment affect actual decision structures and processes, and Bourgeois, McAllister, and Mitchell (1978) found that when faced with more turbulent environments, managers preferred more tightly organized structures. Javidan (1984) found that PEU did not affect long-range planning, a form of decision making, but that interpretations of the permanence of environmental change did. Leblebici and Salancik (1981) found that higher levels of environmental complexity were associated with more specialized decision structures and processes. Finally, and of special relevance given the subject of this volume, Brown and Utterback (1985) found a positive correlation between PEU and externally directed communications activity, and interpreted this finding to mean that higher levels of PEU led to increases in decision-related information-seeking communication directed toward the organization's external environment. A summary model relating organizational environments, managerial perceptions of these environments, and organizational structures has been developed by Yasai-Ardekani (1986).

In this section we have examined the determinants and some of the effects of perceived environmental uncertainty. The next two sections concern the activities that organizations (and their members) undertake to deal with uncertainty. In the first we describe how organizations reduce uncertainty by acquiring and internally distributing information about the environment. In the subsequent section we describe how organizations reduce uncertainty when the information acquired is ambiguous, that is, when it may have multiple meanings.

INFORMATION LOGISTICS

In several disciplines and practices, information and information-conveying communications are viewed almost as physical objects that an organization acquires, sometimes reconfigures, and distributes internally to users, all in a rather mechanistic manner. We will call this view the information logistics view. Much of the related literature deals in intraorganizational information processing (Galbraith, 1973, 1977; Huber, 1982; Wilensky, 1967) or organizational communication (Guetzkow, 1965; O'Reilly & Pondy, 1979; Porter & Roberts, 1976; Thayer, 1967), and is described elsewhere in this volume (see Stohl & Redding, Chapter 14; O'Reilly et al, Chapter 17, this volume). To avoid overlap with these descriptions, but still examine the determinants of relationship between the actual external environment and the information that internal organizational units have for constructing their beliefs about the environment, we will deal here with just two topics: (1) the acquisition of information about the external environment, and (2) the process undertaken by the organization's environment-sensing units to convey information about the environment to internal units, especially to the units that decide what actions the organization should take with regard to opportunities and problems posed by its environment.

Information Acquisition

A considerable number of the formal activities that take place within or on behalf of organizations are forms of information acquisition to reduce uncertainty about the external environment, for example, client surveys, research and development activities, industrial intelligence, wage and salary surveys, and economic forecasts. Many informal behaviors also are directed toward obtaining information, for example, reading the *Wall Street Journal* or listening to coffee break "news." Acquisition of information, and the subsequent logistical and interpretive processes, are major organizational endeavors.

Organizational information acquisition occurs in two forms, *scanning* and *probing*. Organizations scan their external (and internal) environments in order to identify problems and opportunities (Aguilar, 1967; Hambrick, 1982; Stubbart, 1982). Scanning or monitoring is often routinized, as when sales people are required to report competitors' sales or car dealerships are required to report observed manufacturing defects. Organizations initiate ad hoc probes of their environments when more information is required than is available. These deeper examinations of the environment are responses to information or concerns about actual or suspected problems or opportunities.

Some information acquisition is for the purpose of identifying alternatives for solving a problem or exploiting an opportunity. Before a problem or opportunity will result in such search, a number of conditions must be present. These conditions were recognized and succinctly articulated by early authorities. The major variable affecting the initiation of search is dissatisfaction— "the organization will search for additional alternatives when the consequences of the present alternatives do not satisfy its goals" (Feldman & Kanter, 1965, p. 622). There seems to be a general reluctance to initiate search unless it is clearly necessary.

> Not until the element of novelty in a problem situation has become clearly explicit will a significant disruption of the relationship between the environment and the organism be sharply felt and a search begin for alternatives to the habitual response. Then and only then does a more or less conscious and deliberate decision-making process get initiated. (Reitzel, 1958, p. 4)

Downs (1966, p. 190) and Ansoff (1975) have suggested that for search-prompting signals to have an effect they must be very "loud" and received from multiple sources.

Apparently it is important not only that the need for problem-motivated search be clear but that effort directed toward resolving the problem (or capitalizing on the opportunity) be viewed as having some probability of success (Glueck, 1976, p. 70; Schwab, Ungson, & Brown, 1985). For example, Kefalas and Schoderbek (1973) found that when an organizational unit perceives that some situation can be controlled in the future, then it is more likely to initiate information-search activities. In particular, they found that managers spent more time acquiring information about "relatively controllable sectors of the external environment than for the relatively uncontrollable sectors" (Kefalas & Schoderbek, 1973, p. 67). Of course not only must the search effort be viewed as having some probability of success, but it must be viewed as not excessively difficult (Culnan, 1983; O'Reilly, 1982).

Together these ideas suggest that some sort of threshold must be exceeded before search will take place, where the threshold is defined both in terms of the costs and payoffs associated with searching versus not searching and in terms of the probabilities that these costs and payoffs will be incurred. Mintzberg, Raisinghani, and Theoret (1976) discussed a search initiation threshold in terms of these variables, as part of their analysis of 25 instances of organizational problem solving.

In aggregate, the literature that addresses the topic suggests that organizations will initiate problem-motivated search when (1) a problem is recognized and (2) some heuristic assessment of the costs, payoffs, and probabilities involved suggests that a search-justifying threshold value has been reached or exceeded. The classic *A Behavioral Theory of the Firm* (Cyert & March, 1963) suggests that these conditions are both necessary and sufficient for search to occur. Problem-motivated search will not be initiated unless such conditions occur and will be initiated if they occur. In his revision and extension of the behavioral theory of the firm, Carter (1971) added the concept of internally initiated search, often a search for opportunities in the environment—"The procedure was for the president to initiate probes by mentioning, either in casual conversation or by explicit memorandum, that Comcor was interested in purchasing certain types of companies. Staff members could then seek companies that fit the requirements" (Carter, 1971, p. 420).

A number of authorities have noted that the information acquisition of individuals is not easily interpreted as rational (O'Reilly, 1980; Shields, 1983). In their provocative article "Information in Organizations as Signal and Symbol," Feldman and March (1981) point out that the information acquisition of organizations is often not clearly rational, and explain this fact with the observation that those who command that the information be sought (for instance, line managers) often do not incur the search costs—the search is conducted by staff units. Our own observation is complementary—staff units are only too glad to take on the task, as it justifies their existence and legitimizes their requests for increased resources.

Although the information acquisition that is motivated by decision-related problems or opportunities has attracted the most attention, and has become conspicuous in the literature, an organization's environment-sensing units also undertake a good deal of information acquisition in order to fulfill information procurement and reporting responsibilities. The idea that information is sought only for the purpose of affecting decisions is

> an overly simplistic view of the incentives for providing technical information to administrative agencies.... A number of other incentives ... point to a perceived duty or responsibility to provide technical information without regard to probable instrumental effect on actual decisions. (Sabatier, 1978, p. 404)

The U.S. Bureau of the Census acquires enormous amounts of information that is not used directly to solve its own problems or exploit its own opportunities, but presumably to satisfy the decision-making and control needs of other organizational units such as the U.S. Congress. Information acquisition to fulfill reporting responsibilities to other units is a major activity of staff units such as purchasing departments and market research groups.

Although only minimally explored in the literature, in many instances organizational participants seek out and acquire external information unrelated to their problem-solving or reporting responsibilities. Whether this is rational is a matter of how broadly one defines rational. Two organizational realities drive this tendency to create a denser or richer information environment. One of these is the need for decision legitimation; the other is the need for preparation.

In many organizational settings, decision makers must legitimate their decisions to others. Sabatier (1978) discusses this point at some length and notes a number of field studies of organizational decision making where information was sought for the explicit purpose of legitimating decisions reached on other grounds. The need to legitimate decisions to others often causes organizational members to search for more information than is necessary to solve the focal problem. This fact may be a partial explanation for the observation that organizational decision makers acquire "too much" information (O'Reilly & Pondy, 1979).

With respect to the need for preparation, organizational members seek information not only to fulfill explicit organizational requirements, such as solving problems or fulfilling assigned tasks, or to legitimate decisions, but also to fulfill the felt need to develop personal information banks. Some of the search for information observed in organizational settings is undertaken by individuals seeking to develop or maintain a better understanding of that portion of the organization's external environment with which they are concerned. Example behaviors include reading technical journals and attending conventions or industry shows. For some people, such as research personnel, this may be a major time-consuming behavior.

> While the information thus obtained may result in the eventual fulfillment of organizational goals, it is obtained for the collector himself, or herself, rather than for the direct use of other units. For example, many officials regularly scan certain data sources (such as *The Wall Street Journal* or *Aviation Week*) without any prior idea of exactly what type of information they are seeking or will find. They do this not because they are dissatisfied, but because past experience teaches them that new developments are constantly occurring that might affect their present level of satisfaction. (Downs, 1966, p. 169)

A related idea is the following:

> It is not always clear what information will be needed or when it might be useful. Hence, the nature of the job might require incumbents to gather large amounts of information with the possibility that a portion of it might be useful at some future time. This may result in an effort to ask for more information than is strictly needed in an effort to avoid mistakes and reduce uncertainty. (O'Reilly, 1980, p. 692)

Information about the organization's external environment is acquired by many members and units, not just those members and units whose primary responsibility is external information acquisition (Leifer & Huber, 1977; Tushman, 1977; Tushman & Scanlan, 1981). Aside from whatever their formal or primary responsibility may be, we will refer hereafter to such information acquiring units as environment-sensing units, or sensor units. Their information acquisition activity is an important determinant of the quality of organizational decisions (Dollinger, 1984; Wilensky, 1967). So also are the four logistical processes in which sensor units typically engage after they acquire external information.

Logistical Processes at
the Organizational Boundary

A number of processes affect the congruence between an organization's environment and the understanding that organizational members have of that environment. In addition to the acquisition process just described, there is the interpretation process, which we will discuss in a subsequent section, and the four logistical processes that we describe here.[4]

Organizations purposefully acquire and internally disseminate information in order to carry out the critical functions of decision making and control. The dissemination task requires the organization's sensor units to create and transmit a large number of information-conveying communications, which we will call "messages." On the other hand, because a large number of messages may overburden the individuals and work groups subsequently involved in processing the messages, the organization's sensor units reduce the potential internal information load by engaging in two key processes, *message routing* and *message summarizing*. Message routing causes a particular communication or message to be distributed to relatively few organizational units. This selective distribution greatly reduces the information processing load both of the many potential receiving units having little or no use for the information and of the many intermediate units involved in summarizing or transmitting the message. Message summarizing plays a similar role. It has as its purpose reproducing the size of the message while at the same time faithfully reproducing its meaning. For example, large sets of numbers are replaced by their average, and multipage reports are replaced by "management abstracts." Summarization can greatly reduce the cognitive or logistical load on the units having to subsequently process the message.

Messages vary considerably in relevance, length, accuracy, timeliness, and other attributes. As a consequence of this fact and the need to control their own work load, sensor units necessarily exercise some discretion in the way they handle messages. Such discretion allows two other information-processing phenomena to occur in parallel with routing and summarizing. These are message delay and message modification.

There is no value judgment or negativism implied in the use of the phrase *message delay*. Since the priority assignment given a message is a principal determinant of the time it will be delayed, and since making such assignments is necessarily (at least in part) a delegated and discretionary act, it would often be difficult to make objective judgments about the excessiveness of individual delays. *Message modification* refers to the distortion of message meaning. Its source may be either the cognitive limitations or the motivations of the sender or receiver. Modifications may be conscious or unconscious, well-intended or malicious. They range from the well-intended correction of minor errors to the extreme modification of substituting one message for another. Message modification differs from message summarization in that it distorts a message's meaning, whereas summarization does not.

In aggregate, the four processes have two important consequences. One of these is the quantity of messages that must be dealt with by internal organizational units.

Quantity of messages to internal units. The literature identifies four variables that affect the routing and delaying of messages from a sensor unit to a particular internal unit, hence affecting the information load on that unit: (1) message relevance and timeliness; (2) work load of message-sending units; (3) difficulty of communicating to the message-receiving unit; and (4) effect on potential sending units of the receiving unit's obtaining the information. The literature pertaining to these variables is voluminous. We summarize its findings in just four paragraphs, as our purpose here is not to review the literature, but rather to identify the determinants of the difference between the organization's actual external information environment and the information environment known to internal organizational units.

Environment-sensing units, in order to achieve organizational rewards and avoid organizational penalties, use the relevance of a message for some other unit as a criterion in determining whether and when to route the message to that unit. For example, with regard to whether a message should be routed to a unit, Tushman (1979) found that for high-performing units the greater the task interdependence between units, the greater was the frequency of communication routed between the units; presumably task interdependence causes messages to be more relevant and thus communication more frequent. With regard to when a message should be routed, Huber and Ullman (1973) and Gerstenfeld and Berger (1980) found that message-sending units tended to delay their messages when premature delivery would reduce the message's impact. In summary, units whose task fulfillment is viewed as more likely with information held by other units will have this information directed to them and consequently will encounter a higher information load.

It is reasonable to expect that the message-sending behavior of sensor units would be affected by their work load. Meier, for example, found that overloaded units "destroy lowest priorities" when carrying out their functions (Meier, 1963), thus precluding any routing at all. With regard to delay, Downs found that "the most common bureau response to communications overload is slowing down the speed of handling messages" (Downs, 1966, p. 270). Thus the information load on a particular unit is determined in part by the work loads of the sensor units most likely to send messages to that unit.

In order to conserve their resources, sensor units tend to communicate more frequently with units easily contacted than with other units. Studies such as those by Brenner and Sigband (1973), Conrath (1973), and Bacharach and Aiken (1977) have found that either physical or structural accessibility is a determinant of the frequency with which subordinates communicated with superiors. The difficulty in communication may be interpersonal as well as physical or structural, as observed by Brenner and Sigband (1973), Goldhar,

Bragaw, and Schwartz (1976), and Jain (1973). Thus the information load of any unit is partly a function of the perceived difficulty of communicating to that unit.

Turning to the last of the four variables that determine message quantity, the effect on the sending units of the receiving units obtaining the information, we note the pervasive finding that messages are suppressed if their transmission is likely to result in the receiver doing harm to the sender (see McCleary, 1977; Read, 1962; Rosen, Johnson, Johnson, & Tesser, 1973). Similarly, the research on bargaining (see Cummings & Harnett, 1980) and power in organizations (see Pfeffer, 1980) indicates that information is a critical resource in joint decision situations and that withholding information from one's competitors is often useful in attainting one's goals in a competitive environment (Eisenberg, 1984). Thus the amount of information received by a unit is a function of the perceptions that sensor units have about the harm they may incur from the unit as a consequence of providing the information.

Together, routing and delaying determine the quantity of messages received by internal units. The next two processes to be examined, summarizing and modifying, determine the form of messages and thus affect the interpretability of the information contained in the messages.

Interpretability of information from sensor units. Even though message summarization is a process purposefully employed by organizations, and tends to have as an outcome a faithful representation of the original content, it may increase the ambiguity of the information environment if the retained content is equivocal, that is, if the summarization reduces the richness of the message and hence some of its interpretability and meaning. We will pursue this idea further in our later discussion of the information interpretation literature.

There is very little literature that deals with message summarizing, perhaps because findings of successful summarization, that is, condensation without distortion, are less titillating than are findings of modification, for example, alteration with distortion. There is in contrast a sizable literature that deals with message modification. We will summarize it in just a few paragraphs in order to highlight the effect of the sensor unit's modifications on the congruence between the organization's external information environment and the understanding that internal units have of that environment. We first discuss the motivational bases for modification, then the perceptual and cognitive bases, and conclude by noting an organizational determinant of message modification.

As a result of his extensive interviews with administrators, Downs concluded that "Each official tends to distort the information he passes upward in the hierarchy, exaggerating this data favorable to himself and minimizing those data unfavorable to himself" (Downs, 1966, p. 266). His conclusion is strongly supported by both laboratory studies (see Cohen, 1958;

O'Reilly & Roberts, 1974) and field studies (see Athanassiades, 1973; Gore, 1956; Kaufman, 1973; O'Reilly, 1978; Read, 1962; Roberts & O'Reilly, 1974). The dependent variables in these studies were quite varied and included revising the message format (the mildest form of modification) and eliminating the message or substituting an incorrect message (the more extreme forms of modification). Related findings are that when senders do not trust the motives of the receivers, they tend to modify the messages more than otherwise and that modification is influenced by the sender's perception of the receiver's influence over the sender and the sender's mobility aspirations (Mellinger, 1956; Roberts & O'Reilly, 1974). O'Reilly (1978) provides a particularly articulate discussion of the variables of trust, influence, and mobility. Altogether such findings make clear that the congruence between the actual external environment and an internal unit's information about that environment is a consequence of the goal attainment that sensor units believe will accrue to them if they distort message content.

Some research suggests that message modifications are made for the purpose of reducing the stress on the receiver (Campbell, 1958; Rosen & Tesser, 1970) and that "information, once evaluated and integrated, will tend to fit the transmitter's perceptions of the recipient's needs" (Ference, 1970, p. B85). Thus if sensor units perceive an internal unit to be stressed, they may modify their messages in ways that decrease the internal unit's stress but that also decrease the validity of the messages as representation of the actual environment.

We turn now to the perceptual and cognitive bases of message modifications. The fact that sensor units are often themselves receivers of messages from the external environment has some interesting implications. In his early review, Campbell (1958) noted that both cognitive limitations and personal motivations cause transmitters to modify messages imperfectly during their own assimilation, stating that the "tendency to distort messages in the direction of identity with previous inputs is probably the most pervasive of the systematic biases" (p. 346), and that "the human transmitter is prone to bias away from input in the direction of the transmitter's own attitudes" (p. 350). These conclusions suggest that information inputs are transformed in the direction of the receiver's prior information, expectations, or wishes. Porter and Roberts (1976), in their review of findings related solely to cognitively based transformations, stated that "these results would indicate that the more tangible and objective the subject matter . . . the more likely it is that subordinates and their superior will feel that they are communicating accurately, whereas when the messages involve more subjective opinions and feelings there is greater doubt about accuracy" (Porter & Roberts, 1976 p. 1574).

It seems reasonable to believe that if the sender is either cognitively or logistically overloaded, message modifications would be greater. "Whenever human beings operate at near maximum capacity, selective information

loss—undesired reduction of message complexity—is apt to be involved "
(Campbell, 1958, p. 336). Additional support is given to this idea by the case
study of Meier (1963) and the reviews by Driver and Steufert (1969) and Staw
et al. (1981). The net effect of these limitations of message transmitting units,
and hence sensor units, is that the congruence between the external
information environment and its representation to internal units is a
consequence of the ambiguity of the messages received by sensor units and by
the ability of sensor units to deal with this ambiguity.

As is well known, the probability and extent of any communication
phenomena, such as message delay or modification, increases with the
organizational distance between the message's originating source and the
message's ultimate receiver. A dramatic example of this effect of organizational structure is the following:

> A reporter was present at a hamlet burned down by the U.S. Army's 1st Air
> Cavalry Division in 1967. Investigation showed that the order from the division
> headquarters to the brigade was: "On no occasion must hamlets be burned
> down."
>
> The brigade radioed the battalion: "Do not burn down any hamlets unless you
> are absolutely convinced that the Viet Cong are in them."
>
> The battalion radioed the infantry company at the scene: "If you think there are
> any Viet Cong in the hamlet, burn it down."
>
> The company commander ordered his troops: "Burn down that hamlet."
> (Miller, 1972, p. 69)

As this example shows, information can reduce uncertainty even if it is
misrepresentative. But some information is ambiguous; information can be
subject to multiple meanings either to one person or across persons. When this
occurs, uncertainty can be reduced (and understanding created) only through
interpretation.

INFORMATION INTERPRETATION

If a sensor unit notes the existence of a new and unanticipated entity in the
organization's environment, we would expect that perceived environmental
uncertainty would increase. Clearly, information can both increase and
decrease perceived environmental uncertainty (see also Harary & Batell,
1978). But what about information whose content is clear but whose meaning
is not?[5] How does such information lead to understanding? How does it get
interpreted? Our answer lies in two ideas: (1) human beings not only receive
information but also give meaning to its content—they interpret it and (2) this
interpretation is affected by communications among members—shared
meanings develop within organizations through interaction. These ideas have

their roots in *symbolic interactionism* and are closely linked to concepts of communication media. In this section we use the ideas of symbolic interactionism and communication media to explain how an organization's internal processes influence how the external environment is interpreted.

Symbolic Interactionism

The internal information environment can be understood within the broad theoretical framework suggested by symbolic interactionism[6] (Stryker & Statham, 1985). In sharp contrast to the information logistics view presented earlier, the imagery of symbolic interactionism conceptualizes the organization as a dynamic web of human interactions. Over time and through communication among organizational members, symbols—including language and behavior—evolve and take on meaning. Symbols provide meaning that can be used to interpret situations and adjust behavior. Thus an adherent of this framework would argue that organizations are composed of people interpreting situations and the actions of people based on those interpretations (Blumer, 1962). Furthermore, since even established and repetitive forms of action must be renewed through interpretation and designation, organizations are fluid and are continuously constructed and reconstructed via definitional and interpretive processes (Blumer, 1962; Haberstroh, 1965, p. 1201).

The basis for interaction among organizational members is a shared system of meaning. With respect to organizational information, the symbolic interactionism framework focuses on the underlying purpose and meaning of messages rather than on their objectively measurable data characteristics. Research into communication environments is concerned with organizational symbols and their meanings and how individuals create and interpret those symbols (Putnam, 1983). Specific research concerns are the cognitive interpretations of messages, the means through which shared interpretations are reached, and the media through which messages are transmitted.

The concept of information equivocality is central to understanding the value of symbolic interactionism (Weick, 1979). Equivocality is similar to PEU except that the multiplicity of possible interpretations of information, rather than the lack of information, is the problem. Without shared understanding, behavior in organizations tends to be disorganized and random (but see Donnellon, Gray, & Bougon, 1986). Problems arise when the meaning of the situation or problem is ambiguous, when individuals are unclear about what an event means or how to translate it into organizational action, or when previously shared definitions are unsuited to a situation. In such cases, meaning is created through social interaction and discussion (Donnellon et al., 1986). When confronted with an equivocal event, managers use language to share perceptions among themselves and gradually define or create meaning through discussion, groping, trial and error, and sounding out. Managers organize cues and messages to create meaning through their discussion and joint interpretation (Smircich, 1983; Weick, 1979).

When viewed within this framework, the contrast between symbolic interactionism and the logistics of information acquisition and transmission described in the previous section becomes clear. When environmental situations are routine or well understood, organizational members have a history of shared interpretation; consequently, information acquisition and transmission are sufficient to make organizational choices that solve problems or exploit opportunities. However, novel and unexpected external events cannot be handled in the same way because existing meanings tend to be less adequate for interpreting the information received. When the equivocality of the environment is high, the problem for managers is to interpret and know the world. The symbolic interactionism view holds that the essence of managerial action is to develop and establish a new shared perspective so that behavior can be defined and established within the organization's regular structure and processes.

Media Richness

The next logical question in this line of argument is, "How do managers process information to interpret the environment?" How can organizations be designed to facilitate reduction of varying degrees of equivocality from the environment? One answer to consider is the way channels or media are used for communication.

Organizations process information through many channels, including face-to-face conversations, electronic mail, telephones, and memos. Recent research indicates that these channels are not equal in their capacity for reducing equivocality. Daft and Lengel (1984) proposed that media selection is closely linked to the amount of equivocality confronting managers. Based on communication channel research (Bodensteiner, 1970; Holland, Stead, & Liebrock, 1976), they further proposed that the media used in organizations can be organized into a richness hierarchy, where richness is the medium's capacity to change understanding (Daft & Lengel, 1986; Lengel, 1983). According to this perspective, face-to-face interaction is the richest medium, followed by video-phone and video-conferencing, telephone, electronic mail, personally addressed documents such as memos and letters, and formal, unaddressed documents such as bulletins and flyers. The information capacity of these media is presented by Daft and Huber (1986) as a function of four features: (1) the opportunity for timely feedback, (2) the ability to convey multiple cues, (3) the tailoring of messages to personal circumstances, and (4) language variety.

Face-to-face discussion is considered the richest medium because it allows immediate feedback so that understanding can be checked and interpretations corrected. This medium also allows the simultaneous communication of multiple cues, such as body language, blush, facial expression, and tone of voice, cues that convey information beyond the spoken message, enhancing understanding of the message beyond its information content (Meherabian, 1971). Face-to-face communications also use high variety and natural language and tend to tailor the message to the receiver (Daft & Wiginton, 1979). Video-phone and video-conferencing are somewhat less rich than face-to-face communication. They have full audio and video capacities, but some cues are restricted; regulating features of mutual gaze are filtered out, and communications are less emotional in tone than face-to-face communications (Argyle & Cook, 1976; Williams, 1978).

The telephone medium is less rich than face-to-face communication, videophone, and video-conferencing because visual cues are screened out. Feedback is fast, however, so individuals may be able to resolve equivocality. The telephone medium is personal and utilizes natural language, but relies on language content and audio cues rather than visual cues to reach understanding. Electronic mail has several characteristics similar to telephone, with the capacity for rapid feedback and the ability to reach a large, geographically dispersed audience. However, cues such as voice inflection are filtered out and feedback may be less spontaneous than when the telephone is used.

Written communications are typically lower in richness than oral communications. Personally addressed documents such as letters and memos are characterized by slow feedback compared to face-to-face and telephone conversations. Visual cues are limited to those on paper, although unaddressed documents are lowest in richness. Examples are flyers, bulletins, rules, and computer reports. These documents are impersonal, are not amenable to feedback, and visual cues are limited to those in the standard format.

The media richness continuum indicates how organizations reduce equivocality. Each medium is not just an information source but is also a complex information-conveying channel. Each medium is unique in terms of feedback, cues, and language variety. As the equivocality confronting managers increases, richer media are needed to resolve differences of opinion and enact shared understandings. However, when events are already well understood and unequivocal, the meaning of information is already shared and a medium low in richness can be used to convey objective message content.

Information-processing research lends support to the idea that media selection is related to the equivocality associated with environmental uncertainty. For example, considering task requirements as a form of environmental input, Van de Ven, Delbecq, and Koenig (1976) studied task uncertainty and coordination modes. When tasks were nonroutine and therefore less familiar and more equivocal, managers preferred face-to-face modes of coordination. When tasks were routine, written rules and procedures were used. Similarly, Meissner (1969) and Randolph (1978) found that when task-related information was objective and certain, impersonal means of communication such as objects, signs, signals, and written documents were used. Personal (face-to-face) means of communication were used more frequently when tasks were high in uncertainty.

Bodensteiner (1970) found that face-to-face media were used more often for information processing when the organization was undergoing change and experienced uncertainty from the environment. Holland et al. (1976) gathered questionnaire data from R&D units and found that personal channels of communication were important when perceived uncertainty was high. They concluded that face-to-face communications enabled participants to learn about complex topics in a short time. Written information sources, such as the professional literature and technical manuals, were preferred when task assignments were well understood. Lengel and Daft (1985) found that managers selected a rich medium when the message was equivocal and created difficulty for reaching mutual understanding. When messages were unequivocal, managers found it more efficient to use media low in richness. For example, Wager (1962) studied the diffusion of information about a unique organizational change. Most executives first learned about the change informally through face-to-face discussions. Written communications about the change provided additional factual details to managers.

SUMMARY AND RESEARCH NEEDS

This chapter has delineated the state of knowledge about information environments and their relationships with organizational communications. The fact that other authors would have addressed subtopics different from the ones we addressed is not surprising; such is the nature of reviews. Differences in the foci or boundaries of reviews, however, are especially likely when the primary topic of interest has no widely accepted definition. This fact introduces the need for research into the nature of the information environment construct.

The information environment is the "sensable" representation of the organization's external environment; it is not the external environment itself, just as a set of photographs is a seeable representation of the object photographed but is not the object itself. Further, the information environment is itself an environment for the organization, just as the photograph is itself an object to the viewer. The construct of information environment, as that which is "sensable" by the organization, stands conceptually between the construct of the actual external environment and the construct of the perceived external environment. In the context of organizational communications, is the information environment construct necessary? Under which conditions might we be able to ignore the construct and when can we not safely ignore it?

We believe that the construct is worthy of further investigation and development. Until this takes place we cannot know the answers to the two questions just posed, but we can offer some speculative responses. It may be, for example, that the quality of the information environment, its unbiasedness, completeness, and clarity, may be predictive of the effectiveness of organizational adaptation or learning. It may also be that the extent to which the external environment creates the known information environment (by imposing information on the organization's environmental sensing units) versus the extent to which the organization creates the known information environment (by scanning and probing the actual external environment) will affect variables such as communication frequency and predictability and the communication media used. These examples are a tiny sampling of the issues that seem more likely to surface if the information environment construct takes a visible position in organization theory and communication research.

Pursuing further the matter of the information environment, it seems that the role of organizational communication as a process through which the information environment comes to be known could be sharpened if the several relevant literatures were looked at simultaneously and an integrative theoretical model developed. As examples, the literatures on technology transfer across organizations (Czepiel, 1975; Sahal, 1982), on industrial intelligence (Gilad & Gilad, 1986; Sammon, Kurland, & Spitalnic, 1984) and on networks of professionals (Freidkin, 1978; Garvey & Griffith, 1967) may well have common threads, linkages, or findings that could lead to a rich integrative theory concerning the role of communication in creating the known information environments. Each of these literatures has a few findings about the importance of personal communications in interorganizational information transfer, but a richer theory about the role of personal communication in creating a more complete information environment could be developed if all three literatures were examined, even if the intended application of the resulting theory were limited to (say) learning about the technological environment. Further, none of these literatures by itself is composed of a large number of empirical studies, so there is room for empirical research as well as a need for conceptual integration.

In our discussion of the three global characteristics of organizational environments (information load, complexity, and turbulence), we noted that each had more than one dimension, for example, turbulence had as components instability and randomness. Although empirical work has investigated relationships between these three global characteristics and variables of interest in organizational science, such as structure, almost no work has involved the use of these more specific dimensions (but see Dess & Beard, 1984). It may be that researchers should begin working with more fine-grained taxonomies in order to develop more specific organization theories, theories that could serve as the bases for operational guidelines for organizational designers.

The nonspecific nature of the variables interferes also with the development of our understanding of information acquisition. Organizations and their members sometimes search for alternatives (with which to address a problem or opportunity), and they sometimes search for information about already known alternatives. These two forms of search or acquisition would seem to have different antecedents at times, and to involve different organizational processes, for example, scanning versus probing. We could find no empirical studies comparing search behavior as a function of which type of search is being conducted, but the possibilities of different determinants and search behaviors seem worth pursuing.

Turning to the subject of the organization's environment sensors, we see two principal research needs. One concerns the need for organizations to be efficient in the handling of routine information and yet to be effective also in the handling of nonroutine information. Given the apparent differences in the appropriate structures and technologies for carrying out these two tasks, how should an organization design its environment-sensing and information-processing system? The second research need is related to the first and concerns the routing of messages. How can sensor units be helped to make wise decisions about to whom to communicate specific items of information? We noted a number of situational variables that do and probably should affect routing decisions, but whether these variables will have an appropriate effect depends on whether the sensor unit "knows the situation," knows, for example, the information needs of potential message receivers. Very little research has been directed at how potential communicators can be helped to make wise decisions about the routing, packaging, and timing of specific messages.

When discussing the organization's external information environment, we noted that the construct of perceived environmental uncertainty could be regarded as either an estimate of some objective property of the environment or as a personal affective response to the environment. We believe this distinction deserves further exploration. It may be, for example, that if the empirical literature on PEU were segmented according to which of the two subconstructs was used, the literature would be less ambiguous and we would learn more than we have. This would be especially true if meta-analysis (Schmidt & Hunter, 1977) could be used to aggregate the results of the studies within the two literature segments separately.

Our review of the literature on information logistics and on perceived environmental uncertainty brought to the surface the issue of the relationship between information and perceived uncertainty. We noted, for example, that information can increase uncertainty if it contradicts previously believed truths. We also noted that variables such as information specificity and intragroup communication might be related to uncertainty and uncertainty reduction in complex ways.

The literature on perceived environmental uncertainty has not been linked to the issues of information interpretation or the development of meaning in organizations. Is uncertainty so different from ambiguity? Should not the research indicating that communication structure affects PEU be drawn upon by those attempting to understand how shared meaning is developed? It seems to us that the work on PEU should be examined by those pursuing the interpretation perspective.

Although the fact is an obvious one, its importance causes us to state it—the information interpretation literature is woeful. Almost any type of research would help. Communication research seems especially appropriate, given both our discussion of media and the start made in the linking of communication structure and PEU. Information interpretation and shared meaning construction will, when better understood, help in the advancement of our understanding of other important new areas such as organization culture (Barney, 1986) and organizational learning (Daft & Huber, 1986; Fiol & Lyles, 1985).

Another matter that deserves attention from organization communication researchers is the impact of the several new electronic media (see Culnan and Markus, Chapter 13, this volume; see also Kiesler, 1986; Kiesler, Siegel, & McGuire, 1984) on information logistics and interpretation. For example, does electronic mail, by reducing the opportunity or propensity for cogitation relative to that provided by regular mail, or by increasing the opportunity or propensity for cogitation relative to that provided by the telephone, affect the quality of information interpretation? Research addressing this question fits nicely within the set of major issues examined in this chapter; the electronic media are a newly identified means of communicating in organizations, their unique properties have a relatively uninvestigated impact on the nature of the information environment of the message receivers, and they seem to pose special problems and opportunities with regard to information interpretation as this is affected by the sharing of information content.

NOTES

1. In this chapter we use the term *information* in its everyday, layperson sense to refer to symbols and other stimuli that affect our awareness of our environments, as contrasted with its technical definition as a measure of uncertainty (see Huber et al., 1975; Shannon & Weaver, 1949). Thus one's information environment consists of that which is sensed, a partial representation of one's actual environment and a principal basis from which one creates a perceived environment.

2. For purposes of edification, we have made a sharp distinction between the two dominant perspectives on organizational environments, the resource-dependency perspective and the information perspective. While much of the literature on external organizational environments falls clearly into one or the other of these perspectives, not all of it does. Of particular interest is the literature concerned with how organizations use communications to affect their environments, and thus attain a favorable resource dependence relationship. Examples are Miles's study of the tobacco industry's response to the findings of the surgeon general and the consequent federal regulation (Miles, 1982) and Van de Ven and Walker's study of interorganizational coordination among child care and health organizations faced with changes in resource availability (Van de Ven & Walker, 1984).

3. When the probabilities of the possible states are near zero or one, uncertainty is less than when the probabilities are more uniformly distributed across the states. The states are those described as possible by the observer and the probabilities are, of course, subjective estimates reflecting the observer's degree of belief that the respective environmental states will occur.

4. This section draws heavily on Huber (1982). See also Stohl and Redding, Chapter 14 in this volume.

5. We are dealing here with the inadequacy of the simple definition of information as "a measure of uncertainty." Data confirming that a senator voted "aye" reduces a lobby group's uncertainty about how the senator voted, and thus is information. But the meaning, explanations, or implications of the "aye" vote often remain to be interpreted, mulled over, and matched with the information and preconceptions of other group members.

6. Linda Trevino provided substantial assistance with the development of this section.

REFERENCES

Aguilar, F. J. (1967). *Scanning the business environment*. New York: Macmillan.

Aldrich, H. (1979). *Organizations and environments*. Englewood Cliffs, NJ: Prentice-Hall.

Aldrich, H., & Mindlin, S. (1978). Uncertainty and dependence: Two perspectives on environment. In *Organization and environment: Theory, issues and reality* (pp. 149-169). Newbury Park, CA: Sage.

Aldrich, H. E., & Pfeffer, J. (1976) Environments of organizations. *Annual Review of Sociology, 2*, 79-105.

Ansoff, H. I. (1975). Managing strategic surprise by response to weak signals. *California Management Review, 18*, 21-33.

Argyle, M., & Cook, M. (1976). *Gaze and mutual gaze*. Cambridge, MA: Cambridge University Press.

Ashby, W. (1956). *An introduction to cybernetics*. London: Chapman and Hall.

Athanassiades, J. C. (1973). The distortion of upward communication in hierarchical organizations. *Academy of Management Journal, 16*, 207-226.

Bacharach, S. B., & Aiken, M. (1977). Communications in administrative bureaucracies. *Academy of Management Journal, 20*, 365-377.

Barney, J. B. (1986). Organizational culture: Can it be a source of sustained competitive advantage? *Academy of Management Review, 11*, 656-665.

Bell, D. (1979). The social framework of the information society. In M. L. Dertovos & J. Moses (Eds.), *The computer age: A twenty-year view* (pp. 163-211). Cambridge, MA: MIT Press.

Benson, J. K. (1978). The interorganizational network as a political economy. In *Organization and environment: Theory, issues and reality.* (pp. 69-101). Newbury Park, CA: Sage.

Blumer, H. (1962). Society as symbolic interaction. In A. M. Rose (Ed.), *Human behavior and social process* (pp. 179-192). Boston: Houghton-Mifflin.

Bodensteiner, W. D. (1970). *Information channel utilization under varying research and development project conditions: An aspect of inter-organizational communication channel usages.* Unpublished doctoral dissertation, University of Texas, Austin.

Bourgeois, L. J., III. (1985). Strategic goals, perceived uncertainty, and economic performance in volatile environments. *Academy of Management Journal, 28*, 548-573.

Bourgeois, L. J., III, McAllister, D. W., & Mitchell, T. R. (1978). The effects of different organizational environments upon decision and organizational structure. *Academy of Management Journal, 21*, 508-514.

Brenner, M. H., & Sigband, N. B. (1973). Organizational communication—An analysis based on empirical data. *Academy of Management Journal, 16*, 323-324.

Brown, J. W., & Utterback, J. M. (1985). Uncertainty and technical communication patterns. *Management Science, 31*, 301-311.

Burns, T., & Stalker, G. (1961). *The management of innovation*. London: Tavistock.

Campbell, D. T. (1958). Systematic error on the part of human links in communication systems. *Information and Control, 1,* 334-369.

Carter, E. E. (1971). The behavioral theory of the firm and top-level corporate decisions. *Administrative Science Quarterly, 16,* 413-428.

Cohen, A. R. (1958). Upward communication in experimentally created hierarchies. *Human Relations, 18,* 41-53.

Conrath, D. W. (1967). Organizational decision making behavior under varying conditions of uncertainty. *Management Science, 13,* 487-500.

Conrath, D. W. (1973). Communications environment and its relationship to organizational structure. *Management Science, 20,* 586-603.

Culnan, M. J. (1983). Environmental scanning: The effects of task complexity and source accessibility on information gathering behavior. *Decision Sciences, 14,* 194-206.

Cummings, L. L., & Harnett, D. L. (1980). *Bargaining behavior: An international study*. Houston: Dame Publications.

Cyert, R. M., & March, J. G. (1963). *A behavioral theory of the firm*. Englewood Cliffs, NJ: Prentice-Hall.

Czepiel, J. A. (1975). Patterns of interorganizational communications and the diffusion of a major technological innovation in a competitive industrial community. *Academy of Management Journal, 18,* 6-24.

Daft, R. L., & Huber, G. P. (1986). How organizations learn: A communication framework. In S. Bacharach & N. Tomasso (Eds.), *Research in sociology of organizations* (Vol. 5). Greenwich, CT: JAI Press.

Daft, R. L., & Lengel, R. H. (1984). Information richness: A new approach to managerial information processing and organizational design. In B. Staw & L. L. Cummings (Eds.), *Research in organizational behavior* (Vol. 6, pp. 191-233). Greenwich, CT: JAI Press.

Daft, R. L., & Lengel, R. H. (1986). Organizational information requirements, media richness, and structural design. *Management Science, 32,* 554-571.

Daft, R. L., & Wiginton, J. C. (1979). Language and organization. *Academy of Management Review, 4,* 179-191.

de Solla Price, D. (1963). *Little science, big science*. New York: Columbia University Press.

Dess, G., & Beard, D. (1984). Dimensions of organizational task environments. *Administrative Science Quarterly, 29,* 52-73.

Dollinger, M. J. (1984). Environmental boundary spanning and information processing effects on organizational performance. *Academy of Management Journal, 27,* 351-368.

Donnellon, A., Gray, B., & Bougon, M. G. (1986). Communication, meaning, and organized action. *Administrative Science Quarterly, 31,* 43-55.

Downey, H. K., Hellriegel, D. H., & Slocum, J. W. (1975). Environmental uncertainty: The construct and its operationalization. *Administrative Science Quarterly, 20,* 613-629.

Downey, H. K., Hellriegel, D. H., & Slocum, J. W. (1977). Individual characteristics as sources of perceived uncertainty variability. *Human Relations, 30,* 161-174.

Downey, H. K., & Slocum, J. W., Jr. (1975). Uncertainty: Measures, research and sources of variation. *Academy of Management Journal, 18,* 562-578.

Downey, H. K., & Slocum, J. W., Jr. (1982). Managerial uncertainty and performance. *Social Science Quarterly, 63,* 195-206.

Downs, A. (1966). *Inside bureaucracy*. Boston: Little, Brown.

Driver, M. J., & Steufert, S. (1969). Integrative complexity: An approach to individuals and groups as information processing systems. *Administrative Science Quarterly, 14,* 272-285.

Duncan, R. B. (1972). Characteristics of organizational environments and perceived environmental uncertainty. *Administrative Science Quarterly, 17,* 313-327.

Duncan, R. B. (1973). Multiple decision-making structures in adapting to environmental uncertainty. *Human Relations, 26,* 273-291.

Duncan, R. B. (1974). Modifications in decision structure in adapting to the environment. Some implications for organizational learning. *Decision Sciences, 5,* 122-142.

Eisenberg, E. M. (1984). Ambiguity as strategy in organizational communication. *Communication Monographs, 51,* 227-242.

Emery, F., & Trist, E. (1965). The causal texture of organizational environment. *Human Relations, 18,* 21-32.

Farace, R. B., Monge, P. R., & Russell, H. M. (1977). *Communicating and organizing.* Reading, MA: Addison-Wesley.

Feldman, J., & Kanter, H. E. (1965). Organizational decision making. In J. G. March (Ed.), *Handbook of organizations* (pp. 614-649). Chicago: Rand McNally.

Feldman, M., & March, J. (1981). Information in organizations as signal and symbol. *Administrative Science Quarterly, 26,* 171-186.

Ference, T. P. (1970). Organizational communications systems and the decision process. *Management Science, 17,* B83-B96.

Fiol, C. M., & Lyles, M. A. (1985). Organizational learning. *Academy of Management Review, 10,* 803-813.

Friedkin, N. E. (1978). University social structure and social network among scientists. *American Journal of Sociology, 83,* 1444-1465.

Galbraith, J. R. (1973). *Designing complex organizations.* Reading, MA: Addison-Wesley.

Galbraith, J. R. (1977). *Organization design.* Reading, MA: Addison-Wesley.

Garvey, W. D., & Griffith, B. C. (1967). Scientific communication as a social system. *Science, 1,* 79-87.

Gerstenfeld, A., & Berger, P. (1980). An analysis of utilization differences for scientific and technical information. *Management Science, 26,* 165-179.

Gifford, W. E., Bobbitt, H. R., & Slocum, J. W., Jr. (1979). Message characteristics and perceptions of uncertainty by organizational decision makers. *Academy of Management Journal, 22,* 458-481.

Gilad, J., & Gilad, B. (1986). Business intelligence—The quiet revolution. *Sloan Management Review, 27,* 53-62.

Glueck, W. (1976). *Business policy: Strategy formation and management action* (2nd ed.). New York: McGraw-Hill.

Goldhar, J. D., Bragaw, L. K., & Schwartz, J. J. (1976). Information lows, management styles, and technological innovation. *IEEE Transactions on Engineering Management, 23,* 51-62.

Gordon, L. A., & Narayanan, V. K. (1984). Management accounting systems, perceived environmental uncertainty and organization structure: An empirical investigation. *Accounting, Organizations, and Society (UK), 9,* 33-47.

Gore, W. J. (1956). Administrative decision-making in federal field offices. *Public Administration Review, 16,* 281-291.

Guetzkow, H. (1965). Communications in organizations. In J. G. March (Ed.), *Handbook of organizations.* Chicago: Rand McNally.

Haberstroh, C. J. (1965). Organization design and systems analysis. In J. G. March (Ed.), *Handbook of organizations* (pp. 1171-1211). Chicago: Rand McNally.

Hambrick, D. C. (1982). Environmental scanning and organizational strategy. *Strategic Management Journal, 3,* 159-174.

Hannan, M. T., & Freeman, J. H. (1977). The population ecology of organizations. *American Journal of Soociology, 82,* 929-964.

Harary, F. D., & Batell, M. F. (1978). The concept of negative information. *Behavioral Science, 23,* 264-270.

Hedberg, B., Nystrom, P. C., & Starbuck, W. H. (1976). Camping on seesaws: Prescriptions for a self-designing organization. *Administrative Science Quarterly, 21,* 41-65.

Hedberg, B., Nystrom, P. C., & Starbuck, W. H. (1977). Designing organizations to match tomorrow: Prescriptive models of organizations. In P. Nystrom & W. Starbuck (Eds.), *TIMS Studies in the Management Sciences* (Vol. V). Amsterdam: North Holland.

Holland, W. E., Stead, B. A., & Liebrock, R. C. (1976). Information channel/source selection as a correlate of technical uncertainty in a research and development organization. *IEEE Transactions on Engineering Management, 23,* 163-167.

Huber, G. P. (1982). Organizational information systems: Determinants of their performances and behavior. *Management Science, 28,* 135-155.

Huber, G. P. (1984). The nature and design of post-industrial organizations. *Management Science, 30,* 928-951.

Huber, G. P., & McDaniel, R. R. (1986). The decision-making paradigm of organizational design. *Management Science, 32,* 572-589.

Huber, G. P., O'Connell, M. J., & Cummings, L. L. (1975). Perceived environmental uncertainty—Effects of information and structure. *Academy of Management Journal, 18,* 725-740.

Huber, G. P., & Ullman, J. C. (1973). *The local job bank program* Lexington, MA: D. C. Heath.

Hunsaker, P. (1973). Incongruity adaptation capability and accomplishment in leadership training for turbulent environments. *Proceedings of 33rd Annual Meeting of Academy of Management* (225-229).

Jain, H. C. (1973). Supervisory communication and performance in urban hospitals. *Journal of Communication, 23,* 103-117.

Javidan, M. (1984). The impact of environmental uncertainty on long-range planning practices of the U.S. savings and loan industry. *Strategic Management Journal, 5,* 381-392.

Jurkovich, R. (1974). A core typology of organizational environments. *Administrative Science Quarterly, 19,* 380-394.

Kaufman, H. (1973). *Administrative feedback.* Washington, DC: The Brookings Institute.

Kefalas, A., & Schoderbek, P. P. (1973). Scanning the business environment—Some empirical results. *Decision Sciences, 4,* 63-74.

Kiesler, S. (1986, January-February). The hidden messages in computer networks. *Harvard Business Review, 64,* 46-59.

Kiesler, S., & Sproull, L. (1982). Managerial responses to changing environments: Perspectives on problem sensing from social cognition. *Administrative Sciences Quarterly, 27,* 548-570.

Kiesler, S., Siegal, J., & McGuire, T. W. (1984). Social psychological aspects of computer-mediated communication. *American Psychologist, 39,* 1123-1134.

Kilman, R. H. (1983). A typology of organization typologies: Toward parsimony and integration in the organizational sciences. *Human Relations, 36,* 523-548.

Lawrence, P. R., & Lorsch, J. W. (1967). *Organization and environment.* Boston: Harvard Business School.

Leblebici, H., & Salancik, G. (1981). Effect of environmental uncertainty on information and decision processes in banks. *Administrative Science Quarterly, 26,* 578-596.

Leifer, R., & Huber, G. P. (1977). Relations among perceived environmental uncertainty, organization structure, and boundary spanning behavior. *Administration Science Quarterly, 22,* 235-247.

Lengel, R. H. (1983). *Managerial information processing and communication-media source selection behavior.* Unpublished doctoral dissertation, Texas A&M University, College Station.

Lengel, R. H., & Daft, R. L. (1985). *The relationship between message content and media selection in managerial communications: Some preliminary evidence.* Working paper, Texas A&M University.

Lorenzi, P., Sims, H. P., & Slocum, J. W., Jr. (1981) Perceived environmental uncertainty: An individual or environmental attribute? *Journal of Management, 7,* 27-41.

McCleary, R. (1977). How parole officers use records. *Social Problems, 24,* 576-589.

Meherabian, A. (1971). *Silent messages.* Belmont, CA: Wadsworth.

Meier, R. L. (1963). Communications overload: Proposals from the study of a university library. *Administrative Science Quarterly, 4,* 521-544.

Meissner, M. (1969). *Technology and order.* San Francisco: Chandler.

Meyer, J. W., & Scott, W. R. (1983). *Organizational environments.* Newbury Park, CA: Sage.

Mellinger, G. (1956). Interpersonal trust as a factor in communications. *Journal of Abnormal Social Psychology, 116,* 695-704.

Miles, R. E., & Snow, C. C. (1978). *Organizational strategy, structure, and process.* New York: McGraw-Hill.

Miles, R. E., Snow, C. C., Meyer, A., & Coleman, H. (1978). Organizational strategy, structure and process. *Academy of Management Review, 3,* 546-562.

Miles, R. E., Snow, C. C., & Pfeffer, J. (1974). Organization-environment concepts and issues. *Industrial Relations, 13,* 244-264.

Miles, R. H. (1982). *Coffin nails and corporate strategies.* Englewood Cliffs, NJ: Prentice-Hall.

Miles, R. H. (1986). *Managing the corporate social environment: A grounded theory.* Englewood Cliffs, NJ: Prentice-Hall.

Miller, J. G. (1972). Living systems: The organization. *Behavioral Science, 17,* 1-82.

Miller, J. G. (1978). *Living systems.* New York: McGraw-Hill.

Mintzberg, H., Raisinghani, D., & Theoret, A. (1976). The structure of "unstructured" decision processes. *Administrative Science Quarterly, 21,* 246-275.

O'Connell, M., Cummings, L., & Huber, G. (1975). The effects of environmental information and decision unit structures on felt tension. *Journal of Applied Psychology, 61,* 493-500.

O'Reilly, C. A. (1978). The intentional distortion of information in organizational communication: A laboratory and field approach. *Human Relations, 31,* 173-193.

O'Reilly, C. A. (1980). Individuals and information overload in organizations: Is more necessarily better? *Academy of Management Journal, 23,* 684-696.

O'Reilly, C. A. (1982). Variations in decision makers' use of information sources: The impact of quality and accessibility of information. *Academy of Management Journal, 25,* 756-771.

O'Reilly, C. A., & Pondy, L. (1979). Organizational communication. In S. Kerr (Ed.), *Organizational behavior* (pp. 119-150). Columbus, OH: Grid.

O'Reilly, C. A., & Roberts, K. (1974). Information filtration in organizations: Three experiments. *Organizational Behavior and Human Performance, 11,* 153-265.

Pennings, J. M. (1981). Strategically interdependent organizations. In P. C. Nystrom & W. Starbuck (Eds.), *Handbook of organizational design* (Vol. 1, pp. 433-455). Oxford: Oxford University Press.

Perrow, C. (1970). *Organizational analysis: A sociological view.* Belmont, CA: Wadsworth.

Pfeffer, J. (1980). *Power in organizations.* Marshfield, MA: Pitman.

Porter, L. W., & Roberts, K. H. (1976). Communication in organizations. In Dunnette, M. D. (Ed.), *Handbook of industrial and organizational psychology.* (pp. 1553-1589). Chicago: Rand McNally.

Porter, M. E. (1985). *Competitive advantage.* New York: Free Press.

Putnam, L. L. (1983). The interpretive perspective: An alternative to functionalism. In L. L. Putnam & M. E. Pacanowsky (Eds.), *Communication and organization: An interpretive approach* (pp. 31-54). Newbury Park, CA: Sage.

Randolph, W. A. (1978). Organizational technology and the media and purpose dimensions of organization communications. *Journal of Business Research, 6,* 237-259.

Read, W. H. (1962). Upward communication in industrial hierarchies, *Human Relations, 15,* 3-15.

Reitzel, W. A. (1958). *Background to decision making.* Newport, RI: U.S. War College.

Roberts, K. H., & O'Reilly, C. A. (1974). Failures in upward communication in organizations: Three possible culprits. *Academy of Management Journal, 17,* 205-215.

Rosen, S., & Tesser, A. (1970). On reluctance to communicate undesirable information: The MUM effect. *Sociometry, 33,* 253-263.

Rosen, S., Johnson, R. D., Johnson, M. J., & Tesser, A. (1973). The interactive effects of news valence and attraction on communications behavior. *Journal of Personality and Social Psychology, 28,* 298-300.

Sabatier, P. (1978). The acquisition and utilization of technical information by administrative agencies. *Administrative Science Quarterly, 23,* 396-417.

Sahal, D. (1982). *The transfer and utilization of technical knowledge.* Lexington, MA: D. C. Heath.

Sammon, W. L., Kurland, M. A., & Spitalnic, M. (1984). *Business competitor intelligence.* New York: John Wiley.

Schermerhorn, J. R. (1975). Determinants of interorganizational cooperation. *Academy of Management Journal, 18,* 846-856.

Schmidt, F. L., & Hunter, J. E. (1977). Development of a general solution to the problem of validity generalization. *Journal of Applied Psychology, 62,* 529-540.

Schmidt, S. M., & Cummings, L. L. (1976). Organizational environment, differentiation and perceived environmental uncertainty. *Decision Sciences, 7,* 447-467.

Schwab, R. C., Ungson, G. R., & Brown, W. B. (1985). Redefining the boundary spanning-environment relationship. *Journal of Management, 11,* 75-86.

Scott, W. R. (1981). *Organizations: Rational, natural, and open systems.* Englewood Cliffs, NJ: Prentice-Hall.

Shannon, C. E., & Weaver, W. (1949). *The mathematical theory of communication.* Urbana: University of Illinois Press.

Shields, M. D. (1983). Effects of information supply and demand on judgment accuracy: Evidence from corporate managers. *Accounting Review, 58,* 284-303.

Simon, H. A. (1971). Designing organizations for an information rich world. In M. Greenberger (Ed.), *Computers, communications, and public interest* (pp. 37-72). Baltimore, MD: Johns Hopkins University Press.

Simon, H. A. (1973). Applying information technology to organization design. *Public Administration Review, 33,* 268-278.

Smircich, L. (1983). Implications for management theory. In L. L. Putnam & M. E. Pacanowsky (Eds.), *Communication and organizations: An interpretive approach* (pp. 221-241). Newbury Park, CA: Sage.

Smircich, L., & Stubbart, C. (1985). Strategic management in an enacted world. *Academy of Management Review, 10,* 724-736.

Starbuck, W. H. (1976). Organizations and their environments. In M. D. Dunnette, (Ed.), *Handbook of industrial and organizational psychology* (pp. 1069-1123). Chicago: Rand McNally.

Staw, B. M., Sandelands, L. E., & Dutton, J. E. (1981). Threat-rigidity effects in organizational behavior: A multilevel analysis. *Administrative Science Quarterly, 26,* 501-524.

Stryker, S., & Statham, A. (1985). Symbolic interaction and role theory. In G. Lindsay & E. Aronson (Eds.), *Handbook of social psychology* (3rd ed.; Vol, 1, pp. 311-378). New York: Random House.

Stubbart, C. (1982). Are environmental scanning units effective? *Long Range Planning, 15,* 139-145.

Terreberry, S. (1968). The evolution of organization environments. *Administrative Science Quarterly, 12,* 590-613.

Thayer, L. (1967). Communication and organization theory. In F.E.X. Dance, (Ed.), *Human communication theory: Critical essays* (pp. 70-115). New York: Holt, Rinehart & Winston.

Thompson, J. (1967). *Organizations in action.* New York: McGraw-Hill.

Tosi, H., Aldag, R., & Storey, R. (1973). On the measurement of the environment: An assessment of the Lawrence and Lorsch environmental uncertainty scale. *Administrative Science Quarterly, 18,* 27-36.

Tung, R. (1979). Dimensions of organizational environments: An exploratory study of their impact in organizational structure. *Academy of Management Journal, 22,* 672-693.

Tushman, M. L. (1977). Communication across organizational boundaries: Special boundary roles in the innovation process. *Administrative Science Quarterly, 22,* 581-606.

Tushman, M. L. (1979). Impact of perceived environmental variability on patterns of work related communication. *Academy of Management Journal, 22,* 482-500.

Tushman, M. L., & Nadler, D. A. (1978). Information processing as an integrating concept in organizational design. *Academy of Management Review, 3,* 613-624.

Tushman, M. R., & Scanlan, T. J. (1981). Boundary spanning individuals: Their role in information transfer and their antecedents. *Academy of Management Journal, 24,* 287-305.

Ulrich, D., & Barney, J. B. (1984) Perspectives in organizations: resource dependence, efficiency, and population. *Academy of Management Review, 9,* 471-481.

Van de Ven, A., Delbecq, A., & Koenig, R. (1976). Determinants of coordination modes within organizations. *American Sociological Review, 41,* 322-338.

Van de Ven, A., & Walker, G. (1984). The dynamics of interorganizational coordination. *Administrative Science Quarterly, 29,* 598-621.

Wager, L. W. (1962). Channels of interpersonal and mass communication in an organizational setting: Studying the diffusion of information about a unique organizational change. *Sociological Inquiry, 32,* 88-107.

Weick, K. E. (1979). *The social psychology of organizing* (2nd ed.). Reading, MA: Addison-Wesley.

Wilensky, H. (1967). *Organizational intelligence: Knowledge and policy in government and industry.* New York: Basic Books.

Williams, E. (1978). Teleconferencing: Social and psychological factors. *Journal of Communication, 28*(3), 125-131.

Yasai-Ardekani, M. (1986). Structural adaptations to environments. *Academy of Management Review, 11,* 9-21.

Zaltman, G., Duncan, R., & Holker, J. (1973). *Innovations and organization.* New York: John Wiley.

6 Corporate Discourse: Public Relations and Issue Management

GEORGE CHENEY
University of Colorado

STEVEN L. VIBBERT
Purdue University

History and Development of Public Relations
   The Beginning Years: A Definition of the Term/Through the Twenties: An Identity for
   the Term/Through the Thirties: The Institutionalization of the Term/The War Years:
   The Integration of the Term/Through the Fifties: Identification with the Term/
   Through the Sixties: Externalization of the Term/Beyond the Oil Embargo: The
   Transformation of the Term/Some Conlcusions from This Analysis
Terms for Corporate Public Discourse
Environmental Monitoring and Management
Internal and External Relations
The Functions of Contemporary Corporate Public Discourse
   The Rhetorical Function/The Identity-Mangement Function/The Political Function
Conclusion

TO Shakespeare's observation that "some are born great, some achieve greatness, and some have greatness thrust upon 'em" (II, v; 1975, p. 83), Boorstin adds, "It never occurred to him to mention those who hired public relations experts and press secretaries to make themselves look great" (Boorstin, 1978, p. 45). Boorstin's concern—that innate and imposed "greatness" blur with the introduction of public relations—is a common and attractive interpretation of the many current manifestations and historical antecedents of corporate public persuasion. Public relations has been a fact of organizational life throughout this century. Today, we find large organizations of many stripes redefining, refining, and expanding their roles in the public arena. These evolving practices, many of which have corresponded to significant cultural transformations, represent a noteworthy shift in the "corporate" communication posture.

This essay examines the broadening involvement of large organizations in shaping public discourse. The perspective adopted here is rhetorical and terminological; that is, the essay assumes that the terms of corporate discourse are powerfully persuasive *in themselves*, and should be analyzed as such.

The essay begins with a history of public relations and its evolution toward what we call "corporate public persuasion." Second, we define and justify our cluster of terms for corporate public discourse: value, issue, image, and identity. Third, we consider how organizations monitor and manage their environments. Following from this, we treat, fourth, the relationship of internal to external organizational relations. Finally, we discern three trends that describe the contemporary functions of corporate public persuasion— relating to rhetoric, identity, and politics.

HISTORY AND DEVELOPMENT
OF PUBLIC RELATIONS

To interpret the historical significance of an event from the surety of hindsight may be to impose order and continuity where none existed. The problems of selection and interpretation are compounded when one begins to account for the development of the public relations tradition. One might begin with the activities of the ancient Sophists; another might choose the activities of a medieval religious propagandist; still others might find that genesis in the activities surrounding the American revolution. Our concerns here will be more limited; we concentrate our discussion on the American corporate public relations tradition as it evolved from the late 1800s forward. Activities that could be identified "in the spirit of public relations" are less important for our purposes here than the evolution, definition, and development of the *term* "public relations" and the activities that evidence these shifts. What we *could* call public relations begins with history. What *was* called public relations begins in the unsettled corporate environment of the late 1800s.

Moreover, the evolution of *public relations* as a term and as a defined activity suggests that public relations reflects (and projects upon) the social-economic-political-technological environment enveloping it. Public relations can be defined broadly as "the art of adjusting organizations to environments and environments to organizations" (Crable & Vibbert, 1986, p. 394). When that environment evidences crisis or undergoes great change, public relations terminology and activity undergoes a concomitant change. When the embracing environment is settled, public relations is likely to be in *stasis*. When the environment is unsettled, public relations is often seen as organizationally desirable, and thus evolves and develops more quickly. Many of the events reviewed here—the railroads, World Wars I and II, the activism of the 1960s, and the "crisis" of the 1970s—offer some support for this interpretation.

The Beginning Years:
A Definition of the Term

To recall the climate in which public relations appeared as an identifiable part of corporate practice one might hold up William Vanderbilt's sentiments, expressed in 1882:

> The public be damned. What does the public care for the railroads except to get as much out of them for as small a consideration as possible! I don't take any stock in this silly nonsense about working for anybody's good but our own because we are not. When we make a move we do it because it is in our interest to do so; not because we expect to do somebody else some good. (Tedlow, 1979, p. 5)

Such is scarcely a sensitive reading of the benefits of public goodwill but in a paradoxical way Vanderbilt's expression contributed to the evolution of public relations as a corporate concern. When confronted with the quotation, Vanderbilt denied using the language attributed to him. This, Tedlow (1979) argues, indicates that "even the infamous Vanderbilt had enough sensitivity to public opinion to understand that it was a serious mistake for him to flaunt his contempt for it if contempt he felt" (p. 5).

The railroads occupied an unparalleled role in late nineteenth-century American life; they were a source of social and technical marvel among the American population. Additionally, they functioned as an important communicative link that joined Americans of distant locations in ways not before possible. The railroads were the most visible manifestation of American corporate life during this time; with their economic and social visibility came a public airing of their activities. Among those activities, in addition to Vanderbilt's expressed arrogance, were kickbacks, payoffs, and a host of other deeds that held them in unfavorable light. The railroads, then, were a first and unsurprising locus of public relations. The Association of American Railroads claimed first stake in the use of the term *public relations* in 1897 (Cutlip & Center, 1982). Public relations began as a curative response to unfavorable public opinion; its initial use implied *the public defense of actions*.

Clearly, this new term for an ongoing activity did not spring up spontaneously. Westinghouse claims to have started the first identifiable public relations department in 1889. Westinghouse, in competition with Edison General Electric over the merits of alternating versus direct current, was faced with a method and a competitor, both more firmly entrenched. Westinghouse hired specialists who took it upon themselves to publicize— quite literally to make public, as opposed to keeping private—the Westinghouse view on this controversy. The Westinghouse public relations "department" dealt with press inquiries, generated publicity, and fended off attacks from their competitor. At Westinghouse, a constellation of public relations activities began to appear; with the railroads, less than a decade later, those activities would receive their entitlement: public relations (Cutlip & Center, 1982).

With these interlocking moments, public relations came to be defined in (even if limited) corporate circles. Public relations at this point consisted primarily of publicity generated to brunt the attack of another, with a somewhat wary eye focused on both the public and the activity adopted to reach them.

Through the Twenties:
An Identity for the Term

Between the years of the introduction of public relations and its development of a recognizable corporate status, crises and challenges in the social, political, and economic environment abetted its acceptance. By 1900 the Publicity Bureau, essentially a publicity agency, was founded; by 1906 the bureau actively represented the publicity interests of the railroads by targeting publications that might present information favorable to their clients' interests (Tedlow, 1979). During the same time, AT&T, Standard Oil, and United States Steel moved to hire or to institute publicity agents. By the end of World War I, Bethlehem Steel, and Du Pont had established publicity or public relations departments. The organizations came to realize "the importance of controlling news they could not avoid generating" (Tedlow, 1979, p. 18).

And the Great War, itself, had substantial influence on the direction that public relations would take. The Creel Committee's experimentation with wartime propaganda stimulated interest in the potential of such propaganda to be used in nonwartime settings. The identity of public relations during the 1920s began to move away from publicity and toward propaganda as its definitive focus. These two poles are personified by Ivy Lee, on the one hand, and Edward Bernays on the other.

For an activity that had a name but needed an identity, Lee offered direction; public relations *was* publicity. He defined the role of the publicist as the "proper adjustment of the interrelationships" of corporate America and its publics, and defined his job as "interpreting the Pennsylvania Railroad to the public and interpreting the public to the Pennsylvania Railroad" (Hiebert, 1966, pp. 11, 49). One is struck by the manifestly rhetorical nature of his operationalization of the public relations publicist's duty; consider Donald Bryant's identification of rhetoric as "the function of adjusting ideas to people and of people to ideas" (Bryant, 1953, p. 413). Lee offered the identity to public relations practice, partly because he held that the rumors the public could generate in the absence of corporate publicity were far worse than anything the corporation might do. By 1916 "Lee frequently used 'public relations' as a blanket phrase to cover all the various activities in which he was engaged . . . [but] even in the early twenties he referred to himself as a 'publicity advisor,' 'publicity expert,' 'publicity director,' and referred to his work as the profession of publicity" (Hiebert, 1966, p. 87).

Bernays saw his mission differently. He called what he did "public relations counsel," and was the first to invoke that term. Bernays is said to have commented that the difference between his public relations counseling and Lee's was that "his was a science and Lee's was an art" (Hiebert, 1966, p. 92). Indeed, Bernays was greatly impressed by the Creel Committee's World War I propaganda machine and sought to impose the burgeoning intellectual matter of social science upon the problems of the public relations "interpreter."

The nephew of Sigmund Freud, Bernays is generally recognized as the father of modern public relations. He sought to integrate his uncle's writing, his own conception of the emotionality of "the herd," and a healthy respect for propaganda into a social scientific theory of the public relations counsel. In 1923 he produced the first book specifically on the topic of public relations, *Crystallizing Public Opinion*, in which he wrote that the public relations counsel "interprets the client to the public, which he is enabled to do in part because he interprets the public to the client" (Bernays, 1923, p. 14). In the same year, 1923, Bernays taught the first course in public relations, at New York University (Cutlip & Center, 1982, p. 86). If Freud had been intrigued by the interpretation of dreams, Bernays's fascination lay in the dream of interpretation. He wanted to "scientize" the study of public opinion, propaganda, and "the mass" into a body of public relations principles. He transformed the terminology, and the identity, of public relations. With Bernays's reformulations leading the way, public relations began to be institutionalized.

Through the Thirties:
The Institutionalization of the Term

The social/political/economic/technical environment of the 1930s was interpreted as threatening by most corporations. Socially, labor unions nettled them; politically, Roosevelt's New Deal was seen as hostile, and "public relations agencies often found themselves battling the government in order to prevent erosion of private management's prerogatives" (Tedlow, 1979, p. 103); economically, the Great Depression posed a threat to survival; and technologically, radio gave conceptions of "mass culture" new meaning. Public relations by this time was recognized, even if not universally, as both a term and a set of corporate activities. During these years, public relations became institutionalized in the large public agencies that arose to meet these several environmental challenges. The 1930s "saw three organizations firmly establish themselves as public relations counselors to large corporate clients. They were Ivy Lee and T. J. Ross, Carl Byoir and Associates, and Hill and Knowlton" (Tedlow, 1979, p. 88). The institutionalization of public relations was furthered, argues Tedlow, because of "conflict between business and government" (p. 89). And the formation of these "agencies" of public relations was an important step in public relations becoming real for the publics it sought to affect. Lee and Ross gave their counsel on the Wheeler-Rayburn Public Utilities Holding Company Bill, which included radio talks, newspaper ads, a write-in campaign, and an attempt to scapegoat President Roosevelt through a "whispering campaign" (Tedlow, 1979, p. 90). Carl Byoir and Associates represented A&P in a public (as opposed to a lobbied) campaign to head off chainstore legislation, while Hill and Knowlton represented the Steel Institute in their battles with unionism. A public relations establishment began to form, aided by and aiding the corporate establishment which was, in its own mind, under attack from a hostile government. With the entrance of the United States into World War II, the public relations establishment found itself in league with the very government it had fought for the better part of a decade.

The War Years: The Integration of the Term

The now-developed public relations establishment brought the skills it had used to confront the home government to bear on the declared enemies of that government during World War II. As during the previous armed conflict, public relations counselors were employed by the government to further home and foreign propaganda. During the war, corporations faced the challenge of denying consumers many of their wares—due to rationing—at the same time that they hoped to preserve the relationship with those consumers for the day the war would be won and reconversion would take place. Scott (1943) identifies five "promotional tasks for wartime advertising": to aid dealers, who no longer had products to market; to maintain demand for a product line that, having been done without, might be seen as expendable; third, to maintain brand preference in the absence of brand choice; fourth, to promote conversion as a show of cooperation with the government; and fifth, to preserve public goodwill through institutional or public relations advertising (pp. 207-229, as cited in Tedlow, 1979, p. 139). The refinement of public opinion polling during this time especially influenced the use of public relations (or institutional) advertising. According to a General Electric commissioned poll in 1942, 90% of the public showed interest in learning from institutional advertising, 85% wanted information on products being sold, and "three quarters were interested in product development and work toward mitigation of the expected postwar unemployment problem" (Tedlow, 1979, p. 139). Public relations had become assimilated as corporate practice by this time to the extent that it was viewed as a means by which to preserve the consumer base at a time of vital challenge. By the end of the war public relations was no longer uncommon; it was integrated into government and business strategy.

Through the Fifties:
Identification with the Term

In the postwar years, "big business" was not feared as it had been in the teens, twenties, and thirties. With the relative threats somewhat smaller in the fifties, the public relations establishment turned its attention to matters of expansion, even if not innovation. If the thirties saw public relations' institutionalization, he fifties saw its professionalization. In 1947, the Public Relations Society of America unified the "professionalist" motive of public relations communicators. Though there were some fears that the economy would not sustain its growth, in general that economy did grow and public relations grew with it. Public relations counselors, with whom Bernays's term had been largely adopted, came to identify themselves as a specialized culture, indeed a profession. Public relations ceased to be merely a term or even an establishment; it had become a way of life and wanted its "professional" status situated. By the 1950s, the "public relations movement had helped to alter permanently the public vocabulary of business" (Tedlow, 1979, p. 163). With that task accomplished, the movement set forth to change its vocabulary about itself.

Through the Sixties:
Externalization of the Term

Through the 1960s the public relations profession faced an extraordinary set of challenges: a spotty economy; an increasingly unpopular war; unrest at home, the stirrings of "consumerism"; a maturing television medium; and activist groups of virtually every sort. During this time public relations entered the vocabulary of the everyday conversation. It was not unusual to hear public relations used to describe talk about civil rights, the war, a public official's statement, and all manner of corporate activity; rarely were these observations positively and approvingly uttered, however.

During this time corporate public relations displayed its own kind of political awakening. Lobbying came to be accepted as a necessary public relations function. For many, the mass media—particularly television—replaced the government as the primary adversary to be loathed and avoided. As a result, many corporations resorted to the increased use of "controlled media" rather than publicity media to relate their positions to their publics. Though more expensive, these outlets gave them control over the content and circulation of their views. Cutlip and Center (1982) encapsulate the public relations environment of this age:

> Thus, imperceptibly in the late 1960s and obviously in the 1970s, there was a shift of public relations tactics by many of the large, pacesetting, multinational corporations and commercial institutions. The shift was away from dependence on public media to present the business story, and toward more use of controlled

media. Booklets, advertising, speech reproductions, and statements of corporate missions and of social concern made their appearance. Selective, well-planned non-public efforts were made to influence legislation, legislators, and the implementation of government programs, social and economic. Associations serving industry and commerce followed suit on behalf of all businesses large and small. (p. 412)

Public relations, paradoxically, became both more and less public. It began to rely less on mass media delivery systems to relay its information and concentrated more vigorously on private lobbying efforts; in this respect, it dealt with only a limited segment of the greater public. But to the extent that the public relations activity undertaken sought to relate directly with what an organization believed was its judging publics, it reflected a closeness of contact not possible with mass media intermediaries.

Much of this controlled contact was an attempt to structure the presentation types of "values," "issues," "images," and "identities" (which are the terms of public relations treated in this chapter). What appears to have taken place is an adaptation, on the part of those who engaged in public relations practice, to the demands imposed upon it by public familiarity. But adaptation must be continual, and there awaited a watershed moment that would alter again what *public relations* would mean.

Beyond the Oil Embargo:
The Transformation of the Term

The oil embargo that first took place during 1973 fundamentally altered the relationships among business and its government and its consuming publics. When the price of oil and gasoline began to rise, consumers were outraged at the escalating prices they were forced to pay at the pump—that is, if they could *find* a pump that was open. At base, many consumers did not believe that there was an oil shortage; they resented long lines, odd- and even-day gas rationing, and the oil companies that they believed had caused them. The government, too, responded. There were calls to "break up" the major oil producers, to nationalize "Big Oil," and there was a spate of "windfall profits" tax legislation. The major oil companies were in something of a quandary: If they chose to be publicly visible, they risked further strain in their public relationships, especially when the messages they sent were filtered through (what they believed to be) adversarial media systems to consumers who thought they were dissembling. If they chose to shrink from public view, they had no forum in which to respond to criticism and they risked long-term, and potentially fatal, harm to their public relationships. These problems faced by the oil companies "represent" in a useful way the constraints and accommodations that have come to structure contemporary public relations in the corporate setting. Thus evolved the "corporate advocacy" or "advocacy advertising" programs of, for example, Mobil Oil (Crable & Vibbert, 1983). These campaigns were described by Sethi (1977) as "the use of paid advertising space to publicize . . . viewpoint[s] on controversial issues of public policy where their vital interests are at stake" (p. 3). They included the hybrid "advertorial," "op-ed" newspaper agenda setting, and more colloquial-popular appeals. Public relations came to be known as a form of "public policy management" that offered "dynamic" proactive possibilities to organizations (Crable & Vibbert, 1985; Jones & Chase, 1979; Sethi, 1977). These public relations practitioners turned increasingly to "issue management" to adjust an organization's relationship with its supporting environment (Crable & Vibbert, 1985; Jones & Chase, 1979. Thus while many organizations *responded* to the conditions of the early 1970s, they began to adopt a stance that would go far beyond their relatively *reactive* position of the past. The new position, in fact, explicitly recognizes the creative power of large organizations in shaping their "environment." Much of the corporate public persuasion we examine in this essay (for example, Mobil Oil, Phillips Petroleum, the "new" Chrysler Corporation, United Technologies) represents the latest transformation of public relations.

Some Conclusions from This Analysis

"Public relations" has occupied a distinctive role in corporate organizational life for nearly a century. The array of activities constituting "public relations," however, has been highly adaptive in response to the necessities and complexities of organized life. Our historical analysis would suggest that neither what public relations means as a *term* nor the kinds of organizational *actions* that are advanced under its aegis are best understood as a set and fixed proposition. Indeed, quite the opposite is the case. As a term and as an activity public relations suggests a foundation of common assumptions about an organization's resources for coping with its environment, while at the same time public relations holds open the prospect for adaptation, change, and the incorporation of new assumptions when that environment undergoes its inevitable changes.

Recent reformulations of public relations suggest that organizations can no longer afford to let others control their communicative agenda; hence, corporate public persuasion attempts to control the terms under which such discussions take place. Public relations today addresses the margins of overlap between an organization and its publics in distinctive and strategic ways. Through public relations communication, corporate actors attempt— admittedly with varying degrees of success—to control the ways internal and external environments discuss such key concepts as values, issues, images, and identities. To "make an issue" of government regulation, for example, promotes some values over others and affects an organization's image and identity. We now turn to a discussion of these four key terms: *image, issue, identity,* and *value.*

TERMS FOR CORPORATE PUBLIC DISCOURSE

The terms *image, identity, issue,* and *value* call to mind many things both in lay thinking and theoretical conceptualization. Moreover, while each of us has an intuitive feel for these terms and their appropriate usage, we would all be hard pressed to offer unequivocal definitions for any of them. Nevertheless, we *do* talk about such notions all the time, as when a company president acknowledges to a troubled staff, "Our image has been tarnished." Such a statement has both significant meaning and rhetorical force for the employees—even though they may not know *precisely what the corporate image is.*

With these difficulties in mind, we would like to make three points before offering working definitions of our four terms. First, we stress the *reflexivity* involved in any thoughtful consideration of images, identities, issues, and values since they are formulated through and in human communication. One's image has substantial meaning only to the extent that it suggests both distinctiveness and commonality with respect to others. A friend may be said to present a "professional image," meaning that she both distinguishes herself from others we know as "unprofessional" and shares qualities with others who are "professional." To discuss what one person values or "has" for an identity is to talk *necessarily* about others, even if the connection is unstated. This principle applies with equal relevance to the treatment of groups, organizations, nations, and so forth. A comment on the "American national character" is at the same time a formulation of what the speaker considers to be "not American" or perhaps "un-American" (see, for example, Devereux, 1975).

People often *act as if* the U.S. government, or General Motors, or the Roman Catholic Church have identities; therefore, it is meaningful to treat the identities of these collectivities within the context of social inquiry because individual actors make such attributions (see, for example, Weber, 1978). Further, McMillan (1985) discusses the importance and power of organizational personae as presented by major corporations. Care must be taken, however, both to avoid reification of such identities and to recognize the primary "place" of the identities in discourse. This we offer as a second preliminary point.

Third, researchers should not always try to eliminate ambiguity in their investigations, but should often examine the "strategic spots at which ambiguities necessarily arise" (Burke, 1969a, p. xviii). Burke (1969b) offers an excellent example of how people often blur the distinction between the *properties we have* as qualities and the *properties we own* as material possessions. This illustrates the "magical" power of words to transcend different domains and put together otherwise different things. So it is when a large conglomerate such as Beatrice conducts an extensive television ad campaign to bring under one symbolic head its otherwise diverse financial interests.

These points provide a sound basis for our articulation and use of working definitions for the four terms—value, issue, identity, and image. Collectively, the terms are useful for explicating and assessing corporate persuasive campaigns. Moreover, each should be understood in its reflexive richness, its full applicability to collectivities, and its creative role in discourse. We define *values* simply as those things treated as important and basic by individuals or groups. A value is, in short, something that is valued or prized by a person or collectivity as revealed primarily in the ongoing discourse of that individual or collectivity. Values may be thought of both as "roots" and "derivatives" in that one can always "trace" implications from a value in a direction more basic or one more specific. For example, one can inquire of a company that values "safety" what that value draws from on a more fundamental level or how it is manifested in more refined terms. Thus safety might be "built" on a concern for people and also be linked specifically to a conservative orientation toward new product development. Of course, how various values are linked is determined *by,* and *in,* the structure of discourse. And any particular value, say efficiency, functions as a "condensed" premise to the extent that merely invoking the idea of efficiency in various contexts implies that "efficiency is a good thing."

Of course, values are appealed to when two or more parties discuss, debate, or come into conflict over an *issue.* "An issue is created when one or more human agents attach significance to a situation or perceived 'problem.' These interested agents create or recreate arguments which they feel will be acceptable resolutions to questions about the *status quo*" (Crable & Vibbert, 1985, p. 5). Issues are focal points in public discourse that never get "solved" in the sense of an absolute termination of discussion, but they do become "resolved" or "managed." The issue of corporate social responsibility persists as an issue because individuals and groups can always raise questions about what corporations ought to be doing for people. While issues can always be linked either implicitly or explicitly to values, occasionally *values* are at issue themselves. For example, a few years ago it was announced by the leadership of General Motors that *quality* was to become its single most important concern. Clearly, some self-examination and discussion preceded that announcement; the issue was what to present publicly as the corporation's primary value.

To manage issues and promote values is also to affect images and identities. Of course, image and identity are closely related. We use them together to stress the interactive way in which people create, find, and use symbolic representations of themselves and others, whether as individuals or as groups.

In everyday discourse, identity conjures up an idea of something an individual or group *has* or possesses, something indicating continuity and distinctiveness. Image, taken in the lay sense, usually indicates something *projected* by an individual or group, something perceived or interpreted by others. Image and identity can be treated together. Our use of each term stresses the centrality of language. Identity is "what is commonly taken as 'representative' of a person or group" (Cheney & Tompkins, 1984, p. 11). As a representation, an identity is developed dialectically and over time by both the focal person (or group) and others. Moreover, much of what one calls "an identity" is composed of words. In a very practical way, this point was demonstrated by a group of oil companies who in the early 1970s invested millions in a search for the new corporate name, Exxon.

These same points apply to the term *image,* with an important exception. An image may be thought to be more temporary, fleeting, and less basic than an identity. Thus people often treat a "negative image" as something to be altered or improved without affecting a basic identity. In making decisions about how to present the "new" Chrysler corporation, Iacocca (1984) made a point of keeping both the company name and its starlike logo while effecting significant changes in other arenas. A decision was made between things considered as *essential* to the corporation's identity and things that were considered to be *changeable.*

Of course, such a distinction is often tough to maintain, particularly when a person or a collectivity is seen to undergo an Eliza Doolittle-type transformation. Employees of small companies that are absorbed both financially and symbolically by larger ones are said to experience difficulty with loss of identity. Cheney (1983a) found that some long-time professional employees of a subsidiary company were nostalgic for "what the company used to be." What was seen from the consuming conglomerate's view as a "simple" change in image for the acquired company (that is, the old personnel, products, facilities, policies, and logos were maintained) was described as a change *in identity* by the company's employees.

This case is a reminder of the interrelationships between and among these four terms. Issues point to values, values often become issues, the discussion of issues affects images, such changes are liked to identities, and so forth. Further, these connections are possible because of the power of words. An issue is not an issue until it is talked about and labeled as such; an identity becomes "what it is" through symbolic means, though it is of course grounded in physical things.

Because of the creative and evocative power of language, the very "essence" and "boundaries" of the organization are things to be managed symbolically; thus the organization's identity is *the* issue for public relations activity. For a public relations department to identify a specific public and target it for a persuasive campaign, the meanings of both "the company" and "the environment" must be managed in the department's discourse. Public relations (and related corporate communication) specialists are "boundary spanners" (Adams, 1976) who not only "sit" on the organizational border, but also *help determine how and where that line will be drawn.* Hence, while the concept of "environment" calls to mind a body of literature usually considered as separate from that of public relations, it must be considered here to explicate more fully the demands of corporate public discourse.

ENVIRONMENTAL MONITORING AND MANAGEMENT

In recent years, a substantial amount of research has concerned "environmental uncertainty" and how this is managed by organizations. To be sure, the increasing social, economic, and technological complexity of western life has made such investigation not only understandable but also desirable on the part of organizational leaders. Krippendorff and Eleey (1986), for example, argue the pressing need for organizations to "monitor their symbolic environment" using a variety of strategies that manifest and project their specific interests. Ironically, however, the proliferation of so-called environmental uncertainty and environmental monitoring studies *adds* to the environments (and perhaps to their uncertainty) for researchers and practitioners. In this section, we review selected examples of environmental uncertainty research that we find particularly germane to the larger discussion of corporate public discourse: Most of these center on the management of meaning in organizational life (see Huber and Daft, Chapter 5, this volume, for a review of the literature on information environments).

That the distinction between organization and environment is often more of a theoretical artifact than an unproblematic "reality" accepted by organizational actors is suggested in the work of Mills and Margulies (1980). In developing and arguing for a typology of service organizations, Mills and Margulies use the *client-organization* interface as a point of departure for their analysis of information flow. It is important that this focus allows them to characterize classes of organizations by the features of interaction that span the traditional boundary between organization and environment, that is, the contact between clients and providers. As a midrange typology of organizational forms, Mills and Margulies's (1980) scheme reminds us that those we call "clients" (and hence "outsiders") act in many instances as contributors to or members of the organization. Moreover, as Cheney, Block, and Gordon (1986) explain, in applying the Mills-Margulies typology to the study of organizational communication, the nature of the "interface" tells us something about communication processes *both* inside and outside of the organization.

Public relations officers, of course, are necessary contributors to the interface between organization and client. Their communication activities simultaneously represent the organization to the client and the client to the organization. As "boundary spanners" whose job is *defined as communica-*

tion, public relations officers are continually involved in making symbolic connections between organization and environment, even as they "say" what each of the linked domains *is.* In public relations activity, then, we find a symbolically rich focus for the understanding of the organizational-environmental relationship. Grunig (1984) finds that many public relations specialists are beginning to appreciate the complex, interactive, and creative nature of their activity—that it is not only boundary spanning but boundary controlling.

With the problematic nature of the organization-environment boundary in mind, we can consider one of the most important and extensive works on the subject, Howard Aldrich's (1979) *Organizations and Environments.* There Aldrich elaborates a "population ecology model of organizational change" and then treats specific issues of organizational stability and adaptability. In developing his approach, Aldrich criticizes the traditional, bureaucratic model and describes how any organization must be seen within an ever-changing population of organizations vying for scarce resources. Further, Aldrich lays out three main assumptions about the organization's relationship to its environment: (1) "goals may be imposed on an organization by the environment"; (2) "organizational boundaries are not fixed"; and (3) "activity systems [that is, organizations] are not equally adapted to all environments" (pp. 14-17). With these assumptions as a guide, Aldrich attempts to counter an overly rationalistic view of organizations forcefully acting toward self-selected and clearly articulated goals and at the same time acknowledge the power of "other" organizations, those in the "environment." In this way, Aldrich's position offers a needed corrective to previous research, much of which treated the individual organization as an actor without a setting and other actors. Aldrich's principles are directly relevant to the work of public relations where the "proper stance" toward the environment must continually be reassessed.

Building on his "natural selection" model, Aldrich (1979) emphasizes the degree of "fit" between an organization and an environment, which can be known in a rather objective fashion. These terms and concepts, while useful on one level, also effectively prevent Aldrich from enlarging his scope of vision to appreciate more fully that *what is called* the environment is in fact socially constructed (see, for example, Berger & Luckmann, 1967) and that large, dominant organizations "enact" a good deal of it (see, for example, Weick, 1979). The perspective of Weick (1979) and others with a related orientation (e.g. Daft & Lengel, 1984; Smircich & Stubbart, 1985) may be offered as a rounding out of Aldrich's (1979) analysis of organizations and environments, moving the discussion toward implications for corporate public persuasion.

Though accepting some assumptions of a natural selection model, Weick (1979) prefers the term "enactment . . . over variation because it captures the more active role that we presume organizational members play in creating the environments which then impose on them" (p. 130). With this shift in terminology and emphasis, Weick reminds us that "experience is the consequence of activity. The manager [the public relations specialist] literally wades into the swarm of 'events' that surround him and actively tries to unrandomize them and impose some order" (p. 148). With the term *enactment* as a centerpiece, Weick tries to explain how individuals (alone and in organization) "actively *put* things out there that they then perceive and negotiate about perceiving" (p. 165). It follows, then, that the large and powerful organization may be a major contributor to the environment it "faces." "As an organization becomes larger it literally becomes more of its own environment and can hardly avoid stumbling into its own enactments" (Weick, 1979, p. 167).

Certainly this is the case with the massive public campaigns of numerous large organizations: for example, Mobil, General Motors (GM), the National Rifle Association (NRA), Johnson & Johnson, and NASA. Johnson & Johnson so profoundly influenced its own sociopolitical environment after the Tylenol poisonings of the early 1980s that it now successfully presents itself as a market leader in enacting safety measures. In a different arena, NASA finds itself under unprecedented public scrutiny, intensified partly because of the symbolic emphasis the agency (and Washington) placed on the ill-fated *Challenger* mission. For better or for worse, organizations such as these must come to terms with their own enactments.

Working within a Weickian perspective, Smircich and Stubbart (1985) outline their view of "strategic management." Stressing that "organizations and environments are convenient labels for patterns of activity" (p. 726), Smircich and Stubbart describe *the task of strategic management in this view [as] organization making—to create and maintain systems of shared meanings, that facilitate organized action* "(p. 724). An appropriate substitute for the term *strategic management* here is *corporate public persuasions*: The makers and shapers of such campaigns must "make" and "remake" the organization for their various publics. This is especially true in the age of issued advocacy when organizations such as the NRA strategically seek specific political outcomes.

The implications of this line of discussion about organizational-environmental relations can be summed up as follows: First, is the power of the terms organizational actors used to order their world. A strict division between "inside" and "outside" can prevent lay persons or researchers from appreciating the necessary connections between internal and external discourse. Public relations specialists deal directly with these two domains of discourse in such a way as to make them mutually influential. Second, is the effect of the sheer volume of findings and reports through which contemporary organizations monitor their environments. These bodies of discourse necessarily become part of what is perceived and enacted by organizations. Third, is the complex interaction of persuasive campaigns by the dominant organizations of our society; for, on a very important level, the management of an environment of discourse (within which a particular organization is "located") is equal to the management of the environment. Of course, as boundary spanners public relations specialists manage the organization as well and therefore must be concerned with internal *and* external communication.

INTERNAL AND EXTERNAL RELATIONS

Given the problematic and often wavering line between organization and environment and hence between internal and external relations, it is important to turn attention briefly to the kinds of corporate communications usually treated as outside the province of public relations. Specifically, these are house organs, newsletters, reports to stockholders, and various other messages to those considered to be members of the organization in one way or another. It is important to note that many of the principles that apply to external persuasive campaigns apply to internal ones (and vice versa): both types are directed at specific "publics" and both represent the organization in particular ways.

Levinson (1972) explains in powerful terms the need to examine house organs and other periodicals in any thorough investigation of an organization's functioning. In outlining his method of "organizational diagnosis," Levinson (1972) argues that house organs are usually "newsy," but "tend to hide the realities of the organization and place a smiling organizational facade before the readers" (p. 223). A recent study of the house organs of two corporations supported Levinson's claim that house organs are often "disguises for paternalism that, in turn, veils underlying authoritarian attitudes" (Axley, 1983, p. 223).

Despite the significance accorded written corporate communications by these observers, there has been little formal research conducted on either their content or their impact. A number of early studies in organizational communication focused on employee handbooks, company newsletters, memoranda, and "information racks" (see Beach, 1950; Mahoney, 1954; Zelko, 1953). Most of these studies stressed the *informative* dimension of communication, a perspective that was consistent with the orientation of most of the corporate publications before World War II. Dover (1959) observed that during the late 1940s and 1950s, the content of in-house written communications broadened to include discussions of company plans, operations, and policies. Thus employee publications "became the arm of management" (see the review by Putnam & Cheney, 1985, p. 133). As Levinson (1972) explains: "Usually house organs are relegated to editors who are well controlled by several administrative layers above them. Dissent, debate, criticism are rarely found" (p. 223).

From our perspective, the internal corporate communications, such as house organs, should be considered in conjunction with external communications that are traditionally labeled as public relations. Paonessa (1984) supports this point well in noting General Motors's concern for how employees respond to the combination of internal messages and messages to the general public. The company's advocacy programs (for example, on the issues of safety) became more coordinated over time as communication officers explicitly recognized that their messages to employees might well translate into advocacy with respect to the public at large. The company began to recognize the potential for "corporate advocacy" by GM employees themselves, because they collectively came in contact with millions of people. Particularly for the large corporation (or other organization) that creates as well as influences its environment, an understanding of these relationships is of obvious importance. To conduct research and criticism effectively, researchers in organizational communication must be attuned to this relationship as well.

Internal corporate communications, particularly those that are disseminated widely, serve to promote select values, foster select images, create select identities, and determine the status of select issues. Further, they can be seen in the larger context of messages from the organization to the individual. Cheney (1983b) explains how the publications manifest numerous, diverse strategies that symbolically identify the individual with the organization. Such strategies range from direct appeals (for example, *Donnelly Printer's* frequent and specific praise of "Donnelly people") to the often-unnoticed use of "we" to promote managerial values as values of all employees (for instance, a comment by a State Farm chief executive officer that "I'm just glad we built our future together, on the same side of the fence"; cited in Cheney, 1983b, pp. 149-156). To the extent that corporate rhetors can set the terms for discussion in such internal campaigns as well as in external ones, they can effect persuasion on a grand scale.

Nowhere is the strategic significance of an integrative strategy with respect to internal and external communications better illustrated than in Kaufman's (1960) thorough case study of the U.S. Forest Service. As Kaufman found, the federal agency intentionally blended public relations and employee communications so as to reinforce the power of each. Public relations materials were *always* sent to employees, and in many cases rangers were required to serve as representatives to community and state organizations. Kaufman (1960) captures the persuasive force of U.S. Forest Service communication strategies this way:

> Public relations is designed to reduce resistance from outside the Service, win support when possible, and counteract centrifugal tendencies that might induce field men to deviate from promulgated policy. It is intended to affect the external forces acting *on* the Rangers while it strengthens "*inside*" them, by heightening their identification with the organization, [and with] tendencies toward conforming with agency decisions. (pp. 196-197)

Of course, this case not only reveals the importance of linking internal and external relations but also the multifaceted nature of many corporate persuasion efforts. Kaufman's (1960) analysis highlights at least three vital functions of U.S. Forest Service communications: to persuade on several levels, to establish a "corporate identity" for insiders as well as outsiders, and to act politically in and on the larger environment. These functions are increasingly applicable to today's corporate rhetors, as they become more strategic, comprehensive, and proactive in their persuasive campaigns. Hence, we employ the three functions—rhetorical, identity-management, and political—to structure the next sections.

THE FUNCTIONS OF CONTEMPORARY CORPORATE PUBLIC DISCOURSE

Based on our survey of extant literature and contemporary corporate public discourse, we observe that the latter serves three functions, the cumulative effect of which is to blur the publicly shared distinctions between organization and environment. This blurring of "us" and "them" and inside and outside is important strategically because it presents the organization with the opportunity to resolve these ambiguities according to its own designs rather than in simple response to the demands of environmental actors. Specifically, "proactive" public relations strategies serve rhetorical, identity-management, and political functions as large contemporary organizations attempt to mediate among vocal corporate rhetors, uncertain environments, and an ambiguous nexus of their interests.

The Rhetorical Function

First, *organizational "campaigns" are designed to influence both internal and external publics, and therefore function as multifaceted rhetorical acts.* In one of the first studies of organizational discourse from a rhetorical perspective, Knapp (1970) concluded that we have "relatively little information available concerning business rhetoric" (p. 248). Our review of the literature reveals little change in this situation, despite the broadening persuasive activities of large corporations and other organizations. Thus we highlight instances of corporate public persuasion and their rhetorical power while incorporating references to relevant pieces of research.

The "court" of public opinion is a rhetorical arena. As McMillan (1982) notes, most organizations are both subject to and the source of multiple rhetorical influences. Those who enter that arena manifest "the rationale of informative and suasory discourse" (Bryant, 1953, p. 408). Corporate public persuasion may be examined profitably by locating, in the Aristotelian sense, the types of audiences to which messages are addressed and the types of judgments they are asked to make. The publics for corporate persuasive campaigns are judges in the court of public opinion; the object of their judgment is situated rhetoric.

The rhetorical aspects of corporate communication campaigns can be illustrated by treating "image-building" advocacy as epideictic discourse—that which reinforces and sometimes "establishes" values.

According to Aristotle, it is in the epideictic genre that the speaker "praises and blames, and his speech relates to the worthy and unworthy" (Perelman, 1982, p. 19). Because the epideictic was never associated with either the assembly or the courts, but instead with ceremony, it occasionally has been characterized as "a degenerative kind of eloquence with no other aim than to please" (Oravec, 1976, pp. 162-164; Perelman & Olbrechts-Tyteca, 1969, p. 48).

However, the administration of praise and blame is at base "a question of . . . recognizing values" (Perelman & Olbrechts-Tyteca, 1969, p. 48). "In my view, " writes Perelman (1982), "the epideictic genre is central to discourse because its role is to intensify adherence to values, adherence without which discourses that aim at provoking action cannot find the lever to move or inspire their listeners" (p. 19). Crable and Vibbert (1983), in their analysis of Mobil Oil's "epideictic advocacy," further explain that the consensual values that are established in epideictic messages can become the argumentative materials that are used in other, more overtly partisan, appeals.

The margins of overlap between the epideictic and corporate campaigns are illustrated by the efforts of Phillips Petroleum. Phillips, as the eleventh largest oil company in the United States, turned to a non-product-oriented, image-building campaign for a very practical reason, but their use and refinement of the format "is an instructive case in the persuasive potential of shared value premises" (Vibbert, 1984, p. 5).

In the wake of the 1973 oil embargo, Phillips found it had little need to advertise traditionally for the consumption of its product, since there was so little product to consume. Phillips's options, at minimum, were to (1) avoid contact with the public by ceasing all advertising and thus run the risk that they would fade from public memory once the crisis had passed; (2) continue their contact with the public on a business-as-usual basis and run the risk that their contact with the public would create frustration and hostility; and (3) adopt an image-building rhetoric that would search for positive areas of agreement with the public, even if they did not center on consumer-available products. This last strategy would work to keep the Phillips name in the public marketplace, would create an alliance between Phillips and consumers based on shared values (instead of direct product experience), and would become the basis for postcrisis strategies of public opinion redemption through other advocacy efforts (Phillips Petroleum Company, 1980).

Phillips Petroleum (1980) chose the third option and created a campaign they christened "The Performance Story." That campaign included the case of

Becky Sharp, whose Alaskan helicopter rescue was made possible by a Phillips fuel additive; Phillips's production of a blood filter for use by kidney patients; their research in plastics, which led to a shatterproof highway barrier; and their "petro-mat," which led to fewer road repairs (and, they point out, taxpayer savings) in Oklahoma City. These became the evidence of Phillips's "performance." They produced, said their campaign, "good things for cars and the people who drive them." The campaign stressed that Phillips and their consumers shared the values of innovation, research, technological discovery, and conservation. It asked the public not to buy their products, but to celebrate their and others' "performance."

Phillips claims rightly that such campaigns cannot be judged by product sales alone; they report that from 1973 to 1979 (a time during which they aired not one traditional product ad) that their brand recall among their target audience increased 90%. Advertising recall was up 2100%. And Phillips's research indicated that they were "in the top" of favorable public reaction to oil companies (Phillips Petroleum Company, 1980). Apparently the epideictic value premises used in the Phillips image campaign (innovation, discovery, conservation) met with shared acceptance and functioned to bolster the company's public standing in the process.

A later Phillips campaign, which centered on their support of the Olympics (a not uncommon corporate epideictic campaign, to judge from the sponsorship of the 1984 games), points up interesting irony. Perelman (1982) notes that "it was the oratorical competitions held during the [ancient] Olympic Games" that inspired Aristotle's insights into the epideictic (p. 19). The current manifestation of ancient performance is the "Performance Story" of a major oil producer.

A related manifestation of the rhetorical nature of corporate "campaigns" is the attempt to use these efforts to establish key symbolic linkages or identifications that "locate" the corporation in the domain of public discourse. Mobil Oil, for example, coordinated a multifaceted campaign around its explicit and implicit identification *with* the common sense of common people, technology, and conversation and its antithetical opposition to regulation, irresponsible mass media, and an unresponsive Congress. In this way, Mobil came to stand as a modern-day Prometheus, the contemporary bringer of fire (Crable & Vibbert, 1983).

Such symbolic linkages are profoundly rhetorical in nature. They are fundamental efforts at adjusting the relationships between the organization and its publics, its environments. Du Pont's house organ, *Context*, makes extensive use of antithetical identifications concerning "government regulation" in an apparent attempt to situate Du Pont and its employees vis-à-vis a shared perceived threat (Cheney, 1983b, p. 153). Sethi (1977) describes the advocacy efforts of the American Electric Power Company to stand "for" coal and "against" dependence on foreign energy sources. Dionisopoulos (1984) details the advocacy efforts of the nuclear power industry after the Three Mile

Island accident. Their campaign centered on the "need for power," argued that "no one had died at Three Mile Island," and situated the nuclear industry as the solution to America's growing energy needs. The Kaiser Aluminum & Chemical Corporation, in response to unfavorable coverage on ABC's *20/20*, began an advocacy campaign that included full-page ads, case-study booklets for college classes, and extensive use of other controlled media to demonstrate their opposition to "trial by television" (Kaiser Aluminum & Chemical Corporation, 1981).

Rhetorically, these symbolic linkages and unique placements are important because they come to *stand for* the corporation synecdochially. They represent or encapsulate the activities of the larger campaign and the sponsoring corporation, and encourage identification by demonstrating that the corporate rhetor is "separated from big government" or "aligned with the interests of the people." Corporate persuasive campaigns, then, are viewed as multifaced rhetorical artifacts with strategic structures.

The Identity-Management Function

To manage one's audience in discourse is also to manage one's identity in discourse, whether that "one" be an individual or some kind of group. The most profound challenge to advocacy by any organization is *to develop a distinct identity while at the same time being recognized as part of the cultural "crowd."* This kind of balance affords the greatest opportunity for achieving favorable responses from various publics. To a great extent, this dilemma is tied into the paradox of identity itself: the fact that an individual or a group must fashion something distinctive out of symbolic resources that are socially shared (Mackenzie, 1978). In this way, identity (and, we would add, images) are both individually held and socially accomplished, whether that "individual" be a person or a collectivity (see the review in Cheney, 1985).

For the corporate rhetor, the challenge is intensified by two factors. First, the organization must work in the realm of collective representations, usually complicated by an array of internal and environmental issues. Because of this, *external* corporate communications may present an image that is rejected by the employees of the organization. Concern about this possibility has led General Motors to strive for consistency between its internal and external communications (Paonessa, 1984). A second issue is of course the commitment of capital and human resources to large-scale persuasive campaigns. Organizations usually seek some kind of assurance of success before making great investments in image making, issue advocacy, and so forth.

Given the challenge of presenting themselves as "the same, yet different," many large organizations (1) make use of the unquestioned pervasiveness of certain cultural premises and (2) foster their "own" premises linked to the broader ones. To be heard, any speaker or writer must use some fact or opinion that is known and accepted by the audience. What is already shared between rhetor and persuadees then becomes a fulcrum upon which the larger persuasive process is balanced. It is important to note that this capsulizes the philosophy of Aristotle's (1954) *Rhetoric* as well as elaborations of it by Burke (1969b) and others. In persuasive campaigns, organizations draw upon cultural resources—shared values such as freedom, individualism, entrepreneurialism, efficiency, growth—in order to enhance audience approval. At the same time, however, corporate rhetors try to offer something "special" in the way of their own translations of these key values into more specific premises that work for corporate distinctiveness and advantage.

For example, United Technologies (1984a, 1984b) has presented as part of its image-and-issue campaign a series of essays in major news and editorial magazines. In 1984 alone, the conglomerate that changed from the name United Aircraft in the 1970s at the urging of an advertising firm (Margulies, 1977), attempted to identify itself with a range of issues (some of them predictably related to technology, others quite separate). The issues addressed by the corporation in its full-page essay-ads during 1984 included the mechanization of work, defense weaponry, the progress of technology, political action committees, racial equality, governmental spending, democracy, and the Orwellian vision of the year. In one of the corporation's ads, "Technology and Jobs" (United Technologies, 1984b), the corporate rhetor builds upon the value premise of progress (that is, technological advance is per se a good thing) and historical examples to make the case that each new technological step yields more jobs rather than eliminating them. In a weave of inductive and deductive reasoning, the essay leads to the conclusion that "the greatest threat to the labor force today is—lack of technology." In this way, the piece of issue advocacy turns the traditional proworker argument against automation upside down. The most interesting aspects of the ad for our purposes are that (1) it draws upon the often unbridled American confidence in material progress; (2) it works to create and support attitudes favorable to the installation of new technologies in the workplace by big business; and (3) it offers support for the name of the corporation itself by identifying United Technologies with valued technology.

The advocacy advertising by United Technologies, as well as that of other large organizations, reminds us of what Aristotle (1954) called the substance of persuasion: the *example* and the *enthymeme*. The example, being the rhetorical use of inductive reasoning, is self-explanatory. More complex and subtle, and ultimately more important, is the enthymeme: a syllogism drawing on at least one premise held by the audience (see, for example, Bitzer, 1959; Conley, 1984; Delia, 1970). Bitzer (1959) argued that the enthymeme "succeeds as an instrument of rational persuasion because its premises are always drawn from the audience" (p. 408). The rhetor (whether an individual or a group) can either express or suppress shared premises as preference dictates. We also stress, following Delia (1970), that the enthymemic process builds on the universal psychological tendency toward consistency maintenance; thus an audience will often find desirable premises in line with already accepted ones (though this point should not be carried to the degree of committing the logic fallacy). Because of the need to account for the varying strengths within the plurality of "corporate voices" in contemporary society, Tompkins and Cheney offer a second conceptualization of the enthymeme. They define enthymeme$_2$

> as a syllogistic decision-making process, individual or collective, in which a conclusion is drawn from premises (beliefs, values, expectations) inculcated in the decision makers by the controlling members of the organization. One or more parts of enthymeme$_2$ may be suppressed. . . . Organizationally appropriate decisions, once the premises are inculcated, are motivated by the universal psychological process of consistency maintenance and the individual's desire to "behave organizationally." (Tompkins & Cheney, 1985, pp. 188-189)

This formulation is useful in the present discussion because it can easily be applied to the large-scale socializing effects of campaigns by many organizations today. Organizations such as Mobil, General Motors, the National Rifle Association, and others do more than simply rely on the premises already held by their audiences; they work to maintain and to foster certain premises that may then be built upon in ongoing persuasive efforts. Along with Tompkins and Cheney (1985), we underscore the point that enthymemes 1 and 2 are not different processes; they are different ways of handling the sources of major premises (quality, efficiency, freedom, and so forth). With enthymeme$_1$, such premises are treated as *given*, as "belonging" to the audience in question. With enthymeme $_2$ the organization is identified as an important socializing force in itself; that is, it advances one or several major premises in order to generate a more receptive climate for other messages.

A good illustration of this can be found in a discussion and augmentation of the analysis of Mobil Corporation's issue advocacy by Crable and Vibbert (1983). Besides explaining how Mobil's "observations" (half-page ads in Sunday newspaper magazine sections) function as epideictic discourse, Crable and Vibbert show how Mobil worked to establish and reinforce certain premises through its treatment of six major issues: governmental regulation, the Congress, the media, technology, conservation, and American "common sense." Presenting its ads as a forum for "discussing" and "sharing views," Mobil took the opportunity to make strong argumentative cases of its own. In this way, the corporation's treatment of each issue "contributes in an important way to Mobil's role as a corporate rhetor, and thus makes possible an identification and argumentative alliance between Mobil and the readers of 'Observations'" (Crable & Vibbert, 1983, p. 387).

For example, on the subject of regulation, Mobil describes it as costly, inefficient, stifling, and just plain ridiculous. Moreover, the corporation treats regulation as a problem for both business and individuals. "In short regulation is depicted as a problem for corporate America, but also for all America and all Americans: regulation constrains both corporate and individual activity" (Crable & Vibbert, 1983, p. 387).

This discussion and application of the enthymemic process brings us back to the terms we offered at the outset of our theoretical explication. The enthymeme, which draws on and fosters key value premises, is a way of expressing the necessary symbolic connection between persuader and persuadee in communication. Further, the enthymeme both points to and is grounded in some kind of identification of rhetor and audience, whether they be individuals, groups, or organizations. As Burke (1969b) explains: "True, the rhetorician may have to change an audience's opinion in one respect; but he can succeed only insofar as he yields to that audience's opinions in other respects. Some of their opinions are needed to support the fulcrum by which he would move other opinions" (p. 56). Here we find the link between Aristotle's rhetoric and Burke's identification; moreover, the connection helps us to see how it is that the persuasive process is inextricably tied to questions of identity and image. In making a case for a position on a particular issue, a rhetor (individual or corporate) necessarily supports some values over others and effectively assumes a commonality with the audience or public. This point of "sharing," be it actual or simply believed, nevertheless "resides" in the discourse and says something about how both rhetor and audience are represented (Cheney, 1985). Issues, values, images, and identifications thus converge in the practical reality of persuasive discourse.

To be sure, the recent "I'm the NRA" ads by the National Rifle Association demonstrate a highly pragmatic awareness of the interrelationships of these terms and concepts. The full-page magazine ads typically depict smiling Americans from various walks of life holding a gun and framed with a personal statement. Shared identity and issue positions thus merge quite completely in these discursive and visual messages. This kind of merger was just as true, though accorded greater public attention, in the case of Chrysler's revitalization. As Broms and Gahmberg (1982) explain, the portrayal of Chrysler's plight as touching on central values of American society was an important feature of both the discourse of the auto manufacturer itself and the relevant coverage by the news media. The troubled company was granted great symbolic importance by its role as part of the "great American auto industry" and by the "threatening" stance of Japanese manufacturers. Thus the effort to help Chrysler became publicly identified with the restoration of the American dream as a whole. Issue and identity became essentially one, as the corporation and its advocates wrestled for control of public and political discourse.

The Political Function

As can be inferred from the discussion above and from even a causal observation of the sociopolitical landscape, *numerous large organizations today explicitly act in a political manner and "see" themselves as doing so.* "Corporate advocacy" of "corporate issue management" thus refers not only to the messages of *corporations* in the strict sense, but also to a variety of large, influential, and resourceful corporate bodies. Heath (1980) explains that "corporate advocacy consists of the research, analysis, design, and mass dissemination of arguments on issues contexted in the public dialogue in an attempt to create a favorable, reasonable, and informed public opinion which in turn influences institutions' operating environments" (p. 371). This broad formulation includes within its conceptual parameters major persuasive efforts by businesses, unions, religious organizations, and associations of various types. In entering the political arena, however, these organizations are confronted with the dilemma of achieving direct political influence without being identified as political groups. They must proclaim political messages *without at the same time being represented as political bodies* in the discourse of other corporate and individual rhetors. Not to maintain such a balance would jeopardize the boundary-spanning position of these groups; they would risk a total identification with the political order and they would have to deal with politics completely on *its terms*. This dilemma of course parallels that of many boundary-spanning persons and groups as they attempt to meet conflicting expectations (see, for example, the review by Adams, 1976).

The R. J. Reynolds Tobacco Company's recent advocacy campaign demonstrates how an organization can come to terms with political issues but retain perceptions that the group is outside the political establishment (R. J. Reynolds Tobacco Company, 1986). The campaign addresses several issues that are of interest to both smokers and nonsmokers: proposed or actual bans on smoking in public places; the effects of "environmental tobacco smoke" ("secondhand smoke"); the ethical dimensions of cigarette advertising viewed by young people; and workplace smoking restrictions, among others. Each of these has been the object of political, even legislative, action. Yet the Reynolds campaign, aimed at a popular audience through mass circulation magazines, is framed in decidedly nonpolitical terms. To allay the friction between smokers and nonsmokers when public smoking is the issue, Reynolds's offers what is calls a "radical" proposal: "common courtesy." Reynolds's advice to young people who would take up the habit: "Don't smoke" since smoking is an "adult custom." On the issue of secondhand smoke, Reynolds offers the following alternatives: "Confrontation? Segregation? Legislation? No. We think annoyance is neither a governmental problem nor a medical problem. It's a people problem" (R. J. Reynolds Tobacco Company, 1986). Consistently, the R. J. Reynolds campaign defines political, public policy issues as matters of social convention or even as matters of etiquette. In this way, Reynolds's public posture features "grassroots" lobbying, rather than its more private and tainted cousin, the direct appeal for legislative redress. Thus Reynolds is able to come to terms with an industry-threatening set of issues in ways that hold both consuming and consumerist publics responsible for the resolution of the "social" conflict. At the same time, Reynolds's political action is distanced from the political order.

Indeed, we find many examples of corporate bodies who proclaim political messages, but who shy away from the implication that they are political actors. The National Rifle Association's advocacy on behalf of the Second Amendment right to bear arms is couched in a slice-of-life campaign that proclaims of Everyman and Everywoman, "I'm the NRA." The highly successful Mothers Against Drunk Driving have clearly political ends, but their means are premised on grassroots social—rather than overtly political—action. American automobile manufacturers proclaim that import quotas are a matter of "fair competition," an economic explanation, but also a political one. The Reverend Jerry Falwell's Moral Majority, Inc. may stand as an object lesson in reverse here; as the Moral Majority came to be seen as an overtly political body rather than merely the expression of conservative "family" values, its actions came under increasing public and media scrutiny.

Meadow (1981) underscores what we have called the political function of corporate public discourse—the desire to make political messages but to stand outside of politics. Through a content analysis of non-product advertisements that were published in major newspapers and mass magazines in 1979 and 1980, Meadow divined a 10-category typology for the analysis of advocacy advertising. Only 3 of Meadow's 10 discovered categories of non-product advocacy advertisements evidenced overtly political characteristics. Of the non-product advertisements that Meadow located in five-week samples of the *New York Times* and the *Wall Street Journal* during 1980, only 20.5% and 22.8%, respectively, were *overtly* political (Meadow, 1981). Thus it appears that not only do corporate rhetors *desire* political efficacy without political effigy, they in fact structure their corporate public discourse such that political actions are framed in less partisan, nonpolitical terms.

Nowhere is this challenge and its associated problems better seen than in the recent public activity of the U.S. Catholic bishops. In an unprecedented manner, the National Conference of Catholic Bishops (NCCB) has been engaging in corporate advocacy since the early 1980s. In just a half-decade the bishops have openly tackled such controversial and weighty issues as nuclear arms control, U.S. policies in Central America, the role of Hispanic peoples in U.S. society, and the moral and social aspects of this nation's economy. Widely publicized from its inception in 1980 to its final point of development in 1983, the NCCB's pastoral letter on war and peace marked the bishops' full-scale entrance into the arena or organized issue advocacy.

As Goldzwig and Cheney (1984) observe, an interesting irony about this pastoral letter is that the bishops were arguing for their nonpolitical status while taking political action. The bishops were making "necessary application [of moral principles] to public policy, seeing these as a calling of the Church" (Hesburgh, 1984, personal communication). Yet they were also taking great care not to be identified with any particular political group or position—such as the Reagan administration or the "freeze" advocates (Malone, 1983, personal communication). The maintenance of this delicate balance was necessary for a group whose discourse "places" it both *in* the world and to a large degree *outside* it; the stance was required for the preservation of the group's moral authority. Such is the dilemma of advocacy by a religious group on specific political concerns, and acceptance of the challenge opened the bishops to charges of being too political and too technical (Cheney, 1985).

Although the challenges faced by the bishops have unique facets because of their particular sociopolitical and religious contexts, they underscore the difficulties faced by all corporate advocates who seek to operate from the boundaries of the explicitly political arena. In a very real sense, groups in this position must maintain two different identities simultaneously: their traditional, nonpolitical identity and their identity as political advocates. As a task evoking paradox, this challenge reveals something important about the organizational environment of contemporary American society: that advocates are struggling to hold on to some of their "own" terms while confronting the terms of political discourse. Choosing to be "both-and" rather than "either-or," organizations as political actors must not only distinguish themselves through the force of their advocacy but also must keep their discourse at least partly outside the political sphere.

CONCLUSION

We offer three general conclusions from this analysis. First, public opinion is perceived as a valuable corporate ally. As Tedlow (1979) notes, it is perhaps not incidental that public relations was born and grew best in America; the key is American "faith in public opinion as the arbiter of value" (p. xiv). Public relations has evolved from Vanderbilt's sentiments on the public's damnability to the public's near deification. This essay suggests that corporations view public opinion as a valuable collective resource, one much desired and not to be squandered. Corporate public persuasion, in this sense, is communicative resource management.

Our second conclusion is that the stance of public relations is moving increasingly away from reactive accommodation and toward proactive formation. The widespread interest in environmental monitoring, corporate advocacy, issue management, and public policy involvement by corporate persuaders signals a potentially important shift. "Public relations" may have been born in reaction to charges made by others, but corporate public persuasion is increasingly strategically offensive in nature.

Our final conclusion, consistent with the emphasis we have followed throughout, is that corporate actors have become vitally concerned with controlling the terms of their presentation to various publics, both "inside" and "out there." Proactive public relations strategies are attempts to control value, issue, image, and identity as *terms* that also control discussion and enactment of these corporate concepts. This constellation of terms may function rhetorically, politically, or in the interests of organizational identity, and as Burke (1966) notes, such terms necessarily reflect, select, and deflect what we call "reality." Corporate public persuasion, drawing from vast symbolic and materials resources, incorporates key terms of the larger social order, even as it advocates some of its own. Moreover, these kinds of external persuasive efforts are inevitably linked to internal corporate communication, although the relationship in specific cases may exhibit tension or even contradiction. Thus our concern has been for "corporate public discourse" writ large, so as to understand and explicate the context for what is called "organizational communication." Corporate public discourses and the public relations assumptions that underlie them have a distinctive and vital role to play in the communicative life of an organization.

REFERENCES

Adams, J. S. (1976) The structure and dynamics of behavior in organizational boundary roles. In M. D. Dunnette (Ed.), *Handbook of industrial and organizational psychology* (pp. 1175-1199). Chicago: Rand McNally.

Aldrich, H. E. (1979). *Organizations and environments.* Englewood, Cliffs, NJ: Prentice-Hall.

Aristotle (1954). *Rhetoric* (W. R. Roberts, Trans.). New York: Modern Library.

Axley, S. R. (1983) *Managerial philosophy in organizational house organs: Two case studies.* Paper presented at the annual conference of the International Communication Association, Dallas.

Beach, B. (1950). Employee magazines build morale. *Personnel Journal, 29,* 216-220.

Berger, P. L., & Luckmann, T. (1967). *The social construction of reality.* Garden City, NY: Doubleday.

Bernays, E. L. (1923). *Crystallizing public opinion.* New York: Boni and Liveright.

Bitzer, L. F. (1959). Aristotle's enthymeme revisited. *Quarterly Journal of Speech, 45,* 399-408.

Boorstin, D. J. (1978). *The Image: A guide to pseudo-events in America.* New York: Atheneum.

Broms, H., & Gahmberg, H. (1982). *Mythology in management culture.* Helsinki, Finland: Helsingin Kauppakorkeakoulun Kuvalaitos.

Bryant, C. D. (1953). Rhetoric: Its functions and its scope. *Quarterly Journal of Speech, 39,* 401-424.

Burke, K. (1966). *Language as symbolic action: Essays in life, literature, and method.* Berkeley: University of California Press.

Burke, K. (1969a). *A grammar of motives.* Berkeley: University of California Press.

Burke, K. (1969b). *A rhetoric of motives.* Berkeley: University of California Press.

Cheney, G. (1983a). On the various and changing meanings of organizational membership: A field study of organizational identification. *Communication Monographs, 50,* 342-362.

Cheney, G. (1983b). The rhetoric of identification and the study of organizational communication. *Quarterly Journal of Speech, 69,* 143-158.

Cheney, G. (1985) *Speaking of who 'we' are: The development of the U.S. Catholic bishops' pastoral letter* The Challenge of Peace *as a case study in identity, organization, and rhetoric.* Unpublished doctoral dissertation, Purdue University, West Lafayette, IN.

Cheney, G., Block, B. L., & Gordon, B. S. (1986). Perceptions of innovativeness and communication about innovations: A study of three types of service organizations, *Communication Quarterly, 34,* 213-230.

Cheney, G., & Tompkins, P. K. (1984). Coming to terms with organizational identification and commitment. Paper presented at the annual meeting of the Speech Communication Association, Chicago.

Conley, T. (1984). The enthymeme in perspective. *Quarterly Journal of Speech*, 70, 168-187.

Cox, H. (1984). *Religion in the secular city*. New York: Siman & Schuster.

Crable, R. E., & Vibbert, S. L. (1983). Mobil's epideictic advocacy: "Observations" of Prometheus-bound. *Communication Monographs, 50*, 380-394.

Crable, R. E., & Vibbert, S. L. (1986). *Public relations as communication management*. Edina, MN: Bellweather Press.

Crable, R. E., & Vibbert, S. L. (1985). Managing issues and influencing public policy. *Public Relations Review, 11*, 3-16.

Cutlip, S. M., & Center, A. H. (1982). *Effective public relations* (5th ed.). Englewood Cliffs, NJ: Prentice-Hall.

Daft, R. L., & Lengel, R. H. (1984). Information richness: A new approach to managerial behavior and organization design. In B. M. Staw & L. L. Cummings (Eds.), *Research in Organizational Behavior*, (Vol. 6, pp. 191-233). Greenwich, CT: JAI Press.

Delia, J. G. (1970). The logic fallacy, cognitive theory, and the enthymeme: A Search for the foundations of reasoned discourse. *Quarterly Journal of Speech, 56*, 140-148.

Devereux, G. (1975). Ethnic identity: Its logical foundations and its dysfunctions. In G. deVos and L. Romanucci-Ross (Eds.), *Ethnic identity: Cultural continuity and change* (pp. 42-70). Palo Alto, CA: Mayfield.

Dionisopoulos, G. N. (1984). *Corporate rhetoric of the atomic power industry after Three Mile Island*. Unpublished doctoral dissertation, Purdue University, West Lafayette, IN.

Dover, C. J. (1959). The three eras of management communication. *Journal of Communications, 9*, 168-172.

Goldzwig, S., & Cheney, G. (1984). The U.S. Catholic bishops on nuclear arms: Corporate advocacy, role redefinition, and rhetorical adaptation. *Central States Speech Journal, 35*, 8-23.

Grunig, J. E. (1984). Organizations, environments, and models of public relations. *Public Relations Review & Education, 1*, 6-29.

Heath, R. L. (1980). Corporate advocacy: An application of speech communication perspectives and skills—and more. *Communication Education, 29*, 370-377.

Hesburgh, T. M. (1984, April). Personal Interview with George Cheney.

Hiebert, R. E. (1966). *Courtier to the crowd: The story of Ivy Lee and the development of public relations*. Ames: Iowa State University.

Iacocca, L. (1984) *Iacocca: An autobiography*. New York: Bantam Books.

Jones, B. L., & Chase, W. H. (1979). Managing public policy issues. *Public Relations Review, 7*, 3-23.

Kaiser Aluminum & Chemical Corporation (1981). *Trial by television: A case study*. Oakland, CA: Author.

Kaufman, H. (1960). *The forest ranger: A study in administration behavior*. Baltimore, MD: Johns Hopkins University Press.

Knapp, M. L. (1970). Business rhetoric: Opportunity for research in speech. *Southern Speech Communication Journal, 35*, 244-55.

Krippendorff, K., & Eleey, M. F. (1986). Monitoring an organization's symbolic environment. *Public Relations Review, 12*, 13-36.

Levinson, H. (1972). *Organizational diagnosis*. Cambridge, MA: Harvard University Press.

Mackenzie, W.J.M. (1978). *Political identity*. New York: St. Martin's Press.

Mahoney, T. A. (1954). How management communicates with employees. *Personnel, 31*, 109-114.

Malone, J. W. (1983). Personal Interview with George Cheney.

Margulies, W. P. (1977, May 30). Corporate name change: Points to consider when you switch. *Advertising Age, 41*, 46.

McMillan, J. J. (1982). *The rhetoric of the modern organization*. Unpublished Ph.D. dissertation, University of Texas at Austin.

McMillan, J. J. (1985). *In search of the organizational persona: A rationale for studying organizations rhetorically*. Paper presented at the annual conference of the International Communication Association, Honolulu.

Meadow, R. G. (1981). The political dimensions of non-product advertising. *Journal of Communication, 31,* 69-82.

Mills, P. K., & Margulies, N. (1980). Toward a core typology of service organizations. *Academy of Management Review, 5,* 255-265.

Oravec, C. (1976). 'Observation' in Aristotle's theory of epideictic. *Philosophy & Rhetoric, 9,* 162-174.

Paonessa, K. A. (1984). *Corporate advocacy: An investigation of General Motors' effort.* Paper presented at the annual meeting of the Speech Communication Association, Chicago.

Perelman, C. (1982). *The realm of rhetoric.* (W. Kluback, Trans.). Notre Dame, IN: University of Notre Dame Press.

Perelman, C., & Olbrechts-Tyteca, L. (1969). *The new rhetoric: A treatise on argumentation.* Notre Dame, In University of Notre Dame Press.

Phillips Petroleum Company. (1980). *The Performance Story* [Videotape]. Bartlesville, OK: Author.

Putnam, L. L., & Cheney, G. (1985). Organizational communication: Historical development and future directions. In T. W. Benson (Ed.), *Speech communicaticʔ in the twentieth century.* (pp. 130-156). Carbondale: Southern Illinois University Press.

R. J. Reynolds Tobacco Company. (1986). Reprints of the following advertisements: *"Can we have an open debate about smoking?" "What not to do in bed"; "A message from those who don't to those who do"; "Smoking in public"; "Let's separate fact from fiction"; "Some surprising advice to young people from R. J. Reynolds Tobacco"; "We don't advertise to children"; "Second-hand smoke"; "Let's clear the air"; "Second-hand smoke: The myth and the reality"; "How to handle peer pressure"; "Passive smoking: An active controversy"; "Does smoking really make you look more grown up?"; "Some straight talk about smoking for young people"; "The most inflammatory question of our time"; "Smoking in public: A radical proposal"; "A second-hand smokescreen"; Workplace smoking restrictions: A trend that never was."* Winston-Salem, NC: Author.

Scott, J. D. (1943). Advertising when consumers cannot buy. *Harvard Business Review, 21,* 207-229.

Sethi, S. P. (1977). *Advocacy advertising and large corporations.* Lexington, MA: D. C. Heath.

Shakespeare, W. (1975). Twelfth night or, what you will. *The complete works of William Shakespeare.* New York: Avenel Books.

Smircich, L., & Stubbart, C. (1985). Strategic management in an enacted world. *Academy of Management Review, 10,* 724-736.

Tedlow, R. S. (1979). *Keeping the corporate image: Public relations and business: 1900-1950.* Greenwich, CT: JAI Press.

Tompkins, P. K., & Cheney, G. (1985). Communication and unobstrusive control in contemporary organizations. In R. D. McPhee & P. K. Tompkins (Eds.), *Organizational communication: Traditional themes and new directions* (pp. 179-210). Newbury Park, CA: Sage.

United Technologies. (1984a, May). Technology and jobs. *The Atlantic,* p. 67.

United Technologies. (1984b, December). Beyond the possible. *The Atlantic,* p. 54.

Vibbert, S. L. (1984). *Epideictic advocacy: Value premises and corporate image building.* Paper presented at the annual meeting of the Speech Communication Association, Chicago.

Weber, M. (1978). *Economy and society: An outline of an interpretive sociology* (Vol. 1). G. Roth & C. Wittich, (Eds.), Berkeley: University of California Press.

Weick, K. E. (1979). *The social psychology of organizing* (2nd ed.). Reading, MA: Addison-Wesley.

Zelko, H. P. (1953). Information racks: New frontier in industrial communication. *Management Review, 42,* 75-76.

7   Communication Climate
in Organizations

RAYMOND L. FALCIONE
University of Maryland

LYLE SUSSMAN
RICHARD P. HERDEN
University of Louisville

A S the disciplines and corresponding literatures of psychology and
social psychology have evolved, precious few dicta have achieved
the rarified status of being labeled a law. Two that appear to warrant
this label are Thorndike's Law of Effect (1913), which states that the strength
of a behavior is contingent upon its consequences, and Lewin's observation
that behavior is a function of "life spaces," the interaction between person and
environment (1936). In this chapter, we expand upon the latter law and
explore climate, one of the "richest" constructs in organization theory
generally, and organizational communication specifically.

To characterize a construct as "rich" is to suggest at least three conclusions.
First, the construct has received considerable attention in both the theoretical

and empirical literature. Second, the construct appears to have protean proportions; the process of studying it introduces new things to be discovered. Finally, the construct has far-reaching explanatory powers.

Each of these conclusions can be applied to the climate construct. The attention it has received in the theoretical and empirical literature is most dramatically documented by the number of reviews that have dotted the literature (Campbell, Dunette, Lawler, & Weick, 1970; Falcione & Kaplan, 1984; Forehand & Gilmer, 1964; Hellriegel & Slocum, 1974; Jablin, 1980a; James & Jones, 1974; Litwin & Stringer, 1968; Payne & Pugh, 1976; Poole, 1985; Poole & McPhee, 1983; Tagiuri & Litwin, 1968; Woodman & King, 1978).

The protean proportions of the concept are demonstrated in the commonalities of the reviews. To study these reviews is to develop a discomforting feeling that conceivably no two published studies are operationally defining *climate* in exactly the same way. Woodman and King underscore the perplexing nature of the climate construct: "much speculation about organizational climate is likely to elude science and remain in the realm of organizational folklore" (1978, p. 824).

Finally, the explanatory powers of the construct lie in the fact that it provides a conceptual link between phenomena occurring at the organizational level and individual level. If, as Jelinek, Smircich, and Hirsch (1983) report, culture is the *emerging* "explanation of choice for organization researchers" (p. 331), then climate has *historically* been the "explanation of choice."

The richness of the climate construct is further reflected in the volume of work produced by communication researchers. As will be evident in subsequent sections of this chapter, communication climate appears to have emerged as a deceptively simple explanation and the "explanation of choice" for many interested in communication phenomena occurring in organizational settings. The explanation is "simple" in that climate is a construct possessing intuitively logical explanatory power—it seems to make sense. It is "deceptive" in that the protean nature of climate generally also characterizes communication climate specifically.

Our purpose in this chapter is to explore the "deceptively simple" nature of communication climate. In so doing we will (1) highlight the major issues accounting for how the construct has been constitutively and operationally defined; (2) summarize the data it has generated; and (3) propose a model of its functional dynamics.

This chapter is divided into four sections: The first section consists of a review of theoretical perspectives and concerns when analyzing organizational climate generally, and communication climate specifically. This section focuses on how organizational climate has been defined and how communication climate has been measured. The next two sections review the communication climate construct from subsystem perspectives, specifically interpersonal and small group climates. Thus the first three sections address the previously stated purpose by analyzing how communication climate has been defined and the data it has generated. The last section builds upon the preceding ones and proposes a descriptive model of the functional dynamics of communication climate. After discussing the model, the chapter concludes with key research questions for future investigations of the "deceptively simple" communication climate construct.

ORGANIZATIONAL CLIMATE: THEORETICAL OVERVIEW

Defining the Climate Construct

As indicated in the introduction, the climate construct has received considerable attention over the last 30 years, and much effort has been made to isolate, explain, and determine the construct's place in organizational theory. Numerous definitions are suggested in the literature. Tagiuri (1968, p. 27) offers the following definition:

> a relatively enduring quality of the internal environment of organization that (a) is experienced by its members, (b) influences their behavior, and (c) can be described in terms of the values of a particular set of characteristics (or attributes) of the environment.

Hellriegel and Slocum (1974, p. 256) consider the notion of "subsystem" in their definition of organizational climate:

> a set of attributes which can be perceived about a particular organization and/or its subsystems and that may be induced from the way that the organization and/or its subsystems deal with their members and environment.

Schneider (1975a) offers a definition that represents a more subjective perspective of the climate construct by suggesting that climate perceptions are psychologically meaningful molar descriptions of an organizational system's practices and procedures on which people can agree. In other words, there may be many climates that function as frames of reference for individuals.

Research Approaches

Extensive literature reviews (Hellriegel & Slocum, 1974; James & Jones, 1974) reveal three major approaches toward measuring organizational climate. The first approach treats climate as an attribute or set of attributes belonging to an organization. These attributes are viewed as being possessed by the organization itself, and are independent of the perceptions or attributions made by individual members. James and Jones (1974, p. 109) call this approach the "multiple measurement-organizational attribute approach," which suggests that organizations have some type of "personality."

The underlying assumptions of this approach are that (1) organizations exist and persist despite fluctuations in membership; (2) organizations develop a set of characteristics that may be specified; (3) these specified characteristics are relatively enduring over time; (4) the specification of these organizational characteristics may be accomplished objectively; that is, once the set of characteristics is specified, the quality or values of these characteristics may be found independent of individual members' perceptions of the organization; and (5) consensus across observers as to the quality of the characteristics, and thus the climate of the organization would be expected to be obtained. Several studies support the validity of this approach. Climate score variance tends to be greater across rather than within organizations, suggesting that climate is an organizational element (Paolillo, 1982; Zohar, 1980).

The second approach treats climate as an interaction of an organization's characteristics and the individuals' perceptions of those characteristics. James and Jones (1974) call this approach the "perceptual measurement-organizational attribute approach." When approaching climate from this perspective, researchers again assume that organizations have relatively enduring characteristics that are moderators of performance and attitudes. However, climate is seen as a perceptual measure that describes the organization and is different from attitudinal or evaluative variables (James & Jones, 1974). The underlying assumptions of this approach are: (1) climate is considered a perceptual variable, dependent on self-report measures from individual members; (2) perceptions of climate are descriptive, rather than evaluative; and (3) reports of individual members are expected to exhibit considerable congruence. Thus this approach assumes that climate constitutes a consensual perception of an organization's characteristics.

Again, the issue of consensus among respondents is crucial to an understanding of the climate construct if this latter approach is used because the approach purports to measure climate as an organizational attribute. Additionally, the issue of consensus among respondents relates also to consensus among subgroups. There is considerable evidence that within a given organization, subgroups may differ in their perceptions of climate as a function of such variables as hierarchy (Gorman & Malloy, 1972; Payne & Mansfield, 1973) or location (Pritchard & Karasick, 1973). Concern over subgroup differences has caused Johnston (1976) to argue for a definition of climate based on consensual perceptions of the organization by subgroups.

The third approach to measuring organizational climate is termed the "perceptual measurement-individual attribute approach" by James and Jones (1974). This is essentially an individual, psychological approach to organizational climate. The approach considers what is psychologically important to the individual based on how he or she perceives the work environment.

Climate from this perspective, then, is an individual's summary perceptions of his or her encounters with the organization.

Attempts have been made to distinguish the above approach from the first two by differentiating between "organizational" climate and "psychological" climate (James & Jones, 1974). Essentially, this distinction is based upon the unit of theory to be considered, as well as the assumptions under which the research is to be pursued. Investigators interested in individual perceptions would consider psychological climate as the unit of theory, whereas organizational attributes would be considered if one were investigating organizational climate. Additionally, a number of researchers focus on "subsystem," "subunit," or "group" climate as the unit of analysis (Hellriegel & Slocum, 1974; Howe, 1977; Powell & Butterfield, 1978).

The subsystems perspective argues that perceptions are influenced by the experiences one has with the immediate environment, and it would be inappropriate to assess the global perceptions of an entire organization from employees who interact within a limited subsystem environment. Powell and Butterfield (1978, p. 155) conclude:

(1) Climate is a property of subsystems in organizations. Subsystems may consist of organizational members taken individually, in groups formed on any basis, or as a whole.
(2) As a conceptual construct, climate exists independently for separate subsystems. In fact, the relationships may, but do not necessarily, exist between climate for separate subsystems.

In summary, the appropriate unit of theory is a necessary consideration in climate research. Further, since psychological, subsystem, and organizational climate—while related to some degree—differ empirically, not only should the unit of theory be considered, but it must appropriately correspond with the unit of analysis. Although consistency of unit of theory and analysis is important for climate research, it should not preclude the investigation of cross-level relationships and their separate cross-level analysis employing separate measures (Glick, 1985). Recognizing the importance of the appropriate unit of theory and analysis should be a major consideration in all future climate research. Studies should clearly articulate the level(s) of climate being investigated.

Dimensionality of the Climate Construct

As noted previously, the climate construct is one of protean properties. These properties are exemplified in the dimensions subsumed by the construct. Some researchers have argued that climate has become a generic term referring to a broad class of organizational and psychological characteristics (Glick, 1985; James & Jones, 1974; Johannesson, 1973) and thus has become fuzzy and somewhat useless in its contribution to understanding behavior in organizations. Depending on the perspective employed, the climate construct has been treated as a predictor, a criterion, and a moderating variable (Inkson, Hickson, & Pugh, 1968; Litwin & Stringer, 1968). The climate construct may also overlap with other variables that may or may not be unique to the climate domain, such as leadership characteristics (Payne & Mansfield, 1973); satisfaction (Schneider & Snyder, 1975); structure (Payne & Pugh, 1976); managerial activity (Schneider, Parkington, & Buxton, 1980); as well as communication dimensions such as information flow (Drexler, 1977); and superior-subordinate communication (Bass, Valenzi, Farrow, & Solomon, 1975).

As can be seen from this cursory list, climate tends to overlap with many other constructs. It would seem appropriate, then, to view climate as an intersubjective construct in which there are multiple subsystem climates that can be criterion referenced, such as structure, effectiveness, and safety, and cross-level analyzed over time. This appears to be a Herculean task for anyone inclined to research the climate(s) of an organization, but may be necessary if we are to learn anything new about this elusive construct.

Measuring Organizational Climates

Perceptual measures have been used predominantly to measure the climate construct in organizations, and the distinction made by James and Jones (1974) between organizational and psychological climate can be useful here. As stated earlier, psychological climate consists of individual perceptions of the organization, and organizational climate consists of molar properties of the organization that are meaningful to its members. If an investigator wished to measure psychological climate, then individuals' perceptions of the organization would be collected. If organizational climate were being investigated, then the investigator would check for a high degree of consensus across individuals' scores. This would suggest that there was indeed an organizational property being measured. Another method would be to obtain objective correlates validating individuals' perceptions of certain climate dimensions.

In their literature review, Hellriegel and Slocum (1974) found a fair amount of diversity among organizational climate instruments. Some instruments have fairly narrow perspectives (Halpin, 1967), while others are more encompassing (House & Rizzo, 1972; Jones & James, 1979; Tagiuri, 1968). Campbell et al. (1970) considered some commonalities across the instruments and suggested four major climate dimensions: (1) individual autonomy, (2) degree of structure imposed on the position, (3) reward orientation, and (4) consideration. While we see that a considerable amount of diversity exists among climate instruments, there are some commonalities. However, organizational climate is not without criticism for its overlap with organizational properties such as structure, technology, and so on (James & Jones, 1974). Additionally, psychological climate has been criticized for its conceptual impingement on satisfaction (Guion, 1973; Johannesson, 1973).

Another criticism of the organizational climate instruments is that there appears to be an overemphasis on "people-oriented" scales (Hellriegel & Slocum, 1974). In fact this does appear to be the case. As can be seen in Table 7.1, there are a number of dimensions that appear to be directly related to communication in particular.

Organizational Communication
Climate Dimensions

The notion of "ideal communication climate" was postulated by Redding (1972). The dimensions Redding considered to be of particular importance were (1) supportiveness; (2) participative decision making; (3) trust, confidence, and credibility; (4) openness and candor; and (5) high performance goals. Based on Redding's dimensions, Dennis (1975) developed an organizational communication climate instrument consisting of five dimensions: (1) superior-subordinate communication, (2) perceived quality and accuracy of downward communication, (3) perceived openness of the superior-subordinate relationship, (4) opportunities and degree of influence of upward communication, and (5) perceived reliability of information from subordinates and coworkers. When comparing his communication climate instrument with Taylor and Bowers's (1972) measure of organizational climate, Dennis found a considerable degree of overlap in the two constructs.

Expanding on the research conducted by Read (1962), Roberts and O'Reilly (1974) developed a climate-type measure of organizational communication. It consists of 35 items designed to measure 16 facets of communication: trust, influence, mobility, desire for interaction, directionality-upward, directionality-downward, directionality-lateral, accuracy, summarization, gatekeeping, overload, satisfaction, modality-written, modality-face-to-face, modality-telephone, and modality-other. Muchinsky (1977) found that many of Roberts and O'Reilly's dimensions were significantly correlated with Litwin and Stringer's (1968) organizational climate dimensions.

Another measure developed by Downs, Hazen, Quiggens, and Medley (1973) purports to measure "communication satisfaction," which is defined as individuals' satisfaction with informational and relational communication within the organization. Specifically, the instrument measures employee satisfaction with (1) communication climate, (2) supervisor communication, (3) organizational integration, (4) media quality, (5) horizontal and informal communication, (6) organizational perspective, (7) subordinate communication, and (8) personal feedback. Downs (1979) found that the communication

TABLE 7.1
Organizational Climate Questionnaires

Author	Communication-Oriented Dimension
Likert (1967)	Communication processes Decision making Interaction-influence Goal-setting
Taylor & Bowers (1972)	Communication flow Motivational conditions Decision-making practices
Litwin & Stringer (1968)	Warmth Support Conflict
House & Rizzo (1972)	Communication adequacy Information distortion and suppression Horizontal communication Top management receptiveness Upward information requirements Violations in chain of command Work flow coordination
Pritchard & Karasick (1973)	Conflict versus cooperation Social relations Decision centralization Supportiveness
Downey, Hellriegel, & Slocum (1975)	Decision making Warmth Openness
Jones & James (1979)	Opportunities to deal with others Support Interaction facilitation Upward interaction Confidence and trust up Confidence and trust down Cooperation Friendliness and warmth Openness of expression Organizational communication – Down
Gavin & Howe (1975)	Managerial trust Consideration
Payne & Mansfield (1973)	Open-mindedness
Drexler (1977)	Communication flow

climate, personal feedback, and supervisor communication dimensions showed consistently high correlations with satisfaction across six organizations.

The ICA Communication Audit project developed by members of the International Communication Association represents a major effort to measure the communication climate of an organization. The process used multiple measures including in-depth interviews, questionnaires, network analysis, critical incidents, and diaries. Specifically, the dimensions measured in the survey instrument are information receiving, information sending, communication sources, communication channels, communication follow-up, timeliness, accuracy and usefulness of information, communication relationships, and communication outcomes.

In summary, climate is a multilevel attribute encompassing different units of theory and levels of analysis. While instruments designed to measure organizational climate consider organizational attributes, it appears that many possess specific communication dimensions as well. Conversely, it appears that much of the research on communication climate shares considerable variance with organizational climate.

Emerging Perspectives on
Organizational Communication Climate

Recently, Ashforth (1985) considered climate from an "interactionist" perspective, which argues that perceptions of climate are a function of individuals' efforts to understand and "make sense" of the organization and their roles in it. This perspective relies heavily on symbolic interactionism (Blumer, 1969), the cognitive social learning and interactional psychology literature (James, Hater, Gent, & Bruni, 1978; Schneider, 1983), and the organizational socialization literature (Wanous, 1980). The interactionist perspective would argue that conceptualizing climate as an organizational, subsystem, or individual property would not sufficiently explain the construct. The perspective argues that it is better to conceptualize climate as a *joint* property of both the individual and the organization. Similarly, Poole and McPhee (1983) present a case for the *intersubjectivity* of the construct. This perspective suggests that climate is a phenomenon that is intersubjective in nature and is continuously being structured and restructured by organizational members as they *interact with their environment*.

This essay supports Poole and McPhee's position that climate is an intersubjective phenomenon that in its continuous structuring and restructuring affects individuals' actions and organizational outcomes. Poole and McPhee (1983) present a lucid argument that because communication is the medium for all structurational processes, it is a constitutive force for all climates in an organization, no matter what the unit of analysis.

The organizational communication climate therefore consists of one's perceived expectancies and instrumentalities regarding communication, which are continually interacting and evolving with organizational processes, structured around common organizational practices. This perspective argues that the establishment of climates in an organization is a function of socialization processes, and that to understand the notion of climate one must also understand the notion of *structuration* (Poole & McPhee, 1983). Structuration refers to ongoing development and redevelopment of systems and expectations through the application of rules and organizational resources. Structures, then, are rules and resources used in the production and reproduction of systems, and are both the medium and outcome of organizational action. Systems and structure form a type of reciprocal duality, each affecting the other in a continuous structuration process (Poole, 1985; Poole & McPhee, 1983).

Poole's (1985) perspective of an ongoing dynamic process of structuration and its reciprocal relationship with organizational systems is genuinely exciting and provides an insightful approach to the climate construct. Climate, then, can be viewed as an intersubjective phenomenon that is continuously being structured and restructured by organizational members. This perspective offers an alternative to the traditional attribute approaches and suggests alternative avenues for future research.

In summary, the previous sections outlined the consensus and controversy surrounding the concept of climate in organizations. Three basic approaches to defining the climate construct were discussed: (1) multiple measurement-organizational attribute, (2) perceptual measurement-organizational attribute, and (3) perceptual measurement-individual attribute approaches (James & Jones, 1974). In addition, we posited that communication is the sine qua non of all organizational transactions and that the communication climate construct should be viewed as one that is composed of multiple variations, each of which is continuously evolving. Our discussion now turns to two organizational subsystems in which climate is also an important characteristic: the group and the dyad.

GROUP COMMUNICATION CLIMATE

The concept "group" subsumes a variety of dimensions. For example, groups may be formal or informal (Schein, 1980), permanent or temporary (Browning, 1977) and fulfill various individual and/or organizational needs (Hoffman, 1979; Redding, 1972). Moreover, a group operating independently of organizational constraints is qualitatively different than one operating under such constraints.

These definitional issues have been explored in the Jablin and Sussman (1983) review, which specifically focuses on the organization as the context within which groups function. Their definition of an organizational group will be used in the present analysis thus providing the domain for the review that follows. According to Jablin and Sussman,

an organizational group is a collection of three or more organizational members who interact (more or less regularly) over time, are psychologically cognizant of one another, perceive themselves as a group, and, most important, are embedded within a network of interlocking tasks, roles and expectations. (Jablin & Sussman, 1983, p. 12)

Group Climate: Defined and Differentiated

Our definition of group communication climate emerges from definitions presented in the preceding major sections. Specifically, it is defined as *those molar factors, objective and/or perceived, which affect the message sending and receiving process of members within a given organizational group.* Organizational communication climate provides the context within which group climate emerges; however, the latter is not a direct subset of the former. Group communication climate may share properties in common with the larger context but is more than a smaller analogue of the larger system. Group communication climate develops characteristics directly reflecting the norms, tasks, leadership, and membership composition (Jablin & Sussman, 1983) of the group. Similarly, group climate provides a context within which interpersonal communication emerges, but the latter is neither a direct subset of the former nor a smaller analogue

Construct Validity of Group Climate

The studies cited in this section reflect a body of literature that supports the construct validity of group climate. The "robust" nature of this construct may be further supported by Schneider's (1975a) research indicating that a given organization may contain multiple climates, each reflecting a given subsystem of the organization. In this context subsystem refers not only to the task dimension of the organization, but also to its political and socioemotional dimensions. Hence, group climate differences have been associated with hierarchical level, line or staff position, personality characteristics, and demographic characteristics (Payne & Pugh, 1976). Thus the issue is not *do* groups differ in their perception of climate but what *accounts* for this difference? Moreover, given the communication focus of our review, the question is further: What are the communication phenomena (roles, relationships, processes) most clearly associated with the creation and perception of group climate? To address this question we highlight representative studies conducted from each of three orientations to measuring climate.

Multiple Measurement-Organizational Attribute

Within this perspective we focus on the factors that have an objective reality, are directly linked to communication phenomena (roles, relationship processes), are common to groups in organizational settings, and have been hypothesized to be correlates of communication climate. Given these constraints, the factor that most clearly emerges as a constituent factor defining the essence of group communication is leadership.

Leadership style. Beginning with the seminal work of Lewin, Lippit, and White (1939) until the present, researchers have been intrigued with the effect of leadership style on group processes and outcomes. Comprehensive reviews of the leadership style literature can be found in Korman (1966) and Vroom (1976).

A theoretical link between leadership and climate is provided in Folger and Poole's (1984) concept of "theme." According to these authors, themes represent explicit or implicit questions and/or values that guide the group and serve as the foundation for climate. One dominant theme focuses on questions related to power and authority relationships. Examples of power-related themes are expressed in such questions as: How is power distributed in the group? How rigid is the power structure? How are power and respect distributed among group members? Thus leadership, which is the manifestation of power and authority, is a dominant theme affecting the group's climate. In the present review, we highlight representative studies exploring the relationships among leadership style, climate, and outcomes.

Levine (1973) found that when control is equally distributed among group members (participative style), performance and member satisfaction increases. In a related study, Cooper and Wood (1974) found that perceptions of satisfaction and influence are greatest when members are allowed to participate across the stages of decision making—idea generation, evaluation, and selection. Rosenfeld and Plax (1975) examined members' perceptions of autocratic versus democratic leaders. The former were perceived as "object" oriented, the latter as people oriented. The conceptual link integrating the above findings is that what a leader does to encourage or discourage contributions from and among group members directly affects how those members affectively respond to their group experience.

Finally, the classic studies performed at Michigan and Ohio State universities, which have direct impact on the present review, suggest that the effects of leadership style, although directly affecting the climate of the work group, at best yield mixed results. The participatory style (consideration) is not universally superior across all contexts, nor does it necessarily yield high productivity, lower absenteeism, and higher morale (Fleischman, 1973).

Perceptual Measurement-Organizational Attribute

As discussed earlier, the distinction between this perspective and the multiple measurement perspective is that the latter assumes an objective reality operating independently of actors' perceptions. The studies highlighted in this section examine climate as an interactive effect—the product of organizational traits and members' perceptions of those traits.

Again, given constraints of focusing our review on factors (a) directly related to communication phenomena, (b) found in groups and field settings, and (c) hypothesized as correlates of climate, we necessarily limit our summary to two sets of data. The first examines the relationship between one's position in a communication network and climate. The second highlights studies that have found specific communication behaviors and processes perceived by group members to be directly linked to climate.

Network/Structure. Communication researchers have long been intrigued with the relationship between where one is in a network and how one communicates within it and feels toward it. Most of the network research has been conducted in laboratory settings and is extensively reviewed by Shaw (1976).

Based primarily on sociometric data, network studies provide clear support for the thesis that perceptions relative to positions in a network directly affect the climate of the network. For example, Harsbarger (1971) found that problem solving accuracy was higher in centralized versus decentralized structures. However, subjects *believed* they were more accurate and efficient in the decentralized structures. In a study conducted with Navy personnel, Roberts and O'Reilly (1978) report little association among measures of group structure and group effectiveness. However, significant relationships were found between perceptions of the structural climate (for instance, openness) and information accuracy and group connectedness. Danowski (1979) provides data complementary to those provided by Roberts and O'Reilly; group cohesiveness is positively related to perceived information accuracy.

Two studies suggest that the embeddedness of a network within a given organization has significant effects on the climate and productivity of the network. Danowski (1980) and Danowski and Steinfield (1979) report that the degree of connectivity between a network and the surrounding organization (that is, embeddedness) will have an effect on the members' perceptions of one another and their respective networks.

Finally, in a provocative field study examining the effects of changes in communication structure, Mears (1974) found that when a work group moves from one structure to another, productivity is drastically affected. Members must develop new expectations for one another and develop a sense of how the structure should work and become acclimated to the new structural and psychological milieu. This study empirically addresses the "structuration" perspective developed earlier.

Perceived communication correlates. In a study designed to test the construct validity of group climate, Howe (1977) examined climate measures as a function of group effects, subject effects, and group x subject effects. The primary conclusion of the study was that climate responses were more a function of group membership than either subject characteristics or group x subject effects. What is noteworthy in the present context, however, are the specific climate items that were found to be significant and that led to the conclusion.

Of the 16 items in Howe's questionnaire, 5 discriminated among the groups at a statistically significant level; 3 of these items are communication related—communication accuracy, guarded versus open communication, and participation in decision making. Howe's study is important in the present context because it demonstrates that communication variables play a significant role in the creation of consensually validated group climate. Moreover, the data support the interpretation that group membership is a main effect accounting for differences in perceived group climate along with the interactive effects of person by group interaction.

Data provided by Jones and James (1979) reinforce this conclusion. Their study obtained data from 4315 U.S. Navy enlisted men and compared them to data obtained from samples of fire fighters and health-care managers. Subjects completed a questionnaire assessing six dimensions of organizational climate. Three of these dimensions are a direct reflection of communication practices and policies—conflict and ambiguity; leader facilitation and support; and work group cooperation, friendliness, and warmth. Results suggested that aggregated scores were significantly related not only to division context and structure but also to the characteristics of the personnel in the groups.

Perceptual Measurement-Individual Attribute

This approach to measuring climate rests on the assumption that climate is personalistic, with each perceiver constructing his or her own cognitive map of the group. Thus to apply this approach to group processes presents a crucial methodological dilemma; studies of group communication typically involve the summation of scores across group members and comparison of scores (means, variances) between or among groups. However, if we accept the validity of the individual attribute approach and adopt the James and Jones (1974) thesis that this approach should be labeled *psychological climate*, then we are left with an intriguing conclusion. The individual attribute approach to group processes may be a contradiction in terms.

However, at least one study demonstrates both the construct validity of the individual attribute approach and does so within the context of group communication processes. Downs and Pickett (1977) conducted their study within a theoretical framework of contingency analysis (Morse & Lorsch, 1970) examining the interactive effects of leader's style, group member needs, and group productivity. The authors concluded that leadership style and group compatibility produced interactive effects on satisfaction and productivity. Compatibility of group members—as defined by Schutz's (1966) FIRO-B—had a moderating effect on the relationship between leadership style and the two dependent measures.

Korman's review (1966) of the relative effect of consideration versus initiating structure leadership styles underscores the influence of individual attributes and augments the Downs and Pickett (1977) findings. Korman concluded that the studies assessing the relative effects of consideration versus initiating structures are best understood from a contingency framework wherein one of the key variables is subordinate characteristics.

Summary and Synthesis

The level of analysis examined in this section has been groups generally, and organizational groups specifically. The question we applied to this level was both deceptively simple and frustratingly complex: What communication phenomena (roles, processes, relationships) are most clearly associated with the creation and perception of group climate?

Before summarizing the representative studies cited in this section, an explanatory note is necessary. Groups (and also dyads) when studied in organizational contexts can, and usually are, viewed in a figure-ground relationship wherein the organization represents the ground and the level of analysis (dyad or group) represents the figure. However, as Jablin and Sussman (1983) observe, when researchers focus on their respective unit of analysis, the figure assumes primary importance, the ground secondary importance. Moreover, in far too many studies the ground is virtually ignored and the figure is treated in isolation.

Our review of communication climate must *necessarily* focus on the ground. Failure to do so would be tantamount to violating the premise upon which the entire climate literature is constructed: Lewin's concept of "life space."

For our purposes, acknowledging the ground is synonymous with Porter and Roberts's (1976) concept of embeddedness. Thus a group climate may be analyzed onto itself, but *organizational* group climates are embedded in a larger context, which has interactive effects on those groups. This argument concerning enbeddedness and its influence on climate may be best illustrated in Danowski's studies cited earlier.

From this perspective, we deduce four conclusions based on the studies summarized in this section. First, objective attributes of the organizational communication environment have been associated with the creation and perception of group climate. The attribute receiving the greatest attention is leadership style. These studies suggest that member satisfaction increases to the extent that leadership style allows for participation and equal distribution of control across participants.

Second, network studies provide strong support for the thesis that perceived position within a group of message senders/receivers significantly affects affective response to the group and performance within it. These studies suggest that the *objective* presence of a given network may have less impact on group members than the *perceptual* presence of that network. This finding, which has both significant theoretical and methodological implications, supports Jablin's (1980a) contention that "the characteristics that objective measures tap only indirectly affect organizational behavior, whereas the characteristics that perceptual measures explore directly affect the behavior of organizational participants" (p. 331).

Third, the research conducted by Jones and James (1979) reviewed earlier suggests significant implications regarding our knowledge of group communication climate. Three of their six climate dimensions (conflict and ambiguity, leader facilitation and support, and work group facilitation and warmth) can be interpreted as reflecting communication policies and practices. Although Jones and James do not label these three dimensions "communication climate" per se, their operational definition suggests the central role that communication climate plays in the development and productivity of groups. Similarly, Howe's (1977) research yields three communication factors (communication accuracy, openness, and participation) directly linked to group climate that appear to be an independent validation of the three dimensions isolated in the Jones and James (1979) research.

Finally, the centrality of communication and the importance of the human dimension in the creation of climate (Hellriegel & Slocum, 1974) suggests that regardless of the specific nature of the group, the elements of climate are relatively few in number. Jones and James (1979) underscore this interpretation: "It appears, for example, that individual perceptions of work area conditions may be parsimoniously summarized by a few dimensions that describe a wide range of environments" (p. 244). Our review suggests that these dimensions are one's role within a network, style of the leader within the network, accuracy of communication within the group, warmth, and task facilitation.

INTERPERSONAL COMMUNICATION CLIMATE

The concept "interpersonal climate," unlike group climate, has been discussed and analyzed in the literature but it is based more on inference and extrapolation than on extensive programmatic research. Thus even though the construct validity of "interpersonal climate" would appear to be self-evident, it has yet to be empirically demonstrated over a series of studies.

Definition of Interpersonal Climate

If we treat interpersonal communication as the exchange of messages (verbal, nonverbal, intended, unintended) within a dyad, the following definition of interpersonal communication climate emerges: *those molar factors that represent the setting within which message sending and receiving processes of the members of a dyad occur and that affect those processes.*

Thus the focus of this section is the climate specific to a particular dyadic communication system rather than a general organizational climate or a subsystem of groups. Although interpersonal communication climate would appear to be a function of organizational and group climates, it is not a strict subset of either. Rather, each of the three is conceptualized as a set that intersects each of the other two. Those intersections represent causation. The emerging climate of a particular dyad is influenced by the existing climates of the organization and group to which the dyadic parties belong. However, that dyadic climate is also influenced by factors unique to the particular dyad. Furthermore, the intersections between organizational, group, and interpersonal communication climates represent mutual causation. The existing dyadic climates and the communication they affect also influence the development of the group and organizational climates within which they exist. The present section will address only the set represented by interpersonal communication climate.

The above interpersonal communication climate definition could be operationalized from each of the three approaches discussed previously. From the multiple measurement-organizational attribute approach, climate would be defined as the collection of objectively measured environmental attributes that are related to a dyadic communication system. The perceptual measurement-organizational attribute approach would define climate as the dyadic parties' shared perceptions of those attributes. The perceptual measurement-individual attribute approach would define climate as each dyadic party's perceptions of the attributes.

The above conceptualizations have certain appeal (a "climate" exists for every dyadic system) and Schneider's (1975b) call for criterion-oriented climate studies provides some theoretical support for them. However, a review of the communication climate literature failed to uncover any instances where the climate construct was explicitly conceptualized at the dyad level. A few studies have included organizational communication climate as a variable related to dyadic communication (for instance, Falcione, 1978) but none has explicitly conceptualized or measured the communication climate of a dyad. However, the dyadic communication literature provides many examples of variables that could be hypothesized to be components of an interpersonal communication climate. Most of the research on dyadic communication within the organizational context has focused upon the superior-subordinate relationship and this is reflected in the review. While the emphasis on superior-subordinate communication seems appropriate, it should be noted that many of the potential dyadic communication climate components may have explanatory power for other important organizational dyads.

Thus our review of the literature identifies those variables that have been related to interpersonal communication and could be included in a dyadic climate construct. Because the construct has not previously been defined as we propose, the purpose of the section is simply to demonstrate that the literature contains numerous examples of environmental variables that have been related to dyadic communication and that, taken together, could constitute dyadic communication climate. We conclude this section by assessing the research and the possibilities for developing a dyadic communication climate construct.

The following literature review is not intended to be exhaustive but, rather, to identify variables that have been linked to dyadic communication and are possible candidates for inclusion in an interpersonal communication climate construct. That is, they are descriptive rather than evaluative (Payne, Fineman, & Wall, 1976), they are relatively stable over time (Tagiuri, 1968), and they may have immediate impact upon the dyadic exchange (Jessor & Jessor, 1973). The review will be divided into three sections corresponding to the three approaches to climate previously discussed.

Multiple Measurement-Organizational Attribute

The following variables are representative of potential dyadic communication climate dimensions that are "objective" measures of the dyad environment in the sense that they may be independently verified.

Several studies include organizational structure variables. For example, the hierarchical level of dyadic members has been related to participation in decision making (Jago & Vroom, 1977) and to the subordinate's perception of openness in superior-subordinate communication (Jablin, 1982). Similarly, organizational size and the boundary-spanning role acted out by a superior have been found to interact and be related to frequency of subordinate communication (Bacharach & Aiken, 1977). On the other hand, Young (1978) showed a relationship between a more global characteristic, whether the organizational was classified as a Likert (1967) System 1 versus System 4, and subjects' reports on the appropriateness of and willingness to disclose in dyadic communication.

Variables examined at the individual level include characteristics of the role and demographics of the role occupant. Cohen (1958) found a relationship between the superior's power over advancement of the subordinate and the frequency of noncritical upward communication. The information load of the superior was found to be directly related to inaccuracy and omission in subordinate-initiated messages by Meier (1963). Sussman, Pickett, Berzinski, and Pearce (1980) found that the sex-role composition of dyads was related to the communication ascendancy strategy enacted by individuals. Using a more general demographic category, Fairhurst and Snavely (1983a, 1983b) found that members in numerically imbalanced categories (in this case males in a predominantly female situation) were not socially isolated (self-reports concerning message initiation and reception showed no difference in frequency for male tokens).

A multiple measurement-organizational attribute approach to interpersonal climate could, therefore, include molar structural and role attributes that define the setting for and influence dyadic communication. However, it should be noted in the above sample of attributes that they have been used independently and not collectively. Furthermore, they have in most cases been associated with perceptions or self-reported recollections of communication, not with actual communication behavior. These points will be further developed at the end of this section.

Perceptual Measurement-Organizational Attribute

The following variables represent potential dyadic communication climate dimensions that have measured shared perceptions of the dyadic parties. Few studies have related such shared perceptions to dyadic communication. Therefore, some climate variables are included below that relate to noncommunication criteria (such as satisfaction) but were utilized in an interpersonal communication study.

Infante and Gordon (1979) found that metaperceptions of personal traits (one person's perception of a second person's view of the first person's traits) were related to reciprocity of liking. Subordinate satisfaction has been related to the congruence of superior-subordinate perceptions of their communication (Hatfield & Huseman, 1982) and to the managers' self-descriptions of work-related attitudes (Wexley, Alexander, Greenawalt, & Couch, 1980). Wexley et al. (1980) also found that congruence between managers' descriptions of subordinates and subordinates' self-description of work-related attitudes was related to managers' evaluations of subordinates' job performance. Eisenberg, Monge, and Farace (1984) found that a supervisor's perception of agreement with the subordinate, and his or her accurate perception of a subordinate's view of communication initiation and termination rules were both positively associated with performance evaluation. In addition, they found that a subordinate's perceived agreement with his or her supervisor on the same rules was positively associated with satisfaction with supervision.

The above attributes all address the role of shared perceptions in describing the atmosphere within which dyadic communication takes place and show that they may affect dyadic communication behaviors. It should be noted that no attributes of mere perceptual agreement are included. In other words, the perceptual measurement-organizational attribute approach to interpersonal communication climate deals with those attributes that include an explicit dyadic component. Agreement between the independent perceptions of dyadic parties about a single attribute is included in the third approach, which follows.

Perceptual Measurement-Individual Attribute

The following variables are representative of potential dyadic communication climate dimensions that have been measured at the individual perception level. Included are self-perception and individual's perceptions of others.

A number of studies in this category have utilized individuals' self-reports about their own feelings or beliefs. Trust has been related to affective openness (Mellinger, 1956) and to accuracy of communication (Maier, Hoffman & Read, 1963). Maier et al. (1963) also found a relationship between mobility aspirations and inaccuracy in communication. In a study that used a shared perception criterion, Smircich and Chesser (1981) found that subordinates' assessments of authenticity in their relationships with superiors were related to the congruence of the superior's perception of the subordinate's performance and the subordinate's perception of the superior's rating.

Many studies have utilized individuals' perceptions of others to explain aspects of dyadic communication. Roberts and O'Reilly (1974) found that the subordinate's perceptions of his or her superior's upward influence was related to the estimated accuracy of the superior's communication. Jablin (1980b) found that the same perceived upward influence variable interacted with the subordinate's perception of superior's supportiveness to explain the subordinate's perception of openness in superior-subordinate communication. Subordinates' perceptions of openness has also been found to be explained by the subordinate's perception of the political involvement of the superior (Jablin, 1981). Roberts and O'Reilly (1974) also found that the subordinate's perception of his or her superior's influence over the subordinate was related to the subordinate's desire for interaction. More generally, the sender's perception of the receiver's influence over the sender has been related to message modification (Alkire, Collum, Kaswan, & Love, 1968). Sussman (1974) related the superior's perception of subordinate's trust to perceived communication accuracy, while O'Reilly (1978) reports that subordinates' perceptions of superiors' performances were related to communication distortion. Baird (1974) discovered that one's perception of others' willingness to listen was related to the frequency of and willingness to communicate. Marcus and House (1973) related subordinates' perceptions of superiors' expressive versus instrumental style to the frequency of social approval messages.

The above attributes all address individual perceptions about self or about the other dyadic party and have been related to dyadic communication. Therefore, from a perceptual measurement-individual attribute approach it could be argued that they are potential interpersonal communication climate attributes. To this point, however, they have been examined independently and not collectively within communication studies. Furthermore, they have been related only to perceptions about dyadic communications rather than dyadic communication behaviors, or they have been related only to the communication behaviors of one dyadic party.

Summary and Synthesis

The above literature review was conducted from the perspective of a proposed definition of interpersonal communication climate and organized around three previously identified approaches to the climate construct. A summary view of this literature reveals a number of characteristics, points to some tentative conclusions, and suggests a redirection of research efforts relative to communication climate at the interpersonal level.

First, what is most evident from this review is that research has dealt with single, or, at best, a few independent predictor variables. This has been an often cited deficiency in climate research. Given that an interpersonal communication climate construct has not previously been proposed, the present deficiency is understandable. However, if a research thrust is to develop at this level of analysis, studies must be designed to assess programmatically multidimensional interpersonal climates.

Second, another characteristic of the review is the unequal number of studies within the three approaches. While the review is not exhaustive, the unequal distribution does appear to be representative of the literature. Individual perceptual measures are often used, while "objective" measures and shared perceptual measures appear relatively infrequently in dyadic communication studies. It is clear that one's behavior is a function of what is perceived to be true as opposed to some objective reality. However, the failure to include measures of actual structures and processes in the study of dyadic environments raises questions as to the sources of variation in perceptions. Are differences in perception a function of environmental differences or individual differences? Among other things, the answer to this question is critical for normative prescriptions intended to enhance interpersonal communication climate.

The disparity between instances of individual versus shared perceptual measurement is similarly problematic. On the one hand, there is evidence that the initiation of and receptivity to communication is a function of the individual's perceptions of the environment, regardless of the perceptions of the other party. On the other hand, it seems intuitively clear that dyads may develop shared perceptions of their environment as they interact over time and that these shared perceptions could influence their communication.

In this regard, the degree to which individuals share perceptions (direct perspectives) about objects or other people can be measured and related to their interaction. However, while there is yet no consensus in this regard, the Eisenberg et al. (1984) study cited earlier found that agreement (consensus between direct perspectives) had less effect on dyadic communication behavior than the perception of agreement or the accuracy of one's perception of the other's view. This latter concept of metaperspectives (Laing, Phillipson, & Lee, 1966) would seem to be a fertile field for dyadic communication climate. In essence, this approach argues that the comparison of one person's direct perspective to that of another person's direct perspective on the same issue indicates agreement or disagreement only. This perspective argues that understanding or misunderstanding would be measured by comparing one person's metaperspective (that person's perception of the other person's view on the issue) to the other person's direct perspective on the issue. The feeling of being understood or misunderstood would be measured by comparing one person's meta-metaperspective (that person's perception of the other person's view of the first person's view on an issue) to the person's direct perspective on the issue. Finally, realization or failure of realization (being correct or incorrect in feeling understood or misunderstood) would be measured by comparing one person's meta-metaperspective on an issue to the metaperspective of the other on the same issue. Clearly, interpersonal perception is a much more complex and rich area than current research would indicate.

In addition, the existing research makes the implicit assumption that perceptual congruity enhances the quality of communication. While such an assumption appears valid if quality is defined as efficiency (the accuracy and timeliness of message transference), it may be questionable if quality is defined as effectiveness (what is transferred and the effect of transference). For instance, it may be that perceptual congruity promotes mutual understanding of current work requirements but inhibits creativity in planning appropriate future requirements. In addition, defining quality as efficiency focuses research on unidirectional transference. Defining quality as effectiveness broadens the focus to the ongoing dyadic communication system.

In this regard, one could argue that even defining interpersonal communication climate as dyadic is a restricting concept. In a provocative article, Ricci and Selini-Palazzoli (1984) argue for a focus on "n-adic" communication systems. They argue that interpersonal communication is carried out between two parties within a larger interpersonal system and that the nature of that system influences the meaning of communication. Specifically, they argue that the meaning of a communication is a function of content (message), territoriality (number of other players), relationship (equality/inequality of players), and time (short, medium, long term). Thus the nature of the message, the time frame in which it is conveyed, the relevant others in the environment, and the relationship among them, determines the meaning ("rationality") of the communication. More important, the perceptions of the two primary parties about these elements of the environment may differ. What may be completely rational to the initiator because of the perceived environment within which it was initiated, may be irrational to the receptor because of a different perceived environment. Perhaps interpersonal communication climate constructs should include dimensions of territoriality, relationship, and time when studying the effect of classes of content. For instance, studies of interpersonal communication in performance evaluation could measure each party's perception (and metaperception?) of the time frame (annual merit versus long-term development, for example), territoriality (for example, others influencing performance, comparison others), and the relationship among relevant parties (members of a collegial group versus strict hierarchy). It could be assumed that interpersonal communication concerning performance evaluations and hence the effect on performance, is a function of the congruity of perceptions of such dimensions.

Such a broadening of focus for interpersonal climate would provide a much richer conceptual model for dyadic research. In one sense it would sharpen the role of dyadic communication in the larger context of a social system. At the same time, it dulls the distinction between interpersonal and group communication climate.

Third, a final characteristic of the literature reviewed indicates that the proposed attributes within the multiple measurement-organizational attribute and the perceptual measurement-individual attribute approaches have been primarily associated with perceptions of dyadic communication or with individual behavior. On the other hand, attributes within the perceptual measurement-organizational attribute approach more often have been associated with actual dyadic communication behaviors. This observation points to the possibility that only the attribute type from the latter approach should be considered interpersonal communication climate. What makes the communication climate of a dyad unique are those molar attributes of the situation for which the dyadic parties share perceptions. Objectively measurable "realities" and individual differences may affect the shared perceptions of attributes but it is questionable whether they should be considered to be climate.

From this line of reasoning it would seem more appropriate to define interpersonal communication climate as the shared perceptions of a dyad about molar factors representing the setting within which dyadic message sending and receiving processes occur and which affect those processes. These shared perceptions may include degree of congruity between direct perspectives as well as perceptions of agreement, accuracy of perceived agreement, and feelings of being understood. The perceived molar factors may include elements of content, territoriality, relationship, and time. "Objectively" measured situational variables and individual differences between the parties would then be viewed along with communication processes themselves as determinants of interpersonal communication climate. Thus the communication climate of a dyad evolves as the shared perceptions of the individual parties through their communication experiences within an organizational setting.

ORGANIZATIONAL COMMUNICATION
CLIMATE: A DESCRIPTIVE MODEL

The preceding sections examined organizational communication climate in the dyad and small group. In each of these sections, we highlighted representative studies and summarized/synthesized the major conclusions provided by those studies. In the final section of our analysis, we provide a descriptive model of organizational communication climate. The purpose of this model is to answer these questions: What factors account for the development and perception of organizational communication climate? What does the model tell us regarding our knowledge of organizational communication climate? What do we know? What do we not know?

The model, presented in Figure 7.1, is an adaptation of a model proposed by Field and Abelson (1982). Their model explored climate as a generic construct; our adaptation focuses on organizational communication climate specifically. According to this model, organizational communication climate (as developed and as perceived) emerges from the interaction of three major influences: external, organizational, and people.

The *external* influences include those forces outside the organization likely to have an effect inside the organization. The four influences highlighted in the external environment are economic and political trends, technological developments, and sociocultural norms.

The *organizational* influences include those forces within the organization hypothesized as having the greatest effect on climate. The three factors subsumed by the organizational label represent three of the four elements contained in Leavitt's (1965) organizational diamond model. The three elements are task, structure, and technology.

The third influence is labeled *people* and is the fourth element of Leavitt's model. According to our adaptation, the people variables most likely to have an effect on the creation and perception of communication climate are knowledge, skills, abilities, values, and demographics.

Following the argument presented at the end of the section on interpersonal communication climate, organizational and people influences are the objective of the multiple measurement-organizational attribute approach to climate. Therefore, in this model we view those "objective realities" as the sources of stimuli that may influence the creation of communication climate but not as climate per se.

These three influences interact to create *stimuli*, which provide the developmental and perceptual cues associated with communication climate. Drawing from the dichotomy proposed by Hackman (1976), these stimuli may be classified as ambient or discretionary. The former classification refers to cues in the environment constantly impinging on perceivers that tend to operate unconsciously or subliminally. Discretionary cues, on the other hand, are those that are consciously perceived and/or manipulated.

As the model suggests, the cues (both ambient and discretionary) represent messages related to one or a combination of four climate dimensions: autonomy; degree of structure; rewards; and consideration, warmth, and support (Campbell et al., 1970). Moreover, the model underscores the fact that the cues convey messages *of* and *about* these four dimensions. The *of* dimension are explicit references to one of these dimensions (for example, "As of next week we will assume a new organizational structure and move from centralization to decentralization"). The *about* messages represent implicit references to or abstractions of one of the four dimensions (for example, An open door policy is a nonverbal message indicating warmth and support without a specific reference to warmth and support).

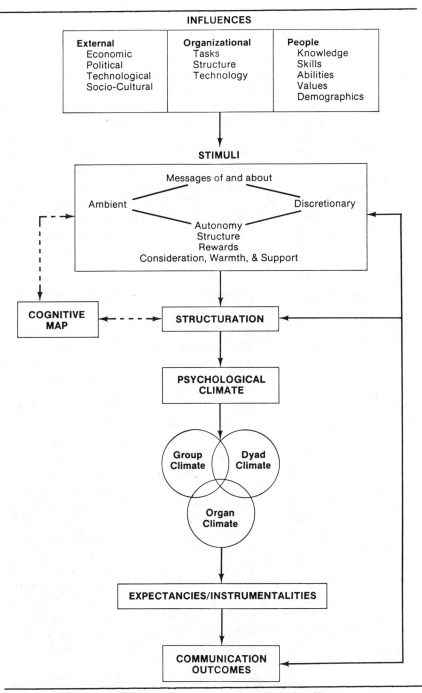

Figure 7.1 A Descriptive Model of Organizational Communication Climate

These four dimensions represent the molar factors that subsume specific communication processes and behaviors addressed in the preceding sections of this chapter. In other words, the essence of communication climate, whether analyzed at the dyadic, group, or organizational level, are messages and metamessages reflecting autonomy, structure, rewards, and consideration, warmth, and support. Moreover, the essence of communication climate is communicated through both ambient and discretionary cues.

These ambient and discretionary cues provide the foundation for structuration, as discussed earlier. Structuration takes place through the establishments of rules and resources used in the production and reproduction of the organizational system (Poole, 1985). The process becomes one of self-maintenance through organizational interaction. These interactions are structured and mediated by the cognitive maps of the organizational members (Guion, 1973; Schneider, 1973). For example, when major policy changes are implemented in organizations, those changes are mediated by employee perceptions of things such as structure, rewards, autonomy, resource availability, and so on.

The cognitive map serves as the interpretive schema for both ambient and discretionary cues. The model depicts this cognitive map as a mediating link between the cues and structuration. In other words, once the map is created it provides the standards or template against which future cues are assessed. Evidence of the role of cognitive maps (expectations, assumptions) in assessing communication practices is found in Jablin's (1984) research on socialization and perceptions of communication practices.

Structuration then serves as the basis of psychological climate, the individual's unique and idiosyncratic perceptions of what is happening in the organization and to him or her. This, then, is the objective of the perceptual measurement-individual attribute approach to climate. Therefore, in this model we view psychological "climate" as the individual perceptual product of structuration. As such, it influences the development of communication climate but it not synonymous with it. These unique perceptions provide the foundation for the development of the communication contexts explored in this analysis: interpersonal, group, and organizational. Moreover, as indicated in the model and as discussed in the preceding sections, each of the contexts provides a distinct view of climate, and each shares a view of organizational communication climate with the other two contexts. Thus we see communication climate as being appropriately measured only through the perceptual measurement-organizational attribute approach. But at the same time, it is essential to recognize that the other two approaches are important to the study of communication climate through their measures of influences and individual perceptions of existing structure.

Thus while it is possible to distinguish unique group and dyad communication climates, each is partially a function of organizational climate. In addition, while a dyadic communication climate is unique to the two primary parties in an interchange, that climate is also a function of the "n-adic" system (territoriality and relationship) in which the dyad is embedded and the influence of group climate structuration on each party present.

In other words, each climate is influenced by the *existing* climate of the larger system of which it is a part and, at the same time, the climate of subsystems influence the *development* of the climate of suprasystems (the intersections of the three sets). For instance, if dyadic climates affect dyadic communication and communication is the vehicle of structuration, then the nature of dyadic climates can be said to influence the development of group and organization climates. That part of each climate which does not intersect the other two represents climate attributes that are not a direct function of a sub- or suprasystem. For instance, Dansereau's (Dansereau, Alutto, & Yammarino, 1984; Nachman, Dansereau & Naughton, 1983, 1985) work with the vertical dyad linkage theory of leadership indicates that a leadership attribute of climate may exist separately at the dyad and group levels. Similarly, group norms regarding communication are clearly a part of group communication climate and, in cohesive groups, affect the climates of dyads within the group. However, different dyads develop distinct shared perceptions about communication rules even within the same cohesive group.

The three types of climate, then, lead to expectancies and instrumentalities directly affecting communication outcomes. These outcomes include those factors affecting the direct continuation, productivity, and growth of the organization. Finally, the outcomes provide feedback used to generate further messages (ambient and/or discretionary) regarding autonomy; degree of structure; rewards; and consideration, warmth, and support; and to reinforce and/or modify the structuration process.

What Do We Know? What Do We Not Know?

Our analysis explored interpersonal, group, and organizational climate. We argued that communication outcomes would be affected by the climate perspective explored in each respective section. However, at no point did we explore the comparative effects of the three climates. In other words, which of the three contexts is likely to have the greatest impact on expectancies and instrumentalities?

Drexler's (1977) research suggests that "climate variances are more attributable to organizations than to organizational sub-units" (p. 40). However, his research did not explore dyads nor did it focus on communication per se. Thus although research suggests that organizational differences are a greater predictor of climate than are subgroup differences, we have yet to explore climate differences across the dyad, small group, and organization as they relate to outcomes.

As suggested in the model, expectancies and instrumentalities are the link between organizational communication climate and outcomes. Our review suggests that we know much more about how climates develop than we do about how these perceived climates affect expectancies and instrumentalities. Perhaps one promising approach is to explore methods and findings of the communication culture literature.

If the stories we tell, the assumptions we develop, and the expectations we share are all a reflection of expectations and instrumentalities, then this element of our model may provide a bridge between the climate literature and the communication culture literature.

The relationship between communication and outcome variables has been explored by Muchinsky (1977), Roberts and O'Reilly (1974), and Dennis (1975). The dominant conclusion arising from these studies is that the variance in performance scores accounted for by climate scores is relatively small. Our model provides an interpretation for this finding.

The link among the climate subsystems and outcome factors is mediated by expectancies and instrumentalities. This suggests that communication climate is *necessary* for member satisfaction and productivity but not *sufficient*. Other factors that are "error terms" or "unaccounted variance" in the studies cited above may be found in the members' expectations concerning communication practices and productivity and instrumentalities between effort and productivity.

As discussed in the introductory section of this chapter, communication climate research has not yet adequately dealt with the issues surrounding the overlap of variables that can be both predictors and criteria or with the issues surrounding level of theory and analysis. It is hoped that the descriptive model developed in this chapter will provide a starting point for resolution of such issues. In particular, the explicit inclusion of structuration as both a producer and product of climate may provide the conceptual basis for determining the proper role of variables in particular studies. By defining climate as the shared perceptions of communicators and specifying the proper approach to measurement as being through perceptual measurement-organizational attributes, the use of the other two approaches and individual perceptions of structure may provide consistency across studies. In addition, by viewing the various communication climates as overlapping constructs, researchers should be more aware of the particular level they are exploring and design their research not only to be consistent for that level but to examine the effects of other levels that overlap their central focus.

At the beginning of this chapter, we labeled communication climate as a deceptively simple construct. There is little doubt that the construct will continue to lure researchers by its simplicity. However, we also hope that these researchers will also be lured by its deceptiveness and in so doing move from our descriptive model of communication climate and generate hypotheses and data resulting in a predictive model.

REFERENCES

Alkire, A., Collum, M., Kaswan, J., & Love, L. (1968). Information exchange and accuracy of verbal behavior under social power conditions. *Journal of Personality and Social Psychology, 9,* 301-338.

Ashforth, B. E. (1985). Climate formation: Issues and extensions. *Academy of Management Review, 10,* 837-847.

Bacharach, S. B., & Aiken, M. (1977). Communication in administrative bureaucracies. *Academy of Management Journal, 20,* 365-377.

Baird, J. W. (1974). An analytical field study of "open communication" as perceived by supervisors, subordinates, and peers. (Doctoral dissertation, Purdue University, 1973). *Dissertation Abstracts International, 35,* 562B. (University Microfilms No. 74-15, 116)

Bass, B. M., Valenzi, E. R., Farrow, D. L., & Solomon, R. J. (1975). Management styles associated with organizational task, personal, and interpersonal contingencies. *Journal of Applied Psychology, 60,* 720-729.

Blumer, H. (1969). *Symbolic interactionism: Perspective and method.* Englewood Cliffs, NJ: Prentice-Hall.

Browning, L. D. (1977). Diagnosing teams in organizational settings. *Group & Organizational Studies, 2,* 187-197.

Campbell, J., Dunette, M., Lawler, E., & Weick, K. (1970). *Managerial behavior, performance, and effectiveness.* New York: McGraw-Hill.

Cohen, A. R. (1958). Upward communication in experimentally created hierarchies. *Human Relations, 11,* 41-53.

Cooper, M. R., & Wood, M. T. (1974). Effects of member participation and commitment in group decision making on influence, satisfaction, and decision riskiness. *Journal of Applied Psychology, 59,* 127-134.

Danowski, J. A. (1979). *Size and environmental uncertainty as predictors of connectivity in organizational and community network groups.* Unpublished manuscript, Annenberg School of Communications, University of Southern California.

Danowski, J. A. (1980). Group attitude-belief uniformity and connectivity of organizational communication networks for production, innovation, and maintenance content. *Human Communication Research 6,* 299-308.

Danowski, J. A., & Steinfield, C. (1979). *Individual network role and network group levels: Cohesiveness and information adequacy.* Paper presented at Communication Networks Conference, East-West Institute, Honolulu.

Dansereau, F., Alutto, J. A., & Yammarino, F. J. (1984). *Theory testing in organizational behavior: The variant approach.* Englewood Cliffs, NJ: Prentice-Hall.

Dennis, H. S. (1975). *The construction of a managerial communication climate inventory for use in complex organizations.* Paper presented at the annual convention of the International Communication Association, Chicago.

Downey, H. K., Hellriegel, D., & Slocum, J. W. (1975). Congruence between individual needs, organizational climate, job satisfaction, and performance. *Academy of Management Journal, 18,* 149-155.

Downs, C. (1979). The relationship between communication and job satisfaction. In R. Huseman, C. Logue, & D. Freshley (Eds.), *Readings in interpersonal and organizational communication* (pp. 363-376). Boston: Allyn & Bacon.

Downs, C., Hazen, M., Quiggens, J., & Medley, J. (1973). *An empirical and theoretical investigation of communication satisfaction.* Paper presented at the annual meeting of the Speech Communication Association, New York City.

Downs, C. W., & Pickett, T. (1977). An analysis of the effect of nine leadership group compatability contingencies upon productivity and member satisfaction. *Communication Monographs, 44,* 220-230.

Drexler, J. (1977). Organizational climate: Its homogeneity within organizations. *Journal of Applied Psychology, 62,* 38-42.

Eisenberg, E. M., Monge, P. R., & Farace, R. V. (1984). Coorientation on communication rules in managerial dyads. *Human Communication Research, 11,* 261-271.

Fairhurst, G. T., & Snavely, B. K. (1983a). A test of the social isolation of male tokens. *Academy of Management Journal, 26,* 353-361.

Fairhurst, G. T., & Snavely, B. K. (1983b). Majority and token minority group relationships: Power acquisition and communication. *Academy of Management Review, 8,* 292-300.

Falcione, R. L. (1978). *Subordinate satisfaction as a function of communication climate and perceptions of immediate supervision.* Paper presented at the annual convention of the Eastern Communication Association, Boston.

Falcione, R. L., & Kaplan, E. A. (1984). Organizational climate, communication, and culture. In R. Bostrom (Ed.), *Communication yearbook 8* (pp. 285-309). Newbury Park, CA: Sage.

Field, R., & Abelson, M. (1982). Climate: A reconceptualization and proposed model. *Human Relations, 3,* 181-201.

Fleischman, E. A. (1973). Twenty years of consideration and structure. In E. A. Fleischman & J. G. Hunt (Eds.), *Current developments in the study of leadership* (pp. 1-40). Carbondale: Southern Illinois University Press.

Folger, J., & Poole, M. S. (1984). *Working through conflict: A communication perspective.* Glenview, IL: Scott, Foresman.

Forehand, G., & Gilmer, B. (1964). Environmental variation in studies of organizational behavior. *Psychological Bulletin, 62,* 361-382.

Gavin, J. F., & Howe, J. G. (1975). Psychological climate: Some theoretical and empirical considerations. *Behavioral Science, 20,* 228-240.

Glick, W. H. (1985). Conceptualizing and measuring organizational and psychological climate: Pitfalls in multilevel research. *Academy of Management Review, 10,* 601-616.

Gorman, L., & Malloy, E. (1972). *People, jobs, and organizations.* Dublin: Irish Productivity Center.

Guion, R. N. (1973). A note on organizational climate. *Organizational Behavior and Human Performance, 9,* 120-125.

Hackman, J. R. (1976). Group influences on individuals. In M. Dunnette (Ed.), *Handbook of industrial and organizational psychology* (pp. 1455-1525). Chicago: Rand McNally.

Halpin, A. (1967). Change and organizational climate. *Journal of Educational Administration, 5,* 5-25.

Harsbarger, D. (1971). An investigation of a structural model of a small group problem solving. *Human Relations, 24,* 43-63.

Hatfield, J. D, & Huseman, R. C. (1982). Perceptual congruence about communication as related to satisfaction: Moderating effects of individual characteristics. *Academy of Management Journal, 25,* 349-358.

Hellriegel, D., & Slocum, J. (1974). Organizational climate: Measures, research, and contingencies. *Academy of Management Journal, 17,* 255-280.

Hoffman, L. R. (1979). Applying experimental research on group problem solving to organizations. *Journal of Applied Behavioral Science, 15,* 375-391.

House, R. J., & Rizzo, J. R. (1972). Toward the measurement of organizational practices: Scale development and validation. *Journal of Applied Psychology, 56,* 388-396.

Howe, J. G. (1977). Group climate: An exploratory analysis of construct validity. *Organizational Behavior and Human Performance, 19,* 106-125.

Infante, D. A., & Gordon, W. I. (1979). Subordinate and superior perceptions of self and one another: Relations, accuracy, and reciprocity of liking. *Western Journal of Speech Communication, 43,* 212-223.

Inkson, J. H., Hickson, D. J., & Pugh, D. S. (1968). *Administrative reduction of variances in organization and behavior.* London: British Psychological Society.

Jablin, F. M. (1980a). Organizational communication theory and research: An overview of communication climate and network research. In D. Nimmo (Ed.), *Communication yearbook 4* (pp. 327-347). New Brunswick, NJ: Transaction Books.

Jablin, F. M. (1980b). Superior's upward influence, satisfaction, and openness in superior-subordinate communication: A reexamination of the "Pelz Effect." *Human Communication Research, 6,* 210-220.

Jablin, F. M. (1981). An exploratory study of subordinates' perceptions of supervisory politics. *Communication Quarterly, 29,* 269-275.

Jablin, F. M. (1982). Formal structural characteristics of organizations and superior-subordinate communication. *Human Communication Research, 8,* 338-347.

Jablin, F. M. (1984). Assimilating new members into organizations. In R. Bostrom (Ed.), *Communication yearbook 8* (pp. 594-626). Newbury Park, CA: Sage.

Jablin, F. M., & Sussman, L. (1983). Organizational group communication: A review of the literature and model of the process. In H. Greenbaum, R. Falcione, & S. Hellweg (Eds.), *Organizational communication: Abstract, analysis, and overview* (Vol. 8, pp. 11-50). Newbury Park, CA: Sage.

Jago, A. G., & Vroom, V. H. (1977). Hierarchical level and leadership style. *Organizational Behavior and Human Performance, 18,* 131-145.

James, L. R., Hater, J. J., Gent, M. J., & Bruni, J. R. (1978). Psychological climate: Implications from cognitive social learning theory and interactional psychology. *Personnel Psychology, 31,* 783-813.

James, L. R., & Jones, A. P. (1974). Organizational climate: A review of theory and research. *Psychological Bulletin, 16,* 74-113.

Jelinek, M., Smircich, L., & Hirsch, P. (1983). Introduction: A code of many colors. *Administrative Science Quarterly, 28,* 331-338.

Jessor, R., & Jessor, S. L. (1973). The perceived environment in behavioral science. *American Behavioral Scientist, 16,* 801-828.

Johannesson, R. E. (1973). Some problems in the measurement of organizational climate. *Organizational Behavior and Human Performance, 10,* 118-144.

Johnston, H. R., Jr. (1976). A new conceptualization of source of organizational climate. *Administrative Science Quarterly, 21,* 95-103.

Jones, A .P., & James, L. R. (1979). Psychological climate: Dimensions and relationships of individual and aggregated work environment perceptions. *Organizational Behavior and Human Performance, 23,* 201-250.

Korman, A. K. (1966). Consideration, initiating structure, and organizational criteria—a review. *Personnel Psychology, 19,* 349-361.

Laing, R. D., Phillipson, H., & Lee, A. R. (1966). *Interpersonal perception: A theory and a method of research.* New York: Springer.

Leavitt, H. (1965). Applied organizational change in industry: Structural, technological, and humanistic approaches. In J. March (Ed.), *Handbook of organizations* (pp. 1144-1170). Chicago: Rand McNally.

Levine, R. L. (1973). Problems of organizational context in microcosm: Group performance and group member satisfaction as a function of differences in control structure. *Journal of Applied Psychology, 58,* 186-196.

Lewin, K. A. (1936). *Principles of topological psychology.* New York: McGraw-Hill.

Lewin, K. A., Lippitt, R., & White, R. (1939). Patterns of aggressive behavior in experimentally created "social climates." *Journal of Social Psychology, 10,* 271-299.

Likert, R. (1967). *The human organization.* New York: McGraw-Hill.

Litwin, G., & Stringer, R. (1968). *Motivation and organizational climate.* Boston: Harvard University Press.

Maier, N.R.F., Hoffman, R. L., & Read, W. H. (1963). Superior-subordinate communication: The relative effectiveness of managers who held their subordinate's position. *Personnel Psychology, 16,* 1-11.

Marcus, P. M., & House, J. S. (1973). Exchange between superiors and subordinates in large organizations. *Administrative Science Quarterly, 18,* 209-222.

Mears, P. (1974). Structuring communication in a working group. *Journal of Communication, 24,* 71-79.

Meier, R. L. (1963). Communication overload: Proposals from the study of a university library. *Administrative Science Quarterly, 4,* 521-544.

Mellinger, G. D. (1956). Interpersonal trust as a factor in communication. *Journal of Abnormal Social Psychology, 52,* 304-309.

Morse, J. J., & Lorsch, J. (1970). Beyond Theory Y. *Harvard Business Review, 48,* 61-68.

Muchinsky, P. M. (1977). Organizational communication: Relationships to organizational climate and job satisfaction. *Academy of Management Journal, 20,* 592-607.

Nachman, S., Dansereau, F., & Naughton, T. S. (1983). Negotiating latitude: A within- and between-groups analysis of a key construct in the vertical dyad linkage theory of leadership. *Psychological Reports, 53,* 171-177.

Nachman, S., Dansereau, F., & Naughton, T. S. (1985). Levels of analysis and the vertical dyad linkage approach to leadership. *Psychological Reports, 57,* 661-662.

O'Reilly, C. A. (1978). The intentional distortion of information in organizational communication: A laboratory and field investigation. *Human Relations, 31,* 173-193.

Paolillo, J. G. (1982). R & D subsystem climate as a function of personal and organizational factors. *Journal of Management Studies, 19,* 327-334.

Payne, R. L., Fineman, S., & Wall, T. D. (1976). Organizational climate and job satisfaction: A conceptual synthesis. *Organizational Behavior and Human Performance, 16,* 45-62.

Payne, R. L., & Mansfield, R. (1973). Relationships of perceptions of organizational climate to organizational structure, context, and hierarchical position. *Administrative Science Quarterly, 18,* 515-526.

Payne, R. L., & Pugh, D. S. (1976). Organizational structure and climate. In M. Dunnette (Ed.)., *Handbook of industrial and organizational psychology* (pp. 1125-1173). Chicago: Rand McNally.

Poole, M. S. (1985). Communications and organizational climates: Review, critique, and a new perspective. In P. Tompkins & R. D. McPhee (Eds.), *Organizational communication: Traditional themes and new directions.* (pp. 79-108). Newbury Park, CA: Sage.

Poole, M. S., & McPhee, R. D. (1983). A structurational theory of organizational climate. In L. Putnam & M. Pacanowsky (Eds.), *Organizational communication: An interpretive approach* (pp. 195-219). Newbury Park, CA: Sage.

Porter, L. W., & Roberts, K. (1976). Communication in organizations. In M. Dunnette (Ed.), *Handbook of industrial and organizational psychology* (pp. 1553-1589). Chicago: Rand McNally.

Powell, G. N., & Butterfield, D. A. (1978). The case for subsystem climates in organizations. *Academy of Management Review, 3,* 151-157.

Pritchard, R., & Karasick, B. (1973). The effects of organizational climate on managerial job performance and job satisfaction. *Organizational Behavior and Human Performance, 9,* 110-119.

Read, W. (1962). Upward communication in industrial hierarchies. *Human Relations, 15,* 3-16.

Redding, W. C. (1972). *Communication within the organization: An interpretive review of theory and research..* New York: Industrial Communication Council.

Ricci, C., & Selvini-Palazzoli, M. (1984). Interactional complexity and communication. *Family Process, 23,* 169-176.

Roberts, K. H., & O'Reilly, C. A. (1974). Failures in upward communication: Three possible culprits. *Academy of Management Journal, 17,* 205-215.

Roberts, K. H., & O'Reilly, C. A. (1978). Organizations as communication structures—an empirical approach. *Human Communication Research, 4,* 283-293.

Rosenfeld, L. B., & Plax, T. O. (1975). Personality determinants of autocratic and democratic leadership. *Speech Monographs, 42,* 203-208.

Schein, E. H. (1980). *Organizational psychology* (3rd ed.). Englewood Cliffs, NJ: Prentice-Hall.

Schneider, B. (1973). The perception of organizational climate: The customer's view. *Journal of Applied Psychology, 57,* 248-256.

Schneider, B. (1975a). Organizational climate: An essay. *Personnel Psychology, 28,* 447-479.

Schneider, B. (1975b). Organizational climate: Individual preferences and organizational realities revisited. *Journal of Applied Psychology, 60,* 459-465.

Schneider, B. (1983). Work climates: An interactionist perspective. In N. W. Feimer & E. S. Geller (Eds.), *Environmental psychology: Directions and perspectives* (pp. 106-128). New York: Praeger.

Schneider, B., Parkington, J. J., & Buxton, V. M. (1980). Employee and customer perceptions of service in banks. *Administrative Science Quarterly, 25,* 252-267.

Schneider, B., & Snyder, R. (1975). Some relationships between job satisfaction and organizational climate. *Journal of Applied Psychology, 60,* 318-328.

Schutz, W. (1966). *The interpersonal underworld.* Palo Alto, CA: Science and Behavior.

Shaw, M. (1976). *Group dynamics.* New York: McGraw-Hill.

Smircich, L., & Chesser, R. J. (1981). Superior's and subordinates' perceptions of performance: Beyond disagreement. *Academy of Management Journal, 24,* 198-205.

Sussman, L. (1974). Upward communication in the organizational hierarchy: An experimental field study of perceived message distortion. (Doctoral dissertation, Purdue University, 1973). *Dissertation Abstracts International, 34,* 5366A. (University Microfilms No. 74-05-055)

Sussman, L., Pickett, T. A., Berzinski, I. A., & Pearce, F. W. (1980). Sex and sycophancy: Communication strategies for ascendance in same sex and mixed sex superior-subordinate dyads. *Sex Roles, 6,* 113-128.

Tagiuri, R. (1968). The concepts of organizational climate. In R. Tagiuri & G. H. Litwin (Eds.), *Organizational climate: Exploration of a concept* (pp. 11-32). Boston: Harvard University Press.

Tagiuri, R., & Litwin, G. H. (Eds.). (1968). *Organizational climate: Exploration of a concept.* Boston: Harvard University Press.

Taylor, J., & Bowers, D. (1972). *Survey of organizations.* Ann Arbor: University of Michigan, Institute of Social Research.

Thorndike, E. H. (1913). *Educational psychology: The psychology of learning* (Vol. 2). New York: Columbia University Teachers College.

Vroom, V. (1976). Leadership. In M. Dunnette (Ed.), *Handbook of industrial and organizational psychology* (pp. 1527-1551). Chicago: Rand McNally.

Wanous, J. P. (1980). *Organizational entry: Recruitment, selection, and socialization of newcomers.* Reading, MA: Addison-Wesley.

Wexley, K. N., Alexander, R. A., Greenawalt, J. P., & Couch, M. A. (1980). Attitudinal congruence and similarity as related to interpersonal evaluation in manager-subordinate dyads. *Academy of Management Journal, 23,* 320-330.

Woodman, R., & King, D. (1978). Organizational climate: Science or folklore? *Academy of Management Review, 3,* 816-826.

Young, J. W. (1978). The subordinate's exposure of organizational vulnerability to the superior: Sex and organizational effects. *Academy of Management Journal, 21,* 113-122.

Zohar, D. (1980). Safety climate in industrial organizations: Theoretical and applied implications. *Journal of Applied Psychology, 65,* 96-102.

8 Organizational Culture: A Critical Assessment

LINDA SMIRCICH
MARTA B. CALÁS
University of Massachusetts

IT is currently popular to discuss organizations in cultural terms. The idea of culture is arousing a great deal of scholarly interest and spawning a "corporate culture" consulting industry. Researchers taken with the idea of culture investigate language, symbols, myths, stories, and rituals as forms of human expression. When a reader encounters an article on stories or corporate myths, he or she identifies it as another "culture" article. But although researchers may use the same terms, they employ these terms differently and for diverse purposes.

In this chapter we assume that the articles and books on organizational culture and symbolism, while not necessarily characterized by tight integration, share enough unity to form a recognizable body called the organizational culture literature. Does it herald something dramatically different in the study of organizations? Or is it just another in a long series of faddish topics that capture the imagination but emerge as disappointing in the end? Is the study of organizational culture a failed project? Or is it a source of inspiration sustaining a revitalized scholarship on organizational life? This chapter explores these issues.

To this end, we subject the organizational culture literature to several forms of review and analysis. We present a thematic framework that stresses the links between anthropology and organizational culture (Smircich, 1983a). This thematic analysis also views the literature from perspectives based on the paradigms and cognitive interests that researchers bring to their work (Stablein & Nord, 1985; Sypher, Applegate, & Sypher, 1985). The diversity and competing views we observe within this literature and those acknowledged by other commentators (Barley, Meyer, & Gash, 1986; Ouchi & Wilkins, 1985), prompt us to take yet another look—from a different vantage point— one that is less concerned with the content of culture literature and more concerned with its meaning and role in organizational theory.

The original impetus behind organizational culture was to counter the dry and overly rational form of traditional theorizing about organizations. It seems that now, however, organizational culture has been appropriated by the rational tradition. Thus to the extent that "culture" has been incorporated into the positivist, technical interest as part of the "traditional organizational literature," the organizational culture literature may be "dominant, but dead" (Habermas, 1983). Our analysis brings us to these questions: How can we revive/revitalize/regain "culture" for organizational studies? And why would we want to do that? To explore these issues we need to understand the role of organizational culture in the broader human sciences. In doing so, we erase the boundaries between disciplines and acknowledge the epistemological unrest that characterizes the human sciences today. We propose that this view will help us to regain culture as a viable alternative for organizational theory and research.

We begin with the conditions that form a context and a pretext for the emergence of an organizational culture literature, conditions of economic turbulence, theoretical debates, and paradigm shifts. At the end of our chapter we return to these issues and examine what kind of organizational culture literature is still possible.

WHY IS CULTURE AN IMPORTANT TOPIC NOW?

The idea of culture is not new; what is new is its widespread popularity in both academic and practitioner circles. There are discussions of corporate myths, rituals, sagas, dramas, legends, and ceremonies in such disparate publications as *Business Week, Fortune,* and *Administrative Science Quarterly.* Anthropologists, folklorists, communication theorists, business school faculty, and corporate managers rub elbows and trade stories at conferences on organizational folklore, symbolism, and culture. This activity represents a major departure from such topics as organization structure and leadership style that dominated research and practice in the seventies. Perhaps even more significant, an interest in culture is reflected in and heightened by management texts appearing on the best seller lists. This eager response to the idea of culture has produced a substantial but diverse and fragmented literature. Why? And what does it mean? Why is there a substantial body of organizational culture literature now?

A constellation of economic and intellectual conditions that arose in the late seventies and early eighties appears to foster receptivity to the idea of culture as an important *subject* and as a *perspective* or *way of seeing* (Jelinek, Smircich, & Hirsch, 1983a). Changes in economic and intellectual discourses reflect a shift in economic power and doubts about managerial capabilities to control organizational life. These changes constitute a context into which culture has surfaced among organizational communication and management theorists.

Shifts in the Perspective of Business

American business managers are beginning to see their roles as members of a global economy in which the dominant players are multinational or transnational organizations. In the United States this "reality" hit home with reports of the stunning economic success of Japan; the surprise of the OPEC oil crisis; and inroads by foreign competitors in steel, shoes, electronics, and so on. These occurrences, mediated by much television and popular press coverage, are making American business take a critical look at itself. The imagery of a "global village" fosters a somewhat less ethnocentric posture in the business world, one that promotes introspection. Within business schools there is considerable interest in international topics, accompanied by efforts to "internationalize" the curriculum.

This introspection has led to disaffection with some major concepts in organization theory. First it was scientific management, then organizational structure, then corporate strategy that seemed to promise business success. In the 1970s a succession of rational planning techniques, such as the Boston Consulting Group's matrix for portfolio management, swept over the business landscape. Disillusionment followed, however, when corporations experienced great difficulties implementing what appeared to be perfectly sound strategies (Keichel, 1982; Schwartz & Davis, 1981). Today General Electric's much heralded strategic planning group is being dismantled. Apparently there is more to business success than a well thought-out strategy. One key answer may be corporate culture ("Corporate Culture," 1980).

Shifts in Organizational
and Communication Theory

Organizational theorists spent the 1960s and the 1970s mining the systems metaphor for insights into organizational life. The systems model stressed attention to inputs-transformation-outputs and dynamic processes, but actual research practice produced static cross-sectional analyses that were more morphological than processual (Pacanowsky & O'Donnell-Trujillo, 1983; Pondy & Mitroff, 1979). Advocates urged organization theorists to move beyond open system approaches to models aimed at the higher mental functions of human behavior, such as language and the creation of meaning (Pondy & Mitroff, 1979).

Organizational behavior in the 1980s, in contrast, reflects two divergent but concomitant trends: (1) a "conservative" path in which researchers focus on improved construct validity, careful selection and measurement of dependent variables, longitudinal and experimental research designs, and use of multivariate statistics; and (2) a "radical" approach that conceptualizes organizations as socially constructed, investigates the symbolic nature of management, and focuses on processes that occur across levels of analysis (Cummings, 1980). Cummings's labeling of these approaches as conservative and radical points out how judgments about knowledge depend on a theorist's perspective. Culture plays an important role in both trends, as will be illustrated in this chapter.

In addition to changes in organizational behavior, communication theory has evolved from linear models of sending and receiving messages to process models that emphasize the way communication is socially constructed and meanings are coproduced (Gerbner, 1983; Putnam & Cheney, 1985). In the linear models, researchers investigate the movement of messages from point to point, paying special attention to the channels, blockages, and filters that hinder effective message transmission. Research centers on such queries as: Does the receiver get the same message that the sender transmitted? If the answer is no, researchers look for breakdowns in the communication channels and for blockages that might inhibit transmission (Putnam, 1983). Gradually research has shifted away from conceptualizing communication as a tangible substance (for example, it flows upward, downward, and laterally within a container organization), and from message barriers, breakdowns, distortion, and frequency (Hawes, 1974; Putnam, 1983).

Current communication theory reflects an interest in the social construction of messages and meaning (Lakoff & Johnson, 1980; Putnam & Pacanowsky, 1983). This orientation attends to the ways that words, symbols, and actions of human actors create and sustain social reality. Meanings do not reside in messages, channels, or filters; rather, they evolve through social interaction and sense-making activities of people. Thus communication is not just another organizational activity that occurs *inside* an organization; rather, it *creates* and *recreates* the social structure that makes organization (Hawes, 1974; Smircich, 1983b). Researchers who espouse this perspective study how reality is performed (Trujillo, 1983) or accomplished through symbolic means (Gronn, 1983).

Shifts in the Human Sciences

Traditionally, *explanation* and *understanding* are framed as opposite ways of knowing and pursuing inquiry. *Explanation*, as evident in positivist science, follows the model of the natural or physical world in which hypothesis testing, experimentation, verification or falsification, and generalizations are expected. *Understanding*, in contrast, relies on interpretations of subjective meanings; thus generalizations are not required or expected. Explanation takes the view of the world from the outside, while understanding takes the view of the world from the inside (Evered & Louis, 1981). The two goals place objective and subjective, the physical world and the social world, in opposition. The ongoing debate between positivism and interpretivism highlights these oppositions.

But regardless of objective/subjective orientation, theorists are beginning to claim that all science is primarily metaphorical (Brown, 1977; Morgan, 1980; Morgan & Smircich, 1980). A researcher's choice of metaphors to frame his or her work reflects implicit assumptions about the nature of the world. Until recently mechanical and organic metaphors from the physical world dominated theorizing about communication and organization. However, as theoretical shifts have occurred so have metaphorical shifts. A movement is under way throughout the human sciences in which the analogies "are coming more and more from the contrivances of cultural performance than from those of physical manipulation—from theater, painting, grammar, literature, law, play" (Geertz, 1983, pp. 22-23). Thus the humanities are providing the analogies for theorizing about organizational culture (Winkler, 1985). The following pages chart the relationship of the organizational culture literature to these shifting economic and intellectual conditions.

ORGANIZATIONAL CULTURE LITERATURE

Since the late 1970s, conferences, books, articles, and special journal issues on cultural have proliferated (Bhagat & McQuaid, 1982; Deal & Kennedy, 1982; Frost, 1985; Frost, Moore, Louis, Lundberg, & Martin, 1985; Jelinek et al., 1983a; Kilmann, Saxton, & Serpa, 1985; Pondy, Frost, Morgan, & Dandridge, 1983; Sathe, 1985; Schein, 1985; Tichy, 1982). Additionally, a new journal, *Dragon*, created by the European-based Standing Conference on Organizational Symbolism, and at least two transatlantic newsletters have been published.[1] With an abundance of culture literature, scholars have used various frameworks to classify research and to create order amidst what appears to be an "organizational culture chaos." Three frameworks illustrate different ways of organizing the cultural literature: by anthropological themes, sociological paradigms, and epistemological interest.

The first framework, *themes*, applies divergent schools of cultural anthropology to organizational culture research (Smircich, 1983a) . Five themes emerge from the intersection of organizational and anthropological literature (see Table 8.1). The five differ in the way they conceptualize culture as a variable or as a "root metaphor." The first two themes, *comparative management* and *corporate culture*, are quite distinct; but they are compatible in that both treat culture as a variable. Both approaches identify organizations and cultures through patterns of relationships across and within boundaries. The research aims to predict contingent relationships that have applicability for managing organizations. The other three themes, cognition, symbolism, and unconscious processes, treat organizations as cultures; research from these perspectives deviates from the contingency framework prevalent in the first two themes. Culture is no longer a characteristic that an organization has; rather, it represents what an organization is (Smircich, 1983a). This use of culture as a root metaphor differs from conceptions of organizations as instruments, tools, or organisms that adapt to their environments. Organizations are understood and analyzed not in economic or materialistic terms, but as expressive, ideational, and symbolic processes (Smircich, 1985).

A second framework applies *paradigms* used by Burrell & Morgan (1979) to link culture and communication to organizational contexts (Sypher et al., 1985). The paradigm framework shares with the themes perspective an interest in sharpening the theoretical distinctions among different organizational culture approaches. The *functionalist paradigm* is characterized by an objectivist vision of social reality, a positivist epistemology, a determinist view of human nature, and a regulatory view of society. Functionalist approaches share a concern for explanation and for producing "useful" knowledge. Useful means generalized lawlike statements that aid in prediction, control, and manageability across situations. The *interpretive paradigm,* in contrast, shares the functionalist's view of society but is differentiated by its subjectivist vision of social reality, its antipositivist epistemology, and its voluntarist view of human nature. Interpretivists do not share the functionalist's concern for prediction and control. Instead, interpretive research centers on documenting processes and experiences through which people construct organizational reality. Thus "useful" knowledge for the interpretivist aims at understanding what is "going on" in a situation, while recognizing that any account of what's going on is dependent on one's viewpoint since no situation can be fully known from only one point of view.

Using an epistemological basis from Habermas's (1970, 1971, 1973, 1975) theory of knowledge, Stablein and Nord (1985) present a third framework, the *interests* embedded in the organizational symbolism literature. They describe three cognitive interests defined by Habermas. First, the *technical interest*, modeled after the concept of science, centers on manipulation and control of the environment represented in research that falls within the functionalist paradigm. Second, the *practical interest* is exemplified by the historical-hermeneutic sciences of interpretation and is motivated by the desire to

TABLE 8.1

Three Frameworks for Analyzing the Organizational Culture Literature

Themes	Paradigmatic Perspective	Theory of Knowledge Perspective
Cultures as Variables	*Culture from a Functionalist Perspective*	*The Technical Interest*
Comparative Management— culture as external variable, synonymous with country. Corporate culture— culture as internal variable, influencing systemic balance and performance.	Organizational culture as a management tool. Managers can control culture through controlling communication practices, and thus influence organizational performance. Some research seeks to define a relationship between objectified cultural events (for example, storytelling, rituals, language) and objective circumstances (productivity, turnover).	Research guided by an interest in manipulation and control of the natural and social environment. Based on a physical science model, features empirical testing of hypotheses and generalizable claims. Success of theory depends on ability to operate on the environment producing predicted effects. Technical knowledge is traditionally what has been called science.
Culture as Root Metaphor.	*Culture from an Interpretive Perspective*	*The Practical Interest*
Organizational cognition— organizations as structures of knowledge; shared frames of reference or rules. Organizational symbolism— organizations as shared meanings; patterns of symbolic discourse. Unconscious processes and organization— organizations as reflections and manifestations of unconscious processes.	Organizations viewed as cultures; focus shifts to the processes of organizing as the enactment of cultural development. Culture is the process through which social action and interaction become constructed and reconstructed into an organizational reality. The symbolic constitutes what is taken for granted as organizational life. Culture and communication are vehicles through which reality is constituted in organizational contexts. Interpretive focus places communication at the center of organizational culture.	Research motivated by the desire to understand meaning in a specific situation so that a decision can be made and action taken. A specific decision, not a generalizable rule, is the goal of knowledge seeking. Literary and historical analysis are models of the practical search of knowledge. Methodology involves the interpretation of the meanings manifest in human interaction. The ultimate claim to validity is consensus of the interested parties on the meaning of the situation. *The Emancipatory Interest* An interest in increasing the level of human autonomy and responsibility in the world. Builds on Freudian and Marxist perspectives in that it stresses the recovery of rationality and responsibility from the blockages of ideology and false consciousness. Methodology of self-reflection that questions assumptions in which the current situation is grounded. It addresses the appropriateness of shared meanings. The validity criterion is the contribution of such knowledge to the potential for autonomous, responsible human action.

SOURCES: Themes drawn from Smircich (1983). Paradigmatic perspective drawn from Sypher et al. (1985); derived from Burrell and Morgan (1979). Theory of knowledge perspective drawn from Stablein and Nord (1985); derived from Habermas (1971).

understand meaning in decision making and action-oriented situations. Finally, the *emancipatory* interest aims to increase the level of human autonomy and responsibility in the world through a critical approach.

Although the three frameworks differ in their assumptions, they represent similar ways of grouping research programs on organizational culture. Specifically, treatments of culture as a variable in the comparative and corporate cultural themes fall into the functionalist paradigm, which derives from technical interests. Similarly, studies on organizational cognition, symbolism, and unconscious processes represent interpretive approaches that typically employ a practical interest. The emancipatory interest in the Stablein and Nord (1985) framework could be developed under any theme but it is more aligned with the radical paradigms that go undiscussed by Sypher et al.

We now examine the organizational culture research with a central focus on the *themes* that emerge in the research, but with insights from the other two frameworks. This approach uncovers patterns and gaps in the literature and shows the close connections between communication and organization theory.

Culture and Comparative Management:
Culture as External Variable

Research on the cross-cultural theme has a long history that builds directly on the bedrock of anthropological studies—the investigation of other cultures. An early cross-cultural project in anthropology established the Human Relations Area Files, a repository of ethnographic data from a wide variety of societies. Researchers organized the data into a generalized yet detailed category scheme; the goal was to accumulate enough comparative data for conducting statistical analyses to achieve cumulative findings (Udy, 1973).

Cross-cultural research in management has not reached the stage of a Human Relations Area Files, although some attempts bear a resemblance (for example, Barrett & Bass, 1970). Organizational research, however, shares comparative anthropology's functionalist view of society by treating culture as an independent, external variable imported into the organization through the membership. Its presence, then, is revealed in the attitudes and actions of individual members. In practice, however, most comparative management research fails to develop the concept of culture; rather, it becomes a background factor that is usually synonymous with country.

The primary goal of this research is to chart variations in managerial and employee practices, attitudes, and perceptions across countries (Haire, Ghiselli, & Porter, 1966; Harbison & Meyers, 1959). There is also an interest in documenting differences among cultures, locating clusters of similarities, and drawing implications for organizational effectiveness (Ronen & Shenkar, 1985). Moreover, these concerns have remained intact over three decades of research (Sekaran, 1981, 1986). Overall, this research theme stresses the importance of national culture over the influence of organizational context (Hofstede, 1980; Kelley & Worthley, 1981). Moves within the area of intercultural communication add to this emphasis by stressing the possibility of cultural translation, an issue that has dominated anthropology for years.

Through deciphering ways that researchers locate similarities and differences across cultures, Adler (1982) develops a typology of cross-cultural research. *Ethnocentric* studies are originally done in one culture by researchers from that culture and are replicated in a different culture. This research, typically conducted by Americans, seeks to know if American theories or practices can be extended to different cultures. These replication studies center on similarities across cultural conditions and aim to demonstrate the universality of research results. *Polycentric* studies are designed to describe, explain, and interpret managerial and organizational practices within specific foreign cultures. They are directed to the broad question, How do managers manage and employees behave in culture X? This approach is often preliminary, followed by an evaluative study aimed at determining which approach is better or more "effective." Adler points out that marketers typically follow polycentric approaches as a way to make their products appeal to diverse groups. *Comparative* research, in contrast, aims to identify the similarities and differences across two or more cultures. By asking, How is culture X different from culture Y?, it seeks to determine which aspects of organization theory are universal and which ones are culturally specific. However, if the researcher either implicitly or explicitly assumes that one culture's approach to organization is superior, then the researcher is doing ethnocentric, not comparative, research.

Most cross-cultural management studies, whether ethnocentric, polycentric, or comparative, fall under the functionalist paradigm; that is, researchers attempt to define and chart relationships among objectifications (such as attitudes, perceptions) within a scientific model. This research has a relatively passive view of human nature and its results are framed as tools for managerial control within a technical interest (Sypher et al., 1985).

Sekaran's (1986) survey of Indian and U.S. employees provides an example of ethnocentric cross-cultural research. Scores on questionnaires were clustered through factor analysis into variables and examined for their similarities and differences across cultures. This study aimed to get a "handle on international differences which might help managers of multinational corporations to adapt or adopt exceptions, management styles, and organizational norms which would attain the desired organizational goals and outcomes" (Sekaran, 1986, p. 19).

The importance of cross-cultural research for multinational organizations is obvious. With the recognition of global interdependence and its concurrent shifts in economic power, this research is of growing interest. The declining economic position of American business in the world has sparked interest in cross-cultural management. At the same time, the expansion of multinational organizations has stimulated enhanced sensitivity to cultural differences and to cultural views of organizations.

Corporate Culture: Culture as Internal Variable

A second research theme linking culture and organization is that of "corporate culture." Although organizations are embedded within a wider cultural context, this theme emphasizes the social-cultural qualities that develop *within* organizations (Smircich, 1983a); hence, culture is conceived of as an internal attribute rather than an external factor that impinges on the organization. Organizations are treated as social instruments that produce goods and services and as social systems that produce distinct cultural artifacts such as rituals, legends, and ceremonies (Dandridge, 1979; Deal & Kennedy, 1982; Harris & Sutton, 1986; Louis, 1980; Martin & Powers, 1983; Tichy, 1982; Trice & Beyer, 1984a, 1984b). Drawing upon anthropology's structural functionalist conception of culture, much corporate culture work implies that the cultural dimension contributes in some way to the systematic balance and effectiveness of an organization (Kilmann et al., 1985; Tichy, 1982; Tunstall, 1983). Thus an internal corporate culture is a possession that gives an organization a competitive advantage (Barney, 1986). The conception of culture as an internal variable leads some researchers to claim that culture is simply organizational climate reborn (Schneider, 1985; see also Falcione, Sussman, and Herden, Chapter 7, this volume).

Researchers have taken the idea of corporate culture in diverse directions. Some adopt a "cultural engineering" approach by stressing the need for a match between internal organizational components, such as culture and reward systems, and external issues, such as strategy (Cummings, 1984; Schwartz & Davis, 1981; Stonich, 1984). Other researchers provide ways of diagnosing organizational culture to help an individual manager negotiate his or her way through an organizational maze or to assist in the management of organizational change (Boje, Fedor, & Rowland, 1982; Sathe, 1983, 1985; Tichy, 1982; Wilkins, 1983). For example, Nicholson & Johns (1985) diagnose problems in absenteeism as tied to an "absence culture" learned by participants. They stress the collective aspects of absence and advise managers to reorient control strategies in light of this new conceptualization of absence.

Other researchers build on the organismic analogy by treating organizations as living or dying systems or as personalities. Taking a psychoanalytic perspective, Kets de Vries and Miller (1985, 1986) present a typology of organizations based on manifestations of pathological personality characteristics. They argue that organizational cultures and strategies often reflect the neuroses of their top management. The death theme surfaces in Harris and Sutton's (1986) examination of the functions of such parting ceremonies as a "wake" for a retrenched academic department. Parting ceremonies help members cope with the affective and cognitive demands of organizational death.

Just as organizational strategy and structure serve as mechanisms for control and effectiveness, the cultural artifacts of stories, rites, and ceremonies are often treated as managerial tools for organizational unification and control. For example, several corporate culture texts argue that organizations with "strong" cultures are apt to be more successful (Deal & Kennedy, 1982; Peters & Waterman, 1982); others points to the critical linkage between leadership and cultural qualities (Peters & Austin, 1985; Schein, 1985). This line of research offers a tantalizing prospect—organization culture may be the lever by which managers influence and direct their organizations (Schwartz & Davis, 1981; Tichy, 1982). Popular books, trade journals, and even academic research emphasize that symbolic devices are used to mobilize the energies of organization members. Managers must find ways to use stories, legends, and other symbolic forms in their unique situations and for their own ends ("Changing a Corporate Culture," 1984; Peters, 1978; Pfeffer, 1981).

Despite the appearance of adopting an interpretive-symbolic approach to communication theory, this work implicitly incorporates mechanistic assumptions and linear models of communication (see Krone, Jablin, and Putnam, Chapter 1, this volume). That is, symbols become a way of transmitting messages that affect organizational practice. Symbols are related to organizational culture in a quasi-causal fashion; researchers see these artifacts of culture as antecedent conditions that affect organizational effectiveness. Stories, legends, and myths, although symbolic in form, project a static and almost "physical" quality in the corporate culture literature.

Several exemplar articles illustrate this theme. Siehl and Martin (1984) discuss how a manager can create, maintain, and transmit a shared culture in order to reap the benefits of increased commitment, cognitive sense-making, and control. These authors envision culture as an essentially unitary concept made up of symbolic tools that fall under the control of management. Their stress on the harmonizing capacity of culture unifies symbolic meaning in a static way, one consistent with the integrationist emphasis of much early anthropology (Allaire & Firsirotu, 1984). In a similar line of research, Trice and Beyer (1984b) discuss why, when, and how managers can use rites to change their corporate cultures. The authors advise managers that existing rites are generally conservative, which can interfere with change efforts; thus managers should eliminate rites that express undesirable ideologies or values. Rites, then, become a managerial tool, a message process for facilitating cultural change efforts (Trice & Beyer, 1984b).

The materialistic treatment of symbols is even more pronounced in Wilkins and Ouchi's (1983) link between organizational culture and economic efficiency. Using the concept of culture to exemplify well-defined social communities, they question how and why organizations attain tight social integration. They focus on culture as a form of economic control, one that substitutes for the marketplace and bureaucratic arrangements. The concept of culture that the authors advance resembles Ouchi's (1981) Theory Z versus Theory A dichotomy more than any broader conception of the term.

Although there is considerable diversity within the corporate culture theme, for example, an "absence" versus a "strong" culture, the literature consistently endorses functionalist assumptions and the pursuit of technical interests. The very raison d'etre of this work is to link corporate culture to organizational and individual performance (Barney, 1986), that is, to evaluate the "psychological and economic value" of cultural dimensions of organizations (Harris & Sutton, 1986). Culture is believed to work mechanically by imprinting individuals with symbolic meaning (Nicholson & Johns, 1985) and by strategic transmission of cultural messages from management to employees (Siehl & Martin, 1984).

What many authors conceive as "cultural knowledge" is actually the value system that management promotes (Siehl & Martin, 1984; Wilkins & Ouchi, 1983). Even though organizational members typically develop shared values and perspectives that counter managerial worldviews, researchers who frame their designs from a managerial perspective are precluded from alternative orientations to "cultural knowledge." The phrase "organizational culture" in the corporate culture literature is often used as a "cookie cutter" placed on the whole fabric of belief systems that pervade organized life. The corporate culture perspective cuts and delimits the range of shared understandings that receive attention from researchers. For example, corporate culture researchers rarely discuss the subcultures of management or workers, shared understandings that unite people on the basis of power or class. Based on the amount of interest in company ceremonies (Dandridge, 1979; Harris & Sutton, 1986; Trice & Beyer, 1984a, 1984b) and the tendency toward "cultural or value engineering" (Meyerson & Martin, 1986), the ultimate research design might be one where participants are connected to galvanic skin meters and alpha wave machines to measure the extent to which they have been emotionally "moved."

Culture is conceptualized and researched differently when researchers treat culture as cognitions, symbolic discourse, or unconscious processes. This view of culture drawn from cognitive, symbolic, and to a lesser extent, structural anthropology is based on different metaphors used to understand cultural dynamics, namely, knowledge systems, dramaturgy, performance, accomplishment, and text (Smircich, 1983a). Sypher et al. (1985) describe the break in the organizational culture literature between themes 1 and 2 and themes 3, 4, and 5 as a shift from the functionalist to the interpretive paradigm. For Stablein and Nord (1985), it signifies different cognitive interests that motivate the conduct of inquiry.

Organizational Cognition—
Culture as Knowledge Structures

From the perspectives of cognitive anthropology or ethnoscience, culture consists of shared knowledge, that is, a system of meanings that accompanies the behaviors and practices of a particular group. The ethnoscience researcher aims to gain an insider's understanding by tapping into the conceptual, ideational system of groups and analyzing the language used to make sense of their worlds. The assumption is that the semantic fields of language contain the natives' worldview and that what people do is related to what they think. This perspective treats organizations communicatively by focusing on language as a route to thought patterns that are maintained through communication.

Increasingly more researchers are applying a cognitive perspective to the study of organizations (Bougon, Weick, & Binkhorst, 1977; Donnellon, Gray, & Bougon, 1986; Gioia, 1986; Gray, Bougon, & Donnellon, 1985; Gregory, 1983; Harris & Cronen, 1979; Huff, 1983; Morey & Luthans, 1984; Shrivastava & Mitroff, 1983; Weick & Bougon, 1986). Researchers view organizations as "knowledge systems," similar to how anthropologists Spradley (1979) and Goodenough (1971) conceive culture. Research from this perspective questions: What are the rules or scripts that guide action? How do people make sense of their situation and how does this sense-making facilitate or hinder coordinated action?

Schall (1983) adopts this perspective in her study of the communication rules that govern power and influence behaviors in two work groups of an investment services corporation. She engages the organizational members in cycles of data collection, interpretation, and reflection about how they enact their organization realities and how their communication rules influence behavior. Akin and Hopelain (1986) frame their research as learning the rules that insiders routinely use to organize their activity and to understand others. They emphasize that this perspective requires spending time with people and observing and documenting how they work. They aim to find the "culture of productivity" among acknowledged high-performing groups by tapping into the concept of "workscape"—the image enacted by workers' actions to affirm what they know is the right thing to do.

Gregory's (1983) study of how Silicon Valley technical professionals understand their careers also departs from functionalist assumptions. She voices an interpretivist's position by criticizing researchers who restrict their vision of culture to the "informal merely social or symbolic side of corporate life" (p. 359). All aspects of corporate experience, including technical ones, are subject to cultural analysis because they are part of a worldview. Gregory, an anthropologist, urges us to consider the corporate world as wondrous, strange, and exotic; and as full of specialized meanings and significance as a remote village on the other side of the Himalayas. In a sense, Gregory is arguing that organization researchers bring an anthropological attitude to the corporate world; they should not take things for granted but instead should maintain an attitude of openness and questioning.

This is much the same stance that ethnomethodologists take toward the patterns of everyday life—making the familiar strange so that everyday routines become the subject of intellectual scrutiny (Sypher et al., 1985). But this attitude is difficult to maintain in one's own surroundings; we tend to be blind to our own cultural understandings. This may account in part for why management theorists doing culture work in corporations adopt restricted views of culture. They look for specialized language or readily identifiable stories instead of the all-pervasive systems of understanding that they themselves share and help create.

Organizational Symbolism—Culture
as Patterns of Discourse

Some anthropologists treat societies or cultures as systems of shared symbols and meanings. They see the anthropologist's task as interpreting the "themes" of culture—those explicit or implicit understandings that underlie cultural activity. To achieve this goal, anthropologists demonstrate how symbols are intertwined in meaningful relationships and how they emanate from the activities of people in a particular setting (Smircich, 1983a). Organizational culture researchers who adopt this perspective frequently embrace the works of anthropologist Clifford Geertz (1973) as a model. However, there are few published accounts in organization studies that carry through with this approach to fieldwork.

When this perspective is applied to organizational analysis, an organization, like a culture, is conceived of as a pattern of symbolic discourse that needs interpreting, deciphering, or reading in order to be understood. Research from this perspective provides vivid descriptive accounts of organizational life, linking meaning to actions. It usually involves the researcher in periods of participant-observation aimed at gathering evidence to piece together a multifaceted and complex picture of symbol systems and their associated meanings. The researcher is also concerned with articulating the recurrent themes that specify the links among values, beliefs, and action in an organization. Additionally this research perspective is distinguished by its attention to the interplay of actions within corporations and the cultural symbols of the broader society.

Following a symbolic approach some researchers treat leadership as the management of meaning (Smircich & Morgan, 1982) or as a cultural performance (Trujillo, 1983, 1985). Other researchers look at the symbolic dynamics of organizational life (Boland & Hoffman, 1983; Smircich, 1983b). For example, Rosen (1985) focuses on the symbolism of an advertising agency's annual breakfast in a luxurious Philadelphia hotel. In surroundings of finery, formality, and food, a dramatic enactment of "communitas" occurs. Executives give pep talks, they tell jokes to the troops, seniority is venerated, and employees are urged to support the United Way a few minutes before they are told of a salary freeze. Rosen sees the ceremony as a social drama, an instrument through which the social order is reinforced and political control sustained. Each part of the dramatic performance of the breakfast rationalizes bureaucracy and neutralizes the stratification of roles, prestige, and remuneration. Culture becomes the terrain of consciousness resting on a foundation of contest and struggle. Management's efforts to exert control and to transmit feelings of harmony, unity, continuity, and order require extraordinary effort; thus culture is "built on the edge of chaos" (Rosen 1985, p. 48).

Rosen's work differs from Trice and Beyer's (1984a, 1984b) approach to the topic of culture. Rosen sees the corporate breakfast as an occasion to reenact and naturalize power differences; Trice and Beyer would see it as a rite of integration. Like those who research corporate culture from a functionalist perspective, Rosen (1985) also sees cultural performances as enabling control, yet he does not reflect a managerial bias. His writing approaches what Stablein and Nord (1985) note is mostly lacking in the organizational symbolism literature, the emancipatory interest. That is, Rosen questions the ideological positions behind the display of enthusiasm and unity to provide a nonmanagerially aligned view of the situation.

Scholars may debate how well Rosen (1985) has succeeded in pursuing the emancipatory interest. However, this question applies to all academicians who gain access to private corporations, who must maintain acceptability to continue their presence on the scene, and who publish their findings in academic journals with an elite readership. We could argue that "true" emancipatory research requires emancipatory change for both *researchers* and the *researched*. Nonetheless, going as far as he did with a critical view marks Rosen as an exception to the norm in the management literature.

Thompson (1983), a sociologist, went even further. He reports on his work in a slaughterhouse and documents the workers' interactions as they cope with danger, strain, and monotony, and as they develop consumer spending norms that trap them in undesirable jobs. He observes how the workers maintain their sanity and worth as human beings in spite of seemingly impossible work situations. Nonverbal gestures are the primary form of communication (for example, knives are beat against tubs used in the plant to communicate time). These gestures symbolize efforts to regain the control that management took from the workers by refusing to install a clock in the work area. Thompson's writing shows how symbols can mobilize the energies of workers in ways that management never planned.

There is actually a dual focus in Thompson's work: an interpretivist concern for the social construction of reality at the plant (Sypher et al., 1985) and an emancipatory concern for the development of false consciousness (Stablein & Nord, 1985). The work reveals an occupational culture that outsiders would regard as dirty and demeaning; it also criticizes society for creating dehumanizing jobs and placing undue value on material goods and property.

In contrast to the optimism and promise in most corporate culture work, Thompson's (1983) message is pessimistic. The workers cope with the domination of the production line and the work setting through their symbolic gestures to gain control, but these efforts (for example, banging tubs to communicate) cannot free them from oppressive jobs. They may transcend the limits of the shop floor, but they end up prisoners of their inability to escape the alienation of a consumer society. Their workplace becomes a trap within a trap.

Ingersoll and Adams (1983) start from the premise that organizations are embedded in a symbolic environment that provides the "raw material" from which organizational symbols develop. Their research seeks to uncover the belief systems or meta-myths that are "situated behind" organizational and managerial practices. Based on samples of literature drawn from business periodicals, management textbooks, and executive biographies, they conclude that the managerial literature is antimythical. It denies myth any status as a form of knowledge. Instead it celebrates rationality through its belief that there is overriding good in the rationalized ordering of activities. Ingersoll and Adams argue that this emphasis on rationality appears in the mass media of the macroculture, in publications of the academic subculture, in consulting and teaching practices, and in understandings of what managers must do in order to succeed. Ingersoll and Adams do not argue that the emphasis on rationality is an accurate portrayal of managerial life; nor do they argue that it should be changed. Instead they are describing a piece of the symbolic landscape to us as participants, creators, and victims of managerial meta-myths. They ask us to turn the research enterprise back on ourselves and to question, "What does it mean?"

Unconscious Processes and Organization—Culture as a Reflection of Mind's Unconscious Operations

Researchers also conceive of culture as expressions of unconscious psychological processes, a view that forms the foundation of structural anthropology (Levi-Strauss, 1963). It also appears in the work of organization theorists who espouse psychodynamic approaches to organizational analysis (Gemmill, 1982; Mitroff, 1982, 1983; Walter, 1982; White & McSwain, 1983). This perspective understands organizational forms and practices as projections of unconscious processes, to be analyzed through the interplay between out-of-awareness processes and their conscious manifestation (Smircich, 1983a). This research may not be recognizable as part of the organizational culture literature and it is comparatively underdeveloped.

What distinguishes this orientation from the psychoanalytic perspective of Kets de Vries and Miller (1986) and Diamond and Allcorn (1984) mentioned in the corporate culture theme is the way an organization is conceptualized. In corporate culture, organizations are places in which personality dynamics (neurotic or otherwise) are acted out. In the unconscious processes theme, all cultural manifestations, including organizations, are seen as displays of unconscious dynamics. The purpose of a cultural study is to reveal the hidden universal dimensions of the human mind. Differernt from the ethnoscience position described above, taking this perspective means that the organizational analyst needs to penetrate beneath the surface level of appearance and to uncover the objective foundations of social arrangements (Deetz & Kersten, 1983; Lucas, 1987).

For example, Smith and Simmons (1983) argue that to understand an organization, it is necessary to enter the system of collective symbolizing that surfaces from organizational members. This collective symbolizing takes the form of meta-metaphors (that is, individual metaphors combined in a particular manner within a context). Myths, fairy tales, and legends are meta-metaphors "that provide clues to the inner links that exist among the basic metaphors that have been mapped into existential contexts to give meaning" (Smith & Simmons, 1983, p. 387). To illustrate these ideas, they present a case study that explores the emergent symbology of a group that plays out a fairy tale (Rumpelstiltskin) while involved in a series of conflicts related to the establishment of their organization.

With a focus on stories or fantasy themes that "spin-out" in groups, Bormann, Pratt, and Putnam (1978) track the development of a female-dominated organizational culture. They conclude that black widow spider fantasies and "mother complex" stories reflect the unconscious oppression that males felt due to the dominant female leadership in the organization. Societal and organizational norms that espouse equal opportunity preclude open rebellion; yet the males deeply resent female control of organizational life.

Broms and Gahmberg (1983) contend that strategic plans are organizational mantras. A strategic plan consists of an image or array of pictures that an organization has of itself. The planning process becomes a chanting or repeating of a mantra in which the organization talks to itself thereby enhancing its image of itself. Mitroff's work (1982, 1983) integrates the psychodynamic theories of Freud and Jung into organization theory. He employs the concept of organizational stakeholder to refer to the psyche, what Jung (1923) called archetypes. Stakeholders are like characters or personages that represent different emotional qualities. Top managers need to deal with stakeholders that are both external and internal to their organizations. This conceptualization of archetype personages provides a fundamentally different way to discuss emotional aspects of corporate life.

The Many Voices and Silences of the
Organizational Culture Literature

Throughout this review we have confronted not only different conceptions of organizational culture but also diverse viewpoints (for example, the natives' versus the researchers' versus the multinationals' point of view) and different purposes for the research (for example, description, emancipation, critique of organizational practices). In effect *the organizational culture literature is full of competing and often incompatible views.* Functionalist, interpretive, and critical voices are all speaking at the same time. It resembles what Burrell and Morgan (1979) would call paradigm wars.

More specifically, Ouchi and Wilkins (1985) describe the proliferation of organizational culture research as a confrontation or a struggle between the dominant view in organizational research (that is, the power holders and their multivariate statistics) and those who advocate naturalistic views of organizational life. They contend that the study of organizations grows through the presence of intellectual tensions that yield theses and antitheses. They believe conflict and confrontation accompanying the interest in culture are essential for good research; dissensus and creativity go together in the pendulum swings of the field.

Sypher et al. (1985), in contrast, see the variations in cultural literature more benignly. Although they advocate interpretive approaches to cultural research, they also urge their colleagues to incorporate the scientific goals of generalizability and replicability into the density and detail of their interpretive analyses. They fail to acknowledge the conflict and incompatibility of these positions; that is, this request places them in opposition to assumptions that underlie the interpretivist position, namely, the belief that "knowledge" of a particular group, even "science," is a social construction.

Stablein and Nord (1985) recognize the confrontation in the cultural literature as more than a struggle between the dominant view and the naturalistic perspective. They emphasize the "silent" confronter, *the unpublished*, as the unacceptable critical view, one that is mostly unrepresented in the organizational symbolism literature.

Ouchi and Wilkins (1985) were very perceptive when they acknowledged the confrontation between the dominant "scientific" view and the more naturalistic perspective. But we see the contest representing more than pendulum swings and paradigm wars within a particular discipline. The organizational culture literature reflects the wider cultural movements in which it is embedded. Thus even the trends that indicate the conditions of possibility for the culture literature are part of the historical situation that must be understood.

THE WIDER CULTURAL CONTEXT: THE POSTMODERN ERA

At present many of the human sciences are characterized by turmoil. The hope for unified fields and accumulated knowledge in each of them has given way to the discomfort provoked by competing views and unresolved differences. This situation can be described as one where "master discourses" are contested by fragmented voices and one where hegemony is constantly questioned (for example, Campbell, 1986).

This situation signals a different historical condition: the movement from the modern to the postmodern (Arac, 1986; Foster, 1983; Huyssen, 1984; Jackson & Carter, 1986; Lyotard, 1984). This condition is spreading across the human sciences and disciplinary borders in a form that amalgamates discourses that were previously separate. In our view, it is necessary to understand the organizational culture literature against the wider historical context of the postmodern era.

The Modernist Challenge: Organizational Culture Literature as Opposition

The notion of "opposition" is central to the labeling of events or activities as "modern." For example, in the fine arts a modernist reaction was the rise of impressionism, cubism, surrealism, and abstract expressionism as ways to counter established forms of representing reality. The idea of opposition applies to other forms of human expression as well (Jameson, 1984; Lyotard, 1984; Rorty, 1979). To summarize, we can say that modernism refers to activities that present an opposition to dominant versions of what is "true" or "good." The problem of modernity is that at some point its opposition (its "less truthful truth") becomes incorporated into the dominant "truth." Thus it is unable to be in opposition anymore. *We argue that the organizational culture literature represents the advent of high modernity in the management field, as an opposition to the "dominant discourse" of positivist/functionalist views in organization theory and research.*

This view goes back to other manifestations, not explicitly "organizational culture" [for example, Burrell & Morgan (1979), Morgan (1980), Morgan & Smircich (1980), Perrow (1981), Pondy & Boje (1975), Pondy & Mitroff (1979)]. Most of these publications are distinguished by their opposition to the "mainstream views" of contemporary social science and their search for better models. At the same time, the possibility of oppositional views was fueled by Kuhn's (1962) widely read "paradigms revolution" and by Berger and Luckmann's (1967) "social construction of reality" view. The "jump" into culture could be understood as a natural outgrowth of these oppositional positions.

However, not all the organizational culture literature is involved in this movement. The first of the five themes, *comparative management*, is not an oppositional type of culture literature. This theme is closely related to post-World War II industrial recovery and to the major role that private and public interests have given to multinational corporations (then called "international business"). Cross-cultural organizational literature has always been and still is "at the service" of traditional functionalist organizational research. Because of its close relations with the practitioners' world, it often shows an even more pragmatic orientation than other organizational research (see, for example, Adler, 1982; Heller & Wilpert, 1981).

The jump into oppositional views, then, begins with the other four themes—a movement inspired by developments in interpretive anthropology that grew during the 1960s and 1970s from the conjunction of Parsonian and Weberian sociology, phenomenology, hermeneutics, structuralism, semiotics, and the Frankfort school of critical theory. They oppose traditional "etic" anthropological approaches with an "emic" approach to culture (Marcus & Fischer, 1986; Pike, 1967). Interpretive anthropology provides new theoretical resources to elicit the natives' point of view and to interpret how different cultural constructions of reality affect social action. This movement, with Clifford Geertz (1973) as its best-known proponent, opposes the positivist vision of anthropologists as "social scientists" with one highlighting their role as "cultural interpreters."

Meanwhile, at the end of the 1970s organizational theory and research was ripe for new views. The theoretical poverty of organizational research was disguised by heavy borrowing from other fields, with little acknowledgment of the borrowing, and a heavy dose of elegant empiricism and statistical wizardry. The borrowing practices, however, were somewhat paralyzed when the "host fields" made opposing philosophies more explicit in their debates. For a field that viewed itself as pragmatic and dominant in the world (look where the crowds of students are going; look whose faculty has the highest salaries), "philosophy" was a useless and foreign word. But soon there were hints of an emerging and different discourse. Many scholars in the organizational sciences were surprised to learn that their view of the world was "positivism/functionalism" and that other views with very different assumptions were beginning to rival the dominant paradigm. Soon the interpretive perspective became the opposition to functionalism, but unfortunately in many cases the debate stayed at the level of technique, confused with the controversy over qualitative versus quantitative methods.

In 1979, *Administrative Science Quarterly* dedicated an issue to qualitative methodology and Pettigrew wrote of "studying organizational cultures." On one hand, the idea of an internal organizational "culture" was not *that* new (see Allaire & Firsirotu, 1984, and Ouchi & Wilkins, 1985, for a genealogy of the use of this term). Since the early 1970s scholars had used terms from symbolic anthropology to *explain* organizational phenomena (see, for example, Mitroff & Kilmann, 1976; Pondy, 1978; Turner, 1971). On the other hand, Pettigrew's (1979) article assembled the pieces in the puzzle. Written within a European tradition accustomed to acknowledging philosophical underpinnings, this article combined the social constructionist perspective and concepts from interpretive, symbolic, and cognitive anthropology with issues in longitudinal research and qualitative methods.

At the same time, American corporations were treated to "orientalizing" discourses. Western culture's fascination with a mythical Orient, as discussed by Edward Said (1978), became very real when clothed in an "economic kimono." But Japan was an unruly subject to study in a conventional cross-cultural mode—a mode that usually aims at "telling others how to do better" and not at "learning how others *do better.*" Not only were the Japanese people different, but their organizations were also different (and more successful). Soon, a connection was made between studying the Japanese culture and studying the Japanese organization culture: theory A, B, or Z?

The "culture" article in *Business Week* ("Corporate culture: The hard-to-change values that spell success or failure," 1980) completed the process. Academia and the business world were suddenly "organizational culture" sensitive and the space between their worlds was filled with a collection of culture books (Deal & Kennedy, 1982; Ouchi, 1981; Pascale & Athos, 1981; Peters & Waterman, 1982). Sensitivity to organizational culture, however, did not imply a "paradigm change." Those who pursued the corporate culture theme stayed within positivist assumptions while using the rhetoric of "myth," "rituals," and "qualitative methods." Rather than opposing the "dominant discourses," they *extended* them for instrumental purposes of prediction and control (Barley et al., 1986). Thus the development of corporate culture was similar to the pattern found in comparative culture research.

The cognitive, symbolic, and unconscious process themes that conceptualize "culture as a root metaphor" are the *real* opposition. Here interpretivists and some critical theorists have pursued an alternative to the "dominant view." To a more naive audience this alternative has arrived, as evidenced by the *Administrative Science Quarterly* "culture issue" (Jelinek et al., 1983b) and *The Journal of Management*'s "symbolism issue" (Frost, 1985). But a less naive observer notices that few interpretivist and critical culture articles are published *outside* "special" issues. The organization culture literature that appears in major journals belongs to the corporate culture theme. Thus "organizational culture" has become dominant (absorbed into the dominant discourses) but dead. . . And what of the opposition—is it in vain?

Postmodernism: Will Organizational Culture Resist?

According to many commentators, "postmodernism" occurs when a modernist project fails. Thus if "organizational culture" represents modernism for the field of organizational research and theory, the "death" of culture indicates that this field is ready for postmodernism. Postmodernism is *resistance,* not opposition. Opposition substitutes one notion of "truth" with an incompatible alternative—for example, advocating one paradigm over another. The postmodern notion of resistance, in contrast, *suspects* and *defers* acceptance of *any* notion of "truth." Resistance means questioning the possibility of attaining truth with the view that the "possibility of attaining truth" is itself an idea, which results from an historical event where "truth or falsity" became a dominant style of thinking (Foucault, 1976; Hacking, 1982; Rorty, 1979). It involves *deconstruction* (Derrida, 1974), as in suspecting, taking apart, or deferring resolution (not as in *destruction*) of our taken-for-granted modes of thinking. Thus in more than one way postmodernism is "postparadigm" thinking.

In postmodernism the "mainstream views" are not the only ones in power anymore. These views may still be dominant, but there are other minor voices that are being heard (the ones that question, the ones in the margin, the resistance). In many ways the nondominant (oppositional) organizational culture literature still around is part of this resistance. In postmodernity, the aim of the minor voices is not to stay around until they become dominant, but *to maintain an opening from which to question the totalitarian attempts (to provide integrative, all-encompassing, worldviews that explain, and explain away, everything) of those who want to become or to stay dominant.*

Postmodernism also questions the authority invested in our categories, fields, and disciplines to determine our bases for knowledge. From this viewpoint, the development and separation of disciplines according to their "inner" logics is an arbitrary practice, mostly sustained by philosophies that are expected to develop "totalizing" and powerful discourses for explaining the world. But in a fragmented world like ours, "totalizing" views are doomed to fail. We need multiple discourses to participate in the many "language games" that we encounter.

Traditionally, the disciplinary core of each field, "the truth of the matter," is believed to be embedded in its literature. The idea of a multiplicity of interpretations (multiple realities, multiple truths) is an uneasy one for "scientific fields" that exemplify a "truth or falsity" style of thinking. Instead, "multiple interpretations" is something pursued by other disciplines, for example, literary theory. But literary theory has news for the "hard" disciplines: any word can have multiple meanings—for different persons, at different times, in different places (Barthes, 1972; Culler, 1982; De Man, 1986; Derrida, 1974; Foucault, 1976). Without implying absolute relativism, the prospect of a single interpretation becomes a very problematic assumption. The idea of multiple interpretations of reality has entered communication theory in the form of "the views of the researched subjects." If we extend the possibility of multiple interpretations to include the research writer and the research reader, we see that no one will ever have the "ultimate truth of the matter" (Astley, 1985). "Truth or falsity" (and the system of inclusion/exclusion created through disciplinary boundaries) is just a "manner of speaking."

In general, oppositional organizational literature has crossed disciplinary boundaries and recognized the contributions of other fields to enhancing our view of organizations. Unlike the mainstream organizational literature, the oppositional literature explicitly acknowledges the source of its ideas. The oppositional culture literature has brought together the discourses of communication theory, sociology, anthropology, philosophy, and linguistics, without attempting to disguise itself as another version of pragmatic organizational discourse. (Here we refer to the works cited in themes 3 to 5, as well as others; for example, Barley, 1983; Conrad, 1985; Deetz, 1985; Ebers, 1985; Evered, 1983; Gray et al., 1985; Hirsch & Andrews, 1983; Huff, 1983; Jermier, 1985; Riley, 1983; Strine & Paconowsky, 1985; Trujillo, 1985). It is a literature that has developed intellectual depth and finesse in the "field," and, consequently, has questioned and suspended the logic of the "field" itself.

To summarize, we emphasize certain themes that characterize post-modernism and draw some connections between these themes and opposi-tional (modernist) organizational culture literature. We argue further that there is another way for this "organizational culture literature" to be understood: *as resistance.* In a sense Ouchi and Wilkins's (1985) analysis of the organizational culture literature as reflecting cycles or swings of a pendulum in which qualitative and quantitative discourses "take turns" or become fashionable, is an understanding heralding under its good will and neutrality the revengeful return of "rigorous scientific organizational research" and the definitive death of oppositional organizational culture literature. But the pendulum will swing to the opposite side only if there *is* an opposite side. The pendulum cannot swing if its movement is *resisted, deferred,* or *suspended rather than opposed.* How is resistance achieved? The issue of *representation* is the site for a lasting attempt at resistance. It points to the ways our work in the organizational disciplines can take a different shape.

POSTMODERNISM, REPRESENTATION, AND CULTURE

Developments in poststructuralism and literary theory (for instance, Derrida's deconstruction, 1974; Foucault's archeology of knowledge, 1976; Barthes's mythologies, 1972) lead to several conclusions. First, if "words" do not necessarily have a fixed meaning, they can be separated from the "things" that they are supposed to represent (that they are *more* than any specific object that they represent); second, even if they had fixed meanings, "words" are different "things"—they have separate identities— from "anything" that they signify. This applies to any sign (which we call "words") that we use to represent anything—be it printed words, sounds, paintings, numbers, photo-graphs, or gestures. Furthermore, the world we know *is* representations we have made and make of it.

A representation is that which stands for something else. To represent is to transform one thing into another through which it can be known; for example, a research project in which one notion of reality (that is, "the world out there") is transformed into another (that is, a written journal article). In any research project, especially those of the empirical variety, there are countless representa-tional transformations that move from the "original idea for the project" to the most recent reader of "the journal article." Representation is also "power to speak in the name of," as when researchers speak as scientific experts in the description of organizational conditions.

In traditional organizational research, representation is not recognized as a problem. The guiding belief is that as long as the correct research techniques and procedures are employed there should not be any problem in capturing the "real world," getting it into a research project, and having other people see it the same way that the researcher sees it. The issues of representation are reduced to problems of technique and to conventions for presenting scientific findings.

Researchers working from interpretivist/social constructionist assumptions acknowledge the problems of representation more readily than traditional researchers. But they address these problems through a "contextualizing strategy," for example, by describing the social/local grounds of that organizational site as experienced by the researcher. This strategy draws its authority and credibility from the presence and experience of the researcher, as opposed to traditional research that draws its authority and credibility from following the conventions of scientific practice in the selection and application of techniques and in the presentation of findings (Calás & Smircich, in press). But the social constructionist does not ask, How is "contextualizing" possible? And how does contextualizing reproduce "reality?" These are central problems that postmodernism highlights through awareness of the "poetic" and "political" dimensions of these questions.

The issue of representation is present in the "paradigm wars," concealed within the modernist oppositional debates. Most organizational theorizing and researching deals with a thematic of presence in its debates about ontology, epistemology, and methodology. Its concerns are with the appropriate ways to approach and apprehend the phenomena *about which* one makes a discourse.

But theorizing of *representing* focuses on a "thematic of absence." That is, it concerns the ways to evoke and maintain *an illusion as a phenomena:* words on a page as organizational realities. With these concerns postmodernism questions the dictums of positivism/empiricism and also phenomenology, which privilege *sensed and experienced presence as reality.* In postmodernism *reality is in the playfulness of presence and absence.* An example may shed some light on this issue.

Imagine that a painter wants to convey a realist image of a "typical object in a room." Her choice is a vase full of roses. Her mastery allows her to paint an image "so real that you can almost smell the roses." She has done a wonderful job of apprehending and representing reality!

Through postmodernist analyses, we understand this situation somewhat differently. The "realist" tradition in painting, which predetermines what is an appropriate subject/object (for example, "real" flowers versus an impressionist bridge, a surrealist "blob," or a "pop" can of soup), shapes the artist's decision to paint typical objects in a room and her choice of a vase of flowers. She uses her mastery to transform a three-dimensional object to a two-dimensional space. Her transformation has to be as close to *reality* as possible; the value of the painting resides in how much it resembles "reality."

But examination of the picture as a painting rather than "as a vase of roses" reveals that it is not "like reality" at all; that is, it's not like the vase of roses that modeled for the painting. Rather, it is flat; it only shows those color differences that are synthetic fictions of light and shadow; and there is no smell of roses. Besides, reality has another context in time and space (the room where the vase is painted, the time when it is painted, and the artist's presence). We could, then, treat this painting not as a representation of reality, but as a present-action of itself or as an allegory/evocation of something else. There are many aspects of reality in the trajectory of this painting that are not evoked in it. Looking at the painting in this way, it becomes a text "to be read," full of indeterminancies. There is much more to the painting than "being like reality."

Another example from a later artistic moment is a collage/montage of real objects pasted together inside a frame—a nice textural arrangement that consists of a cut-up from the *New York Times*, a piece of string, some colored pink and blue cloth, and two soda bottle caps. Each article is a "real whatever." This art piece should be more real than the previous one if we consider the reality of the objects in the composition. Moreover, its title is "Cut-up from the *NYT*, with a Piece of String, Some Colored Cloth, Pink and Blue, and Two Bottle Caps." We may feel some uneasiness. Is it art or is it trash? But, must we see it any differently from the previous example? From a textual point of view, it is as indeterminant as the previous one, except that it "hides" it differently. But, then, in what world is the viewer of a painting participating? Evoked past presence? Present presence? Is evoked past absence, present presence?

How do the problems of representation relate to the organizational culture literature and to maintaining postmodernist resistance in organizational research and theory? Our discussion of roses and bottle caps shows the complexities involved in appreciating and evaluating the worlds we are creating. These complexities have as much to do with "what is seen" as with "how the seeing is done." For us, any literature is as indeterminate as roses and bottle caps. Its meaningfulness stands on the playfulness of presence and absence. Thus appreciating and evaluating the complexities of the organizational culture literature lies in treating it like framed roses and bottle caps.

Reading Our Literature Differently

Traditionally, readings of organizational theory and research focus on the appropriateness of "the model," "the data gathered," and "the results attained." These emphases demonstrate how "science" approaches "reality" to "accumulate knowledge." Oppositional organizational literature questions the paradigmatic assumptions behind these criteria for appropriateness, but its "reality" is still separated from its reconstitution and representation. From a postmodernist point of view, however, if one positions "reality" in representation then the focus of our readings will be different. The first question will be the mastery of effects used in the texts to evoke "presence" in "absence." The second question focuses on the "tradition" (ideology) behind those evocations and the third centers on what kind of world we are constructing with these texts.

The possibility of conducting these readings in organizational theory and research is strengthened by "catching up" with current anthropological writings. Anthropology again is a model for opening new grounds in the organizational literature, this time in a very different context. In a series of related essays, a distinguished group of scholars (Clifford & Marcus, 1986; Marcus & Fisher, 1986; Sass, 1986) recognize the textual practices of "writing culture." These essays explore how ethnography is "just" textutal representations; how ethnographic writing creates fictions in the same sense of "something made or fashioned" by exclusion and rhetoric. (The same can be said for organizational research, whether it occurs in the laboratory or the field.) These anthropologists question not only the social construction of their "scientific" practice but also the textual and political nature of their main research productions. The wide scope of intellectual currents with which they work to critique their own practices reaches a desirable moment of resistance: writing culture as cultured readings of their own written "culture." Similar tasks await organizational researchers.

Let us illustrate what we mean by examining the abstracts and final lines of two recent works on organizational culture (see Table 8.2).

These articles are very different pieces in form and content (Jermier's was published in a special issue, of course!). Which is more real? More truthful? Harris and Sutton's evocation of "reality" in six organizations? Jermier's creation: a dreaming/awake Mike Armstrong? The economic value of Friday beer busts? The meaning of alienation at work?

In reading the abstracts *from the perspective of traditional organizational literature*, respect will be paid to the first article, which uses a cultural perspective to propose generalizations about organizational ceremonies and their psychological and economic values. Science is advanced here. From this viewpoint the second article is an aberration. It is an invented tale, written as a short story with no real data. Its "communist" plot dares to question sacred approaches, developed for the well-being of organizations and their members.

A reading of these abstracts *from an oppositional (modernist) point of view* differs from the traditionalist perspective. The first article combines contradictory assumptions from functionalist and interpretive approaches. The "view from the outside," which guided the project with detailed a priori theoretical categories (despite explicit statements to the contrary), advances a theory of organizational parting ceremonies that can be generalized. However, it overlooks the particular and discrete meanings that these activities have for organizational members in different organizations. It is a clear example of organizational culture literature absorbed by the "dominant discourses."

TABLE 8.2
Abstracts, Final Lines

Abstracts

This paper advances a theory about the functions that parting ceremonies serve for members displaced by organizational deaths. The theory is grounded in data from 11 parties, picnics, and dinners that occurred in six dying organizations. We propose that parting ceremonies create settings in which people can exchange emotional support and can edit self, social system, and event schemata. We also assert that such gatherings provide opportunities for managers to influence the course of organizational demise. (Harris & Sutton, 1986, p. 5).

This is a short story about the two minds of Mike Armstrong, Dialectical Marxist Theory's romantic "everyman" and Critical Theory "anti-hero." The story contrasts day and night versions of Armstrong's worklife as a skilled operator in the control room of a large phosphate plant located in Tampa, Florida. The two versions are presented to illustrate theoretical descriptions of psychic processes engaged when human actors confront an alien world and make sense of it. Alternative forms of subjective alienation, reified consciousness (drawn from Critical Theory), and reflective militancy (drawn from Dialectical Marxism) are developed as deep psychic states through which meaning is constructed in the world. It is proposed that subjective alienation is shaped by mythical forces in the broader symbolic environment and that it profoundly conditions actions and attitudes. Its importance in understanding organizational behavior and the practice of humanistic management is discussed in terms of human meaning-making processes. (Jermier, 1985, p. 67).

Final Lines

This perspective suggests that subsequent theory-building and testing should explore the opportunities and hazards that formal ceremonies hold for the well-being of organizations and their members. Only in this way can we begin to assess the psychological and economic value of Friday beer busts, Christmas parties, sales conventions, and annual company picnics. (Harris & Sutton, 1986, p. 27)

In this study, class-based workplace dynamics have been dramatized in relation to divergent forms of alienated consciousness to illustrate the importance of human meaning-making processes in understanding organizational behavior. Further theoretical analysis and research will clarify and assess the realism of these alternative viewpoints in the meaning of alienation in work. (Jermier, 1985, p. 67).

The second article compares the assumptions of two radical paradigms. Consistent with these paradigms, it proposes political approaches to "reality" and it challenges the status quo with critical views. The novelty of presenting a theoretical piece in the form of a short story provides an interesting illustration of critical issues as well as a concrete example for clarifying radical theoretical perspectives.

From the viewpoint of postmodernism of resistance, both pieces are interesting fictions. The first article parallels the "realistic" tradition. Its mastery of effects resides in how well it works to shock the reader with the "death" metaphor, while at the same time maintaining the illusion of dealing with difficult moments in "real" organizations. It announces its relevance for "the real world" at the end when it comments upon the contribution that it can make to an individual's psychological well-being and to an organization's economic well-being. The second piece is less "realist" since it makes clear that it is "a short story" with no claims of "real" data. It is similar to the collage/montage in our previous example, that is, the "Cut-up from the *NYT*," which announces itself as "itself" in the title. This article announces itself as "a short story." The article presents a collage of generic issues in a consumer society that are seldom acknowledged as important in organizational life. But the article also recognized the difficulty of its position in an organizational world made up of realist texts. In its last sentence it says "further theoretical analysis and research will clarify and assess *the realism* (our emphasis) of these alternative viewpoints."

And Now What Do We Do?

For those of us engaged in organizational research, seeking "truth" has given meaning to what we do. Upon encountering our chapter one may ask, Does it imply that research will be meaningless, for there is no "truth" anyway? If it is all just representations, why bother?

From a postmodernist perspective, the issue of representation in organizational research does not necessarily require a change of style in the research approach. What it requires is the questioning of the research approach as style. Such questioning leads us to enter the postmodern era by addressing the pragmatics, poetics, politics, and ethics of organizational research and theory. Questioning any representation, for example, a journal article, means examining what it does (that is, advance knowledge), how it is said (for instance, the conventions of writing science), who can or should say it (for example, the veteran versus the "novice") and what ideological message it sustains (for instance, the manager's views are privileged over that of other organizational members). These explorations produce disquieting effects over any claim to single straightforward meanings to advance instead the possibility of other meanings.

Thus if we are constituting our world in texts, our resistance to those texts that want to submerge us in a tradition no longer ours has to come not just from "oppositional writings" but from "deconstructive readings"—not just from "organizational culture writings" but from "cultured organizational readings." Cultured organizational readings are those readings that expose and make explicit the representational stratagems ("traditions and effects") in the fictions we call "organizational theory and research"—those readings that allow us to see "scientific discourses" as *just one style of thinking and saying*.

Our readings of Harris and Sutton (1986) and of Jermier (1985) are illustrative of such "postmodernist criticism." They point to the importance of understanding our literature as a cultural practice. Readings such as ours are meta-commentaries (writings) on any text, regardless of field or tradition. They are political statements in their critiques of cultural representation and in their aim to resist the privileging of any representational form as more "truthful." Thus they are representations of representations. They constitute the realm of "textual theory" and "function not as demonstrations within the parameters of a discipline but as redescriptions which challenge disciplinary boundaries ... [and have] the power to make strange the familiar and to make readers conceive of their own thinking, behavior and institutions in new ways . . . [and] their force comes. . .not from the accepted procedures of a particular discipline but from the persuasive novelty of their redescriptions" (Culler, 1982, p. 9).

Few works in organizational research and theory are this type of writing. Some attempt it (for example, Alvesson, 1985; Calás, 1987; Calás & Smircich, in press; Degot, 1985; Stubbart, 1986) by crossing disciplinary boundaries and by situating their critiques of organizational discourses in the wide cultural space of "the world." For our participation in the *postmodernism of resistance depends on our ability to have a much wider and cultured view of the world*, or our ability to see ourselves as participants in the making of this world, and or our ability to speak "culturally" in the multiple voices of "the other participant's" discourse. It means not privileging one form of reading and saying over another. Postmodernism of resistance questions one's own and others' discursive strongholds. It is creating the critical "writing in the margin" of every writing that wants to "center itself on the page."

POSTCULTURE: CULTURED ORGANIZATIONAL LITERATURE AS POSTMODERNIST CRITICISM

In our chapter we have been trying to represent, to create, an illusion of opportunity for the organizational culture literature. Our rhetoric went like this: To the extent that "culture" has been appropriated, incorporated, into the positivist or technical interest—made part of the "traditional organiza-tional literature"—the organizational culture literature may have become dominant but it is dead. Its impetus was as a fresh perspective with which to counter the dry and overly rational forms of theorizing about organizations. Now, organizational culture is *part* of the traditional organizational literature. Its language (myths, stories, rites) has been turned into a fad by traditional approaches in organizational theory and research, which uses its "soft" rhetoric to convey an image of cultural refinement. This chapter argues that interpretive organizational culture literature can be understood as an oppositional/modernist movement in organizational theory and that it has failed to gain any major grounds in its oppositional stance.

How can we regain "culture" for organizational studies? And why would we want to do that? Our answer is to locate the organizational culture literature in a wider historical debate that is taking place in the Western world; a debate that not only opposes traditions but one that questions the very logic and politics of calling something "a tradition"; a debate that conceives of the world as made up in discourses, in textual representations. That debate is the transition from modernism to postmodernism.

We recognize the major contributions of oppositional organizational culture literature, in both its *modern moments and as it stands today in the margins*. As a failed modernist project, its death fulfilled a nascent post-modernity. By creating discourses with which it failed at a strong oppositional movement, it created the conditions of possibility for a postmodernism of resistance. These discourses prompted us to learn more, to become more cultured, and to resist entanglements in disciplinary boundaries. These discourses have enabled us to write this chapter.

The transformation of the organizational culture literature into the *cultured organizational literature* suggests a postmodernism of resistance for organizational theorizing. It will center on issues of representation, pursuing the critical readings of these activities and in a never ending deconstruction of their claims. Thus the organizational culture literature may be "dead" as a revolutionary movement but its traces point to new forms for our work and new tasks for ourselves. "Culture" researchers can examine and question their contexts, instead of providing answers. With these assertions, we close in a postmodernist mode: We ask you the reader to deconstruct this text.

NOTE

1. The *Organizational Symbolism and Culture Newsletter* is edited by Kelley Ott, College of St. Catherine, St. Paul, MN 55105. The other, *Note-Work*, is sponsored by the Standing Conference on Organizational Symbolism and is edited by Antonio Strati, Dipartimento di Politica Sociale, Università degli Studi di Trento, Via Verdi, 26, 38100, Trento, Italy.

REFERENCES

Adler, N. J. (1982). *Understanding the ways of understanding: Cross-cultural management methodology reviewed.* Unpublished manuscript, McGill University, Montreal.

Akin, G., & Hopelain, D. (1986). Finding the culture of productivity. *Organizational Dynamics, 14*(3), 19-32.

Allaire, Y., & Firsirotu, M. E. (1984). Theories of organizational culture. *Organization Studies, 5,* 193-226.

Alvesson, M. (1985). Organizations, image and substance: Some aspects on cultural context of cultural management research. *Dragon,* (2), 45-55.

Arac, J. (Ed.). (1986). *Postmodernism and politics.* Minneapolis: University of Minnesota Press.

Astley, W. G. (1985). Administration science as socially constructed truth. *Administrative Science Quarterly, 30,* 497-513.

Barley, S. R. (1983). Semiotics and the study of occupational and organizational cultures. *Administrative Science Quarterly, 28,* 393-413.

Barley, S. R., Meyer, G. W., & Gash, D. C. (1986, June). *Up against the wall of control: A sociological analysis of the pragmatics of "organizational culture."* Paper presented at the International Conference on Organizational Symbolism, Montreal.

Barney, J. B. (1986). Organizational culture: Can it be a source of sustained competitive advantage? *Academy of Management Review, 11,* 656-665.

Barrett, G., & Bass, B. (1970). Comparative surveys of managerial attitudes and behavior. In J. Boddewyn (Ed.), *Comparative management: Teaching, training, and research* (pp. 179-212). New York: Graduate School of Business Administration, New York University.

Barthes, R. (1972). *Mythologies.* New York: Hill & Wang.

Berger, P. L., & Luckmann, T. (1967). *The social construction of reality.* Garden City, NY: Anchor Books.

Bhagat, R. S., & McQuaid, S. J. (1982). Role of subjective culture in organizations: A review and directions for future research. *Journal of Applied Psychology, 67,* 653-685.

Boje, D. M., Fedor, D. B., & Rowland, K. M. (1982). Myth making: A qualitative step in OD interventions. *Journal of Applied Behavioral Science, 18,* 17-28.

Boland, R. J., & Hoffman, R. (1983). Humor in a machine shop: An interpretation of symbolic action. In L. R. Pondy, P. J. Frost, A. Morgan, & T. C. Dandridge (Eds.), *Organizational symbolism* (pp. 187-198). Greenwich, CT: JAI Press.

Bormann, E. G., Pratt, J., & Putnam, L. (1978). Power, authority, and sex: Male response to female leadership. *Communication Monographs, 45,* 119-155.

Bougon, M., Weick, K. E., & Binkhorst, D. (1977). Cognition in organizations: An analysis of the Utrecht Jazz Orchestra. *Administrative Science Quarterly, 22,* 606-639.

Broms, H., & Gahmberg, H. (1983). Communication to self in organizations and cultures. *Administrative Science Quarterly, 28,* 482-495.

Brown, R. H. (1977). *A poetic for sociology.* New York: Cambridge University Press.

Burrell, G., & Morgan, G. (1979). *Sociological paradigms and organizational analysis.* London: Heinemann.

Calás, M. B. (1987). *Organizational science/fiction: The postmodern in the management disciples.* Unpublished doctoral dissertation, University of Massachusetts, Amherst.

Calás, M. B., & Smircich, L. (in press). Reading leadership as a form of cultural analysis. In J. G. Hunt, D. R. Baliga, H. P. Dachler & C. A. Schriesheim (Eds.), *Emerging leadership vistas.* Lexington, MA: Lexington Books.

Campbell, C. (1986, April 25). Scholarly disciplines: Breaking out. *New York Times,* p. A18.

Changing a corporate culture. (1984, May 14). *Business Week,* pp. 130-138.

Clifford, J., & Marcus, G. E. (Eds.). (1986). *Writing culture: The poetics and politics of enthnography.* Berkeley: University of California Press.

Conrad, C. (1985). Chrysanthemums and swords: A reading of contemporary organizational theory and research. *Southern Speech Communication Journal, 50,* 189-200.

Corporate culture: The hard-to-change-values that spell success or failure. (1980, Oct. 27). *Business Week,* pp. 148-160.

Culler, J. (1982). *On deconstruction: Theory and criticism after structuralism.* Ithaca, NY: Cornell University Press.

Cummings, L. L. (1980). *Organizational behavior in the 1980s.* Unpublished manuscript, Northwestern University, Evanston, IL.

Cummings, L. L. (1984). Compensation, culture, and motivation: A systems perspective. *Organizational Dynamics, 12*(3), 33-44.

Dandridge, L. L. (1979). *Celebrations of corporate anniversaries: An example of modern organizational symbols.* Unpublished manuscript, State University of New York at Albany, New York.

Deal, T. E., & Kennedy, A. A. (1982). *Corporate cultures: The rites and rituals of corporate life.* Reading, MA: Addison-Wesley.

Deetz, S. A. (1985). Ethical considerations in cultural research in organizations. In P.J. Frost, L. F. Moore, M. R. Louis, C. C. Lundberg, & J. Martin (Eds.), *Organizational culture* (pp. 253-269). Newbury Park, CA: Sage.

Deetz, S. A., & Kersten, A. (1983). Critical models of interpretive research. In L. L. Putnam & M. E. Pacanowsky (Eds.), *Communication and organization: An interpretive approach* (pp. 147-171). Newbury Park, CA: Sage.

De Man, P. (1986). *The resistance to theory.* Minneapolis: University of Minnesota Press.

De Man, P. (1979). *Allegories of reading.* New Haven, CT: Yale University Press.

Degot, V. (1985). Some implications of the current trend towards remote referencing of corporate research papers. *Dragon (2),* 125-159.

Derrida, J. (1974). *Of grammatology.* Baltimore: Johns Hopkins University Press.

Diamond, M., & Allcorn, S. (1984). Psychological barriers to personal responsibility. *Organizational Dynamics, 12*(4), 66-77.

Donnellon, A., Gray, B., & Bougon, M. G. (1986). Communication, meaning, and organized action. *Administrative Science Quarterly, 31,* 43-55.

Ebers, M. (1985). Understanding organizations: The poetic mode. *Journal of Management, 11,* 51-62.

Evered, R. (1983). The language of organizations: The case of the navy. In L. R. Pondy, P. J. Frost, G. Morgan, & T. C. Dandridge (Eds.), *Organizational symbolism* (pp. 125-143). Greenwich, CT: JAI Press.

Evered, R., & Louis, M. R. (1981). Alternative perspectives in the organizational sciences: "Inquiry from the inside" and "Inquiry from the outside." *Academy of Management Review, 6,* 385-396.

Foster, H. (Ed.). (1983). *The anti-aesthetic: Essays on postmodern culture.* Port Townsend, WA: Bay Press.

Foucault, M. (1973). *The order of things.* New York: Vintage Books.

Foucault, M. (1976). *The archaeology of knowledge.* New York: Harper & Row.

Frost, P. J. (Ed.). (1985). Organizational symbolism [Special issue]. *Journal of Management, 11,*(2).

Frost, P. J., Moore, L. F., Louis, M. R., Lundberg, C. C., & Martin, J. (Eds.). (1985). *Organizational culture.* Newbury Park, CA: Sage.

Geertz, C. (1973). *The interpretation of cultures.* New York: Basic Books.

Geertz, C. (1983). *Local knowledge.* New York: Basic Books.

Gemmill, G. (1982, August). *Unconscious processes: The black hole in group development.* Paper presented at the meeting of the Academy of Management, New York.

Gerbner, G. (Ed.). (1983). Ferment in the field [Special issue]. *Journal of Communication, 33,*(3).

Gioia, D. A. (1986). Symbols, scripts, and sensemaking. In H. P. Sims & D. A. Gioia (Ed.), *The thinking organization* (pp. 49-74). San Francisco: Jossey-Bass.

Goodenough, W. H. (1971). *Culture, language and society.* Reading, MA: Addison-Wesley.

Gray, B., Bougon, M., & Donnellon, A. (1985). Organizations as constructions and destructions of meaning. *Journal of Management, 11,* 83-98.

Gregory, K. L. (1983). Native-view paradigms: Multiple cultures and culture conflicts in organizations. *Administrative Sciences Quarterly, 28,* 359-376.

Gronn, P. (1983). Talk as the work: The accomplishment of school administration. *Administrative Science Quarterly, 28,* 1-21.

Habermas, J. (1970). *Towards a rational society: Student protest, science and politics.* Boston: Beacon Press.

Habermas, J. (1971). *Knowledge and human interests.* Boston: Beacon Press.

Habermas, J. (1973). *Theory and practice.* Boston: Beacon Press.

Habermas, J. (1975). A postscript to knowledge and human interests. *Philosophy of the Social Sciences, 3,* 157-189.

Habermas, J. (1983). Modernity—an incomplete project. In H. Foster (Ed.), *The anti-aesthetic: Essays on postmodern culture* (pp. 3-15). Port Townsend, WA: Bay Press.

Hacking, I. (1982). Language, truth, and reason. In R. Hollis & S. Lukes (Ed.), *Rationality and relativism* (pp. 185-203). Cambridge, MA: MIT Press.

Haire, M., Ghiselli, E., & Porter, L. (1966). *Managerial thinking: An international study.* New York: John Wiley.

Harbison, F. H., & Myers, C. A. (1959). *Management in the industrial world: An international analysis.* New York: McGraw-Hill.

Harris, L., & Cronen, V. (1979). A rules-based model for the analysis and evaluation of organizational communication. *Communication Quarterly, 27*(1), 12-28.

Harris, S. G., & Sutton, R. I. (1986). Functions of parting ceremonies in dying organizations. *Academy of Management Journal, 29,* 5-30.

Hawes, L. C. (1974). Social collectivities as communication: Perspectives on organizational behavior. *Quarterly Journal of Speech, 60,* 497-502.

Heller, F. A., & Wilpert, B. (1981). *Competence and power in managerial decision-making.* New York: John Wiley.

Hirsch, P. M., & Andrews, J.A.Y. (1983). Ambushes, shootouts, and knights of the roundtable: The language of corporate takeovers. In L. R. Pondy, P. J. Frost, G. Morgan, & T. Dandridge (Eds.), *Organizational symbolism* (pp. 145-155). Greenwich, CT: JAI Press.

Hofstede, G. (1980). *Culture's consequences.* Newbury Park, CA: Sage.

Huff, A. S. (1983). A rhetorical examination of strategic change. In L. R. Pondy, P. J. Frost, G. Morgan, & T. Dandridge (Eds.), *Organizational symbolism* (pp. 167-183). Greenwich, CT: JAI Press.

Huyssen, A. (1984). Mapping the postmodern. *New German Critique,* (33), 5-52.

Ingersoll, V. H., & Adams, G. B. (1983, March). *Beyond organizational boundaries: Exploring the managerial metamyth.* Paper presented at the Organizational Folklore Conference, Los Angeles.

Jackson, N., & Carter, P. (1986). Whither SCOS—Praise and post-modernism. *Note-Work, 5*(2), 4-5.

Jameson, F. (1983). Postmodernism and consumer society. In H. Foster (Ed.), *The anti-aesthetic: Essays on postmodern culture* (pp. 111-125). Port Townsend, WA: Bay Press.

Jameson, F. (1984). Postmodernism, or the cultural logic of late capitalism. *New Left Review, 146,* 53-92.

Jelinek, M., Smircich, L., & Hirsch, P. (Eds.). (1983a). Organizational culture [Special issue]. *Administrative Science Quarterly, 28,*(3).

Jelinek, M., Smircich, L., & Hirsch, P. (1983b). Introduction: a code of many colors. Administrative Science Quarterly, 28, 331-338.

Jermier, J. M. (1985). "When the sleeper wakes": A short story extending themes in radical organization theory. *Journal of Management, 11,* 67-80.

Jung, C. G. (1923). *Psychological types.* London: Routledge & Kegan Paul.

Keichel, W. (1982, December 27). Corporate strategists under fire. *Fortune,* pp. 35-39.

Kelley, L., & Worthley, R. (1981). The role of culture in comparative management: A cross cultural perspective. *Academy of Management Journal, 24,* 164-173.

Kets de Vries, M.F.R., & Miller, D. (1985). *Neurotic organizations.* San Francisco: Jossey-Bass.

Kets de Vries, M.F.R., & Miller, D. (1986). Personality, culture, and organization. *Academy of Management Review, 11,* 266-279.

Kilmann, R., Saxton, M., & Serpa, R. (1985). *Gaining control of the corporate culture.* San Francisco: Jossey-Bass.

Kuhn, T. (1962). *The structure of scientific revolutions.* Chicago: University of Chicago Press.

Lakoff, G., & Johnson, M. (1980). *Metaphors we live by.* Chicago: University of Chicago Press.

Levi-Strauss, C. (1963). *Structural Anthropology* (C. Jacobson & B. G. Schoepf, Trans.). New York: Basic Books. (Original work published 1958)

Louis, M. R. (1980, August). *A cultural perspective on organizations: The need for the consequences of viewing organizations as culture-bearing milieux.* Paper presented at the national meetings of the Academy of Management, Detroit.

Lucas, R. (1987). Political-cultural analysis of organizations. *Academy of Management Review, 12,* 144-156.

Lyotard, J. F. (1984). *The postmodern condition: A report on knowledge.* Minneapolis: University of Minnesota Press.

Marcus, G. E., & Fischer, M.M.J. (1986). *Anthropology as cultural critique: An experimental moment in the human sciences.* Chicago: University of Chicago Press.

Martin, J., & Powers, M. E. (1983). Truth or corporate propaganda: The value of a good war story. In L. R. Pondy, P. J. Frost, G. Morgan, & T. Dandridge (Eds.), *Organizational symbolism* (pp. 93-107). Greenwich, CT: JAI Press.

Meyerson, D., & Martin, J. (1986, June). *Questioning the assumptions of value engineering: Alternative views of the cultural change process.* Paper presented at the International Conference on Organizational Symbolism, Montreal, Canada.

Mitroff, I. I. (1982, August). *Stakeholders of the mind.* Paper presented at the Academy of Management meetings, New York.

Mitroff, I. I. (1983). *Stakeholders of the organizational mind.* San Francisco: Jossey-Bass.

Mitroff, I. I., & Kilmann, R. H. (1976). On organizational stories: An approach to the design and analysis of organizations through myths and stories. In R. H. Kilmann, L. R. Pondy, & D. P. Sleven (Eds.), *The management of organization design* (Vol. 1, pp. 189-207). New York: North Holland.

Morey, N. C., & Luthans, F. (1984). An emic perspective and ethnoscience methods for organizational research. *Academy of Management Review, 9,* 27-36.

Morgan, G. (1980). Paradigms, metaphors, and puzzle solving in organizational theory. *Administrative Science Quarterly, 25,* 605-622.

Morgan, G., & Smircich, L. (1980). The case for qualitative research. *Academy of Management Review, 5,* 491-500.

Nicholson, N., & Johns, G. (1985). The absence culture and the psychological contract—who's in control of absence? *Academy of Management Review, 10,* 397-407.

Ouchi, W. G. (1981). *Theory Z.* Reading, MA: Addison-Wesley.

Ouchi, W. G., & Wilkins, A. L. (1985). Organizational culture. *Annual Review of Sociology, 11,* 457-483.

Pacanwosky, M. E., & O'Donnell-Trujillo, N. (1983). Organizational communication as cultural performance. *Communication Monographs, 50,* 126-147.

Pascale, R. T., & Athos, A. G. (1981). *The art of Japanese management.* New York: Simon & Schuster.

Perrow, C. (1981). Disintegrating social science. *New York University Educational Quarterly, 12,* 2-9.

Peters, T. J. (1978). Symbols, patterns and settings: An optimistic case for getting things done. *Organizational Dynamics, 7*(2), 3-23.

Peters, T. J., & Austin, N. (1985). *A passion for excellence.* New York: Harper & Row.

Peters, T. J., & Waterman, R. H., Jr. (1982). *In search of excellence.* New York: Harper & Row.

Pettigrew, A. M. (1979). On studying organizational cultures. *Administrative Science Quarterly, 24,* 570-581.

Pfeffer, J. (1981). Management as symbolic action: The creation and maintenance of organizational paradigms. *Research in Organizational Behavior* (Vol. 3, pp. 1-52). Greenwich, CT: JAI Press.

Pike, K. L. (1967). *Language in relation to a unified theory of the structure of human behavior* (2nd ed.). The Hague: Mouton.

Pondy, L. R. (1978). Leadership is a language game. In M. McCall & M. Lombaro (Eds.), *Leadership: Where else can we go?* (pp. 87-99). Durham, NC: Duke University Press.

Pondy, L. R., & Boje, D. M. (1975, August). *Bringing mind back in: Paradigm development as a frontier problem in organization theory.* Paper presented at the annual meeting of the American Sociological Association, San Francisco.

Pondy, L. R., Frost, P. J., Morgan, G., & Dandridge, T. C. (Eds.). (1983). *Organizational symbolism.* Greenwich, CT: JAI Press.

Pondy, L. R., & Mitroff, I. I. (1979). Beyond open systems models of organization. In L.L. Cummings & B. M. Staw (Eds.), *Research in Organizational Behavior* (Vol. 1, pp. 3-39). Greenwich, CT: JAI Press.

Putnam, L. L. (1983). The interpretive paradigm: An alternative to functionalism. In L. L. Putnam & M. E. Pacanowsky (Eds.), *Communication and Organizations: An interpretive approach* (pp. 31-54). Newbury Park, CA: Sage.

Putnam, L. L., & Cheney, G. (1985). A critical review of research traditions in organizational communication. In M. Mander (Ed.), *Communications in transition* (pp. 206-224). New York: Prager.

Putnam, L. L., & Pacanowsky, M. E. (Eds.). (1983). *Communication and organizations: An interpretive approach.* Newbury Park, CA: Sage.

Riley, P. (1983). A structurationalist account of political cultures. *Administrative Science Quarterly, 28,* 414-437.

Ronen, S., & Shenkar, O. (1985). Clustering countries on attitudinal dimensions: A review and synthesis. *Academy of Management Review, 10,* 435-454.

Rorty, R. (1979). *Philosophy and the mirror of nature.* Princeton, NJ: Princeton University Press.

Rosen, M. (1985). Breakfast at Spiro's: Dramaturgy and dominance. *Journal of Management, 11,* 31-48.

Said, E. (1978). *Orientalism.* New York: Pantheon Books.

Sass, L. A. (1986, May). Anthropology's native problems. *Harper's,* pp. 49-57.

Sathe, V. (1983). Implications of corporate culture: A manager's guide to action. *Organizational Dynamics, 12*(2), 5-23.

Sathe, V. (1985). *Culture and related corporate realities.* Homewood, IL: Richard D. Irwin.

Schall, M. S. (1983). A communication-rules approach to organizational culture. *Administrative Science Quarterly, 28,* 557-581.

Schein, E. H. (1985). *Organizational culture and leadership.* San Francisco: Jossey-Bass.

Schneider, B. (1985). Organizational behavior. In M. R. Rosenzweig & L. W. Porter (Eds.), *Annual Review of Psychology, 36,* 573-612.

Schwartz, H., & Davis, S. (1981). Matching corporate culture and business strategy. *Organizational Dynamics, 10*(1), 30-48.

Sekaran, U. (1981). Nomological networks and the understanding of organizations in different cultures. In K. H. Chung (Ed.), *Proceedings of the 41st Annual Meeting of the Academy of Management,* 54-58.

Sekaran, U. (1986). Mapping bank employees' perceptions of organizational stimuli in two countries. *Journal of Management, 12,* 19-30.

Shrivastava, P. A., & Mitroff, I. I. (1983). Frames of reference managers use: A study in applied sociology of knowledge. In R. Lamp (Ed.), *Advances in strategic management* (Vol. 1, pp. 161-180). Greenwich, CT: JAI Press.

Siehl, C., & Martin, J. (1984). The role of symbolic management: How can managers effectively transmit organizational culture? In J. G. Hunt, D. Hosking, C. Schrieshelm, & R. Stewart (Eds.), *Leaders and managers: International perspectives on managerial behavior and leadership* (pp. 227-239). New York: Pergamon.

Smircich, L. (1983a). Concepts of culture and organizational analysis. *Administrative Science Quarterly, 28,* 339-358.

Smircich, L. (1983b). Organizations as shared meanings. In L. R. Pondy, P. J. Frost, G. Morgan, & T. Dandridge (Eds.), *Organizational symbolism* (pp. 55-65). Greenwich, CT: JAI Press.

Smircich, L. (1985). Is the concept of culture a paradigm for understanding organizations and ourselves? In P. J. Frost, L. F. Moore, M. R Louis, C. C. Lundberg, & J. Martin (Eds.), *Organizational culture* (pp. 55-72). Newbury Park, CA: Sage.

Smircich, L., & Morgan, G. (1982). Leadership: The management of meaning. *Journal of Applied Behavioral Science, 18,*(3), 257-273.

Smith, K. K., & Simmons, V. M. (1983). A Rumplestiltskin organization: Metaphors on metaphors in field research. *Administrative Science Quarterly, 28,* 377-392.

Spradley, J. P. (1979). *The ethnographic interview.* New York: Holt Rhinehart & Winston.

Stablein, R., & Nord, W. (1985). Practical and emancipatory interests in organizational symbolism: A review and evaluation. *Journal of Management, 11,* 13-28.

Stonich, P. J. (1984). The performance measurement and reward system: Critical to strategic management. *Organizational Dynamics, 12*(3), 45-57.

Strine, M. S., & Pacanowsky, M. E. (1985). How to read interpretive accounts of organizational life: Narrative bases of textual authority. *Southern Speech Communication Journal, 50,* 283-297.

Stubbart, C. I. (1986). *Strategic management research in the age of anti-positive and post-positive turmoil in the social sciences: Rigor or rigor mortis?* Unpublished manuscript, University of Massachusetts, Amherst.

Sypher, B. D., Applegate, J. L., & Sypher, H. E. (1985). Culture and communication in organizational contexts. In W. B. Gudykundst, L. P. Stewart, & S. Ting-Toomey (Eds.), *Communication, culture, and organizational process* (pp. 13-29). Newbury Park, CA: Sage.

Tichy, N. M. (1982). Managing change strategically: The technical, political, and cultural keys. *Organizational Dynamics, 11*(2), 59-80.

Thompson, W. E. (1983). Hanging tongues: A sociological encounter with the assembly line. *Qualitative Sociology, 6,* 215-237.

Trice, H. M., & Beyer, J. M. (1984a). Studying organizational cultures through rites and ceremonials. *Academy of Management Review, 9,* 653-669.

Trice, H. M., & Beyer, J. M. (1984b, October). *Using rites to change corporate cultures.* Paper presented at the conference on Managing Corporate Cultures, Pittsburgh, PA.

Trujillo, N. (1983). Performing Mintzberg's roles: The nature of managerial communication. In L. L. Putnam & M. E. Pacanowsky (Eds.), *Communication and organizations: An interpretive approach* (pp. 73-79). Newbury Park, CA: Sage.

Trujillo, N. (1985). Organizational communication as cultural performance. *Southern Speech Communication Journal, 50,* 210-244.

Tunstall, W. B. (1983). Cultural transition at AT&T. *Sloan Management Review, 25*(1), 1-12.

Turner, B. A. (1971). *Exploring the industrial subculture.* London: Macmillan.

Udy, S. (1973). Cross-cultural analysis: Methods and scope. *Annual Review of Anthropology, 2,* 253-270.

Walter, G. A. (1982, August). *Beneath bureaucratic anarchies: The principle abyss.* Paper presented at the annual meeting of the Academy of Management, New York.

Weick, K. E., & Bougon, M. (1986). Organizations as cognitive maps. In H. P. Sims, Jr. & D. A. Gioia (Eds.), *The thinking organization* (pp. 102-135). San Francisco: Jossey-Bass.

White, O. R., Jr., & McSwain, C. J. (1983). Transformational theory and organizational analysis. In G. Morgan (Ed.), *Beyond method* (pp. 292-305). Newbury Park, CA: Sage.

Wilkins, A. L. (1983). The culture audit: A tool for understanding organizations. *Organizational Dynamics, 12*(2), 24-38.

Wilkins, A. L., & Ouchi, W. G. (1983). Efficient cultures: Exploring the relationship between culture and organizational performance. *Administrative Science Quarterly, 28,* 468-481.

Winkler, K. J. (1985, June 25). Questioning the science in social science: Scholars signal a "turn to interpretation." *Chronicle of Higher Education,* pp. 5-6.

9   Cross-Cultural Perspectives

HARRY C. TRIANDIS
University of Illinois

ROSITA D. ALBERT
University of Minnesota

SOME estimates in the popular press, supported by statistical studies of investments by multinationals (Adler, 1986), suggest that about 80% of what is produced in the United States in 1986 competes in an international market. A typical scenario may well be that an international team of market researchers develops the plan for a particular product by sampling public tastes and markets in a dozen countries; an international engineering team conceives of the technical plans for the production of the product; an international management team gets the resources from banks located in Zurich, London, Hong Kong, and New York, for the construction of plants in France, Brazil, Korea, and Singapore, which eventually send semifashioned products to Mexico, where the products are fitted with computer parts produced in the United States and sold by mass merchandisers in different countries. The accuracy of the specifics of this scenario is not important. The point is that we are living on spaceship earth, in a global village, that satellites and jet travel have changed the way we relate to our fellow humans, and that we are increasingly doing business on a global scale.

Within this network of relationships communication will go from *sources to audiences* and will consist of *messages* delivered through some medium (face-to-face conversation, telex, telephone). As the message travels it suffers from both lack of exact translation and loss of meaning when it is decoded in another culture. The source uses a particular cognitive framework consisting of *categories* and their *associations,* organized into *schemata* that have *affect* attached to them, forming *values, attitudes, expectations, norms, roles,* and reflecting *unstated assumptions.* These are the elements of subjective culture (Triandis, 1972) and they shape the encoding of the message. When the message gets to the other country the local elements of subjective culture shape the decoding. In some cases the message is transmitted well. If it is concrete and specific—for example, send me 1000 widgets, type Z364789—the chances are very good that the message will get there as it was intended. But as soon as the message includes more abstract, nonspecific elements, culture is likely to affect it.

In this chapter we will review what we know about cognitive frames and their elements and how such elements are likely to affect communication. Much of what will be reviewed in the earlier sections will deal with intercultural communication more generally, because many of the basic ideas concerning cognitive frames are the same regardless of setting. In later sections of the chapter we will look more specifically at organizational settings, but even here we will not be able to consider different types of organizational settings (such as multinational corporations, educational, or political organizations) separately, because of the sparseness of the literature.

In sum, the objectives of this chapter are to review the status of the literature on organizational communication that has included a cross-cultural component, and to attempt to look ahead to the research that should be undertaken during the next decade to improve our understanding of organizational communication across cultures.

DEFINITIONS

Organizational communication can take many forms. It can involve communication between two or more individuals, such as supervisors and subordinates (interpersonal communication), between groups, such as managers and workers, labor and management, or customers and marketing departments, or between organizations in different cultures, such as a head office in one country and a subsidiary in another country.

Interpersonal Versus Intergroup Communication

It is worth making a distinction between interpersonal and intergroup communication. In interpersonal communication the participants are aware of the attributes of the individuals participating in the communication, while in intergroup communication they are only aware of some collectivity that is communicating with another collectivity, for example, "the Japanese" and "the Germans." Tajfel (1974) has pointed out that in intergroup relations each group deals with members of the other group as if they are totally interchangeable. Relationships are more likely to be intergroup than interpersonal when (a) there is conflict between the groups, (b) there is a history of conflict, (c) members are strongly attached to their group, (d) there is anonymity of group membership, and (e) movement from group to group is difficult or impossible.

We will define *ingroups* as groups of people who are interdependent, interact over a substantial period of time, and can be identified by others as group members. Within ingroups there is cooperation, mutual support, and reasonable consensus on goals. *Outgroups* are groups toward which particular individuals or groups feel antagonistic or indifferent. Communication is usually rather intensive within ingroups; it may or may not take place with outgroups—to the extent that information is perceived as a resource it may be withheld from outgroups. To the extent that providing the information is a cost to the individual it may also be withheld from ingroup members, but it is generally the case that people are willing to undergo some costs to exchange information with ingroup members, while they are much less likely to do so with outgroup members.

Definition of Culture

Culture has been defined as the human-made part of the environment (Herkovits, 1955). If that broad definition is used, it is helpful to distinguish objective culture (tools, roads, gardens) from subjective culture (norms, roles, belief systems, laws, values). Triandis (1972) showed that aspects of subjective culture form meaningful wholes; they are interrelated in functional ways. Furthermore, there are links between the elements of subjective culture and social behavior (Triandis, 1980b).

When defining a culture *language, time,* and *place* are useful criteria (Triandis, 1980a). Thus in order for a culture to exist it is essential for its members to have the possibility of interaction. If they do not share a language, live in the same time period and in a physical location that permits interaction, it is unlikely that a homogeneous culture will emerge. An important aspect of culture is that it reflects *shared* meanings, norms, and values. Members of the same culture know the "rules of the game" so that their interactions can be effective. Of course, just like when knowing the rules of an athletic game one cannot predict any one play, so knowing a culture cannot allow one to predict what behaviors will take place among members of the culture. One can simply understand such behaviors better.

Communication requires a certain degree of sharing of meanings, linguistic and paralinguistic conventions, and frames of reference. It follows that the more different two cultures are, the more difficult the communication between their members.

The section that follows will describe some dimensions of variation across cultures that appear to have relevance for interpersonal and intergroup communication in organizations. We will examine also how such cultural variations are likely to affect communication within and between culturally different groups and organizations.

DIMENSIONS OF CULTURAL VARIATION

There are probably an infinite number of ways in which cultures differ. However, for a scientific analysis of cultural differences and the systematic study of how culture affects communication, and more generally social behavior, we need to ignore some of the more subtle differences and concentrate on the important ones. A number of theorists have provided indications of dimensions of cultural differences. For example, Kluckhohn and Strodtbeck (1961), Parsons (1951), Glenn (1981), and others have classified cultures or suggested dimensions of cultural differences. Empirical investigations such as Hofstede's (1980) have also provided such dimensions. Since some of the dimensions overlap, and others appear to be conceptually similar, one can try to develop a set that will include the more frequently mentioned dimensions (Triandis, 1984).

Major dimensions of cultural variation that affect communication (see Table 9.1 for details) are perception, cognitive frames people carry with them, and patterns of action acceptable in various societies (for example, physical distances between people involved in conversation, touching). Most important among these are the cognitive frames societies provide their members for processing information that has been perceived. These frames are no doubt constrained by perceptions, learned behaviors about how to communicate, and a variety of organizational factors, such as who reports to whom, who is supposed to do a job, when a job needs to be done, where the communication takes place, how one is supposed to communicate (by letter, on phone), what the expected content of the communication in the particular job setting is, and so on.

Cognitive Frames

Because we believe that these cognitive frames are very important we give them special attention here. Our discussion will focus on emphases on people, ideas, and action; on different values; on process versus goal, and on patterns of information processing.

Emphases on people, ideas, or action. Societies differ in the extent to which they emphasize people, ideas, or actions. In those societies where people are

TABLE 9.1

Major Dimensions of Cultural Variation Affecting Communication

Perception

(1) *Categorization* (Bruner, 1957) is affected by culture (Triandis, 1964).
  (a) Categories are organized into *schemata*. Stereotypes are special schemata.
  (b) Categories can be *broad* or *narrow* (Pettigrew, 1959; Detweiler, 1980).
  (c) Each category domain needs separate analysis in each culture (Frake, 1964).
  (d) Categories can be *concrete* or *abstract;* fall into a complex structure that requires many dimensions to be accounted for (cognitive complexity), be highly or weakly interrelated, form integrated or diffuse cognitive structures (Scott, Osgood, & Peterson, 1979). Dimensions can be very finely or less finely discriminated.
  (e) Of special importance are *person categories.* Attributes of persons, such as ability, personality, attitudes, and demographic categories, are emphasized more or less in different cultures (Triandis, 1967). Achieved versus ascribed status (Parsons, 1951) and attributes that define ingroup versus outgroup membership are especially important dimensions of cultural variation. Cultures differ in the size of ingroups, the basis of ingroup formation, and the ease of becoming an ingroup member.

(2) *Associations, beliefs,* need to be studied in each culture. Techniques to do that have been presented by Szalay et al. (1971), Triandis et al. (1972), and others.

Cognitive Frames

  Emphasis on people, ideas, or action (Glenn, 1981).
  Differences in values (time orientation, individualism-collectivism).
  Emphasis on process versus goal (Glenn, 1981).
  Emphasis on patterns of information processing.

Patterns of Action

  More or less touching; small-large physical distances, loud-soft voices; eye contact; body orientation (Watson, 1970; Donohue, 1985). Emphasis on different kinds of behavior (Mead, 1967; Triandis, 1978); pace of life (Levine & Bartlett, 1984).

emphasized, the interpersonal relationship is paramount. To an Arab what you say is not nearly as important as whether you are a friend or an enemy (Glenn, 1981). It is not the idea that matters but the relationship. On the other hand, for Indians of the correct Hindu persuasion, or for members of the Communist party in the USSR, the idea (ideology) is of crucial significance. If a person has the "right" idea it does not matter who she or he is. Finally, in cultures such as the American one, where action is of great significance, what a person does is much more important than who the person is or what the person says ("hot air"). Thus, for example, good athletes can come from any background and are admired for their actions rather than for their background. One can predict that each of these emphases might result in somewhat different interactions in organizations. For example, reward systems in organizations in societies that emphasize action should be different than those in organizations in societies that emphasize ideas.

In cultures that emphasize people, much time is spent in social interactions that consolidate social networks. In such cultures time tends to be polychronic

(Hall, 1959, 1966, 1976); that is, people interact with others simultaneously and will carry on several conversations in an intertwined manner. In cultures that emphasize ideas, ideology is much more important than reality. If the reality is inconsistent with the ideology, then there is something wrong with the reality. By contrast, in cultures that emphasize action the prevailing philosophy is pragmatism. If it works, it is "obviously" valid (right, correct).

Emphasis on different values. Different societies value time differently. Some societies focus on the past, others on the present, and still others on the future (Kluckhohn & Strodtbeck, 1961). When people come together from societies in which perceptions of time are quite different their interaction may take on a strange quality. Imagine an organization where people from these three kinds of cultures are involved in evaluating the performance of a particular subsidiary. If the members of the subsidiary focus on the past (their brilliant past record), while the members of the headquarters focus on the present (what happened this quarter), their evaluations might be quite different. Or, as another example, if the members of the subsidiary focus on the future and see current losses as as investment that will lead to great profits in five years, while officials at headquarters focus on the present, again there will be considerable disagreements on how to evaluate the performance of the subsidiary.

Societies also differ in the extent to which they value individualism versus collectivism (Hofstede, 1980). For example, in many Japanese companies jobs are assigned to groups, and groups rather than individuals are evaluated by top management. In most U.S. firms the major emphasis is on individual performance.

Emphasis on process versus goal. The traditional Chinese emphasized process, the way to live, while the Western cultures, as well as India, emphasized the goal (the ultimate goal in life, Nirvana) (Glenn, 1981). A consequence of the emphasis on goals is a search for the best ways to reach the goal, which leads to considerable creativity. The major achievements of the Indians and the West in sciences (the Indians invented the concept of zero as well as our numerical system, which the Arabs acquired from them and then passed on to the West) can be traced to the continued search for a path to the ultimate goal. Such a search is unnecessary in a culture where the here and now and the best way to live at this time are emphasized. This contrast also relates to the temporal value orientations (Kluckhonn & Strodtbeck, 1961) of different cultures: orientations emphasizing the future, the present, or the past. The traditional Chinese emphasis was on the present, which must reflect the past as spelled out by Confucius, while the Western orientation is toward the future.

Patterns of information processing. Condon (1978) contrasts the U.S. and Japanese approaches to communication. The American emphasis on "I" contrasts with the Japanese emphasis on "we"; contrast the American emphasis on symmetric relations and minimal status difference with the Japanese emphasis on hierarchy—status, age, and sex differentiation; the American emphasis on verbalization and saying everything that is needed to make the point as clearly as possible with the Japanese emphasis on the unspoken, the context; the American emphasis on logic, proof, linear organization, and precision of definition of terms with the Japanese emphasis on understanding what is implicit, on the associations with what is said, and in not taking specific words at face value; the American emphasis on objective values that can separate the speaker and his or her opinions with the Japanese emphasis on the merging of the objective and subjective, and emphasis on interpersonal values; the American view that silence is negative and indicates a person who is weak, shy, and troubled with the Japanese view that silence indicates strength, and power.

Such observations suggest the need for the development of a generalized theoretical system that can account for them. Glenn (1981) has attempted to develop such a system. He provides a very useful description of differences in communication across cultures that appear to reflect the kind of information that is utilized not only intrapersonally but also interpersonally. His most important dimension concerns associative versus abstractive communication. *Associative communication* focuses on the experience of the individual with the particular entity that is being communicated to another individual. It assumes a good deal of common information and common ways of thinking about that entity so that it occurs in those situations in which people belong to a relatively homogeneous group. Such communication tends to depend on context a great deal. In many traditional societies context is used much more than in the West. However, even in the West there are many conditions under which context is much used. For example, when a NASA official sends a rocket to the moon she or he uses a single command—"Fire"—that has enormous meaning in the particular context in which it is used. While such examples can be found in the West, the complexities of Western societies and the heterogeneity of the countries are such that abstractive communication is much more common.

In *abstractive communication* one defines one's concepts before communicating. Both the West and India utilize abstractive communication much more than associative communication, which is more commonly found in East Asia. Abstractive communication is found in so-called *low-context* cultures where a factual-inductive approach to communication appears to be used rather frequently—that is, a person develops an argument by first listing numerous facts. After listing these facts the person induces a conclusion. Ting-Toomey (1982, cited in Gudykunst & Kim, 1984, p. 58) argues that in low-context cultures, in addition to the factual inductive approach, the axiomatic-deductive style is used (also see Okabe, 1983). In this style the person begins with a broad principle or axiom from which a number of deductions follow, and then presents facts that are consistent with these deductions. In contrast, according to Ting-Toomey, in *high-context* cultures people are more likely to use an affective-intuitive style resembling the style utilized in poetry. Gudykunst and Kim (1984) rank the following countries/cultures from low to high context: Swiss, German, Scandinavian, United States, France, England, Italy, Spain, Greece, Arabia, China, and Japan.

Integrated Model

The cultural differences presented in Table 9.1 interact in some cases with each other. For example, one is more likely to find associative communication in collectivist cultures, because in such cultures there is a higher probability that people will interact frequently with the same other person. Since so many different variables influence communication behavior, we need a theory that will put most of the important variables into the same framework. Such a theory was offered by Gudykunst (1987).

Gudykunst (1987) has developed a general theory of communication behavior that draws on the work of Triandis (1980b). Figure 9.1 reproduces this model. Intentions are defined as "instructions individuals give themselves about how to communicate." Understanding involves "the interpretation of incoming stimuli" and the ability to predict or explain these stimuli, including the others' behavior. Communication is based on understanding, habits, intentions and affect. The link between intentions and communication is affected by facilitating conditions, "the ability of the person to carry out the act, the person's arousal to carry out the act, and the person's knowledge" (Triandis, 1977a, p. 10) which are functions of the communication situation.

The above constructs are all affected by cultural variables. Of special significance are values. In addition, his model draws on cognitive social psychology, for instance, the way ingroups and outgroups are perceived and thought about. He also discusses extensively how cognitive processes influence understanding. Situational factors are examined in terms of norms and roles that determine what communications are possible (communication networks), the environmental setting, and the skills required by the situation. Affect is viewed as making an impact on communication that is not always mediated by cognitive processes. Finally, all these constructs are given some weights that are affected by the situation. For example, Gudykunst argues that people are more conscious of their behavior when they are communicating with people from other social-cultural systems than when they are communicating with people from their own system. Thus he expects greater emphasis on intentions and lesser emphasis on habits in intercultural communication than in intracultural communication.

A good deal of research is needed to operationalize each of the dimensions of cultural variation mentioned above. In addition, such research should ideally utilize a large sample of independent cultures (that is, 50 cultures) to

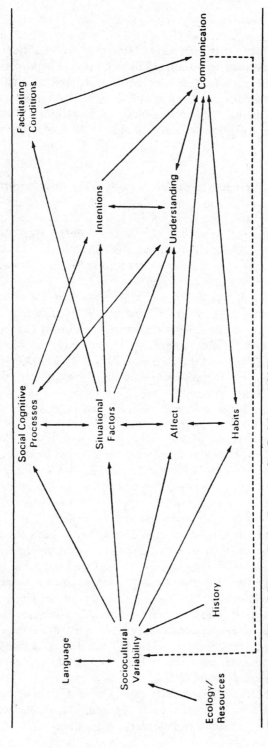

Figure 9.1 Determinants of Communication Behavior after Gudykunst (1987)

study the interrelationships among the various dimensions. In terms of organizational communication specifically, future research needs to consider the dimensions within organization contexts, so that useful data are generated on the relationship between cultural and organizational variables.

In the next section, we turn specifically to issues associated with organizational communication and culture. We find it useful to distinguish between cross-cultural comparisons of organizational communication, in which communication within organizations is examined in two or more cultures, and intercultural communication, in which cross-cultural interactions within a given organization are examined. We will consider each of these topics in turn.

ORGANIZATIONAL COMMUNICATION IN CROSS-CULTURAL PERSPECTIVE

In this section we will address the issue of communication in organizations from a cross-cultural, comparative perspective, that is, we will see how communication behaviors differ in different countries and think about how these differences might influence organizational activities.

We will first consider differences in structural relationships in international organizations. There are, for example, different structures for multinational corporations. Each provides a different ecological environment within which social behavior in general, and communication in particular, takes place.

We will then look at cultural-organizational differences in values and motives. These have received relatively greater attention cross-culturally than other issues and are important contributors to cultural differences in organizational communication.

Next we will examine cultural-organizational differences in communication patterns. And finally we will consider how decision making and conflict resolution differ in organizations in different cultures.

Structural Factors in Multinational Organizations

The relationship between the head office of the corporation and the subsidiaries is one of the most important contextual factors. Adler (1980) has suggested that there are three management models found in organizations within which members differ culturally: cultural dominance, cultural compromise, and cultural synergy. In the cultural dominance model, which is the most prevalent by far, a monocultural style of management is used. Cultural differences are ignored. According to Adler (1980), its strengths are efficiency, consistency, and simplicity. Its weaknesses are the development of resistance from members of the subordinate culture, which may sabotage organizational goals, and result in poor relationships with customers, which may affect sales.

In the cultural compromise model, similarities and differences in management behavior are identified across cultures, but only the similarities among the culturally different managers are used in the formation of organizational policies and practices. Adler (1980) argues its strength is the lack of resistance to management decisions, and its major weakness is the limitation of management behaviors to those that are similar across cultures. This model is more difficult to design and apply consistently than the cultural dominance model.

In the cultural synergy model important cognitive, affective, and behavioral similarities and differences between organization members are recognized and utilized in designing and developing the organization. Its strengths are lack of resistance and a wider range of policies and practices. Its principal weakness is the time commitment required for the cultural analysis of similarities and differences. Some researchers (Dinges & Maynard, 1983; Landis & Brislin, 1983) have expressed concern with the frustration and disappointments that may befall those attempting this ideal, and point out that no well-documented case study or research documenting its usefulness is available.

Jaeger (1983) has argued that some U.S. companies (Type Z) have very clear organizational cultures that they impose throughout the world; other companies (Type A), however, do not impose a uniform culture everywhere. In a study of 22 electronic companies Jaeger found that there were no differences in values between the head office and the subsidiary for the Type Z companies, while there were substantial differences in the case of the Type A companies. The patterns of communication were quite different in these two types of firms. Type Z firms promoted face-to-face contacts (that is, had large travel budgets), used fewer and smaller company manuals, and required fewer reports from the subsidiaries; Type A firms relied heavily on reports and manuals. Specifically, Type A firms sent an average of 42 pages of reports per month to the headquarters; Type Z firms sent an average of 27 pages. Type A firms had 2100 pages of manuals, while Type Z firms had on average 780 pages. Thus this study shows clearly that the policy of the company with respect to having an organizational culture has specific implications for communication.

Heenan and Perlmutter (1979) delineate four types of headquarters orientations toward subsidiaries in a multinational enterprise: ethnocentric, polycentric, regiocentric, and geocentric. Ethnocentric organizations are similar to those included in Adler's cultural dominance model. They tend to put persons from the home country in key positions everywhere and to reward them highly. Authority and decision making tend to rest with headquarters; home standards are applied in evaluating performance; there tends to be a high volume of orders, commands, and advice to subsidiaries; there is a lack of trust of people from other cultures—more from lack of knowledge, according to Heenan and Perlmutter, than due to prejudice.

Polycentric organizations tend to have the attitude that cultures of various countries are quite dissimilar, that foreigners are hard to understand and should be left alone. Local nationals occupy the key positions in their own countries and have control over who gets hired and promoted. With respect to communication, Heenan and Perlmutter mention only that there are few communication difficulties between headquarters and subsidiaries. It seems to us, however, that communication difficulties between headquarters and subsidiaries may well arise in this type of organization.

Regiocentric organizations utilize a regional basis for recruiting, developing, and rewarding people. An example of this would be an American company with regional European headquarters. There may be little information flow to and from headquarters but high communication flow between the regional headquarters and the country subsidiaries.

Geocentric organizations attempt to integrate diverse regions into a global system of decision making. Superiority is not equated with nationality, and headquarters and subsidiaries see themselves as part of the whole. In practice this approach poses a major challenge given the ethnocentric and polycentric pressures that characterize both the home and foreign environments of multinational firms.

The different structures described above reflect different values and motives among the founders and elites of international organizations. In their turn the structures maintain and shape different values and motives. The next section, then, will examine cultural-organizational differences in values and motives.

Cultural-Organizational Differences in Values and Motives

Values and motives are shaped by ecology (Triandis, 1972). Differences in values, worldviews (Porter & Roberts, 1976), or motives can result in messages not being understood (due, for example, to selective perception, distortion), and even if understood, in being ineffective. This is why the study of values and motives is important. Since the literature on cultural differences in values is large (Zavalloni, 1980) it will not be reviewed here. However, a few key studies will provide some indication of the main findings.

The Hofstede dimensions. The most comprehensive study to date of cultural differences in work related values and attitudes has been conducted by Hofstede (1980). He obtained data from 117,000 questionnaires answered by employees of a large multinational corporation in 66 countries. For reasons of stability of data, ecological correlations and factor analyses were limited to 40 countries. Questions were of four types: (1) satisfaction questions, dealing with personal evaluations of aspects of the work situation; (2) perception questions, dealing with the subjective descriptions of aspects of the work situation (according to Hofstede, about half of the perception questions dealt with the behavior of managers); (3) personal goal and belief questions, dealing with beliefs about work and what is desired and desirable; and (4) demographic questions. The four factor-analytically derived dimensions that have emerged from the data (power distance, uncertainty avoidance, individualism, and masculinity), permit comparisons by country and provide a wealth of information about cultural differences in work attitudes. We now turn to discuss these four dimensions.

Power distance is a measure of the interpersonal power or influence between bosses and subordinates. It is based on (a) employees' perceptions that their peers are afraid to disagree with their managers, (b) subordinates' perceptions that their boss makes decisions in an autocratic or paternalistic way, and (c) subordinates' preference for anything but a consultative style of decision making. Hofstede found that high power distances tended to occur in countries with tropical and subtropical climates, larger populations, and greater inequality in wealth. Power distance scores also differed strongly by occupation, being greater between the nonmanagerial and less educated employees and their superiors than between the managerial employees and their superiors. It seems probable that in organizations in high power-distance cultures there is much communication from the top to the bottom of the organization and very little communication from the bottom to the top of the organization. Some communication from the bottom to the top occurs, but mostly through other organizations (such as unions and the church).

Uncertainty avoidance refers to tolerance for uncertainty and it is based on three indicators: rule orientation, employment stability, and stress. Some countries high on uncertainty avoidance were Greece, Portugal, Belgium, Japan, and several Latin American countries. In these countries one is likely to find more written rules, more structure, and lower labor turnover. Along the low end of the continuum were Singapore, Denmark, Sweden, and Hong Kong.

It is likely that in organizations in cultures high in uncertainty avoidance one finds communication centered on rules, norms, and proper behaviors. Many discussions center on what people should or should not do and on how to behave correctly. In organizations in cultures low in uncertainty avoidance there is less clarity on what is proper behavior. Cultures high in uncertainty avoidance will probably have multinationals with Jaeger's (1983) Type Z organizations, and those with low uncertainty avoidance multinationals with Jaeger's Type A organizations.

The *individualism* index reflects the importance that people in various countries place on the individual versus the collectivity. The United States scored highest on individualism (followed by other English-speaking countries), with three Latin American countries (Columbia, Venezuela, and Peru) scoring among the lowest.

It seems probable that organizations in cultures high in individualism will emphasize individual achievement and competition among individuals.

Organizations in cultures high in collectivism will emphasize group achievement (the firm doing well) and cooperation within the organization but competition between the organization and other organizations (for example, between Japanese and American products).

Masculinity refers to the notion that the predominant socialization pattern in many countries is for men to be assertive and woman nurturant. The masculinity index measures to what extent the respondents from a given country tend to endorse goals emphasizing assertiveness interests (such as earnings and advancement) as contrasted to those emphasizing nurturance interests (such as relations with manager, cooperation, and friendly atmosphere). Japan had the highest score for masculinity, followed by the German-speaking countries. Anglo-American countries had scores that were above average, Latin countries had low scores, and the Nordic countries and the Netherlands had the lowest scores.

Organizations in masculine countries find it easy to send employees to different parts of the world, offering higher earnings and advancement as inducements. Organizations in feminine cultures are often unable to use earnings and advancements to induce employees to do jobs that reduce the employees' overall quality of life.

The Hofstede dimensions have already provided a theoretical framework for the prediction of the way people from different cultures will respond to social situations. For example, Bond, Wan, Leung, and Gicalone (1985) found collectivism useful in explaining the behavior of Chinese and U.S. subjects in an insult situation; Forgas and Bond (1985) found collectivism useful in predicting the perceptions of interaction episodes of Chinese and Australian subjects.

These dimensions have several significant implications for ogranizational communication that need to be tested empirically. It is probable that in high power-distance cultures, more so than in low power-distance cultures, communication will be mostly downward, sources will be more influential if they are higher rather than lower in status, and low-status audiences will yield to high-status sources more unquestioningly.

In low power-distance cultures there should be more two-way communication and more careful listening by high-status persons to communications from low-status persons. It is also likely that in high power-distance cultures elegant style will be much more effective than clumsy style, while the effect of style will be nonsignificant in low power-distance cultures. Furthermore, audiences in high power-distance cultures will prefer a serious to a humorous style and message.

In individualistic cultures individuals are more likely to use confrontation than in collectivist cultures. Thus it is likely that in individualistic cultures employees will be more frank than in collectivist cultures, but frankness will be balanced by use of a humorous style, which will be preferred to a serious style.

In individualistic cultures it is probable that subunits of the organization will communicate with each other about matters of mutual interest when (a) members of these subunits are transferred from unit to unit (ingroup boundary is weak), (b) the subunits are unattractive and not cohesive, and (c) there is general trust within the organization (members do not feel that information is a resource that if shared may be used against them). In collectivist cultures, even when these conditions prevail communication may be minimal because people are strongly attached to different collectivities (Hui, 1984), such as family, friends, coworkers, or fellow countrymen, and information is viewed by them as a resource not to be shared with outgroups. When familism is high there may be very little communication with members of the organization who are not part of the family.

Motives and needs. Motives may change over time and members of a culture may emphasize different needs at different times and places. An interesting field study conducted in the British West Indies illustrates this: Aronoff (1967, 1970) found that work organization seemed to be linked to the hierarchy of needs of the workers (Maslow, 1954). Thus he found that cane cutters, who had higher needs for safety, worked in a very authoritarian system and had a pay schedule that rewarded the group but not individuals. Fishermen, on the other hand, who were low in safety and physiological needs but high on affection and esteem needs, had a more democratic work environment and reward system that was based on individual performance. But by 1970 the cane cutters' organization had changed. According to Aronoff, the new group of cane cutters had grown up under dramatically improved health conditions and had had a more secure childhood and consequently had lower safety needs; as a result, a new pay system with individual rewards and a less authoritarian structure was organized. This illustrates how social conditions and cultural factors interact and affect the personality of members of a culture and the traditional structures of work relationships. A replication in the laboratory with U.S. participants (Aronoff & Meese, 1971) showed that in groups composed of persons who were low in safety needs, leadership functions were widely shared among participants, while in groups whose members were safety oriented, leadership was concentrated in a few members. These studies illustrate that motives may change over a relatively short period of time.

In summary, cultural differences in values suggest some differences in organizational communication patterns. We turn now to a closer examination of such communication patterns.

Cultural-Organizational Differences in Communication Patterns

There are few studies of communication patterns per se. We will discuss two studies that are representative. Graves (1972), in a study of English and

French managers and employees in one French and one English light electronics factory, utilized interviews, contact diaries, and communication exercises in which discussions, questionnaires, and written messages were analyzed. Graves found that English managers saw authority as vested in the person, and saw their aim as securing the maximum amount of autonomy, while French managers saw authority as vested in the role, and thus aimed at increasing compliance with the system and rules of the organization. (It is interesting that Kanungo, Gorn, and Dauderis, 1976, invoke the same contrasting perceptions of authority to explain attitudinal differences between Canadian anglophone and francophone managers.) One effect of these findings was that in the English factory, communication problems were created as a result of the managers' preference for using personal networks of communication rather than official channels. In the French factory, conflict was dealt with by submission to a strong central authority. However, a consequence of this was the unwillingness of French managers to assume personal responsibility.

An interesting finding of this research is that only one-third of the written, telephonic, and face-to-face communications were interpreted in the same way by the sender and the receiver, and that proportionately more communication was lost in France than in England (the English use more written communication). Communication problems were often mentioned and there was widespread dissatisfaction with communications in the English factory. The French had a greater number of congruent communications (communications reported identically by both parties). Graves concludes that the business subculture in Europe is radically different from that in United States, has a greater carryover from the social to the business setting, and therefore is more closely linked with the culture as a whole.

In a more recent study, Al-Jafary and Hollingsworth (1983) asked managers in 10 organizations located in the Saudi Arabian area to describe their management system, using Likert's (1967) System 1-to-4 concepts. They found that most managers reported they were using System 3 (Consultative) and would like to use System 4 (Participative). Correlations between system ratings (1 to 4) and other variables showed that communication flow was correlated significantly with system level. In other words, the more the managers reported using consultation or participation, the more they reported that there was much communication in their organization. This finding is not especially remarkable, except for two points:

(1) One would not have expected managers in that part of the world to use systems 3 or 4. There may be a difference between what they say they use and what they actually use. But even so, the fact they consider participation as an ideal reveals something about the impact of Western management perspectives in that area.
(2) There is generality across cultures in the extent to which Likert's systems correlate with other variables. We can use the Likert system variables as indicators of the context of communications in an organization.

It is clear from this review that there are many more studies of values than of communication patterns. This probably reflects the relative costs of the two kinds of research. Whereas one can study values through questionnaire studies and surveys, the study of communication patterns is more demanding of the researcher's time. It is clear that more studies of communication patterns are needed, particularly studies linking communication to the typologies of values outlined above. When discussing the value patterns, we speculated about the communication patterns that are likely to be found in different kinds of cultures. We need studies that will test these speculations.

Communication patterns and values also relate to decision making and conflict resolution, which will be our next topic.

Cultural-Organizational
Differences in Decision Making

While there is very little information about communication patterns and decision making, there is a fair amount on decision making in collectivist cultures, such as Japan, and individualistic cultures such as the United States. E. C. Stewart (1985) argues that decision making, lacking content, acquires much of its character from the culture in which it occurs and suggests different styles of decision making: the technical style, prevalent in the United States, in which the individual is the decision maker; the logical style, modeled on Western European societies, in which the decision maker is the role occupant; the bureaucratic group style, representing universal characteristics of North American bureaucratic decision making, in which a committee makes decisions; and the social collective style, exemplified by the Japanese, in which a (collectivity) group makes the decision. Each style is analyzed by Stewart in terms of three parts of decision making adopted from statistical decision theory: the decision maker, prediction systems, and the criterion. Stewart's sophisticated analysis of culture and decision making cannot be adequately summarized here, but deserves a closer look by those interested in cultural analyses of organizational communication.

Decision-making style has implications for the medium of communication that will be used; when intensive participation is the usual style, face-to-face communication is most likely. When downward, authoritarian decision making is more typical, written communication is most likely. Studies reviewed by Tannenbaum (1980) suggest that participatory decision making is widely considered an ideal. However, there have been exceptions (Whyte & Williams, 1963) and managers in many countries, both socialist and capitalist (Tannenbaum & Cooke, 1978), often believe that lower-rank members of the organization are incapable of making decisions and prefer to be directed and to avoid responsibility (Haire, Ghiselli & Porter, 1966). Thus although managers in seven countries in the study by Barrett and Franke (1969) preferred two-way to one-way communication, one-way communication was more frequently used, particularly in more traditional cultures (Barrett & Bass, 1970; Bass, 1968; Porter & Roberts, 1976; Thiagarajan & Deep, 1970). Such findings, however, may be confounded by the interaction of a country's level of economic development and other variables, such as higher social mobility, higher levels of education and collectivism (Hofstede, 1980). In other words, the more authoritarian and paternalistic styles found in some developing countries (Negandhi, 1973; Tannenbaum, Kovcic, Rosner, Vianello, & Sieser, 1974) may be due to value differences *or* to the lack of social opportunities.

A study by Negandhi and Prasad (1971) compared the attitudes of managers in American subsidiaries in Argentina, Brazil, India, the Philippines, and Uruguay and the attitudes of managers in matched indigenous firms. They found that managers in American subsidiaries are more likely to use delegation than the managers in locally owned firms and to express trust and confidence in the capacities of members. Top executives in locally owned firms in the five countries were less likely than executives in American subsidiaries to share decision making with other members. However, it is important to point out that the differences found were not only due to differences in nationality, since 80% of the executives in American subsidiaries were local nationals and since no differences were found between American managers and native managers in these subsidiaries. Hence it appears in these cases that American cultural norms were affecting the attitudes of local managers in American subsidiaries.

Cultural-Organizational Differences in Conflict Resolution

Conflict resolution is a special aspect of decision making, but because of its importance in intercultural communication it deserves a separate section. Cushman and King (1985) summarized general tendencies regarding organizational values and their implications for conflict resolution strategies in three countries—Japan, the United States, and Yugoslavia—as follows: In Japan, organizational values such as lifelong employment, nonspecialized job assignment, implicit control requiring strong socialization with regard to what behaviors are appropriate, consensual decision making, and collective responsibility reinforce the national culture's preference for collaborative conflict resolution strategies. In the United States, organizational values such as the ability to change jobs based on individual desire, opportunities for rapid promotion, specialized career paths, and individual decision making and responsibility reinforce the culture's preference for competitive conflict resolution strategies. In Yugoslavia, lifelong employment, limited possibility for promotion, intergroup decision making, individual and collaborative responsibility, and respect for diversity reinforce the national culture's preference for compromise as a conflict resolution strategy.

The authors argue that in Japan the main rule to be observed in dealing with interorganizational conflicts is the desire to overcome individual differences by emphasizing group harmony while maintaining face. Cooperation in a conflict situation is achieved by (a) one-on-one consultation designed to persuade all parties that a resolution can be found that maintains group harmony; (b) by the *ringi* system—widely circulating a written proposal for approval and thus making all parties aware of emerging consensus—and (c) by the use of go-betweens (Kume, 1985, describes the Japanese process of decision making in similar terms). In the United States the central values of equality of opportunity, individual rights, competition, and so on lead to generally high initial demands and unyielding positions. This has led over time to the development of an extensive system of third-party interventions in interorganizational conflicts, utilizing conciliation, mediation, fact finding, and arbitration. In Yugoslavia the central values in interorganizational conflict management are respect for diversity, direct democracy, negotiated control, and social concern. Thus disputes are to be settled by worker councils or by sociopolitical communities and the goal of the process is to achieve compromise through collective intervention.

There are studies of the negotiation behavior and conflict resolution styles of members of American culture versus Japanese (Peterson & Shimada, 1978), and versus some samples of Chinese, French, Japanese, Mexicans, Nigerians, and Saudis (Weiss & Stripp, 1985). It is unclear, however, that the findings generalize beyond the specific samples that were used in the particular studies. Also, the results are detailed and difficult to summarize.

Taken together, the cross-national studies of decision making and conflict resolution suggest that culturally determined habits of action in decision making or conflict situations determine the communication patterns that are used in such situations.

INTERCULTURAL COMMUNICATION
WITHIN ORGANIZATIONS

In this section, we focus specifically on intercultural communication, that is, on interactions between culturally diverse persons or groups in organizations. Although comparative research can obviously shed some light on intercultural interactions, we feel that is is important to separate comparative efforts from intercultural efforts and to underscore the importance of the latter for understanding organizational communication.

The primary reason for this importance is that difficulties in communication are more likely to occur and more likely to be problematic, leading at times to overt hostility and conflict when the persons interacting come from different cultures. These difficulties occur for a variety of reasons, including different assumptions made by different cultural groups about what are the appropriate and desirable behaviors in a given situation, different attitudes and values, and different attributions made by persons from different cultures about the same behaviors (Albert, 1983a; Albert & Triandis, 1979, 1985; Triandis, 1975, 1977a).

In addition, with increasing economic interdependence organizations are becoming more and more multicultural in their composition. Consequently, the need for understanding the patterns, processes, and problems of interaction between individuals and groups from different cultures both within and between organizations is becoming increasingly acute.

Research in Intercultural
Organizational Communication

Research on intercultural communication in various organizational settings has been sporadic at best and has varied in terms of the variables investigated, the populations studied, and the scope of the work. We look at some examples in the following paragraphs.

Perceptions of culturally different organizational members. Members of an organization who do not come from the organization's dominant culture may perceive and react to organizational communication behaviors quite differently than members who come from the dominant culture. For example, in an unusual study of Americans in five Japanese plants in the United States, Kume (1985) reported that more than 90% of North American respondents involved in or affected by the decision making replied that there were sharp differences in the decision-making styles of North American and Japanese companies. The management style practiced in these plants was essentially Japanese. Although no numerical data were presented, thus making it difficult to assess the strength of the findings or the degree of agreement among the North American respondents, the author concluded that North Americans had both positive and negative reactions to this style. He indicated that the Japanese way of involving everyone affected by a decision was perceived favorably by some Americans and that most Americans reacted favorably to the open door policy of management and to the social and recreational programs provided. The author claims that the most difficult aspects for Americans to accept were the "sense of commitment, shared responsibility, interdependence and close coordination" (p. 249). Americans also found it hard to accommodate the length of time it took to arrive at decisions. One interesting observation made by the author is that that in the United States to egalitarian and democratic ideals do not carry over into corporate culture: rather, individual competition is stressed within the context of hierarchical power. In Japan the opposite situation seems to prevail: The society is definitely hierarchical yet "management familism" with close and personal communication prevails in the workplace.

Intercultural communication problems. In a study of intercultural communication problems, Adelman and Lustig (1981) presented to Saudi Arabian and American managers employed by a major multinational corporation in Saudi Arabia a list of problems that Saudi Arabians presumably have when communicating with Americans. The subjects were asked to rate the severity of each problem. Saudi Arabian managers were much more likely than their American counterparts to select "know language appropriate for formal and informal situations" and "perform social rituals" as major problems for Saudi Arabians interacting with Americans. Americans perceived that "expressing ideas clearly and concisely" and "displaying forethought and objectivity in decision-making" provided the most difficulties for Saudi Arabians. Both Americans and Saudis felt that repeating, paraphrasing, or clarifying information, identifying main ideas in messages, and organizing ideas for easy comprehension were major problems for Saudi Arabians. Both groups agreed that items that did not present difficulties for Saudi Arabians were use of supportive nonverbal communication, starting conversations, ending conversations, knowing appropriate social rules and forms of address, and knowing when to shift from social to business interaction. The authors concluded that "Saudi Arabians faulted the Americans for their inattention to social ritual as a prelude to task-oriented discussion, while the Americans pointed to the lack of objectivity as the major Saudi Arabian problem" (p. 359). Although it is possible and even likely that Saudi Arabians did feel that way about Americans, it seems to us that the wording used for the rating task, that is, "In communicating with Americans, I think Saudi Arabians have problems in the following area" (p. 355) does not permit the authors to conclude that the Saudis "faulted the Americans." It is clear, nevertheless, that there were significant differences between Americans and Saudis in the perceptions of communication problems. In addition, as the authors pointed out, both groups selected differences in the organization of ideas as a major intercultural problem, and one that needs to be dealt with in intercultural orientation and training programs.

Stereotypes. Although there is a vast literature on the impact of culture on attitudes and stereotypes (see Davidson & Thompson, 1980), there are few studies of intercultural communication and stereotypes in organizations. However, one example of such research is a study of stereotypes of Japanese managers in Singapore (Everett, Stening, & Longton, 1981). The researchers found no significant differences between the stereotypes of the Japanese held by American, British, and Singaporeans who had low contact with Japanese managers. However, the stereotypes held by Singaporeans who had high contact with Japanese managers (that is, who were employees of Japanese companies) were significantly different from the stereotypes of the low-contact managers: high-contact Singaporeans viewed the Japanese managers as more assertive, less methodical and less patient, while low-contact managers saw them as more shy, modest, introverted, and inflexible. The autostereotypes of the Japanese were also different from the stereotypes of them held by managers from the other cultures: The Japanese saw themselves as more frank, extroverted, and flexible, and less ambitious than did persons from other countries who had had either low or high contact with them.

Interactions with cultural minorities in organizations. Fernandez (1975) conducted a survey of 116 Black and 156 White managers or professionals in eight organizations. He found that a substantial majority of both Black and White managers were aware of negative racial attitudes and/or of employees' uncomfortable feelings toward Blacks. One out of five White managers could not answer a question about good and bad characteristics of Black managers because of lack of contact with Black managers. When an index of frequency of contact with Blacks was correlated with an index of negative racial attitudes, White managers who had a lot of contact with Blacks were more likely than those with no contact to have positive racial attitudes. Fernandez warns, however, that this finding should not be misconstrued because many of the White managers who had a lot of contact with Blacks still held negative attitudes toward them. These negative feelings may have been less strong and more subtle, but they were still operative.

Albert (1983a) and Albert and Triandis (1985) have conducted a large-scale program of research on Hispanic-Anglo interactions. The research constitutes one of the first attempts to investigate communication difficulties between Hispanics or Latin Americans and Anglo-Americans in various organizational settings and to identify cultural differences in attributions or interpretations of behavior underlying these difficulties. Analyses of the initial phases of the research, conducted in school settings, indicated that there were four times as many cross-cultural differences in attributions as would be expected by chance alone. In addition to differences due to the cultural backgrounds of the respondents (Hispanic versus Anglo), there were significant findings due to differences in the status of the respondents, and to the interaction of culture and status. Although this research was initially conducted in school settings, many of the fundamental differences found are likely to apply to other organizational settings in which Anglo-Americans, especially Anglo-American managers or supervisors, interact with Hispanics (especially Hispanic subordinates). The following are some examples of such differences: Hispanics tended to emphasize the interpersonal aspects of the situation, to express a more collective orientation and a greater reliance on the family, and to prefer personalized, individualized treatment. Anglo-Americans, on the other hand, tended to focus relatively more on the task rather than on interpersonal relations, to express a more individualistic orientation that favored independence, to emphasize fairness and equality, and to express discomfort with close physical distances and touching.

Methods for Improving
Communication Across Cultures

A number of findings and empirical conjectures presented in this chapter suggest that communication across cultures can often be problematic and ineffective. However, such communication can be improved with cross-cultural training (Landis & Brislin, 1983). The theoretical analysis presented above suggests both the places where difficulties are likely to develop and some way to reduce these difficulties. If a cultural group emphasizes a particular attribute, such as sex, age, or race, it is possible to warn those who will interact with persons from this group. If a culture emphasizes ascription rather than achievement, persons rather than ideas or actions, process rather than goal, field sensitivity versus field independence, it is possible to give trainees opportunities to practice looking at the social environment with different emphases than are typically used in their cultures. If cultures differ on values, it is possible to explicate the implications of such differences. If communication is context dependent or relatively independent, associative, or abstractive, particularistic rather than universalistic, diffuse versus specific, and if grammatical forms differ across languages, it is possible to provide corresponding training.

Much of this kind of training is cognitive. Early developments of this training (Fiedler, Mitchell, & Triandis, 1971) have slowly developed toward a theoretical understanding of what elements should be included in the training (Triandis, 1975), what methods might be used to obtain those elements (Triandis, 1972) and how the effectiveness of such training might be evaluated (Albert, in press b; Triandis, 1977b). A review and discussion of these developments is provided by Albert (1983a). Recent discussions have also focused on conceptual issues (Albert, in press b; Albert & Triandis, 1979), and on short-cut methods for the development of training materials (Triandis, 1984).

Investigations of interactions between Blacks and Whites (Fernandez, 1975; Triandis, 1976), and Hispanics and Anglos (Albert, 1983b, in press a) have resulted in some understandings of why such interactions often result in interpersonal difficulties. One of the major causes of such difficulties is that people from different cultures do not make isomorphic attributions (Triandis, 1975). That is, visitors attribute different causes to the behavior of locals than locals do to their own behavior. Training visitors to make more isomorphic attributions results in visitors and locals understanding the behavior of the locals in more or less similar terms.

Developing such training programs is time-consuming, but evaluations show that the training is helpful. For example, Albert (1984a, 1984b) has utilized the episodes from her research yielding significant differences between Hispanic pupils and Anglo teachers to develop intercultural training materials known as intercultural sensitizers (ICSs) or cultural assimilators (Albert, 1983a; Albert & Adamopoulos, 1976; Fielder et al., 1971). One of these

(Albert, 1984a) is addressed primarily to Americans, especially Americans who work closely with Hispanic pupils. The other (Albert, 1984b) is addressed primarily to Hispanic pupils. Although the episodes depict interactions occurring in school settings, the major themes deal with basic cultural differences that are likely to apply as well to Hispanic-Anglo interactions in other settings.

Two field experiments designed to assess the effectiveness of the first ICS (Albert, 1984a) in sensitizing American teachers to the attributions made by Hispanic pupils have been conducted (Albert & Crespo, 1982; Albert, Triandis, Brinberg, Ginorio, & Anderson, 1979; Crespo, 1982). The results indicated that the ICS and role-playing exercise based on this ICS were both significantly more effective than either a control condition or a training program utilizing "self-insight" training (Kraemer, 1973, 1978) in affecting the attributions made by American teachers about the behaviors of Hispanic pupils.

ICSs have been developed for interactions between Americans and persons from a variety of cultures and countries (Arabs, Iranians, Hondurans, Greeks, and Thais) and for interactions between Black and White and Hispanic and non-Hispanic Americans. There is also an ICS for White nurses interacting with Australian aborigines and a culture general assimilator. These assimilators have been developed for use in organizational contexts as varied as industries, schools, health clinics, and the U.S. armed forces, and they can potentially be developed for persons "from any cultural group interacting with members of any other cultural group anywhere in the world" (Albert, 1983a, p. 191).

In addition to the cognitive training described in some detail above, there are procedures that utilize other forms of training that may be helpful in improving intercultural communication. One important cultural difference is the extent to which cultures allow or encourage the expression of emotion. Persons from a low emotional expression culture interacting with persons from a high emotional expression culture are likely to experience communication difficulties. Usually, the people from the low emotional expression culture see those from the high emotional expression cultures as "uncontrolled," "vulgar," or "undisciplined." Those from the high see those from the low as "well-oiled machines, cold, calculating and unfriendly" (Triandis, 1967). Such uncomplimentary stereotypes and negative emotions are likely to interfere with the accurate decoding of communications. Furthermore, discrepancies in behavior can lead to other kinds of misunderstandings. For example, a person from a low-contact culture may assume that a person from a high-contact culture is either "pushy" or a "homosexual," because of the tendency to touch or hold hands. To reduce such inappropriate emotions and to eliminate inappropriate behaviors requires other kinds of training, such as behavior modification or desensitization (see Triandis, 1977a, chap. 8, for details).

In summary, the literature on cross-cultural training suggests that it is possible to utilize information obtained when designing such training to improve intercultural communication. One can teach about the different meanings of words, actions, and gestures in different cultures; about values and expectations that may distort what information is selected and how information is understood by members of different cultures; about attributions that are made when something is said in certain ways or when someone behaves in particular ways; and so on. Such information can improve the accuracy of communication by making those who are communicating sensitive to the distortions of the communication process that are traceable to cultural differences.

RESEARCH GAPS

There is a great need for research that will test propositions concerning the interaction of cultural variables and communication variables, particularly with respect to behavior in organizations.

The improvement of communication across cultures requires detailed training concerning the meanings of words, actions, and gestures—in short, both the linguistic and paralinguistic behavior of individuals in different cultures. Furthermore, one needs to understand the cultural assumptions that structure communication. Who communicates with whom, when, where, and how are factors that are culturally determined and reflect values, norms, and culturally determined roles likely to distort communication. The kinds of organizational structures that emerge reflect the values, norms, and roles and the structures in turn shape and constrain the kinds of communication behaviors that take place. These general statements need to be explored in detail in future research.

As illustrations of hypotheses that need to be tested, we provide the following:

(1) In high power-distance cultures, sources of communication will make their status, resources, and sources of power more salient than will sources in low power-distance cultures (for example, the boss will say, "It is necessary that you do this job." His or her manner and tone will make it obvious that he or she has great power, and that there should be no discussion about it).

(2) There will be more open conflict and frank discussion during decision making in individualistic than in collectivist cultures.

(3) In cultures high in uncertainty avoidance communications will more frequently be about rules and the proper way to behave than in cultures low in uncertainty avoidance.

(4) In cultures where induction is emphasized, communications that start with facts and end with conclusions will be more effective than in cultures that emphasize deduction, where communications that state a desirable end result

and discuss facts in relation to that result will be more effective. End results that are consistent with broad ideological or religious positions will be especially effective in inducing attitude change.

(4a) In cultures that emphasize induction, organizations will be structured so as to generate many facts relevant to decisions, and leadership will weigh the facts carefully in making decisions. In cultures that emphasize deductive communications, organizations will be so structured as to ensure that people will conform to the decisions of the leadership, particularly when the decisions are consistent with ideology or religion. Thus the first kind of culture will use pragmatic, and the second kind moral, considerations in both patterns of communication and in decision making.

(5) In low-context cultures the more clear and explicit the message is, the more effective it will be. This relationship will not be observed in high-context cultures.

(5a) In low-context cultures organizations are more likely to use explicit messages than in high-context cultures.

(6) In collectivist cultures, where the work group is an important ingroup, organizations will use work group-related messages; such messages will be more effective than messages that are linked to individuals. Conversely, in individualist cultures individual-linked messages will be more effective.

(7) In cultures that emphasize ideology, messages that show how the suggested attitude change is linked to the ideology will be more effective than in pragmatist cultures.

(7a) In cultures that emphasize ideology, organizations that use messages linking desirable organizational behaviors to the ideology will have members that are more satisfied with organizational communications than organizations that use messages not linked to the ideology. Conversely, in pragmatist cultures ideological messages will be ineffective.

(8) In pragmatist cultures messages that show that the attitude change will result in behaviors that have desirable consequences with high levels of probability will be more effective than they would be in ideological cultures.

(9) Messages that utilize the culture's predominant value orientations are more effective than messages that fail to do so (for example, if the culture is future-oriented the message discusses the future).

(10) The more the communicator uses the cognitive-affective framework of the audience, the more effective the communication will be. (The implication is that the communicator must know a great deal about the beliefs and values of the audience to fashion the optimal message).

(11) Communications will be more effective (result in more attitude change, result in desired actions, allow more coordination of action) when there is communication; for instance, in the United States when the source is a distinct individual, who is highly credible, and has achieved much; in Japan when it is a group that is high in the organizational hierarchy, and consists mostly of older males.

(12) Communications will be more effective when the content of the message matches the audience's (a) values; (b) meaning systems; (c) emphasis on

process versus goal; (d) emphasis on people, ideas, or action; (e) use or nonuse of exaggeration; (f) use or nonuse of qualification; (g) use of particularistic or universalistic concepts; (h) use of associative or abstractive style; and (i) use of specific versus general messages.

(13)   Communications will be more effective when the structure of the message matches the audience's use of (a) linear logic and (b) climatic versus anticlimatic structure.

(14)   Communications will be more effective if concrete and specific statements are made in low-context cultures.

(15)   Communications will be more effective in face-to-face situations in cultures that emphasize context. Written communications will be less effective in such cultures.

(16)   Written communications will be more effective in low- than in high-context cultures.

(17)   Organizations that encourage communications that have the characteristics of the effective communications of propositions 11-16 will be more successful than organizations that discourage such communications.

This is a sample of the propositions that are implied in the theoretical sections on culture differences and communications presented in this chapter. Readers should be able to generate many more such hypotheses.

CONCLUDING REMARKS

In looking at the cross-cultural and intercultural organizational literature it is difficult to get a sense of integration. There are many different strands of research, different conceptualizations, and much anecdotal information (see Renwick, 1981) that needs to be investigated more systematically. The dearth of empirical and conceptual work is particularly acute in the intercultural domain.

The studies that have been done differ not only in the degree to which they involve communication-relevant phenomena, but also in the samples used, ranging all the way from data obtained in only one culture to studies with individuals in 66 countries. Most consist of surveys, although there were field studies as well. No doubt the many methodological problems such research must deal with (Adler, 1983; Brislin, Lonner, & Thorndike, 1973), the cost and difficulty of getting cross-cultural and intercultural research conducted, and the burden on colleagues in other countries who do not usually have the time or resources to conduct research are contributing factors to the fragmentary nature of the field.

Albert (in press c) and Albert and Triandis (1985) have delineated a number of psychological, social, and historical factors that seem to have contributed to the general lack of interest in cultural differences among mainstream American individuals. These factors may also be operating within the field of communication. In addition, the lack of professional rewards for cross-cultural investigations in the United States and the relative lack of articles in American journals dealing with organizations in other cultures may reflect the general lack of appreciation for phenomena that may not be as immediate as local phenomena are.

Yet there are indications that this is changing: more and more cross-cultural research is being conducted, and the two main professional associations in the field of communication, the Speech Communication Association and the International Communication Association, now have full-fledged divisions of intercultural communication. Recent work on organizational culture by Schein (1985), Smircich (1983), and others has shown that there is a growing recognition that cross-cultural and intercultural analyses, concepts, and research can contribute to an understanding of organizations. Recent efforts by Bhagat and McQuaid (1982) to examine the role of subjective culture (Triandis, 1972) in organizations, by Lea Stewart (1985) to apply the concept of subjective culture to understanding the conflict between professional employees and their organizations, and by Gudykunst (1985) to extend a typology of intergroup relationships to organizational settings exemplify this trend.

As evidenced by the recent volume edited by Gudykunst, Stewart, and Ting-Toomey (1985) and by the inclusion of this chapter in this book, the field of communication has begun to recognize that the intersection of organizational and intercultural communication provides an especially rich ground for the development of communication theory, research, and informed practice.

There are many avenues that can and probably should be pursued in future research. Some that seem to us to be particularly important are the following: (1) research on the types of communication problems that managers face when they go abroad; (2) investigations of effective culture orientation programs for managers going abroad; (3) research on minority-majority interactions in many cultures and organizations; (4) comparative research on the dimensions of cultural difference as they apply to organizational communication; (5) studies of culturally heterogeneous work teams; and (6) investigations focusing on organizational forms of multicultural organizations not only in industry but also in international professional organizations and international governmental organizations (the World Bank, UNESCO).

Our hope is that this chapter contributes in some small way to stimulate research in the new, increasingly important and promising areas of cross-cultural and intercultural organizational communication.

REFERENCES

Adelman, M. B., & Lustig, M. W. (1981). Intercultural communication problems as perceived by Saudi Arabian and American managers. *International Journal of Intercultural Relations, 5,* 349-363.

Adler, N. (1980). Cultural synergy: The management of cross-cultural organizations. In W. Burke & L. Goodstein (Eds.), *Trends and issues in OD: Current theory and practice* (pp. 163-184). San Diego: University Associates.

Adler, N. J. (1983). Cross-cultural management research: The ostrich and the trend. *Academy of Management Review, 8,* 226-232.

Adler, N. (1986). *International dimensions of organizational behavior.* Boston: Kent.

Al-Jafary, A., & Hollingsworth, A. T. (1983). An exploratory study of management practices in the Arabian Gulf Region. *Journal of International Business Studies, 14,* 143-152.

Albert, R. D. (1983a). The intercultural sensitizer or culture assimilator: A cognitive approach. In D. Landis & R. Brislin (Eds.), *Handbook of intercultural training: Issues in training methodology* (Vol. 2, pp. 186-217). New York: Pergamon.

Albert, R. D. (1983b). Mexican-American children in educational settings: Research on children's and teachers' perceptions and interpretations of behavior. In E. E. Garcia (Ed.), *The Mexican American child: Language, cognition and social development* (pp. 183-194). Tempe: Arizona State University.

Albert, R. D. (1984a). *Communicating across cultures.* Manuscript submitted for publication.

Albert, R. D. (1984b). *Understanding North Americans. A guide for Hispanic pupils.* Manuscript submitted for publication.

Albert, R. D. (in press a). Communication and attributional differences between Hispanics and Anglo-Americans. *U.S. International and Intercultural Communication Annual* (Vol. 10).

Albert, R. D. (in press b). Conceptual framework for the development and evaluation of cross-cultural orientation programs. *International Journal of Intercultural Relations.*

Albert, R. D. (in press c). The place of culture in modern psychology. In P. Bronstein & K. Quina (Eds.), *Teaching the psychology of people: Resources for gender and socio-cultural awareness.* Washington, DC: American Psychological Association.

Albert, R. D., & Adamopoulos, J. (1976). An attributional approach to culture learning: The culture assimilator. *Topics in Culture Learning, 4,* 53-60.

Albert, R. D., & Crespo, O. I. (1982, March). *Cross-cultural sensitization of teachers of Hispanic pupils: New procedures and an experimental evaluation of their effects in naturalistic settings.* Paper presented at the annual meeting of the American Educational Research Association, New York City.

Albert, R. D., & Triandis, H. C. (1979). Cross-cultural training: A theoretical framework and some observations. In H. T. Trueba & C. Barnett-Mizrahi (Eds.), *Bilingual multicultural education and the professional teacher: From theory to practice* (pp. 181-194). Rowley, MA: Newbury House.

Albert, R. D., & Triandis, H. C. (1985). Intercultural education for multicultural societies: Critical issues. *International Journal of Intercultural Relations, 9,* 319-337.

Albert, R. D., Triandis, H. C., Brinberg, D., Ginorio, A., & Anderson, B. (1979). *Measurement procedures for evaluating cross-cultural training programs.* Unpublished manuscript.

Aronoff, J. (1967). *Psychological needs and cultural systems.* Princeton, NJ: van Nostrand.

Aronoff, J. (1970). Psychological needs as a determination in the formation of economic structures: A confirmation. *Human Relations, 23,* 123-138.

Aronoff, J., & Meese, L. A. (1971). Motivational determinants of small-group structure. *Journal of Personality and Social Psychology, 17,* 319-324.

Barrett, G. V., & Bass, B. M. (1970). Comparative surveys of managerial attitudes and behaviors. In J. Boddewyn (Ed.), *Comparative management: Teaching, training and research* (pp. 179-217). New York: Graduate School of Business Administration, New York University.

Barrett, G. V., & Franke, R. H. (1969). Communication preference and performance: A cross-cultural comparison. *Proceedings of the 77th Annual American Psychological Association Convention,* pp. 597-598.

Bass, B. M. (1968). *A preliminary report on manifest preferences in six cultures for participative management.* (Tech. Report 21). University of Rochester Management Research Center, Rochester, NY.

Bhagat, R.S., & McQuaid, S.H. (1982). Role of subjective culture in organizations: A review and directions for future research. *Journal of Applied Psychology Monograph, 67,* 653-685.

Bond, M. H., Wan, K., Leung, K., & Gicalone, R. A. (1985). How are responses to verbal insult related to cultural collectivism and power distance? *Journal of Cross-Cultural Psychology, 16,* 111-127.

Brislin, R. W., Lonner, W. J., & Thorndike, R. M. (1973). *Cross-cultural research methods.* New York: John Wiley.

Bruner, J. (1957). On perceptual readiness. *Psychological Review, 64,* 123-152.

Condon, J. C., Jr. (1978). Intercultural communication from a speech communication perspective. In F. L. Casimir (Ed.), *Intercultural and international communication* (pp. 108-137). Washington, DC: University Press of America.

Crespo, O. I. (1982). *Effects of cross-cultural training on the attributions and attitudes of students in a teacher-training program.* Unpublished doctoral dissertation, University of Illinois, Urbana-Champaign.

Cushman, D. P., & King, S. S. (1985). National and organizational cultures in conflict resolution: Japan, the United States, and Yugoslavia. In W. B. Gudykunst, L. P. Stewart, & S. Ting-Toomey (Eds.), *Communication, culture, and organizational processes* (pp. 114-133). Newbury Park, CA: Sage.

Davidson, A. R., & Thompson, E. (1980). Cross-cultural studies of attitudes and beliefs. In H. C. Triandis & R. W. Brislin (Eds.), *Handbook of cross-cultural psychology* (Vol. 5, pp. 25-72). Boston: Allyn & Bacon.

Detweiler, R. (1980). Intercultural interaction and the categorization process. *International Journal of Intergroup Relations, 4,* 275-293.

Dinges, N. G., & Maynard, W. S. (1983). Intercultural aspects of organizational effectiveness. In D. Landis and R. W. Brislin (Eds.), *Handbook of intercultural training.* (Vol. 3 pp. 50-81). New York: Pergamon.

Donohue, W. A. (1985). Ethnicity and mediation. In W. B. Gudykunst, L. P. Stewart, & S. Ting-Toomey (Eds.), *Communication, culture, and organizational processes* (pp. 134-155). Newbury Park, CA: Sage.

Everett, J. E., Stening, B. W., & Longton, P. A. (1981). Stereotypes of the Japanese manager in Singapore. *International Journal of Intercultural Relations, 5,* 277-289.

Fernandez, J. P. (1975). *Black managers in white corporations.* New York: John Wiley.

Fiedler, F. E., Mitchell, T., & Triandis, H. C. (1971). The culture assimilator: An approach to cross-cultural training. *Journal of Applied Psychology, 55,* 95-102.

Forgas, J. P., & Bond, M. H. (1985). Cultural influences on the perceptions of interaction episodes. *Personality and Social Psychology Bulletin, 11,* 75-88.

Frake, C. O. (1964). Notes on queries in ethnography. *American Anthropologist, 66,* 132-145.

Glenn, E. (1981). *Man and mankind.* Norwood, NJ: Ablex.

Graves, D. (1972). Cultural determinism and management behavior. *Organizational Dynamics, 1*(2), 46-59.

Gudykunst, W. B. (1985). Normative power and conflict potential in intergroup relationships. In W. B. Gudykunst, L. P. Stewart, & S. Ting-Toomey (Eds.), *Communication, culture and organizational processes* (pp. 155-173). Newbury Park, CA: Sage.

Gudykunst, W. B. (1987). Sociocultural variability and communication processes. In C. Berger & S. Chaffee (Eds.), *Handbook of communication science* (pp. 847-889). Newbury Park, CA: Sage.

Gudykunst, W. B., & Kim, Y. Y. (1984). *Communicating with strangers.* Reading, MA: Addison-Wesley.

Gudykunst, W. B., Stewart, L. P., & Ting-Toomey, S. (Eds.). (1985). *Communication, culture, and organizational processes.* Newbury Park, CA: Sage.

Haire, M., Ghiselli, E. E., & Porter, L. W. (1966). *Managerial thinking: An international study.* New York: John Wiley.

Hall, E. T. (1959). *The silent language.* Garden City, NY: Doubleday.

Hall, E. T. (1966). *The hidden dimension.* Garden City, NY: Doubleday.

Hall, E. T. (1976). *Beyond culture.* Garden City, NY: Doubleday.

Heenan, D. A., & Perlmutter, H. V. (1979). *Management in the industrial world.* New York: McGraw-Hill.

Herkovits, M. (1955). *Cultural anthropology.* New York: Knopf.

Hofstede, G. (1980). *Culture's consequences: International differences in work-related values.* Newbury Park, CA: Sage.

Hui, C.C.H. (1984). *Individualism-collectivism: Theory, measurement and its relation to reward allocation.* Unpublished doctoral dissertation, Department of Psychology, University of Illinois, Urbana-Champaign.

Jaeger, A. M. (1983). The transfer of organizational cultures overseas: An approach to control in the multinational corporation. *Journal of International Business Studies, 14,* 91-114.

Kanungo, R. N., Gorn, G. J., & Dauderis, H. J. (1976). Motivational orientation of Canadian anglophone and francophone managers. *Canadian Journal of Behavior Sciences, 8,* 107-121.

Kluckhorn, F., & Strodtbeck, F. (1961). *Variations in value orientations.* New York: Harper & Row.

Kraemer, A. J. (1973). *Development of a cultural self-awareness approach to instruction in intercultural communication.* Alexandria, VA: Human Resources Research Organization.

Kraemer, A. J. (1978). *Teacher training workshop in intercultural communication: Instructor's Guide.* Alexandria, VA: Human Resources Research Organization.

Kume, T. (1985). Managerial attitudes toward decision-making. In W. B. Gudykunst, L. P. Stewart, & S. Ting-Toomey (Eds.), *Communication, culture and organizational processes* (pp. 231-251). Newbury Park, CA: Sage.

Landis, D., & Brislin, R. W. (1983). *Handbook of intercultural training* (Vol. 2). New York: Pergamon.

Levine, R. V., & Bartlett, K. (1984). Pace of life, punctuality and coronary heart disease in six countries. *Journal of Cross-Cultural Psychology, 15,* 233-255.

Likert, R. (1967). The human organization. New York: McGraw-Hill.

Maslow, A. H. (1954). *Motivation and personality.* New York: Harper and Brothers.

Mead, M. (1967). *Cooperation and competition among primitive peoples.* Boston: Beacon.

Negandhi, A. R. (1973). *Management and economic development: The case of Taiwan.* The Hague: Martinus Nijhoff.

Negandhi, A. R., & Prasad, S. B. (1971). *Comparative management.* New York: Appleton-Century-Crofts.

Okabe, R. (1983). Cultural assumptions of East and West: Japan and the United States. In W. B. Gudykunst (Ed.), *Intercultural communication theory: Current perspectives* (pp. 212-244). Newbury Park, CA: Sage.

Parsons, T. (1951). *The social system.* Glencoe, IL: Free Press.

Peterson, R. B., & Shimada, J. Y. (1978). Sources of management problems in Japanese-American joint ventures. *Academy of Management Review, 3,* 796-804.

Pettigrew, T. (1959). The measurement and correlates of category width as a cognitive variable. *Journal of Personality, 26,* 532-544.

Porter, L., & Roberts, K. H. (1976). Communication in organizations. In M. Dunnette (Ed.), *Handbook of industrial and organizational psychology* (pp. 1553-1590). Chicago: Rand McNally.

Renwick, G. W. (1981). *The management of intercultural relations in international business.* Chicago: Intercultural Press.

Schein, E. H. (1985). *Organizational culture and leadership.* San Francisco: Jossey-Bass.

Scott, W. A., Osgood, D. W., & Peterson, C. (1979). *Cognitive structure: Theory, measurement and individual differences.* New York: John Wiley.

Smircich, L. (1983). Concepts of culture and organizational analysis. *Administrative Science Quarterly, 28,* 339-358.

Stewart, E. C. (1985). Culture and decision-making. In W. B. Gudykunst, L. P. Stewart, & S. Ting-Toomey (Eds.), *Communication, culture, and organizational processes* (pp. 177-211). Newbury Park, CA: Sage.

Stewart, L. P. (1985). Subjective culture and organizational decision-making. In W. B. Gudykunst, L. P. Stewart, & S. Ting-Toomey (Eds.), *Communication, culture, and organizational processes* (pp. 212-229). Newbury Park, CA: Sage.

Szalay, L. B., Moon, W. T., Bryson, J., & Paternak, W. P. (1971). *Communication lexicon of three South Korean audiences: Social national and motivational domains* (pp. 1-245). Kensington, MD: American Institute for Research.

Tajfel, H. (1974). Social identity and intergroup behavior. *Social Science Information, 13,* 65-93.

Tannenbaum, A. S. (1980). Organizational psychology. In H. C. Triandis & R. W. Brislin (Eds.), *Handbook of cross-cultural psychology* (Vol. 5, pp. 281-334). Boston: Allyn & Bacon.

Tannenbaum, A. S., & Cooke, R. A. (1978). Organizational control: A review of research employing the control graph method. In C. J. Lammers & D. Hickson (Eds.), *Organizations alike and unlike* (pp. 183-210). London: Routledge & Kegan Paul.

Tannenbaum, A. S., Kovcic, B., Rosner, M., Vianello, M., & Sieser, G. (1974). *Hierarchy in organizations: An international comparison.* San Francisco: Jossey-Bass.

Thiagarajan, K. M., & Deep, S. D. (1970). A study of supervisor-subordinate influence and satisfaction in four cultures. *Journal of Social Psychology, 82,* 173-180.

Triandis, H. C. (1964). Cultural influences upon cognitive process. In L. Berkowitz (Ed.), *Advances in experimental social psychology* (pp. 1-48). New York: Academic Press.

Triandis, H. C. (1967). Towards an analysis of the components of interpersonal attitudes. In C. Sherif & J. Sherif (Eds.), *Attitudes, ego-involvement and change* (pp. 227-270). New York: John Wiley.

Triandis, H. C. (1972). *The analysis of subjective culture.* New York: John Wiley.

Triandis, H. C. (1975). Culture training, cognitive complexity and interpersonal attitudes. In R. Brislin, S. Bochner, & W. Lonner (Eds.), *Cross-cultural perspectives on learning* (pp. 39-78). Newbury Park, CA: Sage.

Triandis, H. C. (1976). *Variations in black and white perceptions of the social environment.* Urbana: University of Illinois Press.

Triandis, H. C. (1977a). *Interpersonal behavior.* Monterey, CA: Brooks/Cole.

Triandis, H. C. (1977b). Theoretical framework for evaluation of cross-cultural training effectiveness. *International Journal of Intercultural Relations, 1,* 19-45.

Triandis, H. C. (1978). Some universals of social behavior. *Personality and Social Psychology Bulletin, 4,* 1-16.

Triandis, H. C. (1980a). Introduction to the handbook of cross-cultural psychology. In H. C. Triandis & W. W. Lambert (Eds.), *Handbook of cross-cultural psychology* (Vol. 1, pp. 1-14). Boston: Allyn & Bacon.

Triandis, H. C. (1980b). Values, attitudes and interpersonal behavior. In H. Howe & M. Page (Eds.), *Nebraska symposium on motivation: 1979* (pp. 195-260). Lincoln: University of Nebraska Press.

Triandis, H. C. (1984). A theoretical framework for the more efficient construction of cultural assimilators. *International Journal of Intercultural Relations, 8,* 301-330.

Triandis, H. C., Kilty, K., Shanmugam, A. V., Tanaka, Y., & Vassiliou, V. (1972). Cognitive structures and the analysis of values. In H. C. Triandis (Ed.), *The analysis of subjective culture* (pp. 181-262). New York: John Wiley.

Watson, O. M. (1970). *Proxemic behavior.* Paris: Mouton.

Weiss, S. E., & Stripp, W. (1985). *Negotiating with foreign business persons: An introduction for Americans with propositions on six cultures* (Working Paper No. 1). New York University Faculty of Business Administration.

Whyte, W. F., & Williams, L. K. (1963). *Supervisory leadership: An international comparison.* Symposium B3, Paper B3c, CIOS XIII.

Zavalloni, M. (1980). Values. In H. C. Triandis & W. W. Lambert (Eds.), *Handbook of cross-cultural psychology* (Vol. 5, pp. 73-154). Boston: Allyn & Bacon.

III

STRUCTURE: PATTERNS OF ORGANIZATIONAL RELATIONSHIPS

In this third part of the book we consider how patterns of communication shape and are shaped by organization structure. The notion of *structure* is probably one of the oldest concepts in organization theory. Organizational theorists have typically used the term to refer to the formal characteristics of organizations that serve to control and coordinate its parts. Research along these lines has tended to focus on how formal structure affects communication processes. In contrast, communication researchers have traditionally explored the nature of emergent, enacted patterns of interaction in organizations. Frequently treating communication as an independent variable, these scholars have attempted to provide a view of how patterns of interaction create and shape organization structure and how individual and organizational goals are achieved through enactment processes. In recent years, however, researchers have recognized that the two approaches are closely intertwined and that formal and informal structures are interactively created over time. As Monge and Eisenberg observe in the opening chapter of this section, "Formal and emergent networks coexist, and each can best be understood in the context of the other."

The four chapters in Part III illustrate the manner in which formal and emergent communication networks/structures coexist in organizations. In addition, these chapters share one major theme: the embeddedness of networks/structures in organizations. The chapters also hold in common the notion of distinguishing among levels of analysis (dyadic, group, organizational, extraorganizational) in exploring communication networks/structures. Yet these chapters stress the necessity of considering the manner in which higher- and lower-order levels of structure interact with each other. Moreover, each chapter emphasizes the embeddedness of communication networks/structures in time. Communication networks/structures are conceived of as dynamic as opposed to static entities.

The chapters included in this part focus on four topics: emergent communication networks, superior-subordinate relationships, formal organizational structure, and information technologies. Thus the order of chapters progresses from a consideration of issues associated with naturally occurring communication patterns in organizations, to communication in prescribed hierarchical dyadic relationships, to an examination of associations between communication and the formal structural features of organizations, to an analysis of how electronic media structure organizational communication processes.

The opening chapter by Monge and Eisenberg attempts to review and integrate research exploring the concept of emergent communication networks. In order to integrate this literature, they place communication network research within the broader field of structural analysis. In particular, they consider how communication structure is conceptualized in three major schools of structural inquiry—the positional, relational, and cultural traditions. This analysis leads Monge and Eisenberg to three conclusions. First, they deem that an integrated framework on emergent networks is feasible. Second, they suggest that formal structure constrains interaction and that the interaction of people shapes social structure. Third, and of major significance to the later theoretical perspective they present, Monge and Eisenberg conclude that the predominance of either a formal or emergent structure is "to some degree a function of where an organization is in its evolutionary cycle." In essence, they argue that formal and emergent networks in organizations are constantly being restructured due to processes associated with the entering and exiting of organizational members. Monge and Eisenberg label this recurrent process of forming, maintaining, and dissolving communication linkages *reorganizing*.

In order to elucidate the reorganizing principle, Monge and Eisenberg examine the nature of emergent network linkages and then propose three types of factors that influence network reorganization: environmental (local and national character, industry and business culture), organizational (organizational culture, climate, and technology) and individual (power and politics, network roles, professional training). They argue, however, that the duration, magnitude, and predictability of the effects of the above factors on network structures and the organizing process may be quite variable. Their review of literature concludes by considering the consequences of network emergence and restructuring. In particular, they explore how network position and group connectivity influence attitudes and how network involvement affects the socialization of newcomers, organizational commitment, innovation, and turnover.

Monge and Eisenberg also suggest a number of critical issues that future emergent network research must address if the area is to progress as a viable arena of study. Their concerns focus on theory building and improved network analysis methodologies. In particular, they foresee the necessity of integrating network theory with organization theory, expanding the notion of organizational network boundaries to include clusters of linkages between the "organization" and broader elements of society, developing sampling techniques that can effectively represent network populations, examining the nature of multiplex (overlapping) linkages among networks, and determining the stability of networks over time.

In concluding their chapter, Monge and Eisenberg place special importance on studying content dimensions of communication networks. They argue that network researchers can provide insights into meaning and interpretation systems in organizations by exploring "semantic" networks. Along these lines, they suggest that by combining a coorientation model to communication content with traditional network analysis methods we can ascertain how patterns of interaction and convergence of meaning among network members are interrelated. According to Monge and Eisenberg, this approach might facilitate studies exploring the cultural tradition of structural inquiry and also potentially serve to integrate the various network traditions by encouraging research examining correspondence in content across types of networks.

In the second chapter in this part, Dansereau and Markham explore what they describe as traditionally one of the "most popular" areas of organizational communication research, communication in formally prescribed superior-subordinate dyads. Their analysis, however, is not merely a review and interpretation of the literature. Rather, they focus on recasting research exploring superior-subordinate communication into four schools of thought with respect to issues associated with levels of analysis. Concluding that the traditions have been isolated both theoretically and empirically from one another, Dansereau and Markham propose that superior-subordinate communication should be studied from multiple levels of analysis and present an approach, which they term "varient analysis," that can test among alternative formulations of superior-subordinate communication. Thus the chapter not only reviews research on superior-subordinate interaction but also presents a method for exploring various modes of communication between members of the dyad.

The first section of the Dansereau and Markham chapter updates recent studies in 10 major areas: interaction patterns and related attitudes, communication openness, upward distortion, upward influence, semantic-information distance, "effective" versus "ineffective" superiors, personal characteristics, feedback, conflict, and systemic variables. In assessing these studies, Dansereau and Markham are encouraged by the recent attention researchers have paid to exploring the processual nature of superior-subordinate communication. However, they do not perceive similar progress with respect to another frequently noted deficiency in the literature: "inattention to the *embeddedness* of superior-subordinate communication relationships within the larger organizational context." Consequently, they devote the remainder of their chapter to considering how higher- and lower-order levels of organizational and communication phenomena affect interaction between subordinates and superiors.

In considering the contemporary literature, they argue that researchers have tended to study superior-subordinate communication from four levels of analysis: the person (individual differences), dyad, group, and collectivity. Further, they observe that within each of these traditions researchers have examined communication issues related to within-entity concerns (for example, differences within dyads) or between whole entities or levels (for example, between pairs of people, dyads). Yet, Dansereau and Markham note, the basis for deciding when to treat phenomena as representing one school of thought or another (or as a within or between entity concern) has not been addressed by researchers. In response to this issue, they propose the following approach: View all levels of analysis a priori as equally likely, and then test among alternative formulations of variables and levels/entities to determine which can be supported and which should be rejected. Along these lines, they describe a conceptualization of multiple levels of analysis and offer a related empirical testing procedure (varient analysis) that can be used to determine which formulation of variables and levels of analysis are more or less likely to apply in any given situation. In addition, they use this conceptualization to show how four multiple-level formulations (or modes) can be used to organize existing studies of superior-subordinate communication.

In concluding their chapter, Dansereau and Markham recognize that levels of analysis have received little attention in previous superior-subordinate communication research. As a consequence, the latter section of their chapter builds upon the 10 categories of research reviewed in the first section to identify opportunities for future research using the varient approach to multiple levels of analysis. Numerous suggestions are offered for refining previous studies of superior-subordinate communication within each topic area and for expanding future research by explicitly considering multiple levels of analysis.

The third chapter in Part III, by Jablin, attempts to synthesize and provide direction for research exploring communication and formal organization structure. Noting that research in this area remains "strewn across a variety of disciplines," Jablin describes his chapter as a "pretheoretical" analysis of the literature—it attempts to "clean up" and interpret communication research associated with formal organization structure. By focusing on those formal characteristics of organizations that serve to control, differentiate, and coordinate its parts, the chapter emphasizes what Monge and Eisenberg earlier termed the "positional" view of structure. However, Jablin's analysis assumes a somewhat broader perspective to formal structure by considering structure a "meta-communicative" constraint on communication processes: "structure communicates about constraints organizational members face in the communication process."

The chapter reviews research examining relationships between communication and four dimensions of structure: configuration, complexity, formalization, and centralization. With respect to configuration, or an organization's shape resulting from the distribution and location of its work roles and units, a number of characteristics are examined, including span of control, hierarchical level, and organizational and subunit size. In turn, organizational complexity, or the division of labor, knowledge, functions, and resources in organizations, is examined in two directions: horizontally and vertically. Research exploring formalization, or the degree to which the requirements of job and work behaviors are explicit in organizations, is then considered. The review section of the chapter subsequently concludes by examining research exploring relationships between communication and organizational centralization. Centralization, or the concentration of decision-making authority at higher (versus lower) levels of management, is considered with respect to two types of decisions: work-related (how and when work is done) and strategic (company policy, organization-environment relations). Overall, the review attempts to distinguish levels of communication phenomena (individual, group, organizational) associated with each of the structure dimensions.

Among the various conclusions that are drawn from the review, several are particularly noteworthy. Jablin emphasizes repeatedly the dearth of research analyzing actual oral and / or written messages in considering communication-structure relationships. The corpus of our knowledge appears based on self-report measures of communication behavior. Further, he observes that the great majority of studies have focused on a very narrow set of communication behaviors: frequency and volume of self-report messages. Moreover, he argues that researchers have tended to study relationships between particular structure dimensions and communication without considering how these relationships may be moderated by other structure characteristics. Like other authors of chapters in this section, Jablin laments the absence of longitudinal research exploring structure-communication relationships. In a brief review of research examining how organizational structure and communication processes vary over organizational life cycles, he illustrates the importance of utilizing time-series research designs and specifying life cycle stages in conducting studies in this area.

In concluding the chapter, Jablin reiterates a theme sounded earlier by Monge and Eisenberg: Formal organization structure and emergent structure are reciprocally interdependent. However, he also acknowledges that while determining the manner in which formal structure and emergent structure shape and are shaped by communication processes represents an exciting area of research, it is also a formidable arena of study.

The fourth and final chapter in Part III by Culnan and Markus considers the notion of structure from a slightly different perspective than the preceding chapters. Specifically, these authors examine how new electronic information technologies or media alter communication processes and thereby influence organizational structure and process. Electronic media are defined as "interactive, computer-mediated technologies that facilitate two-way interpersonal communication" among geographically dispersed individuals and groups. In particular, Culnan and Markus focus on three general types of electronic media: electronic message systems, conferencing systems, and integrated office systems. Their chapter includes a review of studies examining the effects of these media on the individual, group, and to some degree, the organizational levels of analysis. However, they focus solely on the effects of electronic media on intraorganizational communication and exclude from their analysis studies that examine information systems that do not mediate interpersonal and group communication (personal computing, word processing).

In the first half of their chapter, Culnan and Markus review a variety of types of laboratory studies exploring electronic media effects. Their analysis leads them to reject the conceptual framework underlying much of this research, which assumes that electronic media are deficient in comparison to face-to-face communication because they lack various types of communication cues (cues for regulating interaction and forming impressions). Rather, they argue that electronic media "have capabilities not found in face-to-face interaction," such as unique methods to address messages, improved capabilities for controlling access to communication, and new ways of storing and retrieving communication.

The latter half of the chapter explores some of these capabilities by reviewing field studies of the use of electronic media in organizations. Among the studies they review are several suggesting that electronic media undermine authority relationships by overloading the information-processing capability of organizational hierarchies. Culnan and Markus observe that these types of impairments may lead to flattening hierarchies to reduce the need for upward information processing. A summary is made of numerous studies demonstrating that the introduction of electronic media into organizations can result in new and distinctive communication networks, increases in communication linkages among organizational members, and increases in upward and downward hierarchical communication. Additionally, the authors note that the computer storage capabilities associated with electronic media provide new avenues for collecting valid and reliable data for communication network analyses.

In considering this final chapter in Part III, the reader should realize that research exploring electronic communication technologies is still in its infancy. Culnan and Markus's review and analysis of the existing literature clearly demonstrates the important effects these technologies may have on formal and emergent organization structure. Yet, similar to the other authors in this section, they recognize that new communication technologies are embedded within organizational contexts containing older, more traditional forms of structure and communication. The communication structures created by new media cannot be studied or understood in isolation of other forms of structure. Moreover, as Culnan and Markus observe, all communication media were once "new." As a consequence, they conclude that much may be learned about the effects of "new" electronic communication technologies by revisiting earlier organizational communication theory and research.

10   Emergent Communication Networks

PETER R. MONGE
ERIC M. EISENBERG
University of Southern California

THIS chapter reviews research on emergent communication networks in organizations. As a whole, this body of work is fragmented and difficult to synthesize. To integrate these diverse findings, we first place communication network research within the more general context of structural inquiry. Second, we offer some basic definitions to assist the reader in sorting through the network terminology. Third, we present the research findings, organized by causes, consequents, and levels of emergent networks. Fourth and finally, we examine current issues facing communication network research.

AUTHORS' NOTE: We wish to express appreciation to Janet Fulk, Linda Putnam, Ron Rice, and Ev Rogers for their helpful comments and suggestions on earlier drafts of this chapter.

NETWORKS AND THE STRUCTURAL TRADITIONS

Like the concept of formal communication networks to which it is linked, the concept of emergent communication networks can best be understood as a special case of the broader domain of structural analysis. In a classic work, Mitchell (1972) argued that the "recent increase of interest in social networks appears to be due in part to dissatisfaction with conventional modes of structural analysis. In fact, the introduction of the notion of the social network into social analysis seems to have arisen out of exactly such circumstances" (p. 2). It is appropriate, therefore, that we begin this chapter on emergent networks with a brief overview of the field of structural inquiry.

At an abstract level, one conceptualization of structure is a collection of elements or parts and the set of relationships that connects the parts together. Structuralists have studied elements as diverse as people, organizations, and languages. They have also studied many different kinds of relationships such as attraction, kinship, dependency, and communication.[1]

The field of structural analysis has a long and distinguished history. In sociology, Herbert Spencer (1982) and Emile Durkheim (1895/1964) are often credited with introducing structural concepts into sociological thinking. In anthropology, Radcliffe-Brown (1952/1959) incorporated structural-functionalist ideas into his seminal analysis of cultures. And in linguistics, structural thinking can be traced to the pioneering work of de Saussure (1916/1966). Not surprisingly, this wide range of work has led to numerous competing views of structure (Blau, 1981; McPhee, 1985).

Most structural theories of organizations can be placed into one of three major schools of thought. These are the positional, the relational, and the cultural traditions.

The Positional Tradition

The classical view of communication structure in organizations is intellectually rooted in the work of Max Weber (1947), Talcott Parsons (1951), and George Homans (1958). In their conceptualization, structure is a pattern of relations among positions in the social unit (the society, the organization, or the group). Attached to each position is a set of roles that the people occupying the positions are expected to perform. These roles comprise the designated behaviors and obligatory relations incumbent upon the people in the positions. The positions and their roles are formally defined in the organization and exist independently of the individuals who fill them. The individuals who assume these positions are seen as transients who move from position to position; individuals are viewed as less permanent than the positions themselves. When viewed collectively, the positions and attached roles constitute the relatively stable and enduring structure of the organization. Writing within this tradition, James and Jones (1976) define structure as "the enduring characteristics of an organization reflected by the distribution of units and positions within an organization and their systematic relationships to each other" (p. 76). A significant implication of this view of structure is that roles and positions are seen as largely determining to whom people talk and the topics about which they talk. The roles attached to the positions specify the people to whom the person should communicate, the acceptable topics, and the procedural requirements for communication.

This view of communication structure captures an important aspect of organizations. Organizations do have designated positions that people fill, and the roles attached to these positions specify and constrain the behavior of their incumbents (see Jablin, Chapter 12, this volume). However, a number of people have argued that this view of structure is overly simplistic and incomplete (Burt, 1976; Coleman, 1973; Nadel, 1957; White, Boorman, & Breiger, 1976). Specifically, the positional tradition has been criticized for its inability to take into account the active part individuals play in creating and shaping organizational structure.

The Relational Tradition

Writers in the relational tradition focus primarily on the role of human action in forging and maintaining communication linkages and thereby enacting structure. Rather than conceiving of organizational structure in terms of formalization or centralization (which refer more to role and hierarchical relations than to individuals), advocates of the relational school argue that much of what is meaningful to study about structure lies in the emergent interactions between people. In this view, communication structure in organizations may or may not coincide with formal or prescribed structure—individuals may interact in ways that are not dictated by their positions.

Rooted to a large degree in modern systems theory (for example, Buckley, 1967), relational theorists conceive of the relationships among people in a system as worthy of study in their own right. The relational approach has become increasingly popular among students of organizational behavior (Brass, 1984; Roberts & O'Reilly, 1978; Tichy, 1981) and is the most prevalent structural tradition in the communication field (Rogers & Kincaid, 1981). The crucial distinction between the two approaches described so far is that the relational focuses on emergence, while the positional does not. Whereas the positional tradition sees structure as relatively top down, formal, and static, the relational tradition views structure as bottom-up, individually motivated (to a large extent, although not entirely), and dynamic. This shift in emphasis has awakened many researchers to the role of communication networks in promoting goals other than increased efficiency (such as building morale, supporting innovation), as well as to a more general appreciation for the world-building and sense-making processes central to organizational communication (McPhee, 1985; Richards, 1985; Rogers & Kincaid, 1981).

The Cultural Tradition

The cultural tradition represents a third, somewhat related view of social structure. In general, this perspective emphasizes the importance of symbols, meanings, and their transmission throughout social systems. A broad interest in cultural issues in the organizational sciences (Frost, Moore, Louis, Lundberg, & Martin, 1985) has emerged largely due to the assertion that older paradigms (and structural-functionalism in particular) have run their course and need to be revised or replaced. In the 1960s one potential replacement was Levi-Strauss's (1963) structuralism, in which he tried to identify a relatively few underlying mechanisms to account for the more surface aspects of everyday social life. To do so, he made a distinction between surface structures of human action and deep structures, those abstract, cognitive concepts that explained social relations in ways that are for the most part independent of individual human actions or intentions. Blau (1982) summarizes this work:

> For him [Levi-Strauss] and his followers, "deep structure" is a fundamental, unconscious characteristic of the human mind that underlies all empirically observable phenomena, be they kinship arrangements or myths. The deep structure finds various expressions in various cultures—different kinship systems, different mythologies—yet it alone can satisfactorally explain these culturally specific, empirically observable phenomena. (p. 274)

While not all structuralist writers in the cultural tradition emphasize the abstract, cognitive nature of structures to the extent Levi-Strauss did, all share the notion of deep structures subtly related to surface enactments. British anthropologists in particular focused more on "surface" structures and the organization of social relations most akin to the communication field's concern with interaction (see Ortner, 1984). But it was not until the late 1970s that the study of cultures—organizational and otherwise—turned to communication per se as the primary focus of study (see Chapter 15 by Frost, this volume, for a discussion of deep and surface structure as they relate to organizational power). Prior to this point, culture was viewed mainly as a constraint (paralleling the positional tradition) and not as emergent from interaction. According to Ortner, the growing concern with social interaction (or, more broadly, with "practices") reflects "an urgent need to understand where the 'system' comes from—how it is produced and reproduced and how it may have changed in the past or be changed in the future" (p. 146).

Seeing communication in this way requires us simultaneously to reject the view of action as simply the enactment of social rules and norms (associated mainly with de Saussure and Parsons) as well as the other extreme in which social structure is seen as wholly invented by individuals (Thompson, 1978). As Ortner wisely points out, individuals create social reality only in a somewhat ironic sense—the worlds that emerge are rarely the ones they set out to build. In the end, we must pursue a three-pronged approach to social structure, acknowledging all at once that "society is a system, that the system is powerfully constraining, and yet that the system can be made and unmade through human action and interaction" (Ortner, 1984, p. 159; see also Berger & Luckmann, 1966).

Writers who have applied the cultural approach to organizational studies include McPhee (1985), Ranson, Hinings, and Greenwood (1980), and Riley (1983). With few exceptions, these researchers have based their work on Gidden's (1979) writings on structuration, which attempt to account for both the creative and the constraining aspects of social structure. These studies are characterized by an explicit concern for the continual production and reproduction of meaning through communication, examining simultaneously how meanings emerge from interaction and how they act to constrain subsequent interaction.

Integration of the Three Traditions

Various authors have tried to integrate these diverse traditions. Galaskiewicz (1979), for example, combined Homans's (1958) exchange theory with the model of purposive action developed by Coleman (1966, 1973) to address the question of how networks form. Relationships develop, Galaskiewicz says, "out of the purposive action of social actors (whether they be individuals or organizations) who seek to realize their self-interests and, depending on their ability and interest, will negotiate routinized patterns or relationships that enhance these interests" (p. 16). Hence communicative interaction produces structural forms. At the same time, however, "the way in which particular resource networks will be routinized will be determined by the functional needs that the medium of exchange serves in the social organization" (Galaskiewicz, 1979, p. 16). Organization results from a combination of both formal and emergent interdependencies.

Blau (1982) provides a second view of these two positions:

> The focus on the study of the structure of social positions and the study of social relations raises the question of which of the two are the starting points or most primitive concepts. Do we first analyze social relations and distinguish positions on the basis of differences in patterns of relations, or do we start by categorizing people by social position to examine the patterns of relations among them? . . . Implicit in the first procedure is the causal assumption that people's social relations delineate their roles and define their positions in the group, whereas the second procedure implicitly assumes that differences in attributes and positions affect people's social relations. (p. 277)

Blau (1982) argues that both views are true at different times in the development of social structure and that the two must be integrated to provide a complete understanding. He argues, however, that the relational view is most applicable to small, recently formed groups, while the positional view applies to established communities and societies, where social positions are less changeable. More explicitly he states, "When small groups are first formed the social relations that become established in the course of processes of social interaction differentiate the roles of group members, but in lasting organizations or societies persisting differences in social positions rooted in ascribed attributes or available resources govern most social relations"(p. 21).

A third effort attempts to integrate all three rather than just two of the structural traditions. Ranson et al. (1980) criticize the "unhelpful contrasting" of the positional and relational approaches and argue that insights derived from the cultural approach need to be integrated with the other two views. Drawing upon the work of Bacharach and Aiken (1976), Benson (1977), Bourdieu (1977), Giddens (1979), and Rice and Mitchell (1973), they develop a theory of organizational structuring that proposes that three fundamental processes are at work in the development of organizational structures: provinces of meaning, dependencies of power, and contextual constraints. Structure, they argue, can be conceived of as "a complex medium of control which is continually produced and recreated in interaction and yet shapes that interactions: structures are constituted and constitutive" (p. 3).

In sum, the relational and cultural traditions share a common concern with interaction, surface structures, and emergence. This is most clearly seen in contrast with the positional perspective. However, the cultural perspective differs from the relational perspective in two important ways: the increased value placed on meaning and interpretation of communication; and the relationships that are explored between interaction patterns and deep structures that are thought to underlie and explain social life.

These three attempts at integration suggest three principles that we develop in the remainder of this chapter. The first is that an integrated perspective on emergent communication networks is possible. Formal and emergent networks coexist, and each can best be understood in the context of the other. The second point is that both perspectives are valid. This implies that the constraints imposed by an existing structure limit and shape the interactions of people who work in various roles and fulfill various status sets. It also implies the converse, that the interaction of people helps to shape and define the social networks. The third point is that the predominance of either type of structure is to some degree a function of where an organization is in its evolutionary life cycle. In most contemporary organizations both formal and emergent networks are in constant change. This change, however, is not simply the substitution of people in positions as characterized by the positional perspective. Rather, the positions themselves are sometimes altered and the structure significantly changed as a result. As we will argue shortly, restructuring of both the formal and the emergent networks is the predominant phenomenon worthy of study.

Although we have organized this review around the causes and consequents of communication networks, we must emphasize that these are dynamic processes that are at times indistinguishable. To illustrate this perspective before we begin our review of the literature, we invite you to imagine with us how the processes of "reorganizing" communication networks might operate throughout the life cycle of a hypothetical contemporary organization.

REORGANIZING: A HYPOTHETICAL SCENARIO

Imagine for a few moments a group of people that is deciding to form a new organization. They come together in various combinations to discuss their ideas for the new firm. Each person has expertise to contribute to the discussion. They also contribute other resources that can be used to develop the new organization. They talk together at varying times and on varying topics. They make conscious decisions about who will be responsible for what in the newly emerging organization. Some people assume responsibility and authority over others and those others assume more subordinate positions.

Each person has a set of contacts outside the fledgling organization. Frequently, each person draws upon one or more of those contacts to bring those resources and benefits into the organization. As time goes on, relationships change as people discover what works and what does not. New reporting relationships are made, new linkages formed. People discover that they have interests in common, and over time these common interests grow into a set of relatively permanent and stable relationships.

As the organization grows, new people are added. Each person who joins the organization assumes some role or responsibility. Like those who joined the organization before them, new members typically have someone to report to and possibly others who report to them. They have formal, designated responsibilities for conveying and obtaining information. They also bring their unique interests to the organization and as they work they encounter people with similar interests. The amount of time and energy that people can commit to communication, however, is limited. As people forge new linkages they have less time to make contact with others. As newcomers forge linkages with existing members of the organization, existing linkages are modified to accommodate these new contacts.

As people leave the organization, most but not all of their linkages within the company are terminated. If these people are replaced, then some of their linkages (those relevant to their position) will be taken up by new people. Of course, the new people will have the freedom to forge their own personal networks and as a result will develop contact patterns that are different than the ones enacted by their predecessors. If people who leave are not replaced, then those linkages will either be dropped or taken up by others in the organization. Sometimes internal networks will be restructured so that people may either temporarily or permanently assume the responsibilities and linkages of people who have left the firm.

On an individual level we see the process of people forming, maintaining, and terminating their contacts with other people both inside and outside the firm. We can also look at this process from the standpoint of the whole organization. Viewed this way, we may see a collection of people with linkages some of which are highly stable (and perhaps represent the central core of the organization's network) and others of which seem to change quite frequently and to be rather unstable. Not only are new people being added to the network while others leave, but even for those who stay, the communication linkages are constantly being altered in one form or another.

On occasion, organizations are faced with the necessity of making major structural changes. This is most vividly seen at the time of organizational acquisition, merger, and divestiture. In acquisition and merger, two formerly independent firms are blended into one. The new organization has the major task of integrating two existing communication networks. New people, new reporting relationships, and new linkages all need to be formed. In divestiture, a part of the organization is given its independence. Many of the original ties to the parent organization are cut and the newly formed organization must forge its own new linkages. Some of these will be to new people that it must obtain to fill the roles of those who remained with the parent firm. Others will be linkages to the environment to replace those that were maintained by those who remained with the parent firm.

The perspective that we have been describing is characterized by constant change. Organizations continuously add and delete people. And those people constantly forge and dissolve their linkages to one another and to the outside world.

The concept of "reorganizing" best describes this fundamental aspect of organizations. It represents the changes that occur as people join and leave organizations and as they alter their communication linkages with one another. Sometimes this process is deliberate. For example, management may consciously plan a restructuring of the organization to accomplish a new type of work or to increase productivity. At other times, the process occurs naturally without planning. For example, the loss of a key individual or the acquisition of a dynamic leader often has a significant, unanticipated impact on the communication network.

The remainder of this chapter addresses the formation, maintenance, and dissolution of linkages between people and organizations. First, we examine the nature of these linkages: their roles, levels, content, properties, and metrics. Second, we discuss those factors in organizations that affect and are affected by characteristics of networks. Finally, we explore current issues in communication network research and make recommendations for future study.

THE NATURE OF EMERGENT NETWORKS

In this section we examine five crucial issues key to understanding the nature of emergent networks: (1) network articulation and participant roles; (2) levels of analysis; (3) content of linkages; (4) properties of linkages; and (5) individual and network metrics.

Network Articulation and Participant Roles

Network articulation is the process of identifying the various component parts of the network (Farace & Mabee, 1980; Farace, Monge, & Russell, 1977). The three major components of a network are (1) the groups or clusters that make up the networks, (2) the individuals who link the clusters together, and (3) the people not highly involved in the network who do not belong to a group or link groups together. Obviously, work groups such as committees are likely to emerge from a communication network analysis. But at least two other types of emergent clusters are important. The first is coalitions, short-term alliances that typically emerge to accomplish limited political goals. The second is cliques, which are "long-lived and pursue broad ranges of purposes; they are the smallest clusters, and they generally form to meet the expressive and affective needs of organizational members" (Tichy, 1981, p. 228).

Each individual in the network can be thought of as playing a role that corresponds to each of the three categories above. The three roles that any person can fulfill are: a group member, a group linker such as bridge or liaison, and an isolate. Individuals may play different roles in different networks; for example, one can be a group member in the task communication network, but an isolate in the innovation network. Some authors (for example, Tichy & Fombrun, 1979) add an additional role—the star—to describe a person who has many more linkages than most others in a network.

Levels of Analysis

We indicated above that the study of structure can be examined from several different theoretical perspectives. Social networks can also be examined from several levels of analysis. Burt (1978, 1980a) describes three distinct levels: the personal level, the clique level, and the overall network level. Tichy (1981) and Tichy and Fombrun (1979), who adopted a more explicit organizational orientation, add a fourth level, the environmental or interorganizational level.

The study of networks on the individual level, called personal or ego networks, focuses on the relations and patterns of relations that the focal individual has with others in the network. This includes, for example, the number and density of linkages and the number of different networks in which a person is involved. From the positional perspective, analysis centers on the patterns of relations that the focal individual has with all others in the network, including all the people to whom the focal individual is not linked. This includes measures of the degree to which the focal individual is central to the network or occupies a prestigious position in the hierarchy.

The study of networks on the clique level focuses on grouping individuals into different component parts of the network. The components are typically different groups of individuals that are more intensely connected to each other than they are to other members of the overall network. From the relational perspective this usually means that members are grouped by some criterion of cohesion (such as frequency or intensity of communication). From the positional perspective, this level of analysis involves identifying people who are structurally equivalent (Burt, 1978; Sailer, 1978). People are considered to be structurally equivalent when they have the same (or a similar) pattern of relations as other people in the network who occupy their same status. Thus two doctors in a hospital who talk with the same nursing and administrative staff at approximately the same frequency or intensity are considered structurally equivalent even if they do *not* talk to each other.

Research at the network level of analysis centers on describing characteristics and features of the network as a whole. From the relational perspective, a typical network characteristic is density. Network density describes the extent to which the members of the network are interconnected, relative to the criterion of a totally interconnected network, that is, where everyone is connected to everyone else. From a positional perspective, the focus of the analysis is on network stratification. Burt (1980a) explains:

> Extent of stratification is captured by network models of hierarchy and centralization. A system is centralized to the extent that all relations in it involve a single actor. It has hierarchical structure to the extent that a single actor is the direct or indirect object of all relations in it. Hierarchy refers to the prestige of positions. A system is hierarchical to the extent that a single actor has high prestige. (p. 117)

The study of networks on the environmental or interorganizational level centers on two major topics. The first topic addresses the level and kinds of linkages that members of an organization have with people in other organizations. Included here is research on boundary spanning (Adams, 1976, 1980; Tushman & Scanlan, 1981), defined as linkages that organizational members maintain to monitor, exchange with, or represent the organization to its environment. These external linkages are primarily communicative (in that they almost always involve information exchange) and can have significant implications for the effectiveness of the organization and of the individuals who maintain them. The second topic is the degree to which the other organizations to which an organization is linked are themselves interconnected. Interorganizational linkages nearly always involve communication contact at some level in the organizations (see Eisenberg et al., 1985). The constellation of interconnected firms in an organization's environment has been called an organizational set or interorganizational field (Scott, 1983; Turk, 1970; Warren, 1967). Such linkages in an organization's environment can significantly affect a firm's performance. A turbulent, highly interconnected, interorganizational field can threaten an organization's stability and survival. If the organizational set to which an organization is linked is supportive, valuable resources can be supplied that will help the organization. If, on the other hand, the interorganizational field is competitive and not supportive, the organization will probably have greater difficulty surviving. Recent work by Trist (1983) on organizational ecology is noteworthy in its development of "referent organizations"—intermediary groups such as industry associations and labor-management committees—that facilitate more supportive interorganizational networks.

Content of Linkages

The content of a linkage is important in that it defines what flows between people, that is, it specifies the nature of the network. Several alternative but overlapping content typologies have been proposed. Tichy, Tushman, and Fombrun (1979) maintain that four major types of content have been studied in most network research to date. These are exchange of information, exchange of goods and services, expression of affect such as liking and friendship or dislike and animosity, and attempts to influence and control. Farace et al. (1977) examined the research on communication linkages in organizations and concluded that most of the research centered on three types of messages: production, innovation, and maintenance. Production messages deal with getting the work of the organization done. Innovation messages center on solving organizational problems and finding new and better ways to accomplish organizational goals. Maintenance messages focus on individual feelings and social support for personal problems that people encounter both on and off the job. Most recently, Tichy (1981) has developed a taxonomy of perspectives on organizational networks. He identifies three approaches: (1) the technical approach, which deals with communication about production; (2) the political approach, which emphasizes communication regarding individual and group goals; and (3) the cultural approach, which emphasizes messages that transmit shared meanings and values. Because the implications of each type of linkage content for organizational behavior are so various, findings about one type of network may not be generalizable to other types.

Properties of Linkages

There are four major properties of linkages in emergent networks. These properties refer to the ways linkages are conceptualized and operationalized. The four are strength or intensity, symmetricality, reciprocity, and multiplexity.

Historically, linkages are measured by simply determining the presence or absence of a relation between each pair of people in the network. More recent research typically attempts to measure the extent or degree of relationship constituting each linkage. The strength or intensity of a linkage is a reflection of the amount of information, affect, influence, or goods and services that flows through the network. This has been conceptualized and operationalized in many different ways, including amount of interaction that occurs between two people, amount of information that is exchanged, and the frequency and/or duration of contact. It is even possible to include the importance or value of the linkage as a weighting factor in determining the strength or intensity of the relationship (Rice & Richards, 1985).

The symmetricality of a linkage refers to the degree to which both people enter into the same kind of relationship with each other. Linkages may be either symmetrical or asymmetrical. To illustrate, the supervisor-subordinate relationship is asymmetrical since the subordinate "reports to" the boss, but the boss does not "report to" the subordinate. The coworker relationship, on the other hand, is symmetrical because each "works with" the other, that is, they are both in the same kind of relationship. In communication network analysis, a relation such as "talks with" is symmetrical, since it implies that both share the same relationship. A relation like "gives instruction to" is asymmetrical since it implies that one person is giving the information and the other is receiving it.

The reciprocity of a linkage refers to the degree to which two people who are presumed to be linked report the same relationship. While symmetricality focuses on the definition of the relationship, reciprocity centers on the degree to which two people agree about the existence or strength of the linkage. Thus reciprocity is a measurement issue, while symmetricality is a conceptual issue. For example, suppose two people are asked separately to describe their linkage with each other for the symmetrical relationship "communicates with." If both report the same high level of communication (say, several times per day), then the linkage is reciprocated. Likewise, if both report the same low frequency, such as once or twice a month, the linkage is reciprocated. If, however, they report different values, one saying "several times per day" and the other indicating "once or twice a month" (or not at all), the linkage would be unreciprocated. A similar example could be developed for reciprocation about asymmetrical linkages (for example, both superior and subordinate agree that the superior "gives instructions" at least hourly). Obviously, reciprocation is a matter of degree and the researcher must determine the amount of agreement about the nature of the linkages that he or she will accept as constituting reciprocity.

The multiplexity of linkages refers to the degree to which the same people are involved in different networks within the organization. For example, if people in an organization were asked to describe their asymmetrical relations "reports to," the resultant analysis would likely reveal the organization's formal communication networks. Alternatively, if the same people described their communication regarding personal information, a different structure would emerge. As indicated above, networks are distinguishable by communication content areas such as production, innovation, and maintenance topics (see Farace et al., 1977). In each of these topic areas multiple, often overlapping, networks can be obtained, the collection of which provides considerably richer information than analysis of any one of the networks alone. Linkages that encompass more than one topic area or network are said to be multiplex. Historically, communication network analysis has concentrated on *uni*plex networks, or if multiple relations are examined, they are examined separately. This has precluded the examination of the degree to which the networks overlap and are interconnected.

Individual and Network Metrics

Over the years a number of measures have been developed to measure characteristics of networks. Most of them have alternate computational forms that are appropriate for describing characteristics of individual (ego) and organizational networks. The best known and most often used metrics are size, centrality, density, and reachability (see Tichy, 1981, for a list of other metrics).

The simplest metric is size. At the individual level, it refers simply to the number of people to whom a person is linked. At the network level it indicates the total number of linkages in the network.

Centrality is one of the most frequently used network metrics. Freeman (1979) reviewed the research literature that used the concept of centrality and identified three alternative definitions. The first measure of centrality is "degree," the number of direct contacts each person has with other people. In one sense, it is simply a measure of activity. The second measure of centrality is "betweenness." This measure identifies the extent to which a person is directly connected to two other persons who are not typically connected to each other. By being the shortest indirect path between two people, the "between" person has the potential to exercise control over those who he or she is between. The third and most frequently used measure of centrality is closeness or proximity. At the individual level closeness is usually operationalized by summing the length of the shortest path by which an individual typically "reaches" or connects to every other individual. At the organizational level, the extent to which each individual can be reached by everyone else is summed to provide a measure of the closeness/centrality of the entire network; this measure is sometimes called organizational reachability. Freeman (1979) points out that the degree of closeness in a network can be thought of both in terms of individual independence and of the efficiency of the group. Closeness provides a measure of independence in that it indicates the extent to which a person can avoid being controlled by others.

Alternatively, closeness reflects efficiency because it indicates the extent to which a person can reach everyone else (for example, with task-related information) in the shortest number of steps.

A third network characteristic is density or connectedness. Like the other metrics, it can be a property of an individual or a property of the organizational network. Density is defined as the ratio of actual to potential contacts in a network. For an individual, it is the proportion of the total number of people in the network to which that person is directly connected (connectedness). For an entire network, it is the proportion of linkages that exist relative to the total number of contacts that would exist if everyone were linked directly to everyone else.

The final network metric to be discussed is reachability. At the individual level it is defined as the number of steps or linkages it takes to reach another person in the network. At the organizational level it indicates the average number of links separating individuals in the network.

In the next section, we explore some of the factors that lead to reorganization, that is, those factors that seem to bring about change in emergent networks. In doing so, we of necessity cut across many types of networks and levels of analysis.[2] Our presentation is organized from the outside in; we begin with environmental influences on organizational networks, next consider organizational influences, and finally examine individual influences.

FACTORS INFLUENCING EMERGENT NETWORKS

Three types of factors that influence emergent networks are discussed in this section. These are environmental, organizational, and individual.

Environmental Influences on Network Emergence

Since the late 1960s, organizational researchers have increasingly focused their attention on organizational environments (Aldrich, 1979; Pfeffer & Salancik, 1978). Much of this research has structural implications. In this section, we examine research that looks at environmental influences on organizational communication networks.

Changes in the interorganizational field affect the kinds of organizations that emerge and are able to survive. Dense interorganizational networks developed in the United States as a result of the proliferation of a professional management class in the years prior to World War I (Aldrich & Mueller, 1982). Today, a seasoned executive may have thousands of interorganizational contacts (Kaplan, 1984). At the same time, the nature of many of these contacts has changed from face-to-face to mediated as a result of the massive expansion and decentralization of the American work force. Aldrich and Mueller argue that since 1970 environmental changes at the national level have in general favored more formal hierarchies, increased need for interorganizational relations, and increased efforts on the part of organizations to manage their environments.

Some research suggests that national character may be reflected in organizational communication patterns. French employees, for example, tend to avoid close ties at work, whereas Japanese employees tend to seek out such ties (Crozier, 1964; Yoshino, 1968). Organizations exist in social contexts, and aspects of their structure often reflect attitudes at the national level. In the United States, for example, widespread popular interest and appreciation of "excellent strong cultures" (Deal & Kennedy, 1982; Peters & Waterman, 1982) have implications for management style and patterns of employee participation. One implication of this changing cultural awareness has been pressures toward more frequent management-employee communication such as Peters and Austin's (1985) recommendation of management by wandering around. A second implication has been the formation of stronger horizontal linkages as represented in quality circles, participative management, and matrix organizations (Lawler, 1986). Naturally, this tendency has not met with uniform acceptance; individual factors (such as personalities of managers and employees) moderate the effect of national culture on the formation of new network patterns.

Local factors can influence patterns of communication as well. Organizations are constrained structurally by the socioeconomic character of the environment in which they are embedded. For organizations to succeed, their structural forms must be sensitive to the physical and economic characteristics of their local environments (Ranson, Hinings, & Greenwood, 1980). The nature of local government, taxation laws, and the local culture can influence the decision to establish an organization in a community. Once a company is established, these factors encourage (and discourage) the development of certain network configurations. Different structural arrangements are needed to cope with the information-processing requirements associated with different kinds of environments (Tichy, 1981). In general, an organization performs best when there is a good "fit" between the nature of its environment and its formal and informal internal structures. Research shows that diverse, turbulent environments require more flexible, organic structural arrangements, whereas more placid, stable environments can be coped with by more traditional, mechanistic structures (Lawrence & Lorsch, 1967). For example, a bank with a fairly traditional structure may be effective in a small town where there is little pressure from competitors, but might fail in the more competitive environment of a bigger city. Local character and organizational form are variables in a cycle of mutual influence; emergent structures are both causes and consequences of environmental change.

Burt (1979) hypothesizes a similar symbiotic relationship between interorganizational structure and the nature of economic markets. Specifically, he proposes that organizations will forge linkages with firms in other sectors of the economy (via interlocking directorates) to the extent that these sectors constrain the focal organization's profits. Further, an organization's profitability can reflect its successful interlocking with organizations in these problematic sectors. These ideas are in line with interorganizational theory in general (see Eisenberg et al., 1985; Pennings, 1980), which suggests organizations will avoid such ties wherever possible to retain autonomy, but if forced to link, those who do it best will become most successful. A number of empirical studies (Burt, 1980b; Burt, Christman, & Kilburn, 1980) have supported this hypothesis relating market constraints to interorganizational linkages.

Organizational structures differ by industry. While some favor traditional, hierarchical relationships, others tend to be more dynamic and flexible. Meyer and Rowan (1977) argue that institutional organizations such as schools and hospitals are unique in their dependence on environments for legitimacy and survival. This overwhelming need for legitimacy, they contend, leads to predictable structural arrangements. Specifically, institutional organizations must "decouple" their technical and administrative functions so that evaluation of technical functions is avoided whenever possible. In communication network terms, this means that certain people and topics are off limits (for example, school administrators would not in most cases observe a teacher's classroom activities). The loose coupling (Weick, 1976) characteristic of educational organizations can also be translated into network terms; the development of weak ties in an organization can help it maintain stability and survive environmental jolts. Similarly, weak ties across organizational boundaries (Granovetter, 1973) can contribute to organizational development through increased information and resource exchange (Kaplan, 1984).

Industries exist in environments that differ in causal texture (Emery & Trist, 1965). The airline industry, for example, exists in a particularly turbulent field. As a result, organizations in this industry must be highly sensitive to changes on the part of government regulations or competitor marketing strategies. Each major airline has developed a unique structural arrangement for dealing with the environment, ranging from traditional bureaucratic hierarchy to highly participative, profit-sharing programs. As yet, no clear relationships between structure and success have been identified.

Mergers and acquisitions are increasingly common and some literature suggests that their effect on patterns of communication can be dramatic (Riley, 1985; compare Walter, 1985). Clashes in job titles, cultural orientation, compensation practices, reporting relations, and organizational politics can all have a marked impact on their reorganizing. The duration of this impact is important; while one would expect short-term confusion following a merger, over time the new organization must stabilize if it is to survive.

One good example of the effects of merger on communication structure is provided by Danowski and Edison-Swift (1985). Their study focused on changes in communication via electronic mail in a state extension agency as a response to a merger "crisis." The effects of the merger on communication were dramatic—in one month the following occurred: (1) number of messages increased 340%, (2) number of people using the mail system increased 240%, (3) messages became shorter, (4) individual networks became more diffuse, and (5) a large, unified group of communicators emerged. An important finding of this study, however, is that these changes were temporary and short-lived; communication returned to premerger levels a month later.

In sum, the research indicates that various aspects of the environment, including national and local character, changes in the business culture, and the characteristics of specific industries can influence network patterns. In addition, mergers and acquisitions can have a dramatic impact on communication networks, although the duration of this impact may vary. In the next section, we move inside the organization to examine selected organizational-level influences that shape communication network patterns.

Organizational Influences on Network Emergence

The characteristics of jobs, tasks, and the organization as a whole influence patterns of communication. Research has focused on three organizational level influences on structure—size, mode of technical production, and pattern of resource distribution within the organization (Ranson et al., 1980). In addition, the differentiation of jobs, density of people in the work area, and proximity of others have all been found to be positively associated with amount of communication within the organization (Form, 1972; Monge, Edwards, & Kirste, 1978). In a broader consideration of the nature of tasks, Blau (1954) and Wade (1968) observed that total amount of communication was positively correlated with the extent to which employees were given discretion over their work.

Much of the research on organizational-level influences has focused on formal structures rather than on emergent networks. The study of the relationships between size, organizational environments, and formal structure is well established in the literature, and is often summarized as the contingency view of organizations (Miles, 1980). Jablin reviews much of this literature in Chapter 12 of this volume.

Some specific findings relevant to the adoption of new communication technologies are worth mentioning here. For example, the greatest potential benefits and pitfalls associated with electronic messaging systems are associated with the resultant changes in patterns of communication (Montgomery & Benbasat, 1983). In a recent review, Fulk, Power, and Schmitz (1986) presented support for four propositions linking electronic messaging to organizational communication networks. Specifically, they argue that electronic mail facilitates (1) more horizontal linkages across geographical distances thus linking a diversity of people who would otherwise not communicate; (2) more vertical linkages across status levels, leading to a flattening of the hierarchy by encouraging less social inhibition about such contacts; (3) less dense networks, in which a person's contacts are less likely to know each other; and (4) linkages that "spill over" to the relational, nonelectronic communication network in the organization, this having implications for changes in friendship patterns and enduring organizational structures. What Fulk et al. (1986) have done in their review can and should be extended to other new technologies, each of which would be expected to engender somewhat different patterns of communication network participation.

The extent and type of communication patterns that emerge in an organization are partially a function of the perceptions managers and employees have of the organization as a whole (that is, the organizational communication climate). In organizations where the climate is perceived as open and supportive of communication, greater network participation and denser networks can be expected (Goldhaber, Dennis, Richetto, & Wiio, 1979; Roberts & O'Reilly, 1979). It follows that factors affecting climate, such as reorganization, changes in office design, and revised compensation policies, should also affect network participation. Specifically, controversial changes in organizational policies may affect membership in cliques as interaction becomes concentrated within groups advocating specific positions (French & Bell, 1978; Huse, 1975). Whether in reaction to an environmental jolt, or in preparation for an open office design or reorganization, the effective organizational development plan takes into account informal networks that may help or hinder the proposed changes (French & Bell, 1978; Huse, 1975; Zalesny & Farace, 1987). The relationship between networks and organizational-level change is highly contingent; different informal and formal networks may be appropriate for different organizational problems and activities (Allen, 1977; Child, 1972; Tushman, 1977, 1978, 1979).

Research suggests that another excellent predictor of whether or not people will forge linkages is how physically close they are to one another. Following Festinger, Schacter, and Back's (1950) classic housing study, researchers have demonstrated a strong positive relationship between proximity and amount of interaction in organizational and other settings (Allen, 1977; Athanasiou & Yoshioka, 1973; Monge & Kirste, 1980). Especially when an organization is relatively homogeneous in employee characteristics, small differences in proximity may affect linkage formation (Blau, 1977). Given sufficient motivation, linkages may be maintained over long distances, but proximate linkages are more likely to be stable since they require less effort to maintain (Fischer, 1977). Recent developments in the measurement of organizational proximity provide a way to link the dynamics of proximity to the dynamics of reorganizing (Monge, Rothman, Eisenberg, Miller, & Kirste, 1985).

Some changes in network structure can be expected as part of the normal organizational life cycle (Quinn & Cameron, 1983). Quinn and Cameron's model has four organizational "life stages": entrepreneurial, collectivity, formalization, and elaboration of structure. In the early and late stages of development, organizations must focus much of their attention on linkages with the environment, first to develop a market, and later to retain legitimacy and market share in the face of competition.

Adolescence (the collectivity stage) is typically characterized by increased informal communication and talk about innovations. The middle years of an organization's development are characterized by more stable structures. As organizations grow, informal interaction decreases and is replaced by more formalized interaction. Throughout the life cycle, organizations must balance between individual autonomy and interdependence at each stage in their development. Organizational networks that are too dense can be as maladaptive as those that are too diffuse. The challenge is to strike a balance that is effective for coping with the environment at hand.

Other writers have commented on how organizational structures are likely to change over time. In a study of 36 firms, Miller and Friesen (1984) report that over time, authority came to be delegated more often, participative management was used more frequently, but strategy tended to remain centralized. As these firms grew and diversified, greater market heterogeneity and the progressive divisionalization of structure ultimately led to communication linkages between divisions that had become isolated from one another. Also over time, the owner or entrepreneur who founded the company played a less central role in its operations. But Miller and Friesen add some caveats to their conclusions. While general trends in organizational evolution were predictable, there was no deterministic sequence in which all organizations evolved. It is difficult to state with certainty how long an organization will remain at a given stage. Large organizations may have multiple life cycles proceeding concurrently at different levels and in different divisions. Furthermore, the speed at which linkages form and dissolve is difficult to predict. One can imagine certain events engendering a steady rate of change (for example, systematic expansion or phasing out of a program) and others resulting in more dramatic, geometric changes (for example, mass layoffs, movement to a new building, or a takeover). It is wrong to assume that growth or decay in structure is always gradual; contacts may be forged or terminated in fits and starts, depending upon the nature of environmental, organizational, and individual occurrences.

Other research explores organizational-level factors affecting *inter*organizational linkages (see Eisenberg et al., 1985). One common conception of interorganizational relations is the economic exchange model, which suggests that patterns of interorganizational linkages follow patterns of resource dependence. Research has shown that the degree of an organization's dependence on local resources and the degree of domain consensus (agreement on goals and clientele) between organizations are both good predictors of whether interorganizational linkages between members will be established (Galaskiewicz, 1979; Levine & White, 1961).

A variety of other organizational factors have been shown to correlate positively with degree of interorganizational linkage formation. Specifically, size of resource base and staff, control over expendable funds, and a history of complementary relationships between organizations are all positively associated with amount of interorganizational activity (Dillman, 1969). Organization type can also make a difference; in a study of hospitals, Schermerhorn (1977) found that hospital size and type were associated with degree of information sharing, such that individuals from community nonprofit hospitals and from large hospitals were most active in sharing information. Finally, as individuals move from job to job (as is often the case between private companies and government agencies) liaison roles may be created that persist and facilitate interorganizational linkages over time (Edstrom & Galbraith, 1977).

In sum, organizational-level influences on communication are far-ranging and go beyond the more obvious constraints of formal structure. Specifically, we have emphasized the influences of technology, organizational climate and culture, proximity, and stage in an organization's life cycle on the network patterns that are likely to emerge. In addition, we considered how certain characteristics predisposed organizations to participate in interorganizational networks. In the next section, we focus more microscopically on the individual influences shaping organizational communication networks.

Individual Influences on Network Emergence

The emergence of informal structures in organizations depends both on the pursuit of individual preferences and on the organizational and environmental constraints that mitigate against certain linkages being formed. The emergence of informal structure can be thought of as one manifestation of the "inevitable conflict between collective task demands and individual needs" (Katz & Kahn, 1966, pp. 80-81). Within organizational constraints, "People are constantly choosing whom they will begin, continue, or cease to interact with" (Fischer, 1977, p. 3). Often, these linkages result from individuals' motivation either to maintain or to enhance their power position within the organization (Ranson et al., 1980).

From a political perspective, the structuring of communication in ways that limit access to information or resources often leads individuals to form coalitions with specific goals. Political power and organizational structure are highly intertwined (Allen & Porter, 1983; Blair, Roberts, & McKechnie, 1985; McPhee, 1985). Astley and Sachdeva (1984), for example, identify "network centrality," as one of three key sources of organizational power. Attributions of who has power are often more dependent on structural position than member characteristics (Blau & Alba, 1982; Fombrun, 1983).

One well-developed line of research at the individual level focuses on communication network roles. Different individual characteristics are associated with people who are identified as liaisons or isolates. Liaisons are better educated, of higher status, and tend to be of higher cognitive complexity than others (Albrecht, 1979; Amend, 1971; Frost & Whitley, 1971; MacDonald, 1971; Schreiman & Johnson, 1975; Schwartz & Jacobson, 1977). Isolates, on the other hand, have significantly lower rank and tenure (Roberts & O'Reilly, 1974). People with greater informal status in the organization (Monge, Edwards, & Kirste, 1978) and who are better educated (Lincoln & Miller, 1979) tend to be more connected in communication networks. Finally, people who are apprehensive of oral communication tend to be less involved in communication networks (Hurt & Preiss, 1978).

The professional training employees bring to an organization can affect the types of linkages that are formed. Different kinds of training lead to different expectations regarding standard operating procedures and reporting relationships. These expectations are in turn reflected in who professionals are willing to talk to and about what topics. Difficulties often occur when professionals with different training (physicians and social workers) work together on projects (Sproull, 1981).

Individual characteristics and professional training can have an important effect on interorganizational networks as well. Many important linkages cross organizational boundaries; a high-level manager can accumulate literally thousands of contacts in a career (Kaplan, 1984). These linkages may be influenced by personal factors, such as religion and age, or by organizational factors such as professional affiliation (Coleman, Katz, & Menzel, 1966). Sometimes close friendships can facilitate interorganizational activity; other times, "weaker ties" will serve as well or better. As was noted above, characteristics of some groups of professionals mitigate against cooperation since certain kinds of training emphasize status distinctions. Administrator characteristics can make a difference in whether an organization enters into joint programs or informal agreements with other organizations. Administrative tenure has been found to be negatively related to interorganizational network involvement (Schermerhorn, 1977). Perceived homophily (similarity) of administrators is positively related to interorganizational participation (Schermerhorn, 1977), and there is a greater interaction between administrators who share similar ethnic or racial backgrounds (Galaskiewicz, 1979).

Interorganizational linkages are forged and dissolved for personal, selfish, and political reasons as much as they are for reasons favoring the interests of the organization being represented (Galaskiewicz, 1979; Galaskiewicz & Shatin, 1981; Whetten, 1981; White, 1973). Selfish motives, personal ambitions, and kinship can all serve as strong motivations for interorganizational linkages (Aldrich, 1979; Aldrich & Whetten, 1981). Particularistic predispositions are as important an influence on network emergence as is a strict cost-benefit calculation of resource dependency between organizations (Eckstein, 1977; Gillespie & Mileti, 1979; Perrucci & Pilisuk, 1970).

Finally, entrepreneurs play a major role in the restructuring and reorganizing of a business community; moreover, successful entrepreneurs have the advantage of their current organizational position from which they can see possibilities and potential niches. In forming new organizations, entrepreneurs model new structures after existing structures they have seen to be successful (Freeman, 1982).

Caveats

It is helpful to keep three general principles of reorganization in mind when evaluating these research findings. First, many different properties of communication networks can be tracked in observing reorganization and change. Examples include the density of the network, the proportion of individuals playing particular communication roles (liaison, bridge, isolate), and the centrality of individuals.

Second, emergent networks vary in stability. Not all structural arrangements persist for similar amounts of time. For example, an environmental change can radically alter a network (as in the receipt of a new government grant or contract) but once the change has passed, the new network patterns may quickly disappear (Monge, Farace, Miller, & Eisenberg, 1983). We must be sensitive not only to the emergence of a communication pattern but also to the duration of this pattern.

Third, emergent structures may be unpredictable in their responses to change. Small changes in the environment or the organization, if sufficiently disturbing, can have widespread and discontinuous effects on network patterns (Krackhardt & Porter, 1986). In other words, we should not expect that large changes in exogenous factors will have correspondingly large effects on networks; the complex structure of dynamic social systems suggests that such effects can be large or small, discontinuous, and difficult to predict.

CONSEQUENTS OF NETWORK EMERGENCE

A more recent, and in some ways more systematic, body of research has addressed the consequents of network emergence. As indicated earlier, the distinction between determinants and consequents is somewhat artificial, reflecting more a lack of longitudinal research than an important conceptual distinction.

The earliest research on the consequents of network participation focused on the attitudes of people occupying various communication roles. Liaisons have been shown to be more open in their communication (MacDonald, 1976), less trusting of the organization's information system, less satisfied with their jobs, and less committed to their organizations (Roberts & O'Reilly, 1979). In addition, key linkers (bridges and liaisons) tend to see themselves as more central and influential in the organization than others (Albrecht, 1979).

Danowski (1980) conducted a group-level study of connectivity and attitude uniformity in a large organization. Even within broad content categories, Danowski failed to find consistent support for the hypothesized positive relationship between connectivity and attitude uniformity. Instead, groups communicating most about production were *least* homogeneous in attitudes toward the task. Groups that were most connected on innovation topics were most homogeneous in attitudes toward innovation. No relationship was found between connectivity and attitude uniformity for maintenance messages. An important implication of this study is that the precise implications of increased communication contact in organizations is unclear—for certain kinds of messages, more communication may lead to attitudinal consensus or homogeneity—but for other types, greater connectivity may promote uncertainty and attitudinal diversity.

Research is beginning on the role of communication network involvement in the socialization process of new employees. Jablin and Krone (1987) describe organizational entry and assimilation as at least partly one of establishing linkages with a number of relatively stable communication networks (authority, friendship, information, and status). In a recent study of the socialization of new members of churches, Sherman, Smith, and Mansfield (1986) found that greater involvement in information networks facilitated the socialization process.

A recent study by Eisenberg, Monge, and Miller (1984), however, suggests the consequents of network involvement for employee attitudes may not be clear-cut. In their study, communication network involvement was not found to have a direct effect on organizational commitment. Instead, different employee groups (salaried and hourly) had markedly different network patterns. While participation was positively associated with commitment for managers and other salaried employees, only hourly employees who were highly connected were also highly committed to the organization.

Research on what has come to be known as the "strength of weak ties" hypothesis (Granovetter, 1973) also seems counterintuitive at first, but has more than most research programs clarified and explained a variety of organizational phenomena, most notably diffusion, career advancement, and social cohesion (see Weimann, 1983). Weak ties are linkages between people that although infrequent or low in intensity, function to connect individuals with access to significantly different information sources. The importance of weak ties in communication networks lies mainly in their capacity to bring information to groups and individuals who would otherwise not likely receive it. Studies by Friedkin (1980, 1982) of a scientific network and by Weimann (1983) of conversation in a kibbutz community support the notion that weak ties function to facilitate information flow by acting as connectors between diverse groups.

Additional research elaborates the potential benefits of network participation. Research relating structural position to performance has been based on the notion that "being in the right place" in an organization's informal structure can yield positive results for individuals (Fombrun, 1983). In a study of a newspaper publishing company, Brass (1984) examined the relationships between individual influence (as perceived by others in the organization) and position in work flow, communication, and friendship networks. Centrality in all three networks was positively associated with perceptions of influence. Brass argues that these findings provide further support for the operationalization of organizational structure from a relational network perspective. Attributions of influence can be sensitive to connections that cross hierarchical levels or organizational boundaries. For example, research on the "Pelz effect" demonstrates that when a supervisor has greater contact upward in the hierarchy with his or her superiors, he or she will also be more influential with subordinates (see Jablin, 1979). Similarly, individuals who develop contacts that go beyond their immediate work group in an organization are more likely to be influential than their less well-connected counterparts (Brass, 1984). When one considers contacts outside as well as inside of the organization, the most successful boundary spanners turn out to be well connected on both counts—they are internal and external "stars" (Tushman & Scanlan, 1981). Finally, in the interorganizational community, reputation increases in direct proportion to the number of influential extraorganizational ties a person has (Kaplan, 1984). From a practical perspective, such ties can be critical in building a career, finding a new job, or starting a new business (Granovetter, 1973, 1974).

The finding that network position can affect the degree of influence a person has may also apply at the group level or to departments, divisions, and even whole organizations. In separate studies, Hinings, Hickson, Pennings, and Schneck (1974) and Blau and Alba (1982) reported that the group or subunit influence within an organization was positively associated with the degree to which they occupied central positions in work flow and communication networks. In a study of interorganizational networks, Boje and Whetten (1981) found a positive association between centrality in interorganizational networks and influence within the organizational community.

In a related study, Thurman (1979) examined politics and coalition-formation in an office. Thurman demonstrated that "leveling coalitions" (alliances formed to reduce the power of an individual) emerge from existing social relationships, and are hard to identify without the use of network analysis (because they rarely follow any formal rational paths). Further, Thurman argues that the ability of individuals to stave off such attacks is directly related to the breadth and multiplexity of their own social network, from which they draw power to form their own coalition and marshal a counterattack.

Some researchers suggest that individuals who are highly involved in communication networks are also most likely to be innovative (Rogers & Kincaid, 1981). Organizational innovation is a team effort, rarely accomplished by isolated individuals (Kanter, 1983; Rounds, 1984). Albrecht and Ropp (1984) report that individuals who are well linked in innovation networks in an organization are likely to be linked in other ways as well; innovation linkages tend to be multiplex. Communication about innovations seems to flow most naturally between persons who are communicating frequently about routine task and personal matters. Relatedly, those people who are most highly connected in job networks tend to be "opinion leaders" and to talk more about innovation (Parks, 1977).

At the same time, other research suggests that having strong connections may inhibit adoption of certain kinds of innovations. In a study examining the role of networks in blocking or supporting organizational development (specifically, Quality of Work Life studies), Nelson (1986) found that people and organizations with weak or *no* ties to the decision-making community elite were most likely to support the intervention. The most successful interventions involved the "isolated" group—those with strong community ties preferred more technical development efforts that did not challenge existing managerial norms or assumptions.

Research is beginning on the relationship between network involvement and turnover. In a recent study, Krackhardt and Porter (1986) found that turnover in a work group was "concentrated in patterns that can be delineated by role similarities in a communication network" (p. 54). Using the positional approach to network analysis, their research suggests that turnover in organizations may "snowball" and follow discontinuous patterns conditioned by network arrangements.

This section completes our review of the antecedents and consequents of network emergence. In the next section we explore a number of controversial issues in communication network research.

ISSUES IN EMERGENT NETWORK RESEARCH

The past 25 years of research and scholarship has greatly increased our knowledge and understanding of emergent networks. As with most increases in knowledge, this growth has also indicated how little we know and how much more there is to learn. Further advances require us to address several critical issues in future research. We discuss the most important of these issues in this section.

Theory

Our review has amply demonstrated that there is little coherent network theory. Most network research is an ad hoc collection of techniques and procedures driven as much by the options and constraints of computer programs as by theoretical considerations (Rice & Richards, 1985).

Furthermore, most theoretical debates focus on the nature of structure itself rather than the relation of networks to their antecedents and consequents. Blau (1982) makes this point rather forcefully:

There is a danger that the refined methods that network analysis, in particular, has developed will lead to sterile descriptive studies. Factor analysis can illustrate the point by analogy. Although it is a technique that can be most useful in research, factor analysis lends itself to pedestrian studies that merely report the dimensions underlying a set of items without relating these factors to anything else and hence without testing or even exploring contingent propositions, which are the very building blocks of theory. Similarly, there is a danger that blockmodeling, a useful technique, is employed simply to describe the structure of social positions in a group, without relating these to any conditions producing this structure or any of its consequences. Sheer description does not advance social science. (p. 279)

Equally important, however, is tying network analysis and network theory to organizational theory. Little has been done in this area; most theories of organizational structure deal primarily with formal, not emergent, networks. The development of process theories of organizational structuring will provide a useful context for network analysis and improve the quality of network research.

Several efforts have been made to rectify this situation (Blau, 1977; Burt, 1982; Fombrun, 1986; Lorrain & White, 1971). Yet network theories are seldom formally articulated or subjected to empirical tests. Consequently, there is a significant need for more fully developed network theories as well as more empirical research that tests them.

Boundaries

One major problem that network theories will need to address is boundary specification (Laumann, Marsden, & Prensky, 1983). Historically, most research has been conducted in single organizations, where it has been assumed that the network boundary corresponds with the roster of organizational members. More recent research on interorganizational networks (see Eisenberg et al., 1985) and on boundary spanners (Adams, 1980) emphasizes the need to expand our notion of boundaries. Contacts between organizations and between the organization and the family can have significant impact on organizational life. One possibility suggested by Lincoln (1982) is that we may dispense with the traditional notion of organizational boundaries and define network boundaries in terms of dense clusters of linkages wherever they may exist in society.

Sampling

Almost all network research to date has been conducted on "samples" consisting of the members of one organization; often only parts of the organization, such as a department or division, are studied. Rarely is network research conducted in multiple organizations. One reason for this is that most network techniques require a census (that is, all relevant people) rather than a sample. Obtaining an exhaustive census even in one organization is labor intensive and expensive. Recent developments in network sampling theory should make it possible to estimate network parameters on the basis of samples (Frank, 1978). When network researchers can utilize the economy of sampling theory, more comprehensive data that are representative of a broader range of organizational networks will be acquired.

Measurement

Considerable effort needs to be invested in the problems associated with linkage measurement. The preponderance of research findings has been based on the lowest level of measurement, categorical binary data. Improvements need to be made on how to measure linkage strength (Richards, 1985). Further, with the exception of the controversy generated by Bernard and Killworth's (1980) attack on respondent accuracy (see the response by Burt, 1983), little attention has been paid to the problems of validity and reliability of linkage measurement (Monge & Contractor, 1983).

Analysis

The review by Rice and Richards (1985) demonstrates the plethora of analytical techniques available for the analysis of network data. Each technique shares a set of common assumptions with other network algorithms, but also contains its own unique assumptions. Consequently, each technique produces similar though not identical results. This problem is common to a number of statistical procedures as well (for example, factor analysis and multidimensional scaling). The problem can be minimized by comparative research and the establishment of standards. Statisticians who use time series and forecasting routines often publish "contests" between alternative algorithms and programs to determine their relative performance on standard data sets. Other disciplines convene committees to establish conventions and publish standards for conducting and reporting research results. The field of network analysis would profit by developing professional practices like those that have been established in other disciplines.

Multiplexity

Another important issue is multiplexity (Minor, 1983). Traditional techniques have utilized only single relations and have assigned network members to mutually exclusive, nonoverlapping groups. Such procedures, while useful, clearly fail to capture the full complexity of multiple kinds of relations and multiple group membership. Alba (1982) asserts that one of the strengths of the positional (structural equivalence) approach over the relational approach is its ability to handle multiple types of relations. Future research should continue to examine the nature and functions of multiplex linkages (see Albrecht & Ropp, 1984).

Structure and Process

Many authors emphasize the enduring, relatively static nature of communication networks. In this chapter, we have stressed the importance of a dynamic perspective. Cross-sectional studies of organizational communication networks are of limited utility, especially where organizations are undergoing major changes. Fortunately, there is more of a precedent for dynamic, over-time research in network studies than in most other areas of communication study (Rice, 1982). We have argued that reorganizing is the fundamental process in emergent communication networks. Reorganizing is the process by which linkages are continually added and deleted as organizational members respond to external and internal factors. Yet the counterpart of dynamics is stability. Monge (1987) argues that a stable sequence of activities is as much a structure as an arrangement of parts. Every systematic process contains a structure; likewise, as we have emphasized here, every network structure embodies a process. The relation between structure and process, stability and dynamics, or maintenance and change has not yet been carefully explored by organizational communication scholars. Likewise, with rare exceptions (Barnett & Rice, 1985; Rice, 1982) network researchers have yet to design and conduct longitudinal network research that would inform us about the dimensions of stability and change (see Monge, Farace, Eisenberg, Miller, & White, 1984). Identifying the theoretical and empirical coefficients of the structural dynamics of communication networks in organizations will constitute an important test of our collective scholarship.

These seven issues reflect most of the current problems in network research. An eighth issue, the role of communication content, is important enough to discuss separately.

SEMANTIC NETWORKS: OPERATIONALIZING THE CULTURAL TRADITION

Thus far in this chapter we have introduced a framework for thinking about emergent networks that focuses on process conceptualizations and the maintenance of multiple levels and perspectives. While network research has a rich intellectual history, empirical studies have been disconnected theoretically and spread across diverse disciplines, minimizing the cumulative impact of the research. Closer attention to the *content* of what is communicated in network linkages will yield a more comprehensive understanding of the role networks play in organizing. In this section we address the issue of network content, and in so doing offer one operationalization of the cultural perspective on organizational structure.

A significant criticism of network research comes from those who argue that by measuring interaction only in terms of broad content categories, it fails to tap important human factors (see Reynolds & Johnson, 1982). The cultural tradition suggests that much could be gained by probing further into the substantive aspects of linkage content. In this way, network analysis could provide new insights about meaning and interpretation in organizations (Eisenberg, 1986).

Danowski (1986, in press) recently attempted to demonstrate empirically how the message content in communication networks can change over time. He has developed a technique called word network analysis, which provides an automated analysis of work linkages and groupings based upon message content in an electronic mail system. In one such study (Danowski, 1986), he finds support for the hypothesis that as an interpersonal network becomes more interlocked so too will word networks become interlocked. Based on the same data reported in Danowski and Edison-Swift (1985), this study allows for an interesting contrast of contact and word networks. Whereas both were disturbed dramatically by an organizational crisis (in this case, a merger), only the contact network quickly returned to baseline levels. The word network, on the other hand, took a much longer time (nearly six months) to return to "normal," precrisis levels. This suggests that attention to the content of communication networks can provide important information about organizations that contact networks cannot provide. Danowski (in press) suggests that word network analysis may prove useful in mapping the social concepts of a community's culture, and thus integrate interpretive approaches with more traditional quantitative concerns.

Others have also advocated closer investigation of network content (Richards, 1985). The most developed of these is Rogers and Kincaid's (1981) convergence model. In their view, participation in networks is a process through which individuals come to converge (or diverge) on sufficiently shared meanings. Rogers and Kincaid recognize, however, that few studies have actually investigated the relationship between communication patterns and convergence. To do so, more studies must be longitudinal and incorporate communication content. A succinct statement of their argument: "We need to combine the research method of content analysis of communication messages with the technique of network analysis to better understand how individuals give meaning to information that is exchanged through the communication process" (Rogers & Kincaid, p. 77).

It is in this spirit that we suggest combining a familiar approach to communication content—the coorientation model—with traditional network analysis. In contrast with most network research that focuses on the presence or strength of interaction, coorientation research is concerned with the degree to which communicators' meanings have "converged," that is, the level at which they understand and/or agree with one another (see Eisenberg, Monge, & Farace, 1984; McLeod & Chaffee, 1976). Specifically, we propose expanding the notion of network linkages to include not only the presence or intensity of interaction, but also the degree of understanding (do the communicators share a common symbol-referent system?) and agreement (do they agree in opinion on the topics being communicated about?). We are less concerned with frequency of word usage than Danowski, but more concerned with the interpretations and meanings as seen by communicators. By extending network analysis into the semantic domain, we gain the ability to examine various assumptions often left unexamined in network analysis: that messages are in fact received (already addressed to some extent in measures of reciprocity), understood, and agreed with by the recipient. More information in each of these areas will help to specify the implications of being well or poorly connected in an organizational communication network. Furthermore, the degree of convergence on interpretations of key concepts is one potentially effective operationalization of the otherwise elusive notion of organizational culture.

Toward this end, we suggest ways to tap the content of communication linkages. Individuals could be provided with key vocabulary, slogans, or stories, and asked to provide their interpretations; interpretations could be analyzed via content analysis, as could the degree of overlap of interpretations. Linkages would be defined in terms of degree of overlap or convergence of interpretations. Convergence on interpretations is one indication of cultural diversity or homogeneity, and cliques resulting from such an analysis may even provide evidence of subcultures. We would call the resultant configuration a *semantic* network. Similarly, even if people share interpretations for common terms, they may not have similar attitudes, values, or beliefs. For example, a pair of newspaper editors may talk often, share a common understanding of what is meant by "objectivity," and disagree wholeheartedly over whether it is a good thing. Individuals could complete attitudinal scales regarding important issues, and linkages in the resultant *attitudinal* network could be identified based upon degree of similarity across a core set of attitudes. Just as many have argued that single organizations can contain multiple subclimates, so too would we expect clusters or cliques to form around key attitudes or beliefs, which would in turn reflect the nature and homogeneity of the organizational climate.

One interesting issue would be the degree of correspondence between these three types of networks (relational, semantic, and attitudinal) in any given organization. Previous studies have run into difficulty in interpreting results because of the inability to distinguish among linkages that are structurally similar in a positional or relational sense but structurally different in a cultural sense. Research by Danowski (1980) described above suggests an important but complex relationship between connectivity, shared meanings, and attitudinal similarity. Put concretely, while one might find that a top manager and the person who delivers the mail are equally well connected in an organization, we would expect them to occupy radically different positions with a different set of causes and consequents in a semantic or attitudinal network.

The study of semantic or attitudinal networks has other intriguing implications. For example, the meaning of communication role (isolate, liaison) in a semantic or attitudinal network is different from traditional conceptions. Whereas a person may be isolated in terms of frequency of interaction, it would be useful to know if they are "out of touch" attitudinally or if they share a common viewpoint but simply are not talking about it. Perhaps the liaison in a semantic network plays a kind of "translator" role, able to bridge various meaning or cultural systems within the organization.

Finally, semantic network analysis could be used to examine the assumption held by some researchers that organizations are made up of individuals with highly similar core values and beliefs. Organizations could be compared empirically to assess degree of homogeneity of interpretations or core values. Subcultures could be identified around semantic or attitudinal groups or cliques.

THE EMERGENCE OF EMERGENT NETWORKS

In this chapter we have examined the causes and consequents of network emergence in organizations. To contextualize the work in this area, we examined three historical traditions in structural analysis: the positional, the relational, and the cultural. Several scholars, we noted, have attempted to integrate the divergent perspectives.

We presented the idea of reorganizing, which states that people and organizations are continually in the process of forging, maintaining, and terminating their various communication linkages, both inside and outside the organization. To help understand this principle we reviewed the factors that lead people both to maintain or to dissolve their linkages with others. We also examined the effects that changes in networks have on people and organizations. We identified seven critical issues in network research and developed an eighth, the role of communication content, in some detail.

In a sense, emergent network analysis in organizations has a long tradition but a short history. The ideas surrounding the emergence of network structure have been debated for a century. Quantitative empirical research on emergent organizational networks, however, is a relatively recent phenomenon that spans little more than a quarter of that period. While much has been accomplished, even more remains to be done

Research on communication networks needs to progress cumulatively both within and across disciplines rather than in the disjointed fashion that characterizes much of the work to date. Rarely do we find statements on the order of "X showed this and Y showed that; therefore, the next logical step is for us to conduct research Z." Too much network research appears to have been conducted in an intellectual vacuum where researchers are unaware of or fail to integrate the work of their network colleagues in related disciplines.

Network researchers should be pluralistic in their acceptance of work that spans multiple levels and perspectives. At the same time they must also be clear about the levels and perspectives that characterize their own work. For example, research that explores environmental determinants or political maneuvering takes on a decidedly different tone from studies of individual influences on network involvement. Relatedly, differences in emphasis of "structure as constraint" versus "structure as agency," positional versus relational approaches, and formal versus emergent structures need not be resolved by choosing one over the other. Better process research and the important contributions of contemporary structural theorists should allow for a workable resolution of this "unhelpful contrasting" of perspectives (Ranson et al., 1980).

In conclusion, if we have reviewed the rapidly growing field of emergent organizational communication networks accurately, we can predict not only more research but better, more systematic research that integrates the diverse perspectives. The more recent studies reviewed in this chapter have begun to move us in this direction. The integration of the cultural perspective with existing approaches should provide a more complete picture of the role of network emergence in organizational life. If it is to realize its full potential, the study of communication structures in organizations has to take serious account of current developments in communication and organizational theory. We are optimistic that this maturation will occur in the near future.

NOTES

1. In this chapter we focus primarily on communication research conducted in organizational settings. As is well known, network concepts have attained great popularity in many of the social sciences and related applied fields. The reader who is interested in reviews of other network research such as support, friendship, or community networks should look elsewhere (Albrecht & Adelman, 1984; Mitchell, 1969; Monge, 1987; Rogers & Kincaid, 1981).

2. Our discussion of network causes and consequents focuses almost exclusively on informal, emergent interaction. For a discussion of formal networks in organizations, see Dansereau and Markham (Chapter 11) and Jablin (Chapter 12) elsewhere in this book.

REFERENCES

Adams, J. S. (1976). The structure and dynamics of behavior in organizational boundary roles. In M. D. Dunnette (Ed,), *Handbook of industrial and organizational psychology* (pp. 1175-1199). Chicago: Rand McNally.

Adams, J. S. (1980). Interorganizational processes and organizational boundary activities. In L. Cummings & B. Staw (Eds.), *Research in organizational behavior* (Vol. 2, pp. 321-355). Greenwich, CT: JAI Press.

Alba, R. D. (1982). Taking stock of network analysis: A decade's results. In S. B. Bacharach (Ed.), *Research in the sociology of organizations* (Vol. 2, pp. 39-74). Greenwich, CT: JAI Press.

Albrecht, T. L. (1979). The role of communication in perceptions of organizational climate. In D. Nimmo (Ed.), *Communication yearbook 3* (pp. 343-357). New Brunswick, NJ: Transaction Books.

Albrecht, T. L., & Adelman, M. (1984). Social support and life stress: New directions for communication research. *Human Communication Research, 11,* 3-32.

Albrecht, T. L., & Ropp, V. A. (1984). Communicating about innovation in networks of three U.S. organizations. *Journal of Communication, 34,* 78-91.

Aldrich, H. (1979). *Organizations and environments.* Englewood Cliffs, NJ: Prentice-Hall.

Aldrich, H., & Mueller, S. (1982). The evolution of organizational forms: Technology, coordination, and control. In B. M. Staw & L. L. Cummings (Eds.), *Research in organizational behavior* (Vol. 4, pp. 33-87). Greenwich, CT: JAI Press.

Aldrich, H., & Whetten, D. (1981). Organization-sets, action-sets, and networks: Making the most of simplicity. In P. Nystrom & W. Starbuck (Eds.), *Handbook of organizational design* (Vol. 1, pp. 385-408). New York: Oxford University Press.

Allen, R. W., & Porter, L. W. (Eds.). (1983). *Organizational influence processes.* Glenview, IL: Scott, Foresman.

Allen, T. (1977). *Managing the flow of technology.* Cambridge, MA: MIT Press.

Amend, E. (1971). *Liaison communication roles of professionals in a research dissemination organization.* Unpublished doctoral dissertation, Michigan State University, East Lansing, MI.

Astley, W., & Sachdeva, P. (1984). Structural sources of interorganizational power: A theoretical synthesis. *Academy of Management Review, 9,* 104-113.

Athanasiou, R., & Yoshioka, G. (1973). The spatial character of friendship formation. *Environment & Behavior 5,* 43-66.

Bacharach, S. B., & Aiken, M. (1976). Structural and process constraints on influence in organizations. *Administrative Science Quarterly, 21,* 623-642.

Barnett, G. A., & Rice, R. R. (1985). Longitudinal non-Euclidean networks: Applying Galileo. *Social Networks, 7,* 287-322.

Benson, J. K. (1977). Organizations: A dialectical view. *Administrative Science Quarterly, 22,* 1-21.

Berger, P., & Luckmann, T. (1966). *The social construction of reality.* Garden City, NY: Anchor Books.

Bernard, H. R., & Killworth, P. D. (1980). Informant accuracy in social network data IV: A comparison of clique-level structures in behavioral and cognitive network data. *Social Networks, 2,* 191-218.

Blair, R., Roberts, K., & McKechnie, P. (1985). Vertical and network communication in organizations: The present and the future. In R. McPhee & P. Tompkins (Eds.), *Organizational communication: Traditional themes and new directions* (pp. 55-77). Newbury Park, CA: Sage.

Blau, P. M. (1954). Patterns of interaction among a group of officials in a government agency. *Human Relations, 7,* 337-348.

Blau, P. M. (1977). A macrosociological theory of social structure. *American Journal of Sociology, 83,* 26-54.

Blau, P. M. (1981). Introduction: Diverse views of social structure and their common denominator. In P. M. Blau & R. K. Merton (Eds.), *Continuities in structural inquiry* (pp. 1-23). Newbury Park, CA: Sage.

Blau, P. M. (1982). Structural sociology and network analysis: An overview. In P. V. Marsden & N. Lin (Eds.), *Social structure and network analysis* (pp. 273-279). Newbury Park, CA: Sage.

Blau, P., & Alba, R. (1982). Empowering nets of participation. *Administrative Science Quarterly, 27,* 363-379.

Boje, D., & Whetten, D. (1981). Strategies and constraints affecting centrality and attributions of influence in interorganizational networks. *Administrative Science Quarterly, 26,* 378-395.

Bourdieu, P. (1977). *Outline of a theory of practice.* London: Cambridge University Press.
Brass, D. J. (1984). Being in the right place: A structural analysis of individual influence in an organization. *Administrative Science Quarterly, 29,* 518-539.
Buckley, W. (1967). *Sociology and modern systems theory.* Englewood Cliffs, NJ: Prentice-Hall.
Burt, R. (1976). Positions in networks. *Social Forces, 55,* 93-122.
Burt, R. S. (1978). Cohesion versus structural equivalence as a basis for network subgroups. *Sociological Methods and Research, 7,* 189-212.
Burt, R. S. (1979). A structural theory of interlocking corporate directorates. *Social Networks, 2,* 415-435.
Burt, R. S. (1980a). Models of network structure. *Annual Review of Sociology, 6,* 79-141.
Burt, R. S. (1980b). On the functional form of corporate coopation: Empirical findings linking the intensity of market constraint with the frequency of directorate ties. *Social Science Research, 9,* 146-177.
Burt, R. S. (1982). *Toward a structural theory of action: Network models of stratification, perception, and action.* New York: Academic Press.
Burt, R. S. (1983). A note on inferences concerning network subgroups. In R. S. Burt & M. J. Minor (Eds.), *Applied network analysis* (pp. 283-301). Newbury Park, CA: Sage.
Burt, R. S., Christman, K., Kilburn, H., Jr. (1980). Testing a structural theory of corporate cooptation. *American Sociological Review, 45,* 821-841.
Child, J. (1972). Organizational structure, environment, and performance: The role of strategic choice. *Sociology, 6,* 1-22.
Coleman, J. (1966). Foundations for a theory of collective decisions. *American Journal of Sociology, 71,* 615-627.
Coleman, J. S. (1973). *The mathematics of collection action.* Chicago: Aldine.
Coleman J., Katz, E., & Manzel, H. (1966). *Medical innovation: A diffusion study.* Indianapolis, IN: Bobbs-Merrill.
Crozier, M. (1964). *The bureaucratic phenomenon.* Chicago: University of Chicago Press.
Danowski, J. A. (1980). Group attitude uniformity and connectivity of organizational communication networks for production, innovation, and maintenance content. *Human Communication Research, 6,* 299-308.
Danowski, J. A. (1986). *Linking an organization's who-to-whom communication networks and message content networks in electronic mail.* Paper presented at the annual meeting of the International Communication Association, Chicago.
Danowski, J. A. (in press). Organizational infographics and automatic auditing. In G. Goldhaber & G. Barnett (Eds.), *Handbook of organizational communication.* New York: Ablex.
Danowski, J. A., & Edison-Swift, P. (1985). Crisis effects on intraorganizational computer-based communication. *Communication Research, 12,* 251-270.
de Saussure, R. (1966). *Course in general linguistics.* New York: McGraw-Hill. (Original work published 1916)
Deal, T., & Kennedy, A. (1982). *Corporate cultures.* Reading, MA: Addison-Wesley.
Dillman, D. (1969). *Relations between social agencies: A preliminary attempt at measurement and analysis.* Paper presented at the annual meeting of the American Sociological Association.
Durkheim, E. (1964). *The rules of sociological method.* London: Free Press. (Original work published 1895).
Eckstein, S. (1977). Politicos and priests: Iron law of oligarchy in interorganizational relations. *Comparative Politics, 9,* 463-481.
Edstrom, A., & Galbraith, J. (1977). Management transfer as a control strategy. *Administrative Science Quarterly, 22,* 248-263.
Eisenberg, E. M. (1986). Meaning and interpretation in organizations. *Quarterly Journal of Speech, 72,* 88-97.
Eisenberg, E. M., Farace, R. V., Monge, P. R., Bettinghaus, E. P., Kurchner-Hawkins, R., Miller, K., & Rothman, L. (1985). Communication linkages in interorganizational systems. In

B. Derrin & M. Voigt (Eds.), *Progress in communication sciences* (Vol. 6, pp 231-261). New York: Ablex.

Eisenberg, E. M., Monge, P. R., & Farace, R. V. (1984). Coorientation on communication in managerial dyads. *Human Communication Research, 11,* 261-271.

Eisenberg, E. M., Monge, P. R., & Miller, K. I. (1984). Involvement in communication networks as a predictor of organizational commitment. *Human Communication Research, 10,* 179-201.

Emery, F. E., & Trist, E. L. (1965). The causal texture of organizational environments. *Human Relations, 18,* 21-32.

Farace, R. V., & Mabee, T. (1980). Communication network analysis methods. In P. R. Monge & J. N. Cappella (Eds.), *Multivariate techniques in human communication research* (pp. 365-391). New York: Academic Press.

Farace, R. V., Monge, P. R., & Russell, H. M. (1977). *Communicating and organizing.* Reading, MA: Addison-Wesley.

Festinger, L., Schachter, S., & Back, K. (1950). *Social pressures in informal groups: A study of human factors in housing.* Palo Alto, CA: Stanford University Press.

Fischer, C. (1977). *The contexts of personal relations: An exploratory network analysis* (Working paper 281). Berkeley: University of California Institute of Urban and Regional Development.

Fombrun, C. J. (1983). Attributions of power across a social network. *Human Relations, 36,* 493-508.

Fombrun, C. J. (1986). Structural dynamics between and within organizations. *Administrative Science Quarterly, 31,* 403-421.

Form, W. (1972). Technology and social behavior of workers in four countries: A sociotechnical perspective. *Americal Sociological Review, 37,* 727-738.

Frank, O. (1978). Sampling and estimation in large social networks. *Social Networks, 1,* 91-101.

Freeman, J. (1982). Organizational life cycles and natural selection processes. In B. Staw & L. Cummings, *Research in organizational behavior* (Vol. 4, pp. 1-32). Greenwich, CT: JAI Press.

Freeman, L. C. (1979). Centrality in social networks: Conceptual clarification. *Social Networks, 2,* 215-239.

French, W., & Bell, C. (1978). *Organizational development: Behavioral science interventions for organization improvement* (2nd ed.). Englewood Cliffs, NJ: Prentice-Hall.

Friedkin, N. (1980). A test of structural features of Granovetter's strength of weak ties theory. *Social Networks, 2,* 411-422.

Friedkin, N. (1982). Information flow through strong and weak ties in intraorganizational social networks. *Social Networks, 3,* 273-285.

Frost, P., Moore, L., Louis, M. R., Lundberg, C., & Martin, J. (1985). *Organizational culture.* Newbury Park, CA: Sage.

Frost, R., & Whitley, R. (1971). Communication patterns in a research lab. *R & D Management, 1,* 71-79.

Fulk, J., Power, J. G., & Schmitz, J. (1986). *Communication in organizations via electronic mail: An analysis of behavioral and relational issues.* Paper presented at the annual meeting of the American Institute of Decision Sciences, Honolulu.

Galaskiewicz, J. (1979). *Exchange networks and community politics.* Newbury Park, CA: Sage.

Galaskiewicz, J., & Shatin, D. (1981). Leadership and networking among neighborhood human service organizations. *Administrative Science Quarterly, 25,* 434-448.

Giddens, A. (1979). *Central problems in social theory.* Cambridge, MA: Cambridge University Press.

Gillespie, D., & Mileti, D. (1979). *Technostructures and interorganizational relations.* Lexington, MA: D. C. Heath.

Goldhaber, G., Dennis, H., Richetto, G., & Wiio, O. (1979). *Information strategies: New paths to corporate power.* Englewood Cliffs, NJ: Prentice-Hall.

Granovetter, M. (1973). The strength of weak ties. *American Journal of Sociology, 78,* 1360-1380.

Granovetter, M. (1974). *Getting a job.* Cambridge, MA: Harvard University Press.

Hinings, C., Hickson, D., Pennings, J., & Schneck, R. (1974). Structural conditions of intraorganizational power. *Administrative Science Quarterly, 19,* 22-24.

Homans, G. (1958). Social behavior as exchange. *American Journal of Sociology, 62,* 597-606.

Hurt, H. T., & Preiss, R. (1978). Silence isn't necessarily golden: Communication apprehension, desired social choice, and academic success among middle-school students. *Human Communication Research, 4,* 315-328.

Huse, E. F. (1975). *Organization development and change.* St. Paul, MN: West.

Jablin, F. M. (1979). Superior-subordinate communication: The state of the art. *Psychological Bulletin, 86,* 1201-1222.

Jablin, F. M., & Krone, K. J. (1987). Organizational assimilation. In C. Berger & S. H. Chaffee (Eds.), *Handbook of communication science* (pp. 711-746). Newbury Park, CA: Sage.

James, L., & Jones, A. (1976). Organizational structure: A review of structural dimensions and their relationships with individual attitudes and behavior. *Organizational Behavior and Human Performance, 16,* 74-113.

Kanter, R. (1983). *The change masters.* New York: Simon & Schuster.

Kaplan, R. (1984, Spring). Trade routes: The manager's network of relationships. *Organizational Dynamics, 12,* 37-52.

Katz, D., & Kahn, R. (1966). *The social psychology of organizations.* New York: John Wiley.

Krackhardt, D., & Porter, L. (1986). The snowball effect: Turnover embedded in communication networks. *Journal of Applied Psychology, 71,* 50-55.

Laumann, E. O., Marsden, P. V., & Prensky, D. (1983). The boundary specification problem in network analysis. In R. S. Burt & M. J. Minor (Eds.), *Applied network analysis* (pp. 18-34). Newbury Park, CA: Sage.

Lawler, E. E. (1986). *High-involvement management.* San Francisco: Jossey-Bass.

Lawrence, P. R., & Lorsch, J. W. (1967). *Organization and environment: Managing differentiation and integration.* Boston: Graduate School of Business Administration, Harvard University.

Levi-Strauss, C. (Ed.). (1963). The effectiveness of symbols. In *Structural anthropology* (Vol. 1). New York: Basic Books.

Levine, S., & White, P. (1961). Exchange as a conceptual framework for the study of interorganizational relationships. *Administrative Science Quarterly, 5,* 583-601.

Lincoln, J. R. (1982). Intra- (and inter-) organizational networks. In S. B. Bacharach (Ed.), *Research in the sociology of organizations* (Vol. 1, pp. 1-38). Greenwich, CT: JAI Press.

Lincoln, J. R., & Miller, J. (1979). Work and friendship ties in organizations: A comparative analysis of relational networks. *Administrative Science Quarterly, 24,* 181-199.

Lorrain, F., & White, H. C. (1971). Structural equivalence of individuals in social networks. *Journal of Mathematical Sociology, 1,* 49-80.

MacDonald, D. (1971). *Communication roles and communication contents in a bureaucratic setting.* Unpublished doctoral dissertation, Michigan State University, East Lansing.

MacDonald, D. (1976). Communication roles and communication networks in a formal organization. *Human Communication Research, 2,* 365-375.

McLeod, J., & Chaffee, S. (1976). Coorientation and interpersonal perception. *American Behavioral Scientist, 16,* 469-499.

McPhee, R. (1985). Formal structure and organizational communication. In R. McPhee & P. Tompkins (Eds.), *Organizational communication: Traditional themes and new directions* (pp. 149-177). Newbury Park, CA: Sage.

Meyer, J., & Rowan, B. (1977). Institutionalized organizations: Formal structure as myth and ceremony. *American Journal of Sociology, 83,* 340-363.

Miles, R. (1980). *Macro organizational behavior.* Santa Monica, CA: Goodyear.

Miller, D., & Friesen, P. H. (1984). A longitudinal study of the corporate life cycle. *Management Science, 30,* 1161-1183.

Miner, J. B. (1982). *Theories of organizational structure and process.* Chicago: Dryden Press.

Minor, M. J. (1983). New directions in multiplexity analysis. In R. S. Burt & M. J. Minor (Eds.), *Applied Networks Analysis* (pp. 223-244). Newbury Park, CA: Sage.

Mitchell, J. C. (1969). *Social networks in urban situations.* Manchester: University of Manchester Press.

Mitchell, J. C. (1972). Networks, norms and institutions. In J. Boissevain & J. C. Mitchell (Eds.), *Network analysis studies in human interaction* (pp. 15-36). Mouton: The Hague.

Monge, P. R. (1987). Network level of analysis. In C. Berger & S. H. Chaffee (Eds.), *Handbook of communication science* (pp. 239-270). Newbury Park, CA: Sage.

Monge, P. R., & Contractor, N. S. (1987). Communication networks: Measuring techniques. In C. H. Tardy (Ed.), *A handbook for the study of human communication* (pp. 107-138). Norwood, NJ: Ablex

Monge, P. R., Edwards, J., & Kirst, K. (1978). The determinants of communication and communication structure in large organizations: A review of research. In B. Ruben (Ed.), *Communication yearbook 2* (pp. 311-331). New Brunswick, NJ: Transaction Books.

Monge, P. R., Farace, R. V., Eisenberg, E. M., Miller, K. I., & White, L. L.(1984) The process of studying process in organizational communication. *Journal of Communication, 34,* 22-43.

Monge, P. R., Farace, R. V., Miller, K. I., & Eisenberg, E. M. (1983). *Life cycle changes in interorganizational information networks.* Paper presented at the annual meeting of the International Communication Association, Dallas.

Monge, P. R., & Kirste, K. K.(1980). Measuring proximity in human organizations. *Social Psychology Quarterly, 43,* 110-115.

Monge, P. R., Rothman, L. W., Eisenberg, E. M., Miller, K. I., & Kirste, K. K. (1985). The dynamics of organizational proximity. *Management Science, 31,* 1129-1141.

Montgomery, I., & Benbasat, I. (1983). Cost/benefit analysis of computer based message systems. *MIS Quarterly, 7*(1), 1-14.

Nadel, S. F. (1957). *The theory of social structure.* New York: Free Press.

Nelson, R. (1986). Social networks and organizational interventions: Insights from an area-wide labor management committee. *Journal of Applied Behavioral Science, 2,* 65-76.

Ortner, S. (1984). Theory in anthropology since the sixties. *Journal for the Comparative Study of Society and History,* 126-166.

Parks, M. R. (1977). Anomie and close friendship communication networks. *Human Communication Research, 4,* 48-57.

Parsons, T. (1951). *The social system.* New York: Free Press.

Pennings, J. M. (1980). *Interlocking directorates.* San Francisco: Jossey-Bass.

Perucci, R., & Pilisuk, M. (1970). Leaders and ruling elites: The interorganizational bases of community power. *American Sociological Review, 35,* 1040-1057.

Peters, T. J., & Austin, N. (1985). *A passion for excellence.* New York: Random House.

Peters, T., & Waterman, R. (1982). *In search of excellence.* New York: Harper & Row.

Pfeffer, J., & Salancik, G. (1978). *The external control of organizations.* New York: Harper & Row.

Quinn, R. E., & Cameron, K. (1983). Organizational life cycles and shifting criteria of effectiveness: Some preliminary evidence. *Management Science, 29,* 33-51.

Radcliffe-Brown, A. R. (1959). *Structure and function in primitive society.* New York: Free Press. (Original work published 1952)

Ranson, S., Hinings, B., & Greenwood, R. (1980). The structuring of organizational structures. *Administrative Science Quarterly, 25,* 1-17.

Reynolds, E., & Johnson, J. D. (1982). Liaison emergence: Relating theoretical perspectives. *Academy of Management Review, 7,* 551-559.

Rice, L. E., & Mitchell, T. R. (1973). Structural determinants of individual behavior in organizations. *Administrative Science Quarterly, 18,* 56-70.

Rice, R. E. (1982). Communication networking in computer conferencing systems: A longitudinal study of group roles and systems structure. In M. Burgoon (Ed.), *Communication yearbook 6* (pp. 925-944). Newbury Park, CA: Sage.

Rice, R. E., & Richards, W. D., Jr. (1985). An overview of network analysis methods and programs. In B. Dervin & M. Voigt (Eds.), *Progress in communication sciences,* (Vol. 7, pp. 105-165). Norwood, NJ: Ablex.

Richards, W. D., Jr. (1985) Data, models, and assumptions in network analysis. In R. McPhee and P. Tompkins (Eds.), *Organizational communication: Traditional themes and new directions* (pp. 109-128). Newbury Park, CA: Sage.

Riley, P. (1983). A structurationist account of organizational culture. *Administrative Science Quarterly, 28,* 414-437.

Riley, P. (1985). *Culture clash in organizations.* Paper presented at the annual meeting of the International Communication Association, Honolulu.

Roberts, K., & O'Reilly, C. (1974). Measuring organizational communication. *Journal of Applied Psychology, 59,* 321-326.

Roberts, K. H., & O'Reilly, C. A. (1978). Organizations as communication structures: An empirical approach. *Human Communication Research, 4,* 283-293.

Roberts, K. H., & O'Reilly, C. A., III. (1979). Some correlates of communication roles in organizations. *Academy of Management Journal, 22,* 42-57.

Rogers, E. M., & Kincaid, D. L. (1981). *Communication networks: Toward a new paradigm for research.* New York: Free Press.

Rounds, J. (1984). Information and ambiguity in organizational change. In L. Sproull & P. Larkey (Eds.), *Advances in information processing in organizations* (Vol. 1, pp. 111-142). Greenwich, CT: JAI Press.

Sailer, L. D. (1978). Structural equivalence: Meaning and definition, computation and applications. *Social Networks, 1,* 73-90.

Schermerhorn, J. (1977). Information sharing as an interorganizational activity. *Academy of Management Journal, 20,* 148-153.

Schreiman, D., & Johnson, J. D. (1975). *A model of cognitive complexity and network roles.* Paper presented at the annual meeting of the International Communication Association, Chicago.

Schwartz, D., & Jacobson, E. (1977). Organizational communication network analysis: The liaison communication role. *Organizational Behavior and Human Performance, 18,* 158-174.

Scott, W. R. (1983). The organization of environments: Network, cultural, and historical elements. In J. W. Meyer & W. R. Scott (Eds.), *Organizational environments: Ritual and rationality* (pp. 155-175). Newbury Park, CA: Sage.

Sherman, J. D., Smith, H., & Mansfield, E. R. (1986). The impact of emergent network structure on organizational socialization. *Journal of Applied Behavioral Science, 22,* 53-63.

Spencer, H. (1982). *Principles of sociology* (Vol. 2, part 2). New York: Appleton-Century-Crofts.

Sproull, L. (1981). Beliefs in organizations. In P. Nystrom & W. Starbuck (Eds.), *Handbook of organizational design* (Vol. 2, pp. 203-224). New York: Oxford University Press.

Thompson, E. (1978). *The poverty of theory and other essays.* New York: Monthly Review Press.

Thurman, B. (1979). In the office: Networks and coalitions. *Social Networks, 2,* 47-63.

Tichy, N. M. (1981). Networks in organizations. In P. Nystrom & W. Starbuck (Eds.), *Handbook of organizational design* (Vol. 2, pp. 225-249). New York: Oxford University Press.

Tichy, N., & Fombrun, C. (1979). Network analysis in organizational settings. *Human Relations, 32,* 923-965.

Tichy, N., Tushman, M., & Fombrun, C. (1979). Social network analysis for organizations. *Academy of Management Review, 4,* 507-519.

Trist, E. L. (1983). Referent organizations and the development of interorganizational domains. *Human Relations, 36,* 269-284.

Turk, H. (1970). Interorganizational networks in urban society: Initial perspectives and comparative research. *American Sociological Review, 35,* 1-19.

Tushman, M. L. (1977). Communication across organizational boundaries: Special boundary roles in the innovation process. *Administrative Science Quarterly, 22,* 587-605.

Tushman, M. L. (1978). Technical communication in R & D laboratories: The impact of project work characteristics. *Academy of Management Journal, 21,* 624-645.

Tushman, M. L. (1979). Work characteristics and subunit communication structure: A contingency analysis. *Administrative Science Quarterly, 24,* 82-97.

Tushman, M. L., & Scanlan, T. J. (1981). Boundary spanning individuals: Their role in information transfer and their antecedents. *Academy of Management Journal 24,* 289-305.

Wade, L. (1968). Communications in public bureaucracy: Involvement and performance. *Journal of Communication, 18,* 18-25.

Walter, G. (1985). Culture collisions in mergers and acquisitions In P. Frost, L. Moore, M. R. Louis, C. Lundberg, & J. Martin (Eds.), *Organizational culture* (pp. 301-314). Newbury Park, CA: Sage.

Warren, R. (1967). The interorganizational field as a focus for investigation. *Administrative Science Quarterly, 12,* 396-419.

Weber, M. (1947). *The theory of social and economic organization.* New York: Free Press.

Weick, K. E. (1976). Educational organizations as loosely coupled systems. *Administrative Science Quarterly, 21,* 1-19.

Weimann, G. (1983). The not-so-small world: Ethnicity and acquaintance networks in Israel. *Social Networks, 5,* 289-302.

Whetten, D. (1981). Interorganizational relations: A review of the field. *Journal of Higher Education, 52,* 1-28.

White, H. (1973). Everyday life in stochastic networks. *Sociological Inquiry, 43,* 43-49.

White, H. C., Boorman, S. A., & Breiger, R. L. (1976). Social structure from multiple networks. I. Block-models of roles and positions. *American Journal of Sociology, 81,* 730-780.

Yoshino, M. (1968). *Japan's managerial system.* Cambridge, MA: MIT Press.

Zalesny, M. D., & Farace, R. V. (1987). Traditional versus open offices: A comparison of sociotechnical, social relations and symbolic meaning perspectives. *Academy of Management Journal, 30,* 240-259.

11 Superior-Subordinate Communication: Multiple Levels of Analysis

FRED DANSEREAU
State University of New York at Buffalo

STEVEN E. MARKHAM
*Virginia Polytechnic Institute
and State University*

Foci of Research: An Overview and Update
 Interaction Patterns and Related Attitudes/Openness in Communication/Upward
 Distortion/Upward Influence/Semantic-Information Distance/Effective Versus Inef-
 fective Superiors/Personal Characteristics/Feedback/Conflict/Systemic Variables/
 Summary
Assessment of Research Progress
Recasting the Literature in Terms of Levels of Analysis
 The Person Tradition/The Dyad Tradition/The Group Tradition/The Collectivity
 Tradition/Differences Within the Four Traditions/Differences Among Traditions
Conceptualization of Multiple Levels of Analysis
 Single-Level Analysis/Multiple-Level Analysis
Four Modes and Communication
 Personal Mode/Exchange Mode/Leadership Mode/Supervision Mode/Combining
 the Modes
Implications of the Four Modes for Future Research
 Single-Mode Approaches/General Approaches/Multiple Mode Approaches
Summary and Conclusion

T RADITIONALLY, interpersonal superior-subordinate communication has been one of the most popular areas of organizational
communication research. Indeed, in an original and later updated

AUTHORS' NOTE: We would like to thank Joseph A. Alutto, Robert Cardy, Daniel Coleman,
Sanford Ehrlich, Gail McKee, Sidney Nachman, Thomas Naughton, Sheila Puffer, and the
editors of this book, especially Fred Jablin, for their comments on previous versions of this
chapter.

review of the literature, Jablin (1979, 1985) identified 10 relevant topical areas that have been studied in some detail. Given the existence of these reviews, the primary purpose of this chapter is *not* to present an elaborate literature review. Rather, our efforts are directed at: (1) providing a brief orientation to and updating of the 10 areas identified by Jablin (1979, 1985), (2) assessing the degree to which recent research has been successful in overcoming limitations associated with earlier studies of superior-subordinate communication, and (3) based on this assessment demonstrating that future studies need to show greater consideration for the importance of levels of analysis in understanding superior-subordinate interaction.

The greater part of this chapter focuses on the last of the above issues. In particular, we will recast the literature in terms of four major schools of thought (or traditions) that are associated with varying levels of analysis in superior-subordinate communication research. Subsequently, we will suggest and demonstrate how a framework we term the *varient approach*[1] can be used to test theoretically and empirically within and across levels of analysis hypothesized in the four major approaches to superior-subordinate communication. In turn, the final section of this chapter will refine and expand the 10 topical categories of superior-subordinate communication research examined in the first section by explicitly considering multiple levels of analysis for each topic.

FOCI OF RESEARCH: AN OVERVIEW AND UPDATE

Jablin (1979, 1985) identified 10 areas of considerable research activity in superior-subordinate communication. They are: (1) interaction patterns and related attitudes, (2) openness in communication, (3) upward distortion, (4) upward influence, (5) semantic-information distance, (6) effective versus ineffective superiors, (7) personal characteristics, (8) feedback, (9) conflict, and (10) systemic variables. Here we provide a brief orientation to each of these areas by summarizing conclusions drawn in previous literature reviews and discussing the emphasis of more recent investigations associated with each category of research.

Interaction Patterns and Related Attitudes

Jablin (1985, p. 625) has observed, "Probably one of the most consistent findings in superior-subordinate communication research is that supervisors spend from one-third to two-thirds of their time communicating with subordinates." Various researchers have attempted to support this conclusion and the notion that most supervisory communication is verbal and occurs in face-to-face contexts (Luthans & Larsen, 1986; Whitely, 1984, 1985). In addition, these investigators suggest that (1) about one-third of managerial communication is consumed in "routine" communication (writing and reading reports, receiving and sending requested information, answering procedural questions; see Luthans & Larsen, 1986); (2) with the exception of contacts with subordinates, managers often communicate more with persons external to their organizations than with others in their organizations (Luthans & Larsen, 1986); (3) interactions with persons external to the organization and with superiors are viewed as most challenging and important to managers, while contacts with subordinates are viewed as least important and challenging (Whitely, 1984); and (4) the social context (leader-member goal interdependence) of superior-subordinate communication can directly affect interaction and message exchange patterns (Tjosvold, 1985a). Relatedly, other researchers have focused on methods of assessing superior-subordinate interaction, and suggest that coding relational communication patterns (Fairhurst, Rogers, & Starr, 1987) and forms of operant conditioning (Komaki, Zlotnick, & Jenson, 1986) may provide valuable insights into characteristics of communication between superiors and subordinates.

Openness in Communication

Openness in superior-subordinate communication is often conceptualized in terms of two interrelated dimensions: openness in message-sending and openness in message-receiving (Redding, 1972). Similarly, Jablin (1979, p. 1204) stated that "in an open communication relationship between superior and subordinate, both parties perceive the other interactant as a willing and receptive listener and refrain from responses that might be perceived as providing negative relational or disconfirming feedback." In turn, other investigators report that subordinates' perceptions of openness are positively related to their job satisfaction, and in particular their satisfaction with supervision. Not surprisingly, Wheeless, Wheeless, and Howard (1984) and Pincus (1986) suggested that subordinates' perceptions of supervisory "receptivity" (essentially openness in message receiving) are also a powerful predictor of workers' job satisfaction. On the other hand, in a recent laboratory study, Tjosvold (1984) reported that subordinates' perceptions of openness are also related to the nonverbal warmth (communicated through eye gaze, posture, facial expression, and voice tone) displayed by superiors in their interactions with subordinates.

Upward Distortion

The propensity of persons of lower hierarchical rank to distort messages transmitted to persons in higher organizational levels has been frequently noted in the literature. As a consequence, the moderating effects of numerous superior and subordinate characteristics (mobility aspirations, security needs, gender), message factors (message importance, relevance, content, favorableness to superior/subordinate), relational issues (trust, influence), and organizational variables (organizational structure, technology, and climate) have been related to upward message distortion (see Glauser, 1984; Jablin, 1979). Of the various findings of studies in this area, one of the more frequently reported results is that subordinates are often hesitant to communicate upward information that is unfavorable or negative to themselves. Most recently, Fulk and Mani (1986) examined the degree to which supervisors' downward communication affects the accuracy and frequency of subordinates' upward communication distortion. They suggest a reciprocal relationship between superiors' and subordinates' communication behaviors such that "subordinates reported withholding information and generally distorting communication sent upward when their supervisors were seen as actively withholding information" (p. 503).

Upward Influence

Generally speaking, studies of upward influence in superior-subordinate communication have concentrated on exploring variations of the "Pelz Effect" (Pelz, 1952) or the message strategies that subordinates use to influence their superiors. In brief, the Pelz Effect suggests that "subordinates' satisfaction with supervision is a by-product not only of an open, supportive relationship between the two parties, but also of the supervisor's ability to satisfy subordinates' needs by possessing influence with those higher in the organization hierarchy" (Jablin, 1985, p. 627). Overall, most research has been interpreted as supportive of the Pelz Effect and has not been interpreted as uncovering any major moderators of the relationships it suggests (Jablin, 1980). For example, Trempe, Rigny, and Haccoun (1985) recently examined the notion that supervisor gender might moderate the basic tenets of the Pelz Effect. Testing this hypothesis among French-speaking Canadian blue-collar workers, they did not report any sex differences.

Along with reexamining the validity of the Pelz Effect, the last decade has evidenced a resurgence of interest in exploring the dynamics of political activity in organizations (see Frost, Chapter 15, this volume), and especially the communication strategies that subordinates use in their attempts to influence their superiors. Unfortunately, the reports are somewhat inconsistent, with some investigators suggesting that subordinates most commonly use covert message tactics, and other investigators indicating that logical/rational presentation of ideas is most frequently employed. As a consequence, it is not surprising that after reviewing this literature, Jablin (1985, p. 628) concluded that "a subordinate's selection and use of a message strategy in an influence attempt . . . [appears] dependent on a wide array of situational factors (such as decision type, organizational climate and structure, and perceived power of the target)." Attempts to identify situational variables persist. For instance, Richmond, Davis, Saylor, and McCroskey (1984) assert that subordinates perceive their use of power/influence strategies (what they

term *behavior alteration techniques*) to be highly related to the
their supervisors use to influence them. On the other hand, K₁ ͜
suggests that subordinates' level in the hierarchy, sex, and perceptions oı
centralization of authority all significantly affect the types of messages they
use in attempting to influence their bosses.

Semantic-Information Distance

The term *semantic-information distance* describes the gap in information
and understanding that exists between superiors and subordinates (or other
groups within an organization) on specified issues (Jablin, 1979, p. 1207).
Researchers exploring this phenomenon suggest that superiors and subordinates frequently have large gaps in understanding on even such deceptively
simple topics as subordinates' basic job duties (Jablin, 1979) and the degree to
which subordinates participate in decision making (Harrison, 1985). While
many studies in this area have focused on exploring the degree to which
superiors and subordinates agree/disagree with each others' views of specified
topics (direct perspectives), a number of recent investigations have emphasized
differences in "meta-perceptions" (one's views of the other person's perspective; see Laing, Phillipson, & Lee, 1966). The meta-perceptions literature
suggests that superiors and subordinates differ not only in their direct
perspectives of issues, but also often in their meta-perspectives (Smircich &
Chesser, 1981).

Extending upon the notion of meta-perspectives and Newcomb's (1961)
co-orientation model, Eisenberg, Monge, and Farace (1984) recently explored
superiors' and subordinates' perceptions of the communication rules (initiation
and termination rules) that guide their interaction, and subordinates'
satisfaction with supervision and performance. They suggest that the more a
subordinate or supervisor perceives agreement between his or her own
attitudes and his or her *predictions* about the others' attitudes, the higher their
evaluation of the other party. Further, they state: "The accurate perception of
a subordinate's view of these rules by a supervisor is positively associated with
performance evaluation" (Eisenberg et al., 1984, p. 267).

Effective Versus Ineffective Superiors

Although "the identification of effective as compared to ineffective
communication behaviors of superiors has received more investigation than
any other area of organizational communication" (Jablin, 1979, p. 629), we
are still unable to state whether or not there is an ideal set of communication
characteristics associated with "effective" supervisors. In other words, at
present there are researchers who believe that there is a considerable amount
of evidence suggesting that "effective" leader communication behaviors are
contingent on numerous situational factors including organizational climate,

task type, gender and work-unit size. Moreover, Graen and his colleagues (Dansereau, Graen, & Haga, 1975) have suggested that superiors do not develop the same types of exchange patterns with all of their subordinates ("average leadership style"), but rather develop communication relationships that may vary from one superior-subordinate dyad to another ("vertical dyad linkage" model). On the other hand, still other researchers point to a common communication style across "effective" leaders. In particular, "good" supervisors are considered to be: (1) "communication minded" (enjoy communicating), (2) approachable, open, willing, and empathic listeners, (3) oriented toward asking or persuading in contrast to demanding or telling, (4) sensitive to the needs and feelings of subordinates, and (5) open in communicating information to subordinates and willing to explain "why" policies and regulations are being enacted (Redding, 1972, p. 443).

Findings of recent studies do not resolve the somewhat contradictory perspectives described above. For example, Manz and Sims (1984) reported that effective "unleaders" (leaders/coordinators of self-managed groups) display distinctive types of communication behaviors (encouraging open discussion of problems, acting as a communication link with other groups). On the other hand, Komaki (1986, p. 276), in an observational study of effective supervision, suggested that "effective managers conducted essentially the same activities as the marginal managers: they spent approximately the same amount of time interacting, discussing the work, talking about performance-related matters, delivering performance antecedents [expectations], and providing positive, negative, and neutral performance consequences" (knowledge of performance). The only significant difference between the two sets of managers she reported was with respect to the frequency with which they monitored performance, and in particular the extent to which they used work sampling (direct observation).

Personal Characteristics

Numerous personal characteristics of superiors and subordinates have been suggested as affecting the character of their communication relationships (see Jablin, 1979). Consistent with this tradition of research, recent studies have focused particular attention on how interactants' gender affects their communication behavior and attitudes (for a complete review, see Fairhurst, 1986). Along these lines, Steckler and Rosenthal (1985) recently examined potential sex differences in the nonverbal and verbal communication of workers with their bosses, peers, and subordinates. In their laboratory experiment, Steckler and Rosenthal (1985, p. 157) suggested that "females' voices were rated as sounding more competent verbally and nonverbally when they were speaking to their peers." On the other hand, in a study exploring perceptions of female managers and their communication competencies, Wheeless and Berryman-Fink (1985) suggested that regardless of respondents' experiences in working for a female manager, women perceive female managers as more competent communicators than do males. In turn, Serafini and Pearson (1984) reported that perceptions of psychological femininity tend to be associated with the "consideration" component of leadership behavior, while psychological masculinity is related to "initiating structure."

Recent studies have also explored relationships between a number of superiors' and subordinates' communication-related characteristics and subordinates' levels of job satisfaction. For instance, Infante and Gordon (1985) examined the hypothesis that subordinates' satisfaction with supervision will be positively related to the degree to which they perceive their superiors as high in argumentativeness (tendency to advocate positions on issues and to refute the positions others take) and low on verbal aggressiveness (tendency to "attack" the other's self-concept versus position). Relatedly, Johnson, Luthans, and Hennessey (1984) reported that "internal" (with respect to locus of control) supervisors tend to use persuasion more with subordinates than "external" leaders, and that supervisor persuasiveness is positively related to subordinate satisfaction with supervision. In a similar vein, Richmond, McCroskey, and Davis (1986) suggested that subordinate satisfaction is related to their supervisors' use of power and affinity-seeking strategies. On the other hand, Remland (1984) reported that perceptions of leader "consideration" are positively related to the degree to which supervisors display less status nonverbally and subordinates exhibit more status nonverbally. Sypher and Zorn (1986) suggested that communication abilities generally (and cognitive differentiation in particular) are related to the job level and upward mobility of organizational members.

Feedback

Although a considerable amount of recent research has been directed at exploring feedback in superior-subordinate communication, the two major conclusions that Jablin proposed in his 1979 review are still of interest today: (1) "feedback from superiors to subordinates appears related to subordinate performance and satisfaction," and (2) "a subordinate's performance to a large extent controls the nature of his/her superior's feedback" (Jablin, 1979, p. 1214).

Researchers focusing on feedback within the last few years (for a complete review, see Cusella, Chapter 18, this volume) have also suggested (1) "subordinates receiving feedback from sources high versus low in credibility judge the feedback as more accurate, the source as more perceptive, tend to express greater satisfaction with the feedback, and are more likely to use the performance suggestions offered in the feedback" (Bannister, 1986; Earley, 1986); (2) "supervisors may often be reluctant to give subordinates negative performance feedback and . . . this reluctance can affect both the content and frequency of the feedback they give" (Larson, 1986, p. 405); (3) a supervisor's goal interdependence with his or her subordinates and the supervisor's attributions of performance affect the feedback given to poor performers (Tjosvold, 1985b); (4) supervisors with limited authority and informal influence in decision making do not often use confrontative tactics (oral warnings) in disciplining subordinates (Beyer & Trice, 1984); (5) positive supervisory feedback to new employees is negatively related to their turnover (Parsons, Herold, & Leatherwood, 1985); (6) supervisors tend to exhibit positive verbal reward behaviors more frequently in response to high performers, as opposed to goal-setting, punitive, and task information behaviors in response to low performers (Sims & Manz, 1984); (7) managers tend to probe for the causes of failure among poor performers by asking attribution-seeking ("why") questions, while they tend to ask high performers "what-do-you-think" or "how" questions (Gioia & Sims, 1986); and (8) managers either initially assume a punitive approach to controlling poor performers or quickly adopt this approach after attempting to control poor performers through asking questions and problem solving (Fairhurst, Green, & Snavely, 1984a, 1984b).

Conflict

As Jablin (1985) suggested, within the last 10 years the study of the role of communication in superior-subordinate conflict has become increasingly popular (for a complete review, see Putnam & Poole, Chapter 16, this volume). Though some investigators suggest that several factors may moderate the manner in which supervisors may manage conflict with subordinates (for example, supervisor's organizational level, self-confidence), other investigators suggest that superiors may favor the use of "forcing" or "confronting" strategies in managing conflicts with subordinates. At the same time, still other investigators suggest that the particular communication strategies utilized by superiors and subordinates to manage conflict are to some degree reciprocally related to the behaviors exhibited by the other party (Goering, Rudick, & Faulkner, 1986). With respect to more general role problems in superior-subordinate interaction, Gerloff, and Quick (1984) reported that subordinates in "high distortion" relationships with their superiors (low agreement on feedback issues) show significantly higher levels of role conflict with their superiors than persons in "low distortion" relationships.

Systemic Variables

In comparison to the other areas of research discussed in this section, relatively few studies have examined how systemic organizational variables (organizational structure, environment, technology) affect the dynamics of superior-subordinate communication (for a complete review, see Jablin, Chapter 12, this volume). In fact, at this time about all we can even *tentatively* conclude is that (1) organizational size and work group size have not been shown to moderate the quality of communication in superior-subordinate relationships, and (2) the communication behaviors and perceptions of superiors may be somewhat dependent on their hierarchical positions or roles in organizations. Support for this latter conclusion is offered by Hannaway (1985), who concluded that task uncertainty affects managers at lower levels of the hierarchy differently than managers at higher levels. Specifically, lower-level managers were viewed as displaying less assertiveness and information search behavior (self-initiated verbal interaction) under conditions of high uncertainty than were higher-level managers.

Summary

Jablin noted in his 1979 review of the literature that three items seem to be consistently studied with respect to the nature of superior-subordinate interaction: power and status, trust, and semantic-information distance. The preceding "update" of the literature indicates that this conclusion is probably still valid. However, it also seems apparent that recent investigations have increasingly focused on examining the behavioral and cognitive characteristics of communication in the upward influence and feedback processes. Moreover, one of the most frequent themes discernible in the results of these and related studies is that the communication behaviors of superiors and subordinates are often viewed as reciprocally interrelated.

ASSESSMENT OF RESEARCH PROGRESS

An examination of extant reviews of superior-subordinate communication research (Jablin, 1979, 1985; Porter & Roberts, 1976) suggests at least two major criticisms of the literature. First, research in the area has been chided for inattention to the *processual* nature of superior-subordinate communication and the related tendency to study superior-subordinate communication processes through "one-shot" versus longitudinal research designs. Second, studies of superior subordinate communication have been berated for their failure to consider adequately how the *embeddedness* of these relationships within the larger organizational context affects their characteristics. Essentially, this latter issue focuses on the importance of considering levels of analysis in exploring superior-subordinate communication phenomena (Farace & MacDonald, 1974; Jablin, 1979; Jablin & Krone, 1987; Roberts, O'Reilly, Bretton, & Porter, 1974; Thayer, 1968).

To what degree have recent research efforts come to terms with the above inadequacies in previous studies? With respect to the first criticism, that is, insufficient attention to the *processual*, interactive nature of superior-subordinate communication, we can report a partial reversal of previous trends. Some researchers are directly focusing on the dynamics of the process of communication between members of the dyad. Several recent lines of research focusing on coding the sequential exchange of messages between superiors and subordinates illustrate this shift in focus. For example, recent studies by Sims and his associates (Gioia & Sims, 1986; Sims & Manz, 1984) exploring the nature of verbal interaction patterns in the performance appraisal context have focused on the nature of reciprocal determinism and feedback processes in superior-subordinate communication. Similarly, Fairhurst et al. (1987) have suggested various issues that arise when focusing on the dynamics of relational communication patterns in superior-subordinate interaction. In addition, it is also evident that researchers are beginning to explore superior-subordinate communication processes through longitudinal rather than one-shot, static research designs. Along these lines, for example, is the research of Jablin (1984) and Graen, Liden, and Hoel (1982) investigating the assimilation of newcomers into organizations and the development of their related superior-subordinate communication relationships. In turn, the research of Fairhurst et al. (1984a, 1984b) exploring "chains" of control episodes in managers' attempts to discipline and change the performance of subordinates represents another line of longitudinal superior-subordinate communication research. In short, it is apparent that scholars are now starting to devote more attention to the dynamics of the process of superior-subordinate communication. Moreover, analytic techniques for focusing on processual communication data have been considered (see Monge, Farace, Eisenberg, Miller, & White, 1984).

Unfortunately, we have not made similar progress in focusing on the second deficiency noted above in extant superior-subordinate communication research: inattention to the *embeddedness* of superior-subordinate communication relationships within the larger organizational context. Even a cursory analysis of the research reviewed in the preceding section indicates that most studies have focused on examining the communication traits, perceptions, and behaviors of superiors and subordinates in isolation of the social and organizational contexts in which they occur. In short, we currently know little about how higher- and lower-order levels of communication and organizational phenomena affect and relate to interaction between superiors and subordinates. Though we can take some solace in realizing that we are not alone among the organizational sciences in coming to terms with dilemmas associated with levels of analysis in research (see Cummings, 1981; Glick & Roberts, 1984; Kimberly, 1976; Klauss & Bass, 1982; Mossholder & Bedian, 1983; Roberts, Hulin, & Rousseau, 1978; Rousseau, 1985), that does not diminish our responsibility in confronting and overcoming these problems. As Weick (1969, p. 45) argued in discussing levels of analysis in organizational research, "the only way we can learn much about any of these levels is if we know how they are tied together, that is, how one level interacts with another level."

The remainder of this chapter represents an effort to confront problems associated with levels of analysis in superior-subordinate communication research. In particular, in the following sections we will (1) recast the literature in terms of four schools of thought that are associated with varying levels of analysis in superior-subordinate communication research, (2) provide a brief description of a general conceptualization of multiple levels of analysis that responds to critical issues identified by the four schools of thought, (3) use this general conceptualization to show how four multiple-level modes can be used to organize the literature on superior-subordinate communication, and (4) refine and expand the 10 topic categories of research reviewed in the first section of this chapter by explicitly considering multiple levels of analysis for each topic.

RECASTING THE LITERATURE IN TERMS OF LEVELS OF ANALYSIS

In order to come to terms with issues associated with levels of analysis in superior-subordinate communication research, it is first necessary to identify the levels of analysis (or entities) that have been the traditional foci of study. In this section, we attempt to demonstrate that the contemporary literature seems to view superior-subordinate communication from four basic levels of analysis: (1) the person, (2) the dyad, (3) the group, and (4) the collectivity. Moreover, each of these "schools of thought" (traditions) appears to view the issue of level of analysis in the following two ways. First, a school of thought may focus on variables and their relationships that reflect differences *between* whole entities. For example, differences in the communication patterns between dyads (in which pairs of people are considered as one unit) might be a focus of research interest. Second, a school of thought may focus on variables and their relationships *within* entities. For example, communication may be thought of as a process that differentiates superiors and subordinates in dyads. Therefore, two views of superior-subordinate communication—within and between entities—must be considered for each of the four perspectives on hierarchical communication.

The Person Tradition

In terms of the person level of analysis, one way that superior-subordinate communication has been viewed is as a reflection of differences between individuals. The focus of research within this perspective often is on individual differences and perceptions. Much of the research reviewed earlier exploring openness in communication, upward influence and distortion, and the effects of superiors' and subordinates' personal characteristics on communication behavior seems to use this approach. For example, Penley and Hawkins

(1985) analyzed the relationships among variables such as the degree to which subordinates perceived their superiors to be responsive, personal, career-, performance-, and task-oriented as well as the subordinates' perceptions of the degree to which their superiors were considerate and provided structure as defined by responses to the Leader Behavior Description Questionnaire (LBDQ). In this view only the perceptions of subordinates about superiors are of interest; therefore, Penley and Hawkins (1985) analyzed responses only from subordinates.

Research on superior-subordinate communication has also focused on variables and relationships that reflect characteristics inside or within persons. For example, Fulk and Mani (1986) present a model of upward distortion that presumably provides an internal framework that subordinates use in communicating with superiors. Likewise, Broms and Gahmberg (1983) use the notion of "autocommunication" to reflect the idea that communication occurs within individuals. To summarize, two views of persons appear to be asserted in the literature. Specifically, superior-subordinate communication is viewed first as reflecting differences *between* individuals and second as reflecting processes *within* individuals. Moreover, the person tradition views superiors and subordinates as independent of each other.

The Dyad Tradition

In contrast to the person tradition, a second school of thought appears to assert that superiors and subordinates should be viewed as dependent pairings (dyads). In this approach it is necessary to consider simultaneously a superior and each subordinate who reports to a supervisor. Some recent studies exploring semantic-information distance and feedback between superiors and subordinates seem to use this approach. For example, Dansereau, Alutto, and Yammarino (1984) suggested that entire dyads can be characterized by an exchange of attention by a superior in return for good performance by a subordinate. In other words, some dyads can be characterized as richer and others as less rich in terms of leadership attention and subsequent performance. In this approach dyads are viewed as intact entities in which superiors and subordinates are very similar. Thus, for example, Dansereau et al. (1984) focused on scores that reflected differences among dyads rather than on the separate scores of superiors and subordinates. In contrast, a second view of dyads is that superiors and subordinates, although interdependent within the context of the dyad, differ from each other. In this case the focus is on differences within dyads. For example, Watson (1982) argues that superiors within dyads showed resistance to and subordinates showed compliance with each others' attempts to control the relationship. To summarize, previous research has focused on superior and subordinate communication as reflecting the differences *between* dyads and as reflecting the differences *within* dyads. Nevertheless, the focus in these two approaches is on dyads, each composed of one superior and one subordinate.

The Group Tradition

A third approach to superior-subordinate communication appears to focus on the potential impact of a superior on the entire group of individuals who report to that superior. From one perspective, a superior is viewed as displaying a similar style (or characteristic) to all subordinates who report to that superior. Moreover, subordinates are viewed as responding in a homogeneous fashion to a superior. Thus the focus here is not on individual perceptions and internal processes or on superiors and subordinates in pairs but rather on the relationship of a superior's style to his or her work group's performance. In particular, studies examining the communication characteristics of "effective" supervisors (Redding, 1972) often assume this perspective. This view is also typified in many studies focusing on initiation of structure and consideration as measured by the Leader Behavior Description Questionnaire (LBDQ). For example, Ayman and Chemers (1983) aggregated the responses of employees into work group averages that they believed reflected differences *between* superiors.

On the other hand, a second perspective within the group tradition focuses on the variation among subordinates *within* groups (Graen et al., 1982; Lesniak, 1981; Vecchio, 1985). This view suggests that superiors form teams by differentiating among the members of their work groups. For example, one might hypothesize that each superior may direct the communication in a work group differently based on his or her assessment of one subordinate relative to another. In this school of thought, superiors have been viewed as individuals whose personal characteristics or internal processes forge differentiated links with their subordinates within the context of the work group.

The Collectivity Tradition

A fourth school seems to focus on superiors and subordinates as members of large collectivities (for example, departments or organizations). Research exploring systemic variables often uses this view. From one perspective, superior-subordinate communication has been viewed as largely a characterization of either organizational or structural factors in a setting that supersedes individuals. For example, the research of Snyder and Morris (1984) suggested two communication variables—the quality of supervisory communication and information exchange of peer work groups—may be related to revenue and work load measures of overall organization performance. In this study the responses of employees were aggregated to form averages that were thought to reflect the differences *between* organizations (collectivities), rather than differences between employees or differences between dyads or work groups. A somewhat different perspective focuses on differences *within* collectivities. In this approach the focus is on the differences within a collective. For example, Miller (1978) focuses on the interdependencies within systems.

Differences Within the Four Traditions

Each of the traditions we have gleaned from the literature offers some latitude to conceptualize superior-subordinate interaction as a between- or within-entity concern. These traditions, however, fail to provide ways to decide when such views are appropriate. Specifically, how should superiors and subordinates be viewed? At the person level, should each superior and subordinate be viewed in terms of his or her personality characteristics and communication style and/or in terms of the communication processes that occur within a superior and/or a subordinate? At the dyad level, should a superior and subordinate be viewed in terms of a balanced and/or unbalanced exchange between two individuals? In terms of a group level, should a superior be viewed in terms of a style that affects the group and/or as an individual who behaves differently toward individual subordinates? Finally, at the collective level should superiors and subordinates be viewed as similar within collectivities and/or as interdependent but differentiated within organizations?

The importance of the two views within each school can be illustrated by considering the theoretical, empirical, and applied issues that can arise within one school of thought—the group tradition. In one theoretical view of the group tradition, a process within superiors is hypothesized that results in differentiation among subordinates within a group. This raises theoretical questions about the sources and consequences of such discrimination. From an empirical perspective, a proponent of this view would not attempt to measure a superior's style as seen by a whole work unit. Rather, a leader's separate actions and reactions toward each subordinate would be captured. From an applied perspective this focus would lead to training leaders to build teams by "capitalizing" on the relative differences between subordinates (perhaps by varying the type of message depending on a subordinate's strengths relative to other group members). In contrast, from another theoretical perspective, a superior is viewed as being characterized in terms of a single style or personality trait, and interest is focused on the impact of these characterizations (variables) on intact work groups. From an empirical perspective, one need not measure the behavior of the superior toward each subordinate; one need only obtain one characterization of a superior. In this approach, when there are multiple scores from one superior, these scores are aggregated to form one score for each leader. From an applied perspective, leaders would not be trained to "capitalize" on relative differences of specific subordinates but rather to engage them all with a single "effective" communication style.

On the other hand, although the distinction between the two views within any one school of thought is important, it should be noted that when one allows for the possibility that more than one school of thought is plausible, an additional concern arises, as described below.

Differences Among Traditions

The four schools of thought tend to view one set of individuals in very different ways, as the following definitions (adapted from Miller [1978]) illustrate. At the person level, individuals are viewed as independent of each other. At the group and dyad levels, individuals are interdependent based on their *direct* interactions. (The dyad level, of course, is a special case of groups—only two individuals form a dyad.) Finally, at the collectivity level, individuals are connected *indirectly* through hierarchies and echelons. The term *individual* is used in a generic sense in these definitions because individuals can be viewed from any one of these four levels of analysis. Moreover, for ease of presentation the levels are hierarchically organized such that the person is the lowest and the collectivity the highest level of analysis. From an empirical perspective, the schools of thought seem to influence data analysis. For example, when a proponent of the collectivity tradition observes individuals, he or she views them as somewhat irrelevant because individual differences are viewed as a reflection of collectivity differences. From this perspective, as described previously, Snyder and Morris (1984) collapsed scores from hundreds of individuals into a dozen scores that they believed reflected differences between organizations (collectivities). Clearly, a proponent of the school person of thought would analyze the person-level scores and not aggregate them. A proponent of the dyad or group school would aggregate the scores to reflect the number of dyads or groups and not the collectivities. Therefore, from an empirical perspective, one must ask a key question: On what basis is the decision made to treat scores as representing one school of thought or another? Clearly, such decisions to date have not generally been made based on data and/or on the variables of interest (see, for example, Ayman & Chemers [1983], where subordinate reports on the LBDQ were aggregated, and Penley & Hawkins [1985], where the scores on the LBDQ were not aggregated).

In summary, given the growing awareness that multiple levels of analysis should be considered in organizational settings, particularly because individuals (a person-level view) typically report to a superior (dyadic-level view), and are members of work groups (group-level view), and are members of departments and organizations (collectivity-level view), the question naturally follows: How do we determine the appropriate level(s) of analysis for studying superior-subordinate communication phenomena? Our response to this query is relatively straightforward: View levels of analysis (the four traditions in this case) a priori as equally likely. From this perspective each school of thought can be viewed as making somewhat different assertions about the four levels of analysis as the following example illustrates. To a proponent of the person tradition, the dyad, group, and collectivity levels are irrelevant and need not be considered because individuals are viewed as independent of each other. In contrast, to a proponent of the collective tradition, the person level should not be considered independently of collective-level processes. From this example it should be obvious that the two traditions make very different assertions about the degree of importance of the collectivity level. Therefore, the schools of thought seem to require that even when only one level of analysis is of interest, consideration should also be given to the possibility of rejecting that level as inappropriate. In other words, it should be possible to hypothesize that a set of variables, and their relationships, apply to one level of analysis and not to another level. For example, the person tradition may be appropriate for some communication variables even though it focuses on only one level (person) and rejects another level (collectivity). Furthermore, it also seems necessary to allow for hypotheses in which variables (and their relationships) might apply at multiple levels when data support such an induction (as in the collectivity tradition). The next section of this chapter presents a brief review of a conceptualization of multiple levels of analysis that is designed to respond to these requirements.

CONCEPTUALIZATION OF MULTIPLE LEVELS OF ANALYSIS

In this section we review, in simplified terms, one major approach to levels of analysis that seems to address the key issues presented in the last section by (1) considering each level of analysis separately (single-level analysis), and (2) simultaneously considering all levels, taken two at a time (multiple-level analysis). (For a complete discussion, see Dansereau et al., 1984.)

Single-Level Analysis

As suggested earlier, at any level of analysis (for example, the dyad) it is necessary to be able to distinguish on a theoretical and empirical basis between two alternative views of that level—"within" and "between" entity concerns. Below we describe a conceptualization of these two views. The former we term a "parts" perspective and the latter a "wholes" perspective.

When a variable (for example, amount of interaction between two individuals) is measured, a score is sometimes assigned to each of several similar entities (for example, dyads). The assumption that underlies this assignment is that a score characterizes a whole object (for example, one dyad). Thus we can say that systematic variation across scores should occur between objects and that variation within objects on that variable is error. In this way we allow for the possibility that we may be interested in the differences between whole collectivities, whole groups, whole dyads, and/ or whole persons, and that each of the "wholes" can be represented by a single, representative score. In contrast to the wholes condition, the *parts* condition requires that meaningful variation for a given variable occur within an entity and error variation occurs between entities. In this case the focus is on differences within an object. For example, we might be interested in differences that occur within persons, dyads, groups, and/or collectivities. Thus for any particular level of analysis we can *generally* assert that either a part or whole condition applies.[2]

Multiple-Level Analysis

Thus the above conceptualization permits a decision as to whether wholes or parts are of interest at any one level of analysis, and it also permits the rejection of a particular level of analysis. The need for an ability to reject a level of analysis becomes apparent when multiple levels of analysis are of interest. Specifically, suppose we define the person level (as in traditional work) as reflecting differences between independent individuals. As a result, the dyad, group, and collectivity levels are rejected as not relevant. This case—where variables and relationships are hypothesized not to hold at a higher level of analysis—is called a *level-specific* formulation. In contrast, suppose one asserts that variables and relationships hold at the person and dyad level. Then the person level is redefined as reflecting the interdependencies between pairs of individuals and as reflecting differences between or within dyads. This case—where variables and their relationships are hypothesized to hold at two or more levels—is called a *cross-level* formulation. In addition, we could assert that variables and relationships hold only at a collectivity level. This case—where variables and relationships hold at a higher but not a lower level of analysis—is called an *emergent* formulation. Finally, to form a complete set of plausible alternatives, one allows for the hypothesis that variables and relationships do not hold at two levels, which is called a *null* formulation.

To summarize the alternatives for considering two levels of analysis, we should consider four alternatives at each of the two levels simultaneously. To simplify the presentation of this summary, however, only two conditions at each of the two levels are shown in Table 11.1. First an emergent view is indicated in Table 11.1 by the selection of wholes at the higher level and the rejection of the lower level of analysis. This emergent formulation asserts variation and covariation at the lower level is error and that variation and covariation at the higher level is systematic. Second, a level-specific view is indicated by the selection of wholes at the lower level and the rejection of the higher level of analysis. This level-specific formulation asserts that systematic variation and covariation at the lower level remains (that is, it is not error) at the higher level but the higher level does not organize this variation and covariation from the lower level. Third, a cross-level view is indicated by the selection of wholes at the higher *and* lower levels of analysis. This cross-level formulation asserts that variation and covariation is systematic across both levels. Finally, a null condition is indicated by the rejection of both levels of analysis. Table 11.1 illustrates how this conceptualization permits the selection among multiple levels of analysis. In this approach, one theorist may select one formulation (for example, level-specific), while another may select a different formulation (for example, cross-level). This conceptualization is also used to visualize how to perform data analysis to show which of the formulations is more likely. The question to be addressed in the next section is how this conceptualization enhances the four schools of thought about superior-subordinate communication.

FOUR MODES AND COMMUNICATION

The conceptualization from Table 11.1 permits the selection among a number of theoretical formulations that encompass different ways of combining levels of analysis simultaneously (where levels are considered two at a time). In this section four multiple-level formulations will be presented. Each formulation is called a "mode" because each represents a way to characterize superior-subordinate communication and each contains assertions about *four levels* of analysis (persons, dyads, groups, collectivities). Thus our use of the term *mode* provides a simple way to indicate a selected combination of variables in conjunction with selected levels of analysis. In making these selections we attempted to define four modes, each of which we believe is compatible with one of the four traditions described earlier. We view the alignment between the traditions and the modes, to be discussed in this section, as follows:

Tradition	Multiple-Level Communication Mode
Person	Personal
Dyad	Exchange
Group	Leadership
Collective	Supervision

In the above table, the personal mode is aligned with the traditional use of persons in communication. Why not simply use the label of "person level" in lieu of creating a new term, *mode*? Our use of the term *mode* is meant to convey more information than the term *person level of analysis*. To describe a mode, one must also specify (1) a potentially relevant domain of variables, (2) which of two inferences (parts, wholes) do or do not apply to a single-level model, (3) the implied referent for such communication (or sampling frame), and (4) the impact of higher and lower levels of analysis (dyads, groups, and so on) on the previously defined and selected entities and variables. Our purpose here is not to present all possible ways to combine multiple levels in each

TABLE 11.1
Simplified Illustration of Alternative Formulations
of Levels of Analysis for Two Levels

	Emergent	*Level Specific*	*Cross-Level*	*Null*
Higher level				
Wholes	yes	no	yes	no
Parts	no	no	no	no
Lower level				
Wholes	no	yes	yes	no
Parts	no	no	no	no

NOTE: To simplify the presentation, two rejection conditions are not shown in the table. Thus the table assumes that if either or both parts and wholes are selected at one level of analysis for one variable, the level is rejected. See Dansereau et al. (1984) for more precise illustrations.

tradition or all possible ways to use the conceptualization but rather to illustrate some of the consequences of selecting specific combinations of levels of analysis and variables for understanding superior-subordinate communication. Therefore, in this section each mode will be described in terms of (1) the key level of analysis that is selected (a single-level analysis), (2) the selections that are made about multiple levels of analysis (a multiple-level analysis), and (3) the consequences of the selections for each mode for superior-subordinate communication. After the four modes are presented, their characteristics and consequences are compared, contrasted, and integrated.

Personal Mode

The primary focus of the personal mode of superior-subordinate communication is on the "person" as viewed in traditional communication research. In terms of communication, two questions arise: First, how are persons, as the entity of interest, viewed: as parts or wholes? Second, in what ways are higher levels of analysis relevant?

Single-level analysis. The personal mode views individuals as persons who are *independent* of each other. From the perspective of wholes, the personal mode is compatible with the individual difference tradition in industrial psychology (Campbell, Dunnette, Lawler, & Weick, 1970). For example, individuals may be viewed as varying in their locus of control (see, for example, Durand & Nord, 1976; Mitchell, Smyser, & Weed, 1975). From this perspective, the locus of control variable characterizes individuals as whole persons. Persons with different propensities for control may be hypothesized to use different types of communication. Thus from this perspective communication can be viewed as a function of the personal style of the communicator. A second perspective of the personal mode still focuses on individuals, with a concern for "parts," that is, processes that occur within individuals. For example, communication by superiors with their subordinates may be viewed as a reflection of various decisions made within a superior. To capture this process, many scores can be gathered from the superior over time. From the perspective of internal decision making this framework is expected to be applicable to each individual (see, for example, Vroom & Yetton, 1973).

Multiple-level analysis. From the perspective of multiple levels of analysis, in the personal mode superiors and subordinates are viewed as independent of each other; therefore, communication reflects either the personal characteristics of individuals (a wholes perspective) or the interdependencies *within* individuals (a parts perspective). Hence this mode makes the assertion that higher levels of analysis (that is, dyads, groups, and collectivities) are not relevant. In other words, from a multiple-level perspective, the personal mode is specific to the person level (that is, it is a level-specific formulation).

Illustration. To show the link between the personal mode and traditional communication concepts such as intrapersonal communication, think of an individual who focuses exclusively on himself or herself independently of other individuals when a decision is being formulated. As this person communicates, there is no need to interact with others, and, perhaps, a potential harm from so doing might occur because a distraction in the decision formulation may be introduced in the form of an implied reference group other than the solitary decision maker. Thus when the person is considering a decision, his or her (internal) messages are based on his or her point of view. In common parlance, he or she may say "*I* think that . . ." or "*I* believe that a certain decision will be beneficial for me." (Furthermore, regardless of whether such internal messages are or are not made explicit by sharing them with other individuals, they remain in the domain of the personal mode.) Note that these words can deflect consideration away from what other individuals think (that is, the dyad and group levels are irrelevant here) and from what "they" say and think (the collectivity level is irrelevant). Thus this view of personal communication is associated only with the person level of analysis.

Exchange Mode

The exchange mode presumes a focus on superior-subordinate dyads and information that is exchanged between them. Two questions arise: What does it mean for traditional dyadic communication to be viewed in terms of parts or wholes? How do other levels of analysis affect dyads?

Single-level analysis. As noted, the exchange mode focuses exclusively on the dyad. In this mode communication is a reflection of the transactions between two individuals. When whole dyads are considered, the two individuals in an exchange are viewed as identical with respect to the variables that are associated with the exchange. For example, each member of a dyad may get and receive an equal amount of valued outcome (see, for example,

Homans, 1974; Nachman, Dansereau, & Naughton, 1985). When a dyad is viewed in terms of its parts although its two individuals are linked, one individual may receive more and the other less from an exchange. Hollander's (1978) idiosyncrasy credit theory, for example, suggests that a superior tends to have resources that are not available to a subordinate. These credits are then used by a superior to gain other resources or to engage in communication behavior that is not expected. In this parts view, the flows of a particular resource are viewed as unbalanced. Although the debt owed by one individual to another can be offset by exchanging other resources, an imbalance remains for each resource which may result in superior-subordinate communication to establish an equilibrium. However, this dynamic can only be understood within the context of the dyad, which is why a parts perspective on dyadic communication processes may be valuable.

Multiple-level analysis. From the perspective of multiple levels of analysis, in the exchange mode superiors and subordinates are interdependent. In a sense, at the person level a person's individuality is "lost" as the two individuals become interdependent. Although it is possible to assert that the person level is relevant to exchanges, such an assertion would delete the notion that the two individuals can form totally unique relationships beyond their personal characteristics. Thus the exchange mode as we define it rejects the person level of analysis. Moreover, the group level also can be rejected because the relationship between the two individuals is *not* viewed as dependent on their relationships with others. Thus from a multiple-level perspective, the exchange mode is an *emergent* and *level-specific* formulation.

Illustration. To illustrate further the link between the exchange mode and communication, think of an individual in an organization whose primary focus (and therefore the implied frame of reference) is on himself or herself as well as on the other person with whom he or she is communicating. As this individual communicates with others, he or she may base messages not only on his or her own particular needs and goals but also on the desires of the other individual. In common parlance, he or she may say "*We* should . . ." or "*We* agree that certain actions should be taken." Note that these words emphasize the dyad as an implied referent and at the same time they deflect the direction of the communication away from what others may say. In other words, the importance of the dyad as a unit is highlighted without the direct consideration of the characteristics of larger groups. (Ergo, the group and collectivity levels are rejected.) Moreover, attention is deflected away from what an individual might prefer if he or she was to consider his or her own needs separately. Thus the person level is rejected. In this mode, we allow for the consideration of the possibility of a type of communication pattern that has an implied dyadic referent, that goes beyond the separate individuals, and that is identifiably distinct from groups larger than the two people.

Leadership Mode

The leadership mode extends the traditional concern with the supervisory group as the level of analysis. Although the group can be an implied referent for communication messages, specification of a parts versus wholes condition still needs to be considered, as does the effect of other levels of analysis.

Single-level analysis. Even though the leadership mode views an individual (often a superior) as a separate entity, there is a difference when this mode is compared to the personal mode. Here the leader, as a person, directly impacts his or her followers who in turn are viewed as an entire entity or whole group. In the leadership mode the relationship of superiors to a group of followers is of interest. From the perspective of wholes, leaders display a style toward their groups that distinguishes them from their whole group. An individual's leadership style links the leader to his or her group of followers (see, for example, Stogdill, 1974). The work of Redding (1972) and his students on identifying the communication style of leaders that relates to the performance of work groups seems to include a focus on whole persons and whole work groups. From the perspective of parts, a leader can distinguish among followers, one relative to another. Thus a leader is viewed as forming a team by capitalizing on the relative strengths and weaknesses of his or her followers (see, for example, Dansereau et al., 1975).

Multiple-level analysis. From the perspective of multiple levels of analysis, in the leadership mode dyads are viewed as simply reflections of group-level processes. For example, in terms of group parts some dyads may be richer in resources than others. Such differences between dyads are viewed as resulting from a superior comparing and distinguishing among a set of subordinates and *not* from one-to-one relationships that form independently of others outside a superior-subordinate dyad. Moreover, at the person level, individuals (superiors and subordinates) are viewed as interdependent components of a group of individuals and not as independent of each other. It is therefore possible to obtain results that when viewed from a single level of analysis appear to represent the traditional person or dyadic levels. However, consideration of multiple levels simultaneously reveals a cross-level process. Thus the leadership mode involves a cross-level formulation because effects at lower levels of analysis (persons, dyads) are viewed as based on higher-level processes. Furthermore, the leadership mode is level-specific because interdependencies between superiors and subordinates are based on direct interactions and not indirect connections. One can reasonably conclude from a multiple-level perspective that the leadership mode is level-specific (that is, rejects a higher level of analysis—collectivities) and cross-level (that is, applies to persons and dyads—the lower levels of analysis).

Illustration. Leadership seems to be compatible with what we label "personal/group communication." As leaders communicate with others, they may base their messages on (1) the unique set of individual goals (formed by personal communication and introspection) on the leader's agenda and (2) his or her concern about the welfare of the group of followers (derived from the group aspect of the interaction). Note that the leader in this case deflects the basis of the communication away from larger collectivities to highlight his or her perspective *and* to highlight the views of other members of the group. From a leader's perspective, communication is personal, whereas from the follower's perspective this mode of communication is group based.

Supervision Mode

While the entity of interest in the supervision mode is the collectivity, the term also implies an explicit consideration of parts versus wholes and possible cross-level effects.

Single-level analysis. In contrast to the direct linkages between individuals in the exchange and leadership modes, in the supervision mode the linkages between individuals are indirect. These indirect linkages are based on echelons or hierarchies and are indirect because individuals with whom neither superiors nor subordinates interact directly can influence their interaction. For one example of this somewhat difficult concept of indirect linkages, think of superiors and subordinates viewing their interaction as based on what "they" say. In this case "they" refers to members of collectivities that share expectations about what an individual in that collectivity is expected to do. From the perspective of whole collectivities, individuals as members of a collectivity should be virtually identical on relevant characteristics or variables. From the perspective of collectivity parts, individuals may vary but that variation occurs because of the differences between groups within each collectivity.

Multiple-level analysis. The supervision mode should also be viewed from multiple levels of analysis. In this mode, at the person level, individuals are viewed as members of collectivities who are expected to understand what is required of other individuals in a collectivity. For example, individuals may be expected to have a certain facility with a language that is shared by collectivity members. At the person level individuals can *play* their roles, much like actors who do not write their own role(s). In the supervision mode, superior-subordinate interactions do not develop from interpersonally based interactions; rather, dyadic relationships are circumscribed by collectivized demands. In other words, at the dyad and group levels individuals *take* their roles, as expected by others of anyone in a particular role. To show this notion of indirect linkages further, in supervision the basis of any interaction shifts from the person, dyad, and group level to the collectivity level. For example, in supervision at the person level an individual may state, "I don't personally believe in this requirement." At the dyad level an individual may state, "This is not the kind of thing you and I would come up with." At the group level an individual may state, "Our team would not come up with this idea." Nevertheless, in the supervision mode the individuals will focus on what "they" require. Although the supervision mode seems most compatible with the collectivity level of analysis, it also views the lower levels of analysis as relevant. Thus, from a multiple-level perspective, it is a cross-level formulation that is compatible with past work on organizational structure and roles (see, for example, Katz & Kahn, 1978; Weber, 1947).

Illustration. To explain the connection between the supervision mode and communication further, think of an administrator in an organization who controls, monitors, and enforces actions relative to generally accepted regulations. As this individual communicates with other individuals, he or she bases messages on something beyond those individuals who directly interact. In common parlance, he or she may say, "When I enforce these rules, I am only doing my job, which is to say that I am doing what *they* say." Note that these words will deflect the responsibility for the communication away from the administrator as a person, for the administrator becomes an impersonal representative of something larger. These words will also deflect the direction of the communication away from a consideration of the unique characteristics of the individuals who interact because such consideration may be irrelevant, annoying, or costly to the larger collective. In this case we allow for the possibility that communication between two individuals might have very little to do with their respective individuality. Instead, various types of *impersonal* communication at this level are viewed as a reflection of the collectivity's social/technical system in which the individuals are embedded.

Combining the Modes

To illustrate how the four modes may be summarized, compared, and contrasted it is helpful first to visualize the modes from two vantage points. First, from an individual perspective, as employees communicate the modes may appear as straightforward superior-subordinate interactions. Second, from the perspective of formal networks, such seemingly straightforward interactions may be better visualized as forming different organizational configurations. Both vantage points will be highlighted below.

Superior-subordinate perspective. Figure 11.1 presents one way to visualize the four modes from the perspective of superior-subordinate interactions. In this illustration two individuals (A and B) are represented by the amoeba-shaped figures. The personal mode, with an emphasis on a lack of interaction between individuals, is represented by a channel beginning and ending in each individual. In this mode, communication begins and ends with an individual and can reflect his or her own idiosyncrasies. The exchange mode, with an emphasis on direct one-to-one relationships, is represented by a channel connecting only the two individuals. In this mode communication requires an explicit consideration of pairs of individuals. The leadership mode is also represented by a channel between individuals A and B; however, in order to reflect the dependency of the two individuals' interaction on other individuals, a channel connects the two individuals with a third individual. Communication is understood here as influenced by group referents and interactions. Finally, the supervision mode is illustrated in the same way as the leadership mode, except that in order to reflect indirect linkages an additional individual is added who is indirectly connected with the two focal individuals through another individual. In this mode, communication includes considerations beyond superiors and their immediate work groups. In this figure individuals are viewed as *potentially* able to function in all four modes.

Two ways that these modes can be combined are illustrated in Figure 11.2. It is helpful to think of the amoeba-shaped diagrams in Figure 11.2 as two different overlays of one individual from Figure 11.1. As such, the lines inside the amoeba represent two ways in which the modes may be processed within an individual. Specifically, in the *multiplexed* view modes are defined as independent of each other. Thus there are no connections between the lines representing each of the modes that might be used by an individual. For example, any information that is carried by the supervision mode would not influence exchanges. Alternatively, in the *contingent* view, the various modes interact. This is represented by the interconnections between the lines. For example, information that is carried by the supervision mode may trigger certain types of exchanges.

Formal networks perspectives. Figures 11.1 and 11.2 illustrate the way levels of analysis are included in each mode. A simplified, general picture of the modes is presented in Figure 11.3, where (1) the modes are extended to an organizational setting, (2) values for variables are assigned to individuals, and (3) parts and wholes are illustrated for each mode. (See Dansereau et al., 1984, for details on the graphic representation of organizational processes.) As shown in Figure 11.3, by considering the four modes in terms of parts and wholes, eight different networks are constructed. In each of the eight networks, seven individuals are represented by the amoeba-shaped figures. For each mode, the level of analysis is represented by the box-shaped figures and is identical for parts and wholes. The differences that occur within each mode are represented by the line segments representing variables. Specifically, the appearance of a line segment regardless of length indicates a substantial amount of communication (a high score on a variable) and the lack of a line segment indicates a lack of communication (a low score on a variable). We will now describe each mode before considering the meaning of each network for the two individuals represented by A and B in Figure 11.3.

The supervision mode is illustrated in the top of Figure 11.3. In the collectivity-wholes box on the left side, the seven individuals are viewed as linked together into one unit by the line segments. Thus there is a substantial

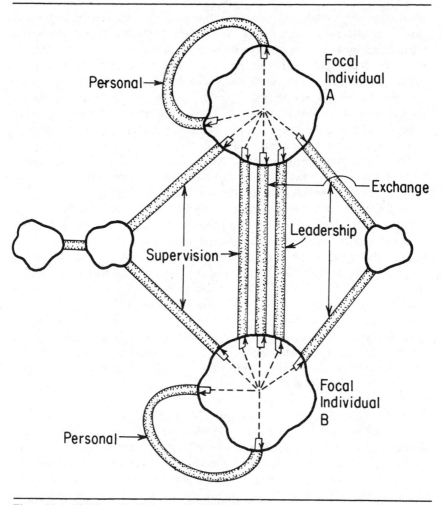

Figure 11.1   The Four Modes for Two Individuals

amount of communication and a lack of variation between individuals in the collectivity. To illustrate differences *between* collectivities, it would be necessary to consider another collectivity in which there was less communication. For example, one might find that impersonal communication (with an emphasis on rules and regulations) is higher in the collectivity shown in the diagram and is almost nonexistent in another collectivity. In terms of collectivity parts as shown on the right side of the diagram, a higher degree of impersonal communication is indicated by the line segments connecting individuals into groups in the lower portion of the figure—those at the bottom of the hierarchy consistently receive more impersonal communication—as compared to the remaining individuals that are not connected into groups. Although the differences in communication occur *within* collectivities, the

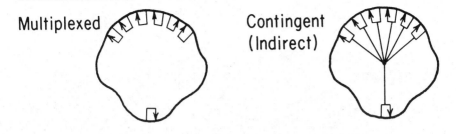

Figure 11.2   Alternative Ways the Four Modes Are Combined by Individuals

same differences within each of several collectivities are expected in a collectivity parts case because, as suggested earlier, parts means systematic variation within rather than between collectivities.

The leadership mode is also illustrated in Figure 11.3. In the illustration of wholes, two of the superiors communicate more with their entire work group, whereas one superior communicates less (no line segment is shown). In this case, the two supervisors differ from the other superiors with respect to the degree to which they communicate. Thus variation occurs between superiors and between their work groups (where work groups are defined as the individuals who report to a superior). From a parts perspective each superior is viewed as communicating on an interpersonal basis with only one of their two subordinates. Thus differences occur *within* each superior and work group.

In terms of a wholes perspective of the exchange mode, of the six possible dyads in Figure 11.3, four are characterized with the line segments as showing more interpersonal communication. In this case, the variation occurs *between* dyads rather than work groups because communication differs both within and between work groups. From a parts perspective, the superiors in each dyad are viewed as providing more interpersonal communication than subordinates. Thus, in the parts case, the communication varies *within* the dyads. This is indicated in Figure 11.3 by the two half line segments associated with each superior (which indicate that superiors systematically differ from their subordinates within each dyad).

In terms of the personal mode, superiors and subordinates are simply not linked. In the case of wholes, the seven individuals display more or less of a particular characteristic and tend to vary in the degree to which they communicate personal views as illustrated by the directed line segments that are not linked with other individuals. Thus valid variation occurs mainly *between* persons. From the perspective of parts, the seven individuals are viewed as displaying more communication in some cases, and less communication in other cases. This is illustrated in Figure 11.3 by the association of a line segment with each individual (these are meant to indicate a display of more communication by all individuals). At the same time the individuals (given the lack of a second line segment) are also viewed as capable of not communi-

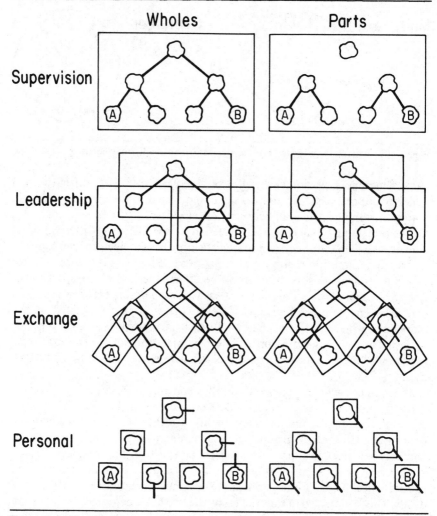

Figure 11.3   The Four Modes as Parts and Wholes in an Organizational Setting

cating. For example, the degree of personal communication may depend on a comparison made *within* the person of the individuals with whom he or she might target for communication. In the example in Figure 11.3 the direction of the line segments indicates a lack of linkage with other individuals in the organizational setting.

Despite the fact it is greatly simplified, Figure 11.3 illustrates that when all of the networks are operating simultaneously, the experiences of individuals may differ. To illustrate this point, let us consider the situation faced by the two individuals represented by the letters A and B in Figure 11.3. We can see that in the supervision mode individual A receives an amount of impersonal communication associated with membership in the collectivity. In terms of leadership, individual A faces a situation where the superior's leadership style does not involve a great deal of communication, and, from a parts perspective, individual A receives less communication from the superior than that received by a colleague in the work group. In terms of exchange, individual A does not form an exchange relationship with the superior that includes a substantial amount of interpersonal communication. In addition (from a personal perspective), individual A has a style that does not include a substantial amount of communication; however, there is communication with some individual—perhaps with an individual who is not the superior. To summarize, individual A—although experiencing a large amount of impersonal communication—is isolated in terms of interpersonal communication, and perhaps withdrawn as a person.

The situation of individual B is quite different from that of individual A. In addition to impersonal communication, he or she has a superior who engages in leadership, which permits the individual and his or her colleague to communicate. Within the work group individual B also receives relatively more communication than the other colleague. In terms of exchange from a wholes perspective, individual B also forms a balanced exchange on some aspects of his relationship with the superior that may include substantial interpersonal communication. From a parts perspective, other aspects of the exchange are unbalanced. Finally, in terms of the personal mode, individual B communicates his or her personal views more often and communicates more with the superior than with others. Clearly, individual B is in a rich communication network that includes personal, interpersonal, and impersonal communication. In contrast, individual A is included only in the impersonal network.

Figure 11.3 illustrates a situation where all of the modes, from the parts and wholes perspectives, are viewed as possible descriptions of communication networks. In examining the figure, different variables are associated with each network. The figure does *not*, however, illustrate the possibility that variables at different levels may interact. For example, the figure does not illustrate that groups with less of a certain type of impersonal communication may be conducive to interpersonal communication. In this case, interpersonal exchange may be operational in one group but not in another, contingent upon a communication process at a higher level.

Summary. We have defined four levels—collectivity, group, dyad, person—that in turn can be characterized in two ways: wholes and parts. To simplify the presentation the eight alternatives listed in Table 11.2 represent only half of all possible combinations. Nevertheless, the four modes—supervision, leadership, exchange, personal—may be characterized as shown in Table 11.2 by the location of double lines along what Dansereau et al.

(1984) call the "entity axis." The partial axis shown in Table 11.2 contains two alternatives for each level of analysis. For the purpose of this illustration, each column in Table 11.2 contains different selections for each level of analysis. In this way, Table 11.2 illustrates that the selection of one alternative at each level implies the rejection of any other alternative selection. For example, the double lines located in the column under the heading "Supervision Wholes" indicate the assertion that supervision reflects differences between whole groups, whole dyads, and whole persons. The double lines under the column labeled "Leadership Parts" indicate the assertion that the within-group differentiation at the group level (parts) is not applicable to the collective level and that at the dyad level the differentiation applies. Finally, at the person level individuals (superiors) are viewed as differentiating among the individuals with whom they may interact. Thus person-level parts are selected. The formulation of the four modes in Table 11.2 highlights the fact that the four modes represent assertions about multiple levels of analysis, and they differ from each and from all other possible ways of making choices among the conditions for each level. Thus Table 11.2 illustrates the similarities and differences among the modes in more specific terms. The assertion of the modes based on the levels of analysis in this way permits the selection of a hypothetical position and the testing of such a position. For example, one initially may assert that two communication variables reflect the supervision mode and then find empirically that these variables are modeled by the personal mode.

The analytical/statistical method that empirically tests among hypothetical positions such as those described above is called *varient* analysis. The term *varient* indicates that *vari*ables and *ent*ities should be considered simultaneously in the research process, and the modes discussed above illustrate eight of these combinations. Unfortunately, an explication of the empirical procedures used to test for the association between variables and levels of analysis is beyond the scope of this chapter. Nevertheless, these procedures are described in Dansereau et al. (1984) and have recently been computerized. They are discussed in detail in Dansereau et al. (1986).

IMPLICATIONS OF THE FOUR
MODES FOR FUTURE RESEARCH

From the discussion thus far it should be apparent that levels of analysis (and thus modes) have been only tangentially addressed in previous research. Therefore, it would be inappropriate to criticize any one study or set of previous studies for an inadequate consideration of levels of analysis. Instead, our approach in this section will be to attempt to identify some of the opportunities for future research that may arise from the varient approach to multiple levels of analysis.

TABLE 11.2
Simplified Illustration of the Four Modes
in Terms of Levels of Analysis

Entities	Mode							
	Supervision		*Leadership*		*Exchange*		*Personal*	
	Wholes	*Parts*	*Wholes*	*Parts*	*Wholes*	*Parts*	*Wholes*	*Parts*
Collectivities								
Wholes	W							
Parts		P						
Group								
Wholes	W	W	W					
Parts				P				
Dyads								
Wholes	W	W	W	W	W			
Parts						P		
Person								
Wholes	W	W	W				W	
Parts				P				P

NOTE: Double lines indicate that a level of analysis is selected (that is, parts or wholes are selected); W = wholes, P = parts. To simplify the presentation, two conditions are not shown for each level. Thus the lack of selection of wholes or parts at any level for any mode means the selection of a rejection condition. See Dansereau et al. (1984) for precise illustrations.

In discussing these research opportunities we will build upon the 10 topical categories of superior-subordinate communication research reviewed in the first part of this chapter. For our purposes, however, it seems useful to group these categories into three sets. Each of the three topical categories in the first set—systemic variables, effective and ineffective superiors, and personal characteristics—seems to include only one of the modes. The second set of two topical categories—interaction patterns and related attitudes, and semantic information distance—seems to include a consideration of general issues surrounding superior-subordinate communication. The studies in this category tend to focus on all modes (variable and level combinations) and attempt to describe communication in a more general or comprehensive sense. The third set of five topical categories—openness in communication, feedback, upward distortion, upward influence, and role concepts—seems to consider multiple modes but focus on specific variables. Besides illustrating the opportunities that these sets of studies provide for including an explicit consideration of levels of analysis in future theoretical and data analytic work, the first set of categories illustrates opportunities to refine single-mode theories by considering more than one level of analysis. The second set illustrates the potential benefits of considering each mode separately and then in combination. The final set of studies illustrates the opportunity to define variables in new ways by considering multiple modes. Thus our purpose in this section is to show how previous work might be refined and expanded by future research that explicitly considers multiple modes and multiple levels of analysis.

Single-Mode Approaches

Three topical categories discussed earlier—systemic variables, effective versus ineffective superiors, and personal characteristics—seem to focus individually on different modes. Because single-mode approaches include assertions about multiple levels of analysis, these approaches might be refined by considering not only one level of analysis in more detail but also by considering multiple levels of analysis. They may be expanded by considering how other modes may influence the mode of interest.

Systemic variables. In general, Jablin (1979) suggests that work on systemic variables has focused on the relationship of technology and organizational structure with superior-subordinate communication. Technology has been viewed as a work group (Hunt, 1970) and organizational-level variable (Jablin, 1982). Although the work group may seem to be the appropriate level of analysis, technology may actually be associated with collectivities that cut across work groups (and organizations). In a similar fashion, structural factors including hierarchical level in an organization can be viewed as collectivized in the sense that expectations are held by many individuals for those at a particular hierarchical level. In this way, systemic variables can be viewed as perhaps reflecting differences between collectivities.

Even though the temporal ordering of systemic variables and communication needs additional research attention, a second set of issues arise concerning the way systemic variables may influence communication. Specifically, what types of communication (variables) tend to be directly related to systemic variables, and what types tend not to be influenced in this way? In a cross-level view, when data are collected at the person, dyad, or work group-level, what is observed at all three levels should be differences between collectivities. In other words, obtained data should not reflect leadership, exchange, or personal modes but rather only supervision. Of course, real data may show the leadership, exchange, and personal modes as being supported regardless of one's theoretical preferences. Thus when considering systemic variables an opportunity clearly exists to refine this approach by empirically demonstrating that a cross-level formulation is appropriate. In other words, to refine this approach one must ask which variables (communication and systemic) tend to be associated with the combination of multiple levels of analysis specified for the *supervision* mode. Finally, these approaches might be expanded by considering whether, for example, in two different collectivities with different types of technology and structure, the leadership, exchange, and personal modes vary, and with what outcomes.

Effective versus ineffective superiors. A second topical category identified earlier includes two approaches to studying effective and ineffective superiors. The first approach, labeled "average leadership style" (see Dansereau et al., 1975), seeks to identify the (communication) styles of superiors that are related to more effective work groups. (See, for example, Redding, 1972.) Moreover, because superiors are viewed as displaying a single style across subordinates as a group, whole superiors and subordinate work groups seem to be of interest in this approach. The second approach, labeled the "vertical dyad linkage approach" (Dansereau et al., 1975), seems to focus on group "parts" because variables tend to be considered in terms of their variation within work groups and superiors (see Graen et al., 1982). In this approach a superior's differential treatment of (or communication with) subordinates is expected to lead to more effective performance of individuals and perhaps work groups.

The temporal ordering of the relationships between superiors' action and subordinates' performance is of course an open empirical question for both approaches. Nevertheless, the approaches are similar because they both reject the notion that differences between superiors or work groups are reflections of differences between collectivities. Instead, these approaches favor the assertion that a superior or leader, not the collective, affects followers. Likewise, both approaches favor the assertion that differences between superior-subordinate dyads are actually reflections of differences between or within superiors and work groups. In the average leadership style, work groups are viewed as whole units, whereas in the vertical dyad linkage approach work groups are viewed as differentiated into parts. Therefore, both approaches are compatible with the *leadership* mode and provide an opportunity to consider multiple levels of analysis as a means of testing whether the variables hypothesized in each approach are in fact associated with the leadership mode or are associated with the personal, exchange, or supervision modes.

For example, Nachman et al. (1983, 1985) tested whether a key variable—negotiating latitude—used in the vertical dyad linkage approach to leadership reflected differences within or between superiors and groups. The results suggested that the variables specified in this model may not reflect differences at the work group level at all but rather may reflect differences between dyads or persons. The importance of theoretically and empirically considering multiple levels of analysis in this approach can also be illustrated with the dyad-level results presented by Dansereau et al. (1984). It was precisely because the work group level of analysis was rejected in these analyses that an exchange rather than leadership formulation was indicated from the data. This approach to associating variables and entities relies on the rejection of the leadership mode to induce exchange. It should be obvious that this type of analysis does not preclude the identification of variables that may be more compatible with the leadership mode. Moreover, it is possible to consider wholes and parts simultaneously at one level of analysis. For example, one might assert that different styles based on differences between superiors (wholes) may moderate the degree to which superiors differentiate between subordinates on a relative basis (parts). This formulation obviously allows for wholes and parts and their interaction. Nevertheless, each variable is associated with specific levels (cross level, level specific, emergent) and tests are made for these levels. Problems concerning levels of analysis with the traditional measurement of average leadership styles have been investigated by Markham and Scott (1983) and Markham, Dansereau, Alutto, and Dumas (1983).

Finally, it should be apparent that contingency formulations (involving wholes or parts at other levels) may expand these leadership approaches. For example, in previous leadership research attention has been focused on the consequences of different styles within different conditions (see, for example, Fiedler, 1967; House, 1971). Although the levels of analysis associated with the hypothesized contingency variables have not been empirically tested, the average leadership and vertical dyad linkage approaches can be expanded to include such considerations. For example, one might ask how different degrees of collectivity-based supervisory communication might influence the relationship between a superior's style and the performance of his or her work group? Likewise, one could consider how the exchanges or personal modes vary when supervisors' styles vary. For example, one might ask: Are persons who prefer more of a particular type of communication more satisfied than others (who prefer less of a particular type of communication) when a superior engages in a particular style?

Therefore, it should be apparent that substantial research opportunities exist to refine these approaches to the topic of effective and ineffective superiors by considering multiple levels of analysis, even though only the leadership mode is of interest. Obviously, there are also substantial opportunities to expand these approaches by considering the indirect contingencies between the leadership mode and other modes.

Personal characteristics. A third topical category reviewed earlier— personal characteristics—seems most compatible with the personal mode. One set of studies in this category focuses on the relationship between individual differences and different degrees of a particular type of communication (see, for example, Durand & Nord, 1976; Mitchell et al., 1975). Yeakley (1982) has suggested that personal preferences for communication styles can be identified on the basis of the four Jungian functions (thinking, feeling, sensing, intuition) as identified by the Myers-Briggs Type Inventory (Briggs-Myers, 1980). Another set of studies in this category focuses on person parts or the relationships within individuals. For example, Fulk and Mani (1986) developed a model of upward communication from subordinates to superiors in which changes within an individual on a variable are followed by changes in a second variable. In this approach the theoretical assertion seems to be that the linkage between individuals is not important but rather the relationships among perceptual variables *inside* individuals are of importance. Although the variables considered by studies in this topical category are quite diverse, they do seem to refer to personal characteristics that are viewed as reflections of individuals (wholes) independent of others or as reflecting processes within persons (parts). Because the studies in this category seem to assert that levels above the person level can be rejected, it should be apparent that there are substantial opportunities to refine these studies of the *personal* mode by testing such an assertion.

In addition, studies of this type might be expanded by considering other modes. For example, collectivities where a certain type of impersonal communication is less prevalent may enhance the relationship between the personality characteristics of individuals and their personal communication. Likewise, certain leadership styles may enhance the emergence of certain relationships inside individuals. To summarize, because studies in this category appear to focus on the personal mode, there is ample opportunity to refine these approaches by focusing on the indirect relationships between the personal mode and other modes.

Summary. For the three topical categories—systemic variables, ineffective and effective superiors, and personal characteristics and associated modes (supervision, leadership, and personal)—we have asserted that empirical tests have not been performed for levels of analysis. Why is this criticism important? From a theoretical perspective, it is possible to assert that any type of communication (or other variable) is associated with any combination of levels of analysis. When individuals are embedded in multiple levels of analysis, from an empirical perspective any level or combination of levels could be associated with variables. Thus empirical tests of the assertions should be performed at the implied levels of analysis. To illustrate this point, consider a case where a proponent of the average leadership style might assert a hypothesis about the individual communication differences of superiors. This assertion implies that the differences between superiors do not reflect differences between collectivities. When levels are not considered empirically, obtained differences between superiors may reflect not only differences between superiors but also differences between collectivities. In other words, a researcher may interpret data as reflecting the leadership mode when the data reflects the supervision mode. Therefore, a consideration of multiple levels of analysis (at least two) is required to test the predictions implied by these approaches. Because the approaches themselves seem to imply predictions about multiple levels of analysis, they can be refined by considering multiple levels of analysis. The long-run consequences of failing to consider multiple levels can be illustrated by the following example. Suppose the leadership mode is inferred by a researcher but the supervision mode is empirically more likely. If a researcher attempts to replicate the results of the study and does not include the differences between collectivities, the replication will fail.

Therefore, a consideration of multiple levels of analysis becomes critical in testing *even when only one mode is of interest.* A consideration of multiple modes, although perhaps not essential for those one-mode perspectives, can expand these approaches. Indeed, the need to consider multiple modes seems to be the focus of the next set of categories that take a more general view of superior-subordinate communication.

General Approaches

Two of the topical categories discussed by Jablin (1979) and reviewed earlier—interaction patterns and related attitudes, and semantic-information distance—suggest a need to consider superior-subordinate communication from an integrated or general multiple mode perspective.

Interaction patterns and related attitudes. As suggested in our review, probably one of the most consistent findings in superior-subordinate communication research is that superiors spend between one-third and two-thirds of their time communicating with subordinates (see Porter & Roberts, 1976). Moreover, Jablin (1979, p. 1203) states that "the majority of this communication concerns task-related issues and is conducted in face-to-face meetings." This statement might be interpreted as suggesting that the supervision mode occurs most frequently in organizations. However, communication about tasks is compatible with the supervision, leadership, exchange, and personal modes. Therefore, an intriguing opportunity arises to assess how the various modes combine to form "total" superior-subordinate communication. In other words, how do all the modes simultaneously contribute to understanding superior-subordinate communication? For example, for our illustration in Figure 11.3, we described multiple communication networks that can combine to form a multivariable, multiple-mode view of "total" superior-subordinate communication.

From this perspective, one might attempt to develop a set of propositions about various types of communication in terms of multiple modes so as to explain the variability in "total" superior-subordinate communication. Such an approach could attempt to specify outcomes from different mixtures of communication under different conditions, as well as specify the independent variables that might influence communication over time. Thus an analysis of research in this topical category suggests that tremendous opportunities may exist for refining previous work to include a consideration of multiple modes and types of communication variables that may explain the variation in the "total" amount of superior-subordinate communication.

Semantic-information distance. Jablin (1979, p. 1207) suggests that semantic-information distance focuses on "the gap in information and understanding that exists between superiors and subordinates (or other groups within an organization) on specified issues." In a somewhat similar way, the "distances" within and between entities were of major concern in our consideration of multiple modes. The way these difference are viewed when wholes and parts are considered is of particular interest. From a wholes perspective, the components of an entity are viewed as homogenized and a lack of difference between them is asserted. Therefore, for wholes, differences and distances occur between entities. In contrast, the parts view suggests that the components of an entity are interdependent but differ from each other (for example, superiors across dyads tend to have consistently more information than subordinates). For parts, differences (and distances) occur within entities. When distances are viewed in this way, it is possible to examine the differences on a measure of the degree of understanding on some matter and then to correlate these differences with another variable. In this way the differences between individuals on a particular matter may be assessed at any number of levels of analysis.

Summary. In a sense, the studies of interaction patterns and related attitudes raise questions about the mix of variables that may contribute to "total" communication. The semantic information distances studies suggest the need to consider the variation between and within units at a *level of analysis.* Inherent in this approach is a simultaneous consideration of *multiple* variables. Thus studies in these two topical categories suggest the importance of variables and levels of analysis and point to extensive opportunities for future research. Although it may appear at this point that most studies have not focused on multiple modes, the final set of studies to be considered seem to suggest that multiple levels of analysis are important.

Multiple Mode Approaches

Although the single-mode approaches might be refined by a consideration of multiple levels of analysis, one advantage of these approaches is that the level of analysis of interest is somewhat easy to identify. In contrast, substantial opportunities seem to exist to refine and expand studies that consider multiple modes by (1) clearly defining each mode in terms of multiple levels of analysis and (2) empirically examining the indirect contingencies among modes.

Openness in communication. As noted earlier, openness in communication typically includes openness in message sending and openness in message receiving. Openness is defined in several ways. For example, Redding (1972) describes openness in message sending as the candid disclosure of feelings, bad news, and important company facts. Likewise, Baird (1974) adds that distinctions should be made among different types of openness. We believe openness might be viewed differently when each of the four modes are considered. For example, openness may reflect collectivity requirements such that greater openness on certain issues may be required by organic as opposed to mechanistic collectivities. Superiors may also display openness in an undifferentiated or differentiated fashion relative to followers. Moreover, openness may be viewed from an exchange perspective, where individuals are open to each other on a interpersonal basis. Finally, openness may simply be an individual difference characteristic.

Although openness can be described with respect to the four modes, as the following questions suggest, the different variables that may be appropriate for each mode may vary. For example, is openness with "important company facts" a supervision mode variable? Is openness, with regard to a "feeling," a personal mode variable? (That is, are some individuals more private about their feelings than others? Or is openness a reflection of person parts, as suggested by Baird [1974], where a change in a person's willingness to talk is a function of that person's perception of another's willingness to listen?) Is openness about the resources one could give to another a reflection of an exchange mode variable? If openness takes on a somewhat different meaning depending on the mode or levels of analysis, then different variables may be used to measure openness.

Furthermore, the interactions of modes can be quite important. For example, does impersonal communication result in the interpretation of openness in one mode (for example, supervision) and a lack of openness in another mode (for example, exchange)? It seems clear that substantial opportunities exist to formulate theories that define openness from the perspective of multiple modes and to consider interactions between different types of openness.

Feedback. In feedback the message is not about the sender but about the potential receiver. As with openness, feedback may be defined differently depending on whether the supervision, leadership, exchange, and/or personal modes are of interest. Specifically, depending on the mode different types of feedback may occur. For example, in the supervision mode feedback might be about the extent to which another individual meets collectivized requirements. In the leadership mode feedback might be about the extent to which another individual fits into the leader's team. In the exchange mode feedback might be about the extent to which another individual "lives up" to an interpersonal agreement. In the personal mode the feedback might focus on the personal characteristics of another individual (wholes) and/or the way in which the other individual might change over time (person parts). Here again, there is ample opportunity to define feedback in different ways depending on the mode of interest. Likewise, the variation in the degree to which individuals provide different types of feedback may be related to other variables defined at multiple levels of analysis.

In addition, different types of feedback may be more or less effective under differing conditions. For example, leadership feedback may be viewed as quite dysfunctional in some collectivities, whereas it may be viewed as quite functional in other collectivities. Thus ample opportunities exist to define the notion of feedback by considering multiple modes and their interactions.

Upward distortion. The topical category of distortion seems to be the converse of openness and feedback. According to Fulk and Mani (1986), at least four types of distortion can be defined from the work of Roberts and O'Reilly (1974): *Gatekeeping* occurs when not all information that has been received is passed upward. *Summarization* involves changing the emphasis given to various parts of the message. *Withholding* of useful information from superiors is a third selective distortion process. *General distortion* involves actively changing the information transmitted.

Although it is possible to view each type of distortion in terms of the four modes, it is also possible to speculate about the level of analysis that may be associated with each type of distortion. From a theoretical perspective one might hypothesize that gatekeeping is a requirement of managerial roles, and therefore a part of the supervision mode. Indeed, as March and Simon (1958) suggest, managers, as part of their jobs, may be required to absorb uncertainty by withholding information and thereby preventing information overload of a superior by providing only key information. Summarization, in contrast, may be used to develop or maintain an interpersonal relationship with a superior by essentially playing to a superior's preferences. In contrast, withholding and general distortion may be a personal matter. From an applied perspective it may be critical to determine the level of analysis that is associated with different types of information. For example, withholding or distorting information about oneself, even though potentially useful to a superior, may be less problematic than withholding or distorting information that is required to be communicated at the collectivity level. Clearly, the modes that may be associated with different types of distortion are open to theoretical and empirical questioning.

According to Jablin (1985), two variables are typically considered as correlates of distortion. First, a lack of trust is viewed as an antecedent of distortion. Clearly, one can ask what does trust mean and what are the levels of analysis associated with trust? One can think of situations where a lack of trust is created by mixing levels. For example, subordinates may perceive their work as based on their personal characteristics (personal mode variable), and a superior, in the leadership mode, may attribute the work to himself or herself as a leader. This situation may lead a subordinate to mistrust the superior. Furthermore, a superior may trust a subordinate with collectivity-level information, but not with personal information. Thus trust also takes on a different meaning depending on the mode associated with it. A second set of variables—the propensity to seek status and be career oriented—has also been related to distortion (see, for example, Mellinger, 1956). Whole persons seems to be asserted in this approach because persons with a higher propensity to seek status are hypothesized to distort. Likewise, at the person level Fulk and Mani (1986) imply that processes within persons (person parts) may influence the degree of distortion that occurs.

To summarize, upward distortion and its correlates may be associated with the supervision, leadership, exchange, and personal modes. As different types of distortion are associated with different modes, the concept of distortion may be able to be defined more clearly. Such formulations should assist our ability to develop contingency models of distortion.

Upward influence. One of the major foci of studies of upward influence has been on a superior's influence with his or her boss and the consequences for a superior's subordinates. Influence, of course, can also be viewed from the perspective of multiple modes. For example, in terms of power (French & Raven, 1968), from a supervision perspective, a superior may have more or less influence with his boss based on his or her title as compared to other superiors who report to that boss (for example, legitimate power). From a leadership perspective, a superior may have greater or less influence given the style of his boss (for example, referent power). From an exchange perspective, a superior may have more or less influence based on his or her exchanges with the boss (for example, reward power). Finally, from a personal perspective, a superior may have greater or less influence due to his or her personal characteristics (for example, expert power). Even when superiors have substantial influence on their bosses, there may be varied consequences for the subordinates who report to these superiors. For example, boss-superior influence based on one mode (for example, legitimate power) may mediate the emergence of other modes (for example, reward power) in the superior's work group. Clearly, the seminal study by Pelz (1952) suggested that there is a need to consider how the relationships between superiors and bosses affect superior-subordinate interactions. We believe, however, that substantial opportunities remain to develop multiple mode models of how superior-boss interactions in turn influence superior-subordinate interactions.

Role concepts (conflict and ambiguity). Earlier we noted that there has been increasing interest in the notion of conflict and ambiguity as applied to superior-subordinate communication. Because the relationship of role theory and levels of analysis has been discussed elsewhere (see Dansereau et al., 1984), we will focus on different ways to view conflict and ambiguity in this section. As should be obvious, the content of the supervision, leadership, exchange, and personal modes can vary in their ambiguity and in the degree to which they contradict each other. For example, a collectivity requirement may contradict the interpersonal understanding that develops between individuals. From this perspective, ambiguity and conflict can be viewed as characterizations or outcomes of the modes. It is also possible that different types of ambiguity and conflict may be associated with different modes. For example, consider a matrix organization where a certain type of conflict actually may be explicitly required as part of supervision. Likewise, conflict and ambiguity may be a reflection of leadership and exchange processes and/or a characterization of persons (for example, some individuals may have a propensity for conflict and ambiguity). Thus there is ample opportunity to develop a variety of definitions of ambiguity and conflict associated with different levels of analysis and relate them to different types of communication.

Summary. As should be apparent, these multiple mode approaches show substantial opportunities for refinement. Different variables, when associated with different modes, can be developed that define constructs with greater precision, permitting tests for contingencies. To summarize, previous single-mode studies might be refined by considering multiple levels of analysis and expanded by considering the interactions among multiple modes. Previous multiple-mode studies might be refined by considering multiple levels of analysis and expanded by considering the interactions among multiple modes. Previous multiple-mode studies might be clarified by defining the modes associated with a variety of new variables and expanded by considering their interaction. The outcome of this process presumably would provide a way to begin to develop general approaches that include explicit formulations of multiple variables and multiple entities that can be tested.

SUMMARY AND CONCLUSION

In this chapter we have used the varient approach to levels of analysis to define four modes of superior-subordinate communication. Although we have illustrated the implications of the approach for performing research and for developing future research, these modes are clearly not exhaustive of the possibilities—a number of other combinations of variables and levels are possible. In fact, when data are analyzed in line with this approach (see Dansereau et al., 1984, and Dansereau et al., 1986) the results may not support any of the four modes but some other combination of multiple levels of analysis. This is possible because varient matrices are determined by the number of variables and levels of analysis that are of interest. As such, the varient matrix is a way to summarize alternative formulations of variables and entities. Obviously, this is a strong inference approach (see Platt, 1964) to understanding superior-subordinate interactions because the results in one study are derived from the rejection of other alternative formulations that could have been supported in that study. By identifying empirically in each of several studies the most likely associations of variables and entities, each study's contribution to the body of knowledge about superior-subordinate interactions should be apparent. In this chapter we have attempted to provide an approach for theoretically and empirically testing among alternative formulations of superior-subordinate interactions that includes multiple variables and multiple levels of analysis.

NOTES

1. The term *varient* was coined to reflect the notion that variables and entities are considered simultaneously in this approach.

2. Logic dictates that two other conditions in addition to wholes and parts must be plausible. Both of these other conditions indicate the rejection of a level of analysis. In one of these conditions scores are found to vary both within and between groups so that no specific condition (wholes or parts) can be induced; in a sense, in this condition the "grouping" of individual scores at the particular level of analysis does not effectively organize the scores. We label this an "equivocal" condition, since it might appear that *either* a parts or a wholes condition can be asserted as appropriate. In addition, an "inexplicable" condition can also exist in which individual scores do not vary within or between groups. Thus in the inexplicable condition *neither* a parts nor whole condition can be asserted as appropriate. For a detailed discussion of these conditions and ways of testing for them, see Dansereau et al. (1984).

REFERENCES

Ayman, R., & Chemers, M. (1983). Relationship of supervisory behavior ratings to work group effectiveness and subordinate satisfaction among Iranian managers. *Journal of Applied Psychology, 68,* 338-341.

Baird, J. E. (1974). *An analytical field study of "open communication" as perceived by supervisors, subordinates, and peers.* Unpublished doctoral dissertation, Purdue University, Lafayette, IN.

Bannister, B. D. (1986). Performance outcome feedback and attributional feedback: Interactive effects on recipient responses. *Journal of Applied Psychology, 71,* 203-210.

Beyer, J. M., & Trice, H. M. (1984). A field study of the use and perceived effects of discipline in controlling work performance. *Academy of Management Journal, 27,* 743-764.

Briggs-Myers, I. (1980). *Gifts differing.* Palo Alto, CA: Consulting Psychologist Press.

Broms, H., & Gahmberg, H. (1983). Communication to self in organizations and cultures. *Administrative Service Quarterly, 28,* 282-295.

Campbell, J. P., Dunnette, M. D., Lawler, E. E., & Weick, K. E. (1970). *Managerial behavior, performance, and effectiveness.* New York: McGraw-Hill.

Cummings, L. L. (1981). State of the art: Organizational behavior in the 1980's. *Decision Sciences, 12,* 365-377.

Dansereau, F., Alutto, J. A., & Yammarino, F. J. (1984). *Theory testing in organizational behavior: The varient approach.* Englewood Cliffs, NJ: Prentice-Hall.

Dansereau, F., Chandrasekeran, B., Dumas, M., Coleman D., Ehrlich, S., & Bagachi, D. (1986). *DETECT, Data enquiry that tests entity and correlational/causal theories: Application and user's guide.* Williamsville, NY: Institute for Theory Testing.

Dansereau, F., Graen, G., & Haga, W. J. (1975). A vertical dyad linkage approach to leadership within formal organizations: A longitudinal investigation of the role-making process. *Organizational Behavior and Human Performance, 13,* 46-78.

Durand, D. E., & Nord, W. R. (1976). Perceived leader behavior as a function of personality characteristics of supervisors and subordinates. *Academy of Management Journal, 19,* 427-438.

Earley, P. C. (1986). Supervisors and shop stewards as sources of contextual information in goal setting: A comparison of the United States with England. *Journal of Applied Psychology, 71,* 111-117.

Eisenberg, E. M., Monge, P. R., & Farace, R. V. (1984). Coorientation of communication rules in managerial dyads. *Human Communication Research, 11,* 261-271.

Fairhurst, G. T. (1986). Male-female communication on the job: Literature review and commentary. In M. L. McLaughlin (Ed.), *Communication yearbook 9* (pp. 83-111). Newbury Park, CA: Sage.

Fairhurst, G. T., Green, S. G., & Snavely, B. K. (1984a). Managerial control and discipline: Whips and chains. In R. N. Bostrom (Ed.), *Communication yearbook 8* (pp. 558-593). Newbury Park, CA: Sage.

Fairhurst, G. T., Green, S. G., & Snavely, B. K. (1984b). Face support in controlling poor performance. *Human Communication Research, 11,* 272-295.

Fairhurst, G. T., Rogers, L. E., & Sarr, R. A. (1987). Manager-subordinate control patterns and judgments about the relationship. In M. L. McLaughlin (Ed.), *Communication yearbook 10* (pp. 395-415). Newbury Park, CA: Sage.

Farace, R. V., & MacDonald, D. (1974). New directions in the study of organizational communication. *Personnel Psychology, 27,* 1-15.

Fiedler, F. E. (1967). *A theory of leadership effectiveness.* New York: McGraw-Hill.

French, J. R., Jr., & Raven, B. (1968). The bases of social power. In D. Cartwright & A. Zander (Eds.), *Group dynamics* (3rd ed., pp. 259-269). New York: Harper & Row.

Fulk, J., & Mani, S. (1986). Distortion of communication in hierarchical relationships. In M. L. McLaughlin (Ed.), *Communication yearbook 9* (pp. 483-510). Newbury Park, CA: Sage.

Gerloff, E. A., & Quick, J. C. (1984). Task role ambiguity and conflict in supervisor-subordinate relationships. *Journal of Applied Communication Research, 12,* 90-102.

Gioia, D. A., & Sims, H. P. (1986). Cognition-behavior connections: Attribution and verbal behavior in leader-subordinate interactions. *Organizational Behavior and Human Decision Process, 37,* 197-229.

Glauser, M. J. (1984). Upward information flow in organizations: Review and conceptual analysis. *Human Relations, 37,* 613-643.

Glick, W. H., & Roberts, H. H. (1984). Hypothesized interdependence, assumed independence. *Academy of Management Review, 9,* 722-735.

Goering, E. M., Rudick, K. L., & Faulkner, M. M. (1986). *The validity of a self-reported conflict management scale in measuring conflict management behaviors.* Paper presented at the annual meeting of the International Communication Association, Chicago.

Graen, G. B., Liden, R. C., & Hoel, W. (1982). Role of leadership in the employee withdrawal process. *Journal of Applied Psychology, 67,* 868-872.

Hannaway, J. (1985). Managerial behavior, uncertainty and hierarchy: A prelude to a synthesis. *Human Relations, 38,* 1085-1100.

Harrison, T. M. (1985). Communication and participative decision making: An exploratory study. *Personnel Psychology, 38,* 93-116.

Hollander, E. P. (1978). *Leadership dynamics: A practical guide to effective relationships.* New York: Free Press.

Homans, G. C. (1974). *Social behavior: Its elementary forms* (rev. ed.). New York: Harcourt Brace Jovanovich.

House, R. J. (1971). A path-goal theory of leader effectiveness. *Administrative Science Quarterly, 16,* 321-339.

Hunt, R. (1970). Technology and organization. *Academy of Management Journal, 13,* 236-252.

Infante, D. A., & Gordon, W. I. (1985). Superiors' argumentativeness and verbal aggressiveness as predictors of subordinates' satisfaction. *Human Communication Research, 12,* 117-125.

Jablin, F. M. (1979). Superior-subordinate communication: The state of the art. *Psychological Bulletin, 86,* 1201-1222.

Jablin, F. M. (1980). Subordinates' sex and superior-subordinate status differentiation as moderators of the Pelz Effect. In D. Nimmo (Ed.), *Communication yearbook 4* (pp. 349-366). New Brunswick, NJ: Transaction.

Jablin, F. M. (1982). Formal structural characteristics of organizations and superior-subordinate communication. *Human Communication Research, 8,* 338-347.

Jablin, F. M. (1984). Assimilating new members into organizations. In R. N. Bostrom (Ed.), *Communication yearbook 8* (pp. 594-626). Newbury Park, CA: Sage.

Jablin, F. M. (1985). Task/work relationships: A life-span perspective. In M. L. Knapp & G. R. Miller (Eds.) *Handbook of interpersonal communication* (pp. 615-654). Newbury Park, CA: Sage.

Jablin, F. M., & Krone, K. J. (in press). Organizational assimilation and levels of analysis in organizational communication research. In C. R. Berger & S.M. Chaffee (Eds.), *Handbook of communication science.* Newbury Park, CA: Sage.

Johnson, A. L., Luthans, F., & Hennessey, H. W. (1984). The role of locus of control in leader influence behavior. *Personnel Psychology, 37,* 61-75.

Katz, D., & Kahn, R. L. (1978). *The social psychology of organizations* (2nd ed.). New York: John Wiley.

Kimberly, J. R. (1976). Issues in the design of longitudinal organizational research. *Sociological Methods and Research, 4,* 321-347.

Klauss, R., & Bass, B. (1982). *Interpersonal communication in organizations.* New York: Academic Press.

Komaki, J. L. (1986). Toward effective supervision: An operant analysis and comparison of managers at work. *Journal of Applied Psychology, 71,* 270-279.

Komaki, J. L., Zlotnick, S., & Jenson, M. (1986). Development of an operant-based taxonomy and observational index of supervisory behavior. *Journal of Applied Psychology, 71,* 260-269.

Krone, K. J. (1985). *Subordinate influence in organizations: The differential use of upward influence messages in decision making contexts.* Unpublished doctoral dissertation, University of Texas at Austin.

Laing, R. D., Phillipson, H., & Lee, A. R. (1966). *Interpersonal perception: A theory and method of research.* New York: Springer.

Larson, J. R. (1986). Supervisors' performance feedback to subordinates: The impact of subordinate performance valence and outcome dependence. *Organizational Behavior and Human Decision Processes, 37,* 391-408.

Lesniak, R. (1981). *The role of vertical communication relationships in traditionally structured, complex organizations.* Unpublished doctoral dissertation, State University of New York at Buffalo.

Luthans, F., & Larsen, J. K. (1986). How managers really communicate. *Human Relations, 39,* 161-178.

Manz, C. C., & Sims, H. P. (1984). Searching for the "unleader": Organizational members' views on leading self-managed groups. *Human Relations, 37,* 409-424.

March, J. G., & Simon, H. A. (1958). *Organizations.* New York: John Wiley.

Markham, S. E. (1978). *Leadership and motivation: An empirical examination of exchange and its outcomes.* Unpublished doctoral dissertation, State University of New York at Buffalo.

Markham, S. E., Dansereau, F., Alutto, J. A., & Dumas, M. (1983). Leadership convergence: An application of within and between analysis to validity. *Applied Psychological Measurement, 7,* 63-72.

Markham, S. E., & Scott, K. D. (1983). A component factor analysis of the initiating structure scale of the LBDQ Form XII. *Psychological Reports, 52,* 71-77.

Mellinger, G. D. (1956). Interpersonal trust as a factor in communication. *Journal of Abnormal Social Psychology, 52,* 304-309.

Miller, J. G. (1978). *Living systems.* New York: McGraw-Hill.

Mitchell, T. R., Smyser, C. M., & Weed, S. E. (1975). Locus of control: Supervision and work satisfaction. *Academy of Management Journal, 19,* 623-631.

Monge, P. R., Farace, R. V., Eisenberg, E. M., Miller, K. I., & White, L. L. (1984). The process of studying process in organizational communication. *Journal of Communication, 34,* 22-43.

Mossholder, K. W., & Bedian, A. C. (1983). Cross-level inferences and organizational research: Perspectives on interpretation and application. *Academy of Management Review, 8,* 547-559.

Nachman, S., Dansereau, F., & Naughton, T. J. (1983) Negotiating latitude: A within and between groups analysis of a key construct in the vertical dyad linkage theory of leadership. *Psychological Reports, 53,* 171-177.

Nachman, S., Dansereau, F., and Naughton, T. J. (1985). Levels of analysis and the vertical dyad linkage approach to leadership. *Psychological Reports, 57,* 661-662.

Newcomb, T. M. (1961). *The acquaintance process.* New York: Holt, Rinehart & Winston.

Parsons, C. K., Herold, D. M., & Leatherwood, M. L. (1985). Turnover during initial employment: A longitudinal study of the role of causal attributions. *Journal of Applied Psychology, 70,* 337-341.

Pelz, D. C. (1952). Influence: A key to effective leadership in the first-line supervisor. *Personnel, 29,* 3-11.

Penley, L., & Hawkins, B. (1985). Studying interpersonal communication in organizations: A leadership application. *Academy of Management Journal, 28,* 309-326.

Pincus, J. D. (1986). Communication satisfaction, job satisfaction, and job performance. *Human Communication Research, 12,* 395-419.

Platt, J. R., (1964). Strong inference. *Science, 146,* 347-353.

Porter, L. W., & Roberts, K. H. (1976). Communication in organizations. In M. Dunnette, (Ed.) *Handbook of industrial and organizational psychology* (pp. 1553-1590). Chicago: Rand McNally.

Redding, W. C. (1972). *Communication within the organization: An interpretive review of theory and research.* New York: Industrial Communications Council.

Remland, M. S. (1984). Leadership impressions and nonverbal communication in a superior-subordinate interaction. *Communication Quarterly, 32,* 41-48.

Richmond, V. P., Davis, L. M., Saylor, K., & McCroskey, J. C. (1984). Power strategies in organizations: Communication techniques and messages. *Human Communication Research, 11,* 85-108.

Richmond, V. P., McCroskey, J. C., & Davis, L. M. (1986). The relationship of supervisor use of power and affinity-seeking strategies with subordinate satisfaction. *Communication Quarterly, 34,* 178-193.

Roberts, K. H., Hulin, C. L., & Rousseau, D. M. (1978). *Developing an interdisciplinary science of organizations.* San Francisco: Jossey-Bass.

Roberts, K. H., & O'Reilly, C. A. (1974). Failures in upward communication: Three possible culprits. *Academy of Management Journal, 17,* 205-215.

Roberts, K. H., O'Reilly, C. A., Bretton, G. E., & Porter, L. W. (1974). Organizational theory and organizational communication: A communication failure? *Human Relations, 24,* 501-524.

Rousseau, D. M. (1985). Issues of levels in organizational research: Multi-level and cross-level perspectives. In B. Staw & L. Cummings (Eds.), *Research in Organizational Behavior* (Vol. 7, pp. 1-37). Greenwich, CT: JAI Press.

Serafini, D. M., & Pearson, J. C. (1984). Leadership behavior and sex role socialization: Two sides of the same coin. *Southern Speech Communication Journal, 49,* 396-405.

Sims, H. P. , & Manz, C. C. (1984). Observing leader verbal behavior: Toward reciprocal determinism in leadership theory. *Journal of Applied Psychology, 69,* 222-232

Smirich, L., & Chesser, R. J. (1981). Superiors' and subordinates' perceptions of performance: Beyond disagreement. *Academy of Management Journal, 24,* 198-205.

Snyder, R., & Morris, J. (1984). Organizational communication and performance. *Journal of Applied Psychology, 69,* 461-465.

Steckler, N. A., & Rosenthal, R. (1985). Sex differences in nonverbal and verbal communication with bosses, peers, and subordinates. *Journal of Applied Psychology, 70,* 157-163.

Stogdill, R. M. (1974). *Handbook of leadership.* New York: Free Press.

Sypher, B. D., & Zorn, T. E. (1986). Communication-related abilities and upward mobility: A Longitudinal investigation. *Human Communication Research, 12,* 420-431.

Thayer, L. (1968). *Communication and communication systems.* Homewood, IL: Irwin.

Tjosvold, D. (1984). Effects of leader warmth an directiveness on subordinate performance on a subsequent task. *Journal of Applied Psychology, 69,* 422-427.

Tjosvold, D. (1985a). Power and social context in superior-subordinate interaction. *Organizational Behavior and Human Decision Processes, 35,* 281-293.

Tjosvold, D. (1985b). The effects of attribution and social context on superiors' influence and interaction with low performing subordinates. *Personnel Psychology, 38,* 361-376.

Trempe, J., Rigny, A. J., & Haccoun, R. R. (1985). Subordinate satisfaction with male and female managers: Role of perceived supervisory influence. *Journal of Applied Psychology, 70,* 44-47.

Vecchio, R. (1985). Predicting employee turnover from leadership member exchange: A failure to replicate. *Academy of Management Journal, 28,* 478-485.

Vroom, V. H., & Yetton, P. W. (1973). *Leadership and decision-making.* Pittsburgh: University of Pittsburgh Press.

Watson, K. (1982). Analysis of communication patterns: A method for discriminating leader and subordinate roles. *Academy of Management Journal, 25,* 107-120.

Weber, M. (1947). *The theory of social and economic organization.* New York: Oxford University Press.

Weick, K. E. (1969). *The social psychology of organizing.* Reading, MA: Addison-Wesley.

Wheeless, L. R., Wheeless, V. E., & Howard, R. D. (1984). The relationships of communication with supervisor and decision-participation to employee job satisfaction. *Communication Quarterly, 32,* 222-232.

Wheeless, V. E., & Berryman-Fink, C. (1985). Perceptions of women managers and their communicator competencies. *Communication Quarterly, 33,* 137-148.

Whitely, W. (1984). An exploratory study of managers' reactions to properties of verbal communication. *Personnel Psychology, 37,* 41-59.

Whitely, W. (1985). Managerial work behavior: An integration of results from two major approaches. *Academy of Management Journal, 28,* 344-362.

Yeakley, F. R. (1982). Communication style preferences and adjustments as an approach to studying effects of similarity in psychological type. *Research in Psychological Type, 5,* 30-49.

12 Formal Organization Structure

FREDRIC M. JABLIN
University of Texas at Austin

I N their 1976 analysis of organizational communication research Porter and Roberts state that "the total configuration of an organization undoubtedly exerts a strong influence on the characteristics of communication within it" (p. 1570). At the same time, however, they observe that knowledge about the impact of various formal organization characteristics, such as size, shape, and authority structure on communication behavior and attitudes, is extremely limited. Although Porter and Roberts's (1976) assessment still tends to portray accurately the state of knowledge in this area, the number of studies (directly or indirectly) exploring relationships between formal organization structure and communication has grown greatly in the last several decades. This literature, however, is strewn across a wide variety of disciplines; has rarely been synthesized; and, in those instances where it has been reviewed, the analyses have been fairly selective in focus (e.g., McPhee, 1985; Monge, Edwards, & Kirste, 1978). As a consequence, the major purposes of this chapter are to (1) synthesize and interpret this literature, and (2) suggest a number of directions for future research in the area of formal organization structure and communication. Similar to Berger and Cummings's (1979) recent review of the organization structure-job attitudes literature, this chapter is a "pretheoretical" analysis; that is, "it aims

AUTHOR'S NOTE: I wish to express appreciation to Arthur G. Bedeian and Linda Putnam for their comments and suggestions on an earlier draft of this chapter.

toward a 'cleaning-up' and interpretation of the relevant literature" (p. 170).

Although there are numerous organization characteristics that affect communication, this chapter focuses on a select group of variables: formal structural characteristics—that is, formal features of an organization that "serve to control or distinguish its parts" (Miles, 1980, p. 18). Thus, in terms of the structural traditions discussed earlier by Monge and Eisenberg (Chapter 10, in this volume), this chapter attempts to review and interpret literature emphasizing the "positional" (versus "emergent" or "cultural") view of organization structure and communication. However, structure will not be viewed only as an "empirical object" (McPhee, 1985; Weber, 1922/1947) but also frequently as an "information processing/coordination mechanism" (e.g., Galbraith, 1973).

At this juncture, several conceptual and empirical issues associated with the purposes of this chapter require elaboration. First, this chapter does not directly consider the causal links between organization structure, strategy, technology, and environment. Organization theorists have researched and debated the nature of these linkages for decades with little resulting consensus (e.g., Aldrich, 1972, 1979; Astley & Van de Ven, 1983; Bedeian, in press; Blau & Schoenherr, 1971; Chandler, 1962; Child, 1972; Gerwin, 1981; Hickson, Pugh, & Pheysey, 1969; Hilton, 1972; Hrebiniak & Joyce, 1985; Pfeffer, 1986; Thompson, 1967; Woodward, 1965; Yasai-Ardekani, 1986); a discussion of the patterns of causation among these variables and their impact on communication is beyond the scope of this chapter (for a discussion of relationships between organization environments and organizational communication, see Huber & Draft, Chapter 5, in this volume). Second, it is essential to recognize that because of inconsistencies in the conceptualization of formal organization characteristics across studies (e.g., Blackburn, 1982; James & Jones, 1976), most research generalizations suggested in this chapter should be viewed tentatively. Additionally, it should be noted that even when structure characteristics are conceptualized similarly across studies, variation in measurement methods often makes it difficult to generalize findings. In particular, research has shown low convergence between survey and institutional (key informant) measures of structure (Ford, 1979; Powers & Huber, 1982; Sathe, 1978; Walton, 1981).

The following analysis is also limited by the general absence of longitudinal research exploring the formal structures of organizations. Since the greater part of this chapter focuses on the formal characteristics of organizations at single points in time, the attending discussion will largely emphasize the role of structure as a problematic constraint on communication behaviors and attitudes. Specifically, structure is considered a meta-communicative "object" or constraint: Structure communicates about constraints that organization members face in the communication process (McPhee, 1985; Watzlavick, Beavin, & Jackson, 1967).

To achieve its purposes, this chapter is divided into two sections. The first section describes the set of structure dimensions that are explored in this chapter, and reviews the results of studies examining relationships between these dimensions and organizational communication. This discussion is followed by various conclusions concerning state-of-the-art research exploring formal structure-communication relationships. Recommendations for future research are proffered at various summary points throughout the chapter, as well as in the chapter's concluding section.

STRUCTURAL DIMENSIONS AND COMMUNICATION

Although there is no clear consensus in the organization literature, four key structural dimensions predominate in most theoretical analyses: (1) configuration (e.g., span of control, organizational size), (2) complexity (vertical and horizontal), (3) formalization, and (4) centralization (see Berger & Cummings, 1979; Blackburn, 1982; Dalton, Todor, Spendolini, Fielding, & Porter, 1980; James & Jones, 1976; Miles, 1980; Porter & Lawler, 1965). Since these dimensions are cited most frequently in the organization literature and encompass almost all of the structural dimensions that have been included in communication-related research, they provide the focus and framework for the ensuing literature review. Additionally, this review attempts (when feasible) to distinguish between levels of communication phenomena (individual, group, organizational) that are associated with various structural dimensions (e.g., Mossholder & Bedeian, 1983).

CONFIGURATION

A number of basic structural characteristics constitute what is commonly referred to as organizational configuration, or the shape of an organization resulting from the location and distribution of its formal roles and work units. In particular, five structural characteristics are frequently associated with organizational configuration: (1) span of control, (2) hierarchical level, (3) organizational size, (4) sub-unit size, and (5) administrative intensity (i.e., the portion of individuals in administrative or support roles). The following review, however, does not consider relationships between administrative intensity and communication attitudes and behaviors since these relationships have been so infrequently investigated.

Span of Control

Span of control, typically defined as the number of subordinates reporting *directly* to a superior, is one of the oldest concepts in organization theory (e.g.,

Fayol, 1916/1949; Graicunas, 1937; House & Miner, 1969; Van Fleet & Bedeian, 1977). Little empirical research, however, has been conducted exploring relationships between span of control and communication. This research void is particularly ironic since one of the primary explanations theorists often supply for altering span of control is based on communication principles. As Meyer (1968, p. 950) reasons, "Intuition tells one that where spans of control are low, supervisors and subordinates have better access to one another than where spans of control are high. . . . Where working conditions are such that two-way interchange between supervisors and workers is not needed, spans of control will be quite large." Essentially, most theorists assume that the need for frequent communication between contiguous hierarchical levels is an important determinant of span of control.

In addition, it is often assumed that the narrower the span, the greater the potential for communication between individuals at upper and lower hierarchical levels; the wider the span, the less potential for interaction. This assumption, however, is problematic, since a concomitant of narrow spans of control is typically an increase in number of hierarchical levels (e.g., Bedeian, 1984). In other words, while narrow spans may increase the probability of interaction between supervisors and their immediate subordinates, narrow spans can also increase the number of levels separating upper- from lower-level organization members, thereby inhibiting cross-level vertical communication. Conversely, while wider spans may decrease the probability of interaction between superiors and immediate subordinates, the probability of communication between persons at the top and bottom of the organization may be facilitated because fewer hierarchical levels separate them.

The few existing empirical studies exploring communication and span of control suggest the following conclusions: (1) Span of control is unrelated to the extent to which a supervisor communicates with his or her subordinates via oral versus written means (Udell, 1967); (2) span of control does not appear related to closeness of supervision (Bell, 1967) or subordinates' perceptions of role clarity (Follert, 1982); (3) narrow spans of control are associated with increased amounts of upward and downward communication between superiors and subordinates (Brewer, 1971); and (4) spans of control do not differentially affect subordinates' perceptions of communication openness with their immediate superiors (Jablin, 1982). Thus while these research results provide some support for the notion that frequency of communication may be affected by span of control, they also indicate that mode and quality of communication are not necessarily affected.

These conclusions, however, should be viewed cautiously. In particular, it is important to realize that the above investigations vary in their operationalization of span of control (for a discussion of conceptual and empirical distinctions associated with measurement of span of control, see Ouchi & Dowling, 1974) and generally do not consider the effects of such variables as job autonomy, routineness of work, and formalization on results. Moreover, with the exception of the Jablin (1982) study, these investigations do not consider possible interaction effects between span of control and either hierarchical level or organizational size (e.g., Dewar & Simet, 1981; Van Fleet, 1983). In addition to the above issues, it seems clear that future studies in this area need to (1) explore relationships between span of control and a wider set of communication variables (for instance, various types of message content, and source accessibility), and (2) gather *behavioral* as compared to self-report assessments of communication activities.

Hierarchical Level

Hierarchical level refers to an individual's position in a scalar chain and ranges from nonsupervisory workers at the lower end of the scale to chief executive officers at the upper extreme (Berger & Cummings, 1979). Consistent with previous reviews of level as a structural dimension (e.g., Porter & Lawler, 1965), only studies examining two or more levels are reviewed here. (Studies of subordinate-immediate superior communication are excluded unless they consider how these dyadic relationships vary at different hierarchical levels.)

Generally speaking, studies exploring relationships between individuals' levels in their organizations and communication-related behavior have operationalized level by asking respondents for a self-report of position in their organization's scalar chain of authority (chain of command). In addition, most investigations have tended to focus on relationships between variations in hierarchical level and (1) formal and informal communication patterns, (2) decision-making behavior and influence strategies, or (3) information adequacy.

Communication patterns. Studies exploring relationships between communication patterns (including volume of message sending/receiving and mode of communication) have produced a variety of findings. It seems apparent that higher-level organization members spend more time in message sending and receiving activities than their lower-level counterparts, thus likely generating a greater volume of communication (Bacharach & Aiken, 1977; Dubin, 1962; Hannaway, 1985; Hinrichs, 1964; Putnam & Sorenson, 1982; Thomason, 1966, 1967). However, the exact form this increase in communication assumes as one moves higher in a hierarchy appears quite variable across organizations and work environments. For example, with respect to the impact of level on frequency of superior-subordinate communication, research has produced equivocal findings. Some studies have shown the ratio of superior to subordinate communication increases the higher one's position in the hierarchy (e.g., Dubin & Spray, 1964), while other investigations report the opposite pattern (e.g., Burns, 1954; Dubin, 1962), and still others have found no consistent relationship (e.g., Martin, 1959). Similarly, findings from studies examining the effect of hierarchical level on peer (horizontal) communication contacts have shown that with ascent in rank peer interactions may increase (Marting, 1969), decrease (Bacharach & Aiken, 1977; Burns, 1954; Martin, 1959), or remain invariant (Dubin & Spray, 1964; Wickesburg, 1968).

In contrast to the above findings, research exploring hierarchical level as related to use of staff conferences and frequency of extra-organizational communication have produced more consistent results. Specifically, it appears that upper-level managers employ staff conferences more than lower-level managers, though the perceived quality of communication occurring in these conferences does not seem to vary between levels (Brinkerhoff, 1972; Wager & Brinkerhoff, 1975). In addition, most studies indicate that extra-organizational communication contacts increase the higher one's rank (Burns, 1954; Dubin & Spray, 1964; Shartle, 1956).

Recent studies also provide evidence suggesting that the communication behavior of organization members may be affected by the interaction of hierarchical level and environmental uncertainty. Along these lines, Hannaway's (1985) research indicates that, under conditions of high uncertainty, upper-level managers initiate more verbal interactions (conversations and meetings) than lower-level managers. Likewise, Brinkerhoff (1972) reports that upper-level managers may use staff conferences more than lower-level managers when confronted by crises and task variability; his results, however, do not reveal strong associations among these variables (*gamma* = .16). Finally, in a study involving an organizational simulation (*n* = 51), Putnam and Sorenson (1982) found that upper levels tend to respond to equivocal messages by searching for actions or solutions whereas lower levels focus on adding interpretations.

Although a relatively new area of study, research findings also indicate that use of electronic mail systems may vary with hierarchical level. In particular, a recent investigation by Sproull and Kiesler (1986) is noteworthy. The results of their study revealed that volume of messages (sent and received) via electronic mail does not vary across levels but the nature of messages is distinctive. Specifically, they discovered that the messages of managers were longer (especially salutations/openings), focused more on work-related topics, and more frequently contained negative affect (words or simple phrases expressing negative sentiment) than the messages of professionals and non-exempt employees.

In summary, the results of the above studies provide tentative support for Daft and Lengel's (1984) argument that upper level-managers use "richer" media (e.g., face-to-face communication, telephone calls) for communication than their lower-level counterparts. However, these studies also suggest the possibility that an individual's hierarchical level and perceptions of environmental uncertainty may interact to affect communication attitudes/behaviors and predominant modes of sending and receiving messages. To conclude, research exploring relationships between hierarchical level and communication patterns has produced a rather diverse, often contradictory set of findings. These results would seem to indicate that a variety of factors jointly affect or moderate relationships between hierarchical level and interaction patterns. In particular, future research might benefit from exploring the joint/moderating effects of work dependency, technology, organizational size, and environmental uncertainty on relationships between hierarchical level and communication (e.g., Daft & Lengel, 1984; Monge et al., 1978).

Decision-making and influence. Unfortunately, only a handful of studies have examined relationships between hierarchical level and communication-related activities associated with decision making. The results of these investigations indicate that (1) upper-level managers tend to involve their subordinates in decision making more than do lower-level managers, and (2) lower-level managers tend to have decisions initiated for them by their superiors (e.g., Blankenship & Miles, 1968; Jago & Vroom, 1977). Consistent with these findings, Jablin (1982) reports that lower-level organization members tend to perceive less openness in superior-subordinate communication than do higher-level members. He hypothesizes that it may be the more open communication climate at higher levels that causes subordinates to become more involved in decision making (Jablin, 1982).

The types of message strategies that individuals at different hierarchical levels use in their efforts to influence others have also been the focus of several recent studies. Kipnis, Schmidt, and Wilkinson (1980) report that persons in higher as compared to lower hierarchical levels use more "rationality" and "assertiveness" tactics when attempting to influence both subordinates and superiors, and use "sanctions" more frequently when trying to influence their subordinates. Similarly, Krone (1985) discovered a tendency for subordinates at higher versus lower hierarchical levels to use more "open persuasion" in attempting to influence their superiors' decisions. In essence, the results of these studies lend credence to the notion that persons at higher hierarchical levels tend to use more "direct" message tactics in their influence attempts.

Information adequacy. In spite of the fact that basic organizational communication texts frequently stress the concepts of "executive isolation" and "uncertainty absorption" in upward communication (March & Simon, 1958), scant recent research has explored the impact of hierarchical level on the degree to which individuals are adequately informed of relevant organizational events, policies, and tasks. Since some of the earliest studies of organizational communication were concerned with these issues (see Redding, 1972, for a review of this literature), the scarcity of recent research in this area is somewhat puzzling. Exceptions to this trend, however, are investigations by Spiker and Daniels (1981) and Penley (1982). Consistent with the results of many earlier studies, their findings provide little evidence of a strong relationship between individuals' perceptions of task/organization-related information adequacy and their hierarchical level. Penley's (1982) results led him to conclude that hierarchical level may not directly affect task-related information adequacy, but rather that level "may moderate relationships between other variables and adequacy" (p. 362). Future research should consider this possibility, and in addition more carefully explore how the content of task/organization information (e.g., production, benefits, policies) may be moderating the impact of hierarchical level on perceived information adequacy (e.g., Davis, 1968; Redding, 1972).

As is the case with information adequacy associated with "sanctioned" task and organization issues, only a minimal amount of research has explored relationships between knowledge of informal, "grapevine" communication items and hierarchical levels. However, the results of the few studies that have examined these issues do paint a consistent picture: Higher-level managers tend to be better informed than lower-level managers (Davis, 1953; Sutton & Porter, 1968). At the same time, it is important to realize that these studies were conducted in relatively small organizations (sample sizes of less than 80) and that their results may not generalize to larger settings.

In closing, two basic issues should be recognized in attempting to generalize the hierarchical level literature reviewed above. First, although most studies initially operationalize hierarchical level via ordinal scaling methods, many studies eventually collapse the resulting distinctions into fairly abstract, somewhat arbitrary nominal groups (for instance, "managerial" and "non-managerial") when conducting data analyses. As a consequence, it is often difficult to compare results across studies. Second, the failure of many studies to consider the effects of other structural characteristics, especially organizational size on results, is a major hindrance in generalizing research findings.

Organizational Size

Although there is considerable disagreement with respect to the conceptual and empirical definition of organizational size (e.g., Kimberly, 1976), it generally refers to the total number of full-time (and some percentage of part-time) employees within an organization. As Porter and Roberts (1976, p. 1571) state, "most observers commonly believe that greater size has deleterious effects on the quality of communication" in organizations. At the same time, however, it is also frequently assumed that as organizational size increases coordination problems increase and organizational members must devote more of their time to communication (e.g., Kasarda, 1974). Unfortunately, with respect to each of these assumptions, the empirical research evidence is mixed.

A number of studies have examined relationships between organizational size and volume, frequency, and mode of communication. Ingham (1970) found that workers in small British industrial organizations (less than 100 workers) have significantly more non-work-related conversations with their bosses on a daily basis than workers in large companies (over 3,000 employees). Negative correlations between organizational size and amount of communication have also been reported by Indik (1965) and Drazin and Van de Ven (1985). However, Bacharach and Aiken (1977) found organizational size to be positively related to the amount of upward, downward, lateral, and total communication of subordinates, but not their superiors (department heads). In contrast, Hage (1974), in a study of 16 health and welfare organizations, discovered only 1 marginally significant relationship among 26 correlations computed between organizational size and various measures of scheduled (planned) and unscheduled oral, task-related communication. In like fashion, Hall, Hass, and Johnson (1967) detected very weak associations between organizational size (ranging from less than 100 employees to over 1,000) and degree of emphasis on written communication and use of established channels of communication.

Research exploring the relationship of organizational size to quality of communication has also produced a rather mixed set of results. On the one hand, Mahoney, Frost, Crandall, and Weitzel (1972), in a study of 19 organizations ranging in size from 200 to over 10,000 employees, found no relationship between organizational size and the degree to which information and organizational communication flow freely. On the other hand, in a study of 12 public sector service agencies, Snyder and Morris (1984) discovered that as agency size increased, employees' perceptions of adequacy of information about agency policies and procedures decreased ($r = -.42$). Several studies report that, as organizational size increases, the quality of communication (e.g., exchange pattern, openness) between superiors and subordinates decreases. However, most of these investigations have not found these relationships to be statistically significant (Green, Blank, & Liden, 1983; Jablin, 1982; Klauss & Bass, 1982; Snyder & Morris, 1984). Finally, initial evidence also suggests that upward influence tactics used by employees to influence their superiors may vary with organizational size. Specifically, Erez and Rim (1982) present data showing that middle managers in very large organizations (6,000 or more employees) tend to use "rational" tactics more with their bosses than managers in small organizations (less than 599 employees).

In sum, the above studies provide limited support for the notion that organizational size is negatively related to quality of communication. Furthermore, the proposition that frequency and volume of communication increases with organizational size has produced an extremely inconsistent set of research findings. While inconsistent findings among studies may be a result of differences in the operationalization of organizational size, these disparate findings also suggest that communication behavior and attitudes may be more directly associated with frequent consequences of organizational size (such as horizontal complexity; Hage, 1974) than with the fairly global concept of size.

Sub-Unit Size

For purposes of this review a sub-unit is defined "as any clearly delineated intraorganizational work unit" (Berger & Cummings, 1979, p. 187). While the impact of sub-unit size on communication attitudes and behaviors has been a frequent focus of study in laboratory research (e.g., Hare, 1976; Shaw, 1981), the manner in which sub-unit size affects these processes in the organizational context has received minimal research attention. Essentially, most researchers assume that the relationships discovered in laboratory research generalize to organizational settings. The validity of this assumption, however, seems highly suspect, since organizational sub-units typically differ in numerous ways from groups found in other contexts (for example, they have formally appointed leaders, are embedded within formal organizations, and operate within formal status hierarchies; see Heinen & Jacobson, 1976; Jablin & Sussman, 1983). As a consequence, only research exploring workgroups within organizational contexts is reviewed here.

Generally, most theorists posit that as sub-unit size increases interaction among unit members will decrease "because of limitations on the amount of effort that an individual can spend interacting with an increasing number of others" (Bass, 1960, p. 677). Findings from several studies are somewhat supportive of this notion. Collecting data from U.S. Naval personnel, O'Reilly and Roberts (1977) found a negative correlation ($r = -.67$) between workgroup size (sociometrically determined) and degree of group connectedness. Similarly, Klauss and Bass (1982) report that as department size increases subordinates tend to perceive less open and two-way communication with their superiors. However, relationships between sub-unit size and a variety of dimensions of managerial communication style (e.g., openness, careful message sending and receiving), while negative in direction, were not statistically significant.

Consistent with the results of the above studies, Van de Ven, Delbecq, and Koenig (1976) discovered that as sub-unit size increases (range: 2-21) the use of impersonal coordination modes (e.g., rules, plans, policies, and procedures) and vertical communication/coordination channels increases (though the use of vertical channels tended to decrease in use when sub-units contained 11 or more members). However, their results also showed that the use of horizontal communication/coordination channels and group meetings remained invariant with increases in sub-unit size. Kipnis et al. (1980) report that as sub-unit size increases, supervisors employ more impersonal influence strategies— assertions, appeals to upper hierarchical levels for support, and sanctions. In turn, Campbell (1952) found that as subunit size increased (from 20 to 100 or more), employees perceived that their level of knowledge about the operation of their incentive pay plan decreased.

To summarize, although only a handful of studies have explored relationships between sub-unit size and communication attitudes and behaviors, their results generally indicate that as sub-units become larger, communication becomes more impersonal and/or formal. In addition, some evidence suggests that communication quality is negatively affected by increases in sub-unit size. Obviously, future research should explore a wider array of communication processes as they relate to sub-unit size. In particular, studies might employ interaction process analysis variables (e.g., giving information, offering opinions, stating agreement; Bales, 1950) used to study group communication processes in laboratory settings. In addition, research exploring the effects of changes in sub-unit size, group development, and communication processes would add considerably to our understanding of the effects of sub-unit size on communication (e.g., Wanous, Reichers, & Malik, 1984).

As the preceding review indicates, it is extremely hazardous to draw generalizations about organizational configuration-communication relationships. Regrettably, relatively few studies have explored issues associated with communication and organizational configuration. Moreover, almost all of the reported research has collected perceptual as compared to behavioral indicators of communication behavior and attitudes. It seems clear that if our understanding of relationships between communication processes and organizational configuration is to progress, researchers must place greater emphasis on collecting *behavioral* communication data.

In addition, an examination of the literature reviewed in the preceding sections suggests that (1) the results of most studies are either inconclusive or contradicted by findings from other investigations, and (2) when consistent relationships are uncovered between organizational configuration and communication behaviors and attitudes these relationships are frequently weak, accounting for small amounts of shared variance. The second of these observations, however, is not particularly surprising and may merely represent a research limitation in this area. Specifically, since configuration dimensions represent physical attributes of an organization's structure that are fairly distal to individuals' immediate task environments, they probably have only *indirect* effects on communication behavior and attitudes (e.g., Jablin, 1980; James & Jones, 1976). As a consequence, they are unlikely to account for huge amounts of variance in communication.

The first observation represents a more serious problem. Why are research findings so inconsistent and contradictory? As repeatedly noted in the preceding sections, it is quite likely that inconsistencies across studies with respect to conceptual definitions and operationalizations of various structural configuration dimensions may be one factor accounting for divergent research findings. In addition, two other factors are worthy of consideration. First, it seems apparent that many studies have explored particular structural configuration dimensions in isolation from other dimensions, and thus the interaction of dimensions is not always accounted for in research designs. The structural characteristics discussed in this section are termed "configuration dimensions" because of their amalgamated (versus isolated) impact on the structural form/configuration of an organization; consequently, our research should consider how the interaction of dimensions affects communication attitudes and behaviors. Second, inconsistent results imply that other organizational variables, such as production technologies and environments, may be interacting with configurational dimensions of structure, and, hence, be confounding research findings. Future research should consider this possibility.

COMPLEXITY

At a very basic level, all organizations can be described in terms of their division of labor, functions, knowledge, and resources. *Complexity* depicts the structural components/units into which organizations and their employees may be categorized (Miles, 1980; Zey-Ferrell, 1979). Differentiation describes the process by which these units evolve, typically occurring in two directions: vertically and horizontally. The result of vertical differentiation is usually referred to as vertical complexity and is an indication of the number of different hierarchical levels in an organization relative to its size. Like organizational configuration, vertical complexity provides an index of an organization's shape: The more managerial levels there are, the taller and more peaked a structure, the fewer the managerial levels, and the flatter a structure. In contrast, the consequence of horizontal differentiation is referred to as horizontal complexity and measures the number of department divisions in an organization. Although a variety of methods are used to determine horizontal complexity, it is typically assessed by determining the number of different occupational specialties or specialized sub-units at a given hierarchical level. To some degree horizontal complexity provides an indication of an organization's width.

To summarize, in very simple terms, complexity represents the number of separate "parts" within an organization as reflected by the division of labor and by the number of both hierarchical levels and departments (Bedeian, 1984). Since many theorists assume that as organizations become more differentiated, coordination and control become more problematic (Blau, 1970; Zey-Ferrell, 1979), and given that communication is usually considered to be an intrinsic element in coordination, the manner in which vertical and horizontal complexity are related to communication represents an important area of research. As the following literature review reveals, however, it remains relatively underresearched.

Vertical Complexity

When considering research exploring vertical complexity it is important to realize the close relationship between this concept and the notion of span of control. As Porter and Lawler (1965, p. 43) observe, "the degree to which a structure is tall or flat is determined by the *average* span of control within [an] organization" (emphasis added). In addition, the tendency for organizational size to be positively related to vertical complexity (e.g., Zey-Ferrell, 1979) is noteworthy, since effects of vertical complexity on communication processes can be confused for effects between size and communication.

Only a limited number of studies have examined relationships between vertical differentiation and communication behaviors and attitudes. Of these investigations, Rousseau (1978) reports that the greater the number of hierarchical levels (range: 3-10) in a department the less performance feedback individuals perceive receiving from supervisors and coworkers. In a similar vein, Klauss and Bass (1982) discovered that as the number of hierarchical levels separating individuals from "focal" others in an organization increases, the more frequently they report sending memos to these persons, the less frequently they have group interactions with them, the more frequently their communications focus on task-related issues and the less frequently on social-personal areas of content. On the other hand, in a study exploring leadership styles Ghiselli and Siegel (1972) determined that "sharing information" with subordinates is positively related to managerial success in tall organizations but negatively related to success in flat organizations.

In contrast to the results of the above investigations, Bacharach and Aiken (1977) found positive correlations between number of hierarchical levels and frequency of subordinates' upward, downward, lateral, and total communication, and with their department heads' frequency of lateral communication. However, when entered into a regression analysis containing several other structural variables, the effects of vertical complexity on communication were found to be nonsignificant. Since organizational size and number of hierarchical levels were strongly correlated ($r = .64$) and size was a significant predictor in the regression analysis, it would appear that organizational size accounted for much of the explained variance associated with vertical complexity. In related research, O'Reilly and Roberts (1977) examined the structure of sociometrically derived task groups and found vertical differentiation (number of different levels independent of group size) to be positively correlated with members' perceptions of information accuracy. However, when entered into a regression analysis that included a variety of other variables (e.g., group connectedness, percentage reciprocal linkages), the relationship between vertical differentiation and perceived information accuracy was not significant.

In brief, findings from the above investigations do not suggest a consistent set of relationships between vertical complexity and communication. As a consequence, it would seem that relationships between complexity and communication may be moderated by other factors. For example, Zey-Ferrell (1979) notes that the effects of vertical differentiation on upward communication may be moderated by the extent to which professionals or "experts" are employed at lower hierarchical levels (also, see Brewer, 1971). Moreover, as noted earlier, organizational size seems to moderate associations between complexity and communication frequency. In addition, the above studies suggest that vertical complexity may have differential effects on modes of communication (e.g., oral vs. written), interaction context (e.g., dyadic vs. group), and message content (e.g., task vs. social). Future research should explore these issues and attempt to examine relationships between vertical complexity and communication with behavioral versus self-report measures of communication (heretofore the predominant measurement approach).

Horizontal Complexity

The work of Hage (1974) and his associates (Hage, Aiken, & Marrett, 1971) represents the earliest major attempts to explore relationships between horizontal complexity and communication. These researchers operationalized horizontal complexity in several ways: number of occupational specialties, degree of extra-organizational professional activity, and number of organizational departments. Data were collected in 16 health and welfare organizations and included self-reports on both scheduled (planned) and unscheduled oral communication. Although the pattern and direction of results were fairly consistent across measures of complexity, the statistical significance of findings did vary considerably across measures. When number of occupational specialties was used as a complexity index, complexity was found to be significantly correlated with average number of scheduled organizationwide committee meetings attended, frequency of department heads' unscheduled communication with other department heads and supervisors in parallel work units, supervisors' communication with workers in various units, workers' communication with colleagues in other units, and overall rate of unscheduled communication. In contrast, no significant relationships were discovered between professional activity and communication, while the only significant correlation ($r = .62$) between number of departments and communication was for department heads' unscheduled communication with supervisors in other work units (see Hage, 1974). In interpreting their results, Hage et al. (1971) conclude that the "volume of communication is higher in more complex organizations" and, in particular, "it is the flow of communication with people *on the same status levels in different departments* that is most highly associated with . . . measures of complexity" (p. 867).

Building on the Hage et al. (1971) research, Bacharach and Aiken (1977) explored relationships between complexity, operationalized as number of departments (in government bureaucracies), and self-reports of frequency of oral communication. Results of their study revealed negative correlations between horizontal complexity and the frequency of subordinates' upward, lateral, and total communication. No significant relationships were found between supervisors' communication and complexity. Moreover, when complexity was entered into a regression analysis with several other structures dimensions (including decentralization), complexity was found to be significantly related ($r = -.33$) to only one communication variable: frequency of subordinates' upward communication. In like fashion, O'Reilly and Roberts (1977) in their study of communication in sociometrically derived task groups discovered a significant correlation between complexity (measured as number of different occupational specialties divided by group size) and perceptions of communciation openness, but found this relationship to be nonsignificant when entered into a regression analysis with other predictor variables.

In considering the above investigations, several issues need to be recognized. First, with increases in size, organizations usually exhibit increases in horizontal complexity—they have more departments and occupational specialties (e.g., Blau & Schoenherr, 1971; Child, 1973; Zey-Ferrell, 1979). Thus research exploring complexity-communication relationships should consider the moderating effects of organizational size on reported results. Second, as the results described above demonstrate, relationships between horizontal complexity and communication may vary with the manner in which complexity is operationalized. Thus, for example, we should not be surprised that Hage et al. (1971) report complexity (number of occupational specialties) positively related to frequency of horizontal communication, and Bacharach and Aiken (1977) find complexity (number of departments) negatively correlated with lateral communication. Not only may the two measures be conceptually distinct (e.g., the latter measure more an index of segmentation or clustering of like specialties while the former is a simple measure of division of labor), but it is possible that the Hage et al. (1971) measure is confounded by organizational size. In summary, while the specific direction of the relationship between horizontal complexity and communication frequency may be unclear, there is little doubt that complexity and communication (albeit self-reported communication behavior) are significantly interrelated.

To conclude, while not typically considered "pure" studies of organizational complexity, the work of Lawrence and Lorsch (1967) and associates (Morse & Lorsch, 1970; Walker & Lorsch, 1968) warrants mention because of the manner in which it operationalized differentiation and the research tradition it helped spawn (contingency theory). Specifically, Lawrence and Lorsch (1967) examined the effects of varying levels of environmental uncertainty on organizational differentiation and integration. However, in contrast to the studies reviewed above, these researchers viewed differentiation in broader terms, as "differences in attitude and behavior, not just the simple fact of segmentation and specialized knowledge" (Lawrence & Lorsch, 1967, p. 9). In particular, their measure of differentiation assessed differences in cognitive and emotional orientation (managers' goals, time and interpersonal orientations) as well as variations in formality of structure. In turn, Lawrence and Lorsch (1967) describe integration as the "quality of the state of collaboration that exists among departments that are required to achieve unity of effort by the demands of the environment" (p. 11).

Among other findings, Lawrence and Lorsch's (1967) research revealed that highly differentiated organizations frequently require elaborate personal, face-to-face communication/coordination modes to achieve "effective" integration (e.g., integrating teams, integrator roles, cross-function teams). In other words, reliance on formal rules, role specifications, written procedures, and the like (attributes of high formalization; discussed below), were found to be inadequate integrating devices in highly differentiated organizations. Thus the research of Lawrence and Lorsch (1967), though distinct from the other studies of differentiation/complexity reviewed earlier, lends further support to the notion that communication processes in organizations (especially with respect to interdepartmental relations; see McCann & Galbraith, 1981) are associated with varying levels of organizational complexity.

FORMALIZATION

The notion of formalization is typically credited to Max Weber (1922/1947), who conceived it as a method for enhancing organizational efficiency and control. In general terms, formalization refers to the degree to which the behaviors and requirements of jobs are explicit—that is, codified into policies, rules, regulations, customs, and so forth (Hage, 1980; Miles, 1980). However, as Zey-Ferrell (1979) observes, research definitions and operationalizations of formalization vary considerably in scope. For example, some operationalizations focus solely on *written* rules, policies, and the like, while others also include unwritten customs and norms that govern behavior (standardization). In addition, definitions vary with respect to their emphasis on the existence of written and unwritten practices *and* enforcement-related issues. In other words, some researchers argue that an organization is highly formalized only when it is characterized by specificity as well as high compliance with and enforcement of expectations (e.g., Hage, 1965). Moreover, operationalizations of formalization differ in their focus on operative (work-related) and regulative practices (customs, rules, procedures associated with internal organizational control and coordination—e.g., hiring, allocation of resources, communication). Finally as with many of the other structural characteristics previously discussed, measures of formalization vary with respect to their reliance on data supplied from employees' self-reports (perceptions) and institutional sources (official records, documents, key informants). As repeatedly demonstrated (e.g., Pennings, 1973), these two measurement methods do not necessarily yield similar results.

Despite the obvious relevance of the concept of formalization to research in organizational communication, very few studies have examined relationships between formalization and communication. Further, the few investigations that have been conducted in this area have focused their attention solely on formalization of operative practices and have not considered relationships between regulative, organizationwide formalization and communication variables. In addition, it should be noted that since many formalization measures include a dimension assessing employees' perceptions of the degree of emphasis on written communications, research exploring formalization-communication relationships has emphasized the effects of formalization of formal and informal oral communication.

The most prominent research investigating formalization and communication is that of Hage (1974) and his associates (Hage et al., 1971). Collecting self-report data from employees in 16 social welfare organizations, they operationalized formalization with two measures: (1) the extent to which respondents reported complete job descriptions for their positions, and (2) employees' perceptions of degree of job specificity. This latter measure was designed to reflect "the programming of jobs, such as the existence of specific procedures for various contingencies, written records of job performance, and well-defined communication channels" (Hage et al., 1971, p. 868). Results of the research revealed statistically nonsignificant associations between formalization and frequency of scheduled communication with the exception of a negative correlation between job specificity and attendance at departmental meetings, $(r = -.57)$. However, with respect to unscheduled communication, analyses indicated a number of significant relationships with the job description measure of formalization, including negative associations between formalization and overall unscheduled interactions $(r = -.50)$, unscheduled communication with persons at the same level but in different departments $(r = -.61)$, and unscheduled interactions with persons at lower status levels in different departments $(r = -.45)$. In addition, it is important to note the overall pattern of Hage et al.'s (1971) results: Negative (though not necessarily statistically significant) associations were found between most categories of frequency of scheduled and unscheduled communication and formalization. Similarly, Rousseau (1978) discovered formalization (operationalized as the extent to which written rules and procedures govern job activities; see Pugh, Hickson, Hinings, & Turner, 1968) to be negatively correlated with individuals' perceptions of the amount of performance feedback they receive from supervisors and coworkers.

In summary, given the limited amount of research that has explored formalization and communication, it is very difficult to suggest generalizations about their relationship. Perhaps the only proposition that can even be tentatively proposed is that formalization of operative (work-related) rules and procedures and frequency of oral, horizontal, unscheduled communication are inversely related. To suggest that additional research exploring associations between formalization and communication is sorely needed is to state the obvious. A more important issue is the direction and manner in which such research should proceed.

Although a number of approaches to research in this area are viable, structuration theory (e.g., Giddens, 1981, 1983; McPhee, 1985; Poole & McPhee, 1983) may provide the most useful perspective for understanding and empirically examining formalization-communication relationships. "Structuration's major argument is that every action bears a *dual* relation to structure: It both *produces* and *reproduces* structure and the related social system" (McPhee, 1985, p. 164). As applied to the study of formalization and communication, structuration theory implies a focus on the communicative process of producing and, in particular, reproducing legitimation in the form of operative and (especially) regulative rules and procedures. Structuration provides a means for explaining the process by which informal "standards" (practices such as rules and procedures that exist in employees' minds but not on paper; Zey-Ferrell, 1979) become formal, and outdated, and are subsequently revised or disregarded. In essence, a structuration approach to the study of formalization moves us beyond measuring how written practices affect the frequency of various forms of oral communication and leads us to consider how communication processes function in the creation, interpretation, legitimation, and transformation of organizational formalization. While research along these lines may require different methodological approaches than traditional studies of formalization and communication (e.g., Poole & McPhee, 1983), enhanced understanding of formalization-communication relationships may be dependent on such changes.

CENTRALIZATION

Generally speaking, an organization is considered centralized to the degree that authority is not delegated but concentrated at higher levels of management. Thus "an administrative organization is centralized to the extent that decisions are made at relatively high levels in the organization; decentralized to the extent that discretion and authority to make important decisions are delegated by top management to lower levels of executive authority" (Simon, Guetzkow, Kozmetsky, & Tyndall, 1954). While organizations become decentralized for a variety of reasons, most frequently it is as a consequence of expansion and growth (e.g., Chandler, 1962; Morris, 1968). In other words, as a small owner-operator enterprise grows and the owner is no longer able to make all decisions, a decentralized structure may develop in which certain decisions are delegated to departments and their respective heads (e.g., production, marketing). If the organization continues to expand, a departmentalized structure may eventually be enacted in which different work units are responsible for a unique product/service or process. However, though each work unit may be managed independently from others, a "top-management group still determines long-range strategies and coordinates divisional activities so as to promote overall goals" (Jennergren, 1981, p. 42).

Various degrees of decentralization are possible as a firm continues to expand and/or needs to adapt to internal and external exigencies.

In empirical research, decentralization is frequently operationalized in one of two ways: (1) the hierarchical level at which decision making takes place, or (2) the extent to which subordinates participate in making decisions (without consideration of hierarchical level; Jennergren, 1981). Although both operationalizations are clearly related, they are only moderately correlated (Khandwalla, 1973, 1977). In addition, it is important to realize that decentralization may occur with regard to only certain types of decisions. Frequently, studies distinguish between two basic types of decisions: work-related and strategic (see Hage, 1980). Work-related decisions concern issues such as how, when, and who performs work assignments. Strategic decisions concern policy-related issues and focus on an organization's long-term relationship to its environment. Since work-related decisions are typically delegated to lower hierarchical levels (Grinyer & Yasi-Ardekani, 1980), measures of decentralization should distinguish between work-related and strategic decisions.

The relationship generally hypothesized between centralization and communication is succinctly stated by Hage et al. (1971):

> There is less need for feedback when power is concentrated at the top of the organization hierarchy, since the role of subordinates is to implement decisions rather than to participate in the shaping of decisions. Therefore, as the concentration of power becomes greater, and consequently as the degree of participation in decision-making by lower participants becomes less, we would expect inhibitions on communications in an organization. (p. 863)

Hage et al. (1971) explored the above proposition by utilizing a self-report index of decentralization that focused on participation in strategic decisions. Results drawn from a sample of health and welfare organizations revealed positive correlations between decentralization and frequency of attending scheduled organizationwide committee meetings ($r = .60$) and departmental meetings ($r = .45$), and between decentralization and frequency of unscheduled interaction with persons in different departments at the same status level ($r = .53$) and at higher levels ($r = .51$). These and related results led the researchers to conclude, in support of their hypothesis, that "if power is dispersed in [an] organization, not only does volume of communication increase, but the flow of communications across departmental boundaries is also increased" (p. 869).

Hage (1974), in a later study of the same organizations investigated above, failed to find support for the notion that intensity of communication is negatively correlated with centralization. However, in this research he used a differrent measure of centralization the index of hierarchy of authority (essentially a measure of control over *work-related* decisions). Utilizing this index his analyses revealed only one significant correlation from among some 26 computed: a likely nonchance positive correlation between centralization and workers' frequency of unscheduled communication with their supervisors ($r = .52$). Thus the results of the two Hage studies suggest that relationships between centralization (participation in decision making) and frequency of communication may vary by decision type (i.e., work-related versus strategic).

With respect to strategic decisions, several studies report results supportive of the Hage et al. hypothesis that decentralization of strategic decision making is positively correlated with frequency of communication. In their study of government bureaus, Bacharach and Aiken (1977) found significant, positive correlations between decentralization and volume of (self-reported) oral upward, downward, lateral, and total communication of subordinates, and between decentralization and frequency of upward, lateral, and total communication of department heads. Moreover, when decentralization was entered into a regression analysis with several other variables (boundary spanning and routinization of work), it remained a significant predictor of subordinates' downward and total communication, and the upward communication of department heads. In turn, Rousseau's (1978) research also supports the notion of a positive relationship between decentralization of strategic decisions and communication. However, in contrast to the studies described above, Rousseau (1978) operationalized centralization as the extent to which the locus of authority to make strategic decisions is confined to the upper levels of a hierarchy (Pugh et al., 1968). Consistent with the findings of Hage and his associates, Rousseau (1978) discovered a negative relationship between centralization and respondents' perceptions of the amount of performance feedback they receive from superiors and coworkers (assessed via the Job Diagnostic Survey, Feedback from Agents scale; Hackman & Oldham, 1975).

A recent study by Krone (1985) represents the only research to date exploring relationships between centralization and communication characteristics other than volume/frequency of message sending and receiving. Utilizing measures of strategic and work-related participation in decision making (Hage, 1974), Krone classified respondents from five organizations into four centralization situations: (1) low work-related and low strategic decision-making authority, (2) low work-related but high strategic decision-making authority, (3) high work-related but low strategic decision-making authority, and (4) high work-related and high strategic decision-making authority. She then investigated the degree to which subordinates in each of these centralization situations used a variety of message strategies to influence their superiors' decision-making behavior. Among other findings, her analyses revealed that subordinates who perceived high amounts of strategic and work-related centralization were the least likely to use open persuasion (influence attempts that are open with respect to means and desired outcomes); conversely, subordinates who perceived low levels of both strategic and work-related centralization used open persuasion more frequently than did subordinates in the other situations.

To summarize, the studies reviewed in this section suggest that centralization of strategic decision making is negatively related to the volume of oral (albeit self-report) communication in organizations. In addition, evidence exists indicating that subordinates' message sending strategies may vary under different forms of centralization. Given the limited amount of research exploring centralization and communication, these conclusions should be viewed in a tentative manner. As Ouchi and Harris (1976) have observed, centralization "is by far the least understood of the major dimensions of structure" (p. 111).

In addition, it is important to recognize the associations that exist between centralization and other structural characteristics, and how these relationships may affect communication attitudes and behaviors. For example, there is considerable evidence that in certain types of organizations, centralization is negatively related to formalization and standardization (for review of this literature, see Jennergren, 1981). In other words, as some types of organizations become more decentralized they increase the use of standardized practies and formal modes and channels of communication. As Meyer (1972), Lammers (1978), and others have argued, managers often feel unsure about decentralizing decision-making and thus build control mechanisms into decision-making processes by creating high degrees of standarization and formalization. Since some of the research discussed earlier suggests that variations in formalization are associated with distinctive forms of communication, it is possible that communication processes in organizations are affected by the interaction of levels of centralization *and* formalization.

Future research should also more carefully explore the effects of physical decentralization on communication processes. As several studies conducted in Europe have shown, physical decentralization (e.g., physically distant regional offices) can have important effects on communication processes, including the frequency of face-to-face interactions, telephone usage, and the communication characteristics of meetings (e.g., Goddard, 1973; Goddard & Morris, 1976; Nilles, 1975; Pye, 1976; Thorngren, 1970). Obviously, these communication effects may be more pronounced in multinational organizations that are physically decentralized (Egelhoff, 1982; Herbert, 1984). Moreover, it should be recognized that organizations that are located at a single site may decentralize certain functions (e.g., production) and not others (e.g., finance). While such simultaneous variations in centralization may be cost efficient, they can create coordination/communication problems between functional groups. For example, Goldhaber, Yates, Porter, and Lesniak (1978) suggest that in situations where a production or service group is decentralized and staff or managerial functions are centralized, interactions between members of the two groups may be stressful and likely "have an impact on participants' willingness and ability to engage in such interactions" (p. 87).

Finally, the effect of new communication technologies on the degree to which organizations adopt centralized or decentralized structural designs requires investigation. This subject has already aroused considerable debate among researchers and theorists (see Culnan & Markus, Chapter 13, in this volume). For example, Whisler (1970a, 1970b) argues and presents evidence to support the notion that computerized information/communication systems enhance the decision-making capacity of upper-level managers and as a consequence result in increased levels of centralization. In contrast, some researchers argue that computerized information technologies promote decentralization (e.g., Blau, Falbe, McKinley, & Tracy, 1976; Pfeffer, 1978; Pfeffer & Leblebici, 1977), while still others maintain that information technologies can enhance centralization or decentralization depending on the nature of an organization's external environment (e.g., Hiltz & Turoff, 1978; Robey, 1977). Clearly, further research will be necessary before these contradictions can be resolved.

CONCLUSIONS

A number of conclusions about research exploring relationships between formal organization structure and communication can be extrapolated from the preceding review. *First*, it seems quite evident that studies exploring formal structure-communication relationships have focused on gathering perceptual and attitudinal self-report measures of communication behavior. Few studies have collected and analyzed *actual* oral and/or written messages. Moreover, most studies have examined a very narrow band of communication behaviors: frequency and volume of communication. Thus while we may be informed about the perceived quantity of communication associated with various dimensions of formal structure, we know little of other communication behaviors and attitudes associated with variations in these dimensions. In addition, our understanding of the manner in which structural dimensions affect message characteristics (e.g., message content, function, formality/informality, medium) is extremely limited. Hence, it is recommended that future studies focus on collecting both behavioral and attitudinal communication data, as well as broaden the features of communication phenomena investigated.

Second, the preceding review indicates that researchers have inadequately considered how the relationships between communication and the particular structure dimensions under examination may be affected by other organization structure characteristics. In other words, simple unidirectional relationships have typically been assumed between particular structure dimensions and communication variables. Ironically, such studies have been pursued despite a number of published admonitions against this practice (e.g., Berger & Cummings, 1979; Porter & Lawler, 1965). In sum, it seems clear that marked increases in our understanding of formal structure-communication relationships will not occur until researchers explore *sets* of conceptually relevant structural characteristics in interaction with one another rather than in isolation. Research along these lines might profit from a thorough analysis of the various structure relationships posited by early organization theorists (e.g., Barnard, 1938; Weber, 1922/1947), whose theoretical propositions with respect to communication and formal structure remain to be adequately tested. Concomitantly, research exploring the *effectiveness* of various communication processes in frequently identified structural gestalts is required (e.g., the structural forms identified by Mintzberg, 1979). However, it seems clear that such studies must either control for or directly consider the effects of other organizational variables, and in particular external environments, when examining structure-communication relationships (e.g., Burns & Stalker, 1961; Lawrence & Lorsch, 1967).

Third, it is apparent from this literature review that some structural dimensions may have stronger relationships with communication behavior and attitudes than do other dimensions. In particular, the structural dimensions of formalization, centralization, and complexity may account for more variability in communication than do other dimensions because they represent practices that directly influence behavior (consequently, they are sometimes referred to as "structuring" properties of organizations; Campbell, Brownas, Peterson, & Dunnette, 1974). Other structural dimensions discussed in this review represent physical attributes of an organization's structure. The effects of these attributes on communication may be conspicuous only after a particular characteristic has exceeded an unknown threshold. The following example suggested by Dalton et al. (1980) lucidly explicates this notion: "Presumably, the difference between a room of 2000 vs 2400 square feet would not substantially affect the behavior of its occupants; however, individuals who work in an 800 square-foot room may behave quite differently in a 4800 square-foot room" (p. 61). Determination of the thresholds at which various structural dimensions begin to measurably effect communication behavior and attitudes represents a potentially important focus for future research. Studies investigating this issue might also consider the manner in which other physical attributes of organizations, including architectural design, open versus closed office systems, physical/symbolic artifacts, and the like, affect communication processes (e.g., Davis, 1984; Morrow & McElroy, 1981; Oldham & Brass, 1979; Steele, 1973).

Fourth, an examination of available studies suggests that researchers have tended to explore formal structure-communication relationships more frequently in service and government-related organizations than in manufacturing and industrial concerns. In addition, data have more frequently been collected from managers and professionals than from nonprofessional and blue-collar workers (Dalton et al., 1980). The extent to which existing research findings generalize to different types of organizations and accurately reflect the communication-related experiences and attitudes of broader occupational samples remains to be tested.

Fifth, even a cursory examination of the literature reviewed in this chapter indicates a paucity of longitudinal research on formal structure-communication relationships. Most studies have utilized cross-sectional research designs. As a consequence, few claims can be made concerning issues of causality in structure-communication relationships. In addition, the stability of associations between structure and communication across time has been infrequently investigated. Recent empirical and theoretical research depicting the characteristics of organizations across their life cycles, including changes in their formal structures and communication priorities, represents an important exception to this trend (e.g., Gray & Ariss, 1985; Kimberly & Miles, 1980; Miller & Friesen, 1983, 1984; Mintzberg, 1984; Smith, Mitchell, & Summer, 1985).

The theoretical literature on organizational life cycles suggests that "organizations progress through an orderly succession of stages as they grow, age, and change their strategies" (Miller & Friesen, 1983, p. 339). Most empirical studies indicate, however, that while life cycle phases are identifiable as well as internally coherent and different from one another, all organizations do *not* necessarily progress through the same pattern of phases (e.g., in one organization "maturity" may be followed by "growth," while in another organization it may be followed by "decline"). As Miller and Friesen (1984) conclude from the results of their research, "While the life cycle pattern is roughly borne out, it merely represents a very rough central tendency rather than an evolutionary imperative" (p. 1176).

Since the empirical study of organizational life cycles is still in its formative stages, most published investigations suffer from methodological limitations (e.g., many are retrospective analyses of organizations and tend to focus on large, successful "survivor" organizations). However, these studies do provide initial insights into potential differences in formal organization structures and communication processes across phases of an organization's development. Thus, for example, Miller and Friesen (1984) report that as organizations in their sample moved through five different life cycle stages (birth, growth, maturity, revival, and decline), openness and fidelity of internal communication increased from birth to growth, remained fairly stable between growth and maturity, increased markedly in the revival period, and decreased significantly in the decline phase. At the same time, their analyses showed that centralization of strategic decision making and organizational differentiation both increased from birth through the revival phase, then decreased in the decline phase. While the generalizability of Miller and Friesen's (1984) results are questionable due to various methodological limitations, they do illustrate an important point: Formal organization structure and related communication processes may vary over time. In fact, these variations over time may represent another explanation for the numerous contradictory findings evident in the studies reviewed earlier in this chapter. Consequently, it is imperative that future studies of formal structure-communication relationships attempt to utilize longitudinal research designs and specify the life cycle stages of the organizations being studied.

To summarize, although for the greater part of the twentieth century theorists have advanced hypotheses concerning the nature of formal organization structure and its relationship to various communication behaviors and activities, relatively little research has actually been conducted exploring this relationship. Regrettably, for some formal structure-communication relationships (e.g., formalization) our knowledge rests on as few as two or three investigations. Generally speaking, researchers have rarely collected behavioral communication data when exploring structure-communication relationships. Moreover, in some studies communication behaviors and attitudes are never observed or measured but are postulated to occur in certain forms, and these "assumed" forms of communication are used as explanations for other research findings (e.g., Blau, Heydebrand, & Stauffer, 1966). While it may not be currently in vogue to study formal structure-communication relationships, it is clear that such research is sorely needed. Either we should study these issues empirically or stop making assumptions about them.

In conclusion, although the preceding discussion has focused on reviewing research and issues associated with formal organization structure and communication, it is essential to recognize that the relationship between formal organization structures and emergent "network structures is complex and reciprocal" (Lincoln, 1982, p. 16). In other words, there is an interdependence between formal organization structure and emergent structure (e.g., McPhee, 1985). Hence, structure is conceived of "as a complex medium of control which is continually produced and recreated in interaction and yet shapes that interaction: structures are constituted and constitutive" (Ranson, Hinings, & Greenwood, 1980, p. 3). The specific manner in which emergent network structure and formal organization structure are interrelated and, in turn, shape and are shaped by communication processes represents an exciting though formidable area of research.

REFERENCES

Aldrich, H. E. (1972). Technology and organizational structure: A reexamination of the findings of the Aston group. *Administrative Science Quarterly, 17,* 26-43.

Aldrich, H. E. (1979). *Organizations and environments.* Englewood Cliffs, NJ: Prentice-Hall.

Astley, W. G., & Van de Ven, A. H. (1983). Central perspectives and debates in organization theory. *Administrative Science Quarterly, 28,* 245-273.

Bacharach. S. B., & Aiken, M. (1977). Communication in administrative bureaucracies. *Academy of Management Journal, 20,* 356-377.

Bales, R. F. (1950). *Interaction process analysis: Method for the study of small groups.* Reading, MA: Addison-Wesley.

Barnard, C. I. (1938). *The functions of the executive.* Cambridge, MA: Harvard University Press.

Bass, B. M. (1960). *Leadership, psychology and organizational behavior.* New York: Harper & Row.

Bedeian, A. G. (1984). *Organizations: Theory and analysis* (rev. ed.). Hinsdale, IL: Dryden Press.

Bedeian, A. G. (in press). Organization theory: Current controversies, issues, and directions. In C. L. Cooper & I. Robertson (Eds.), *International review of industrial and organizational psychology* (Vol. 2). London: John Wiley.

Bell, G. D. (1967). Determinants of span of control. *American Journal of Sociology, 73,* 100-109.

Berger, C. J., & Cummings, L. L. (1979). Organizational structure, attitudes, and behaviors. In B. M. Staw (Ed.), *Research in organizational behavior* (Vol. 1, pp. 169-208). Greenwich, CT: JAI Press.

Blackburn, R. S. (1982). Dimensions of structure: A review and reappraisal. *Academy of Management Review, 7,* 59-66.

Blankenship, L. V., & Miles, R. E. (1986). Organizational structure and managerial decision behavior. *Administrative Science Quarterly, 13,* 106-120.

Blau, P. M. (1970). A formal theory of differentiation in organizations. *American Sociological Review, 35,* 201-218.

Blau, P. M., Falbe, C. M., McKinley, W., & Tracy, P. K. (1976). Technology and organization in manufacturing. *Administrative Science Quarterly, 21,* 20-40.

Blau, P. M., Heydebrand, W. V., & Stauffer, R. E. (1966). The structure of small bureaucracies. *American Sociological Review, 31,* 179-191.

Blau, P. M., & Schoenherr, R. A. (1971). *The structure of organizations.* New York: Basic Books.

Brewer, J. (1971). Flow of communications, expert qualifications and organizational authority structure. *American Sociological Review, 36,* 475-484.

Brinkerhoff, M. B. (1972). Hierarchical status, contingencies, and the administrative staff conference. *Administrative Science Quarterly, 17,* 395-407.

Burns, T. (1954). The direction of activity and communication in a departmental executive group: A quantitative study in a British engineering factory with a self-recording technique. *Human Relations, 7,* 73-97.

Burns, T., & Stalker, G. M. (1961). *The management of innovation.* London: Tavistock.

Campbell, H. (1952). Group incentive payment schemes: The effects of lack of understanding and of group size. *Occupational Psychology, 26,* 15-21.

Campbell, J. P., Brownas, D. A., Peterson, N. G., & Dunnette, M. D. (1974). *The measurement of organizational effectiveness: A review of the relevant research and opinion* (Report Tr-71-1, Final Technical Report). San Diego, CA: Navy Personnel Research and Development Center.

Chandler, A. D., Jr. (1962). *Strategy and structure.* Cambridge: MIT Press.

Child, J. (1972). Organizational structure, environment and performance: The role of strategic choice. *Sociology, 6,* 1-22.

Child, J. (1973). Predicting and understanding organization structure. *Administrative Science Quarterly, 18,* 168-185.

Daft, R. L., & Lengel, R. H. (1984). Information richness: A new approach to managerial behavior and organization design. In B. M. Staw & L. L. Cummings (Eds.), *Research in organizational behavior* (Vol. 6, pp. 193-233). Greenwich, CT: JAI Press.

Dalton, D. R., Todor, W. D., Spendolini, M. J., Fielding, G. J., & Porter, L. W. (1980). Organization structure and performance: A critical review. *Academy of Management Review, 5,* 49-64.

Davis, K. (1953). Management communication and the grapevine. *Harvard Business Review, 31*(5), 43-49.

Davis, K. (1968). Success of chain-of-command oral communication in a manufacturing group. *Academy of Management Journal, 11,* 379-387.

Davis, T. R. (1984). The influence of the physical environment in offices. *Academy of Managment Review, 9,* 271-283.

Dewar, R. D., & Simet, D. P. (1981). A level specific prediction of spans of control examining the effects of size, technology, and specialization. *Academy of Management Journal, 24,* 5-24.

Drazin, R., & Van de Ven, A. H. (1985). Alternative forms of fit in contingency theory. *Administrative Science Quarterly, 30*, 514-539.

Dubin, R. (1962). Business behavior *behaviorally* viewed. In G. B. Strother (Ed.), *Social science approaches to business behavior* (pp. 11-56). Homewood, IL: Dorsey Press.

Dubin, R., & Spray, S. (1964). Executive behavior and interaction. *Industrial Relations, 3*, 99-108.

Egelhoff, W. G. (1982). Strategy and structure in multinational corporations: An information-processing approach. *Administrative Science Quarterly, 27*, 435-458.

Erez, M., & Rim, Y. (1982). The relationships between goals, influence tactics, and personal and organizational variables. *Human Relations, 35*, 871-878.

Fayol, H. (1949). *General and industrial management* (C. Storrs, Trans.). London: Pitman. (Original work published 1916)

Follert, V. F. (1982). Supervisor accessibility and subordinate role clarity. *Journal of Applied Communication Research, 10*, 133-147.

Ford, J. D. (1979). Institutional versus questionnaire measures of organizational structure: A reexamination. *Academy of Management Journal, 22*, 601-610.

Galbraith, J. K. (1973). *Designing complex organizations*. Reading, MA: Addison-Wesley.

Gerwin, D. (1981). Relationships between structure and technology. In P. C. Nystrom & W. H. Starbuck (Eds.), *Handbook of organizational design* (Vol. 2, pp. 3-38). London: Oxford University Press.

Ghiselli, E. E., & Siegel, J. (1972). Leadership and managerial success in tall and flat organization structures. *Personnel Psychology, 25*, 617-624.

Giddens, A. (1981). *A contemporary critique of historical materialism*. Berkeley: University of California Press.

Giddens, A. (1983). *Profiles and critiques in social theory*. Berkeley: University of California Press.

Goddard, J. B. (1973). Office linkages and location: A study of communications and spatial patterns in central London. *Progress in Planning, 1*(Pt. 2), 111-232.

Goddard, J. B., & Morris, D. (1976). The communications factor in office decentralization. *Progress in Planning, 6*(Pt. 1), 1-80.

Goldhaber, G. M., Yates, M. P., Porter, D. T., & Lesniak, R. (1978). Organizational communication: 1978. *Human Communication Research, 5*, 76-96.

Graicunas, V. A. (1937). Relationship in organization. In L. Gulick & L. F. Urwick (Eds.), *Papers on the science of administration* (pp. 183-187). New York: Institute of Public Administration, Columbia University.

Gray, B., & Ariss, S. S. (1985). Politics and strategic change across organizational life cycles. *Academy of Management Review, 10*, 707-723.

Green, S. G., Blank, W., & Liden, R. C. (1983). Market and organizational influences on bank employees' work attitudes and behaviors. *Journal of Applied Psychology, 68*, 298-306.

Grinyer, P. H., & Yasai-Ardekani, M. (1980). Dimensions of organizational structure: A critical replication. *Academy of Management Journal, 23*, 405-421.

Hackman, J. R., & Oldham, G. R. (1975). Development of the job diagnostic survey. *Journal of Applied Psychology, 60*, 159-170.

Hage, J. (1965). An axiomatic theory of organizations. *Administrative Science Quarterly, 10*, 289-320.

Hage, J. (1974). *Communication and organizational control: Cybernetics in health and welfare settings*. New York: John Wiley.

Hage, J. (1980). *Theories of organizations: Form, processes, and transformation*. New York: John Wiley.

Hage, J., Aiken, M., & Marrett, C. B. (1971). Organization structure and communications. *American Sociological Review, 36*, 860-871.

Hall, R. H., Hass, J. E., & Johnson, N. J. (1967). Organizational size, complexity and formalization. *American Sociological Review, 32*, 903-912.

Hannaway, J. (1985). Managerial behavior, uncertainty and hierarchy: A prelude to synthesis. *Human Relations, 38*, 1085-1100.

Hare, A. P. (1976). *Handbook of small group research* (2nd ed.). New York: Free Press.

Heinen, J. S., & Jacobson, E. (1976). A model of task group development in complex organizations and a strategy of implementation. *Academy of Management Review, 1*(4), 98-111.

Herbert, T. T. (1984). Strategy and multinational organization structure: An interorganizational relationships perspective. *Academy of Management Review, 9*, 259-271.

Hickson, D. J., Pugh, D. S., & Pheysey, D. C. (1969). Operations technology and organization structure: An empirical reappraisal. *Administrative Science Quarterly, 14*, 378-397.

Hilton, G. (1972). Causal inference analysis: A seductive process. *Administrative Science Quarterly, 17*, 44-54.

Hiltz, S. R., & Turoff, M. (1978). *The network nation.* Reading, MA; Addison-Wesley.

Hinrichs, J. R. (1964). Communication activity of industrial research personnel. *Personnel Psychology, 17*, 193-204.

House, R. J., & Miner, J. B. (1969). Merging management and behavior theory: The interaction between span of control and group size. *Administrative Science Quarterly, 14*, 451-464.

Hrebiniak, L. G., & Joyce, W. F. (1985). Organizational adaptation: Strategic choice and environmental determinism. *Administrative Science Quarterly, 30*, 336-349.

Indik, B. P. (1965). Organization size and member participation. *Human Relations, 18*, 339-349.

Ingham, G. K. (1970). *Size of industrial organization and worker behavior.* Cambridge: Cambridge University Press.

Jablin, F. M. (1980). Organizational communication theory and research: An overview of communication climate and network research. In D. Nimmo (Ed.), *Communication yearbook 4* (pp. 327-347). New Brunswick, NJ: Transaction Press.

Jablin, F. M. (1982). Formal structural characteristics of organizations and superior-subordinate communication. *Human Communication Research, 8*, 338-347.

Jablin, F. M., & Sussman, L. (1983). Organizational group communication: A review of the literature and model of the process. In H. H. Greenbaum, R. L. Falcione, & S. A. Hellweg (Eds.), *Organizational communication: Abstracts, analysis and overview* (Vol. 8, pp. 11-50). Newbury Park, CA: Sage.

Jago, A. G., & Vroom, V. H. (1977). Hierarchical level and leadership style. *Organizational Behavior and Human Performance, 18*, 131-145.

James, L. R., & Jones, A. P. (1976). Organizational structure: A review of structural dimensions and their conceptual relationships with individual attitudes and behavior. *Organizational Behavior and Human Performance, 16*, 74-113.

Jennergren, L. P. (1981). Decentralization in organizations. In P. C. Nystrom & W. H. Starbuck (Eds.), *Handbook of organizational design* (Vol. 2, pp. 39-59). London: Oxford University Press.

Kasarda, J. D. (1974). The structural implications of social system size: A three-level analysis. *American Sociological Review, 39*, 19-28.

Khandwalla, P. N. (1973). Viable and effective organizational design of firms. *Academy of Management Journal, 16*, 481-495.

Khandwalla, P. N. (1977). *The design of organizations.* New York: Harcourt Brace Jovanovich.

Kimberly, J. R. (1976). Organizational size and the structuralist perspective: A review, critique, and proposal. *Administrative Science Quarterly, 21*, 571-597.

Kimberly, J. R., & Miles, R. H. (1980). *The organizational life cycle.* San Francisco: Jossey-Bass.

Kipnis, D., Schmidt, S. M., & Wilkinson, I. (1980). Intraorganizational influence tactics: Explorations in getting one's way. *Journal of Applied Psychology, 65*, 440-452.

Klauss, R., & Bass, B. M. (1982). *Interpersonal communication in organizations.* New York: Academic Press.

Krone, K. J. (1985). *Subordinate influence in organizations: The differential use of upward influence messages in decision making contexts.* Unpublished doctoral dissertation, University of Texas at Austin.

Lammers, C. J. (1978). The comparative sociology of organizations. In R. H. Turner, J. Coleman, & R. C. Fox (Eds.), *Annual Review of Sociology* (Vol. 4, pp. 485-510). Palo Alto, CA: Annual Reviews.

Lawrence, P., & Lorsch, J. (1967). *Organization and environment: Managing differentiation and integration.* Boston: Division of Research, Graduate School of Business, Harvard University.

Lincoln, J. R. (1982). Intra- (and inter-) organizational networks. In S. B. Bacharach (Ed.), *Research in the sociology of organizations* (Vol. 1, pp. 1-38). Greenwich, CT: JAI Press.

Mahoney, T. A., Frost, P., Crandall, N. F., & Weitzel, W. (1972). The conditioning influence of organization size upon managerial practice. *Organizational Behavior and Human Performance, 8*, 230-241.

March, J., & Simon, H. (1958). *Organizations.* New York: John Wiley.

Martin, N. H. (1959). The levels of management and their mental demands. In W.L. Warner & N. H. Martin (Eds.), *Industrial man* (pp. 276-294). New York: Harper.

Marting, B. J. (1969) A study of grapevine communication patterns in a manufacturing organization. *Academy of Management Journal, 12*, 385-386.

McCann, J., & Galbraith, J. R. (1981). Interdepartmental relations. In P. C. Nystrom & W. H. Starbuck (Eds.), *Handbook of organizational design* (Vol. 2, pp. 60-84). London: Oxford University Press.

McPhee, R. D. (1985). Formal structure and organizational communication. In R. D. McPhee & P. K. Tompkins (Eds.), *Organizational communication: Traditional themes and new directions* (pp. 149-178). Newbury Park, CA: Sage.

Meyer, M. W. (1968). Expertness and span of control. *American Sociological Review, 33*, 944-951.

Meyer, M. W. (1972). *Bureaucratic structure and authority.* New York: Harper & Row.

Miles, R. H. (1980). *Macro organizational behavior.* Santa Monica, CA: Goodyear.

Miller, D., & Friesen, P. H. (1983). Successful and unsuccessful phases of the corporate life cycle. *Organization Studies, 4*, 339-356.

Miller, D., & Friesen, P. H. (1984). A longitudinal study of the corporate life cycle. *Management Science, 30*, 1161-1183.

Mintzberg, H. (1979). *The structuring of organizations: A synthesis of research.* Englewood Cliffs, NJ: Prentice-Hall.

Mintzberg, H. (1984). Power and organization life cycles. *Academy of Management Review, 9*, 207-224.

Monge, P. R., Edwards, J. A., & Kirste, K. K. (1978). The determinants of communication and communication structure in large organizations: A review of research. In B. D. Ruben (Ed.), *Communication yearbook 2* (pp. 311-331). New Brunswick, NJ: Transaction Press.

Morris, W. T. (1968). *Decentralization in management systems.* Columbus: Ohio State University Press.

Morrow, P. C., & McElroy, J. C. (1981). Interior office design and visitor response: A constructive replication. *Journal of Applied Psychology, 66*, 646-650.

Morse, J. J., & Lorsch, J. W. (1970). Beyond theory Y. *Harvard Business Review, 48*(3), 61-68.

Mossholder, K. W., & Bedeian, A. G. (1983). Cross-level inference and organizational research: Perspectives on interpretation and application. *Academy of Management Review, 8*, 547-558.

Nilles, J. M. (1975). Telecommunications and organizational decentralization. *IEEE Transactions on Communication, 23*, 1142-1147.

Oldham, G. R., & Brass, D. J. (1979). Employees' reactions to an open-plan office: A naturally occurring quasi-experiment. *Administrative Science Quarterly, 24*, 267-284.

O'Reilly, C. A., & Roberts, K. H. (1977). Task group structure, communication, and effectiveness in three organizations. *Journal of Applied Psychology, 62*, 647-681.

Ouchi, W. G., & Dowling, H. B. (1974). Defining the span of control. *Administrative Science Quarterly, 19*, 357-365.

Ouchi, W. G., & Harris, R. T. (1976). Structure, technology and environment. In G. Strauss, R. E. Miles, C. C. Snow, & A. S. Tannenbaum (Eds.), *Organizational behavior: Research and issues* (pp. 107-140). Belmont, CA: Wadsworth.

Penley, L. E. (1982). An investigation of the information processing framework of organizational communication. *Human Communication Research, 8*, 348-365.

Pennings, J. M. (1973). Measures of organizational structure: A methodological note. *American Journal of Sociology, 79*, 686-704.

Pfeffer, J. (1978). *Organization design.* Arlington Heights, IL: AHM.

Pfeffer, J. (1986). Organizations and organization theory. In G. Lindzey & E. Aronson (Eds.), *Handbook of social psychology* (3rd.; Vol. 1; pp. 379-440). New York: Random House.

Pfeffer, J., & Leblebici, H. (1977). Information technology and organization structure. *Pacific Sociological Review, 20*, 241-261.

Poole, M. S., & McPhee, R. D. (1983). A structuration theory of organizational climate. In L. L. Putnam & M. Pacanowsky (Eds.), *Organizational communication: An interpretive approach* (pp. 195-219). Newbury Park, CA: Sage.

Porter, L. W., & Lawler, E. E., III (1965). Properties of organization structure in relation to job attitudes and job behavior. *Psychological Bulletin, 64*, 23-51.

Porter, L. W., & Roberts, K. H. (1976). Communication in organizations. In M. Dunnette (Ed.), *Handbook of industrial and organizational psychology* (pp. 1553-1589). Chicago: Rand McNally.

Powers, D. J., & Huber, G. P. (1982). Guidelines for using key informants and retrospective reports in strategic management research. *Proceedings of the American Institute for Decision Science, 2*, 29-31.

Pugh, D. S., Hickson, D. J., Hinings, C. R., & Turner, C. (1968). Dimensions of organization structure. *Administrative Science Quarterly, 13*, 65-105.

Putnam, L. L., & Sorenson, R. (1982). Equivocal messages in organizations. *Human Communication Research, 8*, 114-132.

Pye, R. (1976). Effect of telecommunications on the location of office employment. *OMEGA, 4*, 289-300.

Ranson, S., Hinings, B., & Greenwood, R. (1980). The structuring of organizational structures. *Administrative Science Quarterly, 25*, 1-17.

Redding, W. C. (1972). *Communication within the organization: An interpretive review of theory and research.* New York: Industrial Communication Council.

Robey, D. (1977). Computers and management structure: Some empirical findings re-examined. *Human Relations, 30*, 963-976.

Rousseau, D. M. (1978). Characteristics of departments, positions, and individuals: Contexts for attitudes and behaviors. *Administrative Science Quarterly, 23*, 521-540.

Sathe, V. J. (1978). Institutional versus questionnaire measures of organizational structure. *Academy of Management Journal, 21*, 227-238.

Shartle, C. L. (1956). *Executive performance and leadership.* Englewood Cliffs, NJ: Prentice-Hall.

Shaw, M. E. (1981). *Group dynamics: The psychology of small group behavior* (3rd ed.). New York: McGraw-Hill.

Simon, H. A., Guetzkow, H., Kozmetsky, G., & Tyndall, G. (1954). *Centralization vs. decentralization in organizing the controller's department.* New York: Controllership Foundation.

Smith, K. G., Mitchell, T. R., & Summer, C. E. (1985). Top level management priorities in different stages of the organizational life cycle. *Academy of Management Journal, 28*, 799-820.

Snyder, R. A., & Morris, J. H. (1984). Organizational communication and performance. *Journal of Applied Psychology, 69*, 461-465.

Spiker, B. K., & Daniels, T. D. (1981). Information adequacy and communication relationships: An empirical examination of 18 organizations. *Western Journal of Speech Communications, 45*, 342-354.

Sproull, L., & Kiesler, S. (1986). Reducing social context cues: Electronic mail in organizational communication. *Management Science, 32*, 1492-1512.

Steele, F. I. (1973). *Physical settings and organization development.* Reading, MA: Addison-Wesley.

Sutton, H., & Porter, L. W. (1968). A study of the grapevine in a governmental organization. *Personnel Psychology, 21*, 223-230.

Thomason, G. F. (1966). Managerial work roles and relationships. *Journal of Management Studies, 3*, 270-284.

Thomason, G. F. (1967). Managerial work roles and relationships, part II. *Journal of Management Studies, 4*, 17-30.

Thompson, J. D. (1967). *Organizations in action.* New York: McGraw-Hill.

Thorngren, B. (1970). How do contact systems affect regional involvement? *Environment and Planning, 2*, 409-427.

Udell, J. G. (1967). An empirical test of hypotheses relating to span of control. *Administrative Science Quarterly, 12*, 420-439.

Van de Ven, A. H., Delbecq, A. L., & Koenig, R. (1976). Determination of coordination modes within organizations. *American Sociological Review, 41*, 322-338.

Van Fleet, D. D. (1983). Span of management research and issues. *Academy of Management Journal, 26*, 546-552.

Van Fleet, D. D., & Bedeian, A. G. (1977). A history of the span of management. *Academy of Management Review, 2*, 356-372.

Wager, L. W., & Brinkerhoff, M. (1975). Conferences in context: Status, communication, and evaluation. *Sociometry, 38*, 32-61.

Walker, A. H., & Lorsch, J. W. (1968). Organizational choice: Product vs. function. *Harvard Business Review, 46*(6), 129-138.

Walton, E. J. (1981). The comparison of measures of organization structure. *Academy of Management Review, 6*, 155-160.

Wanous, J. P., Reichers, A. E., & Malik, S. D. (1984). Organizational socialization and group development. *Academy of Management Review, 9*, 670-683.

Watzlavick, P., Beavin, J., & Jackson, D. (1967). *Pragmatics of human communication.* New York: Norton.

Weber, M. (1947). *The theory of social and economic organization.* New York: Free Press. (Original work published 1922)

Whisler, T. L. (1970a). *Information technology and organizational change.* Belmont, CA: Wadsworth.

Whisler, T. L. (1970b). *The impact of computers on organizations.* New York: Prager.

Wickesberg, A. K. (1968). Communication networks in the business organization structure. *Academy of Management Journal, 11*, 253-262.

Woodward, J. (1965). *Industrial organization: Theory and practice.* London: Oxford University Press.

Yasai-Ardekani, M. (1986). Structural adaptations to environments. *Academy of Management Review, 11*, 7-21.

Zey-Ferrell, M. (1979). *Dimensions of organizations: Environment, context, structure, process, and performance.* Santa Monica, CA: Goodyear.

13 Information Technologies

MARY J. CULNAN
American University

M. LYNNE MARKUS
University of California, Los Angeles

THE development of new communication media, such as voice messaging, electronic mail, and teleconferencing, has been stimulated by technological advances in digital information technology. Familiar communication technologies such as the telephone, the telegraph, photography, and printing represent sounds, symbols, and images in analog form. Digital representation of the units of communication considerably enhances their storage, processing, and transmission in space and time. Consequently, the older analog and newer digital technologies are converging, resulting in new electronic communication media that resemble familiar ones but with qualitatively different capabilities. This chapter reviews the conceptual arguments and empirical research that provide a basis for assessing the effects of electronic media on intraorganizational communication.

Proponents of the new electronic media claim that these technologies make communication more efficient, thereby increasing the productivity of the

AUTHORS' NOTE: We acknowledge the helpful comments of Ronald E. Rice on an earlier version of this chapter.

organizations that adopt them and the individuals who use them. For example, electronic media are said to reduce the necessity for and difficulty of transforming a communication from one medium to another (e.g., dictation to typed text) and the nonproductive microactivities (called "shadow functions"; e.g., redialing a busy telephone number) that often impede the completion of communication activities. Further, electronic media are said to reduce the constraints imposed by geographic location and temporal availability (Culnan & Bair, 1983; Rice & Bair, 1984; Uhlig, Farber, & Bair, 1979).

History suggests that the new media may ultimately exert as profound an influence on organizations as traditional media did when they were introduced; some of these effects may be predictable from historical data on the use of older technologies (Carey, 1982). Chandler (1977) for example, argues that the ability of telegraph to facilitate coordination enabled the emergence of the large, centralized railroad firms that became the prototype of the modern industrial organization. Pool (1983) credits the telephone with the now traditional physical separation of management headquarters from field operations, and in particular with the development of the modern office skyscraper as the locus of administrative business activity. The telephone is also believed responsible for the near demise of the formerly substantial occupational category of office boy or messenger: Their functions of physical message delivery were replaced by the transcription activities of switchboard operators and secretaries (Pool, 1983). Rotella (1981a, 1981b) argues that the typewriter and other office equipment created a division of labor in secretarial work that, among other things, allowed women to enter the clerical work force in large numbers. Yates (1982; Markus & Yates, 1982) asserts that the invention of the vertical filing cabinet in the late 1800s led to the development of the now institutionalized interoffice memorandum as well as to the creation of new administrative structures such as the centralized filing department.

Organizational information processing theory also provides a basis for suggesting that the new media will have a major effect on organizations (Galbraith, 1973; Tushman & Nadler, 1978). Organizations use communication activities to make sense of their environments, to coordinate and control internal activities, and to make decisions (O'Reilly & Pondy, 1979). The introduction of new technologies that alter these communication activities has the potential to influence key aspects of organizational structure and process.

Furthermore, communication activities account for a significant portion of the time of individual white-collar workers. For example, in a sample of top executives, Mintzberg (1973) found that 75% of their time was spent in communication-related activities. Mintzberg's findings are consistent with other studies of managerial use of time (e.g., Engel, Groppuso, Lowenstein, & Traub, 1979; Kotter, 1982; Poppel, 1982; Rice & Bair, 1984). Given the pervasiveness of organizational communication, the effect of the new media on organizational communication is potentially significant (Bair, 1979; Culnan & Bair, 1983; Tapscott, 1982).

The purpose of this chapter is to examine the evidence and theoretical arguments relevant to the potential effects of electronic media on intraorganizational communication. While we realize that the new media have important potential implications for mass communication and extraorganizational communication (e.g., Carey, 1982; Rice, 1984c), this chapter will focus entirely on electronic communication technology used to support communication within organizations.

The plan for the chapter is as follows: We first define electronic media and give brief descriptions of some common instances of this technology as it is currently employed in organizational communication. We then review studies of media effects. The majority of these studies focus on individual, rather than organizational, processes and attributes. Although there is a reasonable degree of convergence in the cumulative findings of these studies, a number of issues arise in the attempt to apply them at the organizational level of analysis. We explore these problems and the available empirical work that addresses them. We conclude with an agenda for future research.

The Electronic Media

We define electronic media as interactive, computer-mediated technologies that facilitate two-way interpersonal communication among several individuals or groups. An electronic medium may facilitate communication via written text, recorded or synthesized voice messages, graphical representation of communicators and/or data, or moving images of the communicators and/or message content. Generally, the people who communicate via these new media are geographically dispersed in at least two different locations, which may be next door or on different continents; the media may connect people in several hundreds of physical locations. Two-way interaction via an electronic medium may occur at the same time (synchronously) as in a telephone call, or at different times (asynchronously) as in writing and answering a mailed letter.

Many of the electronic media resemble familiar technologies such as the telephone and the typewriter. However, the convergence of digital with analog technology has endowed the new media with significantly different capabilities. For example, one of the new electronic media is computer conferencing. In this technology, people may participate in a "meeting" at any time of the day or night from any place in which they have access to a computer terminal. A complete written transcript of their public deliberations is maintained online for consultation at any time. In many computer conferencing systems, participants may also send private messages to individuals and subgroups at any point throughout the duration of the conference, which, unlike face-to-face meetings, may last months or even years.

The electronic media that are the focus of this chapter may be categorized into three general types: electronic message systems, conferencing systems, and integrated office systems. Some key instances and attributes of each type are summarized in Table 13.1. For more detailed descriptions of the technical features and characteristics of these systems, the reader is referred to Rice and Associates (1984) or Hirschheim (1985).

Although many people have noted the important communicative role played by data-oriented management information and decision support systems (Huber, 1984), we explicitly exclude from our focus here those systems in which the processing of information content outweighs the mediation of interpersonal and group communication. Our framework, then, excludes (1) information technologies that are primarily oriented to data processing; (2) office automation technologies, such as "standalone" personal computing for word processing, that do not primarily support intraorganizational communication (see, for example, Bikson & Gutek, 1983); and (3) information systems and electronic media that are used primarily for *inter*organizational communication (Hiltz, 1984; Markus, 1984).

Two Perspectives on Electronic Media

We turn now to the research on the effects of the electronic media. The majority of this research has been conducted in controlled laboratory settings. The studies in this tradition assume that (1) communication mediated by technology filters out communicative cues found in face-to-face interaction, (2) different media filter out or transmit different cues, and (3) substituting technology-mediated for face-to-face communication will result in predictable changes in intrapersonal and interpersonal variables.

While these studies have yielded some replicable results and valuable insights into the nature of media use, their underlying assumptions limit their generalizability to the organizational level of analysis. For example, while it is certainly true that face-to-face interaction has many qualities that mediated communication lacks, it is also true that the new electronic media have capabilities and functions not found in face-to-face communication. Research studies that start from the assumption that electronic media have new capabilities are comparatively rare and are not, in general, as carefully crafted theoretically and methodologically. In several respects, they simply are not comparable to the bulk of the literature on media effects, but they address a large void in it. The next section of this chapter reviews studies that assume that the electronic media filter out important communicative cues. The following sections examine reasons for believing that electronic media possess important new capabilities and review the related field research.

CUES FILTERED OUT

A novice user of teleconferencing or messaging technologies becomes aware almost immediately that these new media screen out or diminish sources of information present in face-to-face communication. These sources

TABLE 13.1

Features of Various Electronic Media

Type of Media	Brief Description	Type of Communication Supported	Timing and Geography	Typical Features
Messaging Systems				
(1) Voice messaging	Augmentation for telephone communication Ability to leave and retrieve voice of synthesized voice messages	One-to-one One-to-many	Asynchronous Time independent Geographic distribution	Message forwarding Distribution lists Message storage and retrieval Message editing
(2) Electronic messaging (EMS)	Substitution for telephone or face-to-face User creates a written document using a computer terminal or the equivalent	One-to-one One-to-many	Asynchronous Time independent Geographic distribution	Message creation and editing User receives messages in an electronic in-basket; messages may be answered, filed and/or discarded Message storage and retrieval Distribution lists Message forwarding
Conferencing Systems				
(1) Audio and audiographic	Similar to telephone conference call Participants cannot see each other May have visual aids Substitution for face-to-face meeting, travel	Group	Synchronous Geographic distribution	Ability to transmit graphic materials accompanying a meeting

	Description	Participants	Characteristics	Features
(2) Video	Substitution for face-to-face meeting, travel Transmits voice and images of participants Can be one-way or two-way	Group	Synchronous Geographic distribution One-way in multiple locations Two-way in two locations only	Images of speaker and images of other participants displayed simultaneously Graphical materials also displayed
(3) Computer	Substitution for face-to-face meeting, travel Meetings conducted using text (no audio, no video)	Group One-to-one	Synchronous or Asynchronous Time independent Geographic distribution	Text editing, storage and retrieval Transcript of proceedings maintained Ability for private communication among participants Ability to poll conference participants and collect results of a vote Bulletin boards Preparation and editing of shared documents
Integrated Systems	Substitution for telephone or face-to-face Augmentation of traditional written communication Provides support for messaging, word processing, data processing, and administrative activities using a single interface	One-to-one One-to-many	Asynchronous Time independent Geographic distribution	Same features as electronic messaging Ability to create, edit, store and retrieve, and transmit formal documents Electronic calendars and scheduling Ability to retrieve shared documents Support for traditional data processing

of information fall into at least three categories based upon their nature and the communicative functions they serve: regulation of interaction, perception of communication partners, and awareness of the social context of communication.

Regulation of Interaction

A number of researchers have explored the role of nonverbal cues such as eye gaze (Kendon, 1967) and shifts in voice pitch and loudness (Duncan, 1972) in regulating interaction—for example, in indicating that a speaker is finished and willing to yield the floor to the listener. Audio-only and written media filter out progressively more of these nonverbal cues. Even video teleconferencing does not permit true eye contact because of slight displacements between cameras and viewing screens. Several researchers have hypothesized that the absence of such cues would lead to increases in interruptions and pauses, breakdowns in the rules for taking speaking turns, and other indicators of deregulated interaction.

Empirical research has largely failed to confirm these hypotheses. Interruptions and pauses are more frequent in face-to-face communication than in audio-only or audio-video modes (Short, Williams, & Christie, 1976; Williams, 1978). Furthermore, the physical presence or absence of a speaker seems to account for a greater portion of the so-called media effect than does attenuation of nonverbal visual cues. One explanation is that communicative cues are merely helpful, not essential, for regulating communication. Physical presence and visual cues enable participants to interrupt and speak simultaneously without deregulating the interaction (Williams, 1978). In mediated situations, communicators find ways to compensate for the absence of interaction regulating cues (Short et al., 1976; Schegloff, 1981).

However, research on computer conferencing technology has identified significant changes in interaction patterns under certain conditions. In small, leaderless face-to-face groups, individuals' rates of participation in a discussion are highly unequal, generally following a negative exponential curve called the "Zipf curve" (Vallee, 1984). But in synchronous computer conferencing, in which participants type their comments simultaneously via computer terminals, Hiltz and Turoff (1978) found that participation rates decrease linearly, producing a substantial *decrease* in the *inequality* of participation. They attributed this to the anonymity that the medium affords to low status individuals, women, and people with communication anxiety, who typically defer to others in face-to-face interaction. Rice (1984b) summarized several additional studies with similar results. Vallee (1984) replicated these findings with *synchronous* computer conferences but found that *asynchronous* computer conferences follow the negative exponential pattern typical of face-to-face small group interaction.

These findings are of interest because the frequency and duration of speaking are empirically linked to the emergence of leadership and consensus in small groups. Findings like these would have major implications for intraorganizational communication if they were also found to occur in field settings.

Perception of Communication Partners

Nonverbal cues not only serve the function of regulating social interaction, they also provide valuable information about the communication partner. This information is useful in forming impressions, in evaluating how partners understand and respond to messages, in determining the truthfulness of the partners' communication, and so forth. Short et al. (1976) found no effect of medium on the accuracy of factual information exchanged, although subjects had more confidence in the accuracy of information communicated in face-to-face interaction. They found, however, that communication tasks involving interpersonal conflict (such as bargaining) and interpersonal relations (such as getting to know someone and forming impressions) are highly sensitive to medium, unlike tasks involving simple information exchange. They proposed a theory of social presence to account for these media effects.

According to the theory of social presence, media differ in their "capacity to transmit information about facial expression, direction of looking, posture, dress and non-verbal, vocal cues" (Short et al., 1976, p. 65). But social presence is not an objective property of a medium, derived solely from technical constraints. It also depends on two additional factors (Rice, 1984c). The first of these concerns the subjective perceptions of media by individuals due to their "preexisting attitudes, familiarity, and preferences" (Rice, 1984c, p. 58). The second is the context of the task for which the medium is used. "For example, consider two official organizational tasks: a routine request for updated information and a strategic negotiation between two executives. These very different contexts affect the appropriateness of any given medium" (Rice, 1984c, pp. 58-59). Thus the social presence theory of media posits a complex interaction of technical capabilities, personal perceptions, and contextual characteristics.

The findings of many experimental studies are generally consistent with the theory of social presence. These studies are reviewed in considerable detail in Short et al. (1976) and Rice and Associates (1984) and have been summarized in an annotated bibliography in Johansen, Vallee, and Spangler (1979). Two of the more intriguing findings, discussed below, include the ability of mediated communication to inhibit the emergence of leadership in a group (which in turn inhibits the evolution of consensus), and the tendency of mediated communication to foster the formation of coalitions.

The emergence of a group leader. Direction of eye gaze and eye contact are important sources of feedback and reinforcement to the emerging leader in a small leaderless group. Because video technology attenuates these cues,

Strickland, Guild, Barefoot, and Paterson (1978) expected that video-mediated groups would have less dramatic leadership emergence and stabilization than do face-to-face groups. They found that intragroup processes are strongly affected by media: A strong leader is much more likely to emerge and to continue to monopolize discussions in face-to-face groups than in video-mediated groups. Only in face-to-face groups did Strickland et al. find that frequency and duration of speaking (two relatively stable personality characteristics related to leadership in small groups, according to Rice, 1984c) are related to others' perceptions of the speaker's idea quantity, quality, and attractiveness.

In interpreting their findings, Strickland et al. (1978) note that media appear to reduce consensus about leadership and to increase the focus of participants on the task at hand rather than on the individual members of the group. In related studies, Hiltz and Turoff (1978) and Kiesler, Siegel, and McGuire (1984) found that synchronous computer conferencing increases the amount of time required to achieve group consensus on the task and in some cases prevents the group from reaching task consensus.

The formation of coalitions. The importance of media impact on consensus is open to some question. Consensus is often an artifact of group norms and is not highly correlated with correctness of group decisions (Janis, 1972). However, media also appear to foster the formation of coalitions or subgroups. Laboratory studies reviewed in Jull et al. (1976) found evidence of polarization of opinions between teleconferencing participants in physically separated locations. Polarization is more likely to occur in audio than video conferencing, although it has also been observed in video conferencing (Johansen, 1977).

In a similar vein, Williams (1975, 1977) and Short et al. (1976) found that, in both audio- and video-mediated experimental groups, participants showed a significant tendency to support the person who shared the same physical location and teleconferencing equipment. In the audio mode, participants are also significantly more likely to disagree with the ideas of people at the other end of the link. The tentative conclusions from these studies is that "telecommunications systems can, by separating the group into subgroups, affect the lines along which coalitions form" (Short et al., 1976, p. 139).

In explaining these findings, Williams (1977) drew heavily on studies that show that audio-only conversation (and, by extension, written as well) are "more depersonalized, argumentative, and narrow in focus, compared with face-to-face conversations" (p. 972) and concluded that "any process or phenomenon that depends on the interactors' attitudes toward each other is likely to be affected" (p. 973). The only experimental finding that fails to conform to this general rule concerns attitude change, which is less likely to occur in face-to-face communication. Short et al. (1976) found more opinion change via audio-only media. Kiesler et al. (1984) found significantly higher choice shift in computer-conferencing groups, although Hiltz and Turoff (1978) present contradictory evidence. Short et al. (1976) conclude that, whatever the benefits of face-to-face communication, it also distracts communicators from the task and from vocal cues that might indicate lying. By directing too much attention toward the communicators, face-to-face interaction may lead to ineffective task outcomes.

Awareness of Social Context

Mediated communication filters out a third source of information in addition to the cues that help regulate interaction and create impressions of the communication partner. This third source provides information about the social context of the communication, such as the setting of the communication (i.e. cafeteria versus boardroom) and the hierarchical status of the communication partner. Sproull and Kiesler (1986) have reviewed the literature on the effects of social context information on communication in organizational settings. They argue that if a medium such as computer conferencing or electronic messaging inhibits awareness of social context information, social context will have less effect on individuals and their communication behavior than is normal in face-to-face interaction.

In a field study of electronic messaging in an office equipment manufacturing firm, Sproull and Kiesler (1986) found some support for their hypotheses that the absence of social context information would increase uninhibited communication (i.e., swearing and "flaming"), increase self-absorption as opposed to other-orientation, equalize status differentials among communicators, and blur the boundaries between work and non-work (for example, when employees work at home using telecommunications equipment). They found, for instance, that users of electronic messaging did not know the gender of 40%, or the hierarchical position of 32%, of those who sent messages to them. They also found a large number of non-work-related communications and consistently overestimated their involvement in electronic communication.

Assessing the Literature
on Cues Filtered Out

In summary, this section has reviewed a sizable number of research studies on media effects, mostly experimental in methodology. Taken as a whole, this work has identified and replicated many interesting findings about the effects of media on individuals and interpersonal communication in small, leaderless groups. In addition, it has suggested and provided support for theoretical explanations of the effects, such as the social presence theory of media.

However, from the viewpoint of our purpose in this chapter, the cues-filtered-out literature is something of a disappointment. There are numerous obstacles in the way of generalizing from these studies to the question with which we started: What are the effects of electronic media on intraorganizational communication?

In the first place, theories such as the social presence of media theory have few natural linkages to theories of information processing and organizational communication, a point to which we will return in a later section. This means that however well the theory of social presence has been established, the empirical research has failed to invalidate rival explanations for the same phenomena. Kiesler et al. (1984) have noted "that our own data do not provide any evidence to distinguish among these tentative and somewhat limited potential explanations" (p. 1130), a statement we believe applies to this entire body of work.

Second, the findings of the cues-filtered-out studies are most likely to occur in actual organizational settings to the extent that the laboratory conditions resemble those settings closely. In most of the laboratory studies, for example, the communicators did not know each other before communicating via the new medium, did not have any choice about using the medium, had no alternative ways to communicate with other participants, and were unfamiliar with the communication technology used (Shulman & Steinman, 1977). In addition, they experienced no differences among each other in task or status. This suggests that the findings of the experimental literature are most likely to occur in field settings where participants with equal status and similar tasks are geographically remote from each other, and so have never met, have few opportunities to meet, and few alternative communication media.

Now, it is true that the new electronic media give organizations the ability to design themselves in this way, and that a few firms (mainly high technology firms composed largely of computer professionals) have chosen to do so (Olson & Primps, 1984). However, in the vast majority of organizations, communication takes place under very different conditions, and these conditions are unlikely to change (Olson, 1985). Organizations typically co-locate, both physically and organizationally, individuals who need to work together. Thus interdependent workers often know each other and have the option of communicating in person. In addition, organizations often provide numerous other vehicles for communication—phones, memos, bulletin boards—without imposing severe restrictions on what purposes or tasks for which each medium is to be used. Often, though not invariably, when organizations provide advanced communications technologies to their employees, they also provide training and other opportunities to develop proficiency. Lastly, and perhaps most important, organizational work groups usually have a known and designated leader of higher status than the rest of the participants.

Under conditions like these, use of an electronic medium will never entirely replace other means of communication. And individuals will have other sources of information about each other and about the task than those filtered through an electronic medium. Consequently, the findings from the cues-filtered-out literature are likely to occur less frequently and with less severity than the laboratory studies might seem to indicate.

A number of field studies lend support to this conclusion. Use of electronic media tends to reduce use of telephone and memos and occasionally reduces the need for meetings, but sometimes actually increases face-to-face and written communication (Conrath & Bair, 1974; Edwards, 1978; Johansen, 1984; McKenney, 1985; Palme, 1981; Rice, 1980; Rice & Case, 1983). Thus in most field settings the electronic media do not replace communication via other media but rather exist as new media side-by-side with more traditional ones.

There is still a third conceptual issue that limits the ability to generalize from the findings of these experimental studies. The previously cited research assumes that face-to-face communication is the standard against which mediated communication should be compared and that interaction mediated by electronic technology *filters out* important communicative cues. This ignores the possibility, which we will attempt to justify below, that the electronic media have capabilities not found in face-to-face communication. These new capabilities may be as or more influential in their consequences for intraorganizational communication than the presence or absence of various communicative cues.

NEW CAPABILITIES OF ELECTRONIC MEDIA

Descriptions of electronic media frequently emphasize the power of these technologies in terms of the speed of message delivery, the efficiency of asynchronous communication (because all parties need not participate at the same time), and the number and geographic spread of participants (no longer constrained by physical location and size of meeting facilities) (Rice & Bair, 1984). We do not believe that such descriptions adequately capture the qualitative as well as quantitative differences between these media and traditional media.

For example, synchronous computer conferencing, in which participants communicate at the same time by sending written public and private messages, has virtually no analog in traditional communication modes. The closest situation we can think of—in which people pass written private notes during a formal presentation—differs in two respects: In the traditional situation, the public communications are verbal, not written; and the existence, if not the content, of the private communications can be observed by at least some of the other participants.

Electronic media differ qualitatively from traditional communication modes in several ways. Below, we consider the following: ways of addressing communication; memory, storage and retrieval of communication; and control over access to and participation in communication.

Addressing Communication

In general, most forms of communication in organizations require the sender to specify the identity and physical location of the intended recipient. This is true, albeit to a lesser extent, even for communications to "mailing lists." But some forms of electronic media, such as computer conferencing and the bulletin board features of many electronic messaging systems, allow a sender to address a communication to a "communication space" (sometimes called a "file," a "conference," or a "bulletin board") that can be read by any interested or authorized person. This feature allows individuals to "meet" other like-minded people, whom they might not otherwise have come to know because of differences in geographic location or position in the organizational structure.

The potential consequences of such a feature can be seen in a description of the unintended use of an electronic messaging system within a large corporation. Employees disgruntled by an unpopular management decision used the system to communicate their gripes to peers in other company locations, many of whom they did not previously know. They even circulated resumes and job hunting plans via the network (Emmett, 1981). In a recapitulation of this incident, Kiesler et al. (1984) label this use of the system "uninhibited behavior" and appear to attribute it solely to social-psychological processes: "Whether this behavior was caused specifically by a lack of shared etiquette, by computer culture norms, or by the impersonal and text-only form of communication is not clear" (p. 1130). But this analysis, we believe, lacks an adequate appreciation for the novel capabilities of a new medium that facilitates the grouping of people by what they are interested in rather than by geography, social position, and prior acquaintance.

Palme (1981) offers some support for the contention that addressing communication by topic rather than by the name and/or organizational position of the intended recipient differs sharply from traditional communication. A communication system used in the Swedish Department of Defense had two communication modes: electronic messaging, in which the sender specified an addressee or a distribution list, and conferencing, in which individuals created and participated in open conferences on the basis of their interest in the topic. Palme prepared frequency distributions of both messages and conference entries according to the organizational distance among senders and receivers (i.e., within one department, between two departments, outside the organization). The distribution of addressed messages was quite consistent with distributions reported by Conrath (1973) for face-to-face, written, and even telephone communication. The distribution of conference entries was significantly different, with a much higher percentage of messages crossing departmental and organizational boundaries. This suggests that usage of at least some types of electronic media stimulates communication patterns very different from those usual for traditional media.

Memory, Storage, and Retrieval

The complete written transcript of proceedings that is automatically maintained by some computer conferencing systems is another feature of electronic media that has no analog in face-to-face or telephonic communication. In recurring intraorganizational meetings, organizational participants frequently prepare and publish "minutes" summarizing key decisions and action items. We argue that complete written transcripts differ from minutes in several important respects. Minutes are generally written by a single individual (although the position of secretary may rotate) and so are more likely to represent a single person's understanding of the consensus than does a transcript, which records each participant's observations as they occur. Minutes rarely capture the initial positions of each participant or the interim postures taken as the consensus evolves. A transcript turns each utterance into a public stand to which others can easily refer at later points in time.

We believe that the availability of transcripts could have profound effects on intraorganizational communication and decision-making processes, although we can only speculate on the nature and direction of these effects. For example, transcripts of proceedings might be useful in reducing the experience gap of new organizational members. On the other hand, they may inhibit opinion change and prevent the formation of consensus. The availability and awareness of public stands may make a reinterpretation of the past impossible, thus altering workgroup processes in incalculable ways.

The ability of these systems to maintain accurate transcripts and other records of communication conducted via an electronic medium has important data collection implications (Sproull, 1986). For example, computer-based monitoring can provide objective, longitudinal data on the user population, amount and frequency of use, and communication patterns within a network (Rice, 1984c; Rice & Borgman, 1983; Rice & Rogers, 1984). The advantages of computer-monitored data for understanding user behavior compared to self-reports are obvious. The use of computer-monitored data also raises issues of individual privacy and close monitoring of employee work behavior. If data are collected without the prior consent of the individuals who are being monitored, a decline in morale and productivity could result.

Control Over Access and Participation

Electronic media also present a potential to control and manipulate communication that is almost inconceivable in traditional intraorganizational communication modes. An example can be found in one of the simplest implementations of audio teleconferencing—speakerphones. Many of these devices have so-called "cough" or mute buttons, which allow the speaker(s) at one location to make private remarks unheard by the listener(s) at the other end. Similarly, "freeze frame" or still motion video conferencing transmits snapshotlike images of participants at intervals selected by the participants.

This allows them to compose the appearance of socially correct behavior, which may contrast sharply with their actual behavior.

Further, most commercial offerings of electronic media possess certain features not fully specified by their developers or vendors. The final system configuration is left to the adopting organization and, in some cases, to the ultimate user. For electronic messaging, matters of organizational policy can include such issues as who has access to electronic mailboxes; who can send, read, delete, or alter messages; whether and how message traffic and content is monitored. Singly and in combination, these choices may present new possibilities to control and channel organizational communication. Rice (1984b) makes a similar point with respect to minor variations in the design features of computer conferencing systems, such as the allocation of "air time" to participants, the order of presenting participants' comments, and the capability for private messaging. Although not explicitly addressing the control and manipulation potential of these features, he concludes that small differences in system design features can have noticeable, if limited, effects on group process.

Because electronic media have capabilities not found in face-to-face and other traditional forms of communication, we believe that a theoretical perspective that assumes that these media are deficient compared to face-to-face communication is inadequate. The fact that electronic media may lack cues for regulating interaction, forming impressions of communicators, and apprehending the social context of communication simply cannot account for the findings of a small but growing number of field studies of electronic media use, summarized in the next section. Although many of these studies can be challenged on methodological grounds, they consistently report changes in the quantity, connectivity, and direction of communication via the new media.

In summary, the conceptual framework underlying much of the existing research on media effects assumes that face-to-face communication is the standard against which new media are to be evaluated and that the electronic media are deficient compared to face-to-face communication because they lack important communicative cues. We believe that these assumptions are too limited to support research on the organizational, as opposed to individual or interpersonal, impacts of these technologies. The electronic media have capabilities not found in face-to-face interaction, such as novel ways to address communication, new modes of communication storage and retrieval, and enhanced capabilities for the control over access to and participation in communication.

FIELD RESEARCH ON NEW MEDIA EFFECTS

As we mentioned earlier, a major difficulty in generalizing from the literature on media effects to their consequences for intraorganizational communication is the lack of natural conceptual linkages between theories of media and theories of organizational communication and information processing. In this respect, the media effects research is subject to some of the same criticisms that have been leveled at traditional research on organizational communication (Porter & Roberts, 1976; Roberts, O'Reilly, Bretton, & Porter, 1974).

A perspective on organizational communication developed by O'Reilly and Pondy (1979) offers an approach to resolving this theoretical deficiency. In their framework, *communication outcomes*, such as group relations (consensus, leadership emergence, and coalition formation), emerge from *communication process*, a conceptual category that includes filtering (cues filtered out), accuracy, and overload, among others. Communication process, in turn, is strongly constrained by *communication structure*, which is formed of networks, communication directionality, information channels (including communication media), and roles. As previously discussed, electronic media have new capabilities that appear able to alter dimensions of communication structure as well as to influence the elements of communication process. Finally, communication structure is the outcome, in part, of *organizational variables*, such as organizational structure and information processing needs.

Thus the theory and literature on media effects lacks adequate attention to theoretical concepts, such as organizational variables and communication structure, which shape and constrain the communication processes and outcomes. In the sections that follow, we review field studies of electronic media use in intraorganizational settings organized by the categories of O'Reilly and Pondy's (1979) framework.

Organizational Variables

Information processing theory (Galbraith, 1973) posits strong relationships between two important organizational variables: organizational structure and information processing requirements. According to this theory, electronic communication media may represent one strategy among several others (developing lateral relations or vertical information systems) for increasing the organization's ability to process information. On the other hand, use of electronic media may promote increased communication that overloads the information processing capability of the hierarchy. This may undermine hierarchical authority relationships in organizations.

In a field study of electronic messaging, McKenney (1985) found that increased use of electronic messaging caused a formal reporting system to atrophy. The hypothesis that electronic media may undermine hierarchical authority relations is consistent with the data of Sproull and Kiesler (1986) that these media diminish intraorganizational status differentials. It is also consistent with contentions that earlier media, specifically the telephone and telegraph, have bypassed formal authority and democratized social relations (Pool, 1983).

Deterioration in the information processing potential or the perceived authority of the hierarchy may encourage organizations to adopt strategies that reduce the need for information processing. Thus organizations may change their structures by creating self-contained units (thus flattening the hierarchy) or may simply reduce organizational size. Strassman (1985) finds evidence of a trend away from large organizational units and contends that changes in the economics of information technology "will give the same advantages to small enterprises as have so far been enjoyed only by large organizations" (p. 276).

Communication Structure

As defined by O'Reilly and Pondy (1979), communication structure includes the dimensions of networks, roles (i.e., participant versus isolate), directionality, and information channels (including communication media), each of which we discuss below.

Networks and roles. Virtually every field study of electronic media has identified the outcome of new and increased communication linkages among individuals (Rice, 1984b). For example, the users of a Swedish electronic messaging and conferencing system reported that 50% of the messages they wrote and 75% of the messages they received were new communications that would not have occurred without the system (Palme, 1981). Similarly, Rice and Case (1983) found an increase in new communications among university administrators within two to five months after their introduction to an integrated office system that included electronic messaging. Of the surveyed managers 43% reported exchanging messages with people who were not previously telephone partners or written correspondents, and an additional 14% reported receiving such new communication (Rice & Case, 1983, p. 139). In a survey of users of public video conferencing facilities, Fulk and Dutton (1984) found an increase in the number of communication partners.

The hypothesis that electronic media may create new intraorganizational communication networks raises concerns about the individuals and groups excluded either intentionally through organizational policy and politics or accidentally through inadequate access to technical resources. Few field studies have examined nonparticipants as carefully as participants. In a cross-organizational study of research scientists who used a computer conferencing system, however, Hiltz (1984) found evidence that system use increases communication with colleagues both on and off the network. Apparently, "system members become indirect links between the online and off-line worlds" (Hiltz, 1984, p. 153); "thus, there is an expansion of indirect communication ties, rather than an 'encapsulation' of the online group" (1984, p. 161).

Communication direction. Field investigations also provide evidence about the ability of electronic media to affect the direction of intraorganizational communication. Lippitt, Miller, and Halamaj (1980) found an increase in upward and downward hierarchical communication within a marketing department in which electronic messaging was used. Conrath and Bair (1974) found an increase in the upward flow of communication among users of an integrated office system in two units of a computer software development firm. Rice and Case (1983) also found an increase in upward communication through the use of an integrated office system by university administrators. They noted that this additional communication was not always desired by the recipients. Other research found that initial increases in communication volume in a computer conferencing system resulted in overload for the participants. Ultimately, as users gained experience with the system, they also developed screening skills to prevent overload (Hiltz & Turoff, 1981).

Leduc (1979) studied the use of an integrated office system with messaging capabilities in an intact subunit of Bell Canada at two time periods, 6 and 22 months after the system was introduced. The system was used for internal administrative and project communication as well as for interacting with external consultants to the unit. At the first time period, communication over the system occurred primarily vertically, between bosses and their respective subordinates. At time two, communication approached an "all-channel structure, where everyone communicated with everyone else" (Leduc, 1979, p. 238). Because Leduc did not report on communication flows outside the system, it is unclear whether the changes between the two time periods can be attributed entirely to the system.

Information channels. As previously discussed, electronic media exist side-by-side with traditional media in organizational settings. This raises questions about the circumstances under which an individual will choose a new electronic medium over an available traditional medium. Prior research on media choice suggests that task-related variables and the accessibility of the channel will be major factors in the selection process.

Two task-related variables likely to influence media choice are the purpose of the communication and the communicator's perceptions of the task and the task environment. The relation of task perceptions to the use of electronic media has only begun to receive attention (e.g., Steinfield, 1985a). But research on horizontal communication in organizations suggests that channel selection should be related to the analyzability and equivocality of particular tasks (Daft & Lengel, 1984; Daft & MacIntosh, 1981). According to this view, richer media, such as face-to-face, will be preferred for situations characterized by the need for immediate feedback, interpersonal cues, and variety of language (Daft & Lengel, 1984). This is consistent with the theory of the social presence of media, which argues that individuals will select an electronic medium for communication activities that are low in affective content, such as sharing information or making assignment.

Limited empirical evidence, however, suggests that individuals perceive electronic media to be appropriate for a wider variety of communication activities as they gain experience with them (Hiltz & Turoff, 1981; Rice, 1984c; Steinfield, 1985b). Rice and Love (in press), for example, found that 30% of the total electronic message content in a cross-organizational study of medical professionals was emotive. This empirical evidence suggests that the theory of social presence alone cannot account for media choice in organizations.

The accessibility of electronic media is another important determinant of media choice and information channel selection (Culnan, 1983a; O'Reilly, 1983; Svenning & Ruchinskas, 1984). Culnan (1983b) investigated perceptions of the accessibility of computer-mediated communication and found accessibility to be a multidimensional concept encompassing physical access to both a terminal and the system, the command language, and the ability to retrieve the desired information. A follow-up study found a significant positive relationship between the ability of a user to master the command language of an integrated office system and initial use of the system (Culnan, 1985). While accessibility is apparently an important component of the initial decision to use a new medium (Kerr & Hiltz, 1982; Steinfeld, 1985a), the relationship between accessibility and ongoing use of electronic media remains unexplored.

FUTURE RESEARCH

In the course of this chapter, we have identified a number of issues that have not been adequately addressed by prior theory and research. These include the relationship between theories of media effects with theories of organizational communication and information processing; the critical dimensions of organizational context that moderate the effects of media cue filtering; the significant new capabilities of electronic media and their effects on key aspects of organization, communication structure, and communication process; and the relationship over time among dimensions of organizational context, media accessibility, and media use. All of these are important candidates for future research on the electronic media.

One additional topic is notably absent from much prior research and has not been addressed directly in the earlier sections of this chapter. This topic, implementation decisions and processes, will be discussed next.

Implementation

Our discussion has emphasized the characteristics of electronic media that appear to be related to their usage and effects in intraorganizational settings. Many of these characteristics are inherent in the technical design of the media—for example, the fact that the telephone conveys audio but not video signals. In actual organizational settings, however, some media characteristics are products of organizational choice—for example, which individuals have access to the medium, how convenient their access is, whether or not individuals must pay for this access from personal funds or departmental budgets, and so on. These choices, made at the time when an organization adopts or physically implements an electronic medium, are as likely to influence media choice, ongoing use, and media effects as are the inherent characteristics of the medium (Markus, 1987).

Thus people are likely to avoid electronic media if the media are physically inaccessible, hard to use, costly, insufficiently useful, or fail to connect users with a "critical mass" of friends or coworkers (Culnan & Bair, 1983; Kerr & Hiltz, 1982; Steinfield, 1985a; Uhlig et al., 1979). For example, Rice and Manross (1986) observed strikingly different reactions to the same telephone technology introduced into two units of a single organization. Prior to implementation, both user groups had reported similar attitudes about the anticipated usefulness of the technology. After the fact, researchers attributed differences in use to implementation decisions and activities: poor documentation, inadequate training, and faulty technical support systems.

The effects of implementation decisions and processes on the use and outcomes of traditional information technologies, such as management information systems, have been widely recognized (Markus, 1984). But the literature on electronic media has paid much less attention to the topic of implementation. For example, implementation decisions and activities have gone relatively unrecognized in the literature on media choice (e.g., Daft & Lengel, 1984). A more complete understanding of the intraorganizaional effects of electronic media will clearly require additional theory and research on the topic of media implementation.

CONCLUSION

The literature reviewed in this chapter makes considerable progress toward the goal of understanding the effects of the new electronic media on intraorganizational communication. However, early research and theory on electronic media exhibit a number of significant limitations. First, theories of media effects have not been clearly linked to existing theories of organizational communication and information processing. Second, much of the research has been conducted in the laboratory or in extra-organizational settings. Because such studies exclude or simplify important dimensions of organizational context, the results may not generalize to communication in organizations. In addition, many studies have been conducted at one point in time in a single organization. Longitudinal studies and multiple-site studies are few and far between. Third, much of this research has ignored the new capabilities that distinguish electronic media from traditional modes of communication and that may be central to their intraorganizational effects.

On the other hand, criticisms similar to these have been directed at research on organizational communication via traditional media (Porter & Roberts,

1976). Rice (1984c) points out that all communication media were seen as "new" when they were introduced—"newness" is really quite relative. Consequently, the real conclusion of our review may be the need to revisit theory and research on intraorganizational communication. In this task, the characteristics that make the electronic media seem new to us may be both a challenge and an opportunity.

REFERENCES

Bair, J. H. (1979). Communication in the office of the future: Where the real payoff may be. *Business Communication Review, 9,* 3-11.

Bikson, T. K., & Gutek, B. A. (1983). *Advanced office systems: An empirical look at utilization and satisfaction* (Report N-1970-NSF). Santa Monica, CA: Rand Corporation.

Carey, J. (1982). Videotex: The past as prologue. *Journal of Communication, 32,* 8-87.

Chandler, A. D., Jr. (1977). *The visible hand: The managerial revolution in American business.* Cambridge, MA: Harvard University Press.

Conrath, D. W. (1973). Communications environment and its relationship to organizational structure. *Management Science, 20,* 586-603.

Conrath, D. W., & Bair, J. H. (1974). The computer as an interpersonal communication device: A study of augmentation technology and its apparent impact on organizational communication. *Proceedings of the Second International Conference on Computer Communications,* Stockholm, Sweden.

Culnan, M. J. (1983a). Environmental scanning: The effects of task complexity and source accessibility on information gathering behavior. *Decision Sciences, 14,* 194-206.

Culnan, M. J. (1983b). The dimensions of accessibility to online information: Implications for implementing office information systems. *ACM Transactions on Office Information Systems, 2,* 141-150.

Culnan, M. J. (1985). *The impact of perceived accessibility on the use of an integrated office information system.* Paper presented at the annual meeting of the Academy of Management, San Diego.

Culnan, M. J., & Bair, J. H. (1983). Human communication needs and organizational productivity: The potential impact of office automation. *Journal of the American Society for Information Science, 34,* 215-221.

Daft, R. L., & Lengel, R. H. (1984). Information richness: A new approach to managerial behavior and organizational design. In L. L. Cummings & B. M. Staw (Eds.), *Research in organizational behavior* (Vol. 6, pp. 191-233). Greenwich, CT: JAI Press.

Daft, R. L., & MacIntosh, N. B. (1981). A tentative exploration into the amount and equivocality of information processing in organizational work units. *Administrative Science Quarterly, 26,* 207-224.

Duncan, S. (1972). Some signals and rules for taking speaking turns in conversations. *Journal of Personality and Social Psychology, 23,* 283-292.

Edwards, G. C. (1978). Organizational impacts of office automation. *Telecommunications Policy, 2,* 128-136.

Emmett, R. (1981). Vnet or gripenet? *Datamation, 27*(11), 48-58.

Engel, G. H., Groppuso, J., Lowenstein, R. A., & Traub, W. G. (1979). An office communication system. *IBM Systems Journal, 18,* 402-431.

Fulk, J., & Dutton, W. (1984). Videoconferencing as an organizational information system: Assessing the role of electronic meetings. *Systems, Objectives and Solutions, 4,* 105-118.

Galbraith, J. (1973). *Designing complex organizations.* Reading, MA: Addison-Wesley.

Hiltz, S. R. (1984). *Online communities: A case study of the office of the future.* Norwood, NJ: Ablex.

Hiltz, S. R., & Turoff, M. (1978). *The network nation: Human communication via computer.* Reading, MA: Addison-Wesley.

Hiltz, S. R., & Turoff, M. (1981). The evolution of user behavior in a computerized conferencing system. *Communications of the ACM, 24*(11), 739-751.

Hirschheim, R. S. (1985). *Office automation: Concepts, technologies and issues.* Reading, MA: Addison-Wesley.

Huber, G. P. (1984). Issues in the design of group decision support systems. MiS Quarterly, 8(3), 195-204.

Janis, I. (1972). *Victims of groupthink.* Boston: Houghton-Mifflin.

Johansen, R. (1977). Social evaluations of teleconferencing. *Telecommunications Policy, 1*(5), 395-419.

Johansen, R. (1984). *Teleconferencing and beyond: Communications in the office of the future.* New York: McGraw-Hill.

Johansen, R., Vallee, J., & Spangler, K. (1979). *Electronic meetings: Technical alternatives and social choices.* Reading, MA: Addison-Wesley.

Jull, G. W., McCaughern, R. W., Mendenhall, N. M., Storey, J. R., Tassie, A. W., & Zalatan, A. (1976). *Research report on teleconferencing.* Ottawa: Communications Research Center.

Kendon, A. (1967). Some functions of gaze direction in social interaction. *Acta Psychologica, 26,* 1-47.

Kerr, E. B., & Hiltz, S. R. (1982). *Computer-mediated communication systems.* New York: Academic Press.

Kiesler, S., Siegel, J., & McGuire, T. W. (1984). Social psychological aspects of computer-mediated communication. *American Psychologist, 39,* 1123-1134.

Kotter, J. P. (1982). What effective messages really do. *Harvard Business Review, 60*(6), 156-167.

Leduc, N. F. (1979). Communicating through computers: Impact on a small business group. *Telecommunications Policy, 4,* 235-244.

Lippitt, M. E., Miller, J. P., & Halamaj, J. (1980). Patterns of use and correlates of adoption of an electronic mail system. Prepared for *Proceedings of the American Institute of Decision Sciences,* Las Vegas, Nevada. ADD P. NOS.

Markus, M. L. (1984). *Systems in organizations: Bugs and features.* Marsfield, MA: Pitman.

Markus, M. L. (1987). Chargeback as an implementation tactic for office communication systems. *Interfaces 17,* (3), 54-63.

Markus, M. L., & Yates, J. (1982, June). Historical lessons for the automated office. *Computer Decisions, 14,* 116-119, 260.

McKenney, J. (1985). *The influence of computer based communication on the organization.* Unpublished working paper 9-785-053, Harvard Business School.

Mintzberg, H. (1973). *The nature of managerial work.* New York: Harper & Row.

Olson, M. H. (1985). Do you telecommute? *Datamation, 31*(10), 129-132.

Olson, M. H., & Primps, S. B. (1984). Working at home with computers: Work and nonwork issues. *Journal of Social Issues, 40*(3), 97-112.

O'Reilly, C. A. (1983). The use of information in organizational decision making: A model and some propositions. In L. L. Cummings & B. M. Staw (Eds.), *Research in organizational behavior* (Vol. 5, pp. 103-140). Greenwich, CT: JAI Press.

O'Reilly, C. A., & Pondy, L. R. (1979). Organizational communication. In S. Kerr (Ed.), *Organizational behavior* (pp. 119-150). Columbus, OH: Grid.

Palme, J. (1981). *Experience with the use of the COM computerized conferencing system.* Stockholm, Sweden: Forsvarets Forskningsanstalt.

Pool, I. de Sola. (1983). *Forecasting the telephone: A retrospective assessment.* Norwood, NJ: Ablex.

Poppel, H. L. (1982). Who needs the office of the future? *Harvard Business Review, 60*(6), 146-155.

Porter, L. W., & Roberts, K. H. (1976). Communication in organizations. In M. Dunnette (Ed.), *Handbook of industrial and organizational psychology* (pp. 1153-1589). Chicago: Rand McNally.

Rice, R. E. (1980). The impacts of computer-mediated organizational and interpersonal communication. In M. E. Willaims (Ed.), *Annual review of information science and technology* (Vol. 15, pp. 221-249). White Plains, NY: Knowledge Industry Publications.

Rice, R. E. (1984a). New media technology: Growth and integration. In R.E. Rice & Associates (Eds.), *The new media: Communication, research and technology* (pp. 33-54). Newbury Park, CA: Sage.

Rice, R. E. (1984b). Mediated group communication. In R. E. Rice & Associates (Eds.), *The new media: Communication, research and technology* (pp. 129-154). Newbury Park, CA: Sage.

Rice, R. E. (1984c). Evaluating new media systems. In J. Johnstone (Eds.), *Evaluating the new information technologies: New directions for program evaluation* (No. 23, pp. 53-71). San Francisco: Jossey-Bass.

Rice, R. E., & Associates. (Eds.). (1984). *The new media: Communication, research and technology.* Newbury Park, CA: Sage.

Rice, R. E., & Bair, J. H. (1984). New organizational media and productivity. In R. E. Rice & Associates (Eds.), *The new media: Communication, research and technology* (pp. 185-216). Newbury Park, CA: Sage.

Rice, R. E., & Borgman, C. L. (1983). The use of computer-monitored data in information science and communication research. *Journal of the American Society for Information Science, 34,* 247-254.

Rice, R. E., & Case, D. (1983). Electronic message systems in the university: A description of use and utility. *Journal of Communication, 33,* 131-152.

Rice, R. E., & Love, G. (in press). Electronic emotion: Socio-emotional content in a computer-mediated communication network. *Communication Research.*

Rice, R. E., & Manross, G. (1986). The case of the intelligent telephone: The relationship of job category to the adoption of organizational communication technology. *Communication yearbook 10* (pp.). Newbury Park, CA: Sage.

Rice, R. E., & Rogers, E. M. (1984). New methods and data for the study of the new media. In R. E. Rice & Associates (Eds.), *The new media: Communication, research and technology* (pp. 81-100). Newbury Park, CA: Sage.

Roberts, K. H., O'Reilly, C. A., Bretton, G. E., & Porter, L. W. (1974). Organizational communication and organizational theory: A communication failure? *Human Relations, 24,* 501-524.

Rotella, E. J. (1981a). The transformation of the American office: Changes in employment and technology. *Journal of Economic History, 41,* 51-57.

Rotella, E. J. (1981b). *From home to office: U.S. women at work, 1879-1930.* Ann Arbor, MI: UMI Research Press.

Schegloff, E. A. (1981). Identification and recognition in interactional openings. In I. de Sola Pool (Ed.), *The social impact of the telephone* (pp. 415-450). Cambridge: MIT Press.

Short, J., Williams, E., & Christie, B. (1976). *The social psychology of telecommunications.* New York: John Wiley.

Shulman, A. D., & Steinman, J. I. (1977). Interpersonal teleconferencing in an organizational context. In M. C. Elton, W. A. Lucas, & D. W. Conrath (Eds.), *Evaluating new telecommunications services* (pp. 399-424). New York: Plenum Press.

Sproull, L. (1986). Using electronic mail for data collection in organizational research. *Academy of Management Journal, 29,* 159-169.

Sproull, L., & Kiesler, S. (1986). Reducing social context cues: The case of electronic mail. *Management Science, 32,* 1492-1512.

Steinfield, C. (1985a). Computer mediated communication: Explaining task and socioemotional uses. In M. L. McLaughlin (Ed.), *Communication yearbook 9* (pp. 777-804). Newbury Park, CA: Sage.

Steinfield, C. (1985b). Dimensions of electronic mail use in an organizational setting. *Proceedings of the Academy of Management*, 239-243.

Strassman, P. (1985). *Information payoff: The transformation of work in the electronic age*. New York: Free Press.

Strickland, L. H., Guild, P. D., Barefoot, J. C., & Paterson, S. A. (1978). Teleconferencing and leadership emergence. *Human Relations, 31*, 583-596.

Svenning, L. L. & Ruchinskas, J. E. (1984). Organizational teleconferencing. In R. E. Rice & Associates (Eds.), *The new media: Communication, research and technology* (pp. 217-248). Newbury Park, CA: Sage.

Tapscott, D. (1982). *Office automation: A user-drive method*. New York: Plenum Press.

Tushman, M. L., & Nadler, D. A. (1978). Information processing as an integrating concept in organizational design. *Academy of Management Review, 3*, 613-624.

Uhlig, R. P., Farber, D. J., & Bair, J. H. (1979). *The office of the future: Communication and computers*. New York: North-Holland.

Vallee, J. (1984). *Computer message systems*. NY: McGraw-Hill.

Williams, E. (1975). Coalition formation over telecommunications media. *European Journal of Social Psychology, 5*, 503-507.

Williams, E. (1977). Experimental comparisons of face-to-face and mediated communication: A review. *Psychological Bulletin, 84*, 963-976.

Williams, E. (1978). Visual interaction and speech patterns: An extension of previous results. *British Journal of Social and Clinical Psychology, 17*, 101-102.

Yates, J. (1982). From press book and pigeonhole to vertical filing: Revolution in storage and access systems for correspondence. *Journal of Business Communication, 19*, 5-26.

IV

PROCESS: COMMUNICATION BEHAVIOR IN ORGANIZATIONS

In this final part of the handbook we turn from looking at organizational structure factors that both affect and are affected by communication to *processes* within organizations that relate to communication. These processes are crucial in any attempt to gain a more comprehensive grasp of organizational communication. Also, a focus on process helps to provide a dynamic as opposed to a static view of communication in the organizational context. Indeed, as March and Shapira (cited in O'Reilly & Chatman, Chapter 17, in this volume) have observed, "outcomes are generally less significant than process. It is . . . process that gives meaning to life, and meaning is the core of life."

The six chapters in this part are arranged in a somewhat arbitrary order, but the section as a whole is designed to emphasize the *behavioral* dimension of communication in organizations. Further, these chapters, collectively, reinforce the necessity of considering the links that exist among processes across individual-group-organization-environment levels of analysis. In doing so, the chapters employ a wide variety of concepts—for example, message, power, games, conflict, information processing, feedback, anticipatory socialization, and organizational assimilation—that are vital in advancing our thinking and suggesting directions for future research about the broad topic that constitutes the domain of this handbook.

The opening chapter in Part IV, by Stohl and Redding, addresses a process issue that must occupy center stage in any analysis of organizational communication: the exchange of messages. As the authors succinctly assert, "the fulcrum of research in organizational communication [is] the study of messages." The difficulty in organizing and assessing what is known about messages and their exchange is the fact that, as Stohl and Redding indicate, "the study of messages . . . in the organizational context, rather than constituting a major segment of the literature in organizational communication, is actually strewn across a wide range of literatures, lacking coherence or integration." Thus this topic area is not easily reviewed or summarized despite its obvious importance.

As with other key terms relating to the broad field of communication, there is not total consensus on the definition of "message." For this chapter, the authors have chosen to restrict their use of the term to mean intentional ("nonrandom") verbal language. Of course, "intent" in this definition is purposefulness that an observer attributes to the sender and that may or may not directly correspond to the motivational state of a sender. The authors go on to make a useful distinction between "ostensibly displayed messages," those that "are represented in physical, observable form," and "internally experienced messages," which are "inferred to 'exist' as internal semantic events within the minds of message users (senders, receivers, observers)."

Several commonly used schemes for categorizing messages, such as "formal-informal" and "task-nontask," are summarized in Table 14.2 of the Stohl and Redding chapter. However, the authors believe that the most pervasive and perhaps most useful categorization system involves the *functions* of messages. They present their own set of functional classification systems in Table 14.3 and describe these five systems—individual, relational, instrumental, contextual and structural—in the chapter's text. After reviewing these systems, Stohl and Redding conclude that "researchers need to combine different levels of analysis and different systems of categories" if advances are to be made in understanding "actual organizational experience" in the process of message exchange. To do this, they advocate directing attention to the "multiple functions" of messages. Viewing messages from a functional perspective also leads the authors of this chapter to take a close look at the literature involving three familiar but serious potential problems related to the outcomes of message exchange: overload, distortion, and ambiguity.

In the concluding portion of their chapter, Stohl and Redding identify four issues they consider important for future research dealing with messages. The first of these is a proposal for a four-level categorization system for analyzing messages: the "desired" message, the "intended" message, the "enacted" message, and the "interpreted" message. The second issue concerns recognition of the "observer-inference problem" and its associated hazards of incorrect observer deductions. The third issue revolves around the need for researchers to devote more concentrated attention to the actual, verbatim text of messages, and the need to embed that kind of scrutiny in well-developed conceptual frameworks. The fourth issue is a call for continued efforts to develop improved message taxonomies that can be subjected to rigorous research testing and refinement.

In the second chapter in this part, Frost makes a strong case for adopting an explicitly political perspective if we are to gain an understanding of communication in organizational settings that goes beyond the merely superficial. His basic thesis is that the pursuit of power and the exercise of power constitute the heart of political behavior in organizations. Such behavior or activity, from his viewpoint, is strongly linked to communication because of the latter's role in the development and the uses of power. Communication, for Frost, is both an independent and a dependent variable. The critical elements of communication for his analysis are its rules and structures (the features of the *medium*); and the content, symbols and meaning (the characteristics of the *message*). These, in turn, are intimately connected with what Frost labels as "the fundamental activities of organizations": *contests* among actors motivated by self-interests vying "for the ability to determine the means/ends of doing organizational work," and *struggles for collaboration* "in the performance of organizational work when the means/ends . . . are unclear."

The first section of Frost's chapter elaborates on the nature of organizational power and especially on the notion that there is a "dual nature" of power in that it "exists both on the surface of an organization and beneath it." It is particularly the latter—deep structure power—that Frost finds critically important for analysis. These deeper (more hidden) aspects of power influence the ways in which the communication medium is constructed in an organization even though such influence is often not recognized by participants. Thus for Frost there is a reciprocal relationship between power and the communication medium: Power relationships determine the nature of the communication medium—"which is never neutral"—and the communication medium in turn "itself serves to influence the nature of power in the organization and has implications for subsequent arrangements of this medium." The clear import, as the author points out, is that the features of the communication medium are themselves "contestable" and thus can serve as the object of organization games. The meaning component of communication also becomes a part of the game and closely connected to the development and implementation of power.

Later sections of Frost's chapter expand on these basic ideas and focus specifically on organizational politics, "the embodiment of the exercise of power," and on "organization games," which are the "concrete mechanisms that actors use to structure and regulate their power relations while preserving some freedom to act in their own best interests." Frost devotes considerable attention to "locating" organization games and to identifying the types that exist at both the surface and deep levels. He believes that a game perspective provides a valuable "means of looking at communication [both] as medium and as message" and a useful way to "examine organizational power and communication in a systematic framework." Further, he contends that attention to the "historical evolution" of games within organizations will increase our understanding of how power and communication interact over time. Frost concludes by reemphasizing how the adoption of a deliberately political perspective for analysis—one that focuses on the origins and uses of power—will enhance our knowledge of organizational communication on both the macro as well as the micro level.

The third chapter in Part IV, by Putnam and Poole, deals with conflict and negotiations—certainly types of behavior often closely connected to political behavior that Frost discussed in the preceding chapter—and shows how these critical organizational activities can be approached from a communication perspective. The authors point out that although communication is, for example, "an important theme" of recent books and texts on these topics, *research* on conflict and negotiations largely ignores communication. As they put it, "[communication] appears as part of the taken-for-granted backdrop that shapes the way other forces impinge on organizational conflict." Their basic proposition is that a specific focus on communication can help to advance research on conflict because "communication is the basic constituent of conflict." Such a focus, they state, can "generate innovative research questions and explanatory schemes" in this area.

The role of communication in conflict and negotiations in the Putnam and Poole chapter is analyzed in four contexts or "arenas": interpersonal, bargaining and negotiations, intergroup, and interorganizational. Thus the authors highlight the particular impact of each type of context while at the same time acknowledging the importance of certain similarities that exist across them. Throughout, critical attention is given to how communication is involved in conflict processes: in the formation of issues, the perceptions of conflict, the enactment of conflict behavior, and the residual impressions that form following the conclusion of conflict episodes. Central to their analysis is how specifically different views of communication—mechanistic, psychological, interpretive-symbolic, and system-interaction—have been utilized in conflict literature and research. The chapter also examines four key variables that are useful in understanding the role of communication in conflict situations: actor attributes, conflict issues, relationship (among the actors) variables, and context factors. As was the case in the general approach adopted by Frost in the preceding chapter, communication is viewed as having a reciprocal relationship to each of these four variables: It can influence them and it also can be influenced by them.

In the final section of their chapter, Putnam and Poole summarize the similarities and differences uncovered in their review of the literature with regard to the treatment of communication across the four major contexts (i.e., interpersonal, bargaining, intergroup, and interorganizational). They also advocate utilizing a wider array of approaches (i.e., mechanistic, psychological, etc.) for attacking research problems in any given context. They conclude with some specific suggestions for enhancing the value of future research on the communication aspects of conflict and negotiations.

The chapter by O'Reilly, Chatman, and Anderson on "Message Flow and Decision Making" leads us to consider how communication relates to still another crucial organizational process: information processing. In their chapter these authors argue that there have been two rather independent "streams" of research relating to information processing. One, involving the acquisition and flow of information, has utilized an explicitly communication-oriented approach. The other, involving the use of information, has by and large ignored communication and instead has viewed organizations as "decision making entities." As O'Reilly, Chatman, and Anderson stress, researchers in these two areas typically tend to employ quite different methodologies: The former investigate problems for the most part through the use of field studies, while the latter almost always arrive at their findings through laboratory experiments. The authors further point out that the contextual differences inherent in these two approaches often have significant impacts on the types of results obtained.

The chief contention of this chapter is that an understanding of information processing requires consideration of *both* communication *and* decision making. Thus literature from each area is seen as helpful in gaining that understanding and in illuminating the other area. The bulk of the chapter is devoted to demonstrating the inadequacies of concentrating on either one of these two areas to the exclusion of the other, and to explication of how research in the two areas can usefully be merged. The authors essentially argue that findings from communication research "can add context and realism to the decision-making research" and, similarly, "the decision-making literature can help to make the outcome variables of communication research more concrete and measurable."

The following chapter, by Cusella, also has an information focus—in this case, information about performance. The chapter is developed around the concept of *performance and feedback*, defined by the author as "information conveyed to a receiver about his, her, or its (group) task performance." Performance feedback is viewed as a type of communication process that can have powerful effects on the subsequent motivation and performance of organizational members. The key variables to be considered in examining these effects are the context and content of the feedback and how that content is communicated.

Cusella begins by providing a review of how the feedback concept has been defined somewhat differently by those in cybernetics and those in the behavioral sciences, especially with respect to the notions of positive and negative feedback. The author argues that for purposes of viewing feedback in the organizational context, the latter approach is probably more useful. Thus rather than considering "positive" and "negative" in the error correction sense, as is done in classical cybernetics, positive feedback is defined as information that is regarded as favorable from the recipient's standpoint and negative feedback is unfavorable information. The following section of the chapter examines five specific feedback characteristics: goals, types, dimensionality, source, and functions (outcomes).

The latter portions of the Cusella chapter provide an extensive review of the impacts of feedback on motivation and performance, organized around three major situational contexts within which the feedback takes place: impersonal (i.e., feedback emanating directly from performance of the task or feedback provided by an impersonal source such as a computer or other type of instrument), dyadic, and group. Throughout, considerable emphasis is placed by the author on the communication aspects of the administration of rewards and incentives as they affect both dependent variables. Attribution theory is also given prominent attention in several places, particularly with respect to the performance appraisal as a type of feedback. The chapter concludes with a set of summary observations that tie together this large and diverse literature.

The final and exiting chapter in this part and in the handbook is by Jablin and is, appropriately, on "Organizational Entry, Assimilation, and Exit." The chapter is structured around these three organizational processes, which the author believes have been treated by researchers as separate phenomena for too long when in fact (in his view) they are related parts of a "singular, developmental phenomenon." The focus of the chapter is on the role of communication in each element of this overall process.

Although issues relevant to entry, assimilation, and exit have received a great deal of attention in the organizational literature, especially in recent years, this chapter represents the first time that the literature in these three areas has been jointly examined from an explicitly *communication* perspective. Hence, a major purpose of this review is to draw the attention of communication researchers to these topics and their interrelationships and likewise to alert organizational scholars to the connections of these processes to communication.

In the opening section of his chapter, Jablin shows how such communication-type variables as "source characteristics," "message characteristics," and "receiver characteristics" relate to vocational and organizational anticipatory socialization. A good example of these relationships, which is developed by the author in some detail, is the selection interview, a topic researched for many years but seldom looked at from quite this angle. Also in this section Jablin raises the issue, based on research findings, of the potential consequences for individuals and organizations of the "job candidates' inaccurate job/organizational beliefs" that can arise in the anticipatory socialization phase. The following section on "assimilation" separately considers the subprocesses of "encounter" and "metamorphosis." A basic point that underlies the analyses in this section is that it is the "proactive and reactive communication of expectations" that forms the core of the assimilation process, a process in which both the member and the organization are mutually involved. The final major section in this chapter deals with "exit" and highlights the communication factors related to member turnover and withdrawal from organizations. As the author stresses, communication can be viewed both as an antecedent factor in exit and also as a symptom of other problems that may be involved in generating this behavior. In concluding this chapter, Jablin returns to his main theme: "One of the keys to understanding communication processes and behaviors in organizations is to recognize their *developmental* nature."

14 Messages and Message Exchange Processes

CYNTHIA STOHL
W. CHARLES REDDING
Purdue University

I T is an axiom that organizations cannot exist without communication. And communication, of course, cannot occur in the absence of messages—whether the messages be verbal or nonverbal, intentional or unintentional. Indeed, the fulcrum of research in organizational communication can be described as the study of messages, both "actual" and "perceived." Every chapter that follows in the process section deals, either directly or indirectly, with some form of message-sending, message-receiving, or message-interpreting behavior. Thus to assert that messages are at the core of organizational communication may belabor the obvious.

Curiously enough, however, the study of messages qua messages in the organizational context, rather than constituting a major segment of the literature in organizational communication, is actually strewn across a wide range of literatures, lacking coherence or integration. Recognizing this state of affairs, the present chapter is built around four main purposes: (1) to define what is meant by "message" in the organizational context; (2) to review and evaluate various ways of categorizing messages that have been used in organizational research (the bases on which scientific taxonomies may be built); (3) to provide an integrated analysis of one of the most basic approaches to the study of messages, the "functional"; and (4) to consider three problem areas associated with message exchange: overload, distortion, and ambiguity. The chapter concludes with a summary of implications and suggestions for future research dealing with messages in the organizational setting.

DEFINING "MESSAGE"
IN THE ORGANIZATIONAL CONTEXT

An organization can plausibly be defined as an assemblage of messages if we subsume under "message" any stimulus whatever that triggers a "meaning" in someone's head. Thus we can think of such nonverbal or artifactual messages as carpeted flooring, executive dining rooms and parking areas, keys to the washroom, pay raises, and much more. We can also include the vast universe of verbal (including numeric) messages, such as utterances in face-to-face or telephone conversations, remarks in structured interviews, articles in "house organs," notices on bulletin boards, statistical reports, memoranda, computer printouts, videotape presentations, instructions in employee handbooks, and so on.

Clearly, if we were to adopt the broadest signification of message, the present chapter could conceivably embrace every topic contained in this book; some boundaries must be drawn. An obvious place to start is with etymology. *Message* can be traced to the Latin participle *missus,* derived from the verb *mittere,* "to send." This implies the existence of senders and receivers (which is not to deny that the same agent may function, in a given context, as both sender and receiver—that is, transceiver).

Although indispensable, the foregoing falls far short of delimiting the subject matter to manageable proportions. In the present context, we arbitrarily restrict the term "message" to denote *nonrandom verbal symbolization*—in other words, *language.* We shall examine only that research that deals with verbal messages per se, or with phenomena unequivocally associated with such messages. For present purposes, we define "message" as follows:

> An identifiable unit of oral or written discourse, emitted in a context leading one or more observers to believe that, in all probability, the utterance is related to some sort of conscious intent on the part of the message-sender.

An ironic fact must be noted: Actual messages have rarely been the object of the kind of intensive scrutiny that investigators have accorded such topics as leadership, motivation, organizational structure, group dynamics, or reward systems. Communication specialists have generally chosen to study correlates or perceptions of message activity rather than actual messages; consider, for example, the research on networks, supervisory supportiveness, information diffusion, and communication climate. Even when a leadership construct such as "consideration" is explicitly defined in communication terms—"allowing subordinates more participation in decision making and encouraging more two-way communication" (Fleishman & Harris, 1962, p. 43)—researchers nevertheless omit any examination of the *words* that might be spoken by a "considerate" boss. Indeed, an exhaustive analysis of everyday speech in the work place, such as that undertaken by Meissner (1976), remained almost a unique event in our field until culturally-oriented investigators such as Trujillo (1983) began reporting conversations among organizational members.

Recalling that many speech communication scholars have been indoctrinated in rhetorical theory, one might expect to find an impressive corpus of rhetorical criticism applied to corporate or bureaucratic prose. A few critics have examined the public discourse of managers (for example, Crable & Vibbert, 1983; Fisher, 1965, 1966; Myers & Kessler, 1980), but close analysis of "internal" rhetoric is rare (for exceptions see Cheney, 1983; Huff, 1983). The commendable dissections of "doublespeak" language commonly emitted by organizational spokespersons have been the work of English teachers, not professional rhetorical critics.

Thus, the preparation of this chapter posed a problem. If we restricted ourselves to studies focusing on actual words spoken or written in organizations, the list of relevant titles would be embarrassingly brief. But had we attempted to include all the work casting some light on message phenomena, we would have drowned in a sea of data. The result has perforce been selectivity, guided by decisions conceded to be arbitrary.

The Locus of "Message"

If a message is something that can be sent and received, a question arises: Where does a message exist? Obviously, only the physical manifestations of a message can be literally transferred between sender and receiver; meanings cannot be conveyed from one mind to another. This issue has plagued content analysts from the earliest days of modern communication research. Pioneers in content analysis, such as Berelson (1952) and Lasswell (Lasswell, Leites, & Associates, 1949), long ago grappled with the basic problem arising from the differences between "lexical" (or "sign-vehicle") coding and "semantic" coding. In the former, the analyst merely counted the literal occurrences of specified words or phrases; in the latter, he or she assigned textual units to categories purporting to describe the meanings of words. Semantic coding, therefore, required high levels of inference, exercised at a great cognitive distance from the verbal sign-vehicles presented on the printed page.

The semantic/lexical issue produces an inescapable tension inherent in all research involving message analysis: One can buy either high validity with low conceptual significance (lexical coding), or low validity with high conceptual significance (semantic coding). There is no completely satisfactory way of resolving this dilemma. Each investigator must simply decide what kind of coding or interpretation is appropriate in an individual case. We contend, however, that the research literature offers numerous examples of apparently treating a lexical message as if it were *the* semantic message. We propose, therefore, whenever there is room for doubt, to be explicit about the locus of the message being analyzed. To avoid the narrow terminology of "lexical" and "semantic" we prefer the following designators:

> *Ostensively Displayed (OD) Messages*: those that are represented in physical, observable form
>
> *Internally Experienced (IE) Messages*: those that are inferred to "exist" as internal semantic events within the minds of specified message users (senders, receivers, observers); hence not observable, except by introspection

For example, the locus of the OD message "Starting next Monday, Parking Area No. 4 will be closed for a week for resurfacing" would be these typed words on a sheet of paper. As an IE message, its locus is the interpretation given these words in the mind of Receiver X. Strictly speaking, there will be as many loci of IE messages as there are interpreters of a specified OD message. Confusion results whenever a researcher falls into the trap of equating "the meaning" of a given OD message with his or her own IE version of that message. Later in the chapter, when we discuss such topics as message distortion and ambiguity, the importance of making explicit the distinction between OD and IE messages will be especially obvious. We will also return to this issue under the rubric "the observer-inference problem."

TYPES OF SCHEMES
FOR CATEGORIZING MESSAGES

If investigators are to make real progress toward the goal of understanding message phenomena in the organizational context, they must bring order out of chaos by inventing and applying descriptive categories. "Classification is a basic procedure of science" (Duncan, 1984, p. 137), and the ultimate outcome of categorizing is ideally the construction of a scientific taxonomy, central to the formation of hypotheses as to the nature of things. Perusal of the relevant literature demonstrates that, although there is a proliferation of miscellaneous category schemes, nothing has yet emerged that would merit (in its technical sense) the label "taxonomy." A few researchers have, however, taken the first steps toward generating a single set of categories, purporting to be universally applicable to all kinds of organizational messages.

Comprehensive Category Schemes:
An Overview

An ambitious and provocative "taxonomy of communications" (i.e., messages) was proposed almost twenty years ago by a British professor of industrial engineering, Eilon (1968). Eilon first postulated a set of four dimensions for describing all organizational messages: (1) "kind" of message, such as routine vs. special, and time-triggered vs. event-triggered; (2) areas of organizational activity referred to in the content of a message, such as finance or sales; (3) importance of the message; and (4) "intent and impact" of the message, such as encourage or rebuke.

The major portion of Eilon's (1968) article was devoted to developing subcategories under just the first dimension: kinds of messages. He began by classifying all message kinds according to three media categories: written, oral (face-to-face), and oral (via telephone). He then offered a set of six categories incorporating features of content, form, purpose, and receiver-response (see Eilon, 1968, pp. 271-278). The message-kinds included routine reports, memoranda, inquiries, queries, proposals, and decisions. Each of these six was then described under the three media headings, suggesting differences one would expect to find according to whether a message occurs in written form, in face-to-face interaction, or in a telephone conversation.

Surprisingly, Eilon (1968) did not address specifically the ubiquitous formal/informal message dichotomy. However, Melcher and Beller (1967) had earlier hypothesized a "theory of organization communication" based primarily on the formal/informal distinction, with special emphasis on what they called "channel (i.e., media) selection." The Melcher and Beller scheme encompassed the following message categories: written vs. oral; official vs. unofficial channels; types of message, such as giving orders or requesting information; "legitimacy," referring to whether a message is perceived as falling within the "authorized scope of the office (of the message source)"; goal-oriented vs. means-oriented; and sequences of message-presentation (here they were referring to such arrangements as a written message followed by an oral, or an oral followed by a written).

It is both obvious and regrettable that hypothesized dimensions such as legitimacy, goal vs. means orientation, and the sequencing of different media have largely escaped the notice of communication researchers. As one example of neglected possibilities, we cite the case of message legitimacy; in the words of Melcher and Beller (1967, p. 46),

> a manager's effectiveness may rest upon actions that might not be approved by higher management . . . if some question exists about the legitimacy [of an order or a request for information], the receiver may ask that the message be transmitted along formal channels and be written so that he is protected if a question ever arises.

The legitimate/nonlegitimate distinction is clearly a facet of the familiar (but seldom defined) formal/informal dichotomy. However, so basic and so pervasive in the literature is the terminology of formal and informal that we now single it out for special attention.

The formal/informal dichotomy. Although theorists can never ignore the important conceptualization of this distinction proposed by Barnard (1938), for present purposes the analysis of Downs (1967) is especially pertinent. He has suggested what amounts to a four-dimensional analysis of message activity, expanding formal and informal to (1) formal, (2) subformal, (3) personal, and (4) informal. According to Downs, organizational members, when acting formally, are individuals behaving in conformity with officially stipulated roles; hence, their messages are "explicitly recognized as 'official'" (1967, p. 113). The subformal messages are those "arising from the informal authority structure" and are of two types:

> those that flow along formal channels, but not as formal communications [i.e., not as official messages]; and those that flow along purely informal channels. Both types have the great advantage of not being official; hence they can be withdrawn, altered, adjusted, magnified or canceled without any official record being made. As a result, almost all new ideas are first proposed and tested as subformal communications. In fact, the vast majority of all communications in large organizations are subformal. (Downs, 1967, p. 113)

Subformal messages are distinguished, in turn, from personal—those messages transmitted by officials acting as persons rather than as office holders—whereas subformal messages are transmitted by "individuals acting in their official capacity, but not for the record" (Downs, 1967, p. 115). The categories and distinctions proposed by Downs merit careful study by communication researchers.

Although the Downs four-way analysis of the formal/informal dichotomy is a provocative conceptual advance over the conventional view, we suggest that there are at least nine ways in which the terms "formal" and "informal" have been interpreted in the fields of management theory, organization theory, and communication. These are identified, described, and illustrated in Table 14.1.

The categories in Table 14.1, designated "A" through "I," represent an attempt to incorporate the concepts proposed by both Downs (1967) and Melcher and Beller (1967), along with other approaches—most of which, in fact, have received only casual attention from empirical researchers. Thoughtful perusal of the items described in Table 14.1 is almost sure to stimulate fruitful suggestions for future research, even within the relatively restricted boundaries of the formal/informal dichotomy.

It should be obvious, however, that the formal/informal dichotomy is but one of many frames of reference within which systems of message analysis can

TABLE 14.1
The Formal/Informal Dichotomy

According to	Formal	Informal
(A) Message source	Linked to a role and position of source Example: "House organ," job instruction	Not linked to role or position of source Example: Gossip or grapevine talk, golf-course conversation
(B) Channel by which message is routed	Official, as shown on an organization chart Example: Manager talking to a subordinate, or to a managerial peer	Unofficial, not shown on an organization chart Example: Manager A talking to Manager B's secretary
(C) Physical and social setting in which message is transmitted	Identified with the organization qua organization Example: Manager's office; shop floor; committee meeting	Not identified with the organization qua organization Example: Parking lot; wash room; golf course; cocktail lounge
(D) Authoritativeness (authentication) of content	"Official" Example: Policy announcement; job instructions or orders; invitation to attend a meeting	"Unofficial" Example: Stories, myths, anecdotes, etc. (even when uttered by an officer or manager); "inside dope," rumors about office politics, etc.
(E) Structure (in the larger sense)	Prepared in advance; carefully organized; deliberate; rehearsable	Not prepared in advance; spontaneous; not rehearsable
(F) Usage	Memoranda, reports, speeches "Formal" style Example: "You are hereby notified;" "It has been determined;" "The company will not permit"	Conversational talk: hasty, handwritten notes, etc. "Informal" style Example: "Hey, don't forget to come to that meeting today;" "After hashing it over, we've decided;" "I don't want you to do that"
(G) Presence or absence of public commitment (see Melcher & Beller, 1967)	Formal, public proposal or statement (expectation that it will be defended) Example: Any statement issued in such a manner as to indicate commitment	Private, tentative, exploratory remarks and suggestions ("withdrawable") Example: "Trial balloons" and brainstorming talk; informal group discussion
(H) Media (whether identified with organization or not)[a]	Formal Example: Typed letters on letterhead; announcements released to newspapers, TV, etc.; bulletin boards; "house organs," employee handbooks	Informal Example: Ordinary conversation, whether face-to-face or by telephone; handwritten memos or notes; personal notes
(I) "format"[a]	Routine Example: Committee meetings; form letters; certain bulletin board announcements; certain interviews (especially employment and performance-appraisal; also surveys); graphics of various kinds	Nonroutine Example: Ordinary conversation, whether face-to-face or by telephone; many letters and memoranda; many speeches; some graphics

a. Media and formats can also be analyzed, of course, without reference to the formal/informal dichotomy. The potential list is almost endless (in the 1960s there was circulated a popular pamphlet listing no fewer than 100 different ways of transmitting a message). Recently media have been classified according to cuelessness (Rutter, 1984), social presence (Short, Williams, & Christie, 1976) and information richness (Daft & Macintosh, 1981; Daft & Lengel, 1984). It must be noted also that the dividing line between "medium" and "format" is admittedly fuzzy; for example, between telephone, print, and oral media on the one hand; and conversations, interviews, committee meetings, letters, and in-house TV presentations—all formats— on the other hand.

be constructed. Illustrating this point, Table 14.2 offers at least eight rationales in addition to the formal/informal. Some of these are admittedly rather narrow in scope. Nevertheless, each entry in the table represents a "conceptual foundation" on which can be built a useful scheme for categorizing organizational message phenomena. It should be understood that the list is illustrative, not exhaustive, of the possibilities.

We hasten to acknowledge that boundary lines between entries in Table 14.2 are fluid, and that some of the headings could be regarded as subheads under others. This is especially true of the second entry, "task/nontask." Within this dichotomy is embedded the tacit assumption that all organizations serve some sort of basic task function. Given the widely accepted view of organizations as purposeful systems (Ackoff & Emery, 1972), it is not surprising that of all approaches to the analysis of organizational messages, the most pervasive are those called "functional." Functional refers to the generalized and specific purposes messages serve within the organizational context.

FUNCTIONAL APPROACHES:
AN INTRODUCTION

Within functional approaches people are typically viewed as intentional agents who actively create their environments. Organizations are composed of functional interrelationships, coordinated by communication (Miller, 1972). From this perspective messages are seen to be more than mechanisms through which predetermined actions are exhibited; they serve to define the system itself. Clearly, this is a critical perspective for communication scholars. When we regard messages as purposeful rather than as random acts, messages must be explicable in terms of the functions they purportedly serve. As Katz and Kahn (1978, p. 429) suggest:

> Communication needs to be seen not as a process occurring between any sender of messages and any potential recipient, but in relation to the social system in which it occurs and the particular function it performs in that system.

Several researchers have identified "fundamental" functions to be served by the organization, which can be used as bases for categorizing messages. For example, Redding (1964, pp. 43-44) proposed that all message events in the organizational setting could be classified according to three hypothesized organizational functions: task, maintenance, and human. As somewhat modified twenty years later, the descriptions exemplify one widely accepted view of organizational functions:

- The *task* function: the need to accomplish the prime purpose—providing goods or services to society—that justifies the [organization's] existence.

TABLE 14.2
Some Conceptual Foundations of
Message Classification Schemes

(1)	*Formal vs. informal* (roughly equivalent to official vs. unofficial; see Table 14.1)
(2)	*Task vs. non-task* (referring to messages relevant or not relevant to the job–or to the organization)
(3)	*Purpose, intent, function* (using these terms, not synonymously, but with overlapping significations; see Table 14.3. In terms of

- the sender(s)
- the receiver(s), both intended and unintended
- interested third party observers, inside or outside the organization– especially researchers and content-analysts

(4) *Substantive content vs. relational content* ("relational" is interpreted by Watzlawick, Beavin, & Jackson, 1967, pp. 51-54, as those components of a message–frequently nonverbal–that define the interpersonal relationship between two communicants)

(5) *Mediated vs. nonmediated* (a nonmediated message is one whose ostensive display reaches a listener or reader directly, without the intervention of one or more human "relays"; see Smith, 1973)

(6) *Medium* (referring to the physical "carrier" of a message, such as an oral presentation, an employee newspaper, or in-house TV)

(7) *Initial vs. feedback* (i.e., the first message in an arbitrarily identified sequence of message exchanges vs. those messages considered to be feedback responses to preceding messages)

(8) *Original vs. edited* ("edited" refers to changes made in an original message, by the sender or by others in a chain of serial transmissions, including summaries, abstracts, corrected revisions, addenda, etc.)

(9) *Routine (programmed or programmable) vs. ad hoc or innovative (non programmable)*

- The *maintenance* function: the need to maintain the organization as a going concern, as an entity per se. This need is instrumental to the first. . .
- The *human* function: the need to create conditions in which all members of the organization utilize their talents, realize their potential as human beings, and achieve as high a level of satisfaction as possible. (Redding, 1984, p. 54)

Berlo (1969) proposed a triadic typology retaining task and maintenance as the first two categories but substituting "innovation" as the third category. However, our own preference is to consider innovation as a subcategory under each of the other three (Redding, 1984, p. 54).

Farace, Monge, and Russell (1977) synthesized past taxonomic attempts, and proposed five broad categories of "communication functions": (1) work, (2) maintenance, (3) motivation, (4) integration, and (5) innovation (pp. 56-57). Although the terminology varied widely from author to author, Farace et al. indicate that three of the categories—work, maintenance, and integration—reflected conceptual agreement among the overwhelming majority of theorists reviewed. "Work" corresponds to what many investigators have called "task"; "maintenance," to activities required to sustain the existence of the organization qua organization; "integration," to a rather diffuse set of activities ranging from indoctrination to self actualization.

Recently Goldhaber (1983) has presented a set of four categories, under the heading of "message purpose": task, maintenance, human, and innovation. What must be understood here is that these four message purposes—like the five communication functions of Farace et al.—represent a commingling of at least four potentially separate components: (1) organizational function, (2) communication function, (3) message function, and (4) message content. In other words, when one deals with specific typologies, it may be impossible to identify firm boundary lines among these four. Thus, for example, "function" imperceptibly spills over into "content."

In the next section, we elaborate on a general set of functions transcending message content and incorporating the notion that messages serve to define and constrain a communication system as well as to regulate the flow of interaction within that system. Message contents are typically generated in relation to purposes: both the specific purposes that grow out of a specific occasion and the generalized (tacit) purposes that are hypothesized to cut across all human communication acts (O'Keefe & Delia, 1982).

We need to make clear that not all functions relevant to human interaction are included in our list; for example, we omit the utterance—formulation functions, i.e., those derived from the lexical, syntactic, or articulatory requisites for generating intelligible utterances (Greene, 1984). Rather, we examine functions of messages relating to a wide range of interaction goals— including situation-specific objectives, the creating or enhancing of desires for relationships, and needs for establishing personal identity. Even within this more limited domain, however, this functional category schema is meant to be suggestive rather than definitive.

A Proposed Set of Categories
Based on Message Functions

We suggest that within organizations, messages establish functional relationships through which individuals manage and coordinate their activities as they strive to accomplish personal, group, or organizational goals. In order to attain personal goals (*individual message functions*) organizational members must establish mutually acceptable relational arrangements (*relational message functions*). In turn, these relational arrangements influence the coordination of interdependent individuals toward common task objectives (*instrumental message functions*). Then, as the transactions stabilize (*structural message functions*), the organization is able to pursue its primary objectives and to utilize the available human, material, financial, and technical resources.

Overall, this functional categorization provides a fruitful framework for identifying both strategic and tactical features of message phenomena. Messages that, at first blush, appear to be mismanaged or dysfunctional, may later be found to serve the purpose of a sender or receiver. Mitchell (1979, pp.

TABLE 14.3
Category Systems Based on Message Functions

System 1:	*Individual Functions:* Categorization of messages as the embodiment of the intentional, personal goals of the sender
System 2:	*Relational Functions:* Categorization of messages in terms of how they serve to define the structuring of communication relationships
System 3:	*Instrumental Functions:* Categorization of messages in terms of how they contribute to or detract from the pragmatic goals involved in achieving a group task
System 4:	*Contextual Functions:* Categorization of messages in terms of how they serve to mediate other messages, within a relevant context of interaction
System 5:	*Structural Functions:* Categorization of messages in terms of how they contribute to a regularly patterned system of communication

142-144), discussing bureaucratic prose, presents an example of a complicated official definition of "exit." If we view the function of that message as merely to inform—i.e., describe an exit—such a clumsy, detailed, and seemingly redundant message would be ridiculous. However, if we consider that the most important function of the message (in that context) is to stipulate the legal parameters for what constitutes an exit in a construction contract (the control function), then the message "serves its aim perfectly" (Mitchell, 1979, p. 143). Messages may be intended either to impress or express, create mystery or clarify (Burke, 1969; Tompkins, Fisher, Infante, & Tompkins, 1975). Whenever we examine message functions, then, we must bear in mind that seemingly incompetent messages, as viewed from one perspective, may indeed be highly competent when viewed from a different perspective.

There are three other important qualifications regarding functional classifications. First, the functions of any message (or set of messages) are dependent on whose analytic perspective we adopt. Guetzkow (1965), recalling Burns's (1954) classic study of managers and subordinates, points out that "whether a message is regarded as transmission of a command or merely information is a matter of interpretation" (p. 544).

Second, any single message may serve multiple functions, both within and across the five functional systems. For example, within system 1, the analyst may interpret a message as one of both information and control; but across systems, the same message may be interpreted as establishing dominance (system 2), while also contributing to the accomplishment of a group task (system 3).

Third, to analyze functions of messages we must often go beyond what is actually contained in the OD message. Typically, functions (or purposes) must be *inferred* by the process of constructing a sensible interpretation of what a message is saying and why it was exchanged. Inferential processes are affected by the position of the interpreter, the style of the message (Sanders, 1984), and by the time frame in which the analysis is done; that is, if we focus on messages within an ongoing stream of interaction, we may find functions quite different from those identified when we study messages retrospectively.

The functional category system proposed in Table 14.3 incorporates a variety of functions, postulated as lying on a continuum moving from individual intentions (that is, the idiosyncratic and personal origins of message production), then through the dyadic structuring of a relationship, the accomplishment of a group task, the metacommunicative function of messages within the larger context, concluding with the creation of organizational communication structures. We suggest that categorizing messages within this system can help us understand why a message may be sent, how the message may be interpreted, how the message helps to structure the interaction or relationship, and what is accomplished by the transmission of the message. The schema comprises five identifiable systems of analysis and provides a framework for identifying and analyzing message problems. Considering a variety of perspectives, we can identify over 35 functions, grouped under the five overall systems (see Table 14.4). Even such a lengthy category system does not, however, capture all potential message functions.

Individual Message Functions

The seven individual functions reflect the *intentional* nature of message production. In speech-act theory, every utterance is defined by its "illocutionary point," that is, an *intended* immediate goal to be satisfied by the communication (Jacobs, 1985). Hence, we pose as an appropriate starting point for our taxonomy the work of speech-act theorists.

Searle (1979) argues that the best basis for a taxonomy of speech acts is "differences in the point (or purposes) of the (type of) act." Searle distinguishes among the following: *assertives,* which commit the speaker to the truth of an expressed proposition; *directives,* which are attempts by the speaker to get the hearer to do something; *commissives,* which commit the speaker to a future course of action; *expressives,* which express the speaker's psychological state regarding whatever is specified in the propositional content; and *declarations,* which bring about some alteration in the status or condition of the object (or objects) being referred to.

Issues of power, control, and interpersonal influence are obviously central to the functioning of all organizations. Hence, it is not surprising that, within the organizational context, the message intentions (illocutionary points) and effects (perlocutionary effects) that have most often been studied can be regarded as forms of persuasion. Perlocutionary effect differs from illocutionary effect in that the former includes the totality of actual outcomes associated with a message, while the latter is based on what the receiver understands to be the sender's intention when producing an utterance.

Empirical research has traditionally focused on the types of *directives* organizational members use in their efforts to obtain intended perlocutionary effects. These include the regulative function (messages intended to affect behavior) and the persuasive function (defined here as messages intended to affect opinion, attitudes, or beliefs; Halliday, 1973).

TABLE 14.4
A Sampling of Functional Typologies

Individual Functions		
(1)	Assertives	Searle, 1979
(2)	Directives[a]	Searle, 1979
(3)	Commissives	Searle, 1979
(4)	Expressives	Searle, 1979
(5)	Declarations	Searle, 1979
(6)	Informatives	Halliday, 1973
(7)	Affiliatives	
Relational Functions		
(1)	Relational control	Rogers & Farace, 1975
		Fisher & Hawes, 1971
(2)	Message response	Jablin, 1978
(3)	Face-support	Kline, 1981
(4)	Interaction management	Wiemann, 1977
(5)	Feedback	Cusella, 1980
Instrumental Functions		
(1)	Integration	Parsons, 1951, Bales, 1950
(2)	Pattern maintenance	Parsons, 1951
(3)	Goal attainment	Parsons, 1951; Gioia & Sims, 1986
(4)	Adaptation	Parsons, 1951
(5)	Orientation	Bales, 1950
(6)	Information	Bales, 1950; Gioia & Sims, 1986
		Hatfield, 1976
(7)	Control	Bales, 1950
(8)	Decision	Bales, 1950
(9)	Tension management	Bales, 1950, Hatfield, 1976
(10)	Task opinion	Gioia & Sims, 1986, Hatfield, 1976
(11)	Task direction	Gioia & Sims, 1986, Hatfield, 1976
(12)	Attributions	Gioia & Sims, 1986
(13)	Evaluation	Gioia & Sims, 1986
(14)	Comparisons	Gioia & Sims, 1986
(15)	Provides help	Gioia & Sims, 1986
(16)	Rationale	Hatfield, 1976
Contextual Functions		
(1)	Repeat	Knapp, 1972
(2)	Contradict	Knapp, 1972
(3)	Substitute	Knapp, 1972
(4)	Complement	Knapp, 1972
(5)	Accent	Knapp, 1972
(6)	Verify	Knapp, 1972
Structural Functions		
(1)	Maintenance	Farace, Monge, & Russell, 1977;
		Redding, 1964; 1984
(2)	Task	Farace, Monge, & Russell, 1977;
		Redding, 1964; 1984
(3)	Human	Redding, 1964; 1984
(4)	Innovative	Farace, Monge, & Russell, 1977;
		Greenbaum, 1974
(5)	Political	Tichy, 1981

(continued)

TABLE 14.4   Continued

(6)	Technical	Tichy, 1981
(7)	Cultural	Tichy, 1981
(8)	Authority	Guetzkow, 1965
(9)	Friendship	Guetzkow, 1965
(10)	Information-exchange	Guetzkow, 1965; Greenbaum, 1974
(11)	Task expertise	Guetzkow, 1965
(12)	Status	Guetzkow, 1965
(13)	Regulative	Greenbaum, 1974
(14)	Integrative	Greenbaum, 1974,
		Farace, Monge, & Russell, 1977

a. See also compliance-gaining typologies.

Although there have been but a few attempts to ground the study of organizational messages in speech-act theory, we believe this is a promising avenue to pursue (see Drake & Moberg, 1986; Ewald & Stine, 1983). Specifically, speech-act theory posits conditions regarding the nature of social relations between interactants that go beyond typical content/relational distinctions (Watzlawick, Beavin, & Jackson, 1967). Preparatory conditions associated with the performance of specific illocutionary acts and perlocutionary effects include status, rights, and obligation (Austin, 1962; Searle, 1979). Analysis of the ways in which requests assume willingness on the part of the respondent, whereas directives assume obligation, would greatly enrich our understanding of message phenomena in the organizational context.

Interpersonal influence. Most of the work on organizational *directives* has been done under the rubric of interpersonal influence or compliance gaining rather than speech acts. Comprehensive reviews of the literature (Cody & McLaughlin, 1980; Siebold, Cantrill, & Meyers, 1985; Wheeless, Barraclough, & Stewart, 1983) identify four interwoven strands of research: (1) taxonomic classifications of directives, (2) effects of situational and individual differences on message choice, (3) relationships between source characteristics and types of strategy chosen, and (4) methodological critiques of data analysis and instruments. Many of the taxonomic systems have been developed within the interpersonal context.

A core set of message strategies, developed specifically within the organizational setting, is presented in the Frost chapter (Chapter 15, in this volume) and so will not be detailed here. Briefly, these strategies are assertiveness, ingratiation, rationality, threats, exchange, upward appeal, blocking, and coalitions (Kipnis, Schmidt & Wilkinson, 1980; Schilit & Locke, 1982). However, it is important to note that with the exception of a few scattered examples, organizational researchers have made no effort to construct a catalog of OD *messages* that could be used in actually carrying out each of the influence dimensions identified. But we can point to two studies that have constructed typologies focusing explicitly on compliance-gaining messages in the organizational setting: McCallister (1981) and Richmond, Davis, Saylor, and McCroskey (1984).

McCallister (1981), in a simulated experimental setting, analyzed samples of actual *discourse* produced *by the respondents* themselves in a *specified* work setting. The category system (developed directly from the verbal data) identified messages that conveyed empathy, intolerance, solution, company needs, responsibility, home and work obligations, or information requests. McCallister found that most messages were solution-oriented, containing a mixture of considerate and threatening utterances, but that messages expressing intolerance represented a significant minority of the total. Richmond et al. (1984) also dealt with verbatim messages; however, in this case, the researchers supplied the messages (in clusters) representing 18 a priori compliance-gaining techniques. Two groups of respondents (teachers and bank employees) indicated how frequently they thought they had used each of the messages. Significantly, the investigators reported that very few of the 18 techniques had been used frequently by any of the respondents in dealings with their supervisors.

Throughout the literature there is consistent evidence to suggest that the type of directive chosen is crucially influenced by the hierarchical positions of message senders and message targets. However, evidence indicating which types of messages are associated with which hierarchical level is mixed. Some studies suggest that the higher a person is within the hierarchy, the greater is the diversity of strategies he or she utilizes; whereas people with less power communicate in less diverse, more structured ways. In these studies subordinates' messages were based predominantly on appeals to rationality and expertise (Kipnis et al., 1980; Schilit & Locke, 1982). Richmond et al. (1984) conclude that subordinates do not feel they are in very influential positions and hence (understandably) rarely use directives to influence their supervisors. However, other evidence suggests that subordinates use a wide variety of strategies, including covert messages (Porter, Allen, & Angle, 1981; Weinstein, 1979).

Rim and Erez (1980), Erez and Rim (1982), and Kipnis et al. (1980) indicate that in situations where the target is in a relatively low position, the sender uses more assertive and sanction-oriented messages. However, even within the organizational context, some investigations report a bias toward choosing positive influence strategies (Greenberg & Leventhal, 1976; Tedeschi, Gaes, & Riveria, 1977). Managers have testified that they use coercive messages only when there is a very serious problem and the subordinate is not trusted (Kipnis & Cosentino, 1969; Ricillo & Trenholm, 1983). However, Fairhurst, Green, and Snavely (1984) found that most managers used a punitive approach for controlling poor performance. Kipnis (1976) declares that "of all the bases of power . . . the power to hurt others is possibly most often used" (p. 77). Clearly research findings in this area are so uncertain and contradictory that firm generalizations are hazardous.

Unfortunately, we can also draw few conclusions regarding the actual effects of utilizing these messages. Whether specific messages or generalized strategies actually fulfill their intended functions remains an unanswered question—largely because of the narrow methodology and unidirectionality of past research efforts. There is some evidence to suggest, however, that both supervisors and subordinates attribute successful influence attempts to the content of the message (Schilit & Locke, 1982).

Communicative *responses* to compliance-gaining strategies also have been virtually ignored (an exception is the research by McCallister, 1981); yet these response messages are patently as critical to organizations as are the directive messages. The effectiveness of any directive inevitably depends, to a great extent, on the target's perceptions. Employees may respond to a directive in any of numerous ways, including outright defiance, subterfuge, inattention, hostile acceptance, and gracious compliance. There is a vast range of possible commissives, each of which may invoke different interpersonal and organizational responses. Researchers need to address the reciprocal relationship between type of directive issued and subsequent commissives, subsequent directive, and so on. Clearly, the compliance-*giving* message is as critical to understanding the double interact of control as is the compliance-gaining message. The multiple goals of actors and the reciprocal nature of message influence need to be included in any analysis of organizational directives.

Empirical researchers have traditionally ignored influence attempts among individuals occupying the same hierarchical level, or in situations maximizing equality—such as autonomous work groups, worker participation programs, and union meetings—thus creating a serious gap in the range of organizational messages that are studied. Unlike influence attempts across organizational levels, the basis of peer compliance is not rooted in the authority structure, yet peer compliance is just as important and commonplace. We suggest that influence messages exchanged in "horizontal" contexts be the focus of concerted attention among researchers.

Furthermore, Siebold et al. (1985) have argued that the simplified rational model—assuming a singularly purposive, reflexive, and competent communicator, on which this body of research is based—is extremely problematic. Paradoxically, the model also overemphasizes nonrational manipulative strategies. Indeed, speech communication scholars—who have been prominent contributors—would profit by a generous infusion of concepts drawn from rhetorical theory.

Information exchange. Although the primary focus of functional-message research in the organizational context has been on directives, *information-giving* and *information-seeking* functions have also been studied by sociolinguists and those interested in the development of competence (Monge,

Bachman, Dillard, & Eisenberg, 1982; Stohl, 1983). Encoding and decoding functions (which comprise competence) include the ability to request information and to formulate messages that inform. From a functional vantage point, perspective-taking and the ability to adapt messages to listener characteristics are important components to communication effectiveness (Delia, O'Keefe, & O'Keefe, 1982; Sypher & Zorn, 1986).

Affiliative function. The final individual message function, the *affiliative,* has rarely been addressed directly in the research literature. It can be viewed, however, as the communicative enactment of inclusion needs (Schutz, 1958) and of identification processes (Tompkins & Cheney, 1982). Affiliative messages are intended to link the speaker with the "in-group." Unlike affinity-seeking messages, which are designed to get other people to like or to feel positively toward the speaker (Bell & Daly, 1984), the purpose of an affiliative message is to gain recognition from significant other(s), affirming that the speaker is a legitimate organizational member. Affiliative tactics may frequently include the utterance of jargon-filled messages, telling the latest and hottest gossip, utilizing culturally acceptable forms of address, choosing appropriate pronouns, and so on. Affiliative messages are used to demonstrate power, solidarity, and position within the organization (Brown & Gilman, 1960; Slobin, Miller, & Porter, 1968).

A particularly interesting type of message exchange exemplifying the affiliative function is a "routine." Defined by sociologists as "a sequence of utterances which is regular and procedural and which communicates as much by its form as by its content" (Ervin-Tripp, 1969), routines are commonplace in organizational interaction. An example of an organizational routine was encountered repeatedly by one of the authors while serving as a consultant in a large aerospace company:

Employee A: "How about a leisurely lunch?"
Employee B: "Sure, just what the doctor ordered."
Employee A: "Let's go!"

The ostensive messages displayed here are (1) a simple invitation to lunch, (2) an acceptance of the invitation, and (3) a confirmation of the acceptance. But, in that context, the purpose of the routine actually went far beyond either gastronomic desires or sociability. Employee A intended to let B know that A was aware of a much-discussed controversial memo from management deploring "leisurely" lunch hours. Possible functional interpretations by B may have included either a simple *request* for an extended lunch or an *expressive* message indicating lack of respect for management. The response indicated that B did understand the dual nature of the message and that she too was thumbing her nose at management. Thus the double interact served an affiliative function for the speaker while also testing the respondent's corporate knowledge and group affiliation. A naive or poorly socialized employee would probably have focused on the denotative meaning of "leisurely"—by soberly explaining whether or not she actually had time for a long lunch. We are convinced that since such routines are a common communicative phenomenon in organizations and play a significant part in the socialization process, they deserve close scrutiny by researchers.

Relational Functions

Communication theorists contend that messages convey information (content level) and simultaneously define the relationship between the communicators (relational level; Watzlawick et al., 1967). In the words of Millar and Rogers (1976), "people do not relate and then talk, but they simultaneously relate in talk" (p. 89). This perspective portrays the communication process as a negotiation whereby individuals reciprocally define their relationship.

Within organizations, a fundamental dimension of relationships is control. Thus any functional categorization of messages must include a set of categories pertaining to the control aspects of interactions. These functions include *establishing control/submission, providing positive/negative face support, providing feedback responses, and managing interactional sequences.* Empirical evidence suggests that the nature of the relationships that emerge through message patterns influences an individual's ability to process messages, affects the probability that a particular request or command will be carried out, constrains the communication system, and mediates judgments of appropriateness and competence.

As previously noted, in much of the research on organizational messages only rarely do we find the use of actual messages as data. In contrast, recent work dealing with relational functions has focused specifically on verbal discourse. In the typical study, conversations are recorded and transcribed, a system is devised for assigning relational codes to messages, and the nature of the relationship is identified from the emergent patterns.

Relational control. Relational control refers to communicative acts indicating the right to direct, structure, or dominate the interpersonal communication system (Rogers, 1983). Providing an exemplar of this type of research, Fairhurst and her colleagues have applied Rogers and Farace's (1975) relational communication-control perspective to management-subordinate interactions. The researchers assume that message-exchange patterns provide evidence of the manner in which interactants reciprocally define their control positions. Through a series of steps interacts are translated into one of three control moves: one-up (attempts to control the definition of the relationship), one-down (requests or acceptance of others' definition of the relationship), and one-across (nondemanding, nonaccepting, leveling movements). Three basic transactional types are then assigned to each interaction: symmetry, complementarity, or transition (see Rogers-Millar & Millar, 1979, for a more detailed description of the coding system).

Fairhurst, Rogers, and Sarr (1987) found that manager dominance was associated with negative judgments by the subordinate about the relationship. However, in their sample, they found an unexpectedly high frequency of one-across symmetrical verbal exchanges. Dominant/submissive interchanges were avoided, and only rarely was there disagreement with or direct submission to another's control maneuvers. In contrast, Watson (1982a, 1982b), using Fisher and Hawes's Interact System Model (1971), found that leaders often controlled interactions and resisted subordinates' attempts at control, while subordinates usually submitted to leaders' dominance attempts. Perhaps, as Fairhust et al. (1987) suggest, the pressure in their particular organization to create greater participative environments had caused managers to abandon blatantly autocratic message styles. However, the patterns they found could actually have been interpreted by the interactants as dominance-oriented. There is no way of knowing. Relational-control research, thus far, has been limited by the absence of any systematic attempt to *understand* the interactants' perspectives or to blend the relational and content domains. Unfortunately the coding system treats OD and IE messages as equivalent. Triangulating methods, along with concern for various message levels, should help to enrich this area of research.

Message responses. Using a different research strategy, Jablin (1978) also expanded on Watzlawick et al.'s (1967) relational system, but he focused on message-response categories. He studied three properties of the relationship and content aspects of messages (positive, negative, or irrelevant) and developed five possible message responses: confirmation, accedance, repudiation, disagreement, and disconfirmation.

Jablin was concerned with what types of message responses characterized "open" and "closed" communication relationships between managers and subordinates. He found that regardless of the perceived degree of openness, disconfirming messages (i.e., those perceived as irrelevant to the preceding message) were almost always perceived as destructive of interpersonal relationships. Furthermore, disagreement messages (positive relational/negative content) were preferred to messages containing negative relational substance—even when the content expressed verbal agreement with the speaker's position.

Overall, Jablin suggested that "in open relationships superiors and subordinates possess a greater freedom in their response repertory than do subordinates and superiors in closed communication relationships" (1978, p. 305). However, Jablin conceded that most subordinates are restrained in the type of responses they give to superiors' messages. In his study most subordinates did not use acceding or disconfirming responses, regardless of the type of message received from their superior. Similarly, Watson (1982a, 1982b) found that across all types of antecedent message conditions, leaders exhibit a greater degree of choice among alternative message types than do subordinates.

Face-support. Fairhust et al. (1984) focused on how a subordinate's identity was negotiated, and relational control shared, in an interaction designed to rectify a subordinate's poor performance. Managers were asked to recall what they had said to an employee in such a situation. After transcripts had been prepared from the taped responses, each conversation was evaluated according to the degree to which the manager's communication supported the employee's self-image and granted the employee choice of action. Based on a coding scheme developed by Kline (1981), each message was scored for the dominant level of positive face-support and autonomy. Fairhurst et al. found that the managers used punitive and problem-solving styles of control. The use of positive face-support messages was positively correlated with the employee's overall performance rating; autonomy, was associated with length of time between problem recurrences.

Interaction management and feedback. In a somewhat different vein, Eisenberg, Monge, and Farace (1984) note that all organizations have both implicit and explicit rules regulating interactions and that, based on the degree of compliance with these message rules, members of the organization make evaluations about the appropriateness of one another's behavior. Thus interaction management also implies a relational function of messages. Interaction management skills allow individuals to create and sustain acceptable social transactions and to provide feedback within interactions (Wiemann, 1977). An excellent discussion of the functions of relational feedback messages is found in Cusella (Chapter 18, this volume) and need not be detailed here. However, it is important to note that the predominant concern in the empirical literature on feedback has been with the instrumental nature of communication, especially relationships among various characteristics of feedback messages, motivation, and subsequent task performance.

Instrumental Functions

Instrumental-function systems categorize OD messages in terms of how they contribute to, or detract from, the pragmatic goals involved in attempting to accomplish a task. Whereas the focus of the first two systems was on the interpersonal relationship, the focus now is on the workgroup or organization. Jablin and Sussman (1983) have identified five functions of communication that serve the formal organization: (1) to generate information, (2) to process information, (3) to share information necessary for the coordination of interdependent organizational tasks, (4) to disseminate decisions, and (5) to reinforce a group's perspective/consensus.

Much of the work associated with instrumental functions has focused on communication in work groups and among coworkers. Hackman (1976) distinguishes between two types of messages members receive in their work groups: ambient and discretionary. Ambient messages are often random, unintentional, and available to all group members. Discretionary messages, on the other hand, are sent selectively to specific group members. Our concern here is with discretionary messages.

Most instrumental-category schemes are derived from the functional perspective developed by Parsons (1951) and Bales (1950). The fundamental idea in functional theory is that all groups, regardless of size, must meet four basic needs if they are to survive: (1) integration—how the parts of the system fit together as a whole; (2) pattern maintenance—how the major patterns of culture and interaction in the system are maintained; (3) goal attainment—how a system organizes and controls the pursuit of its tasks and goals; and (4) adaptation—how a system relates to its environment. Basic distinctions are made between task-related vs. socioemotional messages, and between messages that are positively oriented toward a particular functional problem vs. those that are negatively oriented (Bales, 1950; Hare, 1976).

Interaction process analysis. Although heavily criticized, the most frequently encountered system (see Fisher, 1980; Hatfield, 1976) for categorizing instrumental functions of messages is that proposed by Bales (1950): Interaction Process Analysis (IPA). Used primarily in small task-group settings, the Bales system comprises 12 categories (actually 6 bipolar pairs) dealing with problems of orientation, information, control, decision, tension management, and integration. Message categories are the following: gives orientation, asks for orientation, gives opinion, asks for opinion, gives suggestion, asks for suggestion, agrees, disagrees, shows tension release, shows tension, shows solidarity, and shows antagonism. All categories are claimed to be mutually exclusive. Within the IPA system six categories are classified as socioemotional and six as task-related. Applying this system to observations of small group discussions, Bales and Strodtbeck (1951) found a 2-to-1 ratio (in frequencies of occurrence) between task-related and socioemotional messages.

The Hatfield taxonomy. A detailed taxonomy of the instrumental functions of messages exchanged between managers and subordinates was developed by Hatfield (1976). Collecting raw data in the form of written transcripts of tape-recorded oral interactions between managers and their subordinates (in a corporate setting), Hatfield (1976) analyzed a sample of 530 utterances. From an initial tentative set of 106 categories, Hatfield's taxonomy finally included a total of 46 categories, subsumed under five abstract headings: direction, rationale, opinion, information, and expression.

As with most coding schemes of instrumental functions, none of Hatfield's categories refers to any specific topic or subject matter, such as job instructions or job rationale. The category set represents a rather vaguely conceived combination of managerial and communication functions, intended to "represent as accurately as possible the universe of communication behaviors which might occur in the superior/subordinate dyad" (p. 99).

Task functions. The instrumental functions of messages are often used as the basis on which to differentiate sequential phases as groups or develop over time (Bales & Strodtbeck, 1951; Fisher, 1980; Poole, 1980; Tuckman, 1965). Poole (1981), for example, utilizing both IPA and Fisher's (1970) Decision Proposal System, has distinguished among phases by identifying specific interacts, clustered according to the functions they serve in the decision process. All phasic models, whether they be unitary or multiple-sequence, assume that the needs of the group (at any given time) determine the types of messages that are exchanged.

Indeed a strong and consistent relationship exists between communication behavior and task. Jablin (1985) suggests that "the most influential factors affecting interpersonal communication patterns and relationships among group members are the characteristics of the task on which they are working" (p. 636). As investigators take greater cognizance of the fact that groups occupy central positions within organizations (Jablin & Sussman, 1983; Payne & Cooper, 1981) and begin to link typically "small group" topics—such as group development and organizational socialization (Wanous, Reichers, & Malik, 1984)—with organizational phenomena, we can expect an even greater research emphasis on the instrumental function of messages.

Organizational verbal-behavior categorization. The integration of cognitive theories into organizational studies has also resulted in an expanded interest in the instrumental functions of messages. The Organizational Verbal Behavior (OVB) categorization system, recently developed by Sims and Manz (1984) and Gioia and Sims (1986), is similar to Bales's and Hatfield's systems; but it also attempts to identify verbal evidence of cognitions (especially attributional statements and requests). Furthermore, the OVB system includes message categories derived from goal-setting theory (e.g., qualitative goal statement, quantitative goal statement), and social learning theory (e.g., self-evaluation).

Gioia and Sims (1986) have investigated managerial attributions and verbal behaviors of both managers and subordinates in response to varying information about subordinates' work history and current performance. Using the OVB system, they coded transcripts derived from over 70 hours of simulated performance-appraisal interviews. There was strong evidence that performance failure evoked attribution-seeking messages, but no evidence that poor work history or inconsistent information led to the seeking of causes. Interactions with poor performers were characterized by more task-related messages, more attribution-seeking questions, and more punitive utterances. Low-performing subordinates tended to make more task-related statement and attributional statements than did high performing subordinates. Gioia and Sims concluded that "the combined use of attributions and observed verbal behaviors represents a step toward understanding of cognition, behavior, and their relationships within organizations" (p. 224). We agree.

For other examples of coding schemes created to study instrumental message functions we refer the reader to the chapter on conflict in this volume (Putnam & Poole, Chapter 16) as well as to studies of ambiguity (Kreps, 1980; Putnam & Sorenson, 1982) and reviews of the bargaining and negotiating literature (Donohue & Diez, 1985; Putnam & Jones, 1982).

Contextual Functions

Categorizing messages according to contextual function permits us to see how different message systems interrelate and how they affirm or disconfirm other messages. For example, some directive messages may contradict those given to inform, and some messages within the authority network may repeat what is being said in the friendship network. Focusing on contextual interrelationships among messages provides a system of analysis for linking the study of actual messages with important organizational constructs, such as role conflict, goal clarity, and communication climate.

The six contextual functions are adapted from Knapp's (1972) list of ways in which nonverbal communication can support verbal communication (the categories can be usefully applied to verbal as well as nonverbal communication): (1) *repeat,* (2) *contradict,* (3) *substitute,* (4) *complement,* (5) *accent,* or (6) *verify* other messages. The fascinating work on double binds in organizations (Putnam, 1986; Roethlisberger, 1945; Wagner, 1978) provides an excellent example of ways in which to incorporate the analysis of contextual functions into the study of organizational messages. Unfortunately, such incorporation is rare.

Structural Functions

The structural functions of messages refer to the ways in which messages contribute to a regularly patterned system of communication. Organizations become organized by developing patterns of message transactions appropriate to the accomplishment of organizational objectives (Katz & Kahn, 1978). Greenbaum (1974) defines organizational communication as "the sum of a group of subsystems or *functional* communication networks, each of which is related to one or more organizational goals" (p. 741). Guetzkow (1965) assigns to the network concept a central place in his synthesis of theory and research in organizational communication, explaining that as messages are sent and received throughout the organization, "message flows become regularized, so that one may speak of communication nets" (Guetzkow, 1965, p. 539).

Communication networks are not observable, tangible objects. Rather, as specific messages are systematically sent and received, patterns of interrelationships develop, which analysts can then conceptualize as networks. Distinctions among various networks are often made on the basis of the predominant function that a cluster of messages supposedly serves. For example, Guetzkow (1965) specified that the authority network includes the linkages involved in the exercise of power relations within the organization. Authority messages typically flow downward and are viewed as directives or commands. In contrast, the friendship network is composed of messages expected to furnish emotional and social support to the interactants. The information-exchange network represents messages typically concerned with knowledge about activities related to the internal operations of the organization. Verification and repetition are important characteristics of messages within this type of network. Therefore, although networks are the subject of the Monge and Eisenberg chapter (Chapter 10, in this volume), we should not ignore them in the context of any functional message typology.

The close linkage among networks, message functions, and message content is made unmistakably clear in models proposed by Thayer (1968) and Tichy (1981). Tichy (1981), focusing his analysis on networks, presents two different orientations as bases on which to construct category systems. On the one hand, he identifies three kinds of "problems" that are said to "typify different challenges faced by an organization": (1) technical strategies, (2) political allocations, and (3) organizational culture (pp. 231-236). On the other hand, however, he also speaks explicitly of three kinds of message contents: (1) information, (2) affect, and (3) influence (see Tichy, 1981, pp. 226-227, 235). We suggest that these two triads can best be visualized as orthogonal dimensions of a matrix representing nine message categories. This system would provide a useful framework for explicating the relationship between networks and OD and IE messages.

Recognizing that messages are the building blocks of networks, we contend that if more attention were paid to actual messages constituting networks, the contributions of network research would be greatly enhanced. Network studies could move from a relatively static, highly quantified, atheoretical position, to a more interpretive construction of organizational reality.

In summary, the identification of message functions has been the focus of many research endeavors. However, most studies have dealt with only one level of interpretation and one system of categorization. We propose that researchers need to combine different levels of analysis and different systems of categories if our cognitive maps of messages within organizations are to be reasonably isomorphic representations of actual organizational experience. A focus on multiple functions would allow us to explore the different (and frequently contradictory) rationalities found in most organizations.

OUTCOMES OF MESSAGE EXCHANGE:
POTENTIAL PROBLEM AREAS

The very vocabulary of "function" inevitably triggers consideration of the outcome dimension of functional relationships: When X is said to be a "function of Y," we typically examine the way in which changing values of X are correlated with changes in the value of Y. Hence, when we study message functions, it is a natural transition to examine what we call message outcomes. Three areas of potential problems associated with message exchange are dominant in the literature: overload, distortion, and ambiguity. The attention devoted over the years to these three topics reflects the practical concerns of management—concerns that are now recognized as sources of most research topics in the field, through at least the 1960s (see Redding, 1985). However, interest in these problem areas has continued for reasons beyond the utilitarian. The following section illustrates the ways in which each area incorporates a wide range of communication concepts, involving both ostensive and internally experienced messages.

Message Overload

One of the most talked about message problems, if not the most pervasive, is message overload. *Message overload refers to the transmission of new information at a rate that far exceeds the input-processing and output-generating capabilities of organizational actors.* Overload is best conceived as occurring by degrees, varying in intensity, clarity, and disruptiveness. Obviously, response-time demands and the duration of overload affect whether massive or minor disorganization will occur in the response to the overload situation (Churchill, 1965).

The study of overload necessitates a greater focus on internally experienced (IE) rather than ostensively displayed (OD) messages. The potential for overload is increased by the existence of a large number of complex messages within a system, but for overload to occur there must be an attempt to process the OD messages. Thus although communication textbooks exhort speakers to take receivers' capabilities into account, and a few authors define effective messages in terms intended to reduce overload (such as conciseness and brevity; see Redding, 1984), the primary empirical focus has been on receiver responses to overload.

Most research efforts have been directed at identifying adaptive and maladaptive mechanisms of adjustment (Katz & Kahn, 1978). A large body of literature explores ways that scientists, in both academic and research-and-development organizations, cope with the information explosion in various technical fields (see, e.g., Abelson, 1966; Chapanis, 1971; Licklider, 1966; Mullins, 1968; Platt, 1962). More germane to our interests, however, is the work on organizational responses to message inputs (Churchill, 1965; Daft &

MacIntosh, 1981; Huber, 1982). For example, in the 1960s a series of highly influential papers dealing with mechanisms of adjustment to information overload were published (Miller, 1960, 1961, 1964). A classic study by Meier (1963) investigated the effects of information overload on the functioning of an academic research library (see Katz & Kahn, 1978, for a review).

Experimental researchers have also studied the effects of message overload. The detrimental effects of overload on group performance are well documented (Christi, 1954; Lanzetta & Roby, 1957; Leavitt, 1951); however, terms such as "saturation," used to describe the effects of overload, have been criticized on the grounds of poor operationalizations and lack of empirical analyses to test hypotheses directly (Guetzkow, 1965). In general empirical studies of overload can be said to suffer from conceptual as well as measurement problems. Surveys purporting to measure overload typically use a small number of items, all of questionable validity (see Roberts & O'Reilly, 1974; O'Reilly, 1978). Furthermore, survey questions usually ignore message frequency, valence, quality, and content, creating an impoverished view of the phenomenon. In other words, the research on overload rarely includes a study of either OD or IE messages.

Weick (1970) offers a receiver-oriented view of overload that is far richer and less dependent on OD messages than are most conceptualizations. He defines overload as "the perceived inability to maintain a one-to-one relationship between input and output within a realizable future, given an existing repertoire of practices and desires" (p. 56). From this perspective overload is primarily a judgment or appraisal, and the base line is the actor's assessment of his or her own response capabilities. Thus overload is situated in the cognitive responses (IE messages), resulting in a focus on the adaptive response called "twigging"—that is, the modification and balancing of an actor's need for knowledge against his or her capacity to absorb it.

In the more traditional literature, coping mechanisms have been classified in at least six ways: (1) specialization of work, (2) sampling of available information, (3) omission of messages, (4) development of a priority system, (5) development of networks, and (6) modification of messages.

Specialization of work. Work specialization as a response to overload includes the narrowing of attention frames (Paisley, 1981) and the redefining of situations regarding what is relevant for a particular person or work unit (Weick, 1970). Meier (1963) found the following responses in the library: (1) the creation of branch facilities, (2) the delegation of functions to outside agencies, and (3) the creation of rigid regulations whereby some services were reduced or eliminated. Miller (1960, 1961, 1964) highlighted decentralization, or delegation of information processing to others, as a primary coping mechanism for overload.

More recently, Huber (1982) has discussed the process of "message routing," a procedure whereby the organization determines that particular messages are sent to relatively few organizational members. Selective transmissions narrow the scope of messages that a given group may receive, hence reducing the group's information-processing demands and increasing its specialized identity. Huber (1982) identifies six variables that affect the routing and transmission of organizational messages: (1) costs of communicating, (2) workload of the message-sending unit, (3) message relevance, (4) repercussions from communicating bad news, (5) relative power and status of the sender and receiver, and (6) frequency of prior communication.

Sampling of available information. Instead of systematically reviewing all available information that may result in message overload, individuals may sample the content domain (Paisley, 1981). Extreme forms of message sampling include approximation, lowering the standards of precision (Miller, 1960), and lowering performance standards to tolerate higher rates of errors (Meier, 1963). A less dramatic form of sampling is message summarization (Huber, 1982). Summaries reduce the quantity of content while reproducing the essential meaning of messages, thereby greatly reducing the receiver's processing requirements.

Computer-mediated communication may help reduce overload in two ways. First, the ability to store large quantities of information allows the work unit to sample only those bits of information perceived to be most relevant (Paisley, 1981). Second, because electronic messaging is low in social presence, the number of social cues and multiple levels of meaning that must be processed are reduced (Steinfeld & Fulk, 1986). Other sampling practices include a reliance on secondary rather than primary sources and the use of gatekeepers to gather and transmit information (Weick, 1970).

Omission of messages. Omission of messages includes both behavior by the receiver (e.g., failing to handle some input information) and intentional or unintentional behavior by the sender (e.g., ignoring or failing to correct errors [Miller, 1961]; restricting the size of memoranda). Overload may, of course, be avoided by the refusal to handle input at all (Miller, 1961) as well as by the transfer or resignation of personnel (Meier, 1963).

In general, as a quantity-reduction technique, omission consists of applying nonselective criteria to overload: The problem of too many messages is resolved by simply reducing the number of messages indiscriminately. As a strategy for dealing with overload, omission has been criticized because of the likelihood that both relevant as well as irrelevant messages will be excluded (Katz & Kahn, 1978; Weick, 1970).

Development of priority systems. Unlike the omission tactics described above, the development of a priority system consists of the intentional application of selective criteria, which results in adjustments to the perceived relevance or importance of messages. A revised set of priorities enhances the possibility that the messages being processed will be coherent.

If the overload is not very severe, a queuing procedure is often enacted whereby messages are allowed simply to pile up (Miller, 1960). As overload becomes more severe, priority rules may be established, resulting in the storing of incoming requests, in creating waiting lines, and in selecting gatekeepers (Meier, 1963). Low-priority evaluations indicate that some messages are downgraded, delayed, or ignored (Gerstenfeld & Berger, 1980; Meier, 1963; Miller, 1960; Ullman & Huber, 1973). In general, a slowdown in message processing is an inevitable result of message overload (Downs, 1967).

Development of interpersonal networks. Another potential response to overload is the revision of organizational networks. This response may take place in at least two ways: decentralizing one's position in the network, or creating new resource networks that can buffer the unit from message overload.

First, message overload may result from a unit being highly integrated and central to the organizational network. Decentralizing networks by the creation of multiple channels (Miller, 1960) makes a unit less sensitive to overload or saturation because it limits the number of OD messages any single link must process (Shaw, 1981). In general, decentralized communication patterns are associated with a greater ability to deal with work-related uncertainty, which is also associated with greater message generation (Conrath, 1967; Duncan, 1973; Weick, 1979).

Second, the creation of special-purpose networks may help manage overload. Research on "invisible colleges" (Crane, 1972), diffusion of innovation processes (Rogers & Shoemaker, 1971), and gatekeeping and boundary-spanning roles (Tushman, 1977, 1979) illustrate clearly how specific network links may provide the unit with relevant, accurate, and timely messages only when a felt need arises.

Network development and modification often are the result of other strategies for dealing with overload. For example, specialization of work presents an opportunity for new interpersonal relationships to form. Weick (1979) suggests that if a scientist reacts to overload by specialization and new information search practices, bonds between persons may be loosened, dissolved, or redefined, and new attachments may be developed.

Modification of messages. The final type of response to information overload involves the modification of messages themselves. Message transformations can be rooted in the cognitive limitations and motivations of senders and receivers, or in the structural constraints of serial transmission. Modifications may be purposeful or random, well intended or malicious. Message modification differs from message summarization in that it changes the meaning of the message whereas summarization does not. Most studies of message modification fall under the rubric of message distortion. It is important to note that emphasis on the OD message makes this response qualitatively different from those discussed previously. However, with a few notable exceptions identified below, researchers have virtually ignored the actual messages that supposedly are being modified.

Message Distortion

As suggested above, one of the most common forms of message distortion is that associated with "serial transmission." This will be discussed first.

Serial transmission. Messages need to travel up and down and across the organizational hierarchy. As in the familiar game of telephone, messages may get modified or distorted because (1) the goal of one or more of the players is to change intentionally the message, (2) the mere number of people in the game makes it likely that the message will be transformed through subtle changes in each transmission, and (3) a sender or receiver may be unable to reproduce the identical message because of cognitive, physical, or social limitations.

As a message moves through the organization, transformations may also take place as a result of "uncertainty absorption," a concept referring to situations in which messages contain only inferences drawn from a body of evidence rather than the evidence itself (March & Simon, 1958). As a result of uncertainty absorption, recipients are often severely limited in their ability to judge the correctness of presented information. Hence, in such cases the sender's credibility plays a large role in the acceptance of messages.

Ackoff and Emery (1972) distinguish between passing intermediaries, whose only interventions are structural, and active intermediaries, who do more than modify the structure of the message. Specialization, technical vocabulary, and time and spatial factors all increase the likelihood that some members of the organization will act as relays for messages coming into the organization. The relay person may *duplicate* the message without change; *translate* by converting the message from one modality to another; *simplify* a single complex message; *reduce* multiple messages; *combine* reductions; or *summarize* (Smith, 1973).

Campbell's (1958) classic work on types of distortion (biases) occurring as a result of serial transmission provides us with an excellent transition for understanding message transformations within the organization that are not necessarily a result of overload. The most general level of distortion is characterized as message simplification. This includes the abbreviations, condensations, and loss of detail that occur as message units travel through the organization.

Cognitive processes. Another type of distortion occurs because of the tendency to "assimilate messages to prior input"; Campbell (1958) suggests this as the most common of the systematic biases, relating it to features of associative memory. The result is a pervasive bias toward the ordinary and the typical. Similarly, the conservative, repetitive nature and mundane content of "memorable" messages have been discussed elsewhere (Knapp, Stohl, & Reardon, 1981; Stohl, 1986). In these studies the long-term value of organizational memorable messages was found to be enhanced by the consistency of content with other organizational messages and by employees' perceptions of congruence between message content and organizational culture (Stohl, 1986).

Distortion may also occur as a result of assimilation of messages to expected input and to one's own attitudes. In other words, distortion will generally be in the direction of making input look like what was expected to be input or consistent with the sender's or receiver's own attitudes.

Other causes of distortion stem from the tendency to shift coding in the direction of affective evaluation (e.g., the halo effect) and associating a given message with other messages that have often varied together (stereotyping). O'Reilly (1978) also suggests that the probability of distortion increases when group conformity is high and when rewards and punishments are made clear.

In summary, message modification is an inevitable part of serial transmission and information processing. The relationship between the original message and the subsequent ostensive message displays will vary depending on a multitude of circumstances.

Although most work on message transmission/modification is not grounded in the study of OD messages, there is one class of messages that has been extensively studied—rumors. Rumors are defined as messages that are a part of the informal communication network (grapevine) and are specific to persons, situations, or both.

Rumors. The earliest organizational studies of rumor transmission were conducted in a military setting by Caplow (1947). Using both observational and interview methods, Caplow found that (1) rumors traveled along intrafunctional lines rather than interfunctional; (2) comparatively few rumors occurred in the system; (3) rumor information was more often accurate than inaccurate; (4) diffusion rate was rapid; (5) most rumors consisted of three associated statements; (6) distortion appeared mainly through attempts to simplify statements (rather than additions or subtractions); and (7) there were positive relationships between rumor survival time and diffusion and veracity.

Davis (1952, 1953) devised a method for studying communication in the informal grapevine. He called this ECCO analysis (Episodic Communication Channels in Organizations), a technique for identifying the source, method of transmission, and accuracy of transmission of specific messages. Unlike conventional network approaches, in which organizational members are asked to generalize their communication activities, the ECCO survey asks respondents to indicate whether and from whom they have heard specific messages. The advantages of the ECCO methodology are many. Besides being one of the few methods that focuses on actual messages, it takes a minimal amount of time to collect the data, produces results quickly, and is more reliable than other self-report measures of network activity. Unfortunately, each message survey describes a unique diffusion pattern that may or may not approximate a more stable and generalized communication network.

In many organizations rumor and distortion are often (unfortunately) viewed as correlated terms. The grapevine is an inherent part of any organization, but many managers look upon rumors as a problem (Rosnow & Kimmel, 1979). Individuals are less likely to be held accountable for message distortion in the informal than in the formal system (Davis, 1953). Thus many think that information from the grapevine is less likely to be accurate. Research, however, indicates that although sharpening, leveling, and assimilation are common processes of distortion (Allport & Postman, 1947; Davis & O'Conner, 1977), the grapevine usually carries more accurate than inaccurate information (Caplow, 1947; Rosnow & Fine, 1976; Rudolph, 1973). Furthermore, grapevine communication travels faster than most other forms of transmission. Thus the grapevine is not nearly so problematic as is commonly thought.

Rumors appear to emerge to explain situations that are perceived as both confusing and important; that is, the amount of rumor activity varies according to perceived thematic importance and ambiguity. There is a high correlation between frequency of messages in formal and informal systems. In general, rumors are grounded in a combination of uncertainty and anxiety, and are not seriously distorted as they travel through the organization.

Distortion within hierarchical relationships. Another type of distortion is distortion to please the receiver. This is especially common when the message is rooted in the organizational hierarchy and the recipient of the message has power over the sender. The types of subordinate message distortion are quite similar to the strategies used to address message overload. They include gatekeeping, summarization, changing emphasis within a message, withholding, and changing the nature of information (Fulk & Mani, 1986).

Situational antecedents grounded in an instrumental (functional) theory of communication have been extensively investigated. Specifically, there is a significant amount of empirical research to suggest that people in lower power positions suppress information that is detrimental to their own welfare. Studies by Read (1962), Cohen (1958), Watson (1965), and O'Reilly and Roberts (1974) suggest that intentional message omission (gatekeeping) occurs especially when messages are sent to higher status individuals who are also perceived as powerful. Distortion is also positively related to workers' achievement needs and sense of insecurity (Athanassiades, 1973; Mellinger, 1956). Subordinates' trust in supervisors is inversely related to information distortion (Mellinger, 1956; Read, 1962). Under conditions of high trust, the information transmitted is more accurate (Komsky & Krivonos, 1980; O'Reilly & Roberts, 1974) than under conditions of low trust.

By exploring perceptions of role stress and supervisory downward communication, Fulk and Mani (1986) have attempted to ground the study of distortion in a dynamic model by linking subordinates' communicative behavior to the communication of the supervisor. The individual's communication is viewed both as response and stimulus to the partner's communication. Fulk and Mani (1986) found that role stress was not strongly linked to distortion. However, subordinates reported less gatekeeping, withholding, and distortion when they perceived supervisors to be supportive and to be communicating accurate messages. There was one exception: Subordinates reported more summarizing in messages from supervisors who were seen as accurate communicators.

Future research on distortion needs to explore interlocking patterns of behavior and focus on actual messages. There has been a serious neglect of the study of messages, per se; with few exceptions (Komsky & Krivonos, 1980; Sussman, 1974) most of the work reflects subordinate perceptions. Single items of distortion also need to be replaced with richer operationalizations reflecting the complexity of message transmission and interpretation.

Distortion of information may, of course, be rooted in other factors besides the power dimension. In some cases normative assumptions about what kinds of information can be related results in distortion.

Distortion and normative factors. Tesser and Rosen (1975) call the tendency to distort information based on normative assumptions the MUM effect: To keep mum about unpleasant messages. The MUM effect is said to be the result of a pervasive bias impelling communicators to encode (transmit) messages that are thought to be pleasant for the recipient, and to avoid encoding those that are unpleasant.

In a series of experiments Tesser and his colleagues have found that suppression of bad news occurs more often than enhancement of good news, and that the greater reluctance to communicate bad news is restricted to those situations in which the recipient is the person whose fate is altered by circumstances described in the message. The MUM effect has been found across situations and across relationships (intimate, stranger). Generality or specificity of message content does not change the effect nor does the means of transmission.

Studies of the MUM effect are interesting for several reasons. First, they examine actual messages. Second, they look to the subjects to explain their own communicative behavior. Third, the interactive nature of message transmission is considered. However, embedded within this research program is a dangerous assumption, common to almost all distortion work: that there is an objective message "out there," which has a single, definitive meaning.

Thus the distance between what a message "actually says" and what is transmitted is the embodiment of distortion. However, as we have emphasized throughout this chapter, there is always a range of interpretations; the assumption of one objectively "correct meaning" of a message cannot be sustained.

Message Ambiguity

Interpreting messages is a dirty business. From the simplest greeting to the most complex rationalization, messages are inherently ambiguous and sometimes intentionally misleading. (Hewes, Graham, Doelger, & Pavitt, 1985, p. 299)

For anyone attempting to analyze message ambiguity, the dirtiness of message interpretation is magnified by the fact that the concept of ambiguity is itself ambiguous (see Empson, 1930/1963, p. 6). This no doubt helps to account for the paucity of empirical studies on a topic of such obvious importance. So basic is the problem of agreeing on a set of criterial attributes for the term *ambiguity* that, before reviewing the small body of empirical research, we shall address the questions "What is ambiguity?" and "In what respects (if any) may ambiguity be considered as a quality inhering in the words of an OD message?"

At first blush, identifying the critical attributes of the term *ambiguity* should be easy. Everyday usage, as reflected in dictionaries, consistently focuses upon "susceptibility to multiple interpretation" as the basic requirement. The *American Heritage Dictionary* (1969) adds to this a closely related, but not identical, feature when it stipulates that an ambiguous message is one whose meaning is "doubtful or uncertain." A safe inference is that the doubt or uncertainty is a subjective response, induced in the mind of a reader or listener, as a consequence of characteristics discoverable in the wording of a message.

Before proceeding further, we need to take into account the term *equivocality,* frequently encountered as an approximate synonym for *ambiguity*. The *American Heritage Dictionary* (1969) draws an important distinction: *ambiguous* is used to denote "the presence of two or more possible meanings [in a message]"; *equivocal,* to denote "deliberately unclear or misleading usage"—thus introducing the message sender's intentions (a topic to be considered later). In contrast, Weick (1979) seems at times to use the term *equivocality* as an umbrella term covering "ambiguity," "uncertainty," and "other forms of indeterminacy" (1979, p. 174). However, he also writes,

It is important to realize that an input [i.e., a message] is not equivocal because it is devoid of meaning or has confused meaning (both of these connotations are associated with the words ambiguity and uncertainty). Instead, equivocal inputs have multiple significations. . . . The image we want to capture is not that of an environment that is distorted, indeterminate, and chaotic. (Weick, 1979, p. 174)

To this point, one could conclude that (1) an ambiguous message contains specifiable qualities inducing a reader or listener to perceive two or more plausible ways of interpreting the message, and that (2) as a result, the receiver experiences a state of doubt or uncertainty. Although no one would deny that these two attributes are commonly associated with ambiguity, close inspection reveals that they fail to appear in some instances of supposedly "ambiguous messages." As an example there is a venerable case, always presented as a paradigmatic instance of message ambiguity (especially in supervisory-communication workshops): A foreman tells a machine operator, "Better clean up around here," whereupon the operator drops what he is doing and busies himself sweeping the floor; but it turns out that the foreman actually wanted the operator to spend only a few moments cleaning up some oily waste and then to return promptly to the job he was working on (see Haney, 1960, pp. 41-42). The foreman's words, although admittedly open to more than one interpretation, obviously did not produce multiple meanings in the mind of the machine operator; nor is there any evidence to suggest that he experienced doubt or uncertainty. The message receiver in this episode clearly believed that his interpretation of the message was correct.

That the employee "misinterpreted" or "misunderstood" the foreman's remark is undebatable. Hence, we can say that since the sender's message was actually interpreted in two ways—that is, the foreman's and the employee's—it was "susceptible to multiple interpretation" in this particular context. However, neither the sender nor the perceiver, at the time of the message transaction, was aware of this fact. During the episode itself neither communicant experienced subjective doubt or uncertainty (or equivocality). What all this demonstrates is that in some cases a supposedly ambiguous message is not ambiguous at all as far as the communicants' perceptions are concerned.

This line of reasoning encourages us to propose that one solution to the definitional problem is to recognize a distinction between two kinds of experienced ambiguity. By "experienced ambiguity" we refer to a receiver's state of mind as contrasted with the linguistic or structural features of an OD message itself that cause it to be labeled "ambiguous." We designate these as Type 1 and Type 2:

Type 1 ambiguity: a receiver's mental state of doubt, confusion, or uncertainty, resulting either from (a) inability to select a single interpretation from two or more plausible options—that is, multiple interpretations are perceived; or (b) inability to construct any plausible interpretation whatever—that is, the message is perceived as "meaningless" in a particular context.

Type 2 ambiguity: a receiver's mental state of clarity, free from serious doubt or uncertainty, regarding his or her single interpretation; however, this interpretation differs from the sender's intended meaning, and it may differ from the interpretations created by other receivers ("Having selected and imposed a single meaning on any display in front of them, people often discover with regret that additional meanings are just as plausible"; Weick, 1979, p. 173).

"Experienced ambiguity"—whether of Type 1 or Type 2—has been contraposed to the ambiguity commonly thought to reside somehow in the words of a message itself. Although word meanings cannot be legislated, we believe it regrettable that some such label as "potential" or "predicted ambiguity" has never gained currency as a modifier for the ambiguous term *ambiguity*. Eisenberg (1984) is correct in reminding researchers that they are engaged in a fruitless endeavor when they attempt to assign degrees of ambiguity to specific messages:

> more than one researcher has glossed the issue by remaining vague about the locus of ambiguity, i.e., whether it resides in the source's intentions, the receiver's interpretations, or in the message itself . . . Clarity (and conversely, ambiguity) is not an attribute of messages; it is a *relational* variable, which arises through a combination of sources, message, and receiver factors. (p. 229)

To Eisenberg's three factors should be added the fourth essential component of any communication episode: the situation, or context (Bavelas & Smith, 1982; Weick, 1979). In short, researchers dealing with message ambiguity (or equivocality) should be careful to specify their criteria for identifying examples of ambiguity, to make clear the sources of perceptions (senders, receivers, members of rating panels, or the analysts themselves) used in establishing the presence of ambiguity, and to frame the message in clearly described contexts ("equivocality . . . is embedded in the total situation"; Weick, 1979, p. 182).

All these definitional issues provide an essential perspective from which one may view the modest body of published research dealing explicitly with message ambiguity or equivocality in the organizational setting. Especially familiar to students of organizational communication is the Weick (1979) model of organizing, a model that places communication processes at the very center of organization theory. One of his most fundamental hypotheses is that, as equivocality (ambiguity) increases, organizational members will use fewer "assembly rules" but more "communication cycles" (double interacts) than they would in situations of low ambiguity. Three influential studies reflect efforts to conduct empirical "tests" of selected aspects of Weick's theory: Bantz and Smith (1977), Kreps (1980), and Putnam and Sorenson (1982).

In an ingenious but highly contrived experimental situation, Bantz and Smith (1977) presented ad hoc triads of adult subjects with the task of selecting adjectives (from a prepared list) perceived to be useful in clarifying brief literary passages. High, medium, and low equivocality ratings for the passages were based on perceptions of undergraduate student raters, using cloze procedure as the measurement technique. As Kreps (1980) has pointed out, serious questions arise concerning the composition and structure of the triads (supposedly analogous to real-life organizations), the nature of the task (selecting adjectives from a list vs. choosing or composing realistic messages), and the strategy of equating word selection acts with "cycles" (which actually are three-part sequences of act, response, and response to the response: double interacts). These limitations should be kept in mind in noting that Bantz and Smith (1977) reported no significant relationship between number of cycles and degree of equivocality in the messages.

Kreps (1980), attempting to rectify certain shortcomings he had identified in the Bantz and Smith (1977) experiment, content-analyzed utterances made in decision-making meetings of a university faculty senate. Specifically, he focused on "three of the underlying dimensions of informational equivocality as explained by Weick": complexity, unpredictability, and ambiguity (Kreps, 1980, p. 382). He concluded that, consistent with Weick's hypothesizing, high-equivocality messages were associated with higher frequencies of "cycles" than were low-equivocality messages—a conclusion at sharp variance with that of Bantz and Smith (1977).

Putnam and Sorenson (1982) carried out an experiment designed to overcome certain limitations in the Kreps (1980) study. They established two independent variables, communicants' hierarchical position (in a simulated organization) and perceived message equivocality; their two dependent variables were communication cycles (double interacts) and assembly rules. College students, participating in a classroom simulation exercise, were required—acting in small groups—to respond to two sets of four messages, one set determined to be high in ambiguity; the other, low. Results were interpreted as supporting Weick's prediction about assembly rules but not about cycles.

In the light of definitional issues discussed earlier, three features of the Putnam and Sorenson (1982) study warrant special attention. First, the investigators explicitly differentiated between what we have called OD and IE messages; more specifically, they made clear that "ambiguous cues" (in the wording of a message) and "equivocality engendered in the receiver should exist in a parallel relationship"; hence, "the structure of an ambiguous message influences the probability of multiple meanings [in the mind of a receiver]" (p. 117). Moreover, they reminded their readers that "meanings are not restricted to the sender's intentions" (p. 117). Second, in the specific messages that Putnam and Sorenson composed as experimental stimuli, three elements were incorporated as critical conditions of "structural" message ambiguity: (1) the inclusion of "at least one high abstraction term," (2) the omission of certain specific details, and (3) the absence of any "explicit or implicit course of action" to be adopted by the receivers (p. 117). Third, equivocality (that is, ambiguity) was measured in terms of the perceptions of message receivers (actually, two groups: "independent raters" in a pre-test, and the experimental subjects themselves in a post-test; pp. 117-120).

These three studies were all examining what we have designated as Type 1 ambiguity. Message receivers in every case were described as experiencing subjective doubt or uncertainty (at least in some measurable degree) as a consequence of certain qualities of message wording that made it easy to construct multiple interpretations. Sometimes, however, it is hard to know which type of ambiguity is denoted in a research report. For example. Ruchinskas (1982), on the basis of a literature review, concluded that ambiguous work environments are more effectively clarified (not surprisingly) through face-to-face rather than written communication; and that as one moves up the typical hierarchy, the environment becomes more equivocal and the messages more ambiguous. This latter finding is congruent with March and Simon's famous concept of "uncertainty absorption," postulating that as messages travel from lower to upper echelons, details are dropped out or "absorbed" (March & Simon, 1958, pp. 155, 165-167).

Some researchers have worked with the concept of "richness," a term denoting the "potential information-carrying capacity" of a medium (Daft & Lengel, 1984). Thus it has been found that as situations become more ambiguous, the "richer" the available information must be if receivers are to reduce ambiguity, but the type of ambiguity is not specified (Daft & Lengel, 1984). Face-to-face communication—with its advantages of instant, two-way feedback, combined with the availability of both visual (bodily) and linguistic symbol systems—is richer than written media (Daft & Lengel, 1984; for applications of richness to electronically mediated messages, see Steinfield & Fulk, 1986). We should not forget, however, that supplying greater richness of detail can also serve to confuse rather than to clarify; hence, the "richness" concept needs further analysis.

Two older studies, although not focusing on message ambiguity per se, yield findings relevant to Type 2 ambiguity—in which variant ("incorrect") interpretations of a message occur but without the receivers being aware of this at the time of message reception (as in the episode of the foreman and the machine-operator). An important part of the famous Burns (1954) study of British executives revealed that, of 165 outgoing messages classified by the executives as "directives," about half were perceived as mere "information" by the receiver-subordinates. The ambiguity in this case concerned not the "propositional content" of the messages but, rather, what modern speech-act theorists would call "illocutionary" intent (Sanders, 1984; see also Austin, 1962; Searle, 1979).

Building (in part) on the early work of Odiorne (1954), Tompkins (1962) investigated a wide range of communication activities between the national headquarters and selected locals of a major labor union. He generated the concept of "semantic/information distance," conceptualized as measurable differences in either factual knowledge or evaluative interpretation between message senders at national headquarters and receivers in the locals (Tompkins, 1962, pp. 222-226). He concluded that significant distances existed between national headquarters and the locals, but that these gaps apparently produced serious communication problems only when they were "not perceived by the people involved" (Tompkins, 1962, p. 223).

Calculated ambiguity. To this point it has been assumed that ambiguity, whether of Type 1 or Type 2, is the outcome of ineptness or of inability to adapt to the audience situation on the part of a message sender. This kind of ambiguity we shall refer to as *inadvertent.* But there is also another genre of ambiguity, which we shall call *calculated ambiguity.* This occurs by conscious intent on the part of a message sender.

Although William Empson (1963) was a literary critic writing for literary critics, his classic *Seven Types of Ambiguity* (first published in 1930) should not be neglected by modern scholars. It was Empson who demonstrated, in exhaustive detail, that ambiguity can contribute to, as well as detract from, a receiver's understanding or enjoyment of a message. The best poets, Empson (1930/1963) argued, are masters of intentional ambiguity. It could be that the same may be said of "effective" managers. Guetzkow (1965) long ago observed,

> Because ambiguous messages are open to multiple interpretations, meanings more agreeable to the receiver may be attached. Although at times ambiguity results in slippage between sender and receiver such slippage also may promote consensus and agreement. (p. 557)

Recently Eisenberg (1984) devoted a major paper to an elaboration of a similar thesis, proposing the category of "strategic ambiguity" to denote "instances where individuals use ambiguity purposefully to accomplish their goals" (p. 230). Eisenberg identified the functional utility of strategic ambiguity in terms of three outcomes: the promotion of a "unified diversity," the facilitation of "organizational change," and the preservation of "existing positions" (1984, pp. 230-236). As Eisenberg has pointed out,

> Strategic ambiguity fosters the existence of multiple viewpoints in organizations. This use of ambiguity is commonly found in organizational missions, goals, and plans. . . . It is a political necessity to engage in strategic ambiguity so that different constituent groups may apply different interpretations to the symbol. (1984, p. 231)

Weick (1979) also has supported the position that high-equivocal (ambiguous) "inputs" can serve constructive purposes in the organization, especially by preventing creative ideas from being "sealed off from discussion" (p. 186). It is important that communication researchers keep in mind the benefits accruing from ambiguity and resist the temptation of regarding all message ambiguity as an obstacle to be overcome.

Nevertheless, a problem arises here: that of locating a boundary between strategic ambiguity and the subtly deceptive ambiguity commonly known as "double talk." In a now classic essay, Roethlisberger (1945) described the paradigmatic foreman as an individual who is compelled to be both "master and servant of double talk" in order to survive in an environment of incompatible pressures. The editors of *Fortune,* deploring the ubiquity of double talk among corporate managers, quoted an anonymous executive to define what they meant by this term:

> All you have to remember is . . . let the language be ambiguous enough that if the job be successfully carried out, all credit can be claimed, and if not, a technical alibi [can] be found. (Whyte et al., 1952, p. 52)

Earlier in the chapter we mentioned the recent critiques of organizational doublespeak; and a few years ago an organizational sociologist, reflecting on his field studies of four modern corporations, came to the conclusion that the typical "bureaucratic world" encourages "profoundly ambiguous" ethical guidelines, so that a manager is frequently evaluated not by "his willingness to stand by his actions but [by] his agility in avoiding blame" (Jackall, 1983, p. 130). Despite the obvious difficulties confronting the investigator, methodological ingenuity can surely be applied to the study of calculated ambiguity in the organizational context.

Conclusions: ambiguity, equivocality, uncertainty. Theoretical issues, rather than mere semantic quibbles, are involved in attempts to distinguish among the three closely related terms *ambiguity, equivocality,* and *uncertainty.* On these issues, and on these distinctions, no consensus has yet emerged. This may be especially the case with *uncertainty.* After completing a review of the literature on uncertainty in organizational decision making—especially as it relates to "objective" message characteristics—Gifford, Bobbitt, and Slocum (1979) concluded that "there is little commonality among researchers or theorists regarding the precise meaning of uncertainty" (p. 459).

In developing a psychometric instrument for measuring degrees of uncertainty in terms of message characteristics, and limiting themselves to messages received by decision makers, Gifford et al. (1979) identified three areas of uncertainty: the "state of nature," the range of available solutions, and the values ("payoffs") adhering to these solutions. These were all interpreted as falling under the general category of "information adequacy," with ambiguity ("lack of clarity" and presence of multiple interpretations) omitted as a major variable standing by itself (Gifford et al., 1979, p. 460).

Communication researchers, therefore, should be wary of regarding *ambiguity* and *uncertainty* as synonymous terms. We suggest that, at least when referring to messages and message-related events, researchers are well-advised to restrict the term *ambiguity* to situations involving multiple interpretations and/or subjective confusion triggered by the perception of equally probable interpretations—in other words, what we have proposed as Type 1 and Type 2. In addition, it makes sense for researchers to be explicit whenever they use *equivocal* as a term interchangeable with *ambiguous*.[1]

At the beginning of the section we posed the question "In what respects (if any) may ambiguity be considered as a quality inhering in the words of an OD message?" Like Eisenberg (1984), we conclude that strictly speaking, no such attribution is justified. However, this puristic position admittedly clashes with conventional usage, and usage cannot be legislated by researchers' fiat. Indeed, there is no disputing the fact that, in specified contexts, stylistic or syntactical features make some locutions more vulnerable to being perceived as ambiguous than are others. For example, it is difficult to reject the conviction that there must be *something* in the wording that makes the old textbook chestnut "I hope that you the enemy will slay" an "inherently ambiguous" message (Hewes et al., 1985). In their empirical study of "disqualification," a concept closely related to ambiguity, Bavelas and Chovill (1986, p. 70) acknowledge this problem and cite as an example of a highly ambiguous message the following classified ad:

> FOR SALE. 1966 VOLKSWAGEN. VERY CHEAP. PERSON WHO LIKES WORKING ON CARS WOULD BE WISE TO BUY THIS CAR.

Our suggestion is that researchers emphasize the concept of *probability* when referring to ambiguous messages. Thus, the Volkswagen ad could be described as a high-probability ambiguous message—assuming that no further contextual information is provided. In short, those who venture to conduct research on message ambiguity in the organizational setting will inevitably find themselves struggling to reduce unwanted ambiguity (of both Type 1 and Type 2) in their own thinking and writing.

IMPLICATIONS FOR FUTURE RESEARCH

To reduce at least some of the unwanted ambiguity in this chapter, the final section focuses on four areas of concern we have identified as crucial issues for researchers interested in messages: (1) exploring the potentialities of a four-level analysis of messages; (2) recognizing the observer-inference problem; (3) exploiting the actual texts of messages; and (4) developing message taxonomies.

Exploring the Potentialities
of a Four-Level Analysis of Messages

Throughout the chapter we have distinguished between OD (ostensively displayed) and IE (internally experienced) messages. We believe, however, that it is both feasible and useful to carry this line of reasoning a bit further by distinguishing among four levels of a message. The unelaborated IE level on the sender's side fails to identify multiple "layers" of goals and intentions governing the construction of a message. We hypothesize that, especially in the organizational world of power and status differentials, there are important differences between (1) what communicators would really like to say—in the absence of all constraints—and (2) what they decide they should say, and (3) what they actually do say. Suppose that Joanne Doe, a middle manager, is convinced that her boss has made a serious mistake in issuing a certain policy directive to the sales force. Her *desired* message—the one she would like to utter, were there no inhibiting factors whatever—might be "Joe, you really goofed." But, given all the circumstances, Joanne may decide that such a forthright remark would be less than expedient. Therefore, she frames in her mind (perhaps with the aid of jottings on scratch paper) an *intended* message, couched in more diplomatic terms. But what she actually says—the *enacted* message—may be "Joe, how are the sales people responding to that directive you sent out last month?" Finally, the boss's *interpreted* message could be, "There she goes again, always finding fault with anything I do."

To formalize the structural relations among these different versions of "one" message, we offer the following schema of message levels:

Level 1: the *desired* message (an IE message, in the mind of the sender)
Level 2: the *intended* message (again, an IE message in the mind of the sender; sometimes, however, an OD message in the form of a rough draft)
Level 3: the *enacted* message (the OD message actually uttered)
Level 4: the *interpreted* message (always an IE message, existing in the mind of any specified receiver or observer)

By adopting this four-level analysis, researchers should be able to enhance their understanding of what is "really going on" in episodes such as the one involving Joanne Doe and her boss.

We suggest that, unless they attempt to discover the desires and intentions of message-senders, and the divergent interpretations of different message-receivers, researchers will produce impoverished accounts of message phenomena in the organizational setting; for example, when they are concerned with identifying message "functions," or with determining the criteria of message "distortion," or with distinguishing among the variant manifestations of message "ambiguity." Clearly, the study of messages at Levels 1, 2, and 4 will call for the exercise of ingenuity, especially in conducting depth interviews with communicants. And there is no denying that multiple-level message analysis will always entail inferential leaps on the part of the researcher. But the observer-inference problem—the next topic to engage our attention—is inherent in any kind of message-focused inquiry.

Recognizing the
Observer-Inference Problem

Whenever an analyst codes OD messages into categories—such as compliance-gaining—he or she is making a decision based on an inference, an inference that the message represents certain "meanings." The inference problem is especially underscored if a researcher attempts to identify IE messages at Levels 1, 2, or 4, or if a researcher is dealing with ambiguity in any of its manifestations.

Unfortunately, as we have suggested earlier, researchers all too often fail to acknowledge their own inference processes. Categories such as "tell/sell/consult" (for example) are sometimes presented as if they were "objective" descriptors of OD messages. But who assigns the messages to these categories? Almost never is it the actual message-users, whether senders or receivers. Typically, the assignment is made by the observer-analyst.

Computing reliability scores to determine consistency of coding among analysts, useful though this procedure surely is, fails to get to the heart of the inference problem. Such computations address the *range* of interpretations among a group of analysts; but they shed no light whatever on the question "To what degree does any analyst's interpretation correspond with the interpretations of the communicants themselves?" Traditional variable-analytic research designs can yield valuable insights about organizational messages, but they will attain their maximum potential only when they are coupled with techniques designed to reveal the communicants' sense-making processes. Researchers need to present appropriate concrete samples of specific OD messages, along with the data on which they base their interpretations of message meanings. These data will typically emerge from a variety of sources: self-reports, direct observation, documents, interviews, and so on. The observer-inference problem can never be erased, but it can be acknowledged and steps can be taken to reduce the hazards. Above all, analysts must refrain from treating their inferences about messages as though they were the messages themselves.

Exploiting the Actual
Texts of Messages

By exploiting the text we mean engaging in the close study of the actual words contained within oral and written OD messages—wherever verbatim records can be made available. Such intensive scrutiny, to be meaningful, must be carried out in terms of carefully developed conceptual or theoretical rationales. Mere textual analysis for its own sake would be pointless. For illustrative purposes we shall mention several promising frames of reference within which textual-analytic research may be conducted.

We have already observed that the "functional" approach to understanding organizational messages represents an especially fruitful research strategy. We agree with Weick when he suggests that

> Analyses of functions are unusually good starting points in organization theory. Looking for unexpected functions and dysfunctions is a useful pretext to become absorbed in a phenomenon and to think about it carefully. (Weick, 1979, p. 55)

The five message functions proposed earlier in this chapter—individual, relational, instrumental, contextual, structural—provide innumerable opportunities for undertaking close textual analysis, as a basis for exploring relationships between functions and actual messages.

Among the lines of inquiry wide open to exploration are investigations of OD messages as they are related to well-known management "styles"—such as those commonly associated with the names of Likert (1967), Blake and Mouton (1964), and Fleishman, Harris, and Burtt (1955). Likewise, provocative studies can be designed to examine message correlates of power, control, and influence (including "compliance-gaining" communication). One of the most significant areas to explore is that of "unobtrusive control" (see Perrow, 1979; Tompkins & Cheney, 1985); moreover, to our knowledge, no one has yet examined actual OD messages in terms of Barnard's famous set of four conditions for accepting management directives (Barnard, 1938, p. 165).

A second frame of reference is suggested by the broad concept "information adequacy." Under this rubric would be included such topics as dimensions of "message quality" (e.g., relevance, timeliness, comprehensiveness, usability), credibility, redundancy, and logical validity.

A third area to be explored, in terms of message texts, lies within the general concept of "organizational cultures"; for example, content-analytic studies can focus on decision premises, rules, ideological assumptions, stories, jokes, ritualistic messages, and other manifestations of organizational culture. Closely related to cultural studies are those commonly labeled sociolinguistic, psycholinguistic, or semantic. For example, the pioneering study of forms of address by Slobin et al. (1968) merits imaginative follow-up work. We also include here investigations generated within the frames of general semantics and speech-act theory (Ewald & Stine, 1983; Haney, 1984; Sanders, 1984).

An especially promising field of message analysis, one which has barely been mentioned by organizational communication specialists, is that of deception, including outright falsehoods (lies). Perry and Barney (1981) have made a promising start in their discussion of "performance lies" in organizations, and Sissela Bok's *Lying* (1978) is a rich source of ideas for organizational researchers.

Another area of study is that of messages that are not sent, or at least those that are disseminated to a selective "inner circle." This raises issues of suppression, withholding information, and secrecy in general (the proposed four-level model would be particularly relevant here). *Secrets* (Bok, 1983) provides a comprehensive conceptual overview invaluable for anyone attempting to apply contextual analysis to this unconventional category of messages. (See also Chapter 16, by Putnam & Poole, in this volume.)

Finally, we remind potential researchers that exploitation of the text is not to be overlooked by those investigating that elusive phenomenon called "ambiguity."

Developing Message Taxonomies

To advocate close textual analysis of OD messages is fruitless in the absence of reliable and valid categories. Mere catalogs of miscellaneous entities do not get us very far until they are ordered in conceptually meaningful taxonomies. Hence, we acknowledge the urgency with which communication scholars need to generate and test scientifically based message taxonomies. But we also acknowledge that, as categories and taxonomies proliferate, researchers face the monumental problem of trying to make sense of "a great motley list of variables," that may result in "unmanageable interaction" (Mohr, 1982, pp. 23-24).

Not wishing to conclude on a note of gloom, however, we reaffirm our conviction that both quantitative and qualitative modes of inquiry will advance our understanding of the complex universe of organizational messages. It is essential that the language of our research fit the nature of the phenomena being investigated (Daft & Wiginton, 1979). Moreover, we do not wish to leave the impression that scientific methods are the only ones that will improve our understanding. Systematic, sustained programs of rhetorical criticism, whether carried out in terms of the traditional or the new rhetorics, should long ago have been turned on organizational discourse. The most important imperative is that researchers devote much more energy than they have in the past to a close study of *messages themselves.*

NOTE

1. Space will not permit a discussion of subtle, but important, distinctions that can be made between ambiguity and vagueness — the latter roughly correlative with generalized uncertainty. See, for example, Black (1949).

REFERENCES

Abelson, P. H. (1966). Coping with the information explosion. *Science*, No. 3745.
Ackoff, R. (1967). Management misinformation systems. *Management Science, 14,* 147-156.
Ackoff, R. L., Emery, F. E. (1972). *On purposeful systems.* Chicago: Aldine/Atherton.
Allport, G. W., & Postman, L. (1947). *The psychology of rumor.* New York: Henry Holt.

American heritage dictionary. (1969). (W. Morris, Ed.). New York: Houghton Mifflin/ American Heritage.

Athanassiades, J. C. (1973). The distortion of upward communication in hierarchical organizations. *Academy of Management Journal, 16,* 207-226.

Austin, J. L. (1962). *How to do things with words.* Oxford: Clarendon.

Bales, R. F. (1950). *Interaction process analysis: A method for the study of small groups.* Reading, MA: Addison-Wesley.

Bales, R. F., & Strodtbeck, F. (1951). Phases in group problem-solving. *Journal of Abnormal and Social Psychology, 46,* 485-495.

Bantz, C. R., & Smith, D. H. (1977). A critique and experimental test of Weick's model of organizing. *Communication Monographs, 44,* 171-184.

Barnard, C. I. (1983) *The functions of the executive.* Cambridge: Harvard University Press.

Bavelas, J. B., & Chovill, N. (1986). How people disqualify: experimental studies of spontaneous written disqualification. *Communication Monographs, 53,* 70-74.

Bavelas, J. B., & Smith, B. J. (1982). A method for scaling verbal disqualification. *Human Communication Research, 8,* 214-227.

Bell, R. A, & Daly, J. A. (1984). The affinity-seeking function of communication. *Communication Monographs, 51,* 91-115.

Berelson, B. (1952). *Content analysis in communication research.* New York: Free Press.

Berlo, D. K. (1969). *Human communication: The basic proposition.* Unpublished paper, Michigan State University, Department of Communication.

Black, M. (1949). Vagueness: an exercise in logical analysis. In M. Black (Ed.), *Language and philosophy* (pp. 23-58). Ithaca, NY: Cornell University Press.

Blake, R. R., & Mouton, J. S. (1964). The managerial grid. Houston: Gulf Publishing Company.

Bok, S. (1978). *Lying: Moral choice in public and private life.* New York: Random House.

Bok, S. (1983). *Secrets: On the ethics of concealment and revelation.* New York: Random House.

Brown, R. W., & Gilman, A. (1960). The pronouns of power and solidarity. In K. Sebeok (Ed.), *Style in language* (pp. 253-276), Cambridge: MIT Press.

Burke, K. B. (1969). *A rhetoric of motives.* Berkeley: University of California Press.

Burns, T. (1954). The directions of activity and communication in a departmental executive group. *Human Relations, 7,* 73-97.

Campbell, D. T. (1958). Systematic error on the part of human links in communication systems. *Information and Control, 1,* 334-369.

Caplow, T. (1947). Rumors in war. *Social Forces, 25,* 298-302.

Chapanis, A. (1971). Prelude to 2001: Explorations in human communication. *American Psychologist, 26,* 949-961.

Cheney, G. (1983). The rhetoric of identification and the study of organizational communication. *Quarterly Journal of Speech, 69,* 143-158.

Christi, L. S. (1954). Organization and information handling in task groups. *Journal of Operations Research, 2,* 188-196.

Churchill, L. (1965). Some sociological aspects of message load: Information input overload and features of growth in communications-oriented institutions. In F. Massarrik & P. Ratoosh (Eds.), *Mathematical explorations in behavioral science* (pp. 274-284). Homewood, IL: Irwin.

Cody, M. J., & McLaughlin, M. L. (1980). Perceptions of compliance-gaining situations: A dimensional analysis. *Communication Monographs, 47,* 132-148.

Cohen, A. R. (1958). Upward communication in experimentally created hierarchies. *Human Relations, 11,* 41-53.

Conrath, O. W. (1967). Communication environment and its relationship to organizational structure. *Management Science, 20,* 586-603.

Crable, R. E., & Vibbert, S. L. (1983). Mobil's epideictic advocacy: "Observations" of Prometheus-bound. *Communication Monographs, 50,* 380-394.

Crane, D . (1972). *Invisible colleges: Diffusion of knowledge in scientific communities.* Chicago: University of Chicago Press.

Cusella, L. P. (1980). The effects of feedback on intrinsic motivation. In D. Nimmo (Ed.), *Communication yearbook 4* (pp. 367-387). New Brunswick, NJ: Transaction.

Daft, R. L., & Lengel, R. H. (1984). Information richness: A new approach to manager information processing and organization design. In B. Staw & L. L. Cummings (Eds.), *Research in organizational behavior* (pp. 191-233). Greenwich, CT: JAI Press.

Daft, R. L., & MacIntosh, N. B. (1981). A tentative exploration into the amount and equivocality of information processing in organization work units. *Administrative Science Quarterly, 26,* 207-224.

Daft, R. L., & Wiginton, J. C. (1979). Language and organization. *Academy of Management Review, 4,* 179-191.

Davis, K. (1952). *Channels of personnel communication within the management group.* Unpublished doctoral dissertation, Ohio State University, Columbus.

Davis, K. (1953). A method of studying communication patterns in organizations. *Personnel Psychology,* 301-312.

Davis, W. L., & O'Conner, J. R. (1977). Serial transmission of information: A study of the grapevine. *Journal of Applied Communications Research, 5,* 61-72.

Delia, J. G., O'Keefe, B. J., & O'Keefe, O. J. (1982). The constructivist approach to communication. In F.E.X. Dance (Ed.). *Comparative human communication theory* (pp. 177-191). New York: Harper & Row.

Donohue, W. A., & Diez, M. E. (1985). Directive use in negotiation interaction. *Communication Monographs, 52,* 305-318.

Downs, A. (1967). *Inside bureaucracy.* Boston: Little, Brown.

Drake, B. H., & Moberg, D. J. (1986). Communicating influence attempts in dyads: Linguistic sedatives and palliatives. *Academy of Management Review, 11,* 567-584.

Duncan, O. D. (1984). *Notes on social measurement.* New York: Russell Sage.

Duncan, R. B. (1973). Multiple decision-making structures in adapting to environmental uncertainty. *Human Relations, 26,* 273-291.

Eilon, S. (1968). Taxonomy of communications. *Administrative Science Quarterly, 13,* 266-288.

Eisenberg, E. M. (1984). Ambiguity as strategy in organizational communication. *Communication Monographs, 51,* 227-242.

Eisenberg, E. M., Monge, P. R., & Farace, R. V. (1984). Coorientation on communication rules in managerial dyads. *Human Communication Research, 11,* 261-271.

Empson, W. (1963). *Seven types of ambiguity* (3rd ed.). London: Chatto & Windus. (Original work published 1930)

Erez, M., & Rim, Y. (1982). The relationships between goals, influence, tactics, and personal and organizational variables. *Human Relations, 35,* 871-878.

Ervin-Tripp, S. M. (1969). Sociolinguistics. In L. Berkowitz (Ed.), *Advances in experimental social psychology* (Vol. 4, pp. 91-165). New York: Academic Press.

Ewald, H. R., & Stine, D. (1983). Speech act theory and business communication conventions. *Journal of Business Communication, 20,* 13-25.

Fairhurst, G. T., Green, S. G., & Snavely, B. K. (1984). Face support in controlling poor performance. *Human Communication Research, 11,* 272-295.

Fairhurst, G. T., Rogers, L. E., & Sarr, R. A. (1987). Manager-subordinate control patterns and judgments about the relationship. In M. McLaughlin (Ed.) *Communication yearbook 10,* (pp. 395-415). Newbury Park, CA: Sage.

Farace, R. V., Monge, P. R., & Russell, H. M. (1977). *Communicating and organizing.* Reading, MA: Addison-Wesley.

Fisher, B. A. (1970). Decision emergence: Phases in group decision-making. *Speech Monographs, 37,* 50-63.

Fisher, B. A. (1980). *Small group decision making: Communication and the group process* (2nd ed.). New York: McGraw-Hill.

Fisher, B. A., & Hawes, L. C. (1971). An interact system model: Generating a grounded theory of small group decision making. *Quarterly Journal of Speech, 58,* 444-453.

Fisher, R. M. (1965). Modern business speaking: A rhetoric of "conventional wisdom." *Southern Speech Journal, 30,* 327-334.

Fisher, R. M. (1966). A rhetoric of over-reaction. *Central States Speech Journal, 17,* 251-256.

Fleishman, E. A., & Harris, E. F. (1962). Patterns of leadership behavior related to employee grievances and turnover. *Personnel Psychology, 15,* 43-56.

Fleishman, E. A., Harris, E. F., & Burtt, H. E. (1955). *Leadership supervision in industry* (Monograph No. 33, Bureau of Educational Research). Columbus: Ohio State University.

Fulk, J., & Mani, S. (1985). Distortion of communication in hierarchical relationships. In M. McLaughlin (Ed.), *Communication yearbook 9* (pp. 483-510). Newbury Park, CA: Sage.

Gerstenfeld, A., & Berger, P. (1980). An analysis of utilization differences for scientific and technical information. *Management Science, 26,* 165-179.

Gifford, W. E., Bobbitt, H. R., & Slocum, J. W., Jr. (1979). Message characteristics and perceptions of uncertainty by organizational decision makers. *Academy of Management Journal, 22,* 458-481.

Gioia, D. A., & Sims, H. P. (1986). Cognition-behavior connections: Attribution and verbal behavior in leader-subordinate interactions. *Organizational Behavior and Human Decision Processes, 37,* 197-229.

Goldhaber, G. M. (1983). *Organizational communication* (3rd ed.). Dubuque, IA: Wm. C. Brown.

Greenbaum, H. H. (1974). The audit of organizational communication. *Academy of Management Journal, 27,* 739-754.

Greenberg, J., & Leventhal, G. S. (1976). Equity and the use of over-reward to motivate performance. *Journal of Personality and Social Psychology, 34,* 179-190.

Greene, J. O. (1984). A cognitive approach to human communication: An action assembly theory. *Communication Monographs, 51,* 289-306.

Guetzkow, H. (1965). Communication in organizations. In J. March (Ed.), *Handbook of organizations* (pp. 534-573). Chicago: Rand McNally.

Hackman, J. R. (1976). Group influences on individuals. In M. D. Dunnette (Ed.), *Handbook of industrial and organizational psychology* (pp. 1455-1525). Chicago: Rand McNally.

Halliday, M.A.K. (1973). *Explorations in the functions of language.* London: Edward Arnold.

Haney, W. V. (1960). *Communication: Patterns and incidents.* Homewood, IL: Irwin.

Haney, W. V. (1984). *Communication and interpersonal relations* (5th ed.). Homewood, IL: Irwin.

Hare, A. P. (1976). *Handbook of small group research* (2nd ed.). New York: Free Press.

Hatfield, J. D. (1976). *The development of a category system for analyzing superior-subordinate communication behavior.* Unpublished doctoral dissertation, Purdue University, West Lafayette, IN.

Hewes, D. E., Graham, M. L., Doelger, J., & Pavitt, C. (1985). Second guessing: Message interpretation in social networks. *Human Communication Research, 11,* 299-334.

Huber, G. P. (1982). Organizational information systems: Determinants of their performance and behavior. *Management Science, 28,* 135-155.

Huff, A. S. (1983). A rhetorical examination of strategic change. In L. R. Pondy, P. J. Frost, G. Morgan, & T. C. Dandridge (Eds.), *Organizational symbolism* (Monographs in Organizational Behavior and Industrial Relations, Vol. 1, pp. 167-183). Greenwich, CT: JAI Press.

Jablin, F. M. (1978). Message-response and "openness" in superior-subordinate communication. In B. Ruben (Ed.), *Communication yearbook 2* (pp. 293-309). New Brunswick, NJ: Transaction Books.

Jablin, F. M. (1985). Task/work relationships: A life-span perspective. In M. L. Knapp & G. R. Miller (Eds.), *Handbook of interpersonal communication* (pp. 615-654). Newbury Park, CA: Sage.

Jablin, F. M., & Sussman, L. (1983). Organizational group communication: A review of literature and model of the process. In H. H. Greenbaum, R. L. Falcione, & S. A. Hellweg (Eds.), *Organizational communication: Abstracts, analysis, and overview* (Vol. 8, pp. 11-50). Newbury Park, CA: Sage.

Jackall, R. (1983). Moral mazes: bureaucracy and managerial work. *Harvard Business Review, 61*(5), 118-130.

Jacobs, S. (1985). Language. In M. L. Knapp & G. R. Miller (Eds.), *Handbook of interpersonal communication* (pp. 313-343). Newbury Park, CA: Sage.

Janis, L. (1972). *Victims of groupthink: A psychological study of foreign policy decisions and fiascos.* Boston: Houghton Mifflin.

Katz, D., & Kahn, R. L. (1978). *The social psychology of organizations* (2nd ed.). New York: John Wiley.

Kipnis, D. (1976). *The powerholders.* Chicago: University of Chicago Press.

Kipnis, D., & Cosentino, J. (1969). Use of leadership powers in industry. *Journal of Applied Psychology, 53,* 460-466.

Kipnis, D., Schmidt, S. M., & Wilkinson, I. (1980). Intraorganizational influence tactics: Explorations in getting one's way. *Journal of Applied Psychology, 65,* 440-452.

Kline, S. L. (1981). *Construct system development and face support in persuasive messages: Two empirical investigations.* Paper presented at the annual meeting of the International Communication Association, Minneapolis, MN.

Knapp, M. L. (1972). *Nonverbal communication in human interaction.* New York: Holt, Rinehart & Winston.

Knapp, M. L., Stohl, C., & Reardon, K. (1981). Memorable messages. *Journal of Communication, 31,* 27-42.

Komsky, S. H., & Krivonos, P. D. (1980). *Perceived downward message distortion in hierarchical organizations.* Paper presented at the annual meeting of Academy of Management, San Diego, CA.

Kreps, G. L. (1980). A field experimental test and reevaluation of Weick's model of organizing. In B. Ruben (Ed.), *Communication yearbook 4* (pp. 389-398). New Brunswick, NJ: Transaction Books.

Lanzetta, J. T., & Roby, T. B. (1957). Group learning and communication as a function of task and structure "demands." *Journal of Abnormal Social Psychology, 55,* 121-131.

Lasswell, H. D., Leites, N., & Associates. (1949). *Language of politics.* New York: George W. Stewart.

Leavitt, H. J. (1951). Some efforts of certain communication patterns on group performance. *American Journal of Sociology, 46,* 38-50.

Licklider, J. C. (1966). A crux in scientific and technical communications. *American Psychologist, 21,* 1044, 1051.

Likert, R. (1967). *The human organization.* New York: McGraw-Hill.

March, J. G., & Simon, H. A. (1958). *Organizations.* New York: John Wiley.

McCallister, L. (1981). *"Rhetorical sensitivity," sex of interactants, and superior-subordinate communication.* Unpublished doctoral dissertation, Purdue University, West Lafayette, IN.

McPhee, R. D., & Tompkins, P. K. (Eds.). (1985). *Organizational communication: Traditional themes and new directions.* Newbury Park, CA: Sage.

Meier, R. L. (1963). Communication overload: Proposals from the study of a university library. *Administrative Science Quarterly, 4,* 521-544.

Meissner, M. (1976). The language of work. In R. Dubin (Ed.), *Handbook of work, organization, and society* (pp. 205-279). Chicago: Rand McNally.

Melcher, A. J., & Beller, R. (1967). Toward a theory of organization communication: Consideration in channel selection. *Academy of Management Journal, 10,* 39-52.

Mellinger, G. D. (1956). Interpersonal trust as a factor in communication. *Journal of Abnormal Social Psychology, 52,* 304-309.

Millar, F. E., & Rogers, L. E. (1976). A relational approach to interpersonal communication. In G. Miller (Ed.) *Explorations in interpersonal communication* (pp. 87-104). Newbury Park, CA: Sage.

Miller, J. G. (1960). Information input, overload, and psychopathology. *American Journal of Psychiatry, 116,* 695-704.

Miller, J. G. (1961). Sensory overloading. In B. E. Flaherty (Ed.), *Psychophysiological aspects of space flight* (pp. 216-224). New York.

Miller, J. G. (1964). Psychological aspects of communication overload. In R. W. Waggoner & D. J. Carke (Eds.), *International psychiatry clinics: Communication in clinical practice* (pp. 201-224). Boston: Little Brown.

Miller, J. G. (1972). Living systems: The organization. *Behavioral Science, 17*(1), 1-82.

Mitchell, R. (1979). *Less than words can say.* Boston: Little, Brown.

Mohr, L. B. (1982). *Explaining organizational behavior.* San Francisco: Jossey-Bass.

Monge, P. R., Bachman, S. G., Dillard, J. P., & Eisenberg, E. M. (1982). Communicator competence in the workplace: Model testing and scale development. In M. Burgoon (Ed.), *Communication yearbook 5* (pp. 505-528). New Brunswick, NJ: Transaction Books.

Mullins, N. C. (1968). The distribution of social and cultural properties in informal communication networks among biological scientists. *American Sociological Review, 33,* 786-797.

Myers, R. J., & Kessler, M. S. (1980). Business speaks: A study of the themes in speeches by America's corporate leaders. *Journal of Business Communication, 17,* 5-17.

Odiorne, G. S. (1954). An application of the communication audit. *Personnel Psychology, 7,* 235-243.

O'Keefe, B. J., & Delia, J. G. (1982). Impression formation and message production. In M. E. Roloff & C. R. Berger (Eds.), *Social cognition and communication* (pp. 33-72). Newbury Park, CA: Sage.

O'Reilly, C. A. (1978). The intentional distortion of information in organizational communication: A laboratory and field approach. *Human Relations, 31,* 173-193.

O'Reilly, C. A., & Roberts, K. H. (1974). Information infiltration in organizations. Three experiments. *Organizational Behavior and Human Performance, 11,* 253-265.

Paisley, W. (1981). Information and work. In B. Dervin & M.J. Voigt (Eds.), *Progress in communication sciences* (Vol. 2, pp. 114-165). Norwood, NJ: Ablex.

Parsons, L. (1951). *The social system.* New York: Free Press.

Payne, R., & Cooper, C. L. (Eds.). (1981). *Groups at work.* New York: John Wiley.

Perrow, C. (1979). *Complex organizations* (2nd ed.). Glenview, IL: Scott, Foresman.

Perry, L. T., & Barney, J. B. (1981). Performance lies are hazardous to organizational health. *Organizational Dynamics, 9*(3), 68-80.

Platt, J. R. (1962). *The excitement of science.* Boston: Houghton Mifflin.

Poole, M. S. (1981). Decision development in small groups I: A comparison of two models. *Communication Monographs, 48,* 1-24.

Porter, L. W., Allen, R. W., & Angle, H. L. (1981). The politics of upward influence in organizations. In L. L. Cumming & B. Staw (Eds.), *Research in organizational behavior* (Vol. 3, pp. 109-149). Greenwich, CT: JAI Press.

Putnam, L. L. (1986). Contradictions and paradoxes in organizations. In L. Thayer (Ed.), *Organizational communication: Emerging perspectives I* (pp. 151-167). Norwood, NJ: Ablex.

Putnam, L. L., & Jones, T. S. (1982). The role of communication in bargaining. *Human Communication Research, 8,* 262-280.

Putnam, L. L., & Sorenson, R. L. (1982). Equivocal messages in organizations. *Human Communication Research, 8,* 114-132.

Read, W. H. (1962). Upward communication in industrial hierarchies. *Human Relations, 15,* 3-15.

Redding, W. C. (1964). The organizational communicator. In W. C. Redding & G. A. Sanborn (Eds.), *Business and industrial communication* (pp. 29-58). New York: Harper & Row.

Redding, W. C. (1984). *The corporate manager's guide to better communication.* Glenview, IL: Scott, Foresman.

Redding, W. C. (1985). Stumbling toward identity: The emergence of organizational communication as a field of study. In R. D. McPhee & P. K. Tompkins (Eds.), *Organizational communication: Traditional themes and new directions* (pp. 15-54). Newbury Park, CA: Sage.

Richmond, V. P., Davis, L. M., Saylor, K., & McCroskey, J. C. (1984). Power strategies in organizations: Communication techniques and messages. *Human Communication Research, 11,* 85-108.

Ricillo, S. C., & Trenholm, S. (1983). Predicting managers' choice of influence mode: The effects of interpersonal trust and worker attributions in managerial tactics in a simulated organizational setting. *Western Journal of Speech Communication, 47,* 323-339.

Rim, Y., & Erez, M. (1980). A note about tactics used to influence superiors. *Journal of Occupational Psychology, 53,* 319-321.

Roberts, K. H., & O'Reilly, C. A. (1974). Measuring organizational communications. *Journal of Applied Psychology, 59,* 321-326.

Roesthlisberger, F. J. (1945). The foreman: Master and victim of double talk. *Harvard Business Review, 23,* 283-298.

Rogers, E. M., & Shoemaker, F. F. (1971). *Communication of innovations: A cross-cultural approach.* New York: Free Press.

Rogers, L. E. (1983). *Analyzing relational communication: Implications of a pragmatic approach.* Paper presented at the annual meeting of the Speech Communication Association, Washington, DC.

Rogers, L. E., & Farace, R. V. (1975). Analysis of relational communication in dyads: New measurement procedures. *Human Communication Research, 1,* 222-239.

Rogers-Millar, L. E., & Millar, F. E. (1979). Domineeringness and dominance: A transactional view. *Human Communication Research, 5,* 238-246.

Rosnow, R. L., & Fine, G. A. (1976). *Rumor and gossip: The social psychology of hearsay,* Holland: Elsevier.

Rosnow, R. L., & Kimmel, A. J. (1979, August). Lives of a rumor. *Psychology Today,* pp. 88-92.

Ruchinskas, J. (1982). *Communicating in organizations: The influence of context, job, ask, and channel.* Unpublished doctoral dissertation, Annenberg School of Communications, University of Southern California.

Rudolph, E. E. (1973). Informal human communication systems in a large organization. *Journal of Applied Communications Research, 1,* 7-23.

Rutter, D. R. (1984). *Looking and seeing: The role of visual communication in social interaction.* New York: John Wiley.

Sanders, R. E. (1984). Style, meaning and message effects. *Communication Monographs, 51,* 154-167.

Schilit, W. K., & Locke, E. (1982). A study of upward influence in organizations. *Administrative Science Quarterly, 27,* 304-316.

Schutz, W. C. (1958). *FIRO: A three dimensional theory of interpersonal behavior.* New York: Holt, Rinehart & Winston.

Searle, J. R. (1979). *Expression and meaning: Studies in the theory of speech acts.* Cambridge: Cambridge University Press.

Shaw, M. E. (1981). *Group dynamics: The psychology of small group behavior* (3rd ed.). New York: McGraw Hill.

Short, J., Williams, E., & Christie, B. (1976). *The social psychology of telecommunications.* London: John Wiley.

Siebold, D. R., Cantrill, J. G., & Meyers, R. A. (1985). Communication and interpersonal influence. In M. L. Knapp & G. R. Miller (Eds.), *Handbook of interpersonal communication* (pp. 551-611). Newbury Park, CA: Sage.

Sims, H., & Manz, C. G. (1984). Observing leader verbal behavior: Toward reciprocal determinism in leadership theory. *Journal of Applied Psychology, 69,* 222-232.

Slobin, D. I., Miller, S. H., & Porter, L. W. (1968). Forms of address and social relations in a business organization. *Journal of Personality and Social Psychology, 8,* 289-293.

Smith, A. G. (1973). The ethic of the relay men. In L. Thayer (Ed.), *Communication: Ethical and moral issues* (pp. 313-324). London: Gordon & Breach.

Steinfield, C., & Fulk, J. (1986). *Information processing in organizations and media choice.* Paper presented at the annual convention of the International Communication Association, Chicago.

Stohl, C. (1983). Developing a communicative competence scale. In R. N. Bostrom (Ed.), *Communication yearbook 7* (pp. 685-716). Newbury Park, CA: Sage.

Stohl, C. (1986). The role of memorable messages in the process of organizational communication. *Communication Quarterly, 34,* 231-249.

Sussman, L. (1974). Upward communication in the organizational hierarchy: An experimental field study of perceived message distortion (Doctoral dissertation, Purdue University, 1973). *Dissertation Abstracts International, 34,* 5366A.

Sypher, B. D., & Zorn, T. E. (1986). Communication-related abilities and upward mobility: A longitudinal investigation. *Human Communication Research, 12,* 420-431.

Tedeschi, J. T., Gaes, G. G., & Riviera, A. N. (1977). Aggression and the use of coercive power. *Journal of Social Issues, 133,* 101-125.

Tesser, A., & Rosen, S. (1975). The reluctance to transmit bad news. In L. Berkowitz (Ed.), *Advances in experimental social psychology* (Vol. 8, pp. 193-232). New York: Academic Press.

Thayer, L. (1968). *Communication and communication systems.* Homewood, IL: Irwin.

Tichy, N. M. (1981). Networks in organizations. In P. Nystrom & W. Starbuck (Eds.), *Handbook of organizational design* (Vol. 2, pp. 225-249). New York: Oxford University Press.

Tompkins, P. K. (1962). *An analysis of communication between headquarters and selected units of a national labor union.* Unpublished doctoral dissertation, Purdue University, West Lafayette, IN.

Tompkins, P. K., & Cheney, G. (1982). *Toward a theory of unobtrusive control in contemporary organizations.* Paper presented at the annual convention of the Speech Communication Association, Washington, DC.

Tompkins, P. K., & Cheney, G. (1985). Communication and unobtrusive control in contemporary organizations. In R. D. McPhee & P. K. Tompkins (Eds.), *Organizational communication: Traditional themes and new directions* (pp. 179-210). Newbury Park, CA: Sage.

Tompkins, P. K., Fisher, J. Y., Infante, D. A., & Tompkins, E. L. (1975). Kenneth Burke and the inherent characteristics of formal organizations: A field study. *Speech Monographs, 42,* 135-142.

Trujillo, N. (1983). "Performing" Mintzberg's roles: The nature of managerial communication. In L. L. Putnam & M. E. Pacanowsky (Eds.), *Communication and organizations* (pp. 73-97). Newbury Park, CA: Sage.

Tuckman, B. W. (1965). Developmental sequences in small groups. *Psychological Bulletin, 63,* 384-399.

Tushman, M. L. (1977). Communication across organizational boundaries: Special boundary roles in the innovation process. *Administration Science Quarterly, 22,* 587-605.

Tushman, M. L. (1979). Work characteristics and subunit communication structure: A contingency analysis. *Administration Science Quarterly, 24,* 82-98.

Ullman, J.C.M., & Huber, G. P. (1973). *The local job bank program: Performance, structure and directions.* Lexington, MA: D. C. Heath.

Wagner, J. A. (1978). The organizational double bind: Toward an understanding of rationality and its complement. *Academy of Management Review, 3,* 786-795.

Wanous, J. P., Reichers, A. E., & Malik, S. D. (1984). Organizational socialization and group development: Toward an integrative perspective. *Academy of Management Review, 9*, 670-683.

Watson, D. (1965). Effects of certain power structures on communication in task-oriented groups. *Sociometry, 28*, 322-336.

Watson, K. M. (1982a). A methodology for the study of organizational behavior at the interpersonal level of analysis. *Academy of Management Review, 3*, 392-403.

Watson, K. M. (1982b). An analysis of communication patterns: A method of discriminating leader and subordinate roles. *Academy of Management Journal, 25*, 107-120.

Watzlawick, P., Beavin, J. H., & Jackson, D. D. (1967). *Pragmatics of human communication.* New York: Norton.

Weick, K. (1970). The twigging of overload. In H. B. Pepinsky (Ed.), *People and information* (pp. 67-129). New York: Pergamon Press.

Weick, K. E. (1979). *The social psychology of organizing* (2nd ed.). Reading, MA: Addison-Wesley.

Weinstein, D. (1979). *Bureaucratic opposition: Challenging abuses in the workplace.* New York: Pergamon.

Wheeless, L. R., Barraclough, R., & Stewart, R. (1983). Compliance-gaining and power in persuasion. In R. N. Bostrom (Ed.), *Communication yearbook 7* (pp. 105-145). Newbury Park, CA: Sage.

Whyte, W. H., Jr., et al. (1952). *Is anybody listening?* New York: Simon & Schuster.

Wiemann, J. A. (1977). Explication and test of a model of communicative competence. *Human Communication Research, 3*, 195-213.

15 Power, Politics, and Influence

PETER J. FROST
University of British Columbia

The Nature of Organizational Power
    Organizational Power and Communication/The Origins of Organizational Power/Predisposition Toward Power
Organizational Politics
    Political Behavior as Intentional, Self-Interested, and Nonconsensual/Political Activity in Disguise/The Legitimacy of Organizational Politics/Organizational Politics: Power in Action and in Conception/Surface Politics/Deep Structure Politics
Organization Games
    Locating Organizational Games/Surface Games/Deep Structure Games/Penetrating the Deep Structure Game/Examining Outcroppings of the Deep Structure Game/Interlinking Games/Organization Games: A Reprise
Communication and Power? Looking to the Future

Six months later—after a media onslaught that finally forced David Begelman (head of Movie and Television Operations Columbia Pictures Industries) out of the company for good; after Hirschfield (President, Columbia Pictures) plotted secretly but vainly with several outsiders in an attempt to buy control of Columbia (Pictures) and overthrow Herbert Allen (Board Chairman, Columbia Pictures); after Begelman was sentenced to probation and a fine for his crime (embezzlement); . . . after Hirschfield accused the board in a formal letter of trying to discredit and harass him, improperly challenging his authority in breach of his contract, after the heads of Columbia's divisions assembled overnight in New York from two continents to confront the board of directors on his behalf—Alan Hirschfield was fired. (McClintick, 1982, p. 56)

AUTHOR'S NOTE: I wish to express my sincere appreciation to Lyman Porter, Linda Putnam, and Fred Jablin for their insightful editorial input, and to Tirthankar Bose, L. L. Cummings, Elaine Darquin, Stan Deetz, Jill Graham, Sue Koch, Michele and Don Ley and the class of '85, Phil Mirvis, Walter Nord, Ralph Stabelin, for their thoughtful contributions to my preparation of this manuscript.

The playing out of organizational games is one of the functions of power, politics, and communication in organization. In order to study these phenomena we may start with the following assumptions:

(1) Organizational life is significantly influenced by the quest for and exercise of power by organizational actors, which constitute the political activity of organization.
(2) Power exists both on the surface level of organizational activity and deep within the very structure of organizations.
(3) Communication plays a vital role in the development of power relations and the exercise of power.
(4) The manipulation and exercise of power is expressed, in the sense both of actions and relations, as organizational games.

The Columbia Pictures incident cited above provides a glimpse of some of the aspects of organization familiar to investigators viewing organizations from a political perspective. From this perspective, the fundamental activities of organization are the following:

contests among interdependent actors operating within different interpretive frames and led by different self-interests and preferences for *control* of resources, for the ability to determine the means/ends of doing organizational work (Baldridge, 1971; Cyert & March, 1963; Uttal, 1985);

struggles for *collaboration* in the performance of organizational work when the means/ends of its accomplishment are unclear and/or subject to dispute (Barnard, 1938; Pfeffer, 1981; Thompson, 1967; Wilkinson, 1983).

Power relations, the exercise of power, and communication largely influence how such contests and struggles develop, are managed, and are resolved. The task of this chapter is to elaborate on the nature of the linkages between these elements of organizational life. We will do this by first examining the nature of organizational power and politics and then discussing the way in which power and politics both shape and are themselves influenced by the communication medium (the rules and structures of communication) and message (the content, the language, symbols, meaning) in organizational settings.

Several interesting treatments of organizational power and communication exist in the literature (e.g., Conrad, 1983; Conrad & Ryan, 1985; Deetz & Kersten, 1983; Koch, 1984; Mumby, 1984; Pfeffer, 1981). Our approach in this chapter will be to emphasize and integrate important insights from such research as well as from works dealing more exclusively with organizational power (e.g., House, 1984) and politics (Allen & Porter, 1983; Mintzberg, 1983). We treat power and influence as synonymous terms in this chapter, to avoid the semantic tangle that results from trying to distinguish them (House, 1984; Kanter, 1977; McCall, 1979; Mintzberg, 1983; Pfeffer, 1981). Building on these earlier treatments and introducing the construct of the organizational game with its political orientation, its rules of communication, and its meaning (the content of communication), we shall examine how power and communication interrelate and function in the multiple and overlapping organizational games that take place both on the surface of organizations and on the deep structure level. We will use the organization game construct as a mechanism for demonstrating how communication interacts with power and politics in a variety of ways, at different organizational levels and over time.

THE NATURE OF
ORGANIZATIONAL POWER

The fundamental concept in social science is power, in the same sense in which energy is the fundamental concept in physics. (Russell, 1983, p. 12)

Even though it is a basic concept of organizational life, power remains an inchoate and elusive concept, a "messy" one, the subject of much controversy and debate (March, 1966). It is difficult to describe and analyze, in part because it is a multifaceted phenomenon that has surface, visible characteristics as well as hidden ones, whose interrelations must be carefully teased out if one is to fully grasp their meaning (Astley & Sachdeva, 1984; Lukes, 1974). In a sense power in organizations is well understood. Administrators asked to describe power distributions in organizations seem to have little trouble agreeing that they exist and can identify what they look like (Allen, Madison, Renwick, & Mayes, 1979; Gandz & Murray, 1980; Madison, Allen, Porter, Renwick, & Mayes, 1980; Pfeffer, 1981). But in another sense power is a more subtle phenomenon, its origins and impact being embedded in the symbols and systems that evolve out of contests and struggles among organizational actors. Such contests are in many cases preserved and renewed through the perpetuation of earlier power relations, hidden beneath the surface of current organizational functioning.

Several writers have noted the multifaceted nature of power (Astley & Sachdeva, 1984; Lukes, 1974; McClelland, 1970). Most important to our discussion here is the notion of the dual nature of power, which exists both on the surface of an organization and beneath it. A first overt manifestation of surface power can be seen, for example, in the direct confrontation between Hirschfield (backed by his supporters, the Division Heads) and the board at Columbia Pictures, and seen even more clearly in the board's ability to force Hirschfield to rescind his initial decision to fire Begelman. This operation of power is captured in Dahl's (1957) definition of power as the capacity of actor A to get actor B to do what actor B would not otherwise do. The focus of this aspect of power is on decision making, on the capacity to exercise power when decisions are made on crucial or contentious issues. Furthermore, the arguments that Hirschfield and his opponents use to justify their positions and to persuade one another reflect this struggle for power. Examination of such arguments will likely reveal some of the important surface aspects of power (Conrad, 1983).

A second, less visible—though still surface—manifestation of power in a relationship is the capacity of an actor in that relationship to prevent the emergence, for discussion and decision making, of anything other than "safe," uncontroversial issues (Bachrach & Baratz, 1962). In such cases the exercise of power is not seen; rather, its impact is revealed in the absence of challenge. Actors who have power in this sense are able, without protest from fellow-actors, to leave contentious items off the agenda of decision-making meetings. To the extent that such power exists in a relationship, the contentious items or concerns will not be raised for discussion during such a meeting. In his reflections on the meetings of President Kennedy and his cabinet that produced the decision to support an invasion of Cuba by Cuban expatriots to overthrow President Castro (i.e., the 1961 Bay of Pigs invasion), Arthur Schlesinger notes with some bitterness his own unwillingness to speak up, to raise the grave doubts he felt about the wisdom of such a venture. He attributes his reticence to an unwillingness to create a disturbance of the consensus he assumed to have developed in the meeting. He was reluctant to challenge the situation, to make a nuisance of himself (Schlesinger, 1965). His action—or inaction—in this case appears to be a product of covert power of the sort identified here.

But power also exists on a far deeper level, where it is actually embedded in the very structure of organization. It resides in the "socially structured and culturally patterned behavior of groups and practices of institution" (Lukes, 1974, p. 22). Power in this case is a structural aspect of organization rather than a matter of a relationship between actors. This deep structure power is so deeply embedded in the organizational system that issues and challenges to the power holder are unlikely to arise at all. Under these conditions, there is no need for actors with power stemming from the system to wield power in the system, in the surface sense of acting directly or indirectly on decisions. Precisely because such power is embedded in organizational structuring and is therefore a real but unperceived part of the interpretive framework of actors (Brown, 1978), it is virtually impossible for some of the actors to recognize that their interests are not being met, that the sectarian interests of those with power are disguised as universal interests serving all the members of the organization (Deetz, 1985). There is no perception of a need to contest for control or to struggle for collaboration (Brown, 1984). Schlesinger's experience of recognizing, with reflection, that his disagreement on the Cuban invasion decision was subtly controlled would not easily be duplicated, given this kind of power. "The power holders have constituted and institutionalized their provinces of meaning in the very structuring of organizational interactions so that assumptions, interpretations and relevances become the interpretive frame, the cognitive map, of organizational members (Ranson, Hinings, & Greenwood, 1980, p. 8).

The manipulations on which this power rests are "fundamentally tacit procedures that cannot ordinarily be discussed in social discourse" (Molotch & Boden, 1985, p. 73). They cannot readily be identified through organizational analysis. While little research has addressed the question of how this facet of organizational power can be identified and studied, several possible avenues for doing so are discussed later in the chapter.

We shall also discuss later in the chapter the notion that this form of power likely originates in relationships between actors at an earlier point in the history of organization. It becomes invisible and taken for granted with the passage of time and with continued efforts to keep it embedded by actors who benefit from its existence.

Once we recognize organizational power of this structural kind, it becomes evident that the surface level decision making (and "non-decision making") type of power has its roots actually in the deep structure of organization. These different kinds of power are thus interrelated as facets of the same basic element. However, both in terms of actual operation and of analytical identification there is a duality involving surface and deep structure aspects of power. In order to reveal the nature of this duality it is necessary to examine how power is understood. This is where the relationship between power and communication becomes an essential subject for study.

Organizational Power and Communication

The key concept regarding communication in organizations is that it exists as both medium and meaning. It is a medium because power flows along its channels. Communication provides the means through which power can be exercised, developed, maintained, and enhanced. Communication structures, channels, networks, and rules are avenues of power. For their part, the existence of power relations and the exercise of power create the communication structures and rules. Both processes go on simultaneously and sequentially in organizations. The specific nature of the communication medium in an organization grows out of power relationships established at earlier points in the organization's history and is modified as power relationships continue to unfold in the ongoing organization. The use of communication channels, networks, and rules itself serves to influence the nature of power in the organization and has implications for subsequent arrangements of this medium.

Thus the communication medium is never neutral. The structures and rules of communication established in an organization favor some actors over others (Deetz & Kersten, 1983; Mechanic, 1962; Pfeffer, 1981; Putnam, 1983). Furthermore, the medium is itself contestable, can be manipulated by actors who, in the pursuit of their interests, may try to distort the communication medium. Their tactics may include overloading, expanding, constricting, circumventing, and reinterpreting the structures and channels of communication (Caro, 1983; Kanter, 1977; Perrow, 1970; Porter, Allen, & Angle, 1981; Strauss, 1962).

Bower (1970) provides an example of the political nature of the communication medium. He decribes the way in which division managers of a company built almost an entire manufacturing plant without senior executives at the corporate office knowing about it. The managers broke the cost of this large capital project into small enough amounts for its funding to be smuggled through the division's operating budget. This budget permitted managers in the field to spend up to $50,000 dollars on an expense item without having to get permission for the action from the top officers in the company. Corporate policy in this case was circumvented when the divisional managers reinterpreted the communication rules so as to get their project in place. Communication in this case was a medium for the exercise of power.

As meaning, communication is an important part of the ongoing development and exercise of power in organizations. Actors attribute meaning to the material, active and verbal symbols that exist in organization settings (Dandridge, Mitroff, & Joyce, 1980; Riley, 1983). In part, this meaning derives from the interpretive schemes actors bring to organizations (Schutz, 1972). In part, the meaning derives from the surface distribution and exercise of power. In part, in the deep structure of organization this meaning is the representation of power. Power in the latter case acts through the language and complex symbols of organization—the myths, metaphors, rituals, and stories of organization (Conrad, 1983; Deetz & Kersten, 1983; Mumby, 1984).

At the surface level of organization, power and communication (as meaning) are linked through the labeling and sense-making of day-to-day organizational life "as well as through the development of social consensus around labels and definitions of decisions and actions" (Pfeffer, 1981, p. 188). In their attempts to gain or maintain advantage in organizational contests and struggles, actors exercise power while creating meaning around statements, actions, and material aspects of organization (Conrad & Ryan, 1985; Deetz, 1985; Pfeffer, 1981). In some cases the link between power and meaning is overt. Actors label, frame, and invoke meaning around decisions, and other actors respond to such acts of power, either by accepting the meanings and their organizational implications or by countering with more persuasive meaning creations of their own.

In the Columbia Pictures case the decision of whether Begelman should be fired for embezzlement was contested, in part, in terms of the meaning of his actions. Hirshfield labeled Begelman's actions as dishonest and wanted to fire him. Begelman's supporters on the board attributed his actions to temporary insanity and recommended that he only be reprimanded and suspended. Hirschfield saw this latter, relatively favorable labeling of intention as a direct attempt to influence the direction of the decision. On the other side, some of Begelman's supporters attached connotations of dishonesty and unethical conduct to earlier behavior by Hirschfield and his wife and attempted to create a consensus around these meanings. Their goal was to undermine Hirshfield's credibility and force him to retreat from a decision to fire Begelman.

Surface manifestations of power and meaning also occur covertly. In such cases, meanings are invoked in attempts to mobilize support for intentions in ways that minimize the challenge or resistance to these actions and intentions (Pfeffer, 1981). Such manipulations of meaning belong also in the realm of political activity, specifically the exercise of power, which we shall consider later in the chapter.

One consequence of the close links between power and meaning at the level of deep structure of organizations is that the distinction between communication as meaning and as message blurs at this level. This is because the language of organization, which not only describes and insures but also disguises the power relation between and among interest groups, creates the structure of communication even as it creates the patterns and rules of interaction and their meanings (which are taken for granted). Before we take our investigation to this deep structural level of organization, it would be useful to examine the origins of power in organizations and to discuss in some detail what we currently know about the exercise of power.

The Origins of Organizational Power

A resource dependency perspective of power. The most widely known and extensively researched models of organizational power are based on Emerson's (1962) notion of power as the obverse of dependency where the "dependence of Actor A upon Actor B is (1) directly proportional to A's motivational investment in goals mediated by (B) and (2) inversely proportional to the availability of these goals to (A) outside the A-B relations" (Emerson, 1962, p. 32). An actor (B) has power over another actor (A), and can get A to do what B wishes accomplished to the extent that A needs and wants what B has to offer and cannot get easily elsewhere. Similar exchange relationship views of power have been articulated by Blau (1964) and Homans (1974).

From a communicative perspective, actor B can attempt to get actor A to do something B wants accomplished by invoking one or other of a variety of communication strategies (Roloff, 1976). Such communicative behaviors by an actor are invoked with the intention of getting some or other reward from the relationship with other actors, of affecting others with whom he or she interacts. Communication strategies that attempt to influence others can range widely and include those that involve promises and rewards for compliance, threats of punishment for noncompliance, appeals to the other person's feelings ("You will feel better/worse if you comply/do not comply") to the morality of the request, to altruism, or to debts owed to the person making the request. Communication strategies used by individuals to influence others in a relationship can be aggressive or passive, can be prosocial (allowing a relationship to grow in a noncompetitive, win-win manner) or antisocial (endangering the long-term viability of a relationship that is constructive). (See Roloff, 1976, for a comprehensive discussion of such communicative strategies.)

When this definition of power is applied in organizations viewed as systems of interdependencies among social actors, with the work of the organization divided up and allocated to the different actors, power emerges from the dependencies that exist among the actors as they do their work in the organization (Hickson, Hinings, Lee, Schneck, & Pennings, 1971; Pfeffer, 1981; Pfeffer & Salancik, 1974; Salancik & Pfeffer, 1974). Exchanges between actors in this context are unlikely to be equal, although given a diversity of resources in organizations that can enter an exchange and given also the ongoing nature of such interdependencies, there will be conditions under which reciprocity exists among organizational actors. (For example, workers may depend on managers for long-range planning, managers may yield to workers unions on hiring and firing decisions.)

The resource based, relational view of organizational power predicts that power will accrue to those actors who control and can provide critical resources to other actors in the system that the latter cannot get elsewhere. Actors provide critical resources when what they have to offer is *irreplaceable* inside the system (in this case the organization) and is *central* to work carried out in the system. Actors' contributions are central when they are *pervasive*— that is, are linked to the activities of many other actors and have *immediate* impact such that the withdrawal of the resources will seriously and rapidly impede progress in the rest of the organization (Bagozzi & Phillips, 1982; Hambrick, 1981; Hickson et al., 1971; Hinings, Hickson, Pennings, & Schneck, 1974).

An example of this critical resource dependency perspective on power is provided in Crozier's (1964) study of French tobacco plants. As Pfeffer (1981) notes,

> Not only did the maintenance engineers control the one remaining uncertainty confronting the organization, the breakdown of machinery, but the capacity of the engineers to cope with the uncertainty could not readily be replaced. The engineers developed the practice of training new engineers verbally, and over time, documentation that would have made the repair of machinery easy for newcomers had disappeared. (p. 113)

Power relationships based on dependency develop, change, and decline over time (Blau, 1964; Homans, 1974). As noted above, such power reflects structural relationships of organizations (Brass, 1984; Kanter, 1977; Pfeffer, 1981). In Crozier's (1964) tobacco plant study, engineers gained power because they had technical expertise that enabled them to control the functioning of machinery, a critical and central operation of the plant.

Relationship power stems also from more dynamic elements of organization. In part, it is a function of the willingness and ability of actors to transform resource dependency based power into exercised power (House, 1984; Mintzberg, 1983; Pettigrew, 1973). Engineers in the tobacco plants exercised and maintained their power by demonstrating their expertise and by ensuring, through their training techniques, that machine repair remained a nonsubstitutable function that *only they* could do.

Again, in part, relationship power is a function of the meaning's introduced into an exchange between actors (Edelman, 1977). In the tobacco plants, the status of expert is attributed to those maintaining the machinery. Such status, as a resource, enhances the value attributed to the engineers in exchanges with other organizational members. Attributions such as this can be intentionally managed by actors to maintain as well as alter the balance of power in a dependency relationship. Actors such as the tobacco engineers can act to keep their status intact by frequently reasserting, and when necessary demonstrating, their expertise and by actively blocking or countering any move by others to change the way work is done that might diminish that status.

But these are not the only ways in which relationship power emerges. It is also a function of the actor's ability to create uncertainty, to develop a consensus around that definition of uncertainty and its importance, and to manage or eliminate that uncertainty for others.

Resource dependency power essentially develops around areas of critical uncertainty in organizations, around decisions as to what important factor is at the same time uncertain, and who can effectively manage or eliminate that uncertainty for the actors to whom it matters. Power may develop in this manner whenever there are contests and struggles around control of organizational means and ends and whenever collaboration is needed to get interdependent work done. As such, this process has most relevance to the surface level of organization, to the development of power that centers on overt decision making and covert non-decision making, the first two facets of power. The assumption here is that the resource dependency model of potential power applies whenever we are looking at the playing out of organizational decision making, whether we are examining present time organizational actions or historical ones.

Such playing out of decision making includes as important elements the conscious negotiation and persuasion attempts made by actors attempting to gain outcomes they value. Thus actors are likely to seek ways to trade desired outcomes with other actors to seek a mutually beneficial result. Also, actors who wish to influence the decision-making process and its outcomes may code and aim their important messages (those that bear on their interests and agendas) in ways they believe will have the greatest impact on others involved in the process that might persuade others to support them. The self-interested core of such messages can be dressed up in the language of organizational rationality ("This will make us all more efficient"), of expertise ("Test results by professional scientists prove . . . "), and/or of ideology ("This choice will fit with the way we have always done things around here!").

The resource dependency model is relevant also to the development of deep structure power. While deep structure power at one point in time is embedded in the systems of influence that exist in organizations and operates below awareness levels of most organizational members, its origins lie in part in the development of some resource dependency relationship between actors at an earlier point in time. As we shall discuss in the next section of this chapter, organizational actors representing major interest groups in a culture or society (such as the ruling elite, managers, workers, technical and military communities) gain power from dependency relationships at a given point in time. Successful efforts by these actors to reproduce and perpetuate that power, but in a disguised form (so that its sectional nature, benefiting powerful actors at the expense of other actors, is hidden from view), create deep structure power that operates beyond the time of the initiating dependency relationship.

While some theorists have attempted to incorporate the notion of institutional power into the relationship model (Blau, 1964; Pfeffer, 1981), the political antecedents to the development of organizational structures and interdependent systems, which influence present time resource dependencies, are not addressed in this model. They are largely taken as given (Clegg, 1981; Comstock, 1982). To understand such aspects of the development of power we must turn to a sociohistorical perspective of power. While the resource dependency perspective allows us to analyze the immediate aspects of power relationships, it is through the sociohistoric perspective that we see how the relationships are embedded in the deep levels of organizational structure.

A sociohistoric perspective on power. The development of power stems in part from surface level dependency relationships among actors, based on the distribution of resources in the organization and the willingness and skill of actors to create and mobilize perceptions of other actors around interpretations of uncertainty and of the importance of resources. Power develops also from a sociohistorical process in which the outcomes of contests and struggles among actors (interest groups) over the control and management of the work process become incorporated in systems of influence in the form of rules and interpretations of reality, which shape subsequent activities of actors (Clegg, 1981; Mintzberg, 1983; Ranson et al., 1980).

Such contests and struggles take place when systems of influence and the underlying power relations previously ordered become problematic. This occurs around uncertainty when political and economic changes in the environment of organizations pose challenges, threats, or opportunities to actors in those power relationships (and actors looking to join relationships) and stimulate them to reexamine and attempt to reorder/rearrange the relationships (Clegg, 1981).

In such encounters, which lead to deep structure power and reordered power relations, the actors represent major interest groups (Clegg, 1981; Noble, 1984).[1] The political nature of such encounters and of the resulting relationships among actors is frequently disguised so that outcomes are represented as inevitable technical or economic progress (Noble, 1984) beneficial to all interest groups (Deetz, 1985). The sociopolitical nature of the outcome and its relative benefit to some interest groups is rarely self-evident in the language explaining such outcomes, or in the systems of influence that proceed from it. The rules and structures of organization reflected in such systems are found in terms of authority, technical and economic rationality, and of moral (ideological) correctness (Mintzberg, 1983). Over time the role of power relations and of political activity in producing current arrangements, such as the division of labor, distribution of resources, and interpretations of legitimacy is even more extensively covered over, as new actors in organization take as natural and directive that which was, at its inception, political and problematic.

In his analysis of the social history of technological developments in the United States in the decades following World War II, Noble (1984) shows how power and social relations have not only influenced development of current forms of production technology but engendered current beliefs that such forms are the inevitable, natural progression of science rather than the product of the social order of events. He illustrates the process by examining in one detailed analysis the survival of one of two competing technologies, each equally viable but each based on a different philosophy and a different vision of the desired relationship between worker and machine. One technology, record playback (R/P), was designed to permit programming by drawing on and expanding the skills of machinists who were treated in this model as an important store of inherited intelligence in metal-working production. The other technology, numerical control (N/C), was designed to permit programming that eliminated the need for skills and experience input from the machinist.

In time, the N/C technology survived, the R/P technology did not. Noble (1984) identifies as central to this outcome the ideas, actions, and intentions of interest groups from technical, managerial, and military communities. The technical group was represented by engineers who expressed an interest in and a preference for "formal, abstract, quantitative approaches to formulation and solution of problems, an obsession with control, certainty and predictability and a corresponding desire to eliminate as much as possible . . . all human error" (Noble, 1984, p. 191). Within the management community the central preoccupation was with control of the physical and human aspects of production both as a means to greater efficiency and profit and as an end to reduce the control of production by workers and their unions. The dominant preoccupations within the military community arose out of the traditions of command and control that demanded a search for "centralized computer-based command-and-control systems and communication networks"(Noble, 1984, p. 192).

The converging of these three sets of ideas, preoccupations, and preferences, combined with the particular way in which power relations emerged and power was exercised during the development of the R/P and N/C technologies, produced an outcome that favored the latter. Given the preferences of the key actors (engineers, managers, and military personnel) in the game being played out, no funds were made available for R/P development while manufacturers were encouraged by government contracting policies to develop their own N/C capabilities. Workers and unions were excluded from the game. In the circumstances, the shifting of power away from the R/P players was not a surprising outcome.

One important perception offered by the sociohistoric perspective is that deep-level power is dynamic and influential rather than static and deterministic. Historical analysis reveals how the development of deep-level power influences not only current actions but a chain of subsequent actions. At the same time, the social analysis of the development of deep-level power shows its dialectical nature (Benson, 1977). Briefly, such power, in a system of influence, is subject to challenge by actors in the system as contradictions in its implementation occur over time. Such challenges are formed according to the idiosyncratic nature and preferences of the contesting actors. This will be so even though the actors who implement the system of influence may strive to produce consensus through the power in the system (Gray, Bougon, & Donnellon, 1985).

In summary, power exists at the surface and in the deep structure of organizations. Its surface existence (as a potential force) derives from critical resource dependencies between and among organizational actors. Contemporary resource dependencies derive in part from the resolution of earlier, historically based interactions of major actors. Such interactions produce systems of influence in which the unequal distribution of power becomes unnoticed and is hidden under the garb of a legitimate system of influence. Present-time resource dependencies, particularly those of actors who are or will become major actors in organization settings, contribute through their interactions with existing systems of influence to the nature and composition of future deep-level power arrangements.

Much of what we have discussed about power and communication thus far has focused explicitly on power as a potential force[2] in organizations and only implicitly on the exercise of power. It is important before turning directly to the interaction of power and communication that we examine power in action. In this context we will discuss power first in terms of the dispositions of actors to use power and then in terms of enacted power itself, of political activity in organizations.

Predispositions Toward Power

Much of the scholarly attention given to organizational power in recent years has focused on resource dependencies and power in the context of relationships and to an extent on power located in systems of influence. The nature and role of the organizational actor, individual or group, involved with power has been somewhat overlooked. Yet actors are vital components of the contests and struggles for controlling resources and for getting interdependent work done collaboratively. What do we know about such actors?

Some individuals are more disposed than other to want power, to seek it out and to wield it (House, 1984; Jongbloed & Frost, 1985).[3] Individuals differ in their need for power and in their ability to seek and use it. They also differ according to the nature of their expectations of power and what they learn from such experiences. Those with a need and a willingness to use power are likely to use communication more consciously than others as a means to get what they want, to gain control over situations. Their communicative behavior will likely emphasize conscious influence strategies. Those who succeed in gaining desired outcomes through persuasive communication are likely to repeat such efforts in the future. Individuals who are skilled in the use of power are more likely than others to embed that power in their communications with others.

Personality attributes. Most notable motivational antecedents to an individual's predisposition toward power are high needs for power and dominance. Individuals with a high need for dominance are more likely to acquire and exercise power than are those with a low need (Borgatta, 1961; Dyson, Fleitas, & Scioli, 1972; Gough, 1968; Johnson & Fraudson, 1962; Megargee, Bogart, & Anderson, 1966).

Similarly, a high need for power appears linked to the acquisition and use of power (McClelland, 1975; McClelland & Watson, 1973; Uleman, 1972). McClelland's (1970) notion of personal power (people seeking to compete and win at the expense of others) and socialized power (people seeking to collaborate and win, while enhancing the power of others) is an important contribution to this literature. One implication is that people do not necessarily wield power in a destructive manner, so that it is possible to explore and develop the use of power in ways that are beneficial to those doing interdependent work in organizations. (The communicative approaches and behaviors of such power wielding are likely to be similar to those noted by Kanter in the next paragraph.) His insight has implications for understanding leadership and empowerment in organization (Howell, 1986). We address these implications in a discussion of power sharing and empowerment in the final section of the chapter.

Furthermore, recent research on intrapreneurs (individuals behaving innovatively in large, complex organizations; Kanter, 1983; Peters & Waterman, 1982; Pinchot, 1985) suggests a link between need for achievement (McClelland, Atkinson, Clark, & Lowell, 1953) and the use of power. Case studies of intrapreneurs reveal that typically they have a high need for achievement and a willingness to acquire and use power as a means to ensure that their ideas, inventions, innovations become accepted within their organizations (Pinchot, 1985). The intrapreneurs studied by Pinchot appeared interested in power as instrumental for task accomplishment and as something they shared with others rather than as a basis for personal enhancement and advancement in their organizational hierarchies. Kanter (1983) describes such individuals as "quiet entrepreneurs" who communicate in a collabora-tive/participative fashion,

> **persuading much more than ordering** (although threats, direct orders, or pressure from a bigger boss might be used as a last resort); **team building,** including creation of formal task forces or committees, frequent staff meetings, frequent sharing of information, use of regular brain-storming sessions; **seeking input from others,** including needs of users, suggestions from subordinates, review by peers; **showing "political" sensitivity** to the interests of others, their stake or potential in the project, and last but not least, **willingness to share rewards and recognition.** (1983, p. 237)

Machiavellianism is another well-recognized personality characteristic associated with power (Christie & Geis, 1970). Individuals high on the Machiavellianism scale are resistant to social influence, are concerned with task accomplishment rather than with emotional and moral considerations, are strongly inclined to initiate action and to control interactions with others (Drory & Gluskinos, 1980; Epstein, 1969; Weinstein, Beckhouse, Blumstein, & Stein, 1968). Machiavellian behavior includes the use of deception, bluffs, and other manipulative strategies and tactics. These behaviors are more noticeable in such individuals in competitive situations, contexts where uncertainty is likely to prevail and the use of power is likely to be prevalent (Christie & Geis, 1970; Drory & Gluskinos, 1980).

Abilities. Several abilities (and skills) appear linked to the acquisition and use of power. Self-confidence, which may be a personality characteristic but can be induced in individuals (Instone, Major, & Bunker, 1983; Mowday, 1980), cognitive complexity (Zajonc & Wolfe, 1966), linguistic ability (Bucher, 1970; House, 1984), and formal (professional expertise) and informal (physical, intellectual or social) competence (Daft, 1983; Hollander, 1960) appear to be skills associated with power. Self-confidence increases the willingness of individuals to make influence attempts. Cognitively complex individuals are able to identify power relationships, can seek out and handle more information, appear to be more tolerant of situational uncertainty and better able to predict future-related events than those low in such complexity (House, 1984). High communicative competence enhances individuals to articulate arguments, advocate positions, and persuade others—all useful skills for acquiring and using power (Monge, Bachman, Dillard, & Eisenberg, 1982; Parks, 1985; Sypher & Zorn, 1986). Individuals with high professional (technical) expertise or with informal expertise, which is relevant in organizational settings, are more likely to acquire power than those who lack such competence. In their four-year study of insurance company employees, Sypher and Zorn (1986) found strong positive relationships between cognitive complexity in individuals and their persuasive ability. They also found that persons with more developed social cognitive abilities were promoted more often within the organization than those in whom such abilities were less developed.

Previous experience of power. Predispositions of individuals toward the acquisition and use of power appear to be relatively enduring but are also "subject to modification through future learning" (House, 1984, p. 34). Individuals who observe the successful exercise of power or who are rewarded for exercising power are likely to increase their predisposition toward power and to seek opportunities to exercise it in organizations. Opportunities include positions of authority over others and positions involving management of uncertainty where resolution of the uncertainty and maintenance of collaborative effort require actor intervention (House, 1984, pp. 35-36).

The interaction of actor predispositions and organizational conditions influence the opportunities and progress of actors seeking and wielding power. Keeping in mind the duality of power as a surface and deep structure phenomenon, it is possible to see the probable nature of such interactions. On the one hand, actors with relevant abilities, skill, and personality characteristics, positive experiences in the use of power, and with access to and the ability to create resources are likely to impact on surface activities in organizations (Kanter, 1983). They may also be more likely than other actors in an organization to influence the nature of the systems of influence based on deep structure power (Caro, 1983).

Clearly, then, power can be located not only in resource dependencies and in systems of influence but also in the personality, skill, and experience factors that actors bring to the organizational setting. But with respect to actors it remains as potential power "until someone makes a bid for it and then invests it in activities and people that will produce results" (Kanter, 1983, p. 402). Because the strategic actions of actors can thus transform potential into enacted power, we shall now turn our attention to the exercise of power, to organizational politics.

ORGANIZATIONAL POLITICS

Power dynamics . . . are inevitable and needed to make organizations function well. (Kotter, 1979, p. 17)

Organizational politics is the embodiment of the exercise of power. It is represented in the strategies and tactics actors use to get their way in the day-to-day, ongoing, present-time functioning of organization—it is power in action. In addition, keeping in mind our notion of the duality of power, politics can also be found in the intentional building of frameworks, of communication rules and meanings that compose systems of influence; it is power in conception.[4] Once established, such rules and meanings have a deep-seated political impact on day-to-day organizational functioning, an impact that extends beyond the initial act of their creation.

Political Behavior as Intentional,
Self-Interested, and Nonconsensual

Organizational politics is commonly depicted as the intentional self-interested activities of actors. It is activated under conditions of contest for control and in struggles to get collaboration given uncertainty over means-ends linkages and differences in beliefs about desired outcomes (Pfeffer, 1981). It is nonconsensual in the sense that political activity threatens the self-interests of other actors in a power relationship. It is an activity that is likely to arouse the thought or the overt attempt to resist on the part of other actors, were its true intent to be recognized (Frost & Hayes, 1979; Porter et al., 1981).

While it is possible for such nonconsensual activity to produce win-lose outcomes between actors, it is not necessary that this be so. In the Columbia Pictures incident cited earlier, for example, the covert activities of Hirschfield to overthrow Allen and the (initially) disguised efforts of the board members to discredit Hirschfield were self-interested activities likely to produce win-lose outcomes. On the other hand, political activities such as those of the French tobacco plant maintenance engineers who wanted to keep control of a strategic uncertainty (keeping all repair instructions verbal so as to prevent standardization and unrestrained communication of the activity), would not necessarily produce win-lose outcomes. In the latter case, other organizational members did not necessarily suffer from the outcomes of the engineers. The central work of the plant was accomplished. Management in the plant may not have been able to exert as much control over maintenance and the engineers as they wished, but the interdependent work of the organization was accomplished.

The example of the maintenance engineers suggests that an important aspect of the self-interest aspect of organizational politics in organizations is its effect on the choice of an actor's strategy in the initiation and carrying out of that strategy (House, 1984). While actor A's intention may include a concern for the "well-being" and development of actor B, toward or against whom the activity is directed, actor B is excluded from playing an active, knowing role in deciding how his or her self-interest might be accomplished when actor A defines and implements actor A's political strategy. Extrapolating from the tobacco plant case to illustrate this point, we might speculate that although managers/administrators, as one group of actors in the organizational setting, probably benefitted from and accepted the engineer's political strategy (at least in the short run), they may have preferred a different approach and outcome (such as solutions incorporating cost reductions arising from standardized procedures carried out by semiskilled operators). While both parties may win in such an encounter, the intention of the engineers' political strategy is that the game be played on their own grounds and in terms of their own definition of a win-win outcome.

The clearest examples of this type of intentional, self-interested, nonconsensual activity in organizations can be found amongst intrapreneurs. One important characteristic of intrapreneurs appears to be their willingness to engage in communicative acts that involve bending or breaking organizational rules so as to pursue the development of new ideas and products that interest them. Pinchot (1985) describes the activities of several successful intrapreneurs, including a member of the Hewlett Packard organization, a design engineer who developed a new and subsequently profitable oscilloscope monitor in the 1960s. To complete the project this particular intrapreneur gathered critical customer information, in the process violating a rule forbidding employees to show prototypes to customers and expanding his activities well beyond those intended for engineers in the company. Furthermore, he disobeyed—or, more accurately, reinterpreted—a senior manager's communication to "get the project out of the laboratory" (that is, to terminate it) before the manager's next laboratory inspection as an order to get the project completed before the inspection. The senior manager was both angry at being disobeyed and pleased at the success of the outcome (Pinchot, 1985, pp. 23-29). Such strategies include a considerable amount of political flexibility in the construction, use, and interpretation of communications and communicative acts.

Political Activity in Disguise

Political activity may be explicit, but like power at rest, it can have hidden facets and may be, at times, something of a "wooden horse." Like the Trojan horse of legend, the real self-interest of actors represented in the activity can be hidden, disguised, dressed up as non-self-interested, nonpolitical activity.

Koch (1984) describes how one unit in an organization resisted participation in a reorganization that threatened its autonomy. Members of the unit gave lip service to the change while working actively behind the scenes to resist and subvert it. "The foremost aim was to maintain the appearance of cooperation; without it they had no credibility to stand on" (1984, p. 182). Their passive resistance revolved around "quietly demonstrating that it [the reorganization] would compromise their ability to meet the overriding goal of productivity"

(1984, p. 182). Pettigrew (1973, 1985) and Frost and Hayes (1979) offer similar examples of recourse to legitimacy in the service of political intent. Several examples of the hidden face of political activity exist in the literature (Caro, 1983; Kanter, 1977, 1983; Kearns, 1976; Kidder, 1982; Kotter, 1977, 1979; Maccoby, 1976).

The effort to mask real intent appears to be inherent in political activity, even though astute actors may recognize such an effort as an exercise in concealment. The effort stems, at least in part, from a desire to minimize the cost of engaging in the activity. Such costs stem from the disapproval of those whose self-interests are threatened or are ignored by the activity and from mobilization of energy by others to counter the political activity. They are due also to the need for political actors to continue to do interdependent work over extended periods of time.

Disguise of real intent in organizational politics is typically a language game (Edelman, 1977; Pfeffer, 1981). It is likely that the language of disguise will be that of the prevailing system of influence and invoke legitimacy, ideology, expertise, or whatever mix of these values exists in the organization (Mintzberg, 1983).

The Legitimacy of Organizational Politics

Organizational politics is frequently defined as illegitimate activity (House, 1984; Mintzberg, 1983). To label it as such, without specifying that it is illegitimate only from one or the other perspective rather than being unequivocally so, is to introduce an unfortunate bias into our treatment of it. Typically in our models the description of political activity as illegitimate appears to mean activity that threatens the self-interests of the dominant or ruling coalitions (Mintzberg, 1983).

However, to bias our interpretation of it in this way would merely blind us to the political nature of many of the activities of dominant coalitions and to the political underpinnings of the systems of influence that sustain them. It also serves to take our enquiring eye off the political (that is, intentional, self-interested, contestable, opaque) nature of a great deal of activity that goes on in organizations (Allen et al., 1979; Kotter, 1985; Pfeffer, 1981). Political activity is likely to occur wherever and whenever the interests of some organizational actors are threatened by those of other actors. It occurs around uncertainty and involves contest and struggle. Illegitimacy is more useful as a label that members of one interest group stick on the intentions and activities of members of another, opposite, interest group (Alinsky, 1971). The label should not be assigned by scholars as an unqualified evaluation of political activity.

It is difficult, for example, to imagine innovation and change, management of conflict, or "tinkering" with the system taking place in organizations in the absence of political activity (Kotter, 1985; Peters & Waterman, 1982;

Pettigrew, 1985). Organizational politics in such instances becomes necessary when old alignments in the organization (arrangements that balance actors' interests and the doing of organizational work) no longer function, so that new alignments are needed that are not accommodated or anticipated by existing structures, systems, and practices (Culbert & McDonough, 1985; Kotter, 1985). Principled dissent (whistle-blowing; Graham, 1983, 1985), negotiation and bargaining strategies and tactics (Bacharach & Lawler, 1980), and leadership (Pondy, 1978) all involve political activity by organizational members working to get objectives and intentions accomplished in the face of resistance from other members.

Organizational Politics:
Power in Action and in Conception

Organizational politics is a mix of *power in action* (that is, political activity carried out within and through the existing structures of organization) and *power in conception* (that is, political activity directed at framing and reframing (surface) aspects of structure so as to pursue self-interested intention). The case of reorganization noted earlier (Koch, 1984) provides an example of power in action. Power in conception is political activity designed to create structures and channels that will permit the self-interested intentions of the actor to proceed. An illustration of this political activity is provided in the following description of Gurney's interrogation of Dean during the Watergate hearings of 1973:

> In the course of his three-and-one-half-hour close interrogation, Gurney [Edward J. Gurney, U.S. Senator] attempts to discredit Dean [John Dean III, Counsel to President Nixon] in various ways. His most pervasive strategy is to suspend practical ethics, to remove Dean's access to the routine procedures by insisting on literal accounts of "facts," not "impressionistic" ones. He tries to impose a courtroom format that permits a witness to speak only in reply to a question.... Gurney offers only questions that seem to require "simple facts" as their answers. In this way, Dean's incapacity to respond with simple, literal reporting of White House events can discredit the substance of his testimony.... Dean's counterstrategies vary, from insistent efforts to provide details of relevant contexts to offering, as time goes on, his own "theories" of how meaning is constructed through talk and how the legitimacy of accounts of such talk should be judged. (Molotch & Boden, 1985, p. 276)

In this case, the exercise of power is directed at establishing, in an overtly rational but covertly self-interested way, the ground rules for the process of interrogation. Both actors, Gurney and Dean, are engaged in the politics of conception. To the extent that Gurney is successful in his activity of structuring the dialogue, his politically motivated procedures will appear legitimate to the "judges" of the encounter, the taxpaying, voting public.

Surface Politics

Organizational politics on the surface of organizations involves the exercise of power by an actor to get what that actor wants from decision situations, negotiations, and interpersonal interactions. It involves strategies by an actor to confront others so as to gain compliance with his or her intentions and objectives, strategies to avoid resistance and challenge to those intentions and objectives (by preventing the emergence of controversial issues and attention instead to safe ones) and strategies the actor uses to resist influence attempts of others.

Political or influence strategies have been studied in both the interpersonal communication and organizational literature (e.g., Jablin, 1981; Jensen, 1984; Kipnis & Schmidt, 1983; Kipnis, Schmidt, & Wilkinson, 1980; Krone, 1985; Marwell & Schmitt, 1967; Porter et al., 1981; Roloff, 1976; Wiseman & Schenck-Hamlin, 1981). Political strategies in organizations are involved in downward relationships (managing subordinates), lateral relationships (interacting with peers and other actors not in the individual's unit or organization), and upward relationships (managing actors at higher levels in organizations). While there are a variety of strategies of influence available to the political actor, they are not all equally applicable to these three relationship directions. Choice of strategies will vary also depending on the goal of the actor, the characteristics of the actor, and the context within which she or he operates (Jensen, 1984; Porter et al., 1981).

Political communication strategies. A core set of seven influence strategies useful to our discussion of surface politics is provided by Kipnis and his associates (Kipnis & Schmidt, 1983; Kipnis et al., 1980). Many of the strategies in this set have correspondence with strategies identified in interpersonal communication research (see Jensen, 1984, for a discussion of these linkages). The influence strategies developed empirically by Kipnis et al. (1980) are the following: reason (use of facts and data to support the development of a logical argument), coalition (mobilizing other people in the organization), ingratiation (use of impression management, flattery, and the creation of goodwill), bargaining (use of negotiation through exchange of benefits and favors), assertiveness (use of a direct and forceful approach), higher authority (gaining support of people in higher levels in the organization), and sanctions (use of organizationally derived rewards and punishments; Kipnis & Schmidt, 1983, p. 307). Other strategies available to political actors include appeals to altruism ("do it for me," "do it for the good of the company"; Marwell & Schmitt, 1967; Wiseman & Schenck-Hamlin, 1981) and circumvention strategies such as deceit (Wiseman & Schenck-Hamlin, 1981). Exploitation of one's charisma, when an actor is perceived to have this quality, is likely to be recognized as a distinct influence strategy as more is learned about its transformational role in organizational interactions (Bass, 1985; Howell, 1986).

Political strategies involve actors in manipulative communicative actions. Reasoning as a political strategy, for example, is likely to include tactics such as selection of objective criteria that favor the position advocated by the political actor, bringing in outside experts who support the actor's case, and controlling the agenda and the order of appearance of items on the agenda so as to draw attention away from controversial issues and/or toward "safe" issues (Pfeffer, 1981). It may also involve use of information to swamp the other actors (Allen et al., 1979). Coalition building requires developing constituencies external to the organization and building internal alliances, and can involve consciously developing friendships, trading favors and goodwill, and so on. (The overlap of the coalition strategy with other strategies such as bargaining and ingratiation is clear. However, the focus and use of coalitions is likely to be oriented more toward lateral relationships than to supervisor-subordinate relationships, where these other strategies are typically found.) Impression management as a strategy includes attention and adherence to the norms and behaviors thought to be desirable by powerful actors in the organization, sensitivity to dress, appearing to be successful at organizational tasks, and so on (Allen et al., 1979).

Important sources of influence strategies with links to the deep structure of organizations (discussed later) are associated with language, ceremonies, symbols, and settings (Pfeffer, 1981). These strategies are manifested in semantic indirectness, cognitive scripts, and speech acts that frame influence attempts (Drake & Moberg, 1986). Political actors can consciously use these communicative devices as part of their strategies to legitimate decisions, to disguise power relationships, to produce shared meanings and definitions of "the way things are" (as desired by the political actors; see Pfeffer, 1981, pp. 205-229 for a discussion of this material).

Choosing strategies. Raven (1974, p. 192) notes that to the extent that people are rational we would expect them "to use influence strategies which would most likely lead to successful influence." There are many factors which will affect the choices actors make in this regard. One important category of choice discussed in the literature is the direction of influence involved. Actors involved in managing downward (supervisor-subordinate) have perhaps the fullest array of influence strategies available to them, since power flows more easily downward than in other directions in organizations. Supervisors nevertheless appear to use some strategies rather than others: They report use of assertiveness and sanctions to a high degree and only moderate use of ingratiation, bargaining, and appeals to upward authority when dealing with subordinates (Kipnis et al., 1980). Different objectives apparently call for different strategies: Supervisors report the use of ingratiation when assigning work to others, reasoning and assertiveness when trying to improve the performance of others, and reasoning tactics to gain acceptance of change (Kipnis et al., 1980).

Self-confidence of supervisors seems to make a difference to the strategies chosen. Those who feel confident in their ability to influence others are likely to use reward strategies whereas supervisors who lack self-confidence are more likely to use coercion (Goodstadt & Kipnis, 1970; Kipnis & Lane, 1962). Supervisors of large groups are likely to choose impersonal strategies such as assertiveness, sanctions, and appeals to higher authority rather than more personal ones such as ingratiation and bargaining (Kipnis et al., 1980).

Actors involved in managing upward have a more restricted range of strategies available to them since they are operating from a position of less (formal) power than their targets. Actors are likely to engage in manipulative persuasion (the actor is open about the existence of his or her influence attempt but hides the true objectives) or to use manipulation (the actor conceals both the intent and the fact that he or she is making an influence attempt; Porter et al., 1981). Strategies of reason, ingratiation, and coalition are likely to be used to get things accomplished (Kipnis et al., 1980). Sanctions (positive or negative) are less likely to be adopted as these are not typically available to lower-level actors (relative to the power of their targets). However, negative sanctions such as withholding or delaying services, blocking progress, or even simply "working to rule" are tactics available to actors when managing upwards (Mechanic, 1962; Porter et al., 1981). Such tactics are particularly viable when actors are buttressed by union power (Kipnis et al., 1980).

An important aspect of effective leadership is the capacity of the leader to "go to bat" for his or her subordinates. Such upward management is likely to include resort to political strategies. Jablin (1981) notes that such political action can create problems for supervisors. He reports a study in which subordinates who see their supervisors as highly political are both less open in their communication and less satisfied with those supervisors than those who perceive their supervisors as less political. Given that supervisors must resort to influence strategies for at least part of their upward management, they need to find ways to communicate the meaning of such political activity (which can be a way of "going to bat" for subordinates) to their subordinates to maintain effective contact with them.

Organizational actors involved in successfully managing lateral relationships are likely to focus on establishing networks (Kotter, 1985) and developing coalitions (Kanter, 1983) so as to deal effectively with the interdependencies such lateral linkages imply. Reasoning strategy (involving actions such as appealing to the rules so as to persuade other actors to settle territorial differences, or judicious education of actors to persuade them to comply with the political actors' intent) and use of appeals to higher authority are also likely to be common ways to manage lateral relationships.

Implementing one or more political strategies to get things accomplished and to meet an actor's self-interest appears to be commonplace in organizational settings. It occurs whether an individual is managing up, down, or laterally. As Kipnis et al. (1980, p. 22) suggest, "everyone is influencing everyone else in organizations, regardless of job title. People seek benefits, information, satisfactory job performance, the chance to do better than others, to be left alone, cooperation and many outcomes too numerous to mention." Such strategies take place in the context and in interaction with the politics of the deep structure of organizations and we turn now to a discussion of that topic.

Deep Structure Politics

Organizational politics in the deep structure of organizations is focused on the system of influence, the structure and meanings within which organizational life proceeds. It is thus primarily activity concerned with the politics of conception and as such the mechanism is the same as that noted in the Gurney vs. Dean contest. The difference is partly one of scope and duration. Creation of the power embedded in the system of influences is initiated by actors representing an interest group to influence whole patterns of thinking, feeling, and behaving of other interest groups without the latter recognizing the political nature of the system. The time needed to develop this facet of power and the time span of its impact are lengthy, extending far beyond that associated with surface political activity.

The difference between surface and deep structure politics in organizations is partly a qualitative one, however. In the latter case we are not dealing with a simple extrapolation of surface level power dynamics. Deep structure power is embedded in a complex terrain. It is coded in cultural values, beliefs, and practices in and around organizations and in the collective unconscious of organizational actors (Mitroff, 1983; Smith & Simmons, 1983). Thus management of cultural and unconscious aspects of organization so as to manipulate deep structure power can sometimes be imprecise and its outcomes difficult to predict and control. Furthermore, some aspects of this kind of power are likely to be so deeply buried that they cannot be understood, tapped, and manipulated from the surface of organizations. We may be able to explicate deep structure power, but there may be some residual that is so much a part of us that we cannot gain enough "distance" to discover and understand it all.

There is, nevertheless, a connection between the two levels of power and the two kinds of politics. In a sense, Gurney's political attempts to create a framework for action taps the organizational politics in the deep structure of organizations. Politics is sometimes deep structure power in action. This is most clearly so when political activity at the surface level of organization includes attempts to harness the power embedded in the system of influence. This is clearly illustrated in Rosen's (1985) ethnographic study of an advertising agency, which shows how the dominant coalition (that is, the senior management) manipulated language, gestures, and the context of a breakfast ritual to ensure employer acceptance of the structure, goals, and practices of the company, thereby reinforcing and reaffirming the bureaucratic scheme of organization and, indeed, the entire array of capitalistic values.

We argue in this chapter that communication and power are interrelated, that meaning, which is at the heart of communication, is often politically shaped, and that power is itself influenced and given form through communication frameworks and content. We argue for the inclusion in any discussion of power and communication of attention to actors with self-interests, intentions, and strategic actions. One useful metaphor for coming to grips with these various complex concepts and their relationships is the political organization game. Interrelationships between power and communication are reflected in the structuring and enactment of such games. Communication is the medium that ensures the playing of the game since it provides ground rules and channels for action. As a medium it is an important currency in such games. Power itself is embedded in the medium and the meanings of games. Power relations and the exercise of power can influence the development and use of the game's communication rules and structures (Brown, 1978). They also impact on the meanings actors give to the game while it is in play (Pfeffer, 1981). Given the duality of power and the structuring processes that take place in organizations (Giddens, 1979; Riley, 1983), we should expect to find both surface and deep structure games that link the two levels of organization. We turn now to a fuller discussion of the notion of organization games.

ORGANIZATION GAMES

Formal structure has no rationality of its own. The operational significance of the formal structure derives from its relation to the power structure and the rules of the organizational game . . . which prevail in the system of action underlying the organization. (Crozier & Friedberg, 1980, p. 54)

The association between organizational power and game playing is noted in a variety of writings on organization. Language games are used by organizational actors to disguise their political intentions, to mobilize support and quiet opposition (Pfeffer, 1981). The images of sports and war games are prevalent in the political cultures of some organizations (Riley, 1983) and in the processes of merger and acquisition between and among organizations (Hirsch & Andrews, 1983). Political games of insurgency and counterinsurgency, of budgeting, empire building, and sponsorship are among many played out in organizational settings (Mintzberg, 1983). Workers in some organizations play "making out" games to compensate for loss of control over the labor process (Burawoy, 1979). Managers in most organizations play "making it" games involving tactics and strategies and rule following to facilitate their upward mobility in organizations (Harragan, 1977; Korda, 1975; Schrank, 1978).

Political games in organizations are "intricate and subtle, simultaneous and overlapping" (Allison, 1971, p. 216). They are a kind of "multiple ring circus" (Mintzberg, 1983, p. 187). They reveal much about the interplay of power and communication in organizations. The interdependence of such games enables us to examine the surface and deep structure manifestations of power and communication. We will illustrate this point later in the chapter.

Organizational games are concrete mechanisms that actors use to structure and regulate their power relations while preserving some freedom to act in their own best interests (Crozier & Friedberg, 1980, p. 56). Players in these games must exercise their discretion to act, to accomplish their objectives through adopting rational strategies that conform to the nature of the game. People wield power in the context of the structures and rules of the games in which they are involved. However, their strategic actions also have an impact on the structures and rules of these games. The structure and rules in political games are thus flexible rather than rigid and deterministic (Crozier & Friedberg, 1980). There need be no consensus about the rules for organizational games to proceed. Nor is it necessary or even likely that all the rules will be clear or always known to all the players (Allison, 1971; Lukes, 1974; Ranson et al., 1980).

An organizational game thus involves social actors, payoffs, and a set of interpretive strategies that specify the rules, data, and successful outcomes in the game. Given the social construction around power that is involved in such games, there is a degree of elasticity in the way the game is constructed and played. Invention and adaptation enter into the development and enactment of game rules and meanings because they come alive in the service of actors' strategic actions in the game.

An actor's strategy in an organization game is one of bounded intentionality. (That is, while constrained, it is never directly determined. Even passivity can represent choice.) Actors' objectives are

> diverse, more or less ambiguous, more or less explicit, and more or less contradictory. Some will be changed in the course of action, some rejected, others discovered during the process or even after the fact, if only because the unforeseen and unforeseeable consequences of [their] actions require them to reconsider their positions and adjust their aims. (Crozier & Friedberg, 1980, pp. 24-25)

While such behavior cannot be linked to clear, predetermined, fixed objectives, it is rational with respect to "opportunities and through them to their defining context" and with respect to the "behavior of other actors—to the decisions they make and to the game which is thus established among them" (Crozier & Friedberg, 1980, p. 25).

Strategic action in organizational games can be understood in relation to power structures in the game that provide opportunities in and constraints on the game. Furthermore, given that actors take part in simultaneous, overlapping games and the possibility exists for them to develop and encounter other games over time, strategic action must be understood in relation to power structures between and among organizational games.

For example, individuals may join organizations with the intention of being highly productive, thus playing in one (managerial) game and finding themselves pressured by other workers to engage in featherbedding and banking work so as to meet lower performance levels—desired actions in another (worker) game. They then have to choose their strategy: to stay in the former game (sometimes earning a "ratebuster" label from workers; Dalton, 1974), join the latter game (Schrank, 1978), or try to develop or join other games. Possible other games include those in which actors in effect straddle the other two, trying to "play it both ways" (Culbert & McDonough, 1980), or to span boundaries so that they might ultimately resolve the tension between the two games. Actors may also leave the arena in an attempt to avoid engaging in organizational games.

Locating Organizational Games

Organizational games involve individuals and groups. They are played out on the surface and through the deep structure of organization. It is possible to separate analytically several kinds of games played out among different organizational actors engaged in surface activities as well as to identify deep-level games. Table 15.1, while by no means exhaustive, shows something of the rich possibilities in the games arena.

Given the interrelationships among and interpenetration of games, the nature of the exercise of power and the characteristics of communication involved in some games will recur in many other games. Nevertheless, there appear to be some political processes and communication structures and meanings that are particularly associated with specific kinds of games. We shall identify these briefly and then focus in some detail on the games that link surface and deep structure levels of organization so as to more clearly reveal the nature of the relationship between power and communication.

Surface Games

Individual games. Political games played between individual actors and other actors (individuals and groups) appear to be largely focused on gaining and maintaining *context* in organizations (Culbert & McDonough, 1985). Context is the frame of reference that accurately reflects what an individual has in mind when taking an action in an organization. "Few behaviors [in organizations] stand on their own . . . most require an interpretation . . . and context is . . . the frame of reference that underlies any particular interpretation [of behavior]" (Culbert & McDonough, 1985, p. 23). Being able to have one's actions viewed in an appropriate context, enables actors to

TABLE 15.1

Political Organization Games

Focus	Political and Communicative Strategies and Tactics	Primary Emphasis
	SURFACE GAMES*	
Individual Games		
Sponsorship Mentoring Making it Empire building Lording Upward influence	Ingratiation Impression management Networking Gatekeeping Reasoning Rule citing Labeling Managing sanctions Higher authority appeals Covering up Persuading (manipulative persuasion) Assertiveness	Gaining/maintaining/ withholding context
Intraorganizational Games		
(a) Competitive games Budgetting Expertise Line versus staff Rival camps Making out Whistle blowing Young Turks Insurgency- counterinsurgency	Cooptation Coalition building Agenda controlling Using outside experts Managing committees Selective use of objective criteria Bargaining Leaking information Withholding support Scapegoating/defaming Isolating/terminating	Controlling resources; Managing territory; Managing/resisting change
(b) Collaborative games Strategic candidates	Developing champions Building consensus/ support Framing perspectives	
Interorganizational Games		
Mergers-acquisitions Union-management Industry control	Striking/locking out Bargaining/negotiation Interlocking directorates Contracting Bidding, challenging	Controlling resources; Managing territory

(continued)

TABLE 15.1 Continued

DEEP STRUCTURE GAME

Interest Groups Game		
Reality distortion	Naturalization	Gaining/preserving privilege
	Neutralization	for sectional interests
	Legitimation	
	Socialization	

NOTE: This table provides a sample of games and political and communicative activities at different levels of organization. It is intended to stimulate further thinking on the issue of identifying and studying games and their associated political and communicative underpinnings. Mintzberg (1983, 1985) provides a discussion and tabulation of games which provided an important stimulus for the development of the surface games in this table.

merge self-interests with their organizational work. Absence of such a context reduces their power in the organization. The game is played around the meaning of an actor's actions, and an actor wins when that meaning is established in a way that meets his or her self-interests. To illustrate:

> Context is the difference between being viewed as an overly gregarious engineer who is no longer a technically creative performer and the engineer who has the technical know-how to head "Customer Relations" and just the right personality to go along with it. (Culbert & McDonough, 1985, p. 23)

The contest in such games is over competing interpretations of the meaning of a player's actions. Every action is open to critique by another player, every intended meaning can be contested and even destroyed. Strategic action, the exercise of power in the game, involves "self-interested structuring of reality to get context" (Culbert & McDonough, 1985, p. 33). While the game is frequently one of competition and conflict it is not inevitably so. The intent of actors, of players in the game to gain context, is so that they can pursue interdependent work in organizations in a way that meets their needs. This is not necessarily *at the expense* of other players. Collaborative outcomes are possible depending on how the game is defined and played. We will deal with this issue further when we discuss empowerment later in the chapter.

Specific individual games include "making it" (moving up the ladder of success, mentoring, sponsorship, and empire building and upward influence). This appears to be a game in which players seek context that will allow them to increase their power in organizations so as to participate in other organizational games. Some games, such as "lording" (Kanter, 1977; Mintzberg, 1983), are played by actors with little power in the game and who see little opportunity to expand their level of power. They "lord it over" those subject to their influence. Such players hold onto existing power by establishing a context in which it is their role to give literal meaning to the rules and routines of organizations to see that they are enforced rigidly. They attempt to get their way, to resist change by invoking the rule book and the bureaucracy, and by threatening to go to their boss for a ruling.

Activities in individual games include managing impressions (Goffman, 1959, 1974; Zerbe & Paulhus, 1985), staying within boundaries (Biggart & Hamilton, 1984), building and joining networks between and among organizational actors (Kanter, 1983), managing information (Porter et al., 1981), and managing rewards and punishments (French & Raven, 1959). The work of Kipnis (1976), Kipnis et al. (1980), Schmidt and Kipnis (1984), and of Culbert & McDonough (1980, 1985), among others, are particularly relevant to the analysis of individual games.

Intraorganizational games. These games typically involve individuals and groups in collaboration (win-win) or in competition (win-lose) with other groups or with the dominant coalition and the prevailing systems of influence of an organization. Emphasis in these games is on issues such as maintaining the status quo versus introducing change, on rate and kind of innovation, on control over the direction and nature of organizational outcomes.

Several competitive games take place between groups of organizational actors, and many of these are quite readily recognized. Emphasis in these games is on controlling resources and occupying and protecting territory while trying to keep others in the game at a disadvantage. Political activities relevant to such games are likely to include negotiation, bargaining, coalition building, controlling decision premises and agendas, and the selective use of objective criteria to support arguments. The nature and development of such activities is revealed in considerable detail in the work of scholars such as Bacharach and Lawler (1980), Kanter (1983), Mintzberg (1983, 1985), Pfeffer (1981), Stevenson, Pearce, and Porter (1985), and Tompkins and Cheney (1985).

Collaborative games are perhaps best exemplified by the strategic candidate game identified and described by Mintzberg (1983, pp. 205-209). This game involves players in promoting, supporting, and opposing proposals or projects for change in the way things are done in the organization. Such proposals or projects will ultimately be decided by actors in the dominant coalition (comprising actors such as the chief executive, executive board members, appointed review committees, and so on). This game draws on other organizational games and incorporates their rules, meanings, and player's strategies. Mintzberg (1983) provides some of the flavor of this interpenetration of games:

> Strategic candidates are often promoted in order to build empires, and they often require alliances; rivalries frequently erupt between line and staff or between rival camps during the game; expertise is exploited in this game and authority lorded over those without it; insurgencies sometimes occur as byproducts and are countered; capital budgets often become the vehicles by which strategic candidates are promoted; and sponsorship is often a key to success in this game. (p. 206)

Detailed analyses of the strategic contingencies game are provided in the work of Pettigrew (1973, 1985), and Zald and Berger (1978). The intrapreneurial game is closely allied to the strategic candidate game (Kanter, 1983; Pinchot, 1985).

Interorganizational games. Organizations, or the actors representing such organizations, typically engage in political games for the same reasons as do groups inside organizational settings: to control resources and to gain and protect territory. Political processes, in addition to those mentioned for intraorganizational games, are focused on defining, establishing, and challenging the rules of the game as well as competition over meaning that involves actors with interpretive frames more different from one another than is likely to be the case for intraorganizational games. Likely political action in these games includes creation of interlocking boards of directorates (Ornstein, 1984; Pennings, 1980) and the maneuvering that goes on between and among actors in establishing legal contracts and developing legislative policies and procedures.

Deep Structure Games

There is little in the literature that explores deep structure in terms of the games construct. However, the writings of organizational scholars in the critical theory tradition (Astley & Rosen, 1985; Benson, 1977; Braverman, 1974; Conrad & Ryan, 1986; Deetz, 1985; Edwards, 1970; Habermas, 1970a, 1970b; Mumby, 1984; Rosen, 1985; Stablein & Nord, 1985) and those focused on the structuring of organizations (Clegg, 1975; Giddens, 1976, 1979; Ranson et al., 1980; Riley, 1983) provide a basis for developing a sense of what these organizational games might look like. The treatment of games here is, nevertheless, more speculative than is the case for surface games. The primary deep structure game currently recognizable appears to be a systematic distortion of communication so as to maintain and enhance power relations that favor one social reality over other possible alternatives, that favor some interest groups at the expense of others (Deetz, 1985; Habermas, 1974, 1975; Stablein & Nord, 1985). Such distortions of communication occur "when certain groups' expression, certain types of information, or certain forms of expression become arbitrarily privileged" (Deetz, 1985, p. 126). While communication is distorted—almost by definition—in any political game, it is the central focus of political action in the deep structure game. The most encompassing deep structure game—the *mega game,* if you will—involves the establishment of rules and meanings for a whole social system. Power is injected into and becomes embedded in the rules and meanings of government and law (Lindblom, 1977).

The political processes involved in the playing of this game by actors who are primarily representatives of major interest groups in a society are the following:

Naturalization, through which "historically" chosen forms and privileges become defined as the way things are. Their "chosen" quality is no longer open to inspection and discussion, and change is not considered" (Deetz, 1985, p. 126). Taken as a rule in the communication distortion game, this process serves to depict existing relations as the natural outgrowth of events, as part of natural law, and prevents discussion of them. The rule fuctions primarily to preserve prevailing power relationships.

Neutralization, through which "value positions become hidden and value laden activities are treated as if they were value free. A singular position is universalized as a position shared by everyone, thus becoming one of fact rather than choice" (Deetz, 1985, p. 126). One particular way to do this is to embed value positions inherent in assessing work activities and outcomes in abstract, quantitative formulations defined as rational and thus value free. Examination of the criteria underlying the development of the "objective" assessment formulations are removed by defining the formulations as neutral (Conrad & Ryan, 1985).

Legitimation, through which decisions and actions that distort communication are rationalized by invoking "higher-order explanatory devices" (Deetz, 1985, p. 127). Invoking such devices serves to maintain the activities and actions of lower power players at levels and in directions that are not necessarily in their own best interests but serve the interests of those with high power. The real explanation for the direction and level of activities of players with less power is not apparent and cannot be examined even if questioned, since the reason advanced by power holders is in terms of some device such as the Protestant work ethic, loyalty, sacrifice, and so forth.

Socialization, particularly through the mechanisms of learning and orientation that direct and shape desired attitudes, behaviors, and interpretive schemes of some players to the benefit of others.

The historical analysis of the political forces underlying the development of industrial automation by Noble (1984) provides detailed evidence of this game and these processes. Studies also appear in the work of other scholars (Edwards, 1970; Habermas, 1975). In the specific example noted earlier of the respective fates of the numerical control and record playback technologies, the processes of naturalization (the "scientific inevitability" of the survival of numerical control technology) and neutralization (disguising the value positions of managers, engineers, and the military for control of human action in the abstract, quantitative models that supported numerical control technology) were particularly evident.

Penetrating the Deep Structure Game

Almost by definition the precise nature of the deep structure game, whenever it is found in any society, is hard to pin down. The exercise of power, the origins of meaning, the nature and impact of the rules of the game are extensively disguised. It is likely that there are aspects of the game that can never be identified, at least not by anyone who is involved in any other game within the framework of a particular version of the deep structure game.

Nevertheless, if we accept the concept of political games in, among, and around organizations, then it is important to try to understand the nature of the mega game and its relationship to surface games.

Examining Outcroppings of the Deep Structure Game

Looking at the historical antecedents and evolution of the deep structure game is an important path toward discussing the nature of the mega game. In this context, examination of systems of government (Lindblom, 1977; Murdock, 1982) and religion (Nord, Brief, Atich, & Doherty, 1985) and a search for organizational archetypes (Krefting & Frost, 1985, Mitroff, 1983) ought to provide useful insights to the nature of deep-level power.

Other avenues exist that lead to the symbolic processes constituting the surface manifestations of the meaning and the power operating in the deep structure game. Analysis of rituals (Conrad, 1983; Meyer & Rowan, 1977), metaphors (Krefting & Frost, 1985; Pondy, 1983), humor (Boland & Hoffman, 1983; Burawoy, 1979; Coleman, 1974; Frost, Mitchell & Nord, 1986; Roy, 1960), dreams (Smith & Simmons, 1983), stories (Ebers, 1985; Jermier, 1985; Mumby, 1984), and mass media news (Tuchman, 1978; Turow, 1985) are potentially rich sources of information about the nature of the game.

The attachment of meaning to organizational events so that they become part of the currency of the deep-level game is facilitated by the narrative structure of such stories. Organizational stories, told in the context of their cultural settings, are intended to present in the telling a view of what life is really like in organizations. Furthermore, they are often easier to recall and more persuasive than is a set of statistics presenting the same information (Martin & Powers, 1983). By being told and retold, events in a story become taken for granted, become part of the members' interpretive frame, and are accepted uncritically. "Even in the case of apocryphal tales, the division between fiction and reality is blurred to the point where an event becomes a fact if it is retold enough times" (Mumby, 1984, p. 120).

Stories carry potent meaning. They are a potential resource in the development of the rules and as currency in playing out organizational games. Stories are developed and distributed as part of an actor's strategy during a specific phase of a game. When the game involves attacks on the dominant coalition in an organization (e.g., Young Turks, Whistle-Blowing, Insurgency/Counterinsurgency games), stories that are part of the process, such as those featuring defamation, discounting, aggrandizement, and heroism, may well reveal in code the rules and currency of the game.

Interlinking Games

Stories that emerge in the playing of one game can tell us something about that game and about other games with which it is linked. As a general approach to understanding the nature of power and communication in organizations, studying the rules, processes, and contents of one game in the context of other games, and investigating the nature of the relationships between the games should prove instructive. In a search for greater precision about the nature of the deep structural game, surface-level games that contradict and challenge the prevailing system of influence are relevant. Such games include those noted earlier, such as the Whistle-Blowing, Young Turks, Insurgency/Counter-Insurgency, and Union-Management games.

In addition, surface games in which actors through their strategic action demonstrate their understanding of the system of influence and their ability to manipulate it to their advantage (Porter, 1985) will likely provide a valuable source of information on the mega game. Games, such as the strategic candidates game, that focus on innovation and on the "orderly" management of change fall into this category. In a study of the successful introduction of microcomputers into a school system in Chicago, Pondy and Huff (1985) attribute the success of the move to the way in which administrators, key players in the game, consciously constructed a repertory of routines and a language that deemphasized the novelty of what was being proposed, thereby minimizing opposition and securing support from other players in the game. Careful analysis of the way such routines were constructed and the mechanism by which other actors were influenced to accept the reality presented to them should add to our understanding of both this surface game and the deep structure game in which it is embedded.

Similarly, it should be useful to look for games between interest groups where the balance in power relations shifts without any overt signs of struggle and resistance from those "losing" power as a result of the game. Such "small wins" (Weick, 1984) are a possible source of the information we seek about the nature of the deep structure game. An illustration of such a game is provided by Weick (1984, p. 42):

> The feminist campaign against sexism has been more successful with the smaller win of desexing English than with the larger win of desexing legislation (ERA). The success of attempts to make people more self-conscious about words implying sex bias is somewhat surprising, because it represents an imposition of taboos at a time when taboos in general are being removed. "For even as books, periodicals and dictionaries (not all, to be sure) are liberally opening their pages to obscenities and vulgarisms, they are unliberally leaning over backward to ostracize all usage deemed offensive to the sexes" (Steinmetz, 1982, p. 8). This hypocrisy notwithstanding, the reforms have been adopted with little objection, due in part to their size, specificity, visibility, and completeness. As one commentator on Steinmetz's essay put it, "winning equality in the language was necessary; and while the winning shouldn't be overestimated, it will work—the drops of water on the rock—to change consciousness, and in time, unconsciousness." (Williams, 1982, p. 46)

Much of what we have discussed so far in this chapter about organizational politics has focused on power in action and power in conception. An interesting aspect of the small wins concept is that it demonstrates one way in which power develops from "successful" action. When people judge as successful the small win of another, they label the latter actor a winner. Simultaneously, that actor gains power for use in subsequent interactions that would not have been available had the actor not engaged in a win, or had failed in an attempt to register a win. Small wins thus create meanings that carry with them a degree of power that in turn influences subsequent actions and outcomes.

A third source of information about surface organizational games and their links with each other and with the deep structure game resides in the reflexive statements and analyses of key players in a set of related games. Systematic examples of such opportunities present themselves infrequently, but they do occur and provide a basis for analysis of games. Recent examples from within the organizational sciences themselves include reflexive analysis on the publishing process (Cummings & Frost, 1985) and descriptions of the practice of research (Lawler, Mohrman, Mohrman, Ledford, & Cummings, 1985).

Finally, major changes in organizational games can provide a basis for players in those games to begin to understand the deep structure game and the sectional interests they hide. For example, in the current era of technological change, engineers, executives, managers and other major players may have thought they were in a game in which job security and upward mobility were essential meanings within one game; those who now find themselves unemployed, obsolete, and largely powerless may recognize, on reflection and on reframing of their past experience, the political nature of both their current and former statuses in the deep-level game.

Organization Games: A Reprise

The political game construct provides a means of looking at communication as medium and as message (or content) and at its interrelationship with power and political action. It is a way to examine organizational power and communication in a systematic framework. It is a construct that ensures that we attend to both agency and constraint, to the intentions and strategies of organizational actors and to the way actors deal with contingencies in and around the organizational games they are in. It alerts us to the pluralistic nature of organizational life at all levels and to the inequality of that pluralism in many organizational activities. We are encouraged by this perspective to look for victories and losses, to explore the nature of both the victories and the losses, and to try to understand the alternative outcomes that might have emerged had the players been different in terms of the amount or use of their resources or had other players joined the game. Some games have a finite ending, many others do not. Paying attention to historical evolution of organization games ought to produce for us a better understanding of how power and communication function over time.

Given that much political activity is disguised, we ought to investigate the nature of the disguises and to probe for underlying meanings in the communication content of players in the organizational games. Penetrating politically motivated disguises will entail searching for answers to questions such as who the key players and stakeholders are in a given game, what their values and self-interests are, what costs they might incur in revealing those self-interests to other players, what language and symbols are associated with success in the game (e.g., couching self-interests in terms of rationality of ideology because one or the other is the powerful currency in the game), and what hidden agendas are contained within rationally presented arguments. It will require us to examine, where possible, the transcripts and texts of communications between actors, looking for discrepancies between what actors say and what they do and conducting detailed and probing interviews with key players during and after the activities we identify as political. None of these approaches to penetrating political disguises is easy, but they may provide paths to this important knowledge about organizational communication.

There are aspects of the game construct that must be recognized and examined as it is developed and studied further. One aspect is that of the unintended consequences of intentionality. The game notion makes explicit the possible equifinality of the political process in organizations, of actors adjusting intentions, and of the importance of power relations and the exercise of power in the unfolding of the play. So we would expect to observe unintentional outcomes of players' strategies, given that the players are in a dynamic and contingent process. An understanding of these outcomes ought to help us clarify the way the game works.

A second aspect to be acknowledged and clarified is the limits of the game construct itself for helping us to understand organizational life. We have argued that political games are most likely where contests for control, struggles for collaboration, and uncertainty about organizational means and ends are in existence. Other organizational conditions are likely to be more usefully analyzed using other constructs, other metaphors (Bolman & Deal, 1984; Morgan, 1985).

A final note on the utility of political games for studying organizations is to recognize the cost of asserting them as inevitable and pervasive in organizational life. To do so is to risk having them seen as part of the natural order—as the way things are—and as a neutral fact—something we have to accept, and thus cannot do anything about (Deetz, 1985). To make, in this way, the concept of political organizational games part of the very systems of influence we wish to understand, perhaps, is to rob it of its usefulness. It is important, therefore, to leave open the possibility, however remote it may seem at present, that political activity and political games could be eliminated in organizational life. It is conceivable that accomplishing the ideal of undistorted communication, of communicative competence as envisioned by Habermas (1970b), would require a strategic action to eliminate all strategic action. While it is our position in this essay that power, politics, and game playing are the way things are and the way they are likely to continue to be, we recognize the importance of acknowledging the possibility of an alternative condition.

A note on communicating about organizational power. Much of the discussion in this chapter has focussed on research—on the study of organization power and communication. Many of us also teach these topics to others. As communicators about organizations we educators wield power. We conceive and play political games. This is neither good nor bad, it is simply so. We teach topics about leadership, about conflict and conflict management, about persuasive communication and organizational design. All involve political activity. Our actual topics are often about political activity, skills, and games, whether we recognize this or not. Most of us teach these things to future managers rather than to all players in the game. We tend to reinforce the play of many games that disproportionately empower some players over other players. The point is not that we should necessarily teach all players but that should we recognize the political act we perform whenever we communicate knowledge to one interest group rather than another. The pervasiveness of political activity in organizations makes the search for a condition of undistorted communication an ideal rather than an attainable reality (Stablein & Nord, 1985). However, the recognition that we are political agents contributing in a particular way to the formulation of systems of influence ought to free our minds to do so with a greater attention to critical reflection, over time, of what games we are in and how we play them (Gouldner, 1970).

COMMUNICATION AND POWER:
LOOKING TO THE FUTURE

The only way to bring about lasting change and to foster an ability to deal with new situations is by influencing the conditions that determine the interpretation of situations and the regulation of ideas. (Normann, 1977, p. 161)

Scholars in the fields of organizational behavior and communication are becoming more interested in the nature of power and of communication and of their interrelationships in organizations. Realization of the pervasiveness of power, politics, and communication in, among, and around organizations is likely to direct our attention to macro issues in organizations and between organizations. Our research efforts will be increasingly directed toward understanding the origins, nature, and impact of power and communication involved in developing, challenging, and protecting policies that affect large groups of people in an organization and in society. Such studies will focus on—among other phenomena—the dominant coalitions of organization, government, business, and civic groups that are responsible for policymaking in a society. Studies such as those of Noble (1984) on technological change and of Pettigrew (1985) on continuity and change through two decades in a major corporation, and of natural accidents in the nuclear industry (Perrow, 1984) are exemplars of studies that include, as important research questions, the role of power and meaning in the unfolding of the organizational event being investigated and in definitions of organizational effectiveness (Nord, 1983).

Focus on strategic actors in the policymaking realm is also likely to direct our attention, if not our investigative skills, to the large political issues of the era, such as toxic wastes, nuclear arms buildup, the human costs arising from the major changes in the nature of work that are being linked to the introduction of computer technology, energy and environmental conservation debates, and so on (Morgan & Ramierez, 1984). One concern here is whether we possess, in playing our game as researchers, the skills, the motivation, and the legitimating reward structures to permit us to direct our energies in the direction of studying controversial issues and organizations so that we may provide for ourselves, and for others who would learn from us, an understanding of what goes on in those typically interorganizational games.

At the other end of the scale, it will become increasingly important to study the linkages between power, communication, and organization in everyday organizational life. People in organizations and people studying organizations frequently fail to see the magnitude of politics in ongoing organizational transactions (Frost, Mitchell, & Nord, 1986). Most individuals in organizations underestimate "how many [of their] actions will meet with opposition from someone else . . . how political their actions and justifications appear to others with different motives" (Culbert & McDonough, 1985, p. 18).

Looking again to the future, there is a need to examine and understand more clearly than we do at present the nature of organizational politics. We know little about the way in which potential power is transformed into power in action. Nor do we yet know a great deal about the characteristics of the players who are involved in the transformation. The work of House (1984) and Kipnis (1976) among others provides a beginning to this endeavor. We know little about the way in which communication as a medium and as meaning enters into the transformation of power into action. Given a concern about how power is implemented in organizations, these would seem to be important research questions to be answered in the future.

Current writings and research on empowerment (treating empowerment as the use of power to create opportunities and conditions through which other actors can gain power, can make decisions, can use and expand their abilities and skills, can create and accomplish organizational work in ways that are meaningful to them; e.g., Louis, 1985; Roberts, 1985; Thomas & Velthouse, 1985) ought to shed light on the role of the constructive use of power and politics in organizations. Given the pervasiveness of power and politics, such writings will also be meaningful when one examines and deals with the development of trust in organizations (Culbert & McDonough, 1985; Kanter, 1983; Torbert, 1985). Torbert (1985) introduces the concept of action inquiry—the conscious choice by an actor of a particular kind of power from a variety of power types that she or he believes will produce a common political language and understanding among the organizational actors involved in a relationship—to convey this constructive sense of political action. Culbert and McDonough (1985) operationalize the notion of a strategic orientation to action in a similar way, as acting to gain context for one's own organizational concerns. Such efforts to deal with the constructive aspects of power and politics convey the subtlety of the process and the importance of communication in that process.

It is important to recognize that introducing new formulations of power, such as empowerment, signals an awareness of an organizational game that has rules and intentions (of empowering) different from those envisaged in many games where power is exercised in a more competitive, controlling manner. Given the prevailing competitive nature of most games, the empowerment game and its players are vulnerable and can be undermined. Furthermore, players from competitive games may adopt and distort the empowerment concept and see it as another tool to get less powerful players to play the game the way the "empowerer" wants it played. Empowerment may develop meaning not intended by those who "invented" it. These matters need to be kept in mind when we study the way it is applied in real organizational games, assuming its robustness as a theoretical construct.

A broad perspective from which to view the transformation of power into action, and its relationship to meaning in organizations, is likely provided through the concept of organizational culture. Within this framework, studies of ideology (Astley & Rosen, 1985; Mumby, 1984), of charisma (Beyer & Trice, 1985; House, 1977; Howell, 1986), of leadership and followership (Martin, Sitkin, & Boehm, 1985; Siehl, 1985; Smircich, 1983), of political cultures (Riley, 1983), and strategic management (Pettigrew, 1985; Smircich & Stubbart, 1985) are relevant to developing an understanding of this process.

A power struggle of importance to future researchers has developed around the escalating introduction and use of computer technology in organizations. Dismissed from the work scene and propelled into different games (played out around unemployment, welfare, and obsolescence) are workers from many different professions. Elevated to work games are representatives of many specialties associated with computing who will or have doubtless already created new games with their attendant communication rules and languages.

As current power struggles are being played out in, among, and around organizations, it seems likely that the complexity of the process creates conditions in which the outcomes of some games swamp their players and/or those in other games. Organizational games can go out of control. Understanding how these conditions arise and what might be done about them will be an intriguing area of research in the future. What we may predict is that the fallout of such chaos will produce opportunities for new games and new players not yet identified by current writings and research. The current attention given to entrepreneurial and intrapreneurial managers and their behavior indicates that new games are developing in which they will be important players. Studying which new games are legitimated by the deep structure game, which challenge it and are undermined, and which games produce changes in the deep structure game ought to prove a fruitful area of research.

Finally, a realization of the political nature of organizations and the games played in them ought to alert us to the inevitable ongoing roles of communication and power in those organizations. There are few simple, nonpolitical, static outcomes in organizations. Unlike the game of baseball, where Yogi Berra observed, "the game is never over till it's over," in organizational life "the game is never over!"

NOTES

1. At the point of such struggles lie shifts, attempted or accomplished, in definitions of critical resources and dependencies.

2. Before moving on to this discussion, we should note that we believe it is misleading to regard potential power, sometimes referred to as power at rest, as a static, natural phenomenon. There is a dynamic to potential power, given its social origins. It must be enacted by actors from time to time or it will erode and eventually cease to exist for them (Crozier & Friedberg, 1980).

3. House (1984) provides a comprehensive and insightful review and presents a series of testable propositions relevant to the social psychology of power.

4. I am grateful to Phil Mirvis for his insights. They helped me clarify this notion of power.

REFERENCES

Alinsky, S. (1971). *Rules for radicals.* New York: Vintage.

Allen, R. W., & Porter, L. W. (Eds.). (1983). *Organizational influence processes.* Glenview, IL: Scott, Foresman.

Allen, R. W., Madison, D. L., Renwick, P. A., & Mayes, B. T. (1979). Organizational politics: Tactics and characteristics of its actors. *California Management Review, 22*(1), 77-83.

Allison, G. T. (1971). Essence of decision: Explaining the Cuban missile crisis. Boston: Little, Brown.

Astley, W. G., & Rosen, M. (1985). *Power and culture in organizations: A politoco-symbolic dialectic.* Unpublished manuscript, Wharton School, University of Pennsylvania.

Astley, W. G., & Sachdeva, P. S. (1984). Structural sources of intraorganizational power: A theoretical synthesis. *Academy of Management Review, 9,* 104-113.

Bachrach, P., & Baratz, M. (1962). Two faces of power. *American Political Science Review, 56,* 947-952.

Bacharach, S., & Lawler, E. (1980). *Power and politics in organizations.* San Francisco: Jossey-Bass.

Bagozzi, R. P., & Phillips, L. W. (1982). Representing and testing organizational theories: A holistic construal. *Administrative Science Quarterly, 27,* 459-489.

Baldridge, J. V. (1971). *Power and conflict in the university.* New York: John Wiley.

Barnard, C. (1938). *The functions of the executive.* Cambridge, MA: President and Fellows of Harvard University.

Bass, B. M. (1985). *Leadership and performance beyond expectations.* New York: Free Press.

Benson, J. K. (1977). Organizations: A dialectical view. *Administrative Science Quarterly, 22,* 1-21.

Beyer, J. M., & Trice, H. M. (1985). *The communication of power relations in organizations through cultural rates.* Paper presented at the annual meeting of the International Communication Association, Honolulu.

Biggart, N. W., & Hamilton, G. G. (1984). The power of obedience. *Administrative Science Quarterly, 29,* 540-549.

Blau, P. M. (1964). *Exchange and power in social life.* New York: John Wiley.

Boland, R. J., Jr., & Hoffman, R. (1983). Humor in a machine shop: An interpretation of symbolic action. In L. R. Pondy, P. J. Frist, G. Morgan, & T. C. Dandridge (Eds.), *Organizational symbolism* (pp. 187-198). Greenwich, CT: JAI Press.

Bolman, L. G., Deal, T. E. (1984). *Modern approaches to understanding and managing organizations.* San Francisco: Jossey-Bass.

Borgatta, E. F. (1961). Role-playing specifications, personality and performance. *Sociometry, 24,* 218-233.

Bower, J. L. (1970). Planning within the firm. *The American Economic Review: Paper and Proceedings of the 82nd Annual Meeting* (pp. 186-194).

Brass, D. J. (1984). Being in the right place: A structural analysis of individual influence in an organization. *Administrative Science Quarterly, 29,* 518-539.

Braverman, H. (1974). *Labor and monopoly capital: The degradation of work in the twentieth century.* New York: Monthly Review Press.

Brown, L. D. (1984). *Power outside organizational paradigms: Lessons from community partnerships.* Paper presented at the conference on the Functioning of Executive Power, Case Western Reserve University, Cleveland.

Brown, R. H. (1978). Bureaucracy as praxis: Toward a political phenomenology of formal organizations. *Administrative Science Quarterly, 23,* 365-382.

Bucher, R. (1970). Social process and power in a medical school. In M. N. Zald (Ed.), *Power in organizations* (pp. 35-89). New York: Academic Press.

Burawoy, M. (1979). *Manufacturing consent: Changes in the labor processes under monopoly capitalism.* Chicago: University of Chicago Press.

Caro, R. A. (1983). *The path to power.* New York: Random House.

Christie, R., & Geis, F. L. (1970). Studies in Machiavellianism. New York: Academic Press.

Clegg, S. (1975). *Power, rule and domination.* London: Routledge & Kegan Paul.

Clegg, S. (1981). Organization and control. *Administrative Science Quarterly, 26,* 545-562.

Coleman, J. R. (1974). *Blue collar journal: A college president's sabbatical.* New York: Harper & Row.

Comstock, D. E. (1982). Power in organization. *Pacific Sociological Review, 25*(2), 139-162.

Conrad, C. (1983). Organizational power: Faces and symbolic forms. In L. Putnam & M. Pacanowsky (Eds.), *Communication and organizations: An interpretive approach* (pp. 173-194). Newbury Park, CA: Sage.

Conrad, C., & Ryan, M. (1985). Power, praxis and self in organizational communication theory. In R. D. McPhee & P. K. Tompkins (Eds.), *Organizational commumnication: Traditional themes and new directions* (pp. 235-257). Newbury Park, CA: Sage.

Crozier, M. (1964). *The bureaucratic phenomenon.* Chicago: University of Chicago Press.

Crozier, M., & Friedberg, E. (1980). *Actors and systems.* Chicago: University of Chicago Press.

Culbert, S. A., & McDonough, J. J. (1980). *The invisible way: Pursuing self interest and work.* New York: John Wiley.

Culbert, S. A., & McDonough, J. J. (1985). *Radical management.* New York: Free Press.

Cummings, L. L., & Frost, P. J. (1985). *Publishing in the organizational sciences.* Homewood, IL: Richard D. Irwin.

Cyert, R. M., & March, J. G. (1963). *A behavioral theory of the firm.* Englewood Cliffs, NJ: Prentice-Hall.

Daft, R. L. (1983). *Organizational theory and design.* St. Paul, MN: West.

Dahl, R. (1957). The concept of power. *Behavioral Science, 2,* 201-215.

Dalton, M. (1974). The ratebusters: The case of the saleswoman. In P. L. Stewart & M. G. Cantor (Eds.), *The social control of occupational groups and roles R (pp. 206-214). Cambridge, MA: Schenkman.*

Dandridge, T. C., Mitroff, I., & Joyce, W. (1980). Organizational symbolism: A topic to expand organizational analysis. *Academy of Management Review, 5,* 77-82.

Deetz, S. (1985). Critical-cultural research: New sensibilities and old realities. *Journal of Management, 11*(2), 121-136.

Deetz, S., & Kersten, A. (1983). Critical models of interpretive research. In L. Putnam & M. Pacanowsky (Eds.), *Communication and organizations: An interpretive approach* (pp. 147-171). Newbury Park, CA: Sage.

Drake, B. H., & Moberg, D. J. (1986). Communicating influence attempts in dyads: Linguistic sedatives and palliatives. *Academy of Management Review, 11,* 567-584.

Drory, A., & Gluskinos, U. M. (1980). Machiavellianism and leadership. *Journal of Applied Psychology, 65,* 81-86.

Dyson, J. W., Fleitas, D. W., & Scioli, F. P. (1972). The interaction of leadership personality and decisional environments. *Journal of Social Psychology, 86,* 29-33.

Ebers, M. (1985). Understanding organizations: The poetic mode. *Journal of Management, 11*(2), 51-62.

Edelman, M. (1977). *Political language: Words that succeed and policies that fail.* New York: Academic Press.

Edwards, R. C. (1970). *Contested terrain: The transformation of the workplace in the twentieth century.* New York: Basic Books.

Emerson, R. M. (1962). Power-dependence relations. *American Sociological Review, 27,* 31-41.

Epstein, G. F. (1969). Machiavelli and the devil's advocate. *Journal of Personality and Social Psychology, 11,* 38-41.

French, J.R.P., Jr., & Raven, B. (1959). The bases of social power. In D. Cartwright (Ed.), *Studies in social power* (pp. 150-167). Ann Arbor: University of Michigan Press.

Frost, P. J., & Hayes, D. E. (1979). An exploration in two cultures of a new model of political behavior in organizations. In G. W. England, A. R. Negandhi, & B. Wilpert (Eds.), *Organizational functions in a cross-cultural perspective* (pp. 251-272). Kent, OH: Kent State University Press.

Frost, P. J., Mitchell, V. F., & Nord, W. R. (1986). *Organizational reality: Reports from the firing line* (3rd ed.). Glenview, IL: Scott, Foresman.

Gandz, J., & Murray, V. V. (1980). The experience of workplace politics. *Academy of Management Journal, 23,* 237-251.

Giddens, A. (1976). *New rules of sociological method.* New York: Basic Books.

Giddens, A. (1979). *Central problems in social theory.* Berkeley: University of California Press.

Goffman, E. (1959). *The presentation of self in everyday life.* Garden City, NY: Doubleday.

Goffman, E. (1974). *Frame analysis.* New York: Penguin.

Goodstadt, B. E., & Kipnis, D. (1970). Situational influences on the use of power. *Journal of Applied Psychology, 54,* 201-207.

Gough, H. G. (1968). *California Psychological Inventory: An interpreter's syllabus.* Palo Alto, CA: Consulting Psychologists Press.

Gouldner, A. (1970). *The coming crisis in western sociology.* New York: Basic Books.

Graham, J. W. (1983). *Principled organizational dissent.* Unpublished doctoral dissertation, Northwestern University.

Graham, J. W. (1985). *The profit of prophesy: Organizational response to principled organizational dissent.* Unpublished manuscript, Faculty of Commerce and Business Administration, University of British Columbia.

Gray, B., Bougon, M. G., & Donnellon, A. (1985). Organizations as constructions and destructions of meaning. *Journal of Management, 11*(2), 83-98.

Habermas, J. (1970a). On systematically distorted communication. *Inquiry, 13,* 205-218.

Habermas, J. (1970b). Toward a theory of communicative competence. *Inquiry, 13,* 360-375.

Habermas, J. (1974). *Theory and practice* (J. Viertel, Trans.). Boston: Beacon Press.

Habermas, J. (1975). *Legitimation crisis* (T. McCarthy, Trans.). Boston: Beacon Press.

Hambrick, D. C. (1981). Environment, strategy and power within top management teams. *Administrative Science Quarterly, 26,* 253-276.

Harragan, B. L. (1977). *Games mother never taught you.* New York: Warner.

Hickson, D. J., Hinings, C. R., Less, C. A., Schenck, R. J., & Pennings, J. M. (1971). A strategic contingencies theory of intraorganizational power. *Administrative Science Quarterly, 16,* 216-229.

Hinings, C. R., Hickson, D. J., Pennings, J. M., & Schneck, R. J. (1974). Structural conditions of intraorganizational power. *Administrative Science Quarterly, 19,* 22-44.

Hirsch, P. M., & Andrews, J.A.Y. (1983). Ambushes, shootouts and knights of the roundtable: The language of corporate takeovers. In L. R. Pondy, P. J. Frist, G. Morgan, & T. C. Dandridge (Eds.), *Organizational symbolism* (pp. 145-155). Greenwich, CT: JAI Press.

Hollander, E. P. (1960). Competence and conformity in the acceptance of influence. *Journal of Abnormal and Social Psychology, 61,* 365-369.

Homans, G. C. (1974). *Social behavior in its elementary forms* (2nd ed.). New York: Harcourt Brace Jovanovich.

House, R. J. (1977). A 1976 theory of charismatic leadership. In J. G. Hunt & L. L. Larson (Eds.), *Leadership: The cutting edge* (pp. 189-207). Carbondale: Southern Illinois University Press.

House, R. J. (1984). *Power in organizations: A social psychological perspective.* Unpublished manuscript, University of Toronto.

Howell, J. M. (1986). *Charismatic leadership: Effects of leader's style and charisma on individual adjustment and performance.* Unpublished doctoral dissertation, University of British Columbia.

Instone, D., Major, B., & Bunker, B. B. (1983). Gender, self-confidence and social influence strategies: An organizational simulation. *Journal of Personality and Social Psychology, 44,* 322-333.

Jablin, F. M. (1981). An exploratory study of subordinates' perceptions of supervisory politics. *Communication Quarterly, 29,* 269-275.

Jensen, A. D. (1984). *Compliance-gaining and resisting between supervisors and subordinates: A review of the literature and an alternative theoretical approach.* Paper presented at the annual meeting of the International Communication Association, San Francisco.

Jermier, J. (1985). When the sleeper wakes: A short story illustrating themes in radical organizational theory. *Journal of Management, 11*(2), 67-80.

Jongbloed, L., & Frost, P. J. (1985). Pfeffer's model of management: An expansion and modification. *Journal of Management, 11*(3), 97-110.

Johnson, R. T., & Fraudson, A. N. (1962). The California Psychological Inventory profile of student leaders. *Personnel Guidance Journal, 41,* 343-345.

Kanter, R. M. (1977). *Men and women of the corporation.* New York: Basic Books.

Kanter, R. M. (1983). *The change masters.* New York: Simon & Schuster.

Kearns, D. (1976). *Lyndon Johnson and the American dream.* New York: Harper & Row.

Kidder, T. (1982). *The soul of a new machine.* New York: Avon Books.

Kipnis, D. (1976). *The powerholders.* Chicago: University of Chicago Press.

Kipnis, D., & Lane, W. (1962). Self-confidence and leadership. *Journal of Applied Psychology, 46,* 291-295.

Kipnis, D., & Schmidt, S. M. (1983). An influence perspective on bargaining within organizations. In M. H. Bazerman & R. J. Lewicki (Eds.), *Negotiating in organizatons* (pp. 303-319). Newbury Park, CA: Sage.

Kipnis, D., Schmidt, S. M., & Wilkinson, I. (1980). Intra-organizational influence tactics: Explorations in getting one's way. *Journal of Applied Psychology, 65,* 440-452.

Koch, S. E. (1984). *The political negotiated order of computer implementation planning.* Unpublished doctoral dissertation, University of Texas at Austin.

Korda, M. (1975). *Power! How to get it, how to use it.* New York: Random House.

Kotter, J. P. (1977, July/August). Power, dependence and effective management. *Harvard Business Review, 55,* 125-136.

Kotter, J. P. (1979). *Power in management.* New ˙ ork: Amacom.

Kotter, J. P. (1985). *Power and influence.* New York: Free Press.

Krefting, L. A, & Frost, P. J. (1985). Untangling webs, surfing waves and wildcatting: A multiple mataphor perspective on managing organizational culture. In P. J. Frost, L. F. Moore, M. R. Louis, C. C. Lundberg, & J. Martin (Eds.), *Organizational culture* (pp. 155-168). Newbury Park, CA: Sage.

Krone, K. J. (1985). *Subordinate influence in organizations: The differential use of upward influence messages in decision making contexts.* Unpublished doctoral dissertation, University of Texas at Austin.

Lawler, E. E., III, Mohrman, A. M., Jr., Mohrman, S. A., Ledford, G. E., Jr., & Cummings, T. G. (1985). *Doing research that is useful for theory and practice.* San Francisco: Jossey-Bass.

Lindbloom, C. E. (1977). *Politics and markets: The world's political and economic systems.* NY: Basic Books.

Louis, M. R. (1985). Reconfiguring our notions of power: An action-in-context approach. In S. Srivasta (Ed.), *The functioning of executive power* (pp. 111-131). San Francisco: Jossey-Bass.

Lukes, S. (1974). *Power: A radical view.* London: Macmillan.

Maccoby, M. (1976). *The gamesman.* New York: Bantam.

Madison, D. L., Allen, R. W., Porter, L. W., Renwick, P. A., & Mayes, B. T. (1980). Organizational politics: An exploration of manager's perceptions. *Human Relations, 33,* 79-100.

March, J. G. (1966). The power of power. In D. Easton (Ed.), *Varieties of political theory* (pp. 39-70). Englewood Cliffs, NJ: Prentice-Hall.

Martin, J., & Powers, M. E. (1983). Truth or corporate propaganda: The value of a good war story. In L. R. Pondy, P. J. Frost, G. Morgan, & T. C. Dandridge (Eds.), *Organizational symbolism* (pp. 93-107). Greenwich, CT: JAI Press.

Martin, J., Sitkin, S. B., & Boehm, M. (1985). Founders and the elusiveness of a cultural legacy. In P. J. Frost, L. F. Moore, M. R. Louis, C. C. Lundberg, & J. Martin (Eds.), *Organizational cultures* (pp. 99-124). Newbury Park, CA: Sage.

Marwell, G., & Schmitt, D. (1967). Dimensions of compliance-gaining behavior: An empirical analysis. *Sociometry, 30,* 350-364.

McCall, M. W., Jr. (1979). Power, authority and influence. In S. Kerr (Ed.), *Organizational behavior* (pp. 185-206). Columbus, OH: Grid.

McClelland, D. C. (1970). The two faces of power. *Journal of International Affairs, 24,* 29-47.

McClelland, D. C. (1975). *Power: The inner experience.* New York: Irvington.

McClelland, D. C., Atkinson, J., Clark, R., & Lowell, E. (1953). *The achievement motive.* New York: Appleton-Century-Crofts.

McClelland, D. C., & Watson, R. I. (1973). Power motivation and risk taking behavior. In D. C. McClelland & R. S. Steel (Eds.), *Human motivation* (pp. 164-180). Morristown, NJ: General Learning Press.

McClintick, D. (1982, September). Boardroom politics at Wall Street and Vine. *Esquire,* 41-56.

Mechanic, D. (1962). Sources of power and lower participants in complex organizations. *Administrative Science Quarterly, 7,* 349-364.

Megargee, E. I., Bogart, P., & Anderson, B. J. (1966). Production of leadership in a simulated industrial task. *Journal of Applied Psychology, 50,* 292-295.

Meyer, J., & Rowan, B. (1977). Institutionalized organizations: Formal structure as myth and ceremony. *American Journal of Sociology, 83,* 340-363.

Mintzberg, H. (1983). *Power in and around organizations.* Englewood Cliffs, NJ: Prentice-Hall.

Mintzberg, J. (1985). The organization as a political arena. *Journal of Management Studies, 22,* 133-154.

Mitroff, I. I. (1983). *Stakeholders of the organizational mind.* San Francisco: Jossey-Bass.

Molotch, H. L., & Boden, D. (1985). Talking social structure: Discourse, domination and the Watergate hearings. *American Sociological Review, 50,* 273-288.

Monge, P. R., Bachman, S. G., Dillard, J. P., & Eisenberg, E. M. (1982). Communicator competence in the workplace: Model testing and scale development. In M. Burgoon (Ed.), *Communication yearbook 5* (pp. 505-527). New Brunswick, NJ: Transaction.

Morgan, G. (1985). *Images of organization.* Unpublished manuscript, York University.

Morgan, G., & Ramierez, R. (1984). Action learning: A holograph metaphor for guiding social change. *Human Relations, 37,* 1-27.

Mowday, R. (1980). Leader characteristics, self-confidence, and methods of upward influence in organization decision situations. *Academy of Management Journal, 44,* 709-724.

Mumby, D. K. (1984). *Ideology and power in organizations: A radical theory of organizational cultures.* Unpublished doctoral dissertation, Southern Illinois University, Carbondale.

Murdock, G. (1982). Large corporations and the control of communication industries. In M. Gurevitch, T. Bennett, J. Curran, & J. Woolacott (Eds.), *Culture, society and the media* (pp. 118-150). London: Methuen.

Noble, D. F. (1984). *Forces of production.* New York: Knopf.

Nord, W. R. (1983). A political-economic perspective on organizational effectiveness. In K. S. Cameron & D. A. Whetten (Eds.), *Organizational effectiveness: A comparison of multiple models* (pp. 95-133). New York: Academic Press.

Nord, W. R., Brief, A. P., Atich, J. M., & Doherty, E. M. (1985). *Work values and the conduct of organizational psychology.* Unpublished manuscript, Washington University.

Normann, R. (1977). *Management for growth.* New York: John Wiley.

Ornstein, M. C. (1984). Interlocking directorates in Canada: Intercorporate or class alliance. *Administrative Science Quarterly, 29,* 210-231.

Parks, M. R. (1985). Interpersonal communication and the quest for personal competence. In M. L. Knapp & G. R. Miller (Eds.), *Handbook of interpersonal communication* (pp. 171-201). Newbury Park, CA: Sage.

Pennings, J. M. (1980). *Interlocking directorates: Origins and consequences of connections among organizations' boards of directors.* San Francisco: Jossey-Bass.

Perrow, C. (1970). *Organizational analysis: A sociological review.* Belmont, CA: Wadsworth.

Perrow, C. (1984). *Normal accidents: Living with high-risk technologies.* New York: Basic Books.

Peters, T. J., & Waterman, R. J. (1982). *In search of excellence.* New York: Harper & Row.

Pettigrew, A. M. (1973). *The politics of organizational decision making.* London: Tavistock.

Pettigrew, A. M. (1985). *The awakening giant.* Oxford: Basil Blackwell.

Pfeffer, J. (1981). *Power in organizations.* Marshfield, MA: Pitman.

Pfeffer, J., & Salancik, G. R. (1974). Organizational decision making as a political process: The case of a university budget. *Administrative Science Quarterly, 19,* 135-151.

Pinchot, J., III (1985). *Intrapreneuring.* New York: Harper & Row.

Pondy, L. R. (1978). Leadership is a language game. In M. W. McCall, Jr., & M. M. Lombardo (Eds.), *Leadership: Where else can we go?* (pp. 87-99). Durham, NC: Duke University Press.

Pondy, L. R. (1983). The role of metaphors and myths in organizations and in the facilitation of change. In L. R. Pondy, P. J. Frost, G. Morgan, & T. C. Dandridge (Eds.), *Organizational symbolism* (pp. 157-166). Greenwich, CT: JAI Press.

Pondy, L. R., & Huff, A. S. (1985). Achieving routine in organizational change. *Journal of Management, 11*(2), 103-116.

Porter, L. W., Allen, R. W., & Angle, H. L. (1981). The politics of upward influence in organizations. In L. L. Cummings & B. M. Staw (Eds.), *Research in organizational behavior* (Vol. 3, pp. 109-149). Greenwich, CT: JAI Press.

Porter, M. (1985). *Competitive advantage.* New York: Free Press.

Putnam, L. L. (1983). The interpretive perspective: An alternative to functionalism. In L. L. Putnam & M. E. Pacanowsky (Eds.), *Communication and organizations: An interpretive approach* (pp. 31-54). Newbury Park, CA: Sage.

Ranson, S., Hinings, B., & Greenwood, R. (1980). The structuring of organizational structures. *Administrative Science Quarterly, 25,* 1-17.

Raven, B. H. (1974). The comparative analysis of power and influence. In J. T. Tedeschi (Ed.), *Perspectives on social power* (pp. 172-198). Chicago: Aldine.

Riley, P. (1983). A structurationist account of political culture. *Administrative Science Quarterly, 28,* 414-437.

Roberts, N. (1985). *A new topology of power: Distributive, intercursive and collective power.* Paper presented at the annual meeting of the Academy of Management, San Diego.

Roloff, M. E. (1976). Communication strategies, relationships and relational change. In G. R. Miller (Ed.), *Explorations in interpersonal communication* (pp. 173-195). Newbury Park, CA: Sage.

Rosen, M. (1985). Breakfast at Spiro's: Dramaturgy and dominance. *Journal of Management, 11*(2), 31-48.

Roy, D. F. (1960). Banana time: Job satisfaction and informal interaction. *Human Organization, 18,* 156-168.

Russell, B. (1983). *Power: A social analysis.* New York: Norton.

Salancik, G. R., & Pfeffer, J. (1974). The bases and use of power in organizational decision making: The case of a university. *Administrative Science Quarterly, 19,* 453-473.

Schrank, R. (1978). *Ten thousand working days.* Cambridge: MIT Press.

Schlesinger, A. M., Jr. (1965). *A thousand days: John F. Kennedy in the White House.* Boston: Houghton Mifflin.

Schmidt, S. M., & Kipnis, D. (1984). Managers' pursuit of individual and organizational goals. *Human Relations, 37,* 781-794.

Schutz, A. (1972). *The phenomenology of the social world.* London: Heinemann.

Siehl, C. (1985). After the founder: An opportunity to manager culture. In P. J. Frost, L. F. Moore, M. R. Louis, C. C. Lunberg, & J. Martin (Eds.), *Organizational culture* (pp. 125-140). Newbury Park, CA: Sage.

Smircich, L. (1983). Organizations as shared meanings. In L. R. Pondy, P. J. Frost, G. Morgan, & T. C. Dandridge (Eds.), *Organizational symbolism* (pp. 55-65). Greenwich, CT: JAI Press.

Smircich, L., & Stubbart, C. I. (1985). Strategic management in an enacted world. *Academy of Management Review, 10,* 724-736.

Smith, K. K., & Simmons, V. M. (1983). A Rumpelstiltskin organization: Metaphors on metaphors in field research. *Administrative Science Quarterly, 28,* 377-392.

Stablein, R., & Nord, W. (1985). Practical and emancipatory interests in organizational symbolism: A review and evaluation. *Journal of Management, 11*(2), 13-28.

Steinmetz, S. (1982, August 1). The desexing of English. *The New York Times Magazine,* 6, 8.

Stevenson, W. B., Pearce, J. L., & Porter, L. W. (1985). The concept of "coalition" in organizational theory and research. *Academy of Management Review, 10,* 256-268.

Strauss, G. (1962). Tactics of lateral relationship: The purchasing agent. *Administrative Science Quarterly, 7,* 161-186.

Sypher, B. D., & Zorn, T. E., Jr. (1986). Communication-related abilities and upward mobility. *Human Communication Research, 12,* 420-431.

Thomas, K. W., & Velthouse, B. A. (1985). *Cognitive elements of empowerment.* Paper presented at the annual meeting of the Academy of Management, San Diego.

Thompson, J. D. (1967). *Organizations in action.* New York: McGraw-Hill.

Tompkins, P. K., & Cheney, G. (1985). Communication and unobtrusive control in contemporary organizations. In R. D. McPhee & P. K. Tompkins (Eds.), *Organizational communication: Traditional themes and new directions* (pp. 179-210). Newbury Park, CA: Sage.

Torbert, Q. (1985). *Transforming management*. Unpublished manuscript, Boston College.

Tuchman, G. (1978). *Making news*. New York: Free Press.

Turow, J. (1986). Learning to portray institutional power: The socialization of creators in mass media organizations. In R. D. McPhee & P. K. Tompkins (Eds.), *Organizational communication: Traditional themes and new directions* (pp. 211-234). Newbury Park, CA: Sage.

Uleman, J. S. (1972). The need for influence: Development and validation of a measure and comparison of the need for power. *Genetic Psychology Monographs, 85,* 157-214.

Uttal, B. (1985, August). Behind the fall of Steve Jobs. *Fortune,* 20-24.

Weick, K. E. (1984). Small wins. *American Psychologist, 39,* 40-49.

Weinstein, E. A., Beckhouse, L. S., Blumstein, P. W., & Stein, R. B. (1968). Interpersonal strategies under conditions of gain or loss. *Journal of Personality, 36,* 616-634.

Wilkinson, B. (1983). *The shopfloor politics of new techology*. London: Heinemann.

Williams, C. T. (1982, September 5). Letter to the editor about "Desexing the English language." *The New York Times Magazine,* 46.

Wiseman, R. L., & Schenk-Hamlin, W. (1981). A multidimensional scaling validation of an inductively-derived set of compliance gaining strategies. *Communication Monographs, 48,* 251-270.

Zajonc, R. B., & Wolfe, D. M. (1966). Cognitive consequences of a person's position in a formal organization. *Human Relations, 19,* 139-150.

Zald, M. N., & Berger, M. A. (1978). Social movements in organizations: Coup d'etat, insurgency, and mass movements. *American Journal of Sociology, 83,* 823-861.

Zerbe, W. J., & Paulhus, D. L. (1985). *Socially desirable responding in organizational behavior.* Unpublished manuscript, University of British Columbia.

16 Conflict and Negotiation

LINDA L. PUTNAM
Purdue University

M. SCOTT POOLE
University of Minnesota

Overview
　Arenas of Organizational Conflict/Definition of Conflict/The Importance of Communication in Conflict/Alternative Perspectives on Communication in Conflict/Components of Conflict Situations
Interpersonal Conflict
　Role of Communication in Interpersonal Conflict/Links Between Communication and Components of Conflict/Communication and Interpersonal Conflict Management/Assessment of Communication and Interpersonal Conflict Research
Bargaining and Negotiation
　The Role of Communication in Bargaining/Links Between Communication and Components of Bargaining
Communication and Third Party Conflict Management
　Assessment of Communication and Bargaining Research
Intergroup Conflict
　The Role of Communication in Intergroup Conflict/Links Between Communication and Components of Intergroup Conflict/Intergroup Conflict Management/Assessment of Intergroup Conflict Research
Interorganizational Conflict
　The Role of Communication in Interorganizational Conflict/Links Between Communication and Components of Interorganizational Conflict/Interorganizational Conflict Management/Assessment of Communication and Interorganizational Conflict Research
Conclusion
　Similarities and Differences in Conflict Research/Improving Research on Organizational Conflict: Borrowing Dominant Approaches from Other Areas/The Role of Communication in Organizational Conflict

CONFLICT is a pervasive aspect of organizational life. It surfaces in dyadic relationships, between organizational and interorganizational fields. It penetrates competition for resources, coordination

AUTHORS' NOTE: The authors wish to express their appreciation to Barbara Gray, Fred Jablin, Lyman Porter, and Karlene Roberts for their constructive suggestions on an earlier draft of this chapter.

of systems, work distribution, decision making, and many other aspects of organizational behavior. As an intrinsic part of organizational life, its roots tap into structural variables, systemic processes, and individual differences (Renwick, 1975a).

Conflict has become an essential topic in the research and teaching of organizational behavior. A content analysis of MBA course syllabi reveals that conflict is ranked 5th among the 65 topics most frequently taught (Rahim, 1981). Consistent with this growth in pedagogy, organizational conflict research has mushroomed in the past decade, particularly in the areas of superior-subordinate conflict, intraorganizational disputes, and negotiations. The number of review essays on conflict in organizations reflects this increasing interest (see Brett, 1984; Miles, 1979; Pondy, 1967; Putnam, 1985a; Ruble & Cosier, 1983; Thomas, 1976; Thomas, 1979; Van de Vliert, 1984; also see Katz, 1978, special section of the *California Management Review* and Lewicki & Bazerman, 1985, special issue of the *Journal of Occupational Behavior*). Moreover, several books on conflict, negotiation, and conflict management in organizations have surfaced (Bazerman & Lewicki, 1983; Blake, Shepard, & Mouton, 1964; Bomers & Peterson, 1982; Brown, 1983; Byrnes, 1986; Lewicki & Litterer, 1985; Lewicki, Sheppard, & Bazerman, 1986; Rahim, 1986a; 1986b; Rhenman, Stromberg, & Westerlunch, 1970; Robbins, 1974; Tjosvold & Johnson, 1983).

Because of its centrality in the conflict process, communication is an important theme in these texts. Communication underlies the sources, goals, strategies, tactics, relationships, and contact systems that shape the nature of conflict and conflict management. As Thomas and Pondy (1977, p. 1100) observe, "It is communication with which we are most concerned in understanding conflict management among principal parties." However, in most of the research on conflict, communication holds only tangential interest. It appears as part of the taken-for-granted backdrop that shapes the way other forces impinge on organizational conflict.

This chapter focuses specifically on the role of communication in conflict. It aims to integrate the communication studies on organizational conflict and the "bits and pieces" that can be learned about communication in conflict situations from organizational, social psychological, industrial relations, and sociological research. Focusing on communication can lead to significant advances in conflict research because communication is the basic constituent of conflict. That is, the activity of having or managing a conflict occurs through communication. More specifically, communication undergirds the setting and reframing of goals; the defining and narrowing of conflict issues; the developing of relationships between disputants and among constituents; the selecting and implementing of strategies and tactics; the generating, attacking, and defending of alternative solutions; and the reaching and confirming of agreements. Moreover, a communication perspective on organizational conflict can generate innovative research questions and explanatory schemas that provides useful complements to other approaches.

OVERVIEW

Arenas of Organizational Conflict

This chapter considers the role of communication in four arenas of organizational conflict: interpersonal, bargaining and negotiations, intergroup, and interorganizational. These arenas not only represent different contexts for conflict but they also exhibit different processes. That is, relationships between disputants, issues, contextual features, and treatment of communication differ somewhat across the four arenas. For instance, since interpersonal conflicts typically center on individuals and interorganizational disputes generally involve collectivities, the message form, substance, and patterns of communication would typically reflect these diverse parties and their unique features.

Our claim that organizational arena shapes the role of communication in conflict does not preclude cross-arena similarities. We concur with Thomas (1976) that many propositions about conflict generalize across the four levels, although we do not believe this to be uniformly true. More important, what happens in one arena can often be explained in terms of other arenas. For example, interorganizational conflict can be analyzed as interpersonal relationships between boundary-role spanners.

This chapter is divided into six sections. The first is an overview that lays out the basic framework and assumptions of the chapter. The next four cover the conflict literature in the four organizational arenas with specific attention to the following: (1) the role of communication in each conflict arena; (2) links between communication and other components of conflict situations in each arena; (3) communication and conflict management in each arena; and (4) an assessment of the adequacies and inadequacies of the treatment of communication within a given arena. The conclusion or sixth section of the chapter highlights similarities and differences among the four arenas and points out ways that research in one arena could be used to glean insights at other levels.

The literature on organizational conflict is voluminous, quite disparate, and difficult to integrate. Research in different fields, especially across arenas, typically focuses on diverse variables, themes, and topics. This review attempts to ascertain what the disparate fields have in common and how they differ in their treatments of organizational conflict. Since no previous review has covered all four arenas, this chapter represents a first attempt to track similarities and differences among the organizational levels; hence our review uncovers many loose ends, unanswered questions, and unpursued leads. For us, this "untidiness" is attractive since it suggests avenues in which new advances are possible. The remainder of this overview section addresses three other important concerns: a definition of conflict, the significance of communication in conflict, and the components or sets of variables that link communication to conflict.

Definition of Conflict

Conflict, in this chapter, is defined as the interaction of interdependent people who perceive opposition of goals, aims, and values, and who see the other party as potentially interfering with the realization of these goals. This definition equates conflict with its action component; conflict antecedents such as motives, abilities, and social pressures are treated as different phenomena. Moreover, our definition highlights three general characteristics of conflict: interaction, interdependence, and incompatible goals. Social interaction is the way that conflicts are formed and sustained (Folger & Poole, 1984, p. 4). Thus conflicts are shaped in large part by the actions and reactions of conflict participants. The parties in conflict situations are interdependent in that each party has the power to constrain or to interfere with the goals of the other. Finally, at least one of the parties must perceive the conflict situation as an opposition of goals, aims, and values. Thus an individual's perceptions, whether accurate or not, begin to shape the conflict. Even though conflict is typically defined in this manner, researchers in a given arena may focus on specific dimensions of conflict.

The Importance of Communication in Conflict

Like all specialists, communication researchers are sometimes guilty of academic provincialism, of exaggerating the importance of communication in human behavior. However, it is difficult to overstate the impact of communication in conflict. It is important to study the psychology of conflict, the economic or social forces that create divergent interests, and the outcomes of conflict. However, without research on communication and conflict processes, our theories of conflict would be seriously incomplete. Interaction mediates the influence of social psychological and economic antecedents on conflict outcomes. The study of interaction, in turn, necessitates a focus on communication since communication is the *sine qua non* of human interaction.

Communication constitutes the essence of conflict in that it undergirds the formation of opposing issues, frames perceptions of the felt conflict, translates emotions and perceptions into conflict behaviors, and sets the stage for future conflicts. Thus communication is instrumental in every aspect of conflict, including conflict avoidance or suppression, the open expression of opposition, and the evolution of issues. Conflict strategies and tactics are also manifested through communication. Even "physical" strategies such as violence depend on communicative and symbolic processes (Burgess, 1973). Sequences of communicative strategies build into an interaction system that acquires a momentum of its own, moving the conflict toward escalation, avoidance, or constructive management (Folger & Poole, 1984). Moreover, third-party conflict intervention, particularly mediation, relies heavily on communication skills.

Studies of communication in conflict are relatively scarce. This scarcity stems, in part, from the difficulties and time involved in studying communication processes. Logistical concerns, however, should not blind researchers to the fact that conflict cannot be reduced to contextual and individual determinants. Conflict is an emergent process, one that is greater than either party's mental processes. To understand conflict we must examine the entire system of interaction between disputants in a specific context.

Alternative Perspectives on Communication in Conflict

This review adopts the communication perspectives proposed by Fisher (1978) and adapted by Krone, Jablin, and Putnam in Chapter 1 of this volume. Hence it seeks to understand the extent to which the conflict literature has employed a mechanistic, psychological, interpretive-symbolic, or systems-interactional view of communication. Our goal is to ascertain which perspectives dominate the research in a given conflict arena and what we have or have not learned about communication and conflict as a result of the perspectives employed. Rather than repeat information in Chapter 1 of this handbook, our chapter highlights the way a given perspective has been applied to the organizational conflict literature.

The *mechanistic view* of communication, with its emphasis on transmission and its attendant breakdowns and barriers, is dominant in several lines of research. Studies that trace conflict to misunderstandings that result from failure to communicate, gatekeeping, or withholding information exemplify the mechanistic view by centering on the channels and transmission of messages as the essence of conflict (Alexander, 1977). In the mechanistic approach, misunderstanding stems from a lack of fidelity in information flow between sender and receiver. A second group of studies that adopts a mechanistic view tests for the effects of type of channel, amount of information, and distortion in communication flow on conflict outcomes. Thus the researcher manipulates medium or mode of communication to see if disputants are more cooperative in face-to-face, as opposed to audio or written, communication (Short, 1974; Turnbull, Strickland, & Shaver, 1974, 1976; Wichman, 1970).

A third group of studies that espouses the mechanistic perspective casts hostility as noise in the channel that blocks communication between disputants (Hunger & Stern, 1976). This approach treats both conflict and communication as materialistic substances that flow through identifiable channels. A fourth and final group of studies that embrace mechanistic assumptions center on networks as communication contact systems. These studies rarely examine messages or information flow; rather, they depict the webs of affiliations that determine who is in contact with whom in conflict situations and the coalitions that shape conflict emergence (Corwin, 1969; White, 1961; Zald, 1962).

The *psychological approach* to communication is prevalent in research that treats conflict as semantic misunderstanding or as differences in perceptions and cognitive abilities of conflicting parties (Brehmer, 1971; Brehmer & Hammond, 1977). This orientation is also evident in studies on perceptions of completeness or accuracy of information in conflicts (Druckman & Zechmeister, 1973) and on the effects of bargaining orientation on the use of conflict strategies (Lewis & Pruitt, 1971; Radlow & Weidner, 1966). The psychological approach also considers the way in which group differentiation affects stereotyping and simplification of the opponent's position (Coser, 1956; Deutsch, 1973).

The *interpretive-symbolic perspective* centers on the role of shared meanings in conflicts. In this orientation conflict emerges from incongruent meanings of organizational events or from conflicting actions in creating and maintaining organizational reality. Research on the formation of reference groups in organizational conflicts exemplifies the interpretive-symbolic approach to communication in that group ideologies are derived through social interaction (Burawoy, 1979; Whyte, 1955).

The *systems-interaction approach* to communication is evident in research on conflict cycles, phases of conflict development, and sequences of messages and tactics (Bednar & Curington, 1983; Donohue, 1981b; Putnam & Jones, 1982a). These studies analyze patterns of sequential messages that evolve over time into a communication system. These patterns demonstrate reciprocity of conflict behaviors, "locking-in" to cooperative and competitive choices, and stages of escalation-deescalation (Blake et al., 1964; Druckman, Zechmeister, & Solomon, 1972; Pilisuk & Rapoport, 1964).

This review adds a *fifth* perspective, related to the interpretive-symbolic approach, but not covered by Fisher (1978): *critical theory* (Putnam & Pacanowsky, 1983). Critical theory also focuses on meaning, but more specifically on the structures of meaning that embody and reinforce domination. It delves further into the meanings of symbols to discover the hidden structure of domination. Communication enters into critical theory as the cumulative effect of multiple messages that form consensual meanings, constitute the hidden structures, and provide critical insights into the subtle patterns of domination.

Critical theory impacts on confict situations in five ways. First, it defines the knowledge each party has of its world through the symbols and conceptual frames that define social reality for particular disputants. These symbols and conceptual frames typically conceal distorted information that creates psychic prisons for some organizational members. Second, it shapes the roots of conflict by defining a party's interests (Lukes, 1974). Researchers examine how communication creates "false interest" or pseudo-consensus among parties in a dispute. Critical theories seek to understand if rational debate is a genuine endeavor rather than a pseudo-activity. Third, the critical perspective defines the scope of a conflict by determining which issues can be raised and which ones are illegitimate. It attempts to understand the rationales used to constrain some issues and to make others "appropriate" topics for debate. Fourth, it defines the alternatives available to members and the range of moves and outcomes that are appropriate. Unlike the symbolic-interpretive, it aims to penetrate everyday practices to uncover political controversies and social battlefields rooted in the history of these organizational experiences. Fifth, the critical perspective dictates the form that behavior takes when performed by a competent communicator. For example, the normative form of making threats influences how disputants phrase and execute threats to make them acceptable to a particular audience. In these five ways, communication maintains what Gramsci (1971) calls hegemony. Studies of intergroup and interorganizational conflict frequently espouse critical approaches to communication.

Components of Conflict Situations

The communication perspective that a researcher adopts also affects the interface between communication and other components of conflict. This chapter examines four general types of independent variables that interact with communication in organizational conflict. The four are (1) *actor attributes,* for example, predispositions, needs, personality traits, beliefs, attitudes, skills, and cognitive styles; (2)*conflict issues,* specifically, substantive aspects of the conflict, emergence of conflict, the interests or "root issues" of those in conflict; (3)*relationship variables,* for instance, trust, power, target of conflict, and interdependency between communicators; and (4) *contextual factors,* for example, organizational climate, precedent or past history, organizational norms, standard operating procedures, organizational complexity, marketplace factors, and legal-political constraints. Obviously all four elements are present in most organizational conflicts; however, the specific variables subsumed under a given component vary across arenas.

The relationship between communication and these four components is bidirectional. In some cases actor attributes, relationships, issues, or context variables influence communication processes, whereas in other cases communication constitutes and shapes one or more of the four components. Patterns of influence vary across the four arenas. This review identifies which components are researched more frequently than others and which ones yield significant findings for the role of communication in a given conflict arena. In addition, this review delineates the specific variables that researchers examine for a given component and compare and contrast these variables across organizational arenas. The next portion of this chapter reviews the literature on communication and conflict in four organizational arenas: interpersonal conflict, bargaining and negotiation, intergroup, and interorganizational.

INTERPERSONAL CONFLICT

Interpersonal conflict refers to disputes between two organizational members. Although any individual can engage in a dyadic dispute, research on interpersonal conflict has centered primarily on *conflict styles in superior-subordinate relationships*. This focus stems in part from the need to improve the skills of practicing managers, especially since superiors spend approximately 20% of their time managing conflicts (Thomas & Schmidt, 1976).

Conflict style refers to a characteristic mode or a habitual way that a person handles a dispute (Blake & Mouton, 1964). Some research in this area, however, also treats style as either (1) an orientation toward conflicts, (2) categories of conflict strategies and tactics, or (3) planned strategies aimed at attaining a particular goal (Folger & Poole, 1984). The styles under study emanate from a five-category scheme based on concern for self and concern for others (Rahim & Bonoma, 1979). These dimensions represent an expansion of the competitive-cooperative dichotomy that underlies early conflict research (Ruble & Thomas, 1976). These are the five styles: (1) confronting or problem solving—collaborating, working for an integrative solution, and facing conflict directly; (2) forcing or competing—use of position power, assertiveness, verbal dominance, and perseverance; (3) smoothing or accommodating—glossing over differences, playing down disagreements, trivializing the conflict; (4) avoiding or withdrawing—physical or psychological removal from the scene, refraining from arguing, failure to confront; and (5) compromising—searching for an intermediate position, splitting the difference, and meeting the opponent halfway (Blake & Mouton, 1964).

Role of Communication in
Interpersonal Conflict

The psychological perspective has dominated research on communication in interpersonal conflict. Both communication and conflict styles are examined through the conceptual filters of organizational members. In studies on conflict styles communication is equated with perceptions of verbal and nonverbal messages that enact a particular style. For example, forcing in conflict situations is measured as the extent of *perceived* verbal dominance—using a loud voice, asserting one's opinion forcefully, prolonging the discussion of issues, holding firm on a proposed alternative, and using power and influence to win one's position (Putnam & Wilson, 1982; Rahim, 1983a; Riggs, 1983; Ross & DeWine, 1982). Thus, in most studies, perception of message behaviors is substituted for the actual communication of a style.

Consistent with the psychological approach, researchers in this area have created a number of measuring instruments aimed at conflict orientations or typical strategies used in conflicts (see, for example, Blake & Mouton, 1964; Hall, 1969; Lawrence & Lorsch, 1967; Putnam & Wilson, 1982; Rahim, 1983a;

Renwick, 1975a; Riggs, 1983; Ross & DeWine, 1982; Thomas & Kilmann, 1974). Item content ranges from the use of proverbs and internal motivations for handling conflicts (Lawrence & Lorsch, 1967) to the use of verbal messages that enact or typify conflict styles (Putnam & Wilson, 1982; Ross & DeWine, 1982). The instruments report a wide range of diversity in reliability, validity, and social desirability of both item and scale content (Thomas & Kilmann, 1978). Some of the scales demonstrate problems with internal reliabilities (Blake & Mouton, 1964; Lawrence & Lorsch, 1967), with high intercorrelations among the five styles (Putnam & Wilson, 1982; Rahim, 1983a; Ross & DeWine, 1982); with ipsative data unsuitable for tests with inferential statistics (Thomas & Kilmann, 1974), and with social desirability of the item and scale constructs (Blake & Mouton, 1964; Lawrence & Lorsch, 1967; Renwick, 1975a; Thomas & Kilmann, 1975). In addition to problems with reliability and social desirability, the nine measuring instruments also demonstrate disparity in conceptualizing and measuring the five styles, a problem that is often endemic to the psychological perspective.

Some studies on conflict styles treat breakdowns in superior-subordinate communication as one of the primary sources of conflict, thus combining the mechanistic with the psychological perspective (Phillips & Cheston, 1979; Renwick, 1975a). Communication then becomes a channel for transmitting information between sender and receiver and conflict is a breakdown in achieving message fidelity. Several studies on superior-subordinate conflict styles also track the sequence of conflict behaviors over time, thus combining the psychological approach with the systems-interaction perspective (Cosier & Ruble, 1981; Goering, Rudick, & Faulkner, 1986; Ruble & Cosier, 1982). In summary, in the majority of research on interpersonal conflict both communication and conflict styles are treated as if they reside in the disputants' conceptual filters. Both are measured through the use of psychological scales that attempt to determine an individual's habitual or dominant approach to interpersonal conflict.

Links Between Communication and Components of Conflict

In interpersonal conflict research, variables categorized as relational components are examined more frequently and tend to yield more significant findings about the role of communication in interpersonal conflicts than do actor, issue, and context variables.

Relational variables. The relational variables that link communication and conflict styles are organizational position and interdependency in perceptions, attributions, and behaviors. Conflict varies in frequency, acceptance, and style across organizational levels (Thomas & Schmidt, 1976). The higher the position, the more frequent the occurrences of conflict and the more likely that disagreements will surface (Evan, 1965). Managers in high-level positions also view conflict more favorably than do those in lower subordinate roles (Tompkins, Fisher, Infante, & Tompkins, 1974). These differences in frequency and attitude toward conflict suggest that hierarchical role influences the use of communication strategies and conflict styles.

Even though Burke (1970) and London and Howat (1978) report that confrontation is the preferred conflict style for all organizational members, most studies reveal differences in conflict strategies across organizational levels. These differences surface in studies on the characteristic mode of conflict management, on the target of the conflict, and on perceptions of the effectiveness and desirability of each style. Research demonstrates that superiors rely on forcing as their most characteristic mode of handling conflicts (Phillips & Cheston, 1979; Howat & London, 1980; Putnam & Wilson, 1982; Morley & Shockley-Zalabak, 1986). Forcing through reference to position power is particularly characteristic of managers who demonstrate low levels of supervisory expertise (Conrad, 1983). One exception to this general finding is that first-line supervisors, in comparison with middle and upper managers, rely on confronting or problem-solving messages more frequently than they do on forcing strategies (Putnam & Wilson, 1982). This dependence on forcing strategies is particularly characteristic of line managers as opposed to staff and support personnel (Morley & Shockley-Zalabak, 1986). Subordinates, in contrast, prefer to avoid (London & Howat, 1978), to smooth (Putnam & Wilson, 1982), or to compromise (Renwick, 1975b) when placed in conflict situations with their superiors. In effect, preference for conflict strategies differs across hierarchical level, with superiors exhibiting forcing styles and subordinates preferring avoidance, smoothing, and compromise. These disparities in perceived use of style may reflect power and status differentials in handling conflicts.

Choice of style may also hinge on the organizational position of the opponent in a conflict. Superiors at different organizational levels reflect an interest in different targets of disputes. CEOs center their concerns on conflicts with subordinates; vice-presidents, on controversies with peers; and middle managers, on disagreements with superiors (Thomas & Schmidt, 1976).

Studies that test for the effects of target of conflict on choice of style yield inconsistent findings. Putnam and Wilson (1982) report that managers prefer forcing strategies with subordinates, confronting and smoothing styles with superiors, and smoothing and avoiding behaviors with peers. Rahim (1983b, 1986a), using a different conflict instrument, finds that managers use confronting with subordinates, smoothing with superiors, and compromise with peers. Hence these studies concur that smoothing strategies are employed with superiors, but they differ on the dominant modes used with other targets. Despite these discrepancies, both studies demonstrate that managers adapt their conflict strategies to fit particular targets.

Superiors and subordinates also differ in their assessments of the effectiveness, desirability, and satisfaction of a particular conflict style. Subordinates rate confrontation as the most effective and most satisfying strategy (Burke,

1970; Lawrence & Lorsch, 1967; Renwick, 1975a), while superiors report that confrontation is effective only in situations that stem from communication difficulties, low conflicts of interest, and negotiable issues (Phillips & Cheston, 1979; Thomas, 1979). Forcing, although rated by subordinates as less desirable than other styles (Burke, 1970), emerges as the most effective strategy in conflict situations characterized by incompatible goals, past failures to reach agreement, and organizational endorsement of a particular solution (Robbins, 1978). Subordinates rate smoothing and compromise as desirable, but managers view frequent use of these strategies as hindering goal achievement and productivity (Lawrence & Lorsch, 1967). Both superiors and subordinates see avoidance as the least effective and least desirable of the five styles (Burke, 1970; Renwick, 1975b).

Another relational variable that has an impact on choice of conflict strategy is interdependency—particularly perceptual congruence, attributions of intent, and reciprocity in actual behaviors. Congruence tests on perceptions of conflict style reveal that when both the superior and subordinate concur on the superior's tendency to use forcing strategies the subordinate is more satisfied with his or her work than when the two individuals differ in their perceptions of the superior's style (Howat & London, 1980; Richmond, Wagner, & McCroskey, 1983). Congruence in perceptions also relates to projection of one's own style onto the other person. Even when superiors and subordinates are incongruent in their descriptions of one another's conflict style, respondents tend to impose their own style onto the other person, especially for self-descriptions of avoiding, forcing, and confronting (Renwick, 1975b). This finding suggests that when organizational members use avoiding, forcing, or confronting, they typically perceive the other party as using a similar strategy. Perceived reciprocity, then, is a key contributor to choice of conflict style (Thomas & Walton, 1971).

Perceptions are closely tied to attributions that each party makes about causes of the conflict. Superiors and subordinates typically hold incongruent attributions of intent in conflict; namely, competitive intentions are attributed to the other party while problem-solving and compromising causes are typically attributed to self (Thomas & Pondy, 1977). Attribution of intent, unlike perceived use of conflict style, stems from divergent biases that polarize opposing parties and set up the boundaries of a dispute.

Reciprocity of actual conflict behaviors is another variable linked to interdependency between disputants. Research reveals that choice of conflict strategy hinges to a great extent on the other party's tactic. Specifically, disputants reciprocate their opponent's use of forcing, confronting, smoothing, and compromise behaviors in kind; avoiding tactics, however, typically follow a forcing strategy (Cosier & Ruble, 1981; Ruble & Cosier, 1982). In a study that compares actual messages with perceptions of dominant styles, Goering et al. (1986) conclude that the opponent's message behavior, not the self-report style as measured through a questionnaire, accounts for the majority of variance in use of conflict situations.

Conflict issues. The component that emerges as the second most significant link between communication and interpersonal conflict style is the conflict issue itself. Research on interpersonal conflict issues in organizations has focused on four variables: the source, the topic, the frequency, and the importance of a dispute. In conflicts caused by power struggles and incompatible values, organizational members appear to rely on forcing strategies, whereas in controversies that stem from scarce resources, personality differences, and disagreements in attitudes and opinions, individuals choose compromising and smoothing tactics (Phillips & Cheston, 1979; Renwick, 1975a). Problem-solving approaches surface in the management of conflicts that stem from misunderstandings, ambiguous meanings, and discrepancies in reward allocation (Phillips & Cheston, 1979; Renwick, 1975a). Unlike the source of a dispute, topic or subject matter of the conflict fails to exhibit a characteristic conflict mode for disagreements about equipment usage, professional activities, organizational policies, and community involvement (London & Howat, 1978; Renwick, 1975a).

The frequency and salience of an interpersonal conflict, however, may mitigate findings on sources of conflict. Specifically, when conflicts are important and agreement is likely, organizational members rely on confronting tactics to handle the disagreement. Forcing strategies are used in conflict situations characterized by high importance, low probability of agreement, and a high frequency (Blake & Mouton, 1964; Howat & London, 1980). Since conflict management consumes considerable time and energy, organizational members choose to avoid disagreements that rate low in importance, particularly when an agreement is unlikely (Blake & Mouton, 1964; Rahim & Bonoma, 1979).

Actor attributes. In contrast to the research on relational and issue components, studies that focus on actor attributes, although frequent in number, account for only a modicum of variance in predicting choice of conflict strategy. Specifically, such personality or need traits as Machiavellianism (Kilmann & Thomas, 1977), aggression (Bell & Blakeney, 1977), introversion-extroversion (Kilmann & Thomas, 1975), need for achievement (Bell & Blakeney, 1977), and need for control and inclusion (Ross & DeWine, 1984) account for an average of 9% of the total variance in choice of conflict strategies (Waltman & Wilson, 1986).

Similarly, studies on sex differences as predictors of conflict style yield contradictory findings. Jamieson and Thomas (1974) report that males use forcing styles while females employ compromising strategies, but other investigations reveal no gender differences in choice of conflict mode (Bigoness, Grigsby, & Rosen, 1980; Renwick, 1977; Shockley-Zalabak, 1981). When sex role interacts with target of conflict, however, females who demonstrate high commitment to their jobs and to their supervisors and who report to female supervisors are more likely to confront and less likely to force than are their male counterparts. Moreover, males who report to female superiors and who also have high commitment to their jobs are more likely to confront, to smooth, or to compromise than are females in the same conditions (Zammuto, London, & Rowland, 1979).

Context variables. In comparison with the other three components, context factors demonstrate the least predictive power in choice of conflict strategies, with the exception of organizational commitment and conflict history. High organizational commitment is positively related to the use of problem-solving approaches in interpersonal conflicts, if commitment to the profession and to the community is low (London & Howat, 1978). A company's history in managing conflicts also impacts on the message strategies that organizational members use. Specifically, members of organizations characterized by a problem-solving history ask more questions, integrate issues, and identify the opponent's arguments more frequently than do members in companies typified by competitive and avoidance traditions (Tjosvold, 1982, 1983). These studies suggest that asking questions, pointing out weak arguments, and spending time on issues shape the development of an *organizational* rather than an *individual* style for managing conflicts. Further evidence that organizations develop normative strategies for handling conflicts surfaces in the finding that members of volunteer organizations use avoidance as the primary mode for handling conflicts (Howell, 1981; Temkin & Cummings, 1985). Other context variables—for example, organizational climate (Bigoness et al., 1980), leadership style (Bernardin & Alvarez, 1976), goal agreement, open communication channels, and existence of problem-solving mechanisms (Begley, 1983)—do not affect the selection of conflict strategies.

Communication and Interpersonal Conflict Management

Differences in assessing conflict styles suggest that no one style fits all situations. Effectiveness of a particular strategy, as Phillips and Cheston (1979) found, hinges on the disputants' abilities to adapt to the situation, their fairness and objectivity in approaching the conflict, and the way in which they communicate the strategy. Successful use of a particular strategy also hinges on mutual awareness of the conflict, open-minded attitudes, willingness to ignore power issues, and existence of problem-solving procedures (Phillips & Cheston, 1979; Robbins, 1978). Executives also note that early intervention aids in conflict management—the longer the delay, the more unfavorable the conflict (Phillips & Cheston, 1979). Certain modes for handling conflict—for example, compromise and confrontation—often require continuous investment of time, energy, and emotions. Organizational members must be willing to follow through with conflict interventions and to spend the time in interpersonal communication that is necessary to reach an effective settlement (Rahim & Bonoma, 1979; Robbins, 1978).

Assessment of Communication and Interpersonal Conflict Research

Earlier in this chapter we defined conflict as the interaction of interdependent people who perceive opposition in goals, aims, and values, and who see the other party as potentially interfering with the realization of these goals. The literature on interpersonal conflict reframes this definition by concentrating on misunderstandings that *do not necessarily* reflect perceived opposition in goals, aims, or values. Although some studies focus on the causes of conflict (Phillips & Cheston, 1979; Renwick, 1975a), this work presumes an opposition of goals. Rarely do researchers check for perceptions of this opposition in autonomy and control relationships between superiors and subordinates. Hence we conclude that conflict style research has confounded misunderstandings with conflicts rooted in distribution of power and resources. Moreover, social interaction as a characteristic of conflict is relegated to perceptions and cognitions of one person rather than the actions and reactions of interdependent parties. Predispositions toward conflict become more central than do enacted behaviors.

This definition of conflict limits communication research in this area in the following ways: It (1) treats communication either as a source of disagreement or as a means of handling disputes rather than as a fundamental dimension that pervades conflict development and management, (2) reduces communication to indicators of individual predispositions rather than to message patterns that enact a conflict process, (3) treats both communication and conflict as static phenomena rather than dynamic processes, and (4) centers on the perceptions of one person rather than on the series of actions that make communication a joint production of both parties.

Research on conflict styles also incurs problems in the conceptualization of conflict style. First, a particular conflict style—forcing, for example—can be communicated in a variety of ways. That is, individuals can argue persistently, use high vocal volume, and refer to organizational position with a wide range of words, nonverbal cues, and conversational patterns (some may be more desirable than others). Thus the way in which an individual forces a decision may be more significant than the use of forcing as a strategy or dominant style.

A second problem stems from inattention to the way interaction produces a shift in the use of style strategies. Most researchers acknowledge that a dominant orientation to conflict is frequently altered once the interaction progresses. Focusing on shifts in conflict modes during a controversy may yield more insights about effective and ineffective ways of handling conflict than current efforts to uncover predispositions for a particular style.

Finally, reducing communication to misunderstandings or ambiguities oversimplifies the role of interaction in conflict situations. A more complex treatment of communication stems from applying the symbolic-interpretive perspective to an understanding of role-taking and the development of shared meanings. Thus the way individuals take the role of the other person and build a consensus on interpretations of the conflict may ultimately determine how effective each party is in managing an interpersonal dispute. These interpretations may reside in the organizational context or the system level of interaction rather than in the isolated cognitive systems of each disputant. Hence studies that incorporate intergroup and interorganizational levels of analysis may yield more insights about choice of conflict style than do studies that center exclusively on the interpersonal level.

In addition to redefining conflict and to formulating narrow conceptualizations of communication, this research incurs difficulties in measuring conflict styles. First, the five styles may not be exhaustive of all conflict management techniques. Riggs (1983) reports that managers create superordinate goals, coordinate positions, and develop other structural techniques that do not fall into the traditional five styles. Second, conflict style research typically operates in a theoretical vacuum that leads to random and sometimes arbitrary testing of actor, issue, context, and relationship variables. Thus researchers need to develop and test theoretical models for prioritizing and explaining relationships among variables in interpersonal conflict research. Although Musser (1982) and Kabanoff (1985) posit models for choice of conflict strategies, both frameworks lack empirical testing and lack theoretical grounding. Finally, conflict style research has demonstrated an overreliance on self-report surveys, ones confounded with problems in reliability, factor structure, and social desirability. Use of multiple methods, including content analyses of actual messages, interviews with respondents, case studies, and participant observation, could serve as valuable supplements to questionnaire data.

BARGAINING AND NEGOTIATION

Research on bargaining shifts the focus of conflict from styles to proposal exchanges as ways of reaching mutual agreements. Thus in one sense bargaining is the manifestation of a compromise style, but in a larger sense bargaining encompasses all five styles of conflict management (Lewicki & Litterer, 1985). Bargaining constitutes a unique form of conflict management in that participants negotiate mutually shared rules and then cooperate within these rules to gain a competitive advantage over their opponent (Schelling, 1960). Bargaining, then, differs from other forms of conflict in its emphasis on proposal exchanges as a basis for reaching a joint settlement in cooperative-competitive situations. Even though some theorists differentiate between bargaining and negotiation (Rubin & Brown, 1975), the two terms will be used interchangably in this review.

Negotiation has gained considerable appeal as both a formal and an informal fact of organizational life. As a formal activity bargaining is a recurring event aimed at settling disputes over the distribution of scarce resources, contractual relationships, and policy issues. Both parties acknowledge the process as bargaining and both agree to follow formal rules and procedures. Participants in informal bargaining, in contrast, are not overtly aware of negotiating with the other party. They may tacitly agree on the rules and practices of interaction, but they rarely formalize them (Bacharach & Lawler, 1980; Tedeschi & Rosenfeld, 1980).

Research on bargaining stems from political models of organizations that treat negotiating over multiple, frequently incongruent goals and values as important and pervasive forms of decision making (Bacharach & Lawler, 1980; Cyert & March, 1963; Pfeffer, 1981). Informal bargaining surfaces in role making, task coordination, budget allocations, protection of departmental turf, contracts with vendors and customers, and many other organizational activities. Organizational coalitions also engage in informal bargaining in their efforts to attain specific political objectives and to be protected from other interest groups (Bacharach & Lawler, 1980). Despite the pervasiveness of informal bargaining, most of the research has centered on formal negotiations. However, the theories, processes, and findings on formal bargaining may be relevant to the study of informal negotiations.

Since chapters in other publications summarize the research findings on communication and bargaining (Hawes & Smith, 1973; Johnson, 1973, 1974; Putnam, 1985a, 1985b; Putnam & Jones, 1982b; Steinfatt & Miller, 1974; Tedeschi & Rosenfeld, 1980), this review concentrates on the assumptions that underlie these studies and on the variables that affect the links between communication and negotiated outcomes. Specifically, this review examines the communication perspectives that undergird bargaining research, links between communication and related components of bargaining, communication research and third-party conflict management, and an assessment of the treatment of communication in bargaining research.

The Role of Communication in Bargaining

Research on bargaining spans four of the five communication perspectives delineated in this chapter; the majority of studies, however, embrace the psychological and mechanistic perspectives. A type of study that adopts a psychological perspective tests for the effects of bargainer orientation on message tactics and negotiated outcomes. For instance, researchers have examined cooperative versus competitive (Krauss & Deutsch, 1966; Sermat, 1970), individualistic versus problem solving (Lewis & Fry, 1977), tough versus soft (Chertkoff & Conley, 1967; Siegel & Fouraker, 1960), firm versus flexible (Walton & McKersie, 1965), and high conflict versus low conflict (Stern, Sternthal, & Craig, 1975) orientations as they influence such tactics as initial offers, patterns of concessions, commitment statements, use of threats and promises, and use of positive and negative tone of messages.

Psychological views of communication also underlie research on access to information about the opponent's intentions and relative gains (Cummings & Harnett, 1969; Lamm, 1976; Radlow & Weidner, 1966), amount of information exchanged during the bargaining (Saine, 1974), and deception in information disclosure (Crott, Kayser, & Lamm, 1980; Gruder, 1971; Lewicki, 1983). Bargaining research based on a purely mechanistic view of communication typically compares the effects of medium of communication on cooperative-competitive outcomes and on the timing of message exchanges (Morley & Stephenson, 1969, 1970; Voissem & Sistrunk, 1971). This work concentrates on the materialistic quality of message channels and on the presence or absence of explicit communication in bargaining transactions. With an emphasis on the functions of bargaining messages and the characteristics of information exchange, these studies differ from the psychological approach that underlies research on interpersonal conflict and focuses on perceptions of conflict styles.

Bargaining research that adopts a systems-interactional view, in contrast, concentrates on the reciprocity of distributive and integrative tactics (Dono-hue, 1981b; Donohue, Diez, & Hamilton, 1984; Putnam & Jones, 1982a), the escalation or deescalation of tactical maneuvers (Putnam & Jones 1982a), discourse analysis of negotiations (Donohue, 1982; Donohue, Diez, & Stahle, 1983; Weiss, 1985), question-answer sequences in information management (Donohue & Diez, 1983), and the development of bargaining phases (Bednar & Curington, 1983; Douglas, 1962; Stephenson, Kniveton, & Morley, 1977; Gulliver, 1979). These studies examine the processual and developmental nature of communication in bargaining. Other studies that adopt a developmental model from a cultural-interpretive view center on the symbolic or ritualistic function of bargaining and on the stories, myths, and language patterns that establish the historical significance of this event (Kerr, 1954; Putnam & VanHoeven, 1986; Trice & Beyer, 1984). Hence, although the psychological and mechanistic perspectives dominate research on communication and bargaining, studies that adopt developmental and processual views of communication are more prominent in bargaining than in the interpersonal conflict literature.

Links Between Communication and Components of Bargaining

Although a number of variables have shaped research on communication and negotiations, most of the literature centers on the way bargaining issues and relationships affect the use of message strategies and tactics. At the issue level this review focuses on distributive versus integrative bargaining, and at the relational level this review concentrates on bargaining power, organizational role, and negotiator-constituent relationships.

Bargaining issues. In a classic text on bargaining, Walton and McKersie (1965) draw upon Mary Parker Follett's (1941) distinction between compromise and integration to set forth the concepts "distributive" and "integrative" bargaining. In their view, the two types of bargaining exhibit different goals, issues, communication processes, and outcomes. This review focuses on the way assumptions of distributive and integrative bargaining guide research on communication processes. The goal of distributive bargaining is to maximize individual gains and minimize losses while the aim of integrative bargaining is to maximize joint gains. Distributive negotiations center on fixed-sum issues (such as wages, hours, and distribution of limited resources) characterized by mutually exclusive positions and by an inherent conflict of interest between the two sides. Integrative bargaining, in turn, focuses on variable-sum problems (such as rights and obligations) shaped by overlapping interests and flexible initial positions. Both the goals and the perceptions of issues, however, change during the negotiation process (Walton & McKersie, 1965); hence the classification of an issue as distributive and integrative becomes an empirical question.

Bargaining outcomes are also classified as distributive and integrative. Settlements characterized by compromises, trade-offs, and win-lose results fall into the distributive realm whereas creative proposals that cannot be traced back to specific bargaining concessions are treated as integrative settlements (Pruitt, 1983; Pruitt & Lewis, 1977; Walton & McKersie, 1965). Distributive and integrative bargaining are also distinguished by their communicative processes; that is, the techniques for fostering one are believed to work against the development of the other (Pruitt, 1981; Walton & McKersie, 1965). Assumptions underlying distributive and integrative bargaining guide the research on information exchange, negotiation strategies and tactics, issue development, and phase analysis.

The goals of distributive and integrative bargaining impact on information seeking, withholding of data, and deception in making disclosures. In distributive bargaining, negotiators typically aim to keep their opponents from gaining accurate information about their own position while they learn as much as possible about the other party's resistance point (the point at which the bargainer cannot back down any further). Hence bargainers often simultaneously withhold or screen information while they misrepresent or even exaggerate the disclosures they make (Lewicki & Litterer, 1985). Bargainers typically withhold information about the strength of their position, their ultimate preferences, and the values attached to these preferences (Rubin & Brown, 1975). This information is usually gleaned through inferences made about bargaining moves (Lewicki & Litterer, 1985) or through subtle, indirect disclosures made in gradual increments (Daniels, 1967; Pilisuk & Skolnick, 1968). Use of questions rather than imperative demands for information obligates the opponent to reveal data through a series of questions followed by abrupt responses that expand on the topic (Donohue & Diez, 1983).

Direct disclosures of information in distributive bargaining generally obscure a negotiator's true objectives, distort the meaning of messages, reduce options, or manipulate perceptions of costs (Lewicki, 1983). Negotiators disguise their "true" objectives by leading the opponent to draw incorrect conclusions about their resistance point. If a bargainer views his or her opponent as an enemy, he or she is likely to make deceptive arguments, bargain for longer periods, and make fewer concessions (Gruder, 1971). Also, bargainers may distort the meaning of their disclosures by exaggerating their emotional states, by couching messages in coded language systems, and by using incongruent verbal and nonverbal cues (Johnson, McCarty, & Allen, 1976; Lewicki & Litterer, 1985). They may reduce options and manipulate perceived costs through the use of bluffs, exaggerated demands, and threats (Chertkoff & Baird, 1971; Lewicki, 1983). Even though bluffing may increase a bargainer's competitive edge, it may embarrass the opponent and can have a negative impact on the final settlement (Lewicki, 1983). Bluffing can also exacerbate a conflict, particularly when bargaining centers on value issues (Lewis & Pruitt, 1971; Pruitt & Lewis, 1975). The use of face-to-face oral communication between bargainers, however, appears to decrease frequent use of bluffs (Crott et al., 1980).

In contrast, integrative bargaining employs maximum sharing of information and open, accurate disclosure of negotiator's needs and objectives (Walton & McKersie, 1965). Information serves as fact-finding aimed at redefining problems, exploring causes, and generating alternative solutions that meet the goals of both parties (Lewicki & Litterer, 1985). Negotiators drop their defensive barriers and listen to comprehend their opponents' affective and substantive meanings. Bargaining teams use multiple formal and informal channels of communication rather than relying solely on the chief spokesperson for each side (Lewicki & Litterer, 1985; Walton & McKersie, 1965).

The frequency, clustering, and sequencing of bargaining strategies and tactics also distinguish distributive from integrative negotiations. A strategy refers to a broad plan that encompasses a series of moves while tactics are the specific messages that operationalize the strategies (Putnam & Jones, 1982b; Wall, 1985). For example, tough bargaining is a strategy that uses extreme opening bids, few concessions, and firmly worded commitments as tactics to implement this plan (Siegel & Fouraker, 1960). Studies that code actual bargaining talk center on the frequency, clustering, and sequencing of integrative and distributive tactics (see, for example, Hopmann & Walcott, 1976; Lewis & Fry, 1977; Morley & Stephenson, 1977; Zechmeister & Druckman, 1973). For example, bargainers with integrative strategies elicit more reactions from their opponents, make more offers after a settlement is imminent, initiate more alternative solutions, use more soft that hard tactics, and make more references to self and the opponent rather than to party identity (Putnam & Jones, 1982b, p. 174).

Factor analysis of bargaining tactics also suggest ways of classifying tactics. For instance, use of acceptance statements, other-supporting arguments, and exploratory problem-solving messages typify integrative strategies (Putnam & Jones, 1982a) while the use of threats, putdowns, irrelevant arguments, commitments, demands, and charge fault statements are linked to distributive maneuvers (Putnam & Jones, 1982b; Walton & McKersie, 1965). Distributive tactics also cluster into offensive and defensive moves with the use of attacking arguments, rejections, requesting information, and threats aligning with offensive behaviors and the use of self-supporting arguments, demands, retractions, and commitments representing defensive messages (Donohue, 1981a, 1981b; Putnam & Jones, 1982a).

Another approach to the study of integrative and distributive strategies centers on conflict spirals, the degree to which conflict escalates into a destructive cycle out of the control of either party (Blake & Mouton, 1964; Folger & Poole, 1984; Thomas, 1976). This research, similar to the work on competitive and cooperative sequences in matrix games (Rubin & Brown, 1975; Wilson, 1969), examines sequential messages to identify patterns that recur over time. Negotiators in distributive bargaining appear to offset the development of destructive cycles by countering offensive with defensive tactics or by balancing offensive tactics with integrative responses (Donohue, 1981b; Donohue et al., 1984; Putnam & Jones, 1982a). However, when negotiators begin to match tactics, in an offensive-offensive or defensive-defensive pattern, message patterns become tightly structured leading to an escalating conflict that frequently results in impasse (Donohue et al., 1984; Putnam & Jones, 1982a). For example, matching a threat with a counterthreat and a commitment with an equally firm stance often leads to a "lock in" pattern in which both parties freeze into their respective positions (Rubin & Brown, 1975; Walton & McKersie, 1965).

Distributive and integrative processes also differ in issue development and argumentation processes. Distributive issues develop through the addition of facts and the accentuation of positions, while integrative items evolve from separating and establishing priorities among subissues to redefine and clarify the problem (Putnam & Bullis, 1984). As negotiators drop agenda items, simplify subissues, and build packages of items, bargainers initiate creative proposals (Gulliver, 1979). The creation of new proposals is facilitated by changing the type of claim initially argued and by adding qualifiers to proposals rather than by providing additional evidence to support an initial position (Putnam & Geist, 1985). Analysis of arguments for and against proposals also suggests that disagreements over the definition and the causes of a bargaining issue generate frequent use of harm and workability statements (Putnam & Wilson, in press). Making harm and workability arguments, in turn, leads to a longer search process that results in developing creative solutions (Putnam, Wilson, Waltman, & Turner, 1986). Thus integrative solutions emerge only after differences in perceptions of the problem are openly discussed (Walton & McKersie, 1965).

Issue development through the exchange of distributive and integrative tactics also has an impact on bargaining phases, that is, on the evolution of negotiations over time. In naturalistic negotiations it is often difficult to separate distributive from integrative bargaining; hence mixed bargaining may be more commonplace than pure forms of either type (Walton & McKersie, 1965). Since it may be difficult for negotiators to shift back and forth from distributive to integrative orientations, phase analyses of bargaining sessions seek to understand how integrative solutions emerge from distributive orientations (Walton & McKersie, 1965). Phase analysis breaks bargaining sessions into "recognizable, sequential periods marked by different behaviors and sequences of behaviors" (Folger & Poole, 1984, p. 20). Although research differs as to whether bargaining falls into three (Bednar & Curington, 1983; Douglas, 1957; Morley & Stephenson, 1977), eight (Gulliver, 1979), or five phases (Carlisle & Leary, 1981), negotiation moves from a high conflict, distributive stage to a narrowing of differences and a search for an acceptable bargaining range. As the negotiation progresses, bargainers also reduce their use of attacking arguments and their references to party affiliation and increase their use of self- and other-supporting statements (Douglas, 1962; Morley & Stephenson, 1977). Thus although negotiations may cycle back and forth through stages or may develop at different rates, bargaining interaction appears to evolve from posturing and firm stances on initial positions, to exploring alternatives, and to creating a formula for a mutually satisfactory solution. "Movement, orderly and progressive in nature, stands out as a staid property of a collective-bargaining situation which terminates in agreement" (Douglas, 1957, p. 70).

Bargaining relationship. Integrative and distributive bargaining, whether treated as separate orientations or viewed as processes that emerge over time, are intrinsically tied to power relationships between bargainers and to negotiator-constituent relationships. This review treats power as a social relationship determined by the other party's dependence on the bargainer and his or her constituents (Bacharach & Lawler, 1980). Communication plays a central role in the management of impressions used to define each party's dependence (Bacharach & Lawler, 1981). Mutual dependence reduces the use of tough, distributive tactics, especially in conditions of formal bargaining with explicit lines of communication, restricted time limits, and increased information sharing (Bacharach & Lawler, 1980).

Since power is composed of both positional authority and influence, a bargainer's role and his or her relationship with constituents also affects communication processes. Researchers have examined the effects of role imbalance, reward structure, and persuasive ability on such variables as communication frequency, use of threats, and size of concessions (see, for example, Bonoma, 1976; Donohue, 1978; Leusch, 1976; Tedeschi & Bonoma,

1977; Tjosvold, 1974; Wall, 1977b). Bargainer role is frequently linked to organizational position. Labor and management appear to specialize in their use of bargaining tactics with labor assuming the offensive role and management taking the defensive position. Specifically, labor negotiators use more threats, rejections, initiations, requests, attack sequences, and assertive responses than do management bargainers. Management, in turn, aims to protect the status quo through the use of commitments, self-supporting arguments, statistical facts and examples, and high confidence statements (Donohue et al., 1984; Haire, 1955; Morley & Stephenson, 1977; Putnam & Jones, 1982a).

In most instances, however, bargainers function as representatives of constituent groups; hence a negotiator's role is shaped in large measure by the visibility, trust, accountability, and formality of his or her constituent relationships. Bargainers who are under close surveillance, asked to defend and justify their behaviors, and governed by highly formalized rules typically increases their toughness, reduces their search for alternatives, reduces perspective taking, and inhibits communication with their opponent (Bacharach & Lawler, 1980; Carnevale, Pruitt, & Britton, 1979; Rubin & Brown, 1975; Wall, 1977a). Negotiators, then, act as boundary-role spanners who experience considerable role conflict in linking organizational interfaces (Adams, 1976). This boundary role function, however, is not necessarily reactive. Negotiators can play an active role in managing their constituents through tacit communication that capitalizes on language differences between the sides, information control, positive impression management, and shaping interpretations of the bargaining process (Walton & McKersie, 1965).

Actor attributes. Although a number of studies link personality traits to cooperative-competitive bargaining (Rubin & Brown, 1975), only a few studies focus on the impact of actor characteristics on communication processes. These studies identify perspective-taking, credibility, and face-saving abilities as attributes that enhance bargaining effectiveness. Perspective-taking is "the ability to adopt the opponent's viewpoint in structuring bargaining strategies" (Neale & Bazerman, 1983, p. 380). Negotiators with high perspective-taking abilities experience greater success, elicit more concessions, and express greater understanding of the values and expectations of their opponents than do bargainers with low perspective-taking skills (Neale & Bazerman, 1983).

Credibility, in turn, refers to the image or reputation of the bargainer as attained through his or her expertise and reliability in past negotiations (Tedeschi & Rosenfeld, 1980). Credibility increases with past successes in winning concessions for one's team. Successful as opposed to unsuccessful bargainers exhibit a higher degree of information recall from previous sessions (Donohue, 1978; Reiches & Harral, 1974); more vocal excitement (Donohue, 1978); more questioning behavior (Carlisle & Leary, 1981); a stronger tendency to avoid conflict spirals (Carlisle & Leary, 1981); greater frequency of topic changes, rejections, and charge fault statements (Donohue, 1981a, 1981b); and more diversity in arguments (Donohue, 1981a, 1981b). Also, negotiators with high credibility enhance the believability of threats, commitments, and promises (Schlenker, Helm, & Tedeschi, 1973). Face-saving is a means of protecting a credible image or avoiding a weak one (Brown, 1977). To protect an image of strength, bargainers have employed disclaimers, hedging, vague language, omissions, and bluffing. To regain lost strength and to respond to past threats, they have relied on retractions, modifications of erroneous information, qualifiers, and warnings (Borah, 1963; Brown, 1968).

Context variables. Unlike actor attributes, context has not been a dominant variable in bargaining and communication research. Kochan (1980) points out the need to consider the economic, social, and political environment in which negotiations occur as well as the history of labor-management relations. These contextual features frame the bargaining activity and influence motivation levels of participants. They also account for the significant role that audiences and publics play in obtaining settlements. The history of bargaining relationships often shapes the integrative or distributive nature of negotiator orientations. Expectations of conflict-laden relationships establish predispositions that can perpetuate defensive, win-lose bargaining (Lewicki & Litterer, 1985). History also sanctions normative rules and procedures. Normative rules function as moral obligations that potentially limit the range of tactics and type of communication deemed acceptable in the bargaining (Thomas, 1976). Informality and the use of unwritten rules increases flexibility and reduces reliance on precedence (McKersie, 1964). History in the form of stories, myths, and rituals also serves as a means of defining acceptable behaviors and a way of unifying opposing sides against an outside enemy (Putnam & Van Hoeven, 1986).

COMMUNICATION AND THIRD-PARTY CONFLICT MANAGEMENT

Mediation and arbitration extend or elaborate on the negotiation process through the intervention of impartial third parties (Moore, 1986). In mediation a third party assists the disputants in reaching a settlement but he or she has no decision power, whereas in arbitration the third party makes formal decisions based on proposals and supporting evidence generated in the bargaining sessions. Although both processes rely on communication to manage information and exert social influence, mediation is a type of facilitation that hinges almost exclusively on communication for its success (Douglas, 1962).

Research that focuses on the communication patterns of mediators, however, is quite sparse. This review draws from texts, surveys, and naturalistic studies of mediation that concentrate on the mediator's role in regulating communication between the sides. Mediator tactics can be categorized into directive, nondirective, procedural, and reflexive techniques (Carnevale & Pegnetter, 1985; Hilltrop, 1985). Directive or substantive tactics place the mediator in the role of initiating recommendations for proposals, giving opinions about positions, assessing costs of a demand, synchronizing concessions, and inducing compliance (Kolb, 1983b). These tactics are more effective in the latter stages of mediation than in early sessions (Hilltrop, 1985).

Nondirective tactics capitalize on the mediator's role in securing information for the parties and in clarifying misunderstandings. In controlling information flow, the mediator can function as a conduit that passes information between the sides, as a surrogate that adds justifications for positions, as an embellisher who alters or accents information, and as a clarifier who answers questions for each side (Kolb, 1983b). Mediators exercise these tactics by paraphrasing messages, narrowing topics of discussion, and reducing unnecessary repetition of arguments (Douglas, 1962; Wall, 1981). Procedural tactics entail organizing separate or joint sessions, establishing protocol for the sessions, regulating the agenda, and setting timetables and deadlines for specific agreements (Wall, 1981). Finally, reflexive tactics regulate the affective tone of the mediation by developing rapport with participants, using humor, and speaking the language of each side.

Mediators report that reflexive tactics may be more effective than directive and nondirective ones in facilitating joint collaboration between the sides (Carnevale & Pegnetter, 1985). But a comparison of mediators who succeeded in getting settlements and those who failed suggests that directive tactics, including the use of mediator interruptions to reframe arguments, to create alternatives, and to develop new interpretations of proposals, are vital to a mediator's success (Donohue, Allen, & Burrell, in press; Kolb, 1983a).

Mediators indicate that they use directive, nondirective, and reflexive tactics in equal proportion with both labor and management teams (Carnevale & Pegnetter, 1985). Mediators, however, use the reflexive tactic of "helping blow off steam" more frequently with the union and the nondirective tactic of "clarifying the needs of opponents" more frequently with management than with the union (Carnevale & Pegnetter, 1985). This summary of research findings on mediation tactics reaffirms the centrality of communication in the mediation process. Mediators, as Kolb (1985) recognizes, are like the directors of a drama, who set the scene, manage impressions, orchestrate the script, and maintain dramatic inquiry throughout the process.

Assessment of Communication and
Bargaining Research

Unlike research on conflict styles, the work on communication and bargaining for the most part holds consistently to the definition of conflict presented in this chapter. This research focuses on a formal event in which the opposition of goals and values is pursued; it stresses interdependence between disputants, and highlights social interaction as the essence of conflict enactment and management.

Although the psychological perspective of communication also dominates research in this arena, the dependent variables—for example, information distortion, message functions in bargaining, issue and stage development— are directly tied to communication; hence message effects rather than perceived behaviors constitute the primary indice of communication. Moreover, a growing number of studies examine sequential patterns of messages, thus moving communication and bargaining research into the systems-interaction perspective.

Despite these strengths, bargaining research, and particularly studies on information exchange and message strategies and tactics, often employ static models of communication and global analyses of message categories. For example, research on information withholding and deception often examines one bargainer in a highly controlled situation. Information centers on knowledge of intentions and payoffs rather than on values and attitudes that might alter a bargainer's stance. In addition, categories of bargaining tactics frequently group message behaviors into global functions. The category of exploratory problem solving, for instance, encompasses a wide range of search activities and ways of generating alternative proposals. Global categories, in turn, offer minimal insights as to how creative problem solving actually occurs. To rectify this problem, researchers need to center on the wording and content of bargaining tactics, as has been done in work on types of threats.

Also, communicative statements do not fit neatly into discrete categories of integrative and distributive bargaining. Since messages perform multiple functions through a variety of verbal and nonverbal cues, a given utterance may serve both distributive and integrative goals simultaneously. For example, commitments can be worded in vague, ambiguous ways conveyed through firm yet friendly vocal overtones and simultaneously signal firmness and flexibility (Lewicki & Litterer, 1985). Adopting the view that messages serve a variety of functions that can fulfill contradictory goals might yield more insights about bargaining interaction than does a reliance on discrete, dichotomous categories.

Message analysis also needs to be integrated with cognitive processes of bargainers, namely, with the way preferences and expectations change as a result of bargaining interaction (Gulliver, 1979). More research is needed on the way negotiators and team members make interpretations about their opponent's messages and about the bargaining activities. Finally, research on communication and bargaining has concentrated too narrowly on micro-analyses of bargaining interaction. Few studies have attempted to integrate such contextual features as bargaining laws, organizational structures, and economic factors into investigations of information processing, message tactics, and bargaining phase development (Putnam, 1985a).

INTERGROUP CONFLICT

Unlike research on interpersonal conflict and bargaining, the study of intergroup conflict centers on aggregates rather than individuals. Although bargaining research treats constituents as groups, this work focuses primarily on the bargainer-constituent relationship rather than on interactions between opposing groups. Intergroup conflict, in contrast, tends to reify groups or organizational units, treating them as homogeneous entities. This practice, however, ignores the fact that group members are independent actors. Often, groups have a multiplicity of views about conflict and express multiple, even contradictory, messages. One key question in intergroup conflict, then, is how groups become and remain homogeneous in order to present a coherent voice and to engage in unified action. Communication is critical to the process of building coherence and maintaining homogeneous groups.

The Role of Communication in
Intergroup Conflict

A combination of the mechanistic and the psychological perspectives dominates research on intergroup conflict. Studies of the effects of intergroup conflict on the organization as a whole typically reflect a mechanistic view. This research relates the emergence and intensity of conflict to such aspects of organizational structures as complexity, size, and unit interdependence. Centering on these global, almost distant and abstract characteristics aligns this arena with mechanistic information transmission. Analyses of interaction and meaning, in turn, require a closer focus than has emerged in the intergroup research. Conflict in the intergroup arena results from communication barriers and breakdowns in networks linked to organizational structures. Since communication channels can be used to unify group members against other groups, blockage of the channel is both the cause and the effect of intergroup polarization.

The psychological perspective supplements this mechanistic analysis by examining micro-level influences on communication. For example, complex, multilevel salary grades at the organizational level represent an extension of micro-level interpersonal conflict at the intergroup level. This psychological view of communication operates from the following assumptions of intergroup conflict: (1) Opposing groups have divergent images or perceptions of each other's needs, beliefs, and intentions—differences created and maintained by communication; (2) these divergent images unite groups against one another through negative evaluations of the opposing group and through assumptions that the opposition wishes them ill; (3) polarization causes groups to break off communication, thereby reaffirming polarization and divergent images.

Psychological images also act as perceptual filters that distort communication by creating barriers, misunderstandings, and misinterpretations of the other group's desires and beliefs. By focusing on perceptions and images, the research on intergroup conflict has generally ignored the interaction and the symbolic processes exchanged between groups. Hence past research has yielded insights on the inputs and outcomes of intergroup interaction but has added only a modicum to our understanding of the conflict process itself. Participant observation studies of intergroup conflicts, such as Gouldner's (1954) *Wildcat Strike,* Dalton's (1959b) *Men Who Manage,* and Burawoy's (1979) *Manufacturing Consent,* however, represent notable exceptions to this claim.

Links Between Communication and Components of Intergroup Conflict

Context and relationship emerge as the more dominant components in research on intergroup conflict. The lack of attention to actor characteristics in this arena is surprising given the psychological bent of most intergroup conflict theories. However, since researchers typically cast *the group* rather than the individual as the primary actor, individuals represent stereotypes or coordinated components of generally solid phalanxes.

Context. The larger organization itself, as embodied in such global structural variables as complexity, unit interdependence, and status differences, serves as the primary contextual determinant of intergroup conflict. The effects of complexity and unit interdependence on intergroup conflict are intertwined. Complexity, defined as the number of different units or specialties in the organization, has a positive relationship with level of conflict and with the number of different issues (Corwin, 1969; Hage, 1974; Thomas, 1976). As complexity increases, communication networks fragment and lead to different perspectives within units. If this condition is combined with high interdependence, conflict between units increases (Corwin, 1969; Lawrence & Lorsch, 1967; Putnam & Wilson, 1982; Thomas, 1976; Walton & Dutton, 1969; White, 1961; Zald, 1962). Matrix organizations, in contrast, are characterized by permanent and pervasive lateral conflicts; hence they are designed to carry high communication loads that aid in managing conflicts caused by complex tasks and turbulent environments (Galbraith, 1971; Mintzberg, 1979).

Complex and stabilized organizational structures also favor the use of forcing to manage interdepartmental conflict, primarily as a way of convincing those who hold different viewpoints to accept the other party's preferences (Putnam & Wilson, 1982). The use of forcing, in turn, can exacerbate conflict;

considerable energy must be expended to get participants to use problem solving rather than forcing (Delbecq & Filley, 1974; Galbraith, 1971; Stein & Kanter, 1980). This energy, in the form of high interaction rates, encourages open expression of conflict, therefore making disputes less severe. For example, Corwin's (1969) study of a school system indicates that more conflicts, but less intense ones, emerge in systems with higher levels of interaction. A correlate of complexity—dispersion of facilities—also relates to intergroup conflict. For example, physical barriers, such as walls between units or a two-hour drive between facilities, may cause communication breakdowns and prevent the resolution of problems (Dalton, 1959a; Sebring 1977; Walton & Dutton, 1969). When problems occur under these conditions, interaction tends to escalate a conflict.

Other factors that affect communication and intergroup conflict are status differences among units. Research suggests that the greater the status differences, the more interunit conflict (Dalton, 1959a; Walton & Dutton, 1969; Zald, 1962). In an effort to gain control over their own destinies, organizational units increase their concern for equity in the distribution of resources and rewards (Zald, 1981). Among workers a comparison of such rewards as wages and hours can become a symbolic root of conflict among units (Whyte, 1955). Impending changes in resource allocations or power structures can also foment conflict, as units attempt to benefit from these changes (Dalton, 1959b). For example, "destabilizing" incidents, such as the departure of an executive or a financial crisis, often trigger struggles over the redistribution of power (Gouldner, 1954; Hage, 1974).

Just as structure influences conflict interaction, conflict can restructure the organization. Conflict occasions shifts in the relative status or power of groups, changes in alliances, and alterations in formal structure. Hage (1974) characterizes conflict as a "deviation-amplifying process" that increases communication and causes an organization to change in an effort to regain stability. He documents how a conflict about an innovation program in a medical organization facilitates a shift from a mechanistic to an organic structure. Moreover, attempts to regulate conflict among professional groups can lead to greater specialization between organizational units (Ritti & Gouldner, 1969).

Intergroup relationships. Intergroup relationships are the "interfaces between two systems" (Brown, 1983). Interfaces differ in the degree of their organization. Tightly organized interfaces exhibit well-defined group boundaries and communication channels; intergroup relationships are rigidly defined; communication is closed; and differences between units "produce suppression or harmonizing that prevent exploration of issues or constructive conflict [management]" (Brown, 1983, p. 30). In contrast, at loosely organized interfaces group boundaries are open; relationships are more fluid and less hierarchical; and communication is open. Conflict at these interfaces leads to withdrawal or to escalation that threatens survival of the ties between groups (Brown, 1983). Given these two extremes, Brown advocates an intermediate level of connectivity between units.

The degree of organization among units may hinge on the type of lateral relationship between each of them. Consistent with the literature on bargaining, units who see their relationship as competitive or *distributive* exhibit selective misrepresentation, withholding information, commitment to position, and use of threats in interactions between groups (Walton, Dutton, & Cafferty, 1969; Walton, Dutton, & Fitch, 1966). These patterns, which often become rigidly circumscribed and formalized, foster negative attitudes, suspicion, and disassociation between groups, even when they lead to effective agreements. In contrast, units who see their relationship as cooperative or *integrative* employ problem solving, informality, openness, and flexibility in intergroup communication. These patterns facilitate more positive and trusting intergroup attitudes than do distributive patterns.

Distributive patterns often lead to relational deterioration through negative responses to intergroup competition, including (1) an increase in expression of loyalty toward the group; (2) discourse slanted in favor of ingroup positions and demeaning of outgroup positions; (3) minimization of intergroup agreements and exaggeration of differences; (4) a lack of understanding of outgroup positions; and (5) charges of disloyalty if group members see validity in the outgroup's position (Blake et al., 1964).

Issue definition. Distributive and integrative relationships often overlap with the way issues become defined in intergroup conflict. Participant observation studies provide valuable insights on issue definition in intergroup conflicts (see, for example, Dalton, 1959b; Gouldner, 1954). Consistent with issue development in bargaining, issues are redefined throughout intergroup interaction. Indeed, controlling the final definition of an issue is one route to power within and between groups (Bachrach & Baratz, 1962; Lukes, 1974). Distinctions exist, however, between issues defined *within* a group and those that emerge *between* conflicting groups.

The definitions of issues within a group are rarely divulged, for fear that openness would give the other group an advantage (Dalton, 1959b). But within-group issue definition can exert an impact on intergroup behavior. For example, Gouldner (1954) notes how management's privately held definition of a workers' wildcat strike escalated conflict between management and labor. Management defined the strikes as an attempt to seize control of the firm while the workers defined them as a reaction to unfair labor policies.

Issues that are defined openly between groups are the terrain on which the conflict takes place. Issue definition, as noted in the section on bargaining, often functions as a bargaining tactic. As a result, issues are often transformed by moving them from private to public domains. Rather than divulge motives and intentions that could be viewed as self-serving, groups define issues in ways that sanction their legitimacy. For example, issues linked to economic transactions, such as contracts, hiring, and plant operations, might be regarded as legitimate whereas ones based on labor rights or rights by custom might be viewed as illegitimate (Gouldner, 1954). Hence groups typically express legitimate issues and reframe other demands in light of these legitimate ones. Another tactic used in issue definition is to ignore the other group's expression of issues or to rephrase their issues in ways consistent with your own. Gouldner (1954) reports that because management was afraid of losing status, they ignored items raised by the union; the union acceded to this avoidance strategy by dropping issues. Each side persistently redefined the other party's claims.

Intergroup Conflict Management

Researchers have approached the management of intergroup conflict through the use of structural and process interventions. A good intervention prevails if the solution is both efficient (reasonable amount of time spent on a resolution) and high in quality (actually solves the problem; Brett & Rognes, 1986). Structural interventions realign organizational structures and formally reallocate resources. One common strategy is to develop formal rules that regulate intergroup relations, constrain communication networks, limit strategies and tactics, and impose process guidelines. Increased formalization, however, can inadvertently upset stable networks, create more conflict (Dalton, 1959b), and allow both sides to manipulate rules for their own ends (Crozier, 1964). A second structural intervention is the use of departments or positions to manage intergroup relations (Lawrence & Lorsch, 1967; Walton & Dutton, 1969). Individuals in these positions, however, must have good communication skills (Brett & Rognes, 1986) and they must sometimes suppress conflict in order to appear to be successfully managing it (Dalton, 1959a).

Process interventions, in contrast, redirect conflict behavior and reframe the participant's perspectives. Since other theorists discuss this approach (Blake et al., 1964; Brett & Rognes, 1986; Brown, 1983), we present only a brief summary of this work. Two generic strategies underlie these interventions: either eliminating group boundaries or recognizing the boundaries and working around them. Blake et al. (1964) argue that the second approach is much easier, but they stress that a "mental reorientation" is necessary to avoid problems that stem from group differentiation.

The most widely known process intervention is the use of superordinate goals to unify opposing groups. Much of the early research on superordinate goals (Sherif, Harvey, White, Hood, & Sherif, 1961; Wehr, 1979) confounds goal introduction with conflict removal. Thus superordinate goals appear to reduce perceived but not underlying conflict (Hunger & Stern, 1976). Other researchers question the value of this intervention and claim that unless groups develop a culture for understanding one another and a different set of communication patterns, superordinate goals are not likely to work (Billig, 1976; Blake et al., 1964; Deschamps & Brown, 1983).

Assessment of Intergroup Conflict Research

Four general problems characterize the research on intergroup conflict in organizations. First, most of the research centers on perceptions and outputs of communication, with little attention to communication. Psychological dynamics and "concrete" structural characteristics become the major determinants of intergroup conflict. Studies often center on attribution processes and ignore the communication patterns that lead to these attributions. With research that adopts a mechanistic view, communication becomes a channel for other forces or a property of the network, such as density or rate of interaction. Message effects, fidelity, and intergroup interaction are rarely examined as discrete variables. Exceptions to this claim are the participant observation studies that provide a wealth of detail about interaction processes but draw very few explicit conclusions about communication; the reader must extrapolate propositions about intergroup interaction from these reports.

A second problem with this research is a tendency to treat groups as univocal, as if they were analogous to individuals. Although it is certainly true that group members often act in concert, sometimes there are differences between members and divisions in a group. In the latter case, a "group" is less an entity and more a collection of individuals, each of whom should be considered in the analysis of intergroup conflict (Campbell, 1958). To avoid simplifying groups, researchers need to assess how organizational members define groups and how group boundaries occur. Third, current studies have no way to determine which groups will oppose one another. An adequate theory of intergroup conflict must explain which groups will develop into conflict and on what grounds (Billig, 1976). Fourth, intergroup conflict research has not dealt with the relationship between the interpersonal, the intergroup, and the cultural-institutional levels. Interpersonal interaction constitutes the vehicle for much of intergroup conflict while the cultural and institutional environment establishes general assumptions and terms of discourse for intergroup moves.

A focus on communication can aid in addressing these criticisms. Communication is valuable in creating and maintaining homogeneity amidst pressures for divergence, in defining the opposition and issues through an elaboration of shared beliefs, in unifying groups, and in shaping relationships at different social levels. In addition to these functions, communication underlies three interlocking processes that are fundamental to the development of intergroup conflict: social categorization, group differentiation, and group ideologies (Folger & Poole, 1984).

These three processes in conjunction with communication also mediate the creation and maintenance of group homogeneity, the definition of opposing groups and issues, the unification of groups, and the shaping of interpersonal and cultural-institutional levels. Social categorization relates to both the development and the solidifying of a group. Organizations are divided into a number of social categories, including male-female, old-young, veteran-newcomer, labor-management, staff-line, educated-uneducated, exempt-nonexempt, union-nonunion, and types of departments. Research on social categorization details the processes by which groups become salient (Billig, 1976; Doise, 1978; Tajfel, 1980). Sources of categories include general societal divisions (race, gender, class), organizational structures and processes (division of labor, incentive systems), and informal communication and negotiation (clique development). Communication is instrumental in determining which sources develop into which social categories that lead to intergroup conflict.

Group differentiation refers to the polarization and stereotyping of the opposition. Differentiation processes realize the potential of symbolic social categories to stimulate conflict. Research summarized above has explored the communicative dynamics underlying the group polarization and stereotyping of the opposition that characterize group differentiation (Coser, 1956; Blake et al., 1964; Janis, 1972; Deutsch, 1973). Group differentiations and oppositions, in turn, are rationalized through the development of group ideologies (Billig, 1976). The term *ideology* refers to the beliefs a group holds about the "structure of action" in the social system and about itself and other groups. An ideology organizes a group's relationship to other groups, influences whether conflicts develop or not, and determines why groups choose the enemies that they do. To the extent that all members hold the same ideology, a group will be more likely to act as a unit. General social climate, organizational structure, and interaction between units influence the development of ideologies through communication processes that are amenable to the dominant groups. In their role as opinion leaders and controllers of group structure, dominant groups may shape the organization's ideologies in ways advantageous to them. For example, the existence of multilevel salary grades redirects labor-management conflicts laterally, so workers compete with one another for raises (Burawoy, 1979; Edwards, 1979; Kanter, 1977; Whyte, 1955).

In considering processes of ideological development in concert with group categorization and differentiation, it is necessary to go beyond mechanistic and psychological views of communication to symbolic and critical analyses. Incorporating these concerns would substantially enhance theories of intergroup conflict. The three processes—categorization, differentiation, and ideological development—mediate many of the effects mentioned above. For example, a large part of the influence of contextual features such as interdependence, complexity, and communication barriers comes from their effects on group differentiation and ideology. For example, the redefinition of issues into legitimate terms is strongly influenced by ideologies. Critical analyses show how issue development is constrained by "hidden faces of power," which determine which issues are open for debate (Bachrach & Baratz, 1962; Lukes, 1974). Since the dominant ideology is typically taken for granted, it sets the limits of discourse for all organizational members. By determining what can be discussed, an ideology limits the issues that can be formulated or even imagined (Burawoy, 1979; Clegg, 1975; Edwards, 1979; Gouldner, 1954). A critical perspective in conjunction with an emphasis on the symbolic aspects of communication could uncover how the "hidden faces of power" control the legitimacy of issues for intergroup conflicts.

INTERORGANIZATIONAL CONFLICT

Many of the same dynamics that operate in intergroup conflict also have an impact on interorganizational conflict. Specifically, the role of structure in shaping and being shaped by conflict interaction, the importance of tightly and loosely connected linkages, and the effects of within-group issue definition on between-group controversies also apply to interorganizational conflict. However, unlike intergroup conflict, the institutional environment in interorganizational conflict assumes a significant role since it is the arena in which conflict is played out (Van de Ven, Emmett, & Koenig, 1980). Moreover, conflict, in turn, can reshape the relationships that make up the institutional environment (Assael, 1969).

The Role of Communication in
Interorganizational Conflict

Studies of interorganizational conflict typically adopt either a mechanistic or a critical perspective of communication. Since these studies rarely examine communication directly, interaction is embedded within interorganizational relationships. Conflict between organizations occurs primarily in the market-place, where organizations attempt to carve out and maintain "niches" or domains. Within these markets legal and contractual structures govern interorganizational interaction. Public and private agencies typically act as "linking pins" to mediate these organizational networks. This use of interaction networks to model organizational linkages and market transactions exemplifies the mechanistic view of communication. Studies that adopt the critical-symbolic view, in contrast, center on the way discourse functions in legal and contractual structures and the way hidden faces of power affect institutional environments.

Mechanistic and critical views of communication also function differently within interorganizational theories. Four different models of interorganizational relationships emerge in the literature: social exchange (Levine & White, 1961; Marrett, 1971; White, Levine, & Vlasak, 1980), organizational relationships as a holistic system (Gray, 1985; Gray & Hay, 1986), organizational relationships as networks that center on links between focal organizations and their organization sets (Aldrich, 1971; Aldrich & Whetten, 1981; Evan, 1966; Hirsch, 1972), and interorganizational relationships as political economies (Benson, 1975; Zald, 1981). The first three theoretical perspectives tend to embrace a more mechanistic view of communication while the latter approach relies on critical-symbolic notions of communication.

Links Between Communication and Components of Interorganizational Conflict

Only two of the four components of conflict emerge as significant in research on interorganizational conflict: *context* and *relationships*. Since the predominant element of context is the relationship among members of an organizational set, these two components will be discussed together. Interorganizational interaction, as noted above, occurs in the context of markets in which organizations that are typically in competition for scarce resources must coordinate and control an uncertain environment (Molnar & Rogers, 1979). Hence the structures and processes that organize market transaction influence the creation and monitoring of interorganizational conflict (Chatov, 1981). For example, governmental regulations both reveal and monitor conflict networks. The existence of legal codes that help ensure a resolution that protects all parties, such as the Antitrust Act, bring out conflicts that powerful organizations might have otherwise squelched. The process of negotiating ideologies also regulates conflict networks. For instance, the development of common institutionalized "interpretive schemes" among antipoverty organizations with high conflict potential enabled institutions to act in concert, stake out exclusive domains, pressure deviant organizations back in line, and generally avoid conflict (Warren, Rose, & Bergunder, 1974).

Interorganizational contexts can be divided into four different types of networks: unitary, federative, coalitional, and social choice (Warren, 1967). The four networks differ in the degree to which relationships among the parties are organized, their network density, and their power distribution (Brown, 1983). In his discussion of interorganizational interfaces, Brown (1983) spells out some potential problems with the four contexts. Unitary networks, which are tightly organized, can result in collusion and suppression of conflict. In coalition and social choice networks, which are loosely organized, conflict can result in fragmentation, isolation, and sometimes uncontrolled escalation.

These studies rarely address how organizations behave in conflict and how this behavior relates to communication. One exception to this pattern is Benson's (1975) action orientations and corresponding strategies for changing interorganizational networks. The action orientations are Weberian ideal types that specify the motivations of agencies, the issues they focus on, the communication strategies they adopt, and the types of subsequent actions they take. For example, some agencies adopt an orientation toward fulfilling program requirements. An administrator with this orientation justifies resources on the basis of immediate benefits and tends to see other agencies with similar programs as threats. These orientations, along with network change strategies, could form the basis for research on communication in interorganizational conflict.

Interorganizational Conflict Management

The management of interorganizational conflict typically focuses on network regulation. This regulation takes the forms of keeping conflict within acceptable bounds while maintaining some controversy to prevent mergers (Litwak & Hylton, 1962) and developing strategies for managing interorganizational conflict (Brown, 1983). Conflict management can also be facilitated by building integrative and cooperative networks between organizations (Metcalfe, 1976) and successful movement through the problem-solving, direction-setting, and structuring phases of interorganizational coordination (McCann, 1983; Gray, 1985). Communication is embedded in each of these approaches since it defines the nature of network exchanges.

Assessment of Communication and Interorganizational Conflict Research

Empirical studies of interorganizational conflict have adopted static, structural descriptions of interaction. Moreover, this research focuses too much on cross-sectional samples, formal quantifiable types of transactions, and individual organizations while it typically ignores power distributions and the environmental system as a whole (Rogers & Whetten, 1982). Although these shortcomings are understandable in view of the complexities inherent in organizational interaction, ignoring these features leads to one-dimensional theories of interorganizational conflict.

To address these shortcomings, more research is needed on interpersonal interactions that bridge organizations and on micro processes that compose institutions. Such an analysis is necessary to understand the operative influence in interorganization relations—members' actions. In addition, this research needs a more sensitive and far-reaching critical-symbolic analysis of interorganizational conflict than is exemplified in the political economic perspectives. Although studies like Benson's (1975) are insightful, they tend to reify resources and relationships by ignoring the social processes that produce and maintain these structures. Interaction is critical to the production and reproduction of market conditions and power distributions that underlie these conditions (Clegg, 1975; Giddens, 1979). These social processes are part of the hegemony that cultural communication helps to create and maintain.

Moreover, to understand interorganizational conflict, researchers need to grapple with symbolic forms, with their multiple meanings and shifting frames of reference. Legal and economic codes are an important part of the language of interorganizational relations. As in intergroup conflict, these legitimate "languages" can transform issues and serve as tools for prosecuting and redefining conflict. For example, issues may be legitimated by casting them in legal terminology that "cleanses" them of prejudice and provides an air of objectivity. To understand issue legitimation and the importance of symbolic analysis, it is necessary to consider the mingling of multiple codes—legal, economic, public relations, corporate responsibility, and everyday language.

CONCLUSION

Although this chapter clusters the organizational conflict literature into four seemingly distinct arenas, we recognize that the four levels are not mutually exclusive. This section summarizes the similarities and differences across arenas by highlighting (1) the unique research foci within each, (2) similarities across arenas in links between communication and conflict components, and (3) the common themes that emerge across arenas. We then suggest ways that research topics characteristic of one particular arena could be used to yield insights in other organizational arenas. Finally, we conclude with a critique of the role of communication in organizational conflict research.

Similarities and Differences in Conflict Research

A comparison across organizational arenas reveals two striking differences in the treatment of communication and conflict. First, as Table 16.1 reveals, context variables are more dominant in the research on intergroup and interorganizational conflict than they are in the interpersonal and bargaining arenas. This observation is scarcely surprising since it reflects the unique foci of macro and micro organizational research, but it also indicates the difficulty that researchers face in selecting salient context variables for studies of interpersonal conflict and bargaining and in choosing actor and issue variables that directly affect intergroup and interorganizational conflict. Such context variables as goal consensus, organizational climate, and formal conflict management procedures exert minimal influence on the choice of conflict strategies at the interpersonal level. Research on actor and issue components in interorganizational conflict is virtually nonexistent. Hence each arena appears to specialize in links between communication and components that are central to organizational research at that particular level.

The four arenas are similar in their reliance on the mechanistic and psychological perspectives as the dominant modes for studying communication; however, each arena frames communication quite differently for a given perspective. Mechanistic approaches at the interpersonal and the intergroup

TABLE 16.1
Significant Variables

Links Between Communication and Components of Organizational Conflict

Arena	Actor	Issue	Relationship	Context
Interpersonal conflict	(1) Personality traits (2) Interpersonal needs (3) Sex-role differences	(1) Source of conflict* (2) Topic of conflict (3) Frequency of occurrence (4) Importance of dispute	(1) Organizational position (2) Target of conflict* (3) Perceptual congruency* (4) Attributions of intent (5) Reciprocity of behaviors*	(1) Organizational commitment* (2) Precedent–conflict history* (3) Organizational climate (4) Goal consensus (5) Formal communication channels

Bargaining and negotiations	(1) Perspective-taking ability
	(2) Credibility*
	(3) Face-saving ability
		(1) Distributive and integrative goals and issues*
		  (a) Information exchange
		  (b) Negotiation strategies*
		  (c) Issue development
		  (d) Phase analysis
			(1) Power-dependency
			(2) Bargainer role*
			(3) Bargainer-constituent relationship*
				(1) Economic, social, and political environment
				(2) Bargaining history
				(3) Normative rules

Intergroup conflict		(1) Issue definition*
		  (a) Within groups
		  (b) Between groups
		(2) Transformation and legitimacy*
			(1) Connectivity*
			(2) Distributive-integrative lateral relationships
				(1) Organizational complexity*
				(2) Unit interdependence*
				(3) Unit status differences*

Interorganizational conflict			(1) Types of networks (2) Action orientations	(1) Marketplace* (2) Governmental regulations*

* Denotes strongest predictors of role of communication based on research findings from a number of different studies.

levels treat communication barriers, misunderstandings, and channel block-ages that cause conflicts. This view of communication differs markedly from casting communication as a network system at the interorganizational level and as a medium for exchanging proposals in bargaining. All four of these orientations, however, embody assumptions of the mechanistic tradition. In like manner, research that adopts psychological views of communication also varies across arenas. Studies at the interpersonal level cast communication as the perceived behaviors that typify predispositions of conflict styles. These perceptual schemes take the form of images or stereotypes that distort communication at the intergroup level. In bargaining, negotiators' perceptions have an impact on their communicative strategies, which in turn shape final outcomes; hence the treatment of communication as a psychological phe-nomenon shifts roles from input stimuli at the interpersonal level to output of perceptual filters at the intergroup level and to message effects at the bargaining level.

Other similarities across levels also reflect slight differences in the treatment of communication and conflict. Relational variables emerge as significant at all four levels, particularly such variables as power, organiza-tional role, and linkages between individuals and groups. At the intergroup and interorganizational levels, however, these variables focus on ties between collectivities—for example, network types and degree of connectivity between units; reciprocity of behaviors and perceptions, in turn, are more prominent variables at the interpersonal and bargaining levels. In like manner, actor variables, even in interpersonal and bargaining research, have yielded limited insights in understanding the role of communication in conflict. Perhaps conflict issues and context variables such as group support and organizational structure may "wash out" the effects of actor characteristics. Moreover, the significance of research findings on relational variables suggests that combina-tions of personal types are more important than characteristics of a single actor, particularly for communication-related concerns. Research that ad-vances combinations of personal attributes between senders and receivers holds greater promise to detect which individual attributes affect the management of organizational conflict than does current work on isolated variables.

Issue definition is another significant similarity among the four arenas. The bargaining and intergroup levels are congruent in their treatment of conflict issues as outgrowths of communication patterns that evolve over time. At the interpersonal and interorganizational levels, however, issues are treated as static variables defined by fixed characteristics such as type, source, and importance of conflict issues. In like manner, context variables are treated as organizational fixtures, projecting an aura of objectivity and immutability. Market transactions, government regulations, unit interdependence, conflict history, and organizational climate are treated as permanent features of intergroup and interorganizational relationships with little attention to contingencies that alter these context elements.

In addition to similarities and differences across arenas, two conflict themes emerge as common within each: conflict styles and integrative and distributive processes of conflict. Analogs of *conflict style* appear at all four levels. Researchers have identified five conflict styles at the interpersonal level that have also been applied to bargaining research (Lewicki & Litterer, 1985), particularly under the more global distinction of competitive and cooperative styles. Conflict styles at the interunit level affect ingroup and outgroup relationships and shape issue definition within and between groups (Walton & Dutton, 1969; Walton, Dutton, & Cafferty, 1969). Action orientations at the interorganizational level reflect different conflict styles or predispositions toward conflict behavior (Benson, 1975). Hence all four arenas demonstrate an interest in linking conflict styles to communicative behaviors.

Integrative and distributive approaches to conflict are explicitly addressed at the bargaining and the intergroup levels (Walton & McKersie, 1965). The other two organizational arenas, however, include aspects of integrative and distributive goals or strategies in their research on conflict. Specifically, interpersonal research incorporates integrative and distributive approaches as characteristics of confrontation and forcing styles. The confrontation style of conflict management aims for maximizing joint gains, disclosure of disputant needs, exploring causes, and generating alternative solutions—patterns that parallel integrative bargaining. In contrast, forcing is aligned with winning, concealing information, and repeated use of attacking arguments and commitment statements that also typify distributive bargaining. Network linkages at the intergroup level reflect distributive and integrative processes even though these relationships are typically cast as stable patterns in the research literature. Groups that develop competitive relationships exhibit selective misrepresentation and threats that resemble distributive bargaining, while units that develop cooperative linkages employ flexibility and openness through integrative modes of communication. Since integrative and distributive approaches to conflict encompass goals, issues, processes, and outcomes, this theme offers considerable potential in investigating the role of communication in each conflict arena.

Improving Research on Organizational Conflict: Borrowing Dominant Approaches from Other Arenas

Research on the role of communication in organizational conflict could be improved by borrowing four approaches that dominate only one of the arenas. The bargaining arena could serve as a model for investigating *arguments, influence strategies, and persuasive messages* in conflict interaction and for studying the phasic development of conflict. Treating conflict styles as ways of gaining compliance or clusters of arguments might aid in translating predispositions into enacted message behaviors. For example, smoothing might be viewed as an ingratiation strategy that serves as a prelude for confrontation. Distributive and integrative relationships in intergroup conflict may emerge from the way that opposing groups use influence strategies. Thus messages exchanged between group members might reflect inflexibility or unwillingness to shift argument positions or might reveal how members reframe issues and shift claims within and between groups. And viewing issue definition and network patterns as both private and public persuasive campaigns might reshape research on intergroup and interorganizational conflict.

Conflict theorists (Pondy, 1967) have also called for *developmental models of conflict,* but bargaining is one of the few organizational arenas that incorporates a stage analysis of the development of conflict. By using a developmental model, interpersonal research could track changes in the choice and use of conflict strategies across the stages of a dispute. The intergroup level, with its intrinsic focus on the emergence of conflict, is particularly appropriate for studying the evolution of group relationships or changes in unit interdependence and status differences during conflicts. For example, researchers could track the emergence of conflict issues between groups, the way communication of these issues shapes relationship definitions between groups, and the way influence strategies affect status differences between and within groups. Finally, interorganizational conflict researchers could apply a developmental model to the study of conflict episodes that emerge from and define market transactions, types of network patterns, and action orientations. Hirsch's (1969, 1971) study on the rise and fall of giants in the popular music industry and Turow's (1985) analysis of socialization and organizational power in mass media organizations provide developmental models of message exchange in interorganizational networks.

Research in intergroup conflict on the *latency or formation stages of conflict* could provide a model for the other three arenas. Communication plays a significant role in the way conflicts emerge. The thrust of the research at the interpersonal and bargaining arenas centers on communicative strategies for managing conflicts. Both arenas could gain additional insights on strategies used in conflict management by tracking the formation of controversial issues back to their inception. For example, researchers could examine message exchanges that shape how organizational members become aware of scarce resources and how this awareness evolves into a dispute through social information processing.

Moreover, intergroup and interorganizational arenas could serve as models for studying the impact of *organizational structure* on conflicts. For the most part, organizational structure has been underemphasized in studies of conflict behavior. Although a number of studies tap structural variables (Corwin, 1969), they fail to capture how structure enters into conflict or how structure is enacted through conflict. Studies by Dalton (1959b) and Burawoy (1979), however, provide excellent models for understanding the way deviant or resistant structures emerge within and reshape bureaucratic procedures and hierarchical relationships through intergroup conflicts.

The Role of Communication in Organizational Conflict

Our analysis of the role of communication in organizational conflict suggests two general conclusions. First, there is no one-to-one relationship between communication and organizational conflict. Simple formulas such as "more communication will reduce conflict" or "ambiguities in communication lead to conflict" have been refuted in research. Communication sometimes reduces conflict, sometimes exacerbates it, and sometimes has no effect on it. The way conflict interactions unfold within organizational contexts, issues, and relationships plays a major role in determining how communication affects conflict (Folger & Poole, 1984; Hawes & Smith, 1973). Second, the communication perspective a researcher employs has an impact on the role communication plays in conflict situations. Mechanistic and psychological orientations restrict communication to channel and transmission effects, fidelity issues, perceptions of verbal and nonverbal behaviors, and message effects. These perspectives lead the researcher to ignore the role of communication in constituting and defining conflicts. More research is needed that embraces the symbolic, systems-interactional, and critical perspectives of communication in organizational conflicts. Yet, regardless of the perspective employed, communication emerges as a significant factor in the development, enactment, and management of organizational conflict.

In addition to broadening our perspectives on communication, future studies on communication and organizational conflict need to focus on the processual and dynamic aspects of communication. Even the work on conflict strategies and tactics often treats messages as general descriptors rather than enacted behaviors. Researchers in intergroup and interorganizational conflict view communication as a static channel for other processes that affect conflict. Many of the dynamics of conflict are communication processes. While we do not maintain that communication is all that happens in conflict situations, it is much more important than most research suggests. Additional work is needed on the role of cultural communication in placing boundaries on conflict and in determining which issues are legitimate, which moves and countermoves are conceivable, and which aspects of social reality are negotiable.

Finally, more contextual and structural variables need to be incorporated into the design of organizational conflict research. Variables such as environmental uncertainty, mergers and acquisitions, and economic fluctuations often influence interpersonal and labor-management conflicts as well as interorganizational ones. The rise of dispute resolution centers that mediate community and interorganizational disputes will influence conflict processes throughout the organization. We anticipate that interest in dispute practices will continue to grow and will infuse managerial training, company practices, and organizational structure. These changes will have a dramatic shift on conflict resarch and conflict management in organizations. Given the importance of conflict in effective decision making, understanding the role of communication in conflict is essential to the survival of overall effectiveness of any organization.

REFERENCES

Adams, J. S. (1976) The structure and dynamics of behavior in organizational boundary roles. In M. Dunnette (Ed.), *Handbook of industrial and organizational psychology* (pp. 1175-1199). Chicago: Rand McNally.

Aldrich, H. (1971). Organizational boundaries and interorganizational conflict. *Human Relations, 24,* 279-293.

Aldrich, H., & Whetten, D. (1981). Organization-sets, action-sets, and networks: Making the most of simplify. In W. Starbuck & S. Nystrom (Eds.), *Handbook of organizational design* (Vol. 1, pp. 385-408). Oxford: Oxford University Press.

Alexander, E. R., III (1977). Communication and conflict resolution. In R. C. Huseman, C. J. Logue, & D. L. Freshley (Eds.), *Readings in interpersonal and organizational communication* (3rd ed., pp. 287-304). Boston: Holbrook Press.

Assael, H. (1969). Constructive role for interorganizational conflict. *Administrative Science Quarterly, 14,* 573-581.

Bacharach, S. B., & Lawler, E. J. (1980). *Power and politics in organizations.* San Francisco: Jossey-Bass.

Bacharach, S. B., & Lawler, E. J. (1981). *Bargaining: Power, tactics, and outcomes.* San Francisco: Jossey-Bass.

Bachrach, P., & Baratz, M.S. (1962). Two faces of power. *American Political Science Review, 56,* 947-952.

Bazerman, M. H., & Lewicki, R. J. (Eds.). (1983). *Negotiating in organizations.* Newbury Park, CA: Sage.

Bednar, D. A., & Curington, W. P. (1983). Interaction analysis: A tool for understanding negotiations. *Industrial and Labor Relations Review, 36,* 389-401.

Begley, T. M. (1983, August). *Factors affecting the use of conflict management strategies.* Paper presented at the annual meeting of the Academy of Management Association, Dallas, TX.

Bell, E., & Blakeney, R. (1977). Personality correlates of conflict resolution modes. *Human Relations, 30,* 849-857.

Benson, J. K. (1975). The interorganizational network as a political economy. *Administrative Science Quarterly, 20,* 229-249.

Bernardin, H. J., & Alvarez, K. (1976). The managerial grid as a predictor of conflict resolution method and managerial effectiveness. *Administrative Science Quarterly, 21,* 84-92.

Bigones, W. J., Grigsby, D. W., & Rosen, B. (1980, August). *Effects of organizational climate, locus of control, and target of confrontation upon individual's willingness to confront conflict.* Paper presented to the annual meeting of the National Academy of Management Association, Detroit, MI.,

Billig, M. (1976). *The social psychology of intergroup relations.* New York: Academic Press.

Blake, R. R., & Mouton, J. S. (1964). *The managerial grid.* Houston: Gulf Publishing.

Blake, R. R., Shepard, H., & Mouton, J. S. (1964). *Managing intergroup conflict in industry.* Houston: Gulf Publishing.

Bomers, G.B.J., & Peterson, R. B. (Eds.). (1982). *Conflict management and industrial relations.* Boston: Kluwer-Nijhoff.

Bonoma, T. V. (1976). Conflict, cooperation, and trust in three power systems. *Behavioral Science, 6,* 499-514.

Borah, L. A. (1963). The effects of threat in bargaining: Critical and experimental analysis. *Journal of Abnormal and Social Psychology, 66,* 37-44.

Brehmer, B. (1971). Effects of communication and feedback on cognitive conflict. *Scandinavian Journal of Psychology, 12,* 205-216.

Brehmer, B., & Hammond, K. R. (1977). Cognitive factors in interpersonal conflict. In D. Druckman (Ed.), *Negotiations: Social psychological perspectives* (pp. 79-103). Newbury Park, CA: Sage.

Brett, J. M. (1984). Managing organizational conflict. *Professional Psychology: Research and Practice, 15,* 664-678.

Brett, J. M., & Rognes, J. K. (1986). Intergroup relations in organizations. In P. S. Goodman (Ed.), *Designing effective work groups.* San Francisco: Jossey-Bass.

Brown, B. R. (1968). The effects of need to maintain face on interpersonal bargaining. *Journal of Experimental Social Psychology, 4,* 107-122.

Brown, B. R. (1977). Face-saving and face-restoration in negotiation. In D. Druckman, (Ed.), *Negotiations* (pp. 275-299). Newbury Park, CA: Sage.

Brown, L. D. (1983). *Managing conflict at organizational interfaces.* Reading, MA: Addison-Wesley.

Burawoy, M. (1979). *Manufacturing consent.* Chicago: University of Chicago Press.

Burgess, P. G. (1973). Crisis rhetoric: Coercion vs. force. *Quarterly Journal of Speech, 59,* 61-73.

Burke, R. J. (1970). Methods of resolving superior-subordinate conflict: The constructive use of subordinate differences and disagreements. *Organizational Behavior and Human Performance, 5,* 393-411.

Byrnes, J. F. (1986). *Managing and resolving conflict.* New York: American Management Association.

Campbell, D. T. (1958). Common fate, similarity, and other indices of the status of aggregates of persons as social entities. *Behavioral Science, 3,* 14-25.

Carlisle, J., & Leary, M. (1981). Negotiating groups, In R. Payne & C. L. Cooper (Eds.), *Groups at work* (pp. 165-188). New York: John Wiley.

Carnevale, P.J.D., & Pegnetter, R. (1985). The selection of mediation tactics in public sector disputes: A contingency analysis. *Journal of Social Issues, 41,* 65-81.

Carnevale, P.J.D., Pruitt, D. G., & Britton, S. D. (1979). Looking tough: The negotiator under constituent surveillance. *Personality and Social Psychology Bulletin, 5,* 118-121.

Chatov, R. (1981). Cooperation between government and business. In W. Starbuck & S. Nystrom (Eds.), *Handbook of organization design* (Vol. 1, pp. 409-437). Oxford: Oxford University Press.

Chertkoff, J. M., & Baird, S. L. (1971). Applicability of the big lie technique and the last clear chance doctrine in bargaining. *Journal of Personality and Social Psychology, 20,* 298-303.

Chertkoff, J. M.,& Conley, M. (1967). Opening offer and frequency of concessions as bargaining strategies. *Journal of Personality and Social Psychology, 22,* 31-50.

Clegg, S. (1975). *Power, rule, and domination.* London: Routledge & Kegan Paul.

Conrad, C. (1983). Power and performance as correlates of supervisors' choice of modes of managing conflict: A preliminary investigation. *Western Journal of Speech Communication, 47,* 218-228.

Corwin, R. G. (1969). Patterns of organizational conflict. *Administrative Science Quarterly, 14,* 507-520.

Coser, L. S. (1956). *The functions of social conflict.* New York: Free Press.

Cosier, R. A., & Ruble, T. L. (1981). Research on conflict-handling behavior: An experimental approach. *Academy of Management Journal, 24,* 816-831.

Crott, H., Kayser, E., & Lamm, H. (1980). The effects of information exchange and communication in an asymmetrical negotiation situation. *European Journal of Social Psychology, 10,* 149-163.

Crozier, M. (1964). *The bureaucratic phenomenon.* Chicago: University of Chicago Press.

Cummings, L., & Harnett, D. (1969). Bargaining behavior in a symmetric bargaining triad: The impact of risk-taking propensity, information, communication, and the terminal bid. *Review of Economic Studies, 36,* 485-501.

Cyert, R. M., & March, J. G. (1963). *A behavioral theory of the firm.* Englewood Cliffs, NJ: Prentice-Hall.

Daniels, V. (1967). Communication, incentive and structural variables in interpersonal exchange and negotiation. *Journal of Experimental Social Psychology, 3,* 47-74.

Dalton, M. (1959a). Conflicts between staff and line managerial officers. *American Sociological Review, 15,* 342-351.

Dalton, M. (1959b). *Men who manage.* New York: John Wiley.

Delbecq, A. L. & Filley, A. (1974). *Program and project management in a matrix organization: A case study.* Madison, WI: Bureau of Business Research and Service.

Deschamps, J. C., & Brown, R. (1983). Superordinate goals and intergroup conflict. *British Journal of Social Psychology, 22,* 189-195.

Deutsch, M. (1973). *The resolution of conflict: Constructive and destructive processes.* New Haven, CT: Yale University Press.

Doise, W. (1978). *Groups and individuals.* Cambridge: Cambridge University Press.

Donohue, W. A. (1978). An empirical framework for examining negotiation processes and outcomes. *Communication Monographs, 45,* 247-257.

Donohue, W. A. (1981a). Analyzing negotiation tactics: Development of a negotiation interact system. *Human Communication Research, 7,* 273-287.

Donohue, W. A. (1981b). Development of a model of rule use in negotiation interaction. *Communication Monographs, 48,* 106-120.

Donohue, W. A. (1982, May). *A conversational analysis of negotiation interaction: The structure of opening moves.* Paper presented at the annual meeting of the International Communication Association, Boston.

Donohue, W. A., Allen, M., & Burrell, N. (1985). Communication strategies in mediation. *Mediation Quarterly, 10,* 75-89.

Donohue, W. A., & Diez, M. E. (1983, May). *Information management in negotiation.* Paper presented at the annual meeting of the International Communication Association, Dallas, TX.

Donohue, W. A., Diez, M. E., & Hamilton, M. (1984). Coding naturalistic negotiation interation. *Human Communication Research, 10,* 403-425.

Donohue, W. A., Diez, M. E., & Stahle, R. B. (1983). New directions in negotiation research. In R. Bostrom (Ed.), *Communication yearbook 7* (pp. 249-279). Newbury Park, CA: Sage.

Douglas, A. (1957). The peaceful settlement of industrial and intergroup disputes. *Journal of Conflict Resolution, 1,* 69-81.

Douglas, A. (1962). *Industrial peacemaking.* New York: Columbia University Press.

Druckman, D., & Zechmeister, K. (1973). Conflict of interest and value dissensus: Propositions in the sociology of conflict. *Human Relations, 26,* 449-466.

Druckman, D., Zechmeister, K., & Solomon, D. (1972). Determinants of bargaining behavior in a bilateral monopoly situation: Opponent's concession rate and relative defensibility. *Behavioural Science, 17,* 514-531.

Edwards, R. C. (1979). *Contested terrain: The transformation of the workplace in the 20th century.* New York: Basic Books.

Evan, W. M. (1965). Superior-subordinate conflict in research organizations. *Administrative Science Quarterly, 10,* 52-64.

Evan, W. M. (1966). The organization-set: Toward a theory of interorganizational relations. In J. D. Thompson (Ed.), *Approaches to organizational design* (pp. 175-191). Pittsburgh: University of Pittsburgh Press.

Fisher, B. A. (1978). *Perspectives on human communication.* New York: Macmillan.

Folger, J. P., & Poole, M. S. (1984). *Working through conflict.* Glenview, IL: Scott Foresman.

Follett, M. P. (1941). Constructive conflict. In H. C. Metcalf & L. Urwick (Eds.), *Dynamic administration: The collected papers of Mary Parker Follett* (pp. 30-49). New York: Harper & Brothers.

Galbraith, J. R. (1971). Matrix organization designs. *Business Horizons, 14,*(1), 29-40.

Giddens, A. (1979). *Central problems in social theory.* Berkeley: University of California Press.

Goering, E. M., Rudick, K. L., & Faulkner, M. M. (1986, May). *The validity of a self-reported conflict management scale in measuring conflict management behaviors.* Paper presented at the annual meeting of the International Communication Association, Chicago.

Gouldner, A. (1954). *Wildcat strike.* Yellow Springs, OH: Antioch Press.

Gramsci, A. (1971). *Selection from prison notebooks.* London: Lawrence & Wishart.

Gray, B. (1985). Conditions facilitating interorganizational collaboration. *Human Relations, 10,* 911-936.

Gray, B., & Hay, T. M. (1986). Political limits to interorganizational consensus and change. *Journal of Applied Behavioral Science, 22,* 95-112.

Gruder, L. (1971). Relationships with opponent and partner in mixed-motive bargaining. *Journal of Conflict Resolution, 15,* 403-416.

Gulliver, P. H. (1979). *Disputes and negotiations.* New York: Academic Press.

Hage, J. (1974). *Communication and organizational control.* New York: John Wiley.

Haire, M. (1955). Role-perceptions in labor-management relations: An experimental approach. *Industrial and Labor Relations Review, 8,* 204-216.

Hall, J. (1969). *Conflict management survey: A survey of one's characteristic reaction to and handling of conflicts between himself and others.* Monroe, TX: Telemetrics International.

Hawes, L. C., & Smith, D. H. (1973). A critique of assumptions underlying the study of communication in conflict. *Quarterly Journal of Speech, 59,* 423-435.

Hilltrop, J. M. (1985). Mediator behavior and the settlement of collective bargaining disputes in Britain. *Journal of Social Issues, 41,* 83-99.

Hirsch, P. M. (1969). *The structure of the popular music industry.* Ann Arbor: University of Michigan Survey Research Center.

Hirsch, P. (1972). Processing fads and fashions: An organization-set analysis. *American Journal of Sociology, 77,* 639-659.

Hopmann, P. T., & Walcott, C. (1976). The impact of international conflict and detente on bargaining in arms control negotiations: An experimental analysis. *International Interactions, 2,* 189-206.

Howat, G., & London, M. (1980). Attributions of conflict management strategies in supervisor-subordinate dyads. *Journal of Applied Psychology, 65,* 172-175.

Howell, J. L. (1981). The identification, description and analysis of competencies focused on conflict management in a human services organization: An exploratory study (Doctoral dissertation, University of Massachusetts, 1980). *Dissertation Abstracts International 42,*(3-a), 933.

Hunger, R., & Stern, L. W. (1976). Assessment of the functionality of superordinate goals in reducing conflict. *Academy of Management Journal, 16,* 591-605.

Janis, I. L. (1972). *Victims of groupthink.* Boston: Houghton-Mifflin.

Jamieson, D. W., & Thomas, K. W. (1974). Power and conflict in student-teacher relationships. *Journal of Applied Behavioral Science, 10,* 321-336.

Johnson, D. W. (1973). Communication in conflict situations: A critical review of the research. *International Journal of Group Tensions, 3,* 46-67.

Johnson, D. W. (1974). Communication and the inducement of cooperative behavior in conflicts: A critical review. *Speech Monographs, 41,* 64-78.

Johnson, D. W., McCarty, H., & Allen, K. (1976). Congruent and contradictory verbal and nonverbal communication of cooperativeness and competitiveness in negotiations. *Communication Research, 3,* 275-292.

Kabanoff, B. (1985). Potential influence structures as sources of interpersonal conflict in groups and organizations. *Organizational Behavior and Human Decision Processes, 36,* 113-141.

Kanter, R. M. (1977). *Men and women of the corporation.* New York: Harper & Row.

Katz, R. N. (Ed.). (1978). Conflict and the collaborative ethic [special section]. *California Management Review, 21*(2).

Kerr, C. (1954). Industrial conflict and its mediation. *American Journal of Sociology, 60*, 230-245.

Kilmann, R. H., & Thomas, K. W. (1975). Interpersonal conflict-handling behavior as reflections of Jungian personality dimensions. *Psychological Reports, 37,* 971-980.

Kilmann, R. H., & Thomas, K. W. (1977). Developing a forced-choice measure of conflict-handling behavior: The MODE instrument. *Educational and Psychological Measurement, 37,* 309-325.

Kochan, T. A. (1980). Collective bargaining and organizational behavior research. In B. M. Staw & L. L. Cummings (Eds.), *Research in organizational behavior* (Vol. 2, pp. 129-176). Greenwich, CT: JAI Press.

Kolb, D. M. (1983a). Strategy and the tactics of mediation. *Human Relations, 36,* 247-268.

Kolb, D. M. (1983b). *The mediators.* Cambridge: MIT Press.

Kolb, D. M. (1985). To be a mediator: Expressive tactics in mediation. *Journal of Social Issues, 41,* 11-26.

Krauss, R. M., & Deutsch, M. (1966). Communication in interpersonal bargaining. *Journal of Personality and Social Psychology, 4,* 572-577.

Lamm, H. (1976). Dyadic negotiations under asymmetric conditions: Comparing the performance of the uninformed and the informed party. *European Journal of Social Psychology, 6,* 255-259.

Lawrence, P. R., & Lorsch, J. W. (1967). *Organization and environment.* Boston: Harvard University Press.

Leusch, R. F. (1976). Sources of power: Their impact on interchannel conflict. *Journal of Marketing Research, 4,* 382-390.

Levine, S., & White, P. E. (1961). Exchange as a conceptual framework for the study of interorganizational relationships. *Administrative Science Quarterly, 5,* 583-601.

Lewicki, R. J. (1983). Lying and deception: A behavioral model. In M. H. Bazerman & R. J. Lewicki (Eds.), *Negotiating in organizations* (pp. 68-90). Newbury Park, CA: Sage.

Lewicki, R. J. & Bazerman, M. H. (Eds.). (1985). Negotiating in organizations [special issue]. *Journal of Occupational Behavior, 6,*(1).

Lewicki, R. J., & Litterer, J. (1985). *Negotiation.* Homewood, IL: Irwin.

Lewicki, R. J., Sheppard, B. H., & Bazerman, M. H. (1986). *Research in negotiation in organizations: A series of analytical essays and critical reviews* (Vol. 1). Greenwich, CT: JAI Press.

Lewis, S. A., & Fry, W. R. (1977). Effects of visual access and orientation on the discovery of integrative bargaining alternatives. *Organizational Behavior and Human Performance, 20,* 75-92.

Lewis, S. A., & Pruitt, D. G. (1971). Orientation, aspiration level, and communication freedom in integrative bargaining. *Proceedings of the 79th Annual Convention of the American Psychological Association, 6,* 221-222.

Litwak, E., & Hylton, L. (1962). Interorganizational analysis: A hypothesis on coordinating agencies. *Administrative Science Quarterly, 6,* 395-415.

London, M., & Howat, G. (1978). The relationships between employee commitment and conflict resolution behavior. *Journal of Vocational Behavior, 13,* 1-14.

Lukes, S. (1974). *Power: A radical view.* New York: Macmillan.

Marrett, C. B. (1971). On the specification of interorganization dimensions. *Sociology and Social Research, 61,* 83-99.

McCann, T. (1983). Design guidelines for social problem solving interventions. *Journal of Applied Behavior Science, 19,* 177-189.

McKersie, R. B. (1964). Avoiding written grievances by problem solving: An outside view. *Personnel Psychology, 17*(4), 367-379.

Metcalfe, J. L. (1976). Organizational strategies and interorganizational networks. *Human Relations, 29,* 327-343.

Miles, R. H. (1979). Organizational conflict and its management. In R. Miles & W. A. Randolph (Eds.). *The organizational game* (pp. 204-222). Glenview, IL: Scott, Foresman.

Mintzberg, H. (1979). The structuring of organizations. Englewood Cliffs, NJ: Prentice-Hall.

Molnar, J., & Rogers, D. A. (1979). A comparative model of interorganizational conflict *Administrative Science Quarterly, 24,* 405-424.

Moore, C. W. (1986). *The mediation process: Practical strategies for resolving conflict.* San Francisco: Jossey-Bass.

Morley, D. M., & Shockley-Zalabak, P. (1986). Conflict avoiders and compromisers: *Toward an understanding of their organizational communication style. Group and Organizational Behavior, 11*(4), 387-402.

Morley, I., & Stephenson, G. (1969). Interpersonal and interparty exchange: A laboratory simulation of an industrial negotiation at the plant level. *British Journal of Psychology, 60,* 543-545.

Morley, I., & Stephenson, G. (1970). Strength of case, communication systems, and the outcome of simulated negotiations: Some social psychological aspects of bargaining. *Industrial Relations Journal, 1,* 19-20.

Morley, I., & Stephenson, G. (1977). *The social psychology of bargaining.* London: Allen and Unwin.

Musser, S. J. (1982). A model for predicting the choice of conflict management strategies by subordinates in high-stake conflicts. *Organizational Behavior and Human Performance, 29,* 257-269.

Neale, M. A. & Bazerman, M. H. (1983). The role of perspective-taking ability in negotiating under different forms of arbitration. *Industrial and Labor Relations Review, 36,* 378-388.

Pfeffer, J. (1981). *Power in organizations.* Marshfield, MA: Pitman Publishers.

Phillips, E., & Cheston, R. (1979). Conflict resolution: What works? *California Management Review, 21,*(4), 76-83.

Pilisuk, M., & Rapoport, A. (1964). Stepwise disarmament and sudden destruction in a two-person game: A research tool. *Journal of Conflict Resolution, 8,* 36-49.

Pilisuk, M., & Skolnick, P. (1968). Inducing trust: A test of the Osgood proposal. *Journal of Personality and Social Psychology, 8,* 121-133.

Pondy, L. R. (1967). Organizational conflict: Concepts and models. *Administrative Science Quarterly, 12,* 296-320.

Pruitt, D. G. (1981). *Negotiation behavior.* New York: Academic Press.

Pruitt, D. G. (1983). Integrative agreements: Nature and antecedents. In M. H. Bazerman & R. J. Lewicki (Eds.), *Negotiating in organizations* (pp. 35-50). Newbury Park, CA: Sage.

Pruitt, D. G., & Lewis, S. A. (1975). Development of integrative solutions in bilateral negotiation. *Journal of Personality and Social Psychology, 31,* 621-633.

Pruitt, D. G., & Lewis, S. A. (1977). The psychology of integrative bargaining. In D. Druckman (Ed.)., *Negotiations* (pp. 161-192). Newbury Park, CA: Sage.

Putnam, L. L. (1985a). Bargaining as organizational communication. In R. D. McPhee & P. K. Tompkins (Eds.), *Organizational communication: Traditional themes and new directions* (pp. 129-148). Newbury Park, CA: Sage.

Putnam, L. L. (1985b) Bargaining as task and process: Multiple functions of interaction sequences. In R. L. Street, Jr., & J. N. Cappella (Eds.), *Sequence and pattern in communicative behaviour* (pp. 225-242). London: Edward Arnold.

Putnam, L. L., & Bullis, C. (1984, May). *Intergroup relations and issue redefinition in teachers' bargaining.* Paper presented at the annual meeting of the International Communication Association, San Francisco.

Putnam, L. L., & Geist, P. (1985). Argument in bargaining: An analysis of the reasoning process. *Southern Speech Communication Journal, 50,* 225-245.

Putnam, L. L., & Jones, T. S. (1982a). Reciprocity in negotiations: An analysis of bargaining interaction. *Communication Monographs, 49,* 171-191.

Putnam, L. L., & Jones, T. S. (1982b). The role of communication in bargaining. *Human Communication Research, 8,* 262-280.

Putnam, L. L., & Pacanowsky, M. E. (Eds.). (1983). *Communication and organizations: An interpretive approach.* Newbury Park, CA: Sage.

Putnam, L. L., & Wilson, S. R. (in press). Argumentation and bargaining strategies as discriminators of integrative and distributive outcomes. In A. Rahim (Ed.), *Managing conflict: An interdisciplinary approach.* New York: Praeger.

Putnam, L. L., & Van Hoeven, S. A. (1986, April). *Teacher bargaining as a cultural rite of conflict reduction.* Paper presented at the annual meeting of the Central States Speech Association, Cincinnati, OH.

Putnam, L. L., & Wilson, C. E. (1982). Communicative strategies in organizational conflicts: Reliability and validity of a measurement scale. In M. Burgoon (Ed.), *Communication yearbook 6* (pp. 629-652). Newbury Park, CA: Sage.

Putnam, L. L., Wilson, S. R, Waltman, M. S., & Turner, D. (1986). The evolution of case arguments in teacher's bargaining. *Journal of American Forensic Association, 23,* 63-81.

Radlow, R. , & Weidner, M. F. (1966). Unenforced commitments in "cooperative" and "non-cooperative" non-constant sum games. *Journal of Conflict Resolution, 10,* 497-505.

Rahim, M. A. (1981). Organizational behavior courses for graduate students in business administration: Views from the tower and the battlefield. *Psychological Reports, 49,* 583-592.

Rahim, M. A. (1983a). A measure of styles of handling interpersonal conflict. *Academy of Management Journal, 26,* 368-376.

Rahim, M. A. (1983b, August). *How managers handle interpersonal conflict with superiors, subordinates, and peers.* Paper presented to the annual meeting of the Academy of Management, Dallas, TX.

Rahim, M. A. (1986a). Referent role and styles of handling interpersonal conflict. *Journal of Social Psychology, 126,* 79-86.

Rahim, M. A. (1986b). *Managing conflict in organizations.* New York: Praeger.

Rahim, A., & Bonoma, T. V. (1979). Managing organizational conflict: A model for diagnosis and intervention. *Psychological Reports, 44,* 1323-1344.

Reiches, N. A., & Harral, H. B. (1974). Argument in negotiations: A theoretical and empirical approach. *Speech Monographs, 41,* 36-48.

Renwick, P. A. (1975a). Impact of topic and source of disagreement on conflict management. *Organizational Behavior and Human Performance, 14,* 416-425.

Renwick, P. A. (1975b). Perception and management of superior-subordinate conflict. *Organizational Behavior and Human Performance, 13,* 444-456.

Renwick, P. A. (1977). Effects of sex-differences on the perception and management of conflict: An exploratory study. *Organizational Behavior and Human Performance, 19,* 403-415.

Rhenman, E., Stromberg, L., & Westerlunch, G. (1970). *Conflict and cooperation in business organizations.* New York: John Wiley.

Richmond, V. P., Wagner, J. P., & McCroskey, J. C. (1983). The impact of perceptions of leadership style, use of power, and conflict management style on organizational outcomes. *Communication Quarterly, 31,* 27-36.

Riggs, C. J. (1983). Dimensions of organizational conflict: A functional analysis of communication tactics. *Communication yearbook 7* (pp. 517-531). Newbury Park, CA: Sage.

Ritti, R. R., & Gouldner, F. (1969). Professional pluralism in an industrial organization. *Management Science, 16,* B233-B246.

Robbins, S. P. (1974). *Managing organizational conflict: A nontraditional approach.* Englewood Cliffs, NJ: Prentice-Hall.

Robbins, S. P. (1978). "Conflict management" and "conflict resolution" are not synonymous terms. *California Management Review, 21,*(2), 67-75.

Rogers, P. L., & Whetten, D. A. (1982). *Interorganizational coordination.* Ames: Iowa State University Press.

Ross, R., & DeWine, S. (1982, November). *Interpersonal conflict: Measurement and validation.* Paper presented at the annual meeting of the Speech Communication Association, Washington, DC.

Ross, R., & DeWine, S. (1984, November). *Interpersonal needs and communication in conflict: Do soft words win hard hearts?* Paper presented at the annual convention of the Speech Communication Association, Chicago.

Rubin, J., & Brown, B. (1975). *The social psychology of bargaining and negotiation.* New York: Academic Press.

Ruble, T. L., & Cosier, R. A. (1982). A laboratory study of five conflict-handling modes. In G.B.J. Bomers & R. B. Peterson (Eds.), *Conflict management and industrial relations* (pp. 158-171). Boston: Kluwer-Nijhoff.

Ruble, T. L., & Cosier, R. A. (1983). Conflict processes. In D. Hellriegel, J. W. Slocum, & R. W. Woodman (Eds.), *Organizational behavior* (pp. 456-485). St. Paul: West.

Ruble, T. L., & Thomas, K. W. (1976). Support for a two-dimensional model of conflict behavior. *Organizational Behavior and Human Performance, 16,* 143-155.

Saine, T. A. (1974). Perceiving communication conflict. *Speech Monographs, 41,* 49-56.

Schelling, T. C. (1960). *The strategy of conflict.* Cambridge, MA: Harvard University Press.

Schlenker, B. R., Helm, B., & Tedeschi, J. T. (1973). The effects of personality and situational variables on behavioral trust. *Journal of Personality and Social Psychology, 32,* 664-670.

Sebring, R. (1977). The five million dollar misunderstanding: A perspective on state government-university Interorganizational conflicts. *Administrative Science Quarterly, 22,* 505-523.

Sermat, P. G. (1970). Is game behavior related to behavior in other interpersonal situations? *Journal of Personality and Social Psychology, 16,* 121-132.

Sherif, M., Harvey, O. J., White, B. J., Hood, W. R., & Sherif, C. W. (1961). *Intergroup conflict and cooperation: The robbers cave experiment.* Norman, OK: University Book Exchange.

Shockley-Zalabak, P. S. (1981). The effects of sex differences on the preference of utilization of conflict styles of managers in a work setting: An exploratory study. *Public Personnel Management, 10*(3), 289-294.

Short, J. A. (1974). Effects of medium of communication on experimental negotiation. *Human Relations, 27,* 225-234.

Siegel, S., & Fouraker, L. E. (1960). *Bargaining and group decision making.* New York: McGraw-Hill.

Stein, B. A., & Kanter, R. M. (1980). Building the parallel organization: Creating mechanisms for permanent quality of work life. *Journal of Applied Behavioral Science, 16,* 371-388.

Steinfatt, T., & Miller, G. (1974). Communication in game theoretic models of conflict. In G. Miller & H. Simon (Eds.), *Perspectives on communication in social conflicts* (pp. 14-75). Englewood Cliffs, NJ: Prentice-Hall.

Stephenson, G. M., Kniveton, B. K., & Morley, I. E. (1977). Interaction analysis of an industrial wage negotiation. *Journal of Occupational Psychology, 50,* 231-241.

Stern, L. W., Sternthal, B., & Craig, S. C. (1975). Strategies for managing inter-organizational conflict: A laboratory paradigm. *Journal of Applied Psychology, 60,* 472-482.

Tajfel, H. (1980). *Differentiation between social groups: Studies in the social psychology of intergroup relations.* New York: Academic Press.

Tedeschi, J. T., & Bonoma, T. V. (1977). Measures of last resort: Coercion and aggression in bargaining. In D. Druckman (Ed.), *Negotiations* (pp. 213-241). Newbury Park, CA: Sage.

Tedeschi, J. T., & Rosenfeld, P. (1980). Communication in bargaining and negotiation. In M. E. Roloff & G. R. Miller (Eds.), *Persuasion: New directions in theory and research* (pp. 225-248). Newbury Park, CA: Sage.

Temlin, T., & Cummings, H. W. (1985, November). *An exploratory study of conflict management behaviors in voluntary organizations.* Paper presented at the annual meeting of the Speech Communication Association, Denver.

Thomas, K. W. (1976). Conflict and conflict management. In M. Dunnette (Ed.), *Handbook of industrial and organizational psychology* (pp. 889-936). Chicago: Rand McNally.

Thomas, K. W. (1979). Conflict. In S. Kerr (Ed)., *Organizational behavior* (pp. 151-181). Columbus, OH: Grid Publications.

Thomas, K. W., & Kilmann, R. H. (1974). *Thomas-Kilmann conflict MODE instrument*. New York: XICOM, Tuxedo.

Thomas, K. W., & Kilmann, R. H. (1975). The social desirability variable in organizational research: An alternative explanation for reported findings. *Academy of Management Journal, 18,* 741-752.

Thomas, K. W., & Kilmann, R. H. (1978). Comparison of four instruments measuring conflict behavior. *Psychological Reports, 42,* 1139-1145.

Thomas, K. W., & Pondy, L. R. (1977). Toward an "intent" model of conflict management among principal parties. *Human Relations, 30,* 1089-1102.

Thomas, K. W., & Schmidt, W. H. (1976). A survey of managerial interests with respect to conflict. *Academy of Management Journal, 19,* 315-318.

Thomas, K. W., & Walton, R. E. (1971). *Conflicting-handling behavior in interdepartmental relations* (Research Paper No. 38, Division of Research, Graduate School of Business Administration, UCLA). Los Angeles: University of California.

Tjosvold, D. (1974). Threat as a low-power person's strategy in bargaining: Social face and tangible outcomes. *International Journal of Group Tensions, 16,* 494-510.

Tjosvold, D. (1982). Effects of approach to controversy on supervisors' incorporation of subordinates' information in decision making. *Journal of Applied Psychology, 67,* 189-191.

Tjosvold, D. (1983). Effects of supervisor's influence orientation on their decision making controversy. *Journal of Psychology, 113,* 175-182.

Tjosvold, D., & Johnson, D. W. (Eds.), (1983). *Productive conflict management: Perspectives for organizations.* New York: Irvington.

Tompkins, P. K., Fisher, J. Y., Infante, D. A., & Tompkins, E. L. (1974). Conflict and communication within the university. In G. R. Miller & H. W. Simons (Eds), *Perspectives on communication in social conflict* (pp. 153-171). Englewood Cliffs, NJ: Prentice-Hall.

Trice, H. M., & Beyer, J. M. (1984). Studying organizational cultures through rites and ceremonials. *Academy of Management Review, 9,* 653-669.

Turnbull, A. A., Strickland, L., & Shaver, K. G. (1974). Phrasing of concessions, difference of power, and medium of communication. *Social Psychology Bulletin, 1,* 228-230.

Turnbull, A. A., Strickland, L., & Shaver, K. G. (1976). Medium of communication, differential power, and phrasing of concessions: Negotiating success and attributions to the opponent. *Human Communication Research, 2,* 262-270.

Turow, J. (1985). Learning to portray institutional power: The socialization of creators in mass media organizations. In R. D. McPhee & P. K. Tompkins (Eds.), *Organizational communication: Traditional themes and new directions* (pp. 211-234). Beverly Hills, CA: Sage.

Van de Ven, A. H., Emmett, D., & Koenig, R. (1980). Frameworks for interorganizational analysis. In A. R. Negandhi (Ed.), *Interorganizational theory* (pp. 19-38). Kent, OH: Kent State University Press.

Van de Vliert, E. (1984). Conflict: Prevention and escalation. In P.J.D. Drenth, H. Thierry, P. J. Willems, & C. J. deWolff (Eds.), *Handbook of work and organizational psychology* (pp. 521-551). New York: John Wiley.

Voissem, N. H., & Sistrunk, F. (1971). Communication schedule and cooperative game behavior. *Journal of Personality and Social Psychology, 19,* 160-167.

Wall, J. A. (1977a). Intergroup bargaining: Effects of opposing constituent's stance, opposing representative's bargaining, and representative's locus of control. *Journal of Conflict Resolution, 21,* 459-474.

Wall, J. A. (1977b) Operantly conditioning a negotiator's concession making. *Journal of Experimental Social Psychology, 13,* 431-440.

Wall, J. A. (1981). Mediation: An analysis, review, and proposed research. *Journal of Conflict Resolution, 25,* 157-181.

Wall, J. A. (1985). *Negotiation: Theory and practice.* Glenview, IL: Scott, Foresman.

Waltman, M. S., & Wilson, S. R. (1986, April). *Communication and dyadic conflict management in organizations: A review of instrumentation, individual and situational influences, and an alternative theoretical conceptualization.* Paper presented at the annual meeting of the Central States Speech Association, Cincinnati, OH.

Walton, R. E., & Dutton, J. M. (1969). The management of interdepartmental conflict: A model and review. *Administrative Science Quarterly, 14,* 73-84.

Walton, R. E., Dutton, J. M., & Cafferty, T. P. (1969). Organizational context and interdepartmental conflict. *Administrative Science Quarterly, 14,* 522-542.

Walton, R. E., Dutton, J. M., & Fitch, H. G. (1966). A study of conflict in the process, structure, and attitudes of lateral relationships. In A. H. Rubenstein, S. Haberstroh, & J. Chadwick (Eds.), *Some theories of organization* (pp. 444-465). Homewood, IL: Irwin.

Walton, R. E., & McKersie, R. B. (1965). *A behavioral theory of labor negotiations: An analysis of a social interaction system.* New York: McGraw-Hill.

Warren, R. (1967). The interorganizational field as a focus for investigation. *Administrative Science Quarterly, 12,* 397-419.

Warren, R. L., Rose, S. M., & Bergunder, A. F. (1974). *The structure of urban reform.* Lexington, MA: D. C. Heath.

Wehr, P. V. (1979). *Conflict regulation.* Boulder, CO: Westview.

Weiss, S. E. (1985). *The language of successful negotiators: A study of communicative competence in intergroup negotiation simulations.* Unpublished doctoral dissertation, University of Pennsylvania, Philadelphia.

White, H. (1961). Management conflict and sociometric structure. *American Journal of Sociology, 67,* 185-199.

White, P., Levine, S., & Vlasak, G. (1980). Exchange as a conceptual framework for understanding interorganizational relationships: Application to nonprofit organizations. In A. R. Negandhi (Ed.), *Interorganization theory* (pp. 166-181). Kent, OH: Kent State University Press.

Whyte, W. F. (1955). *Money and motivation.* New York: Harper & Brothers.

Wichman, H. (1970). Effects of isolation and communication on cooperation in a two-person game. *Journal of Personality and Social Psychology, 16,* 114-120.

Wilson, W. (1969). Cooperation and cooperativeness of the other player. *Journal of Conflict Resolution, 13,* 110-117.

Zald, M. (1962). Organizational control structures in five correctional institutions. *American Journal of Sociology, 68,* 335-345.

Zald, M. (1981). Political economy: A framework for comparative analysis. In M. Zey-Ferrell & M. Aiken (Eds.), *Complex organizations: Critical perspectives* (pp. 237-262). Glenview, IL: Scott, Foresman.

Zammuto. R. F., London, M., & Rowland, K. W. (1979). Effects of sex on commitment and conflict resolution. *Journal of Applied Psychology, 64,* 227-231.

Zechmeister, K., & Druckman, D. (1973). Determinants of resolving a conflict of interest: A simulation of political decision-making. *Journal of Conflict Resolution, 17,* 63-88.

17 Message Flow and Decision Making

CHARLES A. O'REILLY
JENNIFER A. CHATMAN
University of California, Berkeley

JOHN C. ANDERSON
UNICEF

F OR several decades there has been considerable theoretical interest in organizations as information processing entities (e.g., Daft & Macintosh, 1981; Ference, 1970; March & Simon, 1958; Thompson, 1967; Weick, 1969). This view has focused attention both on the flow of information within organizational settings as well as the use of information by organizational members. Jay Galbraith (1973) for example, has proposed that one of the central mechanisms by which organizations adjust to shifting environmental pressures is through changes in the information processing capacity of the organization's structure. Tushman and Nadler (1978) have suggested that as complexity and uncertainty increase, organizations have a greater need for information processing. Karl Weick (1969), also using an information processing perspective, suggests that one of the central tasks faced by all organizations is that of importing and processing signals from the environment. Weick suggests that the internal processing of this information will depend on the perceived equivocality in the original signals.

AUTHORS' NOTE: We wish to thank Bill Barnett, Tom Biddle, Rick Boettger, Nancy Euske, and Jerry Goodstein for their helpful comments on earlier drafts of this chapter.

COMPARING MESSAGE FLOW
AND DECISION-MAKING RESEARCH

The emphasis on information and its importance in organizations is reflected in two streams of empirical research: (1) message flow (e.g., Monge, Edwards, & Kirste, 1978; Roberts & O'Reilly, 1978), and (2) decision making (e.g. Cyert & March, 1963). The former research tradition has examined the flow of messages within organizations, and the individual and organizational effects associated with the accurate flow of messages (e.g., O'Reilly & Pondy, 1979). The relative strength of this research program has been its realism or external validity. Researchers have often operationalized their independent variables to be directly relevant to organizations in the real world. This has been accomplished through the use of field setting methodologies to test hypotheses (e.g., Monge et al., 1978; Tushman & Scanlan, 1981). Additionally, this perspective has taken a dynamic view of information processing rather than a more traditional static or outcome view. Thus the emphasis is on the *process* of information transmission and acquisition. This is an important shift in focus because, as March and Sapira (1982, p. 30) argue, "outcomes are generally less significant than process. It is the process that gives meaning to life, and meaning is the core of life."

The weakness of this approach has been researchers' relative lack of precision and consensus both in how they define messages (see Stohl & Redding, Chapter 14, in this volume) and in what the appropriate boundaries of the concept of communication are (Porter & Roberts, 1976; Roberts & O'Reilly, 1974; Weick, 1983). Part of this problem can be attributed to the fact that communication is a complex process that sometimes becomes a circular phenomenon. For example, communication variables may influence subsequent communication patterns, which in turn influence those initial variables. Since communication is a process, communication research must reflect the inherent circularity of the process. The task of comparing between research studies is made more challenging, however, because some researchers treat message processes as a dependent variable while others treat them as an independent variable (see Jablin, 1982, as an example of the former; see Kapp & Barnett, 1983; and Eisenberg, Monge, & Miller, 1983, as examples of the latter).

In contrast, the decision-making research has provided insights about how information is used in organizational decision making. Pfeffer and Salancik (1977), for instance, have shown that organizational subunits will often use power to emphasize decisional criteria on which the subunit does comparatively well. Janis and Mann (1977) provide numerous examples of how decision makers may selectively seek out information to bolster a preferred position or defensively avoid negative information. The strength of decision making research has been that the dependent variables have been relatively tractable (e.g., use of information, decision quality, time elapsed to make decision). However, because the predominant method used in decision making research is laboratory experimentation (e.g., Abelson & Levi, 1986), realism is often sacrificed for precision (Tetlock, 1985). Thus issues arise about how generalizable such findings are for understanding organizational decision making.

Lab Versus Field Studies

A salient difference between decision-making and message transmission research exists in the methodologies used. The substantial literature on decision making and human information processing has relied almost exclusively on various types of laboratory experiments. For instance, a rough examination of 319 references cited in Slovic, Fischoff, and Lichtenstein (1977) suggests that at least 85% were *not* in field settings (also see Abelson & Levi, 1983; Nisbett & Ross, 1980). This chapter is not meant to be a critique of the use of laboratory experiments as a means for productively exploring information processing and decision making. Nor is it the purpose of this paper to explore the pros and cons of laboratory versus field research. Excellent coverage of these methodological issues is available elsewhere (e.g., Aronson & Carlsmith, 1968; Bouchard, 1976; Cook & Campbell, 1979; Winkler & Murphy, 1973; Zelditch, 1969). What is worthy of consideration here, however, is the extent to which there are important differences between laboratory studies of decision making and the message transmission that takes place in organizational settings. Figure 17.1 highlights some of the more important distinctions between laboratory and field studies used in decision-making and message flow research.

In addition to understanding message flow and decision-making processes, an accurate picture of organizational decision making should incorporate an assessment of the contextual pressures on decision makers; that is, in order to understand how information is used by real-world decision makers, studies need to account for the pressures that affect decision makers' willingness and ability to search for and use information in the actual performance of their duties. This is an important consideration since a number of studies suggest that decisions made under laboratory conditions may not correspond with the same decision made *in vivo*. For instance, Ebbesen and Kocnecni (1975) found that felony court judges, when presented with fictitious case histories containing all the relevant information, were most influenced by the nature of the crime and previous criminal records. However, when the researchers examined *actual* decisions made by these same judges, they found the decisions to be based almost exclusively on the district attorney's recommendations, which, in turn, were based primarily on the severity of the crime.

Differences between laboratory and field studies have also been reported by Gorman, Clover, and Doherty (1978) in a provocatively titled paper, "Can We Learn Anything About Interviewing Real People from "Interviews" of Paper People?" Judges in this experiment were required to make predictions

In laboratory studies, the decision makers usually:	In field studies, the decision makers usually:

-are passive receivers
-are focused on a limited set of cues
-have little experience with the task
-have no "rules" for coding and processing
-have little vested interest in long term
  except for the one set by experimenter
-operate with artificial time pressures
 	
-have little vested interest in long term
  results
-are clearly identified
-are unconcerned with interpersonal
  relationships
	-are senders as often as receivers
	-are concerned with multiple cues
	-are well experienced with the task
	-have response sets developed
	-have potentially conflicting goals
	
	-operate with a variety of time
	  pressures
	-are responsible for long term
	  results
	-are often unidentified
	-must deal with interpersonal
	  as well as task relationships

In laboratory studies, the information cues typically:	In field studies, the information cues typically:

-are present, absent, or available at
  a specified cost
 	
-are quantifiable
-are obtrusive and reactive
-are written
-are relevant only to the set of tasks
  at hand; the experiment creates its
  own context
-emanate from a "neutral" source with
  which the subject is unfamiliar
 	
-are not verifiable through feedback
-are limited in the number of cues
  which are methodologically feasible
  in any one study
-have no interpersonal content
	-are often difficult to distinguish,
	  available but not easily accessed,
	  or without a specifiable cost
	-are qualitative
	-are unobtrusive and nonreactive
	-are verbal
	-are relevant to a broad set of
	  tasks
	
	-emanate from sources with varying
	  saliences and credibilities to
	  the receiver
	-can be checked for accuracy
	-are socially, culturally, and
	  sequentially embedded

Figure 17.1 Differences Between Laboratory and Field Studies

based solely on the files of subjects and then from actual interviews of the same subjects. These investigators found substantial differences in the two conditions. Actual interviews often resulted in different decisions, increased confidence in the decision, and the use of different informational cues. These findings are consistent with a number of other studies that call attention to the artificiality of the laboratory situations and to the binding constraints that often affect decision makers in actual organizations (e.g., Beach, 1975; Svenson, 1979; Winkler & Murphy, 1973). An illustrative list of some of the potentially important differences in laboratory and field experiments is suggested by Figure 17.1. Obviously, if we are to develop a valid descriptive theory of message transmission and decision making in organizations (as opposed to a normative theory of decision making) that also possesses external validity, the research base must include the impact of contextual or situational influences on decision makers' propensities to seek out and use information.

INTEGRATING MESSAGE TRANSMISSION
AND DECISION MAKING

If the two approaches are integrated and both method and theory are shared, we gain an ability to use the strengths and minimize the weaknesses of each. This enhances our ability to depict how these processes operate and interact in organizational settings. Although message transmission research has explored information acquisition processes, generally it has not concentrated on how information is used for decision making; rather it has emphasized the individual and organizational effects of accurate or inaccurate information flow. The decision-making research has stressed how information and other structural and power variables interact to affect the *outcomes* of organizational decisions. This research has not typically focused on how actual decision makers acquire the information they need to make decisions. As Connolly (1977, p. 207) has noted in his review of decision making, "the limitation of research based on the individual decision-event model is that the decision maker is considered largely in isolation from the organizational environment which provides his input information, and to which he communicates his output." Tetlock (1985, p. 298) expresses a similar sentiment: "Most important decisions are not, after all, the product of isolated information processors; they are the product of intensive interactions among members of groups."

By considering decision making and message transmission in organizations as integrated processes, researchers will be in a better position to study information processing in organizations. In this chapter we will argue that the message flow literature can add context and realism to the decision-making research. Likewise, the decision-making literature can help to make the outcome variables of message flow more concrete and measurable. If we define "information processing" as the overarching process, and message transmission and decision making as elements of that process, then a full understanding of information processing requires an understanding of both its component processes.

Figure 17.2a illustrates the components of information processing in organizations. Currently, the majority of research on either message flow or decision making is conducted within the vertical boundaries of the respective areas. While these studies have been useful in illuminating the respective processes of message transmission and decision making as they have been previously bounded, they have not provided us with a well-developed picture of how the processes fit together. We do not mean to underestimate the contributions of either stream of research, as both have added important insights into organizational behavior. For example, message flow researchers have appropriately examined a number of outcome variables that have little to do with decision making (e.g., Albrecht, 1979; Stohl, 1986). Likewise, the decision-making research has generated interesting analyses of individual information use involving process tracing methods such as recording eye movements and recording verbal protocols (e.g., Abelson & Levi, 1986). While interesting, the research so far has largely failed to link the transmission of information to its actual use by organizational decision makers (e.g., O'Reilly, 1982).

Figure 17.2b shows how one could conceptually link the decision-making and message flow perspectives. This link, we believe, would continue to add important insights and help to further refine conceptualizations of information processing in organizations.

To explore some of these issues the rest of this chapter will (1) discuss the shortcomings of considering message acquisition and decision making, or information use, in isolation from each other; (2) demonstrate how the streams could be linked by looking at some of the common variables used by each stream; and (3) illustrate the importance of considering contextual characteristics that may affect decision making in organizations.

Distinction Between the Acquisition
and Use of Information

Basically, a decision involves the use of information to assess the results of a future course of action, given that some future states of the world are more desirable than others. This implies that a decision maker either has the requisite information available to make the choice or will obtain information through a process of search. The distinction between the use of information by decision makers as contrasted to its acquisition is an important one for understanding organizational information processing. Arrow (1973, p. 48) noted that "decisions, wherever taken, are a function of information received.... In turn, the acquisition of information must be analyzed, since it is itself the result of decisions." Arrow goes on to make explicit the distinction between the two kinds of decisions: decisions to act in some concrete sense, and decisions to collect information. Cyert and March (1963, p. 10) make a similar distinction between the need for a "theory of choice" and a "theory of search." Thus in order to understand how individuals in organizations typically make decisions we must understand both how they acquire information and how, once acquired, they process or use this information. It is recognized that on some occasions the link between information search and use may be tenuous—as with Cohen, March, and Olsen's garbage can model (1972). In general, however, information used for making decisions must be sought out by decision-making entities. Therefore, it is interesting to note that the

(A) SEPARATE MODELS

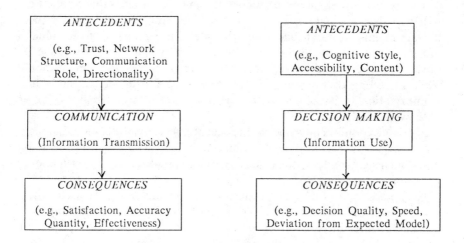

(B) INTEGRATED MODEL

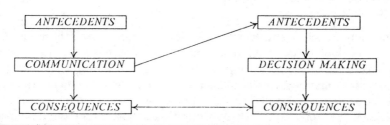

Figure 17.2(A)(B)   Separate (A) and Integrated (B) Models of Message Flow (left) and Decision Making Stages

literature on the acquisition of information by decision makers comes primarily from field studies of message flow, while our knowledge of information use comes almost entirely from laboratory studies of decision making.

Linking Research Literatures

Since we have established the importance of integrating message flow and decision making, our next task is to suggest how this integration might actually be accomplished. In this section, we will consider some of the variables that have been examined by the two perspectives. It should be noted that our intent is not to present an exhaustive review of either approach. Excellent reviews of these literatures are available in this volume and elsewhere (e.g., Monge & Eisenberg, Chapter 12, in this volume; Stohl & Redding, Chapter 14, in this volume; Abelson & Levi, 1983; Blair, Roberts, & McKechnie, 1985). Rather, we will choose a few illustrative variables for the purpose of demonstrating how these streams might be linked in practice.

Figure 17.3 shows a number of the more thoroughly researched variables used in each perspective. As one can see, although decision making and message flow are closely related by their mutual emphasis on information processing, there is some distinction between the types of variables focused on. In Figure 17.3 we suggest ways of linking variables across approaches—that is, linking quadrants I to IV and II to III.

In order to make these linkages more explicit, we provide a few examples of how the variables in Figure 17.3 could be integrated. For example, one interesting analysis might begin with the "accessibility" or "salience" of information (e.g., Culnan, 1984; Tversky & Kahneman, 1973), often used as independent variables in decision-making research, and look at the influence of these on the distortion of messages. One prediction is that the less accessible information is, the more likely it is that it will be distorted by the message sender. This may occur because of the difficulty in validating information that is not easily accessible. Therefore, a sender may feel free to interpret the information in a way that strengthens the decision he or she would like to see made (e.g., Lerner, 1976; Meltsner, 1976). The opposite prediction could be made for information that is highly salient or accessible, since users can more easily validate it and distortion can be more easily detected.

Another chain of variables that could be studied might begin with performance or decision outcomes (e.g., Staw & Ross, 1980) and examine the impact of these on the subsequent role and status of the message sender. Elements that could be incorporated in this analysis are directionality of the message transmission and personal ambition of the receiver and sender (e.g., Delehanty, Sullo, & Wallace, 1982; Huber, 1982). Thus, one could imagine a case where a previously low status decision maker makes a "good" decision or series of decisions. This may change the organizational status of that person, both formally and informally. One could then investigate whether the decision maker's credibility is enhanced and whether the patterns and content of messages exchanged between him or her and others change (Lerner, 1976; O'Reilly & Roberts, 1976). The point of such a study would be to clarify the factors that influence message transmission, in terms of the content, direction, and form of the message sent.

A third and slightly more complex case could be imagined. One could argue that an organization's structure determines the number of boundary spanners in that organization (e.g., Leifer & Huber, 1977; Tushman, 1977). The network position of the boundary spanners in turn may determine who among them has access to particular types of information—both the information

Representative Independent Variables	Representative Dependent Variables
Decision making I	Decision making II

Salience of information
Vividness of information
Heuristics for processing
  information:
    availability
    accessibility
    representativeness
    anchoring and adjustment
Structure of the problem
	Decision outcome
	Individual and group
	  performance
	Organizational effectiveness
	Information use
	Decision recognition

Communication III	Communication IV

Form of information
Content of information
Accessibility of information
Credibility of sender
Role of sender/receiver
Status of sender/receiver
Trust between participants
Power of participants
Proximity of participants
Personal ambition of participants
Directionality of information
Structure of organization:
  group processes
  task specialization
  hierarchy (number of levels)
  incentive structure
Network position
Norms of the organization
	Distortion of information
	Accuracy of information
	Filtering of information
	Quantity and direction of
	  communication
	Amount of subsequent
	  communication
	Number of boundary spanners
	Number of rules
	Power of participants
	Decision making quality
	Organization performance

Figure 17.3 Variables in Decision Making and Communication Research

used to make the decisions as well as information about what decisions are going to be made. Thus the boundary spanners may use information about the possible decision outcomes to determine which decisions should be made predicated on expected effects on future status in the network. This case illustrates the highly circular nature of the phenomenon, and could explore the mechanism by which communication and decision making interact in organizational settings. While the above examples are only illustrative, they suggest the richness and importance of research that incorporates both decision-making and message characteristics. In the next section, we suggest some ways in which the context, in the form of communication variables, can influence decisions in organizations.

Contextual Effects on Decision Making

In this section we continue to consider ways in which message transmission and decision-making variables may be integrated, concentrating explicitly on the group or organizational level. As suggested by several authors, laboratory evidence about information use and decision making may not be an adequate representation of the real world (e.g., Connolly, 1977; Slovic et al., 1977; Winkler & Murphy, 1973). O'Reilly (1983), for example, has observed that in actual organizational decision making, unlike most laboratory simulations, information may be ambiguous, may come from sources with varying degrees of credibility, and information users (decision makers) may be subject to a variety of pressures while pursuing multiple goals. Clausen (1973), for instance, has described the pressures on members of Congress and observed that most of their decision making with respect to voting is "uninformed" in the sense that they have little time to properly acquire and assimilate the information necessary to assess the issues carefully. Instead, votes are cast using a simplifying heuristic, such as the party line or the position of a respected colleague. Mintzberg (1973) has made similar observations about the pressures and time constraints on executives, noting that very little time is available to these decision makers to adequately search for and use large amounts of information. Further, even if a great deal of information is collected decision makers may not be able to use such information efficiently (Feldman & March, 1981; Nisbett & Ross, 1980). Studies of decision making could, therefore, benefit by considering those communication variables that may make real-world decision makers behave in ways that are quite different from those of laboratory decision makers.

One dominant contextual characteristic of organizations often ignored in laboratory experiments is the constant press in organizations for uniformity, conformity, and predictability. In order for an organization to perform successfully, the independent contributions of its members must be directed and coordinated toward sanctioned ends. This means that a variety of pressures and inducements will be used to regularize the behavior of individuals (e.g., March & Simon, 1958). Several salient characteristics of organizations that serve these homogenizing ends may be postulated, and message characteristics function prominently in each of these:

(1) *organizational structure*, which acts to restrict and channel information flows and establish a system of roles, authority, and expertise;
(2) *incentive systems*, which act to encourage the pursuit of certain goals and discourage others; and

(3) *group pressures*, which are both formal and informal and which make salient desired attitudes and behaviors.

These factors, which can be seen in the form of reward and punishment systems, hierarchy and authority, coordination and control, task design, and others, all have the result of securing conformity and compliance from organizational participants. Figure 17.4 (adapted from O'Reilly, 1983) presents a simplified model of the decision-making process that may characterize how decisions are made in organizations. These and other pressures may easily influence any of the stages of decision making outlined in Figure 17.2 (right). Incentive systems, for example, operate to make certain outcomes salient and desirable. Members are socialized to accept organizational goals and practices, which usually reflect the norms of the organization (Scott, 1981). Communication networks exist to ensure the presence of certain types of information. Specialization and task design encourage the development of expertise in the handling of only certain types of problems. Each of these factors (incentive system, structure, and norms) may affect (1) the *quantity* of information available to the decision maker, and (2) the *quality* of information available. The quantity and quality of information may then have direct effects on the types of decisions to be made and on how decision makers behave.

Organizational structure. If a decision maker requires information to define a problem and to generate a list of alternative solutions, it logically follows that the quantity and quality of information available will be related to the alternatives considered, estimates of probabilities made, and outcomes seen as desirable. In the organizational context it is important that relevant information be available to the appropriate decision makers. One mechanism by which the total information available to the organization is parceled is through the structuring of activities. Hierarchy and specialization are primary tools of this endeavor. Insofar as the information requirements match the task, this solution is efficient (Galbraith, 1973; Scott, 1981; Tushman & Nadler, 1978). Under some circumstances, however, the presence of hierarchy and specialization may lead to severe constraints on the information available to decision makers.

The literature offers some explicit variables concerned with the transmission of information that are relevant to the structural constraints of information flows. For example, O'Reilly (1978) has addressed the issue of the impact of organizational structure on the distortion of information in organizational communication. Drawing on the earlier works of Wilensky (1967), Janis (1972), Kaufman (1973), and others, O'Reilly suggests that hierarchy and specialization may act to encourage the distortion of information among organizational members by decreasing the trust between senders and receivers. Roberts and O'Reilly (1974) document the impact of hierarchy on the

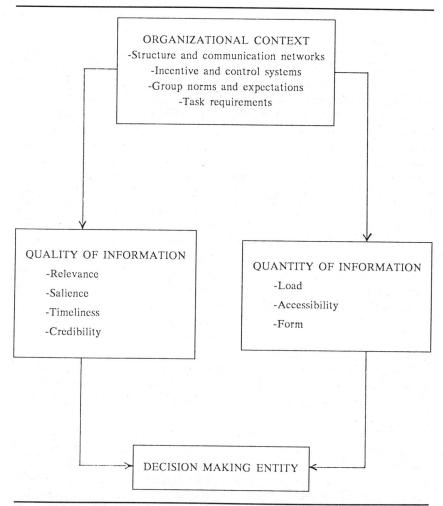

Figure 17.4 Simplified Model of Decision Making Process (adapted from O'Reilly, 1983)

quantity and quality of information being passed to higher echelon decision makers. Read (1962) also demonstrates the restraining effect hierarchy and status impose on the transmission of information by subordinates to superiors. More recently, researchers have found other effects of hierarchy and status differences on information flow. For example, Bradley (1978) found that high power and high status people receive more upward communication than high power but low status people. Slobin, Miller, and Porter (1968) found that individuals in middle-level positions are much more willing to communicate self-disclosure information upward than they are to divulge it downward. Additionally, numerous communication studies have shown that the level of trust between sender and receiver affects both the amount and type of information transmitted (Gains, 1980; Jablin, 1982; O'Reilly, 1977).

Since many important decisions in organizations are made at higher levels, these decision makers need accurate, reliable, and relevant information to define problems, generate alternatives, and ultimately make choices. This information is often acquired through messages exchanged from subordinates to superiors. Therefore, the variables that influence this relationship also influence the decision outcome by affecting the content and quality of information transmitted. In general, research findings demonstrate that subordinates attempt to present themselves in a favorable light to those above them in the hierarchy and are willing to suppress certain important pieces of information while transmitting unimportant information if it reflects favorably on themselves (e.g., Gains, 1980; O'Reilly & Pondy, 1979; Wilensky, 1967). This phenomenon is intensified when a subordinate is providing information to a superior who has control over his fate (Bradley, 1978; Monge et al., 1978). Additionally, information that reflects positively on the subordinate is more likely to be passed upward, and information that reflects negatively on the subordinate is less likely to be transmitted to the superior. In fact, this tendency is so strong that subordinates who do not trust their superior are willing to suppress unfavorable information even if they know that such information is useful for decision making (O'Reilly, 1978).

Other investigations have shown similar results. For instance, Pettigrew (1972) documented how a single individual, acting as a gatekeeper for information flowing to a policymaking group, was able to determine the outcome of a purchasing decision by carefully allowing only certain types of information through to the decision makers. Plott and Levine (1978) demonstrated how, through the arrangement of a meeting's agenda, outcomes could be determined in advance. Lowe and Shaw (1968) provided evidence that departments systematically inflate and bias budget requests to support claims for increased resources. In a slightly different vein, Kaufman (1973) showed how subordinates learned not to pass certain items of information upward in the hierarchy because superiors, on learning of these, would be required to act in ways contrary to their self-interest. A classic example of this system induced distortion is provided by McCleary (1977) in a study of how parole officers underreported deviant behavior to their supervisors. As noted by Kaufman (1973) this resulted in incidents being reported only when the information sent upward would result in enhancing the subordinates' career.

A number of investigations provide evidence about the influence of specialization on information flow. Hage, Aiken, and Marrett (1971), Brewer (1971), and others report that structure, while serving to channel information flows, may also act under some circumstances to deny decision makers relevant data. For example, Brewer found that a narrow span of control tends to increase the total amount of upward and downward communication between superiors and subordinates, while Jablin (1982) found that span of control has no differential impact on subordinates' perceptions of openness in communication between superiors and subordinates. Janis and Mann (1977, p. 122) describe the attack on Pearl Harbor and note that Admiral Kimmel assumed that the army had been notified to activate their defenses when, due largely to the lack of horizontal information flow produced by unconnected hierarchies, no such message had been sent. Gouran (1976) describes a similar lack of information available to President Nixon about the extent of people's involvement in the early stages of the Watergate cover-up.

Organizational structure has also been found to influence organizational roles and status. Zucker (1977), for example, showed how in a laboratory experiment the mere designation of an individual as having status resulted in the perpetuation of inaccurate judgments as successive generations of subjects continued to accept the estimates of the putative expert. Lerner (1976) in another laboratory experiment found that merely labeling some subjects as "experts" resulted in significant differences in their behavior. These results are consistent with the large body of research on conformity, which clearly demonstrates that individuals tend to perceive information as more credible if it comes from authority figures (e.g., Milgram, 1963; Zucker, 1977).

Finally, a related issue is how lack of consensus or ambiguity is dealt with in organizations. Putnam and Sorenson (1982) examined the impact of ambiguous messages and hierarchical level on the processing of equivocality. They found that with messages that were highly ambiguous, organization members used fewer rules and fewer people to process the information than when the messages were not ambiguous. There was also an effect of organizational level on how members attempted to reduce ambiguity. Foremen and workers were more likely to add interpretations, while managers tended to propose specific action steps. Eisenberg (1984) also discusses the importance of ambiguity as a strategy for message transmission in organizations. He claims that ambiguity, rather than being a deviant occurrence, is actually quite common and can have such diverse consequences as promoting versatility, facilitating organizational change, and preserving current positional structures. In summary, it seems clear that organizational structure may affect communication variables that, in turn, directly have an impact on the decision-making process.

Incentive systems. A related contextual pressure on decision makers' use of information can also be seen in the impact of organizational incentive systems. Decision makers are rewarded for pursuing certain ends and punished for others. The pervasive impact of incentive systems is difficult to overestimate. Kerr (1975) provides a number of instances in which employees behaved in seemingly contradictory ways, often appearing to do the opposite of the espoused goals. For example, directors of orphanages were found to establish policies that worked against the placement of children in foster homes, and acted to keep them in the orphanage; universities routinely established incentive systems that mitigated against encouraging high quality teaching; sport teams often rewarded individual performance when a team-oriented effort was required. Upon analysis, these results were seen not to be contradictory but rather were entirely consistent with the operative incentive systems; that is, people in organizations typically do those things for which they are rewarded. In Kerr's (1975) example, orphanage directors who succeeded in placing children in foster homes would be "rewarded" by cuts in staff, resources, and prestige among peers. In a direct test of the hypothesis that decision makers would respond to the operative control system, Harrell (1977) demonstrated that subordinate decision makers would follow their superior's lead and make decisions using similar criteria, even when superiors began making decisions which were contrary to the official policy.

Hence there is evidence that incentive systems may influence information use and decision making in two important ways: First, incentive systems may operate to encourage the transmission of certain types of information and discourage the transmission of other types. This may reflect an attempt on the part of the information sender to obtain rewards and avoid punishments. It may also act as a clear signal from the receiver that only certain types of information are desired (e.g., Halberstam, 1972; Janis & Mann, 1977). Second, incentive systems may act to focus the decision makers on a few, highly rewarded outcomes to the exclusion of others. Under these circumstances, there may be a tendency to ignore other important outcomes and alternatives in the pursuit of the single, highly salient consideration. Distortions referred to as goal displacement or means-ends reversal are examples. For example, Blau (1964) in his study of job placement personnel described how a change in the incentive system produced a dramatic change in the criteria used for decision making by the placement personnel. Additionally, Staw's work (e.g., 1982) on the escalation of commitment is relevant to the extent that decision makers may persist in a losing course of action (e.g., throwing good money after bad) in the hopes of eventually making a good decision out of a bad one. This seemingly nonrational behavior may become quite rational from the decision makers perspective if the incentive system is set up to reward good decisions and to punish poor decisions.

Group pressures. A number of specific issues must be considered regarding the impact of group pressures on organizational decision making. Decision makers are subject to formal and informal norms, operate within a role set, and are usually required to "live with" the results of the decisions they make. In this setting, a decision maker can seldom focus on a single problem and a single set of informational cues. Instead, there may be increased reliance on the group both for the information necessary to make the decision and their acceptance and compliance with the decision. Vroom and Yetton (1973), Maier (1967), Janis and Mann (1977) and others have pointed out in some detail how decision making in organizational settings is often characterized by a need to arrive at a mutually acceptable decision rather than an optimal one. This constraint may often require decision makers to avoid seeking certain information, being biased toward outcomes, and generally arriving at the decisions with a sensitivity to the divergent interests within the group (see

Murnighan, 1985, for an interesting lab experiment addressing this issue).

Janis and Mann (1977), for instance, describe numerous instances in which groups may selectively seek out supportive information to bolster a preferred position and defensively avoid contradictory or unfavorable information. Janis (1972), calling this "groupthink," provides a number of retrospective accounts in which groups acted to bolster desired opinions and exclude contrary ones. For instance, decision making by President Kennedy's advisory committee during the Bay of Pigs incident was characterized afterward by the suppression of doubts, creation of feelings of unanimity and invulnerability, and an unwillingness to risk conflict within the group. Johnson (1974) provides a nice example of this tendency to seek unanimity and avoid conflict in decision making. She hypothesized that executives would make a less desirable but acceptable short-run decision to avoid generating conflict with others in the group. Using 49 businessmen across ten situations she discovered that although subjects could identify the ideal decision for each situation, their overwhelming tendency was to make sub-optimal decisions in order to avoid conflict (also see Putnam & Poole, Chapter 16, in this volume).

The group process literature is especially interesting because it brings decision-making research closer to communication research by acknowledging that decision making includes an important process element. This literature again underscores the importance of integrating organizational analyses to include both process and outcome elements. In fact, the inclusion of process analyses in organizational research is argued to be one way of integrating micro- and macro-level organizational behavior (March & Olsen, 1984).

Summary. The operation of contextual factors such as organizational structure, incentive systems, and group pressures may affect both the acquisition and processing of information by decision makers. Decision makers in actual organizational settings may be subject to a variety of pressures and constraints not easily investigated in laboratory settings. However, unless these contextual effects are investigated, findings about information processing and decision-making behavior may not possess the external validity necessary to be useful in understanding organizational decision making. The methods and variables that are examined in the communication literature could help to guide future studies of decision making in organizations.

ACQUIRING AND USING INFORMATION IN DECISION MAKING

Consider how the above contextual factors might affect decision makers' acquisition and use of information in organizational settings. In an ideal world decision makers would seek out the information that is known to be accurate and relevant to the decision at hand. But how does this process actually occur?

First, there is good evidence that decision makers in organizations are noticeably biased in their procurement of information. Instead of relying on the most accurate sources of information (Naylor, 1964), decision makers, for a variety of reasons, rely on more accessible sources. For example, O'Reilly (1982) found that although decision makers recognized information sources of high quality, they used sources that provided lower quality information but were more accessible. He explains these results in terms of the costs involved in obtaining information from less accessible sources. Given that the decision makers were under time constraints and subject to numerous interruptions, it may have been that they were simply unable to seek out higher quality information when it came from less accessible sources. Similar findings have been reported about the information seeking behavior of physicians (Menzel & Katz, 1955), scientists (Gerstberger & Allen, 1968), policymakers (Clausen, 1973) managers (Mintzberg, 1973), and college students (Culnan, 1984).

The bias toward accessible information is also reflected in managers' strong preferences for oral as opposed to written information (Dewhirst, 1971) and for information from trustworthy or credible sources (e.g., Beach, Mitchell, Deaton, & Prothero, 1978; Giffin, 1967; Mintzberg, 1973). Research in these areas has shown that managers typically prefer shorter, oral reports to longer written ones. Interestingly, there is also evidence that, when obtaining information in this manner, managers may judge the validity of the information based on the credibility of the source, not the facts of the matter. This may lead to the acceptance of a piece of information as "true" or "false" depending on how much the recipient trusts the sender. The research on source credibility also suggests that it may be the "safeness" or trustworthiness of the source, more than expertise, that determines whether information is believed (O'Reilly & Roberts, 1976). Thus information may be acquired from accessible, trustworthy sources rather than from potentially higher quality sources that, while being perceived of as having the requisite expertise, are not considered trustworthy. These tendencies may reflect structural barriers that make information sources sanction the use of some sources but not others. They may also reflect the structural barriers that are created by group pressures and can act to limit the range of "acceptable" information seeking.

Aside from information acquisition biases, similar contextual influences may be seen on decision makers' use of information. For example, given that decision makers are able to make sense of a relatively small amount of information, it becomes difficult to determine which items of information, of the total quantity available, a decision maker will focus on and use. Studies are consistent in finding that subject matter experts typically use different information in making judgments (e.g., Fiske & Taylor, 1984; Slovic et al., 1977). This suggests that decision makers, when presented with a large quantity of data, may interpret and weight the information differently.

Hawkins, Hoffman, and Osborne (1978), for example, in a drug evaluation study, showed that various actors were weighting information differently according to the evaluation criteria they were using. Other studies have demonstrated variation in preference for types of information across decision makers (Kilmann & Mitroff, 1976), as well as how stress reduces one's ability to process information (cf. Janis & Mann, 1977; Nisbett & Ross, 1980; Wright, 1974). Since, as Mintzberg (1973) has shown, managers' work is characteristically fragmented and subject to distractions and time pressures, it is likely that users of information will be unable to assimilate fully all of the available information. This interpretation is consistent with studies showing that over time, details are forgotten and the reconstructed meaning is often less ambiguous than originally portrayed and interpreted as offering support for a favored position (Feldman & March, 1981; Ross, 1977). Information contained in the original signal that is unfavorable is likely to be either forgotten or reinterpreted so as to minimize its negative consequences.

On the other hand, when decision makers are attempting to reach a negative decision, evidence is available suggesting that decision makers may seek out and overweight negative evidence; that is, when the incentives are to reach a negative conclusion, there is a tendency to use whatever negative information is available to say no (Fiske & Taylor, 1984; Kanouse & Hansen, 1972). Selection interviewers, when presented with a large number of positive cues and very few negative ones have been shown to systematically attend to the negative information and use it to reject applicants. Miller and Rowe (1967), for example, found that when subjects were required to make assessment decisions, there was a significant tendency to be influenced by negative rather than positive adjectives used to describe a candidate. Other corroborative evidence is available from studies of personal perception, investment decisions and gamblers (Kanouse & Hansen, 1972). When decision makers favor a position, the bias has been shown to operate toward the selection of favorable information as well (cf. Morlock, 1967).

It should be noted that this bias does not necessarily suggest that decision makers truncate their search for information having once obtained data that can be used to support a desired position or oppose an undesired one. The apparent tendency is to seek out selectively information that bolsters one's position and avoid unsupported information in either acquisition or processing, but not necessarily to avoid searching. In fact, a number of laboratory studies have demonstrated an interesting propensity among decision makers to desire more information than can be effectively used (Chervany & Dickson, 1974; Feldman & March, 1981; Oskamp, 1965). The paradox is that decision makers appear to seek more information than is required, even to the point of inducing overload (O'Reilly, 1980). While the overload may actually impair performance, the additional information has been shown to increase the decision makers' confidence. The net result may be that decision makers arrive at poorer decisions but are more confident in their choices.

Thus it appears that decision makers will selectively seek out information that supports or opposes a position, acquire as much of this information as possible, and be increasingly confident in their decision although such decisions may be substantially biased. Meltsner (1976), in a book on policy analysts in bureaucratic settings, makes a relevant distinction between two categories of information sought by decision makers: information used to *make* decisions and information used to *support* decisions. Clearly, there are incentives in organizations to be "correct" in decision making. Because of this, it is reasonable for decision makers to seek information that is supportive of a particular position, as well as information that undermines opposing views. Information use of this type is commonplace in organizations, but seldom examined in laboratory settings.

In summary, both the information transmitted to the decision maker and the decision maker's framing of it can act to affect the decision outcomes. Both message transmission and decision making need to be examined if an adequate understanding of organizational decision making is to be had.

CONCLUSION

This chapter has argued that two very distinct research perspectives exist; one focuses on message flow in organizations, and the other examines decision making. While each of these approaches has obvious strengths, comparatively little cross-tradition research has been undertaken. Instead, the former perspective has focused primarily on the process of information transmission in organizational settings, without paying much detailed attention to how individuals actually use acquired information, while the latter approach has concentrated on how individuals use cues in choice and judgment once information has been acquired. These traditions differ sharply in focus (the process of information transmission versus the outcomes of using cues) and methodology (field versus laboratory).

In an excellent review of decision making, Tetlock (1985) observed, "A pervasive feature of natural decision environments—but not of laboratory experiments on cognitive processes—is the fact that people are potentially accountable for the judgments and decisions they express" (p. 297). The crucial point is that studies of judgment and choice would be enriched if more attention were paid to the context in which decisions are made. In contrast, communication researchers have often failed to examine the outcome variables most logically related to message transmission—that is, the *use* of information by individuals or groups to make choices. Clearly, studies that bridge the two research streams are needed. The successful integration of these two important literatures will, in our estimation, offer the potential of significantly advancing our understanding of both organizational communication and decision making.

REFERENCES

Abelson, R. P., & Levi, A. (1986). Decision-making and decision theory. In G. Lindzey and E. Aronson (Eds.), *Handbook of social psychology* (3rd., Vol. 1, pp. 231-310). Reading, MA: Addison-Wesley.

Albrecht, T. L. (1979). The role of communication in perceptions of organizational climate. In D. Nimmo (Ed.), *Communication yearbook 3* (pp. 343-357). New Brunswick, NJ: Transaction.

Aronson, E., & Carlsmith, M. (1968). Experimentation in social psychology. In E. Aronson & G. Lindzey (eds.), *Handbook of social psychology* (2nd ed., Vol. 2, pp. 1-79). Reading, MA: Addison-Wesley.

Arrow, K. J. (1973) *The limits of organization.* New York: Norton.

Beach, B. (1975). Expert judgment about uncertainty: Bayesian decision making in realistic settings. *Organizational Behavior and Human Performance, 14,* 10-59.

Beach, L. R., Mitchell, T. R., Deaton, M. D., & Prothero, J. (1978). Information relevance, content and source credibility in the revision of opinions. *Organizational Behavior and Human Performance, 21,* 1-16.

Blair, R., Roberts, K., & McKechnie, P. (1985) Vertical and network communication in organizations: The present and the future. In P. Tompkins & R. McPhee (Eds.), *Organizational communication: Traditional themes and new directions* (pp. 55-77). Newbury Park, CA: Sage.

Blau, P. (1964). *Exchange and power in social life.* New York: Wiley.

Bouchard, T. (1976). Field experiment methods: Interviewing, questionnaires, participant observation, systematic observation, unobtrusive measures. In M. Dunnette (Ed.), *Handbook of industrial and organizational psychology* (pp. 1553-1596). Chicago: Rand McNally.

Bradley, P. (1978). Status and upward communication in small decision-making groups. *Communication Monographs, 45,* 33-43.

Brewer, J. (1971) Flow of communication, expert qualifications and organizational authority structure. *American Sociological Review, 36,* 475-484.

Chervany, N., & Dickson, G. (1974). An experimental evaluation of information overload in production environment. *Management Science 20,* 1335-1344.

Clausen, A. (1973). *How congressmen decide: A policy focus.* New York: St. Martin's.

Cohen, M., March, J., & Olsen, J. (1972). A garbage can model of organizational choice. *Administrative Science Quarterly, 17,* 1-25.

Connolly, T. (1977). Information processing and decision making in organizations. In B. Staw & G. Salancik (Eds.), *New directions in organizational behavior* (pp. 205-243). Chicago: St. Clair.

Cook, T., & Campbell, D. (1979). *Quasi-experimentation: Design and analysis issues for field settings.* Chicago: Rand McNally.

Culnan, M. (1984). The dimensions of accessibility to online information: Implications for implementing office information systems. *ACM Transactions on Office Information Systems, 2,* 141-150.

Cyert, R., & March, J. (1963). *A behavioral theory of the firm.* Englewood Cliffs, NJ: Prentice-Hall.

Daft, R., & Macintosh, N. (1981). A tentative exploration into the amount and equivocality of information processing in organizational work units. *Administrative Science Quarterly, 26,* 207-224.

Delehanty, T., Sullo, P., & Wallace, W. (1982). A method for the prescriptive assessment of the flow of information within organizations. *Management Science, 28,* 910-923.

Dewhirst, H. D. (1971). Influence of perceived information-sharing norms on communication channel utilization. *Academy of Management Journal, 14,* 305-315.

Ebbesen, E., & Kocnecni, V. (1975). Decision making and information integration in the courts: The setting of bail. *Journal of Personality and Social Psychology, 32,* 805-821.

Eisenberg, E. (1984). Ambiguity as strategy in organizational communication. *Communication Monographs, 51,* 227-242.

620 PROCESS: COMMUNICATION BEHAVIOR IN ORGANIZATIONS

Eisenberg, E., Monge, P., & Miller, K. (1983). Involvement in communication networks as a predictor of organizational commitment. *Human Communication Research, 10,* 179-201.

Feldman, M., & March, J. (1981). Information in organizations as signal and symbol. *Administrative Science Quarterly, 26,* 171-186.

Ference, T. (1970). Organizational communications systems and the decision process. *Management Science, 17,* B83-B96.

Fiske, S., & Taylor, S. (1984). *Social cognition.* Reading, MA: Addison-Wesley.

Gains, J. (1980). Upward communication in industry: An experiment. *Human Relations, 33,* 923-942.

Galbraith, J. (1973). *Designing complex organizations.* Reading, MA: Addison-Wesley.

Gerstberger, P., & Allen, T. (1968). Criteria used by research and development engineers in the selection of an information source. *Journal of Applied Psychology, 52,* 272-279.

Giffin, K. (1967). The contribution of studies of source credibility to a theory of interpersonal trust in the communication process. *Psychological Bulletin, 68,* 104-120.

Gorman, C., Clover, W., & Doherty, M. (1978). Can we learn anything about interviewing real people from "interviews" of paper people? Two studies of the external validity of a paradigm. *Organizational Behavior and Human Performance, 22,* 165-192.

Gouran, D. (1976). The Watergate coverup: Its dynamics and its implications. *Communication Monographs, 43,* 176-186.

Hage, J., Aiken, M., & Marrett, C. (1971). Organization structure and communications. *American Sociological Review, 36,* 860-871.

Halberstam, D. (1972). *The best and the brightest.* New York: Random House.

Harrell, A. (1977). The decision-making behavior of air force officers and the management control process. *Accounting Review, 52,* 833-841.

Hawkins, J., Hoffman, R., & Osborne, P. (1978). Decision makers' judgments: The influence of role, evaluative criteria and information access. *Evaluation Quarterly, 2,* 435-454.

Huber, G. (1982). Organizational information systems: Determinants of their performance and behavior. *Management Science, 28,* 138-155.

Jablin, F. (1982). Formal structural characteristics of organizations and superior-subordinate communication. *Human Communication Research, 8,* 338-347.

Janis, I. (1972). *Victims of groupthink.* Boston: Houghton Mifflin.

Janis, I., & Mann, I. (1977). *Decision making: A psychological analysis of conflict, choice, and commitment.* New York: Free Press.

Johnson, R. J. (1974). Conflict avoidance through acceptable decisions. *Human Relations, 27,* 71-82.

Kanouse, D. E., & Hansen, L. R. (1972). Negativity in evaluations. In E. E. Jones, D. E. Kanouse, H. H. Kelley, R. E. Nisbett, S. Valins, & B. Weiner (Eds.), *Attribution: Perceiving the causes of behavior* (pp. 47-62). Morristown, NJ: General Learning Press.

Kapp, J., & Barnett, G. (1983). Predicting organizational effectiveness from communication activities: A multiple indicator model. *Human Communication Research, 9,* 239-254.

Kaufman, H. (1973). *Administrative feedback.* Washington, DC: Brookings Institution.

Kerr, S. (1975). On the folly of rewarding A, while hoping for B. *Academy of Management Journal, 18,* 769-783.

Kilmann, R., & Mitroff, I. (1976). Qualitative versus quantitative analysis for management science: Different forms for different psychological types. *Interfaces, 6,* 17-27.

Leifer, R. P., & Huber, G. P. (1977). Relations among perceived environmental uncertainty, organizational structure, and boundary-spanning behavior. *Administrative Science Quarterly, 22,* 235-247.

Lerner, A. W. (1976). *The politics of decision making: Strategy, cooperation and conflict.* Newbury Park, CA: Sage.

Lowe, E., & Shaw, R. (1968). An analysis of managerial biasing: Evidence from a company's budgeting process. *Journal of Management Studies, 5,* 304-315.

Maier, N.R.F. (1967). Assets and liabilities in group problem solving. *Psychological Review, 74,* 239-249.

March, J., & Olsen, J. (1984). The new institutionalism: Organizational factors in political life. *American Political Science Review, 78,* 734-749.

March, J., & Sapira, Z. (1982). Behavioral decision theory and organizational decision theory. In G. Ungson & D. Braunstein (Eds.), *New directions in decision making: An interdisciplinary approach to the study of organizations* (pp. 1-54). Boston: Kent.

March, J., & Simon, H. (1958). *Organizations.* New York: John Wiley.

McCleary, R. (1977). How parole officers use records. *Social Problems, 24,* 576-589.

Meltsner, A. J. (1976). *Policy analysts in the bureaucracy.* Berkeley: University of California Press.

Menzel, H., & Katz, E. (1955). Social relations and innovation in the medical profession. *Public Opinion Quarterly, 19,* 337-352.

Milgram, S. (1963). Behavioral study of obedience. *Journal of Abnormal and Social Psychology, 67,* 371-378.

Miller, J. W., & Rowe, P. M. (1967). Influence of favorable and unfavorable information upon assessment decisions. *Journal of Applied Psychology, 51,* 432-435.

Mintzberg, H. (1973). *The nature of managerial work.* New York: Harper & Row.

Monge, P., Edwards, J., & Kirste, K. (1978). The determinants of communication and communication structure in large organizations: A review of research. In B. Ruben (Ed.), *Communication yearbook 2*(pp. 311-331). New Brunswick, NJ: Transaction Books.

Morlock, H. (1967). The effect of outcome desirability on information required for decisions. *Behavioral Science, 12,* 296-300.

Murninghan, J. K. (1985). Coalitions in decision-making groups: Organizational analogs. *Organizational Behavior and Human Decision Processes, 35,* 1-26.

Naylor, J. (1964). Accuracy and variability of information sources of determiners and source preference of decision makers. *Journal of Applied Psychology, 48,* 43-49.

Nisbett, R., & Ross, L. (1980). *Human inference: Strategies and shortcomings of social judgment.* Englewood Cliffs, NJ: Prentice-Hall.

O'Reilly, C. A. (1977). Superiors and peers as information sources, work group supportiveness, and individual decision making performance. *Journal of Applied Psychology, 62,* 632-635.

O'Reilly, C. A. (1978). The intentional distortion of information in organizational communication: A laboratory and field approach. *Human Relations, 31,* 173-193.

O'Reilly, C. A. (1980). Individuals and information overload in organizations: Is more necessarily better? *Academy of Management Journal, 23,* 684-696.

O'Reilly, C. A. (1982). Variations in decision makers' use of information sources: The impact of quality and accessibility of information. *Academy of Management Journal, 25,* 756-771.

O'Reilly, C. (1983). The use of information in organizational decision making: A model and some propositions. In L. Cummings & B. Staw (Eds.), *Research in organizational behavior* (Vol. 5, pp. 103-139). Greenwich, CT: JAI.

O'Reilly, C., & Pondy, L. (1979). Organizational communication. In S. Kerr (Ed.), *Organizational behavior* (pp. 119-150). Columbus, OH: Grid.

O'Reilly, C., & Roberts, K. (1976). Relationships among components of credibility and communication behaviors in work units. *Journal of Applied Psychology, 61,* 99-102.

Oskamp, S. (1965). Overconfidence in case study judgments. *Journal of Consulting Psychology, 29,* 261-265.

Pettigrew, A. (1972). Information control as a power resource. *Sociology, 6,* 187-204.

Pfeffer, J., & Salancik, G. (1977). *The external control of organizations: A resource dependence perspective.* New York: Harper & Row.

Plott, C., & Levine, M. (1978). A model of agenda influence on committee decisions. *American Economic Review, 68,* 146-160.

Porter, L., & Roberts, K. (1976). Organizational communication. In M. Dunnette (Ed.), *Handbook of industrial and organizational psychology* (pp. 1553-1589). Chicago: Rand McNally.

Putnam, L., & Sorenson, R. (1982). Equivocal messages in organizations. *Human Communication Research, 8,* 114-132.

Read, W. (1962). Upward communication in industrial hierarchies. *Human Relations, 15,* 3-16.

Roberts, K., & O'Reilly, C. (1974). Failures in upward communication in organizations: Three possible culprits. *Academy of Management Journal, 17,* 205-215.

Roberts, K., & O'Reilly, C. (1978). Organizations as communication structures: An empirical approach. *Human Communication Research, 4,* 283-293.

Ross, L. (1977). The intuitive psychologist and his shortcomings: Distortions in the attribution process. In L. Berkowitz (Ed.), *Advances in experimental social psychology* (pp. 173-220). New York: Academic Press.

Scott, W. R. (1981). *Organizations: Rational, natural, and open systems.* Englewood Cliffs, NJ: Prentice-Hall.

Slobin, D., Miller, S., & Porter, L. (1968). Forms of address and social relations in a business organization. *Journal of Personality and Social Psychology, 8,* 449-468.

Slovic, P., Fischoff, M., & Lichtenstein, S. (1977). Behavioral decision theory. In M. Rozensweig & L. Porter (Eds.), *Annual review of psychology,* (Vol. 28, pp. 1-39). Palo Alto: Annual Reviews.

Staw, B. (1982). Counterforces to change. In P. Goodman (Ed.), *Change in organizations* (pp. 87-121). San Francisco: Jossey-Bass.

Staw, B., & Ross, J. (1980). Commitment in an experimenting society: A study of the attribution of leadership from administrative scenarios. *Journal of Applied Psychology, 65,* 249-260.

Stohl, C. (1986). The role of memorable messages in the process of organizational socialization. *Communication Quarterly, 34,* 231-249.

Svenson, O. (1979). Process descriptions of decision making. *Organizational Behavior and Human Performance, 23,* 86-112.

Tetlock, P. (1985). Accountability: The neglected social context of judgment and choice. In B. Staw & L. Cummings (Eds.), *Research in organizational behavior* (Vol. 7, pp. 297-332). Greenwich, CT: JAI.

Thompson, J. D. (1967). *Organizations in action.* New York: McGraw-Hill.

Tushman, M. (1977). Special boundary roles in the innovation process. *Administrative Science Quarterly, 22,* 587-605.

Tushman, M., & Nadler, D. (1978). Information processing as an integrating concept in organizational design. *Academy of Management Review, 3,* 613-624.

Tushman, M., & Scanlan, T. (1981). Boundary scanning individuals: Their role in information transfer and their antecedents. *Academy of Management Journal, 24*(2), 289-305.

Tversky, A., & Kahneman, D. (1973). Availability: A heuristic for judging frequency and probability. *Cognitive Psychology, 5,* 207-232.

Vroom, V., & Yetton, P. (1973). *Leadership and decision making.* Pittsburgh: University of Pittsburgh Press.

Weick, K. (1969). *The social psychology of organizing.* Reading, MA: Addison-Wesley.

Weick, K. (1983). Organizational communication: Toward a research agenda. In L. Putnam & M. Pacanowsky (Eds.), *Communication and organizations: An interpretive approach* (pp. 13-29). Newbury Park, CA: Sage.

Wilensky, H. (1967). *Organizational intelligence.* New York: Free Press.

Winkler, R., & Murphy, A. (1973). Experiments in the laboratory and the real world. *Organizational Behavior and Human Performance, 10,* 252-270.

Wright, P. (1974). The harassed decision maker: Time pressures, distractions, and the use of evidence. *Journal of Applied Psychology, 59,* 555-561.

Zelditch, M., Jr. (1969). Can you really study an army in the laboratory? In A. Etzioni (Ed.), *A sociological reader on complex organizations* (pp. 528-529). New York: Holt, Rinehart & Winston.

Zucker, L. (1977). The role of institutionalization in cultural persistence. *American Sociological Review, 42,* 726-743.

18 Feedback, Motivation, and Performance

LOUIS P. CUSELLA
University of Dayton

TO anyone who has spent time working in or observing organizations, there can be little dispute that the feedback concept—information about the results of actions taken by individuals, groups, or organizations—is central to our understanding of organizational behavior in general and of organizational communication specifically. As a consequence, it should be of little surprise that feedback is a widely used concept in management decision making, planned organizational change, management

AUTHOR'S NOTE: I wish to thank Teresa L. Thompson, Dan Slater, and Fred Jablin for their helpful comments on earlier drafts of this chapter.

control, organizational design, training, performance appraisal, motivation, and organizational communication (e.g., Cusella, 1980, 1986; Ramaprasad, 1983).

Even a cursory review of writings in the organizational sciences suggests that an impressive amount of feedback research has been conducted. However, nearly all the feedback-motivation and feedback-performance research has been conducted in the areas of organizational psychology and organizational behavior. A paucity of feedback research has been conducted by organizational communication scholars. This fact is startling, considering the prominence of feedback in any organizational communication process (Redding, 1972). As a result, almost all models of feedback and feedback research emphasize the internal psychological processes involved in feedback sending (e.g., Larson, 1984) and feedback receiving (e.g., Ilgen, Fisher, & Taylor, 1979).

The emphasis of extant research on internal/psychological processes represents a crucial line of study in the effort to explore feedback processes, rather than a limitation per se, since no research perspective can be all things to all people. However, it should be recognized that researchers adopting the psychological approach have employed cognitive models to explain phenomena (i.e., feedback-motivation and feedback-performance) that are also fundamentally *pragmatic communication processes.* In communication theory *pragmatics* signifies more than the lay notion of "practical"—the pragmatics of communication concerns the manner in which symbols affect behavior. As such, a pragmatic communication approach to the study of feedback focuses on the feedback sender-feedback receiver *relationship*, as mediated by their communication activity (Watzlawick, Beavin, & Jackson, 1967). In other words, from a communication perspective, feedback processes consist of an exchange of behaviors that emphasize the (1) symbolic; (2) relational; and (3) systemic aspects to feedback-motivation/performance relationships.

Although to date little feedback research has come from the area of organizational communication, the prospects for feedback research via a communication perspective are outstanding. A research agenda of this sort would, for example, explore issues related to the context in which feedback is administered and received, the relational control and definitional aspects of feedback messages, patterns of control in feedback systems, the study of the content of feedback messages, the symbolic quality of feedback messages as recurrent signs embedded in an organizational culture, and ultimately how these phenomena affect motivation and performance. Moreover, as the following discussion will demonstrate, a communication perspective to feedback processes, while representing a clear conceptual separation from cognitive models of feedback is, nevertheless, interdependent with them.

In light of the above issues, the central purposes of this chapter are to examine and integrate the relevant literature and demonstrate how the context and manner in which performance feedback is communicated, plus the nature of the feedback per se, affects a receiver's (task performer's) subsequent motivation and performance. This examination considers the nature of the feedback process in the following contexts: (1) feedback conveyed via a receiver's work environment not directly mediated by another actor (impersonal feedback); (2) feedback delivered to a receiver by another person (dyadic feedback); and (3) feedback delivered to a group about the group's performance (group feedback).

Additionally, the research reviewed here generally focuses on studies exploring the subsequent effects of feedback on task motivation and/or task performance and not on investigations of learning per se. Feedback-learning research, however, is both important and voluminous (Adams, 1968) and will be considered briefly in discussing impersonal feedback.

The general definition of feedback advocated in this chapter—*messages conveyed to a receiver about his, her, or its (group) task performance*—also serves to focus the analysis. For example, while it can be argued that incentives and rewards possess information qualities for their recipients, very little incentive/reward research is included; incentives and rewards are seldom conceived, either theoretically or operationally, as messages conveyed within a communication context. For the purpose of conceptual clarity, however, the constructs of incentive and reward will be defined.

Lastly, instead of compartmentalizing communication variables relevant to traditional communication models (e.g., source → message → channel → receiver → feedback), this essay examines the process dynamics of feedback transmission and reception by exploring traditional communication model variables in the context of feedback sending and receiving attributional processes. Prior to this discussion, however, basic constitutive and operational issues associated with the constructs of feedback, motivation, and performance are briefly considered.

DEFINING FEEDBACK

Despite wide usage of the feedback concept, there is little consensus on its definition either inside or outside of organizational studies (Ashby, 1956; Buckley, 1967; Clement & Frandsen, 1976; Ramaprasad, 1983; Wilden, 1972) where definitions of feedback vary in both their breadth and depth (Ramaprasad, 1983). While there is little consensus on a definition, there is little question that the feedback construct originated in the science of cybernetics.

Feedback Concept: Cybernetics

Wiener (1948) coined the term feedback from the science of cybernetics as it referred to the report aspect of output energy that was returned to a system as input. In a later work, Wiener (1954) defined feedback as "a method of controlling a system" (p. 61). Following the work of Wiener (1948), Powers (1973, p. 352) proposed a modified version of a prototypic feedback loop in a human behavior system. According to Powers, the loop begins when a stimulus, or disturbance, occurs in the social field, generating an input signal. Between this signal and its response a number of important "unseen" (hypothetical) operations occur (Powers, 1973). Though only the stimulus and response are seen, Powers (1973) intimates that a *sensor function* receives an input signal from the stimulus and transmits its own sensor signal on toward the system as a whole, altering it to the quality of the input signal. This sensor signal is then compared with a *reference signal* (goal) of unspecified origin, which states the system's desired states of regulation (level of activity). In turn, a *system comparator* emits an error signal, which is based on the discrepancy between the sensor signal and reference signal. This error signal activates the system's *effector function* to produce the system's response to the original stimulus in the social field. Consequently, the output, a part of the environment, provides a feedback link to the input stimulus.

It is also important to recognize that feedback in cybernetics is viewed in two different senses: positive and negative. Negative feedback is the technical term used to denote those feedback signals a system uses to maintain its stability while progressing toward a predetermined goal (reference signal). Theoretically, negative feedback serves as a corrective signal to prevent a system from overshooting its mark (goal) and self-destructing. A negative feedback loop is generally understood as an error-activating process designed to maintain constancy or a steady state in response to environmental alterations (Kantor & Lehr, 1975). Alternatively, positive feedback denotes information that does not return corrective signals to the system; the system continues to self-accelerate, thus increasing deviations from a predetermined goal. From a systems theory perspective, every organization unit (macro or micro) must at times change its basic structure and adapt to environmental change.

Further, because of their integral role in system regulations, the nature and origin of cybernetic *reference signals* (system goals) warrant elaboration. In a sense, feedback loops are action loops (interconnected activities) that occur when an activity entails a chain of other activities that, in turn, ultimately recreate the original situation (Masuch, 1985). They are called negative or positive feedback loops, depending on whether they are moving away from or approaching the reference point. Here it must be emphasized that the reference signal or reference point in any feedback loop can be determined in two different ways: (1) by making value judgments (i.e., by defining some desired standard) or (2) by assessing facts (Masuch, 1985). Along these lines Masuch (1985) suggests the following:

Negative feedback loops are called "deviation-counteracting" when related to normative standards (value judgments) and "self-correcting" when related to a factual point of reference. Positive feedback loops, on the other hand, are called "deviation amplifying" when related to norms and "self-reinforcing" when related to facts. (p. 16)

Figure 18.1 (adapted from Masuch, 1985, p. 16) outlines this perspective.

For example, to the extent that the factual state of organizational affairs reflects it, the relationship between organizational change and organizational stability is *self-correcting* (Pondy, 1967): Increases in change decrease stability while increased stability diminishes change. Similarly, the relationship between task sharing and task specialization is *self-correcting* (Muto & Cusella, 1984): The more coworkers share tasks, the less they specialize; while the less coworkers specialize, the more they share task activities. On the other hand, the relationship between liking and interaction (Homans, 1961) is *self-reinforcing* (liking leads to interaction and vice versa). If a noncompetitive relationship is the norm, the perspective of Watzlawick et al. (1967) suggests that escalating symmetrical interaction ("one-upping" each other) is *deviation amplifying*, whereas rigidly complementary interaction (where A regularly seeks control and B acquiesces) is *deviation counteracting* (stabilizing), given the goal of a noncompetitive relationship.

Feedback Concept: Behavioral Science

It is important to note that behavioral scientists have not consistently used the terms "positive feedback" and "negative feedback" as cybernetic theorists originally defined them (Cusella, 1980; Nadler, 1979). As Nadler (1979) observes, such inconsistencies exist because the cybernetic view of feedback has limitations in its application to human behavior. To understand how feedback affects behavior, researchers, especially in the areas of learning and task performance, have developed a variety of perspectives to move beyond simple error correction cybernetic models.

Distinctions between cybernetic and behavioral science approaches to feedback are epitomized in their definitions of basic constructs, including such deceptively simple notions as positive and negative feedback. In contrast to cybernetic definitions of positive and negative feedback, behavioral science definitions are not as precise. For instance, a task performer may be rewarded verbally (praise) and monetarily (pay) for successful task completion. From a theoretical standpoint, are such verbal and monetary rewards a part of a negative or a positive feedback loop? Their *purpose* is clearly that of a negative feedback loop. But while almost certainly perceived as attractive, the praise and pay are not "positive" in the *technical* sense, in that both probably will fail to increase deviations from the predetermined goal (successful task completion). Additionally, while praise and pay may maintain successful task performance, they cannot in the *ordinary* sense of the word be construed as "negative." To eliminate this conceptual, empirical, and semantic confusion, some adjustments have been made by behavioral scientists. For example,

		Point of Reference (Goal)	
		Value Based ("Normative")	Empirically Based ("Factual")
Impact on System	Increase System Disequilibrium (Movement away from goal)	Deviation - Amplifying Loop	Self-Reinforcing Loop
	Decrease System Disequilibrium (Movement toward goal)	Deviation - Counteracting Loop	Self-Correcting Loop

SOURCE: Reprinted from "Vicious circles in organizations" by M. Masuch, published by *Administrative Science Quarterly, 31* (1), p. 16, by permission of *Administrative Science Quarterly*. © Administrative Science Quarterly, 1985.

Figure 18.1 Types of Feedback Loops

Kantor and Lehr (1975) suggest that social scientists use the term "constancy loops" in place of negative loops and "variety feedback loops" in place of positive loops. In this way feedback and its component processes may be redefined in ways that overcome the cybernetic conceptualization.

In addition, definitions of feedback vary somewhat depending on the particular level of analysis that behavioral scientists are exploring. For instance, in the dyadic context, Ilgen et al. (1979) define feedback from a *source* to a *recipient* as information about the *appropriateness* of the recipient's past performance. When considering the effects of feedback on task group behavior, Nadler (1979) views feedback as information about the actual performance or actions of a task group used to affect subsequent changes in group member motivation and changes in group performance strategies. On the other hand, at the organizational systems (macro) level, Ramaprasad (1983) states that feedback is information about the gap between the actual level and the reference level of a system parameter that is used to alter the gap in some way. While variance in the above definitions may seem minor, each definition is somewhat distinct, thus making it difficult to translate knowledge generated about feedback processes from numerous disciplines into the context of organizational communication.

In order to cope with the types of operational and conceptual definitional problems described above, Cusella (1980) has argued that organizational communication scholars may best contribute to an understanding of feedback in organizations by focusing on *verbal feedback*, either orally delivered messages directed face-to-face or written or mediated messages directed in a non-face-to-face manner, regarding the actions of receivers who have been performing an assigned organizational task. From this perspective, positive feedback denotes "favorable" feedback or praise, while negative feedback typically refers to "unfavorable" feedback or criticism.

FEEDBACK CHARACTERISTICS

Simultaneous to the attention given to refining definitional aspects of feedback, numerous efforts have been undertaken to distinguish among various characteristics of feedback in the organizational setting. In particular, researchers have focused on explicating five key factors: (1) feedback purposes (goals); (2) types of feedback; (3) dimensions of feedback; (4) sources of feedback; and (5) functions (outcomes) of feedback. Findings of research exploring each of these characteristics is briefly summarized below.

Feedback Goals

Based on the work of learning theorists and Vroom's (1964) theory of motivation, Cusella (1980) concluded that the purposes of feedback may be to

(1) reward (strengthen habits of behavior); (2) inform (evoke already established habits); (3) cue (increase the probability of arousal of correct effort-to-performance expectations concerning the consequences of actions for successful task performance); (4) motivate (increase the perceived value of successful performance and decrease the perceived value of unsuccessful performance); (5) regulate (keep goal-directed behaviors on course); (6) learn (increase the strength of correct and decrease the strength of incorrect effort-to-performance expectations concerning the consequences of actions for successful performance).

Feedback Types

Bogart (1980) suggests that three types of strategic information about system situations can be fed to points in the system where it can be employed in determining system responses: *feedback, feedforward,* and *feedwithin.* Characterizing the flow of strategic information about system conditions as "feed processes" (p. 238), Bogart (1980) views *feedback* in the traditional sense as information about system output or performance (past results) that is fed back into the system. Student response to an instructor's lecture is an example of this feed process. On the other hand, *feedforward* enables systems to scan environmental situations to forecast trends, and to adjust performance in anticipation of changing environmental circumstances. In organizational terms, feedforward is essentially "organizational knowledge," as in the example of a budget planning process. Thus feedforward generates an expectation, while feedback confirms or disconfirms it. In turn, *feedwithin* is defined as "information about the flow of information or resources between parts of the system; it is information about thruput" (Bogart, 1980, p. 240). In the organizational context, feedwithin is internal intelligence, or information of events, or circumstances within the system. The use of television cameras in a maximum security prison is an example of a feedwithin sensor. Any disturbance within the prison, transmitted via images to a monitor receiver, would provide feedwithin.

With respect to *feedback* specifically, Bourne (1966) argues that, at its most basic level, feedback provides some information about the correctness, accuracy, or adequacy of an individual's past behavior. Early researchers viewed feedback this way (Arps, 1917). Ilgen et al. (1979) suggest that feedback also possesses an "information value" that they assert depends on "the incremental increase in knowledge about performance that the feedback provides the recipient (p. 351). Based on Social Judgment Theory, Hammond, McClelland, and Mumpower (1980) propose the notions of "outcome feedback" and "cognitive feedback" as parallels to the concept of "accuracy of response" and "information value" (p. 228).

Outcome feedback and cognitive feedback are analogous to the notions of *knowledge of results* (KR) and *knowledge of performance* (KP) offered some years ago by Annett and Kay (1957). KR is feedback provided in terms of end scores, numerical results, test numbers, or output yield figures. KP is information that serves as a performance index within the task itself that conveys to the individual reasons why he or she performed a task in a particular way. KP is thus a more complete type of feedback in an information theory sense.

Feedback Dimensionality

In contrast to feedback type, feedback dimensionality refers to the form or dimensional/factor structure of feedback. Recently, a study of the dimensional structure of feedback suggests that feedback is composed of at least the following conceptual dimensions: (1) the sign of the feedback (+/-); (2) its timeliness; (3) its specificity; (4) its frequency; and (5) its sensitivity (Larson, Glynn, Fleenor, & Scrontrino, 1985). While these feedback dimensions may not be empirically distinct (Ilgen, Peterson, Martin, & Boeschen, 1981; Larson et al., 1985), consideration of their conceptual distinctions does facilitate an understanding of feedback processes.

Typically, the sign or *valence* levels of feedback are distinguished into one of two categories, positive and negative, and may be the most important message characteristic influencing feedback acceptance (Ilgen et al., 1979). Conceptually, feedback valence refers to the perceived attractiveness or value of the information conveyed in the message. Operationally, positive feedback consists of messages that connote acceptance of the behavior or comparative statements that indicate satisfactory or higher performance, while negative feedback consists of messages that refer unfavorably to the recipient's behavior or comparative statements that indicate unsatisfactory performance. While this perspective implies that all performance feedback contains either a favorable (+) or an unfavorable (-) evaluation of task behavior, Cusella (1984a) argues that there also exists a point midway on the sign continuum where feedback may be characterized as neither positive nor negative but *neutral.* This type of feedback resembles Gibb's (1961) characterization of message neutrality, in the sense of connoting detachment.

The four remaining aspects of feedback dimensionality can be characterized as components of positive (favorable) and negative (unfavorable) performance feedback. Feedback *timeliness* centers on how quickly a feedback source provides feedback after the performance occurs, and has been conceptualized by Miller (1953) and Annett and Kay (1957) in terms of either "action feedback," which tells the recipient what should be done while continuing the current task behavior, or "learning feedback," which tells the recipient only what has just been done. By telling the recipient what to do next, action feedback allows the recipient to modify his or her present response. By occurring after the termination of the task behavior, learning feedback can only indicate what the recipient should have done or how the next set of task behaviors should be modified. By comparison, feedback *specificity* refers to the extent to which the feedback provides specific (detailed) as opposed to general (nondetailed) information about performance. Feedback *frequency* denotes the number of times or rate of occurrence at which feedback is given. Finally, feedback *sensitivity* describes whether or not the feedback source exhibits concern for the recipient's feelings when conveying the feedback.

Feedback can also vary in all the ways that information is perceived by receivers. Swanson (1974) measured perceived usefulness of information in terms of numerous characteristics (e.g., timeliness, accuracy) while Larcker and Lessig (1980) measured information usefulness in terms of perceived importance and clarity. These findings are pertinent, since Lucas (1975) found that useless information distracted task performers. In this regard usefulness may also be affected by the *mode* of information presentation (Lucas & Nielsen, 1980). Thus other factors may moderate the various feedback dimensions.

Feedback Source

The feedback *source* conveys or sends a feedback message to a recipient. Numerous efforts have been made to characterize the various sources from which feedback can be conveyed. Annett (1969) proposed two general sources of feedback (KR): *intrinsic* KR and *extrinsic* KR. Intrinsic KR is feedback that is naturally present and is not subject to experimenter manipulation. Instrinsic KR consists of stimuli perceived by the individual that arise inherently from carrying out that task (e.g., an individual's perceptions of his or her own performance). Extrinsic KR consists of any stimuli manipulated by a source other than the individual performer, such as a test score. While the intrinsic-extrinsic distinction has been found to be important (Greller, 1975), it is by no means the only way of categorizing the source of feedback (Herold & Greller, 1977).

For example, Greller and Herold (1975; and Hanser & Muchinsky, 1978, 1980) investigated five sources of feedback (self, task, supervisor, coworkers, company) and found that individuals find feedback from the task and from themselves to be most useful when determining whether they have met job requirements. Herold and Greller (1977) examined feedback from (1) sources above the recipient in the organizational hierarchy; (2) nonhierarchical others; (3) the independent internal observations of the recipient; and (4) work flow feedback. Finally, Greller (1980) evaluated six sources of feedback: (1) formal organizational rewards; (2) informal assignments from one's supervisor; (3) the immediate supervisor; (4) coworkers; (5) comparisons to the work of others; and (6) task feedback. An important finding of Greller (1980) is that supervisors and subordinates disagree on the importance and usefulness attached to these six feedback sources.

By contrast, Ilgen et al. (1979) in an abbreviated category system classify sources of feedback into three distinct sets: (1) other individuals who have observed the recipient's behavior (e.g., supervisors, coworkers, subordinates, and customers); (2) the task environment (e.g., working on the task itself, augmented feedback—auditory feedback during a visual tracking task, quickened feedback reported before the actual result has occurred); and (3) individuals who judge their own performance and therefore serve as their own source of feedback (self-feedback). Ilgen et al. (1979) stress, however, that their (and by implication any) classification scheme of feedback sources is of little value for suggesting the extent feedback from a source affects a recipient unless two communication concepts are considered: *source credibility* and *power*. Source credibility is determined by a recipient's perception of the source's expertise to judge the recipient's behavior accurately and the perceived trustworthiness of the source. The power of a feedback source centers on his or her ability to control the rewards and sanctions received by the recipient.

Finally, a recent series of studies (Ashford, 1986; Ashford & Cummings, 1983; Herold & Parsons, 1985) warrants discussion because it attempts to clarify the degree to which individuals can be *proactive sources* of their own feedback. Researchers exploring this notion argue that the organizational literature on feedback has been constrained, tending to treat task performers as passive "receivers" of feedback and focusing on external feedback sources and message "sending" processes. Thus the role of the individual performer as an active monitor, seeker, and even generator of feedback has been largely ignored. Moreover, as Herold and Parsons (1985) observe, while much discussion exists concerning the task versus "self" distinction of feedback sources, the more important issue may not be whether one's task is a different feedback source from one's "self," but rather that the *self* and *task* function as a feedback source stimulus system in which the *self* mediates feedback from the *self/task* system by initiating, perceiving, and interpreting processes. What may follow, therefore, is that *self* and *task* form a cybernetic feedback system in which some degree of mutual control is exhibited by self and task as feedback sources. Clearly, this perspective lends itself to an analysis of the self-task feedback complex as a type of "action loop" (Masuch, 1985), previously discussed. Operationalizing the self/task feedback complex as an action loop, however, remains a challenge for future feedback investigators.

Feedback Functions (Outcomes)

Numerous researchers have sought to identify distinctions among feedback functions (outcomes). For example, Payne and Hauty (1955) propose that feedback may serve (1) a directional function, keeping goal directed behavior on course; or (2) an incentive function, stimulating greater effort by the feedback recipient. In organization contexts, the directional and incentive functions of feedback are central to the motivation process (Campbell &

Pritchard, 1976) and will be elaborated in a subsequent section.

The distinction between feedback goals, discussed earlier, and feedback outcomes can be illuminated by comparing them as they emerge along a spatial/temporal continuum. The purpose (goal) of feedback is frequently (although not always) ascertained before feedback is transmitted. Essentially, feedback goals serve as the starting point of the feedback process. The feedback that is transmitted functions to produce certain outcomes—to provide direction or stimulate greater effort in the receiver. A feedback outcome is, in a sense, the end result of the feedback process—either it does or does not enhance directionality or stimulate greater effort. Feedback outcomes, therefore, represent the eventual impact of the feedback process, and are ascertained retrospectively (Weick, 1979).

Summary

To recapitulate, feedback may vary in terms of its (1) purpose (goals); (2) types; (3) dimensions; (4) sources; and (5) functions (outcomes). Recognizing that feedback may vary in these ways is essential for understanding the nature of specific feedback research studies and in comparing results across investigations. Without this foreknowledge (a form of feedforward), readers of reviews of feedback research may be asked, albeit unwittingly, to compare apples and oranges—studies where feedback has not been similarly conceived or operationalized.

As the preceding discussion suggests, when considering feedback from both a theoretical and practical standpoint, it is essential to be cognizant that the information about the difference between the actual level of performance and the reference level is feedback *only* when it is used to *alter* the gap. If the information received is stored in memory, it is not feedback (Ramaprasad, 1983). In other words, unless the information about the actual performance or actions of a system is "used to control future actions, simply providing feedback information is insufficient for defining feedback in the classic sense" (Jacoby, Troutman, Muzursky, & Kuss, 1984, p. 538). As Annett (1969) observes, the information value of feedback depends, at least in part, on the incremental increase in knowledge about performance that the feedback provides the recipient. However, Ilgen et al. (1979) add an important caveat to this:

> the degree to which feedback provides information can only be judged subjectivity—from the recipients' frame-of-reference. The amount of information it provides depends upon the incremental increase in information about the behavior over and above the information already possessed by the individual. (p. 351)

In essence, it seems clear that in conducting feedback research, investigators must assess the utility of the feedback information conveyed to the recipient.

This, in turn, depends on the relationship between feedback message and receiver (Ilgen et al., 1979). Feedback source and recipient must share similar codes if the systemic necessity of requisite variety (Ashby, 1956) is to be maintained. As Weick (1969) explains, Ashby's Law of Requisite Variety states, "that processes must have the same degree of order or chaos as there is in the input to these processes. . . . Accurate registering requires the matching of processes to the characteristics of their inputs. Only if this prior matching occurs is transformation possible" (pp. 40, 42).

The research considered in the remainder of this chapter focuses primarily on the feedback-motivation relationship and the feedback-performance relationship within the impersonal, dyadic, and group contexts and, to a lesser extent, on the feedback-learning relationship that has been discussed admirably and at length elsewhere (e.g., Adams, 1968). While *verbal feedback* will be the principal focus of reviewing feedback-motivation/performance relationships, commentary on incentives also will be included where necessary. There are several reasons for this. First, research suggests that behavior is essentially shaped through control of incentive allocation (Annett, 1969). Second, the distinctions between incentives, reinforcers, and feedback are not always clear (e.g., Bilodeau & Bilodeau, 1961). Third, it seems apparent that in the context of work organizations, a highly salient influence on individuals' levels of motivation and satisfaction is the organization's power to give tangible rewards (e.g., pay, promotion, status symbols). Thus, while we will discuss incentives, our major emphasis will be on the *communicative* dynamics associated with the administration of tangible, verbal, and symbolic incentives and their effect on *either* motivation *or* performance. The basics of each of these potential outcomes of feedback are briefly explained in the next section.

MOTIVATION AND PERFORMANCE

In reviewing the research stemming from motivation theory in organizational psychology, Campbell and Pritchard (1976) contend that defining motivation can be a painful intellectual endeavor: "The primary reason for such pain seems to be the felt need to equate 'motivation' with a particular behavior or physical state" (p. 64). Terms used synonymously with motivation are deprivation level, general activity level, degree of satisfaction, and effort expended toward the completion of a task.

The first step in explaining motivation is to understand its relationship with the psychometric variables of performance and ability. Lawler (1973) observes a frequently appearing equation that concisely describes the relationship of motivation (M) and ability (A_b) to performance (P_f): $P_f = f(A_b \times M)$. In other words, performance is a multiplicative combination of ability and motivation. Performance is defined as virtually any behavior a person exhibits directed toward the accomplishment of a task or goal, and ability refers to how the person can perform at the present time. The construct of motivation is more difficult to explain, though Campbell and Pritchard (1976) posit that it is most meaningful to view motivation as a multiplicative function of (1) the choice to expend or initiate effort on a certain task; (2) the choice to expend a certain amount or degree of effort; and (3) the choice to persist in expending a certain amount of effort.

Campbell and Pritchard's (1976) work illustrates three points. First, motivation is not synonymous with performance, aptitude, or ability. An important implication here is that not all performance problems that occur in organizations are the result of low motivation. If low motivation is the cause of poor performance, the corrective action required will be different than corrective action required to remedy poor performance caused by low ability.

Second, although a worker can control his or her motivation, ultimately the worker cannot completely control his or her performance. Performance is almost always organizationally defined both quantitatively in terms of "output" and qualitatively in terms of "how well" a person accomplishes a task (Guion, 1965). Also, an individual cannot control the variables of aptitude or organizational environment.

Third, the above arguments serve to point out the extremely complex nature of motivation and the demands placed on those who study motivation. Anyone interested in communication and motivation in the organization would do well to heed the words of McGuire (1973), "to demand simplicity condemns one to an inadequate theory" (p. 225).

As a way of managing this complexity, current research on motivation has drawn a distinction between two broad categories of motivation strategies: extrinsic motivation and intrinsic motivation (Campbell & Pritchard, 1976). Extrinsic motivation (EM) refers to performing an activity because it leads to rewards external to, or independent of, the actual activity itself (e.g., money, praise, food, status, etc.). Festinger (1967) proposed that extrinsic rewards affect a person's concept of why he or she is working and lead the person to believe that the "working" is for the rewards. Intrinsic motivation (IM) attempts to arrive at a situation where a person desires to be a high performer because being a high performer is viewed as *valuable for its own sake* (Young, 1961) and is self-sustaining.

Since the notion of "reward" (reinforcer) occupies a central position in motivation theory, it is important to recognize distinctions between the reward construct and other motivational factors, particularly the concept of "incentives." Annett (1969) argues that such a distinction should be based on the dependent variable of concern in any study. Essentially, rewards "are said to reduce drive, (while) incentives appear to increase drive" (Annett, 1969, p. 35). In this view, incentives enhance energy expenditure while rewards induce "more or less permanent changes in behavior" (Annett, 1969, p. 36).

Communication, Motivation and
Performance: General Issues

A considerable amount of research suggests that performance feedback (1) motivates the receiver through the information/reinforcement it provides about one's competence, and (2) directs behavior so as to be in line with appropriate goal-directed activity (Annett, 1969; Cusella, 1980; Deci, 1975; Ilgen et al., 1979; Payne & Hauty, 1955). Moreover, readers need to accept, *within limits,* the generally accepted view that the impact of feedback on performance is virtually always positive (Jacoby et al., 1984). Thus it should also be recognized that there is increasing evidence (Einhorn & Hogarth, 1978; Hammond & Summers, 1972; Jacoby et al., 1984; Steinman, 1976) that the feedback-performance relationship depends on the *type* of feedback that is involved. For example, Jacoby et al.'s work (1984) suggests that outcome feedback, as opposed to cognitive feedback, may be especially dysfunctional in a complex, dynamic task environment. Jacoby et al. (1984) also report that, in contrast to poorer performing decision makers, better performing decision makers are more likely to ignore outcome-only feedback when that feedback lacks predictive and/or explanatory value.

Several issues with respect to feedback/incentive research also warrant elaboration. First, it is important to realize that most studies in this area have investigated *either* the various relationships between feedback/incentives and motivation *or* the various relationships between feedback/incentives and performance. Because there are some conceptual and empirical differences between motivation and performance, readers would do well to keep the theoretical assumptions of individual feedback studies clearly in mind. This will help guard against false claims about what the research allegedly shows.

Second, it seems clear that, to date, researchers exploring relationships between incentive/rewards and motivation/performance have not adequately considered the potential effects of the *communicative* aspects of incentive/reward administration on the results. In fact, we are aware of no studies that have systematically explored the communication dynamics that surround reward administration. Furthermore, there appears to be no application of the principles of the classic reinforcement schedules to the administration or delivery of verbal feedback in work organizations. Few incentive studies provide verbatim accounts of the instructions given to subjects prior to the conduct of the research. However, extrinsic rewards are seldom administered in an informational or relational vacuum. We have yet to see studies that report what is said by the "rewarder" to the "rewardee." On its face, it would appear that the act of administering a reward is a "one-up" relational activity (Cusella, 1980). Yet unless we see detailed reports of the communication of rewards, we cannot assume that this is always the case.

Finally, as one considers the need to explore verbal feedback as an incentive, one must, of necessity, also consider which of the classic reinforcement schedules should be utilized to reflect the complexities of the giving of feedback in organizations. One could imagine positive or negative feedback manipulated along a fixed ratio (e.g., piecerate) or a fixed interval (e.g. hourly rate, or annual performance appraisal meeting), or a variable ratio (where a person could not predict the amount of feedback he or she would receive). For example, Pritchard, Hollenback, and DeLeo (1980) argue that a variable ratio-variable amount schedule—where not every response is reinforced and where the amount of reinforcement varies—occurs frequently in organizations, especially in supervisory recognition and peer approval (p. 338), both obvious forms of verbal organizational feedback. In short, the possibilities abound when one considers applying the principles of incentive research to the process of verbal feedback in organizations (Ostrove, 1978).

With the above issues in mind, the remainder of this chapter will summarize and interpret research on feedback source-recipient relationships within the impersonal, dyadic, and group contexts and present directions for future *communication-oriented* feedback research. Within each of these sections, where appropriate, the impact of feedback on performance and extrinsic/intrinsic levels of motivation will be discussed.

IMPERSONAL FEEDBACK

Feedback is not necessarily something that another person must introduce into a task situation. It may be inherent in a task situation. This notion is not inconsequential. As Ashford (1986) suggests, individuals actively monitor their environment by observing various situational cues and observing others in an effort to infer how well they are doing. Knowledge of results, as it is classically viewed, may take many forms and may emanate from various sources—some personal and others impersonal, depending on the nature of the feedback source-recipient relationship. Feedback that is not delivered or mediated by another person will be called impersonal feedback. Annett (1969) labels this intrinsic KR. This feedback typically arises from carrying out the task and is most common in research on performance-tracking tasks, where the research subject is regularly informed via a visual display screen of the discrepancy between desired and actual behavior. Since the manner in which individuals process and respond to variations in feedback is of primary interest in this research tradition, studies exploring tracking behavior are somewhat analogous to those research approaches in organizational communication that view organization members as information processors (e.g., Poole, 1978; Thayer, 1967; Tushman & Nadler, 1978).

Feedback-Performance Relationships

Research on tracking has been summarized by Poulton (1966) and will only be highlighted here. The typical tracking involves at least two intrinsic sources of feedback: the operator's awareness of his or her response and the external display screen (Bilodeau & Bilodeau, 1961). The foundational research on the impact of feedback on tracking behavior can be divided into three broad areas: (1) transformation (manipulation of the form of the feedback); (2) temporal delay (immediate vs. delayed feedback); and (3) supplements to the standard (extra cues; Bilodeau & Bilodeau, 1961). For example, it has been shown repeatedly that there is no improvement in the operator's tracking behavior without knowledge of results, progressive improvement with it, and deterioration after its withdrawal (Bilodeau, 1953; Bilodeau, Bilodeau, & Schumsky, 1959; Conklin, 1959; Kinkade, 1963; Smode, 1958; Taylor, 1957).

The *timing* of feedback delivery during tracking tasks is an extremely relevant area for organizational communication scholars, because verbal performance feedback is always delivered either during the actual performance or at some time after the performance. Both Ammons (1956) and Holland and Henson (1956) report that immediate feedback improves performance while delayed feedback is less effective. However, it is important to recognize that there are numerous studies in the feedback literature that have found no differences in performance levels between individuals receiving immediate and receiving delayed feedback (e.g., Denny, Allard, Hall, & Rokeach, 1960; Noble & Alcock, 1958; Saltzman, Kanfer, & Greenspoon, 1955). In attempting to resolve these discrepancies Bilodeau and Bilodeau (1961), in their analysis of the literature, suggest, "All in all, it is clear that to delay or to give immediate KR can be quite immaterial for learning to make relatively simple Rs (responses)" (p. 254). For complex responses, however, the *timing* of feedback delivery appears to be an entirely different matter.

Another issue of relevance in the feedback-performance relationship, as yet not thoroughly explored (Adams, 1964), is the impact a receiver's *anticipation* of feedback has on future performance. "On-going feedback must be interpreted as a function of responses preceding the immediate past and as cues related to future events" (Bilodeau & Bilodeau, 1961, p. 256). From this perspective it is clear that received feedback interacts with a receiver's expectations that are, in part, affected by feedback received previously. Thus it becomes apparent that theories concerning feedback should incorporate a cyclic temporal perspective. Here, Locke's (1968) work on goal setting, discussed below, is particularly relevant.

The conclusion to be drawn from feedback/motor skills research is clear: In order to be effective, feedback must refer in some way to the degree to which one's task behavior has not met one's goal, since the fundamental purpose of feedback is to control behavior, even though an unlimited variety of responses are always possible (Bilodeau & Bilodeau, 1961). In other words, the *referent* (Cusella, 1980; 1982; 1984a) of feedback messages must be the receiver's task performance and not characteristics of the receiver unrelated to task activity. Further, it appears that controlling behavior requires that feedback inform receivers of where they have failed more so than where they have succeeded. For a further discussion of issues related to the feedback training/task performance relationship the reader is directed to reviews and critiques by Adams (1964), Ammons (1956), Annett (1969), Bilodeau (1966), Noble (1968), and Payne and Hauty (1955).

Feedback-Motivation Relationships

Arnold (1976, 1985) has studied the effects on IM of "impersonal" task-related feedback. Similar to tracking experiments, Arnold has studied performance feedback in the form of a performance summary delivered to subjects on a computer terminal video display unit. His findings suggest that in situations where receivers possess high levels of IM to complete a task, informational feedback on task performance—specifically, detailed reports regarding levels of performance related directly to the task—can have a potent effect on receivers' perceived feelings of competence and hence IM.

As organizations increase their use of electronic communication systems (Steinfield, 1985), Arnold's (1976, 1985) research on computer-generated performance feedback, as well as the results of studies exploring tracking behavior, will take on added relevance for the study of communication in organizations. As Siegel, Dubrovsky, Kiesler, and McGuire (1986) observe, computer-mediated communication may become a mainstay of organizational communication and will likely have major effects on work and the organization of work. Recently, Kiesler (1986) has argued that computer-mediated organizational communication affects the "content" of messages by limiting information communicators get about the communicative relationship (e.g., message "tone," nonverbal cues) to the point that "people focus their attention on the message rather than on each other" (p. 48). This suggests that organizations sanction computer-mediated task feedback when concerns regarding individuality, empathy, comparisons, and group norms are not salient.

Directions for Communication Research

From a communication theory perspective, one gap in the nonmediated feedback research, in general, is the effect that *context* has on the feedback performance/motivation relationship. As Bateson (1935) has firmly established, the context in which communication behaviors occur determines the meaning of those behaviors. With notable exceptions (e.g., Larson, 1984), what has yet to be fully considered is the role that one's social environment plays as it interacts with the task feedback one receives in a typical modern organizational context. It appears that when nonmediated feedback is received in the presence of others (e.g., subordinates, peers, or supervisors) context would play an important role in determining the impact of that feedback. This would especially be the case if the valence (+/−) of the feedback were both conspicuous and salient to the task performer and to those around him or her. What may emerge, theoretically, is a private-public continuum that describes a performer's social environment: the presence of others, or lack thereof, while a task performer receives nonmediated feedback. Future research should explore these notions.

Moreover, if we can view work as an information environment (Hanser & Muchinsky, 1978) where a variety of feedback sources are available to feedback recipients, then the information search behavior of feedback recipients (Ashford, 1986; Ashford & Cummings, 1983) needs to be considered as an independent and dependent variable in impersonal feedback research. Nearly all existing feedback models take for granted that the recipient is given feedback information—the recipient is a passive information receptacle. However, as Jacoby et al. (1984) observed, "When the source of feedback is the task environment itself, the individual must actively engage in the search for and accessing of this information" (p. 543). In a broader sense, the recipient's interest in and willingness to seek out performance feedback will most certainly influence the feedback reception process (Ashford, 1986).

These issues represent directions for future communication research in the nonmediated feedback context. We turn now to a review of research in the dyadic feedback context.

DYADIC FEEDBACK

This section reviews research within the dyadic context, where feedback directed to a task performer has been mediated by another individual. The traditional analog of the dyadic feedback context is the superior (feedback source)/subordinate (feedback receiver) relationship. Given the central place of superior-subordinate communication in organizations (Jablin, 1979), it is not surprising that much research has focused on the dyadic feedback context. In particular, researchers have focused on the following topics: (1) feedback-performance relationships; (2) feedback-motivation relationships; (3) feedback and attributional processes; and (4) the use of rewards and punishments.

Feedback-Performance Relationships

The primary concern of this section is the work of Locke (1968) and his associates on Goal Setting Theory, which is founded on four basic tenets (Pinder, 1984). First, an individual's conscious ideas—goals and intentions—regulate his or her actions. Second, if goals determine human effort, it follows that higher or harder goals will result in higher levels of performance than will easy goals. Third, specific goals (such as "writing four research papers within 12 months") are seen as resulting in higher levels of effort than vague goals (such as "let's increase research productivity"). Fourth, "incentives" such as money, feedback, or competition will not affect behavior unless they lead to the setting and/or acceptance of specific, hard goals. Relatedly, goal difficulty, not task difficulty, determines effort (Pinder, 1984). In sum, goal setting theory proposes that for incentives to successfully motivate or enhance performance they must alter the task performer's goals and intentions, or build the task performer's commitment to currently held goals and intentions (Pinder, 1984).

With respect to the critical role of feedback in goal setting contexts,[1] early goal setting studies attempted to ascertain whether feedback directly affected performance or whether the effects of feedback were mediated by the process of goal setting (Locke, 1967; Locke & Bryan, 1968, 1969a, 1969b; Locke, Cartledge, & Knoeppel, 1968). Results of these investigations demonstrated that feedback by itself was insufficient as a mechanism to improve task performance. What emerged was an interest in testing specific combinations of goal level and variations in feedback, as depicted in Figure 18.2. In this figure, Cell 1 represents explicit, difficult goals combined with performance feedback; Cell 2, explicit, difficult goals without performance feedback; Cell 3, performance feedback with no explicit goals (or essentially "do the best you can" types of goals considered by researchers as tantamount to no assigned goals); and Cell 4, neither explicit goals nor performance feedback. Generally, studies based on this matrix have included at least three of these four cells in their research designs, and can be characterized as falling within two distinct clusters of studies (Locke et al., 1981).

One cluster of studies involves comparisons among Cells 1, 3, and 4. Overall, these studies suggest that although feedback alone is not sufficient to increase performance (Cell 3 = Cell 4), feedback plus goals produces improved performance (Cell 1 > Cell 3; Bandura & Simon, 1977; Dockstader, 1977; Latham, Mitchell, & Dossett, 1978; Locke et al., 1981; Nemeroff & Consentino, 1979). Another cluster of studies utilizes comparisons between Cells 1, 2, and 4 and shows that goals, regardless of type, without feedback are insufficient to improve performance (Cell 2 = Cell 4); but when goals are present, feedback is sufficient to affect increases in performance (Cell 1 > Cell 2; "At Emery Air Freight," 1973; Becker, 1978; Komaki, Barwick, & Scott, 1978; Locke et al., 1981; Strang, Lawrence, & Fowler, 1978). In turn, related research has shown that when goals are present, providing specific and frequent feedback clearly facilitates performance (e.g., Frost & Mahoney, 1976; Kim & Hamner, 1976; Locke et al., 1981). Thus goal setting-feedback research indicates that *both* goals and feedback to the individual about his or her performance vis-à-vis those goals are necessary in order to foster high performance levels (Bandura & Cervone, 1983, 1986; Locke et al., 1981; Pinder, 1984).

In summary, feedback and incentives work to increase motivation or performance only if they change a person's goal and intentions, or build commitment to those they already hold (Pinder, 1984). Moreover, as Annett (1969) argues, feedback can be the means by which a standard or goal is

Feedback Condition

		Performance Feedback	No Performance Feedback
	Difficult and Explicit Goal	1	2
Goal Condition	Non-Explicit Goal ("Do the best you can")	3	4

SOURCE: Reprinted from Locke, E. A., Shaw, K. N., Saari, L. M., & Latham, G. P. (1981). Goal setting and task performance: 1969-1980. *Psychological Bulletin, 90,* p. 133, *Figure 1.1 Model for analyzing goal-KR studies.* Copyright 1981 by the American Psychological Association. Reprinted/adapted by permission of the author.

Figure 18.2 Matrix for Classifying Goal-Setting/Feedback Research

specified and a means by which a subject can relate his or her performance to the goal, but feedback per se does not necessarily have any motivational effect. Put another way, feedback interacts with a subject's performance goal, providing the subject with information pertaining to where he or she stands in relation to the goal (Annett, 1969); or it provides information to the receiver regarding his or her competence and self-determination (Deci, 1975).

Directions for communication research. While a considerable amount of research has been generated about goal setting theory, a number of issues in this area deserve further study (Locke et al., 1981). First, few studies have included a complete 2 × 2 design with Feedback/No Feedback and Explicit-Difficult Goals/"Do Best" Goals, or No Goals as the independent variables. Second, investigators should explore whether feedback, subsequent to its reception, has an effect on the level of goal difficulty set by performers on future tasks. As Cummings, Schwab, and Rosen (1971) discovered, in some instances providing feedback can lead to the setting of higher goals than when feedback is not provided. Third, *the issue of how information from feedback is processed by the receiver warrants further study.* Consistent with this, Campion and Lord (1982) have developed a control systems model of motivation that considers a goal as a referent or desired state to which performance is compared. According to the model, feedback conveys information regarding any discrepancy between goal and performance, thus creating a corrective motivation. In turn, the model suggests that specific goals produce better performance than ambiguous goals because they permit the use of more precise feedback from the environment (Campion & Lord, 1982). Studies by Matsui, Okada, and Inoshita (1983) and Thomas and Ward (1983) support this view.

The methodological ramifications of the influence of feedback on subsequent goals also warrant research attention. In particular, researchers need to examine if it is impossible to separate the constructs of goal setting and feedback, since "it is almost impossible to give individuals feedback regarding their performance in such an innocuous way that it does not become a cue, establish a standard of performance, or simply create a demand characteristic" (Tolchinsky & King, 1980, p. 464). Seemingly, the only area of research where this danger of feedback-goal confounding may be controlled is when feedback is impersonal. Unfortunately, however, the studies that have even indirectly addressed the differential impact of externally versus internally generated feedback in the goal setting paradigm have produced inconsistent results (e.g., Ivancevich & McMahon, 1982; Kim & Hamner, 1976). Yet it is also clear that this issue is of major importance to communication researchers interested in goal setting theory. Most goal setting and MBO programs have emphasized externally generated, formal superior-subordinate feedback meetings (Ivancevich & McMahon, 1982). But, because the form and content of feedback can vary (Cusella, 1984a), it is conceivable that external feedback and internal feedback, presented in different forms and with different amounts of information, may affect performance or motivation differently. Regrettably, however, little effort has been taken to standardize feedback messages across levels either within individual studies or across studies. Thus the nature of the information embedded in the feedback is almost always unmeasured and unreported. From an information processing perspective, it is difficult to propose relationships between feedback from different loci (internal versus external) and subsequent performance when locus is only one consideration. Perceived information content, quality, and meaning must also be considered. It may be that during the receiver's processing of feedback, the relative distance (either psychological or temporal) between the information received and the dependent measure in question shapes the potential impact of the feedback. Some dependent variables (outcomes) may be more important to receivers than are others. Consequently, feedback may vary in its perceived salience, in terms of the importance attached to it, as it refers to different organizational outcomes.

Finally, a recent series of impressive field studies conducted by Pritchard and his colleagues (cited below) exploring feedback and goal setting are of interest since many of their findings either contradict feedback/motivation theory or are counterintuitive. Specifically, one would not expect the finding by Pritchard and Montagno (1978) that nonspecific feedback would have strong positive effects on productivity while specific feedback would have no such effects. On the other hand, while Pritchard, Montagno, and Moore (1978) found that, in general, high specificity feedback was superior to low specificity feedback, they also found that, in general, impersonal feedback was superior to personal feedback and that delayed feedback was superior to immediate feedback. In contrast, Pritchard, Bigby, Beiting, Coverdale, and Morgan (1981) discovered that impersonal feedback was not superior to personal feedback but was equally effective. Pritchard et al. (1981) also found that absolute feedback was as effective as comparative feedback, *unlike* Pritchard and Montagno (1978) but *similar to* Pritchard et al. (1978). In a related study, Chhokar and Wallin (1984) found that more frequent feedback (once a week) did not result in more effective performance (job safety) than less frequent feedback (once every two weeks). While a number of reasons can be postulated for these inconsistent results (for instance, variation in the operationalization of feedback), the emergence of such contradictory findings clearly suggests that many answers remain to be found to questions regarding the manner in which receivers process feedback messages.

Feedback-IM Relationships

Deci (1975) has developed cognitive evaluation theory (CET) to account for the reduction in a person's IM to perform a task when that task is tied to contingent extrinsic (monetary) rewards. For Deci and Ryan (1980) "intrinsically motivated behaviors are those that are motivated by the underlying need for competence and self-determination" (p. 42). There are two processes by which extrinsic rewards can affect IM. One process changes a person's perceived locus of causality from within him or her to certain features of the external environment, thus decreasing IM. The second process alters a person's feelings of competence and self-determination. Feelings of competence and self-determination enhance IM while diminished feelings of competence and self-determination decrease IM. While several elements of CET have received empirical support (Deci, 1975; Deci & Ryan 1980; Fisher, 1978; Notz, 1975) other hypotheses have not been supported (e.g., Boal & Cummings, 1981; Calder & Staw, 1975; Hamner & Foster, 1975; Pate, 1978; Salancik, 1975; Scott, 1976).

The relevance of CET for communication scholars emerges when considering the tenet of CET that every reward (including feedback) has two aspects: (1) to *control* the reward-receiver's behavior, and (2) to *inform* a person about his or her competence and self-determination. According to CET, a more salient controlling aspect will initiate the change in the perceived locus of causality and diminish IM. A more salient informational aspect will initiate changes in feelings of competence and self-determination and will enhance IM. Fisher (1978) observed that both informational aspects (competence and self-determination) must be operative. Addressing the *valence* of rewards/feedback, Deci (1972) argued that positive verbal feedback should not diminish a person's level of IM because it is not phenomenologically distinct from the task itself. Rather, positive feedback should enhance a person's feelings of competence and self-determination because the informational aspect is more salient. Negative feedback, on the other hand, is predicted to decrease IM through decreasing one's feelings of competence and self-determination in relation to the task activity.

Communication-IM research. While CET focuses on the internal states of intrinsically motivated subjects, more and more research is attempting to explore the myriad communication variables surrounding the feedback administration and feedback reception processes. For example, in their review and revision of CET, Deci and Ryan (1980) discuss more than a dozen experiments variously utilizing children, college students, and adults that have investigated the effects of positive feedback on IM. Nearly all the studies support the contention that positive competence feedback should always increase IM and that negative feedback will decrease IM if it signifies that the receiver is incompetent (Deci & Ryan, 1980).

Other research has explored the effects variations in other aspects of verbal feedback have on the IM of task performers (Harackiewicz, 1979; Harackiewicz & Larson, 1986; Harackiewicz & Manderlink, 1984; Harackiewicz, Manderlink, & Sansone, 1984; Harackiewicz, Sansone, & Manderlink, 1985). From this research it is clear that a feedback source may influence IM (1) through competence information, and (2) whether or not feedback is given in a controlling manner (Harackiewicz & Larson, 1986). Positive performance feedback based on social norms can enhance IM (Boggiano & Ruble, 1979; Deci, 1972; Harackiewicz, 1979). Yet feedback perceived as controlling can reduce IM (Deci & Ryan, 1980; Pittman, Davey, Alafat, Wetherill, & Kramer, 1980; Ryan, 1982). Additionally, positive feedback may not always enhance IM, depending on the objectivity and the timing of the feedback and the achievement orientation of the receiver (Harackiewicz et al., 1985). Some observers have concluded that feedback receivers vary such that high performers need feedback that emphasizes their competency and personal control, while average to low performers need the emphasis to be placed on extrinsic rewards resulting from performance (Cummings, 1976; Ilgen et al., 1979).

A number of studies have explored the effects that variations in other aspects of actual verbal feedback have on the IM of task performers. For example, Cusella (1980) offered a propositional extension to CET citing as independent variables certain factors relevant to the communication process and the administration of feedback messages. The 14 propositions and five related constructs he derived (see Table 18.1) suggest relationships among (1) Message/Relational characteristics, (2) Context-Setting and Communication

Rules, (3) Feedback Source characteristics, and (4) Receiver characteristics, as feedback affects the IM of receivers. For example, positive verbal feedback can be salient on the control dimension ("one-up") and therefore negatively affect IM.

In an empirical effort to test some of these predictions, Cusella (1982) manipulated two dimensions of post-performance feedback: (1) Expertise of the feedback source—high versus low, and (2) Valence of the feedback—positive versus neutral. Results indicated that high expertise of the feedback source enhanced IM. Valence alone did not enhance a receiver's level of IM, but the data demonstrated an Expertise × Valence interaction such that subjects receiving positive feedback from a highly expert source exhibited greater levels of IM than did receivers in any other condition.

In another study, Cusella (1984a) predicted that four variables would moderate the impact of verbal feedback on IM: (1) the Valence of the feedback (positive versus neutral); (2) the Expertise of the source (expert versus nonexpert); (3) the Referent of the feedback (task behavior versus personal); and (4) the Sex of the feedback recipient. Results of an experimental simulation indicated that positive feedback increases IM more than does neutral feedback, and that Valence, Referent, and Expertise interact such that positive, task-behavior feedback administered by an expert source increases IM more than any other combination of these three variables.

While not manipulating feedback per se, some researchers have explored the effect of expected evaluative feedback on performance. For example, Shalley and Oldham (1985) found that individuals exhibited high IM when (1) they attained an easy goal and expected an evaluation, and (2) they attained a difficult goal and expected no evaluation. This finding suggests that goal difficulty and the expectation of external evaluative feedback interact to affect IM (Shalley & Oldham, 1985). This could arise because the low performer acts as a feedback source and self-administers negative feedback concerning his or her competence. Here is a striking example of how internal nonmediated feedback may diminish performance. Other research in this area reflects the complexities of the feedback-motivation-performance relationship (Janz, 1982). For example, the expectation of performance evaluation (positive or negative) may enhance performance (Jackson & Zedeck, 1982; White, Mitchell, & Bell, 1977) while negatively affecting IM (Harackiewicz et al., 1984).

For the organizational communicator, this conundrum presents a substantial challenge. Evaluation, or the expectation of it, is frequently perceived as threatening to one's self-esteem (Gibb, 1961) and is likely to produce a defensive communication climate, a decidedly unappealing prospect for any supervisor. Thus, in utilizing performance evaluation, managers may need to balance possible short-term gains in performance against the long-term negative consequences of diminished subordinate IM and defensive communication barriers between themselves and their subordinates. In terms of

TABLE 18.1
Predictors of the Effect of Feedback on Intrinsic Motivation (IM)

Type of FB	Salient Aspect		Locus		Self Determination	Competence	IM	
	Control	Info	Ext.	Int.			Increase	Decrease
Message/Relational Characteristics								
One-up strategy	X		X				X	
One-down strategy	X			X			X	
One-across strategy		X		X		X	X	
Equitable administration		X		X		X	X	
Content: KR		(X)		X		X	X	
Content: KP	X maybe	X	X			X		X
Evaluation comparative		X	X		X	X	X	
Manipulation (perceived)	X		X		X			X
Timing: Delayed and financial reward	X		X		X			X
Private vs. public	X		X		X		X	
Referent: Behavioral		X			X	X	X	
Personal	X							X
Specific (if not too detailed and person is highly involved in task)		X			X	X	X	
Rules shared							X	
Source Characteristics								
Intrapersonal		X		X	X	X	X	
External	X		X					X
High credibility		X			X	X	X	
Low credibility	X		X					X
High status to low status	X		X					X
Receiver Characteristics								
Perception-reception								

*Individual Differences: (demographics; achievement needs). Rural individuals more easily motivated intrinsically. Achievement oriented individuals more responsive to individual/task feedback.

**Acceptance: (believability–discrepancy–performance/feedback congruence). The congruence between feedback and a receiver's view of his or her formance may affect the phenomenological nature of the feedback and its believability and acceptance.

***Goals: (specific vs. nonspecific–hard vs. easy). Self-set goals would result in higher IM than assigned goals when the goals are equal.

feedback research, these phenomena can only be explored through longitudinal research efforts focusing on enduring superior-subordinate relationships.

Yet, given the human organism's drive to evaluate his or her abilities (Festinger, 1954), it may be impossible to construct superior-subordinate feedback systems that do not inherently possess a perceived evaluative component. The pivotal issue may be the relative merits of a sender emphasizing evaluation during actual feedback delivery, as opposed to describing job performance with an emphasis on future task improvements. Gibb (1961) found that describing another person's actions does not produce defensive reactions.

Conclusions and research directions. Based on these studies, a number of points can now be made about the feedback-IM relationship not specified in CET (Deci & Ryan, 1980). First, in order for positive competence feedback to enhance IM, feedback valence (+/–) probably interacts with aspects of source credibility (i.e., expertise). Further, although it has yet to be tested empirically, it can be predicted with confidence that perceptions of source trustworthiness would also interact with feedback valence in order for positive feedback to enhance IM. Because trustworthiness is an essential element of feedback source credibility (Ilgen et al., 1979), a recipient's perceptions of the expertise and trustworthiness of a feedback source would enhance the feedback's believability and the recipient's acceptance (Cusella, 1980).

In the dyadic context, the findings are mixed concerning whether positive feedback must convey information regarding a receiver's *task performance* to effect an increase in IM. Although not formerly tested, Cusella (1982) failed to find a significant difference between feedback referents (i.e., task-related favorable feedback versus person, non-task-related favorable feedback). However, in a later study Cusella (1984a) did find a three-way interaction such that subsequent levels of IM were highest for individuals receiving positive *task-related* feedback administered by an expert source, although this finding emerged for the pencil-and-paper measure of IM and not for a behavioral measure. In interpreting these results, work from attribution theory was used to explain the likelihood that feedback receivers make different attributions about their different behaviors at different times during their work experience. This again suggests that feedback is most effective when it is frequent and specifically refers to micro-behavioral components of task performance. However, a caveat to this proposition is the reminder that there is evidence suggesting that, as message receivers, task performers react personally to *all* organizational feedback they receive, *regardless* of whether it is intended to target on task behavior or the individual (Cusella, 1982).

What may be most important for communication research is for feedback-IM researchers to be sensitive to both content and relationship dimensions of feedback messages. The sending of feedback messages not only conveys information (the content dimension) but, at the same time, imposes behavior on the feedback receiver because of the command components of the relationship dimension (Watzlawick et al., 1967). The content dimension of this perspective is similar to the informational aspect (Deci, 1975) of feedback. Likewise, the relationship dimension resembles the control aspect (Deci, 1975) of feedback. The relationship perspective of a source-recipient dyad is particularly relevant to the motivation process, where incoming feedback messages have an impact not only on a subordinate's feelings of competence and self-determination but also on his or her performance success.

Since attributions appear to play a role in the feedback-motivation-performance process, research on attribution theory, in the feedback context, is the focus of the following section.

Receiver/Sender Attributions and Feedback

Numerous feedback-motivation writers have implied that individuals' attributions of the causes of their performance interact with the performance feedback they receive (e.g., Arnold, 1976, 1985; Brophy, 1981; Deci, 1975). The logic of this view emanates from attribution theory. Attribution theory is specifically concerned with how individuals assign enduring traits or dispositions to themselves and other persons (Heider, 1958; Kelley, 1972, 1973). It assumes that individuals have a need to understand and explain the events around them, and that, based on this need, individuals will develop a lay or "naive" theory of behavior (Heider, 1958; Staw, 1975). The implication of this view for feedback research is evident. If attribution theory is valid, then a feedback recipient or sender may very well possess a "theory" of the relationship between the feedback received and subsequent performance (e.g., Staw, 1975).

Leadership research. An important body of research, closely associated with the feedback-attribution-motivation area, uses attribution theory to study leadership. In particular, these investigations have studied the processes underlying *feedback sending*, attributions, and their effects on leader behavior. For example, Mitchell and Green (1978) and Green and Mitchell (1979; see also, Mitchell, Green, & Wood, 1981) have developed a model that shows how attributions may be used to help describe how leaders communicate with poor performers. The Green and Mitchell (1979) model posits a two-part process (subordinate behavior → leader attribution → leader behavior). At the attributional stage a leader becomes aware of an incident of poor subordinate performance and then attempts to understand the cause of the poor performance. Then, there is a feedback stage where a leader must choose a course of action and respond communicatively to the subordinate. Leader attributions involve one of two judgments. Either the cause is attributed as internal to the subordinate (e.g., aptitude, skill, or motivation), or the cause is attributed as external to the subordinate (e.g., work environment, nature of task difficulty). Internal attributions direct the leader to change the subordinate's behavior through feedback, punishment, or training. External attributions direct the leader to change the situation or task (e.g., altering the task, providing assistance, or providing superior information).

The communication implications of this model are compelling. Green and Mitchell (1979) found that supervisors tend to see poor subordinate performance as more internally than externally caused, and that when confronted with poor subordinate performance supervisors tend to emphasize the relationship dimension of feedback—that is, to praise, blame, punish or train rather than redesign work, alter work environments, or increase information flow (the content dimension of feedback). In a study of nursing supervisors' behavior and subordinate poor performance, Mitchell and Wood (1980) found the following: (1) Internal attributions of poor nurse performance led supervisors to punitive responses (what could be considered "one-up" messages—see Stohl & Redding, Chapter 14, in this volume); and (2) when the consequences of poor performance were perceived by supervisors as serious, as compared to not serious, supervisors used more internal attributions *and* punitive responses. Similarly, Green and Liden (1980) found that when the subordinate was seen as the cause of poor performance (1) control responses were directed at the subordinate, (2) were more punitive, and (3) included more change to the subordinate's job. In turn, Mitchell and Kalb (1981) also found that the outcomes of a subordinate's ineffective behavior have an impact on the attributions and evaluations made by the supervisor. Additionally, Brown and Mitchell (1986) confirmed that observers tend to blame people rather than environments for performance problems.

In summarizing this section, it is useful to review Larson's (1984) model of supervisory feedback sending as it relates to the communication process. Larson's (1984) model includes both the determinants and consequences of supervisory feedback and suggests a causal psychological/communication model where (1) situational (i.e., internal) variables affect (2) a supervisor's feedback behavior (communication), which in turn affects (3) a subordinate's self-perceived competence (internal) and thereby influences (4) a subordinate's motivation (behaviorally manifested). Noting that informal performance feedback from supervisors can have beneficial effects on subordinates' performance and their work-related attitudes, Larson (1984) discusses factors that influence this feedback sending behavior and the impact that feedback sending can have on both the subordinate and supervisor. Among the many benefits of this approach is the implication that the feedback process is dynamic, such that the results of a feedback episode at Time 1 serve as part of the antecedent conditions of a feedback episode Time 2, and so on. Recent research by Larson (1986) has revealed that supervisors give subordinates feedback less often about instances of poor performance, but when they do it is more specific (content dimension) than their feedback about good performance. Larson (1986) also found that supervisors give feedback more often under conditions of high rather than low outcome dependence (whether a supervisor's organizational rewards are dependent on their subordinates' performance) only when the subordinate exhibited a pattern of gradually worsening performance.

Performance appraisal. As one of the most popular areas of organization research, the (formal) performance appraisal emphasizes the need to provide employees with accurate feedback about their job performance (Cummings & Schwab, 1973). In recent years researchers have devoted particular attention to the role of feedback and attributions in the appraisal process. In general, studies in this area indicate that (1) supervisors distort negative information when it must be given to low performers; and (2) when subordinate performance is attributed to ability rather than effort, supervisors give less appropriate feedback (Fisher, 1979; Ilgen & Knowlton, 1980). These findings are striking, since it appears that a number of processes converge on the problem of poor performance to suggest that, even if there is a belief in the need for performance feedback, that feedback will be inappropriate if increased motivation and performance are desired. Thus we see that it is not only feedback recipients who have an aversion to negative feedback (Redding, 1972); senders of feedback are similarly averse. This process is muddled further when subordinate perceptions of performance feedback are included, since receivers (subordinates) perceive negative feedback to be more positive than it actually is (Ilgen et al., 1979). When this is combined with supervisors' tendencies to positively distort performance feedback to subordinates (Fisher, 1979; Ilgen & Knowlton, 1980) it is likely that feedback recipients may hold positively inflated views of their organizational performance. This is compounded by the fact that feedback that one is "satisfactory" is disconfirming for many feedback recipients (Pearce & Porter, 1986). This may result from the very best of intentions, yet "to improve the accuracy of subordinate perceptions, it would seem that both superiors and subordinates need to be made more aware of the tendencies to inflate feedback and factors that affect it" (Ilgen & Knowlton, 1980, p. 453).

Directions for communication research. Organizational communication scholars familiar with current communication theory, with its view of communicative interaction as a stochastic process (e.g., Hawes, 1973), will no doubt appreciate the Larson (1984) model of the feedback process discussed earlier. Nonetheless, there has been a paucity of feedback that incorporates this dynamic/process perspective theoretically. While some writers have suggested that feedback loops be viewed as a dynamic process (e.g., Larson, 1984; Masuch, 1985), there is also a paucity of feedback research that utilizes the methodological tools necessary to operationalize feedback loops as process phenomena. Communication scholars have long argued that the *communication interact* should be the fundamental unit of analysis in the study of communication systems (Hawes, 1973) and that "given that interdependence is the crucial element from which a theory of organizations is built, *interacts* rather than acts are the crucial observables that must be specified" (Weick, 1969, p. 33). Weick (1969) extends this perspective further by arguing that, as the appropriate unit of analysis, a series of interacts are

> contingent response patterns, patterns in which an action by actor A evokes a specific response in actor B which is then responded to by actor A. This is the pattern designated a "double interact" by Barker and Wright (1955), and it is proposed by Hollander and Willis (1967) as the basic unit of describing interpersonal influence" (p. 33)

For Weick, organizational interaction (1969, p. 33; 1979) involves control, influence, and authority—processes central to performance feedback administration. We can concur with his argument that "a description of organizing must use the double interact as the unit of analysis for specifying observable behaviors" (p. 33). Essentially, this perspective offers a theoretical model on which superior-subordinate *feedback loops* can be investigated. B. A. Fischer (1978) argues that a "pragmatic perspective" (p. 298) of human communication envisions feedback as a social process constituting a holistic system of interactants. In this view, feedback "is then discernible within the patterns of interaction as a minimal sequence of three acts (double interact). The feedback process becomes not simply a response but a circular closed loop of interaction" (p. 298). When the feedback process is conceptualized in this manner, it is clear that both internal psychological and external communicative processes are operative. For example, Ilgen, Mitchell, and Fredrickson (1981) found that supervisors who believed their own rewards were dependent on their subordinates' performances responded more positively toward the subordinates who performed poorly. Additionally, Mitchell and Liden (1982) found that supervisors rated poor performers more positively and good performers more negatively when the poor performer was high in social and/or leadership skills than when he or she was low on these factors.

Clearly, the feedback process that emerges between subordinates and supervisors, with its series of interconnected events (e.g., subordinate performance[1]—supervisory feedback[1]—subordinate performance[2]—supervisory feedback[2] . . .), lends itself to stochastic analysis. The theoretical work of Larson (1984) and the research of Fairhurst, Green, and Snavely (1984) and Gioia and Simms (1986) suggest the possible beginning of this type of feedback research. This process approach to organizational feedback loops is compatible with Watzlawick et al.'s (1967) analysis of "positive" and "negative" feedback *"relationships"* (p. 31), which conforms to the notions of deviation amplifying and counteracting loops, where *feedback interacts* serve as *inputs* into the superior-subordinate communication *system*. If, as Larson (1984) strongly suggests, the feedback process is dynamic, it behooves feedback researchers to employ methods that tap the process. For example, Green, Fairhurst, and Snavely (1986) identified three tactics managers use to control ineffective subordinate performance and concluded "that the *meaning* of any single" (p. 23) control (one-up) action (i.e., feedback) "was affected by its relationship to other actions" (p. 23) preceding and following it. Alternatively, the subordinate's communicative behavior affects supervisor attributions and feedback. For example, Wood and Mitchell (1981) found that poor performers could differentially manage the appraisals and responses of a manager such that if they offered *excuses* to a supervisor he or she would attribute less responsibility, be less personal, and be less punitive toward the subordinate. Supervisors did not characteristically act in this manner when subordinates offered *apologies* for their poor performance. These findings correspond to the view that supervisor-subordinate feedback processes are best understood as a system of interaction, which can be described as an interconnected series of double interacts.

It is also worthy to note the complementarity of Laing's (1961) work on attributions and injunctions, which falls within the broad purview of communication theory, and the attributional model of feedback sending in organizational behavior. Essentially, Laing (1961) argues that when attributions are repeated frequently they take on the force of injunctions about *how* to behave. The applicability of this perspective to feedback-control mechanisms should be explored since one of the goals of supervisory feedback is influencing workers to expend effort to perform a task successfully. In other words, do subordinates perceive regular performance feedback as efforts to control their behavior? And, how does this affect their performance? Beyond this, communication researchers should also explore how patterns of feedback between a supervisor and subordinate affect the subordinate's definition of him- or herself and his or her subsequent task performance. As Watzlawick et al. (1967) observe, messages (e.g., performance feedback) may confirm (accept), reject, or disconfirm (ignore) a receiver's self-definition, and will most certainly affect the receiver's subsequent behavior. This aspect of communication theory connects well with the attribution model and offers numerous feedback research opportunities.

Finally, it is important to recognize that, to date, the attribution research reviewed here sheds more light on the underlying processes and reasons why certain forms of feedback are sent by supervisors to subordinates than about the impact of actual feedback messages on subordinates' motivation or performance. Future investigations, therefore, need to explore the effects supervisory attributions have on actual supervisory feedback behavior and, subsequently, the effects of this feedback on subordinate behavior. In turn, it should be realized that most research in this area has required "supervisors" to *select* a feedback message *strategy*—not send a *message per se*—from a pool of strategic feedback options. Obviously, actual supervisory feedback behavior in the field may vary from research contexts and, thus, may change the effect of feedback on subsequent subordinate response. In essence, what may be needed is a *conjoint* attributional/behavioral model that seeks to explain, across time and in relation to each other, (1) the attribution processes of feedback senders and their feedback sending behavior, and (2) the attribution processes of feedback receivers and actual subsequent receiver task behavior, and vice versa.

Rewards, Punishments, Warnings, Reprimands

As if the feedback literature were not in itself immense, there is also a substantial body of literature in the area of leader reward and punishment behavior and its effects on subordinate performance (Farris & Lim, 1969; Lowin & Craig, 1968). This literature is too substantial to review in detail, yet because of the conceptual overlap between the variables of reward/punishment and feedback, a review of the essential aspects of the research is appropriate. Recall that Wiener (1948) described a "feedback loop" by which information about actual performance is used to control future actions toward a predetermined goal. A reward is any attractive phenomenon that, when presented following a response, increases the frequency of that response. Alternatively, Kazdin (1975) defines punishment as "the presentation of an aversive event or the removal of a positive event following a response which decreases the frequency of that response" (pp. 33-34).

Rewards and punishments, then, possess informational cues, in an information theory sense (Shannon, 1948), while feedback, either the expectation of it or subsequent to it, may encourage or discourage the continuation of an activity. The difference between feedback per se, on the one hand, and rewards or punishments, on the other, seems to center on the establishment of an "if-then" contingency between an established action and a future action or outcome. With rewards, a nonrandom contingency exists between some defined response and some attractive or aversive consequence (Sims & Szilagnyi, 1975). A major portion of the leader reward research has been directed at the impact of monetary rewards on motivation and performance (Arvey & Ivancevich, 1980). But such a contingency has never been included in any conceptualization of feedback.

In an effort to make sense of the research on leader reward/punishment behavior and its impact on performance, a number of excellent studies, reviews, and critiques have emerged and warrant specific mention. In their review of the research, Arvey and Ivancevich (1980) offer six propositions regarding the effective use of punishments in organizations:

(1) Punishment is more effective in organizational contexts if the aversive stimuli or events are delivered immediately after the undesirable response occurs than if the delivery is delayed (p. 126).

(2) Moderate levels of punishment are more effective than low or high levels (p. 127).

(3) Punishment procedures are more effective when the agent administering the punishment has relatively close and friendly relationships with the employee being punished (p. 127).

(4) Punishment of undesired behavior is more effective if (a) it consistently occurs after every undesirable response, (b) it is administered consistently across different employees by the same managers, and (c) different managers are consistent in their application of punishment for the same undesirable response (p. 128).

(5) Punishment is more effective when clear reasons are communicated to employees concerning why the punishment occurred, what the contingency is, and what the consequences of the behavior are in the future (p. 129).

(6) To the extent that alternative desirable responses are available to employees and these responses are reinforced, punishment is enhanced (p. 129).

In addition, Sims (1980) suggests two other propositions that can be drawn from the literature: (1) In most studies that contrast positive and punitive leader behavior, reward behavior tends to have a much stronger effect on employee performance; and (2) both longitudinal field and laboratory studies seem to support the idea that punishment tends to be more a *result* of employee behavior (i.e., managers tend to increase punishments in response to poor employee performance) than a cause. This point clearly supports our argument for a double-interact, conjoint, relational model of feedback loops.

Recently, Podsakoff, Todor, and Skov (1982) found that (1) only performance-contingent reward behavior affected subordinate performance significantly; (2) leader contingent reward behavior and employee satisfaction were positively correlated; and (3) contingent punishment had no effect on subordinate performance or satisfaction. Studies by Ilgen and his colleagues (1981), Liden and Mitchell (1985), and Sims (1977) also failed to reveal a significant relationship between types of negative feedback and subsequent behavior, while Sims and Szilagnyi (1975) found that when leaders' "punishment" of subordinates was communicated it was negatively related to subsequent employee performance. Here the critical issue may be whether the *type* (e.g., specific vs. nonspecific) of negative feedback provided is differentially related to receiver performance (Liden & Mitchell, 1985). From a communication perspective the credibility of the feedback source plays a crucial role in receiver *responsiveness* to and *satisfaction* with the feedback (Bannister, 1986; Cusella, 1980, 1982, 1984a; Ilgen et al., 1979).

One thing is clear from this research: Positive feedback and negative feedback are used by supervisors to shape future subordinate performance. Recently two field-observational studies of the role of supervisory feedback in controlling subordinate performance have appeared. In the first of these studies Fairhurst et al. (1984) explored managerial use of "face support" (positive feedback) in controlling subordinate poor performance. Essentially,

Fairhurst et al. (1984) utilized an expanded view of performance feedback and focused their research on how a subordinate's identity is negotiated and how relational control between supervisors and subordinates is shared when managers deal with subordinate poor performance. They found that when confronted with a poor performer, many managers tended either to revert to criticism, reprimands, threats, or orders from the start of a control sequence, *or* they initially attempted a "problem solving" style but would quickly abandon it for the punitive approach described above. In the second study, Gioia and Sims (1986) found distinctly different patterns of managerial attribution and verbal behavior for subordinate performance failures as compared to success. Here face-to-face superior-subordinate interaction resulted in an attributional shift toward leniency by the managers, who assigned less blame of failure and more credit for success after the interaction (Gioia & Sims, 1986).

In sum, these two studies suggest, as might be expected, that managers vary their feedback as a function of their perceptions of subordinate task performance. Furthermore, the *context* of the interaction (face-to-face vs. other) affects both the manager's attributions of subordinate performance and the nature of the feedback he or she conveys to subordinates. The generalization to be drawn from these two studies is that despite one's best intentions to approach subordinate low performance as a "problem" to be "solved," managers place a high valence on the relational control of their subordinates. The goal of *relational control*, in turn, may influence the type of feedback managers send subordinates. Additionally, it may be the case that even when managers revert to punitive control (one-up) attempts (Fairhurst et al., 1984) they continue to search for reasons to be lenient (one-across or one-down) (Gioia & Sims, 1986) in their evaluation of their subordinates.

Conclusions and research directions. Among the conclusions to be drawn from the leader reward/punishment research, the following are of particular interest. First, as style of communication may vary across interactants (Norton, 1983), so may differences emerge in (1) one's approach to evaluating performance, and (2) the styles employed when conveying types of sanctions and performance feedback to subordinates. Second, as one begins to classify, for example, verbal warnings as punishment and verbal praise as reward (e.g., O'Reilly & Weitz, 1980), the conceptual distinctions between rewards/punishments, on the one hand, and positive/negative feedback, on the other, become blurred to the point where it may be conceptually and operationally irrelevant to distinguish between rewards/punishments and feedback. Both have informational properties and the potential to encourage or discourage continued action. Third, while it is clear that a leader's reward/feedback behavior influences the behavior of subordinates, the reverse is also true to the extent that leader feedback behavior and subordinate performance are mutually causal (Greene, 1973, 1976; Sims, 1977; Sims & Manz, 1984; Sims &

Szilagnyi, 1979). For example, Herold (1977) demonstrated that leader behavior and attitude varied as a function of subordinate behavior. Fourth, it may well be the case that a supervisor's orientation in giving feedback (his or her *feedback style*) influences the type of feedback given to subordinates, which also affects supervisory attributions of subordinates; in turn, this series results in a favorable or unfavorable evaluation of performance (e.g., Kipnis, Schmidt, Price, & Stitt, 1981). Finally, it appears that in order to make valid knowledge claims about the relationship between contingent and noncontingent reward and punishment behaviors (including feedback) and subordinate responses, the whole spectrum of reward/punishment behaviors must be studied systemically (Hunt & Schuler, 1976; Podsakoff, 1982; Podsakoff, Todor, Grocer, & Huber, 1984; Podsakoff et al., 1982).[2]

In closing, probably no other area lends itself more to future communication research than does the area of supervisor-subordinate reward/punishment behavior. Research opportunities range from the development of typologies of the verbal rewards and punishments used in real-life organizations, which would address both linguistic structure and information content, to the utilization of stochastic time-series analyses of the complex variety of patterned supervisory verbal rewards/punishments and subordinate performance interaction (and vice versa). The context (e.g., public vs. private) in which reward/punishment behavior occurs and its impact on supervisor-subordinate interaction should certainly be explored further. Finally, researchers have yet to investigate fully the relationship or command (Watson, 1982; Watzlawick et al., 1967) dimensions of verbal rewards/punishments, even though it is clear that all verbal rewards/punishments possess degrees of relational dominance or submissiveness (Cusella, 1980) to which feedback receivers respond in a variety of ways (Fairhurst et al., 1984; Green et al., 1986).

Affiliated Research Areas

As the length of the preceding section suggests, probably more research has explored feedback processes in dyadic relationships than in any other context. Moreover, the reader should realize that the preceding presentation has not covered all variations of feedback studies in this area but has included those most relevant to the focus of this chapter. Readers interested in other areas of research are directed to the following research, listed by topic area: training, feedback, and motivation/performance (Komaki, Collins, & Penn, 1982; Komaki, Heinzmann, & Lawson, 1980); feedback and persistence of change (Clarke, 1972; Conlon, 1980; French, 1955, 1958); feedback and source characteristics (Frey, 1981; Halperin, Snyder, Shenkel, & Houston, 1976; Tuckman & Oliver, 1968); method of feedback presentation in the appraisal interview (Ivancevich, 1982; Lawler & Rhode, 1976; Nadler, 1977; Nadler, Mirvis & Cammann, 1976; Nadler, Cammann, & Mirvis, 1980); and in general a variety of feedback-related factors that may be relevant to the appraisal process (e.g., Burke, Weitzel, & Weir, 1980; Cummings & Schwab, 1973; DeCotiss & Petit, 1978; DeNisi, Cafferty, & Meglino, 1984; Feldman, 1981; Hobson, Mendel, & Gibson, 1981; Ilgen & Feldman, 1983; Ilgen et al., 1979; Ivancevich, 1982; Landy & Farr, 1980; Redding, 1972).

GROUP FEEDBACK

To this point the discussion has covered motivation and performance in the impersonal and dyadic feedback contexts. In both of these contexts, feedback research has focused on feedback directed at individuals. Indeed it is within the impersonal and dyadic contexts that most feedback research has been conducted. Although Nadler (1977, 1979) has called for more feedback-group research relative to the dyadic context, fewer researchers have responded to this call. This is somewhat unfortunate because it is common to find feedback being administered to work units as a whole. This is especially true with the increasing popularity of quality circles (Marks, 1986; Marks, Mirvis, Hackett, & Grady, 1986). It is important to note that while some of the group feedback research has displayed a communication focus, most of it has been variable specific rather than oriented toward the group process of feedback reception and sense making. It is the feedback research conducted within the group context to which we now turn our attention.

Feedback and Group Functioning

In his 1979 review of feedback and group functioning, Nadler distinguished three types of feedback: (1) individual feedback, (2) individual feedback administered in a group, and (3) feedback administered to an entire group. Group feedback is different than individual feedback because the information is confounded by the actions of other group members—the individual wonders if the feedback is directed toward him or her, or toward the whole group. Additionally, the individual is limited by the group in how much he or she may act on the feedback because any one individual's behavior may have only a small effect on overall group performance.

Just as in individual and dyadic feedback, group feedback has some rather specific effects on several dependent variables. For instance, a number of studies have associated feedback with increased group performance or productivity (Cook, 1968; Erez, 1977; Forward & Zander, 1971; Kim & Hamner, 1976; Zander & Forward, 1968), leading Nadler (1979) to conclude that feedback can affect group performance and that this effect occurs through some cuing effects or some motivational effects or a combination of the two (e.g., Berkowitz & Levy, 1956; Hunt & Ebeling, 1983; Payne & Hauty, 1955; Pryer & Bass, 1959; Siegel & Ruh, 1973). Other research has examined the impact of performance feedback on members' ratings of group process.

(Binning & Lord, 1980; Downey, Chacko, & McElroy, 1979). For example, Staw (1975) found that groups that received feedback indicating good performance, as opposed to poor performance, rated their group as possessing more cohesiveness, communication, motivation, ability, satisfaction, role clarity, and influence.

Similar to Nadler's (1979) review of feedback in group contexts, the following discussion will focus on a number of specific feedback variables/factors that have frequently been studies by researchers: (1) feedback aggregation level; (2) task vs. process feedback; (3) the evaluative content of feedback; (4) the nature of the group feedback process; (5) individual differences in responding to group feedback; and (6) the moderating effects of task structure on the impact of group feedback.

Feedback Aggregation Level

Within the group structure, feedback can be administered to an individual within a group or to the group as a whole. Group feedback has been found to increase group pride (Berkowitz & Levy, 1956), task motivation (Berkowitz & Levy, 1956; Nadler, 1979), team accuracy (Rosenberg & Hall, 1958), group attraction and group esteem (Frye, 1966), and involvement (Nadler, 1979). Individual feedback, on the other hand, generally has been shown to be associated with increased individual performance and aggregated group performance (Zajonc, 1962; Zander & Wolfe, 1964), individual levels of self-esteem (Frye, 1966), and participation rates (Smith, 1972). Stone (1971) found some marginally significant effects, indicating higher satisfaction and performance with individual as opposed to group feedback. Madsen and Finger (1978) found no differences between individual brainstorming with or without feedback, but found that both of these were more effective than group brainstorming.

While group feedback traditionally is studied within the superior-subordinate setting, two studies have explored the nature and effects of *peer* feedback in groups. In the first of these studies, Ogilvie and Haslett (1985) examined *how* peer feedback typically is communicated in groups. Results of their research revealed the following dimensions to peer feedback: dynamism, trust, clarity, mood, and criticism. Judgments of the effectiveness of feedback were related to dynamism and to a verbally assertive style. Both feedback form and content influenced judgments of feedback effectiveness. On the other hand, DeNisi, Randolph, and Blencoe (1982) concluded that both negative group-level feedback from a peer and negative group-level feedback from a supervisor influenced their measure of students' objective performance. They also observed that individual peer feedback was more effective than group supervisor feedback in creating differences on (1) evaluations of perceived group performance and (2) evaluations of perceived motivation, both individual and group.

In summary, it is important to realize that a wide variety of individual difference variables have emerged in response to feedback aggregation levels; these individual difference variables will be discussed in a following section. Additionally, the results of research on feedback aggregation levels indicate that task-group structure may moderate the impact of aggregation level, such that group feedback does not improve group performance if the task requires minimal interdependence (Glaser & Klaus, 1966; Klaus & Glaser, 1970). As Nadler (1979) suggests, if group feedback is no more than a sum of individual feedback, then individual feedback is preferable.

Feedback Task Versus Process Focus

Just as individual or dyadic feedback can have various foci, group feedback can focus on either task performance or group process. Two studies have found no differences between task and process feedback (Bouchard, 1969; Lucas, 1965), although both had severe methodological limitations (Nadler, 1979). In other research, process feedback has been found to lead to less defensiveness and higher task efficiency (Gibb, Smith, & Roberts, 1955), to increased involvement, consensus, solidarity, and supportiveness (Weber, 1971), and to increased goal achievement and rational problem solving (Weber, 1972). In Weber's studies, however, process feedback typically consisted of groups simply viewing videotapes of themselves in action. Walter and Miles (1972; see also Walter, 1975) found that viewing of videotapes was not effective without providing group members an opportunity to also observe a social model.

Generally, it appears that

(1) feedback must provide clear information about errors and how to correct them;
(2) task feedback can enhance performance if it clarifies goals and how to reach them;
(3) process feedback can enhance performance if it is augmented, such as with models, and
(4) process feedback provides a cuing rather than motivational function (Nadler, 1979).

Feedback Evaluative Content

The valence of the feedback, favorable or unfavorable, positive or negative, moderates the impact of feedback in groups just as it does when feedback is directed toward individuals. Favorable feedback leads groups to rate themselves as more cohesive, motivated, and open to change (Staw, 1975), leads to more attraction (Berkowitz, Levy, & Harvey, 1957), to more participation (Bavelas, Hastorf, Gross, & Kite, 1965), and to a greater readiness to reduce status incongruence (Burnstein & Zajonc, 1965). Those in no feedback and favorable feedback conditions show greater consistency between individual and group aspirations (Zander & Wulff, 1966). Generally, favorable feedback is accepted more readily than is unfavorable feedback (Jacobs, 1974), even when it is presented in the form of personality profiles (Schaible, 1970). On the other hand, Morran and Stockton (1980) suggest that favorable feedback is seen as more desirable and effective but not necessarily more credible than unfavorable feedback.

Unfavorable feedback, however, is needed in order to unfreeze habits or change problem behaviors (Stoller, 1968). Yet other research indicates that unfavorable feedback may lead to defensiveness (Gibb et al., 1955), less pride and more task-oriented behavior (Berkowitz & Levy, 1956), lower aspiration level (Dustin, 1966), less attraction to the group (Schlenker, Soraci, & McCarthy, 1976), and more distortion of team scores and attributions of cause of behavior to outside factors (Dustin, 1966; Johnson, 1967; Schlenker et al., 1976). With unfavorable feedback, lower status group members try to reduce the control given to high status members (Michener & Lawler, 1971). Criticism seems to stimulate coping and attributional processes among group members (Varca & Levey, 1984).

Other variables also interact with feedback valence. There is less defensiveness to group than to individual unfavorable feedback (Berkowitz & Levy, 1956). High initial motivation groups show more task-oriented behavior after unfavorable feedback, while low motivation groups respond better to favorable feedback (Berkowitz, Levy, & Harvey, 1957). Those with high self-concepts rate unfavorable feedback as more desirable than do those with moderate self-concepts, but not as more credible or effective (Morran & Stockton, 1980). A recent study by Guzzo, Wagner, Maguire, Herr, and Hawley (1986) concluded that implicit theories about group process combined with negative but not positive information affect people's reports about groups. Binning, Zaba, and Whattam (1986) found that observers' ratings of specific behaviors and global evaluations were biased in the direction of performance cues. These findings support Phillips and Lord's (1982) theory of the biasing effects of performance cues in terms of an observer's cognitive categorization. Finally, it is critical to note the finding of Smith (1972) that feedback is *more* important than actual behavior in determining ratings of participation, the quality of ideas, and leadership.

Generally, then, the research in this area is fairly consistent: Positive feedback leads to favorable outcomes for the group while negative feedback leads to less favorable outcomes. But the impact of valence is moderated by several other variables.

The Nature of the Feedback Process in Groups

At various points in this chapter reference has been made to factors relating to how feedback is processed. In particular, some research has examined how feedback is processed or used by groups. Feedback, of course, may be ignored by a group. Or feedback may serve a cuing function to help groups develop strategies for improving performance (Ellsworth, 1973; Nadler, 1976). And as mentioned repeatedly in this chapter, feedback may be used motivationally, although many have argued that goal setting is the critical process that enables feedback to have motivational effects (Kim & Hamner, 1976; Locke, 1968; Locke et al., 1968; Spoelder-Claes, 1973; Zander, 1971). Most research thus focuses on the goal setting properties of group feedback. Zander (1971) has argued that aspiration levels become meaningful only when a group has feedback about its performance. Shelley (1954) and Zander and Medow (1965) found that goals are raised after success and maintained or lowered after failure, although Poythress and Spicer (1976) found no such differences.

Several authors have suggested PDM—Participatory Decision Making (Lowin, 1968)—to enhance goal acceptance (Vroom & Yetton, 1973). Although Hannan (1975) found that PDM did, in fact, increase goal acceptance, three other studies found no significant differences in the acceptance of assigned and participative goals (Dossett, Latham, & Mitchell, 1979; Latham, Mitchell, & Dossett, 1978; Latham & Saari, 1979). However, Erez and Kanfer (1983) argued that participation in goal setting increases goal acceptance beyond externally assigned goals by increasing an individual's feelings of control over the goal setting process. Their most recent study found participative and representative groups outperforming assigned-goal groups (Erez, Earley, & Hulin, 1985). They further argued that, as goal acceptance increases, the influence of goal setting on performance increases, and that participation is particularly effective at enhancing goal acceptance when the goal is unreasonable or difficult. In partial substantiation of this, Becker's (1978) field study found the best performance in groups that had both a difficult goal and feedback about their performance. Most research, then, supports the importance of goal acceptance in the feedback process and indicates that participation can help increase goal acceptance. What has been lacking is an investigation of the communicative dynamics among group members during the participation process, especially the emergence of intra-group feedback loops as the group makes sense of the performance feedback. Furthermore, research should also explore the effect that a leader's communicative behavior, especially on a relational level, has on the group's acceptance of assigned and participative goals. For example, do one-up, one-down, or one-across leader descriptions of assigned or participative goals differentially affect group acceptance?

Differences in Individual Group Members

All members within a particular group, of course, are not likely to respond to feedback in the same way. To date the research has identified several individual difference variables that moderate the effect of feedback: motivation level, task- vs. self- or other-orientation, self-esteem, and need achievement vs. need affiliation. More particularly, differences in individual vs. group feedback do not affect high need achievers; high need affiliators, however, function more effectively when they have received group feedback (French, 1958). High motivation group members are more affected by individual feedback in their attraction to other group members, with performance feedback playing the largest role in determining attraction (Berkowitz et al., 1957). On the other hand, high motivation groups appear to respond better to unfavorable feedback than do those lower in motivation (Berkowitz et al., 1957). Frye (1966) reports that those who are task-oriented, as opposed to self- or other-oriented, respond more positively to performance feedback. Generally, then, achievement- or task-oriented individuals are more sensitive to feedback, especially individual feedback, and respond more positively to negative feedback.

Finally, in a test of Byrne's (1961, 1964) repression-sensitization construct, Varca and Levey (1984) assessed the impact of feedback on coping strategies and found that a direct threat from individual feedback increases defensiveness among repressors, while an indirect threat from group feedback increases defensiveness among sensitizers.

Task Structure

One final variable that moderates the impact of feedback in groups is task structure. Hackman and Morris (1975) define structure as the process of how individual roles and behavior combine to create group performance. Thus one variable included in task structure is interdependence. Although Nadler (1979) argues for the importance of task structure as a factor in the group feedback process, only two studies have included it as a variable. As was mentioned earlier, Glaser and Klaus (1966) and Klaus and Glaser (1970) concluded that groups do not respond well in situations of minimal interdependence where group feedback is received.

Directions for Communication Research

As within the impersonal and dyadic contexts, feedback within the group setting is no less complex a process. Yet in comparison to the dyadic context the paucity of research on group feedback is apparent. Nadler's (1979) schema and the various moderating influences outlined above provide a point of departure for researchers interested in exploring this increasingly important setting for the delivery of feedback in organizations.

As noted earlier, with the increasing popularity of quality circles (Marks, Mirvis, Hackett, & Grady, 1986) and such structures as worker-owned and other cooperative organizational arrangements, researchers in the future should investigate the role of feedback in the group setting. For example, it is clear that quality circles are dependent on performance feedback regarding the success of their problem solving efforts if they are to function effectively. Yet no research to date has systematically explored variations in feedback sent to quality circles and its effect on subsequent quality circle performance.

In addition, research is needed on the role of groups in creating an organization's embedded feedback environment. This research is called for since workgroups function as core units in any organization's informational feedback system, where individuals are immersed in workgroups. These workgroups may themselves serve as embedded sources and recipients of feedback. Along these lines recent research by Herold and Parsons (1985) is relevant. They report on the development of a 95-item instrument used to assess the amount and type of feedback information available to individuals in work settings. What emerged from their factor analyses of two different "feedback environments" (hospital nurses and electric utility supervisors) were 15 dimensions reflecting various sources of feedback and the type of information they convey. Since the research of Herold and Parsons (1985) clearly indicates that organizations contain multifaceted feedback environments, future group-level feedback studies should aim at determining how workgroups function as embedded recipients and sources of feedback.

A focus on group feedback environments may also lead feedback researchers to further explore groups as organizational *sub-cultures* (Smircich, 1983). In their analysis of corporate cultures, Deal and Kennedy (1982) present a structure for analyzing organizational environments based on two dimensions: (1) the amount of risk associated with organizational action; and (2) the speed with which organizational members receive feedback on results. In their research, Thompson and Browning (1986) found considerable support for the Deal and Kennedy (1982) framework.

In the area of group feedback research one of the most promising, and as yet untapped, areas for communication researchers is the manner in which group members, functioning as a communication system, verbally process amongst themselves the performance feedback they receive. While an impressive number of studies have tapped the psychological dynamics involved during the reception of group feedback (Bowen & Siegel, 1973; Nadler, 1979) little research has investigated how group members, as a unit, verbally react, interpret, define, and make sense out of the feedback they receive, through group discussion and interaction. If we apply Weick's (1979) "sense making recipe" to the group context, then communication researchers are aptly suited to inspect the group's communication behavior, reflectively and retrospectively, after the reception of group performance feedback. Weick's (1979, p. 64) model of knowing, thinking, seeing, and *saying* can be expressed in a group context in the following manner: "How can we know what we think till we see what we say?" The manner in which group members discuss feedback pertaining to the group's performance may influence the "meaning" the feedback has for the group and the group's subsequent effort to accomplish its work. Communication researchers have a long history of small group research (Fisher, 1980) and the observational and analytical tools they have employed could be used while conducting group feedback-motivation-performance research.

POSTSCRIPT

Based on the preceding review of the feedback, motivation, and performance literature, we end this chapter as we began—with the idea that the context and manner in which performance feedback is communicated, plus the nature of the feedback per se, affects a receiver's (task performer's) subsequent motivation and/or performance. As this examination has demonstrated, the feedback, motivation, and performance triad contains numerous opportunities for *pragmatic* (Watzlawick et al., 1967) and *symbolic* (Cusella, 1984b) communication research. Researchers should also strive to ascertain a *grammar of social contexts* that reflects the various organizational settings in which feedback is administered and processed. If developed further, this needed research will add much to our knowledge and understanding of the critical role that feedback plays in the motivation and performance of organization members.

NOTES

1. This discussion follows the work of Locke, Shaw, Sarri, and Latham (1981).
2. Readers interested in leader reward/punishment behavior and subordinate performance are encouraged to pursue a number of exhaustive and incisive reviews of the literature (Ashour, 1982; House & Baetz, 1979; McCallister, 1984; McFatter, 1982; Podsakoff, 1982; Podsakoff et al., 1984).

REFERENCES

Adams, J. A. (1964). Motor skills. In P. Farnsworth, O. McNemar, & Q. McNemar (Eds.), *Annual review of psychology* (Vol. 15, pp. 181-202). Palo Alto: Annual Reviews Inc.

Adams, J. A. (1968). Response feedback and learning. *Psychological Bulletin, 70,* 486-504.

Ammons, R. B. (1956). Effects of knowledge of performance: A survey and tentative theoretical formulation. *Journal of General Psychology, 54,* 279-299.

Annett, J. (1969). *Feedback and human behavior.* Middlesex, England: Penguin.

Annett, J., & Kay, H. (1957). Knowledge of results and "skilled performance." *Occupational Psychology, 31,* 72-83.

Arnold, H. J. (1976). Effects of performance and extrinsic reward upon high intrinsic motivation. *Organizational Behavior and Human Performance, 17,* 275-288.

Arnold, H. J. (1985). Task performance, perceived competence, and attributed causes of performance as determinants of intrinsic motivation. *Academy of Management Journal, 28,* 876-888.

Arps, G. F. (1917). A preliminary report on "work with knowledge of results vs. work without knowledge of results." *Psychological Review, 24,* 449-455.

Arvey, R. D., & Ivancevich, J. M. (1980). Punishment in organizations: A review, propositions, and research suggestions. Academy of Management Journal, 5, 123-132.

Ashby, W. R. (1956). *An introduction to cybernetics.* New York: Wiley.

Ashford, S. J. (1986). Feedback seeking in individual adaptation: A resource perspective. *Academy of Management Journal, 29,* 465-487.

Ashford, S. J., & Cummings, L. L. (1983). Feedback as an individual resource: Personal strategies for creating information. *Organizational Behavior and Human Performance, 32,* 370-398.

Ashour, A. S. (1982). A framework of a cognitive-behavioral theory of leader influence and effectiveness. *Organizational Behavior and Human Performance, 30,* 407-430.

At Emery Air Freight. (1973). *Organizational Dynamics, 1,* 41-50.

Bandura, A., & Cervone, D. (1983). Self-evaluative and self-efficacy mechanisms governing the motivational effects of goal systems. *Journal of Personality and Social Psychology, 45,* 1017-1028.

Bandura, A., & Cervone, D. (1986). Differential engagement of self-reactive influences in cognitive motivation. *Organizational Behavior and Human Decision Processes, 38,* 92-113.

Bandura, A., & Simon, K. M. (1977). The role of proximal intentions in self-regulation of refractory behavior. *Cognitive Therapy and Research, 1,* 177-193.

Bannister, B. D. (1986). Performance outcome feedback and attributional feedback: Interactive effects on recipient responses. *Journal of Applied Psychology, 71,* 203-210.

Barker, R. G., & Wright, H. F. (1955). *Midwest and its children.* Evanston, IL: Row-Peterson.

Bateson, G. (1935). Culture contact and schismogenis. *Man, 35,* 178-183.

Bavelas, A., Hastorf, A. H., Gross, A. E., & Kite, W. R. (1965). Experiments on the alteration of group structure. *Journal of Experimental Social Psychology, 1,* 55-70.

Becker, L. J. (1978). Joint effect of feedback and goal setting on performance: A field study of residential energy conservation. *Journal of Applied Psychology, 63,* 428-433.

Berkowitz, L., & Levy, B. I. (1956). Pride in group performance and group task motivation. *Journal of Abnormal and Social Psychology, 53,* 300-306.

Berkowitz, L., Levy, B. I., & Harvey, A. R. (1957). Effects of performance evaluations on group integration and motivation. *Human Relations, 10,* 195-208.

Bilodeau, E. A. (1953). Acquisition of two lever-positioning responses practiced over several periods of alteration. *Journal of Experimental Psychology, 46,* 43-49.

Bilodeau, E. A. (Ed.). (1966). *Acquisition of skill.* New York: Academic Press.

Bilodeau, E. A., & Bilodeau, I. M. (1961). Motor-skills learning. In P. Farnsworth, O. McNemar, & Q. McNemar (Eds.), *Annual review of psychology,* (Vol. 12, pp. 243-280). Palo Alto: Annual Reviews, Inc.

Bilodeau E. A., Bilodeau, I. M., & Schumsky, D. A. (1959). Some effects of introducing and withdrawing knowledge of results early and late in practice. *Journal of Experimental Psychology, 58,* 142-144.

Binning, J. F., & Lord, R. G. (1980). Boundary conditions for performance cue effects on group process rating: Familiarity versus type of feedback. *Organizational Behavior and Human Performance, 26,* 115-130.

Binning, J. F., Zaba, A. J., & Whattam, J. C. (1986). Explaining the biasing effects of performance cues in terms of cognitive categorizations. *Academy of Management Journal, 29,* 521-535.

Boal, K. B., & Cummings, L. L. (1981). Cognitive evaluation theory: An experimental test of processes and outcomes. *Organizational Behavior and Human Performance, 28,* 289-310.

Bogart, D. H. (1980). Feedback, feedforward, and feedwithin: Strategic information in systems. *Behavioral Science, 25,* 237-249.

Boggiano, A. K., & Ruble, D. N. (1979). Competence and the over-justification effect: A developmental study. *Journal of Personality and Social Psychology, 37,* 1462-1468.

Bouchard, T. J. (1969). Personality, problem solving procedure and performance in small groups. *Journal of Applied Psychology, 53,* 1-29.

Bourne, L. E., Jr. (1966). Comments on Prof. I. M. Bilodeau's paper. In E. A. Bilodeau (Ed.), *Acquisition of skill* (pp. 297-313). New York: Academic Press.

Bowen, D. D., & Siegel, J. P. (1973). Process and performance: A longitudinal study of the reactions of small task groups to periodic performance feedback. *Human Relations, 26,* 433-448.

Brophy, J. (1981). Teacher praise: A functional analysis. *Review of Educational Research, 51,* 5-32.

Brown, K. A., & Mitchell, T. R. (1986). Influence of task interdependence and number of poor performers on diagnoses of causes of poor performance. *Academy of Management Journal, 29,* 412-424.

Buckley, W. (1967). *Sociology and modern systems theory.* Englewood Cliffs, NJ: Prentice-Hall.

Burke, R. J., Weitzel, W., & Weir, T. (1980). Characteristics of effective interviews reviewing performance: Do supervisors and subordinates agree? *Psychological Reports, 47,* 643-654.

Burnstein, E., & Zajonc, R. B. (1965). The effect of group success on the reduction of status incongruence in task-oriented groups. *Sociometry, 28,* 344-362.

Byrne, D. (1961). The repression-sensitization scale: Rationale, reliability, and validity. *Journal of Personality, 29,* 334-349.

Byrne, D. (1964). Repression-sensitization in experimental personality research. In B. A. Maher (Ed.), *Progress in experimental personality research* (pp. 170-220). New York: Academic Press.

Calder, B. J., & Staw, B. M. (1975). The interaction of intrinsic and extrinsic motivation: Some methodological notes. *Journal of Personality and Social Psychology, 31,* 76-80.

Campbell, J. P., & Pritchard, R. D. (1976). Motivation theory in industrial and organizational psychology. In M. D. Dunnette (Ed.), *Handbook of industrial and organizational psychology.* (pp. 63-139). Chicago: Rand McNally.

Campion, M. A., & Lord, R. G. (1982). A control systems conceptualization of the goal setting and changing process. *Organizational Behavior and Human Performance, 30,* 265-287.

Chhokar, J. S., & Wallin, J. A. (1984). A field study of the effect of feedback frequency on performance. *Journal of Applied Psychology, 69,* 524-530.

Clarke, D. E. (1972). The effects of simulated feedback and motivation on persistence at a task. *Organizational Behavior and Human Performance, 8,* 340-346.

Clement, D. A., & Frandsen, K. D. (1976). On conceptual and empirical treatments of feedback in human communication. *Speech Monographs, 43,* 11-28.

Conklin, J. E. (1959). Linearity of the tracking performance function. *Perceptual and Motor Skills, 9,* 387-391.

Conlon, E. J. (1980). Feedback about personal and organizational outcomes and its effects on persistence of planned behavioral changes. *Academy of Management Journal, 23,* 267-286.

Cook, D. M. (1968). The impact on managers of frequency of feedback. *Academy of Management Journal, 11,* 263-277.

Cummings, L. L. (1976). *Appraisal purpose and the nature, amount, and frequency of feedback.* Paper presented at the meeting of the American Psychological Association, Washington, D.C.

Cummings, L. L., & Schwab, D. P. (1973). *Performance in organizations.* Glenview, IL: Scott, Foresman.

Cummings, L. L., Schwab, D. P., & Rosen, M. (1971). Performance and knowledge of results as determinants of goal setting. *Journal of Applied Psychology, 55,* 526-530.

Cusella, L. P. (1980). The effects of feedback on intrinsic motivation. In D. Nimmo (Ed.), *Communication yearbook 4* (pp. 367-387). New Brunswick, NJ: Transaction.

Cusella, L. P. (1982). The effects of source expertise and feedback valence on intrinsic motivation. *Human Communication Research, 8,* 17-32.

Cusella, L. P. (1984a). The effects of feedback source, message, and receiver characteristics on intrinsic motivation. *Communication Quarterly, 32,* 211-221.

Cusella, L. P. (1984b). Conceptual issues in organizational communication research: Elements of a model of conceptual authenticity. *Communication Quarterly, 32,* 293-300.

Cusella, L. P. (1986). *Feedback, motivation and performance.* Paper presented at the annual meeting of the Academy of Management, Chicago.

Deal, T. E., & Kennedy, A. A. (1982). *Corporate cultures.* Reading, MA: Addison-Wesley.

Deci, E. L. (1972). Effects of contingent and non-contingent rewards and controls on intrinsic motivation. *Organizational Behavior and Human Performance, 8,* 217-229.

Deci, E. L. (1975). *Intrinsic motivation.* New York: Plenum.

Deci, E. L., & Ryan, R. M. (1980). The empirical exploration of intrinsic motivational processes.

In L. Berkowitz (Ed.), *Advances in experimental social psychology* (Vol. 13, pp. 39-80). New York: Academic Press.

DeCotiss, T., & Petit, A. (1978). The performance appraisal process: A model and some testable propositions. *Academy of Management Review, 3*, 635-646.

DeNisi, A. S., Cafferty, T. P., & Meglino, B. M. (1984). A cognitive view of the performance appraisal process: A model and research proposition. *Organizational Behavior and Human Performance, 33*, 360-396.

DeNisi, A. S. Randolph, W. A., & Blencoe, A. G. (1982). Level of source of feedback as a determinant of feedback effectiveness. *Academy of Management Proceedings*, 175-179.

Denny, M. R., Allard, M., Hall, E., & Rokeach, M. (1960). Supplementary report: Delay of knowledge of results, knowledge of task, and the intertrial interval. *Journal of Experimental Psychology, 60*, 327.

Dockstader, S. L. (1977). *Performance standards and implicit goal setting: Field testing Locke's assumptions.* Paper presented at the meeting of the American Psychological Association, San Francisco.

Dossett, D. L., Latham, G. P., & Mitchell, T. R. (1979). The effects of assigned versus participatively set goals, knowledge of results, and individual differences when goal difficulty is held constant. *Journal of Applied Psychology, 64*, 291-298.

Downey, H. K., Chacko, T. I., & McElroy, J. C. (1979). Attribution of the "causes" of performance: A constructive, quasi-longitudinal replication of the Staw (1975) study. *Organizational Performance and Human Performance, 24*, 287-299.

Dustin, D. (1966). Members reactions to team performance. *Journal of Social Psychology, 69*, 237-243.

Einhorn, H. J., & Hogarth, R. M. (1978). Confidence in judgment: Persistence of the illusion of validity. *Psychological Review, 85*, 395-416.

Ellsworth, R. B. (1973). Feedback: An asset or liability in improving treatment effectiveness? *Journal of Consulting and Clinical Psychology, 40*, 383-393.

Erez, M. (1977). Feedback: A necessary condition for the goal setting-performance relationship. *Journal of Applied Psychology, 62*, 624-627.

Erez, M., Earley, P. C., & Hulin, C. L. (1985). The impact of participation on goal acceptance and performance: A two-step model. *Academy of Management Journal, 28*, 50-66.

Erez, M. & Kanfer, F. H. (1983). The role of goal acceptance in goal setting and task performance. *Academy of Management Journal, 8*, 454-463.

Fairhurst, G. T., Green, S. G., & Snavely, B. K. (1984). Face support in controlling poor performance. *Human Communication Research, 11*, 272-295.

Farris, G. F., & Lim, F. G. (1969). Effects of performance on leadership cohesiveness, influence, satisfaction, and subsequent performance. *Journal of Applied Psychology, 53*, 490-497.

Feldman, J. M. (1981). Beyond attribution theory: Cognitive processes in performance appraisal. *Journal of Applied Psychology, 66*, 127-148.

Festinger, L. A. (1954). A theory of social comparison processes. *Human Relations, 7*, 117-140.

Festinger, L. A. (1967). *The effects of compensation on cognitive processes.* Paper presented at the annual meeting of the McKinsey Foundation of Managerial Compensation, Tarrytown, NY.

Fisher, B. A. (1978). *Perspectives on human communication.* New York: Macmillan.

Fisher, B. A. (1980). *Small group decision making.* New York: McGraw Hill.

Fisher, C. D. (1978). The effects of personal control, competence, and external reward systems on intrinsic motivation. *Organizational Behavior and Human Performance, 21*, 273-288.

Fisher, C. D. (1979). Transmission of positive and negative feedback to subordinates: A laboratory investigation. *Journal of Applied Psychology, 64*, 533-540.

Forward, J., & Zander, A. (1971). Choice of unattainable group goals and effects on performance. *Organizational Behavior and Human Performance, 6*, 184-199.

French, E. G. (1955). Some characteristics of achievement motivation. *Journal of Experimental Psychology, 50*, 232-236.

French, E. G. (1958). Effects of the interaction of motivation and feedback on task performance. In J. W. Atkinson (Ed.) *Motives in fantasy, action and society* (pp. 400-408). Princeton, NJ: Van Nostrand.

Frey, D. (1981). The effect of negative feedback about oneself and cost of information on preferences for information about the source of feedback. *Journal of Experimental Social Psychology, 17*, 42-50.

Frost, P. J., & Mahoney, T. A. (1976). Goal setting and the task process. *Organizational Behavior and Human Performance, 17*, 328-350.

Frye, R. L. (1966). The effect of orientation and feedback of success and effectiveness on the attractiveness and esteem of the group. *Journal of Social Psychology, 70*, 205-211.

Gibb, J. (1961). Defensive communication. *Journal of Communication, 11*, 141-418.

Gibb, J. R., Smith, E. E., & Roberts, A. H. (1955). Effects of positive and negative feedback upon defensive behavior in small problem solving groups. *American Psychologist, 10*, 335.

Gioia, D. A., & Sims, H. P. (1986). Cognitive-behavior connections: Attribution and verbal behavior in leader-subordinate interactions. *Organizational Behavior and Human Decision Process, 37*, 197-229.

Glaser, R., & Klaus, D. A. (1966). Reinforcement analysis of group performance. *Psychological Monographs: General and Applied, 80*, Whole No. 621.

Green, S. G., Fairhurst, G. T., & Snavely, B. K. (1986). Chains of poor performance and supervisory control. *Organizational Behavior and Human Decision Processes, 38*, 7-27.

Green, S. G., & Liden, R. C. (1980). Contextual and attributional control decisions. *Journal of Applied Psychology, 65*, 453-458.

Green, S. G., & Mitchell, T. R. (1979). Attributional process in leader-member interactions. *Organizational Behavior and Human Performance, 23*, 429-458.

Greene, C. N. (1973). Causal connections among managers' merit pay, job satisfaction, and performance. *Journal of Applied Psychology, 58*, 95-100.

Greene, C. N. (1976). A longitudinal investigation of performance-reinforcing leader behavior and subordinate satisfaction and performance. *Proceedings of the Midwest Academy of Management Meetings*, 157-185.

Greller, M. M. (1975). The consequences of feedback. *Dissertation Abstracts International, 36*, 25118. (Univ. Microfilms No. 75-24, 539).

Greller, M. M. (1980). Evaluation of feedback sources as a function of role and organizational level. *Journal of Applied Psychology, 65*, 24-27.

Greller, M. M., & Herold, D. M. (1975). Sources of feedback: A preliminary investigation. *Organizational Behavior and Human Performance, 21*, 47-60.

Guion, R. M. (1965). *Personnel testing*. New York: McGraw-Hill.

Guzzo, R. A., Wagner, D. B., Maguire, E., Herr, B., & Hawley, C. (1986). Implicit theories and the evaluation of group process and performance. *Organizational Behavior and Human Decision Processes, 37*, 279-295.

Hackman, J. R., & Morris, C. G. (1975). Group tasks, group interaction process, and group performance effectiveness: A review and proposed integration. In L. Berkowitz (Ed.), *Advances in experimental social psychology* (Vol. 8, pp. 45-99). New York: Academic Press.

Halperin, K., Snyder, C. R., Shenkel. R. J., & Houston, B. K. (1976). Effect of source status and message favorability on acceptance of feedback. *Journal of Applied Psychology, 61*, 85-88.

Hammond, K. R., McClelland, G. H., & Mumpower, J. (1980). *Human judgment and decision making*. New York: Praeger.

Hammond, K. R., & Summers, D. A. (1972). Cognitive control. *Psychological Review, 79*, 58-67.

Hamner, W. C., & Foster, L. W. (1975). Are intrinsic and extrinsic rewards additive: A test of Deci's CET of task motivation. *Organizational Behavior and Human Performance, 14*, 398-415.

Hannan, R. L. (1975). *The effects of participation in goal setting on goal acceptance and performance: A laboratory experiment*. Unpublished doctoral dissertation, University of Maryland, College Park.

Hanser, L. M., & Muchinsky, P. M. (1978). Work as an information environment. *Organizational Behavior and Human Performance, 21*, 47-60.

Hanser, L. M., & Muchinsky, P. M. (1980). Performance feedback information and organizational communication: Evidence of conceptual convergence. *Human Communication Research, 7*, 68-73.

Harackiewicz, J. M. (1979). The effects of reward contingency and performance feedback on intrinsic motivation. *Journal of Personality and Social Psychology, 37*, 1352-1361.

Harackiewicz, J. M., & Larson, J. R. (1986). Managing motivation: The impact of supervisor feedback on subordinate task interest. *Journal of Personality and Social Psychology, 51*, 547-556.

Harackiewicz, J. M., & Manderlink, G. (1984). A process analysis of the effects of performance-contingent rewards on intrinsic motivation. *Journal of Personality and Social Psychology, 20*, 531-551.

Harackiewicz, J. M., Manderlink, G., & Sansone, C. (1984). Rewarding pinball wizardry: Effects of evaluation and cue value of intrinsic interest. *Journal of Personality and Social Psychology, 47*, 287-300.

Harackiewicz, J. M., Sansone, C., & Manderlink, G. (1985). Competence, achievement orientation, and intrinsic motivation: A process analysis. *Journal of Personality and Social Psychology, 48*, 493-508.

Hawes, L. C. (1973). Elements of a model for communication process. *Quarterly Journal of Speech, 59*, 11-21.

Heider, F. (1958). *The psychology of interpersonal relationships.* New York: John Wiley.

Herold, D. M. (1977). Two-way influence processes in leader-follower dyads. *Academy of Management Journal, 20*, 227-237.

Herold, D. M., & Greller, M. M. (1977). Feedback: The development of a construct. *Academy of Management Journal, 20*, 142-147.

Herold, D. M., & Parsons, C. K. (1985). Assessing the feedback environment in work organizations. *Journal of Applied Psychology, 70*, 290-305.

Hobson, C. J., Mendel, R. M. & Gibson, F. W. (1981). Clarifying performance appraisal criteria. *Organizational Behavior and Human Performance, 28*, 164-188.

Holland, J. G., & Henson, J. B. (1956). Transfer of training between quickened and unquickened tracking systems. *Journal of Applied Psychology, 40*, 362-366.

Hollander, E. P., & Willis, R. H. (1967). Some current issues in the psychology of conformity and nonconformity. *Psychological Bulletin, 68*, 62-67.

Homans, G. C. (1961). *Social behavior: Its elementary forms.* New York: Harcourt, Brace & World.

House, R. J., & Baetz, J. L. (1979). Leadership: Some empirical generalizations and new research directions. In B. M. Staw & L. L. Cummings (Eds.), *Research in organizational behavior* (Vol. 1, pp. 341-424). Greenwich, CT: JAI Press.

Hunt, G. T., & Ebeling, R. E. (1983). The impact of a communication intervention on work-unit productivity and employee satisfaction. *Journal of Applied Communication Research, 11*, 57-58.

Hunt, J. G., & Schuler, R. S. (1976). *Leader reward and sanctions behavior in a public utility: What difference does it make?* Working paper, Southern Illinois University.

Ilgen, D. R., & Feldman, J. M. (1983). Performance appraisal: A process focus. In B. M. Staw & L. L. Cummings (Eds.). *Research in organizational behavior* (Vol. 5, pp. 141-197). Greenwich, CT: JAI Press.

Ilgen, D. R., Fisher, C. D., & Taylor, M. S. (1979). Consequences of individual feedback on behavior in organizations. *Journal of Applied Psychology, 64*, 349-371.

Ilgen, D. R., & Knowlton, W. A. (1980). Performance attributional effects on feedback from supervisors. *Organizational Behavior and Human Performance, 25*, 441-456.

Ilgen, D. R., Mitchell, T. R., & Fredrickson, J. W. (1981). Poor performers: Supervisor's and subordinate's response. *Organizational Behavior and Human Performance, 27*, 386-410.

Ilgen, D. R., Peterson, R. B., Martin, B. A., & Boeschen, D. A. (1981). Supervisor and subordinate reactions to performance appraisal sessions. *Organizational Behavior and Human Performance, 28*, 311-330.

Ivancevich, J. M. (1982). Subordinates' reactions to performance appraisal interviews: A test of feedback and goal-setting techniques. *Journal of Applied Psychology, 67*, 581-587.

Ivancevich, J. M., & McMahon, J. T. (1982). The effects of goal setting, external feedback, and self generated feedback on outcome variables. *Academy of Management Journal, 25*, 359-372.

Jablin, F. M. (1979). Superior-subordinate communication: The state of the art. *Psychological Bulletin, 86*, 1201-1222.

Jackson, S. E., & Zedeck, S. (1982). Explaining performance variability: Contribution of set task characteristics, and evaluative contexts. *Journal of Applied Psychology, 67*, 759-768.

Jacobs, A. (1974). The use of feedback in groups. In A. Jacobs & W. W. Spradlin (Eds.), *Group as an agent of change* (pp. 408-448). New York: Behavioral Publications.

Jacoby, J., Troutman, T., Muzursky, D., & Kuss, A. (1984). When feedback is ignored: Disutility of outcome feedback. *Journal of Applied Psychology, 69*, 531-545.

Janz, T. (1982). Manipulating subjective expectancy through feedback: A laboratory study of the expectancy-performance relationship. *Journal of Applied Psychology, 67*, 480-485.

Johnson, W. A. (1967). Individual performance and self evaluation in a simulated team. *Organizational Behavior and Human Performance, 2*, 309-328.

Kantor, D., & Lehr, W. (1975). *Inside the family*. New York: Harper & Row.

Kazdin, A. E. (1975). *Behavioral modification in applied settings*. Homewood, IL: Dorsey.

Kelley, H. H. (1972). *Attribution in social interaction*. Morristown, NJ: General Learning Press.

Kelley, H. H. (1973). The processes of causal attribution. *American Psychologist, 28*, 107-128.

Kiesler, S. (1986). The hidden messages in computer networks. *Harvard Business Review, 64*, 46-60.

Kim, J. S., & Hamner, W. C. (1976). Effect of performance feedback and goal setting on productivity and satisfaction in an organizational setting. *Journal of Applied Psychology, 61*, 48-57.

Kinkade, R. G. (1963). *A differential influence of augmented feedback on learning and on performance* (WADC Air Force Systems Command Tech. Report. AMRL-TDR-63-12). Dayton, OH: Wright Patterson Air Force Base.

Kipnis, D., Schmidt, S., Price, K., & Stitt, C. (1981). Why do I like thee: Is it your performance or my orders? *Journal of Applied Psychology, 66*, 324-328.

Klaus, D. J., & Glaser, R. (1970). Reinforcement determinants of team proficiency. *Organizational Behavior and Human Performance, 5*, 33-67.

Komaki, J., Barwick, K. D., & Scott, L. R. (1978). A behavioral approach to occupational safety. *Journal of Applied Psychology, 64*, 434-445.

Komaki, J. L., Collins, R. L., & Penn, P. (1982). The role of performance antecedents and consequences in work motivation. *Journal of Applied Psychology, 67*, 334-340.

Komaki, J., Heinzmann, A. T., & Lawson, L. (1980). Effect of training and feedback: Component analysis of a behavioral safety program. *Journal of Applied Psychology, 65*, 261-270.

Laing, R. D. (1961). *The self and others*. London: Tavistock.

Landy, F. J., & Farr, J. L. (1980). Performance rating. *Psychological Bulletin, 87*, 72-107.

Larcker, D. F., & Lessig, V. P. (1980). Perceived usefulness of information: A psychometric examination. *Decision Science, 11*, 121-134.

Larson, J. R., Jr. (1984). The performance feedback process: A preliminary model. *Organizational Behavior and Human Performance, 33*, 42-76.

Larson, J. R., Jr. (1986). Supervisors' performance feedback to subordinates: The effect of performance valence and outcome dependence. *Organizational Behavior and Human Decision Processes, 37*, 391-408.

Larson, J. R., Glynn, M. A., Fleenor, C. P., & Scrontrino, M. P. (1985). *Exploring the dimensionality of manager's performance feedback to subordinates*. Paper presented at the annual meeting of the Academy of Management, San Diego.

Larson, J. R., & Skolnik, Y. (1982). *The effect of giving performance feedback on memory based performance ratings*. Paper presented at the annual meeting of the Academy of Management, New York.

Latham, G. P., Mitchell, T. R., & Dossett, D. L. (1978). Importance of participative goal setting and anticipated rewards on goal difficulty and job performance. *Journal of Applied Psychology, 63*, 163-171.

Latham, G. P., & Saari, L. M. (1979). The effect of holding goal difficulty constant on assigned and participatively set goals. *Academy of Management Journal, 22*, 163-168.

Lawler, E. E. (1973). *Motivation in work groups*. Monterey, CA: Brooks/Cole.

Lawler, E. E., & Rhode, J. G. (1976). *Information and control in organizations.* Santa Monica, CA: Goodyear.

Liden, R. C., & Mitchell, T. R. (1985). Reactions to feedback: The role of attributions. *Academy of Management Journal, 28,* 291-308.

Locke, E. A. (1967). Motivational effects of knowledge of results: Knowledge or goal setting? *Journal of Applied Psychology, 51,* 324-329.

Locke, E. A. (1968). Toward a theory of task motives and incentives. *Organizational Behavior and Human Performance, 3,* 157-189.

Locke, E. A., & Bryan, J. F. (1968). Goal-setting as a determinant of the effect of knowledge of score on performance. *American Journal of Psychology, 81,* 398-406.

Locke, E. A., & Bryan, J. F. (1969a). The directing function of goals in task performance. *Organizational Behavior and Human Performance, 4,* 35-42.

Locke, E. A., & Bryan, J. F. (1969b). Knowledge of score and goal level as determinants of work rate. *Journal of Applied Psychology, 53,* 59-65.

Locke, E. A., Cartledge, N., & Knoeppel, J. (1968). Motivational effects of knowledge of results: A goal-setting phenomenon? *Psychological Bulletin, 70,* 474-485.

Locke, E. A., Shaw, K. N., Saari, L. M., & Latham, G. P. (1981). Goal setting and task performance: 1969-1980. *Journal of Applied Psychology, 90,* 125-152.

Lowin, A. (1968). Participative decision-making: A model, literature critique, and prescriptions for research. *Organizational Behavior and Human Performance, 3,* 68-106.

Lowin, A., & Craig, J. R. (1968). The influence of level of performance on managerial style: An experimental object-lesson in the ambiguity of correlational data. *Organizational Behavior and Human Performance, 3,* 440-458.

Lucas, C. (1965). Task performance and group structure as a function of personality and feedback. *Journal of Social Psychology, 66,* 257-270.

Lucas, H. C. (1975). Performance and the use of an information system. *Management Science, 21,* 908-919.

Lucas, H. C., & Nielsen, N. R. (1980). The impact of the mode of information presentation on learning and performance. *Management Science, 26,* 982-993.

Madsen, D. B., & Finger, J. R. (1978). Comparison of a written feedback procedure, group brainstorming, and individual brainstorming. *Journal of Applied Psychology, 63,* 120-123.

Marks, M. L. (1986). The question of quality circles. *Psychology Today, 20,* 36-46.

Marks, M. L., Mirvis, P. H., Hackett, E. J., & Grady, J. F. (1986). Employee participation in a quality circle program: Impact on quality of work life, productivity, and absenteeism. *Journal of Applied Psychology, 71,* 61-69.

Masuch, M. (1985). Vicious circles in organizations. *Administrative Science Quarterly, 30,* 14-33.

Matsui, T., Okada, A., & Inoshita, A. (1983). Mechanisms of feedback affecting task performance. *Organizational Behavior and Human Performance, 31,* 114-122.

McCallister, L. (1984). *The punishment process in organizations.* Paper presented at the Southern Academy of Management Convention, New Orleans.

McFatter, R. M. (1982). Purpose of punishment: Effects of utilities of criminal sanctions on perceived appropriateness. *Journal of Applied Psychology, 76,* 225-267.

McGuire, W. J. (1973). Persuasion, resistance, and attitude change. In I. O. Poole, F. W. Frey, W. Schramm, N. Maccoby, & E. Parker (Eds.)., *Handbook of communication* (pp. 216-252). Chicago: Rand McNally.

Michener, H. A., & Lawler, E. J. (1971). Revolutionary coalition strength and collective failure as determinants of status reallocation. *Journal of Experimental Social Psychology, 7,* 448-460.

Miller, R. B. (1953). *Handbook of training and equipment design* (WADC Technical Report, 53-136). Dayton, OH: Wright Patterson Air Force Base.

Mitchell, T. R., & Green, S. G. (1978). *Leader responses to poor performance: An attributional analysis.* Paper presented at the annual meeting of the American Psychological Association, Toronto.

Mitchell, T. R., Green, S. G., & Wood, R. (1981). An attributional model of leadership and the poor performing subordinate. In L. L. Cummings & B. M. Staw (Eds.), *Research in organizational behavior* (Vol. 3, pp. 197-234). Greenwich, CT: JAI Press.

Mitchell, T. R., & Kalb, L. S. (1981). Effects of outcome knowledge and outcome valence on supervisor's evaluation. *Journal of Applied Psychology, 66*, 604-612.

Mitchell, T. R., & Liden, R. C. (1982). The effects of social context on performance evaluations. *Organizational Behavior and Human Performance, 29*, 241-256.

Mitchell, T. R., & Wood, R. E. (1980). Supervisor's responses to subordinate poor performance: A test of an attributional model. *Organizational Behavior and Human Performance, 25*, 123-138.

Morran, D. K., & Stockton, R. A. (1980). Effect of self-concept on group member reception of positive and negative feedback. *Journal of Counseling Psychology, 27*, 260-267.

Muto, J., & Cusella, L. P. (1984). *An alternative theory of organizational communication grounded in empirical data.* Paper presented at the annual convention of the International Communication Association, San Francisco.

Nadler, D. A. (1976). Using feedback for organizational change: Promises and pitfalls. *Group and Organizational Studies, 1*, 177-186.

Nadler, D. A. (1977). *Feedback and organizational development: Using data based methods.* Reading, MA: Addison-Wesley.

Nadler, D. A. (1979). The effects of feedback on task group behavior. *Organizational Behavior and Human Performance, 23*, 309-338.

Nadler, D. A., Cammann, C., & Mirvis, P. H. (1980). Developing a feedback system for work units: A field experiment in structural change. *Journal of Applied Behavioral Science, 16*, 41-62.

Nadler, D. A., Mirvis, P. H., & Cammann, C. (1976). The ongoing feedback system: Experimenting with a new managerial tool. *Organizational Dynamics, 4*, 63-80.

Nemeroff, W. F., & Consentino, J. (1979). Utilizing feedback and goal setting to increase performance appraisal interviewer skills of managers. *Academy of Management Journal, 22*, 566-576.

Noble, C. E. (1968). The learning of psychomotor skills. In P. R. Farnsworth, M. R. Rosensweig, & J. T. Polefka (Eds.), *Annual review of psychology* (Vol. 19, pp. 203-250). Palo Alto: Annual Reviews, Inc.

Noble, C. E., & Alcock, W. T. (1958). Human delayed-reward learning with different lengths of task. *Journal of Experimental Psychology, 56*, 407-412.

Norton, R. (1983). *Communicator style.* Beverly Hills, CA: Sage.

Notz, W. W. (1975). Work motivation and the negative effects of extrinsic rewards: A review with implications for the theory and practice. *American Psychologist, 30*, 884-891.

Ogilvie, J. R., & Haslett, B. (1985). Communicating peer feedback in a task group. *Human Communication Research, 12*, 79-98.

O'Reilly, C. A., & Weitz, B. A. (1980). Managing marginal employees: The use of warnings and dismissals. *Administrative Science Quarterly, 25*, 467-484.

Ostrove, N. (1978). Expectations for success on effort-determined tasks as a function of incentive and performance feedback. *Journal of Personality and Social Psychology, 36*, 909-916.

Pate, L. E. (1978). Cognitive versus reinforcement views of intrinsic motivation. *Academy of Management Journal, 20*, 505-514.

Payne, R. B., & Hauty, G. T. (1955). Effects of psychological feedback upon work decrement. *Journal of Experimental Psychology, 50*, 342-351.

Pearce, J. L., & Porter, L. W. (1986). Employee responses to formal performance appraisal feedback. *Journal of Applied Psychology, 71*, 211-218.

Phillips, J. J., & Lord, R. G. (1982). Schematic information processing and perceptions of leadership in problem-solving groups. *Journal of Applied Psychology, 67*, 486-492.

Pinder, C. C. (1984). *Work motivation.* Glenview, IL: Scott, Foresman.

Pittman, T. S., Davey, M. E., Alafat, K. A., Wetherill, K. V., & Kramer, N. A. (1980). Informational versus controlling verbal rewards. *Personality and Social Psychology Bulletin, 6*, 228-233.

Podsakoff, P. M. (1982). Determinants of a supervisor's use of rewards and punishments: A literature review and suggestions for further research. *Organizational Behavior and Human Performance, 29,* 58-83.

Podsakoff, P. M., Todor, W. D., Grocer, R. A., & Huber, V. L. (1984). Situational moderators of leader reward and punishment behaviors: Fact or fiction? *Organizational Behavior and Human Performance, 34,* 21-63.

Podsakoff, P. M., Todor, W. D., & Skov, R. (1982). Effects of leader contingent and non-contingent reward and punishment behaviors on subordinate performance and satisfaction. *Academy of Management Journal, 25,* 810-821.

Pondy, L. R. (1967). Organizational conflicts: Concepts and models. *Administrative Science Quarterly, 12,* 296-320.

Poole, M. S. (1978). An information-task approach to organizational communication. *Academy of Management Review, 3,* 493-504.

Poulton, E. C. (1966). Tracking behavior. In E. A. Bilodeau (Ed.), *Acquisition of skill* (pp. 361-410). New York: Academic Press.

Powers, W. T. (1973). Feedback: Beyond behaviorism. *Science, 179,* 351-356.

Poythress, M., & Spicer, C. (1976). *Effects of feedback concerning success and failure on group aspirations and individual coping behavior in classroom work groups.* Paper presented at the annual convention of the International Communication Association, Portland, Oregon.

Pritchard, R. D., Bigby, D. G., Beiting, M. Coverdale, S., & Morgan, C. (1981). *Enhancing productivity through feedback and goal setting* (AFHRL-TR-81-7). Brooks AFB, TX: Occupation and Manpower Res. Div., Air Force Human Resources Laboratory.

Pritchard, R. D., Hollenback, P., & DeLeo, P. J. (1980). The effects of continuous and partial schedules of reinforcement on effort, performance, and satisfaction. *Organizational Behavior and Human Performance, 25,* 336-353.

Pritchard, R. D., & Montagno, R. V. (1978). *The effects of specific vs. non-specific and absolute vs. comparative feedback on performance and satisfaction* (AFHRL-TR-78-12, AD-A055-693). Brooks AFB, TX: Occupation and Manpower Res. Div., Air Force Human Resources Laboratory.

Pritchard, R. D., Montagno, R. V., & Moore, J. R. (1978). *Enhancing productivity through feedback and job design* (AFHRL-TR-78-44, AD-A061 703). Brooks, AFB, TX: Occupation and Manpower Res. Div., Air Force Human Resources Laboratory.

Pryer, N. W., & Bass, B. M. (1959). Some effects of feedback on behavior in groups. *Sociometry, 22,* 56-63.

Ramaprasad, A. (1983). On the definition of feedback. *Behavioral Science, 28,* 4-13.

Redding, W. C. (1972). *Communication within the organization.* New York: Industrial Communication Council.

Rosenberg, S., & Hall, R. L. (1958). The effects of different social feedback conditions upon performance in dyadic teams. *Journal of Abnormal and Social Psychology, 57,* 271-277.

Ryan, R. (1982). Control and information in the intrapersonal sphere: An extension of cognitive evaluation theory. *Journal of Personality and Social Psychology, 43,* 450-461.

Salanick, G. R. (1975). Interaction effects of performance and money on self-perception of intrinsic motivation. *Organizational Behavior and Human Performance, 13,* 339-351.

Saltzman, I. J., Kanfer, F. H., & Greenspoon, J. (1955). Delay of reward and human motor learning. *Psychological Reports, 1,* 139-142.

Schaible, T. K. (1970). *Group cohesion, feedback acceptance and desirability: Functions of the sequence and valence of feedback.* Unpublished master's thesis, West Virginia University.

Schlenker, B. R., Soraci, S., & McCarthy, B. (1976). Self-esteem and group performance as determinants of egocentric perceptions in cooperative groups. *Human Relations, 29,* 1163-1187.

Scott, W. E. (1976). The effects of extrinsic rewards on "intrinsic motivation": A critique. *Organizational Behavior and Human Performance, 15,* 117-129.

Shalley, C. E., & Oldham, G. R. (1985). The effects of goal difficulty and expected external evaluation in intrinsic motivation. *Academy of Management Journal, 28*, 628-640.

Shannon, C. E. (1948). A mathematical theory of communication. *Bell Systems Technical Journal, 27*, 379-423, 623-656.

Shelley, H. P. (1954). Level of aspiration phenomena in small groups. *Journal of Social Psychology, 40*, 149-164.

Siegel, A., & Ruh, R. A. (1973). Job involvement, participation in decision-making, and job behavior. *Organizational Behavior and Human Performance, 9*, 318-327.

Siegel, J., Dubrovsky, V., Kiesler, S., & McGuire, T. W. (1986). Group processes in computer-mediated communication. *Organizational Behavior and Human Decision Processes, 37*, 157-187.

Sims, H. P. (1977). The leader as a manager of reinforcement contingencies: An empirical example and a model. In J. E. Hunt & L. L. Larson (Eds.), *Leadership: The cutting edge* (pp. 121-137). Carbondale: Southern Illinois Press.

Sims, H. P. (1980). Further thoughts on punishment in organizations. *Academy of Management Review, 5*, 133-138.

Sims, H. P., & Manz, C. C. (1984). Observing leader verbal behavior: Toward reciprocal determinism in leadership theory. *Journal of Applied Psychology, 69*, 222-232.

Sims, H. P., & Szilagnyi, A. D. (1975). Leader reward behavior and subordinate satisfaction and performance. *Organizational Behavior and Human Performance, 14*, 426-438.

Smircich, L. (1983). Concepts of culture and organizational analysis. *Administrative Science Quarterly, 28*, 339-358.

Smith, K. H. (1972). Changes in group structure through individual and group feedback. *Journal of Personality and Social Psychology, 24*, 425-428.

Smode, A. F. (1958). Learning and performance in a tracking task under two levels of achievement information feedback. *Journal of Experimental Psychology, 56*, 297-304.

Spoelder-Claes, R. (1973). Small group effectiveness on an administrative task as influenced by knowledge of results and sex composition of the group. *European Journal of Social Psychology, 3*, 389-402.

Staw, B. M. (1975). Attribution of the "causes" of performance: A general alternative interpretation of cross-sectional research on organizations. *Organizational Behavior and Human Performance, 13*, 414-432.

Steinfield, C. W. (1985). Computer-mediated communicating in an organizational setting: Explaining task-related and socioemotional uses. In M. L. McLaughlin (Ed). *Communication yearbook 9* (pp. 777-804). Newbury Park, CA: Sage.

Steinman, D. L. (1976). The effects of cognitive feedback and task complexity in multiple cue probability learning. *Organizational Behavior and Human Performance, 15*, 168-179.

Stoller, F. H. (1968). Focused feedback with videotape: Extending the group's functions. In G. M. Gazda (Ed.), *Innovations to group psychotherapy* (pp. 207-255). Springfield, IL: Charles C Thomas.

Stone, T. H. (1971). Effects of mode of organization and feedback level on creative task groups. *Journal of Applied Psychology, 55*, 324-330.

Strang, H. R., Lawrence, E. C., & Fowler, P. C. (1978). Effects of assigned goal level and knowledge of results on arithmetic computation. *Journal of Applied Psychology, 63*, 446-450.

Swanson, E. B. (1974). Management information systems: Appreciation and involvement. *Management Science, 21*, 178-188.

Taylor, F. V. (1957). Simplifying the controller's task through display quickening. *Occupational Psychology, 31*, 120-125.

Thayer, L. (1967). Communication and organizational theory. In F.E.X. Dance (Ed.), *Human communication theory* (pp. 70-115). New York: Holt.

Thomas, E., & Ward, W. (1983). The influence of own and other outcome on satisfaction and choice of task difficulty. *Organizational Behavior and Human Performance, 32*, 399-416.

Thompson, M., & Browning, L. (1986). *Risk and feedback: An examination of the dimensions of process culture.* Paper presented at the annual meeting of the International Communication Association, Chicago.

Tolchinsky, P. D., & King, D. C. (1980). Do goals mediate the effects of incentives on performance? *Academy of Management Review, 5,* 455-467.

Tuckman, B. W., & Oliver, W. F. (1968). Effectiveness of feedback to teachers as a function of source. *Journal of Educational Psychology, 59,* 297-301.

Tushman, M. L., & Nadler, D. A. (1978). Information processing as an integrating concept in organizational design. *Academy of Management Review, 3,* 613-624.

Varca, P. E., & Levey, J. C. (1984). Individual differences in response to unfavorable group feedback. *Organizational Behavior and Human Performance, 33,* 100-110.

Vroom, V. (1964). *Work and motivation.* New York: John Wiley.

Vroom, V. H., & Yetton, P. W. (1973). *Leadership and decision making.* Pittsburgh, PA: University of Pittsburgh Press.

Walter, G. A. (1975). Effects of video tape feedback and modeling on the behaviors of task group members. *Human Relations, 28,* 121-138.

Walter, G. A., & Miles, R. E. (1972). Essential elements for improving task-group membership behaviors. *Proceedings of the American Psychological Association Annual Convention, 7,* 461-462.

Watson, K. (1982). An analysis of communication patterns: A method of discriminating leader and subordinate roles. *Academy of Management Journal, 25,* 107-120.

Watzlawick, P., Beavin, J., & Jackson, D. (1967). *The pragmatics of human communication.* New York: Norton.

Weber, R. J. (1971). Effects of videotape feedback on task group behavior. *Proceedings of the American Psychological Association Annual Convention, 6,* 499-500.

Weber, R. J. (1972). Effects of process feedback, consultation, and knowledge of results on perceptions of group process. *Proceedings of the American Psychological Association Annual Convention, 7,* 449-460.

Weick, K. E. (1969). *The social psychology of organizing.* Reading, MA: Addison-Wesley.

Weick, K. E. (1979). *The social psychology of organizing* (2nd ed.). Reading, MA: Addison-Wesley.

White, S. E., Mitchell, T. R., & Bell, C. H. (1977). Goal setting, evaluation apprehension, and social cues as determinants of job performance and job satisfaction in a simulated organization. *Journal of Applied Psychology, 62,* 665-673.

Wiener, N. (1948). *Cybernetics: On control and communication in the animal and the machine.* New York: John Wiley.

Wiener, N. (1954). *The human use of human beings: Cybernetics and society.* Garden City, NY: Doubleday Anchor.

Wilden, A. (1972). *System and structure.* London: Tavistock.

Wood, R. E., & Mitchell, T. R. (1981). Manager behavior in a social context: The impact of impression management on attributions and disciplinary actions. *Organizational Behavior and Human Performance, 28,* 356-378.

Young, P.T. (1961). *Motivation and emotion.* New York: John Wiley.

Zajonc, R. B. (1962). The effects of feedback and probability of group success on individual and group performance. *Human Relations, 15,* 149-161.

Zander, A. (1971). *Motives and goals in groups.* New York: Academic Press.

Zander, A., & Forward, J. (1968). Position in group, achievement motivation and group aspirations. *Journal of Personality and Social Psychology, 8,* 282-288.

Zander, A., & Medow, H. (1965). Strength of group and desire for attainable group aspirations. *Journal of Personality, 33,* 122-139.

Zander, A., & Wolfe, D. (1964). Administrative rewards and coordination among committee members. *Administrative Science Quarterly, 9,* 59-69.

Zander, A., & Wulff, D. (1966). Members' test anxiety and competence: Determinants of a group's aspirations. *Journal of Personality, 34,* 55-70.

19 Organizational Entry, Assimilation, and Exit

FREDRIC M. JABLIN
University of Texas at Austin

ALTHOUGH variability certainly exists, it is probably reasonable to estimate that most people spend between thirty and forty years of their lives working in occupations within some form of organizational setting. Given statistics suggesting that the median monthly turnover of persons employed in the United States is approximately 2% (Bureau of National Affairs, 1980), and that even in the most stable industries individuals usually average less than ten years on the job (Bureau of Labor Statistics, 1975), the experience of entering, becoming assimilated into, and exiting work organizations is a quite common phenomenon in our society. Thus it is not surprising to discover that researchers have devoted a considerable amount of effort to exploring the nature of these processes. Unfortunately, however, most of this attention has focused on examining specific elements of the organizational entry, assimilation, and exit process in relative isolation of one another, and has not considered the process as a singular, developmental phenomenon. As a consequence, the primary purpose of this chapter is to present an integrated and, it is hoped, heuristic discussion of the nature and functions of communication in the organizational entry, assimilation, and exit process.

The developmental nature of the organizational entry-assimilation-exit process is perhaps best illustrated by tracing from childhood through employment in one's chosen vocation the development of an individual's work career. Consequently, the first section of this chapter examines how communication functions in the vocational and organizational entry processes. As will be seen, these processes serve as a form of "anticipatory socialization" for new organizational recruits, providing them with certain expectations (often of questionable accuracy) of the communication characteristics of their occupations and work environments. This discussion will be followed by an examination of the organizational assimilation process, and in particular, how people become socialized into the communication cultures of their organizations and concomitantly attempt to change these environments to better suit their needs and goals. Subsequently, attention will be focused on the role of communication in the organizational disengagement process, including an examination of both the causal and symptomatic characteristics of communication in the turnover process. Directions for future research will be suggested within each of these sections.

ANTICIPATORY SOCIALIZATION

Socialization to work and preparation to occupy organizational positions commences in early childhood (Crites, 1969). As part of this conditioning most of us have developed, prior to entering any particular organization, a set of expectations and beliefs concerning how people communicate in particular occupations and work settings. Jablin (1985a) proposes that this anticipatory socialization contains two related phases: (1) the process of vocational choice/socialization, and (2) the process of organizational choice/entry. Moreover, as Wanous (1977, p. 602) observes, vocational choice usually precedes organizational entry, and "it is almost always true that organizational entry follows occupational entry for those on their first full-time job." As a consequence, research exploring the vocational anticipatory socialization process is discussed below, followed by an analysis of the organizational anticipatory socialization process.

Vocational Anticipatory Socialization

Although a number of theories have been proposed to explain the vocational development process (e.g., Brown, Brooks, & Associates, 1984; Osipow, 1983; Walsh & Osipow, 1983), the most widely accepted approaches assume that as an individual matures from childhood to young adulthood he or she is intentionally and unintentionally gathering occupational information from the environment, comparing this information against his or her self-concept, "weighing the factors and alternatives involved in choosing an occupation and finally making a series of conscious choices which determine the direction of his [or her] career" (Van Maanen, 1975, p. 82). As noted in

Figure 19.1, there are a number of sources through which people acquire vocational information during the occupational choice/socialization process that are likely to affect their perceptions of how people communicate in work settings. These sources of information include (1) family members, (2) educational institutions, (3) part-time job experiences, (4) peers and friends (including nonfamilial adults), and (5) the media (Jablin, 1985a). Research related to each of these sources is considered briefly below.

Family. Given that family members, and in particular parents, are almost always considered by young children and adolescents as "significant others" in their lives (Blyth, Hill, & Thiel, 1982), it should be of no surprise that parents are often quite influential in the career choices of their offspring (e.g., Brown et al., 1984). As Leifer and Lesser (1976, p. 38) observe, adolescents and young adults frequently report that their "parents were the primary determiners of their occupational choices." Ironically, however, our knowledge of what children learn from their parents and siblings about the nature of work, and in particular the communication characteristics of occupations and work relationships, is quite limited.

However, several forms of ancillary evidence suggest that family members may be important sources of communication-related occupational and organizational information for their children. First, research findings indicate that the family setting provides children with opportunities to learn about and participate in task-oriented organizing activity (Goldstein & Oldham, 1979; Larson, 1983; White & Brinkerhoff, 1981). Relatedly, Goldstein and Oldham (1979) have found that children not only regularly participate in organized task activities in the family setting but also have developed stereotypes of the interaction patterns of persons in superior-subordinate relationships. In turn, other research suggests that by the age of three children have developed sex stereotypes of the behaviors of persons in different occupations (e.g., Kirchner & Vondracek, 1973).

Though children may implicitly learn about the communication characteristics of work relationships by participating in family-related organizing activity, discussions with their parents about work and careers provide such information in a more explicit fashion (Laska & Micklin, 1981). For example, a recent *Wall Street Journal*/Gallup poll (Crossen, 1985, p. 33) found that 36% of 313 children (between the ages of 14 and 22) of a sample of senior executives of U.S. firms reported that "their fathers frequently talk about work at home." Moreover, respondents indicated that such discussions tend to concern people and relationships at work and not information about the specifics of their fathers' work. In essence, these results suggest that the occupational information children obtain from discussions with their parents does not necessarily focus on the nature of their parents' work, but rather on interaction styles and "human relations" problems that are experienced in the work setting.

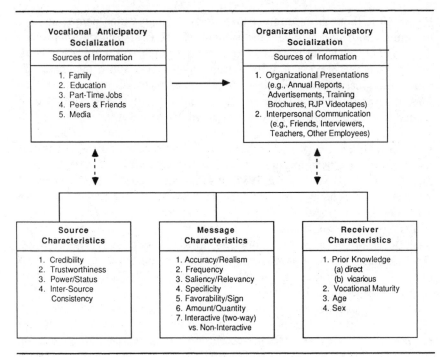

Figure 19.1 Communication in the Anticipatory Socialization Process

Educational institutions. Of the five major sources from which individuals obtain vocational information, educational institutions are probably one of the most significant (e.g., Jablin, 1985a). Though at present our understanding of what students learn in school about communication attributes of occupations is constrained, research in the area does suggest that the information educational institutions (prior to professional or trade school) directly and indirectly disseminate to students focuses more on the way (style) people communicate in different occupational/organizational roles than with the specific content characteristics of such roles (e.g., DeFleur & Menke, 1975; Jablin, 1985a; Leifer & Lesser, 1976). In addition, it seems clear that once a student has selected a vocation and receives specific education in that field, the manner in which he or she communicates with other members of the field, clients, and the like is somewhat regulated by implicit interaction norms learned during their vocational education (Bucher & Stelling, 1977; Moore, 1969; Van Maanen & Barley, 1984).

Part-time employment. Statistics suggest that at any given point in time approximately one-half of all persons of high school age are employed in part-time jobs, and that about 80% of the nation's youth will have been employed in part-time jobs prior to graduating from high school (Rotchford & Roberts, 1982; Steinberg, 1982). Studies examining the nature of adolescents' part-time jobs suggest a number of interesting conclusions about the communication characteristics of these work experiences and what may be learned from them.

First, findings indicate that adolescent part-time workers do not have very close communication relationships with their coworkers or supervisors (Greenberger, Steinberg, Vaux, & McAuliffe, 1980) and spend considerable amounts of time at work unsupervised (Ruggiero, Greenberger, & Steinberg, 1982). In fact, Greenberger et al. (1980) report that adolescent part-time workers are less likely to talk to their supervisors about a personal problem than they are to talk to their fathers, mothers, siblings, and work-related and non-work-related friends. Second, research indicates that adolescents' part-time jobs differ substantially among one another with respect to the opportunities they provide for workers to communicate on the job, as well as with respect to the nature of these interactions (Greenberger, Steinberg, & Ruggiero, 1982). For instance, Greenberger et al. (1982) found that of six jobs commonly held by adolescents—retail sales and cashier work, clerical work, food service work, cleaning, manual labor, and operative/skilled labor—food service, retail, and operative/skilled workers spend more time attempting to influence others (giving instructions or commands, offering advice or suggestions, stating opinions) than do persons employed in the other jobs. Further, results of the behavioral coding of adolescents in part-time jobs indicates that part-time jobs differ in the opportunities they provide adolescents for communication with adults and peers (Greenberger et al., 1982; Ruggiero & Steinberg, 1981). As Greenberger et al. (1982, p. 93) observe, "all jobs do not provide young workers with identical experiences and as such are not likely to be equally facilitative of adolescents' development and socialization." Third, studies suggest that while part-time jobs do not necessarily have a great impact on adolescents' career plans (Steinberg, Greenberger, Vaux, & Ruggiero, 1981; Wijting, Arnold, & Conrad, 1977), "adolescents who work are learning a good deal about relationships" (Greenberger et al., 1980, p. 200).

In summary, it would appear that because of limited relationships between the types of part-time jobs in which adolescents are employed and their occupational goals, adolescents do not acquire large repertoires of specific, career-related skills as a result of their work experiences. On the other hand, it also seems apparent that certain types of part-time jobs provide adolescents with opportunities to learn and apply relational communication skills that may generalize to other work contexts. Clearly, the specific manner and extent to which these early job experiences may contribute to the relational communication styles individuals adopt when they eventually enter their chosen occupations represents an area deserving of future research attention.

Peers and friends. Although most adolescents spend over 50% of their time during a typical week with their peers (Csikszentmihalyi & Larson, 1984) and usually consider peers "significant others" in their lives (Blyth et al., 1982;

Montemayor & Van Komen, 1980), our knowledge of what adolescents and younger children learn from their interactions with peers and friends about the nature of communication in work relationships and occupations is essentially nonexistent. Yet it should be realized that related studies suggest that there is a positive relationship between the career aspirations of adolescent friendship pairs (Brown, 1980; Kandel, 1978) and that best friends and age-mates are often consulted by adolescents with respect to their educational and occupational aspirations or choices (Haller & Butterworth, 1960; Herriot, Ecob, & Hutchinson, 1980; Simpson, 1962; Wallace, 1965). Moreover, Brown (1980) reports that the more adolescents discuss among one another sex-roles and career plans the less likely they are to choose occupations that are traditionally sex-role stereotyped (e.g., Tangri, 1972). As Peterson and Peters (1983, p. 81) observe, "peers function as significant others who confirm or disconfirm the desirability of occupations." The specific nature of the effects of peer interaction and socializing on adolescents' perceptions and expectations of communication in work contexts or occupations, however, awaits determination by future research.

Media. As is frequently noted in the literature, "the mass media, and in particular television, often transmit an inaccurate, stereotypic image of how people behave/communicate in various occupations" (Jablin, 1985b, p. 618). Further, it has been asserted that the distorted occupational images that television creates for children "may well persist into adulthood" (Christenson & Roberts, 1983, p. 88). Television has been criticized for representing people in sex-role stereotyped occupations (e.g., Beuf, 1974; Freuh & McGhee, 1975; Morgan, 1980), for overrepresenting managerial and professional occupations and underrepresenting jobs of lesser prestige (DeFleur, 1964; DeFleur & DeFleur, 1967; Greenberg, 1982; Katzman, 1972), and for frequently portraying persons who are successful in their occupational roles as spending the bulk of their conversational time giving orders and/or advice to others and generally engaging in fairly aggressive communication behaviors (DeFleur, 1964; Theberge, 1981; Turow, 1974, 1980). In turn, findings from other investigations indicate that in television representations of the workplace little of the content of conversations among role occupants concerns work-related issues; rather, discussions focus on such topics as romantic relationships, family and marriage problems, and similar forms of small talk (Katzman, 1972; Turow, 1974). In essence, "television's representation of occupational roles, as with other roles, is both a wider perspective than everyday experience and a caricature of the actual world of work" (Peterson & Peters, 1983, p. 81).

Though some studies suggest that frequent exposure to television may influence how children and adolescents view occupational roles, and in particular their beliefs about actual interpersonal behavior in the work setting (e.g., Bogatz & Ball, 1971; DeFleur & DeFleur, 1967; Dominick, 1974; Siegel,

1958), additional study of these issues will be required before definitive conclusions about causality can be drawn (e.g., Christenson & Roberts, 1983; Faber, Brown, & McLeod, 1979). In particular, given research findings that suggest the influence of television representations of occupations on childrens' beliefs may be most potent for occupations or jobs that are outside of their everyday contacts (e.g., DeFleur & DeFleur, 1967), the extent to which television characters provide children with "surrogate experience" to know how to behave and communicate in work situations before such situations have been encountered in real life should be a focus of future research (Noble, 1983).

Summary. Research exploring the vocational organizational communication socialization (VOCS) process is still in its infancy. Consequently, at this point we are not able to (1) indicate the degree to which various information sources reinforce or conflict with one another, or (2) draw conclusions about their long-term effects on organizational communication behaviors and attitudes. However, two generalizations do appear tenable about the VOCS process. First, while individuals probably are not learning a great deal about the specific communication behaviors/skills that are required of various occupations and organizational positions during their vocational development, they are receiving information and developing beliefs about the communication styles (ways of communicating, e.g., friendly, relaxed, contentious, dominant, animated) associated with occupations and work relationships. Second, it seems clear that one of the stylistic attributes of work-related communication that we learn about early in life is that "'power' is an integral element of interpersonal communication in work/organizational relationships" (Jablin, 1985b, p. 619). In conclusion, based on the preceding discussion Figure 19.1 suggests a number of source, message, and receiver characteristics that might be important factors to consider in future research exploring both the VOCS process and its effects.

Organizational Anticipatory Socialization

In the process of seeking jobs individuals concomitantly develop expectations about the organizations and respective positions for which they have applied for employment. As suggested in Figure 19.1, job seekers typically acquire information which may affect their job/organizational expectations from two basic sources: (1) organizational literature (for example, job advertisements, annual reports, training brochures, job preview booklets), and (2) interpersonal interactions with other applicants, organizational interviewers, teachers, current employees, and the like. Generally speaking, studies exploring each of these sources of information have focused on one of three broad areas of research: (1) the relative effectiveness of various information sources in recruiting/attracting newcomers, (2) the realism or accuracy of job/organizational expectations that result from contacts with each source, and (3) the role of the employment interview as a recruiting and selection device. Research findings relevant to each of these areas of study are reviewed briefly below.

Recruiting source effects. Studies exploring the relative effectiveness of recruiting sources in attracting and subsequently retaining newcomers have produced mixed results. Basically research results have varied depending on the manner in which recruiting source effectiveness has been operationalized.

Comparing such recruiting sources as newspaper advertisements, employee referrals, "walk-ins," and employment agencies, a number of studies have found that newcomers who are recruited informally as a result of employee referrals tend to have lower job turnover rates than persons recruited through more formal sources, such as newspaper advertisements (Breaugh & Mann, 1984; Decker & Cornelius, 1979; Gannon, 1971; Reid, 1972; Taylor & Schmidt, 1983). However, Caldwell and Spivey (1983) report that employee referrals are a good recruiting source with respect to employee retention for white employees but not for black employees, for whom they found employment agencies the best recruiting source.

Results of studies in which the job performance and absenteeism rates of newcomers have been employed as indicants of recruiting source effectiveness, however, have produced more equivocal results. Specifically, Taylor and Schmidt (1983) report no significant differences among recruiting sources in relation to later levels of employee job performance, while findings from Breaugh's research (Breaugh, 1981; Breaugh & Mann, 1984) indicate that persons who contact organizations on their own initiative receive higher performance ratings than individuals who are recruited from college placement centers, newspaper advertisements, or employee referrals. Further, in terms of absenteeism, Breaugh (1981) reports persons recruited through newspaper advertisements missed more work days than individuals recruited through other sources. In contrast, Taylor and Schmidt (1983, p. 349) found rehire sources to be more effective with respect to attendance than other sources, including employee referrals.

Two basic explanations have been posited for the recruiting source effects described above. The "individual differences" hypothesis (Schwab, 1982) suggests differential source effectiveness is linked to individual differences in the applicant populations that are attracted to each communication or recruiting source. On the other hand, the "realistic information" hypothesis proposes that "individuals recruited via sources which provide more accurate information will be able to self-select out of jobs which do not meet their needs" (Breaugh & Mann, 1984, p. 261). In essence, this latter position suggests that recruiting sources vary with respect to the degree to which they provide realistic job previews (see discussion below). To date, only a handful of studies have explored these two explanations for recruiting source effects.

Of these investigations, Quaglieri's (1982) and Breaugh and Mann's (1984) findings are supportive of the realistic information hypothesis in that they suggest formal sources provide less accurate job information than do more informal sources. On the other hand, with respect to the individual differences hypothesis, Breaugh (1981) and Breaugh and Mann (1984) found limited support for the supposition, while Taylor and Schmidt (1983) report source differences for employee characteristics such as sex, age, and previous pay. However, as Breaugh and Mann (1984) observe, in the Taylor and Schmidt (1983) research there were no differences among any of the sources except for rehires, who differed from all of the other sources.

In summary, since most personnel experts do not consider rehires to be major recruiting sources (Breaugh & Mann, 1984), the results of the above studies seem to suggest greater support for the realistic information hypothesis as an explanation for recruiting source effects than the individual differences hypothesis. At the same time, until additional research exploring relationships between individual difference characteristics other than demographic variables (e.g., motivation) and recruiting sources have been conducted, this conclusion should be viewed in a tentative manner (Breaugh & Mann, 1984).

Realism of job/organizational expectations. Generally speaking, job applicants have unrealistic, typically positively inflated expectations about the organizations in which they are seeking employment (e.g., Jablin, 1984; Wanous, 1980). In part, it has been suggested that job candidates' expectations are unrealistic because organizations tend to follow traditional recruitment strategies in which they focus on primarily communicating the positive features of organizational membership to applicants (Wanous, 1977, 1980). Thus, for example, it is not surprising to discover that the recruitment literature organizations provide to college placement centers usually attempts to project companies as exciting and prestigious places to work (attraction) and typically focuses on extrinsic versus intrinsic job features (Hayes, 1969; Herriot & Rothwell, 1981; "Recruiting Literature," 1981; Shyles & Ross, 1984). The desirability of recruits developing inflated job/organizational expectations, however, is problematic since the more inflated job candidates' preentry expectations, the more difficult it usually is for them to meet these expectations once on the job. Moreover, it has been posited that to the extent that recruits expectations are unmet, the greater will be their job turnover and the lower their levels of job satisfaction and organizational commitment (Porter & Steers, 1973).

In order to provide job seekers with more realistic job/organizational expectations and concomitantly to reduce turnover and increase employee job satisfaction and commitment, Wanous (1977) and others have proposed what is termed the "realistic job preview" (RJP). According to Popovich and Wanous (1982, p. 571),

The RJP functions very much like a medical vaccination in its attempt to deflate newcomer expectations. . . . The typical medical vaccination injects one with a small, weakened dose of germs, so that one's body can develop a natural resistance to disease. The RJP functions similarly by presenting job candidates with a small dose of 'organizational reality.'

Thus it is believed that by presenting job applicants with RJPs their expectations will be deflated to more realistic levels, self-selection will occur among "marginal" applicants, and recruits will be better prepared to cope once they start work; and because they are provided with accurate job/organizational information prior to making their employment decisions, recruits will feel greater commitment to their jobs, exhibit higher levels of job satisfaction and lower turnover.

Findings from studies exploring the reasons why RJPs should work, as well as the relative effectiveness of RJPs in reducing turnover and enhancing the job attitudes of recruits, however, have produced inconsistent results. While studies have clearly shown that RJPs can significantly lower recruits' initial job expectations (Dean & Wanous, 1984; Dugoni & Ilgen, 1981; Krausz & Fox, 1981; Wanous, 1973; Youngberg, 1963), support for the notion that expectations will be inversely related to newcomers' postemployment levels of job satisfaction and commitment has been equivocal (Dean & Wanous, 1984; Dugoni & Ilgen, 1981; Katzell, 1968; Krausz & Fox, 1981; Miceli, 1985; Reilly, Brown, Blood, & Malatesta, 1981). Similarly, results from studies examining the relationship between RJPs and turnover have been very inconsistent and in general suggest that RJPs can be expected to improve employee retention rates only roughly 9% over rates experienced without their use (McEvoy & Cascio, 1985). Hence, while RJPs can lower expectations, "lowered expectations may be a necessary but not sufficient condition for RJPs to affect turnover" (Colarelli, 1984, p. 640).

A number of reasons have been posited for inconsistencies in research findings among RJP studies. Among other factors that have been suggested as causes of variant results are inconsistent operational definitions of "realism" across studies, variability among the organizational roles in which RJPs have been tested, differences across studies in methods and modes of presenting RJPs, and the general failure to adequately consider source, message, and audience (receiver) characteristics in preparing RJPs (e.g., Breaugh, 1983; Greenhalgh & Okun, 1984; Popovich & Wanous, 1982; Reilly et al., 1981). Thus, for example, across RJP studies message sources frequently vary or are not clearly stated. Yet, as Popovich and Wanous (1982) argue, consideration of the source of an RJP message is crucial since some company sources are likely to be perceived as less credible than other sources. Along these lines, Colarelli (1984) provides empirical evidence showing that when RJPs are administered by job incumbents, the information they provide is perceived as more trustworthy ($p < .06$) and as more personally relevant to applicants than is information communicated in RJP brochures.

The Colarelli (1984) study is of further interest in that it, like several other investigations (Reilly et al., 1981; Zaharia & Baumeister, 1981), examined how method of communication contributes to the effectiveness of RJPs. However, the Colarelli (1984) research is somewhat distinct from these other studies in that it not only considered the effects of the method (e.g., oral, videotape, brochure) on the effectiveness of RJPs but also the one-way versus two-way character of communication during the presentation. Interestingly, unlike other studies that have examined the effectiveness of oral RJP presentations in reducing turnover (Dugoni & Ilgen, 1981; Gomersall & Myers, 1966; Krausz & Fox, 1981), Colarelli's results showed oral RJPs, albeit two-way in nature and presented by job incumbents (high credibility sources), to be significantly more effective in reducing turnover than written presentations. In short, the results of this study reiterate the notion that generalizable conclusions will not be possible about the effects of RJPs until researchers control for source, message, and receiver communication characteristics in conducting RJP experiments.

The selection interview. Although, surprisingly, it is rarely conceptualized as such, the employment interview is probably the most common form of job preview that applicants receive from organizations (see Arvey & Campion, 1982; Jablin & McComb, 1984). While we can only speculate as to why the interview is not frequently considered a form of job/organization preview, it seems likely that this is due largely to the tendency among RJP researchers to focus on the preview as a formal, standardized, one-way form of communication. In contrast, the interview is typically considered a semi-structured, somewhat unreliable (with respect to inter-rater reliability) form of two-way communication. Yet, as Jablin and McComb (1984) observe, the interview is also an information-sharing, expectation-matching communication event and as such plays a key role in the assimilation of organizational newcomers. Additionally, although the validity and reliability of the interview as a selection device may be questioned (Mayfield, 1964; Schmitt, 1976; Ulrich & Trumbo, 1965), it nevertheless serves important organizational recruiting and public relations functions (Arvey & Campion, 1982).

The selection interview should be considered, in part, a form of job preview because of (1) the content of conversation that occurs within it, and (2) the manner in which "talk time" is distributed between the participants. More specifically, research suggests that a considerable amount of conversational content within interviews focuses on job/organizational issues (Keenan & Wedderburn, 1980; Reinsch & Stano, 1984; Taylor & Sniezek, 1984; Teigen, 1983). For example, Teigen (1983) reports that about 38% of the talk (operationalized by word count of actual interview transcripts) and 18% of the various topics discussed in screening interviews are devoted to exchanges about organizational climate issues (job duties and responsibilities, pay and benefits, coworker relations, supervision, advancement potential). With respect to the distribution of talk time in selection interviews, studies indicate that interviewers tend to hold the floor for longer periods of time than applicants (Cheatham & McLaughlin, 1976; Reinsch & Stano, 1984; Tengler & Jablin, 1983). In fact, Tengler and Jablin (1983) found in analyzing videotapes of screening interviews that applicants speak for only about 10 minutes in the average 30-minute interview. Seemingly, interviewers are spending their talk time answering applicants' questions, which typically focus on job/organizational topics (Babbitt & Jablin, 1985), or telling candidates about themselves or the job/organization. In short, given the frequent discussion of job/organizational topics in screening interviews and the domination of talk time by recruiters, it would appear that the "interview is important not only as an interpersonal communication event, but because of the role it plays in communicating job/organizational expectations to potential employees" (Jablin, 1985b, p. 621).

While the interview may play important expectation-sharing functions, it is also important to recognize that applicants and recruiters do not necessarily share similar expectations or perceptions about the nature of the interview. For instance, with respect to relationships between expectations and actual experiences, Herriot and Rothwell (1983) report that interviewees expect their interviewers to talk more about what the job entails, promotion prospects and benefits, and to ask more about the applicant's education, reasons for applying for the job, and knowledge of the company than they actually experience, while interviewers expect applicants to talk more about themselves, their educations, reasons for applying, and to tell applicants more about the job and organization than they actually experience. Relatedly, findings reported by Cheatham and McLaughlin (1976, p. 13) suggest that applicants tend to rate themselves and their interviewers as more "verbally communicative" (talkative, questioning, vocal) than do their recruiters, while their interviewers perceive "applicants are more talkative and less effective in listening and questioning-answering behaviors" than do applicants. In summary, based on the findings of these and other studies (Harlan, Kerr, & Kerr, 1977; Heriott & Rothwell, 1981; Posner, 1981; Taylor & Sniezek, 1984), it seems apparent that applicants and interviewers possess differential expectations and perceptions of their communication behaviors in selection interviews. Additionally, while at this time it is difficult to draw firm conclusions, exploratory research suggests that interview expectation-experience discrepancies may affect both applicants' and interviewers' employment decisions (Heriott & Rothwell, 1981, 1983).

Given the important information and expectation-sharing functions of the selection interview, it should be of no surprise to discover that over the years numerous studies have examined the communication properties of the interview. Along these lines, in a recent literature review Jablin and McComb (1984) found that 30 of 53 employment interviewing studies (57%) conducted between 1976 and 1982 explored communication-related variables. Moreover, their review revealed that of the studies investigating communication issues,

70% focused solely on interviewer communication, 17% examined interviewee communication exclusively, while only 13% involved the study of the interviewer-interviewee message-exchange process. Clearly, this bias toward exploring the interview*ers'* behaviors and attitudes is indicative of a general tendency to view the interview as a selection/decision-making tool for the organization, which unfortunately often causes us to "lose sight of the fact that it is also a communication event in which the interviewee is recruited by the organization and evaluates the organization and its representative with respect to potential employment" (Jablin & McComb, 1984, p. 151).

The long tradition of research examining communication in the selection interview has produced a multitude of findings (e.g., Daly, 1978; Freiberg & Hellweg, 1984; Goodall & Goodall, 1982; Jablin & McComb, 1984). However, Jablin (1985b, pp. 620-621) has recently suggested a number of generalizations that can be extrapolated from this literature, several of which are elaborated below:

(1) Generally, applicants' interview outcome expectations (including likelihoods of accepting job offers) appear related to their perceptions of their recruiters as trustworthy, competent, composed, empathic, enthusiastic and well-organized communicators (see Alderfer & McCord, 1970; Fisher, Ilgen & Hoyer, 1979; Jablin, Tengler, & Teigen, 1982; Rynes & Miller, 1983; Schmitt & Coyle, 1976; Teigen, 1983).

(2) Applicants do not particularly like or trust interviewers and appear hesitant to accept job offers if their only sources of information are recruiters; however, interviewers who are job incumbents are perceived as presenting more realistic job/organizational information than are interviewers who are personnel representatives (see Downs, 1969; Fisher et al., 1979; Jablin, Tengler, & Teigen, 1985).

(3) Interviewee satisfaction appears related to the quality and amount of organizational and job information the recruiter provides, the degree to which the recruiter asks the interviewee open-ended questions that are high in "face validity," and allows him or her sufficient talk time (see Herriot & Rothwell, 1983; Karol, 1977; Tengler, 1982).

(4) Most questions applicants ask their interviewers are closed-ended, singular in form, typically not phrased in the first person, asked after interviewers ask applicants for inquiries, and seek job-related information (see Babbitt & Jablin, 1985; Einhorn, 1981).

(5) Applicants' perceptions of their interviewers as empathic listeners appear to be negatively related to the degree to which interviewers interject interruptive statements while the interviewees are speaking (see McComb & Jablin, 1984).

(6) Interviewees who display high versus low levels of nonverbal immediacy (operationalized by eye contact, smiling, posture, interpersonal distance, and body orientation) and are high in vocal activity tend to be favored by interviewers (Byrd, 1979; Forbes & Jackson, 1980; Imada & Hakel, 1977; Keenan, 1976; Keenan & Wedderburn, 1975; McGovern & Tinsley, 1978; Trent, 1978).

(7) Recruiters find interviewees more acceptable if they receive favorable information about them prior to or during their interviews; however, recruiters do not necessarily adopt confirmatory question strategies to validate their expectancies (see Constantin, 1976; Herriot & Rothwell, 1983; Sackett, 1979; Tucker & Rowe, 1979).

(8) Interviewers tend to employ inverted funnel question sequences (they begin with closed questions and then progress to more open-ended questions), thus limiting applicant talk time during the opening minutes of interviews (see Tengler & Jablin, 1983).

(9) Interviewers tend to rate more highly and be more satisfied with applicants who talk more of the time in their interviews (though this talk is not necessarily in response to interviewers' questions), who elaborate on answers, and whose discussion on topics more nearly matches interviewers' expectations (see Einhorn, 1981; Herriot & Rothwell, 1983; Tengler & Jablin, 1983).

(10) Applicant communication ability/competence (e.g., fluency of speech, composure, appropriateness of content, ability to express ideas in an organized fashion) is frequently reported by interviewers to be a critical factor in their decisions (see Hollandsworth, Kazelskis, Stevens, & Dressel, 1979; Kinicki & Lockwood, 1985; Posner, 1981).

Although the above generalizations have received empirical support in the literature, due to the myriad methodological problems that have historically plagued interview studies (e.g., Arvey & Campion, 1982; Jablin & McComb, 1984; Schmitt, 1976) the reader is advised to exercise caution in overgeneralizing these findings. In particular, it should be noted that most studies have focused on examining the screening interviews of college students (initial career entrants) occurring in placement centers, apply to screening versus second on-site interviews (which have been infrequent objects of study), often utilize paper-and-pencil interviews (e.g., Gorman, Clover, & Doherty, 1978) or college students as interviewers in simulated interview situations, tend to be fairly microanalytic in nature (Schmitt, 1976), rarely consider the effects of situational variables on results (e.g., job markets), frequently employ outcome measures of questionable validity (Jablin & McComb, 1984), and in general have relied on collecting and analyzing perceptual as compared to behavioral data.

Suggestions for future research abound in the many literature reviews and analyses that have been published concerning the selection interview (see Arvey & Campion, 1982; Herriot, 1984; Jablin, 1975; Jablin & McComb, 1984; Schmitt, 1976). As a consequence, only three directions for future research are advanced here. First, as noted earlier, it is apparent that studies need to place greater emphasis on examining the nature of interview message-exchange processes and their corresponding effects on applicant and interviewer attitudes and employment decisions. Second, our understanding of the interview might be enhanced by viewing it in broader terms, as part of the process of seeking employment. In other words, research needs to explore how applicants prepare for interviews, the effects of interview preparation on interview performance (e.g., Stumpf, Austin, & Hartman, 1984), potential interaction effects that may exist between recruitment sources and interview processes, and how success and failure (rejection) in interviews affects job seekers' subsequent interviewing behavior and attitudes (e.g., Herriot, Ecob, & Hutchinson, 1980; Jablin & Krone, 1984). Finally, it is recommended that future studies begin to examine how selection processes in general, and employment interviews in particular, affect the sense-making activities of organizational insiders (Sutton & Louis, 1984). For instance, how does the interviewing process (such as applicants' questions and remarks) affect how organizational insiders feel about themselves and their companies?

Summary. The preceding discussion has provided an overview of communication processes relevant to anticipatory organizational socialization. Intrinsic to this presentation has been the notion that job seekers develop expectations about jobs/ organizations and their communication characteristics as a result of the interaction of their vocational socialization and the sources of information with which they come into contact in the job search process. As stressed in the preceding pages, regardless of the method of employer-applicant information exchange, an outgrowth of this process is the emergence within recruits of somewhat distorted (typically inflated) expectations of what jobs and organizations will be like. Whether job candidates' tendencies to develop inaccurate job/ organizational expectations are caused by organizational recruiting/ selection practices, or person-perception processes associated with applicants, or the interaction of the two is at this time a matter of speculation. However, the consequences of job candidates' inaccurate job/ organizational beliefs and expectations seems very clear: Discrepancies between expectations and reality will increase the surprise (Louis, 1980) associated with organizational entry and make the organizational assimilation process more difficult for the newcomer.

ORGANIZATIONAL ASSIMILATION

Organizational assimilation can be thought of as the process by which an individual becomes integrated into the "reality" or culture of an organization (Jablin, 1982). The process is generally considered to be composed of two reciprocal dimensions: (1) deliberate and unintentional efforts by the organization to "socialize" employees (see Van Maanen, 1975), and (2) workers' attempts to "individualize" or modify their roles and organizational environments to better satisfy their needs, ideas, and values (see Schein, 1968). Moreover, as dynamic, interactive processes, organizational socialization and employee individualization are also fundamental elements of the organizational "role-making" process (Graen, 1976; Jablin, 1982). Viewed in this manner, assimilation processes become amenable to empirical study since it is through the proactive and reactive communication of expectations to and from an individual by members of his or her "role set" (Katz & Kahn, 1966) that organizational roles are negotiated and individuals share in the socially created "reality" of organizations (Berger & Luckmann, 1967).

A variety of models have been proposed explaining the phases or stages through which the process of assimilating new organizational recruits progresses (Feldman, 1976; Porter, Lawler, & Hackman, 1975; Van Maanen, 1975). While each of these models is somewhat unique from the others, when integrated they suggest the assimilation of newcomers typically proceeds through three basic phases: (1) some form of anticipatory socialization; (2) an "encounter" phase, which includes the organizational entry period and the "reality shock" (Hughes, 1958) that is often associated with such boundary passages; and (3) a "metamorphosis" stage during which the newcomer acquires organizationally "appropriate" attitudes and behaviors, resolves intra- and extra-organizational role conflicts, and commences efforts to individualize his or her organizational role. Further, it should be realized that the metamorphosis stage is generally considered to be a ubiquitous feature of organizational membership since organizational socialization requirements will vary over time (resocialization) as will employees' efforts to individualize their organizational roles (Jablin, 1982; Porter et al., 1975).

Since the preceding section of this chapter has already outlined communication processes and outcomes associated with anticipatory socialization, the remainder of this section will focus on the characteristics of communication in the encounter and metamorphosis stages of the assimilation process. In addition, this analysis will suggest a number of communication-related outcomes typically associated with organizational assimilation. Consistent with the earlier discussion of anticipatory socialization, the following review will focus on the nature and effects of newcomers' interactions with various communication sources as they progress through the encounter and metamorphosis stages of organizational assimilation. In particular, two basic message characteristics—whether a message is "ambient" (pervasive, noncontingent) or discretionary (intentional, transmitted selectively) in nature (see Hackman, 1976; Jablin, 1982)—will be considered as they apply to newcomers' communications with three essential sources of information (the "organization"/management, supervisors, and coworkers) during the assimilation process (Jablin, 1982, 1985b). Figure 19.2 presents an overview of the assimilation processes and communication variables, issues, and outcomes that are central to the following discussion.

Encounter

It is during the encounter stage of assimilation, or what is frequently referred to as the "breaking-in" period (Van Maanen, 1975), that the newcomer confronts the reality of his or her organizational role (Berlew &

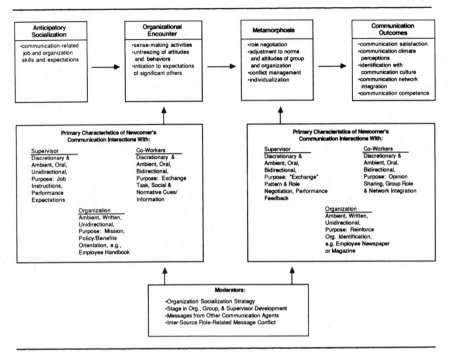

Anticipatory Socialization
- communication-related job and organization skills and expectations

Organizational Encounter
- sense-making activities
- unfreezing of attitudes and behaviors
- initiation to expectations of significant others

Metamorphosis
- role negotiation
- adjustment to norms and attitudes of group and organization
- conflict management
- individualization

Communication Outcomes
- communication satisfaction
- communication climate perceptions
- identification with communication culture
- communication network integration
- communication competence

Primary Characteristics of Newcomer's Communication Interactions With:

Supervisor
Discretionary & Ambient, Oral, Unidirectional, Purpose: Job Instructions, Performance Expectations

Co-Workers
Discretionary & Ambient, Oral, Bidirectional, Purpose: Exchange Task, Social & Normative Cues/ Information

Organization
Ambient, Written, Unidirectional, Purpose: Mission, Policy/Benefits Orientation, e.g., Employee Handbook

Primary Characteristics of Newcomer's Communication Interactions With:

Supervisor
Discretionary & Ambient, Oral, Bidirectional, Purpose: "Exchange" Pattern & Role Negotiation, Performance Feedback

Co-Workers
Discretionary & Ambient, Oral, Bidirectional, Purpose: Opinion Sharing, Group Role & Network Integration

Organization
Ambient, Written, Unidirectional, Purpose: Reinforce Org. Identification, e.g. Employee Newspaper or Magazine

Moderators:
- Organization Socialization Strategy
- Stage in Org., Group, & Supervisor Development
- Messages from Other Communication Agents
- Inter-Source Role-Related Message Conflict

Figure 19.2 Communication and the Organizational Assimilation Process

Hall, 1966; Schein, 1968; Van Maanen, 1975). If the newcomer has not accurately anticipated his or her new job and organization this stage can be a very traumatic period and involve "a destructive phase (analytically similar to the Lewinian concept of unfreezing) which serves to detach the individual from his [or her] former expectations" (Van Maanen, 1975, p. 84). However, while this encounter can be a reality or role shock (Hughes, 1958; Minkler & Biller, 1979), more often than not it is less intense and merely "involves a pattern of day-to-day experiences in which the individual is subjected to the reinforcement policies of the organization and its members" (Porter et al., 1975, p. 164). Thus rather than experience a series of shocks the newcomer will experience a sequence of surprises (Louis, 1980) or discrepancies between expectations and reality. In turn, these surprises will stimulate cognitive sense-making processes within the newcomer (Louis, 1980) as he or she attempts to attribute meaning to unexpected experiences by reformulating existing work-related cognitive scripts and attributional models (Jablin, 1982). In summary, during the encounter period the newcomer learns the requirements of his or her role and what the organization and its members consider to be "normal" patterns of behavior and thought (Van Maanen, 1975).

Clearly, the process by which one learns about what the organization considers to be acceptable behaviors and attitudes is essentially communicative in nature. In other words, "the recruit develops initial interpretation schemes for his or her new work environment primarily from formal and informal communication received from others" (Jablin, 1982, pp. 266-267). Three key sources of such communication are the "organization"/management, the newcomer's immediate supervisor, and his or her coworkers/workgroup members.

Organization/management. Upon entry into an organization newcomers are typically barraged with a variety of mediated and nonmediated forms of communication from management. Further, most of these messages tend to be "ambient" in nature, that is, provided on a noncontingent, nonselective basis to all newcomers. For example, recruits may be exposed to an orientation by members of the organization's personnel department in which they receive a wide variety of written publications and an oral briefing on a variety of topics including work rules, insurance, employee services, and the like (St. John, 1980).

While statistics on the number of organizations that provide formal orientation programs to newcomers are unavailable, survey findings do suggest that over 50% of companies present newcomers with some form of presentation or "indoctrination" booklet (Woodward, 1968). At the same time, it is noteworthy that we know little of the relative effectiveness of these documents in orienting newcomers or whether or not they provide accurate depictions of their respective organizational environments. In turn, the employee handbook also appears to be a vital part of most organizational orientation programs (Cowan, 1975; St. John, 1980). As Jones (1973, p. 138) observes, "the handbook is the most widely used written medium for downward communication" in organizations. With respect to content, most handbooks appear to focus on three basic issues: (1) organizational history, mission, and policies; (2) work rules and related procedures and practices; and (3) employee benefits and services (Cowan, 1975; Jones, 1973). For example, in a recent content analysis of a sample of employee handbooks distributed to newcomers in organizations that Peters and Waterman (1982) identify as "excellent" or "near excellent," Wolfe and Baskin (1985) found approximately 21% of content (word count) focusing on issues related to company history, philosophy, and mission, 16% devoted to explication of work rules, and 44% explaining compensation and benefit plans. Unfortunately, however, while the information contained in employee handbooks appears to have face validity with respect to orienting newcomers to organizational operations and practices (though little empirical assessment data exist on this subject), other evidence suggests that "most employee handbooks are not yet adequately readable for the audience for which they are intended" (Davis, 1968, p. 419). Related findings have also shown that while organizations spend large sums of money attempting to communicate benefits information to new (and continuing) employees, employee awareness and understanding of their benefits are quite low (Driver, 1980; Holly & Ingram, 1973; Huseman & Hatfield, 1978; Sloane & Hodges, 1968).

Though the relative effectiveness of organizations in communicating various types of policy-related information to newcomers is either unknown or of limited success (e.g., Redding, 1972), it should also be noted that several studies do provide support for the notion that such information may be more effectively communicated to newcomers (but not necessarily continuing employees) via mediated rather than nonmediated means. For instance, findings of Dahle's (1953) research suggest that benefits-related information is more effectively communicated to new (less than one year in the company) versus continuing employees by written as opposed to oral modes of communication. Similarly, Putnam, Murray, and Hill (1981), in a laboratory study of the relative impact of oral and written communication of organizational policies on employee performance and retention of information during organizational encounter, found that written communication was superior to oral communication with respect to its effects on both newcomers' performance and their knowledge of policies. In interpreting their results these researchers propose that because recruits often experience information overload and lack a frame of reference for classifying information, "written information provides a reference point for making sense out of the massive array of facts that newcomers receive" (Putnam et al., 1981, p. 14). Alternatively, the position that written forms of communication may be more effective than oral mediums in orienting newcomers to organizational, policy-related information is also consistent with Daft and Lengel's (1984) argument that information mediums low in "richness" (slow in feedback, visual in channel, impersonal, simple in language) are sufficient for communicating routine, straightforward, and fairly unequivocal types of information to employees.

Interestingly, few empirical studies have explored the nature of the oral orientation programs that organizations present, typically through their personnel departments, to newcomers. In fact, essentially all we know about these programs is that they are frequently available to newcomers. For example, Louis, Posner, and Powell (1983) report that 64% of newcomers (MBA college graduates) participate in such activities and that newcomers view them as moderately helpful in learning about their organizations. Unfortunately, the nature of the content of these programs has yet to be empirically examined, though prescriptive essays on this subject indicate that programs often focus on issues similar to those covered in employee handbooks (St. John, 1980). On the other hand, in a rather rare experimental study of the effects of organizational orientation programs on newcomers' subsequent levels of job performance, Gomersall and Myers (1966) suggest that informal "anxiety-reduction" sessions following formal, conventional personnel department orientation briefings can dramatically improve the length of time it takes for employees to obtain minimal job competency levels. Of particular interest is the fact that these anxiety-reduction sessions focused primarily on communication-related issues, urging newcomers to disregard "hall talk" (hazing by old-timers and rumors) and to "take the initiative in communication" with their supervisors (especially to feel free to ask questions).

In turn, the specific effects of "formal" (occurring away from the work setting and presenting newcomers with experiences specifically designed for them), typically "collective" (group) organizational training-socialization programs on new employee assimilation remains relatively unexplored (Louis et al., 1983; Van Maanen & Schein, 1979). However, numerous possibilities exist for research in this area, including (1) determining the short- and long-term effects of isolating newcomers in formal training programs from communication sources other than those sanctioned by the organization, (2) ascertaining the effects of group interaction processes in collective training experiences on newcomers' sense-making efforts, and (3) examining the degree to which recruits apply what they have been taught in training programs to the "reality" of the work setting (Jablin & Krone, 1987; Van Maanen, 1977; Van Maanen & Schein, 1979).

In summary, to date little research has been conducted exploring the functions or effects of organizational/management communication during the encounter phase of assimilation. This lack of study, however, should not be assumed to indicate that such communication does not play a vital role in the assimilation process. In fact, from the organization's perspective, the effective communication of policy-related information is essential, if for no other reason than that the organization is often legally bound to communicate such information to employees (e.g., entitlements such as social security, worker's compensation). However, it is also important to realize that this information is not likely to create many surprises for newcomers since it is relatively concrete and extrinsic in nature and, as Wanous (1980) observes, newcomers tend to have fairly accurate expectations of concrete job matters. In essence, it appears that organizational/management communication with newcomers during the encounter stage is fairly one-way in nature, ambient in form, and directed primarily at *informing* employees about "what is customary and desirable" (Van Maanen, 1977, p. 28) rather than with changing their attitudes and behaviors.

Supervisor. A newcomer's communication relationship with his or her initial supervisor is a crucial factor in determining the nature of the employee's encounter experience, since

(1) the supervisor frequently interacts with the subordinate and thus may serve as a role model (Weiss, 1977), (2) the supervisor has the formal power to reward

and punish the employee, (3) the supervisor mediates the formal flow of downward communication to the subordinate (for example, the supervisor serves as an interpreter/filter of management messages), and (4) the supervisor usually has a personal as well as formal role relationship with the recruit. (Jablin, 1982, p. 269)

Moreover, findings of studies consistently indicate a newcomer's relationship with his or her initial supervisor can have long-term consequences on the success of the individual's organizational and professional career (Graen & Ginsburgh, 1977; Kanter, 1977; Katz, 1980; Thompson & Dalton, 1976; Vincino & Bass, 1978).

While a recruit's relationship with his or her initial supervisor may play an important role in the newcomer's assimilation into the organization, it is also apparent that newcomers frequently are not satisfied with their first bosses (Katz, 1985). In part, this dissatisfaction is due to the newcomer's high level of dependency on the supervisor for job information and resources, but more often dissatisfaction develops because the supervisor is not sensitive to the problems of the new employee (for instance, the high level of uncertainty he or she is experiencing) and/or is deficient in the skills required to supervise or "coach" newcomers (Dunnette, Avery, & Banas, 1973; Gomersall & Myers, 1966; Kotter, 1973; Livingston, 1969). In particular, supervisors who successfully manage newcomers appear to be highly skilled in communication, especially in "giving and receiving feedback, articulating expectations and performance criteria, explaining realistically decisions passed down from above, coaching, and helping" (Kotter, 1973, p. 98). Unfortunately, while some supervisors possess these skills and are sensitive to the encounter needs of newcomers, others are not, and as a result newcomers are often advised to "seek the help and information they need to do their work effectively instead of waiting or wishing their bosses to provide it" (Katz, 1985, p. 122). However, while the results of empirical investigations do suggest that newcomers often take this advice, findings also indicate that the willingness of newcomers to initiate communication interactions with their supervisors develops gradually and is not necessarily immediate in nature. For example, Jablin (1984), examining the communication logs of nursing assistants during their third week of work (first week on the job after training), discovered that almost two-thirds of recruits' communication interactions with their supervisors were initiated by the other party. It was not until the ninth week of work that the log data showed recruits and supervisors initiating interactions at equal rates.

Although the results of extant studies suggest that it may be beneficial for newcomers to seek information and feedback from their supervisors during the encounter period (e.g., Ashford, 1986; Feldman & Brett, 1983; Jablin, 1984), almost no research exists exploring the specific communication strategies that recruits use in acquiring "knowledge" from their bosses. In fact, to date, only two basic strategies have been explored as mechanisms by which newcomers seek information and feedback from their supervisors: (1) *monitoring* (the newcomer observes the reactions of his or her supervisor and coworkers to his or her behavior and/or the newcomer compares his or her own behavior to the behavior of other subordinates), and (2) making *direct inquiries* or explicitly asking for information and feedback (Ashford, 1986; Ashford & Cummings, 1983, 1985).

While the above information/feedback-seeking strategies represent two means by which newcomers may obtain information from their supervisors, they are not necessarily inclusive of all the major knowledge acquisition strategies recruits utilize. Other approaches seem just as viable, and may be preferable since they possess fewer psychological costs and tendencies for making erroneous attributions (a danger of monitoring strategies; Ashford & Cummings, 1983). For example, extrapolating from research exploring information-seeking strategies in nonwork contexts (Berger & Bradac, 1982), we might speculate that manipulation of what Jourard (1971) has labeled the "dyadic effect" (or "norm of reciprocity") may be frequently used by organizational newcomers. Thus if a newcomer wanted to discover if his or her supervisor expected employees to work weekends to complete assignments, the newcomer might disclose during an appropriate conversation that while in school rather than turn projects in late he or she often "pulled all-nighters." In this context, the norm of reciprocity would predict that the supervisor (all things being equal) will respond with a disclosure about his or her work style in similar situations. To summarize, future research exploring how newcomers acquire information and feedback from their supervisors needs to focus on developing and verifying broader typologies of (1) newcomers' information-seeking strategies, and (2) the related content areas in which newcomers seek information and feedback from their superiors.

Similarly, while there is a considerable amount of theoretical speculation as to the purposes of the (unsolicited) messages that newcomers receive from their supervisors during the encounter period, almost no empirical research has directly explored this issue. However, Jablin's (1984) analysis of the communication logs of newly hired nursing assistants does support the often expressed notion that such messages tend to be directed at setting work-related goals and expectations for newcomers (e.g., Katz, 1980). Specifically, his findings indicate that of the messages newcomers received from their superiors, 51.8% involved job instructions and 23.2% job-related information, and that recruits had fairly positive attitudes toward these types of interactions. Thus, in the parlance of Schein's (1971) taxonomy of the behaviors and norms newcomers acquire during the assimilation process, it would appear that the communications that recruits receive from their immediate supervisors during the encounter period focus on matters related to the acquisition of "pivotal" role behaviors and attitudes (job rationale, task skills, procedures or practices, and supervisors' performance expectations of workers) and tend to be fairly directive in nature. The frequency of such feedback, however, may be moderated by the degree to which the newcomer is high or low in "role orientation" (considers the job relevant to his or her career; Graen, Orris, & Johnson, 1973).

In summary, interactions between newcomer and superior during the encounter period appear to focus on the supervisor communicating task, performance, and interpersonal expectations or goals to the recruit, and to some degree on the newcomer's seeking feedback about his or her performance and the meaning of unclear, ambiguous events and expectations. Further, it should be realized that the expectations and goals that a supervisor communicates to a newcomer are not only a result of direct, face-to-face interactions with the recruit (discretionary message exchanges) but also a byproduct of (1) the newcomer's modeling of the superior's style, values, and behaviors (Weiss, 1977, 1978), and (2) the recruit's monitoring of coworkers interactions with the superior (essentially a form of vicarious learning; see Bandura, 1977), and (3) the superior's oral and written communication with the workgroup as a whole (ambient messages). In turn, the relative impact of a superior's communication of expectations to a newcomer on the newcomer's subsequent job performance should not be underestimated. As findings from several studies have shown (e.g., Berlew & Hall, 1966; Eden & Shani, 1982), the communication of high performance expectations from a first supervisor to a recruit can have positive effects on the newcomer's immediate performance as well as long-term career success. Finally, it should be noted that research findings indicating that newcomers possess fairly positive attitudes toward "directive," task-structuring communications they receive from their superiors during the encounter period are supportive of the notion that newcomers may initially prefer to be assigned goals by their superiors rather than to participate in goal setting. As Katz (1980) argues, consistent with the path-goal model of leadership (House, 1971), newcomers (especially persons in their first jobs) may respond favorably to supervisor assigned goal-setting and structuring since these activities tend to reduce ambiguity, clarify the relationship between task performance and rewards, and in general provide greater definition of their supervisors' expectations.

Workgroup/coworkers. Although organizations rarely *consciously* involve peers in the assimilation of newcomers, research consistently supports the notion that newcomers' daily interactions with coworkers/peers are one of the most important factors affecting their assimilation (Evan, 1963; Feldman, 1977; Van Maanen, 1975). As Louis et al. (1983, pp. 863-864) discovered in a survey of recent MBA graduates and the socialization practices they experienced in their new jobs and organizations, "interactions with peers was available to more respondents than any other aid, and was significantly correlated with job satisfaction, commitment and tenure intention."

During the encounter period, interactions of newcomers with the members of their workgroups may serve a variety of functions: (1) They may serve an informative function by helping the newcomer interpret "the events they experience, to learn many nuances of seemingly clearcut rules, and to learn the informal networks" (Feldman, 1981, p. 314); (2) an affective-psychological function by providing emotional support against the stresses of the organization's socialization initiatives and the uncertainties of the new work setting (Becker, Geer, Hughes, & Strauss, 1961; Dornbush, 1955; Feldman, 1977); (3) a normative function by affecting newcomers' work-related attitudes (Weiss & Nowicki, 1981; White & Mitchell, 1979); and (4) a job performance function resulting from newcomers modeling the work behaviors and methods of peers (Rakestraw & Weiss, 1981).

While only a handful of empirical studies have examined the types, frequencies, and contexts of newcomers' communication interactions with coworkers/peers during the encounter period, the results of these investigations are fairly supportive of the notion that a considerable amount of activity is directed toward information exchange and sense-making (Louis, 1980). For example, Feldman and Brett (1983) report that one of the major coping strategies of new hires is seeking information from coworkers. Similarly, Jablin (1984), in his analysis of the communication logs of nursing assistants during their third week of work, discovered newcomers and coworkers initiating interactions with one another at roughly equal rates with the primary purpose of information exchange (80% of interactions).

Since the actual content characteristics of discretionary message exchanges between newcomers and incumbent coworkers have rarely been studied in the organizational setting, theorists frequently extrapolate to the organizational context from related findings of social psychological laboratory investigations of newcomer assimilation into problem-solving groups (e.g., Feldman, 1984). In particular, it is assumed that a considerable amount of encounter period communications from coworkers to newcomers focuses on content related to educating recruits to selective group norms and obtaining conformity to "shared" values, attitudes, and behaviors (e.g., Feldman, 1984; Hackman, 1976). In addition, given the role ambiguity, psychological stress, and need for coworker acceptance that newcomers often experience (Feldman, 1977; Katz, 1980), it is generally believed that rather than deviate from group norms recruits typically acquiesce to the attitudes and behaviors implied in the messages sent by peers (e.g., Berkowitz & Howard, 1959; Festinger, 1954; Schachter, 1951).

While the above position has intuitive appeal, it should be recognized that empirical research exploring how and the extent to which newcomers adopt their group's norms is extremely rare. Further, recent studies are not completely supportive of the notion that newcomers are passive recipients of group norms. Among these investigations several studies by Ridgeway (1978, 1981) are noteworthy, since their results bring into question the efficacy of portions of Hollander's (1958, 1960) "idiosyncratic credit" theory, on which many of our assumptions about communication, deviance, and conformity in groups are based. In turn, research examining the process of norm development in groups suggests that while newcomers may often willingly accept their group's interpretations of reality, "they may also raise objections and challenge their group's understandings of what constitutes appropriate behavior" (Bettenhausen & Murnighan, 1985, p. 370). In particular, this may be the case when a newcomer is knowledgeable and entering a workgroup that does not have a history of success (Ziller & Behringer, 1960).

On the other hand, recent studies exploring the effects of "social information processing" on employees' job attitudes suggest that newcomers may also learn about acceptable behaviors and attitudes in their new work environments from the ambient messages they receive from coworkers (e.g., Caldwell & O'Reilly, 1982; Griffin, 1983; O'Reilly & Caldwell, 1979; Roberts & Glick, 1981; Salancik & Pfeffer, 1978; Weiss & Nowicki, 1981). Basically, the social information processing approach to job attitudes proposes that an individual's work attitudes are partially constructed from informational cues provided by others in the work place, particularly coworkers. In other words, the model suggests that the job attitudes of a newcomer will be a result of not only "objective" task characteristics (see Hackman & Lawler, 1971), but also of the dimensions of the work environment that peers (and others) draw attention to, create meaning for, and evaluate in the course of their daily interactions. Thus, for example, a comment by an old-timer to a newcomer "that a job does not give a person a chance to think implies not only that the job has a certain feature but that the presence or absence of that feature should be important to the person" (Salancik & Pfeffer, 1978, p. 230).

While studies of social information processing have produced somewhat mixed results (e.g., Thomas & Griffin, 1983), the notion that social information plays an important role in workers' perceptions and attitudes has generally been supported. Consequently, the argument that coworker-generated ambient messages have important effects on newcomers' developing job attitudes seems reasonable. Unfortunately, to date no investigation has explicitly explored the role and effects of social information processing in the assimilation of newcomers to workgroups (and organizatons). Unquestionably, future studies along these lines should be initiated. In particular, investigations exploring the characteristics of the stories, myths, and humor that old-timers generate in the workgroup setting might provide insight into the nature and effects of ambient, socially available messages on newcomers' attitudes and behaviors (see Brown, 1985; Mitroff & Kilmann, 1976; Wilkins, 1978).

Though the discussion to this point has focused on the nature of newcomer-incumbent communication during the encounter period, a newcomer's assimilation into a workgroup and organization can also be affected by what these parties strategically *avoid* communicating about. As Feldman (1977, p.

989) reports, "Until such time as employees feel they are trusted by coworkers, they are often not able to get information which is essential to doing their jobs well." Similarly, the creation of "strategic ambiguity" (Eisenberg, 1984) about performance standards, or failing to provide newcomers with feedback about enacted work behaviors can affect the nature of the assimilation process (Roy, 1955).

Concomitantly, while the above analysis has focused on the nature and effects of a newcomer's interactions with members of his or her immediate workgroup on the newcomer's assimilation, the potential influence of interactions with members of other "secondary" organizational groups on the nature of the newcomer's encounter experience must be acknowledged. As Shibutani (1962, pp. 138-139) argues, "For any individual, there are as many reference groups as there are channels of communication in which a person regularly becomes involved." Moreover, the more reference groups with which a newcomer interacts the greater the probability that some of the role-defining messages communicated to the recruit will conflict with one another. In turn, the more role and interpersonal conflict the newcomer experiences, the more stressful the encounter period, the more difficult the process of developing schemas for understanding the work environment, and the longer the time required to develop friendships with members of the role-set (Feldman, 1977; Kahn, Wolfe, Quinn, Snoek, & Rosenthal, 1964; Katz, 1985).

In summary, as with newcomers' interactions with their superiors, the communication of expectations dominates transactions between newcomers and coworkers during the encounter period. However, in contrast to interactions with superiors, newcomer-incumbent interactions seem to focus on the communication of a broader set of expectations, that is, the exchange of expectations concerning "relevant" (desirable but not necessary), "peripheral" (permitted by not necessarily even desirable), as well as "pivotal" values and behaviors (Schein, 1971). As Schein (1968, p. 7) observes,

> the more subtle types of values which the organization holds, which indeed may not even be well understood by the senior people, are often communicated through peers. . . . They can communicate the subtleties of how the boss wants things done, how higher management feels about things, the kinds of things that are considered heroic in the organization, the kinds of things which are taboo.

In turn, the willingness of newcomers to initiate discretionary interactions with their coworkers to obtain and give information appears significantly greater than their willingness to initiate similar types of interactions with their superiors. Research findings suggest also that a major concern of newcomers is in achieving acceptance by members of their workgroups, and that to some extent it is necessary for newcomers to feel accepted by their coworkers before they can feel and be competent on the job (Feldman, 1977). However, it also seems likely that newcomers do not always spontaneously adopt the norms communicated to them as "appropriate" by members of their workgroups, but rather under certain circumstances attempt to influence their peers to modify their informally accepted values and behaviors. Finally, although a relatively new focus of study, social information processing theory and research suggests that ambient messages from incumbent employees to newcomers may play a vital role in the ability of newcomers to make sense of their new work environments.

Concluding issues. Prior to addressing the nature of communication processes in the metamorphosis stage of assimilation, several caveats with respect to the preceding discussion warrant consideration:

(1) This discussion focused on only three of the many sources with whom newcomers exchange role-defining messages during the encounter period. Other sources include subordinates (e.g., Crowe, Bochner, & Clark, 1972; Graen, 1976), mentors or sponsors (e.g., Daniels & Logan, 1983; DeWine, Casbolt, & Bentley, 1983; Boster, Wigand, & Collofello, 1984), clients and customers (e.g., Danet, 1981; Mills, & Morris, 1986; Witlatch, 1985), professional organizations, unions, and family members (e.g., Feldman, 1976).

(2) Though the preceding analysis has tended to isolate the various sources with whom newcomers exchange role-defining messages, it is essential to realize that newcomers will often be exchanging messages with multiple sources and that these messages may present conflicting perspectives.

(3) This discussion has viewed organizational socialization strategies in general rather than specific terms and has not considered the effects of particular types of socialization strategies (see Jones, 1986; Van Maanen, 1978; Van Maanen & Schein, 1979) on communication processes.

(4) The preceding analysis has not considered how the point in "developmental" time at which a newcomer enters an organization, workgroup, and superior-subordinate relationship affects the nature of communication in his or her assimilation experience. In other words, this discussion did not directly address the impact of organizational life cycles (e.g., Jablin & Krone, 1987; Jick & Greenhalgh, 1981; Smith, Mitchell, & Summer, 1985), phases of group development (e.g., Katz, 1980; Wanous, Reichers, & Malik, 1984), or newcomers' and superiors' career stages (e.g., Baird & Kram, 1983) on communication and assimilation processes. Clearly, these are all important issues and need to be considered in research exploring communication and organizational assimilation processes.

Metamorphosis

During the metamorphosis stage of assimilation the newcomer "attempts to become an accepted, participating member of the organization by learning new attitudes and behaviors or modifying existing ones to be consistent with the organization's expectations" (Jablin, 1984, p. 596). Thus, as a result of the various reinforcements that a newcomer experiences during and subsequent to his or her initial organizational encounter, he or she begins the gradual process of using, accepting, and eventually internalizing a set of appropriate "constitutive rules through which organizational meanings are established and regulative rules through which members coordinate their everyday interaction" (Harris & Cronen, 1979, p. 14). At the same time, however, it is essential to recognize that, "It is those present organizational members involved in the incoming employee's new relationships who transmit the organization's norms and who thus, in effect, determine when the individual has acquired the 'proper' socialized role" (Porter et al., 1975, p. 166). In turn, the metamorphosis period is also when newcomers often initiate efforts to individualize their organizational roles (achieve acceptable levels of "coorientation" with others about their roles), as well as endeavor to resolve intra- and extra-organizational role conflicts (Feldman, 1976).

Consistent with the preceding discussion of the encounter phase of assimilation, the following section will consider the nature of a newcomer's communication relationships with three key message sources during the metamorphosis stage: the organization/management, the worker's immediate superior, and the employee's coworkers/workgroup members. Several parameters will guide this analysis: (1) The discussion focuses primarily on the first "wave" of the metamorphosis experiences of newcomers, concentrating on the first few years of organizational tenure (regrettably, this emphasis reflects the paucity of long-term longitudinal research conducted in this area); (2) the communication processes and functions that are elucidated apply primarily to newcomers who are initially entering organizations and/or are beginning their first jobs in their respective occupational areas (for discussions of the assimilation of job transferees and job/organization changers see Brett, 1980, 1984; Jablin, 1985b); and (3) this discussion does not focus on the effects of macro-level variables on communication and assimilation processes since these relationships have recently been elaborated elsewhere (Jablin & Krone, 1987).

Organization/management. The barrage of ambient, typically written, mass media, one-way communications that newcomers receive from management during their initial organizational encounters usually continues during the metamorphosis period. However, while during the encounter phase these messages served primarily an orientation function, these communications begin to serve another important purpose during the metamorphosis period: reinforcing a sense of organizational identification and commitment. At the same time, the relative effectiveness of these communications in reinforcing feelings of organizational identification will likely be moderated by at least two major factors: (1) the extent to which newcomers have already developed (through interpersonal interactions with superiors and coworkers) interpretive schemas consistent with the attitudes expressed in the newsletters, memoranda, videotape broadcasts, and so forth that they receive from management, and (2) the degree to which newcomers actually attend to and perceive as credible the communications they receive from management (McGuire, 1968; Redding, 1972; Weiss, 1968).

While no research to date has directly explored the nature of mass media, management-newcomer communication during the metamorphosis period of assimilation, results of studies exploring the characteristics of employee publications (especially employee newsletters/newspapers) distributed by organizations lend support to the notion that they are often designed to encourage organizational identification. Specifically, studies examining the characteristics of employee newsletters/newspapers suggest that these publications inspire workers to identify with their respective organizations through two closely interrelated methods: (1) strategic selection of content to be published, and (2) utilization of a variety of rhetorical tactics in presenting content.

With respect to the content of employee publications, most surveys and content analyses of "house organs" indicate that they heavily reflect their respective management's philosophies, are typically mailed directly to employees' homes so that family members can share company news, contain numerous photographs of employees, and devote the majority of their stories to topics concerning employee and department/division recognition and general company news such as new benefits and policies, forthcoming projects, and the financial status of the organization (e.g., Axley, 1983; Clampitt, Crevcoure, & Hartel, 1986). According to Cheney (1983a), content of this type, combined with a variety of rhetorical tactics in writing related stories (e.g., McMillian, 1982) fosters organizational identification through one of three basic strategies: (1) the "common ground" technique, which focuses on the close association between the employee and the organization (for example, stories stress the notion that people "belong to the organization rather than on the organization as a collection of people" (p. 150) and include testimonials by employees "expressing dedication, commitment, even affection with regard to the organization" (p. 152); (2) identification through antithesis (disassociation) in which employees are encouraged to unite against a common enemy; (3) frequent use of an assumed or transcendent "we" in stories (essentially a form of strategic ambiguity; Eisenberg, 1984); and (4) utilization of "unifying symbols" such as logos and trademarks in publications. In short, house organs are one means by "which the formal organization presents its interests as the interests of the employee member" Cheney (1983a, p. 156).

During this phase of assimilation newcomers also begin to develop schemas for distinguishing the relative importance of the various written memoranda and notices they receive from "upper" management. While the manner in which newcomers acquire this skill has yet to be explored by researchers, it does seem apparent that employees are socialized to attend to certain "cues" in the written messages they receive. For example, Harvey and Boettger (1971) report that managers attend more carefully to memos they receive from their superiors than from other sources, while studies by Langer and her colleagues on "mindlessness" and attentional processes suggest that the structural properties of memos can affect the extent to which individuals attend to the semantic communication contained within them (Langer, 1978; Langer, Blank, & Chanowitz, 1978). Clearly, the processes by which newcomers are socialized to consume some of the messages they receive from management sources in "mindful" versus "mindless" states should be a focus of future research. Relatedly, future studies should consider how the characteristics of the written messages newcomers send to others in the organization change as employees move through the metamorphosis period. For example, it seems likely that as newcomers become assimilated into their organizations their written messages should become briefer, since "insider" terms, organizational vernacular, and "taken for granted" assumptions (Hopper, 1981) will be used for what earlier might have required elaborate explication (e.g., Daft & Lengel, 1984; Pfeffer, 1981a).

In summary, as in the encounter stage of assimilation, during the metamorphosis phase management-newcomer communication tends to be one-way and written in form, ambient, and frequently directed at informing employees about various elements of their organization's operations and culture. However, many of these communiques also serve the additional, often implicit function of reinforcing workers' feelings of organizational identification. On the other hand, it also seems apparent that as newcomers become assimilated within their organizations many messages they receive from management are unattended, which may diminish the effectiveness of these communications.

Supervisor. While during the encounter stage of assimilation interactions between a newcomer and his or her immediate superior focus on exploring initial work, organizational, and personal role expectations, during the metamorphosis period members of the dyad begin the process of testing, negotiating, and defining the nature of their communication relationship (Graen, 1976; Jablin, 1982). In particular, studies by Graen and his colleagues (Cashman, Dansereau, Graen, & Haga, 1976; Dansereau, Graen, & Haga, 1975; Graen & Cashman, 1975; Graen, Cashman, Ginsburgh, & Schiemann, 1977; Graen & Ginsburgh, 1977; Graen et al., 1973; Haga, Graen, & Dansereau, 1974) suggest that newcomers develop one of two basic types of communication relationships or exchanges with their superiors: (1) leadership or (2) supervision. Leadership exchanges, in contrast to supervision exchanges, have been found to be characterized by higher amounts of trust, attention/concern, influence, inside information, confidence, and negotiating latitude from the superior, as well as greater involvement by the subordinate in workgroup communication and administration activities. Or, as Dansereau et al. (1975, p. 73) propose, "The key distinction between leadership and supervision in the organization is in the way in which a superior uses his [or her] formal authority. In supervision, a superior uses his [or her] authority to force the member to comply with some prescribed role." Thus it appears that supervision exchanges are typified by fairly "closed" superior-subordinate communication relationships whereas leadership exchanges are characterized by "open" climates of communication (e.g., Jablin, 1979).

In addition, findings from the Graen et al. studies indicate that newcomers who experience leadership exchanges with their supervisors tend to be more successful in individualizing their work roles than newcomers who develop supervision exchanges (e.g., Dansereau et al., 1975). However, results of these investigations also suggest that the success of a subordinate's individualization efforts may be moderated by the type of exchange the subordinate's boss has with his or her superior (essentially a variant of the "Pelz Effect"; see Pelz, 1952; Jablin, 1980a). Specifically, regardless of the quality of their relationships with their immediate supervisors, it seems evident that newcomers reporting to superiors who do not have leadership exchanges with their boses complain of resistance, unresponsiveness, and inertia in their attempts to make desired changes (Cashman et al., 1976; Graen et al., 1977).

Though findings from Graen et al.'s research on the development of superior-subordinate relationships have greatly increased our knowledge of the types of communication exchanges that evolve between members of the dyad, these studies provide limited information concerning how and why particular interaction patterns emerge. In other words, we have little understanding of what initial communication behaviors and attitudes lead newcomers and their superiors to develop leadership or supervision exchanges. In turn, the potential effects of newcomers' prior superior-subordinate communication relationships and of their initial expectations of their relationships with their new superiors on the type of communication exchange that develops during the metamorphosis period have not been explored. Further, while the work of Graen and his colleagues places heavy emphasis on the importance of negotiating latitude in leadership exchanges, to date no research has explored exactly how from a communicative perspective newcomers negotiate their roles with their bosses. For example, it might be productive if studies were initiated exploring the message strategies newcomers use in their upward influence attempts during the role negotiation process (e.g., Kipnis, Schmidt, & Wilkinson, 1980; Krone, 1985; Porter, Allen, & Angle, 1981; Schilit & Locke, 1982). On the other hand, since other studies suggest that as newcomers become assimilated into their organizations they become less active in seeking feedback from their superiors and others (e.g., Ashford, 1986; Ashford & Cummings, 1985), the issue of whether or not this tendency is moderated by the type of exchange that evolves between subordinate and superior needs to be considered.

In addition, it seems imperative that we begin to examine the implicit assumption of most research that superior-subordinate communication relationships, once formed, are somehow fixed. The possibility that over the course of metamorphosis exchange patterns may change needs to be considered. In particular, studies might examine the types of interpersonal actions (for example, violations of constitutive and regulative communication rules) that cause a superior-subordinate relationship to shift toward a new level of exchange. By contrast, if the level of exchange in superior-subordinate communication is found to be a stable phenomenon, the question of "how to ensure that the stabilized interpersonal contract remains appropriate given changes that subsequently occur in the task, the business's environment, or individual aspirations and needs" requires investigation (Gabarro, 1979, p. 22).

In summary, interactions between newcomers and their immediate superiors during the metamorphosis period appear to focus on negotiating the nature of their communication relationships. However, as the above discussion indicates, at present we have only a limited understanding of (1) how and why particular types of communication exchange patterns develop, and (2) the communication processes associated with superior-subordinate role negotiations. In addition, it seems apparent that most studies have focused on the exchange of discretionary messages within the superior-subordinate dyad and have not considered the effects of a superior's communication with his or her workgroup as a whole (i.e., ambient communication) on the development of individual superior-subordinate exchange patterns. In other words, our understanding of the types of interaction patterns that develop between newcomers and their superiors during the metamorphosis period would profit by examining (1) the nature of the discretionary messages at the content and relational levels (e.g., Jablin, 1978) exchanged between newcomers and their superiors, (2) the nature of a superior's group-directed (ambient) communication, and (3) potential effects of the interaction of discretionary and ambient message forms on the development of leader-subordinate relationships (e.g., Schriesheim, 1980).

Workgroup/coworkers. As noted earlier, during the encounter phase coworkers' interactions with newcomers serve a variety of functions. Similar communication functions are also served during the metamorphosis period, but to differing degrees. For example, coworker interactions will likely perform less of an informational/sense-making function as an employee's tenure in an organization and workgroup increases (Katz, 1980). As Jablin (1982, p. 273) suggests, it seems reasonable to expect that "once a recruit obtains a basic perspective for interpreting the work environment, he or she may become less reliant on the group (an external source) for the construction of events and shift to more personal (internal) explanations." Jablin's (1984) analysis of the communication logs of nursing assistants during their third and ninth weeks of work provides indirect support for this notion in that results revealed a trend showing that over time recruits perceived their interactions with coworkers as less valuable, interesting, and satisfying.

Not only might we expect newcomers during the metamorphosis period to become less dependent on coworkers for interpretatons of their work environments but also to become more oriented to sharing their own interpretations of organizational reality with their coworkers. In other words, it is likely that as newcomers become more aware of their work environments they will increasingly give information and feedback to their coworkers rather than seek information and feedback from them. Initial support for this proposal is found in the results of two recent studies. In the first of these investigations, Ashford and Cummings (1985) discovered that as tenure within an organization increases employees seek feedback less from their coworkers and supervisors. On the other hand, Jablin's (1984) investigation of the organizational assimilation of nursing assistants revealed that the frequency with which newcomers were giving information or instructions to coworkers increased over 20% between their third and ninth weeks of work. Future research should explore whether or not such changes in communication behavior apply to all content areas/topics that typify newcomers' interactions with coworkers as well as various forms of coworker relationships (e.g., Jablin & Sussman, 1983).

In turn, the tendency of newcomers during the metamorphosis stage to increasingly share their views of group and organizational activities with their peers may account for feelings frequently expressed among old-timers that newcomers pose a threat to group integrity (Ziller, 1965). As Mooreland and Levine (1982, p. 160) observe, "newcomers often have a fresh and relatively objective view of the group, which enthuses them to ask questions or express opinions that are unsettling to older members." As a consequence, it is not surprising that related research has shown that over time newcomers become increasingly involved in conflicts with coworkers and other groups with which they interact in their organizations (Graen et al., 1973). Further, as Feldman (1976, p. 986) reports, newcomers "who do not feel accepted by coworkers tend to get into more arguments with their peers, and generate more conflict than those workers who feel more comfortable socially."

Regardless of the degree to which newcomers are accepted by their coworkers, some degree of group redevelopment will occur to accommodate the needs of newcomers. As Wanous et al. (1984, p. 671) argue, "the groups joined are themselves changed during the assimilation process . . . the newcomer must take on a particular role, and the newcomer's role may necessitate some role changing on the part of established group members." Thus while we can expect newcomers to generally adapt their attitudes and behaviors to be consistent with those of their coworkers (e.g., Festinger, 1957; Newcomb, 1958), they will also change the groups they enter to better accommodate their individual needs (e.g., Fine, 1976; Ziller & Behringer, 1960). However, it is also likely that the degree to which groups will accommodate newcomers will be moderated by other group characteristics, including level of group cohesiveness, the length of time group members have worked together, and the frequency with which new members enter the group (e.g., Katz, 1980; Ziller, Behringer, & Jansen, 1961).

At present, while numerous studies have explored the manner in which groups attempt to influence and obtain conformity from newcomers (e.g., Hackman, 1976; Levine, 1980; Shaw, 1981), almost no research has investigated the particular communication strategies that newcomers use to negotiate their roles with their workgroups. However, it does seem likely that one means newcomers utilize to enhance their bargaining positions is to join existing informal group communication networks that, acting as coalitions, may possess considerable power and influence in their groups (e.g., Pfeffer, 1981b). As studies have shown, the presence of even one supporter for a "deviate" position can dramatically reduce conformity (e.g., Allen, 1975). The manner in which newcomers use other political tactics to influence their groups and how the presence of newcomers affects their groups' "pecking orders" represent fruitful areas for future study.

While almost no research exists exploring processes associated with the development of newcomers' group and organizational communication network roles (e.g., Jablin, 1980b), it seems likely that such factors as group task, job assignment, proximity to other workers, interpersonal attraction, group network centrality, and the like will influence the types of group-level networks (e.g., friendship, task networks) in which they become integrated (e.g., Jablin & Sussman, 1983). In particular, the extent to which newcomers conform to group norms may be greater in decentralized networks, since in these types of network configurations all group members can directly communicate with and exert pressure on the newcomer (Shaw, 1981). The influence of coworkers on newcomers may also be affected by the degree to which newcomers are integrated into organizational-level as compared to group-level networks and the degree to which newcomers receive conflicting, inconsistent messages among the networks in which they participate. In turn, we might expect that the greater the overlap between the membership in the organizational networks in which newcomers participate with the membership of the networks in which newcomers are involved external to the organization, the less difficulty they will experience with role conflict during the metamorphosis period (e.g., Feldman, 1976).

Finally, it seems reasonable to hypothesize that as newcomers progress through the metamorphosis period the ambient messages they receive from coworkers about their tasks and work environments will have less of an effect on newcomers' job and task attitudes than these messages did during the encounter stage. Along these lines, Vance and Biddle (1985), in a laboratory study exploring the interactive effects of task experience and coworker generated social cues on job-related attitudes, found that as workers gained experience in their tasks relative to receiving social information, social cues had less impact on job-related attitudes. In interpreting their findings the researchers suggest that social cues may have a large impact on task-related attitudes early in work experience "because they interfere with (or short-circuit) the experience-based attitude formation process by providing an alternative source of task information" (Vance & Biddle, 1985, p. 263). However, given that the task involved in this experiment was relatively short in duration (about 30 minutes), the generalizability of the results of this study to actual organizational settings may be suspect. Clearly, future studies of social information processing theory need to be of longer duration and involve more complex tasks if their results are going to be valid representations of attitude formation processes newcomers experience during organizational assimilation.

In summary, while only a handful of studies have explored newcomers' communication interactions with coworkers during the metamorphosis stage of assimilation, this period can be characterized as one in which newcomers become less dependent on their peers for information about and interpretations of their work environments. In fact, during this stage newcomers may increase the frequency with which they give information and feedback to their coworkers and decrease their efforts in seeking information from them. Additionally, newcomers may become involved in conflict with their peers in the process of negotiating their workgroup roles and becoming integrated into group-level communication networks. In brief, although newcomers will likely conform to most of the behavioral and attitudinal norms communicated to them by members of their workgroups, their mere presence will result in some form of redevelopment of group task roles and communication patterns.

Communication-Related Outcomes

In addition to the numerous noncommunication outcomes posited to result from the assimilation process (e.g., Feldman, 1981), a number of communication outcomes can be postulated, including newcomers' (1) feelings of organizational communication satisfaction, (2) perceptions of organizational communication climate, (3) degree of understanding and sharing in the communication culture of the organization, (4) participation in emergent organizational communication networks, and (5) levels of organizational communication competence (Jablin, 1982, 1985b). As the following discussion will reveal, some of these outcomes have received more research attention than others though none has been thoroughly examined within the context of the organizational assimilation process. In general, the order in which the outcomes are discussed below reflects the relative degree to which they have been investigated in previous research.

Communication satisfaction. As newcomers become assimilated into their organizations they will experience some form of affective response to their communication environments (e.g., Jablin, 1982). While our understanding of how and why newcomers arrive at these affective states is limited, two explanations are usually posited: (1) The communication predispositions or "needs" of workers are being satisfied to varying degrees (Downs, 1977; Hecht, 1978), and (2) job incumbents are cuing newcomers to those aspects of their communication environments in which they should and should not be satisfied (Salancik & Pfeffer, 1978). Currently, however, no research has directly compared the explanatory power of these two theories in relation to newcomers' emergent levels of communication satisfaction.

Although the specific "causes" of newcomers' varying levels of communication satisfaction await determination, a number of related generalizations concerning communication satisfaction and the assimilation process can tentatively be drawn from the literature. First, it seems quite evident that upon entry into organizations newcomers often have fairly inflated expectations of the degree to which they will be satisfied with their jobs and communication environments, and that their actual levels of satisfaction are much lower once they gain experience on the job (e.g., Jablin, 1984). Second, though the research of Graen and his colleagues has shown the same decreasing levels of satisfaction noted above, their studies also indicate that newcomers' success in negotiating their roles (developing leadership or supervision exchanges) to some extent moderates the magnitude of this attenuation in feelings (Cashman et al., 1976; Dansereau et al., 1975). In other words, a major factor that may contribute to newcomers' levels of satisfaction are their communication relationships with their superiors. As a consequence, studies exploring the development of newcomers' levels of communication satisfaction might benefit from closer scrutiny of the communication processes and variables that lead subordinates and superiors to develop particular types of exchange patterns. Third, it seems likely that the communication characteristics that are most potent in predicting newcomers' levels of communication satisfaction vary as they gain experience in their organizations and become less reliant on others for information. Consistent with this position, for example, are data from a study by Katz (1977) in which he discovered that over the first year of work the strength of association between feedback from superiors/subordinates and newcomers' levels of job satisfaction steadily decreased (from .40 to .22).

Communication climate. Based on theories of social informational influence (e.g., Ashforth, 1985; Deutsch & Gerard, 1955; Festinger, 1954; Salancik & Pfeffer, 1978), it is expected that newcomers' communication climate perceptions should over time converge to become similar to incumbents in their workgroups and organizations. Unfortunately, "little research exists exploring how perceptions of overall (or superior-subordinate, or peer) communication climates develop over time" (Jablin, 1985b, p. 637). In fact, at present our knowledge of this process is limited to one study, the results of which suggest that newcomers (nursing assistants) enter organizations with inflated communication climate expectations (for almost all dimensions of communication), that subsequent to their organizational encounters these perceptions are extremely deflated, and that perceptions plateau at this lower level for at least the first six months of employment (Jablin, 1984). While the results of this study provide some seminal information about the development of communication climate perceptions during the assimilation process, they do not, however, provide data concerning whether or not newcomers' climate perceptions converge to become similar to incumbents' perceptions. Clearly, if this issue is to be adequately explored future research will need to collect data from recruits and group incumbents prior to the entry of newcomers into workgroups. These data can then be compared to newcomers' and incumbents' subsequent communication climate perceptions to ascertain if newcomers' perceptions actually begin to conform to those of their peers.

Communication culture. In a general sense, all of the communication outcomes discussed in this section are closely related to one omnibus consequence of a newcomer's organizational assimilation: some degree of understanding and sharing in the communication culture of the organization. As relates to the assimilation process culture can be conceived of as the set of shared, taken-for-granted *assumptions* that underlie an organization's communication ideology. In other words, culture informs employees of organizational values, beliefs, and issues that are important and provides cues to the paradigms and decision premises that guide communication behavior and attitudes within the organization and its subunits (see Smircich & Calás, Chapter 8, in this volume). Thus from the organization's perspective the identification of newcomers with its communication culture serves as an implicit and powerful form of organizational control (e.g., Pfeffer, 1981a; Tompkins & Cheney, 1985), while for newcomers developing an understanding of their organization's communication culture is a requisite for determining successful strategies for individualizing their organizational roles.

Unfortunately, the processes by which newcomers "come to appreciate pivotal organizational values, role-related abilities and missions and interpretation schemes appropriate to the local culture [of organizations] have not been adequately explored" (Louis, 1980, p. 233). Two recent studies, however, suggest viable avenues for such research. In the first of these investigations, Brown (1985) used stories told by organizational members to explore how storytelling acts as a form of sense-making during the organizational assimilation process. Results of this interview study revealed that "as members moved through the socialization process, story-use changed to become more closely associated with organizational values and cultures" (Brown, 1985, p. 38). On the other hand, Stohl (1986), in an analysis of interviews with members of a small company, examined the role of memorable messages (messages capsulizing how one should behave) in the process of organizational socialization. Among other findings, her results suggest that when one is learning a new organizational culture, messages "about how things get done, what meanings may be ascribed to behavior, and actual evaluation by members of the culture are as important as information regarding how to behave"(Stohl, 1986, pp. 243-244). While these studies provide strong foundations for future research in this area, the generalizability of their findings are, however, limited by their static research designs and collection of retrospective data from respondents. Hopefully future studies exploring how newcomers share and learn to understand the communication cultures of their organizations will examine the process in a longitudinal fashion.

Communication network participation. As newcomers are assimilated into their organizations they will become not only "links" in various overlapping emergent communication networks but will also assume a variety of communication network roles (see Monge & Eisenberg, Chapter 10, in this volume). While to date no research has directly explored how newcomers join and assume various roles in organizational networks, related research showing that workers' levels of job satisfaction, job/work identification, group attitude uniformity, and in some cases organizational commitment are positively related to the degree to which they are integrated into their organizations' communication networks (Albrecht, 1979, 1984; Danowski, 1980; Eisenberg, Monge, & Miller, 1983; McLaughlin & Cheatham, 1977; Roberts & O'Reilly, 1979) suggests that the degree to which newcomers eventually become connected to their organizations' communication systems may represent one index of how "effectively" they have been assimilated (Jablin, 1985b). Future research should explore this possibility, as well as the notion that persons who eventually assume "linker" roles (liaisons, bridges) may be more effectively assimilated into their organizations than individuals who become "isolates" in networks (perhaps with the exception of "weak ties"; see Granovetter, 1973).

Future investigations in this area might also build on the findings of other recent network studies, and in particular the notions that (1) supervisors who are liaisons in networks may serve as "network builders" for newcomers (Katz & Tushman, 1983); (2) as an individual's tenure in an organization increases and as the number of positions that an individual occupies in an organization increases, the "radiality" (dispersion) of communication links within the organization for that individual increases (Lester & Willer, 1984); and (3) newcomers may be attracted to initiating network links with persons they perceive as high in work competence and status (Stohl, 1986; Tushman & Scanlan, 1981a, 1981b).

Communication competence. Since to some degree communication competence is context bound, a byproduct of the assimilation process will be the emergence within newcomers of varying degrees of organizational communication competence. While there are a wide variety of definitions of communication competence (e.g., Parks, 1985), in a general sense it can be thought of as "the ability to attain relevant interactive goals in specified social contexts using socially acceptable means and ways of speaking [or writing] that result in positive outcomes with significant others" (Stohl, 1983, p. 688). Though it is evident that individuals vary with respect to the degree to which they are competent organizational communicators (e.g., Monge, Bachman, Dillard, & Eisenberg, 1982), no research has yet considered communication competence as an important and relevant outcome of the assimilation process. As a consequence, it is recommended that future studies begin to explore what variables and processes lead some newcomers to become optimal organizational communicators, others to become satisfactory communicators, and still others to become only minimally competent communicators. In addition, consistent with Harris and Cronen's (1979) conceptualization of communication competence, investigators should probably explore the construct at two interrelated levels: *strategic* competence (accurate knowledge of organizational meanings or constitutive rules) and *tactical* competence (knowledge of regulative rules that guide cooperative interaction to bring about outcomes).

Summary. In this section a number of communication outcomes of the organizational assimilation process have been proposed. In considering these consequences the reader is cautioned to remain cognizant of the dynamic nature of these outcome variables; rather than remain stable over time, shifts will occur in their corresponding levels as individuals are perennially being assimilated into their organizations.

ORGANIZATIONAL EXIT

Although people exit jobs and organizations just as frequently as they enter them, the investigation of communication processes associated with job/organizational disengagement (in comparison to entry processes) have been fairly infrequent objects of study. While there are numerous reasons why communication scholars have been remiss in studying organizational disengagement processes, two explanations are prominent. First, generally speaking, organizational communication researchers have historically focused on demonstrating relationships between communication and job/organizational satisfaction and performance, to the neglect of other "outcome" variables. Second, and perhaps more important, communication processes associated with organizational exit are often difficult to interpret because at once they may be causal antecedents of employee turnover *and* symptomatic manifestations of other problems and activities. For instance, certain types of communication behaviors that often precede employee turnover (for example, curtailing communication contacts) may be caused by an individual's dissatisfaction with his or her work relationships, or may be a symptom of another work-related problem and/or represent correlates of organizational "leave-taking." Thus, while communication-related problems at work may be a cause of employee turnover, they may also be (1) illustrative of what Hirschman (1970) describes as an alternative to organizational exit—"voice" (efforts at confronting the organization), or (2) exemplify communication correlates of organizational withdrawal/disengagement.

Since to a considerable degree voice-associated communication behaviors are manifestations of employees' individualization efforts, this section will focus on elucidating relationships between communication as an antecedent of turnover and as a symptom of organizational withdrawal. A number of communication-related consequences of turnover will also be proposed. This discussion will be organized around the preliminary model of communication and turnover processes depicted in Figure 19.3. In considering this model it is important to realize that (1) communication problems, dissatisfactions, and so forth typically are not the sole reasons for employee turnover, but represent just one of a host of factors (e.g., Bluedorn, 1982; Mobley, Griffeth, Hand & Meglino, 1979; Mowday, Porter & Steers, 1982; Muchinsky & Tuttle, 1979; Price, 1977); (2) not all of the causal variables suggested in the model have been thoroughly investigated (that is, the model should be viewed in a tentative manner); and (3) the model is intended to represent the nature of communication in the *voluntary* turnover process and may not be applicable to other forms of turnover (e.g., Bluedorn, 1978).

Communication as an
Antecedent of Turnover

As indicated in Figure 19.3 and consistent with most recent conceptualizations of the turnover process (e.g., Mowday et al., 1982), communication factors are considered to be antecedents of employees' affective responses to the work environment (particularly job/communication satisfaction and organizational commitment), which subsequently are posited to be directly related to intentions to terminate employment. In turn, intentions to leave have been shown to be strongly predictive of actual turnover (e.g., Mowday et al., 1982). Given the preliminary nature of the model, and the limited amount of research exploring many of the variables within it, no direct causal links between specific communication variables and turnover are proposed. Research relevant to each communication factor in Figure 19.3 is reviewed briefly below.

Organizationwide communication. Earlier, in the analysis of organization/management communication during the metamorphosis period of assimilation, it was suggested that an important function of these messages

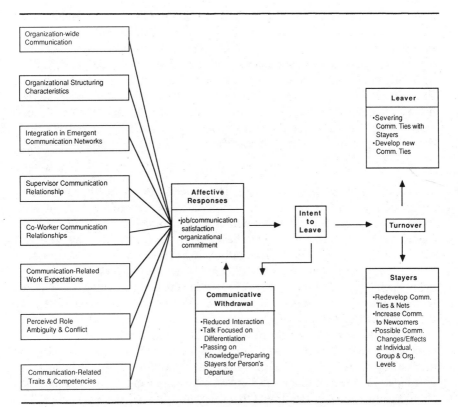

Figure 19.3 Communication and Turnover: A Preliminary Model

(particularly as communicated through house organs) is to reinforce employees' feelings of organizational identification. While no research to date has directly explored this relationship or the effects of organizationwide (oral and written) communication on employees' feelings of organizational commitment and turnover, relationships among these variables seem plausible. Specifically, it seems reasonable to expect that the more organizationwide communication reinforces employees' feelings of organizational identification the greater will be their commitment and the lower their turnover. Some tentative support for this position is available in the results of a recent study by Cheney (1983b), in which he found that (1) employees' levels of organizational identification were positively associated with company communication orientation, and (2) employees' general feelings of organizational identification were negatively related to job search activity.

Structuring characteristics. Extant research also supports the notion that organizational formalization (codification of work-related rules and procedures) is positively associated with organizational commitment and related attitudes (Bluedorn, 1980; Morris & Steers, 1980). On the other hand, with respect to centralization of authority, research findings are inconsistent; several studies have reported negative associations between centralization and organizational commitment (Morris & Steers, 1980; Rhodes & Steers, 1981), while other studies have uncovered no relationships (Bluedorn, 1980; Stevens, Beyer, & Trice, 1978). In essence, while organizational structuring characteristics appear related to employees' affective responses to their work environments, the strength of these relationships is quite variable, suggesting that their influence on commitment may be moderated by other factors (e.g., Stevens et al., 1978).

Network integration. Although it is frequently proposed that increased integration within *organizational* communication networks is positively related to organizational commitment (e.g., Buchanan, 1974; Kanter, 1968; Salancik, 1977), only one study has *directly* explored this hypothesis. Moreover, the results of this investigation did not reveal a simple relationship between involvement in work-related communication networks and commitment. Specifically, Eisenberg et al. (1983) discovered that employees who were highly connected in task-related networks and who were also *un*involved in their jobs (little psychological identification with the work) were more committed than workers who were moderately job involved (regardless of level of network connectedness). Thus it appears that for employees who are uninvolved in their jobs "affiliation and other relational needs may be met via participation in communication networks at work, and this alone may be enough to encourage commitment to the organization" (Eisenberg et al., 1983, p. 193). Future research should replicate this finding and attempt to determine other variables that may moderate relationships between network involvement and organizational commitment. Such studies might also explore the notion that the more employees are integrated into intra- as compared to extra-organizational networks, the greater their organizational commitment and the lower their turnover propensity (Katz & Tushman, 1983).

Supervisory communication. A considerable amount of research supports the position that the superior-subordinate communication relationship is an important determinant of an employee's level of organizational commitment and likelihood of turnover. In particular, studies indicate that the frequency with which superiors and subordinates communicate (Dansereau et al., 1975; Graen & Ginsburgh, 1977; Graen et al., 1973; Katz & Tushman, 1983; Krackhardt, McKenna, Porter, & Steers, 1981; Louis et al., 1983) and the extent to which supervisors provide feedback to subordinates are negatively related to employee turnover (Dansereau, Cashman, & Graen, 1973; Parsons, Herold, & Leatherwood, 1985; Wells & Muchinsky, 1985). While there are some exceptions (e.g., Vecchio, 1985), research exploring the types of exchange patterns that subordinates develop with their supervisors suggests that employees who report "leadership" as compared to "supervision" exchanges with their bosses tend to have lower turnover rates and higher levels of job satisfaction (Ferris, 1985; Graen, Liden, & Hoel, 1982; Katerberg & Hom, 1981; Liden & Graen, 1980).

On the other hand, it should be noted that findings from several investigations indicate that increases in supervisory initiating structure may be positively associated with employees' levels of organization commitment (Brief, Aldag, & Wallden, 1976; Morris & Sherman, 1981). While at first this relationship may appear inconsistent with the results of studies reported above, this is not necessarily the case. As Mowday et al. (1982, p. 59) suggest, when leader initiating structure involves clarifying job expectations and task goals such behaviors can increase employees' felt responsibility and commitment. In addition, as argued earlier, high levels of initiating structure may be perceived in a positive fashion by new employees but not by more tenured workers. In summary, the quality of an employee's communication relationship with his or her superior appears to be consistently and often strongly related to commitment and turnover.

Coworker communication. While studies examining relationships between coworker relations and turnover propensity have usually produced nonsignificant results (Mobley et al., 1979), research exploring relationships between levels of coworker interaction and organizational commitment have generally shown positive associations (e.g., Buchanan, 1974; Louis et al., 1983; Rotondi, 1975; Sheldon, 1971). In addition, as discussed earlier, investigations examining the impact of coworker-generated social information on employees' attitudes suggests that coworkers' attitudes can rub off on one another (e.g., White & Mitchell, 1979). As a consequence, while the nature of an employee's communication relationships with coworkers may not directly impact his or her turnover propensity, these relationships likely impact his or her affective responses to the work environment, which in turn are associated with intent to leave.

Communication expectations. Although there are some exceptions (see Mobley et al., 1979), findings from most investigations of the "met expectations" hypothesis have been fairly supportive of its validity (e.g., Cotton & Tuttle, 1986; Muchinsky & Tuttle, 1979; Porter & Steers, 1973). Essentially, this hypothesis proposes that "when an individual's expectations—whatever they are—are not substantially met, his [or her] propensity to withdraw [will] increase" (Porter & Steers, 1973, p. 152). As relates to communication, several studies have explored whether or not employees who leave their organizations and those who stay differ in their initial expectations of the communication climates of their organizations (Jablin, 1984; Wilson, 1983). In this regard, Jablin (1984) found that the communication climate expectations of nursing assistants who remained in their new jobs were consistently lower than those of newcomers who voluntarily terminated their employment. In addition, his results revealed that newcomers who quit their jobs had more positive perceptions of the communication climate of their last jobs than did recruits who remained on the job, suggesting that "job withdrawers' exaggerated perceptions of their jobs may have served to inflate their expectations of the communication climates of their new organizations" (Jablin, 1984, p. 621).

Role ambiguity and conflict. Several studies have suggested that high levels of role conflict and role ambiguity may retard newcomers' assimilation into organizations and are negatively associated with organizational commitment and related work attitudes (Ashford & Cummings, 1985; Bluedorn, 1980; Kemery, Bedeian, Mossholder, & Touliatos, 1985; Lyons, 1971; Morris & Koch, 1979; Morris & Sherman, 1981; Stevens et al., 1978). Similarly, a recent meta-analysis of the turnover literature by Cotton and Tuttle (1986) lends support to the notion that role clarity is negatively related to turnover.

Communication traits and competencies. While a wide variety of communication-related traits have been suggested as moderators of newcomers' abilities to adapt successfully to their organizations (e.g., Jablin, 1982), almost no research exists testing these propositions. Among the individual difference factors most relevant to newcomers' organizational assimilation and related affective responses to their work environment are attributional tendencies, self-perceptions of locus of control, self-efficacy, predispositions toward high or low self-monitoring, cognitive complexity, communication apprehension, and tolerance for ambiguity (e.g., Ashford & Cummings, 1983, 1985; Jablin, 1982; Jones, 1983, 1986). In addition, it would seem likely that the degree to which newcomers master their communication environments—that is, become competent organizational communicators—would facilitate their ability to satisfy their needs and thereby have an impact on their affective responses to their jobs/organizations.

Summary. In this section a number of communication-related variables have been postulated to be indirect causal antecedents of voluntary turnover. As should be clear to the reader by this point, research exploring the role of communication variables as causal factors in the turnover process is still in its infancy. In particular, our understanding of the nature of the interrelationships between communication antecedents of turnover, and how these variables interact with other elements of the turnover process are essentially non-existent. It is hoped that future research will begin to explore these issues.

Communication Correlates of Withdrawal

As suggested in Figure 19.3, as employees' affective responses to their jobs/organizations become more negative and their intent to leave increases, they will typically exhibit various withdrawal behaviors (e.g., Beehr & Gupta, 1978). Basically, "withdrawal" refers "to a variety of behaviors that are intended to place physical and psychological distance between employees and aversive work environments" (Rosse & Hulin, 1985, p. 325). To date most research has focused on two basic manifestations of withdrawal, absenteeism (e.g., Steers & Rhodes, 1978) and lateness (e.g., Adler & Golan, 1981). Although it has been an infrequent object of study, numerous communication-related behaviors are also likely correlates of the withdrawal process and warrant investigation.

At present only two studies have either directly or indirectly explored possible communication correlates of withdrawal. In the first of these inquiries, Wilson (1983), in an interview study, reports that as individuals disengage from organizations their talk initially reflects a differentiation of self from others, followed by a circumscription of communication activities, which subsequently leads to a period emphasizing concern for the future of the organization and its members. On the other hand, in a more indirect exploration of communication correlates of withdrawal, Rosse and Hulin (1985) discovered that dissatisfied workers tend to engage in "avoidance" behaviors as a form of withdrawal. However, it should be noted that their avoidance measure included communication- and non-communication-related items.

Building on the above studies and related research exploring leave-taking processes in interpersonal relationships (e.g., Duck, 1985; Knapp, 1978), a number of communication correlates of withdrawal can be postulated. First, it seems likely that in the initial stages of the withdrawal process employees will increasingly avoid communication with others; that is, they will reduce the rates at which they initiate interactions with others, the variety of topics they discuss, and the degree to which they are integrated into organizational communication networks. Concomitantly, when they do interact with others their talk will likely emphasize differences or distinctions between themselves and other organizational members. Moreover, such differentiation-focused talk will later probably serve a useful purpose for "stayers," since it may provide them with data they can use in making attributions to explain their colleague's departure and thereby reduce the dissonance they may experience by remaining in their jobs/organizations (e.g., Steers & Mowday, 1981). In turn, it seems reasonable to expect that the final stage of withdrawal communication will focus on the leaver's preparing fellow employees for his or her departure from the organization. In particular, talk will emphasize a concern for the welfare of remaining members, the passing on of important job/organization knowledge to others, and attempts at recruiting stayers to replace (at least temporarily) the leaver in critical task-related communication networks. In addition, as Figure 19.3 indicates, it seems likely that a reverse causality cycle will exist between communication-related withdrawal behaviors and feelings about work, since each stage of withdrawal should influence ensuing affective responses, which in turn will influence subsequent behaviors, and so on (Rosse & Hulin, 1985).

In summary, although to date almost no research exists exploring communication correlates of withdrawal, the value of identifying such behaviors should not be underestimated. Given that supervisors in organizations have been shown to be relatively unaware of which of their subordinates are likely to leave their jobs (Parsons et al., 1985), identification of the communication correlates of withdrawal might provide supervisors with behavioral cues to use in recognizing employees who are moving toward turnover and allow them to intervene to ameliorate sources of dissatisfaction before it's too late.

Communication Consequences of Turnover

The final elements in Figure 3 depict possible communication consequences of the turnover process for the person leaving the organization and for those remaining. As with other aspects of the nature and functions of communication in the turnover process, little empirical research has directly explored the communication consequences of turnover. However, a number of propositions have been suggested in the literature and are worthy of review. First, at the individual level of analysis, turnover may affect the communication behaviors and attitudes of the leaver's coworkers and supervisor. For example, if the leaver was a close communication tie of an employee, the loss of this link in the employee's communication network(s) may impact his or her ability to obtain and send information, as well as his or her affective responses to the organization (e.g., Krackhardt & Porter, 1985; 1986). For a supervisor, the exit of a subordinate (especially a high performer) may require him or her to make changes in his or her supervisory communication behaviors, particularly if communication problems existed in the leaver-supervisor relationship.

On the other hand, at the workgroup level high turnover may require members to spend more of their time communicating group norms and values to newcomers, and/or lead the group to increase the structure of their communication relationships to compensate for the loss of "informal understandings" that previously existed among group members (Bluedorn, 1982). In contrast, if the group member leaving was a communication isolate or deviate, group cohesiveness may increase and internal group conflict decrease as a result of the individual's exit (Mowday et al., 1982).

Turnover can also have several major communication consequences at the organizational level of analysis. The instability associated with high levels of turnover may lead the organization to increase its centralization of authority and extent of formalization (Price, 1977). As Pfeffer (1983, p. 333) observes, "a work force with shorter average tenure in the organization has less routinized behavioral and communication patterns, requiring more formalized coordination and communication structures to ensure effective control." Further, high levels of turnover may result in very active informal organizational communication networks and grapevine communication. Moreover, since turnover often results in missing links in communication networks, message flows within networks will likely "detour" around vacant links, adding linkages to networks and increasing information loss or distortion in transmission (Bluedorn, 1982).

Finally, it should be realized that the person leaving will also experience some communication consequences. Paramount among these consequences is that it will be necessary for the leaver to develop a whole new set of communication relationships and network ties at his or her new job and organization. In addition, it is likely that the leaver will either desire to or be compelled to break his or her communication ties with previous coworkers. According to Steers and Mowday (1981), this is likely to occur under one of two conditions. First, communication contacts will probably be severed in situations where the leaver was satisfied with the job/ organization that he or she left, since interaction with previous coworkers may create dissonance for the leaver about his or her choice to leave. Conversely, in situations where the leaver wishes to maintain communication contacts with former coworkers, his or her previous colleagues may not want to engage in communication since receipt of information about an attractive alternative (the leaver's new job) may cause them to experience dissatisfaction about their jobs. In summary, while the propositions and related model reviewed in this section make intuitive sense, their validity awaits to be determined by empirical research.

CONCLUDING STATEMENT

This chapter has attempted to present an integrated and heuristic discussion of the nature, functions, and effects of communication in the organizational entry, assimilation, and exit process. In considering this analysis, however, the reader should realize that this discussion has focused on reviewing the nature of the organizational entry, assimilation, and exit process through only one cycle, and that most individuals will experience the process numerous times in their work careers. As a consequence, the knowledge, skills, and experiences they collect through any one cycle will incrementally become a part of their anticipatory socialization for subsequent cycles. Essentially, the perspective presented in this chapter reiterates the often expressed notion that regardless of level of analysis, one of the keys to understanding communication processes and behaviors in organizations is to recognize their *developmental* nature.

REFERENCES

Adler, S., & Golan, J. (1981). Lateness as a withdrawal behavior. *Journal of Applied Psychology, 66*, 544-554.

Albrecht, T. L. (1979). The role of communication in perceptions of organizational climate. In D. Nimmo (Ed.), *Communication yearbook 3* (pp. 343-357). New Brunswick, NJ: Transaction.

Albrecht, T. L. (1984). Managerial communication and work perception. In R. N. Bostrom (Ed.), *Communication yearbook 8* (pp. 538-557). Newbury Park, CA: Sage.

Alderfer, C. P., & McCord, C. G. (1970). Personal and situational factors in the recruitment interview. *Journal of Applied Psychology, 54,* 377-385.

Allen, V. L. (1975). Social support for nonconformity. In L. Berkowitz (Ed.), *Advances in experimental social psychology* (Vol. 8, pp. 1-43). New York: Academic Press.

Arvey, R. D., & Campion, J. E. (1982). The employment interview: A summary and review of recent research. *Personnel Psychology, 35,* 281-322.

Ashford, S. J. (1986). Feedback-seeking in individual adaptation: A resource perspective. *Academy of Management Journal, 29,* 465-487.

Ashford, S. J., & Cumming, L. L. (1983). Feedback as an individual resource: Personal strategies of creating information. *Organizational Behavior and Human Performance, 32,* 370-398.

Ashford, S. J., & Cummings, L. L. (1985). Proactive feedback seeking: The instrumental use of the information environment. *Journal of Occupational Psychology, 58,* 67-79.

Ashforth, B. E. (1985). Climate formation: Issues and extensions. *Academy of Management Review, 10,* 837-847.

Axley, S. R. (1983). *Managerial philosophy in organizational house organs: Two case studies.* Paper presented at the annual meeting of the International Communication Association, Dallas.

Babbitt, L. V., & Jablin, F. M. (1985). Characteristics of applicants' questions and employment screening interview outcomes. *Human Communication Research, 11,* 507-535.

Baird, L., & Kram, K. (1983, Spring). Career dynamics: Managing the superior/subordinate relationship. *Organizational Dynamics, 11,* 46-64.

Bandura, A. (1977). *Social learning theory.* Englewood Cliffs, NJ: Prentice-Hall.

Becker, H. S., Geer, B., Hughes, E. C., & Strauss, A. (1961). *Boys in white: Student culture in medical school.* Chicago: University of Chicago Press.

Beehr, T., & Gupta, N. (1978). A note on the structure of employee withdrawal. *Organizational Behavior and Human Performance, 21,* 73-79.

Berger, C. R., & Bradac, J. J. (1982). *Language and social knowledge: Uncertainty in interpersonal relationships.* London: Edward Arnold.

Berger, P., & Luckmann, T. (1967). *The social construction of reality.* Garden City, NY: Doubleday.

Berkowitz, K., & Howard, R. C. (1959). Reactions to opinion deviates as affected by affiliation need (*n*) and group member interdependence. *Sociometry, 22,* 81-91.

Berlew, D. E., & Hall, D. T. (1966). The socialization of managers: Effects of expectations on performance. *Administrative Science Quarterly, 11,* 207-233.

Bettenhausen, K., & Murnighan, J. K. (1985). The emergence of norms in competitive decision-making groups. *Administrative Science Quarterly, 30,* 350-372.

Beuf, A. (1974). Doctor, lawyer, household drudge. *Journal of Communication, 24,* 142-145.

Bluedorn, A. C. (1978). A taxonomy of turnover. *Academy of Management Review, 3,* 647-651.

Bluedorn, A. C. (1980). A unified model of turnover from organizations. In R. C. Huseman (Ed.), *Proceedings of the 40th annual meeting of the Academy of Management,* 268-272.

Bluedorn, A. C. (1982). The theories of turnover: Causes, effects, and meaning. In S. B. Bacharach (Ed.), *Research in the sociology of organizations* (Vol. 1, pp. 75-128). Greenwich, CT: JAI Press.

Blyth, D. A., Hill, J. P., & Thiel, K. S. (1982). Early adolescents' significant others: Grade and gender differences in perceived relationships with familial and nonfamilial adults and young people. *Journal of Youth and Adolescence, 11,* 425-450.

Bogatz, G. A., & Ball, S. J. (1971). *The second year of Sesame Street: A continuing evaluation.* Princeton, NJ: Educational Testing Service.

Boster, F. S., Wigand, R. T., & Collofello, P. M. (1984). *Mentoring, social interaction and commitment: An empirical analysis of a mentoring program.* Paper presented at the annual meeting of the International Communication Association, San Francisco.

Breaugh, J. A. (1981). Relationships between recruiting sources and employee performance, absenteeism, and work attitudes. *Academy of Management Journal, 24,* 142-147.

Breaugh, J. A. (1983). Realistic job previews: A critical appraisal and future research directions. *Academy of Management Review, 8,* 612-619.

Breaugh, J. A., & Mann, R. B. (1984). Recruiting source effects: A test of two alternative explanations. *Journal of Occupational Psychology, 57,* 261-267.

Brief, A. P., Aldag, R. J., & Wallden, R. A. (1976). Correlates of supervisory style among policemen. *Criminal Justice and Behavior, 3,* 263-271.

Brett, J. M. (1980). The effect of job transfer on employees and their families. In C. L. Cooper & R. Payne (Eds.), *Current concerns in occupational stress* (pp. 99-136). New York: John Wiley.

Brett, J. M. (1984). Job transitions and personal and role development. In K. M. Rowland & G. R. Ferris (Eds.), *Research in personnel and human resources management* (Vol. 2, pp. 155-185). Greenwich, CT: JAI Press.

Brown, D., Brooks, L., & Associates. (1984). *Career choice and development.* San Francisco: Jossey-Bass.

Brown, J. D. (1980). *Adolescent peer group communication, sex-role norms and decisions about occupations.* Paper presented at the annual meeting of the International Communication Association, Acapulco.

Brown, M. H. (1985). That reminds me of a story: Speech action in organizational socialization. *Western Journal of Speech Communication, 49,* 27-42.

Buchanan, B. (1974). Building organizational commitment: The socialization of managers in work organizations. *Administrative Science Quarterly, 19,* 533-546.

Bucher, R., & Stelling, J. G. (1977). *Becoming professional.* Newbury Park, CA: Sage.

Bureau of Labor Statistics. (1975). *Job tenure of workers, January, 1973* (Special Labor Rep. 172). Washington, DC: Bureau of Labor Statistics.

Bureau of National Affairs. (1980). *Job absence and turnover: 1979.* Washington, DC: Bureau of National Affairs.

Byrd, M.L.V. (1979). *The effects of vocal activity and race of applicant on the job selection interview decision.* Unpublished doctoral dissertation, University of Missouri, Columbia.

Caldwell, D. F., & O'Reilly, C. A. (1982). Task perceptions and job satisfaction: A question of causality. *Journal of Applied Psychology, 19,* 51-76.

Caldwell, D. F., & Spivey, W. A. (1983). The relationship between recruiting source and employee success: An analysis by race. *Personnel Psychology, 36,* 67-72.

Cashman, J., Dansereau, F., Graen, G., & Haga, W. J. (1976). Organizational understructure and leadership: A longitudinal investigation of the managerial role-making process. *Organizational Behavior and Human Performance, 15,* 278-296.

Cheatham, T. R., & McLaughlin, M. (1976). A comparison of co-participant perceptions of self and others in placement center interviews. *Communication Quarterly, 24(3),* 9-13.

Cheney, G. (1983a). The rhetoric of identification and the study of organizational communication. *Quarterly Journal of Speech, 69,* 143-158.

Cheney, G. (1983b). On the various and changing meanings of organizational membership: A field study of organizational identification. *Communication Monographs, 50,* 342-362.

Christenson, P. G., & Roberts, D. F. (1983). The role of television in the formation of children's social attitudes. In M.J.A. Howe (Ed.), *Learning from television: Psychological and educational research* (pp. 79-99). New York: Academic Press.

Clampitt, P. G., Crevcoure, J. M., & Hartel, R. L. (1986). Exploratory research on employee publications. *Journal of Business Communication, 23,* 5-17.

Colarelli, S. M. (1984). Methods of communication and mediating processes in realistic job previews. *Journal of Applied Psychology, 69,* 633-642.

Constantin, S. W. (1976). An investigation of information favorability in the employment interview. *Journal of Applied Psychology, 61,* 743-749.

Cotton, J. L., & Tuttle, J. M. (1986). Employee turnover: A meta-analysis and review with implications for research. *Academy of Management Review, 11,* 55-70.

Cowan, P. (1975). Establishing a communication chain: The development and distribution of an employee handbook. *Personnel Journal, 54,* 342-344, 349.

Crites, J. O. (1969). *Vocational psychology.* New York: McGraw-Hill.

Crossen, C. (1985, March 19). Kids of top executives are crazy about dad—especially his money. *Wall Street Journal,* Sec. 2, p. 33.

Crowe, B. J., Bochner, S., & Clark, A. W. (1972). The effects of subordinates' behavior on managerial style. *Human Relations, 25,* 215-237.

Csikszentmihalyi, M., & Larson, R. (1984). *Being adolescent: Conflict and growth in the teenage years.* New York: Basic Books.

Daft, R. L., & Lengel, R. H. (1984). Information richness: A new approach to managerial behavior and organization design. In B. M. Staw & L. L. Cummings (Eds.), *Research in organizational behavior* (Vol. 6, pp. 191-233). Greenwich, CT: JAI Press.

Dahle, T. L. (1953). *An experimental study of methods of communication in business.* Unpublished doctoral dissertation, Purdue University.

Daly, J. A. (1978). *The personnel selection interview: A state of the art review.* Paper presented at the annual meeting of the International Communication Association, Chicago.

Danet, B. (1981). Client-organization interfaces. In P. C. Nystrom & W. H. Starbuck (Eds.), *Handbook of organizational design* (Vol. 2, pp. 382-428). New York: Oxford University Press.

Daniels, T. D., & Logan, L. L. (1983). Communication in women's career development relationships. In R. N. Bostrom (Ed.), *Communication yearbook 7* (pp. 532-552). Newbury Park, CA: Sage.

Danowski, J. A. (1980). Group attitude-belief uniformity and connectivity of organizational communication networks for production, innovation, and maintenance content. *Human Communication Research, 6,* 299-308.

Dansereau, F., Cashman, J., & Graen, G. (1973). Instrumentality theory and equity theory as complementary approaches in predicting the relationship of leadership and turnover among managers. *Organizational Behavior and Human Performance, 10,* 184-200.

Dansereau, F., Graen, G., & Haga, W. J. (1975). A vertical dyad linkage approach to leadership within formal organizations: A longitudinal investigation of the role making process. *Organizational Behavior and Human Performance, 13,* 46-78.

Davis, K. (1968). Readability changes in employee handbooks of identical companies during a fifteen-year period. *Personnel Psychology, 21,* 413-420.

Dean, R. A., & Wanous, J. P. (1984). Effects of realistic job previews on hiring bank tellers. *Journal of Applied Psychology, 69,* 61-68.

Decker, P. J., & Cornelius, E. T. (1979). A note on recruiting sources and job survival rates. *Journal of Applied Psychology, 64,* 463-464.

DeFleur, L. B., & Menke, B. A. (1975). Learning about the labor force: Occupational knowledge among high school males. *Sociology of Education, 48,* 324-345.

DeFleur, M. L. (1964). Occupational roles as portrayed on television. *Public Opinion Quarterly, 28,* 57-74.

DeFleur, M. L., & DeFleur, L. B. (1967). The relative contribution of television as a learning source for children's occupational knowledge. *American Sociological Review, 32,* 777-789.

Deutsch, M., & Gerard, H. B. (1955). A study of normative and informational social influences upon individual judgment. *Journal of Abnormal and Social Psychology, 51,* 629-636.

DeWine, S., Casbolt, D., & Bentley, N. (1983). *Moving through the organization: A field study assessment of the patron system.* Paper presented at the annual meeting of the International Communication Association, Dallas.

Dominick, J. R. (1974). Children's viewing of crime shows and attitudes of law enforcement. *Journalism Quarterly, 51,* 5-12.

Dornbush, S. (1955). The military academy as an assimilating institution. *Social Forces, 33,* 316-321.

Downs, C. W. (1969). Perceptions of the selection interview. *Personnel Administration, 32,* 8-23.

Downs, C. W. (1977). The relationship between communication and job satisfaction. In R. C. Husemen, C. M. Logue, & D. L. Freshley (Eds.), *Readings in interpersonal and organizational communication* (3rd ed., pp. 363-375). Boston: Holbrook Press.

Driver, R. W. (1980). A determination of the relative efficacy of different techniques for employee benefit communication. *Journal of Business Communication, 17,* 23-37.

Duck, S. (1985). Social and personal relationships. In M. L. Knapp & G. R. Miller (Eds.), *Handbook of interpersonal communication* (pp. 655-686). Newbury Park, CA: Sage.

Dugoni, B. L., & Ilgen, D. R. (1981). Realistic job previews and the adjustment of new employees. *Academy of Management Journal, 24,* 579-591.

Dunnette, M. D., Avery, R., & Banas, P. (1973). Why do they leave? *Personnel, 50*(3), 25-39.

Eden, D., & Shani, A. B. (1982). Pygmalion goes to boot camp: Expectancy, leadership, and training performance. *Journal of Applied Psychology, 67,* 194-199.

Einhorn, L. J. (1981). An inner view of the job interview: An investigation of successful communicative behaviors. *Communication Education, 30,* 217-228.

Eisenberg, E. M. (1984). Ambiguity as strategy in organizational communication. *Communication Monographs, 51,* 227-242.

Eisenberg, D. M., Monge, P. R., & Miller, K. I. (1983). Involvement in communication networks as a predictor of organizational commitment. *Human Communication Research, 10,* 179-201.

Evan, W. M. (1963). Peer group interaction and organizational socialization. A study of employee turnover. *American Sociological Review, 28,* 436-440.

Faber, R. J., Brown, J. D., & McLeod, J. M. (1979). Coming of age in the global village: Television and adolescence. In E. Wartella (Ed.), *Children communicating* (pp. 215-249). Newbury Park, CA: Sage.

Feldman, D. C. (1976). A contingency theory of socialization. *Administrative Science Quarterly, 21,* 433-452.

Feldman, D. C. (1977). The role of initiation activities in socialization. *Human Relations, 30,* 977-990.

Feldman, D. C. (1981). The multiple socialization of organizational members. *Academy of Management Review, 6,* 309-318.

Feldman, D. C. (1984). The development and enforcement of group norms. *Academy of Management Review, 9,* 47-53.

Feldman, D. C., & Brett, J. M. (1983). Coping with new jobs: A comparative study of new job hires and job changers. *Academy of Management Journal, 26,* 258-272.

Ferris, G. R. (1985). Role of leadership in the employee withdrawal process: A constructive replication. *Journal of Applied Psychology, 70,* 777-781.

Festinger, L. (1954). A theory of social comparison processes. *Human Relations, 7,* 117-140.

Festinger, L. (1957). *A theory of cognitive dissonance.* Stanford, CA: Stanford University Press.

Fine, G. A. (1976). *The effects of a salient newcomer on a small group: A force field analysis.* Paper presented at the annual meeting of the American Psychological Association, Washington, DC.

Fisher, C. D., Ilgen, D. R., & Hoyer, W. D. (1979). Source of credibility, information, favorability, and job offer acceptance. *Academy of Management Journal, 22,* 94-103.

Forbes, R. J., & Jackson, P. R. (1980). Non-verbal behaviour and the outcome of selection interviews. *Journal of Occupational Psychology, 53,* 65-72.

Freiberg, K. L, & Hellweg, S. A. (1984). *A theoretical and methodological evaluation of organizational interviewing research from a communication perspective.* Paper presented at the annual meeting of the Academy of Management, Boston.

Freuh, T., & McGhee, P. E. (1975). Traditional sex-role development and amount of time spent watching television. *Developmental Psychology, 11,* 109.

Gabarro, J. (1979). Socialization at the top: How CEOs and subordinates evolve interpersonal contracts. *Organizational Dynamics, 7*(3), 2-23.

Gannon, M. J. (1971). Source of referral and employee turnover. *Journal of Applied Psychology, 55,* 226-228.

Goldstein, B., & Oldham, J. (1979). *Children and work: A study of socialization.* New Brunswick, NJ: Transaction.

Gomersall, E. R., & Myers, M. S. (1966). Breakthrough in on-the-job training. *Harvard Business Review, 44*(4), 62-72.

Goodall, D. B., & Goodall, H. L. (1982). The employment interview: A selective review of the literature with implications for communication research. *Communication Quarterly, 30,* 116-123.

Gorman, C. D., Clover, W. H., & Doherty, M. E. (1978). Can we learn anything about interviewing real people from "interviews" of paper people? Two studies of the external validity of a paradigm. *Organizational Behavior and Human Performance, 22,* 165-192.

Graen, G. (1976). Role-making processes within complex organizations. In M. D. Dunnette (Ed.), *Handbook of industrial and organizational psychology* (pp. 1201-1245). Chicago: Rand McNally.

Graen, G., & Cashman, J. F. (1975). A role making model of leadership in formal organizations: A developmental approach. In J. G. Hunt & L. L. Larson (Eds.), *Leadership frontiers* (pp. 143-165). Kent, OH: Kent State University Press.

Graen, G., Cashman, J. F., Ginsburgh, S., & Schiemann, W. (1977). Effects of linking-pin quality on the quality of working life of lower participants. *Administrative Science Quarterly, 22,* 491-504.

Graen, G., & Ginsburgh, S. (1977). Job resignation as a function of role orientation and leader acceptance: A longitudinal investigation of organizational assimilation. *Organizational Behavior and Human Performance, 19,* 1-17.

Graen, G., Liden, R., & Hoel, W. (1982). Role of leadership in the employee withdrawal process. *Journal of Applied Psychology, 67,* 868-872.

Graen, G. B., Orris, J. B., & Johnson, T. W. (1973). Role assimilation processes in a complex organization. *Journal of Vocational Behavior, 3,* 395-420.

Granovetter, M. S. (1973). The strength of weak ties. *American Journal of Sociology, 78,* 1360-1380.

Greenberg, B. S. (1982). Television and role socialization. In D. Pearl et al. (Eds.), *Television and behavior: Ten years of scientific progress and implications for the eighties* (Vol. 2, 179-180). Rockville, MD: Department of Health and Human Services.

Greenberger, E., Steinberg, L. D., Vaux, A., & McAuliffe, S. (1980). Adolescents who work: Effects of part-time employment on family and peer relations. *Journal of Youth and Adolescence, 9,* 189-202.

Greenberger, E., Steinberg, L. D., & Ruggiero, M. (1982). A job is a job is a job . . . or is it? *Work and Occupations, 9,* 79-96.

Greenhalgh, L., & Okun, R. L. (1984). *The realistic construction of job preview material.* Paper presented at the annual meeting of the Academy of Management, Boston.

Griffin, R. W. (1983). Objective and social sources of information in task design: A field experiment. *Administrative Science Quarterly, 28,* 184-200.

Hackman, J. R. (1976). Group influences on individuals. In M. D. Dunnette (Ed.), *Handbook of industrial and organizational psychology* (pp. 1455-1525). Chicago: Rand McNally.

Hackman, J. R., & Lawler, E. E. (1971). Employee reactions to job characteristics. *Journal of Applied Psychology Monograph, 55,* 259-286.

Haga, W. J., Graen, G., & Dansereau, F. (1974). Professionalism and role making in a service organization: A longitudinal investigation. *American Sociological Review, 39,* 122-133.

Haller, A., & Butterworth, C. E. (1960). Peer influences on levels of occupational and educational aspirations. *Social Forces, 38,* 389-395.

Harlan, A., Kerr, J., & Kerr, S. (1977). Preference for motivator and hygiene factors in a hypothetical interview situation: Further findings and some implications for the employment interview. *Personnel Psychology, 30,* 557-566.

Harris, L., & Cronen, V. E. (1979). A rules-based model for the analysis and evaluation of organizational communication. *Communication Quarterly, 27,* 12-28.

Harvey, J. B., & Boettger, C. R. (1971). Improving communication within a managerial workgroup. *Journal of Applied Behavioral Science, 7,* 164-179.

Hayes, J. (1969). Occupational choice and the perception of occupational roles. *Occupational Psychology, 43,* 15-22.

Hecht, M. L. (1978). The conceptualization and measurement of interpersonal communication satisfaction. *Human Communication Research, 3,* 253-264.

Herriot, P. (1984). *Down from the ivory tower: Graduates and their jobs.* Chichester, England: John Wiley.

Herriot, P., Ecob, R., & Hutchinson, M. (1980). Decision theory and occupational choice: Testing some modifications. *Journal of Occupational Psychology, 53,* 223-236.

Herriot, R., & Rothwell, C. (1981). Organizational choice and decision theory: Effects of employers' literature and selection interview. *Journal of Occupational Psychology, 54,* 17-31.

Herriot, R., & Rothwell, C. (1983). Expectations and impressions in the graduate selection interview. *Journal of Occupational Psychology, 56,* 303-314.

Hirschman, A. O. (1970). *Exit, voice and loyalty: Responses to decline in firms, organizations, and the state.* Cambridge, MA: Harvard University Press.

Hollander, E. P. (1958). Conformity, status, and idiosyncrasy credit. *Psychological Review, 65,* 117-127.

Hollander, E. P. (1960). Competence and conformity in the acceptance of influence. *Journal of Abnormal and Social Psychology, 61,* 365-369.

Hollandsworth, J. G., Kazelskis, R., Stevens, J., & Dressel, M. E. (1979). Relative contributions of verbal, articulative and nonverbal communication to employment interview decisions in the job interview setting. *Personnel Psychology, 32,* 359-367.

Holly, W. H., & Ingram, E. (1973). Communicating fringe benefits. *Personnel Administrator, 18,* 21-22.

Hopper, R. (1981). The taken-for-granted. *Human Communication Research, 7,* 195-211.

House, R. J. (1971). A path-goal theory of leader effectiveness. *Administrative Science Quarterly, 16,* 321-338.

Hughes, E. C. (1958). *Men and their work.* New York: Free Press.

Huseman, R. C., & Hatfield, J. D. (1978). Communicating employee benefits: Directions for future research. *Journal of Business Communication, 15,* 3-17.

Imada, A. S., & Hakel, M. D. (1977). Influence of nonverbal communication and rater proximity on impressions and decisions in simulated employment interviews. *Journal of Applied Psychology, 62,* 295-300.

Jablin, F. M. (1975). The selection interview: Contingency theory and beyond. *Human Resource Management, 14,* 2-9.

Jablin, F. M. (1978). Message-response and "openness" in superior-subordinate communication. In B. D. Ruben (Ed.), *Communication yearbook 2* (pp. 293-309). New Brunswick, NJ: Transaction.

Jablin, F. M. (1979). Superior-subordinate communication: The state of the art. *Psychological Bulletin, 86,* 1201-1222.

Jablin, F. M. (1980a). Superior's upward influence, satisfaction and openness in superior-subordinate communication: A reexamination of the "Pelz effect." *Human Communication Research, 6,* 210-220.

Jablin, F. M. (1980b). Organizational communication theory and research: An overview of communication climate and network research. In D. Nimmo (Ed.), *Communication yearbook 4* (pp. 327-347). New Brunswick, NJ: Transaction.

Jablin, F. M. (1982). Organizational communication: An assimilation approach. In M. E. Roloff & C. R. Berger (Eds.), *Social cognition and communication* (pp. 255-286). Newbury Park, CA: Sage.

Jablin, F. M. (1984). Assimilating new members into organizations. In R. N. Bostrom (Ed.), *Communication yearbook 8* (pp. 594-626). Newbury Park, CA: Sage.

Jablin, F. M. (1985a). An exploratory study of vocational organizational communication socialization. *Southern Speech Communication Journal, 50,* 261-282.

Jablin, F. M. (1985b). Task/work relationships: A life-span perspective. In M. L. Knapp & G. R. Miller (Eds.), *Handbook of interpersonal communication* (pp. 615-654). Newbury Park, CA: Sage.

Jablin, F. M., & Krone, K. J. (1984). Characteristics of rejection letters and their effects on job applicants. *Written Communication, 1,* 387-406.

Jablin, F. M., & Krone, K. J. (1987). Organizational assimilation. In C. R. Berger & S. H. Chaffee (Eds.), *Handbook of communication science* (pp. 711-746). Newbury Park, CA: Sage.

Jablin, F. M., & McComb, K. B. (1984). The employment screening interview: An organizational assimilation and communication perspective. In R. N. Bostrom (Ed.), *Communication yearbook 8* (pp. 137-163). Newbury Park, CA: Sage.

Jablin, F. M., & Sussman, L. (1983). Organizational group communication: A review of the literature and model of the process. In. H. H. Greenbaum, R. L. Falcione, & S. A. Hellweg (Eds.), *Organizational communication: Abstracts, analysis, and overview* (Vol. 8, pp. 11-50). Newbury Park, CA: Sage.

Jablin, F. M., Tengler, C. D., & Teigen, C. W. (1982). *Interviewee perceptions of employment screening interviews: Relationships among perceptions of communication satisfaction, interviewer credibility and trust, interviewing experience, and interview outcomes.* Paper presented at the annual meeting of the International Communication Association, Boston.

Jablin, F. M., Tengler, C. D., & Teigen, C. W. (1985). *Applicant perceptions of job incumbents and personnel representatives as communication sources in screening interviews.* Paper presented at the annual meeting of the Academy of Management, San Diego.

Jick, T. D., & Greenhalgh, L. (1981). *Information processing of new recruits in a declining organization.* Paper presented at the annual meeting of the Academy of Management, San Diego.

Jones, D. E. (1973). The employee handbook. *Personnel Journal, 52,* 136-141.

Jones, G. R. (1983). Psychological orientation and the process of organizational socialization: An interactionist perspective. *Academy of Management Review, 8,* 464-474.

Jones, G. R. (1986). Socialization tactics, self-efficacy, and newcomers' adjustments to organizations. *Academy of Management Journal, 29,* 262-279.

Jourard, S. (1971). *Self-disclosure: An experimental analysis of the transparent self.* New York: John Wiley.

Kahn, R. L., Wolfe, D. M., Quinn, R. P., Snoek, J. D., & Rosenthal, R. A. (1964). *Organizational stress: Studies in role conflict and ambiguity.* New York: John Wiley.

Kandel, D. B. (1978). Similarity in real-life adolescent friendship pairs. *Journal of Personality and Social Psychology, 36,* 306-312.

Kanter, R. M. (1968). Commitment and social organization: A study of commitment mechanisms in utopian communities. *American Sociological Review, 33,* 499-517.

Kanter, R. M. (1977). *Men and women of the corporation.* New York: Basic Books.

Karol, B. L. (1977). *Relationship of recruiter behavior, perceived similarity, and prior information to applicants' assessments of the campus recruitment interview.* Unpublished doctoral dissertation, Ohio State University.

Katerberg, R., & Hom, R. (1981). Effects of within-group and between-groups variation in leadership. *Journal of Applied Psychology, 66,* 218-223.

Katz, D., & Kahn, R. L. (1966). *The social psychology of organizations.* New York: John Wiley.

Katz, R. (1977). Job enrichment: Some career considerations. In J. Van Maanen (Ed.), *Organizational careers: Some new perspectives* (pp. 133-147). New York: John Wiley.

Katz, R. (1980). Time and work: Toward an integrative perspective. In B. M. Staw & L. L. Cummings (Eds.), *Research in organizational behavior* (Vol. 2, pp. 81-128). Greenwich, CT: JAI Press.

Katz, R. (1985). Organizational stress and early socialization experiences. In T. Beehr & R. Bhagat (Eds.), *Human stress and cognition in organization: An integrative perspective* (pp. 117-139). New York: John Wiley.

Katz, R., & Tushman, M. L. (1983). A longitudinal study of the effects of boundary spanning supervision on turnover and promotion in research and development. *Academy of Management Journal, 26,* 437-456.

Katzell, M. E. (1968). Expectations and dropouts in schools of nursing. *Journal of Applied Psychology, 52,* 154-157.

Katzman, N. (1972). Television soap operas: What's been going on anyway? *Public Opinion Quarterly, 36,* 200-212.

Keenan, A. (1976). Effects of non-verbal behavior of interviewers on candidates' performance. *Journal of Occupational Psychology, 49,* 171-176.

Keenan, A., & Wedderburn, A.A.I. (1975). Effects of non-verbal behaviour of interviewers on candidates' impressions. *Journal of Occupational Psychology, 48,* 129-132.

Keenan, A., & Wedderburn, A.A.I. (1980). Putting the boot on the other foot: Candidates descriptions of interviewers. *Journal of Occupational Psychology, 53,* 81-89.

Kemery, E. R., Bedeian, A. G., Mossholder, K. W., & Touliatos, J. (1985). Outcomes of roles stress: A multisample constructive replication. *Academy of Management Journal, 28,* 363-375.

Kinicki, A. J., & Lockwood, C. A. (1985). The interview process: An examination of factors recruiters use in evaluating job applicants. *Journal of Vocational Behavior, 26,* 117-125.

Kipnis, D., Schmidt, S. M., & Wilkinson, I. (1980). Intraorganizational influence tactics: Explorations in getting one's way. *Journal of Applied Psychology, 65,* 440-452.

Kirchner, E. P., & Vondracek, S. I. (1973). *What do you want to be when you grow up? Vocational choice in children aged three to six.* Paper presented at the meeting of the Society for Research in Child Development, Philadelphia.

Knapp, M. L. (1978). *Social intercourse: From greeting to goodbye.* Boston: Allyn & Bacon.

Kotter, J. P. (1973). The psychological contract: Managing the joining-up process. *California Management Review, 15,* 91-99.

Krackhardt, D., McKenna, J., Porter, L. W., & Steers, R. M. (1981). Supervisory behavior and employee turnover: A field experiment. *Academy of Management Journal, 24,* 249-259.

Krackhardt, D., & Porter, L. W. (1985). When friends leave: A structural analysis of the relationship between turnover and stayers' attitudes. *Administrative Science Quarterly, 30,* 242-261.

Krackhardt, D., & Porter, L. W. (1986). The snowball effect: Turnover embedded in communication networks. *Journal of Applied Psychology, 71,* 50-55.

Krausz, M., & Fox, S. (1981). Two dimensions of a realistic preview and their impact on initial expectations, expectation fulfillment, satisfaction and intentions to quit. *Journal of Occupational Behavior, 2,* 211-216.

Krone, K. J. (1985). *Subordinate influence in organizations: The differential use of upward influence messages in decision making contexts.* Unpublished doctoral dissertation, University of Texas at Austin.

Langer, E. (1978). Rethinking the role of thought in social interaction. In J. H. Harvey, W. J. Ickes, & R. F. Kidd (Eds.), *New directions in attribution research* (Vol. 2, pp. 35-58). Hillsdale, NJ: Lawrence Erlbaum.

Langer, E., Blank, A., & Chanowitz, B. (1978). The mindlessness of ostensibly thoughtful action: The role of placebic information in interpersonal interaction. *Journal of Personality and Social Psychology, 36,* 635-642.

Larson, R. W. (1983). Adolescents' daily experience with family and friends: Contrasting opportunity systems. *Journal of Marriage and the Family, 45,* 739-750.

Laska, S. B., & Micklin, M. (1981). Modernization, the family and work socialization: A comparative study of U.S. and Columbian youth. *Journal of Comparative Family Studies, 12,* 187-203.

Leifer, A. D., & Lesser, G. S. (1976). *The development of career awareness in young children.* Washington, DC: National Institute of Education.

Lester, R. E., & Willer, L. R. (1984). *Determinants and consequences of organizational communication network patterns: A theoretical formulation and exploratory pilot study.* Paper presented at the annual meeting of the International Communication Association, San Francisco.

Levine, J. M. (1980). Reaction to opinion deviance in small groups. In P. B. Paulus (Ed.), *Psychology of group influence* (pp. 375-429). Hillsdale, NJ: Lawrence Erlbaum.

Liden, R. C., & Graen, G. B. (1980). Generalizability of the vertical dyad linkage model of leadership. *Academy of Management Journal, 23,* 451-465.

Livingston, J. S. (1969). Pygmalion in management. *Harvard Business Review, 47(4),* 81-89.

Louis, M. R. (1980). Surprise and sense-making: What newcomers experience in entering unfamiliar organizational settings. *Administrative Science Quarterly, 25,* 226-251.

Louis, M. R., Posner, B. Z., & Powell, G. N. (1983). The availability and helpfulness of socialization practices. *Personnel Psychology, 36,* 857-866.

Lyons, T. F. (1971). Role clarity, need for clarity, satisfaction, tension, and withdrawal. *Organizational Behavior and Human Performance, 6,* 99-110.

Mayfield, E. C. (1964). The selection interview: A reevaluation of published research. *Personnel Psychology, 17,* 234-260.

McComb, K. B., & Jablin, F. M. (1984). Verbal correlates of interviewer empathic listening and employment interview outcomes. *Communication Monographs, 51,* 353-371.

McEvoy, G. M., & Cascio, W. F. (1985). Strategies for reducing employee turnover: A meta-analysis. *Journal of Applied Psychology, 70,* 342-353.

McGovern, T. V., & Tinsley, H.E.A. (1978). Interviewers evaluations of interviewee nonverbal behavior. *Journal of Vocational Behavior, 13,* 163-171.

McGuire, W. J. (1968). The nature of attitudes and attitude change. In G. Lindzey & E. Aronson (Eds.), *Handbook of social psychology* (2nd ed., Vol. 3, pp. 136-314). Reading, MA: Addison-Wesley.

McLaughlin, M. L., & Cheatham, T. R. (1977). Effects of communication isolation on job satisfaction of bank tellers: A research note. *Human Communication Research, 3,* 171-175.

McMillan, J. J. (1982). *The rhetoric of the modern organization.* Unpublished doctoral dissertation, University of Texas at Austin.

Miceli, M. P. (1985). The effects of realistic job previews on newcomer behavior: A laboratory study. *Journal of Vocational Behavior, 26,* 277-289.

Mills, P. K., & Morris, J. H. (1986). Clients as "partial" employees of service organizations: Role development in client participation. *Academy of Management Review, 11,* 726-735.

Minkler, M., & Biller, R. P. (1979). Role shock: A tool for conceptualizing stresses accompanying role transitions. *Human Relations, 32,* 125-140.

Mitroff, I. I., & Kilmann, R. H. (1976). On organizational stories: An approach to the design and analysis of organizations through myths and stories. In R. H. Kilmann, L. R. Pondy, & D. P. Slevin (Eds.), *The management of organization design: Strategies and implementation* (pp. 189-207). New York: North-Holland.

Mobley, W. H., Griffeth, R. W., Hand, H. H., & Meglino, B. M. (1979). Review and conceptual analysis of the employee turnover process. *Psychological Bulletin, 86,* 493-522.

Monge, P. R., Bachman, S. G., Dillard, J. P., & Eisenberg, E. M. (1982). Communicator competence in the workplace: Model testing and scale development. In M. Burgoon (Ed.), *Communication yearbook 5* (pp. 505-527). New Brusnwick, NJ: Transaction.

Montemayor, R., & Van Komen, R. (1980). Age segregation of adolescents in and out of school. *Journal of Youth and Adolescence, 9,* 371-381.

Moore, W. E. (1969). Occupational socialization. In D. A. Goslin (Ed.), *Handbook of socialization theory and research* (pp. 1075-1086). Chicago: Rand McNally.

Mooreland, R. L., & Levine, J. M. (1982). Socialization in small groups: Temporal changes in individual-group relations. In L. Berkowitz (Ed.), *Advances in experimental social psychology* (Vol. 15, pp. 137-192). New York: Academic Press.

Morgan, M. (1980). *Longitudinal patterns of television use and adolescent role socialization.* Unpublished doctoral dissertation, University of Pennsylvania.

Morris, J., & Koch, J. (1979). Impacts of role perceptions on organizational commitment, job involvement, and psychosomatic illness among three vocational groupings. *Journal of Vocational Behavior, 14,* 88-107.

Morris, J., & Sherman, J. D. (1981). Generalizability of an organizational commitment model. *Academy of Management Journal, 24,* 512-526.

Morris, J., & Steers, R. M. (1980). Structural influences on organizational commitment. *Journal of Vocational Behavior, 17,* 50-57.

Mowday, R. T., Porter, L. W., & Steers, R. M. (1982). *Employee-organization linkages: The psychology of commitment, absenteeism, and turnover.* New York: Academic Press.

Muchinsky, P. M., & Tuttle, M. L. (1979). Employee turnover: An empirical and methodological assessment. *Journal of Vocational Behavior, 14,* 43-77.

Newcomb, T. M. (1958). Attitude development as a function of reference groups: The Bennington study. In E. E. Maccoby, T. M. Newcomb, & E. L. Hartley (Eds.), *Readings in social psychology* (3rd ed., pp. 265-275). New York: Holt, Rinehart & Winston.

Noble, G. (1983). Social learning from everyday television. In M.J.A. Howe (Ed.), *Learning from television: Psychological and educational research* (pp. 101-124). New York: Academic Press.

O'Reilly, C. A., & Caldwell, D. F. (1979). Informational influence as a determinant of perceived task characteristics and job satisfaction. *Journal of Applied Psychology, 64,* 157-165.

Osipow, S. H. (1983). *Theories of career development* (3rd ed.). Englewood Cliffs, NJ: Prentice-Hall.

Parks, M. R. (1985). Interpersonal communication and the quest for personal competence. In M. L. Knapp & G. R. Miller (Eds.), *Handbook of interpersonal communication* (pp. 171-201). Newbury Park, CA: Sage.

Parsons, C. K., Herold, D. M., & Leatherwood, M. L. (1985). Turnover during initial employment: A longitudinal study of the role of causal attributions. *Journal of Applied Psychology, 70,* 337-341.

Pelz, D. (1952). Influence: A key to effective leadership in the first line supervisor. *Personnel, 29,* 209-217.

Peters, T. J., & Waterman, R. H. (1982). *In search of excellence.* New York: Harper & Row.

Peterson, G. W., & Peters, D. F. (1983). Adolescents' construction of social reality: The impact of television and peers. *Youth and Society, 15,* 67-85.

Pfeffer, J. (1981a). Management as symbolic action: The creation and maintenance of organizational paradigms. In L. L. Cummings & B. M. Staw (Eds.), *Research in organizational behavior* (Vol. 3, pp. 1-52). Greenwich, CT: JAI Press.

Pfeffer, J. (1981b). *Power in organizations.* Marshfield, MA: Pitman.

Pfeffer, J. (1983). Organizational demography. In L. L. Cummings & B. M. Staw (Eds.), *Research in organizational behavior* (Vol. 5, pp. 299-357). Greenwich, CT: JAI Press.

Popovich, P., & Wanous, J. P. (1982). The realistic job preview as a persuasive communication. *Academy of Management Review, 7,* 570-578.

Porter, L. W., Allen, R. W., & Angle, H. L. (1981). The politics of upward influence in organizations. In L. L. Cummings & B. M. Staw (Eds.), *Research in organizational behavior* (Vol. 3, pp. 109-149). Greenwich, CT: JAI.

Porter, L. W., Lawler, E. E., & Hackman, J. R. (1975). *Behavior in organizations.* New York: McGraw-Hill.

Porter, L. W., & Steers, R. M. (1973). Organizational, work, and personal factors in employee turnover and absenteeism. *Psychological Bulletin, 80,* 151-176.

Posner, B. Z. (1981). Comparing recruiter, student, and faculty perceptions of important applicant and job characteristics. *Personnel Psychology, 34,* 329-339.

Price, J. L. (1977). *The study of turnover.* Ames: Iowa State University Press.

Putnam, L. L., Murray, E., & Hill, B. (1981). *Mode of communication in the encounter phase of organizational socialization.* Paper presented at the annual meeting of the Central States Speech Association, Chicago.

Quaglieri, P. L. (1982). A note on variations in recruiting information obtained through different sources. *Journal of Occupational Psychology, 55,* 53-55.

Rakestraw, T. L., & Weiss, H. M. (1981). The interaction of social influences and task experience on goals, performance, and performance satisfaction. *Organizational Behavior and Human Performance, 27,* 326-344.

Recruiting literature: Is it accurate? (1981). *Journal of College Placement, 42,* 56-59.

Redding, W. C. (1972). *Communication within the organization: An interpretive review of theory and research.* New York: Industrial Communication Council.

Reid, G. L. (1972). Job search and the effectiveness of job-finding methods. *Industrial and Labor Relations Review, 25,* 479-495.

Reilly, R. R., Brown, B., Blood, M. R., & Malatesta, C. Z. (1981). The effects of realistic previews: A study and discussion of the literature. *Personnel Psychology, 34,* 823-834.

Reinsch, N. L., & Stano, M. (1984). *Student experiences in employment interviews.* Paper presented at the annual meeting of the International Communication Association, San Francisco.

Rhodes, S. R., & Steers, R. M. (1981). Conventional vs. worker-owned organizations. *Human Relations, 34,* 1013-1035.

Ridgeway, C. L. (1978). Conformity, group-oriented motivation and status attainment in small groups. *Social Psychology, 41,* 175-188.

Ridgeway, C. L. (1981). Nonconformity, competence and influence in groups: A test of two theories. *American Sociological Review, 46,* 333-347.

Roberts, K. H., & Glick, W. (1981). The job characteristics approach to task design: A critical review. *Journal of Applied Psychology, 66,* 193-217.

Roberts, K. H., & O'Reilly, C. A. (1979). Some correlates of communication roles in organizations. *Academy of Management Journal, 22,* 42-57.

Rosse, J. G., & Hulin, C. L. (1985). Adaptation to work: An analysis of employee health, withdrawal, and change. *Organizational Behavior and Human Decision Processes, 36,* 324-347.

Rotchford, N. L., & Roberts, K. H. (1982). Part-time workers as missing persons in organizational research. *Academy of Management Review, 7,* 228-234.

Rotondi, T. (1975). Organizational identification and group involvement. *Academy of Management Journal, 18,* 892-897.

Roy, D. E. (1955). Banana time: Job satisfaction and informal interaction. *Human Organization, 18,* 158-168.

Ruggiero, M., Greenberger, E., & Steinberg, L. D. (1982). Occupational deviance among adolescent workers. *Youth and Society, 13,* 423-448.

Ruggiero, M., & Steinberg, L. D. (1981). The empirical study of teenage work: A behavioral code for the assessment of adolescent job environments. *Journal of Vocational Behavior, 19,* 163-174.

Rynes, S. L., & Miller, H. E. (1983). Recruiter and job influences on candidates for employment. *Journal of Applied Psychology, 68,* 147-154.

Sackett, P. R. (1979). *The interviewer as hypothesis tester: The effects of impressions of an applicant on subsequent interviewer behavior.* Unpublished doctoral dissertation, Ohio State University.

St. John, W. D. (1980). The complete employee orientation program. *Personnel Journal, 59,* 373-378.

Salancik, G. R. (1977). Commitment and the control of organizational behavior and belief. In B. M. Staw & G. R. Salancik (Eds.), *New directions in organizational behavior* (pp. 1-54). Chicago: St. Clair Press.

Salancik, G. R., & Pfeffer, J. (1978). A social information processing approach to job attitudes and task design. *Administrative Science Quarterly, 23,* 224-253.

Schachter, S. (1951). Deviation, rejection and communication. *Journal of Abnormal and Social Psychology, 46,* 190-207.

Schein, E. H. (1968). Organizational socialization and the profession of management. *Industrial Management Review, 9,* 1-16.

Schein, E. H. (1971). The individual, the organization, and the career: A conceptual scheme. *Journal of Applied Behavioral Management, 7,* 401-426.

Schilit, W. K., & Locke, E. A. (1982). A study of upward influence in organizations. *Administrative Science Quarterly, 27,* 304-316.

Schmitt, N. (1976). Social and situational determinants of interview decisions: Implications for the employment interview. *Personnel Psychology, 29,* 79-101.

Schmitt, N., & Coyle, B. W. (1976). Applicant decisions in the employment interview. *Journal of Applied Psychology, 61,* 184-192.

Schriesheim, J. F. (1980). The social context of leader-subordinate relations: An investigation of the effects of group cohesiveness. *Journal of Applied Psychology, 65,* 183-194.

Schwab, D. P. (1982). Organizational recruiting and decision to participate. In K. Rowland & G. Ferris (Eds.), *Personnel management: New perspectives.* Boston: Allyn & Bacon.

Shaw, M. E. (1981). *Group dynamics: The psychology of small group behavior* (3rd. ed.). New York: McGraw-Hill.

Sheldon, M. E. (1971). Investments and involvements as mechanisms producing commitment to the organization. *Administrative Science Quarterly, 16,* 142-150.

Shibutani, T. (1962). Reference groups and social control. In A. M. Rose (Ed.), *Human behavior and social processes.* Boston: Houghton-Mifflin.

Shyles, L., & Ross, M. (1984). Recruitment rhetoric in brochures advertising the all volunteer force. *Journal of Applied Communication Research, 12,* 34-49.

Siegel, A. E. (1958). The influence of violence in the mass media upon children's role expectations. *Child Development, 29,* 35-56.

Simpson, R. L. (1962). Parental influence, anticipatory socialization, and social mobility. *American Sociological Review, 27,* 517-522.

Sloane, A. A., & Hodges, E. W. (1968). What workers don't know about employee benefits. *Personnel, 45,* 27-34.

Smith, K. G., Mitchell, T. R., & Summer, C. E. (1985). Top level management priorities in different stages of the organizational life cycle. *Academy of Management Journal, 28,* 799-820.

Steers, R. M., & Mowday, R. T. (1981). Employee turnover and post-decision accomodation processes. In L. L. Cummings & B. M. Staw (Eds.), *Research in organizational behavior* (Vol. 3, pp. 235-281). Greenwich, CT: JAI Press.

Steers, R. M., & Rhodes, F. R. (1978). Major influences on employee attendance: A process model. *Journal of Applied Psychology, 63,* 391-407.

Steinberg, L. D. (1982). Jumping off the work experience bandwagon. *Journal of Youth and Adolescence, 11,* 183-205.

Steinberg, L. D., Greenberger, E., Vaux, A., & Ruggiero, M. (1981). Early work experience: Effects on adolescent occupational socialization. *Youth and Society, 12,* 403-422.

Stevens, J. M., Beyer, J., & Trice, H. M. (1978). Assessing personal, role, and organizational predictors of managerial commitment. *Academy of Management Journal, 21,* 380-396.

Stohl, C. (1983). Developing a communication competence scale. In R. N. Bostrom (Ed.), *Communication yearbook 7* (pp. 685-716). Newbury Park, CA: Sage.

Stohl, C. (1986). The role of memorable messages in the process of organizational socialization. *Communication Quarterly, 34,* 231-249.

Stumpf, S. A., Austin, E. J., & Hartman, K. (1984). The impact of career exploration and interview readiness on interview performance and outcomes. *Journal of Vocational Behavior, 24,* 221-235.

Sutton, R. I., & Louis, M. R. (1984). *The influence of selection and socialization on insider sense-making.* Paper presented at the annual meeting of the Academy of Management, Boston.

Tangri, S. (1972). Determinants of occupational role innovation among college women. *Journal of Social Issues, 28,* 177-199.

Taylor, M. S., & Schmidt, D. W. (1983). A process-oriented investigation of recruitment source effectiveness. *Personnel Psychology, 36,* 343-354.

Taylor, M. S., & Sniezek, J. A. (1984). The college recruitment interview: Topical content and applicant reactions. *Journal of Occupational Psychology, 57,* 157-168.

Teigen, C. W. (1983). *Communication of organizational climate during job screening interviews: A field study of interviewee perceptions, "actual" communication behavior and interview outcomes.* Unpublished doctoral dissertation, University of Texas at Austin.

Tengler, C. D. (1982). *Effects of question type and question orientation on interview outcomes in naturally occurring employment interviews.* Unpublished master's thesis, University of Texas at Austin.

Tengler, C. D., & Jablin, F. M. (1983). Effects of question type, orientation, and sequencing in the employment screening interview. *Communication Monographs, 50,* 245-263.

Theberge, L. (1981). *Crooks, conmen and clowns: Businessmen in T.V. entertainment.* Washington, DC: Media Institute.

Thomas, J., & Griffin, R. (1983). The social information processing model of task design: A review of the literature. *Academy of Management Review, 8,* 672-682.

Thompson, P. H., & Dalton, G. W. (1976). Are R&D organizations obsolete? *Harvard Business Review, 54,* 105-116.

Tompkins, P. K., & Cheney, G. (1985). Communication and unobtrusive control in contemporary organizations. In R. D. McPhee & P. K. Tompkins (Eds.), *Organizational communication: Traditional themes and new directions* (pp. 179-210). Newbury Park, CA: Sage.

Trent, L. W. (1978). *The effects of varying levels of interviewee nonverbal behavior in the employment interview.* Unpublished doctoral dissertation, Southern Illinois University.

Tucker, D. H., & Rowe, P. M. (1979). Relationship between expectancy, causal attributions, and final hiring decisions in the employment interview. *Journal of Applied Psychology, 64,* 27-34.

Turow, J. (1974). Advising and ordering in daytime, primetime. *Journal of Communication, 24,* 138-141.

Turow, J. (1980). Occupation and personality in television dramas: An industry view. *Communication Research, 7,* 295-318.

Tushman, M. L., & Scanlan, T. J. (1981a). Characteristics of external orientations of boundary spanning individuals. *Academy of Management Journal, 24,* 83-98.

Tushman, M. L., & Scanlan, T. J. (1981b). Boundary spanning individuals: Their role in information transfer and their antecedents. *Academy of Management Journal, 24,* 289-305.

Ulrich, L., & Trumbo, D. (1965). The selection interview since 1949. *Psychological Bulletin, 63,* 100-116.

Vance, R. J., & Biddle, T. F. (1985). Task experience and social cues: Interactive effects on attitudinal reactions. *Organizational Behavior and Human Decision Processes, 35,* 252-265.

Van Maanen, J. (1975). Breaking in: Socialization to work. In R. Dubin (Ed.), *Handbook of work, organization and society* (pp. 67-120). Chicago: Rand McNally.

Van Maanen, J. (1977). Experiencing organization: Notes on the meaning of careers and socialization. In J. Van Maanen (Ed.), *Organizational careers: Some new perspectives* (pp. 15-45). New York: John Wiley.

Van Maanen, J. (1978). People processing: Strategies of organizational socializing. *Organizational Dynamics, 7*(1), 18-36.

Van Maanen, J., & Barley, S. R. (1984). Occupational communities: Culture and control in organizations. In B. M. Staw & L. L. Cummings (Eds.), *Research in organizational behavior* (Vol. 6, pp. 287-365). Greenwich, CT: JAI Press.

Van Maanen, J., & Schein, E. H. (1979). Toward a theory of organizational socialization. In B. M. Staw & L. L. Cummings (Eds.), *Research in organizational behavior* (Vol. 1, pp. 209-264). Greenwich, CT: JAI Press.

Vecchio, R. P. (1985). Predicting employee turnover from leader-member exchange: A failure to replicate. *Academy of Management Journal, 28,* 478-485.

Vincino, F. L., & Bass, B. M. (1978). Lifespace variables and managerial success. *Journal of Applied Psychology, 63,* 81-88.

Wallace, W. I. (1965). Peer influence and undergraduates aspirations for graduate study. *Sociology of Education, 38,* 375-392.

Walsh, W. B., & Osipow, S. H. (Eds.). (1983). *Handbook of vocational psychology: Foundations* (Vol. 1). Hillsdale, NJ: Lawrence Erlbaum.

Wanous, J. P. (1973). Effects of a realistic job preview on job acceptance, job attitudes and job survival. *Journal of Applied Psychology, 58,* 327-332.

Wanous, J. P. (1977). Organizational entry: Newcomers moving from outside to inside. *Psychological Bulletin, 84,* 601-618.

Wanous, J. P. (1980). *Organizational entry: Recruitment, selection and socialization of newcomers.* Reading, MA: Addison-Wesley.

Wanous, J. P., Reichers, A. E., & Malik, S. D. (1984). Organizational socialization and group development: Toward an integrative perspective. *Academy of Management Review, 9,* 670-683.

Weiss, H. M. (1977). Subordinate imitation of supervisor behavior: The role of modeling in organizational socialization. *Organizational Behavior and Human Performance, 19,* 89-105.

Weiss, H. M. (1978). Social learning of work values in organizations. *Journal of Applied Psychology, 63,* 711-718.

Weiss, H. M., & Nowicki, C. E. (1981). Social influence on task satisfaction: Model competence and observer field dependence. *Organizational Behavior and Human Performance, 27,* 345-366.

Weiss, W. (1968). Effects of the mass media of communication. In G. Lindzey & E. Aronson (Eds.), *Handbook of social psychology* (2nd ed., Vol. 5, pp. 77-195). Reading, MA: Addison-Wesley.

Wells, D. L., & Muchinsky, P. M. (1985). Performance antecedents of voluntary and involuntary managerial turnover. *Journal of Applied Psychology, 70,* 329-336.

White, L. K., & Brinkerhoff, D. B. (1981). Children's work in the family: Its significance and meaning. *Journal of Marriage and the Family, 43,* 789-798.

White, S. E., & Mitchell, T. R. (1979). Job enrichment versus social cues: A comparison and competitive test. *Journal of Applied Psychology, 64,* 1-9.

Wijting, J. P., Arnold, C. R., & Conrad, K. A. (1977). Relationships between work values, socio-educational and work experiences, and vocational aspirations of 6th, 9th, 10th, and 12th graders. *Journal of Vocational Behavior, 11,* 51-65.

Wilkins, A. (1978). *Organizational stories as an expression of management philosophy: Implications for social control in organizations.* Unpublished doctoral dissertation, Stanford University.

Wilson, C. E. (1983). *Toward understanding the process of organizational leave-taking.* Paper presented at the annual meeting of the Speech Communication Association, Washington, DC.

Witlatch, M. J. (1985). *Exploring client feedback in service organizations.* Paper presented at the annual convention of the Academy of Management, San Diego.

Wolfe, M. N., & Baskin, O. W. (1985). *The communication of corporate culture in employee indoctrination literature: An empirical analysis using content analysis.* Paper presented at the annual meeting of the Academy of Management, San Diego.

Woodward, J. K. (1968). Presentation booklets: How they are used; what they contain. *Public Relations Journal, 24,* 28-29.

Youngberg, C. F. (1963). *An experimental study of job satisfaction and turnover in relation to job expectations and self expectations.* Unpublished doctoral dissertation, New York University.

Zaharia, E. S., & Baumeister, A. A. (1981). Job preview effects during the critical initial employment period. *Journal of Applied Psychology, 66,* 19-22.

Ziller, R. C. (1965). Toward a theory of open and closed groups. *Psychological Bulletin, 64,* 164-182.

Ziller, R. C., & Behringer, R. D. (1960). Assimilation of the knowledgeable newcomer under conditions of groups success and failure. *Journal of Abnormal and Social Psychology, 60,* 288-291.

Ziller, R. C., Behringer, R. D., & Jansen, M. J. (1961). The minority member in open and closed groups. *Journal of Applied Psychology, 45,* 55-58.

AUTHOR INDEX

Abelson, M. 218, 224n
Abelson, P. H. 475, 494n
Abelson, R. P. 602, 605, 607, 619n
Ackoff, R. L. 458, 479, 494n
Adamopoulos, J. 286, 292n
Adams, G. B. 243, 260n
Adams, J. A. 626, 636, 640, 641, 667n
Adams, J. S. 54, 64n, 177, 189, 192n, 313, 329, 335n, 570, 590n
Adelman, M. B. 284, 291n, 335, 336n
Adler, N. J. 236, 246, 257n, 264, 273, 274, 290, 292n
Adler, S. 723, 725n
Agarwala-Rogers, R. 23, 40n
Aguilar, F. J. 142, 158n
Aiken, M. 27, 39n, 147, 158n, 212, 223n, 309, 336n, 393, 394, 397, 401, 402, 403, 405, 407, 408, 413n, 415n, 612, 620n
Akin, G. 240, 257n
Alafat, K. A. 647, 675n
Alba, R. D. 116, 120n, 323, 327, 330, 336n
Albert, R. D. 283, 285, 286, 287, 290, 292n
Albrecht, T. L. 23, 38n, 324, 325, 327, 331, 335, 336n, 605, 619n, 716, 726n
Alcock, W. T. 640, 675n
Aldag, R. J. 139, 163n, 721, 727n
Alderfer, C. P. 691, 726n
Aldrich, H. E. 57, 64n, 131, 158n, 178, 192n, 317, 324, 336n, 390, 413n, 582, 590n
Alexander, E. R. III 553, 590n
Alexander, R. A. 213, 227n
Alinsky, S. 520, 541n
Al-Jafary, A. 279, 292n
Alkire, A. 214, 223n
Allaire, Y. 238, 247, 257n

Allard, M. 640, 670n
Allcorn, S. 243, 259n
Allen, K. 567, 593n
Allen, M. 572, 592n
Allen, R. W. 323, 336n, 465, 499n, 504, 505, 508, 518, 520, 522, 523, 524, 531, 541n, 545n, 547n, 709, 736n
Allen, T. 321, 336n, 616, 620n
Allen, V. L. 712, 726n
Allison, G. T. 527, 541n
Allport, G. W. 481, 494n
Alutto, J. A. 221, 223n, 354, 358, 361, 367, 371, 372, 373, 375, 376, 382, 383, 384, 384n, 386n
Alvarez, K. 561, 590n
Alvesson, M. 256, 257n
Amend, E. 324, 336n
Ammons, R. B. 640, 641, 667n
Anderson, B. 287, 292n
Anderson, B. J. 515, 546n
Andrews, F. M. 119, 122n
Andrews, J. A. Y. 250, 260n, 526, 544n
Angle, H. L. 465, 499n, 508, 518, 522, 524, 531, 547n, 709, 736n
Annett, J. 632, 633, 635, 636, 637, 638, 639, 640, 641, 643, 644, 667n
Ansoff, H. I. 143, 158n
Applegate, J. L. 229, 233, 234, 235, 236, 239, 240, 242, 245, 263n
Arac, J. 246, 257n
Argyle, M. 153, 158n
Argyris, C. 45, 64n, 71, 94n
Ariss, S. S. 412, 415n
Aristotle 78, 79, 80, 94n, 186, 192n
Arnold, C. R. 683, 739n
Arnold, H. J. 641, 651, 667n
Aronoff, J. 278, 292n
Aronson, E. 602, 619n

Arps, G. F. 631, 667n
Arrow, K. J. 606, 619n
Arvey, R. D. 656, 657, 667n, 689, 692, 726n
Ashby, W. R. 135, 158n, 626, 636, 667n
Ashford, S. J. 634, 639, 642, 668n, 699, 700, 709, 711, 722, 726n
Ashforth, B. E. 203, 223n, 714, 726n
Ashour, A. S. 667, 668n
Assael, H. 581, 590n
Astley, W. G. 52, 64n, 118, 120n, 249, 257n, 323, 336n, 390, 413n, 505, 532, 540, 541n
Athanasiou, R. 321, 336n
Athanassiades, J. C. 149, 158n, 481, 495n
Athos, A. G. 248, 261n
Atich, J. M. 534, 546n
Atkinson, J. 516, 545n
Austin, E. J. 693, 738n
Austin, J. L. 464, 487, 495n
Austin, N. 238, 261n, 318, 340n
Avery, R. 699, 729n
Axelrod, R. 98, 120n
Axley, S. R. 23, 38n, 180, 192n, 707, 726n
Ayman, R. 355, 357, 384n

Babbitt, L. V. 690, 691, 726n
Bacharach, S. B. 54, 64n, 147, 158n, 212, 223n, 309, 336n, 393, 394, 397, 401, 402, 403, 408, 413n, 521, 531, 541n, 564, 569, 570, 577, 590n
Bachman, S. G. 467, 499n, 517, 546n, 717, 735n
Bachrach, P. 506, 541n, 581, 590n
Back, K. 321, 338n
Baetz, J. L. 667, 672n
Bagchi, D. 372, 383, 384n

SUBJECT INDEX

ROSITA D. ALBERT (Ph.D., University of Michigan) is an Associate Professor of Speech Communication at the University of Minnesota, where she is also a faculty member in the departments of International Relations and in Latin American Studies. She is originally from Brazil, and taught previously at the University of Illinois. She has directed a large scale program of research on Hispanic-Anglo interactions and cultural differences in attribution. Her research has focused on intercultural communication in different organizational settings and on the development and evaluation of cross-cultural training programs.

JOHN C. ANDERSON received his Ph.D. in organizational behavior from Cornell University in 1977. He has held the positions of Assistant Professor at the Graduate School of Management at UCLA, Assistant Professor at the School of Business, Queen's University (Canada), and Associate Professor at the Graduate School of Business, Columbia University. His teaching and research interests include public sector labor relations, unions as organizations, human resource management, and strategic planning. He has published several books and over 50 articles and chapters in books on these topics. He is currently Senior Manager, United Nations Childrens' Fund, New York.

MARTA B. CALÁS is an Instructor of Organizational Behavior and a doctoral candidate at the School of Management of the University of Massachusetts at Amherst. Born in a Third World country, she has had a longstanding interest in the intersections of culture and management and has been involved with cross- cultural management issues as an academician and consultant. Her current work is directed toward reformulating management writings as cultural critiques in a postmodern Western society.

JENNIFER A. CHATMAN is a doctoral candidate in organizational behavior at the University of California's Graduate School of Business Administration. She received her B.A. degree (1981) in psychology from the University of California at Berkeley. She has published in the areas of commitment, decision making, and impression management in organizations. She is currently conducting her dissertation research, which examines selection and socialization processes in Big Eight accounting firms.

GEORGE CHENEY (Ph.D., Purdue University) is Assistant Professor in the Communication Department at the University of Colorado, Boulder. His research centers on the relationship of the individual to society, particularly as shaped and expressed in the organizational setting. His work has been published in such journals as *Communication Monographs, Quarterly Journal of Speech*, and *Communication Quarterly*.

MARY J. CULNAN is Associate Professor and Director of the Business Management Information Systems Program at the Kogod College of Business Administration, American University, Washington, D.C. Her interests include implementation strategies for office information systems, scholarly communication in applied disciplines, and information processing in the U.S. Senate. Prior to joining the faculty at American University, she served on the faculties of the University of Virginia and the University of California, Berkeley.

LOUIS P. CUSELLA (Ph.D., Purdue University) is Associate Professor of Communication at the University of Dayton, in Dayton, Ohio. He has published articles in *Communication Yearbook, Human Communication Research, Quarterly Journal of Speech, Communication Education*, and *Communication Quarterly*. His principal research interests include the role of feedback in work motivation. Currently he is writing a book on organizational communication for Harper & Row.

RICHARD L. DAFT is Hugh Roy Cullen Professor of Business Administration at Texas A&M University. He has published several articles in the areas of organizational information processing, organizational structure, innovation, and control. He is associate editor of *Administrative Science Quarterly*, and has authored or coauthored five books, including *Organizational Theory and Design* (1986, West). His current research is on communication media, including the relationship of media to information richness and the symbolic value of media within organizations.

FRED DANSEREAU is Associate Professor of Management at the State University of New York, Buffalo. He has published in the areas of role theory, leadership, and exchange and motivation, in journals such as *Organizational Behavior and Human Performance, Academy of Management Journal, Journal of Applied Psychology, American Sociological Review*, and *Applied Psychological Measurement*. He has developed an approach that includes levels of analysis in hypothesis testing, which is described in his book *Theory Testing in Organizational Behavior: The Varient Approach*. Recently he completed a computer package called DETECT for empirical testing at multiple levels of analysis.

ERIC M. EISENBERG (Ph.D., Michigan State University) is Associate Professor of Communications Arts and Sciences at the University of Southern California. He has published articles and book chapters on various aspects of organizational communication, including inter-organizational relations, communication networks, and the strategic use of ambiguity by managers and employees.

NANCY A. EUSKE is a doctoral student in organizational behavior and industrial relations at the School of Business Administration, University of California, Berkeley. Her research interests include the behavioral implications of institutionalization theory. She is currently investigating the relationship between communication networks and newcomer organizational socialization.

RAYMOND L. FALCIONE (Ph.D., Kent State University) is Associate Professor of Communication at the University of Maryland, College Park. Formerly he was the Director of Speech Communication Division at the University of Maryland. He has served in numerous elected offices in the International Communication Association and on the editorial boards of *Human Communication Research, Journal of Applied Communication Research,* and *Communication Quarterly.* His selected publications have appeared in *Human Communication Research, Communication Yearbook 1* and *Communication Yearbook 8, Personnel Journal, Journal of Business Communication,* and *Nursing Research.* He has also been a coauthor/editor of the *Organizational Communication: Abstracts, Analysis and Overview* series of books. He has received a universitywide award for outstanding teaching at the University of Maryland, and has consulted for numerous government and private organizations.

PETER J. FROST (Ph.D., University of Minnesota) is Professor in the Industrial Relations Management Division of the Faculty of Commerce and Business Administration at the University of British Columbia. He is coeditor of several books, including *Organizational Culture* and *Publishing in the Organizational Sciences.* He has edited a special issue on organizational symbolism for the *Journal of Management.* His primary research emphases have been culture, symbolism, organizational politics, and the processes of knowing and understanding organizational life. His current interest is in the concept of intuition and its possible link to choice in organizations.

RICHARD P. HERDEN (Ph.D., University of Pittsburgh) is Associate Professor of Management in the School of Business at the University of Louisville. He received his B.A. and M.B.A. degrees from the University of South Florida. He has served as Acting Director of the Center for Management Development and Acting Associate Dean for Academic Programs in the School of Business at the University of Louisville. His work has been published in the *Academy of Management Review, Business Horizons, Personnel Journal,* and *Human Systems Management.* He is also coauthor of the six-volume series of books entitled *Improving Supervisor Productivity* (1984), published by Dow Jones Irwin. His industrial experience includes positions at Electronic Communications, Inc., and NCR, and he has been a consultant with a variety of industrial, human services, and educational organizations.

GEORGE P. HUBER is the Fondren Foundation Chaired Professor of Business at the University of Texas at Austin. His research focuses on organizational design, decision making, and information systems, and he has written three books and over 70 publications on these topics. In 1983, his pioneering article on the nature and design of postindustrial organizations was awarded First Prize in the International Prize Competition sponsored by the College on Organizations of the Institute of Management Sciences. He has conducted studies of information use in research and development organizations for the National Science Foundation and studies of organization design for the U.S. Army Research Institute for the Behavioral and Social Sciences.

FREDRIC M. JABLIN (Ph.D., Purdue University) is Associate Professor of Speech Communication at the University of Texas at Austin. His research has been published in a wide variety of journals and scholarly books, including *Human Communication Research, Communication Monographs, Communication Yearbook, Human Resource Management, Psychological Bulletin, Handbook of Interpersonal Communication,* and *Social Cognition and Communication.* He is a member of the editorial boards of the *Academy of Management Journal, Human Communication Research,* and *Communication Research.* His research has examined various facets of superior-subordinate communication, group problem solving, interaction in the employment interview, and related organizational entry processes. He is currently completing a book for the Dryden Press exploring organizational communication from an assimilation approach.

KATHLEEN J. KRONE (Ph.D., University of Texas at Austin) is Assistant Professor in the Department of Communication at the Ohio State University. She received her B.S. and M.S. degrees from Illinois State University. Her work has been published in the *Handbook of Communication Science* and *Written Communication.* Her research interests include upward influence in organizations, communicative aspects of organizational assimilation, and interviewing.

STEVEN E. MARKHAM (Ph.D., State University of New York at Buffalo) is Assistant Professor of Management at Virginia Polytechnic Institute and State University. He has published in the *Academy of Management Journal, Journal of Occupational Psychology, Applied Psychological Measurement, Personnel Psychology, Psychological Reports, Personnel Administrator,* and

The Review of Business and Economic Research. His recent work has focused on measurement problems in leadership, field experiments in attendance improvement, and multilevel problems in organizational diagnosis.

M. LYNNE MARKUS is Assistant Professor, Computer and Information Systems, at the Graduate School of Management, University of California, Los Angeles. Her research interests include the organizational effects of electronic communication media, office automation, and information systems. Prior to joining the faculty at UCLA, she worked as a consultant with Arthur D. Little, Inc., and as an assistant professor at the Sloan School of Management at MIT. She is the author of *Systems in Organizations: Bugs and Features* (1984, Pitman Publishing) and is a member of the editorial board of *Office: Technology and People.*

PETER R. MONGE (Ph.D., Michigan State University) is Professor of Communications at the Annenberg School of Communications, University of Southern California. He is coauthor of *Communicating and Organizing* and coeditor of *Multivariate Techniques in Communication Research.* He has published articles on applications of systems theory to communication, the role of emergent communication networks in organizations, the relationship of communication processes to organizational participation, and research procedures for studying communication processes.

CHARLES A. O'REILLY is a Professor in the Graduate School of Business at the University of California, Berkeley. He has published extensively in the areas of communication, decision making, and commitment. He is currently engaged in studies of organizational demography and the impact of corporate culture in high technology firms.

M. SCOTT POOLE (Ph.D., University of Wisconsin—Madison) is Associate Professor of Speech Communication at the University of Minnesota, where he is an Associate of the Strategic Management Research Center and the Management Information Systems Research Center. His areas of interest are group and organizational communication and research methodology. He has recently coedited (with Randy Hirokawa) *Group Communication and Decision-Making* (Sage).

LYMAN W. PORTER is Professor of Management in the Graduate School of Management at the University of California, Irvine. He formerly served as Dean of the Graduate School of Management at UC Irvine. He is past president of the Academy of Management and in 1983 received that organization's award for Scholarly Contributions to Management. His major fields of interest are organizational psychology and management.

LINDA L. PUTNAM (Ph.D., University of Minnesota) is Associate Professor in the Department of Communication at Purdue University. Her research interests include bargaining and negotiations, conflict management in organizations, and interpretive approaches to organizational communication. She has published articles and book chapters that have appeared in such publications as *Human Communication Research, Communication Monographs, Communication Yearbook, Small Group Behavior, Western Journal of Speech Communication,* and *Journal of Business Communication.* She is the coeditor of *Communication and Organization: An Interpretive Approach,* a Sage Focus Edition. She serves on the editorial boards of five journals, including *Human Communication Research, Academy of Management Review, Communication Monographs,* and *Communication Research.*

W. CHARLES REDDING (Ph.D., University of Southern California) is Professor Emeritus of Communication at Purdue University, where, since 1955, he has directed approximately 40 doctoral dissertations in the area of organizational communication. He is a Fellow and Past President of the International Communication Association. Among his numerous publications is *Communication Within the Organization.*

KARLENE H. ROBERTS (Ph.D., University of California) is Professor of Business Administration at the University of California, Berkeley. Her research interests are in organizational communication methodologies for studying organizations, the design and operation of extremely complex systems, and international management. She is Past President of the Organizational Behavior Division of the Academy of Management.

LINDA SMIRCICH (Ph.D., Syracuse University) is Associate Professor of Organizational Behavior at the School of Management of the University of Massachusetts at Amherst. In her teaching and scholarly writing she aims to expand the ways people think about organizations and their possibilities. She has been particularly interested in developing interpretive, radical humanist, and feminist perspectives on organization and management theory issues.

CYNTHIA STOHL (Ph.D., Purdue University) is an Assistant Professor in the Department of Communication at Purdue University. Her research interests focus primarily on formal and emergent communication networks and worker participation programs. Her work has appeared in several journals including *Journal of Communication, Communication Quarterly, International Journal of Intercultural Relations, Peace and Change,* and in *Communication Yearbook 10.*

LYLE SUSSMAN (Ph.D., Purdue University) is an Associate Professor of Management in the School of Business, University of Louisville. He is the author of four books and numerous articles. He has designed and conducted training programs for Fortune 500 companies, nonprofit organizations, and governmental agencies.

PHILLIP K. TOMPKINS (Ph.D., Purdue University) is Professor of Communication at the University of Colorado, Boulder. He recently coedited (with Robert D. McPhee) Volume 13 of the Sage Annual Reviews of Communication, *Organizational Communication: Traditional Themes and New Directions* (1985). His areas of interest, in addition to organizational communication, are those domains in which postmodernist literary and social theory converge. He is the President-Elect of the International Communication Association.

HARRY C. TRIANDIS (Ph.D, Cornell University) is Professor of Psychology in the Department of Psychology and the Institute of Labor Relations at the University of Illinois in Urbana-Champaign. He is the author of *The Analysis of Subjective Culture*, and the editor of the six-volume *Handbook of Cross-Cultural Psychology*. He is Past President of the International Association of Cross-Cultural Psychology, the Divisions of Personality and Social Psychology, and the Society for the Psychological Study of Social Issues of the American Psychological Association, and is currently President of the Interamerican Society of Psychology.

STEVEN L. VIBBERT (Ph.D., University of Iowa) is Associate Professor of Communication at Purdue University. His interests include political public relations and the analysis of corporate issue management strategies. He has recently coauthored (with R.E. Crable) *Public Relations as Communication Management.*

KARL E. WEICK (Ph.D., Ohio State University) holds the Harkins and Company Centennial Chair in Business Administration at the University of Texas at Austin, and is former editor of *Administrative Science Quarterly*. He has been associated with the faculties of Purdue University, University of Minnesota, and Cornell University. He also held short-term appointments at the University of Utrecht in the Netherlands, Wabash College, Carnegie Mellon University, Stanford University, and Seattle University. His research interests include how people make sense of confusing events, the effects of stress on thinking and imagination, techniques for observing complicated events, self-fulfilling prophecies, the craft of applying social science, substitutes for rationality, and determinants of effective managerial performance. His writings on these topics are collected in four books, including *The Social Psychology of Organizing* and the coauthored *Managerial Behavior, Performance and Effectiveness,* which won the 1972 Book of the Year Award from the American College of Hospital Administration. He has also written numerous journal articles, book chapters, and book reviews.

NOTES

NOTES

NOTES